BUSINESS IMMIGRATION
LAW & PRACTICE
SECOND EDITION

VOLUME 1
NONIMMIGRANT CONCEPTS

W0006361

DARYL BUFFENSTEIN
BO COOPER
KEVIN MINER
CRYSTAL WILLIAMS

AMERICAN IMMIGRATION LAWYERS ASSOCIATION

Website for Corrections and Updates

Corrections and other updates to AILA publications
can be found online at:
www.aila.org/publications/books/errata

If you have any corrections or updates to the information in this book,
please let us know by sending a note to the address below, or e-mail us at
books@aila.org

This publication is designed to provide accurate and authoritative information in regard to the subject matter covered. It is distributed with the understanding that the publisher is not engaged in rendering legal, accounting, or other professional service. If legal advice or other expert assistance is required, the services of a competent professional should be sought.

—from a Declaration of Principles jointly adopted by a Committee of the American Bar Association and a Committee of Publishers

Proceeds from the sales of AILA publications are reinvested in the association to help support member programs and services in the areas of federal and state advocacy, government liaison, practice assistance, ethics education, media outreach, and timely dissemination of members-only information via *www.aila.org*. In addition, contributions are made to the American Immigration Council (AIC).

Copyright © 2011, 2017 by the American Immigration Lawyers Association

All rights reserved. No part of this publication may be reproduced or transmitted in any form or by any means, electronic or mechanical, including photocopy, recording, or any information storage retrieval system, without written permission from the publisher. No copyright claimed on U.S. government material or material owned and copyrighted by other entities.

Requests for permission to make electronic or print copies of any part of this work should be mailed to Director of Publications, American Immigration Lawyers Association, 1331 G Street NW, Ste. 300, Washington, DC 20005, or e-mailed to *books@aila.org*.

Printed in the United States of America

ISBN 978-1-57370-407-6
Stock No. 54-07

Summary Table of Contents

Business Immigration: Law & Practice, 2nd Ed.

Copyright © 2017. American Immigration Lawyers Association. All rights reserved.

Copyright © 2017. American Immigration Lawyers Association. All rights reserved.

TABLE OF CONTENTS
BUSINESS IMMIGRATION: LAW & PRACTICE
VOLUME 1

Copyright © 2017. American Immigration Lawyers Association. All rights reserved.

Copyright © 2017. American Immigration Lawyers Association. All rights reserved.

Copyright © 2017. American Immigration Lawyers Association. All rights reserved.

Copyright © 2017. American Immigration Lawyers Association. All rights reserved.

Copyright © 2017. American Immigration Lawyers Association. All rights reserved.

Copyright © 2017. American Immigration Lawyers Association. All rights reserved.

Copyright © 2017. American Immigration Lawyers Association. All rights reserved.

Copyright © 2017. American Immigration Lawyers Association. All rights reserved.

Copyright © 2017. American Immigration Lawyers Association. All rights reserved.

Copyright © 2017. American Immigration Lawyers Association. All rights reserved.

Copyright © 2017. American Immigration Lawyers Association. All rights reserved.

Copyright © 2017. American Immigration Lawyers Association. All rights reserved.

Copyright © 2017. American Immigration Lawyers Association. All rights reserved.

Copyright © 2017. American Immigration Lawyers Association. All rights reserved.

Copyright © 2017. American Immigration Lawyers Association. All rights reserved.

Copyright © 2017. American Immigration Lawyers Association. All rights reserved.

Copyright © 2017. American Immigration Lawyers Association. All rights reserved.

Copyright © 2017. American Immigration Lawyers Association. All rights reserved.

Copyright © 2017. American Immigration Lawyers Association. All rights reserved.

Copyright © 2017. American Immigration Lawyers Association. All rights reserved.

ABOUT THE AUTHORS

Daryl Buffenstein is a past president of the American Immigration Lawyers Association (AILA), and also served a four-year term as AILA's general counsel. He has been a trusted immigration advisor to business for over 35 years. He has testified on numerous occasions before Congress on business immigration issues and has written key business provisions in most major pieces of immigration legislation over the past 25 years. As AILA president, Mr. Buffenstein led a successful national campaign to defend legal immigration. He was the recipient of AILA's Founders Award, which honors the person or entity having the most significant impact on immigration in the preceding year. He was one of the original founders of the Business Immigration Coalition, a predecessor of Compete America, the alliance of major national business organizations dedicated to business immigration reform. Mr. Buffenstein repeatedly has been named one of the country's top immigration lawyers in the Human Resource Executive/ Lawdragon listing of the Most Powerful Employment Lawyers in America, and in numerous other listings such as Best Lawyers in America, Who's Who in American Law, and the International Who's Who in Business Law. Mr. Buffenstein is a partner in the Atlanta office of Fragomen, Del Rey, Bernsen & Loewy, LLP.

Bo Cooper had a prominent career in government before private practice, serving as general counsel of the Immigration and Naturalization Service during two administrations. He was twice the recipient of the Commissioner's Exceptional Service Award, the agency's most prestigious award. On behalf of the United States, Mr. Cooper was involved in negotiating immigration-related agreements with other governments and was frequently a U.S. delegate to international organizations. After leaving government, he headed Paul Hastings' Washington, D.C., immigration practice and now manages the Government Strategies and Compliance Group at Fragomen, Del Rey, Bernsen & Loewy, LLP in the Firm's Washington, D.C., office. Mr. Cooper provides strategic immigration advice and representation to a wide variety of businesses and organizations as well as immigration regulatory and legislative assistance. He is also an expert in compliance, government investigations, and complex asylum and other individual matters. He has testified frequently before Congress, has served as amicus on immigrant matters before the U.S. Supreme Court, and has made many television, radio, and print media appearances. He has taught immigration law at the University of Michigan Law School, the Georgetown

Copyright © 2017. American Immigration Lawyers Association. All rights reserved.

University Law Center, and the Washington College of Law at American University. Mr. Cooper received his Juris Doctorate from Tulane University Law School and clerked for the Chief Justice of the High Court of American Samoa. He also has been recognized repeatedly as one of the nation's top immigration counsel, in the Human Resource Executive/Lawdragon listing of the Most Powerful Employment Lawyers in America, and in other national and global listings.

Kevin Miner is a Partner in the Atlanta office of Fragomen, Del Rey, Bernsen & Loewy, LLP. His practice includes working with clients to develop effective strategies for business immigration, including all aspects of nonimmigrant visas for high-skilled workers, the PERM labor certification process, immigrant petitions, consular processing, and adjustment of status. He also has extensive experience in immigration compliance matters, and has represented Fortune 500 companies in U.S. Department of Labor (DOL) Labor Condition Application compliance audits. Mr. Miner serves as an Elected Director on the Board of Governors of AILA, where he participates in governance of the association and is actively involved with shaping the Association's approach toward high-skilled immigration reform. He has been part of the AILA Liaison Committee with the Department of Labor since 2012, and served as Chair of the committee from 2015 to 2017. Mr. Miner has been listed among the Top 40 Up and Coming Employment Lawyers in 2016 and 2017 by Human Resource Executive/LawDragon, and has been listed in Who's Who Legal and Best Lawyers in America. Mr. Miner holds a JD from The College of William & Mary, Marshall-Wythe School of Law, where he served as Managing Editor of the Administrative Law Review.

Sarah K. Peterson (author of the National Interest Waivers section) is the founder of SPS Immigration PLLC based in Minneapolis, MN. Her employment-based practice focuses on physicians, academia, start-ups, and high-tech companies. Sarah actively participates in the American Immigration Lawyers Association ("AILA") on both a local and the national level. She has served as an Elected Director on the AILA Board of Governors since 2012. She also serves as Vice Chair of AILA's DOL liaison committee and on the Healthcare Professionals/Physicians Committee. Sarah has previously served on AILA Liaison committees with the California and Nebraska USCIS Service Centers and Chaired the Minnesota/Dakotas Chapter of AILA. Sarah has served on the Immigrant Law Center of Minnesota's (ILCM) Public Policy Committee since 2013. Sarah was recognized in 2016 and 2017 as one of 40 Up and Comers in Employment Law by HRE/Law Dragon, is listed in

Copyright © 2017. American Immigration Lawyers Association. All rights reserved.

the International Who's Who of Corporate Immigration Lawyers since 2014, and was selected as one of Minnesota's Lawyer's Up and Coming Attorneys for 2010. She frequently speaks with the press and travels internationally to speak on employment-based immigration. Sarah is scheduled to teach an advanced Immigration Law class at the University of Minnesota Law School in 2018. Sarah holds a joint law degree and master in public policy from the University of Minnesota Law School and the Hubert H. Humphrey Institute of Public Affairs.

Crystal Williams started in the field of immigration law in the early 1980s as an editor and manager of law publications for two private publishers. She then became the first full-time employee of what was then the American Immigration Law Foundation (AILF), and is now the American Immigration Council (the Council), serving as Director of the Legalization Assistance/Appeals Project. She spent the next decade practicing immigration law with Paul, Hastings, Janofsky and Walker in Atlanta during which time she served on numerous AILA committees. Ms. Williams subsequently joined the staff of AILA as Director of Liaison & Information. She served a brief period with the Policy & Planning office of the then-U.S. Immigration and Naturalization Service, before returning to AILA to later serve as Deputy Director for Programs and, eventually, Executive Director. In many of these capacities, she worked with Federal agencies, Congress, and the media to advocate for the need for fair and just immigration laws and policies. She received her JD from Georgetown University Law Center and a BS from State University of New York at Oneonta. Having retired from AILA in 2015, she has moved to North Carolina and has been splitting her time between traveling the world and working on this book. Ms. Williams is the 2017 recipient of the Susan D. Quarles AILA Service Excellence Award.

Copyright © 2017. American Immigration Lawyers Association. All rights reserved.

PREFACE

While this is titled as—and it is—a book addressing "business" immigration law and practice, that term does not do full justice to the process that this book is about. One clear thing we have learned during our time in this field is that "business" immigration law and practice is really about the process by which our country's employers can draw ideas and expertise and drive and intellect from the world's talent pool. This process is far from perfect, and it can be immensely complicated, unpredictable, and difficult to navigate; that's the reason we have produced this book in the first place. But it is a process, we are convinced, that has contributed to the ability of employers in this country to develop new ideas, find better ways to do things, and create jobs. And it is a process that we have found it a privilege to be involved in.

We hope very strongly that this book will be helpful to others involved in the business immigration process. For in-house counsel and human resources professionals and private practitioners, we have tried to create a resource that is useful on different levels: from beginning-level introduction to the issues, to nuts-and-bolts checklists and practice pointers, to in-depth discussion of complex legal and practice issues, to advanced strategic planning and advice.

We also hope that this book will be valuable to those in government service who are involved in the business immigration process. From our combined experience both within and outside of government, we know that grappling with business immigration issues can be just as daunting for government officials as for those in the private sector. We have therefore tried to ensure that this book could be a helpful resource to the lawyers, adjudicators, judges, clerks, and others in public service whose responsibilities require them to deal with business immigration.

We have done our best, consistent with the production schedule, to ensure that the book has incorporated precedent cases, regulations, and guidance through May 1, 2017. As we go to press, the regulation on entrepreneur parole has been finalized, but will not come into effect for another couple of months. Because there is not yet any practice experience with the rule, it is covered instead in an appendix summarizing the regulation.

Finally, even a specialty field like business immigration is too broad to cover every related topic, and some of those have fallen outside the scope of these volumes. Some highly specialized topics, such as the EB-5 program for immigrant investors, physicians (other than National Interest Waivers), Schedule A health care workers, and the crucial considerations surrounding

Copyright © 2017. American Immigration Lawyers Association. All rights reserved.

employment verification, worksite enforcement, and compliance, are addressed in-depth by other excellent AILA publications already in existence.

Daryl Buffenstein
Bo Cooper
Kevin Miner
Crystal Williams
May 2017

ACKNOWLEDGMENTS

Although this book bears our names, it is the result of the hard work, support, encouragement, and advice of many, including those who wrote pieces of the book but whose names do not appear on the cover. Sarah Peterson did a superb analysis of the legal developments on the National Interest Waiver front, and contributed the sections in Volume Two, Chapter Three on both regular and physician NIWs. And the first edition of this book would never have come into existence without Eunice Kim. Her research, drafting, and analysis were indispensable to the core book that has been updated in this edition.

One of the best benefits of spending our careers in immigration is the extraordinary level of generosity and common purpose among so many in this field. This generosity of time and expertise played a huge role in the production of this book. We have been lucky enough to have the chapters reviewed and critiqued by some of the best legal minds in the profession. We are very, very thankful to the following experts, whose time and insights helped to make this book better than we could have made it on our own: Dan Berger, Dagmar Butte, Robert Cohen, Alexander Dgebuadze, Amy Erlbacher-Anderson, Vic Goel, David Grunblatt, Kenneth Harder, Loan Huynh, Jeff Joseph, Jared Leung, Tien-Li Loke-Walsh, Jeanne Malitz, Roger McCrummen, Jennifer Minear, Reginald Pacis, Anthony Weigel, and Palma Yanni.

Finally, we are also deeply indebted to Lisa Waters, Sarah Redzic, Danielle Polen, Mary Johnson, and the professional staff of AILA who spent countless hours and endless patience reviewing, designing, promoting, and providing support for this book.

Our warmest thanks to you all.

About AILA

The American Immigration Lawyers Association (AILA) is a national bar association of more than 15,000 attorneys who practice immigration law and/or work as teaching professionals. AILA member attorneys represent tens of thousands of U.S. families who have applied for permanent residence for their spouses, children, and other close relatives for lawful entry and residence in the United States. AILA members also represent thousands of U.S. businesses and industries that sponsor highly skilled foreign workers seeking to enter the United States on a temporary or permanent basis. In addition, AILA members represent foreign students, entertainers, athletes, and asylum-seekers, often on a pro bono basis. Founded in 1946, AILA is a nonpartisan, not-for-profit organization that provides its members with continuing legal education, publications, information, professional services, and expertise through its 39 chapters and over 50 national committees. AILA is an affiliated organization of the American Bar Association and is represented in the ABA House of Delegates.

American Immigration Lawyers Association
www.aila.org

CHAPTER ONE

INTRODUCTION

I. Purpose and Organization

This book seeks to provide a strong foundation in the practice of business immigration law through two approaches: citation of most available guidance, including statutes, regulations, case law, U.S. Citizenship and Immigration Services (USCIS) and other agency guidance and correspondence, and minutes of liaison meetings between government agencies and stakeholders, as well as explanations and detailed discussion of strategies from a nuts-and-bolts practical perspective. It is hoped that these two approaches will support the practitioner in the following ways:

- To guide reference to the cited materials, so the practitioner may turn readily to original sources where useful;

- To provide detailed explanations and summaries of requirements and interpretations;

- To discuss legislative history and shifts in agency policy and interpretation;

- To flag common pitfalls and explore strategies to avoid them;

- To assist the practitioner in helping the client to form appropriate expectations that can be incorporated into business planning; and

- To guide the practitioner in how to complete the necessary forms.

We hope with this book to answer a need within the business immigration community, for advanced and newer practitioners alike, to provide a "one-stop shop" for practical advice, legal citations, legislative and adjudicative history, detailed guidance on recent developments, and strategic approaches to achieving the best possible results for clients and creating carefully informed expectations. We hope that you find this book to be helpful to you in your practice.

The book addresses both nonimmigrant and immigrant concepts, organized by topic, with relevant cross-references, designed both to present the information with maximum efficiency and to identify the innumerable ways in which choices made at one stage of the immigration process can have potentially decisive ramifications on others. For example, sponsoring a nonimmigrant for permanent residence may have a negative impact on a petitioner's ability to extend the beneficiary's nonimmigrant status in certain circumstances. These topics are therefore discussed in the chapters on nonimmigrant status and cross-referenced in the chapters on labor certification, immigrant visa petitions, and consular processing and adjustment of status.

II. Guide to Using the Book

This book is designed to help the business immigration lawyer help clients to make the best choices, and then to execute those choices with maximum success in a challenging regulatory and adjudicatory environment. Where the practitioner, employer, and employee have agreed upon a choice of nonimmigrant status or path to

1

Copyright © 2017. American Immigration Lawyers Association. All rights reserved.

permanent residence, then the appropriate chapters will help to equip the practitioner with the tools needed to carry out that choice effectively. The chapters are built on the basics but go on to provide more advanced treatment, strategic considerations, practical tips, and references.

Our aim, though, is to also help the practitioner help the client through those choices in the first place. What classification fits? What classification fits *best*? What's on the horizon for the employer and/or the employee, and what choices now will best facilitate that future planning? This book tries to support that structured planning process throughout, but the paragraphs that follow will help to introduce some of those concepts and choices, and provide an early overview of what goes into successful business immigration planning.

When assessing a client's need initially to employ and obtain U.S. employment authorization on behalf of a specific foreign national, there are often several non-mutually exclusive approaches possible, each often with differing advantages and limitations. The inquiry generally begins with the nature of the proposed job duties, as well as the foreign national's educational background and citizenship(s). Most of the nonimmigrant statuses focus on the type of job to be performed, and so discussion with the client should typically begin here.

For example, both the H-1B and TN classifications are generally for professional jobs, so a petition for H-1B or TN status would be unsuccessful if the job does not require an individual with at least a baccalaureate degree.[1] It is important to draw a distinction between the job requirements and the foreign national's qualifications. For example, a foreign national may qualify for an H-1B professional position even if he or she has not earned a bachelor's degree, if he or she possesses three years of progressive experience in a professional position for every lacking year of post-secondary education.[2] But the employer's job requirements, and not the foreign national's qualifications, should be the first and foremost consideration.[3] As another example, if the employer states that the purpose of employment is to train the foreign national, then the J-1 and H-3 categories, which are specifically for training and not employment, could be the more appropriate classifications.

After assessing the nature of the petitioner's need for the beneficiary's services, the practitioner should determine the best nonimmigrant category for the position, through consideration of the foreign national's qualifications and/or citizenship. For example, a foreign national may perform a professional job in H-1B, H-1B1, TN, or E-3 status. The job requirements for these categories are generally similar, but the differences can be determinative. For example, a foreign national may qualify for TN

---

[1] As discussed in Volume 1: Chapter Fourteen, "TN Visas and Status," one exception to this rule is for Scientific Technicians and Technologists.
[2] For further discussion of this exception, see Volume 1: Chapter Seven, "H-1B Visas and Status."
[3] For further discussion of this issue, see Volume 2: Chapter Three, "The Immigrant Visa Petition."

Copyright © 2017. American Immigration Lawyers Association. All rights reserved.

status through foreign licensure, whereas H-1B status generally requires licensure from a U.S. state. In addition, H-1B1 status is available only to citizens of Chile and Singapore, TN status is available only to Mexican and Canadian citizens, and E-3 status is available only to Australian citizens. The foreign national may lack a bachelor's degree entirely, sparking the need to explore other options. Here, the O classification may be an appropriate fit, if the petitioner requires an individual with extraordinary ability and the foreign national can demonstrate the necessary record of experience and success in the industry.

The chapters ahead on nonimmigrant status will provide the resources to help identify and make these kinds of choices, through quick references such as checklists of relevant questions and necessary documents, and through more advanced discussion and analysis.

The practitioner must also help the client and/or foreign national understand the relative advantages and disadvantages of each of the potentially available classifications. A foreign national holding H-1B status can in certain circumstances be eligible for certain extensions of nonimmigrant status well beyond what would otherwise be the limit, until permanent residence is obtained. With green card backlogs stretching for many years in some categories, and especially pronounced for some nationalities, this can be a crucial option. Yet it is not available outside the H-1B classification. In periods of high demand, quotas can also be a decisive issue. There is no quota on TN visas (or on other, less closely analogous but possibly available, classifications such as L), unlike H-1B, H-1B1, and E-3 visas, and which have annual caps. Another consideration is the professional and economic needs of family members. The accompanying spouse may desire U.S. employment authorization, which is available to spouses of E or L nonimmigrants, but not to those of Hs or TNs, for example.

Discussion of benefits and drawbacks should also include any long-term strategy for employment and toward permanent residence, so the practitioner should explore the employer's intended period of employment. For example, if the H-1B quota has been exhausted, then it may make the most sense to request TN status for an initial period and then seek a change of status to H-1B later, when H-1B visa numbers become available again. In the context of permanent residence, one nonimmigrant classification may be more favorable than another from the standpoint of setting up the petition for immigrant classification. A foreign national who qualifies as either an L-1A or an H-1B nonimmigrant might well benefit more from choosing the L-1A classification, since there is a correlative immigrant classification for multinational managers and executives that can be much more easily accessible. As another example, it may be preferable to file an O-1 petition instead of an H-1B petition because the extraordinary ability immigrant classification has many of the same requirements as those for O nonimmigrant status.

These are the kinds of issues and strategies that make up the day of the business immigration lawyer. The variations are as wide as the number of employers and employees who need the lawyer's advice. The chapters ahead are designed to help the

Copyright © 2017. American Immigration Lawyers Association. All rights reserved.

business immigration lawyer identify the often highly complex considerations, crystallize choices and advise the client, and execute the choices successfully.

One of the unique things about immigration law—and one reason why we wrote this book—is that the sources of law are often so scattered and disorganized, and are often "soft" law anyway. It is unlike so many other fields of law, where there is a clear path to the rules that order the behavior of the regulated party: a statute from Congress, more detailed development through thorough regulations from an executive agency, interpretations of those regulations through an orderly set of agency interpretive rulings, and then development through judicial decisions after court challenges. Instead, with immigration, the code has been amended haphazardly and its pieces don't fit well together. The regulations are often incomplete, out of date, or never written. For example, major statutory revisions to Immigration and Nationality Act §212 in 1996 were not ever regulated, leaving complex concepts such as inadmissibility because of unlawful presence—and, yes, this issue does arise in business immigration—undefined by agency regulation.

As a result, the operative guidance is often found in much less formal instruments, such as agency policy memos, agency officer manuals, letters from individual government officials to individual companies or lawyers that get shared around, notes from liaison minutes, and the like. And often they don't fit together and may even directly conflict. These situations can give rise to some very tricky advisory choices. The source of the authority on which the business immigration lawyer is basing a view can therefore be extremely important, and we have tried to refer to the widest possible range of resources throughout this book.

Copyright © 2017. American Immigration Lawyers Association. All rights reserved.

CHAPTER TWO

BASIC NONIMMIGRANT CONCEPTS

This chapter will address several important issues relating to nonimmigrant visas and status as well as the processes of filing a petition, making a visa application, and applying for admission to the United States. Specific issues relating to particular nonimmigrant classifications are discussed in the individual chapters.

I. Key Considerations

The following considerations often form the foundation for any nonimmigrant petition or visa application, so the practitioner should be familiar with these most basic requirements of immigration law.

A. *Employment in the United States vs. Employment Abroad*

The opening point of many business immigration discussions is whether U.S. employment authorization is required. The client and/or foreign national may believe that no separate U.S. employment authorization is necessary because there is no similar requirement in the foreign national's home country. The practitioner should advise on the need to file an employment-based nonimmigrant petition, as there are negative consequences to the foreign national if he or she engages in unauthorized employment,[1] as discussed below, and to the employer under Immigration and Nationality Act (INA) §274A.

U.S. immigration law requires that an individual possess proper U.S. employment authorization in order to "work" in the United States,[2] and the factors to be analyzed for a U.S. employment relationship often differ from those considered by the immigration and/or labor laws of other countries.[3] Although the terms "work" and "employment" are not helpfully defined by statute or regulation, they may be understood as involving labor or service in return for compensation. The practitioner may find the following guidance helpful:

> "The term employment means any service or labor performed by an employee for an employer within the United States."[4]

> "The term employment means any service or labor performed by an employee for an employer within the United States, including service or

---

[1] *See, e.g., Matter of Dukpa,* 18 I&N Dec. 282 (D.D. 1981).

[2] Immigration and Nationality Act (INA) §274A(b)(1)(B)–(D). *See also generally* INA §274A (titled "Unlawful Employment of Aliens").

[3] *See, e.g.,* Citizenship and Immigration Canada, "Business visitors: who can apply," (updated Aug. 3, 2016), http://www.cic.gc.ca/english/visit/business-who.asp (discussing requirements of a visit of fewer than six months and a foreign source of income or profits).

[4] 8 Code of Federal Regulations (CFR) §274a.1(h).

Copyright © 2017. American Immigration Lawyers Association. All rights reserved.

labor performed on a vessel or aircraft that has arrived in the United States and has been inspected, or otherwise included within the provisions of the Anti-Reflagging Act codified at 46 U.S.C. 8704, but not including duties performed by nonimmigrant crewmen defined in sections 101(a)(10) and (a)(15)(D) of the Act. However, employment does not include casual employment by individuals who provide domestic service in a private home that is sporadic, irregular or intermittent."[5]

"In determining whether an alien is engaging in activities consistent with the terms or his or her nonimmigrant status, the [legacy] INS [Immigration and Naturalization Service] has taken a broad-based functional view of what constitutes 'employment,' rather than one based merely on the existence of remuneration.... Although the term 'employment' is not defined in the status the [legacy] INS has defined this term, for purposes of section 274A of the Act, to mean any service or labor performed in the United States by an individual, other than an independent contractor, *for wages or other remuneration*."[6]

"The word 'employment' is a common one, generally used with relation to the most common pursuits, and therefore ought to be received as understood in common parlance. The word 'employment' is also defined as meaning the act of being employed for one's self. It should be self-evident... that any and all types of employment taken without proper authority constitute unauthorized employment."[7]

"Employment as defined by *Webster's New World Dictionary of the American Language*, Second College Edition, means: the thing at which one is employed; work; occupation; profession; job."[8]

Therefore, the first issue to analyze may be whether the foreign national's activities are those which he would ordinarily perform in his or her home country as an occupation, profession, or job, whether for an employer or for himself or herself. For example, if a foreign national has held numerous positions abroad as a software engineer and will perform software engineering duties in the United States, then he or she should obtain U.S. employment authorization, even if he or she will be self-employed and provide the services pursuant to a contract signed by the U.S. client and his or her own foreign company. For this analysis, the length of the foreign

---

[5] 8 CFR §274a.1(h).

[6] Legacy Immigration and Naturalization Service (INS), P. Virtue, "Classification of Visiting University Lecturers" (Aug. 20, 1993), 1 INS and DOJ Legal Opinions §93-61 (citing 8 CFR §274a.1(f) through (h)) (emphasis in original).

[7] *Matter of Tong,* 16 I&N Dec. 593 (BIA 1978) (internal citation omitted).

[8] *Matter of Dukpa,* 18 I&N Dec. 282 (BIA rejected the employer's attempt to term the remuneration "an offering and not a salary").

Copyright © 2017. American Immigration Lawyers Association. All rights reserved.

national's visit to the United States is not as important as the type of anticipated activities, as U.S. employment authorization may be required even if the foreign national will not be based in the United States for a long period of time.[9] In essence, the need for U.S. employment authorization is driven by the nature of the activities to be performed in the United States, even if the source of income is foreign, because the "question of where the beneficiary's paycheck may originate is not a relevant factor in determining the beneficiary's eligibility for the nonimmigrant classification sought in the petition."[10]

Generally, the focus on the remuneration is not on whether it is regular,[11] or specifically termed a salary,[12] but on whether it is provided in exchange for services rendered.[13] The Board of Immigration Appeals (BIA) rejected a foreign national's claim of serving as an unpaid volunteer when he received room and board, "walking around" money, and "full support" from a U.S. entity for medical and transportation expenses:

"He clearly received compensation in return for his efforts on behalf of the Church [employer]. By his own account, he is provided the wherewithal to cover both necessary and nonessential expenses, such an entertainment and recreation…. The [foreign national's] relationship with the Church [employer] in effect guarantees him a standard of living similar to that of many moderate-income wage earners. The fact that he receives no fixed salary or remuneration in an amount proportional to his success as a fund-raiser is, in our view, immaterial."[14]

---

[9] 9 Foreign Affairs Manual (FAM) 401.1-3(C) (noting how a foreign national may seek a B-2 visa "for the purpose of earning money in the United States during the slack season at home and then returning home to resume regular employment" would not be classifiable as a nonimmigrant due to the intent to work in the United States, despite the short period of intended stay).

[10] *Matter of Pozzoli*, 14 I&N Dec. 569 (Reg'l Comm'r 1974) (noting that the beneficiary "will 'render his services' in the United States even if the salary is paid from abroad"). The case also discusses the employment relationship in the context of the L-1 nonimmigrant visa classification, noting that despite the beneficiary's being paid by the Italian company, he was found to be an employee of the U.S. entity based on common law principles governing the master-servant relationship and therefore the employee was eligible for L-1 classification.

[11] *Matter of Hall*, 18 I&N Dec. 203 (BIA 1982).

[12] *Matter of Dukpa*, 18 I&N Dec. 282 (D.D. 1981) (BIA rejected the employer's attempt to term the remuneration "an offering and not a salary").

[13] *Matter of Hall*, 18 I&N Dec. 203 (noting that the foreign national received room and board, "'walking around' money," and "full support" from a U.S. entity for medical and transportation expenses "in return for" fundraising efforts).

[14] *Id.* For a further discussion of the difference between remuneration and incidental expenses, including analysis of standard of living and cost of living expenses, see Volume 1: Chapter Three, "Visitors: B Visas and Status and the Visa Waiver Program" (discussing in detail legacy INS, P. Virtue, "Classification of Visiting University Lecturers" (Aug. 20, 1993), 1 INS and DOJ Legal Opinions §93-61).

Copyright © 2017. American Immigration Lawyers Association. All rights reserved.

In fact, an individual may be deemed an employee even if he or she does not receive a salary or other remuneration,[15] or receives non-monetary compensation.[16] The one exception may be if the foreign national visits the United States to explore investing in the United States.[17] However, the activities of an investor should be generally permissible under the U.S. immigration laws, as they should mainly entail attending business meetings,[18] as discussed in Volume 1: Chapter Three, "Visitors: B Visas and Status and the Visa Waiver Program." As a practical matter, the practitioner should be careful in advising the client against filing an E change of status petition with U.S. Citizenship and Immigration Services (USCIS), as discussed in Volume 1: Chapter Four, "E-1 and E-2 Visas and Status," because change of status is generally not permitted if a foreign national has engaged in unauthorized employment and experience has shown that ambiguity is often resolved against the petition.

For example, for a manager employed by a French company who travels for one week every month to the U.S. subsidiary to discuss marketing efforts for a new product, the practitioner should discuss with the client obtaining L-1A status. Even though such a manager's activities would not be considered "skilled or unskilled labor" and would therefore not be prohibited by the statute on B business visitors,[19] because his or her duties would primarily entail attending business meetings, as a practical matter, the foreign national may face difficulty at the port of entry following multiple trips to the United States:

"The fine line between a temporary visitor for business and an alien seeking local labor or employment is often a difficult one to draw…. Should it be determined … that the alien is receiving 'remuneration,' however, the B-1 business visitor will be in violation of his or her nonimmigrant status and will be engaged in unauthorized employment for purposes of section 274A of the Act."[20]

During the discussion, the practitioner will most likely have to address how the foreign source of income does not automatically preclude L-1 status,[21] as discussed

---

[15] *Matter of Tessel, Inc.*, 17 I&N Dec. 631 (Acting Assoc. Comm'r 1981) (holding that although the foreign national did not "receive a salary as chairman he is nonetheless an employee of the company").

[16] *Matter of Hall*, 18 I&N Dec. 203 (particular attention to room and board).

[17] *Matter of Lett*, 17 I&N Dec. 312 (BIA 1980); 9 FAM 41.31 N9.7.

[18] 9 FAM 402.2-5(C)(7).

[19] INA §101(a)(15)(B).

[20] Legacy INS, P. Virtue, "Classification of Visiting University Lecturers" (Aug. 20, 1993), 1 INS and DOJ Legal Opinions §93-61 (citing legacy INS Operations Instruction (OI) 214.2(b)). For a discussion of the impact of such unauthorized employment on a change of status or extension application, see below in this chapter. For a discussion of permissible activities while in B-1 status, see Volume 1: Chapter Three, "Visitors: B Visas and Status and the Visa Waiver Program."

[21] *Matter of Pozzoli*, 14 I&N Dec. 569 (Reg'l Comm'r 1974).

Copyright © 2017. American Immigration Lawyers Association. All rights reserved.

above, as well as how the inquiry should focus on the activities to be performed in the Unites States and the potential negative consequences.

B. Appropriate Intent

A foreign national should have the appropriate intent regarding his or her visit and/or stay in the United States. Although this is colloquially called "nonimmigrant intent," that term is slightly misleading, because the standard is actually whether the foreign national presents sufficient proof to establish that he or she is entitled to the requested nonimmigrant classification.[22] The immigration statutes discuss what is in essence proving a lack: "The term 'immigrant' means every alien except an alien who is within one of the following classes of nonimmigrant aliens," followed by the statutes listing the nonimmigrant classifications.[23] The relevant statute states:

"Every alien (other than a nonimmigrant described in subparagraph (L) or (V) of section 101(a)(15), and other than a nonimmigrant described in any provision of section 101(a)(15)(H)(i) except subclause (b1) of such section) shall be presumed to be an immigrant until he establishes to the satisfaction of the consular officer, at the time of application for a visa, and the immigration officers, at the time of application for admission, that he is entitled to a nonimmigrant status under section 101(a)(15)."[24]

Similarly, U.S. Department of State (DOS) guidance states:

"With limited exceptions, all visa applicants are presumed to be immigrants (and thus not eligible for a nonimmigrant visa (NIV)) unless and until they satisfy [the consular officer] that they qualify for one of the NIV categories defined in INA Section 101(a)(15). When adjudicating NIV applications, [the officer] must be careful to recognize that the standards for qualifying for an NIV are found in the relevant subsections of 101(a)(15) and corresponding regulations and FAM guidance, not in 214(b) itself."[25]

Specific requirements of nonimmigrant visa classifications are discussed in the individual chapters. A foreign national in H-1B or L-1 status is permitted to have dual intent,[26] *i.e.,* to remain in the United States as a nonimmigrant while actively pursuing permanent residence, and experience has shown that the same standard is typically applied to H-4 and L-2 dependents of H-1B and L-1 nonimmigrants. In general, applicants for B, F, H-2, H-3, J, O-2, P, and Q visas must have a foreign residence and have no intention of abandoning that residence.[27] The foreign residence should be

---

[22] *See* INA §214(b) and 9 FAM 401.1-3(E).

[23] INA §101(a)(15).

[24] INA §214(b).

[25] 9 FAM 403.1-2.

[26] INA §214(h).

[27] 9 FAM 401.1-3(F)(1) and (2).

Copyright © 2017. American Immigration Lawyers Association. All rights reserved.

a "place of general abode … [which] means his principal, actual dwelling place in fact, without regard to intent,"[28] but it does not need to be independently maintained by the visa applicant.[29] For example, experience has shown that a youthful visa applicant may present evidence regarding the foreign residence of his or her parents. In addition, the foreign residence "need not be the alien's former residence," so the foreign national may present evidence of the intent to establish a residence in a third country "after a temporary visit in the United States."[30]

Generally, a broad "desire to remain in this country permanently in accordance with the law, should the opportunity to do so present itself, is not necessarily inconsistent with nonimmigrant status."[31] But stating a desire to immigrate to the United States or to ultimately seek citizenship may prove fatal to a nonimmigrant petition or visa application.[32] Similarly, a federal court accepted a BIA finding of "strong evidence" and upheld denial of the applications to adjust status filed on behalf of foreign nationals who had been admitted as visitors:

> "[They] entered the United States with a 'preconceived' intent to remain permanently…. For in this case, there are a number of factors which, taken together, indicate that the [foreign nationals] had an intention, at the time that they came into the United States, of remaining indefinitely. For example, they had sold their home in Argentina before entering the United States…. Further, the fact that the [foreign nationals] secured employment in this country, and acquired household goods here through the use of credit, constitutes evidence in support of the Board's finding that they had an intention to remain permanently when they entered the United States.[33]

As stated by the BIA: "It is true that a rapid sequence of events by an alien may suggest a lack of bona fide intent…. Yet what constitutes a 'rapid' sequence of events depends on the circumstances of each case."[34] Therefore, an application to adjust status was denied "as a matter of discretion based on [the foreign national's] preconceived intent to remain in the United States," as evidenced by a recommendation letter written before the foreign national's U.S. admission, the foreign national's application for "ministerial recognition" to allow him to conduct

---

[28] INA §101(a)(33); 9 FAM 401.1(F)(2).

[29] 9 FAM 401.1(F)(2).

[30] Id.

[31] Matter of Hosseinpour, 15 I&N Dec. 191 (BIA 1975).

[32] Lauvik v. INS, 910 F.2d 658 (9th Cir. 1990) (denial of E extension by legacy INS, inter alia, based on such a statement by the foreign national). See also Ameeriar v. INS, 438 F.2d 1028 (3d Cir. 1971), reh'g denied (stating that "[a]djustment of status is therefore a matter of administrative grace, not mere statutory eligibility" in upholding denial of adjustment of status, because, inter alia, the foreign national secured employment within five days of his arrival in the United States).

[33] Von Pervieux v. INS, 572 F.2d 114 (3d Cir. 1978).

[34] Matter of Patel, 19 I&N Dec. 774 (BIA 1988).

Copyright © 2017. American Immigration Lawyers Association. All rights reserved.

religious services 11 days after his arrival, and an employment letter confirming his appointment to pastor dated the day before he filed a B-2 extension application, in which he stated that "his reasons for requesting an extension were 'to continue in visitor status, to mingle with friends and church members from Tonga living here.'"[35] Another application to adjust status was denied when it was filed 16 days after the foreign national's admission.[36]

DOS generally applies what is called the "30/60 day rule" to assess, during a subsequent visa application, whether a foreign national misrepresented his or her intention regarding the U.S. stay when initially applying for a visa or for U.S. admission.[37] Under this rule, DOS should analyze whether a foreign national stated a proper intent during the application for a visa or for U.S. admission but then performed acts that contradicted the stated intent, such as:

- "Actively seeking unauthorized employment and, subsequently, becom[ing] engaged in such employment;

- "Enrolling in a program of academic study without the benefit of the appropriate change of status;

- "Marrying and taking up permanent residence; or

- "Undertaking any other activity for which a change of status or an adjustment of status would be required, without the benefit of such a change or adjustment."[38]

Consular officers "may presume that the applicant misrepresented his or her intention in seeking [the initial] visa or entry" if the act occurred within 30 days of the foreign national's U.S. admission.[39] If the act occurred within 30 to 60 days of the U.S. admission, then "no presumption of misrepresentation arises," but the consular officer may, if he or she has "reasonable belief" of a misrepresentation, request "countervailing evidence."[40] If the act occurred at least 60 days after the U.S. admission, then "no presumption of misrepresentation arises," but if a consular officer reasonably believes that intent might have been misrepresented, he or she can request countervailing evidence.[41] If the violation of status occurred more than 60 days after admission, "the Department [of State] does not consider such conduct alone to constitute a basis for an INA 212(a)(6)(C)(i) inadmissibility."[42] Consular

---

[35] *Matter of Lasike*, 17 I&N Dec. 445 (BIA 1980).

[36] *Matter of Ro*, 16 I&N Dec. 93 (BIA 1977).

[37] 9 FAM 302.9-4(B)(3).

[38] 9 FAM 302.9-4(B)(3)(g)(2).

[39] 9 FAM 302.9-4(B)(3)(g)(3).

[40] 9 FAM 302.9-4(B)(3)(g)(4).

[41] 9 FAM 302.9-4(B)(3).

[42] 9 FAM 302.9-4(B)(3)(g)(5).

Copyright © 2017. American Immigration Lawyers Association. All rights reserved.

officers are instructed to seek an advisory opinion from headquarters if they are going to find inadmissibility for conduct inconsistent with stated intent.[43]

Although the rule is technically for DOS, USCIS has been known to apply it as well, especially in family-based cases for foreign nationals who initially entered in B-2 status.[44]

The practitioner is, however, advised against applying the rule mechanically, because the inquiry focuses on the foreign national's intent and on whether a misrepresentation was made during the course of a visa application; so an individual will not necessarily be "in the clear" after the passage of 60, or even 90, days if he or she did not have the proper intent in the first place.

C. Permanent Residence as Long-Term Employment Authorization

As is discussed in detail in the individual chapters, several key nonimmigrant classifications have maximum time limitations. For example, with limited exceptions, a foreign national may hold L-1B status for only five years,[45] so one way to add value to the client and to plan for additional casework is to inform the client of an upcoming deadline and discuss available strategies for sponsoring the foreign national for permanent residence. The practitioner is strongly advised to begin these discussions well in advance, ideally three years before the deadline, as experience has shown that even if the client is ready to undertake sponsorship for permanent residence, the case may not move for some time. The reason to introduce the topic early is to minimize the likelihood of a break in U.S. employment authorization. In our example, if the client is informed of the deadline only one year in advance, then there may be insufficient time to file both a multinational manager immigrant visa petition and a labor certification application, if both become necessary, as discussed in Volume 1: Chapter Eleven, "L-1 Visas and Status." The individual chapters also discuss potential pitfalls with employment-based sponsorship for permanent residence.

II. Obtaining Nonimmigrant Status and Changing Status

A. Petition Filing and Adjudication

Individual chapters discuss the necessary documents for petitions. In order to avoid delays and added expense, it is important to select the correct nonimmigrant visa category from the outset, as USCIS will not allow a later change in the category requested.[46] Instead, a new petition must be submitted and the process started over.

---

[43] 9 FAM 302.9-4(B)(3)(g)(3) and (4).

[44] "ISD Liaison Teleconference," (Dec. 19, 2002), AILA Doc. No. 02122741.

[45] 8 CFR §214.2(*l*)(12)(i).

[46] *E.g., Matter of S-D-P-*, ID# 16750 (May 27, 2016) ("There is no statute, regulation, or precedent that permits a petitioner to change the classification of a petition once the Director has issued a decision.")

Copyright © 2017. American Immigration Lawyers Association. All rights reserved.

This section will address issues generally common to petitions and applications filed with USCIS.

1. *Important Issues for Petition Filing*

First and foremost, USCIS subscribes to the receipt rule rather than the mailbox rule.[47] Under certain circumstances, USCIS may announce that it is excusing the fact that a filing was not received on time, usually because either the USCIS office was closed on what should have been a regular business day,[48] or because of natural disasters or terrorism events affecting the petitioner, applicant, or counsel.[49]

A petition will be deemed properly filed only when it complies with USCIS's filing requirements, which include the following:

- Filing by delivery to the appropriate Service Center with jurisdiction;[50]
- Completed petition form(s)[51] and supporting documents;
- Signature(s);[52]
- Complete payment of the nonrefundable filing fee(s);[53]
- Executed Form G-28, Notice of Entry of Appearance as Attorney or Accredited Representative, for the represented petitioner; and
- Executed Form I-907, Request for Premium Processing, if applicable.

The practitioner should confirm that these filing requirements, which are discussed in detail in the following sections, are satisfied, because if USCIS rejects the petition, then the petition "will not retain a filing date."[54] The practitioner is advised ***not*** to rely on the following USCIS guidance:

---

[47] 8 CFR §103.2(a)(7)(i) (stating that "[a]n application or petition received in a USCIS office shall be stamped to show the time and date of actual receipt and … shall be regarded as properly filed when so stamped"); 8 CFR §103.2(a)(6).

[48] U.S. Citizenship and Immigration Service (USCIS), "Important Information on Form I-129 H-1B, H-2A, and H-2B Petitions" (Oct. 18, 2013), AILA Doc. No. 13101803 (government shutdown due to congressional budget gridlock); "Practice Alert: Severe Weather Closes USCIS Service Centers" (Feb. 4, 2011), AILA Doc. No. 11020371 (Service Centers closed for severe winter weather "will make accommodations for delayed deliveries").

[49] "USCIS Reminds Individuals Affected by Hurricane Sandy of Temporary Relief Measures" (Nov. 2, 2012), AILA Doc. No. 12110243 (extensions for those who could not file because of hurricane); "Post-9/11 Service Center Operations Email" (Sept. 18, 2001), AILA Doc. No. 01091831 (legacy INS directives regarding filing flexibility and other issues in wake of 9/11/01 terrorism attacks).

[50] 8 CFR §§103.2(a)(1) and (a)(6).

[51] 8 CFR §103.2(a)(1).

[52] 8 CFR §§103.2(a)(1), (a)(2), and (a)(7)(i).

[53] 8 CFR §§103.2(a)(1) and 103.7.

[54] 8 CFR §103.2(a)(7)(i).

Copyright © 2017. American Immigration Lawyers Association. All rights reserved.

"Although the instructions for each type of application or petition specify where that application or petition is to be submitted, submission to an incorrect office (or incorrect post office box where more than one box is used by a Service Center to sort cases by application type) is not a reason for rejection. Such cases should be receipted and routed to the appropriate office for processing."[55]

In practice, USCIS routinely rejects applications and petitions filed with a Service Center that lacks jurisdiction. For a discussion of how to address erroneous rejections, see below.

a. Delivery

Nonimmigrant petitions are generally filed on Form I-129 at one of USCIS's Service Centers. Which Service Center depends upon what type of petition is being filed and where the beneficiary's place of employment is located.[56] Some types of nonimmigrant petitions are all filed at only one Service Center.[57] For others, if the beneficiary will work at multiple locations, the filing should be at the Service Center with jurisdiction over the petitioner's primary office.[58] The practitioner should check the USCIS website for the correct filing address.[59]

If the beneficiary is outside the United States, no filings are made for dependent family members. They will obtain visas as part of the consular process, discussed later in this chapter. However, if an extension or change of status application is being filed, then a Form I-539 should be included in the I-129 filing package for a dependent spouse and/or children under age 21.[60] If the dependents' application cannot be filed at the same time because, for example, they are not in the United States at the time of filing or have a different expiration date on their I-94s, their I-539s should be filed independently. Those independent filings must be sent to the appropriate USCIS Lockbox instead of to the Service Center address.[61] Extensions of stay are discussed in greater detail later in this chapter.

Experience has shown that the following courier services may be used for all Service Centers:

---

[55] Adjudicator's Field Manual (AFM) 10.1.

[56] USCIS, "Direct Filing Addresses for Form I-129, Petition for a Nonimmigrant Worker" (updated July 1, 2016), https://www.uscis.gov/i-129-addresses.

[57] Id.

[58] Id.; "AILA/VSC Liaison Practice Pointer: I-129 Jurisdiction—The 'Primary Office' Rule" (Mar. 21, 2011), AILA Doc. No. 11032166.

[59] USCIS, "Direct Filing Addresses for Form I-129, Petition for a Nonimmigrant Worker" (updated July 1, 2016), https://www.uscis.gov/i-129-addresses.

[60] 8 CFR §214.1(c)(2); USCIS, "How do I extend my nonimmigrant stay in the United States?" (May 2016), https://www.uscis.gov/sites/default/files/USCIS/Resources/C1en.pdf.

[61] USCIS, "Filing Addresses for Form I-539, Application to Extend/Change Nonimmigrant Status" (updated July 1, 2016), https://www.uscis.gov/i-539-addresses.

Copyright © 2017. American Immigration Lawyers Association. All rights reserved.

- U.S. Postal Service express mail, with return receipt requested;
- U.S. Postal Service certified mail, with return receipt requested;
- UPS;
- Federal Express.[62]

The practitioner should note, however, that use of express or certified mail may result in delay of delivery, because USCIS may pick up mail from the post office boxes irregularly. If the filing deadline is within a few days, then the practitioner may wish to use a courier service with next-day delivery, such as Federal Express (FedEx) or United Parcel Service (UPS).

b. Complete Petition Documents

(1) Forms and Supporting Documents

Original signed forms should be filed,[63] with a duplicate set of original petition documents, "with original signatures on all forms preferred, as would otherwise be done for consular notification," for DOS's Petition Information Management Service (PIMS) procedure.[64] Be sure to use the most current version of each form, as outdated versions may be rejected.[65]

The petition filing should include original supporting documents where possible,[66] although experience has shown that original I-94 cards, passports, diplomas, and transcripts, as well as birth, marriage, and death certificates, need not be submitted.[67] The practitioner should avoid submitting originals of these official documents because "original documents submitted when not required will remain a part of the record,"[68] and will not be returned.[69] Copies of documents are generally acceptable, unless the original is required by regulation or the form's instructions.[70] The petition filing "need only submit those original documents necessary to support the benefit

---

[62] For additional courier services that may be used for the California Service Center (CSC), *see* "List of Bonded Couriers for CSC" (Mar. 29, 2013), AILA Doc. No. 13032942 and "CSC Update: UPS is an Acceptable Courier" (Mar. 27, 2008), AILA Doc. No. 08032533.

[63] 8 CFR §103.2(b)(4).

[64] "PIMS Processing Update," (Mar. 21, 2008), AILA Doc. No. 08032132.

[65] USCIS, "Revised Form I-129 Now Available" (Jan. 9, 2015), https://www.uscis.gov/news/alerts/revised-form-i-129-now-available. Check under the "Edition Date" tab on the USCIS webpage for the form you are using. Select the form from *https://www.uscis.gov/forms*.

[66] 8 CFR §103.2(b)(4) (stating that "documents issued to support an application or petition … must be submitted in the original unless previously filed with USCIS"); AFM 11.1.

[67] 8 CFR §103.2(b)(4) (stating that "[u]nless otherwise required by the applicable regulation or form's instructions, a legible photocopy of any other supporting document may be submitted").

[68] *Id.*; AFM 11.1.

[69] AFM 11.1.

[70] *Id.*

Copyright © 2017. American Immigration Lawyers Association. All rights reserved.

sought."[71] For example, an H-1B petition should include a copy of the foreign national's university diploma and transcripts in order to demonstrate that the foreign national has earned the education required for the position. The specifics of the forms are discussed in the individual chapters.

It is also not necessary to submit originals of USCIS or legacy INS-issued documents "unless required by USCIS,"[72] but the practitioner is nevertheless strongly encouraged to include evidence of lawful immigration status in the petition filing. Certain documents that are necessary to support a petition "(such as labor certifications, Form DS-2019, medical examinations, affidavits, formal consultations, letters of current employment and other statements) must be submitted in the original unless previously filed with USCIS."[73] For a discussion of a request for an original document in a Request for Evidence (RFE), see below.

Documents in a foreign language "shall be accompanied by a full English language translation which the translator has certified as complete and accurate, and by the translator's certification that he or she is competent to translate from the foreign language into English."[74] For example, the following statement may be used: "I, [insert name], certify that I am competent to translate from [insert foreign language] into English and that the foregoing [or aftergoing] is a true, correct, and accurate translation of the attached document." It is also recommended that the translation certificate be notarized if possible. If the underlying foreign language document is an extract, USCIS may accept it, as long as it "contain[s] all the information necessary to make a decision on a case" and as long as an authorized official prepared the extract.[75] Submissions that have been translated using an online translation tool have been criticized as having "limited" probative value.[76] Also, summary translations are not recommended.[77] For a further discussion of a petition and supporting documents, as well as the standard of review used by USCIS, see below.

(2) Eligibility

Generally, the petitioner "must establish" eligibility "for the requested benefit at the time of filing the application or petition," which means first:

---

[71] 8 CFR §103.2(b)(4); AFM 11.1.

[72] *Id.*

[73] 8 CFR §103.2(b)(4); AFM 11.1.

[74] 8 CFR §103.2(b)(3); AFM 11.3.

[75] *Id.*

[76] *Matter of C-B-&F-, Inc.,* ID# 13701 (AAO Sept. 28, 2015).

[77] 8 CFR §103.2(b)(3); AFM 11.3 (stating that a "summary of a document prepared by a translator is unacceptable"); *Matter of F-I-T-T-,* ID# 16838 (AAO June 23, 2016) (summary translation is of "diminished" value).

Copyright © 2017. American Immigration Lawyers Association. All rights reserved.

"All required application or petition forms must be properly completed and filed with any initial evidence required by applicable regulations and/or the form's instructions. Any evidence submitted in connection with the application or petition is incorporated into and considered part of the relating application or petition."[78]

As stated by the regulations: "If the evidence submitted with the application or petition establishes eligibility, USCIS will approve the application or petition."[79] Specifically, an RFE or a Notice of Intent to Deny (NOID) should not be issued in these circumstances:

"If the record is complete with respect to all of the required initial evidence as specified in the regulations and on the application or petition and accompanying instructions, the USCIS adjudicator is <u>not</u> required to issue a RFE to obtain further documentation to support an approval based on that record."[80]

In addition, as a practical matter, the practitioner who submits as comprehensive a filing package as possible should be able to avoid an RFE, although adjudication without an RFE cannot be guaranteed, as discussed below, because:

"Applicants and petitioners who submit completed applications or petitions will minimize the need for RFE and facilitate faster decision by USCIS. [US]CIS has found that in some cases, the standard [RFE response] timeframe serves to encourage applicants or petitioners to submit incomplete applications or petitions, relying on the RFE process to prompt them to submit the missing documents. The RFE process and the ensuing delays slows down the processing."[81]

The USCIS guidance essentially repudiated the previous practice of issuing "a RFE for additional types of evidence that could tend to eliminate all doubt and all possibility for fraud."[82] Despite acknowledging the basis of this caution "in light of the 'zero tolerance memo' issued by INS Commissioner Ziglar in 2002 in the wake of '9/11,'" the guidance noted that the "zero tolerance memo" had "been rescinded."[83] The adjudication process now has the following policy initiatives: "USCIS is determined to

---

[78] 8 CFR §103.2(b)(1).

[79] 8 CFR §103.2(b)(8)(i).

[80] USCIS, W. Yates, "Requests for Evidence (RFE) and Notices of Intent to Deny (NOID)" (Feb. 16, 2005), AILA Doc. No. 05021810 (emphasis in original).

[81] 72 Fed. Reg. 19100 (Apr. 17, 2007). The guidance references the former 12-week response time.

[82] USCIS, W. Yates, "Requests for Evidence (RFE) and Notices of Intent to Deny (NOID)" (Feb. 16, 2005), AILA Doc. No. 05021810. *See also* 72 Fed. Reg. 19100 (Apr. 17, 2007) (stating that "USCIS is not responsible for advising the applicant or petitioner of the evidence that the applicant or petitioner should submit with each particular case beyond providing general filing guidance via form instructions and regulations").

[83] USCIS, W. Yates, "Requests for Evidence (RFE) and Notices of Intent to Deny (NOID)" (Feb. 16, 2005), AILA Doc. No. 05021810.

Copyright © 2017. American Immigration Lawyers Association. All rights reserved.

protect the integrity of its adjudications, but USCIS must also facilitate lawful immigration, and has a responsibility to process cases efficiently and reasonably."[84]

One exception is this: if "the applicable statute or regulation makes the approval of a petition or application a matter entrusted to USCIS discretion, USCIS will approve the petition or application only if the evidence of record establishes both eligibility and that the petitioner or applicant warrants a favorable exercise of discretion."[85] Another exception is if "evidence justifying a particular concern to support a RFE or a referral to Fraud Detection and National Security (FDNS)."[86]

In contrast, if the evidence of the record "establishes ineligibility, the application or petition will be denied on that basis."[87] As stated by USCIS:

"Clear ineligibility exists when the adjudicator can be sure that an applicant or petitioner cannot meet a basic statutory or regulatory requirement, even if the filer were to be given the opportunity to present additional information. Inability to meet a basic statutory or regulatory requirement includes circumstances where the evidence submitted by the applicant or petitioner clearly establishes that the filing is categorically ineligible for approval ... [and] circumstances where the evidence submitted clearly establishes that a substantive requirement cannot be met."[88]

The regulations were amended to reflect the fact that the forms and USCIS website provide instructions and "complete information regarding evidentiary requirements," so USCIS believes that "filings should be complete at the beginning of the process."[89] Therefore, if "an application or petition lacks the required initial evidence, USCIS may deny the incomplete application or petition, though adjudicators are urged to exercise this option judiciously, or issue a request for evidence (RFE)."[90]

Despite the statement that "United States Citizenship and Immigration Services will continue generally to provide petitioners and applicants with the opportunity to review and rebut derogatory information of which he or she is unaware,"[91] multiple

---

[84] *Id.*

[85] 8 CFR §103.2(b)(8)(i).

[86] USCIS, W. Yates, "Requests for Evidence (RFE) and Notices of Intent to Deny (NOID)" (Feb. 16, 2005), AILA Doc. No. 05021810. The guidance also discusses the process of referring a case to the "local FDNS Immigration Officer." For sample checklists for different types of fraud investigations, see USCIS document, "Fraud Referral Sheet," (Sept. 30, 2004), AILA Doc. No. 10012861.

[87] 8 CFR §103.2(b)(8)(i).

[88] USCIS, W. Yates, "Requests for Evidence (RFE) and Notices of Intent to Deny (NOID)" (Feb. 16, 2005), AILA Doc. No. 05021810.

[89] 72 Fed. Reg. 19100 (Apr. 17, 2007).

[90] AFM 10.1.

[91] 72 Fed. Reg. 19100 (Apr. 17, 2007).

Copyright © 2017. American Immigration Lawyers Association. All rights reserved.

reports indicate that such an opportunity is not always provided, as discussed below. Examples of clear ineligibility provided by USCIS guidance include:

- "A petitioning company seeking to file an L-1 petition clearly states that the petitioner has no relationship to a foreign company abroad;

- "An H-1B petition filed for a position such as a factory machine operator that cannot possibly support the necessary baccalaureate degree (or equivalent) requirement;

- "An E-1 treaty trader or E-2 treaty investor petition filed on behalf of a beneficiary who is not a national of a country with a qualifying treaty with the United States; or

- "An employer seeking to file an H-2B petition on behalf of an H-2B alien who has been physically present in the [United States] in H-2B status for the entirety of the preceding three years without a six-month absence."[92]

(3) Denial Without RFE or NOID

Denial without an RFE or NOID should be limited to "clearly deficient applications or petitions,"[93] and USCIS should "exercise this option judiciously."[94] The practitioner should note that despite the various USCIS guidance, multiple reports discuss how USCIS adjudicators nevertheless deny petitions without RFEs or NOIDs,[95] even though the preamble to the final rule stated:

"USCIS currently intends to limit the application of its discretionary authority to deny an application or petition for lack of initial evidence without an RFE to cases that are filed with little more than a signature and the proper fee, and therefore are substantially incomplete or where the applicant or petitioner has failed to demonstrate a basis for eligibility for the benefit sought (e.g., an application for adjustment of status as an immediate relative), where no information or evidence of a covered relationship is provided. These skeletal applications, or applications that are filed alleging eligibility for a benefit based upon having filed a separate benefit application which has since been denied or of which USCIS has no record, clearly do not establish eligibility."[96]

---

[92] USCIS, W. Yates, "Requests for Evidence (RFE) and Notices of Intent to Deny (NOID)" (Feb. 16, 2005), AILA Doc. No. 05021810 (internal citations omitted).

[93] 72 Fed. Reg. 19100 (Apr. 17, 2007).

[94] USCIS, D. Neufeld, "Removal of the Standardized Request for Evidence Processing Timeframe, Final Rule, 8 CFR 103.2(b)" (June 1, 2007), AILA Doc. No. 07062171.

[95] "AILA Liaison/TSC Meeting Minutes" (Jan. 22, 2009), AILA Doc. No. 09091565 (discussing denial of immigrant visa petitions in successor-in-interest cases); "AILA Liaison/TSC Meeting Minutes" (Nov. 12, 2008), AILA Doc. No. 09021275; "AILA/USCIS Liaison Minutes" (Mar. 19, 2009), AILA Doc. No. 09031920; "AILA/USCIS Liaison Minutes" (Oct. 28, 2008), AILA Doc. No. 08110767.

[96] 72 Fed. Reg. 19100 (Apr. 17, 2007).

Copyright © 2017. American Immigration Lawyers Association. All rights reserved.

In certain situations, the issue appears to have been resolved,[97] but the practitioner should note the following statements:

> "[W]hile USCIS makes every effort to avoid needless denials, USCIS may exercise the authority to deny an incomplete or poorly presented case. What constitutes initial evidence for a particular application or petition is generally set forth either in the applicable forms instructions and/or regulations pertaining to the particular classification or benefit sought."[98]

> "If the case is clearly ineligible, USCIS will not delay adjudication by issuing an RFE."[99]

c. Signatures

The petition must be signed by the petitioner, and this signature "certifies under penalty of perjury that the application or petition, and all evidence submitted with it, either at the time of filing or thereafter, is true and correct."[100] The signature should be "wet ink"[101]—*i.e.*, not a photocopy—or "for applications or petitions filed electronically as permitted by the instructions to the form, in electronic format."[102] For most employment-based nonimmigrant petitions, the form will be signed by the employer's representative. It is generally recommended that signatures be in blue or black ink.[103] A parent may sign an application on behalf of a child, such as Form I-539, Application to Extend/Change Nonimmigrant Status.[104]

---

[97] "AILA Liaison/TSC Meeting Minutes" (Jan. 22, 2009), AILA Doc. No. 09091565 (stating that "the examiner will normally issue an RFE so that the appropriate evidence can be submitted").

[98] "AILA/USCIS Liaison Minutes" (Oct. 28, 2008), AILA Doc. No. 08110767.

[99] "AILA/USCIS Liaison Minutes" (Mar. 19, 2009), AILA Doc. No. 09031920.

[100] 8 CFR §103.2(a)(2). *See also* 8 CFR §103.2(a)(7)(i); AFM 11.4.

[101] An interim guidance memorandum from USCIS seems to allow for photocopies of original signatures, "Signatures on Paper Applications, Petitions, Requirements, and Other Documents Filed with U.S. Citizenship and Immigration Services," PM-602-0134 (June 7, 2016), AILA Doc. No. 16060860. However, where the form's instructions require an original signature, such as for a Form I-129, original, "wet ink," signatures are required. "Practice Alert: Forms Still Require an Original Signature" (Dec. 12, 2016), AILA Doc. No. 16121230.

[102] 8 CFR §103.2(a)(2).

[103] While USCIS previously advised signing documents in blue ink (*See, e.g.*, "TSC Liaison Minutes" (Aug. 13, 2000), AILA Doc. No. 00090703, in recent years it has more frequently stated a preference for black ink (*See, e.g.*, "Instructions for Notice of Entry of Appearance as Attorney or Accredited Representative" (May 5, 2106), *https://www.uscis.gov/sites/default/files/files/form/g-28instr.pdf*; "USCIS FY2016 H-1B Webpage Updated" (Mar. 12, 2015), AILA Doc. No. 15031362. In practice, however, the USCIS mailroom sometimes rejects forms signed in black ink because the signatures are incorrectly concluded to be photocopies, so signing in blue ink can be beneficial despite the USCIS instructions.

[104] 8 CFR §103.2(a)(2).

Copyright © 2017. American Immigration Lawyers Association. All rights reserved.

d. Payment

The filing fees for petitions and applications are stated in the regulations,[105] or the practitioner may check the USCIS website.[106] Generally, filing fees for petitions filed with USCIS, including the premium processing fee, may not be waived.[107] Payment "must be drawn on a bank or other institution located in the United States and be payable in United States currency," and "[f]ees in the form of postage stamps shall not be accepted."[108] The remittance "shall be made payable to the 'Department of Homeland Security,'"[109] and the practitioner should note that abbreviations, such as DHS or USDHS (for the U.S. Department of Homeland Security) should not be used.[110] USCIS will accept "[b]ank drafts, cashier's checks, certified checks, personal checks..., and money orders ... drawn on U.S. financial institutions."[111] The practitioner is encouraged to use a check rather than a money order, because "the receipt notice number will appear on the back of the cancelled check," which allows the practitioner to consult the bank "to see if the check was deposited" but such an approach is unavailable with money orders.[112]

For bank checks, the practitioner should note the following:

- The check "must be pre-printed" with the name of the individual or business, "bank name and address, bank routing number, [] account number and the check number;

- The check should also state an individual's home address and telephone number of the individual or business;

- All fields should be completed, including date, "Pay to the Order of," amount in numerals and words, "For/Memo," and signature blocks.

- The check should be signed by the individual "whose name is authorized for signature on the bank account from which the funds will be drawn" in the case of an individual or "in the case of a business check an authorized signee on the business checking account," and the signature "should be signed with an ink pen and be legible or match the signature card on file at the bank"; and

---

[105] 8 CFR §103.7(b)(1).

[106] USCIS, "Filing Fees," https://www.uscis.gov/fees.

[107] 8 CFR §§103.7(c)(1) and (5); 8 CFR §103.2(f)(3). The exceptions, which do not generally apply to nonimmigrant petitions, are stated in 8 CFR §103.7(c)(5).

[108] 8 CFR §103.7(a)(2).

[109] *Id.*

[110] *See, e.g.,* USCIS, "Instructions for Petition for Nonimmigrant Worker" (updated Aug. 13, 2015), https://www.uscis.gov/sites/default/files/files/form/i-129instr.pdf, and "Instructions for Petition for Alien Workers" (updated Apr. 20, 2016), https://www.uscis.gov/sites/default/files/files/form/i-140instr.pdf.

[111] USCIS, "Paying Immigration Fees" (updated July 7, 2014), https://www.uscis.gov/forms/paying-immigration-fees.

[112] "VSC Practice Pointer: Use Checks for Filing Fees" (Sept. 17, 2008), AILA Doc. No. 08091779.

Copyright © 2017. American Immigration Lawyers Association. All rights reserved.

- Self-printed checks "must conform to banking industry standards in order to allow for proper processing."[113]

A petition that is filed with the incorrect filing fee "shall be rejected as improperly filed."[114] A petition that is filed with payment that is "subsequently returned as non-payable will not retain a filing date."[115] Although the petitioner is allowed a second chance to pay the fee within 14 days after notification from USCIS,[116] the client will most likely wish to avoid the delay. One report states that if "the invoice is paid after the 14 days, USCIS will keep the payment but will not adjudicate the petition."[117]

If the petition or application has been approved but the "charges are not paid the approval shall be automatically revoked because it was improperly filed."[118] There is a fee of $30 for each returned check, and a USCIS receipt "for any remittance shall not be binding upon the Department of Homeland Security if the remittance is found uncollectible."[119] In addition, "legal and statutory deadlines will not be deemed to have been met if payment is not made within 10 business days after notification by the Department of Homeland Security of the dishonored check."[120]

e. Form G-28 and Changing Attorney Information

As stated in the regulations, an "applicant or petitioner may be represented by an attorney in the United States,"[121] where "attorney" is defined as "any person who is a member in good standing of the bar of the highest court of any State, possession, territory, Commonwealth, or the District of Columbia, and is not under any order of any court suspending, enjoining, restraining, disbarring, or otherwise restricting him in the practice of law."[122] For employment-based nonimmigrant petitions, the foreign national beneficiary "is not a recognized party in such a proceeding."[123]

---

[113] "Questions & Answers: USCIS Check Instructions" (June 29, 2009), AILA Doc. No. 09091167.

[114] 8 CFR §103.2(a)(7)(i).

[115] Id.

[116] 8 CFR §103.2(a)(7)(ii).

[117] "Practice Pointer: Refunds and Stopped Checks or Bounced Checks" (May 12, 2017), AILA Doc. No. 09091169. Although the document cites 8 CFR §103.2(a)(7)(ii) for this proposition, it does not appear that the regulation addresses this situation at all, but the prudent practitioner should strive to avoid this situation. This document also discusses the procedure once payment is received, requesting proof of payment, and refund requests. A foreign national may, for example, desire proof of payment in order to establish that an extension of change of status application was timely filed, even if the foreign national departed the United States while the application was pending. AFM 40.9.2.

[118] 8 CFR §103.2(a)(7)(ii).

[119] Id.

[120] Id.

[121] 8 CFR §103.2(a)(3).

[122] 8 CFR §1.1(f).

[123] 8 CFR §103.2(a)(3).

Copyright © 2017. American Immigration Lawyers Association. All rights reserved.

The representation should be stated on Form G-28, Notice of Entry of Appearance as Attorney or Accredited Representative, which should be signed by both the employer's representative and the practitioner, because if "a notice of representation is submitted that is not properly signed, the application or petition will be processed as if the notice had not been submitted."[124] Signatures should be in black ink,[125] although USCIS has indicated that dark blue ink also is acceptable.[126] Facsimile (stamped) signatures are not acceptable.[127]

In 2017, USCIS began notifying customers when a Form G-28 submitted with an application or petition was not accepted at a USCIS Lockbox facility. If the G-28 has not been accepted, customers are notified on the receipt notice issued for the application or petition.[128]

As stated by USCIS: "An original G-28 should be filed with each application."[129] The practitioner is also strongly encouraged to print the G-28 on blue paper, single sided,[130] and to place it at the top of the petition filing,[131] in order to avoid processing delays.[132] Experience has shown that doing so, in addition to stapling the check to the G-28, is usually sufficient. If there is limited time to prepare and file the petition, however, such as if the forms are emailed to and printed by the client, this form may be printed on plain white paper.

Generally, a new, fully complete G-28, stating the petition receipt number, is necessary for any change in representation.[133] The practitioner may also wish to "add[] a brightly colored cover sheet identifying the submission as a new G-28."[134] The practitioner should call the USCIS National Customer Service Center

---

[124] *Id.*

[125] "Instructions for Notice of Entry of Appearance as Attorney or Accredited Representative" (May 5, 2106), *https://www.uscis.gov/sites/default/files/files/form/g-28instr.pdf.*

[126] "AILA FAQs: Completing the New G-28 Form; Answers Provided by USCIS Office of Intake and Document Production" (Oct. 11, 2013), AILA Doc. No. 13101144.

[127] "AILA/SCOPS Liaison Teleconference Q&As" (Nov. 13, 2013), AILA Doc. No. 13120344.

[128] "USCIS Message: Form G-28 Non-Acceptance Notice" (Mar. 7, 2017), AILA Doc. No. 17030860.

[129] "AILA Liaison/SCOPS Q&As" (July 30, 2008), AILA Doc. No. 08082160.

[130] "AILA FAQs: Completing the New G-28 Form; Answers Provided by USCIS Office of Intake and Document Production" (Oct. 11, 2013), AILA Doc. No. 13101144.

[131] *Id.* (noting blue paper and placement "on top of the filing" as ways to ensure the G-28 is found by USCIS contractors). *See also* "AILA Liaison/TSC Meeting Minutes" (Nov. 17, 2009), AILA Doc. No. 10011931; "AILA Liaison/TSC Meeting Minutes" (May 19, 2009), AILA Doc. No. 09052966.

[132] "VSC Practice Pointer: G-28s" (Sept. 4, 2008), AILA Doc. No. 08090469.

[133] "NSC Updates Procedure for Reporting Attorney Change of Address for Pending Petitions" (Jan. 15, 2009), AILA Doc. No. 09011567.

[134] "AILA Liaison/TSC Meeting Minutes" (Nov. 17, 2009), AILA Doc. No. 10011931. Although this guidance specifically addresses new G-28s when the petition or application was filed without representation, the principle should remain the same.

Copyright © 2017. American Immigration Lawyers Association. All rights reserved.

after 30 days to confirm that the G-28 was connected with the petition or application.[135]

USCIS has provided addresses for each of the Service Centers for filing new G-28s, for all purposes, including withdrawing, adding, or substituting as counsel, and for attorneys to provide a change of address when they move.[136] The P.O. boxes are for U.S. postal service delivery, including Express Mail and certified mail, and the street addresses are for courier deliveries:

Texas Service Center (TSC)
P.O. Box 850891
Mesquite, TX 75185-0891
OR
4141 N. St. Augustine Rd.
Dallas, TX 75227

California Service Center (CSC)
P.O. Box 30111
Laguna Niguel, CA 92607
OR
24000 Avila Rd. 2d Floor Room 2312
Laguna Niguel, CA 92677

Nebraska Service Center (NSC)
P.O. Box 82521
Lincoln, NE 68501
OR
850 "S" St.
Lincoln, NE 68508

Vermont Service Center (VSC)
P.O. Box 600
St. Albans, VT 05479
OR

---

[135] *Id.* (discussing remedial measures if "information from a call to the NCSC does not show the new G-28 in the system within 30 days of the filing").

[136] "Practice Pointer: Submitting an Attorney Change of Address" (Apr. 21, 2107), AILA Doc. No. 17042132 (providing P.O. box addresses at the Service Centers for G-28s); "Practice Pointer: Getting USCIS to Recognize the G-28" (June 23, 2015), AILA Doc. No. 08090469 (providing P.O. box addresses at the Service Centers for G-28s); "AILA/SCOPS Teleconference Agenda" (Nov. 12, 2014), AILA Doc. No. 14112160 (providing both P.O. box and courier addresses).

Copyright © 2017. American Immigration Lawyers Association. All rights reserved.

75 Lower Welden St.
St. Albans, VT 05479

It is recommended that the P.O. boxes be used, as they are specifically set aside for issues involving Form G-28. Anything sent to these boxes should not include anything else, not even a cover letter, as that will only slow the process.[137]

When an attorney is changing his or her address, VSC and CSC prefer separate G-28s for each case—USCIS has called this a "best practice"—but all four of the Service Centers will accept a letter from the attorney listing pending cases.[138] Be sure to include the receipt number, beneficiary's Alien Registration Number (A number) if any, and form type.[139]

For VSC, the practitioner may also want to use the VSC G-28 Routing Sheet,[140] and mail it to the attention of the Community Engagement Officer.[141] The sheet should be placed on "top of all general correspondence submitted" to VSC, to "streamline VSC's internal correspondence processes."[142] The following options are available on the sheet:

- "New attorney/representative;
- "Replacing current attorney/representative at same law firm;
- "Change of current attorney/representative's law firm;
- "Change of address of attorney/representative; and
- "Withdrawing G-28."[143]

It is critical to "include the related receipt and/or A number of the case involved on the routing sheet in the space provided."[144] The "VSC G-28 Routing Sheet" should not be used to respond to RFEs or NOIDs.[145]

---

[137] "Practice Pointer: Getting USCIS to Recognize the G-28" (June 23, 2015), AILA Doc. No. 08090469.

[138] "AILA/SCOPS Teleconference Agenda" (Nov. 12, 2014), AILA Doc. No. 14112160.

[139] *Id.*

[140] "Vermont Service Center Routing Sheet Instructions" (undated, posted Dec. 19, 2008), AILA Doc. No. 08121960.

[141] AILA/VSC Liaison Practice Pointer: Attorney Change of Address" (updated Feb. 13, 2012), AILA Doc. No. 11012570.

[142] "Vermont Service Center Routing Sheet Instructions" (undated, posted Dec. 19, 2008), AILA Doc. No. 08121960.

[143] "VSC G-28 Routing Sheet," which can be found under "Related Resources" in the upper right corner of the web page containing "Vermont Service Center Routing Sheet Instructions" (undated, posted Dec. 19, 2008), AILA Doc. No. 08121960.

[144] "Vermont Service Center Routing Sheet Instructions" (undated, posted Dec. 19, 2008), AILA Doc. No. 08121960.

[145] *Id.*

Copyright © 2017. American Immigration Lawyers Association. All rights reserved.

f. Known Employer Pilot Program

In March 2016, USCIS introduced a pilot program with the goals of reducing the amount of paperwork filed with and retained by USCIS, promoting consistency in adjudications, streamlining the process, and providing greater efficiency and consistency between USCIS, DOS, and U.S. Customs and Border Protection (CBP).[146] Under this process, employers can file an application to request USCIS to predetermine whether certain employer requirements relating to "corporate structure, operations and financial health" are met.[147]

Employers create a profile in the web-based "Known Employer Document Library (KEDL) and complete and upload Form I-950, Application for Predetermination under Known Employer Program, along with documents addressing the requirements to be predetermined. If USCIS approves the request, the employer can then file petitions for individual beneficiaries without having to re-document the corporate information. "USCIS will defer to the approved predetermination" unless it finds a material change, a substantial change in circumstances, or new material that adversely affects the validity of the predetermination.[148]

The predetermination in the pilot is available only for the nonimmigrant categories of H-1B, L-1A and B, and TN, as well as the immigrant categories of outstanding professor or researcher and multinational manager or executive.[149]

At launch, five companies were signed on as participants, with room for four more, but USCIS was not accepting applications for any more participants.[150]

g. Premium Processing

Premium processing guarantees a USCIS response, which may be approval, denial, RFE, NOID, or opening of an "investigation relating to the application or petition for fraud or misrepresentation," within 15 calendar days,[151] in exchange for an additional fee of $1,225. The request is made on Form I-907, Request for Premium Processing, and the "processing period begins when USCIS receives Form I-907, with the fee, at the designated address contained in the instructions to the form."[152] If a response is not provided within the processing period, then the $1,225 fee "will be automatically refunded to the petitioner or applicant, and [USCIS] will continue to

---

[146] USCIS, "Known Employer Pilot" (updated Mar. 10, 2016), *https://www.uscis.gov/working-united-states/known-employer-pilot*; "DHS Launches Known Employer Pilot Program" (Mar. 3, 2016), AILA Doc. No. 16030305.

[147] *Id.*

[148] *Id.*

[149] *Id.*

[150] *Id.*

[151] 8 CFR §103.2(f)(1).

[152] *Id.*

Copyright © 2017. American Immigration Lawyers Association. All rights reserved.

process the application/petition on the premium processing track,"[153] which means USCIS "must still expeditiously process the case."[154] The refund will be issued "only after [USCIS] has completed review of the petition," in order to "bar against fraud or misrepresentation."[155]

Questions have arisen as to whether a refund can be obtained if USCIS issues an unwarranted RFE, such as for materials that already were submitted or items unrelated to the case. If a petitioner or applicant believes a refund is in order, a request should be sent to the Service Center where the I-907 was filed, clearly stating why the RFE was in error and providing any documentation that might be helpful. "If the service agrees that the RFE was inappropriate, they will send a refund request to [the Burlington Finance Center]."[156]

Refunds, however, are not processed quickly. "A refund is typically mailed out within 60 days after the Service Center initiates the request.[157]

The premium processing request may be filed concurrently with the nonimmigrant visa petition, or the attorney or the petitioner may request premium processing after the petition has been filed, by submitting Form I-907 with the petition's receipt notice.[158] The practitioner should provide his or her telephone number, facsimile number, and email address "in Part 1 of the Form I-907 and … check the appropriate box," in order to "ensure that any RFE or correspondence … is sent directly to the attorney of record."[159]

E-filing of the Form I-907 is unavailable.[160] The $1,225 check must be separate from any other filing fees.[161] Contact information for the Premium Processing Unit (PPU) should "be provided … on [the] receipt notice,"[162] and the PPU also usually emails receipt notices,[163] although this may be delayed if the USCIS computer system

---

[153] 8 CFR §103.2(f)(3).

[154] "AILA/VSC Practice Pointer: Refund of Premium Processing Fees" (Aug. 3, 2009), AILA Doc. No. 09080368.

[155] *Id.*

[156] "AILA/SCOPS Teleconference Agenda" (July 27, 2016), AILA Doc. No. 16080801.

[157] *Id.*

[158] USCIS, "I-907, Request for Premium Processing Service" (updated Mar. 31, 2017), https://www.uscis.gov/i-907.

[159] "AILA/VSC Practice Pointer: Direct Correspondence with the Premium Processing Unit" (Aug. 26, 2009), AILA Doc. No. 09082663.

[160] USCIS, "How Do I Use the Premium Processing Service?" (updated Mar. 31, 2017), https://www.uscis.gov/forms/how-do-i-use-premium-processing-service.

[161] 8 CFR §103.2(f)(3).

[162] USCIS, "How Do I Use the Premium Processing Service?" (updated Mar. 31, 2017), https://www.uscis.gov/forms/how-do-i-use-premium-processing-service.

[163] "VSC Continues to Experience Problems with Premium Processing E-mails" (Feb. 9, 2009), AILA Doc. No. 09012164.

Copyright © 2017. American Immigration Lawyers Association. All rights reserved.

experiences an "interruption."[164] The practitioner may also call the PPU at 1-866-315-5718 once the receipt notice has been issued.[165] As stated by one commenter, premium processing "is the only way to communicate with the Service Center adjudicators and actually get through to a live person who knows what is going on with [the] application."[166]

The petitioner or the petitioner's attorney may sign the premium processing request,[167] but "neither the beneficiary nor the beneficiary's attorney or accredited representative can request premium processing," so the practitioner should confirm that a Form G-28, signed by the employer's representative, petitioner, or applicant, whichever is applicable, was filed with the underlying petition or application.[168] An attorney "may not sign an I-907 requesting premium processing" if the Form "G-28 is from the beneficiary only."[169] Therefore, the cautious practitioner may wish to have the client representative sign the form, since this step should add only one day in preparation time if the form is emailed directly to the client. Otherwise, time may be lost in mailing the petition and awaiting USCIS receipt before ultimately receiving a rejection notice. If a premium processing request is erroneously rejected for this reason, the request should be submitted to the Case Rejection Unit.[170]

To obtain the approval notice or other USCIS response more quickly, the practitioner should "include a postage paid and self-addressed courier delivery slip" and envelope with the request for premium processing.[171] USCIS should return the results of the adjudication" to the practitioner using the envelope and slip.[172]

The following nonimmigrant visa petitions are eligible for premium processing at the time of this writing:

---

[164] "VSC Acknowledges that Erroneous Notices Were Sent from the Premium Processing Unit" (Nov. 21, 2008), AILA Doc. No. 08112131 (stating a system "shut down" and therefore "left the VSC with a backlog of e-mails").

[165] USCIS, "How Do I Use the Premium Processing Service?" (Mar. 31, 2017), https://www.uscis.gov/forms/how-do-i-use-premium-processing-service. USCIS notes that "this phone number is only for inquiries relating to Premium Processing Service."

[166] "AILA/VSC Practice Pointer: Direct Correspondence with the Premium Processing Unit" (Aug. 26, 2009), AILA Doc. No. 09082663.

[167] "VSC Resumes Accepting Attorney-Signed I-907 Premium Processing Forms" (Feb. 1, 2010), AILA Doc. No. 10012971.

[168] "USCIS on Form I-907 Request for Premium Processing Service Signature Policy" (Dec. 13, 2006), AILA Doc. No. 06121367.

[169] *Id.*

[170] "VSC Resumes Accepting Attorney-Signed I-907 Premium Processing Forms" (Feb. 1, 2010), AILA Doc. No. 10012971.This document has the mailing address for the Case Rejection Unit.

[171] USCIS, "How Do I Use the Premium Processing Service?" (updated Mar. 31, 2017), https://www. uscis.gov/forms/how-do-i-use-premium-processing-service.

[172] *Id.*

Copyright © 2017. American Immigration Lawyers Association. All rights reserved.

- E-1, E-2, H-1B, H-2B, H-3, L-1A, L-1B, Blanket L, O-1, O-2, P-1, P-1S, P-2,; P-2S, P-3, P-3S, Q-1, R-1 (only if a site inspection has been completed for the work location), and TN.[173]

In addition, premium processing is available for the following categories of immigrant visa petitions:

- Aliens of extraordinary ability;

- Outstanding professors and researchers;

- Members of the professions with advanced degrees or exceptional ability who are not seeking a national interest waiver;

- Skilled workers;

- Professionals; and

- Workers other than skilled workers and professionals.[174]

The practitioner should note several exceptions. Premium processing may not be requested for immigrant visa petitions on behalf of professionals, skilled workers, and unskilled workers if any of the following conditions are met:

- The petitioner files a second immigrant visa petition "while an initial Form I-140 remains pending";

- The petitioner will request substitution of a beneficiary on the approved labor certification application;

- The petitioner requests a duplicate copy of the approved labor certification application, "(i.e., cases filed without an original labor certification from the Department of Labor)"; and

- The immigrant visa petition has been adjudicated to "a final decision."[175]

USCIS on occasion temporarily terminates or suspends the availability of Premium Processing Service for certain petitions or applications when it expects or receives a volume of requests that it cannot handle, or for other reasons that arise from time to time. This is announced on USCIS's website.[176] For example, in 2017, USCIS temporarily suspended premium processing for up to six months to "help ... reduce overall H-1B processing times."[177]

In 2015, USCIS temporarily suspended premium processing for extension of stay H-1B petitions so that USCIS could implement its new regulation for H-4 spouses'

---

[173] *Id.*

[174] *Id.*

[175] *Id.*

[176] *Id.*

[177] "USCIS Will Temporarily Suspend Premium Processing for all H-1B Petitions" (Mar. 3, 2017), AILA Doc. No. 17030335.

Copyright © 2017. American Immigration Lawyers Association. All rights reserved.

employment authorization "in a timely manner and adjudicate applications for employment authorization filed by H-4 nonimmigrants under the new regulations."[178]

h. Expedites

A petition may be expedited by USCIS, without payment of the premium processing fee, if the following requirements are met:[179]

- "Severe financial loss" to a company or individual;

- "Emergency situation";

- "Humanitarian reasons";

- An organization designated as nonprofit requests expediting "in furtherance of the cultural and social interests of the United States";

- "Department of Defense or national interest situation," where the request "must come from official U.S. governmental entity and state that [the] delay will be detrimental to the government";

- "USCIS error," although a formal expedite request may not be necessary to correct the error;[180] and

- "Compelling interest of USCIS."

An "extreme emergent situation" and "humanitarian situation" may include "unexpected events in a person's home country," such as natural disasters[181] "or civil war,"[182] although "[s]tandard requirements for security checks remain in place under expedited procedures."[183] A humanitarian situation may also include "[i]mminent events which may affect the eligibility of the applicant or petitioner, such as the termination of a program whose duration is limited by statute or the 'aging out' of a dependent."[184] The final two factors may include the following:

- A USCIS-wide policy for certain types of petitions or applications, "such as the USCIS Director's fiscal year priority that backlogs in a given type of application or petition be reduced to a specified level";

---

[178] USCIS, "How Do I Use the Premium Processing Service?" (updated Mar. 31, 2017), https://www. uscis.gov/forms/how-do-i-use-premium-processing-service.

[179] USCIS, "Expedite Criteria" (updated July 27, 2015), https://www.uscis.gov/forms/expedite-criteria.

[180] Legacy INS, F. Ohata, "Service Center Guidelines for Expedite Requests on Petitions and Applications" (Apr. 20, 2001), 78 Interpreter Releases 1118–20 (July 2, 2001).

[181] USCIS, A. Mayorkas, "Initial Relief Efforts for Aliens Affected by the January 12, 2010, Haiti Earthquake" (Jan. 15, 2010), AILA Doc. No. 10011960; USCIS, "USCIS Reminds Customers of Program Flexibilities" (Sept. 24, 2008), https://www.uscis.gov/archive/archive-news/uscis-reminds-customers-program-flexibilities.

[182] AFM 10.11.

[183] USCIS "Haitian Relief Measures: Questions and Answers" (Jan. 15, 2010), AILA Doc. No. 10011512.

[184] AFM 10.11.

Copyright © 2017. American Immigration Lawyers Association. All rights reserved.

- "A need to coordinate actions with" other DHS branches or "other agencies in order to meet common goals"; and

- "To correct an injustice which may have occurred, or to prevent one which may be about to occur."[185]

Although not properly an expedite, USCIS may prioritize certain petitions and applications based on statutory requirements, such as the one requiring "that L-1 petitions be adjudicated within 30 days of filing."[186]

If the expedite request will be filed concurrently with the nonimmigrant visa petition, then the petition should include "a written explanation as to why the application or petition needs to be expedited," with "EXPEDITE REQUEST" written at the top of the statement, which should in turn be placed on top of all other petition documents.[187] The practitioner should also submit "adequate and relevant" supporting evidence of the need for the expedite request.[188] The expedite request should be bona fide, which is defined as "a request which clearly outlines the eligibility for expedite under one of the criteria listed."[189] In contrast, a "simple notation on the petition, or cover letter, is not sufficient to establish a bona fide request for expedite."[190] The practitioner is strongly encouraged to submit the expedite request with the initial filing of the petition wherever possible. For additional discussion on the explanation of the need for the expedite request, see below.

Alternatively, after the petition has been filed, the expedite request may be made to the National Customer Service Center (NCSC), which "will take a 'service request' and forward [the] expedite request to the office with jurisdiction over the application or petition."[191] Contact information for the practitioner should be provided, because if "any additional information is needed, [the practitioner] will be contacted to send supporting documentation."[192] Other options for requesting the expedite include visiting a USCIS field office with an INFOPASS appointment,

---

[185] *Id.*

[186] *Id.*

[187] USCIS, "Expedite Criteria" (updated July 27, 2015), https://www.uscis.gov/forms/expedite-criteria; legacy INS, F. Ohata, "Service Center Guidance for Expedite Requests on Petitions and Applications" (Nov. 30, 2001), AILA Doc. No. 02011131.

[188] Legacy INS, F. Ohata, "Service Center Guidance for Expedite Requests on Petitions and Applications" (Nov. 30, 2001), AILA Doc. No. 02011131. *Cf.* USCIS, "Expedite Criteria" (updated July 27, 2015), https://www.uscis.gov/forms/expedite-criteria (noting that supporting evidence "may" be submitted).

[189] Legacy INS, F. Ohata, "Service Center Guidelines for Expedite Requests on Petitions and Applications" (Apr. 20, 2001), 78 Interpreter Releases 1118–20 (July 2, 2001).

[190] *Id.*

[191] USCIS, "Expedite Criteria" (updated July 27, 2015), https://www.uscis.gov/forms/expedite-criteria; "AILA Liaison/CSC Meeting Minutes" (Feb. 25, 2009), AILA Doc. No. 09022669.

[192] "AILA Liaison/CSC Meeting Minutes" (Feb. 25, 2009), AILA Doc. No. 09022669.

Copyright © 2017. American Immigration Lawyers Association. All rights reserved.

"writing a letter to the local office or service center,"[193] or contacting a congressional office, law enforcement agency, or "other Government entities."[194]

As stated by CSC: "All expedite requests are reviewed on a case-by-case basis and are granted at the discretion of the Service Center Director."[195] Legacy INS guidance states: "The Service Center Director is responsible to assure that all bona fide expedite requests reviewed promptly by Service Officers qualified to adjudicate such requests…. The Service Center will advise the requestor of the denial of any bona fide expedite request in a timely manner."[196] And there "is no appeal of the denial of an expedite request."[197]

Generally, expediting is unavailable if a petitioner may request premium processing for the nonimmigrant visa petition.[198] The one exception is for organizations "designated as not-for-profit entities" by the IRS; these organizations "have the choice to request discretionary expedited service as they have in the past or they may choose to pay the Premium Processing fee and utilize that service."[199] And if "the criteria for a discretionary expedite are not met, the not-for-profit petitioner still has the option of requesting of Premium Processing upgrade by filing Form I-907 with fee."[200]

---

[193] USCIS, "Expedite Criteria" (updated July 27, 2015), https://www.uscis.gov/forms/expedite-criteria

[194] Legacy INS, F. Ohata, "Service Center Guidance for Expedite Requests on Petitions and Applications" (Nov. 30, 2001), AILA Doc. No. 02011131. This document has the address of the legacy INS Congressional Liaison Unit. For a list of telephone and facsimile numbers, which may not be operable, see legacy INS, F. Ohata, "Service Center Guidelines for Expedite Requests on Petitions and Applications" (Apr. 20, 2001), 78 Interpreter Releases 1118–20 (July 2, 2001). Note that the legacy INS memorandum of November 30, 2001, did not explicitly supersede this April 20, 2001, memorandum.

[195] "AILA Liaison/CSC Meeting Minutes" (Feb. 25, 2009), AILA Doc. No. 09022669.

[196] Legacy INS, F. Ohata, "Service Center Guidelines for Expedite Requests on Petitions and Applications" (Apr. 20, 2001), 78 Interpreter Releases 1118–20 (July 2, 2001).

[197] "AILA Liaison/CSC Meeting Minutes" (Feb. 25, 2009), AILA Doc. No. 09022669.

[198] USCIS, "How Do I Use the Premium Processing Service?" (updated Oct. 26, 2015), https://www.uscis.gov/forms/how-do-i-use-premium-processing-service.; legacy INS, F. Ohata, "Service Center Guidelines for Expedite Requests on Petitions and Applications" (Apr. 20, 2001), 78 Interpreter Releases 1118–20 (July 2, 2001).

[199] USCIS, "How Do I Use the Premium Processing Service?" (updated Oct. 26, 2015), https://www.uscis.gov/forms/how-do-i-use-premium-processing-service.; legacy INS, F. Ohata, "Service Center Guidance for Expedite Requests on Petitions and Applications" (Nov. 30, 2001), AILA Doc. No. 02011131; legacy INS, F. Ohata, "Service Center Guidelines for Expedite Requests on Petitions and Applications" (Apr. 20, 2001), 78 Interpreter Releases 1118–20 (July 2, 2001).

[200] USCIS, "How Do I Use the Premium Processing Service?" (updated Oct. 26, 2015), https://www.uscis.gov/forms/how-do-i-use-premium-processing-service.; legacy INS, F. Ohata, "Service Center Guidelines for Expedite Requests on Petitions and Applications" (Apr. 20, 2001), 78 Interpreter Releases 1118–20 (July 2, 2001).

Copyright © 2017. American Immigration Lawyers Association. All rights reserved.

i. Erroneous Rejection

If the practitioner believes that a petition or application was erroneously rejected by USCIS, then it may be resubmitted. Service-center-specific guidance is discussed below, but generally, "All submissions should include the original filing, original check, rejection notice, reason applicant [or practitioner] feels [the] rejection is incorrect, attached with a brightly colored sheet on the front for faster identification, and double wrapped with the inner envelope labeled: DO NOT OPEN IN MAILROOM."[201]

The address for CSC is:

USCIS California Service Center
Attn: CRU
24000 Avila Road, 2nd Floor
Laguna Niguel, CA 92677.[202]

The address for NSC is:

USCIS Nebraska Service Center
Attn: CRU
850 S Street
Lincoln, NE 68508.[203]

For TSC, the practitioner "should in the first instance resubmit the filing using the 'double-bag' method," which entails placing the rejected petition or application "into a sealed, plain envelope," with "ATTN.: CPAU/Watts. Do Not Open in the Mailroom. Previously Rejected in Error," written on the envelope.[204] The "sealed envelope should then be placed inside a regular mailer envelope (FedEx, Express Mail, etc.)," with "ATTN: CPAU/Watts" written on the outside envelope, sent to the following address:

Texas Service Center
4141 N. St. Augustine Road
Dallas, TX 75227.[205]

TSC stated that the street address is "preferred,"[206] because it "will ensure supervisory review and help TSC track the kinds of improper rejections that have been occurring."[207] The package should contain a copy of the rejection notice(s).[208] In

---

[201] "My Case Was Improperly Rejected By A Service Center—What Should I Do?" (Nov. 26, 2007), AILA Doc. No. 07112661.

[202] Id.

[203] Id.

[204] "AILA-USCIS TSC Liaison Meeting" (Jan. 22, 2009), AILA Doc. No. 09091565.

[205] Id.

[206] Id.

[207] "AILA-USCIS TSC Liaison Meeting Minutes" (Sept. 11, 2008), AILA Doc. No. 09021764.

Copyright © 2017. American Immigration Lawyers Association. All rights reserved.

addition: "TSC acknowledges that its standard rejection cover letters may in some instances not clearly reflect the reason(s) for rejection. The contractors in the Mailroom must choose a rejection reason from a prescribed list, and cannot provide a handwritten reason explaining the rejection."[209]

If a case is erroneously rejected by VSC, then, as stated on the rejection notice, the practitioner should resubmit the petition with "a brightly colored coversheet marked 'Attn: CRU Supervisor' and 'Case Improperly Rejected' in large block letters" and with "a letter setting forth the reason(s) why the case was improperly rejected," to the following address:

USCIS/Vermont Service Center
ATTN: CRU Supervisor/Improper rejection
75 Lower Welden Street
St. Albans, VT 05479-0001.[210]

The practitioner should note that "VSC strongly emphasized that this procedure should only be used for cases that have already been rejected initially and should not be used in instances where the filer anticipates or fears an initial rejection."[211]

If a case was rejected by a USCIS Lockbox, email *lockboxsupport@dhs.gov*, and attach the rejection notice, proof of why the submission was improperly rejected, and the petitioner/beneficiary's name and date of birth.[212]

2. Petition Adjudication

This section will discuss the generalities of petition adjudication. Individual visa classification issues are discussed in the relevant chapters.

Generally, no petition or application may be approved without a security check of the Interagency Border Inspection System (IBIS), which "is a multi-agency effort to improve border enforcement and facilitate inspections of applicants for admission into the United States," and "includes a concurrent check of the NCIC [National Crime Information Center] Hot Files," which "queries the following databases":

- "Wants and Warrants;
- "Missing Persons;
- "Violent Gang and Terrorists;

---

[208] "AILA-USCIS TSC Liaison Meeting" (Jan. 22, 2009), AILA Doc. No. 09091565.

[209] *Id.*

[210] "AILA/VSC Liaison Committee Practice Pointer: Wrongful Rejections from VSC?" (Nov. 4, 2008), AILA Doc. No. 08110466.

[211] *Id.*

[212] "Case Resolution Strategies" (June 1, 2016), AILA Doc. No. 10100873, at 31st page on pdf count.

Copyright © 2017. American Immigration Lawyers Association. All rights reserved.

- "Protection Order File;
- "Registered Sexual Offender;
- "Secret Service Presidential Protection;
- "Foreign Fugitives;
- "Deported Felons; and
- "Supervised Release File."[213]

The name of the petitioner, applicant, or beneficiary, as well as the names of any derivative family members, must be checked.[214] The exceptions are as follows:

- The individual "is under 14 years of age at the time of approval or denial of the application or petition";
- "An IBIS check has been performed and found to be negative on the same application or petition, or a concurrently-filed application or petition, involving such individual within the previous 180 days"; and
- The name of the beneficiary is "are unavailable at the time of adjudication," such as for unnamed H-2 beneficiaries.[215]

a. Standard of Review

(1) Burden of Proof

As noted above, the petitioner bears the burden of establishing eligibility "for the benefit sought,"[216] at the time of filing,[217] which USCIS construes as resulting in denial if there is not a showing of eligibility; USCIS guidance states that the "government is not called upon to make any showing of ineligibility until the alien has first shown that he is eligible."[218] USCIS also reviews whether "disqualifying conditions are not present."[219] But USCIS distinguishes between establishing initial eligibility and final adjudication of the petition, which may rely on discretionary factors or information later learned during the course of adjudication, such that if

---

[213] AFM 10.3.

[214] *Id.*

[215] *Id.*

[216] AFM 11.1 (citing *Matter of Brantigan*, 11 I&N Dec. 493 (BIA 1966)). *See also* USCIS, M. Aytes, "Alternate definition of 'American firm or corporation' for purposes of section 316(b) of the Immigration and Nationality Act, 8 USC 1427(b), and the standard of proof applicable in most administrative immigration proceedings" (Jan. 11, 2006), AILA Doc. No. 06021014.

[217] 8 CFR §103.2(b)(1).

[218] AFM 11.1; AFM 10.3.

[219] USCIS, R. Divine, "Legal and Discretionary Analysis for Adjudication" (May 3, 2006), AILA Doc. No. 06051562.

Copyright © 2017. American Immigration Lawyers Association. All rights reserved.

"such adverse factors do exist, it is again the applicant's burden to overcome these factors."[220]

(2) Standard of Proof

Generally, the "standard of proof applied in most administrative immigration proceedings is the 'preponderance of the evidence' standard," which is interpreted as determining, "even if the director has some doubt as to the truth,"[221] whether "relevant, probative, and credible evidence" has been submitted to "lead the director to believe that the claim is 'probably true' or 'more likely than not.'"[222] "More likely than not" has been defined "as a greater than 50 percent probability of something occurring."[223] More important, petitions "are not required to demonstrate eligibility beyond a reasonable doubt."[224] USCIS confirmed that "[a]djudicators receive training on the appropriate burden of proof standards during their USCIS Academy training."[225]

If "the director can articulate a material doubt," then an RFE should be issued.[226] But "if that doubt leads the director to believe that the claim is probably not true, [the adjudicator may] deny the application or petition."[227] The practitioner should also note USCIS guidance regarding the relationship between the standard of proof and specific evidentiary requirements: "Additionally, the 'preponderance of the evidence' standard does not relieve the petitioner or applicant from satisfying the basic evidentiary requirements set by regulation. Therefore, if the regulations require specific evidence, the applicant is required to submit that evidence."[228]

For RFEs or NOIDs "erroneously includ[ing] phrases such as 'clearly establish' or other language alluding to a standard other than 'preponderance of the evidence,'" USCIS advises that "the most appropriate response is to respond to the RFE, submitting the requested evidence, and note that the adjudicator appears to have referenced the incorrect standard of proof in the notice."[229] USCIS acknowledged, however, that because of "the heavy caseload of [USCIS] adjudicators, there may be instances when the wording of a particular decision or RFE may not have articulated

---

[220] AFM 11.1.

[221] Id.; Matter of Chawathe, 25 I&N Dec. 369 (AAO Oct. 20, 2010), AILA Doc. No. 10102030.

[222] AFM 11.1; Matter of Chawathe, 25 I&N Dec. 369 (AAO Oct. 20, 2010), AILA Doc. No. 10102030.

[223] AFM 11.1 (citing U.S. v. Cardozo-Fonseca, 480 U.S. 421 (1987)).

[224] USCIS, W. Yates, "Requests for Evidence (RFE) and Notices of Intent to Deny (NOID)" (Feb. 16, 2005), AILA Doc. No. 05021810.

[225] "AILA/USCIS Liaison Minutes" (Oct. 28, 2008), AILA Doc. No. 08110767.

[226] AFM 11.1; Matter of Chawathe, 25 I&N Dec. 369 (AAO Oct. 20, 2010), AILA Doc. No. 10102030.

[227] Id.

[228] AFM 11.1.

[229] "AILA/USCIS Liaison Minutes" (Oct. 28, 2008), AILA Doc. No. 08110767.

Copyright © 2017. American Immigration Lawyers Association. All rights reserved.

the appropriate standard of proof" and stated that "USCIS is currently reviewing this issue globally with a special emphasis on quality assurance."[230]

(3) Evidence

USCIS seems to rely upon the "best evidence rule," which generally requires the introduction of the evidence that best proves the fact at issue, as "an external basis for verifying claimed facts":

"The rule states that where the contents of a document are at issue in a case, the document itself must be introduced rather than secondary evidence as to its content. For example, if an issue in an interview is the date on which a divorce decree became final, the divorce decree itself should be introduced, rather than a letter stating when the decree became final or a second marriage certificate stating the date of the first divorce."[231]

The main exceptions allow for acceptance of a certified copy of a public document and for acceptance of a copy as an original if "a document is prepared in carbon or multiple copies (as opposed to photocopies created after the fact)."[232]

For nonimmigrant visa petitions, as a practical matter, almost all evidence submitted to USCIS will be private documentary evidence, such as job descriptions, diplomas, transcripts, credentials evaluations, experience letters, annual reports, support statements, "business records and tax records."[233] Generally, supporting documents "need not comply with the strict rules of evidence."[234] The practitioner should note the following guidance: "Circumstances surrounding the creation of such records, such as evidence that a document was created immediately at the time of the event it purports to record, as part of the regular conduct of business, may affect the weight given to the document."[235]

A petitioner may also wish to provide an expert opinion "on a particular set of facts or circumstances involving scientific, technical, or other specialized knowledge."[236] USCIS guidance states:

"In order to provide such opinion testimony, the witness must be qualified as an expert by knowledge, skill, experience, training or education. When an expert witness is offered, the person offering the testimony of the witness must prove the

---

[230] "AILA/USCIS Liaison Minutes" (Mar. 19, 2009), AILA Doc. No. 09031920.

[231] AFM 11.1 (stating that "[w]hile the best evidence rule is not strictly applicable in an administrative proceeding, [the adjudicator] should adhere to it as closely as [the adjudicator] can").

[232] *Id.*

[233] *Id.* (mentioning "business records and tax records").

[234] *Id.*

[235] *Id.*

[236] *Id.* (stating that a "petitioner or applicant may also occasionally offer testimony from someone claimed to be an expert").

Copyright © 2017. American Immigration Lawyers Association. All rights reserved.

experience and qualifications of the witness and the facts of the case at hand. The testimony of expert witnesses has been accepted by USCIS, and findings based on their testimony have been upheld by the courts."[237]

As stated by USCIS: "Primary evidence is evidence which on its face proves a fact. For example, the divorce certificate is primary evidence of a divorce."[238] As another example, an annual report listing a multinational corporation's parent, affiliates, and subsidiaries may serve as primary evidence of the corporate relationship necessary for an L-1 petition.

The regulations provide that the "non-existence or other unavailability of required evidence creates a presumption of ineligibility,"[239] "which is the applicant or petitioner's burden to overcome,"[240] and which may be rebutted by submitting secondary evidence, which is interpreted as "evidence which makes it more likely that the fact sought to be proven by the primary evidence is true, but cannot do so on its own face, without any external reference."[241] For example, if "a birth or marriage certificate[] does not exist or cannot be obtained, an applicant or petitioner must demonstrate this and submit secondary evidence, such as church or school records, pertinent to the facts at issue."[242] And if secondary evidence is also unavailable, then "the applicant or petitioner must demonstrate the unavailability of both the required document and relevant secondary evidence, and submit two or more affidavits, sworn to or affirmed by persons who are not parties to the petition who have direct personal knowledge of the event and circumstances."[243] In short, "[s]econdary evidence must overcome the unavailability of primary evidence, and affidavits must overcome the unavailability of both primary and secondary evidence."[244]

In order to demonstrate that a government record is unavailable, the petitioner or applicant "must submit an original written statement on government letterhead establishing this from the relevant government or other authority,"[245] attesting to the fact that no record exists or can be located, or that the record sought was part of some segment of records which were lost or destroyed.[246] The "statement must indicate the reason the record does not exist, and indicate whether similar records for the time and

---

[237] Id.

[238] Id.

[239] 8 CFR §103.2(b)(2)(i).

[240] AFM 11.1.

[241] Id.

[242] 8 CFR §103.2(b)(2)(i).

[243] Id.

[244] Id.

[245] 8 CFR §103.2(b)(2)(ii).

[246] AFM 11.1.

Copyright © 2017. American Immigration Lawyers Association. All rights reserved.

place are available."[247] An exception for this governmental statement is if the Foreign Affairs Manual (FAM) "indicates this type of document generally does not exist."[248]

As stated by USCIS: "A petitioner or applicant cannot simply assert that the primary evidence does not exist."[249] The petitioner or applicant who has been unsuccessful in obtaining "the necessary document or statement from the relevant foreign authority may submit evidence that repeated good faith attempts were made to obtain the required document or statement,"[250] such as an affidavit,[251] but USCIS may nevertheless require the document if it "finds that such documents or statements are generally available."[252]

b. Review by the USCIS Adjudicator

Generally, adjudication of a request for immigration benefits entails legal analysis, discretionary analysis, security clearances from law enforcement databases, and analysis of a waiver application,[253] if applicable. Legal analysis for USCIS involves reviewing the requirements of the nonimmigrant visa classification and assessing whether the petitioner has demonstrated eligibility.[254] Discretionary analysis typically follows the legal analysis, because even if the petitioner or applicant has established eligibility, USCIS may rely upon its discretion to deny a petition or application,[255] as discussed below. USCIS guidance directs the adjudicator to consider the following questions:

- "Is the form complete and signed?

- "Is the applicant or petitioner represented by counsel with Form G-28 on file?

- "Are there any responses which require further explanation or indicate there may be a need for additional documentation?

- "Are all necessary supporting documents present and translated into English, if necessary?

- "Is the beneficiary statutorily eligible for the benefit sought?

- "Are all supporting documents authentic and unaltered?

---

[247] 8 CFR §103.2(b)(2)(ii).

[248] Id.; AFM 11.1.

[249] AFM 11.1.

[250] 8 CFR §103.2(b)(2)(ii).

[251] AFM 11.1.

[252] 8 CFR §103.2(b)(2)(ii).

[253] USCIS, R. Divine, "Legal and Discretionary Analysis for Adjudication" (May 3, 2006), AILA Doc. No. 06051562. For details on waiver law and process, see The Waivers Book (AILA 2d Ed. 2017), https://agora.aila.org/product/detail/3208.

[254] Id.

[255] Id.

Copyright © 2017. American Immigration Lawyers Association. All rights reserved.

- "Is there any reason to suspect fraud?
- "Are there any legal precedent decisions or court orders relevant to the case?
- "Are there any ancillary applications which should be filed by the applicant (*e.g.* a waiver application, adjustment application, advance parole request, or employment authorization request)?"[256]

USCIS guidance also states:

"Even in non-discretionary cases, the consideration of evidence is somewhat subjective. For example, in considering an employment-based petition, the adjudicator must examine the beneficiary's employment experience and determine if the experience meets or exceeds, in quality and quantity, the experience requirement stated on the labor certification by the employer. However, a subjective consideration of facts should not be confused with an exercise of discretion. Like an exercise of discretion, a subjective consideration of facts does not mean the decision can be arbitrary, inconsistent or dependent upon intangible or imagined circumstances."[257]

(1) RFEs and NOIDs

This section will address the details of RFEs and NOIDs, as well as the differences between the two. USCIS guidance states that issuance of an RFE or NOID "is usually discretionary but strongly recommended" for that gray area between clear eligibility and clear ineligibility,[258] as discussed above:

"USCIS adjudicators must recognize that our customers find our procedures and requirements sometimes difficult to follow, and denial of a case that ultimately could have been approved can cause significant delay and inconvenience to a customer. Therefore, unless the case is clearly ineligible for approval (i.e., denial decision) or the filer has demonstrated eligibility by the preponderance of evidence without special cause for concern (i.e., approval decision), adjudicators normally should issue a RFE or a NOID, whichever is more appropriate."[259]

---

[256] AFM 10.3.

[257] AFM 10.15.

[258] USCIS, W. Yates, "Requests for Evidence (RFE) and Notices of Intent to Deny (NOID)" (Feb. 16, 2005), AILA Doc. No. 05021810. This memorandum rescinded the previous guidance, USCIS, W. Yates, "Requests for Evidence (RFE)" (May 4, 2004), because "the May 4, 2004 memorandum appears to have created a misimpression that cases could be denied without RFE or NOID even when a RFE or NOID may have given the applicant or petitioner ('filer') a reasonable chance to resolve adjudicators' concerns about lack of evidence or about apparent ineligibility." USCIS, W. Yates, "Requests for Evidence (RFE) and Notices of Intent to Deny (NOID)" (Feb. 16, 2005), AILA Doc. No. 05021810.

[259] USCIS, W. Yates, "Requests for Evidence (RFE) and Notices of Intent to Deny (NOID)" (Feb. 16, 2005), AILA Doc. No. 05021810.

Copyright © 2017. American Immigration Lawyers Association. All rights reserved.

The regulations note the three choices available to USCIS if "all required initial evidence has been submitted but the evidence submitted does not establish eligibility:"

- Deny the petition or application due to ineligibility;

- Issue an RFE; or

- Issue a NOID, stating "the basis for the proposed denial, and requir[ing] that the applicant or petitioner submit a response within a specified period of time as determined by USCIS."[260]

USCIS guidance states the following "five options" if "a case is received with all required initial evidence and the adjudicator cannot decide the case based on the information submitted":

- "Perform research using such internal sources," as discussed below;

- "Request that the applicant or petitioner submit additional documentary evidence";

- "Interview the petitioner, beneficiary, applicant, or other witnesses";

- "Conduct... a field examination," permitted by the local field office policy; and

- "Execute an investigation."[261]

Experience has shown, however, that for employment-based nonimmigrant petitions, the first two options are most frequently used. USCIS guidance also states: "It is possible to combine, in a sense, a RFE and a NOID, requesting additional evidence on certain points and explaining an anticipated basis for denial on others."[262] Experience has shown, however, that these documents tend to be RFEs. In a sense, any RFE indicates that the petition has the potential to be denied, even if it is not specifically worded as a NOID. The preamble to a final rule states: "USCIS cannot, however, issue a NOID based on missing initial evidence if an RFE has not first been issued."[263]

The RFE or NOID must be in writing, stating the following:

- The "type of evidence required";

- The requirement of initial evidence and/or additional evidence to be submitted; or

---

[260] 8 CFR §103.2(b)(8)(iii).

[261] AFM 10.5.

[262] USCIS, W. Yates, "Requests for Evidence (RFE) and Notices of Intent to Deny (NOID)" (Feb. 16, 2005), AILA Doc. No. 05021810.

[263] 72 Fed. Reg. 19100 (Apr. 17, 2007).

Copyright © 2017. American Immigration Lawyers Association. All rights reserved.

- The "bases for the proposed denial" which should be "sufficient to give the applicant or petitioner adequate notice and sufficient information to respond."[264]

(a) RFEs

As stated by USCIS: "A Request for Evidence (RFE) is a notice issued by USCIS to an applicant or petitioner seeking immigration benefits requesting initial or additional evidence to establish eligibility."[265] Generally, an RFE represents USCIS using its discretion to request additional evidence of eligibility for the classification sought, rather than an outright denial based on ineligibility or "for lack of initial evidence,"[266] as noted above. USCIS guidance states that "RFEs should, if possible, be avoided," especially for "'discretionary' evidence," because they "may unnecessarily burden USCIS resources, duplicate other adjudication officers' efforts, and delay case completion."[267]

Instead, "[i]nitial case review should be thorough," and the adjudicator should consult "other USCIS records" and determine whether information is "readily available from external sources" before issuing an RFE.[268] The sources accessed by USCIS adjudicators which are relevant to employment-based nonimmigrant visa petitions include the following:

- The regulations,[269] including preambles to the final rules;[270]

- Federal court decisions;

- Decisions by the BIA and Administrative Appeals Office (AAO);

- Operating instructions;

- "USCIS policies and procedures, field manuals, policy memoranda, the Administrative Manual, and other official policy documents";

- The FAM;

- "Other secondary sources (*i.e.*, legal dictionaries, legal encyclopedias, etc.)";[271]

- Opinions of USCIS and legacy INS general counsel;

- U.S. Department of Labor (DOL) Occupational Outlook Handbook and Dictionary of Occupational Titles;[272]

---

[264] 8 CFR §103.2(b)(8)(iv).

[265] 72 Fed. Reg. 19100 (Apr. 17, 2007); AFM 10.5.

[266] 8 CFR §103.2(b)(8)(ii) and (iii).

[267] AFM 10.5.

[268] *Id.*

[269] AFM 14.1.

[270] AFM 14.3.

[271] AFM 14.1.

[272] AFM 14.6.

Copyright © 2017. American Immigration Lawyers Association. All rights reserved.

- Immigration treatises and reference books;[273]
- USCIS databases and records on the immigration histories of foreign nationals;[274]
- USCIS intranet and the internet;[275]
- The law library of Congress;[276] and
- USCIS's Validation Instrument for Business Enterprises (VIBE) system.[277]

USCIS guidance states that "USCIS may consider other evidence from its files or from other sources when adjudicating an application or petition."[278] The guidance does caution the adjudicator, however, that before an adverse decision is based on such outside or USCIS information, the petitioner or applicant should be provided with "an opportunity to rebut the information, unless the applicant or petitioner was already aware of such information, or could reasonably be assumed to be aware of such information."[279] In response to comments of concerns about how this external information is used, USCIS stated:

> "USCIS adjudicators have the authority to research and confirm the veracity of any relevant information. They are not necessarily 'looking for information outside of the record,' but may only be fact-checking assertions and evidence relating to the petition. For example, they may check a State's online corporate records to confirm that a petitioner actually is incorporated as claimed. They may also be confirming the standing of the attorney of record."[280]

Although previously certain cases were denied without an RFE or NOID based on information outside the record but within public domain, many iterations of the issue seem to have been resolved.[281] For example, RFEs and denials were previously issued

---

[273] AFM 14.7.

[274] AFM 14.8.

[275] AFM 14.9.

[276] AFM 14.10. For a discussion of the weight of the various sources of law, see Volume 1: Chapter One, "Introduction."

[277] USCIS, "New Validation Tool Aids Adjudication of Certain Employment-Based Petitions Questions and Answers" (Jan. 24, 2012), AILA Doc. No. 12012447.

[278] AFM 11.5 (citing 8 CFR §103.2(b)). It does not appear, however, that any section of this regulation actually "provides that USCIS may consider other evidence from its files or from other sources when adjudicating an application or petition," as is stated in the "Outside Sources and Other USCIS Records" section of the AFM at 11.5.

[279] AFM 11.5 (relating to derogatory information).

[280] "AILA/USCIS Liaison Minutes" (Oct. 28, 2008), AILA Doc. No. 08110767.

[281] "AILA Liaison/SCOPS Q&As" (July 30, 2008), AILA Doc. No. 08082160; "AILA/USCIS Liaison Minutes" (Oct. 28, 2008), AILA Doc. No. 08110767 (stating that if external information "yields reliable evidence that may adversely affect the adjudication, then [USCIS] agree[s] that, before relying on the information, a notice of derogatory information is required … to provide a petitioner or applicant the opportunity to rebut any information discovered by an adjudicator from an external source") (internal citation omitted).

Copyright © 2017. American Immigration Lawyers Association. All rights reserved.

based on information from Wikipedia, an online reference guide where "[a]nyone with internet access can write and make changes to Wikipedia articles,"[282] but the issue has been resolved and "there should not be additional RFEs or denials citing Wikipedia."[283]

Another issue regarding an outside source has arisen in recent years. In response to congressional pressure regarding perceived fraud in the petitioning process, USCIS contracted with Dun and Bradstreet, Inc. (D&B) to obtain access to "commercially available data ... to validate and verify information submitted by petitioners."[284] The result is the Verification Initiative for Business Enterprises (VIBE) program:

"Adjudicators will use the information from VIBE to verify the petitioner's qualifications. For example, if a petitioner is seeking L-1 status for a beneficiary, VIBE will help adjudicators confirm that the petitioner has a foreign affiliate, which is a requirement for granting L-1 status.

"Information from VIBE will help confirm petitioners' financial viability in cases where petitioners must establish ability to pay.

"USCIS will not deny a petition based upon information from VIBE without first giving the petitioner the opportunity to respond to the agency's concerns. USCIS will issue an RFE or a Notice of Intent to Deny (NOID) if it is necessary to resolve relevant inconsistencies or other issues that emerge upon review of VIBE-supplied information that are material to the benefit requested."[285]

The 2011 rollout of VIBE resulted in a torrent of RFEs and NOIDs questioning the bona fides of established employers, thus raising concerns about the reliability of the information in the database.[286] As a result, D&B set up a portal for U.S.-based, privately held companies "to create, verify or correct [their] D&B record ... online through the firm's new streamlined process."[287] Note that "U.S.-based publicly traded companies, government entities and foreign companies wishing to create, update or

---

[282] See generally "Wikipedia: About," http://en.wikipedia.org/wiki/Wikipedia:About.

[283] "AILA Liaison/SCOPS Q&As" (July 30, 2008), AILA Doc. No. 08082160.

[284] "USCIS Letter to Senator Grassley on H-1B Fraud Prevention and Detection" (Nov. 10, 2009), AILA Doc. No. 09120161. See also USCIS, "Revised H-1B Anti-Fraud Operational Guidance" (June 13, 2013), AILA Doc. No. 14010245.

[285] USCIS, "Validation Instrument for Business Enterprises (VIBE) Program" (updated Jan. 24, 2012), https://www.uscis.gov/working-united-states/information-employers-employees/employer-information/vibe/validation-instrument-business-enterprises-vibe-program. See also "USCIS Request for Comments on Draft RFE Template for L-1Bs" (July 7, 2015), AILA Doc. No. 15071760.

[286] E.g., "AILA Liaison/USCIS Meeting Questions and Answers" (Apr. 7, 2011), AILA Doc. No. 11040735; "Tips for Submitting VIBE RFE Examples" (Apr. 11, 2011), AILA Doc. No. 11041133.

[287] USCIS, "Validation Instrument for Business Enterprises (VIBE) Program" (updated Jan. 24, 2012), https://www.uscis.gov/working-united-states/information-employers-employees/employer-information/vibe/validation-instrument-business-enterprises-vibe-program. The portal can be found at http://fedgov.dnb.com/webform.

Copyright © 2017. American Immigration Lawyers Association. All rights reserved.

view their report with D&B may use *www.dnb.com*; however, they may be subjected to direct marketing from D&B."[288] While D&B may try to solicit fees for such things as "expediting" records corrections, payment of such fees is not necessary and is likely pointless.[289]

As a practical matter, the practitioner should ensure that complete corporate information is provided in the initial filing, and, if aware of any discrepancies between the submission and the petitioner's D&B information, either correct the D&B or explain the discrepancy from the outset. The information that USCIS accesses through VIBE includes:

- "Business activities, such as type of business (North American Industry Classification System code), trade payment information, and status (active or inactive).

- "Financial standing, including sales volume and credit standing.

- "Number of employees, both on-site and globally.

- "Relationships with other entities, including foreign affiliates.

- "Type of office. (Examples include single entities, branches, subsidiaries and headquarters.)

- "Type of legal entity. For example, LLC, partnership or corporation.

- "Company executives.

- "Date of establishment as a business entity.

- "Current physical address."[290]

For a discussion of derogatory information from other external sources, see the discussion of NOIDs below.

If an RFE is necessary, then "the adjudicator must: (1) determine what evidence is lacking and (2) request that evidence."[291] The guidance cautions against the issuance of multiple RFEs; instead, the adjudicator should be able to "generally avoid this situation by conducting a careful initial case review and then issuing a clearly drawn

---

[288] USCIS, "Validation Instrument for Business Enterprises (VIBE) Program" (updated Jan. 24, 2012), https://www.uscis.gov/working-united-states/information-employers-employees/employer-information/vibe/validation-instrument-business-enterprises-vibe-program.

[289] "VSC Stakeholder Meeting Minutes" (May 6, 2011), AILA Doc. No. 11091463; "AILA/VSC Liaison Practice Pointer: Dealing with VIBE" (Sept. 14, 2011), AILA Doc. No. 11091469; "USCIS Releases Streamlined Process for VIBE Submissions" (Jan. 26, 2013), AILA Doc. No. 12012690.

[290] USCIS, "Validation Instrument for Business Enterprises (VIBE) Program" (updated Jan. 24, 2012), https://www.uscis.gov/working-united-states/information-employers-employees/employer-information/vibe/validation-instrument-business-enterprises-vibe-program.

[291] AFM 10.5.

Copyright © 2017. American Immigration Lawyers Association. All rights reserved.

RFE."[292] But "additional evidence may raise unforeseen new questions that the adjudicator could not have identified during initial case review,"[293] in which case a subsequent RFE may be issued.

Issuance of an RFE is "most appropriate when a particular piece or pieces of necessary evidence are missing."[294] For example, an RFE may be issued if an L-1 petition has evidence of all the regulatory criteria except the corporate relationship. Experience has also shown, however, that RFEs are issued to resolve an adjudicator's questions or doubt. A common example is the request for full job descriptions of subordinate employees of L-1 managers, to confirm that the subordinates are in turn professionals or managers. The USCIS guidance provides this helpful direction about "limited, specific" RFEs:

> "[T]he highest quality RFE is one that limits the request to the missing evidence. Generally, it is unacceptable to issue a RFE for a broad range of evidence when, after review of the record so far, only a small number of types of evidence is still required. 'Broad brush' RFEs tend to generate 'broad brush' responses (and initial filings) that overburden our customers, over-document the file, and waste examination resources through the review of unnecessary, duplicative, or irrelevant documents. While it is sensible to use well articulated templates that set out an array of common components of RFEs for a particular case type, it is not normally appropriate to 'dump' the entire template in a RFE; instead, the record must be examined for what is missing, and a limited, specific RFE should be sent, using the relevant portion from the template. The RFE should set forth what is required in a comprehensible manner so that the filer is sufficiently informed of what is required. If a filing is so lacking in initial evidence that a 'wholesale' RFE from a template seems appropriate, an adjudicator should confirm this with a supervisor before doing so.

> "It can be helpful to customers to articulate how and why information already submitted is not sufficient or persuasive on a particular issue. Customers can become confused and frustrated when they receive general requests for information that they believe they have already submitted. The effort it takes to assess existing evidence helps either to spur the customer to provide persuasive evidence, or to form the basis of a convincing denial notice in the absence of such new evidence."[295]

---

[292] *Id.*

[293] *Id.*

[294] USCIS, W. Yates, "Requests for Evidence (RFE) and Notices of Intent to Deny (NOID)" (Feb. 16, 2005), AILA Doc. No. 05021810.

[295] *Id.*

Copyright © 2017. American Immigration Lawyers Association. All rights reserved.

"In short, an adjudicator should strive to request the evidence needed for thorough, correct decision-making. An adjudicator should not 'fish' for evidence."[296]

Nevertheless, multiple reports also expressed concern about "receipt of requests for information that bear little or no relevance to the benefit being sought and/or are overreaching 'boilerplate' requests."[297] USCIS responded that such RFEs may be because of lack of "immediate access to prior filings,"[298] and acknowledged "that it is neither in the interests of the agency nor those of the regulated public to issue 'boilerplate' RFEs that do not address the specific deficiencies in a request for benefits."[299] Requests for "sensitive financial information about potential employers or employees" should be issued "only when absolutely necessary to adjudicate effectively a pending petition."[300] USCIS agreed with the suggestion to include the following points in adjudicator training:

- "Excessive documentation should not be requested as a routine matter;

- "Only in 'doubtful or marginal cases' should voluminous, non-specific documentation be requested;

- "The Service should recognize established companies with solid records of immigration compliance; and

- "Where additional documentation is necessary, such requests should be limited to the specific issues in question."[301]

Nevertheless, boilerplate and broad-brush RFEs remain common, and experience has shown that this creates a dilemma for the practitioner, both for representing the client before USCIS and for client relations. First, the practitioner may submit all available evidence with the initial filing and struggle to find more documents if an RFE is issued, which is very common for certain nonimmigrant classifications, such as O-1, L-1B, and L-1A function managers. This strategy also has three disadvantages. First, the practitioner may overload the adjudicator with too much potentially irrelevant evidence, as noted below, which, as a practical matter, may make it more difficult for the adjudicator to locate and identify the pertinent evidence. Second, the practitioner may be placed in the awkward position of informing the adjudicator that the documents and information requested in the RFE were already

---

[296] AFM 10.5: Requesting Additional Information.

[297] "AILA Liaison/USCIS Meeting Questions and Answers" (Oct. 27, 2009), AILA Doc. No. 09110664; "AILA/USCIS Liaison Minutes" (Mar. 19, 2009), AILA Doc. No. 09031920; "AILA/USCIS Liaison Minutes" (Oct. 28, 2008), AILA Doc. No. 08110767.

[298] "AILA Liaison/USCIS Meeting Questions and Answers" (Oct. 27, 2009), AILA Doc. No. 09110664.

[299] "AILA/USCIS Liaison Minutes" (Oct. 28, 2008), AILA Doc. No. 08110767.

[300] "AILA Liaison/USCIS Meeting Questions and Answers" (Oct. 27, 2009), AILA Doc. No. 09110664.

[301] *Id.*

Copyright © 2017. American Immigration Lawyers Association. All rights reserved.

provided. Third, the client may be displeased at the delay because of all the work necessary to gather the evidence when preparing to file the petition.

Alternatively, the practitioner may strive to limit the documents submitted with the initial filing, but one drawback is the potential for a denial without an RFE or NOID. In addition, submitting less than a comprehensive filing almost guarantees an RFE or NOID, assuming the case will not be denied outright. The client may be displeased at the delay, especially if the client already provided the information requested to the practitioner.

Generally, the first strategy is recommended, because then the practitioner may inform the client that complete documents were submitted but were overlooked or disregarded by the adjudicator, and the practitioner may delicately inform the adjudicator that the requested documents are being submitted a second time. This approach is supported by USCIS guidance:

> "In responding to an RFE, the petitioner/applicant should make every effort to provide the information requested, or articulate clearly, in its response to an RFE, the reasons why it believes that the RFE is overly broad or fails to address the particular issue or issues identified by the adjudicator.... It is in the strong interest, therefore, of the applicant/petitioner to provide all relevant documentation— including that relating to prior submissions to the agency, if relevant, with its original submission and/or in response to an RFE—in meeting its burden of establishing eligibility for the benefit sought."[302]

USCIS may also request an original document in an RFE, "at any time ... for review,"[303] such as if there is a question of the authenticity of the document,[304] and "[f]ailure to submit the requested original document by the deadline may result in denial or revocation of the underlying application or benefit."[305] USCIS should return the original document to the petitioner "upon completion of the adjudication."[306] If the document is not returned "within a reasonable time after completion of the adjudication, the petitioner or applicant may request return of the original document by submitting a properly completed and signed Form G-884 to the adjudicating USCIS office."[307]

An RFE should not change the "priority date of a properly filed petition," regardless of whether the documents requested are for initial or other evidence, but the practitioner should note that the processing time "will start over from the date of

---

[302] "AILA/USCIS Liaison Minutes" (Oct. 28, 2008), AILA Doc. No. 08110767.

[303] 8 CFR §103.2(b)(5).

[304] AFM 11.1.

[305] 8 CFR §103.2(b)(5); AFM 11.1.

[306] 8 CFR §103.2(b)(5).

[307] *Id.*

Copyright © 2017. American Immigration Lawyers Association. All rights reserved.

receipt of the required initial evidence."[308] This indicates that the time to respond to
the RFE does not count toward the processing time for purposes of case status reports
and inquiries:

> "If USCIS requests that the applicant or petitioner submit additional evidence or
> respond to other than a request for initial evidence, any time limitation imposed on
> USCIS for processing will be suspended as of the date of request. It will resume at
> the same point where it stopped when USCIS receives the requested evidence or
> response, or a request for a decision based on the evidence."[309]

(b) NOIDs

In contrast, a NOID "is designed to provide a poignant taste of denial without its
immediate consequences, so that the filer can understand why the evidence submitted
has not been persuasive and can have the best chance to overcome the deficiency if
possible."[310] A NOID is defined as "a written notice issued by USCIS to an applicant
or petitioner that USCIS has made a preliminary decision to deny the application or
petition."[311] In addition:

> "A NOID may be based on evidence of ineligibility or on derogatory information
> known to USCIS, but not known to the petitioner or applicant.... The NOID
> provides the applicant or petitioner with an opportunity to inspect and rebut the
> evidence forming the basis of the decision to deny the petition or application."[312]

A NOID should not be "broad brush" and the adjudicator should evaluate the
evidence already submitted in the same manner as discussed above regarding
RFEs.[313] An adjudicator should select the NOID over the RFE if "initial evidence is
predominantly present" and one of the following criteria are present:

- The petition "does not appear to establish eligibility by the preponderance of the
  evidence,"[314] such as if initial evidence for all individual regulatory criteria has
  been submitted but the totality of the evidence does not demonstrate eligibility for
  the nonimmigrant classification;

- The petition "appears to be ineligible for approval but not necessarily incurable";
  or

---

[308] 8 CFR §103.2(b)(10)(i). This regulation also discusses rescheduling biometrics appointments, such as for
U nonimmigrant petitions. For a discussion of interim benefits, *See* 8 CFR §103.2(b)(10)(ii).

[309] 8 CFR §103.2(b)(10)(i).

[310] USCIS, W. Yates, "Requests for Evidence (RFE) and Notices of Intent to Deny (NOID)" (Feb. 16, 2005),
AILA Doc. No. 05021810.

[311] 72 Fed. Reg. 19100 (Apr. 17, 2007).

[312] *Id.*

[313] USCIS, W. Yates, "Requests for Evidence (RFE) and Notices of Intent to Deny (NOID)" (Feb. 16, 2005),
AILA Doc. No. 05021810.

[314] *Id.*

Copyright © 2017. American Immigration Lawyers Association. All rights reserved.

- The "adjudicator intends to rely for denial on evidence not submitted by the filer,"[315] as discussed above.

Derogatory information of which the petitioner or applicant is unaware should be disclosed to the petitioner or applicant, with an opportunity to respond through explanation, rebuttal, or provision of other information,[316] except for the following:

- Statutory ineligibility for the classification sought "shall be based only on information contained in the record of proceeding";

- A discretionary determination as part of the adjudication will not be disclosed to the petitioner or applicant if it was "based in whole or in part on classified information not contained in the record and not made available to the applicant, provided the USCIS Director or his or her designee has determined that such information is relevant and is classified … as requiring protection from unauthorized disclosure in the interest of national security"; and

- Classified information will not be provided to the petitioner or applicant, unless the classifying authority has agreed in writing to such disclosure.[317]

- USCIS guidance states that for derogatory outside information, "[n]ormally, 30 days is the shortest time that can be given for response."[318]

(c) Deadline for Response

The RFE or NOID should also state "the deadline for response," which for an RFE should not "exceed twelve weeks" and which for a NOID should not "exceed thirty days."[319] In promulgating the rule on RFE and NOID response times, the "final rule [did] not include a specific presumptive minimum time frame for responses," because the goal was "to give USCIS flexibility to set the timeframes for responding to RFEs as a matter of agency practice and procedure and to more specifically set a reasonable time based upon the nature of the information requested."[320] USCIS also noted that "[c]ertain applicants and petitioners are also exploiting the RFE process to deliberately delay the processing and thus prolong their stay in the United States."[321]

---

[315] *Id.* (citing 8 CFR §103.2(b)(16)(i) ("filing generally"); 8 CFR §§214.2(h)(10)(ii), (k)(10)(iii), (*l*)(8)(i), (o)(7)(i), and (p)(9)(i) ("H, L, O, and P nonimmigrant petitions and K nonimmigrant extension of stay applications")).

[316] 8 CFR §103.2(b)(16). *See also* AFM 10.3.

[317] 8 CFR §103.2(b)(16). *See also* AFM 11.1.

[318] USCIS, W. Yates, "Requests for Evidence (RFE) and Notices of Intent to Deny (NOID)" (Feb. 16, 2005), AILA Doc. No. 05021810.

[319] 8 CFR §§103.2(b)(8)(iv) and (ii) (noting that USCIS may "request that the missing initial evidence be submitted within a specified period of time as determined by USCIS").

[320] 72 Fed. Reg. 19100 (Apr. 17, 2007).

[321] *Id.*

Copyright © 2017. American Immigration Lawyers Association. All rights reserved.

Generally, the response times should fit into the following categories, with days being counted as calendar days:[322]

Type of Documents or Information Requested	# of Days
Initial evidence required by the form	30
Evidence for Form I-539, Application to Extend/Change Nonimmigrant Status	30
Evidence available in the United States	42
Evidence available abroad	84

If the RFE is sent by mail, then the petitioner or applicant "will receive three additional days."[323] The guidance also notes: "Exceptionally unusual applications or petitions may require atypical response times. In all circumstances, adjudicators should try to choose an RFE response timeframe that is appropriate under the facts of the case."[324]

In January 2009, TSC guidance confirmed that its RFE deadlines were conforming to these guidelines, as until then it seemed there was a "blanket policy of 30 days" for RFEs.[325] Experience since then has been that most RFEs provide 84 days, although one will occasionally see one allowing only 30 days. USCIS took care to note that the revised regulations do not "let individual adjudicators determine when to offer less than thirty days to respond to a NOID and how long to give in such instances."[326] But the practitioner should note that the petitioner may be provided only 30 days to respond even if the request is not for initial evidence, as CSC has stated that "in some instances, even if it is additional evidence, [CSC] may only allow 30 days and both the regulation and memo support this practice,"[327] based on the interpretation that the other USCIS guidance "are simply guidelines."[328] USCIS also noted that a potentially

---

[322] AFM app. 10-9.

[323] *Id.* The practitioner should note that the proper citation is 8 CFR §103.5a(b), and not 8 CFR §103.5(b), as stated in the guidance.

[324] AFM app. 10-9.

[325] "AILA Liaison/TSC Meeting Minutes" (Jan. 22, 2009), AILA Doc. No. 09091565; "AILA Liaison/TSC Meeting Minutes" (Nov. 12, 2008), AILA Doc. No. 09021275.

[326] 72 Fed. Reg. 19100 (Apr. 17, 2007).

[327] "AILA Liaison/CSC Meeting Minutes" (Feb. 25, 2009), AILA Doc. No. 09022669; "AILA Liaison/CSC Meeting Minutes" (Jan. 28, 2009), AILA Doc. No. 09012968.

[328] "AILA Liaison/CSC Meeting Minutes" (Feb. 25, 2009), AILA Doc. No. 09022669. *See also* "TSC RFEs Requesting Foreign Documents: Are You Getting the Short Shrift? AILA Wants to Know!!" (Jan. 19, 2010), AILA Doc. No. 10011966 (discussing RFE deadline of 30 days for a request for additional evidence).

Copyright © 2017. American Immigration Lawyers Association. All rights reserved.

shorter response time does not "restrict the applicant's or petitioner's ability to file all of the obviously necessary and relevant documents with the original application,"[329] so the practitioner should file as complete a petition as possible, as discussed above.

The regulations state that USCIS will not grant extensions or additional time to respond to an RFE or NOID.[330] But TSC guidance states that additional time to respond may be requested, "up to the regulatory limit" of 12 weeks, by "submit[ting] a written request explaining the reason more time is needed and asking for additional time."[331] A "'Request for Additional Time' response sheet" may be developed and circulated "to allow requests for additional time to be readily identified in the Mailroom,"[332] although this worksheet remains unavailable to date. The practitioner should note the request from TSC that the practitioner filing the extension request should explain the need for additional time, but should not submit a partial RFE response.[333] Instead, "all evidence" should be filed "at the same time with the response,"[334] presumably by the new deadline. The practitioner should note, however, that this request assumes that the extension is granted; if there is no answer from TSC on the extension request, then all evidence, or as much as may be gathered in time, must be filed by the initial RFE response deadline.[335]

(d) Response to the RFE or NOID

The petitioner's timely response to the RFE or NOID may be one of the following:

- A "complete response containing all requested information at any time within the period afforded;

- A "partial response," which USCIS will construe as a request "for a decision based on the record"; or

- Withdrawal of the petition or application,[336] as discussed below.

USCIS should "hold the case in abeyance while waiting for the applicant or petitioner to respond."[337] Then, upon filing of a response by the petitioner or applicant, or if "the time to submit a response elapses, the case shall be returned to

---

[329] 72 Fed. Reg. 19100 (Apr. 17, 2007).

[330] 8 CFR §103.2(b)(8)(iv).

[331] "AILA Liaison/TSC Meeting Minutes" (Jan. 22, 2009), AILA Doc. No. 09091565; "AILA Liaison/TSC Meeting Minutes" (Nov. 12, 2008), AILA Doc. No. 09021275.

[332] *Id.*

[333] *Id.*

[334] *Id.*

[335] This may be similar to the extension request in the context of responding to an audit of a labor certification application. See Volume 2: Chapter Two, "The Labor Certification Application."

[336] 8 CFR §103.2(b)(11).

[337] AFM 10.11.

Copyright © 2017. American Immigration Lawyers Association. All rights reserved.

its original processing place," which "will normally make the case ready for immediate adjudication."[338]

Failure to timely respond to an RFE or NOID may result in summary denial of the petition due to abandonment, denial "based on the record, or deni[al] for both reasons,"[339] unless the response was affected by a natural disaster, such as the Haiti earthquake in January 2010:

> "USCIS will consider exercising discretion on a case-by-case basis not to deny for abandonment or failure to respond to a Request for Evidence (RFE) if the applicant, petitioner or beneficiary lives in the affected area or if the alien needed to obtain documentation from the affected area or otherwise demonstrates a direct connection between the disaster and the failure to pursue the application or petition."[340]

USCIS will not accept piecemeal responses: "All requested materials must be submitted together at one time, along with the original USCIS request for evidence or notice of intent to deny. Submission of only some of the requested evidence will be considered a request for a decision on the record."[341]

If the evidence submitted in the response "does not establish filing eligibility at the time the application or petition was filed," then the petition or application will be denied, as well as any subsequent petition or application that is based on the underlying initial petition or application,[342] such as an application to adjust status that is concurrently filed with an immigrant visa petition. And if the petitioner fails to provide all of the requested documents "and requests a decision based on the evidence already submitted, a decision shall be issued based on the record."[343] Specifically, "failure to submit requested evidence which precludes a material line of inquiry shall be grounds for denying the application or petition."[344]

(2) Checking the Status of a Pending Petition or Application

The practitioner may check the status of a petition or application online,[345] although "there is a several day delay in the system update to the USCIS Case Status

---

[338] *Id.*

[339] 8 CFR §103.2(b)(13)(i); AFM 10.1.

[340] USCIS, A. Mayorkas, "Initial Relief Efforts for Aliens Affected by the Jan. 12, 2010, Haiti Earthquake" (Jan. 15, 2010), AILA Doc. No. 10011960.

[341] 8 CFR §103.2(b)(11).

[342] 8 CFR §103.2(b)(12).

[343] 8 CFR §103.2(b)(14).

[344] *Id.*

[345] USCIS website, "My Case Status," https://egov.uscis.gov/casestatus/landing.do.

Copyright © 2017. American Immigration Lawyers Association. All rights reserved.

Online," including a delay of up to a week for approvals.[346] But the online system may not provide details about a USCIS office to which a file is transferred or about case status after a file is transferred.[347] Importantly, in the event that "an RFE is sent but not received, and there is no indication of an RFE in the Customer Relationship Interface System (CRIS), the case may be denied due to abandonment, particularly if USCIS records indicate that the notice was mailed to a correct address."[348]

The practitioner may also inquire about the status of a petition or application through the NCSC at 1-800-375-5283, between 8:00 am and 6:00 pm (Eastern time), on Mondays through Fridays.[349] The practitioner should "have available [the] receipt number, alien registration number, type of application filed and date filed." Attorneys and accredited representatives should be able to "quickly connect with an NCSC customer service representative, who will send the inquiry to the appropriate USCIS office for resolution.... The customer service representative will assess the nature of the call and either accept a service request or transfer the call for more in-depth review."[350]

USCIS encourages individuals to "take note of the following information":

- "The name and/or ID number of the NCSC representative;
- "The date and time of the call; and
- "Any service request referral number, if a service referral on a pending case is taken."[351]

Generally, the NCSC representative may assist with the following "tier one inquiries following established USCIS scripts":[352]

- "Getting Ready to File;
- "Need to Order Form;
- "Benefits for U.S. Citizens;

---

[346] "SCOPS Practice Alert: USCIS Case Status Online Notification Delay" (Oct. 22, 2009), AILA Doc. No. 09102221.

[347] "AILA Practice Alert: USCIS on Problems with Online Case Tracking" (Dec. 20, 2010), AILA Doc. No. 10122078.

[348] *Id. See also* "USCIS Q&As from AILA Meeting" (Mar. 29, 2012), AILA Doc. No. 12033045, p. 18.

[349] "AILA/VSC Committee Practice Pointer: Using NCSC and Preparing Your Case for AILA Liaison" (Oct. 16, 2009), AILA Doc. No. 09101664.

[350] "USCIS Alert on Change to NCSC Call Routing Procedures" (Aug. 9, 2013), AILA Doc. No. 13080962.

[351] USCIS, "Case Status Inquiries with the Service Centers" (Aug. 6, 2009), AILA Doc. No. 09081067.

[352] "AILA/VSC Committee Practice Pointer: Using NCSC and Preparing Your Case for AILA Liaison" (Oct. 16, 2009), AILA Doc. No. 09101664; USCIS, "Customer Service Reference Guide" (updated Nov. 25, 2014), https://www.uscis.gov/about-us/electronic-reading-room/customer-service-resource-guide/customer-service-reference-guide (stating that the "guide is a duplicate of the information used by the representatives at the National Customer Service Center to answer calls on [USCIS] toll free numbers").

Copyright © 2017. American Immigration Lawyers Association. All rights reserved.

- "Benefits for Permanent Residents;
- "Nonimmigrants;
- "Refugees and Asylees;
- "Filing for Permanent Residence based on Family;
- "Filing for Permanent Residence based on Employment;
- "Employment Authorization;
- "Temporary Protected Status;
- "Special Programs;
- "Immigration-Related Responsibilities when Hiring an Employee and Completing Form I-9;
- "Hiring a Foreign National for Short-Term Employment;
- "Helping a Foreign National Employee Get Permanent Resident Status; and
- "Treaty Traders and Investors."[353]

The NCSC representative should "escalate" the inquiry "to a tier two USCIS officer in the following circumstances":

- "Approved case: non-delivery of a document or document not received;
- "Explanation needed regarding an RFE;
- "Pending case: Consulate or POE [point of entry] has not received notice of approved I-129;
- "Pending case: Change of information on I-129;
- "Pending case: companion cases have been separated; and
- "Service Center error on a card, approval, or receipt notice."[354]

Then, if "more than *15 days have passed*" since the NCSC inquiry "and the issue has not been resolved or explained," then the practitioner may "email the proper USCIS Service Center" with jurisdiction over the petition or application:

- CSC: csc-ncsc-followup@dhs.gov;
- VSC: vsc.ncscfollowup@dhs.gov;
- NSC: ncscfollowup.nsc@dhs.gov; and
- TSC: tsc.ncscfollowup@dhs.gov.[355]

---

[353] USCIS, "Customer Service Reference Guide" (updated Nov. 25, 2014), https://www.uscis.gov/about-us/electronic-reading-room/customer-service-resource-guide/customer-service-reference-guide.

[354] "AILA/VSC Committee Practice Pointer: Using NCSC and Preparing Your Case for AILA Liaison" (Oct. 16, 2009), AILA Doc. No. 09101664.

Copyright © 2017. American Immigration Lawyers Association. All rights reserved.

The email should contain the same information noted above,[356] including "all the tracking and/or other information about the initial call to NCSC."[357] And if "the NCSC did not issue a service request" following the initial inquiry, then the practitioner should "indicate the reason the NCSC representative did not issue the request,"[358] if known. It is critical that the practitioner first contact NCSC, because "the USCIS Service Center follow-up email boxes are exactly for this purpose: follow-ups."[359] Generally, correspondence of a case status inquiry sent by mail to a Service Center "automatically will be rejected by the Mailroom with the direction for the inquirer to lodge the case status request with NCSC." Therefore, the practitioner should not mail a case status inquiry with an updated G-28.[360]

If there is no response from the Service Center "**within 21 days** of contacting the appropriate Service Center," then the practitioner "may email the USCIS Headquarters Office of Service Center Operations … at: *SCOPSSCATA@dhs.gov,"* and a response should be provided "from this email address *within ten days*."[361] Individuals residing in Canada who cannot contact the NCSC may email "a general inquiry mailbox" at *USCIS.Canada@dhs.gov.*

(3) Final Decision on the Petition

The decision on the petition will be in writing and sent to the petitioner and the attorney.[362] The petitioner or applicant "shall be permitted to inspect the record of proceeding which constitutes the basis for the decision,"[363] except as discussed below. If the petition or application is approved, then usually a detailed analysis of the reasons for approval is not necessary.[364] But in the case of denial, USCIS guidance directs adjudicators to "articulate clearly the legal analysis and then, separately, any discretionary analysis":

---

[355] USCIS, "General Case Inquiries" (July 26, 2013), *http://bit.ly/USCISinquiry* (emphasis in original). *See also* "Case Resolution Strategies" (June 1, 2016), AILA Doc. No. 10100873, pdf p. 25.

[356] USCIS, "General Case Inquiries" (July 26, 2013), http://bit.ly/USCISinquiry.

[357] "AILA/TSC Practice Pointer: USCIS Service Center Liaison Follow-Up Procedures" (Sep. 15, 2009), AILA Doc. No. 09091564.

[358] USCIS, "General Case Inquiries" (July 26, 2013), *http://bit.ly/USCISinquiry.*

[359] "AILA/TSC Practice Pointer: USCIS Service Center Liaison Follow-Up Procedures" (Sep. 15, 2009), AILA Doc. No. 09091564.

[360] "AILA Liaison/TSC Meeting Minutes" (May 19, 2009), AILA Doc. No. 09052966.

[361] USCIS, "General Case Inquiries" (July 26, 2013), *http://bit.ly/USCISinquiry* (emphasis in original). *See also* "Case Resolution Strategies" (June 1, 2016), AILA Doc. No. 10100873, pdf p. 25.

[362] 8 CFR §103.2(b)(19).

[363] 8 CFR §103.2(b)(16).

[364] USCIS, R. Divine, "Legal and Discretionary Analysis for Adjudication" (May 3, 2006), AILA Doc. No. 06051562.

Copyright © 2017. American Immigration Lawyers Association. All rights reserved.

"In cases in which the legal ineligibility is completely clear, an extensive write-up of any discretionary analysis may not be necessary, but the decision should still reflect that the adjudicator did make a discretionary assessment, where applicable. If there is a possibility that the legal analysis could be overturned (such as in an unsettled area of law), or if the legal analysis leads to a finding of eligibility, but the discretionary analysis is negative, then it is critical to articulate carefully the discretionary analysis by setting forth the positive and negative factors considered and the reasons the negative factors outweigh the positive. The rationale should be set forth so that the customer, any administrative reviewer (AAO, BIA, IJ [immigration judge]), and the federal courts can understand it and appreciate its logic."[365]

"Denials may consist mainly of 'boilerplate' paragraphs explaining the legal basis for the adverse decision or they may be entirely original. In all cases, the specific facts of the individual case must be explained in the decision. If a denial is based on precedent decisions, those decisions should be properly cited in the body of the denial notice."[366]

A denial notice should inform the petitioner or applicant of the right to appeal.[367] As stated by USCIS guidance: "Denial decisions are normally sent to a supervisory officer for review and signature prior to mailing."[368] For further discussion of discretionary analysis and security clearances, see Volume 2: Chapter Four, "Consular Processing, Adjustment of Status, and Permanent Residence Issues."

If an RFE or NOID was issued, then:

"[The] adjudicator should review all relevant evidence, which may include evidence previously submitted and now supplemented. It is not normally appropriate to review the response without reference to the existing record. Normally, it should be appropriate to approve or deny a case without further RFE. Sometimes, however, a RFE response opens a new line of inquiry requiring a new RFE or NOID. In other cases, a RFE response may provide the missing initial evidence, but now the combined record requires notice to the filer why the record appears unpersuasive, so that a NOID is required. It should be rare to follow a NOID with a new RFE or NOID, rather than approval or denial."[369]

And if "the response to the NOID is not sufficient, then, after review of the entire record, the preparation of the denial decision often will require limited

---

[365] *Id.*

[366] AFM 10.3. For additional discussion of denial notices, including the "five elements," *see* AFM 10. 7.

[367] AFM 10.7.

[368] AFM 10.3.

[369] USCIS, W. Yates, "Requests for Evidence (RFE) and Notices of Intent to Deny (NOID)" (Feb. 16, 2005), AILA Doc. No. 05021810.

Copyright © 2017. American Immigration Lawyers Association. All rights reserved.

editing of the NOID, although sometimes the response will require more detailed analysis for denial."[370]

(a) Withholding Adjudication of the Petition

USCIS may withhold adjudication if it is determined that:

"[A]n investigation has been undertaken involving a matter relating to eligibility or the exercise of discretion, where applicable, in connection with the application or petition, and that the disclosure of information to the applicant or petitioner in connection with the adjudication of the application or petition would prejudice the ongoing investigation."[371]

If the investigation remains incomplete for "one year of its inception," then USCIS "shall review the matter and determine whether adjudication of the petition or application should be held in abeyance for six months or until the investigation is completed, whichever comes sooner."[372] There are then periodic reviews every six months, conducted by the district director, the regional commissioner, and two associate commissioners.[373]

(b) Withdrawal

A petition or application may be withdrawn "at any time until a decision is issued by USCIS."[374] But the practitioner should note and caution the client that "a withdrawal may not be retracted,"[375] and "USCIS's acknowledgement of a withdrawal may not be appealed."[376] Similarly, a "denial due to abandonment may not be appealed, but an applicant or petitioner may file a motion to reopen,"[377] as discussed below. The regulations also state:

"Withdrawal or denial due to abandonment does not preclude the filing of a new application or petition with a new fee. However, the priority or processing date of a withdrawn or abandoned application or petition may not be applied to a later application petition. Withdrawal or denial due to abandonment shall not itself affect the new proceeding; but the facts and circumstances surrounding the prior application or petition shall otherwise be material to the new application or petition."[378]

---

[370] *Id.*

[371] 8 CFR §103.2(b)(18).

[372] *Id.*

[373] *Id.*

[374] 8 CFR §103.2(b)(6). This regulation also states that withdrawal of an approved petition may take place "until the person is admitted or granted adjustment or change of status, based on the petition."

[375] 8 CFR §103.2(b)(6).

[376] 8 CFR §103.2(b)(15).

[377] *Id.*

[378] *Id.*

Copyright © 2017. American Immigration Lawyers Association. All rights reserved.

3. *Duplicate Approval Notices*

A duplicate approval notice may be requested by the same petitioner or applicant "who filed the original application or petition," on Form I-824, Application for Action on an Approved Application or Petition, with fee and copies of the petition and receipt notice.[379] Alternatively, CSC "will issue a duplicate approval notice if the request is made within 30 days of the petition's approval."[380] The practitioner may contact the PPU if applicable, or call NCSC if the petition "was filed under regular processing" and then send a written request to the CSC at *csc-ncsc-followup@dhs.gov.*[381] If 30 days have passed since the approval date, then the request must be made on Form I-824.[382]

Form I-824 may also be filed to request notification of a new U.S. consulate of the petition approval or of a new port of entry of an approved waiver application, as long as the petition remains valid.[383] A form I-824 "shall be approved if the Service determines the applicant has fully demonstrated eligibility for the requested action."[384] The practitioner should note that there "is no appeal from the denial of an application filed on Form I-824."[385]

Form I-824 should not be necessary if USCIS fails to mail approval notices due to an "interruption" in computer systems; USCIS usually catches the error of its own accord and initiates the production and mailing of approval notices.[386] Similarly, when erroneous notices were "generated" in the past, USCIS "instructed" officers "to respond to any inquiries in this regard that the system was experiencing problems and to disregard any erroneous notices that may have been generated."[387] And if USCIS mails out blank approval notices, the error should be corrected by USCIS, and an individual should not need to contact NCSC.[388] For example, when USCIS issued "approximately 500 incorrect" approval notices, USCIS mailed corrected notices and

---

[379] 8 CFR §§103.5b(a) and (b); USCIS, "Instructions for Form I-824, Application for Action on an Approved Application or Petition" (Oct. 21, 2015), https://www.uscis.gov/sites/default/files/files/form/i-824instr.pdf; AFM 10.6.

[380] "AILA/CSC Liaison Practice Pointer: Requesting a Duplicate Approval Notice" (Sept. 30, 2009), AILA Doc. No. 09093061.

[381] *Id.*

[382] *Id.*

[383] 8 CFR §§103.5b(a) and (b); USCIS, "Instructions for Form I-824, Application for Action on an Approved Application or Petition" (Oct. 21, 2015), https://www.uscis.gov/sites/default/files/files/form/i-824instr.pdf; AFM 10.6.

[384] 8 CFR §103.5b(c).

[385] *Id.*

[386] "VSC Acknowledges Failure to Mail All Notices from the Last Week in October" (Nov. 21, 2008), AILA Doc. No. 08112130.

[387] *Id.*

[388] "VSC Advises AILA of Blank I-539 Approval Notices Sent" (Jan. 28, 2009), AILA Doc. No. 09012868.

Copyright © 2017. American Immigration Lawyers Association. All rights reserved.

directed those who did not receive a corrected notice to contact the NCSC or CSC and VSC at the follow-up email addresses stated above, with "Approval Notice Error" as the subject line of the email.[389]

4. Appeals and Motions to Reopen

Both AAO appeals and motions to reopen and reconsider are filed on Form I-290B, Notice of Appeal or Motion, as discussed in the following sections.

The practitioner should confirm that the proper box is checked for motion or appeal, because only one box can be checked,[390] and although an appeal may be treated as a motion to reopen, as discussed below, a motion will only be reviewed by USCIS as a motion:

> "If the Center determines that the additional materials do not overcome the denial, it will re-affirm the denial, and the case will not be forwarded to the AAO for consideration. A cover letter requesting that the Service Center treat the Form I-290B as a motion, and if denied, as an appeal, will not be effective to correct a mistake on the form. The Petitioner must properly designate whether it is seeking to appeal the decision or request the Service Center to reopen or reconsider its own decision."[391]

If a petition is denied and the petitioner files an appeal or motion to reopen and then files a second petition, the practitioner should warn the client that the second petition will not be processed until the appeal or motion to reopen is adjudicated.[392] USCIS policy is to hold the second petition "in abeyance pending the outcome of appeal."[393] USCIS indicated that this policy went into effect following the issuance of USCIS field guidance in 1989.[394] In response to the comment that the legacy INS memorandum did not dictate this specific policy, USCIS stated:

> "The internal coordination called for in the 1989 Memorandum serves important interests in maintaining consistent adjudication and in preventing fraud and misrepresentation. If the subsequent filing presents, in essence, the exact same

---

[389] "USCIS to Issue Revised Approval Notices for Certain Forms I-129 and I-539" (Feb. 1, 2010), AILA Doc. No. 10020320.

[390] USCIS, "Instructions for Form I-290B, Notice of Appeal or Motion," https://www.uscis.gov/files/form/i-290binstr.pdf, at 4.

[391] "NSC Liaison Committee Practice Tip on Filing I-290B Appeals" (Oct. 15, 2008), AILA Doc. No. 08101571 (emphasis removed).

[392] "AILA Liaison/SCOPS Q&As" (July 30, 2008), AILA Doc. No. 08082160.

[393] *Id.*; "AILA/USCIS Liaison Minutes" (Oct. 28, 2008), AILA Doc. No. 08110767.

[394] "AILA/USCIS Liaison Minutes" (Oct. 28, 2008), AILA Doc. No. 08110767 (citing legacy INS, R. Norton, "Adjudication of Petitions and Applications which are in Litigation or Pending Appeal" (Feb. 8, 1989), AILA Doc. No. 08091267). The legacy INS memorandum also discusses "the potential 'embarrassment' of an inconsistent decision" and the potential "significant financial loss to the Service if an appellant succeeds in recovering legal fees under the Equal Access to Justice Act."

Copyright © 2017. American Immigration Lawyers Association. All rights reserved.

claim as the filing that is on appeal, deferring adjudication of the later filing conserves limited resources and safeguards against 'forum shopping.' These concerns are particularly weighty when the petitioner or applicant does not, in the subsequent filing, disclose the materially relevant fact of the other pending case. In other cases, the internal coordination could result in the expedited adjudication of the appeal."[395]

For a discussion of appeals and motions vis-à-vis the accrual of unlawful presence, see below.

a. Appeals

Denials of most nonimmigrant visa petitions may be appealed to the AAO.[396] A denial notice should inform the petitioner of the right to appeal to the AAO, "which considers cases under the appellate jurisdiction of the Associate Commissioner, Examinations"[397] and attach the appeal form.[398] An appeal must be filed within 30 days of service of the denial decision on Form I-290B, Notice of Appeal or Motion, with fee.[399] If the denial was served by mail, as is usually the case, three days are added, meaning that the appeal must be received by USCIS within 33 days of the date the denial was sent.[400]

An untimely appeal will be rejected, with USCIS retaining any filing fee.[401] An exception is if the "untimely appeal meets the requirements of a motion to reopen" or a motion to reconsider, as discussed below, in which case "the appeal must be treated as a motion, and a decision must be made on the merits of the case."[402] Jurisdiction generally lies with the same official who made the adverse decision, "unless the affected party moves to a new jurisdiction," in which case the appeal should be reviewed with the office with jurisdiction over the new "geographic location."[403]

---

[395] "AILA/USCIS Liaison Minutes" (Oct. 28, 2008), AILA Doc. No. 08110767 (citing legacy INS, R. Norton, "Adjudication of Petitions and Applications which are in Litigation or Pending Appeal" (Feb. 8, 1989), AILA Doc. No. 08091267).

[396] USCIS, "The Administrative Appeals Office (AAO)" (updated June 13, 2016), https://www.uscis.gov/about-us/directorates-and-program-offices/administrative-appeals-office-aao/administrative-appeals-office-aao.

[397] 8 CFR §103.3(a)(1)(iv).

[398] 8 CFR §§103.3(a)(1)(i) and (iii)(A).

[399] 8 CFR §103.3(a)(2)(i).

[400] 8 CFR §103.8(b). *See also* AAO Practice Manual 3.7(c).

[401] 8 CFR §103.3(a)(2)(v)(B)(1).

[402] 8 CFR §103.3(a)(2)(v)(B)(2).

[403] 8 CFR §103.3(a)(2)(ii).

Copyright © 2017. American Immigration Lawyers Association. All rights reserved.

Complete appeal documents must be submitted in the appeal timeframe.[404] Appeals should NOT be sent to the AAO,[405] but instead should be sent to the address appropriate for the type of petition, using the chart on the USCIS website.[406]

When filing the appeal, the practitioner can opt to submit a brief with the appeal form, submit a brief within 30 calendar days, or not submit one at all, by checking the appropriate box on Form I-290B.[407] If more than the additional 30 days is needed, a written request can be submitted to the AAO "for additional time to submit a brief."[408] "[The] thirty-day briefing period is automatically granted by checking the appropriate box on Form I-290B. It does not require additional AAO approval. If, however, an appellant requires additional time beyond the original thirty days, the AAO may extend the deadline for submitting briefs for good cause shown. Appellants may mail or fax extension requests directly to the AAO within thirty calendar days of filing the appeal."[409]

That being said, the AAO encourages filing of the brief with the Form I-290B for practical reasons: "While appellants may submit supplemental materials after filing the appeal, the submission of additional materials complicates USCIS's ability to match the appeal with those materials in time for the field office's initial review of the appeal (initial field review). *Id*. To ensure that the field office has a meaningful opportunity to consider supplemental materials during initial field review, the AAO recommends that appellants submit supplemental materials concurrently with the appeal."[410] However, preparation of an effective brief often takes longer than 30 days, and so filing with the Notice often will not be possible. If the brief is filed later, practitioners should follow up by telephone (at the number noted below) to ensure that the brief and the Notice were matched up at AAO.

The request for additional time and the brief should be filed directly with the AAO[411] at:

U.S. Citizenship and Immigration Services

---

[404] 8 CFR §§103.3(a)(2)(i) and (a)(2)(vi).

[405] USCIS, "Instructions for Form I-290B, Notice of Appeal or Motion," https://www.uscis.gov/files/form/i-290binstr.pdf, at 6.

[406] USCIS, "Direct Filing Addresses for Form I-290B, Notice of Appeal or Motion" (updated Dec. 30, 2015), https://www.uscis.gov/i-290b-addresses.

[407] USCIS, "Form I-290B" (version 1/23/14 N), https://www.uscis.gov/i-290b, Part 3. *See also* AAO Practice Manual 3.8.

[408] 8 CFR §103.3(a)(2)(vii).

[409] "USCIS Answers Questions About Practicing Before the AAO" (Feb. 9, 2016), AILA Doc. No. 16020932 (USCIS response dated Sept. 11, 2015, to inquiry from attorney Naomi Schorr, regarding confusion between the language in the regulations and on the form's instructions). *See also* AAO Practice Manual 3.8(c).

[410] AAO Practice Manual 3.8.

[411] 8 CFR §103.3(a)(2)(viii).

Copyright © 2017. American Immigration Lawyers Association. All rights reserved.

Administrative Appeals Office
20 Massachusetts Avenue, NW, MS 2090
Washington, D.C. 20529-2090[412]

The AAO can be contacted at:
Fax 703-778-7483
Phone 703-224-4501[413]

In addition, "[t]he AAO has the discretion to accept or reject supplemental information submitted after the deadline for submitting briefs. To supplement a pending appeal with new evidence after the deadline, the appellant should add 'SUPPLEMENTAL EVIDENCE' in all capital letters in the subject line of the cover letter,"[414] and provide the appellant's full name, the A number if any, the receipt numbers for the Notice of Appeal and for the underlying petition, and a copy of the G-28 that was submitted with the appeal.[415]

A request may also be made for oral argument before the AAO, generally within the 30-day appeal period, with a written request "specifically" explaining "why oral argument is necessary."[416] USCIS "has sole authority to grant or deny a request for oral argument."[417] If the request is granted, then the AAO "shall set the time, date, place, and conditions of oral argument."[418] Oral argument may be granted "when a case involves an issue of particular significance and the AAO determines that it would benefit from supplemental argument."[419]

AAO will entertain requests for expedited treatment where the requester can show severe financial loss, an "extreme emergent situation," a "humanitarian situation," a nonprofit's request that furthers the country's "cultural and social interests," a Defense Department or national security situation where the request comes from a U.S. government entity and states that a delay will be "detrimental to the government," a USCIS error that created an unreasonable delay, or "a compelling interest of USCIS."[420] The expedite request should be mailed or faxed to the AAO address or fax number above, with a cover clearly marked "EXPEDITE REQUEST." Documentation to support the basis for the request should be included.[421]

---

[412] AAO Practice Manual 6.1.

[413] *Id.*

[414] AAO Practice Manual 3.8(d).

[415] AAO Practice Manual 6.1.

[416] 8 CFR §103.3(b)(1).

[417] 8 CFR §103.3(b)(2).

[418] *Id.*

[419] AAO Practice Manual 6.5.

[420] AAO Practice Manual 6.3.

[421] *Id.*

Copyright © 2017. American Immigration Lawyers Association. All rights reserved.

The beneficiary of a visa petition may not file an appeal.[422] If an appeal is filed by the beneficiary, then the appeal will "be rejected as improperly filed," and "any filing fee the Service has accepted will not be refunded."[423] If an attorney files an appeal without a fully executed G-28, then "the appeal is considered improperly filed," and "any filing fee the Service has accepted will not be refunded regardless of the action taken."[424] But if the appeal "fails to identify specifically any erroneous conclusion of law or statement of fact for the appeal," then the USCIS officer "shall summarily dismiss" the appeal. If an attorney files such an appeal, the officer may make a finding of "frivolous behavior."[425]

A USCIS official "may treat the appeal … as a motion for the purpose of granting the motion"[426] by "decid[ing] whether or not favorable action is warranted," rather than forwarding the appeal to the AAO by taking "favorable action" within "45 days of receipt of the appeal,"[427] although this does not preclude the official from reopening or reconsidering the decision of his own accord, as discussed below. Otherwise, the official "shall promptly forward the appeal and the relating record of proceeding to the AA[O]."[428]

If the USCIS official "decides favorable action is warranted" for an appeal that is properly filed except for a fully executed G-28, then the attorney should be provided 15 days to submit a complete G-28.[429] If the proper G-28 is not submitted by the deadline, then "the official may, on his or her own motion," issue a new favorable decision "without notifying the attorney."[430] For appeals where the official does not take favorable action, the attorney should be directed to file the complete G-28 with the AAO, and the "appeal may be considered properly filed as of its original filing date," as long as the attorney files "a properly executed Form G-28."[431] USCIS should forward the appeal and the related record of proceeding to the AAO.[432]

USCIS may also request "for review of a decision (approval or denial) by an appellate authority," such as the BIA or AAO, by certifying the decision. USCIS guidance states that certification "should be initiated in a case where":

---

[422] 8 CFR §103.3(a)(1)(iii)(B).

[423] 8 CFR §103.3(a)(2)(v)(A)(1).

[424] 8 CFR §103.3(a)(2)(v)(A)(2)(i).

[425] 8 CFR §103.3(a)(1)(v). Attorney sanctions are discussed in 8 CFR §292.3.

[426] 8 CFR §103.5(a)(8).

[427] 8 CFR §103.3(a)(2)(iii).

[428] 8 CFR §103.3(a)(2)(iv).

[429] 8 CFR §103.3(a)(2)(v)(A)(2)(ii).

[430] Id.

[431] 8 CFR §103.3(a)(2)(v)(A)(2)(iii).

[432] Id.

Copyright © 2017. American Immigration Lawyers Association. All rights reserved.

- "Headquarters has directed certification of an individual case, class of cases or cases with particular fact patterns; or

- "The deciding official believes the facts or issues of a case are so novel or complex that review by a higher level of authority is an appropriate means of obtaining guidance."[433]

The USCIS adjudicator "must assemble a complete record of proceedings in the same manner as a record prepared for an appeal, including the 'Board' and 'Public' copies."[434] And a "certified decision is not considered final until the order has been considered by the appellate body."[435] An appeal may be withdrawn, by making the request "in writing, before a decision is made."[436] The AAO applies a de novo standard of review.[437] The appeal decision "must be in writing," with a copy served on the appellant and the attorney, if applicable.[438]

b. *Motions to Reopen and Motions to Reconsider*

A petitioner or applicant may also file a motion to reopen or reconsider, and "the official having jurisdiction may, for proper cause shown, reopen the proceeding or reconsider the prior decision."[439] Both motions to reconsider a USCIS action and motions "to reopen a proceeding before the Service" must be filed within 30 days of the USCIS decision,[440] with "the official who made the latest decision in the proceeding unless the affected party moves to a new jurisdiction," in which case the motion should be filed with the official who has jurisdiction over the "new geographical location[]."[441]

One exception is that USCIS may, in its discretion, excuse a late filing "where it is demonstrated that the delay was reasonable and was beyond the control of the applicant or petitioner."[442] The practitioner may find it helpful to consider how these factors are interpreted in the context of nunc pro tunc requests for extension or change of status, as discussed below.

---

[433] AFM 10.18.

[434] *Id.*

[435] *Id.*

[436] 8 CFR §103.3(a)(2)(ix).

[437] AAO Practice Manual 3.4; "AILA/USCIS Liaison Minutes" (Mar. 19, 2009), AILA Doc. No. 09031920; CIS Ombudsman, P. Khatri, "Recommendation from the CIS Ombudsman to the Director, USCIS" (Dec. 6, 2005), https://www.dhs.gov/xlibrary/assets/CISOmbudsman_RR_20_Administrative_ Appeals_12-07-05.pdf (citing *Dor v. INS*, 891 F.2d 997, 1002 n.9 (2d Cir. 1989); *Spencer Enterprises Inc. v. U.S.*, 229 F. Supp. 2d 1025, 1043 (E.D. Cal. 2001), *aff.'d.* 345 F.3d 683 (9th Cir. 2003)).

[438] 8 CFR §103.3(a)(2)(x).

[439] 8 CFR §103.5(a)(1)(i).

[440] *Id.*

[441] 8 CFR §103.5(a)(1)(ii).

[442] 8 CFR §103.5(a)(1)(i).

Copyright © 2017. American Immigration Lawyers Association. All rights reserved.

The motion should be filed on Form I-290B, Notice of Appeal or Motion, "signed by the affected party or the attorney or representative of record," with the following documents:

- Legal brief, if the practitioner wishes to submit one;

- Filing fee; and

- Statement discussing "whether or not the validity of the unfavorable decision has been or is the subject of any judicial proceeding and, if so, the court, nature, date, and status or result of the proceeding."[443]

The documents should be "[a]ddressed to the official having jurisdiction" and "[s]ubmitted to the office maintaining the record upon which the unfavorable decision was made for forwarding to the official having jurisdiction."[444] A motion that does not comply with the requirements, discussed above and below, "shall be dismissed,"[445] based on "failure to meet those requirements, using a written order describing the deficiencies."[446] If a motion is dismissed on this ground, then the filing fee will not be refunded, "unless is it determined that there was some USCIS error involved in the applicant or petitioner submitting the motion."[447]

All supporting documents for the motion "must be submitted concurrent with the motion."[448] Merely filing a motion to reopen or reconsider "does not stay the execution of any decision in a case or extend a previously set departure date," unless USCIS "directs otherwise,"[449] as discussed below. The form may not be filed by the beneficiary of a petition or the beneficiary's attorney.[450]

The motion to reopen "must state the new facts to be proved in the reopened proceeding and be supported by affidavits or other documentary evidence."[451] If the motion to reopen is granted, then "the proceeding shall be reopened," and the "notice and any favorable decision may be combined."[452] If the motion is being filed after a

---

[443] 8 CFR §103.5(a)(1)(iii).

[444] 8 CFR §§103.5(a)(1)(iii)(D) and (E).

[445] 8 CFR §103.5(a)(4).

[446] AFM 10.17.

[447] Id.

[448] USCIS, "Instructions for Form I-290B, Notice of Appeal or Motion," https://www.uscis.gov/files/form/i-290binstr.pdf.

[449] 8 CFR §103.5(a)(1)(iv). Neither does filing a "subsequent application." 8 CFR §103.5(a)(1)(iv).

[450] USCIS, "Instructions for Form I-290B, Notice of Appeal or Motion," https://www.uscis.gov/files/form/i-290binstr.pdf.

[451] 8 CFR §103.5(a)(2).

[452] 8 CFR §103.5(a)(4). It does not appear that this section is cross-applicable to motions to reconsider, because the regulations specifically mention "proceedings" only for motions to reopen in several places. 8 CFR §§103.5(a)(1)(i), (a)(4), and (a)(5).

Copyright © 2017. American Immigration Lawyers Association. All rights reserved.

petition or application was "denied due to abandonment," then it must include "evidence that the decision was in error because" of one of the following reasons:

- "The requested evidence was not material to the issue of eligibility";

- The filing included the necessary initial evidence, "or the request for initial evidence or additional information" was provided by the deadline, such as a copy of delivery confirmation; or

- The RFE "was sent to an address other than that on the application, petition, or notice of representation," or the petitioner or applicant notified USCIS in writing "of a change of address or change of representation subsequent to filing and before the Service's request was sent, and the request did not go to the new address."[453]

The motion to reconsider "must state the reasons for reconsideration and be supported by any pertinent precedent decisions to establish that the decision was based on an incorrect application of law or Service policy."[454] In addition, a motion to reconsider a decision "must, when filed, also establish that the decision was incorrect based on the evidence of record at the time of the initial decision,"[455] which means that the error should not be based on evidence that was not part of the record of the initial decision.

As stated by USCIS guidance:

"Ordinarily a motion is adjudicated by the same officer who made the original decision. In all cases, the motion must be considered by the same office (district, service center, immigration court, AAO, or BIA) which most recently decided the case.... Consideration of a motion is a two-stage process: the first stage is a determination as to whether the case should be reopened or reconsidered, and the second stage (for those motions that are reopened or reconsidered) is the rendering of a new decision."[456]

The practitioner should note that USCIS generally gives deference to the original decision if the filing entailed "any form of extension or similar benefit" and the original filing and motion featured the same parties: "Deference is required even if there is a precedent or adopted decision. Furthermore, officers may only draw a different conclusion where there is a clear change or distinction in facts. Even in such instances, a supervisor must explicitly concur with the different conclusion."[457]

---

[453] 8 CFR §103.5(a)(2).

[454] 8 CFR §103.5(a)(3).

[455] *Id.*

[456] AFM 10.17.

[457] *Id.*

Copyright © 2017. American Immigration Lawyers Association. All rights reserved.

The USCIS decision on a motion "must be in writing," with a copy … served on the affected party and the attorney or representative of record, if any."[458] The USCIS "official who denied an application or petition may treat the appeal from that decision as a motion for the purpose of granting the motion."[459] If the motion is granted, then the USCIS decision on the motion may be in one of the following formats:

- "To approve the application or petition, if all reasons for the original denial have been overcome and no new reasons have arisen;

- "To deny the application or petition for the same reasons as in the original decisions, but with an explanation as to why the arguments submitted in the motion were not persuasive;

- "To deny the application or petition for reasons not contained in the original decision, provided the applicant or petitioner is given an opportunity to review and rebut any new evidence of which he or she was not already aware; or

- "A combination of the second and third possibilities (reaffirmation of the original reasons plus the addition of new reasons)."[460]

A USCIS denial of a motion may be appealed to the AAO "only if the original decision was appealable" to the AAO.[461] The regulations on oral argument before the AAO for appeals, discussed above, also apply to motions to reopen and reconsider.[462]

USCIS may also reopen a proceeding or reconsider a decision. If the new decision is favorable to the petitioner or applicant, then "the Service officer shall combine the motion and the favorable decision in one action,"[463] and no additional notice of USCIS's reopening or reconsideration need be provided.[464] But if the new decision is unfavorable to the petitioner or applicant, then USCIS may issue a Notice of Intent,[465] and "shall give the affected party 30 days after service of the motion to submit a brief," as well as a "new appeal period."[466]

This time period may be extended "for good cause shown."[467] USCIS may reopen or reconsider a decision, for example, if the adjudicator "determine[s] that a petition

---

[458] 8 CFR §§103.5(a)(7) and 103.3(a)(2)(x).

[459] 8 CFR §103.5(a)(8).

[460] AFM 10.17.

[461] 8 CFR §103.5(a)(6).

[462] 8 CFR §103.5(a)(7).

[463] 8 CFR §103.5(a)(5)(i).

[464] AFM 10.17.

[465] Id.

[466] Id.

[467] 8 CFR §103.5(a)(5)(ii).

Copyright © 2017. American Immigration Lawyers Association. All rights reserved.

should not have been approved but there are no specifically applicable grounds for revocation in the regulations."[468]

If the petitioner or applicant "does not wish to submit a brief, the affected party may waive the 30-day period."[469] But USCIS guidance also cautions: "Unless there is a clear finding of fraud or substantial material misrepresentation, or the facts have clearly and distinctly changed, officers should not reopen a previously approved and valid application or petition. Even in these circumstances, a supervisor must explicitly concur with the different conclusion."[470]

B. Change of Nonimmigrant Status

A foreign national may change nonimmigrant status to a new classification upon approval of a petition which includes a request for change of status by USCIS.[471] To be eligible for change of status, the foreign national must have maintained lawful nonimmigrant status.[472] In addition, as discussed in individual chapters, if the beneficiary of a change of status petition is also the beneficiary of an immigrant visa petition or application to adjust status, then the change of status petition may be denied, depending on the requisite intent of the requested nonimmigrant classification.[473]

Change of status is also unavailable to foreign nationals who received graduate medical education or training in J-1 status, who are subject to the two-year foreign residence requirement after having held J status and who have not obtained the necessary waiver, or who were admitted to the United States in Visa Waiver Program (VWP) status.[474] A foreign national in M status may not change status to H "if the education or training which the student received while an M-1 student enables the student to meet the qualifications for temporary worker classification,"[475] and "[n]o nonimmigrant can be granted M-1 status in order to gain training necessary to qualify for H status."[476]

A change of status application is not necessary if the foreign national was admitted in B-1 status and "intends to remain in the United States temporarily as a

---

[468] AFM 10.17.

[469] 8 CFR §103.5(a)(5)(ii).

[470] AFM 10.17.

[471] INA §248(a).

[472] *Id.*; 8 CFR §248.1(a); *Matter of Lee*, 11 I&N Dec. 601 (BIA 1966). The statute discusses other, rare grounds of inadmissibility arising from accruing unlawful presence. For further discussion of unlawful presence, see below [unlawful presence].

[473] AFM 30.3.

[474] INA §§248(a)(2), (a)(3), and (a)(4); 8 CFR §§248.2(a)(3), (4), and (5).

[475] 8 CFR §248.1(d); AFM 30.3.

[476] AFM 30.3.

Copyright © 2017. American Immigration Lawyers Association. All rights reserved.

visitor for pleasure during the period of authorized admission."[477] Similarly, F-1 change of status is not required of dependent spouses and children of E, H, J, and L nonimmigrants who will attend school.[478]

Although USCIS guidance states that the "purpose is to allow such [a] nonimmigrant, in meritorious situations, to avoid the delay and expense of departing from the United States and returning, in order to engage in activities other than those permitted in his or her original or current nonimmigrant visa category,"[479] the practitioner should discuss with the client whether a change of status is appropriate. For example, change of status is not available if the foreign national has violated or may violate B status by engaging in unauthorized employment, as noted above, because merely filing the change of status request does not grant employment authorization. USCIS guidance notes how a change of status request may indicate an intended employment start date and how a foreign national may engage in unauthorized employment if he or she begins working on that date without petition approval.[480] In such a situation, "USCIS may initiate a motion to reopen the case and deny the change of status decision,"[481] so the practitioner should inform the client that the foreign national may not accept employment until the petition is approved. Another practical reason to request consular notification rather than change of status is if the foreign national will need to travel home in any event to attend to personal matters, such as packing up the foreign residence and accompanying dependents to a visa interview.

A petition requesting change of status to E-1, E-2, H-1C, H-1B, H-2A, H-2B, H-3, L-1, O-1, O-2, P-1, P-2, P-3, Q-1, R-1, or TN must be filed on Form I-129, with appropriate evidence establishing eligibility for the new nonimmigrant status.[482] A passport does not need to be submitted with the change of status petition or application, because passport validity information must be provided on the form, but the foreign national nevertheless "must hold a valid passport at the time of application and is required to maintain validity during the entire period of his or her stay in the United States."[483] The petition on behalf of the principal nonimmigrant should include all required documents, including a copy of the I-94 record with the front and back of the I-94 card if a physical card was issued, because an "application

---

[477] 8 CFR §248.3(e)(1); AFM 30.3.

[478] 8 CFR §248.3(e)(2).

[479] AFM 30.3.

[480] Id.

[481] Id.

[482] 8 CFR §248.3(a); AFM 30.3 (stating that the "applicant must meet all eligibility criteria for the new category").

[483] AFM 30.3.

Copyright © 2017. American Immigration Lawyers Association. All rights reserved.

for a change of status submitted without such required documentation is not considered properly filed, even if the fee was collected and a receipt issued."[484]

If the beneficiary departs the United States while the change of status petition is pending, the change of status request will be deemed abandoned and ultimately denied.[485] However, despite some vague language in the guidance, experience has been that USCIS will generally adjudicate the eligibility for the classification and the eligibility for the requested action as separate issues. Thus, it will treat the request for a change of status as abandoned when it learns a beneficiary has departed the United States, but will adjudicate the merits of the petition separately. If the petitioner establishes eligibility for the classification sought, the petition should be approved for consular notification, but the change of status request will be denied because the beneficiary left the United States and is not eligible to change status.

An application for change of status on behalf of dependent spouse and children of the principal nonimmigrant worker should be filed on Form I-539, Application to Extend/Change Nonimmigrant Status,[486] with evidence of the familial relationship, such as a marriage certificate and/or birth certificate(s);[487] evidence of the principal applicant's valid nonimmigrant status or application for change of status or extension;[488] and copies, front and back, of the Forms I-94, Arrival/Departure Record, for all applicants.[489] Only one application needs to be filed for the dependent family members as long as the change of status petition for the principal nonimmigrant will be filed on Form I-129,[490] or as long as the entire family unit holds

---

[484] *Id.*

[485] Legacy INS, T. Cook, "Travel After Filing a Request for a Change of Nonimmigrant Status, (June 18, 2001), AILA Doc. No. 01081635.

[486] 8 CFR §§248.3(a) and (b); USCIS, "Instructions for Form I-539, Application to Extend/Change Nonimmigrant Status," https://www.uscis.gov/files/form/i-539instr.pdf. Although 8 CFR §248.3(a) notes that the Form I-129 may be used for dependent beneficiaries, if "the form version specifically provides for their inclusion," the form has only one question regarding whether an application for dependent(s) will accompany the petition and the number of dependents. USCIS, "Form I-129, Petition for a Nonimmigrant Worker," https://www.uscis.gov/files/form/i-129.pdf.

[487] 8 CFR §248.3(b) (stating that the extension application must be filed with "any initial evidence specified in the applicable provisions of §214.2," which in turn mention dependents only generally as the spouse and children of the principal nonimmigrant); USCIS, "Instructions for Form I-539, Application to Extend/Change Nonimmigrant Status," https://www.uscis.gov/files/form/i-539instr.pdf. *See also* relevant nonimmigrant definitions for accompanying or following to join spouses and children in INA §101(a)(15); INA §101(b)(1) for a definition of child.

[488] AFM 30.3.

[489] USCIS, "Instructions for Form I-539, Application to Extend/Change Nonimmigrant Status," www.uscis.gov/files/form/i-539instr.pdf; AFM 30.3.

[490] This is the principle of practice when 8 CFR §248.3(a) is read in conjunction with 8 CFR §248.3(b), although neither regulation specifically states so, since "[m]ore than one person may be included in an application where the co-applicants are all members of a single family group and either all hold the same nonimmigrant status or one holds a nonimmigrant status and the co-applicants are his or her spouse and/or

Cont'd

Copyright © 2017. American Immigration Lawyers Association. All rights reserved.

the same nonimmigrant status,[491] such as B-2. But the practitioner should not file a combined request for extension and/or change of status on behalf of multiple beneficiaries on the same Form I-539 if they currently hold different statuses.[492] If only Form I-539 will be filed, then it should be filed with the Service Center with jurisdiction over the applicant's place of residence.[493]

As discussed later in this chapter, an individual who entered through an air or sea port of entry after April 30, 2013, likely would have received only a stamp in the passport, and not a physical I-94 card.[494] USCIS nevertheless requires a copy of the I-94,[495] so it will be necessary to go to the CBP website and print out a copy.[496]

With minor exceptions, all applications to change status must be timely filed, which means they must be received by USCIS before the status expires.[497] Specifically, "USCIS does not consider the package received or timely filed until it is actually on-site at the Service Center."[498] But use of U.S. Postal Service (USPS) mail service to the Service Center's post office box may not guarantee timely filing:

> "The service centers pick up correspondence delivered to the P.O. Box at one or more scheduled times during the day. Therefore, while customers may file applications by USPS at the P.O. Box, delivery to that P.O. Box does not ensure that the filing will be picked up by USCIS the same day it is placed in the P.O. Box by the USPS, and thus, will not be considered timely filed."[499]

Although USCIS stated that it would update the immigration form websites to notify petitioners and applicants of this policy on mailing packages to USCIS post office boxes,[500] it does not appear that this has occurred.[501] For time-sensitive filings,

---

children who hold derivative nonimmigrant status based on the principal's nonimmigrant status." 8 CFR §248.3(b).

[491] 8 CFR §248.3(b); AFM 30.3.

[492] "AILA/VSC Liaison Practice Pointer: Form I-539 and the VSC Helpful Filing Tips" (Jan. 25, 2010), AILA Doc. No. 10012563 (providing the example of a parent seeking change of status from TN to H-4 and children who are already in H-4 status requesting an extension).

[493] AFM 30.3.

[494] 78 Fed. Reg. 18457 (Mar. 27, 2013); USCIS, "Instructions for Form I-539, Application to Extend/Change Nonimmigrant Status," https://www.uscis.gov/files/form/i-539instr.pdf, at 12.

[495] USCIS, "Instructions for Form I-539, Application to Extend/Change Nonimmigrant Status," https://www.uscis.gov/files/form/i-539instr.pdf, at 12.

[496] CBP, "Official Site for Travelers Visiting the United States: Apply for or Retrieve Form I-94," https://i94.cbp.dhs.gov/I94/#/home.

[497] 8 CFR §248.1(b) (stating that "a change of status may not be approved for an alien who failed to maintain the previously accorded status or whose status expired before the application or petition was filed").

[498] "AILA/USCIS Liaison Minutes" (Oct. 28, 2008), AILA Doc. No. 08110767.

[499] Id.

[500] Id.

Copyright © 2017. American Immigration Lawyers Association. All rights reserved.

the practitioner is advised to use an express courier service that will deliver the package to the actual Service Center with next-day delivery. As a practical matter, the very latest date that the change of status application may be shipped to USCIS is the last business day before the nonimmigrant status expires, as long as an express means for next-day delivery is used, because USCIS subscribes to the receipt rule rather than the mailbox rule.[502] For a discussion of nunc pro tunc application requests, see below.

Approval of a change of status request requires a favorable exercise of discretion by USCIS, and the following factors are considered:

- Whether the foreign national possesses the "financial ability to maintain the status sought";
- "[W]hether there was possible deception when the original visa or admission was sought;
- The "ultimate intentions" of the foreign national;
- The "veracity of documentation submitted"; and
- The "overall effects of a positive or negative decision."[503]

USCIS guidance also states:

"It is important to keep in mind that discretionary does not mean arbitrary. Given similar fact patterns, discretionary decisions should yield similar results regardless of where such cases are adjudicated or by whom. There is a significant body of precedent decisions which discuss the appropriate exercise of discretion under a variety of situations. Familiarity and conformity with these precedents are critical to achieving consistent and fair results in such cases."[504]

"An exercise of discretion does not mean the decision can be arbitrary, inconsistent or dependent upon intangible or imagined circumstances. Although regulations can provide guidelines for many of the types of factors which are appropriate for consideration, a regulation cannot dictate the outcome of a discretionary application.... It will be useful, particularly for inexperienced adjudicators, to discuss unusual fact patterns and novel cases requiring an exercise of discretion with peers and supervisors. In particularly difficult or unusual cases, the decision may be certified for review to the Administrative Appeals Office. Such certifications may ultimately result in expansion of the body of precedent

---

[501] USCIS, "Instructions for Form I-539, Application to Extend/Change Nonimmigrant Status," https://www.uscis.gov/files/form/i-539instr.pdf.

[502] 8 CFR 103.2(a)(7)(i) (stating that "[a]n application or petition received in a USCIS office shall be stamped to show the time and date of actual receipt and ... shall be regarded as properly filed when so stamped").

[503] AFM 30.3.

[504] *Id.*

Copyright © 2017. American Immigration Lawyers Association. All rights reserved.

case law. Discretionary decisions or those involving complex facts, whether the outcome is favorable or unfavorable to the petitioner or applicant, require supervisory review."[505]

In the context of employment-based change of status requests, the above-noted factors "are either inapplicable or of considerably less weight."[506] For example, "it is generally not necessary to further explore an applicant's ability to maintain status financially (unless the rate of remuneration is so low that the principal would be unable to support himself or herself and all dependents)."[507] But USCIS may conclude that a "rapid sequence of events between arrival and filing for a change of status may be indicative of the applicant's attempt to avoid consular scrutiny of his or her prior employment," and evidence of prior employment experience "should be explored as part of the petition adjudication, rather than in the context of the change of status request."[508] USCIS guidance states the following regarding assessing deception and intent:

> "Although the facts in such situations could be indicative of actual visa fraud, more often the appropriate course of action may be to deny the application as a matter of discretion. A denial would not be warranted simply because an applicant entered as a visitor, for example, and was later offered an opportunity to attend school, receive specialized training or accept employment. It is necessary to look closely at the facts of the particular case, examining such facts as dates on supporting documents. If necessary, seek additional information from the applicant concerning all facts leading to his or her request."[509]

Much of the case law on this issue addresses change of status from B to F-1.[510] Further discussion of appropriate intent[511] and a rapid sequence of events appears earlier in this chapter.

Generally, RFEs should be "relatively unusual," and personal interview of the applicant "should rarely be required."[512] If the foreign national should have obtained

---

[505] AFM 10.15.

[506] AFM 30.3.

[507] *Id.*

[508] *Id.*

[509] *Id.*

[510] *See, e.g., Matter of Hsu*, 14 I&N Dec. 344 (Reg'l Comm'r 1973). *See also Matter of Le Floch*, 13 I&N Dec. 251 (BIA 1969) (USCIS guidance interprets this case as "rul[ing] that even the applicant's claim that she was misinformed by a consular officer regarding the need for a student visa was insufficient to justify entry as a visitor"); AFM 30.3.

[511] *Matter of Gutierrez*, 15 I&N Dec. 727 (Reg'l Comm'r 1976).

[512] AFM 30.3.

Copyright © 2017. American Immigration Lawyers Association. All rights reserved.

a waiver of inadmissibility for the initial nonimmigrant status, or if the waiver has expired, then the extension may not be granted until a valid waiver is presented.[513]

An approved change of status request will result in the "grant[ing of] a new period of time to remain in the United States without the requirement of filing a separate application and paying a separate fee for an extension of stay."[514] The foreign national's "nonimmigrant status under his new classification shall be subject to the terms and conditions applicable generally to such classification."[515] A replacement I-94 card should be attached to the approval notice, "indicating the new status and extension date."[516] The practitioner should note that an approved change of status may be voided if the change of status was granted for a future effective date and if the foreign national traveled after the petition was approved but before the valid effective date, as discussed in Volume 1: Chapter Seven, "H-1B Visas and Status." In addition, "a dependent's ineligibility for change of status does not preclude approval of the principal's application only."[517] There is no appeal from the denial of a change of status petition or application request, although the denial of the underlying petition may be appealed to the AAO.[518]

USCIS has discretion to approve a change of status request filed after status has expired where the untimeliness was due to circumstances beyond the applicant's or petitioner's control, the delay was commensurate with the circumstances, the individual has not otherwise violated status and remains a bona fide nonimmigrant, and the individual is not in removal proceedings.[519] The reasons for the delay "should be appropriately documented."[520] Explicit exceptions are sometimes made for foreign nationals impacted by natural disasters or civil unrest.[521] The practitioner should note that, unlike untimely filed extension applications, back-dating the validity period is generally not available to untimely filed change of status applications, so an approval

---

[513] *Id.*

[514] 8 CFR §248.3(f).

[515] *Id.*

[516] AFM 30.3.

[517] *Id.*

[518] 8 CFR §248.3(g).

[519] 8 CFR §248.1(b).

[520] "TSC Liaison Meeting Notes" (May 3, 1999), AILA Doc. No. 99050659.

[521] USCIS, "Tips for Foreign Nationals in the United States Impacted by Civil Unrest or Natural Disasters in Their Home Country" (updated Oct. 31, 2013), *https://www.uscis.gov/news/alerts/tips-foreign-nationals-united-states-impacted-civil-unrest-or-natural-disasters-their-home-country. See also, e.g.,* "USCIS Outline Temporary Immigration Relief Measures for Individuals Affected by Typhoon Soudelor" (Aug. 7, 2015), AILA Doc. No. 15080704; "USCIS Reminds Japanese Nationals Impacted by Recent Disaster" (Mar. 17, 2011), AILA Doc. No. 15080794.

Copyright © 2017. American Immigration Lawyers Association. All rights reserved.

notice may be valid from the date of adjudication, even if the late filing is excused,[522] although more recent guidance states that USCIS "does not retroactively change nonimmigrant status via a nunc pro tunc approval."[523] If a change of status application is not adjudicated until after the requested validity end date, then USCIS will generally approve the application for one day.[524]

III. Nonimmigrant Visa Applications

Aside from certain, limited exceptions,[525] it is necessary to have a visa to enter the United States, or when reentering the United States after travel abroad.[526] This section provides a general overview of the nonimmigrant visa application process and related considerations.

A. The Visa Application Process

The process for applying for the visa will vary somewhat from consulate to consulate, so it is important to consult the website of the consulate in question before proceeding with the application process.[527] The essential steps are as follows:

1. Completing the DS-160, Nonimmigrant Visa Electronic Application

As of April 30, 2010, all nonimmigrant visa applicants are required to complete and submit the web-based DS-160 nonimmigrant visa application form prior to their visa application interview.[528] The DS-160 application form can be found on the DOS website.[529] When starting a new DS-160, the user "will be issued a unique application identification (ID) number after selecting and answering a security question."[530] The

---

[522] "AILA Liaison/VSC Meeting Minutes" (Dec. 5, 2007), AILA Doc. No. 07122062. See also "TSC Liaison Meeting Notes" (May 3, 1999), AILA Doc. No. 07122062.

[523] "AILA Liaison/VSC Meeting Minutes" (Jan. 21, 2009), AILA Doc. No. 09012768 (discussion of extended processing time). See also "TSC Liaison Meeting Notes" (May 3, 1999), AILA Doc. No. 99050659.

[524] "AILA Liaison/VSC Meeting Minutes" (Jan. 21, 2009), AILA Doc. No. 09012768 (discussion of extended processing time).

[525] For example, citizens of the 38 countries that participate in the Visa Waiver Program (VWP) who are traveling to the United States for tourism or business purposes for stays of 90 days or less do not require visas to be admitted to the United States. Department of State (DOS), "Visa Waiver Program (VWP)," https://travel.state.gov/content/visas/en/visit/visa-waiver-program.html.

[526] DOS, "About Visas: The Basics," https://travel.state.gov/content/visas/en/general/frequently-asked-questions.html. See also 8 CFR §214.1(a)(3)(i) (discussing necessary travel documents for each application for U.S. admission).

[527] Department of State (DOS), "Temporary Worker Visas," https://travel.state.gov/content/visas/en/employment/temporary.html#howtoapply. A list of the consulates and embassies, with links to their sites, can be found at https://www.usembassy.gov/.

[528] DOS, "Worldwide Deployment of the DS-160," (Nov. 2009), AILA Doc. No. 09120861. The DS-160 form combines all information previously collected on the Forms DS-156 (required of all nonimmigrant visa applicants, DS-157 (required of male nonimmigrant visa applicants between the ages of 16 and 45), DS-158 (required of F-1, F-2, M-1, and M-2 visa applicants), and DS-3052 (required of V visa applicants).

[529] DOS, "Apply for a Nonimmigrant Visa," https://ceac.state.gov/genniv/.

[530] DOS, "DS-160: Frequently Asked Questions," http://bit.ly/DS160FAQ.

Copyright © 2017. American Immigration Lawyers Association. All rights reserved.

application can be saved within the DOS website by clicking the "next" button at the bottom of each page completed.[531] The user can exit a partially completed application, but must have the application ID to return to it. However, after 30 days the application will be removed,[532] so it is advisable to save the application to one's own computer if there is any chance that completion of the form will take longer than 30 days.

When beginning the Form DS-160, the visa applicant should select the location of the U.S. embassy or consulate where the visa application will be made and enter the code shown below that box, then click the "Start a New Application" button.[533] As part of the electronic submission of the Form DS-160, the foreign national will be asked to provide an electronic copy of a photograph, which must meet certain requirements.[534] The foreign national may check if the photograph is acceptable prior to beginning the application form by clicking the "Test Photo" button and uploading an electronic photograph.[535]

The DS-160 application form should be filled in as completely as possible, leaving blank only those fields that are not mandatory or do not apply to the visa applicant's case.[536] Fields marked "Optional" may be left blank, and some fields may also offer the visa applicant the option to state "Does Not Apply."[537] If a mandatory field is left blank or completed incorrectly, a message should advise the visa applicant on how to correct the entry.[538] Experience has shown that, upon completion and submission of the DS-160 application form, the visa applicant should receive an email from the Consular Electronic Application Center, attached to which should be a confirmation page containing the visa applicant's electronically uploaded photo and a unique confirmation number. This confirmation page must be brought to the visa application interview by the applicant, as without it, the U.S. embassy or consulate may be unable to "access" the visa application and "process [the foreign national's] visa case."[539]

---

[531] *Id.*

[532] *Id.*

[533] DOS, "Apply for a Nonimmigrant Visa," https://ceac.state.gov/genniv/.

[534] DOS, "Photo Requirements," https://travel.state.gov/content/visas/en/general/photos.html.

[535] *Id.*

[536] DOS, "Apply for a Nonimmigrant Visa," https://ceac.state.gov/genniv/.

[537] *Id.*

[538] *Id.*

[539] *Id.*

Copyright © 2017. American Immigration Lawyers Association. All rights reserved.

2. Scheduling a Nonimmigrant Visa Application Interview

DOS has been moving to an online visa interview scheduling system, with appointments made through a portal on each consulate's website[540] after the DS-160 has been completed. The practitioner should check the wait time for the next available appointment, because this wait time differs depending on the particular U.S. embassy or consulate.[541] Experience has shown that the length of time to schedule a nonimmigrant visa interview is typically longer during the summer months, during the month of September in years when the H-1B cap is met close to April 1, and around holidays in the home country and in the United States.[542]

3. Paying the Nonimmigrant Visa Application Processing Fee

Nonimmigrant visa applicants are required to pay a nonrefundable nonimmigrant visa application processing fee of $160, $190, or $205 per applicant.[543] As with the procedures for scheduling a nonimmigrant visa application interview, however, the procedure for payment of this fee differs depending on the individual U.S. embassy or consulate, so the practitioner should check the website of the U.S. embassy or consulate. For example, the U.S. Consulate in Amsterdam allows payment of the nonimmigrant visa application processing fee by debit card or bank transfer, but not by credit card.[544]

In contrast, the U.S. embassy in Mexico City requires payment either by credit card on its website or in cash pesos at any Banamex or Scotiabank branch prior to the visa application interview, with the receipt number then entered into the appointment system.[545] The practitioner should also refer to the website of the U.S. embassy or consulate to inform the foreign national of any additional requirements, such as inclusion of the visa applicant's full name and passport number when paying the visa application fee or additional charges for certain types of payments.[546]

---

[540] See, e.g., the portal of the U.S. Embassy in Cameroon, https://ais.usvisa-info.com/en-cm/niv. At the time of this writing, the portals indicate that they are temporary, so this url is subject to change.

[541] Visa wait times for every U.S. embassy or consulate can be found on the DOS website, "Visa Appointment and Processing Wait Times," https://travel.state.gov/content/visas/en/general/wait-times.html.

[542] For a general discussion of visa application delays, see the Government Accountability Office (GAO) Report, "Border Security: Long-Term Strategy Needed to Keep Pace with Increasing Demand for Visas" (July 2007), AILA Doc. No. 07080366. See also "Approved Liaison Minutes for Istanbul Post" (May 27, 2009), AILA Doc. No. 10020553 (late spring and early summer typically have the busiest workloads).

[543] DOS, "Fees for Visa Services," https://travel.state.gov/content/visas/en/fees/fees-visa-services.html.

[544] Visa Information and Appointment system for the Embassy of the United States in The Netherlands, "Visa Fees," https://ais.usvisa-info.com/en-nl/niv/information/fee.

[545] U.S. Embassy in Mexico City, "Visa Services, How to Apply," https://mx.usembassy.gov/visas/petition-based-employment/how-to-apply/.

[546] Visa Information and Appointment system for the Embassy of the United States in The Netherlands, "How to Apply / Visa Overview," https://ais.usvisa-info.com/en-nl/niv/information/niv.

Copyright © 2017. American Immigration Lawyers Association. All rights reserved.

4. *Generally Required Documents for Nonimmigrant Visa Applications*

Although the documents required to be brought to the visa application interview will vary depending on both the particular U.S. embassy or consulate and the type of nonimmigrant visa for which the applicant is applying, the following is a list of documents that are generally required for all nonimmigrant visa applications:

- Passport, valid for valid for at least six months beyond the visa applicant's intended stay in the United States,[547] and with at least two blank pages;[548]

- Form DS-160 confirmation page, as discussed above;

- Nonimmigrant visa interview confirmation letter; and

- Proof of payment of the nonimmigrant visa application processing fee, discussed above.[549]

Experience has shown that, although not required, the following documents should also be brought to the nonimmigrant visa application interview, if applicable:

- Form I-797, evidencing USCIS approval of a nonimmigrant petition on behalf of the visa applicant;[550]

- Copy of the underlying nonimmigrant petition and supporting documents filed with USCIS on behalf of the foreign national;[551]

- Employment verification letter;

- A few paystubs evidencing the visa applicant's continuing employment; and

- Copy of the visa applicant's *curriculum vitae* or résumé.

---

[547] 9 FAM 403.9-3(B)(1). The FAM states exceptions to this requirement under the following circumstances:

(i) where the visa applicant is within the purview of 22 CFR §41.21(b), which provides exceptions from passport validity requirements for certain A, G, and NATO aliens;

(ii) where the passport requirement has been waived pursuant to INA §212(d)(4);

(iii) where the visa applicant holds F international student classification and is granted admission for the period required to complete the course of study indicated on his or her Form I-20, Certificate of Eligibility for Nonimmigrant (F-1) Student Status; or

(iv) where the visa applicant's passport was issued by a country that has entered into an agreement with the United States for the extension of the validity of passports for a period of six months beyond the end date specified in the visa applicant's passport, as discussed below.

[548] "Rome District Chapter Practice Pointer: Visa Refusals Under INA 221(g)" (Dec. 11, 2009), AILA Doc No. 12110930 (noting that if there are no empty pages in the applicant's passport, a §221(g) refusal could be triggered).

[549] Proof of payment will vary depending on the U.S. embassy or consulate where the applicant will apply for his or her nonimmigrant visa, as discussed above.

[550] Prior to the launch of DOS's Petition Information Management Service (PIMS), discussed in detail below, the original Form I-797 was a required document for the visa application interview.

[551] "Rome District Chapter: Updates from U.S. Embassy, London" (Oct. 17, 2008), AILA Doc. No. 08102850 (noting how visa applicants "can 'save themselves an hour or two' of wait time on interview day").

Copyright © 2017. American Immigration Lawyers Association. All rights reserved.

The practitioner may wish to inform the client and/or foreign national that, as part of the visa application process, the majority of nonimmigrant visa applicants are required to be finger-scanned.[552]

5. What to Expect After the Nonimmigrant Visa Application Interview

If the applicant's nonimmigrant visa application is approved,[553] then the U.S. embassy or consulate will retain the visa applicant's passport in order to prepare a nonimmigrant visa stamp and place it in the passport, after which the passport may be mailed back or available for pick up. As with the wait time for the next available appointment, the processing times for visa issuance and passport return vary depending on the individual U.S. embassy or consulate, so the practitioner is encouraged to consult DOS for an estimate of the processing time,[554] as well as the website of the individual U.S. embassy or consulate. The practitioner should note that there is often a fee associated with the return of the passport, which must be paid at the time of the nonimmigrant visa application interview.[555] The practitioner should check the website of the U.S. embassy or consulate for the appropriate procedure on inquiring about pending visa applications. Generally, however, email seems to be preferred over telephone calls or faxes.[556] For a discussion of visa processing delays, see below. An issued visa may also have an annotation, such as to indicate clearance of a security advisory opinion (SAO), or waiver, exemption, or overcoming of ineligibility.[557]

B. Visa Reciprocity

The practitioner should note that a foreign national's country of birth and visa classification may impact the validity period of an issued visa, the number of entries granted, and the reciprocity fee for the visa. Reciprocity fees may be understood as being based on what another country charges U.S. citizens for visas that have similar purposes.[558] When a foreign government imposes such fees on U.S. citizens for certain types of visas, the United States will "impose 'reciprocal' fees to nationals of

---

[552] 73 Fed. Reg. 49091 (Aug. 20, 2008). Initially only two fingerprint scans of nonimmigrant visa applicants were required, but this was later expanded to 10 fingerprint scans. 72 Fed. Reg. 25351 (May 4, 2007).

[553] See below for discussions concerning delays in nonimmigrant visa application processing for administrative processing reasons and denials of nonimmigrant visa applications.

[554] DOS, "Visa Appointment & Processing Wait Times," https://travel.state.gov/content/visas/en/general/wait-times.html/.

[555] Id.

[556] "Approved Liaison Minutes for Istanbul Post" (May 27, 2009), AILA Doc. No. 10020553 (stating that "COs are often not at their desk and may not have the file with them").

[557] 9 FAM 403.9-5(G) and (H).

[558] DOS, "Reciprocity and Civil Documents by Country," https://travel.state.gov/content/visas/en/fees/reciprocity-by-country.html.

Copyright © 2017. American Immigration Lawyers Association. All rights reserved.

that country for similar-type of visas."[559] The reciprocity fee is separate from the visa application fee and "is charged only if the visa is granted."[560]

For example, regardless of the end date listed on the I-797 approval notice issued by USCIS, a Chinese national applying for an H-1B visa will be issued a multiple entry visa valid for only 12 months.[561] A Brazilian national issued an L visa will incur a visa reciprocity fee of USD $100 per applicant in addition to the mandatory USD $190 visa application fee, and the visa will be valid for a maximum of 24 months for multiple entries.[562] Given these considerations, it is highly recommended that the practitioner consult the DOS Reciprocity Schedule for the foreign national's country of citizenship in advance of the visa application interview,[563] in order to properly inform the client and/or foreign national.

C. The Petition Information Management Service (PIMS)

Since November 2007, U.S. consular posts have been able to access the details of H, L, O, P, and Q nonimmigrant petitions approved by USCIS through PIMS.[564] One reason that PIMS was established was "to end consular posts' reliance on paper USCIS approval notices supplied by visa applicants, which were subject to fabrication and alteration, and to enhance fraud detection."[565]

As a result of the advent of PIMS, DOS's Kentucky Consular Center (KCC) ceased its prior practice of emailing scanned copies of approved nonimmigrant petitions to U.S. consular posts.[566] As stated by DOS: "The electronic PIMS record created by the KCC is now the primary source of evidence to be used in verifying petition approval."[567] The PIMS record contains information about the petition and the petitioner. Information about the beneficiary may be unavailable, such as on an

---

[559] Id.

[560] DOS, "Media Note: Proposal for Increase of Nonimmigrant Visa Application Fees" (Dec. 14, 2009), AILA Doc. No. 09121465.

[561] DOS, "China Reciprocity Schedule," https://travel.state.gov/content/visas/en/fees/reciprocity-by-country/CH.html.

[562] DOS, "Brazil Reciprocity Schedule," https://travel.state.gov/content/visas/en/fees/reciprocity-by-country/BR.html.

[563] DOS, "Reciprocity and Civil Documents by Country," https://travel.state.gov/content/visas/en/fees/reciprocity-by-country.html.

[564] DOS, "Accessing NIV Petition Information Via the CCD" (Nov. 25, 2007), AILA Doc. No. 07112560.

[565] "PIMS Update" (Aug. 15, 2008), AILA Doc. No. 08081564.

[566] DOS, "Accessing NIV Petition Information Via the CCD" (Nov. 25, 2007), AILA Doc. No. 07112560.

[567] Id.

Copyright © 2017. American Immigration Lawyers Association. All rights reserved.

H-2 petition for multiple unnamed workers.[568] Blanket L petition information is available in PIMS.[569]

Because U.S. consular posts are able to access the details of approved nonimmigrant petitions through PIMS, a visa applicant is no longer required to bring the original I-797 approval notice to a visa application interview.[570] The practitioner should nevertheless strongly encourage a visa applicant to present the original Form I-797, as it may be relied upon by a consular officer to "initiate adjudication processing through PIMS" and to request confirmation of petition approval if the record cannot be immediately located in PIMS.[571] In addition, DOS requires the USCIS receipt number for the petition in order to access the PIMS record,[572] and a number printed on the Form I-797 may be more readily accepted than the foreign national stating the number verbally. Further, the foreign national will most likely need to present the original approval notice to a CBP officer when seeking admission to the United States.[573]

As discussed in the individual chapters relating to H, L, O, and P status, the practitioner is strongly encouraged to file a duplicate original petition with USCIS to ensure that USCIS sends a copy of the approved petition to the KCC for entry into the PIMS database.[574] This information then becomes available to a consular officer to verify the petition approval.[575] But if a duplicate original petition is not filed and/or there is no record of petition approval in PIMS, then the consular officer must email the KCC for verification,[576] and the visa may not be issued "until the post sees the petition in PIMS."[577]

Filing a duplicate original petition should allow the visa applicant to avoid potential delays in visa issuance based on the need to verify petition approval when "the petition information was not sent to KCC by a USCIS service center …, if KCC

---

[568] "DOS Answers AILA Questions on PIMS" (Nov. 29, 2007), AILA Doc. No. 07112960 (stating that "[w]hen a named beneficiary is not a requirement of the petition category, then [the KCC isn't] looking for a named beneficiary").

[569] *Id.*

[570] DOS, "Temporary Worker Visas," https://travel.state.gov/content/visas/en/employment/temporary. html

[571] DOS, "Accessing NIV Petition Information Via the CCD" (Nov. 25, 2007), AILA Doc. No. 07112560.

[572] DOS, "Temporary Worker Visas," https://travel.state.gov/content/visas/en/employment/temporary. html.

[573] "PIMS Update" (Aug. 15, 2008), AILA Doc. No. 08081564.

[574] DOS, "Temporary Worker Visas," https://travel.state.gov/content/visas/en/employment/temporary. html; "PIMS Update" (Aug. 15, 2008), AILA Doc. No. 08081564; "PIMS Processing Update" (Mar. 21, 2008), AILA Doc. No. 08032132.

[575] DOS, "Accessing NIV Petition Information Via the CCD" (Nov. 25, 2007), AILA Doc. No. 07112560.

[576] *Id.*

[577] "Update: New PIMS System" (Dec. 10, 2007), AILA Doc. No. 07121072.

Copyright © 2017. American Immigration Lawyers Association. All rights reserved.

fails to timely notify the consulate of the verification, or if the consulate fails to check or follow up on positive verification that was sent."[578] In addition, the likelihood of such delays is "increased if a visa applicant's extension, change of status, or amended petition was approved prior to late March 2008, or regardless of petition filing date, if the petitioner did not file a duplicate original with USCIS."[579] The practitioner is not advised to file Form I-824, Application for Action on an Approved Application or Petition, as filing this application "by itself, will not result in a petition being sent to the KCC for scanning into PIMS," and "with the current processing times for I-824s, it is unlikely the information would reach the KCC faster than an email from a consular officer."[580]

Because a foreign national may be informed that the visa application is undergoing "administrative processing" even when the delay is caused by the need for PIMS verification rather than the need for security checks, as discussed below, the practitioner may wish to advise the foreign national to ask the reason for the delay: "This will not do anything to speed visa issuance, but it may help to clarify why the applicant is waiting."[581] If USCIS succeeds in overhauling its computer systems and databases, then consular officers may be able to access petition details through a more efficient system,[582] but such developments remain unavailable to date.

D. Administrative Processing

The practitioner should note and advise the client and/or foreign national of the potential for extended delays in visa application processing because of what is broadly referred to as "administrative processing."[583] This occurs when the interviewing consular officer invokes INA §221(g),[584] which states, in pertinent part:

"No visa or other documentation shall be issued to an alien if:

(1) it appears to the consular officer, from statements in the application, or in the papers submitted therewith, that such alien is ineligible to receive a visa or such other documentation under section 212, or any other provision of law,

(2) the application fails to comply with the provisions of this Act, or the regulations issued thereunder, or

---

[578] "PIMS Update" (Aug. 15, 2008), AILA Doc. No. 08081564.

[579] *Id.*

[580] *Id.*

[581] *Id.*

[582] *Id.* (noting USCIS, "USCIS Transformation Program Concept of Operations" (Mar. 27, 2007), https://www.hsdl.org/?abstract&did=483127).

[583] DOS, "Administrative Processing Information," https://travel.state.gov/content/visas/en/general/administrative-processing-information.html.

[584] *See, e.g.,* U.S. Consulate in Hyderabad, India, "Frequently Asked Questions" *http://bit.ly/indiaFAQ*, Refusals 214(b) and Administrative Processing 221(g).

Copyright © 2017. American Immigration Lawyers Association. All rights reserved.

(3) the consular officer knows or has reason to believe that such alien is ineligible to receive a visa or such other documentation under section 212, or any other provision of law."[585]

Experience has shown that INA §221(g) is primarily invoked by the interviewing officer where a determination has been made that security checks are required before the visa application can be approved.[586] The most common security checks that may result in visa application processing delays are as follows:[587]

- *Visas Condor.* Part of the Security Advisory Opinion (SAO) system, this requires consular officers to refer visa applications "identified by law enforcement and intelligence information (originally certain visa applicants from 26 predominantly Muslim countries), for greater review by intelligence and law enforcement agencies."[588] In practice, experience has shown Visas Condor clearances take between two and four weeks.

- *Visas Mantis.* Part of the SAO system, this requires consular officers to refer visa applications when it is determined that a visa applicant's proposed activity in the United States would involve exposure to any of fifteen sensitive technologies included in the Technology Alert List (TAL).[589] In practice, experience has shown that Visas Mantis clearances take between two and eight weeks.

- *Visas Donkey.* Part of the SAO system, this requires consular officers to refer visa applications with a name match of the visa applicant's name in the Consular Lookout and Support System (CLASS) name-check database.[590] In practice, experience has shown that Visas Donkey clearances take between ten and 14 weeks.

- *NCIC Criminal Hits.* The CLASS name-check database incorporates records from the FBI's NCIC. If there is a "hit" in the system between the visa

---

[585] INA §221(g).

[586] For a discussion of the FBI security procedures, *see* DOJ, "The Federal Bureau of Investigation's Security Check Procedures for Immigration Applications and Petitions" (June 2008), https://oig.justice.gov/reports/FBI/a0824/final.pdf.

[587] For a discussion of joint visa security measures by DOS and U.S. Immigration and Customs Enforcement (ICE), *see* "DHS OIG Report, "U.S. Immigration and Customs Enforcement Visa Security Program" (July 2008), AILA Doc. No. 08081861.

[588] CRS Report for Congress, "Immigration: Terrorist Grounds for Exclusion and Removal of Aliens" (Jan. 12, 2010), https://www.fas.org/sgp/crs/homesec/RL32564.pdf.

[589] DOS, "Visa Approval Backlog Effect on Small Business," (June 4, 2003), https://2001-2009.state.gov/r/pa/ei/othertstmy/32998.htm. *See also* CRS Report for Congress, R. Wasem, "Visa Issuances: Policy, Issues, and Legislation" (Updated Jan. 24, 2007), AILA Doc. No. 07020763. For the last known published version of the Technology Alert List, *see* "State Department Updates Guidance on Technology Alert Checks" (Aug. 1, 2002), AILA Doc. No. 03030449.

[590] "DOs and DON'Ts for Attorneys Representing Applicants (and for Consular Officers Too!)" (Feb. 6, 2012), AILA Doc. No. 08121964.

Copyright © 2017. American Immigration Lawyers Association. All rights reserved.

applicant's name and a record of a prior arrest or conviction, then consular officers are required to submit the applicant's fingerprints to the FBI to request the applicant's record and/or confirm that the applicant has no record.[591] In practice, experience has shown that clearances of false hits, which is where the applicant has the same or similar name to someone with a prior arrest and/or conviction but is not in fact the same person, are resolved the same day, while clearances for positive hits are generally resolved the day after the visa application interview.

In practice, a determination by the interviewing officer that additional supporting documents must be provided by the visa applicant is another common reason for the invocation of INA §221(g).[592] Experience has also shown that nonimmigrant visa applicants may encounter difficulty obtaining a visa in certain situations, including, but not limited to:

- Where the nonimmigrant visa applicant entered the United States in B, F, or J visa status and subsequently changed status to H-1B; and

- Where an immigrant petition or adjustment of status application has been filed on the nonimmigrant visa applicant's behalf and he or she is attempting to obtain any visa other than an H-1B or L-1 visa. The practitioner is advised to inform his or her client of the possibility of a visa application denial or extended period of administrative processing time. As stated by DOS: "All [visa applicants] should keep in mind that if there is an unanticipated delay in visa processing, they will need to spend more time overseas than originally planned."[593]

The DOS Visa Office has set procedures for inquiries regarding nonimmigrant visa applications that have been subjected to administrative processing.[594] Applicants and attorneys must wait at least 60 days before initiating an inquiry.[595] The first step is to contact the consular post where the interview was held.[596] After at least two attempts and 30 days after the last attempt and six months after the administrative processing has been pending, AILA Immigration Lawyers Association (AILA)

---

[591] 22 CFR §41.112(d)(2)(vii).

[592] *See generally*, "DOS Practice Pointer: Administrative Processing" (July 8, 2016), AILA Doc. No. 12091850, quoting Pattison, Stephen R. and Simkin, Andrew T., "Consular Processing in India," *The Consular Practice Handbook*, 2012 Ed. (AILA 2012) ("In [some] cases, it is not the existence of a lookout hit that triggers the decision, but other circumstances that either have arisen during the interview or are based on information in the record…..").

[593] DOS, C. Barry (June 23, 2004), AILA Doc. No. 04063062.

[594] "DOS VO Inquiries" (Dec. 19, 2008), AILA Doc. No. 08121971.

[595] DOS, "Administrative Processing Information," https://travel.state.gov/content/visas/en/general/administrative-processing-information.html.

[596] "DOS Practice Pointer: Administrative Processing" (July 8, 2016), AILA Doc. No. 12091850; "Practice Pointer: Resolving Issues with Cases Pending at Consular Posts" (July 8, 2016), AILA Doc. No. 16070801. *See* DOS's portal for embassy and consular websites, https://www.usembassy.gov/.

Copyright © 2017. American Immigration Lawyers Association. All rights reserved.

members can submit a request for liaison assistance, and nonmembers might pursue congressional assistance.[597]

E. Visa Application Denials and Refusals

The majority of nonimmigrant visa applicants are presumed to be immigrants, and therefore not eligible for a nonimmigrant visa, unless and until they satisfy a consular officer that they qualify for one of the nonimmigrant visa categories.[598] Nonimmigrant visa refusals, however, must be based on legal grounds.[599] Common legal grounds for nonimmigrant visa denials include:

- Grounds related to health, criminality, security, public charge, lack of labor certification and qualification, illegal entry and immigration violations, documentation, ineligibility for citizenship, and previous removal or deportation;[600]

- Failure to comply with a two-year home residency requirement;[601]

- Failure to establish entitlement to a nonimmigrant visa classification;[602]

- INA §221(g) grounds, as discussed above; and

- Having been admitted on the basis of a nonimmigrant visa and remaining in the United States beyond the period of authorized stay.[603]

The practitioner is cautioned that although INA §221(g) is generally invoked by consular officers for administrative processing reasons, nonimmigrant visa applicants must nevertheless answer "Yes" to the Form DS-160 question, "Have you ever been refused a U.S. visa?" because the invocation of INA §221(g) is technically a nonimmigrant visa application refusal.[604]

---

[597] "DOS Practice Pointer: Administrative Processing" (July 8, 2016), AILA Doc. No. 12091850.

[598] 9 FAM 302.1-2(B)(2). The complete list of nonimmigrant visa categories can be found in INA §101(a)(15).

[599] 22 CFR §41.121(a).

[600] INA §212(a).

[601] INA §212(e). This section is applicable to certain nonimmigrant visa applicants who previously held J visa status.

[602] INA §214(b). Section 214(b) denials most frequently occur in cases where B or F visa applicants fail to establish to the satisfaction of a consular officer that they have a residence abroad that they have no intention of abandoning. *See* DOS, "Visa Denials," https://travel.state.gov/content/visas/en/general/denials.html.

[603] INA §222(g).

[604] "Rome District Chapter Practice Pointer: Visa Refusals Under INA 221(g)" (Dec. 11, 2009), AILA Doc No. 12110930. But an applicant who has been refused a visa under §221(g) need not complete a new nonimmigrant visa application form or pay the machine-readable visa fee again if less than one year has elapsed since the last refusal, as this is considered a re-activation of the application and not a new application. 9 FAM 403.10-4(a)c.

Copyright © 2017. American Immigration Lawyers Association. All rights reserved.

If a nonimmigrant visa application is refused, then the consular officer must inform the visa applicant of the grounds for refusal, as well as of any potential ways to overcome the refusal, unless such disclosure is barred.[605] All nonimmigrant visa refusals must be reviewed by consular supervisors.[606] If the consular officer believes that the refusal can be overcome by additional evidence, then a review of the refusal may be deferred for up to 120 days.[607] The consular officer may also initiate a recommendation for waiver of inadmissibility for certain grounds,[608] as long as certain conditions are met.[609] Finally, DOS may request the consular officer in a specific case or in specified classes of cases to submit a report if a nonimmigrant visa application is refused.[610] Upon review, DOS may issue an advisory opinion to the consular officer to assist in further consideration of the case.[611]

F. Third Country National Visa Applications

On July 16, 2004, DOS discontinued its domestic visa reissuance service, also called visa revalidation, for nonimmigrant C, E, H, I, L, O, and P visas.[612] Although DOS recognized the convenience of domestic visa reissuance to the international business community, the program was discontinued "because of increased interview requirements" and the requirement that "U.S. visas issued after October 26, 2004 include biometric identifiers."[613] In order to mitigate the inconvenience to visa applicants, DOS noted that "[a]pplicants not traveling to their home countries may apply for a new visa at a U.S. embassy or consulate in a third country if they are physically present in the consular district and make a visa interview appointment

---

[605] 22 CFR §41.121(b)(1). Disclosure may be barred under INA §§212(b)(2) or (3). 22 CFR §41.121(b)(1).

[606] 22 CFR §41.121(c).

[607] Id.

[608] 9 FAM 305.4-3(A).

[609] 9 FAM 305.4-3(B). These conditions require a determination by the consular officer that:

(i) the applicant is not inadmissible under INA §214(b) (covering the principle that all nonimmigrant visa applicants except for H-1B and L-1 visa applicants are presumed to be immigrants unless they establish to the satisfaction of a consular officer that they are entitled to nonimmigrant status);

(ii) the applicant is not inadmissible under INA §§212(a)(3)(A)(i)(I), (a)(3)(A)(ii), (a)(3)(A)(iii), (a)(3)(C), or (a)(3)(E) (covering criminal, terrorist, foreign policy, and participants in Nazi persecution, genocide, torture, and extrajudicial killing, respectively);

(iii) the applicant is not seeking a waiver of nonimmigrant documentary requirements of INA §212(a)(7)(B), which may be waived only under the provisions of INA §212(d)(4); and

(iv) the applicant is otherwise qualified for the nonimmigrant visa which he or she is seeking.

[610] 22 CFR §41.121(d).

[611] Id.

[612] 69 Fed. Reg. 35121 (June 23, 2004).

[613] Id. (citing Section 303 of the Enhanced Border Security and Visa Entry Reform Act of 2002 (Pub. L. No. 107-173, 166 Stat. 543)).

Copyright © 2017. American Immigration Lawyers Association. All rights reserved.

where necessary" and that "[a]pplicants may apply at U.S. visa processing posts in Canada and Mexico if they have made a visa interview appointment in advance."[614]

In practice, experience has shown that the termination of DOS visa revalidation service led to increased demand for visa applications in Canada and Mexico by these third country nationals (TCNs). The term "third country national" is defined as an individual who "is neither a citizen of the United States nor of the country to which assigned for duty."[615] In the U.S. immigration context, therefore, third country nationals also include individuals who are not nationals in the country in which they will apply for a visa, and third country national visa applications are visa applications made at a U.S. consulate in a country other than the foreign national's home country.

Although it is generally best for a foreign national to apply for a visa in his or her home country, under certain circumstances, a foreign national may wish to consider processing the visa application at a U.S. consular post in Canada or Mexico as a third country national. Reasons for this approach include delays in obtaining visa application appointments in the foreign national's home country, the prohibitive cost of the foreign national traveling to his or her home country, and convenience if the foreign national plans to travel on a business trip to Canada or Mexico anyway.[616]

In addition, certain countries do not have a U.S. embassy or consulate, so citizens of those countries must apply at an embassy or consulate in a different country,[617] and DOS may designate the primary U.S. embassy or consulate or encourage use of certain consulates.[618] An embassy or consulate may have a procedure in place for this type of TCN; for example, the U.S. Consulate in Dubai provides visa appointment slots for Iranian citizens.[619] Although this section will focus on TCN visa applications at consulates in Canada and Mexico, TCNs may be able to make visa applications at other locations.[620]

---

[614] DOS, C. Barry (June 23, 2004), AILA Doc. No. 04063062.

[615] 3 FAM 7271.1.

[616] DOS, "Nonimmigrants in the United States—Applying for Visas in Canada or Mexico," https://travel.state.gov/content/visas/en/general/nonimmigrants-present-visiting-canada-mexico.html (stating that "Nonimmigrants who are already in the United States, have an expired visa, and remain in legal status are encouraged to apply for a new visa at non-border U.S. Embassies and Consulates in conjunction with foreign travel for business or pleasure.").

[617] "Approved Liaison Minutes for Istanbul Post" (May 27, 2009), AILA Doc. No. 10020553.

[618] U.S. Consulate in Istanbul, "Visas to the U.S.: Information for Iranian Nonimmigrant Visa Applicants," https://ais.usvisa-info.com/en-IR (stating that interviews in Farsi are available at consulates in Dubai, UAE; Ankara, Turkey; and Yerevan, Armenia); INA §222(g).

[619] U.S. Consulate in Dubai, "Appointment System for Non-immigrant Visas for Residents of Iran," http://bit.ly/DubaiIran.

[620] See, e.g., "AILA Liaison Questions for U.S. Embassy, London" (Oct. 13, 2010), AILA Doc. No. 10110960, item 4 (stating that it will accept third country nationals' applications, but noting that, for those not resident in the U.K., "Consular Officers may find it difficult to assess applicants' ties outside the UK for those visa categories that require a resident [sic.] abroad to qualify for the visa.").

Copyright © 2017. American Immigration Lawyers Association. All rights reserved.

1. TCNs Who May Apply for Visas in Mexico or Canada

The U.S. Embassy and consulates in Mexico restrict TCN visa applications to those applicants seeking to renew visas in any visa category except B-1/B-2 and H-2, as long as the renewal is in the same visa category.[621] TCNs who reside in Mexico in FM2 or FM3 status may apply for an initial or renewal visa in any category.[622] Also, a TCN whose passport and visa was lost or stolen and who needs a B-1/B-2 visa to return to his or her home country may apply in Mexico.[623]

Although the U.S. Embassy and consulates in Canada do not require that a TCN applicant's initial visa was issued elsewhere, the following caution is stated:

"It is always best to apply for a visa in your home country. However, you may request an appointment for a visa interview at any consular office in Canada.

"Please be aware that demand for visas from those living in the U.S. far exceeds our visa appointment capacity. It is possible that you may experience a long wait for an appointment or that no appointments may be available until others cancel their appointments."[624]

For example, in the summer of 2014, the consulates in Canada made it known that they were "extremely limited in their ability to accept TCN cases during the peak demand period of June, July, and August" and suggested that applicants try elsewhere during that time.[625]

2. TCNs Who May Not Apply for Visas in Mexico or Canada

In general, the following TCNs cannot apply for visas at a U.S. embassy or consulate in either Mexico or Canada:

- TCNs who have been out of status in the United States by having overstayed the validity date indicated on the I-94 card;[626] and

- TCNs of countries which have been determined to be state sponsors of international terrorism, including Syria, Sudan, and Iran.[627]

---

[621] U.S. Consulates in Mexico, "Third Country Nationals," http://bit.ly/MexicoTCN; "DOS Mission Fact Sheet" (Dec. 19, 2012), AILA Doc. No. 12121942.

[622] *Id.*

[623] U.S. Consulates in Mexico, "Third Country Nationals," http://bit.ly/MexicoTCN.

[624] Canada—Official U.S. Department of State Visa Appointment Service, "What Is a Third Country National (TCN)?" https://ais.usvisa-info.com/en-ca/niv/information/tcn.

[625] "DOS Alert: TCN Processing in Canada 'Extremely Limited' This Summer" (June 4, 2014), AILA Doc. No. 14060447.

[626] INA §222(g). Such individuals are required to apply for visas at either a U.S. embassy or consulate in their home country or, if there is no office in such country, in such other consular office as the Secretary of State shall specify. INA §222(g).

[627] Enhanced Border Security and Visa Entry Reform Act of 2002, §306, Pub. L. No. 107-173, 166 Stat. 543 (May 14, 2002). *See also* DOS, "Frequently Asked Questions—Visa Applicants from State Sponsors of
Cont'd

Copyright © 2017. American Immigration Lawyers Association. All rights reserved.

The U.S. Embassy and consulates in Mexico, but not Canada, place the following additional restrictions, such that the following individuals may not make TCN visa applications:

- TCNs applying for B-1/B-2 or H-2 visas, including renewals, who are not resident in Mexico;

- TCNs who entered the United States with a visa issued in their home country, changed immigration status in the United States, and seek a new visa in the new visa category;

- TCNs who entered the United States in one visa category and will apply for U.S. admission in a different visa category;

- TCNs who have fallen out of status in the United States by either having overstayed the validity date indicated on the I-94 card or violating the terms of their immigration status; and

- TCNs who entered the United States under the auspices of the Visa Waiver Program.[628]

In addition, DOS states: "U.S. embassies and consulates routinely do not accept applications for 'E' visas from third country national applicants who are not resident in their consular districts,"[629] although experience has shown that the language on the websites of the U.S. Embassy and consulates in Mexico stating that they will accept visa renewal applications does apply to E visa renewals. However, they no longer accept initial E applications from non-resident TCNs.

3. TCN Visa Applications at U.S. Consulates in Mexico

The following consular posts in Mexico accept TCN visa applications: Ciudad Juarez, Guadalajara, Hermosillo, Matamoros, Merida, Mexico City, Monterrey, Nogales, Nuevo Laredo, and Tijuana.[630] Because individual consular posts vary in terms of rules and policies regarding eligible visa categories, required forms and documentation, attorney representation, and visa issuance processing times, the practitioner is advised to check the website of the particular consulate at which the foreign national will apply for a visa for specific requirements. TCNs who would like

---

Terrorism Countries," https://travel.state.gov/content/visas/en/general/frequently-asked-questions/visa-applicants-from-state-sponsors.html. Cuba, North Korea, Iraq, and Libya were also originally included on the list of countries determined to be state sponsors of international terrorism, but have since been dropped from this list.

[628] U.S. Consulates in Mexico, "Third Country Nationals," *http://bit.ly/MexicoTCN*.

[629] DOS, "Nonimmigrants in the United States—Applying for Visas in Canada or Mexico," https://travel.state.gov/content/visas/en/general/nonimmigrants-present-visiting-canada-mexico.html.

[630] *Id.*

Copyright © 2017. American Immigration Lawyers Association. All rights reserved.

to book a visa application appointment at a U.S. consulate in Mexico may do so online at *https://ais.usvisa-info.com/es-mx/niv.* [631]

4. TCN Visa Applications at U.S. Consulates in Canada

The following consular posts in Canada accept TCN visa applications: Calgary, Halifax, Montreal, Ottawa, Quebec City, Toronto, and Vancouver.[632] Again, because individual consular posts vary in terms of rules and policies regarding eligible visa categories, required forms and documentation, attorney representation, and visa issuance processing times, the practitioner is advised to check the website of the particular consulate at which the foreign national will apply for a visa for specific requirements. TCNs who would like to book a visa application appointment at a U.S. consulate in Canada may do so online at *https://ais.usvisa-info.com/en-ca/niv.*[633]

5. Special Considerations

a. Possibility of Visa Application Denial and Impact of Administrative Processing Delays

The most significant issue facing a TCN applicant is the possibility that the visa application will be denied and the applicant will be unable to apply for U.S. admission until a visa is issued by the embassy or consulate in his or her home country.[634] In practice, experience has shown that TCN visa applications get low priority with respect to consular resources, and that issuance of nonimmigrant visas at U.S. consulates and embassies in Mexico and Canada is discretionary. In the event that a TCN visa application is denied, the TCN visa applicant is not eligible to reenter the United States based on his or her USCIS petition through automatic revalidation, as discussed below, and must instead return to his or her home country to apply for a visa with which he or she may seek admission to the United States.[635]

In addition, the practitioner should caution the client and the foreign national about the possibility that visa issuance may be delayed by administrative processing,[636] as discussed above. In contrast to administrative processing by an embassy or consulate in the visa applicant's home country, a TCN visa applicant may

---

[631] *Id.*

[632] *Id.*

[633] *Id.*

[634] 22 CFR §41.112(d)(2)(vii).

[635] 22 CFR §41.112(d)(2)(vii); "Further Instructions on Change to 41.112(d) Regarding Automatic Extension of Visas" (June 19, 2002), AILA Doc. No. 02061947; DOS, "Nonimmigrants in the United States—Applying for Visas in Canada or Mexico," https://travel.state.gov/content/visas/en/general/nonimmigrants-present-visiting-canada-mexico.html ("Anyone who has applied for and been refused visa issuance at a U.S. Embassy or Consulate is prohibited from re-admission or reentry to the United States in the same visa category, even though they are in possession of a valid admission stamp or paper Form I-94.").

[636] *See, e.g.,* U.S. Consulates in Mexico, "Third Country Nationals," http://bit.ly/MexicoTCN.

Copyright © 2017. American Immigration Lawyers Association. All rights reserved.

be forced to remain in a country where he or she has no support network,[637] and must accrue the costs of a hotel or other housing for a significant period of time.

b. Mexican Visa Requirements

Depending on the citizenship of the TCN visa applicant, an appropriate Mexican visa from a Mexican embassy or consulate may be required to enter Mexico for the purpose of obtaining a U.S. visa stamp at a consular post in Mexico.[638] The following is a list of countries whose citizens are required to have Mexican tourist visas to enter Mexico:

Afghanistan	Grenada	Peru
Albania	Guatemala	Philippines
Algeria	Guinea	Qatar
Angola	Guinea Bissau	Russian Federation
Antigua and Barbuda	Guyana	Rwanda
Armenia	Haiti	Sahrawi Arab Dem. Rep.
Azerbaijan	Honduras	Saint Kitts and Nevis
Bahrain	India	Saint Lucia
Bangladesh	Indonesia	Saint Vincent and the
Belarus	Iran	Grenadines
Benin	Iraq	Sao Tome and Principe
Bhutan	Jordan	Saudi Arabia
Bolivia	Kazakhstan	Senegal
Bosnia and Herzegovina	Kenya	Serbia
Botswana	Kiribati	Seychelles Islands
Brazil	Korea, North	Sierra Leone
Brunei	Kuwait	Solomon Islands
Burkina Faso	Kyrgyzstan	Somalia
Burundi	Laos	South Africa
Cambodia	Lebanon	Sri Lanka

---

[637] Cf. DOS, C. Barry (June 23, 2004), AILA Doc. No. 04063062 (noting that visa applications made in the home country have the benefit of the visa applicant being "in a familiar environment with a support network while the additional processing is completed").

[638] U.S. consulates in Mexico, "Third Country Nationals Who Live in the United States and Who Wish to Apply for Visas in Mexico," https://mx.usembassy.gov/visas/third-country-nationals-non-mexicans-who-wish-to-apply-for-visas-in-mexico.

Copyright © 2017. American Immigration Lawyers Association. All rights reserved.

Cameroon

Cape Verde

Central African Republic

Chad

China

Colombia

Comoros

Congo

Congo, Rep. Dem (Zaire)

Cote d'Ivoire

Cuba

Democratic Republic of the Congo

Djibouti

Dominica

Dominican Republic

Ecuador

Equatorial Guinea

Egypt

Eritrea

Ethiopia

Fiji

Gabon

Gambia

Georgia

Ghana

Lesotho

Liberia

Libya

Macedonia

Madagascar

Malawi

Maldives

Mali

Mauritania

Mauritius

Moldova

Mongolia

Montenegro

Morocco

Mozambique

Myanmar (Burma)

Namibia

Nauru

Nepal

Nicaragua

Niger

Nigeria

Oman

Pakistan

Palestine

Papua New Guinea

Sudan

Surinam

Swaziland

Syrian Arab Republic

Taiwan (China)

Tajikistan

Tanzania

Thailand

Togo

Tonga

Tunisia

Turkey

Turkmenistan

Tuvalu

Uganda

Ukraine

United Arab Emirates

Uzbekistan

Vanuatu

Vietnam

Western Samoa

Yemen

Zambia

Zimbabwe[639]

c. Canadian Visa Requirements

Depending on the citizenship of the TCN visa applicant, an appropriate Canadian visa from a Canadian embassy or consulate may be required to enter Canada for the

---

[639] Mexican National Institute of Immigration, http://www.inm.gob.mx/EN/index.php?page/need_visa.

Copyright © 2017. American Immigration Lawyers Association. All rights reserved.

purpose of obtaining a U.S. visa stamp at a consular post in Canada.[640] The following is a list of countries whose citizens require Canadian tourist visas to enter Canada:

Afghanistan

Albania

Algeria

Angola

Argentina

Armenia

Azerbaijan

Bahrain

Bangladesh

Belarus

Belize

Benin

Bhutan

Bolivia

Bosnia-Herzegovina

Botswana

Brazil

Bulgaria

Burkina Faso

Burundi

Cambodia

Republic of Cameroon

Cape Verde

Central African Republic

Chad

Chile

China, People's Republic of

Guinea-Bissau

Guyana

Haiti

Honduras

India

Indonesia

Iran

Iraq

Israel (only Israeli citizens holding valid Israeli "Travel Document in lieu of National Passport")

Ivory Coast

Jamaica

Jordan

Kazakhstan

Kenya

Kiribati

Korea, North

Kosovo

Kuwait

Kyrgyzstan

Laos

Lebanon

Lesotho

Liberia

Libya

Macao S.A.R.

Palau

Palestinian Authority

Panama

Paraguay

Philippines

Qatar

Romania

Russia

Rwanda

Sao Tomé e Principe

Saudi Arabia, Kingdom of

Senegal

Serbia

Seychelles

Sierra Leone

Somalia

South Africa

South Sudan

Sri Lanka

St. Kitts and Nevis

St. Lucia

St. Vincent and the Grenadines

Sudan

Surinam

Swaziland

Syria

Taiwan (if passport does

---

[640] Government of Canada, "Entry Requirements by Country," http://www.cic.gc.ca/english/visit/visas-all.asp.

Copyright © 2017. American Immigration Lawyers Association. All rights reserved.

Colombia

Comoros

Congo, Democratic Republic of the

Congo, Republic of the

Costa Rica

Cuba

Djibouti

Dominica

Dominican Republic

East Timor

Ecuador

Egypt

El Salvador

Equatorial Guinea

Eritrea

Ethiopia

Fiji

Gabon

Gambia

Georgia

Ghana

Grenada

Guatemala

Guinea

Macedonia

Madagascar

Malawi

Malaysia

Maldives Islands

Mali

Marshall Islands

Mauritania

Mauritius

Mexico

Micronesia, Fed. States

Moldova

Mongolia

Montenegro

Morocco

Myanmar (Burma)

Nauru

Nepa

Nicaragua

Niger

Nigeria

Oman

Pakistan

not include personal identification number)

Tajikistan

Tanzania

Thailand

Togo

Tonga

Trinidad and Tobago

Tunisia

Turkey

Turkmenistan

Tuvalu

Uganda

Ukraine

United Arab Emirates

Uruguay

Uzbekistan

Vanuatu

Venezuela

Vietnam

Yemen

Zambia

Zimbabwe

Others may require completion of an Electronic Travel Authorization (eTA) to enter Canada.[641]

IV. Admission to the United States

Upon arriving in the United States, a foreign national should make an "[a]pplication to lawfully enter the United States … in person to an immigration

---

[641] *Id.* Scroll down to list of countries whose nationals require an eTA.

Copyright © 2017. American Immigration Lawyers Association. All rights reserved.

officer at a U.S. port-of-entry when the port is open for inspection."[642] As stated by CBP:

> "All persons arriving at a port-of-entry to the United States are subject to inspection by U.S. Customs and Border Protection (CBP) Officers. CBP Officers will conduct the Immigration, Customs and Agriculture components of the Inspections process."[643]

As stated by DHS:

> "Inspection and admissibility upon arrival to the United States involves verification of the identity of the alien and a determination that the alien is admissible to the United States, i.e., that the alien has established that the alien has permission to be admitted and is not ineligible for admission by reason of any of the disqualifying provisions in the Immigration and Nationality Act, as enacted and amended by Congress."[644]

In addition to the documentary requirements, discussed below, most foreign nationals also are required to provide biometric identifiers, evidence of identity, evidence of lawful immigration status, and evidence that the immigration status has been properly maintained for the United States Visitor and Immigrant Status Indicator Technology (US-VISIT) program,[645] as discussed below.

A March 2017 Executive Order suspends entry into the United States of nationals of six countries: Syria, Iran, Sudan, Somalia, Libya, and Yemen.[646] The order states that the suspension is for 90 days, but before nationals of the six countries can resume entering the United States, an assessment of each country must be conducted by the DHS Secretary, Secretary of State, and the Director of National Intelligence. The order requires the Secretary of State to request additional information from each country, and if the country does not provide the additional information, or the DHS Secretary does not certify that the country has a plan to provide that information, certain categories of nationals of those countries are to be included in a presidential proclamation prohibiting entry. The Secretary of State, Attorney General or DHS Secretary can at any time recommend that additional countries be added to or taken off the list. Lawful permanent residents are excepted from this version of the order, as are individuals issued visas prior to the effective date of the order or who were admitted or paroled into the United States prior to the date of the order.[647]

---

[642] INA §§235(a)(1) and (3); 8 CFR §235.1(a).

[643] U.S. Customs and Border Protection (CBP), "Applying for Admission into United States" (updated Mar. 10, 2015), https://www.cbp.gov/travel/international-visitors/applying-admission-united-states.

[644] 73 Fed. Reg. 77473 (Dec. 19, 2008).

[645] 8 CFR §235.1(f)(1)(ii).

[646] Exec. Order No. 13780, 82 Fed. Reg. 13209 (Mar. 9, 2017), AILA Doc. No. 17030604.

[647] *Id.*

Copyright © 2017. American Immigration Lawyers Association. All rights reserved.

This order supersedes an earlier Executive Order[648] that had been enjoined by multiple courts.[649] However, the March 2017 order also was enjoined.[650] At the time of this writing, the injunctions are still in effect and are being appealed by the government, and so nationals of the six countries are still allowed entry into the United States.

Inspection and admission may be performed in a foreign territory, if an "aircraft, vessel, or train [will] proceed[] directly, without stopping, from a port or place in foreign territory to a port-of-entry in the United States."[651] These examinations "made immediately prior to such departure at the port or place in the foreign territory ... shall have the same effect under the Act as though made at the destined port-of-entry in the United States."[652] For example, there are pre-flight inspection offices in Toronto and Vancouver.[653] As stated by CBP:

> "Generally, passengers who are inspected at a preclearance facility are permitted to arrive at a U.S. domestic facility and exit the U.S. domestic terminal upon arrival or connect directly to a U.S. domestic flight without further CBP processing. Preclearance facilities primarily serve to facilitate low risk passengers, relieve passenger congestion at Federal inspection facilities in the United States, and enhance security in the air environment through the screening and inspection of passengers prior to their arrival in the United States."[654]

CBP uses primary lookout overrides (PLORs) to update the system to reflect the fact than an individual is not the individual on the target or hit list.[655] For example, the "client Pedro Escobar is not the same person as the drug cartel leader Pedro Escobar."[656] For one way to resolve a recurring problem of being referred to

---

[648] Exec. Order No. 13769, 82 Fed. Reg. 13769 (Feb. 1, 2017), AILA Doc. No. 17012560.

[649] *E.g., State of Washington*, No. C17-0141JLR (W.D. Wash. 2017). *See* "President Trump's Executive Actions on Immigration," AILA Doc. No. 16113030 for ongoing updates on the orders, their status, and the federal court challenges to them.

[650] *E.g., State of Hawaii v. Trump*, CV. No. 17-00050 DKW-KSC (D.Haw. 2017). *See* "President Trump's Executive Actions on Immigration," AILA Doc. No. 16113030 for ongoing updates on the orders, their status, and the federal court challenges to them.

[651] 8 CFR §235.5. *See also* 1 CBP Inspector's Field Manual (IFM) 15: Preinspection and Preclearance, 14-1 Agency Manuals 24.1, General. Note that CBP announced in 2014 that it would no longer be using the IFM, replacing it with an "Officer's Reference Tool" that it considers law enforcement sensitive and will not be made public. While a FOIA request has been filed for it, as of this writing, it has not been released. Nevertheless, many of the procedures in the IFM do appear to still be in place. "Practice Alert: CBP is Replacing Inspectors Field Manual with Officer's Reference Tool" (Feb. 7, 2014), AILA Doc. No. 14020749.

[652] 8 CFR §235.5.

[653] 19 CFR §101.5. This regulation states all the CBP preclearance offices.

[654] 74 Fed. Reg. 64601 (Dec. 8, 2009), AILA Doc. No. 09120860.

[655] "Highlights from the CBP Open Forum at Annual Conference 2009" (June 19, 2009), AILA Doc. No. 09061969. CBP indicated there are 700,000 PLORs.

[656] *Id.*

Copyright © 2017. American Immigration Lawyers Association. All rights reserved.

secondary inspection, see below. A foreign national may be referred to secondary inspection for a variety of reasons, including, but not limited to:

- Incomplete travel documents;

- Lack of proper documents or visa;

- Questions on whether the foreign national "previously violated one of the laws CBP enforces";

- Criminal record of potential concern; and

- Random selection.[657]

CBP generally does not permit attorneys to accompany foreign nationals in the inspection area,[658] although this may be permitted by individual deferred inspection sites or ports of entry (POEs). DHS stated that this is because:

"The introduction of the concept of legal counsel into a secured international inspection area would severely disrupt the efficient processing of the vast majority of international travelers for little, if any, benefit. Inspection of aliens and accompanying luggage is conducted very rapidly in a secured inspection environment for a number of different purposes. Facilities for detailed questioning in secondary inspection are limited. No evidence has been presented to DHS that suggests that any benefit accrues from permitting counsel to consult with clients in this environment when they are free to consult prior to seeking admission to the United States or if they are placed in removal proceedings."[659]

A. Documents Necessary for Application for U.S. Admission

An application for U.S. admission entails "present[ing] whatever documents are required and … establish[ing] to the satisfaction of the inspecting officer that the alien is not subject to removal under the immigration laws, Executive Orders, or Presidential Proclamations, and is entitled … to enter the United States."[660] CBP has a website discussing the inspection procedures at air, land, and sea POEs.[661]

As a practical matter, a foreign national should present a valid passport and a valid U.S. visa,[662] unless the foreign national is exempt from the passport and/or the visa requirement. Documents required for an application for admission as "[p]ermits to enter" include passports, visas, and re-entry permits.[663] A foreign national may

---

[657] CBP, "Comment Card" (Sept. 3, 2009), AILA Doc. No. 09090364.

[658] 8 CFR §292.5(b); 73 Fed. Reg. 77473 (Dec. 19, 2008).

[659] 73 Fed. Reg. 77473 (Dec. 19, 2008).

[660] 8 CFR §235.1(f)(1).

[661] CBP, "Applying for Admission into United States" (updated Mar. 10, 2015), https://www.cbp.gov/travel/international-visitors/applying-admission-united-states.

[662] INA §§212(a)(7)(B)(i)(I) and (i)(II); 8 CFR §212.1.

[663] INA §215(f).

Copyright © 2017. American Immigration Lawyers Association. All rights reserved.

present a valid visa in an expired passport, as long as he or she also presents a valid passport: "The new, valid travel document need not be issued by the same authority which issued the document containing the valid visa."[664] In the example provided by legacy INS guidance, a foreign national "may present an expired Hong Kong Certificate of Identity with a valid nonimmigrant visa plus a valid Hong Kong Special Administrative Region passport."[665]

In general, a passport must be valid for six months beyond the period of initial admission.[666] But DHS and DOS permit waiver of the six-month passport requirement for citizens of certain countries, because the "foreign governments have entered into agreements with the Government of the United States whereby their passports are recognized as valid for the return of the bearer to the country of the foreign-issuing authority for a period of six months beyond the expiration date specified in the passport," which effectively "extend[] the validity period of the foreign passport an additional six months notwithstanding the expiration date indicated in the passport."[667] Colloquially called the "six month club," citizens of the following countries only need to present a passport that is valid through the admission expiration date:[668]

Algeria	Guinea	Panama
Andorra	Guyana	Papua New Guinea
Angola	Haiti	Paraguay
Antigua and Barbuda	Hong Kong (Certificates of Identity and Passports)	Peru
Argentina		Philippines
Armenia	Hungary	Poland
Aruba	Iceland	Portugal
Australia	India	Qatar
Austria	Indonesia	Romania
The Bahamas	Ireland	Russia
Barbados	Israel	San Marino
Belgium	Italy	Saudi Arabia
	Ivory Coast	

---

[664] 1 CBP IFM 15: Nonimmigrants and Border Crossers, 14-1 Agency Manuals, 15.3, Visas; 22 CFR §41.112(b)(3).

[665] 1 CBP IFM 15: Nonimmigrants and Border Crossers, 14-1 Agency Manuals, 15.3, Visas.

[666] INA §212(a)(7)(B)(i)(I).

[667] 1 CBP IFM 15: Nonimmigrants and Border Crossers, 14-1 Agency Manuals, 15.3, Visas.

[668] CBP, "Six Month Club" (June 20, 2016), http://bit.ly/6monthCBP. Countries come and go from this list with some frequency, so it should be checked each time the issue arises.

Copyright © 2017. American Immigration Lawyers Association. All rights reserved.

Belize	Jamaica	Serbia
Bermuda	Japan	Seychelles
Bolivia	Latvia	Singapore
Bosnia-Herzegovina	Lebanon	Slovakia
Brazil	Libya	Slovenia
Bulgaria	Liechtenstein	South Africa
Burma (Myanmar)	Lithuania	South Korea
Canada	Luxembourg	Spain
Chile	Macau	Sri Lanka
Colombia	Macedonia	St. Kitts and Nevis
Costa Rica	Madagascar	St. Lucia
Croatia	Malaysia	St. Vincent and the Grenadines
Cyprus	Maldives	Surname
Czech Republic	Malta	Sweden
Denmark	Mauritania	Switzerland
Dominica	Mauritius	Taiwan
Dominican Republic	Mexico	Thailand
Egypt	Monaco	Trinidad and Tobago
El Salvador	Mongolia	Tunisia
Estonia	Montenegro	Turkey
Ethiopia	Mozambique	Tuvala
Fiji	Nepal	Ukraine
Finland	Netherlands	United Arab Emirates
France	New Zealand	United Kingdom
Gabon	Nicaragua	Uruguay
Georgia	Nigeria	Uzbekistan
Germany	Norway	Vatican (Holy See)
Greece	Pakistan	Venezuela
Grenada	Palau	Zimbabwe
Guatemala		

Copyright © 2017. American Immigration Lawyers Association. All rights reserved.

B. Form I-94, Arrival/Departure Record

Previously, a foreign national arriving at a port of entry was issued a paper Form I-94, Arrival/Departure Record "as evidence of the terms of admission."[669] As stated by CBP:

"Form I-94 (Arrival/Departure Record) and Form I-94W (Nonimmigrant Visa Waiver Arrival/Departure Record) are used to document a traveler's admission into the United States. These forms include date of arrival, visa classification and the date the authorized stay expires."[670]

In 2013, CBP began to roll out an automated process whereby the foreign national receives a stamp in the passport, and the I-94 is recorded electronically and not given to the individual.[671] As of this writing, the automated process is in place for arrivals by air and sea, but not yet for entries by land. Thus, the old process still applies to land entries.

For entries by land, the foreign national still fills out a two-section CBP Form I-94 upon arrival, including the following information:

- Full name;
- Date of birth;
- Country of citizenship;
- Gender;
- Passport number, issuance date, and expiration date;
- Country of residence;
- City and date of visa issuance, if applicable;
- U.S. telephone number and address, including number, street, city, and state; and
- Email address.[672]

The CBP inspector should then endorse the Form I-94 with the class of admission, date of arrival, and authorized length of stay, and stamp the foreign national's passport. The CBP inspector should "retain[] the arrival portion" of the I-94 card. The "bottom" portion should be returned to the foreign national, and surrendered to U.S. officials upon exiting the United States, as discussed below.[673]

A foreign national entering by air or sea no longer has to fill out a paper Form I-94 upon arrival. Instead, CBP collects the information by automated means, primarily

---

[669] 8 CFR §235.1(h)(1).

[670] 74 Fed. Reg. 7243 (Feb. 13, 2009).

[671] 78 Fed. Reg. 18457 (Mar. 27, 2013).

[672] 78 Fed. Reg. 18457 (Mar. 27, 2013), at 18459.

[673] *Id.*

Copyright © 2017. American Immigration Lawyers Association. All rights reserved.

through the Advance Passenger Information System (APIS),[674] an interactive system by which carriers forward passenger information to CBP.[675] Information submitted for each person on the airplane or vessel includes:

- Full name;
- Date of birth;
- Gender;
- Citizenship;
- Country of residence;
- Status onboard the conveyance;
- Travel document type;
- Passport or other DHS-approved document number, country of issuance, and
- expiration date;
- Alien registration number, if applicable; and
- Address while in the United States.[676]

From this information, CBP creates an electronic I-94 record. However, that record usually is not physically provided to the foreign national.[677] Instead, a stamp is placed in the individual's passport.[678] If a physical copy of the I-94 is wanted, which it almost inevitably will be, it is available through a portal on CBP's website.[679] Early experience with the site has been less than perfect, but it is important to persist, as the I-94 will generally be needed for such things as I-9 verification, obtaining a U.S. driver's license, extension and change of status applications, and other circumstances in which proof of status is needed. In any event, the foreign national and attorney should review the I-94 to ensure it is accurate.

In theory, it is possible to obtain a physical I-94 at the air or sea port of entry: "CBP will continue to provide a paper Form I–94 to those who request such form, as well as to certain classes of aliens, such as certain refugees, asylees, and parolees, and whenever CBP determines the issuance of a paper form is appropriate."[680] However,

---

[674] CBP, "APIS: Advance Passenger Information System" (updated Apr. 6, 2016), https://www.cbp.gov/travel/travel-industry-personnel/apis2.

[675] 78 Fed. Reg. 18457 (Mar. 27, 2013), at 18459-60.

[676] 78 Fed.Reg. 18457 (Mar. 27, 2013), at 18460.

[677] Id.

[678] "American Immigration Lawyers Association CBP Liaison Committee Meeting Agenda" (Apr. 11, 2013), AILA Doc. No. 13051655, p. 8.

[679] "Official Site for Travelers Visiting the United States: Apply for or Retrieve I-94," https://i94.cbp.dhs.gov/I94/#/home.

[680] 78 Fed. Reg. 18457 (Mar. 27, 2013), at 18460.

Copyright © 2017. American Immigration Lawyers Association. All rights reserved.

experience has shown a great reluctance on the part of CBP inspectors to provide the form, and in any event, it will only be provided through referral to secondary inspection,[681] thus adding considerable time and headache to the individual's entry into the United States.

Typical I-94 expiration dates are discussed in the individual chapters. Experience has shown that if the passport will expire before the petition expiration date and the foreign national is a citizen of one of the "six month club" countries discussed earlier in this chapter, then the period of admission is typically cut short to match the passport expiration date. If the foreign national is not a citizen of one of the "six month club" countries, however, and the passport will expire before the petition expiration date, then the I-94 expiration date should be the date six months before the passport expiration date. The same principle applies for a foreign national seeking admission without an approved petition, such that the I-94 should be valid through the passport expiration date or six months before the passport expiration date, respectively, instead of the date through which he or she would otherwise be admitted. For a discussion of the consequences of remaining in the United States beyond the expiration date on the I-94, see below.

If the I-94 (or I-94W card for visa waiver entries) is issued at a land POE, then the foreign national will need to pay a fee of $6,[682] and the I-94 card "will be considered issued for multiple entries unless specifically annotated for a limited number of entries."[683] If a foreign national pays this fee using a personal check, then he or she will be required to provide a Taxpayer Identifying Number.[684] A foreign national who is paroled into the United States,[685] such as "for urgent humanitarian or significant public benefit,"[686] will also "be issued a completely executed Form I-94, endorsed with the parole stamp."[687] DHS defines "issue" to include creation of an electronic record,[688] but has indicated that it will continue to provide a physical I-94 to "certain … parolees."[689]

The following foreign nationals may be admitted without issuance of an I-94 card:

- Canadian citizens who are admitted in B status or "admitted to proceed in direct transit through the United States";

---

[681] "American Immigration Lawyers Association CBP Liaison Committee Meeting Agenda" (Apr. 11, 2013), AILA Doc. No. 13051655, p. 8.

[682] 8 CFR §§235.1(h)(1) and 103.7(b)(1).

[683] 8 CFR §235.1(h)(1).

[684] 74 Fed. Reg. 63761 (Dec. 4, 2009).

[685] 8 CFR §235.1(h)(2).

[686] INA §212(d)(5).

[687] 8 CFR §235.1(h)(2).

[688] 8 CFR §1.4(c).

[689] 78 Fed. Reg. 18457 (Mar. 27, 2013), at 18460.

Copyright © 2017. American Immigration Lawyers Association. All rights reserved.

- Residents of the British Virgin Islands who are admitted "only to the U.S. Virgin Islands" in B status, as long as certain requirements are satisfied;
- Mexican citizens who are admitted in B status and who either:
  - Are exempt from the passport and visa requirements and are "admitted for a period not to exceed 30 days to visit within 25 miles of the border"; or
  - Are exempt from the passport and visa requirements or possess a valid visa and a valid passport and are "admitted for a period not to exceed 72 hours to visit within 25 miles of the border"; or
  - Are exempt from the passport and visa requirements and are "admitted at the Mexican border POEs in the State of Arizona at Sasabe, Nogales, Mariposa, Naco or Douglas to visit within the State of Arizona within 75 miles of the border for a period not to exceed 30 days"; or
  - Are exempt from the passport and visa requirements or possess a valid visa and a valid passport and are "admitted at the Mexican border POEs in the State of Arizona at Sasabe, Nogales, Mariposa, Naco or Douglas to visit within the State of Arizona within 75 miles of the border for a period not to exceed 72 hours"; and
  - Mexican citizens who bear "diplomatic or official passports."[690]

1. Correction of an Erroneous Form I-94 or Passport Stamp at the Port of Entry

The practitioner should strongly advise the client and/or foreign national to carefully review the entry stamp, and I-94 card if one was issued, upon receipt from the CBP inspector.

This is because, as discussed in Volume 1: Chapter One, "Introduction," a foreign national's authorized period of admission is governed by the Form I-94/entry stamp, and not the visa. At all possible times, the foreign national should seek correction of an error during the admission process: "Correcting mistakes on the spot is quicker and cheaper than delaying, and it prevents confusion."[691] CBP may correct an I-94 card if a "B-2 visitor[']s stay was limited without signed supervisory approval recording the visa expiration date instead of the petition expiration date as the authorized period of stay."[692]

---

[690] 8 CFR §235.1(h)(1).

[691] ICE, "Fact Sheet: F/M/J Nonimmigrants: Managing Information that the U.S. Government Needs About Nonimmigrants During Their Visit" (May 15, 2006), http://bit.ly/iceFMJfact, and https://www.ice.gov (search for F/M/J nonimmigrants fact sheet"). Although this document specifically discusses F, M, and J nonimmigrants, the principle should apply to other nonimmigrants.

[692] 1 CBP IFM 15: Nonimmigrants and Border Crossers, 14-1 Agency Manuals, 15.12, Correction of Erroneous Admissions.

Copyright © 2017. American Immigration Lawyers Association. All rights reserved.

Alternatively, if contemporaneous correction does not occur, then the foreign national may visit "[a]ny designated deferred inspection location or CBP office located within an international airport … regardless of where the actual document was issued."[693] "Travelers are encouraged to contact sites not located within an international airport to establish an appointment, if necessary. In many instances, the location of your final destination where the discrepancy will be resolved may not be the port of your first arrival into the United States. Mail-in procedures are generally not available."[694]

Before making any changes, the CBP officer should "take the necessary steps to ensure that neither the original error nor the proposed correction are deliberate actions designed for fraudulent purposes."[695] To "correct information beyond biographical and admission data," a CBP officer "must administratively 'depart' the person from the original, erroneous admission to close out the erroneous record, and then 'readmit' [him/her], backdated to the original admission date, using correct information."[696] CBP guidance indicates that this procedure "is required" because of a "system design,"[697] though it is unclear whether this is still the case under the automated system. A new corrected Form I-94 should be issued, backdated "to the original admission date."[698]

A POE at an international airport may also issue an initial I-94 card if the foreign national was not "properly inspected and admitted at a port-of-entry, through an oversight or error on the part of the government."[699] The CBP officer should "[p]repare a memorandum of facts for the Director, Field Operations (DFO) having jurisdiction over the port where the actual entry occurred."[700] The issue may be discussed by facsimile or telephonically, in "the interest of efficiency."[701] If the DFO does not disagree with the "finding that the incident occurred through inadvertence and was not a deliberate act on the part of the alien to avoid inspection," then the CBP officer may complete the admission, including preparation of a[] Form I-94, as

---

[693] *Id.* (stating that in "many instances, the location of [the] final destination where the discrepancy will be resolved may not be the port of [the] first arrival into the United States"); 1 CBP IFM 15: Nonimmigrants and Border Crossers, 14-1 Agency Manuals, 15.12, Correction of Erroneous Admissions.

[694] CBP, "Deferred Inspection," https://www.cbp.gov/contact/deferred-inspection/overview-deferred-inspection.

[695] 1 CBP IFM 15: Nonimmigrants and Border Crossers, 14-1 Agency Manuals, 15.12, Correction of Erroneous Admissions (providing the example that "a correction on a year of birth may be part of an attempt to qualify for social security benefits").

[696] *Id.*

[697] *Id.*

[698] *Id.*

[699] *Id.*

[700] *Id.*

[701] *Id.*

Copyright © 2017. American Immigration Lawyers Association. All rights reserved.

if it occurred in the normal manner."[702] But if an I-94 card will not be issued, then the removal proceedings may be initiated.[703] The procedures discussed above are not available for foreign nationals who entered "without inspection or attempted entry without inspection … at other than a port-of-entry."[704]

In 2008, CBP POEs issued approximately one million I-94 cards, with 10 digits instead of 11, and CBP later "recalled and replaced" the erroneous cards, but if a foreign national did not receive a corrected I-94 card, he or she may visit a POE at an international airport or a Deferred Inspection office.[705] The practitioner should note that "[m]ail-in procedures are not available,"[706] although, as discussed above, an individual may obtain a copy of his or her I-94 through a CBP web portal.[707] In addition, errors on I-94 cards issued by USCIS should be sent to USCIS for correction.[708] For further discussion of deferred inspection sites, see below.

2. Return of Form I-94 upon Departure

Automation of the I-94 includes automation of the departure process. Thus, for air and sea departures, it no longer is required that the individual surrender the I-94. Instead, the carrier "provide[s] passenger information before a plane leaves the ground and again when the plane leaves the ground ('wheels up')…. CBP will use APIS, the passenger manifest, plus DOS information to create the CBP information for the automated I-94…."[709] Those who were issued a paper I-94 should still surrender it to the carrier upon departure.[710]

However, if the departure is by land, the individual "would turn the Form I-94 in to the Canadian authorities, or if departing to Mexico, to CBP. *If a nonimmigrant alien arrives by air or sea and departs at a land border, the departure will not be*

---

[702] *Id.*

[703] *Id.*

[704] *Id.*

[705] "Liaison Update: Requesting a Replacement I-94 Where Original was Misprinted" (May 15, 2008), AILA Doc. No. 08051567.

[706] CBP, "Deferred Inspection," https://www.cbp.gov/contact/deferred-inspection/overview-deferred-inspection; 1 CBP IFM 15: Nonimmigrants and Border Crossers, 14-1 Agency Manuals, 15.12, Correction of Erroneous Admissions.

[707] "Official Site for Travelers Visiting the United States: Apply for or Retrieve I-94," https://i94.cbp.dhs.gov/I94/#/home.

[708] USCIS, "Instructions for I-102, Application for Replacement/Initial Nonimmigrant Arrival-Departure Document," https://*www.uscis.gov/files/form/I-102instr.pdf*, edition 10/15/14N; USCIS, W. Yates, "I-94 Errors Issued by U.S. Citizenship and Immigration Services" (Mar. 30, 2004), AILA Doc. No. 04042769.

[709] "American Immigration Lawyers Association CBP Liaison Committee Meeting Agenda" (Apr. 11, 2013), AILA Doc. No. 13051655, p. 8.

[710] CBP, "Arrival/Departure Process Changes for Foreign Visitors Arriving via Air or Sea" (updated Dec. 20, 2013), https://www.cbp.gov/travel/international-visitors/i-94-instructions/i94-rollout.

Copyright © 2017. American Immigration Lawyers Association. All rights reserved.

recorded."[711] Practitioners should advise clients in this circumstance to keep proof of departure so that, in the future, they can show that they departed timely.

Because an erroneous record of overstay may impact a foreign national's eligibility for admission at a later date, especially for VWP participants, as discussed in Volume 1: Chapter Three, "Visitors: B Visas and Status and the Visa Waiver Program," and may result in visa voidance,[712] the practitioner should strongly encourage the client and/or foreign national to ensure that the government has a record of the departure. It is advisable for clients who departed by land to send the uncollected I-94 to CBP's data processing center[713] at:

> Coleman Data Solutions
> Box 7965
> Akron, OH 44306
> Attn: NIDPS (I-94)
> USA
> (If using U.S. Postal Service)
>
> OR
>
> Coleman Data Solutions
> 3043 Sanitarium Road, Suite 2
> Akron, OH 44312
> Attn: NIDPS (I-94)
> (If using FedEx or UPS)[714]

The I-94 card should be returned to this address, and not to a consulate or an immigration office. The card should be accompanied by proof of the date and fact of the departure such as a used airline ticket or boarding pass, a passport stamp showing date of arrival in the destination country, pay slips from employment outside of the United States subsequent to departure, credit card slips showing purchases made outside of the the United States post-departure, etc. It also is a good idea to include a statement on colored paper identifying clearly the date of departure and requesting that it, rather than the date that the card was received by the processing center, be entered. In addition, practitioners should advise clients to carry copies of this

---

[711] *Id.* (emphasis added)

[712] INA §222(g).

[713] "American Immigration Lawyers Association CBP Liaison Committee Meeting Agenda" (Apr. 11, 2013), AILA Doc. No. 13051655, p. 8.

[714] CBP, "I still have my I-94," https://help.cbp.gov/app/answers/detail/a_id/752/~/i-still-have-my-i-94.

Copyright © 2017. American Immigration Lawyers Association. All rights reserved.

evidence when they seek to re-enter in case the information was not entered or entered incorrectly.[715]

C. Waiver of Documentary Requirements

As noted above, the documentary requirements have been waived for certain individuals.[716] Generally, Canadian citizens do not need visas, except those seeking admission in E, K, S, or V status.[717] Following adoption of the Western Hemisphere Travel Initiative (WHTI), a valid, unexpired passport is now required for Canadian citizens, with the following exceptions,[718] where "adjacent islands" means "Bermuda and the islands located in the Caribbean Sea, except Cuba,"[719] and "contiguous territory" includes Canada and Mexico:

- Participants in the NEXUS Program "may present a valid unexpired NEXUS program card when using a NEXUS Air kiosk or when entering the United States from contiguous territory or adjacent islands at a land or sea port-of-entry."[720] NEXUS is a joint program with Canada[721] that "allows pre-screened travelers expedited processing when entering the United States and Canada. Program members use dedicated processing lanes at designated northern border ports of entry, NEXUS kiosks when entering Canada by air and Global Entry kiosks when entering the United States via Canadian Preclearance airports. NEXUS members also receive expedited processing at marine reporting locations."[722]

- Participants in the Free and Secure Trade (FAST) Program "may present a valid unexpired FAST card at a land or sea port-of-entry prior to entering the United States from contiguous territory or adjacent islands."[723] FAST "is a commercial clearance program for known low-risk shipments entering the United States from

---

[715] *Id. See also* "Practice Tip—Documenting Timely Departures from the U.S." (Dec. 28, 2007), AILA Doc. No. 07122860. Although this tip pre-dates the I-94 automation, the suggested processes are still advisable for those who departed by land.

[716] 8 CFR §235.3(b)(9).

[717] 8 CFR §§212.1(a)(1), (h), (*l*), and (m).

[718] 8 CFR §212.1(a)(1).

[719] 8 CFR §212.0. The islands are Anguilla, Antigua, Aruba, Bahamas, Barbados, Barbuda, Bermuda, Bonaire, British Virgin Islands, Cayman Islands, Cuba, Curacao, Dominica, the Dominican Republic, Grenada, Guadeloupe, Haiti, Jamaica, Marie-Galante, Martinique, Miquelon, Montserrat, Saba, Saint Barthelemy, Saint Christopher, Saint Eustatius, Saint Kitts-Nevis, Saint Lucia, Saint Maarten, Saint Martin, Saint Pierre, Saint Vincent and Grenadines, Trinidad and Tobago, Turks and Caicos Islands, and other British, French, and Netherlands territory or possessions bordering on the Caribbean Sea. 8 CFR §286.1(a).

[720] 8 CFR §212.1(a)(1)(i).

[721] CBP, "How to Renew Your Nexus Membership" (updated Mar. 3, 2016), https://www.cbp.gov/travel/trusted-traveler-programs/nexus/renew-nexus.

[722] CBP, "NEXUS" (updated Sept. 8, 2015), https://www.cbp.gov/travel/trusted-traveler-programs/nexus.

[723] 8 CFR §212.1(a)(1)(ii).

Copyright © 2017. American Immigration Lawyers Association. All rights reserved.

Canada and Mexico," by permitting "expedited processing for commercial carriers who have completed background checks and fulfill certain eligibility requirements."[724]

- Participants in the Secure Electronic Network for Travelers Rapid Inspection (SENTRI) Program "may present a valid unexpired SENTRI card at a land or sea port-of-entry prior to entering the United States from contiguous territory or adjacent islands."[725] SENTRI "allows expedited clearance for pre-approved low-risk travelers," by offering "dedicate[d] commuter lanes into the United States at Southern land border ports."[726] There are not citizenship or age requirements, but in essence, most brushes with the law will render an individual ineligible.[727]

- Canadian Indians may present "a[n] Indian and Northern Affairs Canada (INAC) card issued by the Canadian Department of Indian Affairs and North Development, Director of Land and Trust Services (LTS) in conformance with security standards agreed upon by the Governments of Canada and the United States, and containing a machine readable zone" at a land POE on the Canadian border, as long as DHS designates this to be acceptable.[728]

- Certain children may "present an original or a copy of [the] birth certificate, a Canadian Citizenship Card, or a Canadian Naturalization Certificate when arriving in the United States from contiguous territory at land or sea ports-of-entry," as long as certain requirements are met.[729]

A Mexican citizen who seeks B status at a land POE on the Mexican border with "a Form DSP-150, B-1/B-2 Visa and Border Crossing Card issued by the Department of State, containing a machine-readable biometric identifier" may present that document in lieu of a visa.[730] A member "of the Texas Band of Kickapoo Indians or Kickapoo Tribe of Oklahoma who is in possession of a Form I-872 American Indian Card" may present that document in lieu of a passport when applying for admission at a land or sea POE from contiguous territory or adjacent islands.[731] In addition, the following Mexican citizens may not require visas:

---

[724] CBP, "Free and Secure Trade (FAST)" (updated Sept. 21, 2015), https://www.cbp.gov/travel/trusted-traveler-programs/fast.

[725] 8 CFR §212.1(a)(1)(iii).

[726] CBP, "Secure Electronic Network for Travelers Rapid Inspection (SENTRI)" (updated Sept. 25, 2015), https://www.cbp.gov/travel/trusted-traveler-programs/sentri.

[727] CBP, "Eligibility" (updated Sept. 23, 2015), https://www.cbp.gov/travel/trusted-traveler-programs/sentri/eligibility.

[728] 8 CFR §212.1(a)(1)(iv).

[729] 8 CFR §212.1(a)(1)(v). This section discusses the additional conditions.

[730] 8 CFR §212.1(c)(1)(i). Note that WHTI prohibits using a BCC in lieu of a passport, as discussed below.

[731] 8 CFR §212.1(c)(1)(ii).

Copyright © 2017. American Immigration Lawyers Association. All rights reserved.

- Those with a Border Crossing Card (BCC), "with a biometric identifier, issued by the DOS, and a passport," who seek admission in B status "from other than contiguous territory,"[732] as long as "the biometric identifier contained on the card matches the appropriate biometric characteristic of the alien";[733]

- Crew members "on an aircraft belonging to a Mexican company owned carrier authorized to engage in commercial transportation into the United States";[734] and

- Those bearing Mexican diplomatic or official passports who are military or civilian officials "of the Federal Government of Mexico entering the United States for 6 months or less for a purpose other than on assignment as a permanent employee to an office of the Mexican Federal Government in the United States," as well as "the official's spouse or any of the official's dependent family members under 19 years of age, bearing diplomatic or official passports, who are in the actual company of such official at the time of admission into the United States."[735]

If a Mexican citizen possesses "a combination B-1/B-2 nonimmigrant visa and border crossing card (or similar stamp in a passport), issued by DOS prior to April 1, 1998, that does not contain a machine-readable biometric identifier," then he or she must present a valid passport and "may be admitted on the basis of the nonimmigrant visa only, provided it has not expired and the alien remains admissible."[736]

Bermudan citizens also need not present a valid visa, except for those seeking admission in E, K, S, or V status, but passports are required,[737] following implementation of the Western Hemisphere Travel Initiative (WHTI) program. Bahamian citizens and "British subjects resident in the Bahamas" must present valid passports and visas, "unless, prior to or at the time of embarkation for the United States on a vessel or aircraft, the alien satisfied the examining U.S. immigration officer at the Bahamas, that he or she is clearly and beyond a doubt entitled to admission ... in all other respects."[738]

For "British subjects resident in the Cayman Islands or in the Turks and Caicos Islands," a valid "passport is required," as well as a valid visa, unless the foreign national "arrives directly from the Cayman Islands or the Turks and Caicos Islands

---

[732] 8 CFR §212.1(c)(2)(i).

[733] 8 CFR §212.1(c)(3).

[734] 8 CFR §212.1(c)(2)(ii).

[735] 8 CFR §212.1(c)(2)(iii). Dependent spouses and children seeking F or M status must present passports. 8 CFR §212.1(c)(2)(iii).

[736] 8 CFR §212.1(c)(4).

[737] 8 CFR §212.1(a)(2).

[738] 8 CFR §212.1(a)(3).

Copyright © 2017. American Immigration Lawyers Association. All rights reserved.

and presents a current certificate from the Clerk of Court of the Cayman Islands or the Turks and Caicos Islands indicating no criminal record."[739]

A citizen of "Barbados, Grenada, Jamaica, or Trinidad and Tobago, who has his or her residence in British, French, or Netherlands territory located in the adjacent islands of the Caribbean area, or in Barbados, Grenada, Jamaica, or Trinidad and Tobago" may not require a visa if one of the following conditions are met:

- The foreign national is "proceeding to the United States as an agricultural worker"; or

- The foreign national is "the beneficiary of a valid, unexpired indefinite certification granted by" DOL for employment in the U.S. Virgin Islands and "is proceeding to the Virgin Islands of the United States for such purpose"; or

- Is the dependent spouse or child of one of the above-mentioned individuals.[740]

A citizen of the British Virgin Islands "who has his or her residence in the British Virgin Islands" may be admitted without a visa as long as the following requirements are satisfied:

- The foreign national seeks admission "solely to visit" the U.S. Virgin Islands; or

- Upon embarkation on an airplane in Saint Thomas, U.S. Virgin Islands, the foreign national satisfies each of the following conditions:

  - The U.S. travel, which may be "to any other part" of the United States, will be for the purpose of visiting for business or pleasure in B status;

  - The foreign national "satisfies the examining U.S. Immigration officer at the port-of-entry that he or she is clearly and beyond a doubt entitled to admission in all other respects"; and

  - The foreign national "presents a current Certificate of Good Conduct issued by the Royal Virgin Islands Police Department indicating that he or she has no criminal record."[741]

Visas are not required of foreign nationals eligible to apply for admission under the VWP.[742]

D. Deferred Inspection

CBP may, in its discretion, defer an individual to another CBP office or POE,[743] if the inspection officer at the POE believes that:

---

[739] 8 CFR §212.1(a)(4).

[740] 8 CFR §212.1(b)(1).

[741] 8 CFR §212.1(b)(2).

[742] 8 CFR §212.1(i).

[743] 8 CFR §235.2(a).

Copyright © 2017. American Immigration Lawyers Association. All rights reserved.

- A foreign national may establish admissibility by:
  - Posting a bond; or
  - Obtaining a waiver of ground(s) of inadmissibility; or
  - "Presenting additional evidence of admissibility not available at the time and place of the initial examination";[744] or
- Additional action is necessary, such as:
  - "[F]urther review of the case (including perhaps a review of an existing A file)"; or
  - An "other similar action that can only be conducted at the onward location."[745]

As stated by CBP:

"Deferred inspections are used when an immediate decision concerning the immigration status of an arriving traveler cannot be made at the port of entry due to a lack of documentation. On a case-by-case basis, the port of entry may schedule the traveler to report to a Deferred Inspection Site at a future date in order to present the necessary documentation and/or information. The traveler will be given an Order to Appear-Deferred Inspection, Form I-546, explaining what information and/or documentation is required to resolve the discrepancy."[746]

"The inspecting officer shall defer for a specific purpose, and not as a way to transfer a difficult case to another office. The inspecting officer should normally only use deferrals when it appears the case would probably be resolved in the alien's favor, with limited exceptions. The officer shall not defer an alien who is not expected to establish his or her admissibility."[747]

A CBP inspector at the POE should consider the following factors "when making a decision on whether to defer the inspection":

- "The likelihood that the alien will be able to establish admissibility;
- "The type of documents lacking, and the ability to obtain necessary documentation;

---

[744] 8 CFR §235.2(b). Bonds are discussed in INA §213. Waivers are discussed in INA §§211 (admission of returning permanent residence without required documents), 212(d)(3), and 212(d)(4) (waiver of certain grounds of inadmissibility for nonimmigrants and presenting additional evidence of admissibility not available at the time and place of the initial examination).

[745] 1 CBP IFM 17: Inadmissible Aliens, 14-1 Agency Manuals, 17.1, Deferred Inspection.

[746] CBP, "Deferred Inspection" (updated Aug. 2, 2016), https://www.cbp.gov/contact/deferred-inspection/overview-deferred-inspection.

[747] 1 CBP IFM 17: Inadmissible Aliens, 14-1 Agency Manuals, 17.1, Deferred Inspection.

Copyright © 2017. American Immigration Lawyers Association. All rights reserved.

- "The alien's good faith efforts to obtain necessary documents prior to arrival at the POE;

- "The verification or establishment of the alien's identity and nationality;

- "Age, health, and family ties;

- "Other humanitarian considerations;

- "The likelihood that the alien will appear;

- "The nature of possible inadmissibility (*i.e.*, criminal history, previous violations, etc.); and

- "The potential danger posed to society if the alien were to be paroled."[748]

A foreign national whose inspection is deferred should "be photographed and fingerprinted on Form FD-249,"[749] and this may be separate from the biometrics collection requirements of the US-VISIT program, discussed below. The foreign national should be paroled "for a brief period, generally not to exceed 30 days, sufficient for the paperwork to arrive at the onward office and for the applicant to obtain any necessary evidence to establish admissibility."[750] The issued Form I-94 should contain the following information:

- "Date to which deferred/paroled";

- "DE, Deferred Inspection" in the purpose section;

- "Deferring port code";

- "Action date";

- "The officer's admission stamp number";

- "Onward office code"; and

- The foreign national's "right index fingerprint on the reverse of the departure portion of the Form 1-94."[751]

The "further examination" is generally deferred "to the district director having jurisdiction over the place where the alien is seeking admission, or over the place of the alien's residence or destination in the United States."[752] Deferred inspection should not be considered admission of the foreign national,[753] but should be understood as providing the foreign national with the opportunity to address his or

---

[748] 1 CBP IFM 17: Inadmissible Aliens, 14-1 Agency Manuals, 17.1, Deferred Inspection.

[749] *Id.*

[750] *Id.*

[751] *Id.*

[752] *Id.*

[753] 8 CFR §235.2(c).

Copyright © 2017. American Immigration Lawyers Association. All rights reserved.

her admissibility as soon as possible.[754] In this regard, CBP guidance provides the following direction to CBP inspectors:

> "Appearance for deferred inspection may place additional burdens on the applicant who may, in many cases, be required to spend considerable time and money to comply with the required deferral procedures. Ensure that the information provided to the onward office is sufficient to allow the onward office to complete the deferred inspection in a single appearance."[755]

The practitioner should note that individual deferred inspection offices have differing days and hours of operation, and some offices require appointments, while others do not.[756] If an individual must visit a deferred inspection station, then the practitioner should encourage him or her to contact the specific station to inquire about that station's procedures before appearing.[757] Alternatively, the foreign national may be informed of "a specific reporting date and time block" by the CBP inspector at the POE.[758]

If the ground of potential inadmissibility is medical, the CBP inspector at the POE should "consult with the Public Health Service (PHS) before permitting the alien to proceed."[759] Medical documents should be returned in a sealed envelope to the foreign national if he or she "is required to submit to further medical examination prior to reporting to the onward office," or "forward[ed] … with the deferral papers directly to the onward office" if the foreign national will not need to visit a doctor, medical clinic, or PHS facility first.[760]

The officer at the deferred inspection site "should have received the deferral paperwork in advance of the applicant's appearance" and should have "reviewed [it] prior to the applicant's appearance."[761] A private "attorney may be allowed to be present upon request if the supervisory CBP Officer on duty deems it appropriate,"

---

[754] 8 CFR §235.2(c). This should be the principle when 8 CFR §235.2(c) (stating that "[s]uch deferral shall be accomplished pursuant to the provisions of section 212(d)(5) of the Act for the period of time necessary to complete the deferred inspection") is read in conjunction with INA §212(d)(5) (stating that "when the purposes of such parole shall … have been served the alien … thereafter his case shall continue to be dealt with in the same manner as that of any other applicant for admission to the United States").

[755] 1 CBP IFM 17: Inadmissible Aliens, 14-1 Agency Manuals, 17.1, Deferred Inspection.

[756] CBP, "Deferred Inspection Sites" (July 10, 2012), https://www.cbp.gov/sites/default/files/assets/documents/2016-Nov/deferred_inspection_sites_110316_2.pdf. *See also* 1 CBP IFM 17: Inadmissible Aliens, 14-1 Agency Manuals, 17.1, Deferred Inspection.

[757] CBP, "Deferred Inspection Sites" (updated Nov. 3, 2016), https://www.cbp.gov/document/guidance/deferred-inspection-sites (stating that "[t]ravelers are encouraged to contact sites not located within an international airport to establish an appointment, if necessary").

[758] 1 CBP IFM 17: Inadmissible Aliens, 14-1 Agency Manuals, 17.1, Deferred Inspection.

[759] *Id.*

[760] *Id.*

[761] *Id.*

Copyright © 2017. American Immigration Lawyers Association. All rights reserved.

but the role "in such a situation is limited to that of observer and consultant to the applicant."[762] A foreign national who is deemed admissible should be issued a new I-94 card, "using the office symbol of the onward office and the current date as the date of admission."[763] If a foreign national does not appear before a deferred inspection site as required, then a notice to appear (NTA) "shall be executed using the information listed on the Form I-546 and mailed to the address provided," and "[a]ll information related to the case shall be added to the A-file."[764]

If the district director refuses to allow the foreign national to post bond or to apply for a waiver of a ground of inadmissibility, then the decision "shall be without prejudice to the renewal of such application or the authorizing of such admission by the immigration judge without additional fee."[765] And if a foreign national "is found or believed to be suffering from a disability that renders it impractical to proceed with the examination" at the POE, then the inadmissibility should not be determined at the POE; inspection should be deferred "for such time and under such conditions" as required by "the district director in whose district the port is located," in order to allow family members to testify and to ensure the "protection or guardianship" of "any accompanying aliens."[766] A foreign national may also visit a deferred inspection site to correct an erroneous I-94 card.[767]

As stated by CBP guidance: "Before an alien is deferred, the inspecting officer shall consider the likelihood that the alien will abscond or pose a security risk."[768] Therefore, a foreign national who "is clearly inadmissible or may pose a security risk or danger to society" should be either placed in removal proceedings or permitted to "withdraw his or her application for admission."[769]

E. Inadmissibility, Expedited Removal, and Withdrawal of the Application for Admission

A foreign national may be removed from the United States if he or she is deemed inadmissible because of fraud or misrepresentation, or because of a lack of the proper entry documents, unless these requirements are waived,[770] as discussed above. If the foreign national is placed in expedited removal proceedings, then he or she "will be given a reasonable opportunity to establish to the satisfaction of the examining

---

[762] *Id.*

[763] *Id.*

[764] *Id.*

[765] 8 CFR §235.2(d).

[766] 8 CFR §235.2(e).

[767] CBP, "Deferred Inspection" (updated Aug. 2, 2016), https://www.cbp.gov/contact/deferred-inspection/overview-deferred-inspection.

[768] 1 CBP IFM 17: Inadmissible Aliens, 14-1 Agency Manuals, 17.1, Deferred Inspection.

[769] *Id.*

[770] 8 CFR §235.3(b)(2)(i).

Copyright © 2017. American Immigration Lawyers Association. All rights reserved.

immigration officer that he or she was admitted or paroled into the United States following inspection" to counter the charge:

> "The alien will be allowed to present evidence or provide sufficient information to support the claim. Such evidence may consist of documentation in the possession of the alien, the Service, or a third party. The examining immigration officer will consider all such evidence and information, make further inquiry if necessary, and will attempt to verify the alien's status through a check of all available Service data systems. The burden rests with the alien to satisfy the examining immigration officer of the claim of lawful admission or parole."[771]

If the foreign national "establishes that he or she was lawfully admitted or paroled," then the case should be further reviewed to determine whether a ground of deportability applies, whether the foreign national is inadmissible, "whether such parole has been, or should be, terminated," and whether the foreign national is inadmissible.[772] If the foreign national "cannot satisfy the examining officer that he or she was lawfully admitted or paroled," then he or she "will be ordered removed."[773]

There is generally no "entitlement" to "a hearing before an immigration judge" or "to an appeal of the expedited removal order" to the BIA.[774] The foreign national "shall be detained pending determination and removal," except that the foreign national may be paroled into the United States if "parole is required to meet a medical emergency or is necessary for a legitimate law enforcement objective."[775] These specific provisions on expedited removal do not apply to foreign nationals seeking admission under the VWP.[776]

A foreign national may be permitted to withdraw the application for admission in lieu of removal proceedings or expedited removal proceedings, although there is no right to withdrawal.[777] The withdrawal "must be made voluntarily."[778] Generally, permission is granted only if the foreign national "intends and is able to depart the United States immediately," and the foreign national "shall normally remain in carrier or [DHS] custody pending departure, unless the district director determines that

---

[771] 8 CFR §235.3(b)(6).

[772] 8 CFR §235.3(b)(6). The grounds of deportability are discussed in INA §237(a). The grounds of inadmissibility are discussed in INA §212(a).

[773] *Id.*

[774] 8 CFR §235.3(b)(2)(ii).

[775] 8 CFR §235.3(b)(2)(iii).

[776] 8 CFR §235.3(b)(10).

[777] 8 CFR §235.4.

[778] *Id.*

Copyright © 2017. American Immigration Lawyers Association. All rights reserved.

parole of the alien is warranted" for "urgent humanitarian reasons" or "significant public benefit."[779]

F. DHS Traveler Redress Inquiry Program

DHS established the Traveler Redress Inquiry Program (DHS TRIP) as "a single point of contact for individuals who have inquiries or seek resolution regarding difficulties they experienced during their travel screening at transportation hubs—like airports and train stations—or crossing U.S. borders."[780] DHS TRIP may be used to address the following difficulties and situations:

- "Watch list issues;

- Screening problems at ports of entry;

- Situations where travelers believe they have been unfairly or incorrectly delayed, denied boarding or identified for additional screening at our nation's transportation hubs."[781]

This is the online system to be used, for example, if a foreign national is in fact the same foreign national with a potential ground of inadmissibility, but the foreign national is deemed admissible after extensive interview in secondary inspection.[782] An individual may "file an inquiry to have erroneous information corrected in DHS systems," and the inquiry should be "routed for redress to the appropriate DHS components," which in turn should "review the request and reach a determination about a traveler's status."[783] The foreign national should "be assigned a record identifier or Redress Control Number."[784]

G. Automatic Revalidation

Generally, a foreign national admitted under most visa classifications may visit Canada or Mexico for up to 30 days and "retain" the Form I-94.[785] The foreign national may also be readmitted to the United States even if his or her visa has expired because the "validity of an expired nonimmigrant visa ... may be considered to be automatically extended to the date of application for readmission."[786] In addition, the foreign national may be admitted even if he or she was granted a change

---

[779] 8 CFR §§235.4 and 212.5(b).

[780] Department of Homeland Security (DHS), "DHS Traveler Redress Inquiry Program (DHS TRIP)" (updated Nov. 4, 2016), https://www.dhs.gov/dhs-trip.

[781] Id.

[782] "Highlights from the CBP Open Forum at Annual Conference 2009" (June 19, 2009), AILA Doc. No. 09061969.

[783] DHS, "DHS Traveler Redress Inquiry Program (DHS TRIP)" (updated Nov. 4, 2016), https://www.dhs.gov/dhs-trip.

[784] Id.

[785] CBP, "Automatic Revalidation of Visas" (May 23, 2012), AILA Doc. No. 12052359.

[786] 22 CFR §41.112(d)(1)(i).

Copyright © 2017. American Immigration Lawyers Association. All rights reserved.

of status, because "the validity of an expired or unexpired nonimmigrant visa may be considered to be automatically extended to the date of application for readmission, and the visa may be converted as necessary to that changed classification."[787] This process is known as "automatic revalidation,"[788] or "automatic visa revalidation."

To qualify for automatic revalidation, such an individual must meet the following conditions:

- Possess a valid Form I-94, "endorsed by DHS to show an unexpired period of initial admission or extension of stay,"[789] or a valid Form I-94 and a valid Form I-20 or Form DS-2019 for F and J nonimmigrants, respectively;[790]

- Possess a valid passport;[791]

- Seek "readmission within the authorized period of initial admission or extension of stay,"[792] which means while the I-94 is still valid;

- Seek "readmission after an absence not exceeding 30 days solely in contiguous territory," except for F and J nonimmigrants,[793] as discussed below;

- Have "maintained and intend[] to resume nonimmigrant status,"[794] as discussed below;

- Did not apply "for a new visa while abroad";[795] and

- "Does not require authorization for admission under INA §212(d)(3)."[796]

An individual with an expired F or J visa is eligible for automatic revalidation following travel from contiguous territory and adjacent islands other than Cuba.[797] Such an individual should be able to retain the Form I-94 and Form DS-2019 or Form I-20 and be readmitted for the balance of time required to complete [the] program.[798]

---

[787] 22 CFR §41.112(d)(1)(ii).

[788] CBP, "Automatic Revalidation of Visas" (May 23, 2012), AILA Doc. No. 12052359.

[789] 22 CFR §41.112(d)(2)(i).

[790] 8 CFR §§214.1(b)(1)(iv) and (b)(2)(iv). Note that this regulation still references the old Form IAP-66, but the current document for J nonimmigrants is the DS-2019.

[791] 22 CFR §41.112(d)(2)(v).

[792] 22 CFR §41.112(d)(2)(iv).

[793] 22 CFR §41.112(d)(2)(ii).

[794] 22 CFR §41.112(d)(2)(iii).

[795] 22 CFR §41.112(d)(2)(vii).

[796] 22 CFR §41.112(d)(2)(vi) (concerning applicants otherwise ineligible for nonimmigrant visas who are temporarily admitted under the authority of the Attorney General or Secretary of State).

[797] 22 CFR §41.112(d)(2)(ii).

[798] CBP, "FAQs on the Arrival-Departure Record (I-94 Form) & Crewman Landing Permit (I-95 Form)" (Dec. 31, 2008), https://help.cbp.gov/app/answers/detail/a_id/1218/~/automatic-revalidation-for-certain-temporary-visitors; 22 CFR §41.112(d)(2); 8 CFR §214.1(b). The regulations still reference the old Form
Cont'd

Copyright © 2017. American Immigration Lawyers Association. All rights reserved.

The practitioner should note that the regulation uses the term "apply" when discussing a visa application,[799] so a foreign national should be ineligible for automatic revalidation if the visa application is pending or was denied. Nationals of Iran, Syria, and Sudan, the countries that currently are designated as state sponsors of terrorism, are also not eligible for automatic revalidation.[800] In addition: "Greater scrutiny should be applied to those nationals of countries identified as supporting terrorism. In general, applicants not eligible for automatic revalidation should be allowed to withdraw their application for admission, unless expedited removal is otherwise warranted."[801] The practitioner may wish to advise the foreign national to carry a copy of CBP's Automatic Revalidation Fact Sheet.[802] For a discussion of readmission of VWP travelers, see Volume 1: Chapter Three, "Visitors: B Visas and Status and the Visa Waiver Program."

V. Extending Nonimmigrant Status

If a foreign national's employment assignment will continue after the expiration of the petition initially approved by USCIS, then an extension application should be filed with USCIS on Form I-129, Petition for a Nonimmigrant Worker.[803] Generally, the supporting documents for an extension application are similar to those submitted with the initial petition.[804] Just as for initial petitions, an extension application filed on Form I-129 may be filed up to 180 days in advance.[805] Filing early is highly recommended, because of extended processing times, and because temporary employment authorization pursuant to a timely filed extension application is

---

IAP-66, but the current document for J nonimmigrants is the Form DS-2019, as discussed in Chapter Ten, "J-1 Visas and Status."

[799] 22 CFR §41.112(d)(2)(vii).

[800] 22 CFR §41.112(d)(3); DOS, "Automatic Revalidation," https://travel.state.gov/content/visas/en/general/automatic-revalidation.html. Some other documents cited in this section also mention Cuba as a state sponsor of terrorism, but that designation was rescinded in May 2015 (DOS, "Rescission of Cuba as a State Sponsor of Terrorism" (May 29, 2015), https://obamawhitehouse.archives.gov/blog/2015/05/29/rescission-cuba-state-sponsor-terrorism.

[801] 1 CBP IFM 15: Nonimmigrants and Border Crossers, 14-1 Agency Manuals, 15.3, Visas.

[802] "Highlights from the CBP Open Forum at Annual Conference 2009" (June 19, 2009), AILA Doc. No. 09061969; CBP, "Important Update: Automatic Revalidation of Visas" (May 23, 2012), https://www.cbp.gov/sites/default/files/documents/auto_reva_3.pdf.

[803] 8 CFR §214.1(c)(1). For a discussion of extension of a particular nonimmigrant classification, see the individual chapter.

[804] *Id.* (stating that the "petition must be filed with … the initial evidence specified in §214.2").

[805] USCIS, "Instructions for Form I-129, Petition for a Nonimmigrant Worker," https://www.uscis.gov/files/form/i-129instr.pdf.

Copyright © 2017. American Immigration Lawyers Association. All rights reserved.

generally available for only 240 days,[806] although the practitioner may request premium processing if necessary and available.

An application for extension on behalf of dependent spouse and children of the principal nonimmigrant worker may be filed on Form I-539, Application to Extend/Change Nonimmigrant Status,[807] with evidence of the familial relationship, such as marriage certificate and/or birth certificate(s),[808] evidence of the principal applicant's valid nonimmigrant status or application extension,[809] and copies, front and back, of the Forms I-94 for all applicants.[810]

As a practical matter, the practitioner should endeavor to file the two forms together, with the Service Center with jurisdiction over the principal nonimmigrant's place of employment,[811] in order to maximize the likelihood of an approval being granted before the initial status expires, because experience has shown that extension applications filed independently of the principal nonimmigrant's extension petition have historically been processed more slowly.[812] Although a copy of the passport(s) is necessary "only if requested" by USCIS, because the application form requests information on passport validity,[813] the passport(s) "must be valid at the time of application for extension ... and the alien must agree to maintain the validity of his or her passport and to abide by all the terms and conditions of his extension."[814] Only one application needs to be filed for the dependent family members as long as the

---

[806] 8 CFR §274a.12(b)(20). *See also* 81 Fed. Reg. 2068 (Jan. 15, 2016), AILA Doc. No. 16011402, adding H-1B1, E-3, and CW-1 to the nonimmigrant statuses eligible for the 240-day rule.

[807] 8 CFR §214.1(c)(2); USCIS, "Instructions for Form I-539, Application to Extend/Change Nonimmigrant Status," https://www.uscis.gov/files/form/i-539instr.pdf; AFM 30.2. Although 8 CFR §214.1(c)(1) notes that the Form I-129 may be used for dependent beneficiaries, if "the form version specifically provides for their inclusion," the form has only one question regarding whether an application for dependent(s) will accompany the petition and the number of dependents. USCIS, "Form I-129, Petition for a Nonimmigrant Worker," https://www.uscis.gov/files/form/i-129.pdf.

[808] 8 CFR §214.1(c)(2) (stating that the extension application must be filed "together with any initial evidence specified in the applicable provisions of §214.2," which in turn mention dependents only generally as the spouse and children of the principal nonimmigrant); USCIS, "Instructions for Form I-539, Application to Extend/Change Nonimmigrant Status," https://www.uscis.gov/files/form/i-539instr.pdf. *See also* relevant nonimmigrant definitions for accompanying or following to join spouses and children in INA §101(a)(15); INA §101(b)(1) for a definition of child.

[809] AFM 30.2.

[810] USCIS, "Instructions for Form I-539, Application to Extend/Change Nonimmigrant Status," https://www.uscis.gov/files/form/i-539instr.pdf.

[811] *Id.*

[812] "AILA Liaison/VSC Meeting Minutes" (Jan. 21, 2009), AILA Doc. No. 09012768 (discussion of extended processing time).

[813] AFM 30.2.

[814] 8 CFR §214.1(a)(3)(i).

Copyright © 2017. American Immigration Lawyers Association. All rights reserved.

extension application for the principal nonimmigrant will be filed on Form I-129,[815] or as long as the entire family unit holds the same nonimmigrant status,[816] such as B-2. If only Form I-539 will be filed, then it should be filed with the Service Center with jurisdiction over the applicant's place of residence.[817]

Except as discussed below, all applications to extend status must be timely filed, which means they must be received by USCIS before the status expires.[818] As a practical matter, the very latest date that the extension application may be shipped to USCIS is the last business day before the nonimmigrant status expires, as long as an express means for next-day delivery is used, because USCIS subscribes to the receipt rule rather than the mailbox rule.[819] As stated by USCIS guidance regarding extension petitions: "Approval of a timely-filed I-129 extension is always considered *nunc pro tunc*, effectively forgiving the status violation for overstaying or continuing employment (with the same employer) which may have occurred between the expiration of the original admission period and the approval date of the extension."[820]

In addition, no extension application may be approved if the foreign national "failed to maintain the previously accorded status,"[821] or if the foreign national was admitted in VWP status.[822] For example, B, H-4, TD, O-3, and P-4 nonimmigrants who engage in unauthorized employment will generally be held to have violated their nonimmigrant status.[823] The practitioner should also be aware of the potential need to file a second extension application, with receipt by the requested extension end date, even if the first extension application has not been adjudicated.[824] If the foreign

---

[815] This is the principle of practice when 8 CFR §214.1(c)(1) is read in conjunction with 8 CFR §214.1(c)(2), although neither regulation specifically states so, since "[m]ore than one person may be included in an application where the co-applicants are all members of a single family group and ... one holds a nonimmigrant status and the other co-applicants are his or her spouse and/or children who hold derivative nonimmigrant status based on his or her status." 8 CFR §214.1(c)(2).

[816] 8 CFR §214.1(c)(2).

[817] AFM 30.2.

[818] 8 CFR §214.1(c)(4) (stating that an "extension of stay may not be approved for an applicant ... where such status expired before the application or petition was filed").

[819] 8 CFR 103.2(a)(7)(i) (stating that "[a]n application or petition received in a USCIS office shall be stamped to show the time and date of actual receipt and ... shall be regarded as properly filed when so stamped").

[820] AFM 30.2 (italics in original).

[821] 8 CFR §214.1(c)(4). *See also Matter of Siffre*, 14 I&N Dec. 444 (BIA 1973).

[822] 8 CFR §214.1(c)(3)(i).

[823] "USCIS's SOPs for I-539 Processing" (undated, posted Sept. 7, 2007), AILA Doc. No. 07090760; *Matter of Sparmann*, 11 I&N Dec. 285 (Acting D.D. 1965) (noting that the B-1 nonimmigrant had "continued to maintain his nonimmigrant status").

[824] "AILA Liaison/VSC Meeting Minutes" (Jan. 21, 2009), AILA Doc. No. 09012768 (discussion of extended processing time). *See also Matter of Teberen*, 15 I&N Dec. 689 (BIA 1976) ("reject[ing] counsel's contention that the [foreign national] cannot 'overstay' until he receives a formal denial of an extension from the district director").

Copyright © 2017. American Immigration Lawyers Association. All rights reserved.

national should have obtained a waiver of inadmissibility for the initial nonimmigrant status, or if the waiver has expired, then the extension may not be granted until a valid waiver is presented.[825]

Approval of an extension application requires an exercise of discretion by USCIS,[826] where USCIS "must be satisfied that the applicant will continue to engage only in activities specifically consistent with his or her nonimmigrant status."[827] An extension application may be denied if USCIS determines that the applicant plans to remain in the United States indefinitely.[828] There "is no appeal from the denial of an application for extension of stay filed on Form I-129 or I-539,"[829] although the underlying petition may be approved on behalf of a principal nonimmigrant even if the extension request is denied.[830]

Generally, USCIS states that RFEs should be "relatively unusual,"[831] though experience in recent years in several categories has shown the opposite to be true.[832] Personal interview of the applicant or a "formal investigation for an extension should rarely be required."[833] The validity period of an extension may end on an individual's date of departure from the United States, if the foreign national returned abroad while the application was pending.[834] An approved extension application "granted to members of a family group" will be valid "for the same period of time," such that the "shortest period granted to any member of the family shall be granted to all members of the family."[835] As a practical matter, this means that the validity period for the approved extension for derivative beneficiaries will be the same as the validity period of the principal nonimmigrant's extension application, which in turn may not be granted beyond the date of any labor condition application or temporary labor certification application, if applicable.[836] For situations where all family members hold

---

[825] AFM 30.2.

[826] 8 CFR §214.1(c)(5); AFM 30.2.

[827] 8 CFR §214.1(c)(5); *Matter of Rogalski*, 14 I&N Dec. 507 (D.D. 1973).

[828] *Matter of Safadi*, 11 I&N Dec 446 (BIA 1965).

[829] 8 CFR §214.1(c)(5).

[830] USCIS, W. Yates, "The Significance of a Prior CIS Approval of a Nonimmigrant Petition in the Context of a Subsequent Determination Regarding Eligibility for Extension of Petition Validity" (Apr. 23, 2004), AILA Doc. No. 04050510.

[831] AFM 30.2(c)(4).

[832] National Foundation for American Policy, "Analysis: Data Reveal High Denial Rates for L-1 and H-1B Petitions at U.S. Citizenship and Naturalization Services" (Feb. 2012), *http://bit.ly/2012nfap* (noting fiscal year 2011 RFE rates on extension applications of 63% for L-1Bs, 51% for L-1As, 26% for H-1Bs, and 27% for O-1s).

[833] AFM 30.2(c)(4).

[834] "AILA Liaison/VSC Meeting Minutes" (Jan. 21, 2009), AILA Doc. No. 09012768.

[835] 8 CFR §214.1(c)(2).

[836] AFM 30.2(c)(3)(F).

Copyright © 2017. American Immigration Lawyers Association. All rights reserved.

the same status, such as B-2, the extension validity period for all family members may be truncated by the 21st birthday of a child named on the application,[837] or a passport expiration date, although a regulation requires only that the passport be valid at the time of extension and that the alien maintain a valid passport throughout the period of stay.[838]

A. Form I-539

The most common approach when the extension application is for multiple family members who are dependents of a principal employment authorized nonimmigrant is to name the spouse of the principal nonimmigrant as the primary applicant and list children on the supplement. Experience has also shown that it is helpful to place a tab on the bottom of the page, with "Form I-539" written on it.

Biographic and personal information for the applicant should be provided in Parts 1 and 4, with appropriate answers for the questions in Part 2. In Part 3, the end date of the extension request on this form should match the end date of the request for the principal nonimmigrant's petition extension or the end date of an approved extension petition.[839] If the applicant does not have a valid passport, then an explanation, such as one describing actions taken to renew the passport or explaining why a passport cannot be renewed, should be provided.[840]

Truthful answers should be provided to the questions in Part 4, so these should be highlighted for the client to consider. If the applicant entered the Diversity Visa Lottery, then the practitioner may state this on an addendum, although entering the lottery is not generally considered a proper application for an immigrant visa.[841] If Form I-130, Petition for Alien Relative (for family-based cases); Form I-140, Immigrant Petition for Alien Worker (for employment-based cases); or Form I-360, Petition for Amerasian, Widow(er), or Special Immigrant (for certain special cases) was filed directly on behalf of any of the applicants, then this should be disclosed and the receipt number should be provided, if available, as part of the "[explanation] on a separate piece of paper." But if an immigrant petition was filed only on behalf of a principal foreign national who is not named on the Form I-539, then it should not be necessary to mark "Yes," since the dependent spouse and children filing Form I-539 were not the beneficiaries but only named as a spouse or child of the principal foreign

---

[837] "AILA Liaison/VSC Meeting Minutes" (Jan. 21, 2009), AILA Doc. No. 09012768.

[838] 8 CFR §214.1(a)(3)(i).

[839] USCIS, "Instructions for Form I-539, Application to Extend/Change Nonimmigrant Status," https://www.uscis.gov/files/form/i-539instr.pdf.

[840] Id.

[841] 80 Fed. Reg. 43338 (July 22, 2015), at 43340, stating "Diversity Visa program selectees and their derivatives are not beneficiaries of approved immigrant visa petitions." The context of the statement is different, but the same logic should apply.

Copyright © 2017. American Immigration Lawyers Association. All rights reserved.

national. For a discussion of the grounds of inadmissibility, see Volume 2: Chapter Four, "Consular Processing, Adjustment of Status, and Permanent Residence Issues."

One appropriate explanation on Part 4, #19 of the applicant's source of financial support without working is to explain how the principal nonimmigrant provides the support: "I am fully supported by my [insert familial role of principal nonimmigrant, such as husband, wife, father, or mother], who is employed by Employer in [insert principal's nonimmigrant status] status." The form's instructions state that "[w]illful failure to disclose" information relating to current or previous nonimmigrant J status "can result" in the application being denied.[842]

The form should be signed, preferably in black ink, and dated.

B. Common Issues

1. Previous Petition Approval Does Not Guarantee Extension Approval

The practitioner may wish to warn the client that prior approval of a petition does not guarantee approval of the extension petition, because:

"CIS has the authority to question prior determinations. Adjudicators are not bound to approve subsequent petitions or applications seeking immigration benefits where eligibility has not been demonstrated, merely because of a prior approval which may have been erroneous…. Each matter must be decided according to the evidence of record on a case-by-case basis."[843]

Generally, the prior approval "should be given deference," as long as the extension petition "involve[es] the same parties (petitioner and beneficiary) and the same underlying facts."[844] As stated by USCIS guidance:

"The alien beneficiary of a Form I-129 being filed by his or her employer for an extension has previously been found eligible for nonimmigrant status, either by INS, USCIS or CBP at the time of admission or through an initial petition, or by the Department of State during the visa issuance process."[845]

But the practitioner should note the following USCIS guidance:

"That said, petition extension requests will not be automatically approved, but will be adjudicated on their merits, based on the documentation submitted with the petition. If the documentation submitted is insufficient to meet the petitioner's

---

[842] USCIS, "Instructions for Form I-539, Application to Extend/Change Nonimmigrant Status," https://www.uscis.gov/files/form/i-539instr.pdf.

[843] USCIS, W. Yates, "The Significance of a Prior CIS Approval of a Nonimmigrant Petition in the Context of a Subsequent Determination Regarding Eligibility for Extension of Petition Validity" (Apr. 23, 2004), AILA Doc. No. 04050510 (internal citations omitted) (citing *Matter of Church Scientology International*, 19 I&N Dec. 593 (Comm'r 1988) and 8 CFR §103.8(d), which defines the term "record of proceedings").

[844] *Id.*

[845] AFM 30.2.

Copyright © 2017. American Immigration Lawyers Association. All rights reserved.

burden of proof, or the law does not support approval of the request, an adjudicator lacks the legal authority to approve the request notwithstanding such deficiency, even if the agency may have previously approved a request involving the same petitioner/beneficiary and similar facts."[846]

And no deference is due if:

- "[I]t is determined that there was a material error with regard to the previous petition approval;

- There has been a "substantial change in circumstances"; or

- "[T]here is new material information that adversely impacts the petitioner's or beneficiary's eligibility."[847]

USCIS guidance states that material error "involves the misapplication of an objective statutory or regulatory requirement to the facts at hand" and provides the example of previous approval of an H-1B petition when "the beneficiary's degree is not appropriate to the proffered occupation."[848] The guidance also points out that typically, "adjudicators should not question prior adjudicators' determinations that are subjective, such as the prior adjudicator's evaluation of the beneficiary's education, specialized training, and/or progressively responsible experience in a degree equivalency determination."[849]

A "substantial change in circumstances" in turn "involves any material change to either the petitioner's or the beneficiary's eligibility for the nonimmigrant classification sought."[850] The examples provided include a change in the corporate relationship, the beneficiary's job duties, or the organizational structure of the petitioner for the purposes of L classification; a review of whether the beneficiary possesses valid licensure for the occupation, whether permanent or temporary, for the period of requested petition validity, or a review of whether the petitioner continues to qualify as a U.S. employer or qualifies as an agent if the petitioner relocates abroad, for the purposes of H classification; and a review of whether at least 75

---

[846] "AILA/USCIS Liaison Minutes" (Oct. 28, 2008), AILA Doc. No. 08110767.

[847] USCIS, W. Yates, "The Significance of a Prior CIS Approval of a Nonimmigrant Petition in the Context of a Subsequent Determination Regarding Eligibility for Extension of Petition Validity" (Apr. 23, 2004), AILA Doc. No. 04050510. *See also* AFM 30.2 ("[a]bsent gross error, a change in the circumstances surrounding the alien's stay, or discovery of new information not previously available, the adjudicator should not engage in an in-depth review of issues relating to the initial status").

[848] USCIS, W. Yates, "The Significance of a Prior CIS Approval of a Nonimmigrant Petition in the Context of a Subsequent Determination Regarding Eligibility for Extension of Petition Validity" (Apr. 23, 2004), AILA Doc. No. 04050510.

[849] *Id.*

[850] *Id.*

Copyright © 2017. American Immigration Lawyers Association. All rights reserved.

percent of the entertainment group members have performed with the group for at least one year for the purposes of P classification.[851]

As a practical matter, the practitioner may note that a substantial change in circumstances may be the result of "new material information," because both situations involve a review of whether the petitioner and/or beneficiary remain eligible for the nonimmigrant classification. "New material information" is defined as "any fact not available to the previous adjudicator that would impact the petitioner's or beneficiary's eligibility for the nonimmigrant classification sought."[852] Although the only example stated is "information that affects national security or public safety,"[853] the practitioner should not focus exclusively on this situation. For example, new material information may reveal that a scientific technician or technologist in TN status is not eligible for a TN extension because there is no longer a professional to whom to provide direct support.

If any of these three reasons is the basis for an RFE or denial notice, then the document should "clearly articulate" the factor.[854] Alternatively:

"[I]f the adjudicator has strong reason to believe that the alien was not entitled to a nonimmigrant status in the first place, he or she may seek clarification from the applicant through correspondence or by requiring an interview at the appropriate local office. If it is established that the applicant was not entitled to the status initially, the application should be denied and (if appropriate) the information provided to the visa issuing post or port-of-entry through normal intelligence and liaison procedures."[855]

Following multiple reports of RFEs and denial notices that did not provide a clear explanation, USCIS indicated that adjudicators would be "reminded to include a clear explanation of any finding that there has been a substantial change or material error in the RFEs and denials."[856] And if an adjudicator wishes to issue an RFE or denial notice to an extension petition "where the parties and facts involved have not changed," then the Deputy Center Director "should review and clear in writing, prior to the issuance of an RFE or final decision."[857]

---

[851] Id.

[852] Id.

[853] Id.

[854] Id.

[855] AFM 30.2.

[856] "AILA/USCIS Liaison Minutes" (Mar. 19, 2009), AILA Doc. No. 09031920; "AILA/USCIS Liaison Minutes" (Oct. 28, 2008), AILA Doc. No. 08110767.

[857] USCIS, W. Yates, "The Significance of a Prior CIS Approval of a Nonimmigrant Petition in the Context of a Subsequent Determination Regarding Eligibility for Extension of Petition Validity" (Apr. 23, 2004), AILA Doc. No. 04050510.

Copyright © 2017. American Immigration Lawyers Association. All rights reserved.

2. Nunc Pro Tunc Extensions

The regulations allow for excuse, "in the discretion" of USCIS, of a failure to timely file, as long as the following conditions are met:

- "The delay was due to extraordinary circumstances beyond the control of the applicant or petitioner, and the Service finds the delay commensurate with the circumstances,"[858] which USCIS in turn interprets to mean that the "length of the delay was reasonable";[859]

- The foreign national "has not otherwise violated his or her nonimmigrant status";

- The foreign national "remains a bona fide nonimmigrant"; and

- The foreign national "is not the subject" of deportation or removal proceedings.[860]

It is not necessary to file a separate application for the nunc pro tunc relief in addition to the extension application, and approval of the extension request may be "granted from the date the previously authorized stay expired."[861] When submitting the extension application and the request for nunc pro tunc relief, the practitioner should include a "cover letter explaining the situation" and "a colored sheet of paper" with "NUNC PRO TUNC REQUEST" in capital letters "to ensure that the request receives proper consideration."[862] The practitioner should note that, for dependents who are not eligible for I-688B employment authorization documents (EADs), not violating nonimmigrant status includes not accepting or engaging in unauthorized employment.[863]

A not uncommon example of the need for nunc pro tunc relief is where a principal nonimmigrant's status is extended, but due to an "inadvertent error" by the employer or employer's counsel, a consonant extension application is not filed on behalf of the dependents.[864] It is hoped that USCIS guidance, which indicates that "this type of inadvertently overlooked dependent extension situation may (doesn't have to) qualify

---

[858] 8 CFR §214.1(c)(4)(i).

[859] USCIS, "Instructions for Form I-539, Application to Extend/Change Nonimmigrant Status," https://www.uscis.gov/files/form/i-539instr.pdf.

[860] 8 CFR §214.1(c)(4).

[861] 8 CFR §214.1(c)(4); "AILA Liaison/VSC Meeting Minutes" (Dec. 5, 2007), AILA Doc. No. 07122062.

[862] "AILA/TSC Liaison Minutes" (Nov. 4, 2002), AILA Doc. No. 02111845.

[863] "NSC Business Product Line Teleconference Q&As" (Jan. 25, 2005), AILA Doc. No. 05020162.

[864] "Minutes of AILA USCIS Liaison Meeting" (Mar. 23, 2006), AILA Doc. No. 06060761; "NSC Business Product Line Teleconference Q&As" (Jan. 25, 2005), AILA Doc. No. 05020162; "AILA/TSC Liaison Minutes" (Nov. 4, 2002), AILA Doc. No. 02111845.

Copyright © 2017. American Immigration Lawyers Association. All rights reserved.

as extraordinary circumstances,"[865] represents the "internal policy" that USCIS previously indicated would be forthcoming.[866]

Other potential grounds for a request for nunc pro tunc relief include major catastrophes, family deaths or emergencies, or medical conditions or procedures, and may be accompanied by news articles, a death certificate, or a doctor's letter, as well as a statement from the foreign national. For example, following the Haiti earthquake in January 2010, USCIS issued guidance encouraging the favorable consideration of applications filed late:

> "In accordance with existing guidelines, Service Center directors have authority to accept applications for extension of stay and change of status submitted after the applicant's period of admission has expired. Such applications must include evidence of the applicant's inability to return to Haiti prior to the expiration of his or her authorized period of admission due to the events of January 12, 2010. Haitian nationals and residents in lawful, nonimmigrant status on January 12, 2010, will be excused for filing late up to March 12, 2010. After March 12, 2010, eligibility for delayed filing will be determined on a case-by-case basis."[867]

Following the September 11, 2001, terrorist attacks, Congress enacted a statute extending the nonimmigrant status of foreign nationals who were "disabled as a direct result of a specified terrorist activity" and of their spouses and children, providing for employment authorization, allowing a sort of grace period of one month during which unlawful presence would not accrue, and stating that extension applications by these individuals would be deemed timely filed if received within 60 days of the deadline.[868] Among the permissible "circumstances preventing an alien from timely acting" were "office closures," "mail or courier service cessations or delays," "airline flight cessations or delays," and "other closures, cessations, or delays affecting case processing or travel necessary to satisfy legal requirements."[869]

VI. Dependents

Dependent spouses and children are eligible for derivative nonimmigrant status.[870] These dependents may apply for their visas at the same time as the principal

---

[865] "Minutes of AILA USCIS Liaison Meeting" (Mar. 23, 2006), AILA Doc. No. 06060761.

[866] "NSC Business Product Line Teleconference Q&As" (Jan. 25, 2005), AILA Doc. No. 05020162.

[867] USCIS, A. Mayorkas, "Initial Relief Efforts for Aliens Affected by the January 12, 2010, Haiti Earthquake" (Jan. 15, 2010), AILA Doc. No. 10011960.

[868] Uniting and Strengthening America by Providing Appropriate Tools Required to Intercept and Obstruct Terrorism Act (USA PATRIOT Act), §422, Pub. L. No. 107-56, 115 Stat. 272 (2001).

[869] *Id.*

[870] INA §§101(a)(15)(E), (H)(iii), (J), (L), (O)(iii), and (P)(iv); 8 CFR §214.6(j)(1).

Copyright © 2017. American Immigration Lawyers Association. All rights reserved.

nonimmigrant,[871] or they may "follow to join," which "permits an alien to obtain a nonimmigrant visa (NIV),"[872] after the principal foreign national has been issued a visa and/or been admitted to the United States. As long as the principal nonimmigrant remains alive and maintains nonimmigrant status, and as long as there is an appropriate familial relationship between the principal and dependent foreign nationals, "[t]here is no statutory time period during which the following to join alien must apply for a visa and seek admission into the United States."[873]

Marriage between individuals of the same sex is now recognized under U.S. law,[874] and thus the same rules apply to same-sex spouses as to those of the opposite sex.[875]

The immigration statute excludes from the definition of the term "spouse" those individuals who were not in the physical presence of each other when they married, "unless the marriage shall have been consummated."[876]

Although common law marriage may be viewed as less than a legal marriage in the United States, common law spouses may also be eligible for derivative nonimmigrant visas and status, as long as common law marriage is recognized in the country of visa issuance: "The underlying principle in determining the validity of the marriage is that the law of the place of marriage celebration controls. If the law is complied with and the marriage is recognized, then the marriage is deemed to be valid for immigration purposes."[877] A chief exception is that "[m]arriages, considered to be void under state law as contrary to public policy, such as polygamous or incestuous marriages, cannot be recognized for immigration purposes even if the marriage is legal in the place of marriage celebration."[878] Both parties must have been able to enter into marriage by legal termination of any previous marriages.[879] In order for a marital relationship, such as common law marriage or cohabitation, to be acceptable for immigration purposes in "the absence of a marriage certificate, an official verification, or a legal brief verifying full marital rights," the following conditions must be met:

---

[871] *See, e.g.,* 9 FAM 402.14-11, 402.13-11, 402.9-8(A), 402.9, and 402.10-14, as well as 9 FAM 402.5-6(D)(4) (discussing how dependent spouses and children may accompany or follow to join the principal nonimmigrant).

[872] 9 FAM 102.3-1.

[873] *Id.*

[874] *U.S. v. Windsor*, 133 S.Ct. 2675 (2013); *Obergefell v. Hodges*, 135 S.Ct. 2584 (2015).

[875] USCIS, "Same-Sex Marriages" (updated Apr. 3, 2014), https://www.uscis.gov/family/same-sex-marriages; DOS, "Cable with Post-DOMA Guidance" (Aug. 2, 2013), AILA Doc. No. 13080252.

[876] INA §101(a)(35).

[877] 9 FAM 102.3-1.

[878] *Id.*

[879] *Id.*

Copyright © 2017. American Immigration Lawyers Association. All rights reserved.

- The relationship "bestows all of the same legal rights and duties possessed by partners in a lawfully contracted marriage"; and

- "Local laws recognize such cohabitation as being fully equivalent in every respect to a traditional legal marriage," which means that:

  - "The relationship can only be terminated by divorce;

  - "There is a potential right to alimony;

  - "There is a right to intestate distribution of an estate; and

  - "There is a right of custody, if there are children."[880]

Therefore, if common law marriage bestows the same rights and obligations as a traditional legal marriage in the jurisdiction where it was celebrated and where the visa application will be made, then the common-law spouse should be eligible for a derivative visa.[881] One way to evaluate if the common-law spouse is eligible for a dependent visa is to review the foreign country's statutes regarding common-law marriage. For example, in Guatemala, a de facto union is recognized after it is registered with the Office of the Civil Registry and generally imposes the same obligations and confers the benefits of rights of spouses as through a legal marriage.[882] The practitioner would then need to compare the Guatemalan statutes to confirm that the relationship may be terminated only through divorce, provides for alimony, provides for intestate distribution, and provides for custody rights of children in common.

If, however, common law marriage in the home country does not bestow the same rights and impose the same obligations of a traditional legal marriage or does not satisfy the conditions imposed for immigration purposes, or if common law marriage is not recognized in the home country,[883] then the accompanying foreign national may obtain a B-2 visa, as discussed in Volume 1: Chapter Three, "Visitors: B Visas and Status and the Visa Waiver Program."

For purposes of a visa application, it is irrelevant whether the proposed state of U.S. residence recognizes common law marriage, because the focus of the inquiry is on whether common law marriage is recognized by the jurisdiction where the marriage was celebrated and where the visa application will be made.[884]

---

[880] 9 FAM 102.3-1.

[881] *Id.*

[882] United Nations High Commissioner for Refugees, "Guatemala: Information on Common Law Marriages" (Jan. 2000), http://www.refworld.org/docid/3ae6a6a340.html.

[883] UK, "Marriage, civil partnership and divorce," https://www.gov.uk/browse/births-deaths-marriages/marriage-divorce.

[884] *Adams v. Howerton*, 673 F.2d 1036 (9th Cir. 1982), *cert. denied*, 458 U.S. 1111 (1982); *Matter of Jose Lamas-Soto*, A70 178 883 (BIA 1995), 15 Immig. Rptr. B1-191 (Feb. 28, 1996).

Copyright © 2017. American Immigration Lawyers Association. All rights reserved.

A "child," as defined in the immigration statute, must be unmarried and under the age of 21.[885] The definition includes children born in wedlock, stepchildren who are under the age of 18 when the parent and stepparent marry, children born out of wedlock who are legitimated before the age of 18, children born out of wedlock who have a bona fide parent-child relationship with the principal nonimmigrant-parent, and adopted children.[886] In addition, "[a] child who was born of a marriage which existed at the time of the principal alien's admission to the United States is considered to have been acquired prior to the principal alien's admission."[887]

The practitioner should also consider whether the dependents are citizens of a different country from that of the principal nonimmigrant. Experience has shown that most U.S. consulates will accept visa applications from foreign nationals who reside in the country, even if they are not citizens of that country, so it should be possible for the entire family to apply for their visas at the same U.S. consulate; but the practitioner should confirm that residence in the jurisdiction and/or a familial relationship to a citizen is sufficient for a visa application to be accepted. Also, the practitioner should advise the client of any differing reciprocity fees necessary because of the various citizenships. For example, the principal nonimmigrant may be Zambian and have a reciprocity fee of $300 for an H-1B visa,[888] but his wife and children, as Angolan citizens, may only have to pay $10 each for their H-4 visas.[889]

Generally, dependent spouses and children are ineligible for Social Security numbers (SSNs) unless they independently qualify for employment authorization, because proof of employment eligibility is required for an SSN application.[890] The one exception is if the dependent requires an SSN for "a valid non-work reason,"[891] and presents "a document from a U.S. Federal, State, or local government agency that explains why [the dependent] need[s] a Social Security number and that [the dependent] meet[s] all the requirements for the government benefit."[892] The "card will be marked" to state that the individual does not have employment authorization.[893] The practitioner may also wish to review the government benefit to

---

[885] INA §101(b)(1).

[886] INA §§101(b)(1)(A)–(E).

[887] 9 FAM 102.3-1.

[888] DOS, "Zambia Reciprocity Schedule," https://travel.state.gov/content/visas/en/fees/reciprocity-by-country/ZA.html.

[889] DOS, "Angola Reciprocity Schedule," https://travel.state.gov/content/visas/en/fees/reciprocity-by-country/AO.html.

[890] SSA, "Social Security Numbers for Noncitizens," https://www.ssa.gov/pubs/EN-05-10096.pdf (stating that "To apply for a Social Security number to work in the United States, you must show [the SSA] current immigration documents with work authorization").

[891] Id.

[892] SSA, "Application for a Social Security Card," https://www.ssa.gov/online/ss-5.pdf.

[893] Id.

Copyright © 2017. American Immigration Lawyers Association. All rights reserved.

confirm that the foreign national will not be deemed inadmissible and unable to adjust status by receiving it.[894]

If the principal nonimmigrant wishes to declare a spouse and/or children on his or her federal tax return, then individual taxpayer identification numbers (ITINs) may be obtained for the dependents.[895] As stated by the IRS, "An ITIN does not authorize work in the United States or provide eligibility for Social Security benefits."[896]

VII. Maintaining the Status

Maintaining nonimmigrant status should be viewed in two ways. First, the foreign national should perform only those activities for which the status was granted, and not perform those activities that are prohibited by the status.[897] An example of the first permissible activity is working for an H-1B employer that filed the approved H-1B petition, and an example of the second impermissible activity is working for another employer without the filing of a non-frivolous H-1B petition for change of employer or concurrent employment.[898] As discussed in Volume 1: Chapter Seven, "H-1B Visas and Status," the individual can begin work for the new employer after the petition is properly filed. Other statuses must wait until the petition is approved. Another example is that a B-2 tourist may engage in visiting the United States for pleasure and to spend time with family members and friends, but he or she may not work in the United States while in B-2 status.[899]

The foreign national's activities while in the United States impact whether he or she has complied with the terms of his or her admission,[900] and whether he or she has

---

[894] For a further discussion of this topic, see Volume 2: Chapter Four, "Consular Processing, Adjustment of Status, and Permanent Residence Issues."

[895] IRS, "Individual Taxpayer Identification Number (ITIN)," https://www.irs.gov/individuals/individual-taxpayer-identification-number-itin.

[896] Id.

[897] AFM 30.1; 9 FAM 401.1-3(B) and (C) (generally discussing permissible activities and restrictions on employment); Matter of Taerghodsi, 16 I&N Dec. 260 (BIA 1977) (unauthorized employment in F-1 status constituted failure to maintain status).

[898] For a discussion of H-1B change of employer petitions, see Volume 1: Chapter Seven, "H-1B Visas and Status." See also Matter of Dacanay, 16 I&N Dec. 238 (BIA 1977) (H-1 petition for new employer).

[899] 9 FAM 401.1-3(C) (generally discussing restrictions on employment); Matter of Lee, 11 I&N Dec. 601 (BIA 1966) (noting that the foreign national did not maintain his nonimmigrant status by "ceasing his temporary employment"); Matter of Bennett, 19 I&N Dec. 21 (BIA 1984) (unauthorized employment in B-2 status deemed a failure to comply with the terms and conditions of his status and a failure to maintain status).

[900] INA §237(a)(1)(C) (discussing ground of deportability from violating status or failing to comply with terms and conditions of status); Matter of Bennett, 19 I&N Dec. 21 (BIA 1984); Matter of Yazdani, 17 I&N Dec. 626 (BIA 1981) (noting the need for compliance, rather than "substantial compliance," when the foreign national failed to obtain legacy INS approval to change F-1 schools even though she had mailed in the request and it was lost in the mail); Matter of Kotte, 16 I&N Dec. 449 (BIA 1978) (accepting unauthorized employment in F-1 status deemed failure to comply with the terms and conditions of that status); Matter of Murat-Khan, 14 I&N Dec. 465 (BIA 1973) (foreign national's criminal conviction and incarceration "has not constituted a failure to maintain the nonimmigrant status" of a student since she continued her studies while
Cont'd

Copyright © 2017. American Immigration Lawyers Association. All rights reserved.

violated the underlying status in any way.[901] In addition, "[w]illful failure by a nonimmigrant to register or to provide full and truthful information requested by [DHS] (regardless of whether or not the information requested was material) constitutes a failure to maintain nonimmigrant status."[902] Generally, a foreign national who merely properly files an application to adjust status is not "deemed to have 'otherwise violate[d] the terms of a nonimmigrant visa,'" as long as the application is filed "prior to the expiration of the alien's nonimmigrant status."[903]

Second, maintaining status should also be understood as requiring affirmative filings with USCIS, in order to obtain the appropriate immigration status to remain in the United States beyond the expiration of the authorized period of stay and perform the desired activities.[904] For example, an individual does not obtain employment authorization simply by filing a petition to change status from B-2 to H-1B:

"[I]t is only the formal approval of the change of status application by USCIS that constitutes authorization to engage in activities consistent with that new status. An alien who, prior to approval of a change of status, engages in activities not consistent with his or her present status is at risk of being found to be in violation of status in the event the application is denied, although approval is often retroactive to the date of the original application."[905]

Neither does approval of a labor certification application alone grant the employment authorization that would permit these activities.[906]

And with the exception of foreign nationals who are granted "Duration of Status" periods of admission, as discussed below, most foreign nationals are admitted to the United States for a set period of time.[907] Without an extension or change of status

---

imprisoned); *Matter of A–*, 9 I&N Dec. 100 (BIA 1960) (focus is on the purpose of the foreign national's admission, where a nonimmigrant may be unable to pursue tourism for pleasure while incarcerated but incarceration may not result in failure to maintain student status if the foreign national continues attending school).

[901] INA §237(a)(1)(C) (discussing ground of deportability from violating status or failing to comply with terms and conditions of status).

[902] 8 CFR §214.1(f) (citing INA §237(a)(1)(C)(i)).

[903] Legacy INS, L. Crocetti, "Processing of 245(i) adjustment applications on or after the October 1, 1997, sunset date; Clarification regarding the applicability of certain new grounds of inadmissibility to 245(i) applications" (May 1, 1997), AILA Doc. No. 97050191, 74 Interpreter Releases 791–94 (May 12, 1997).

[904] 9 FAM 401.1-3(B); *Matter of Tong*, 16 I&N Dec. 593 (BIA 1978).

[905] AFM 30.1. *See also* 9 FAM 401.1-3(C); *Oki v. INS*, 598 F.2d 1160 (9th Cir. 1979); DOS, "INA 212(a)(9)(B) and Applications to Change NIV Status or Extend NIV Stay" (May 30, 2000), AILA Doc. No. 00060202.

[906] *Matter of Raol*, 16 I&N Dec. 466 (BIA 1978).

[907] DOS, "P.L. 104-208 Update No. 36: 212(a)(9)(A)–(C), 212(a)(6)(A)–(B)" (Apr. 4, 1998), AILA Doc. No. 98040490.

Copyright © 2017. American Immigration Lawyers Association. All rights reserved.

application timely filed and ultimately approved by USCIS, the time period of the authorized stay will expire, and the foreign national will have "overstayed".[908] "A nonimmigrant alien has the obligation either to depart at the expiration of his authorized period of stay, or to obtain a proper extension of that stay."[909] Therefore, the practitioner should monitor these expiration dates to ensure that an extension or change of status application is timely filed.

Violating the terms of one's status and overstaying one's admission are not mutually exclusive or inclusive.[910] Either or both may be the reason that a foreign national "falls out of status," which is a colloquial term for when an individual fails to maintain valid immigration status.[911]

In addition, USCIS may visit the employment site after an H-1B, L-1, or R nonimmigrant is admitted to see if he or she actually is employed and performing the job as described in the petition package.[912] There generally is no advance notice of such a visit, and the inspector usually will ask to speak to the human resources manager or the person who signed the petition, and may also seek to interview the beneficiary. The inspectors may review payroll records, and compare information found at the site with information on the petition.[913] A Notice of Intent to Revoke status can result from such visits.[914]

Failure to maintain status may render a foreign national ineligible for an extension of status,[915] ineligible for change of status,[916] ineligible to adjust status to that of a

---

[908] *Matter of Varughese*, 17 I&N Dec. 399 (BIA 1980) (using the term "overstay"); *Matter of Teberen*, 15 I&N Dec. 689 (BIA 1976) (using the term "overstay"); *Matter of Lok*, 18 I&N Dec. 101 (BIA 1981) (in the case history, the foreign national was deemed deportable for remaining in the United States beyond his period of authorized stay); *Milande v. INS*, 464 F.2d 774 (7th Cir. 1973).

[909] *Matter of Tong*, 16 I&N Dec. 593 (BIA 1978); *Matter of Teberen*, 15 I&N Dec. 689 (BIA 1976).

[910] 9 FAM 401.1-3(C) (noting example of a foreign national with the intent to depart the United States within the period of authorized stay but also with the intent to engage in unauthorized activities); *Matter of Varughese*, 17 I&N Dec. 399 (BIA 1980) (foreign national deemed deportable for overstaying and for engaging in unauthorized employment); *Matter of Lennon*, 15 I&N Dec. 9 (BIA 1974) (charges of overstay and failing to comply with the terms and conditions of nonimmigrant status).

[911] *Matter of A–*, 9 I&N Dec. 100 (BIA 1960) (using the term "out of status"); *Ghorbani v. INS*, 686 F.2d 784 (9th Cir. 1982) (foreign national failed to obtain school transfer approval from legacy INS and engaged in unauthorized employment).

[912] "Practice Pointer: H-1B and L-1 FDNS Site Visits" (July 26, 2016), AILA Doc. No. 16072604. *See also* "H-1B Compliance Review Report Site Visit Instructions" (Dec. 5, 2008), AILA Doc. No. 09101461; "Sample FDNS Follow-Up E-mail Question After H-1B Site Visits" (Feb. 25, 2011), AILA Doc. No. 11022521; "USCIS FDNS Supplemental Answers to AILA Questions on Site Visits" (Aug. 5, 2011), AILA Doc. No. 11080569. Site visits also can occur prior to USCIS's decision on the petition.

[913] *Id.*

[914] "USCIS FDNS Answers AILA Questions on Site Visits" (June 7, 2011), AILA Doc. No. 11062243.

[915] 8 CFR §214.1(c)(4).

[916] 8 CFR §248.1(b); *Matter of Lee*, 11 I&N Dec. 601 (BIA 1966).

Copyright © 2017. American Immigration Lawyers Association. All rights reserved.

lawful permanent resident,[917] and subject to removal proceedings.[918] One exception to these penalties is if a statute is enacted to provide a new deadline for the filing of petitions or applications under INA §245(i).[919] In addition, if the foreign national's initial nonimmigrant status expires after an application to adjust status is properly filed, then the application to adjust status should "protect[] him from the accrual of unlawful presence,"[920] as discussed below.

As stated by USCIS guidance: "Voluntary departure is not a nonimmigrant status."[921] Therefore, any time spent in the United States pursuant to a grant of voluntary departure (VD) should not be "counted when calculating unlawful presence," as discussed below, but a foreign national who has been given a period of voluntary departure "is not considered to be maintaining status for purposes of receiving an extension or status change."[922]

Finally, a foreign national should notify USCIS "in writing of each change of address and new address within 10 days from the date of such change."[923] The Form AR-11, Alien's Change of Address Card, may be mailed to the address stated on the form[924] or submitted online.[925] If the form is mailed, USCIS recommends using a delivery service that offers delivery confirmation, "in case there should ever be a question."[926] Filing Form AR-11 does not notify USCIS of the new address for purposes of pending petitions or applications, and notifying USCIS of the new

---

[917] INA §245(c); AFM 40.9.2(a)(2); *Matter of Dukpa*, 18 I&N Dec. 282 (Dist. Dir. 1981); *Aiyadurai v. INS*, 683 F.2d 1195 (8th Cir. 1982); *Matter of Hall*, 18 I&N Dec. 203 (BIA 1982). *But see Matter of Lett*, 17 I&N Dec. 312 (BIA 1980) ("self-employment without prior authorization does not have the same meaning as unauthorized and does not preclude adjustment of status … in the case of a qualified nonpreference investor," although an "unsuccessful applicant for an investor exemption runs the risk that work performed in connection with his nonqualifying investment may be considered unauthorized employment"); *Oki v. INS*, 598 F.2d 1160 (9th Cir. 1979); *Matter of Raol*, 16 I&N Dec. 466 (BIA 1978).

[918] INA §237(a)(1)(C). *See, e.g., Matter of Del Risco*, 20 I&N Dec. 109 (BIA 1989) (foreign national deemed deportable for overstaying); *Matter of Varughese*, 17 I&N Dec. 399 (BIA 1980); *Matter of Lok*, 18 I&N Dec. 101 (BIA 1981); *Matter of Kotte*, 16 I&N Dec. 449 (BIA 1978).

[919] *See, e.g.*, Pub. L. No. 106-554 (Dec. 21, 2000). *See also* legacy INS, R. Bach, "Accepting Applications for Adjustment of Status Under Section 245(i) of the Immigration and Nationality Act" (Apr. 14, 1999), 76 Interpreter Releases 652–58 (Apr. 26, 1999).

[920] AFM 40.9.2(a)(2). For a further discussion of maintaining status in the context of adjustment of status applications, see Volume 2: Chapter Four, "Consular Processing, Adjustment of Status, and Permanent Residence Issues."

[921] AFM 30.1.

[922] *Id.*

[923] INA §265(a).

[924] USCIS, "Form AR-11, Alien's Change of Address Card," https://www.uscis.gov/files/form/ar-11.pdf.

[925] USCIS, "Online Change of Address," https://egov.uscis.gov/crisgwi/go?action=coa.

[926] USCIS, "Change of Address Information" (updated Feb. 23, 2016), https://www.uscis.gov/addresschange.

Copyright © 2017. American Immigration Lawyers Association. All rights reserved.

address for a pending petition or application does not satisfy the notification requirement; a foreign national must complete Form AR-11 and separately notify USCIS of the new address for pending petitions or applications.[927]

A. Unlawful Presence

Unlawful presence is one of the consequences of failing to maintain status: "[An] alien is deemed to be unlawfully present in the United States if the alien is present in the United States after the expiration of the period of stay authorized by the Attorney General or is present in the United States without being admitted or paroled."[928]

But the practitioner should note the difference between unlawful status and unlawful presence:

"[I]t is important to comprehend the difference between being in an unlawful immigration status and the accrual of unlawful presence ("period of stay not authorized"). Although these concepts are related (one must be present in an unlawful status in order to accrue unlawful presence), they are not the same.... [T]here are situations in which an alien who is present in an unlawful status nevertheless does not accrue unlawful presence. As a matter of prosecutorial discretion, DHS may permit an alien who is present in the United States unlawfully, but who has pending an application that stops the accrual of unlawful presence, to remain in the United States while that application is pending. In this sense, the alien's remaining can be said to be 'authorized.' However, the fact that the alien does not accrue unlawful presence does not mean that the alien's presence in the United States is actually lawful."[929]

Therefore, although a foreign national must lack lawful immigration status in order to accrue unlawful presence, the fact that a foreign national does not accrue unlawful presence, such as due to an exception, does not mean that the foreign national has valid immigration status. For example, as noted above, VD "is not a nonimmigrant status,"[930] but time in the United States pursuant to a grant of VD

---

[927] Id.

[928] INA §212(a)(9)(B)(ii). This section will not discuss entry without inspection. Generally, a foreign national who is paroled into the United States does not accrue unlawful presence as long as there is no violation of the terms of the parole. AFM 40.9.2(a)(3)(D); "INS General Counsel List of Resolved Issues" (Dec. 22, 1999), AILA Doc. No. 99122271; legacy, P. Virtue, "Advance Parole for Aliens Unlawfully Present in the United States for More than 180 Days" (Nov. 26, 1997), AILA Doc. No. 97120290.

[929] AFM 40.9.2(a)(2). The guidance also notes that the "application of section 245(k) of the Act is a good example of the importance of clearly distinguishing unlawful status from the accrual of unlawful presence." For a discussion of INA §245(k), see Volume 2: Chapter Four, "Consular Processing, Adjustment of Status, and Permanent Residence Issues."

[930] AFM 30.1.

Copyright © 2017. American Immigration Lawyers Association. All rights reserved.

should not be "counted when calculating unlawful presence,"[931] even though it is not lawful nonimmigrant status.[932]

The accrual of unlawful presence may be viewed as requiring both unlawful status and the absence of an applicable exception, such as a tolling period, to cause an interim time period of authorized stay, such as the pendency of a benefit application. Similarly, the "terms 'authorized status' (authorized period of admission or lawful status) and 'period of stay authorized by the Secretary of Homeland Security' are not interchangeable."[933] The practitioner may find it helpful to consider authorized period of stay and authorized status as a circle and its concentric center, respectively, since authorized status means authorized period of stay, but not all authorized periods of stay are authorized status.

For example, USCIS guidance noted how the beneficiary of a timely filed extension application is "in a period of stay authorized by the Secretary of Homeland Security," but the pending application "does not put an individual into valid and authorized nonimmigrant status, *i.e.*, he or she is not in authorized status while the application is pending."[934]

An authorized period of stay includes the following:

- For foreign nationals who are inspected and admitted, through the expiration of the I-94 card, or any extension, or until a "formal finding of a status violation," as discussed below;

- For foreign nationals who are inspected and admitted for "Duration of Status," "any period of presence in the United States, unless DHS, IJ, or the BIA makes a formal finding of a status violation, in which case unlawful presence will only begin to accrue as of the date of the formal finding";

- For foreign nationals granted VD, "the period of time between the granting of VD and the date for their departure";

---

[931] *Id.*

[932] This section will not address voluntary departure vis à vis accrual of unlawful presence. USCIS guidance does address this issue. AFM 40.9.2(b)(3)(H).

[933] AFM 40.9.2(b)(3)(D)(vii).

[934] USCIS, "Consolidation of Guidance Concerning Unlawful Presence for Purposes of Sections 212(a)(9)(B)(i) and 212(a)(9)(C)(i)(I) of the Act" (May 6, 2009), AILA Doc. No. 09051468, pp. 37-38 ("Therefore, if an individual has filed an initial application for EOS or COS and subsequently files additional (untimely) requests for EOS or COS, the subsequently filed request will not stop the individual from accruing unlawful presence, if the initial request is denied."). *See also Bokhari v. Holder*, 622 F.2d 357 (5th Cir. 2010) (240-day automatic extension of work authorization under 8 CFR §274a.12(b)(20) did not confer lawful status, and thus beneficiary ineligible for later adjustment of status). *But see El Badrawi v. DHS*, 579 F. Supp.2 249 (D. Conn. 2008) (extended employment authorization under 8 CFR §274a.12(b)(20) resulted in lawful status, and thus arrest during that period constituted false arrest under the Federal Tort Claims Act).

Copyright © 2017. American Immigration Lawyers Association. All rights reserved.

- For beneficiaries of change of status or extension applications, "who have remained in the United States after expiration of the Form I-94 while awaiting DHS's decision, the entire period of the pendency of the application," as discussed below;

- For foreign nationals who are applicants for adjustment of status, "the entire period of the pendency of the application, even if the application is subsequently denied or abandoned, provided the alien did not file for adjustment 'defensively' (*i.e.*, after deportation proceedings had already been initiated)";

- For foreign nationals "covered by Temporary Protected Status (TPS), the period after TPS went into effect and prior to its expiration; and

- For foreign nationals granted deferred action, "the period during which deferred action is authorized."[935]

USCIS guidance provides the example of a foreign national who is admitted in nonimmigrant status, which is valid until January 1, 2009, and who then remains in the United States beyond that date and files an application to adjust status on May 10, 2009:

"The filing of the adjustment application stops the accrual of unlawful presence. But it does not 'restore' the alien to a substantively lawful immigration status. She is still amenable to removal as a deportable alien under section 237(a)(1)(C) of the Act because she has remained after the expiration of her nonimmigrant admission."[936]

In this example, the foreign national has accrued 129 days of unlawful presence. For a further discussion of how the accrual of unlawful presence is counted, see below.

An individual who remains in the United States beyond the period of authorized stay for more than 180 days but less than one year is subject to a three-year bar against a subsequent admission to the United States.[937] An individual who remains in the United States beyond the period of authorized stay for more than one year is subject to a 10-year bar against a subsequent admission to the United States.[938] Importantly, the bar is triggered upon the foreign national's departure from the United States, since the statutes discuss "seek[ing] admission within 3 [and 10] years of the date of such alien's departure."[939]

---

[935] 9 FAM 302.9-14(B)(1).

[936] AFM 40.9.2(a)(2).

[937] INA §212(a)(9)(B)(i)(I).

[938] INA §212(a)(9)(B)(i)(II).

[939] INA §§212(a)(9)(B)(i)(I) and (II). *See also* 9 FAM 302.9-14(B)(2); AFM 40.9.2(a)(2); AFM 40.9.2(a)(5); *Matter of Rodarte-Roman*, 23 I&N Dec. 905 (BIA 2006); DOS cable, "P.L. 104-208 Update No. 36: 212(a)(9)(A)–(C), 212(a)(6)(A) and (B)" (Apr. 4, 1998), AILA Doc. No. 98040490 (stating that if "an alien
Cont'd

Copyright © 2017. American Immigration Lawyers Association. All rights reserved.

USCIS had previously taken the position that the "inadmissibility period continues to run even if the alien is paroled into the United States or is lawfully admitted as a nonimmigrant" who has obtained a waiver.[940] This meant that time spent physically present in the United States pursuant to parole or an approved waiver could count toward the three– or 10-year period, "even if the alien had been in the United States … during the inadmissibility period."[941]

It is likely that this view regarding waivers continues. However, with respect to advance paroles, a 2012 precedent BIA decision found that a foreign national who leaves after a grant of advance parole has not made a departure and thus has not triggered inadmissibility under the three– and 10-year bars.[942] The State Department applies this holding only to advance paroles obtained in the adjustment of status context.[943] However, the AAO has found in multiple nonprecedent decisions that people in Temporary Protected Status (TPS) who exit on advance parole have not effected a departure, and thus have not triggered inadmissibility under the bars,[944] thus indicating a view that the case applies to all exits under advance parole. Further, the DHS Secretary instructed the DHS General Counsel to issue written legal guidance "which will clarify that *in all cases* when an individual physically leaves the United States pursuant to a grant of advance parole, that individual shall not have made a 'departure' within the meaning of section 212(a)(9)(B)(i) of the INA."[945] That guidance has not yet been forthcoming.

In addition, because the statute specifically references departure "prior to the commencement of proceedings,"[946] the three-year bar "applies only to aliens who left the United States voluntarily before the DHS commenced proceedings against them."[947] Therefore, if the foreign national was placed in deportation or removal proceedings before his or her departure, then he or she would not be inadmissible for

---

accrues the requisite period of unlawful presence but does not subsequently depart the United States (*e.g.*, in the case of an alien applying for adjustment of status with the INS), then 9B would not apply"); legacy INS, P. Virtue, "Advance Parole for Aliens Unlawfully Present in the United States for More than 180 Days" (Nov. 26, 1997), 74 Interpreter Releases 1864–68 (Dec. 8, 1997).

[940] USCIS, L. Melmed (Jan. 26, 2009), AILA Doc. No. 09012874.

[941] USCIS, R. Divine (July 14, 2006), AILA Doc. No. 09012874.

[942] *Matter of Arrabally and Yerrabelly*, 25 I&N Dec.771 (2012).

[943] 9 FAM 302.9-14(B)(2)(c).

[944] *E.g., Matter of [name and case number not provided]* (AAO Jul. 23, 2014), *http://bit.ly/jul141h*; *Matter of [name and case number not provided]* (AAO Oct. 24, 2012), http://bit.ly/oct1214h; *Matter of [name and case number not provided]* (AAO Aug. 7, 2012), http://bit.ly/aug122h.

[945] J. Johnson, "DHS Directive to Provide Consistency Regarding Advance Parole" (Nov. 20, 2014), AILA Doc. No. 14112014.

[946] INA §212(a)(9)(B)(i)(I).

[947] 9 FAM 302.9-14(B)(2)(b).

Copyright © 2017. American Immigration Lawyers Association. All rights reserved.

the three-year period,[948] although he or she could become inadmissible on other grounds, such as being previously ordered removed or failing to attend a removal hearing.[949] In this situation, departing the United States voluntarily should be differentiated from a formal grant of voluntary departure (VD).[950] Although departure pursuant to a grant of VD "is still voluntary because removal proceedings have not yet commenced,"[951] the former may also refer to the foreign national departing the United States of his or her own volition.[952] Departure after issuance and filing of an NTA with an immigration court also should not trigger the three-year bar.[953]

In contrast, the statute regarding the 10-year bar has no language discussing proceedings,[954] so the departure after accrual of at least one year of unlawful presence will trigger the 10-year bar, regardless of "whether the departure was before, during, or after removal proceedings and whether the alien departed on his or her own initiative or under deportation orders."[955] The 10-year bar "applies even if the alien leaves after removal proceedings have commenced; the individual will be inadmissible, even if he or she leaves after the NTA has been filed with the immigration court."[956] As stated by USCIS, the differing treatment "provides the alien with an incentive to end his or her unlawful presence by leaving the United States, rather than contesting removal."[957] Although waivers are available for these bars, this section will not address them.[958]

The statutory definition of unlawful presence generally addresses the situation where a foreign national "stay[s] beyond the date specified on the Form I-94," but a foreign national may also accrue unlawful presence after violating status, through a "formal finding of a status violation made by DHS or an immigration judge in the context of an application for an immigration benefit or in deportation proceedings, whichever comes first."[959]

---

[948] *Id.*; "INS General Counsel List of Resolved Issues" (Dec. 22, 1999), AILA Doc. No. 99122271.

[949] 9 FAM 302.9-14(B)(2)(c).

[950] AFM 40.9.2(a)(4)(C).

[951] *Id.*

[952] DOS, "P.L. 104-208 Update No. 36: 212(a)(9)(A)–(C), 212(a)(6)(A) and (B)" (Apr. 4, 1998), AILA Doc. No. 98040490.

[953] AFM 40.9.2(a)(4)(C).

[954] INA §212(a)(9)(B)(i)(II).

[955] 9 FAM 302.9-14(B)(2)(c). *See also* AFM 40.9.2(a)(4)(D); DOS, "P.L. 104-208 Update No. 36: 212(a)(9)(A)–(C), 212(a)(6)(A) and (B)" (Apr. 4, 1998), AILA Doc. No. 98040490.

[956] AFM 40.9.2(a)(4)(D).

[957] *Id.*

[958] To explore the subject of waivers in detail, see *The Waivers Book* (AILA 2d Ed. 2017), https://agora.aila.org/product/detail/3208, and *Provisional Waivers* (AILA 2d Ed. 2017), https://agora.aila.org/product/detail/3197.

[959] 9 FAM 302.9-14(B)(1).

Copyright © 2017. American Immigration Lawyers Association. All rights reserved.

Therefore, if an extension or change of status application is not timely filed and subsequently approved by USCIS, then the foreign national may begin to accrue unlawful presence in the United States. The timely filing of a change of status or extension application may toll the accrual of unlawful presence, if the following conditions are met:

- The foreign national was "lawfully admitted or paroled into" the United States;

- The foreign national is the beneficiary of a timely filed "nonfrivolous application for a change or extension of status before the date of expiration" of the authorized period of stay; and

- The foreign national has not engaged in unauthorized employment "before or during the pendency of such application."[960]

The tolling should be for "during the pendency" of the filed change of status or extension application,[961] as long as the application is "subsequently approved" or the foreign national departed the United States while the application was pending, even if the application is ultimately denied."[962] Although the statute states that the tolling should be only for up to 120 days,[963] USCIS policy "has extended the 120-day statutory tolling period to cover the entire period during which an application for EOS [Extension of Status] or COS [Change of Status] is pending; this extension is valid for the three-year and the 10-year bars."[964] Even if the foreign national departs the United States while the application is pending, and after the I-94 card has expired, he or she should not be subject to the three-year or 10-year bar, as long as the above-stated requirements were met.[965] But importantly, "the filing of a request for EOS or COS does not put an individual into valid and authorized nonimmigrant status, *i.e.*, he or she is not in authorized status."[966]

---

[960] INA §212(a)(9)(B)(iv). *See also* AFM 40.9.2(b)(2)(G).

[961] INA §212(a)(9)(B)(iv).

[962] 9 FAM 302.9-14(B)(1).

[963] INA §212(a)(9)(B)(iv).

[964] AFM 40.9.2(b)(2)(G). *See also* 9 FAM 302.9-14(B)(5) (stating that "DHS has inferred that the '120 days' limitation was probably predicated on an assumption that they would be able to adjudicate the application within that time frame. Due to DHS backlogs, however, some cases have been pending as long as six months or more, during which the applicants could incur the three or 10-year penalties through no fault of their own if only the first 120 days were tolled and the application was ultimately denied. Therefore, for all cases involving potential inadmissibility under INA 212(a)(9)(B) whether under the three-year bar of 212(a)(9)(B)(i)(I) or the 10-year bar of INA 212(a)(9)(B)(i)(II), DHS has decided to consider all time during which an application for extension of stay (EOS) or change of nonimmigrant status (COS) is pending to be time authorized by the Attorney General (AG)"); DOS, "INA 212(a)(9)(B) and Applications to Change NIV Status or Extend NIV Stay" (June 2, 2000), AILA Doc. No. 00060202.

[965] AFM 40.9.2(b)(3)(C).

[966] AFM 40.9.2(b)(3)(D)(vii). *See also* USCIS, "Consolidation of Guidance Concerning Unlawful Presence for Purposes of Sections 212(a)(9)(B)(i) and 212(a)(9)(C)(i)(I) of the Act" (May 6, 2009), AILA Doc. No. 09051468, pp. 37-38.

Copyright © 2017. American Immigration Lawyers Association. All rights reserved.

If it becomes necessary to file subsequent extension applications because the initial application is not approved before the expiration date on the I-94 card, then the practitioner should ensure that the subsequent applications are timely filed, because untimely filed applications "will not stop the individual from accruing unlawful presence, if the initial request is denied."[967] USCIS guidance terms such multiple applications "bridge filings,"[968] and notes the importance of a timely filing: "The alien does not accrue unlawful presence as long as the timely filed request is pending. However, the filing of a request for EOS or COS does not put an individual into valid and authorized nonimmigrant status, *i.e.,* he or she is not in authorized status. Therefore, if an individual has filed an initial application for EOS or COS and subsequently files additional (untimely) requests for EOS or COS, the subsequently filed request will not stop the individual from accruing unlawful presence, if the initial request is denied."[969]

A "nonfrivolous" application "must have an arguable basis in law and fact and must not have been filed for an improper purpose (*e.g.,* as a groundless excuse for the applicant to remain in activities incompatible with his or her status)."[970] Importantly, however, just because an application is denied does not mean that it was frivolous: "It is not necessary to determine that the DHS would have approved the application for it to be considered nonfrivolous."[971] An example of a frivolous application is where the foreign national engaged in unauthorized employment.[972] But a foreign national's ineligibility for a visa should be differentiated from being the beneficiary of a frivolous application.[973] As stated by USCIS guidance, if the change of status or extension application "is approved, the alien will be granted a new period of authorized stay, retroactive to the date the previous period of authorized stay expired."[974] If the application is denied for being frivolous or because the foreign national accepted unauthorized employment, then "any and all time after the expiration date marked on Form I-94, Arrival/Departure Record, will be considered unlawful presence time,"[975]

---

[967] AFM 40.9.2(b)(3)(D)(vii).

[968] *Id.* The title of this section is "Nonimmigrants—Multiple Requests for EOS Or COS ("Bridge Filings") and Its Effect on Unlawful Presence."

[969] USCIS, "Consolidation of Guidance Concerning Unlawful Presence for Purposes of Sections 212(a)(9)(B)(i) and 212(a)(9)(C)(i)(I) of the Act" (May 6, 2009), AILA Doc. No. 09051468, pp. 37-38.

[970] 9 FAM 302.9-14(B)(5); AFM 40.9.2(b)(3)(C).

[971] 9 FAM 302.9-14(B)(5).

[972] *Id.*

[973] DOS, "INA 212(a)(9)(B) and Applications to Change NIV Status or Extend NIV Stay" (June 2, 2000), AILA Doc. No. 00060202.

[974] AFM 40.9.2(b)(3)(D)(i). The practitioner should note that this may not apply to change of status applications, as discussed above.

[975] AFM 40.9.2(b)(3)(D)(ii); USCIS, "Consolidation of Guidance Concerning Unlawful Presence for Purposes of Sections 212(a)(9)(B)(i) and 212(a)(9)(C)(i)(I) of the Act" (May 6, 2009), AILA Doc. No. 09051468, p. 36.

Copyright © 2017. American Immigration Lawyers Association. All rights reserved.

and a foreign national admitted for duration of status will accrue unlawful presence from the date of the denial.[976] If the application is denied because it was not timely filed, then unlawful presence will accrue from the expiration date on the I-94 card.[977] And if "a timely filed, non-frivolous request for EOS or COS is denied for cause, unlawful presence begins to accrue the day after the request is denied."[978] USCIS guidance also states:

"The filing of a motion to reopen or reconsider does not stop the accrual of unlawful presence.... However, if the motion is successful and the benefit granted, the grant is effective retroactively. The alien will be deemed to not have accrued unlawful presence. If DHS reopens proceedings, but ultimately denies the petition or application again, the petition or application will be considered to have been pending since the initial filing date.... In the case of a timely, non-frivolous application, unlawful presence will accrue from the date of the last denial of the petition or application, not from the earlier, reopened decision."[979]

"The filing of an appeal to the AAO for the denial of the underlying petition, however, has no influence on the accrual of unlawful presence. Unlawful presence starts to accrue on the day of the denial of the request for EOS or COS regardless of whether the applicant or the petitioner appeals the denial of the petition to the AAO. However, if the denial of the underlying petition is reversed on appeal, and the EOS or COS subsequently granted, the individual is not deemed to have accrued any unlawful presence between the denial of the petition and request for EOS or COS, and the subsequent grant of the EOS or COS."[980]

A properly filed application to adjust status may also truncate the accrual of unlawful presence, and the period of time that the application was pending will not count toward the 180-day and one-year markers for unlawful presence, even if the application is ultimately denied.[981] The application must have been properly and affirmatively filed with USCIS.[982]

Generally, the period of unlawful presence is not accrued in the aggregate:

---

[976] *Id.*

[977] AFM 40.9.2(b)(3)(D)(iii); USCIS, "Consolidation of Guidance Concerning Unlawful Presence for Purposes of Sections 212(a)(9)(B)(i) and 212(a)(9)(C)(i)(I) of the Act" (May 6, 2009), AILA Doc. No. 09051468, p.37.

[978] AFM 40.9.2(b)(3)(D)(iv).

[979] AFM 40.9.2(b)(3)(D)(v).

[980] AFM 40.9.2(b)(3)(D)(vi).

[981] AFM 40.9.2(b)(3)(A). *See also Matter of Cano*, A78 131 147 (BIA 2006), 34 Immig. Reptr. B1-14; DOS, "Treatment of Adjustment Applications for Purposes of Determining Unlawful Presence Under INA 212(a)(9)(B)" (June 2, 2000), AILA Doc. No. 00060201.

[982] AFM 40.9.2(b)(3)(A).

Copyright © 2017. American Immigration Lawyers Association. All rights reserved.

"Neither of the ... time frames is cumulative. The unlawful presence must occur in the same trip to the United States, and periods of unlawful presence accrued on separate trips cannot be added together."[983]

"[The bars] only appl[y] to an alien, who has accrued the required amount of unlawful presence during any single stay in the United States; the length of the alien's accrued unlawful presence is not calculated by combining periods of unlawful presence accrued during multiple unlawful stays in the United States. If, during any single stay, an alien has more than one (1) period during which the alien accrues unlawful presence, the length of each period of unlawful presence is added together to determine the total period of unlawful presence time accrued during that single stay."[984]

This means that only individual days within a single U.S. visit are counted toward the 180-day and one-year markers.[985] But the practitioner should note that "separate periods of unlawful presence occurring during the same overall period of stay (e.g., unlawful presence before and after a period of voluntary departure) should be added together to calculate total unlawful presence during a particular stay."[986] In addition, generally "protection from the accrual of unlawful presence under any section of this Adjudicator's Field Manual (AFM) chapter does not cure any unlawful presence that the alien may have already accrued before the alien came to be protected."[987]

To count the accrual of unlawful presence for a foreign national who was admitted until a specific date, which USCIS guidance terms "Date Certain," DHS counts the day after the expiration date on the I-94 card as the first day of unlawful presence.[988] But if "USCIS finds, during the adjudication of a request for immigration benefit, that the alien has violated his or her nonimmigrant status, unlawful presence will begin to accrue either the day after Form I-94 expires or the day after USCIS denies the request, whichever is earlier."[989] Similarly, a determination by an immigration judge of a status violation means that "unlawful presence begins to accrue the day after the immigration judge's order or the day after the Form I-94 expired, whichever is

---

[983] 9 FAM 302.9-14(B)(2). *See also* 9 FAM 302.9-14(B)(1) (noting how unlawful presence "accrued prior to the filing of an application for adjustment of status, or the granting of voluntary departure, or the effective date of TPS is not 'cured' by the subsequent period of authorized stay that these events trigger, and additional unauthorized presence will resume accruing after these authorized periods lapse").

[984] AFM 40.9.2(a)(4)(A). Although the guidance only specifically addresses the three-year bar, it is very likely that it applies to the 10-year bar as well, since the title of the section is "Unlawful Presence for Purposes of the 3-Year and 10-Year Bars Is Not Counted in the Aggregate."

[985] AFM 40.9.2(a)(4)(A). This guidance provides two more examples.

[986] 9 FAM 302.9-14(B)(2).

[987] AFM 40.9.2(b)(4). *See also* DOS, "Treatment of Adjustment Applications for Purposes of Determining Unlawful Presence Under INA 212(a)(9)(B)" (June 2, 2000), AILA Doc. No. 00060201.

[988] AFM 40.9.2(b)(1)(E)(i).

[989] *Id.*

Copyright © 2017. American Immigration Lawyers Association. All rights reserved.

earlier."[990] USCIS guidance took pains to emphasize "that the accrual of unlawful presence neither begins on the date that a status violation occurs, nor on the day on which removal proceedings are initiated."[991] The actual expiration date of the Form I-94 is not counted, and neither is the actual date of departure from the United States.[992] In addition, any time of unlawful presence from before April 1, 1997, is not counted.[993]

F-1 international students and J-1 exchange visitors are typically admitted for duration of status rather than for a period of time.[994] Generally, these foreign nationals therefore cannot "overstay," since an end date to the period of admission was not stated on the Form I-94.[995] Instead, these foreign nationals should be deemed to be in unlawful status only after a determination by an immigration judge or DHS that they have violated their nonimmigrant status, with the accrual of unlawful presence starting on the date of the determination rather than on the date of the underlying violation.[996] The determination may be made in the course of adjudicating a benefit application or at immigration court, with unlawful presence accruing from the date the request is denied or the date the determination is made by the immigration judge, respectively.[997]

The agencies that administer the immigration laws differ in their treatment of Canadian and Mexican citizens who are admitted without Forms I-94 or admission stamps in their passports. USCIS takes the view that these "non-controlled nonimmigrants" should be treated as having been admitted for duration of status in the same manner as F-1 and J-1 nonimmigrants.[998] The State Department is of the view that individuals "who were admitted from Canada or Mexico with an I-68 or DSP-150 Border crossing card, or any other Canadian or Mexican entrants to the

---

[990] *Id.*

[991] *Id.*; "INS General Counsel List of Resolved Issues" (Dec. 22, 1999), AILA Doc. No. 99122271.

[992] 9 FAM 302.9-14(B)(1). *See also* AFM 40.9.2(b)(1)(E)(i); "INS General Counsel List of Resolved Issues" (Dec. 22, 1999), AILA Doc. No. 99122271.

[993] AFM 40.9.2(a)(4)(A); AFM 40.9.2(a)(9); 9 FAM 302.9-14(B)(2); *Matter of Rodarte-Roman*, 23 I&N Dec. 905 (BIA 2006); DOS, "P.L. 104-208 Update No. 36: 212(a)(9)(A)–(C), 212(a)(6)(A) and (B)" (Apr. 4, 1998), AILA Doc. No. 98040490.

[994] 1 CBP IFM 15: Nonimmigrants and Border Crossers, 14-1 Agency Manuals, 15.4 Requirements and Procedures for Nonimmigrant Classes; DOS, "Ref: (a) Montreal 1497, (b) Victars E57819, (c) 97 State 23545, (d) State 60539," 76 Interpreter Releases 1552–53 (Oct. 25, 1999) and AILA Doc. No. 99102090.

[995] 1 CBP IFM 15: Nonimmigrants and Border Crossers, 14-1 Agency Manuals, 15.4 Requirements and Procedures for Nonimmigrant Classes (directing CBP inspectors to admit F and J nonimmigrants for Duration of Status).

[996] AFM 40.9.2(b)(1)(E)(ii); 9 FAM 302.9-14(B)(1); DOS, "Ref: (a) Montreal 1497, (b) Victars E57819, (c) 97 State 23545, (d) State 60539," 76 Interpreter Releases 1552–53 (Oct. 25, 1999) and AILA Doc. No. 99102090.

[997] AFM 40.9.2(b)(1)(E)(ii).

[998] AFM 40.9.2(b)(1)(E)(iii). The text does not explicitly refer to Mexicans, but refers to "Non-controlled Nonimmigrants (e.g., Canadian B-1/B-2), so presumably the guidance applies to both.

Copyright © 2017. American Immigration Lawyers Association. All rights reserved.

United States who were not issued an I-94 (and who were not subsequently formally found to be out of status by USCIS or an immigration judge (IJ)" should be so treated.[999]

CBP, however, takes the opposite view, indicating that the statute and regulations do not support "a determination that any individual who is admitted, but not provided an I-94, is admitted for an indefinite period of time."[1000] Thus, in determining strategy for a Canadian or Mexican in this situation, the practitioner should be mindful of which agency or agencies will have a role in the case.

In any event, a Canadian or Mexican citizen who enters without inspection accrues unlawful presence from the date of unlawful entry, like other foreign nationals who enter without inspection.[1001] But the accrual of unlawful presence for these individuals "may not be counted in the aggregate."[1002] Instead, "there must be an unbroken period of unlawful presence lasting at least six months after April 1, 1997, and following the applicant's eighteenth birthday, before [the] bar could apply."[1003]

A foreign national who was admitted pursuant to the VWP, was subsequently granted a period of "satisfactory departure" from ICE, "and who leaves during the satisfactory departure period, is deemed to not have violated his or her VWP admission."[1004] Therefore, as long as the foreign national departs within the satisfactory departure period, "unlawful presence will not accrue during the satisfactory departure period," but if the foreign national remains in the United States "after the expiration of the grant of satisfactory departure, unlawful presence will begin to accrue the day after the satisfactory departure period expires unless some other provision or policy determination protects the person from accrual of unlawful presence."[1005]

One key exception to the rule is that minors, which are defined as individuals under the age of 18 years, may not accrue unlawful presence,[1006] although unlawful presence will begin to accrue on the foreign national's 18th birthday.[1007]

---

[999] 9 FAM 302.9-10(B)(1)(c)(3).

[1000] "CBP Response to AILA Memorandum on Unlawful Presence" (Apr. 10, 2013), AILA Doc. No. 13041059.

[1001] DOS, "Ref: (a) Montreal 1497, (b) Victars E57819, (c) 97 State 23545, (d) State 60539," 76 Interpreter Releases 1552–53 (Oct. 25, 1999) and AILA Doc. No. 99102090.

[1002] Id.

[1003] Id.

[1004] AFM 40.9.2(b)(3)(N).

[1005] AFM 40.9.2(b)(3)(N).

[1006] INA §212(a)(9)(B)(iii)(I); DOS, "P.L. 104-208 Update No. 36: 212(a)(9)(A)–(C), 212(a)(6)(A) and (B)" (Apr. 4, 1998), AILA Doc. No. 98040490. Other exceptions are noted in INA §212(a)(9)(B)(iii).

[1007] AFM 40.9.2(b)(2)(A).

Copyright © 2017. American Immigration Lawyers Association. All rights reserved.

B. Filing Form I-102, Application for Replacement/Initial Nonimmigrant Arrival Record

A nonimmigrant who entered by air or sea after the April 20, 2013, transition to electronic I-94s should be able to obtain a copy of his or her I-94 at any time from the CBP website.[1008] However, if the individual entered by land, entered prior to the transition, or obtained his or her last I-94 from USCIS through, for example, an extension or change of status application, and loses or misplaces Form I-94, Arrival/Departure Record, then Form I-102, Application for Replacement/Initial Nonimmigrant Arrival Record, may be filed with USCIS.[1009] The application may also be used if the original card was "mutilated," "destroyed," or not issued upon U.S. admission, such as for Canadian citizens, but is now required by the foreign national.[1010] For example, a Canadian citizen may file Form I-102 "with an application for extension of stay or change of status,"[1011] although experience has shown that USCIS may grant the change of status request even if an underlying I-94 card was not issued. However, a foreign national may not file Form I-102 if he or she "was not properly inspected and admitted at a port-of-entry, through oversight or error on the part of the government" in order to correct the "improper inspection."[1012] Instead, the foreign national will need to go to a CBP secondary inspection site,[1013] as discussed earlier in this chapter.

The form should be filed with the USCIS Lockbox based on the state of residence of the foreign national.[1014] The one exception is that an application for an initial I-94 card should be filed with the service center where the extension or change of status application is filed.[1015] If the initial I-94 card is mutilated, then it should be submitted with the filing.[1016] Otherwise, the application should include supporting evidence that the foreign national was admitted to the United States after inspection by a CBP officer, such as "a copy of the passport biographical data page and admission stamp, a copy of the original I-94/I-95, ... [or] a statement explaining the facts of admission

---

[1008] "Official Site for Travelers Visiting the United States: Apply for or Retrieve I-94," https://i94.cbp.dhs.gov/I94/#/home.

[1009] 8 CFR §264.6; AFM 30.4.

[1010] 8 CFR §264.6(b); AFM 30.4.

[1011] AFM 30.4.

[1012] Id.

[1013] CBP, "I-94 Automation Fact Sheet" (Nov. 2015), https://www.cbp.gov/sites/default/files/assets/documents/2016-Mar/i-94-automation-fact-sheet.pdf.

[1014] USCIS, Direct Filing Addresses for Form I-102, Application for Replacement/Initial Nonimmigrant Departure Document" (updated Feb. 22, 2010), https://www.uscis.gov/forms/direct-filing-addresses-form-i-102-application-replacementinitial-nonimmigrant-departure-document.

[1015] USCIS, "Instructions for I-539, Application to Extend/Change Nonimmigrant Status" (Apr. 6, 2015), https://www.uscis.gov/sites/default/files/files/form/i-539instr.pdf.

[1016] AFM 30.4.

Copyright © 2017. American Immigration Lawyers Association. All rights reserved.

and reasons why other evidence is unavailable."[1017] Other relevant documents may include evidence of the foreign national's identity, "a copy of the police report relating to the theft," and "copies of any evidence in [his or her] possession to substantiate [the] claim,"[1018] such as a boarding pass or flight itinerary.

As stated by USCIS guidance, "Although nominally an adjudication, such applications involve little more than a record check to verify the fact of initial inspection and admission."[1019] The process essentially entails confirming the lawful admission of the foreign national through a database or, for foreign nationals who "arrived in the United States prior to January 1, 1983," by manual check of records.[1020] Although a foreign national may be interviewed to confirm his or her admission in the absence of an entry stamp or other evidence or to investigate "doubts about the veracity of the alien's claims," including "[h]onest errors,"[1021] it does not seem that interviews are frequently required.[1022]

More important, "Form I-102 is not a discretionary application, and there is no requirement to verify maintenance of status"; so there should be no "further adjudicative effort" or investigation if "USCIS records or evidence submitted support the claimed nonimmigrant admission."[1023] An issued approval notice should contain a replacement I-94 card.[1024]

There is no appeal from the denial of this application.[1025] Although the form allows an individual to file the application to request correction of an erroneous I-94 card,[1026] it seems that this is only possible for I-94 cards that are issued by USCIS; so the form should not be used to obtain a corrected I-94 card if the error was committed by CBP when issuing the card.[1027] In addition, correcting the I-94 card in person should save the client the filing fee and significant processing times.[1028]

[1017] *Id.*

[1018] USCIS, "Instructions for I-102, Application for Replacement/Initial Nonimmigrant Arrival-Departure Document" (Oct. 15, 2014), https://www.uscis.gov/sites/default/files/files/form/i-102instr.pdf.

[1019] AFM 30.4.

[1020] *Id.*

[1021] *Id.*

[1022] For a discussion of "I-102 fraud," *see* AFM 30.4.

[1023] AFM 30.4.

[1024] *Id.*

[1025] 8 CFR §264.6(c); AFM 30.4.

[1026] USCIS, "Form I-102, Application for Replacement/Initial Nonimmigrant Arrival-Departure Document" (Mar. 9, 2016), https://www.uscis.gov/i-102.

[1027] USCIS, "Instructions for I-102, Application for Replacement/Initial Nonimmigrant Arrival-Departure Document" (Oct. 15, 2014), https://www.uscis.gov/sites/default/files/files/form/i-102instr.pdf.

[1028] USCIS, "Processing Time Information," https://egov.uscis.gov/cris/processTimesDisplayInit.do.

Copyright © 2017. American Immigration Lawyers Association. All rights reserved.

VIII. Western Hemisphere Travel Initiative and United States Visitor and Immigrant Status Indicator Technology Program

Two more recent developments for U.S. admission requirements are the Western Hemisphere Travel Initiative (WHTI) and the US-VISIT program.

A. Western Hemisphere Travel Initiative

WHTI is a joint program between DHS and DOS that changed the documentary requirements for citizens of the United States, Canada, Bermuda, and Mexico[1029] seeking to enter the United States from "the Americas, the Caribbean, and Bermuda."[1030] Following promulgation of the rule, which was published and finalized in response to the Intelligence Reform and Terrorism Prevention Act of 2004 (IRTPA) and the Department of Homeland Security Appropriations Act of 2007, and which sought to shorten the inspection time of CBP officers and increase security, generally when applying for U.S. admission at the port of entry following international travel within the Western Hemisphere, individuals must present valid U.S. passport books,[1031] or passport cards,[1032] or a valid foreign passport and visa,[1033] except as discussed below.

The documentary requirements for U.S. citizens apply to admissions at air, land, and sea ports of entry,[1034] except that a U.S. passport card is only acceptable at a land or sea port of entry; it may not be presented as proof of identity and citizenship at an air POE.[1035] In the context of air ports of entry:

> "The only exceptions to this requirement [are] for United States citizens who are members of the United States Armed Forces traveling on active duty; travelers who present a Merchant Mariner Document traveling in conjunction with maritime business; and travelers who present a NEXUS Air card used at a NEXUS Air kiosk."[1036]

[1029] 71 Fed. Reg. 68412 (Nov. 24, 2006); 73 Fed. Reg. 18383 (Apr. 3, 2008).

[1030] DOS, "FAQs on the Western Hemisphere Travel Initiative" (Feb. 23, 2006), AILA Doc. No. 06022373.

[1031] 71 Fed. Reg. 68412 (Nov. 24, 2006).

[1032] 73 Fed. Reg. 18383 (Apr. 3, 2008).

[1033] 71 Fed. Reg. 68412 (Nov. 24, 2006); 73 Fed. Reg. 18383 (Apr. 3, 2008).

[1034] *Id.*

[1035] 73 Fed. Reg. 18383 (Apr. 3, 2008); 8 CFR §235.1(b)(1).

[1036] 71 Fed. Reg. 68412 (Nov. 24, 2006) (citing the Intelligence Reform and Terrorism Prevention Act of 2004 (IRTPA), Pub. L. No. 108-458, 118 Stat. 3638 (Dec. 17, 2004) and Department of Homeland Security Appropriations Act of 2007, Pub. L. No. 109-295, 120 Stat. 1355 (Oct. 4, 2005)); 73 Fed. Reg. 18383 (Apr. 3, 2008). The final rules also discuss other, extremely limited exceptions, such as certain Outer Continental Shore workers. *See also* 8 CFR §§235.1(b)(2) through (4).

Copyright © 2017. American Immigration Lawyers Association. All rights reserved.

The general passport requirement "may be waived on a case-by-case basis for unforeseen emergencies or 'humanitarian or national interest reasons,'"[1037] such as a local emergency,[1038] "urgent medical issues, first responder situations, and cross-border emergency services."[1039] A U.S. citizen or national does not need to present a passport if he or she traveled "directly between parts of the United States, which includes Guam, Puerto Rico, the U.S. Virgin Islands, American Samoa, Swains Island, and the Commonwealth of the Northern Mariana Islands, without touching at a foreign port or place."[1040] A U.S. passport is also not required if the U.S. citizen boards a cruise ship from a U.S. place for a round-trip cruise that returns to the same port or place of departure,[1041] where "cruise ship" is defined as "a passenger vessel over 100 gross tons, carrying more than 12 passengers for hire, making a voyage lasting more than 24 hours any part of which is on the high seas, and for which passengers are embarked or disembarked in the United States or its territories";[1042] also, a U.S. citizen aboard such a cruise ship under the age of 16 years may present the original or copy of a birth certificate, without accompanying photo identification.[1043] Failure to present a U.S. passport book or card should not result in denial of entry but may cause delays due to the need for "additional inspection and processing until the inspecting officer is satisfied that the traveler is a U.S. citizen."[1044]

An oral declaration of U.S. citizenship is generally insufficient; appropriate document(s) should be provided.[1045] Enhanced driver's licenses for citizens, such as those from Vermont, Michigan, Quebec, Manitoba, British Columbia, Ontario,[1046] New York,[1047] and Washington,[1048] may also satisfy WHTI requirements at land and

---

[1037] 71 Fed. Reg. 68412 (Nov. 24, 2006) (citing the Intelligence Reform and Terrorism Prevention Act of 2004 (IRTPA), Pub. L. No. 108-458, 118 Stat. 3638 (Dec. 17, 2004)); 73 Fed. Reg. 18383 (Apr. 3, 2008).

[1038] 73 Fed. Reg. 18383 (Apr. 3, 2008).

[1039] DHS, "Frequently Asked Questions: Publication of Western Hemisphere Travel Initiative (WHTI) Land and Sea Final Rule" (Apr. 3, 2008), AILA Doc. No. 08032865.

[1040] 71 Fed. Reg. 68412 (Nov. 24, 2006).

[1041] 73 Fed. Reg. 18383 (Apr. 3, 2008); 8 CFR §235.1(b)(5).

[1042] 8 CFR §212.0.

[1043] 73 Fed. Reg. 18383 (Apr. 3, 2008). *See also* 8 CFR §§235.1(b)(8) and 212.1(a)(1)(v) for special treatment of U.S. and Canadian citizen children applying for admission.

[1044] 73 Fed. Reg. 18383 (Apr. 3, 2008). *See also* 8 CFR §235.1(b) (discussing claim of U.S. citizenship during inspection at a POE).

[1045] 72 Fed. Reg. 72744 (Dec. 21, 2007).

[1046] 74 Fed. Reg. 25618 (May 29, 2009).

[1047] 73 Fed. Reg. 73343 (Dec. 2, 2008).

[1048] 73 Fed. Reg. 18421 (Apr. 3, 2008).

Copyright © 2017. American Immigration Lawyers Association. All rights reserved.

sea POEs.[1049] As additional state driver's licenses are accepted by DOS and DHS, notices will be published in the *Federal Register*.[1050]

U.S. permanent residents should use Form I-551, Lawful Permanent Resident Card, and a passport should not be required.[1051] Other foreign nationals must also present a valid passport when departing and entering the United States, as well as a visa or other entry document, except for Canadian and Bermudan citizens.[1052] A foreign national who does not present a valid passport and visa may be admitted "on a temporarily [*sic*] basis in case of a medical or other emergency."[1053]

Permanent residents of Canada must also present a valid passport and visa.[1054] Generally, oral declarations of Canadian or Bermudan citizenship are insufficient,[1055] although CBP may "make individual exceptions in extraordinary circumstances when oral declarations alone or with other alternative documents may be accepted."[1056] U.S. and Canadian citizens may also present "CBP Trusted Traveler cards under the NEXUS, SENTRI, and FAST programs" at "land and sea ports-of entry when traveling from contiguous territory or adjacent islands."[1057]

The Border Crossing Card (BCC) for Mexican citizens may be presented in lieu of a passport at land POEs or when "arriving by pleasure vessel or by ferry from Mexico," as long as the U.S. visit will be "within the border zone for a limited time period."[1058] "Pleasure vessel" is defined as "a vessel that is used exclusively for recreational or personal purposes and not to transport passengers or property for hire," and "ferry" is defined as "any vessel operating on a pre-determined fixed schedule and route, which is being used solely to provide transportation between places that are no more than 300 miles apart and which is being used to transport

---

[1049] 73 Fed. Reg. 18383 (Apr. 3, 2008).

[1050] *Id.*

[1051] *Id.* ("Lawful Permanent Residents (LPRs) of the United States will continue to be able to enter the United States upon presenting a Lawful Permanent Resident card (I–551) or other valid evidence of permanent resident status. There are current regulations that already address the entry of LPRs into the United States, which remain unchanged by WHTI.").

[1052] 71 Fed. Reg. 68412 (Nov. 24, 2006); 8 CFR §§212.1(a)(1) and (2).

[1053] 73 Fed. Reg. 18383 (Apr. 3, 2008).

[1054] *Id.*

[1055] 72 Fed. Reg. 72744 (Dec. 21, 2007).

[1056] 73 Fed. Reg. 18383 (Apr. 3, 2008).

[1057] *Id.*; 8 CFR §§212.1(a)(1)(i) through (iii); 8 CFR §235.1(b)(4). Enrollment in the SENTRI program by a Canadian citizen requires submission of a valid passport and visa. 73 Fed. Reg. 18383 (Apr. 3, 2008).

[1058] 73 Fed. Reg. 18383 (Apr. 3, 2008); 8 CFR §212.1(c)(1)(i). This treatment is based on whether a Form I-94 will be issued.

Copyright © 2017. American Immigration Lawyers Association. All rights reserved.

passengers, vehicles, and/or railroad cars."[1059] All "[a]rrivals aboard all vessels other than ferries and pleasure vessels [will] be treated as sea arrivals."[1060]

The BCC was rejected as an acceptable document in lieu of a passport at air POEs "because the BCC cannot be used with CBP's Advance Passenger Information System (APIS), which collects data from travelers prior to their arrival in and departure from the United States."[1061] Mexican citizens may not present a FAST or SENTRI card "in lieu of a passport or BCC," but "these participants would continue to benefit from expedited border processing."[1062]

U.S. and Mexican citizen members of the Kickapoo Tribe and the Tribe of Oklahoma may depart and enter the United States at land and sea POEs when entering from contiguous territory or adjacent islands by presenting Form I-872, American Indian Card, issued by USCIS, in lieu of a passport.[1063] A Tribal Card in lieu of a passport is acceptable for members of the Pascua Yaqui[1064] and Kootenai[1065] Tribes.

B. Entry/Exit Program

The Office of Biometric Identity Management (OBIM), formerly known as the U.S. Visitor and Immigrant Status Indicator Technology Program (US-VISIT),[1066] requires that nonimmigrant visitors to the United States provide biometrics in the form of digital fingerscans and photographs at the port of entry when applying for admission.[1067] The program was established by DHS in 2004[1068] "in accordance with several statutory mandates that collectively require DHS to create an integrated, automated biometric entry and exit system that records the arrival and departure of aliens; biometrically compares the identities of aliens; and authenticates travel documents presented by such aliens through the comparison of biometric identifiers."[1069] As stated by DHS:

[1059] 8 CFR §212.0.

[1060] 73 Fed. Reg. 18383 (Apr. 3, 2008).

[1061] 71 Fed. Reg. 68412 (Nov. 24, 2006).

[1062] 73 Fed. Reg. 18383 (Apr. 3, 2008).

[1063] *Id.*; 8 CFR §212.1(c)(1)(ii). The final rule also discusses how a tribal document may qualify as an acceptable entry document. *See also* 8 CFR §§235.1(b)(6) and (7); 8 CFR §235.1(e).

[1064] 76 Fed. Reg. 33776 (June 9, 2011).

[1065] 77 Fed. Reg. 4822 (Jan. 31, 2012).

[1066] DHS, "US-VISIT Replaced by Office of Biometric Identity Management (OBIM)" (May 21, 2013), AILA Doc. No. 13052142.

[1067] 73 Fed. Reg. 77473 (Dec. 19, 2008); 8 CFR §235.1(f)(1)(ii).

[1068] 69 Fed. Reg. 468 (Jan. 5, 2004).

[1069] 73 Fed. Reg. 77473 (Dec. 19, 2008) (citing the Immigration and Naturalization Service Data Management Improvement Act of 2000 (DMIA), Pub. L. No. 106-215, 114 Stat. 337 (June 15, 2000); the Visa Waiver Permanent Program Act of 2000, Pub. L. No. 106-396, 114 Stat. 1637 (Oct. 30, 2000); the USA PATRIOT
Cont'd

Copyright © 2017. American Immigration Lawyers Association. All rights reserved.

"DHS views US-VISIT as a biometrically-driven program designed to enhance the security of United States citizens and visitors, while expediting legitimate travel and trade, ensuring the integrity of the immigration system, and protecting the privacy of our visitors' personal information."[1070]

Although the regulation also states that "other specified biometric identifiers" may also be required, DHS stated that there are "no plans to collect biometric identifiers in addition to photographs and fingerprints."[1071] The inclusion of the term was "prophylactic," to address potential "technological development [that] may provide the capacity for use of other biometric identifiers in the future," and because "historically, other biometric identifiers such as height, weight, color of hair, color of eyes, etc., have been recorded."[1072] Other biometric identifiers include "hand geometry measurements, handwriting samples, iris scans, retina scans, voice patterns, and other unique characteristics."[1073] DHS indicated it would "make reasonable efforts that are also consistent with the Government's need to verify an alien's identity to accommodate any person with disabilities which prevent him or her from complying with the requirements of this rule for fingerprinting, photographs or other biometric collections," by following the Americans With Disabilities Act and the Federal Rehabilitation Act."[1074] For example:

"[If] a satisfactory fingerprint… cannot be taken, the inspecting officer may accept another biometric identifier that will reasonably identify the person or sufficient additional information from the alien from which the officer can determine the individual's identity. In some instances where the identity of a person with disabilities does not appear to be truly at issue, the requirement for fingerprints or other biometric identifier may be waived in the discretion of the inspecting officer."[1075]

Initially, program participation was required of foreign nationals seeking admission with nonimmigrant visas.[1076] Later rules expanded the impacted

---

Act, Pub. L. No. 107-56, 115 Stat. 271 (Oct. 26, 2001); the Enhanced Border Security and Visa Entry Reform Act of 2002 (Border Security Act), Pub. L. No. 107-173, 116 Stat. 543 (May 14, 2002); the Intelligence Reform and Terrorism Prevention Act of 2004 (IRTPA), Pub. L. No. 108-458, 118 Stat. 3638 (Dec. 17, 2004); and the Implementing Recommendations of the 9/11 Commission Act of 2007, Pub. L. No. 110-52, 121 Stat. 266 (Aug. 3, 2007)).

[1070] 73 Fed. Reg. 77473 (Dec. 19, 2008).

[1071] *Id.*

[1072] *Id.*

[1073] 69 Fed. Reg. 468 (Jan. 5, 2004).

[1074] *Id.* (citing the Americans With Disabilities Act, 42 USC §12101 *et seq.* and the Federal Rehabilitation Act, 29 USC §701 *et seq.*).

[1075] 69 Fed. Reg. 468 (Jan. 5, 2004).

[1076] *Id.*

Copyright © 2017. American Immigration Lawyers Association. All rights reserved.

individuals to include VWP participants,[1077] lawful permanent residents, foreign nationals with immigrant visas, refugees and asylees, parolees, and Canadian citizens who are issued I-94 cards or who require waivers of inadmissibility.[1078] The program should not later become required of U.S. citizens, because "DHS is limited by statute and regulation to apply US-VISIT to aliens."[1079] There are also "no plans to charge a user fee to those seeking admission to the United States to finance US-VISIT."[1080] Failure to comply with the US-VISIT program requirements "may result in a determination that the alien is inadmissible":[1081]

> "The rule does not attempt to identify every ground of inadmissibility that may apply because each case may present different circumstances that skilled inspectors are trained to assess and adjudicate. The rule does not change any of the existing criteria for inadmissibility, but allows inspectors to consider a failure to provide requested biometric identifiers as a factor in their admissibility determinations. In some circumstances, such as an individual who cannot physically provide clear fingerprints, a failure to do so will not necessarily result in an inadmissibility determination, provided that the inspector is otherwise satisfied that the person is who he claims to be and has appropriate authorization to enter the country."[1082]

Now the only exceptions are Canadian citizens who seek temporary admission in B status and are issued I-94 cards; foreign nationals with A, G, and NATO visas, as well as "certain officials of the Taipei Economic and Cultural Representative Office;[1083] and individuals under the age of 14 years and over the age of 79 years at the time of admission.[1084] Other individuals may become exempt if DHS and DOS jointly determine the requirement should not apply, and an individual foreign national may be exempted if DHS, DOS, and the Central Intelligence Agency (CIA) determine that the requirement should not apply, "based on the interests of the United States in managing its foreign and military affairs."[1085]

[1077] 69 Fed. Reg. 53318 (Aug. 31, 2004).

[1078] 73 Fed. Reg. 77473 (Dec. 19, 2008).

[1079] Id.

[1080] Id.

[1081] 8 CFR §235.1(f)(1)(ii); 69 Fed. Reg. 468 (Jan. 5, 2004).

[1082] 69 Fed. Reg. 468 (Jan. 5, 2004).

[1083] 73 Fed. Reg. 77473 (Dec. 19, 2008) (stating that "[o]ne of the main reasons for exempting Canadians who do not require a separate admissibility determination through Form I-94 in this rulemaking is to coordinate the timing of the WHTI land border port of entry procedures, before DHS can determine what, if any, additional steps should be taken for US-VISIT processing of these aliens at land border ports of entry"); 8 CFR §235.1(f)(1)(iv)(B).

[1084] 8 CFR §235.1(f)(1)(iv)(A).

[1085] 8 CFR §§235.1(f)(1)(iv)(C) and (D).

Copyright © 2017. American Immigration Lawyers Association. All rights reserved.

DHS has run pilot programs to collect biometric information of a foreign national, as well as "documentation of his or her immigration status in the United States, and such other evidence as may be requested to determine the alien's identity and whether he or she has properly maintained his or her status while in the United States," upon a foreign national's departure.[1086] To date, no program has been implemented beyond the pilot stage, and considerable barriers continue to exist that complicate large-scale implementation.[1087]

To the extent an exit biometric program exists, a foreign national who "fails to comply with the departure requirements may be found in violation of the terms of his or her admission, parole, or other immigration status."[1088] The failure to comply with the program upon departure may "be a factor in support of a determination that the alien is ineligible to receive a future visa or other immigration status documentation, or to be admitted to the United States," based on a totality of the circumstances analysis, "including, but not limited to, all positive and negative factors related to the alien's ability to comply with the departure procedures":[1089]

> "The Department intends to focus its enforcement of departure requirements in this rule on cases where the alien willfully and unreasonably fails to comply with this regulation. The rule provides that an alien's failure to follow the departure procedures may be considered by an immigration or consular officer in making a discretionary decision on whether to approve or deny the alien's application for a future immigration benefit. The rule does not, however, state that an alien's failure to comply with departure procedures in every instance will necessarily result in a denial of a future visa, admission or other immigration benefit. For example, no alien will be penalized for failing to provide biometrics on departure where the Department has not yet implemented the departure facilities or procedures at the specific port where the person chooses to depart. There may well be instances where a consular officer or inspector, in his or her discretion and after reviewing the totality of the circumstances, determines that an alien's previous failure to comply with the departure procedures does not result in a finding of inadmissibility or the denial of an immigration benefit."[1090]

The failure to comply may also result in a finding of overstay, "where the available evidence clearly indicates that the alien did not depart the United States within the time period authorized at his or her last admission or extension of stay,"

[1086] 8 CFR §§215.8(a)(1) and 214.1(a)(3)(ii); 69 Fed. Reg. 468 (Jan. 5, 2004).

[1087] GAO, "Actions Needed by DHS to Address Long-Standing Challenges in Planning for a Biometric Exit System" (Jan. 20, 2016), AILA Doc. No. 16012103.

[1088] 8 CFR §§215.8(b) and (c).

[1089] 8 CFR §215.8(b).

[1090] 69 Fed. Reg. 468 (Jan. 5, 2004).

Copyright © 2017. American Immigration Lawyers Association. All rights reserved.

may render the individual inadmissible based on the accrual of unlawful presence, and may result in voidance of the nonimmigrant visa that was used to be admitted.[1091]

In response to comments that lawful permanent residents and foreign nationals with immigrant visas should not be subject to the program, DHS responded that enrollment in the program was necessary in order to address "immigration document fraud," as well as admissibility and security issues.[1092] DHS also noted that "the US-VISIT programmatic statutes all refer to 'aliens' without differentiation between immigrants and nonimmigrants," since the term "alien" includes permanent residents.[1093]

The OBIM program and technology includes biometric data gathered by DOS in the course of a nonimmigrant visa application, in order to confirm identity and visa eligibility.[1094] Since 2004, nonimmigrants have been processed through US-VISIT at all land POEs.[1095] The I-94 card should be marked with the date that the OBIM/US-VISIT processing was completed, and the foreign national should be sent to secondary inspection to renew the OBIM/US-VISIT enrollment approximately every six to eight months.[1096] DHS stated the following regarding the retention of biometric information:

"DHS uses the historical fingerscans to ensure that the best quality prints are matched against watchlists. This 'best print forward' process involves evaluating the quality of the prints each time DHS encounters an alien and using the best quality print from that point on. DHS is less and less likely to receive a 'false positive,' as the quality of prints will improve over a lifetime of encounters—both because of this quality selection process and because of improvements in the hardware and software used in the process."[1097]

DHS indicated that a "false positive" should not result in "negative information [being] associated with the traveler history" and "will not affect future entries into the United States."[1098] Generally, a foreign national should have to submit 10 fingerprints only once, whether at a POE or, for a permanent resident, at an Application Support

---

[1091] 8 CFR §215.8(c); 69 Fed. Reg. 468 (Jan. 5, 2004). See elsewhere in this chapter for a discussion of unlawful presence accrual and visa voidance.

[1092] 73 Fed. Reg. 77473 (Dec. 19, 2008).

[1093] Id.

[1094] 69 Fed. Reg. 53318 (Aug. 31, 2004).

[1095] 73 Fed. Reg. 77473 (Dec. 19, 2008).

[1096] Id.

[1097] Id.; 69 Fed. Reg. 53318 (Aug. 31, 2004).

[1098] 69 Fed. Reg. 53318 (Aug. 31, 2004).

Copyright © 2017. American Immigration Lawyers Association. All rights reserved.

Center (ASC) as part of the application to adjust status; subsequent biometrics, "in whatever environment," should require fewer than 10 fingerprints.[1099]

The biometric information is checked "against government databases to identify suspected terrorists, known criminals, or individuals who have previously violated U.S. immigration laws," to help DHS determine a foreign national's admissibility, identify foreign nationals who "may present security and criminal threats," and combat fraud: "By linking the alien's biometric information with the alien's travel documents, DHS reduces the likelihood that another individual could assume the identity of an alien already recorded in US-VISIT or use an existing recorded identity to gain admission to the United States."[1100]

In addition, DHS, DOJ, and DOS collaborated "to achieve interoperability between IAFIS [Integrated Automated Fingerprint Identification System] and IDENT [Automated Biometric Identification System]," which are "a national fingerprint and criminal history system maintained by the Criminal Justice Information Services Division of the FBI" and DHS's biographic record system, respectively.[1101] Immigration history, criminal history, and terrorist information are shared by DHS and FBI through these and other databases.[1102]

DHS has used the OBIM program to deny U.S. admission; "place [foreign nationals] in expedited removal, or return[foreign nationals] to the country of last departure"; detain foreign nationals; and arrest foreign nationals "pursuant to [] criminal arrest warrant[s]."[1103] In response to a comment, DHS stated in the final rule of December 19, 2008, that none of the adverse decisions were based on false positives.[1104] DHS noted that the program has also "expedited the travel of millions of legitimate entrants."[1105] DHS also provided the following reassurance regarding extensions of status:

> "Biographic data from USCIS are transmitted to the Arrival Departure Information System (ADIS) so that changes to immigration status are reflected in US-VISIT in near-real time. Accordingly, US-VISIT has the capability to ensure

---

[1099] 73 Fed. Reg. 77473 (Dec. 19, 2008).

[1100] *Id.*; 69 Fed. Reg. 468 (Jan. 5, 2004).

[1101] 73 Fed. Reg. 77473 (Dec. 19, 2008). For a list of the agencies and entities that have access to the biometric information gathered, as well as a discussion of measures to protect privacy interests, see 69 Fed. Reg. 468 (Jan. 5, 2004).

[1102] FBI, "Privacy Impact Assessment Integrated Automated Fingerprint Identification Systems (IDENT)/Next Generation Identification (NGI) Biometric Interoperability" (Jan. 18, 2012), http://bit.ly/IAFISimm.

[1103] *Id.*

[1104] *Id.* The rule also discusses the "matching algorithms and thresholds," as well as methods for resolving "close matches."

[1105] 73 Fed. Reg. 77473 (Dec. 19, 2008).

Copyright © 2017. American Immigration Lawyers Association. All rights reserved.

that aliens who are in lawful status are not determined to have stayed past their original periods of admission if that period has been extended by USCIS."[1106]

"Pursuant to CIS policy, the timely and nonfrivolous filing of certain benefit applications will toll unlawful presence time from accruing until the adjudication of that benefit application.... US-VISIT is an interoperable system, which can access data from other DHS systems, including the CIS system responsible for tracking immigration benefit applications. Thus, aliens who fall under this scenario described above will not be adversely impacted by US-VISIT, since the US-VISIT system will have access to the CIS benefit processing information."[1107]

If a foreign national believes that there is an error in the information contained in DHS systems, he or she should utilize the Traveler Redress Inquiry Program (TRIP), discussed earlier in this chapter, to seek correction.[1108]

IX. Export Control[1109]

USCIS changed Form I-129[1110] in December 2010 to add a section on export control, requiring petitioners to certify that they have reviewed both the Export Administration Regulations (EAR) and the International Traffic in Arms Regulations (ITAR) and have determined whether an export license is required for the foreign national beneficiary. If such a license is needed, petitioners must attest that they will prevent the foreign national beneficiary from accessing the controlled technology or technical data until the required license is obtained.

The export control attestations must be completed only for H-1B, H-1B1, L-1, and O-1A petitions. The section can be left blank for all other nonimmigrant categories. It should be noted, however, that the export control requirements still apply to other nonimmigrants,[1111] even though an attestation is required for only four visa categories. Therefore, it is prudent to advise the client regarding the need to obtain export control guidance regardless of the visa classification being sought.

The list of federal agencies involved in international business transactions is long, but the three primary agencies that regulate U.S. imports and exports of goods,

---

[1106] *Id.*

[1107] 69 Fed. Reg. 53318 (Aug. 31, 2004).

[1108] DHS, "Traveler Redress Inquiry Program (DHS TRIP)" (updated Nov. 4, 2016), https://www.dhs.gov/dhs-trip.

[1109] This section is adapted from the article "What Every Immigration Attorney Should Know About Export Controls Regulations and Licensing," by Doreen M. Edelman, David S. Jones, and Kevin Miner, Immigration Practice Pointers (AILA 2012–13 Ed.).

[1110] USCIS, "Form I-129, Petition for a Nonimmigrant Worker" (Aug. 13, 2015 ed.), https://www.uscis.gov/i-129, Part 6.

[1111] ITAR §120.16, defining "foreign person" (to whom the requirements apply) as "Any natural person who is not a lawful permanent resident as defined by [INA §101(a)(20)] or who is not a protected individual as defined by [INA §274B(a)(3)]."

Copyright © 2017. American Immigration Lawyers Association. All rights reserved.

technology, money, and services to and from foreign countries are: Department of Commerce, DOS, and Department of the Treasury. For export control purposes, "deemed exports" to foreign persons within the United States are subject to the same restrictions and licensing procedures as exports that actually leave the United States for export to a foreign destination.[1112]

The U.S. Department of Commerce, Bureau of Industry and Security (BIS) governs the export, deemed export, and re-export from third countries of commercial and dual use items (items with both military and commercial uses) through the EAR.[1113] The EAR requires exporters to obtain a license to export certain items classified on the Commerce Control List (CCL), depending on the ultimate shipment destination. All non-military items fall under the authority of the EAR, although not all items actually require a license for export. If an item or technology is not for military use but is not classified on the CCL, the item is likely considered "EAR99," which means it does not require a classification-based license. However, BIS also maintains a variety of restrictive lists that prohibit certain end uses or end users from receiving U.S. goods or technology. Therefore, even if your item is EAR99, you must check these lists before determining whether you need a BIS export license.[1114]

The U.S. Department of State, Directorate of Defense Trade Controls (DDTC) governs defense articles and services, including military use items, technical data, and space– and satellite-related articles. ITAR defines the licensing rules that regulate the export, re-export, and deemed export of these items which are classified on the U.S. Munitions List (USML).[1115] Like BIS, the State Department also maintains a list of restricted parties, such as the Debarred Parties List and an Embargoed Country List.[1116] It is also required that all U.S. exporters and manufacturers of USML items register with DDTC.[1117]

The Department of the Treasury, Office of Foreign Assets Controls (OFAC) administers and enforces trade sanctions and economic embargoes against hostile countries, entities, and individuals to further U.S. foreign policy and national security objectives. U.S. persons are prohibited from exporting, importing, financing, or otherwise facilitating transactions involving certain countries, individuals, and organizations. Overall, OFAC administers sanction programs of some kind in numerous countries, although many programs focus on specific targets rather than

---

[1112] 15 CFR §734.2(b)(2)(ii).

[1113] 15 CFR §730.

[1114] Dept. of Commerce BIS, "Export Control Classification Number (ECCN)," https://www.bis.doc.gov/index.php/licensing/commerce-control-list-classification/export-control-classification-number-eccn.

[1115] 22 CFR §120.

[1116] DOS, "List of Statutorily Debarred Parties," https://www.pmddtc.state.gov/compliance/debar.html.

[1117] DOS, "Who Must Register," https://www.pmddtc.state.gov/registration/wmr.html.

Copyright © 2017. American Immigration Lawyers Association. All rights reserved.

countrywide embargos.[1118] OFAC sanctions can have a severe impact on foreign nationals attempting to use the EB-5 immigrant and E-2 nonimmigrant visas programs to gain a visa by investing money in the United States. Thus, consultation with an expert on export controls is important if an OFAC-sanctioned country is involved.

Procedures to avoid import and export violations are imperative in order to protect your clients and attain their goals without taking on added liability. The complex system of U.S. government regulations along with the approximately 50 lists of barred parties can make U.S. international trade law appear overwhelming, but these difficulties are manageable and are not an automatic bar to achieving your and your clients' objectives.

Because of renewed focus on deemed exports, companies need to review their export compliance programs. The company manager must know and understand what the technologies are, whether they are used or available in the company, and whether any foreign national has access to the technology. Technology of customers and vendors may qualify if a foreign employee has access to it. Fortunately, only a small percentage of companies actually handle covered technologies. But, for those companies using covered technologies, the consequences of noncompliance are significant. Penalties include civil fines of up to $1,094,010 per violation, criminal penalties of up to $1 million per violation and up to 10 years in prison, a denial of export privileges, and debarment from U.S. government contracts.[1119]

An immigration practitioner without export control background should not take it upon himself or herself to assess whether a client is subject to export control licensing. Counsel should be limited to explaining the export control questions on the Form I-129 and providing an overview of export control so that the client company is pointed in the right direction in assessing the I-129 question. Counsel may also explain that an export license is not required prior to filing, but rather must be obtained before the foreign national gains access to a controlled technology. In addition, counsel should explain the potential liabilities associated with failure to comply with export regulations and ensure that an authorized individual makes the determination of how to answer the I-129.

Still, there are clients who will choose not to obtain separate export control counsel and mark the form as not needing an export license. In such cases, it is important that the immigration practitioner properly document that the client has been made aware of the potential issues such as signing under the risk of perjury, the risks of export violations, and the potential fines and imprisonment, as well as document

---

[1118] Treasury Dept., "OFAC FAQs: General Questions," https://www.treasury.gov/resource-center/faqs/Sanctions/Pages/faq_general.aspx.

[1119] Commerce Dept. BIS, "Penalties," *https://www.bis.doc.gov/index.php/enforcement/oee/penalties;* 81 Fed. Reg. 36791 (June 8, 2016).

Copyright © 2017. American Immigration Lawyers Association. All rights reserved.

that the client has indicated that for the purposes of the I-129, it is not subject to export control. It may be helpful to have a prepared statement to provide to clients, explaining the issues, and to require that the client sign and return the statement before finalizing the I-129.

Sample Language: *The Export Administration Regulations ("EAR") and the International Traffic in Arms Regulations ("ITAR") require U.S. employers to seek and receive authorization from the U.S. Government before releasing to foreign persons in the U.S. controlled technology or technical data. Under both the EAR and ITAR, release of controlled technology or technical data to foreign persons in the U.S. is deemed to be an export to that person's country or nationality. For purposes of completing Part 6 of Form I-129, the U.S. government requires the petitioning entity to certify that it has reviewed the EAR and ITAR and determined whether it will require a U.S. export license to release controlled technology or technical data to the beneficiary. In this regard, please confirm if COMPANY is subject to this regulation. If an export license is required, then COMPANY must further certify (by selecting #2 of Part 6) that it will not release or otherwise provide access to controlled technology to the beneficiary until it has received from the U.S. Government the required authorization to do so.*

One area in which an immigration practitioner can feel more comfortable advising on export control issues is in the employment screening phase. If you know that a client has export control issues, it is advisable to discuss how to address these in the hiring and recruitment process so that pre-emptive measures can be taken. Only U.S. citizens, lawful permanent residents, temporary residents under the Legalization or Agricultural Program of the Immigration Reform and Control Act of 1986, and asylees/refugees are protected classes for the purposes of citizenship discrimination.[1120] Also, there are legal and contract compliance exceptions to citizenship status discrimination.[1121]

Accordingly, it is permissible for an employer to ask carefully worded questions to determine if an export license is required.[1122] For example, a company may explain on its application form that it works with technologies subject to U.S. export control regulations, and therefore must request certain information to determine whether it would be necessary to obtain a U.S. government export license prior to releasing its technologies to that individual. If a company then ascertains that the individual is not a protected person, it can move on to further question nationality and

---

[1120] 8 CFR §274B(a)(3).

[1121] 8 CFR§274B(a)(2)(C).

[1122] *See, e.g.*, "OSC TAL on Requesting Documents from Applicants and New Hires for Export Control Purposes" (Mar. 31, 2016), AILA Doc. No. 16041374; Correspondence between attorney Malcolm K. Goeschl and DOJ Office of Special Counsel (Feb. 25, 2013), https://www.justice.gov/sites/default/files/crt/legacy/2013/02/28/163.pdf. In both pieces of correspondence, attorneys set forth potential wording for questions on the subject and the OSC critiques the approaches.

Copyright © 2017. American Immigration Lawyers Association. All rights reserved.

citizenship. Even then, the employer should be careful of the anti-discrimination provisions regarding national origin discrimination, which apply to all work-authorized individuals.[1123] Also, it is important to separate the employment verification process from the export control compliance process to avoid running afoul of the INA §274B(a)(6) prohibition against unfair documentary practices.[1124]

The employer should then consider the following factors in deciding whether or not to proceed with a hire when licensing will be required: time needed to get a license in relation to the need for the position, whether the candidate is subject to policy of denial (*e.g.*, ITAR license for Chinese national),[1125] the prospect for unacceptable conditions on grant of license, whether the company is able to support the technology control plan, and whether another equally qualified candidate who does not need a license is available. If an employer proceeds with the hire, it is advisable to include export control contingency language in the offer letter or have alternative plans for employment if the employee will begin before a license is obtained or in the event it is not granted.

[1123] *Id.*

[1124] Correspondence between Valorie Aguilar and DOJ Office of Special Counsel (Oct. 6, 2010), https://www.justice.gov/sites/default/files/crt/legacy/2011/06/07/134.pdf.

[1125] 22 CFR §126.1.

Copyright © 2017. American Immigration Lawyers Association. All rights reserved.

CHAPTER THREE

VISITORS: B VISAS AND STATUS AND
THE VISA WAIVER PROGRAM

I. Executive Summary

The "B" visa category allows foreign nationals to visit the United States on short trips for business or pleasure. The foreign national must apply for a visa at a U.S. consulate abroad. Admission at the port of entry usually is for the duration of the foreign national's business activities, although admission for a period of six months is relatively common. Tourists typically will be admitted in B status for six months. Individuals holding B status may not work in the United States, although certain limited employment-like activities may be permissible. The B category is also available for common law spouses, same-sex partners, and extended family members of nonimmigrant visa holders, as discussed below. Extensions of B status are available, as are change of status from B to other nonimmigrant visa categories.

The Visa Waiver Program (VWP) is an alternative to the B visa for nationals of certain approved countries, who may apply for admission to the United States without a B visa to engage in business or tourist activities after registering with U.S. Customs and Border Protection's (CBP) Electronic System for Travel Authorization (ESTA). When seeking admission to the United States, the foreign national should present documents evidencing the reason for his or her visit to the United States and documents evidencing return abroad following completion of the visit. Admission is granted for 90 days, and it is typically not possible to extend or change status once a foreign national has been admitted under the VWP.

A. Checklist of Requirements

- Reason for visit to United States

- Evidence of nonimmigrant intent

  - Residence abroad

  - Employment abroad

  - Social or cultural ties abroad

  - Familial ties abroad

- Specific duration of visit to United States

- Funds to cover expenses during travel to United States

B. Documents and Information Necessary to Prepare an Application

- Description for U.S. assignment

Copyright © 2017. American Immigration Lawyers Association. All rights reserved.

- How long do you intend to stay in the United States?

- Information on corporate relationship between two companies

- Do you have employment, familial, social, or cultural ties to your home country?

- Do you have documents that evidence these ties to your home country?

- Do you have documents that evidence your ability to pay for your own expenses while visiting the United States?

C. *Checklist of Questions to Ask the Client*

- Documents evidencing reason for travel to United States, such as:
  - Agendas for business meetings, professional conference, or meeting of Board of Directors;
  - Evidence of contracts to be negotiated;
  - Evidence of litigation;
  - Documents evidencing the employment relationship with a foreign entity that seeks to provide the foreign national's professional services in the United States while the foreign national is employed abroad;
  - Documents evidencing the employment relationship with a foreign entity that seeks to facilitate training in the United States;
  - Contracts of service, whether for installation, repair, or service of commercial or industrial equipment or machinery purchased abroad, or to train U.S. workers on such installation, repair, or services;
  - Employment contract as a personal or domestic employee of a U.S. citizen or foreign national;
  - Invitation to wedding, family reunion, or other personal event;
  - Schedule and receipt for purchase of tourist package;
  - Documents evidencing the medical procedures to be undertaken in the United States;
  - Documents evidencing the cultural or social events in which the foreign national intends to participate;
  - Documents evidencing the familial relationships with cohabitating partners, common-law spouses, extended family members, and same-sex partners of foreign nationals who hold or who will hold valid nonimmigrant status;
  - Other evidence of the reason for U.S. visit; it is permissible to apply for a B visa for certain narrow situations, as discussed below;

Copyright © 2017. American Immigration Lawyers Association. All rights reserved.

- Copies of biographic page of visa applicant's passport and any pages that have entry/exit stamps to foreign countries;
- Résumé or employment history of visa applicant;
- Recent pay stubs from employer and bank statements of visa applicant; or
- Evidence of residence in home country, such as property title or lease agreement.

II. B Visas and Nonimmigrant Status

A. Introduction

The B nonimmigrant visa category is for foreign nationals who wish to temporarily visit the United States, for either "business" under B-1 status or "pleasure" under B-2 status.[1] The purpose of the visa category is to encourage international travel by nationals of foreign countries to the United States for cultural, social, and economic benefits.[2] As discussed in more detail below, "business" typically includes activities that further international commerce but are non-productive and non-remunerative, and "pleasure" typically includes general tourism of U.S. attractions, familial visits, receipt of U.S. medical services, and participation in social events.[3] The practitioner should note, however, that permissible B activities vary widely in scope, such that detailed discussions with the client may be necessary to identify the most appropriate subset.

The B visa category differs from many other nonimmigrant visa categories in that issuance of the visa does not flow from prior approval of a petition by U.S. Citizenship and Immigration Services (USCIS).[4] Instead, a consular officer reviews a visa application in its entirety and decides whether to issue the visa.[5] There is no USCIS determination of eligibility.[6]

Most importantly, individuals who apply for B visas are subject to close scrutiny regarding nonimmigrant intent under Immigration and Nationality Act (INA) §214(b),[7] which is discussed in detail in Volume 1: Chapter Two, "Basic Nonimmigrant Concepts." Of particular note is that the B visa applicant bears the

---

[1] Immigration and Nationality Act (INA) §101(a)(15)(B); 8 Code of Federal Regulations (CFR) §214.2(b).

[2] 9 Foreign Affairs Manual (FAM) 402.2(F).

[3] 9 FAM 402.2-4(A).

[4] Legacy Immigration and Naturalization Service (INS), M. Creppy, "Documentation and Registration of Nonimmigrant Students" (Dec. 21, 1993), 1 INS and DOJ Legal Opinions §93-74.

[5] *See* "Visitor Visa," Department of State (DOS), https://travel.state.gov/content/visas/en/visit/visitor.html.

[6] USCIS, www.uscis.gov/visit-united-states/visit-us, refers readers to the DOS website.

[7] 9 FAM 402.2-2(C), (D), and (F)(b). *See also* 9 FAM 302.1-2(B); "Visa Denials," DOS, https://travel.state.gov/content/
visas/en/general/denials.html.

Copyright © 2017. American Immigration Lawyers Association. All rights reserved.

burden of proof to demonstrate that he or she meets each of the visa requirements to the consular officer's satisfaction. If the consular officer remains unsatisfied about compliance with one or more of the requirements, then the visa may be denied under INA §214(b).[8] Under the INA, B visa applicants are deemed to be immigrants "until they prove to [the consular officer] that they qualify for nonimmigrant status."[9] Denial of a visa application under INA §214(b) should be distinguished from a determination of inadmissibility for a visa or admission to the United States.[10]

Unlike other countries, which allow "working holidays" where certain visitors to those countries may work and earn money to support ongoing travel and living costs,[11] most B visitors are prohibited from engaging in employment while in the United States.[12] However, one can be a visitor both for business and pleasure on the same trip. Consular officers reviewing B visa applications typically place great emphasis on the foreign national's financial ability to remain in the United States without engaging in unlawful employment.[13] As discussed in more detail below, applicants for B visas must demonstrate possession of funds to cover these expenses at the time the visa application is made, as otherwise the visa application may be denied pursuant to INA §214(b).[14]

B. Requirements and Interpretations

One may apply for a B visa with the intent of using it multiple times over as long a period as the consulate may allow and, in fact, a visa can be issued for multiple entry up to 10 years. However, documentation in support of the application must demonstrate eligibility for at least one specific upcoming trip.

An applicant for a B visa bears the burden of proof to demonstrate the following:

- There is a valid reason for the visit to the United States;[15]

---

[8] 9 FAM 302.1-2(B).

[9] 9 FAM 401.1-3(E).

[10] FAM 302.1-2(B)(3). *See also* "DOS Cable Indicates 214(b) Not Equivalent to Inadmissibility" (Dec. 1, 2004), AILA Doc. No. 05032279. For a detailed discussion of admissibility and waivers of inadmissibility, *see* Volume 1: Chapter Two, "Basic Nonimmigrant Concepts."

[11]   *See,   e.g.,*   "Working   Holiday   Visa,"   New   Zealand   Immigration, https://www.newzealandnow.govt.nz/move-to-nz/new-zealand-visa/work-visa/working-holiday-visa; "Australian Working Holiday Visa Basic Requirements," Australian Visa Bureau, http://www.visabureau.com/australia/australian-working-holiday-visa.aspx; "Working Holiday Scheme," Hong   Kong   Special   Administrative   Region   Immigration   Dept., http://www.immd.gov.hk/eng/services/visas/working_holiday_scheme.html (updated Jan. 1, 2016).

[12] INA §101(a)(15)(B); 9 FAM 402.2(E)(b); 9 FAM 401.1-3(C).

[13] 9 FAM 402.2(E)(b).

[14] 22 CFR §41.31(a)(3); 9 FAM 402.2(E)(b).

[15] 9 FAM 402.2-2(B) and (E).

Copyright © 2017. American Immigration Lawyers Association. All rights reserved.

- The purpose of the U.S. visit is to engage in lawful business or pleasure activities;[16]

- The visit to the United States will have a specific duration of time;[17]

- He or she maintains a residence in a foreign country and does not intend to abandon it;[18]

- He or she has strong ties to his or her foreign residence;[19] and

- He or she has sufficient funds for the expenses of the visit.[20]

Each of the requirements is discussed in detail below. Failure to clearly demonstrate each of the points listed above typically results in denial of the visa application.[21] In these situations, the reason for the visa denial is frequently stated as "INA §214(b)." This means that the visa applicant failed to prove his or her nonimmigrant intent to the satisfaction of the consular officer, and the consular officer did not issue the B visa because the visa applicant might remain in the United States beyond the period of authorized stay.[22] Strategies for visa applications subsequent to such visa denials are discussed below.

For all B visa applications, the reason for the U.S. visit should be the linchpin of the analysis and documents presented to the consular officer. It is critical that the purpose of the U.S. visit be clearly explained because, even if the client satisfies his or her burden of proof to demonstrate nonimmigrant intent with respect to the other three criteria, the visa may ultimately be denied.[23] If the consular officer does not believe the visa applicant has a valid reason for visiting the United States, then he or she may presume that the visa applicant intends to immigrate to the United States, and this will result in denial of the B visa application.[24] The reason for the U.S. visit should be at the forefront of all discussions with the client and be the focus of the supporting documents prepared. The client should be encouraged to provide details

---

[16] 9 FAM 402.2-2(E).

[17] 9 FAM 402.2-2(B)(a)(1)(b) and 402.2-2(D).

[18] 9 FAM 402.2-2(B)(a)(1)(a) and 402.2-2(C).

[19] 9 FAM 402.2-2(C).

[20] 9 FAM 402.2(E)(b).

[21] 9 FAM 402.2-2(B)(a)(2).

[22] 9 FAM 402.2-2(B)(a)(2); 9 FAM 302.1-2(B); DOS, "Visa Denials," https://travel.state.gov/content/visas/en/general/denials.html.

[23] 9 FAM 402.2-2(C)(e) (stating that the consular officer "must be satisfied that the alien's intent in seeking entry to the United States is to engage in activities consistent with B-1/B-2 classification").

[24] 9 FAM 402.2-2(C) and (D).

Copyright © 2017. American Immigration Lawyers Association. All rights reserved.

on the reason for the foreign national's U.S. visit, what the foreign national intends to do during the visit, and what is attractive about visiting the United States.

1. Permitted Activities

As noted above, an individual in B status does not have employment authorization (except for certain very limited situations, discussed below) and should not engage in any hands-on work. The Foreign Affairs Manual (FAM) provides detailed information on the types of permissible B-1 and B-2 activities, and the following is an overview of these activities.

a. Business Visits

The general concept of a "business" visit entails activities that are performed pursuant to an individual's profession, but that are not local employment, labor for hire, or hands-on work,[25] and that do not result in U.S.-based remuneration.[26] The distinction between labor and permissible business activities may be difficult to determine.[27] In many instances, performance of business activities in the United States is an extension of the individual's occupation in his or her country, as the activities in the United States "are incidental to work that will be principally performed outside of the United States and is permitted."[28] The Department of State (DOS) offers general guidance on the B-1 visa category.[29] Individual situations are discussed in more detail below.

The client should be advised of the prohibition of "employment" while in B-1 status.[30] As discussed in detail in Volume 1: Chapter Two, "Basic Nonimmigrant Concepts," U.S. immigration laws and guidance take a "broad-based functional view of what constitutes 'employment,' rather than one based merely on the existence of remuneration."[31] In short, "employment" is considered to be "any service or labor performed in the United States by an individual, other than an independent contractor, for wages or other remuneration,"[32] where "remuneration" is defined as "some kind

---

[25] *Karnuth v. Albro*, 279 U.S. 231 (1929).

[26] INA §101(a)(15)(B); 22 CFR §41.31(b)(1); 9 FAM 402.2-5(A) and (C), 402.2-5(F)(1).

[27] 8 CFR §214.1(e); 9 FAM 402.2-5(A); Legacy INS, P. Virtue, "Classification of Visiting University Lecturers" (Aug. 20, 1993), 1 INS and Department of Justice (DOJ) Legal Opinions §93-61 (citing legacy INS Operations Instructions (OI) 214.2(b)); 58 Fed. Reg. 40024 (July 26, 1993).

[28] 9 FAM 402.2-5(A).

[29] DOS, "Business Travel to the United States," http://bit.ly/DOSbusiness. *See also* 9 FAM 402.2-5(C).

[30] 9 FAM 402.2-5(A) and (C).

[31] Legacy INS, P. Virtue, "Classification of Visiting University Lecturers" (Aug. 20, 1993), 1 INS and DOJ Legal Opinions §93-61 (citing *Matter of Tessel, Inc.*, 17 I&N Dec. 631 (Acting Assoc. Comm'r, Exam. 1981)). Volume 1: Chapter Two, "Basic Nonimmigrant Concepts," also addresses who the immigration authorities consider to be an employer.

[32] Legacy INS, P. Virtue, "Classification of Visiting University Lecturers" (Aug. 20, 1993), 1 INS and DOJ Legal Opinions §93-61 (citing legacy INS OI 214.2(b), citing 8 CFR §9274a.1(f)–(h)).

Copyright © 2017. American Immigration Lawyers Association. All rights reserved.

of payment or exchange in kind to a person for a service, loss or expense."[33] During this discussion and while preparing the client for the visa appointment, as discussed below, it may be wise to emphasize that the interpretation of "business" clearly allows meetings and discussions to gather information,[34] and that other proposed activities may be closely scrutinized to ensure that the B-1 visitor will not engage in employment or perform hands-on work or labor.[35] The practitioner should also advise the client that payment of remuneration abroad will nevertheless be considered remuneration for purposes of determining employment, as discussed below.

However, it is appropriate to engage in certain commercial transactions while in B-1 status, as stated in a Board of Immigration Appeals (BIA) case that was later affirmed by the attorney general.[36] In that case, the visitor took orders for custom-made men's business suits from customers in the United States, and then sent the information, together with measurements, to a tailoring firm in Hong Kong. The principal place of business was Hong Kong, the suits were produced in Hong Kong, and profits from the sales accrued to the Hong Kong firm, and not to the visitor. For these reasons, the BIA and the attorney general agreed that the visitor engaged in permissible commercial activity that fell properly within the definition of "business" and not "gainful employment." In other words, even though the taking of orders and measurements might be considered part of a person's occupation under other contexts, such as a tailor who lives and performs his vocation in the United States, it was not considered "work" in the B-1 visa context, specifically because the principal place of business was abroad, the visitor's activities served to further the interest of the visitor's foreign employer, and the visitor earned no income in the United States.[37]

In another example, an individual who is employed abroad by a computer parts manufacturer may need to travel to the United States in order to further the business of his or her foreign employer, such as if the foreign company has entered into a contract to sell customized computer parts to a U.S. client from abroad. In such a situation, the B-1 visitor may need to visit the United States to meet with representatives of the U.S. client to display the functionality of the prototype computer part that was manufactured based on specifications that had been previously provided by email, meet with U.S. representatives to discuss the finalization of the specifications of the computer parts, and view the U.S. client's

---

[33] Legacy INS, P. Virtue, "Classification of Visiting University Lecturers" (Aug. 20, 1993), 1 INS and DOJ Legal Opinions §93-61 (citing legacy INS OI 214.2(b), citing *U.S. v. Dittman*, Case No. 91000027 (OCAHO July 9, 1990)).

[34] *Matter of Opferkuch*, 17 I&N Dec. 158 (BIA 1979).

[35] 9 FAM 402.2-5(A) and (C); *Karnuth v. Albro*, 279 U.S. 231 (1929).

[36] *Matter of Hira*, 11 I&N Dec. 824 (BIA 1965, 1966; AG 1966).

[37] *Id.*

Copyright © 2017. American Immigration Lawyers Association. All rights reserved.

worksite to see how the customized computer parts will be fitted into the U.S. client's end product.

A third example is where an employee of a foreign subsidiary that was recently acquired by the U.S. parent needs to visit the United States to discuss the shared business plans of the foreign subsidiary and the U.S. parent and the continued integration of the business operations of both companies.

The key factors in all of these situations are that the B visa applicant would remain on the payroll of his or her foreign employer, and all hands-on work, whether to provide deliverables, products, or services, would be performed in the foreign country, following the business visit to the United States. In almost all situations, salary and wage remuneration must be paid from abroad.[38] However, a U.S. company may provide an expense account or reimbursement for expenses that are incidental to the visit.[39] For a discussion of permissible payment of expenses from a U.S. source, see below.

Another way to approach the definition of "business visit" is to consider the common understanding of "traveling for a business meeting," where individuals meet with business associates, whether within the same group of companies, or with existing or potential clients or vendors, to discuss specifications, plan goals, and discuss progress in achieving the objectives. Note that this should be distinguished from "traveling for business," which is a concept, especially with respect to consultants, where employees travel to another worksite to perform hands-on work. Use of the B-1 visa for this purpose is not permitted.

It is perhaps for this reason that executives and senior-level managers may face fewer difficulties in obtaining B-1 visas than professionals. Executives and managers, who are frequently charged with leading and establishing long-term strategies and overall plans, may not even engage in hands-on work in their home countries. All of their "work" activities may be considered "business activities" because they typically provide guidance on how to troubleshoot issues without performing any work to resolve the issues themselves.

In contrast, professionals frequently perform the hands-on work at the direction of executives and managers. A professional is subject to the prohibition on use of the B-1 category to provide labor for hire in the same manner that a skilled or unskilled worker would be subject.[40] For these cases, it is critical to highlight that, although

---

[38] 9 FAM 402.2-5(F)(1). One exception is payment of wages, salary, or other remuneration to certain domestic and personal employees, as discussed below.

[39] *Id.*

[40] *Matter of Neill*, 15 I&N Dec. 331 (BIA 1975). *Cf.* 9 FAM 402.2-5(A) (noting that "[e]ngaging in business activities contemplated for B-1 visa classification generally entails business activities other than the performance of skilled or unskilled labor"); 9 FAM 492.2-5(C) (stating that "[t]he statutory terms of INA
Cont'd

Copyright © 2017. American Immigration Lawyers Association. All rights reserved.

hands-on work is performed in the foreign country, the professional will not perform any hands-on work in the United States. Rather, involvement in hands-on work in the United States will be strictly limited to observation of other employees of the U.S. company performing that work. All of the hands-on work will be performed abroad. Nevertheless, the line between permissible business activities and prohibited employment may be difficult to distinguish. In addition, certain activities which are clearly local employment are by special exception expressly permitted under the B-1 business visitor visa classification, such as the services of certain household employees accompanying their employers who are temporarily in the United States and installation and repair of equipment purchased abroad, as discussed below.

Outside of these exceptions, the most persuasive approach may be to explain how the observation in the United States is directly necessary in order for the hands-on work to be performed abroad. If applicable, this explanation may be supported by evidence of how the hands-on work could not be performed in the United States, whether because of the nature of the contract or a lack of resources, tools, or technologies. Note, however, that in certain limited situations, professionals and trainees may engage in employment-type activities while in B-1 status, as long as they receive no U.S.-based remuneration, as discussed below.

DOS has specifically stated that the following are permissible "business" activities:

- "Engage in commercial transactions, which do not involve gainful employment in the United States (such as a merchant who takes orders for goods manufactured abroad);

- "Negotiate contracts;

- "Consult with business associates;

- "Litigate;

- "Participate in scientific, educational, professional or business conventions, conferences, or seminars; or

- "Undertake independent research."[41]

---

§101(a)(15)(B) specifically exclude from this classification aliens coming to the United States to perform skilled or unskilled labor").

[41] 9 FAM 402.2-5(B).

Copyright © 2017. American Immigration Lawyers Association. All rights reserved.

(1) Engaging in Commercial Transactions

Although the statute does not provide a definition of "commercial transaction," the available interpretative guidance ranges from allowing only "buying or selling,"[42] to "any act (within the confine of the law), which is performed expressly to derive a profit … includ[ing], but … not limited to the purchase, sale, marketing, distribution, advertisement, negotiation, procurement, transmission, or transportation of goods or services."[43]

In addition, a legacy INS opinion offers the following definitions of foreign trade and commerce:

- "[T]rade in goods or services"; and[44]

- "Trade means to engage in commerce or business transactions of bargain and sale; barter; exchange; traffic; hence to deal something, while the word commerce is defined as the exchange of goods, productions, or property of any kind; especially, exchange on a large scale, as between states or nations."[45]

The seminal example of "commercial transactions, which do not involve gainful employment in the United States" and which qualify as business, is *Matter of Hira*, as discussed above. The commercial transaction involved the selling of custom-made business suits from Hong Kong. As noted above, the key requirements are that the principal place of business is abroad, the visitor's activities serve to further the visitor's foreign employer, and the visitor earns no income in the United States.[46]

Other examples of permissible activities include the following:

- The purchase of paper scrap in the United States for sale abroad;[47]

- The delivery of truckloads of meat from abroad to the United States;[48]

- Sale in the United States by foreign farmers of perishable crops at retail;[49]

---

[42] Legacy INS Inspector's Field Manual, 14-1 INS Manuals Scope, Chap. 15.4.

[43] OI 214.2, "Special requirements for admission, extension, and maintenance of status."

[44] Legacy INS, G. Rees III, "Foreign Trade and Commerce Defined" (Feb. 23, 1993), 1 INS and DOJ Legal Opinions §93-15 (citing Opinion of the General Counsel, 83-0202 (July 9, 1984), *reproduced in* 61 Int. Rel. 642 (Aug. 9, 1984) and *In Re Fang Lan Dankowski*, 478 F. Supp. 1203 (D. Guam 1979)).

[45] *In Re Fang Lan Dankowski*, 478 F. Supp. 1203 (D. Guam 1979) (citing *Jeu Jo Wan v. Nagle*, 9 F.2d 309 (9th Cir. 1925) (emphasis, internal text markings, and internal quotations removed)).

[46] *Matter of Hira*, 11 I&N Dec. 824 (BIA 1965, 1966; AG 1966).

[47] *Matter of G–P–*, 4 I&N Dec. 217 (BIA 1950). Also note that in this case, as with *Matter of Cortez-Vasquez*, 10 I&N Dec. 544 (BIA 1964), the foreign national returned to his foreign residence regularly.

[48] *Matter of H– and A–*, 6 I&N Dec. 711 (BIA 1955) (applying principles and analysis of *Matter of G–P–*).

Copyright © 2017. American Immigration Lawyers Association. All rights reserved.

- Sale in the United States of plastic bags on behalf of a foreign employer;[50] and

- Sale of firewood abroad after gathering the firewood in the United States.[51]

Most of the activities listed above entailed sale or purchase, but commercial transactions need not be limited to sales and purchases. As noted above, commercial transactions entail activities that are undertaken with the objective of earning profits, such as advertisements, marketing, procurement, solicitation, negotiations, distribution, or transportation,[52] as long as the commerce is international and all hands-on work will be performed abroad.

In fact, each of the cases discussed above presented facts that demonstrated how the business activity also entailed international commerce. In one case, the BIA focused the analysis on whether the "incidental" sale of crops at retail "to housewives, etc." qualified as commercial transactions of an international nature and, therefore, business.[53] The sale of crops arranged in advance at wholesale was stated to be a "legitimate commercial activity."[54] Although this sale at retail would entail accrual of some profit in the United States, the BIA held that the consideration was whether "the actual place of eventual accrual of profits, at least predominantly, remains in the foreign country."[55]

In another case, the foreign national returned to his foreign residence every night, and it may have been particularly pertinent that he was required to do so in order to sell abroad the goods he had obtained in the United States, that his business was "essentially of an international character" such that he was not competing with U.S. workers, and that all income was earned abroad.[56]

In a third case, the BIA deemed the act of cutting firewood in the United States before transport abroad to be "legitimate activities incidental to their principal business abroad which is intercourse of a commercial character."[57] In addition, it may be particularly important that the BIA commented that, even though the foreign

---

[49] *Matter of B– and K–*, 6 I&N Dec. 827 (BIA 1955).

[50] *Matter of P–*, 8 I&N Dec. 206 (BIA 1958).

[51] *Matter of Cortez-Vasquez*, 10 I&N Dec. 544 (BIA 1964).

[52] Engagement in transportation activities pursuant to the North American Free Trade Agreement (NAFTA) Treaty is permissible for Canadian and Mexican nationals, as discussed in more detail below.

[53] *Matter of B– and K–*, 6 I&N Dec. 827 (BIA 1955).

[54] *Id.*

[55] *Id.*

[56] *Matter of G–P–*, 4 I&N Dec. 217 (BIA 1950). This case is also notable in that it provides an overview of other situations that qualified as "business," including the sale of various goods, customs brokerage, and exhibiting movies.

[57] *Matter of Cortez-Vasquez*, 10 I&N Dec. 544 (BIA 1964).

Copyright © 2017. American Immigration Lawyers Association. All rights reserved.

national entered the United States four times a week, he returned to his residence abroad following each trip to the United States, which lasted only about 12 to 14 hours.[58] It may also be pertinent that the foreign national was not considered to compete with U.S. business, perhaps because of the "expense involved."[59]

If the planned activities are "a necessary incident to international trade or commerce,"[60] then the commercial transaction and the international trade or commerce could be the same. Therefore, a railroad clerk was admitted to the United States to ensure safety protocols of train cars that internationally transported goods.[61] The commercial transaction involved the sale or purchase of goods; the BIA held that the clerk's duties were "in many ways as crucial as the duties performed by the train engineer for the movement of the train and the transportation of the goods across the border."[62] It may have been pertinent that the foreign national spent only a few hours of his daily shift engaged in these activities in the United States.[63] Similarly, transporting commodities or machinery "across the international boundary" was deemed an essential element of and a necessary incident to international trade.[64]

Conversely, B-1 status was denied in the following situations because the foreign nationals did not engage in international trade or commerce or activities that were incidental to international trade or commerce:

- Sale of Christmas trees because the trees were only sold in the United States and because accrual of profits was solely in the United States;[65]

- Truck loading and recording of goods received;[66] and

- Painting and sale of paintings in the United States.[67]

---

[58] *Id.*

[59] *Id.*

[60] *Matter of Duckett*, 19 I&N Dec. 493 (BIA 1987) (citing *Matter of Hira*, 11 I&N Dec. 824 (BIA 1965, 1966; AG 1966)). *See also Matter of Cote*, 17 I&N Dec. 336 (BIA 1980) (stating "an alien need not be considered a 'businessman' to qualify as a business visitor, if the functions he performs is a necessary incident to international trade or commerce"); 51 Fed. Reg. 44266 (Dec. 9, 1986).

[61] *Matter of Duckett*, 19 I&N Dec. 493 (BIA 1987).

[62] *Id.*

[63] *Id.*

[64] *Matter of Camilleri*, 17 I&N Dec. 441 (BIA 1980).

[65] *Matter of M–*, 6 I&N Dec. 533 (BIA 1955).

[66] *Matter of G–*, 6 I&N Dec. 255 (BIA 1954). Note that although the goods were to be transported from the United States to Canada, the Board of Immigration Appeals (BIA) nevertheless held that "it is clear that [the foreign national] is not engaged in any international trade." The ultimate reason for denial was that the work was "of a continuing nature at a fixed and permanent place," and his income derived from work that was 100 percent located in the United States.

Copyright © 2017. American Immigration Lawyers Association. All rights reserved.

In sum, commercial transactions involve many different types of functions, but the crux is that the activities performed in the United States serve to facilitate international trade or commerce and the performance of hands-on work abroad. Thus, in most instances, documenting the link to international trade and commerce is critical to a successful application. For this type of application for a B-1 visa and admission, the supporting evidence should clearly explain how the U.S. activities will further international trade or commerce and how they must be performed outside the United States. Such evidence could include the following:

- To document existence of the foreign employer:
    - Incorporation and license documents;
    - Lease or property title documents for the foreign employer's premises;
    - Corporate tax returns;
    - Print-outs from the foreign employer's website;
    - Employment and payroll records for employees; and
    - Contracts for goods or services provided by the foreign employer in the foreign country.
- To document predominant accrual of profits abroad:
    - Evidence of payment pursuant to contracts for goods or services provided by the foreign employer;
    - Payroll records evidencing salary, wages, or commissions provided to the foreign national; and
    - Job description for the foreign national's position.
- To document international trade or commerce:
    - Contracts for goods or services provided by the foreign employer;
    - Contracts for transportation of goods across international borders;
    - Business plans documenting the planned activities in the United States and their impact on the foreign employer's operations; and
    - Other evidence of sales or purchases abroad.
- To document that the foreign national's activities are incidental to international trade or commerce:
    - Explanations of how the foreign national's activities in the United States are necessary to conduct international trade or commerce; and

---

[67] *Matter of Minei*, 11 I&N Dec. 430 (Reg. Comm'r 1965). Note that a foreign national may engage in artistic activities, as long as no artwork is sold in the United States and as long as the foreign national is not under contract with a U.S. employer, as noted below.

Copyright © 2017. American Immigration Lawyers Association. All rights reserved.

– Job description for the foreign national's position abroad, so as to explain how the U.S. activities comprise only a small fraction of his or her duties overall.

- To document that the hands-on work will be performed abroad:

  – Contracts specifying the worksite of the goods provided or services performed to be in the foreign country;

  – Organizational charts of employees abroad who will perform the work;

  – Organizational charts of employees in the United States who cannot undertake the hands-on work because of other responsibilities; and

  – Documents explaining the lack of resources, tools, or technologies at any worksite in the United States.

(2) Negotiating Contracts

In many cases, negotiation of contracts will fall within the purview of the "business discussions" detailed below. This is because negotiating contracts frequently entails meetings with clients, vendors, or other stakeholders; hands-on work will not be performed until the contract is executed.

It may not be necessary to specify contract negotiation if the B visa applicant will also engage in business meetings and discussions while in the United States. However, if the foreign employer is lesser-known, or if the individual is self-employed, then a better strategy may be to focus on the contract to be negotiated rather than the nature of the B visa applicant's employment abroad. This is because the contract may be more persuasive as the driving reason for the U.S. visit, and documents relating to the contract negotiation activities may be more readily accessible. For these cases, it is helpful to provide the following evidence:

- Any initial contract negotiations previously undertaken by correspondence, telephone, or email;

- Descriptions or summaries of the nature of the products or services to be provided following contract execution;

- Documents evidencing the U.S. company's background and need for the proposed services to be provided by the foreign entity; and

- Documents evidencing the B visa applicant's employment status and authority to negotiate contracts and evidence.

If the B visa applicant is self-employed as a freelancer without a sponsoring incorporated company, then additional care should be taken with respect to each of these types of evidence. It is also recommended that a self-employed B visa applicant also present the following evidence:

- Executed contracts of service for other clients;

Copyright © 2017. American Immigration Lawyers Association. All rights reserved.

- Evidence that all work performed—to provide the services or products detailed in the previous contracts—was performed outside the United States, such as foreign payroll records, bills of lading, correspondence with previous clients to deliver the services or products, and entry and exit stamps in the B visa applicant's passport; and

- Corporate and/or personal tax returns filed by the applicant.

(3) Consulting with Business Associates

As discussed above, business meetings and discussions do not include hands-on work. Although the Foreign Affairs Manual (FAM) allows B-1 visitors to "consult with business associates," it may be more helpful to explain that the business visitor will "engage in business meetings and discussions," because the latter term more clearly describes the activities to be undertaken in the United States. The term "consult with business associates" seems more ambiguous regarding what the visitor will actually do while present in the United States. A B-1 visitor may also "gather pertinent information" on behalf of his or her foreign employer.[68] Appropriate documents to evidence the business meetings and discussion are discussed above.

In addition, consulting with business associates may also include business activities to be performed by a foreign national who will seek investment in the United States.[69] The B-1 visitor may seek an investment that would subsequently qualify him or her for status as an E-2 investor, but it is not required that the B-1 visitor seek an E-2 investment.[70] To evidence this as a reason for the U.S. visit, the documents listed for business meetings and discussions above may be presented. Evidence of the investment may be bank statements, portfolios, wire transfers, contracts, ledgers documenting stock ownership, and shareholder registration.

(4) Litigating

Similar to contract negotiation, litigation frequently entails business meetings with counsel representatives, representatives of the opposing party, or the judge and jury, to review documents, discuss strategy, and present evidence or testimony. It should not, however, be assumed that litigation and preparation for it can never involve labor for hire, because a professional may provide labor for hire just as a skilled or unskilled worker may.[71] Therefore, clients should be counseled against having the foreign national physically retrieve documents, perform investigations, prepare briefs,

---

[68] *Matter of Opferkuch*, 17 I&N Dec. 158 (BIA 1979).

[69] 9 FAM 402.2-5(C)(7).

[70] *Id.*

[71] *Matter of Neill*, 15 I&N Dec. 331 (BIA 1975).

Copyright © 2017. American Immigration Lawyers Association. All rights reserved.

or perform research in the United States, as these activities could be construed as hands-on work.

To demonstrate the litigation, the activities performed abroad, and the activities to be performed in the United States, the B visa applicant could submit the following documents:

- Evidence of the litigation, such as docketing calendars, documents describing the claim filed by the suing party, and filing and reply briefs;

- Retainer agreement between the foreign national and a party to the litigation;

- Documents evidencing why the foreign national would be involved in the litigation as an attorney, such as if the group of companies maintains in-house counsel only abroad;

- Documents evidencing how the foreign national is the representative of his or her employer, who in turn is the plaintiff or defendant;

- Subpoena notices for witnesses;

- Contract for services as an expert witness;

- Evidence of the foreign national's role as defendant;

- Email, facsimile, or letter correspondence discussing the litigation; and

- Telephone logs or notes about the litigation.

(5) Participating in Scientific, Educational, Professional or Business Conventions, Conferences, or Seminars

One key benefit to this subset of the B-1 visa category is that consular officers are directed to expedite B visa applications for "applicants traveling to the United States to attend conferences, conventions, or meetings on specific dates."[72] Possibly due to the understanding that conference dates can rarely be altered for the benefit of a single attendee, this direction may help to prevent a situation in which an applicant is granted a B-1 visa for a specific duration to attend the conference, convention, or seminar, but only after the event has already concluded.

To document attendance at a professional conference, convention, or seminar, the following documents may be provided:

---

[72] 9 FAM 402-2(F)(b).

Copyright © 2017. American Immigration Lawyers Association. All rights reserved.

- Agendas for the event;

- Confirmation of payment for attendance by the foreign national;

- Confirmation of presentation of an article, professional speech, scholarly endeavor, or product showcase, if applicable (note that if a showcase entails physical demonstration of the product, this may be considered hands-on work);

- Approval from the B visa applicant's employer to attend the event; and

- Business plans explaining the objective of the presentation as it relates to the foreign employer's overall goals.

Regarding educational seminars, DOS stated:

> If posts find applicants will be engaged in something other than a week or more of full-time study, and that the course is neither offered for academic credit nor required for completion of an academic program of study, then the activity may be properly classifiable as B-1 as an educational convention or seminar.[73]

For a discussion of permissible payment of conference and related expenses by a foreign and/or U.S. company, see below.

(6) Undertaking Independent Research

The guidance on what qualifies as "independent research" for immigration purposes is minimal. In the university context, independent research or study entails concentration on a designed project, with laboratory research and/or literature review, and ultimately an articulation of the project goals and whether the empirical evidence supported the initial hypotheses.[74] Alternatively, independent research or study may entail a focused inquiry into and analysis of a discrete question of fact, law, or situation, whether in the pursuit of academic or professional achievement.[75] Because this subset is listed among other permissible business visitor activities, it seems appropriate to have the field of study or research be related to the applicant's academic or professional background.

If the B visa applicant seeks to visit the United States in order to engage in independent research, the following evidence may be helpful:

---

[73] DOS, "Student and Exchange Visitor Visa Update" (Apr.1, 2010), AILA Doc. No. 10051363.

[74] *See, e.g.,* "Handbook for Directors of Undergraduate Studies in Yale College," Yale University, http://catalog.yale.edu/dus/.

[75] *See, e.g.,* Association of Independent Research Institutes, https://www.airi.org/about-airi.

Copyright © 2017. American Immigration Lawyers Association. All rights reserved.

- Documents describing the independent research project in which the foreign national is involved;

- Documents describing the ultimate goal or objective of the research project;

- Documents describing the need for the foreign national's independent research project, such as the business plan, academic degree program, or other professional endeavor;

- Documents describing the research already performed for the project;

- Documents describing why the research cannot be performed outside the United States; and

- Documents describing the types of information and documents to be gathered in the United States.

b. Other Permissible Types of Business Visits

The activities discussed above comprise the typical use of the B-1 visa category. However, the DOS provides for other permissible situations and eligible individuals. These situations, discussed below, often seem to reflect a policy determination that certain types of activity which appear to be work, in context, fulfill the requirement of being business rather than local employment.

(1) B-1 in Lieu of H-1 or H-3

If the visa applicant is customarily employed and paid by a foreign entity, with the source of the salary from abroad, he or she may be eligible to visit the United States and provide professional services or receive training.[76] This subset is one of the few exceptions to the prohibition on employment in B-1 status, and the foreign national need not apply for USCIS employment authorization in order to provide services in the United States. Many consular officers and inspectors are skeptical of the category, and thus obtaining a visa and being admitted in this category can at times prove challenging, and the client should be prepared for those challenges.

The requirements are as follows:

- The visa applicant is customarily employed by a foreign firm.[77] The practitioner should note that it may be difficult to establish that the employment is customary if it has been for a period shorter than one month: "It

---

[76] 9 FAM 402.2-5(F).

[77] Id.

Copyright © 2017. American Immigration Lawyers Association. All rights reserved.

may be more difficult for a new hire to establish their employment status with the overseas firm if they are immediately sent to the U.S. to engage in H-1B caliber activity."[78]

- The visa applicant will receive no salary or other remuneration (except for an expense allowance or reimbursement for the costs of the visit) from a U.S. source.[79]

- The foreign firm has an office abroad and disburses its payroll abroad. Note that this requirement does not mean that the foreign company must be entirely separate from a U.S. company. A "foreign branch of a U.S. firm can qualify as a foreign firm."[80] The mere fact of a corporate relationship between the two companies should not result in denial of the B-1 visa based on income from a U.S. source.[81]

- The visa applicant's salary or wages are paid by the foreign company and will continue to be so paid for the duration of the U.S. visit.[82]

- The source of the visa applicant's salary is abroad.[83]

- The visa applicant meets the eligibility requirements of the relevant H-1 or H-3 visa classification.[84] In short, an H-1 professional must possess at least a bachelor's degree or the equivalent in a related field to perform professional activities in the United States (and the activities in the United States must be "H-1B caliber")[85]; and an H-3 trainee's visit must entail training that is not available in his or her home country and that will benefit the B-1 visitor in pursuing a career outside the United States, while not involving any productive employment except that which is "incidental and necessary to the training" and

---

[78] DOS, "B-1 in Lieu of H" (Oct. 12, 2012), AILA Doc. No. 12102246.

[79] 9 FAM 402.2-5(F)(1).

[80] DOS, "B-1 in Lieu of H" (Oct. 12, 2012), AILA Doc. No. 12102246.

[81] 9 FAM 402.2-5(F).

[82] *Id.*

[83] *Id.*

[84] DOS, "B-1 in Lieu of H" (Oct. 12, 2012), AILA Doc. No. 12102246. *See also* "Notes from London Liaison Meeting" (Jan. 7, 1999), AILA Doc. No. 99012958.

[85] DOS, "B-1 in Lieu of H" (Oct. 12, 2012), AILA Doc. No. 12102246.

Copyright © 2017. American Immigration Lawyers Association. All rights reserved.

not involving placement in a position "in the normal operation of the business and in which citizens and resident workers are regularly employed."[86]

- The proposed activity in the United States is not for long-term placement.[87]

With respect to the source of the visa applicant's salary, legacy INS guidance indicates that a U.S. bank or financial institution may arrange payment of the salary, as long as the source of the salary remains abroad.[88] There can be no "chargeback." However, where the foreign firm is ultimately reimbursed by the U.S. company for the costs of the visa applicant's services or training, then use of the B-1 in lieu of an H-1 or H-3 is inappropriate. This is because a chargeback entails income from a U.S. source.[89]

Legacy INS guidance also indicates that if an international group of companies has a centralized payroll system in the United States, such that all foreign employees who perform services abroad receive checks issued in the United States, then the B visa applicant should not be precluded from engaging in proper business activities and should not be deemed to receive income from a U.S. source. In such a situation, the applicant "must demonstrate that he is employed abroad by the foreign-based company and is coming to the United States to perform functions for his employer, not for the U.S. company."[90]

For these visa applications, the following documents may be prepared and submitted:

- Documents evidencing applicant's customary employment abroad;
- Documents evidencing the foreign source of applicant's salary;

---

[86] 9 FAM 402.2-5(F)(9). For more on the requirements of H-1B status, see Volume 1: Chapter Seven, "H-1B Visas and Status." For a detailed discussion of the requirements of H-3 training programs, see Volume 1: Chapter Nine, "H-3 Status."

[87] DOS, "B-1 in Lieu of H" (Oct. 12, 2012), item 6, AILA Doc. No. 12102246. *See also* "AILA/Department of State Liaison Meeting" (Apr. 7, 2016), item 12, AILA Doc. No. 16041133, both indicating that these visas "should generally be issued for activity in the U.S. that is less than six months in duration." *But see* 9 FAM 402.2-5(F)(9), which states with respect to H-3 activities that "the fact that the training may last one year or more is not in itself controlling and it should not result in denial of a visa, provided you are satisfied that the intended stay in the United States is temporary, and that, in fact, there is a definite time limitation to such training."

[88] Legacy INS, R. Miller, 70 No. 7 Interp. Rel. 221 (Feb. 22, 1993).

[89] 58 Fed. Reg. 58982 (Nov. 5, 1993). Although this proposed regulation did not become a final regulation, the discussion of "chargebacks" is helpful. *See also* Legacy INS, J. Bednarz, "CO 214b-C, CO 1815-C" (May 17, 1994), 71 Interp. Rel. 1247 (Sept. 12, 1994), and *Matter of G–*, 6 I&N Dec. 255 (BIA 1954). Although this case addressed B-1 status, as opposed to B-1 in lieu of H-1 or H-3 status, the BIA held that the "work which he does in the United States provides the entire source of his income," even though his salary was entirely paid by a foreign firm.

[90] Legacy INS, J. Bednarz, 71 No. 29 Inter. Rel. 992 (Aug. 1, 1994). *But see* 9 FAM 402.2-5(F), stating that the foreign entity's payroll "must be disbursed abroad."

Copyright © 2017. American Immigration Lawyers Association. All rights reserved.

- Documents evidencing the proposed activities in the United States:
  - The professional services to be provided in the United States; or
  - The training program in the United States;
  - The absence of the training in the foreign country; and
  - How the training program will prepare the trainee for a career abroad.
- Copy of applicant's bachelor's degree, for B-1 in lieu of H-1;
- Copy of applicant's résumé;
- Copies of applicant's pay stubs;
- Statement from U.S. company describing the U.S. activities and confirming that there will be no U.S.-based remuneration; and
- Statement from foreign employer confirming the applicant's customary employment and foreign-based remuneration.

The practitioner is advised to reference the FAM citation in the supporting documents and request that the visa be annotated with the following: "B-1 in lieu of H-1" or "B-1 in lieu of H-3."[91] The foreign national should also be advised to carry copies of the supporting documents when seeking admission to the United States, so they may be presented to the immigration officer at the port of entry if necessary.

For foreign nationals who already possess standard B-1/B-2 visas in their passports, they should be advised of the benefits and drawbacks of applying for a new B-1 visa specifically for the purpose of the H-1 or H-3 visit. The disadvantages are the timing delays and costs of preparing and filing the new B-1 visa application. However, the advantage is the greater likelihood of the foreign national being admitted in B-1 in lieu of H-1B or H-3 status where the B-1/B-2 visa stamp contains the B-1 in lieu of H-1B or H-2 annotation.

First, if the foreign national will make multiple trips to the United States for the project or training program, then having evidence of the separate visa application may prevent the foreign national from experiencing difficulty in entering the United States. As a practical matter, immigration officers at the ports of entry may question whether an individual who has a pattern of frequently seeking admission in B-1 status is truly engaging in business activities. If the immigration officer presumes that the individual has engaged in longer term unauthorized employment and denies admission, then this fact would have to be disclosed on subsequent applications for visas and admission. The individual may face additional difficulty at a later date. Conversely, filing an extension of B-1 in lieu of H-1 or H-3 status may result in a finding that USCIS had not specifically authorized employment.[92] Such an extension

---

[91] 9 FAM 403.9-5(A); *See also* DOS, "B-1 in Lieu of H" (Oct. 12, 2012), AILA Doc. No. 12102246.

[92] "CSC Liaison Minutes" (Mar. 26, 2003), AILA Doc. No. 03040442.

Copyright © 2017. American Immigration Lawyers Association. All rights reserved.

could be considered identical to an extension of B-1 status to engage in business activities, with no consonant extension of employment authorization.[93] However, if USCIS adopts the State Department's current position that the U.S. activity should be no more than six months in duration,[94] an extension beyond those six months could be questionable.

Second, if the foreign national will remain in the United States over a significant period of time, then evidence of the new visa application may be helpful in obtaining a longer period of admission, because the project or training program may then serve to provide the "limited period of stay" that is also longer term.[95] For B-1 in lieu of H-3 trainees in particular, consular officers know that "the fact that the training may last one year or more is not in itself controlling."[96] If the visa is annotated to provide the anticipated length of the U.S. trip, then there may be a higher likelihood of the immigration inspector granting a period of admission of one year.[97]

Finally, if the foreign national later requests another type of nonimmigrant visa or status, then evidence of a proper B-1 in lieu of H-1 or H-3 visa application and visa issuance may prevent questions from the consular officer or immigration officer regarding whether the foreign national engaged in unauthorized employment.

As noted above, B-1 in lieu of H-1 or H-3 status is one exception to the prohibition on employment in B status. For this reason, a client may wish to avoid having these entries grouped with B-1 admissions for business activities that do not involve hands-on work. The additional protection may be particularly helpful given efforts to limit or completely remove availability of a "B-1 in lieu of H-1" category.[98]

Finally, the practitioner should discuss with the client that the consulates have been inconsistent in their reception and approval of these visa applications, and ports of entry have been inconsistent in admitting foreign nationals who present the visas. At least one consular official has provided guidance on how these visa applications are adjudicated,[99] but experience has shown that consulates vary widely in adjudication procedures and likelihood of approval.[100] The practitioner should discuss

---

[93] *Cf.* 8 CFR §274a.12(b)(20) (allowing for a 240-day extension of employment authorization for individuals who have employment authorization for a specific employer incident to status) and 8 CFR §274a.12(c)(17) (noting that personal and domestic employees in B-1 status must apply for employment authorization from USCIS).

[94] DOS, "B-1 in Lieu of H" (Oct. 12, 2012), item 6, AILA Doc. No. 12102246.

[95] 9 FAM 402.2-2(D).

[96] 9 FAM 402.2-5(F)(9).

[97] DOS, "B-2 Classification Appropriate for Cohabitating Partners" (July 2001), AILA Doc. No. 01070031, 6 Bender's Immigr. Bull. 744 (July 15, 2001).

[98] "DOS Responds to Grassley's Concerns over B-1 in Lieu of H-1B" (May 13, 2011), AILA Doc. No. 11052660. *See also* 58 Fed. Reg. 58982 (Nov. 5, 1993); 58 Fed. Reg. 40024 (July 26, 1993).

[99] "Notes from London Liaison Meeting" (Jan. 7, 1999), AILA Doc. No. 99012958.

[100] "DOS Answers to AILA Questions" (Mar. 17, 2005), AILA Doc. No. 05062117.

Copyright © 2017. American Immigration Lawyers Association. All rights reserved.

the risk of this visa classification with the client in detail, as well as the fact that even if the visa is issued by the consulate, the foreign national may nevertheless be denied admission to the United States or may be admitted in B-1 status despite the B-1 in lieu of H-1B or H-3 annotation.

(2) B-1 Status for Personal and Domestic Employees

Certain personal and domestic employees of employers coming to the United States temporarily are also eligible to work in the United States while in B-1 status.[101] Personal and domestic employees include, but are not limited to, housekeepers, chauffeurs, cooks, housemaids, parlor maids, butler, valets, footmen, gardeners, nannies, au pairs, babysitters, caretakers, and paid companions.[102] The employees may accompany their employers to the United States. Alternatively, the employees may submit separate applications for visas and admission at a later date. An application for an Employment Authorization Document (EAD) must be made to USCIS.[103] Unlike many other subsets of the B-1 visa category, the salary, wages, or remuneration may be paid from abroad or from within the United States.[104] The employer and employee will generally be subject to the full scheme of federal, state, and local employment, tax, and insurance obligations applicable to local employment within the United States.[105]

The following section discusses eligibility for B-1 status and employment authorization as a personal and/or domestic employee. In addition to the requirements stipulated in the FAM and by other DOS guidance,[106] individual consulates may require additional information or documents as part of the visa application. Therefore, the practitioner should consult the consulate's website for updated information. For example, a consulate may require that the employment contract specify that the employer provide medical insurance and agree not to withhold the employee's passport.[107] Different consulates may have conflicting conditions: deductions by the employer for food and lodging "must be no more than reasonable and voluntarily agreed to on the part of the employee"[108] or the employer may not make such

---

[101] 9 FAM 402.2-5(D).

[102] *See, e.g.*, U.S. Consulates in La Paz, Bolivia and San Jose, Costa Rica; http://bolivia.usembassy.gov/domesticempl.html, and http://sanjose.usembassy.gov/nivdomestic.html.

[103] 8 CFR §§274a.12(c)(17)(i) and (ii).

[104] 9 FAM 402.2-5(D)(5) (stating "[t]he source of payment to a B-1 personal or domestic employee or the place where the payment is made or the location of the bank is not relevant").

[105] *See, e.g.*, Internal Revenue Service "Publication 926 (2008), Household Employer's Tax Guide," https://www.irs.gov/publications/p926/ar02.html#d0e235, and "Topic 756—Employment Taxes for Household Employees," Internal Revenue Service, https://www.irs.gov/taxtopics/tc756.html.

[106] DOS, "Rights and Protections for Temporary Workers," https://travel.state.gov/content/visas/en/general/rights-protections-temporary-workers.html (updated April 2016).

[107] U.S. Consulate in La Paz, Bolivia, http://bolivia.usembassy.gov/domesticempl.html.

[108] U.S. Consulates in San Jose, Costa Rica, http://sanjose.usembassy.gov/nivdomestic.html.

Copyright © 2017. American Immigration Lawyers Association. All rights reserved.

deductions from the employee's wages.[109] (In fact, under the FAM, such deductions generally are not allowed, as discussed below.) Common issues regarding period of admission to the United States, obtaining an EAD from USCIS, and obtaining a Social Security number (SSN) are discussed below. The issued visa should be annotated with the employer's name.[110] Personal and domestic employees of U.S. lawful permanent residents (LPRs) are not eligible for B-1 status, "as it is contemplated that the employing LPR is a resident of the United States."[111]

Three subsets of individuals are permitted to bring domestic employees to the United States under B-1 status. While the requirements under each subset are similar, some are stated a bit differently, and the FAM applies some requirements to some subsets but not to others.[112] Each category is addressed individually below. However, the practitioner is advised to reference the website of the consulate at which the visa application will be lodged, since many posts lay out a general set of requirements for domestic employee B-1s, and do not differentiate between subsets.

(a) Personal and Domestic Employees of U.S. Citizens Who Reside Abroad[113]

This subset is available when the U.S. citizen employer maintains a permanent home or is stationed abroad, but will visit the United States temporarily.

The following are the requirements for this subset of the B-1 visa category:

- The employee has a residence abroad and has no intention of abandoning this residence;

- The employee demonstrates, through statements from previous employers, that he or she has "at least one year's experience as a personal or domestic employee";

- The employee was employed abroad by the nonimmigrant employer "as a personal or domestic employee, for at least one year prior to the date of the employer's admission to the United States," or the employer can demonstrate that, while abroad, he or she has regularly employed a domestic servant "in the same capacity as that intended" for the employee. If using the latter standard, it

---

[109] U.S. Consulate in La Paz, Bolivia, http://bolivia.usembassy.gov/domesticempl.html.

[110] 9 FAM 403.9-5(C).

[111] 9 FAM 402.2-5(D)(4).

[112] For example, no prohibition against deductions from wages for room and boarding is included for U.S. citizens residing abroad who are visiting the United States (9 FAM 402.2-5(D)(1)), but is part of the requirements for all three other categories (9 FAM 402.2-5(D)(2), 402.2-5(D)(3), and 402.3-9(B)(4)).

[113] 9 FAM 402.2-5(D)(1).

Copyright © 2017. American Immigration Lawyers Association. All rights reserved.

should be noted that the employer-employee relationship nevertheless must exist prior to the commencement of the visit to the United States; and

- The employee possesses an "original employment contract or a copy of the contract," with original signatures, and will present the contract to the immigration officer at the port of entry. The employment contract must be signed and dated by the employer and the employee. It must also stipulate the following additional provisions:

  - The employee will be paid the minimum or prevailing wage, whichever is greater, for an eight-hour work day, and provide "any other benefits normally required for U.S. domestic workers in the area of employment";
  - The employer will provide at least two weeks' notice of intent to terminate the employment; and
  - The employee will not be required by the employer to give more than two weeks' notice of intent to resign.

Given the existence of a subset for U.S. citizen employers who will come to the United States for temporary assignments, it seems that the temporary visits would involve pleasure activities, a shorter duration, and/or business or professional activities that would not give rise to a longer-term assignment. The U.S. consulate, where the employee will apply for a visa, may have guidance on appropriate lengths of visits. Perhaps because this subset anticipates a short-term visit, certain requirements found in other subsets are not explicitly included in the FAM for this one. For example, the subsets for employees of U.S. citizens on temporary assignment in the United States and for employees of nonimmigrant foreign nationals require that the employer provide free room and board and travel expenses, while no such requirements are explicitly stated in the FAM for U.S. citizens merely visiting the United States.

Again, however, as with all visa applications, the practitioner should check the website of the consulate where the employee will apply for a B-1 visa, as individual consulates may have additional requirements or may apply all the requirements for all subsets to all applicants.[114] Other consulates also go beyond parroting the FAM to be more specific about compliance with U.S. wage and hour rules, such as paying time-

---

[114] For example, many consulates do not differentiate among employees of U.S. citizens on temporary U.S. visits, employees of U.S. citizens on temporary assignment in the U.S., and employees of foreign nationals in nonimmigrant status. *See, e.g.,* U.S. Consulates in New Delhi and Guadalajara, http://newdelhi.usembassy.gov/nivdomesemploy.html and http://bolivia.usembassy.gov/domesticempl. html.

Copyright © 2017. American Immigration Lawyers Association. All rights reserved.

and-one-half for overtime,[115] or providing sample contracts that seem to go beyond the stated requirements.[116]

(b) Personal and Domestic Employees of U.S. Citizens on Temporary Assignment in the United States[117]

This subset is available to a narrow class of individuals because of the strict requirements, which are as follows:

- The U.S. citizen employer must be "subject to frequent international transfers lasting two years or more as a condition of the job as confirmed by the employer's personnel office" and must return to the United States for a period of no longer than six years. The initial confirmation should be a statement from the employer's employer. Copies of work visas and permits to other countries, employment contracts for international assignments, and copies of leases and residences in foreign countries may supplement this document.

- The personal or domestic employee must have no other employer in the United States besides the U.S. citizen.

- There must be an employment contract that is signed and dated by the employer and the employee.

- The employer must provide, and the employment contract must confirm provision of, free room and board, as well as round-trip airfare to the United States and return abroad.

- The employment contract must provide for at least the minimum or prevailing wage (whichever is greater) for an eight-hour work day.

- The employment contract must also "reflect any other benefits normally required for U.S. domestic workers in the area of employment."

- In the event of termination, the employer must provide at least two weeks' notice of his or her intent to terminate.

---

[115] *See, e.g.,* U.S. Consulate in Beirut, Lebanon, http://lebanon.usembassy.gov/personal-or-domestic-employees-b1/b1-contract-requirements.html.

[116] *See, e.g.,* U.S. Embassy in Mexico City, https://mx.usembassy.gov/visas/domestic-employees/, which provides a sample contract at http://photos.state.gov/libraries/mexico/1019454/arevaloya/employment-contract.jpg, that includes such specifics as lunch hour, time off on weekends, and the employee not being required to be at the employer's home during time off.

[117] 9 FAM 402.2-5(D)(2).

Copyright © 2017. American Immigration Lawyers Association. All rights reserved.

- In the event of resignation by the employee, the employee must not be required by the employer to give more than two weeks' notice.

- The B-1 visa may be issued only if the consular officer is satisfied that the following conditions are met:
  - The employee has a residence abroad and has no intention of abandoning this residence, as with all B-1 visa applications;
  - The employee was employed abroad by the U.S. citizen "as a personal or domestic servant for at least six months prior to the date of the employer's admission to the United States," or the employer demonstrates that, while residing abroad, he or she "regularly employed a domestic servant in the same capacity as that intended for the applicant." If using the latter standard, it should be noted that the employer-employee relationship nevertheless must exist prior to the commencement of the employer's assignment in the United States;
  - The employee demonstrates that he or she gained "at least one year of experience as a personal or domestic servant by producing statements from previous employers attesting to such experience"; and
  - The employee possesses "an original employment contract or a copy of the contract," with original signatures, and will present the contract to the immigration officer at the port of entry.

Employers must comply with the requirements of federal and state minimum wage laws.[118] The "minimum wage" may be determined federally (by the Fair Labor Standards Act)[119] or by an individual state.[120] The "prevailing wage" is defined as "the average wage paid to similarly employed workers in a specific occupation in the area of intended employment."[121] The prevailing wage may be calculated from the Foreign Labor Certification Data Center Online Wage Library, available at *www.flcdatacenter.com*, by selecting the FLC Wage Search Wizard, the state of intended employment from the drop-down menu, the county of intended employment, and the job code from the drop-down list (or searching by keyword).[122]

---

[118] *See* U.S. Department of Labor, Wage and Hour Division, "Questions and Answers About the Minimum Wage," https://www.dol.gov/whd/minwage/q-a.htm.

[119] *Id.*

[120] *See* U.S. Department of Labor, Wage and Hour Division, "Minimum Wage Laws in the States" (July 1, 2016), https://www.dol.gov/whd/minwage/america.htm.

[121] *See* U.S. Department of Labor, Employment and Training Administration, "Prevailing Wages (PERM, H-2B, H-1B, H-1B1 and E-3)" (Feb. 25, 2016), https://www.foreignlaborcert.doleta.gov/pwscreens.cfm.

[122] For further explanation of how to determine the prevailing wage, *see* U.S. Consulate in New Delhi, http://newdelhi.usembassy.gov/nivdomesemploy.html.

Copyright © 2017. American Immigration Lawyers Association. All rights reserved.

The FAM does not require that the employment must have been for the six months immediately preceding the U.S. citizen's admission to the United States, so a former personal or domestic employee may accompany or join the U.S. citizen in the United States to provide his or her services. The practitioner should note the provision of the FAM which deals with personal and domestic employees of foreign nationals with U.S. nonimmigrant status, and which explains that regular employment is "either year-round or seasonally" and "over a period of several years preceding the domestic employee's visa application."[123]

In addition, the requirement of six months of previous employment seems to mean that the anticipatory filing of a B-1 visa application, before the employee has accrued six months of employment, will result in visa denial. The consular officer may determine that there was failure to demonstrate satisfaction of this requirement, so it is advised that the employee delay filing the visa application until the employer can clearly confirm the mandatory six months of employment, whether through a statement, pay stubs or other evidence of remuneration, or employment contracts.

Alternatively, the employer may demonstrate regular employment of an employee in the same role as the function that the visa applicant will be employed. Appropriate evidence of this previous regular employment may include employment contracts, job descriptions, paystubs, cancelled checks, bank statements, advertisements of job availabilities, and/or statements from staffing agencies or recruiters. Note, however, that the FAM guidance states that this substitute requirement is available only if the U.S. citizen seeks to employ a domestic servant. Although the FAM guidance seems to use the terms "personal" and "domestic" interchangeably, this is one of several instances in this section where only domestic employees are referenced.[124] Therefore, the absence of mention of personal employees should be discussed with the client. If it comes to light that the employee will engage in both personal and domestic activities, then the client may wish to limit the employment to domestic activities. Conversely, more risk-averse clients may wish to forego such a visa application by an intended personal employee, such as a personal assistant, who will engage in no domestic activities.

If this latter alternative is used, it must be remembered that the FAM still requires that the employer-employee relationship have existed prior to the beginning of the U.S. assignment. Thus, while six months' history of employment is not required, some amount—even one day—must be shown.

Although the text of the FAM guidance indicates that the employee may possess a copy of the executed employment contract, the requirement that the employee present

---

[123] 9 FAM 402.2-5(D)(3).

[124] The other omissions of reference to personal employees are discussed below.

Copyright © 2017. American Immigration Lawyers Association. All rights reserved.

a contract with original signatures from both employer and employee seems to mandate that the employee possess the original and not a copy.

(c) Personal and Domestic Employees of Foreign Nationals Who Hold Nonimmigrant Status in the United States[125]

Certain foreign nationals who hold or who will hold nonimmigrant status in the United States are also eligible to sponsor personal and domestic employees for B-1 status. The foreign national employer must hold one of the following nonimmigrant statuses:

- B: business or pleasure visitor

- E: investor or treaty trader

- F: international student

- H: professional in a specialty occupation, nurse in a shortage area, agricultural worker, temporary worker, or trainee

- I: worker in foreign media

- J: trainee

- L: intracompany transferee

- M: international vocational student

- O: individual with extraordinary ability and individual supporting individuals with extraordinary ability

- P: artist; entertainer, whether a member of a reciprocal exchange program or not; and artist with a culturally unique performance

- Q: participant in international cultural exchange program

The following are the requirements for this subset of the B-1 visa category:

- The employee has a residence abroad and has no intention of abandoning this residence, as with all B-1 visa applications;

---

[125] 9 FAM 402.2-5(D)(3). For more detailed discussions of the requirements of each nonimmigrant status category, please see the individual chapters.

Copyright © 2017. American Immigration Lawyers Association. All rights reserved.

- The employee demonstrates that he or she has "at least one year's experience as a personal or domestic employee"; and

- The employee was employed abroad by the nonimmigrant employer "as a personal or domestic employee, for at least one year prior to the date of the employer's admission to the United States," or if the employment relationship "existed immediately prior to the time of visa application, the employer can demonstrate that he or she has regularly employed (either year-round or seasonally) personal or domestic employees over a period of several years preceding the domestic employee's visa application";

- The employer will pay round-trip travel expenses from the foreign country to the United States, and then from the United States to the country of the employer's subsequent and "onward" assignment, or from the United States "to the employee's country of normal residence at the termination of the assignment"; and

- There must be an employment contract. The employment contract must be signed by the employer and the employee. It must also stipulate the following additional provisions:
  - The employee will be guaranteed the minimum or prevailing wage, whichever is greater;
  - The employer will provide free room and board; and
  - The "employer will be the only provider of employment to the employee."

The validity of the B-1 visa issued to a domestic or personal employee of an employer, who holds nonimmigrant status in the United States, may not exceed the validity of the employer's visa.[126] The practitioner is advised to discuss the standard of INA §214(b) with the client in detail, because it may be difficult for a personal or domestic employee to have compelling evidence of a residence abroad, considering if the employee resides in the employer's home abroad and has no property or lease of his or her own. In addition, the nonimmigrant intent standard may be different for the employer and the employee. For example, H-1B, H-4, and L visa applicants may have dual intent to hold nonimmigrant status and pursue permanent residence,[127] so these employers would face no questions regarding nonimmigrant intent. The FAM specifically notes that the employee's requirement to have a residence abroad that he or she has no intention of abandoning applies even if the employer holds a status that

---

[126] 9 FAM 403.9-4(C)(8).

[127] 9 FAM 302.1-2(B)(5).

Copyright © 2017. American Immigration Lawyers Association. All rights reserved.

does not require such a showing. If the employer and employee apply for visas together, then the result may be visa issuance for the employer and visa denial for the personal or domestic employee based on INA §214(b). Thus, if the employee has resided with the employer in the past, the employer may need to maintain a residence abroad, notwithstanding that the requirement does not apply to him or her.

To evidence the required year of experience as a personal or domestic employee, the visa applicant may submit letters from his or her current and/or previous employer(s); an individual consulate may require that the year of qualifying experience have been gained with the sponsoring employer.[128]

If there are specific reasons or conditions that necessitate the services of a domestic or personal employee, it may be helpful to provide the supplementary documents discussed herein. In addition, for situations where the dependent family members may not qualify for derivative nonimmigrant status, it may be particularly helpful to demonstrate how the dependents will be able to accompany the employer, such as in B-2 status, as discussed below, and will, therefore, require the assistance of the personal or domestic employee, by submitting copies of the nonimmigrant visa stamps of the dependent(s). For example, a parent may need to accompany the employer, whether because of infirmity or age. In such cases, it may be helpful to provide documents evidencing the employer's responsibility to provide a home for the dependent, such as doctor's letters or cost estimates for nursing home services, in addition to copies of the dependent's B-2 visa stamp.

Two more terms that are not defined in the FAM are "year-round" and "seasonally," which apply to the alternative for past employment that the employer show that he or she has regularly employed personal or domestic employees for several years. The *Merriam-Webster Dictionary* defines "year-round" as "occurring, effective, employed, staying, or operating for the full year: not seasonal";[129] Board of Alien Labor Certification Appeals (BALCA) has stated that a year-round position should be "continuous or carried out throughout the year."[130] The *Merriam-Webster Dictionary* defines seasonally as "affected or caused by seasonal need or availability."[131] In the context of H-2A temporary agricultural workers, "seasonal" has been defined as follows:

"[O]rdinarily, the employment pertains to or is the kind exclusively performed at certain seasons or periods of the year and which, from its nature, may not be continuous or carried on throughout the year. A worker who moves from one seasonal activity to another, while employed in agriculture or performing

---

[128] U.S. Consulate in Guadalajara, https://mx.usembassy.gov/visas/domestic-employees/.

[129] *Merriam-Webster's Dictionary*, https://www.merriam-webster.com/dictionary/year-round.

[130] *Matter of Twin Industries*, 2007-INA-00270 (BALCA Jan. 18, 2008), AILA Doc. No. 08021378.

[131] *Merriam-Webster's Dictionary*, https://www.merriam-webster.com/dictionary/seasonally.

Copyright © 2017. American Immigration Lawyers Association. All rights reserved.

agricultural labor, is employed on a seasonal basis even though he may continue to be employed during a major portion of the year."[132]

Finally, this FAM guidance explicitly allows for two options for the return airfare that must be provided to the employee following the completion of the U.S. assignment. The employer may provide airfare from the United States to the country of the employer's "onward" assignment, such as if the employee will accompany the employer to a third country. Alternatively, the employer may provide airfare to the country of the employee's "normal residence." Therefore, it seems that the employee may depart the United States with the employer or may return to the home country, even if the employer will travel to a third country without the employee.

(d) Managing Client Expectations: Common Issues with B-1 Visas for Personal and Domestic Employees

Assisting with B-1 visa applications for personal or domestic employees can be challenging, from the perspectives of both the visa application and client management, as the U.S. immigration laws for these employees may be less accommodating than the laws of other countries.[133] The Department of State has a detailed "Know Your Rights" pamphlet available on its website, indicating the focus on ensuring compliance with both U.S. immigration laws and employment laws.[134] The practitioner will need to prepare clients for the potential difficulties—especially those who wish to accompany the employee to the interview, those who believe that the visa application is a matter of course, or those who experience frustration with the B-1 visa application process and wish to attempt to bring domestic or personal employees to the United States without going through the proper channels of visa application, visa issuance, and application for admission to the United States.

In order to facilitate the employee's subsequent application for admission to the United States, and for other reasons, as discussed below, it may be helpful to request, in the statement from the employer, that the visa be annotated with the employer's name and with the applicable section from the FAM.[135] This way, when the immigration officer at the port of entry inspects the employee's application for admission, the employee will have documentary evidence of an accurate representation of the intended U.S. employment. This approach may also help to

---

[132] *Matter of W.A. Maltsberger,* 94-TLC-13, 1994 DOL ARN LEXIS 96 (June 6, 1994).

[133] *See, e.g.,* U.K. Border Agency and Citizenship and Immigration Canada, https://www.gov.uk/domestic-workers-in-a-private-household-visa and http://www.cic.gc.ca/english/ work/caregiver/index.asp.

[134] DOS, "Know Your Rights," https://travel.state.gov/content/dam/visas/LegalRightsandProtections/Wilberforce_Pamphlet_October2016.pdf

[135] 9 FAM 402.2-5(H); 403.9-5(A); 14-1 legacy INS Inspector's Field Manual 15.4, "Requirements and Procedures for Nonimmigrant Classes" (stating the "consular officer will annotate 'personal or domestic servant of … (employer's name)' on the B-1 visa"). The issues surrounding applications for Social Security numbers are discussed in this section as well.

Copyright © 2017. American Immigration Lawyers Association. All rights reserved.

document compliance by the employer and the employee with the relevant immigration laws, such that, in the event that the employee makes multiple trips of extended duration to the United States, the immigration officer does not erroneously conclude that the employee has engaged in unauthorized employment throughout all of those visits. Further, for subsequent B-1 visa applications, these documents may also be submitted to evidence that the employee has the required six months or year of qualifying experience and that the employee has a history of complying with U.S. immigration laws. The third and possibly most relevant point is that such evidence can rebut the presumption of the employee's intent to immigrate pursuant to INA §214(b), because the employee could show a history of returning to his or her home country following the U.S. visits, a record of not overstaying, and a history of not using the B-1 visa to immigrate.

The issued B-1 visa typically has a validity period of six months or a validity period that matches the length of the employer's temporary or nonimmigrant stay, whichever is less.[136] Upon admission to the United States, the employee should be granted B-1 status valid for six months or one year from the date of entry or B-1 status that matches the length of the employer's temporary or nonimmigrant stay, whichever is less.[137]

The challenges continue even after successful B-1 visa application and admission to the United States. The employee must apply for U.S. employment authorization,[138] unlike an employee of a foreign government official,[139] a personal employee of an official or representative of an international organization,[140] or an attendant, servant, or personal employee of a NATO foreign national.[141] Even though the terms of the employment relationship have been disclosed to the consular officer during the visa application, the employee does not have employment authorization incident to status.[142] In addition, the employee may need to apply for an SSN in order for the necessary taxes to be paid or withheld from the employee's income.[143]

---

[136] Note that, as discussed in Volume 1: Chapter Two, "Basic Nonimmigrant Concepts," the validity period of the visa has no bearing on the period of admission granted to the visitor.

[137] 8 CFR §214.2(b)(1); OI 214.2, "Special requirements for admission, extension, and maintenance of status."

[138] 8 CFR §§274a.12(c)(17)(i) and (ii).

[139] 8 CFR §274a.12(b)(2).

[140] 8 CFR §274a.12(b)(8).

[141] 8 CFR §274a.12(b)(18).

[142] 8 CFR §§274a.12(c)(17)(i) and (ii).

[143] See, e.g., Internal Revenue Service "Publication 926 (2008), Household Employer's Tax Guide," https://www.irs.gov/publications/p926/ar02.html#d0e235, and "Topic 756—Employment Taxes for Household Employees," Internal Revenue Service, https://www.irs.gov/taxtopics/tc756.html.

Copyright © 2017. American Immigration Lawyers Association. All rights reserved.

The practical considerations of these employment relationships should be discussed in detail with the client. First, initial admission in B-1 status for these employees is typically for a period between six months and one year from the date of admission.[144] It is possible to request extensions of B-1 status in six-month increments,[145] but premium processing is not available for B-1 extensions.[146]

Then, in this case, the employee will not have employment authorization until USCIS issues an EAD,[147] as "[t]here is no provision in the regulations for such [domestic or personal employee] aliens to work in the U.S. during the first 90 days of the pendency of the I-765, [Application for Employment Authorization]."[148] This process may take up to more than 90 days,[149] which means that the employee may engage in unauthorized employment for a significant period of time. Legacy INS previously stated, "Unofficially HQ indicates they would not hold these domestics to the requirement of waiting for their EADs prior to working and being paid. However, there is no official policy memo on this."[150]

In addition, if the employee engages in unauthorized employment, the employer may violate U.S. immigration laws during this time period and face criminal and civil penalties.[151] Moreover, the employer may have difficulty in completing the Form I-9, Employment Eligibility Verification, because the employee would not have a document authorizing employment. In addition to the potential criminal and civil penalties imposed upon the employer, an employee who has engaged in more than an aggregate of 180 days of unauthorized employment since the date of his or her most recent admission to the United States is ineligible to apply to adjust status to that of an LPR if he or she should apply for adjustment of status on an employment-based ground while physically present in the United States.[152]

The individual would be ineligible to adjust status in the United States for any amount of unauthorized employment[153] if the application's basis is other than

---

[144] 8 CFR §214.2(b)(1).

[145] 8 CFR §214.2(b)(1); 14-1 (Legacy) INS Inspector's Field Manual 15.4, "Requirements and Procedures for Nonimmigrant Classes."

[146] USCIS, "How Do I Use the Premium Processing Service?" https://www.uscis.gov/forms/how-do-i-use-premium-processing-service (updated 10/26/2015).

[147] INA §274A(h)(3); 8 CFR §§274a.12(c)(17)(i) and (ii).

[148] "VSC Liaison Minutes" (Apr. 6, 2000), AILA Doc. No. 00040671.

[149] "AILA Liaison/SCOPS Q&As" (Sept. 17, 2008), AILA Doc. No. 08092369.

[150] "VSC Liaison Minutes" (Apr. 6, 2000), AILA Doc. No. 00040671.

[151] INA §§274A(a)(1) and (2); 8 CFR §274a.3 ("employer who continues the employment of an employee hired after Nov. 6, 1986, knowing that the employee is or has become an unauthorized alien with respect to that employment, is in violation" of U.S. immigration laws); INA §§274A(e)(5) and (f).

[152] INA §245(k)(2)(B).

[153] INA §245(c)(8).

Copyright © 2017. American Immigration Lawyers Association. All rights reserved.

employment, such as through a family relationship or the diversity visa lottery. Although a domestic or personal employee in B-1 status may not be interested in applying to adjust status to that of an LPR and may, therefore, view this prohibition as irrelevant, it is important to note that the criminal and civil penalties remain. It may also be considered a failure to maintain status,[154] and could result in denial of an application to extend stay.[155] Moreover, ensuring that employment is authorized may be one of the aspects of previous employment to confirm compliance with the "conditions of previous contracts" and any applicable U.S. laws, which are explored by the consular officer during subsequent B-1 visa applications, as discussed above.

The issued EAD should have an expiration date that matches the expiration of the employee's authorized stay in the United States, as noted on the employee's I-94 card, Arrival-Departure Record.[156] Although there does not appear to be specific guidance on the validity periods of EADs for domestic or personal employees, legacy INS addressed the situation in the context of another nonimmigrant classification.[157] Based on anecdotal evidence, most B-1 domestic and personal employees are not issued EADs with validity periods that extend beyond the periods of authorized stay. Previously, at least one USCIS Service Center had a practice to issue an EAD with validity of one year,[158] but it appears that this is no longer the case.

In the event that the employee will continue to provide domestic or personal services to the employer for an additional period, beyond the dates of expiration on the I-94 card and the EAD, then the employee will need to request a B-1 extension on Form I-539, Application to Extend/Change Nonimmigrant Status, and a new EAD from USCIS.[159] The new EAD application must be filed and approved in order for the employee to have continued employment authorization.[160] Unlike certain other nonimmigrant statuses, filing this extension does not provide continued employment

---

[154] 8 CFR §214.1(e) (stating "Any unauthorized employment by a nonimmigrant constitutes a failure to maintain status within the meaning of section 241(a)(1)(C)(i) of the Act." The statutory reference in the regulation has not been updated, and should be to INA §237(a)(1)(C)(i), which states that failure to maintain status renders a nonimmigrant deportable. While it could be argued that the reference in §214.1(e) relates strictly to deportability and not to eligibility for change of status, this view has generally not been accepted. *See* "USCIS's SOPs for I-539 Processing" (Mar. 1, 2003), AILA Doc. No. 07090760.)

[155] 8 CFR §214.1(c)(4)

[156] 8 CFR §274a.13(b).

[157] *See, e.g.*, 66 Fed. Reg. 46699 (Sept. 7, 2001) (If the alien's application for employment authorization is approved, the service will grant the alien employment authorization for a period of time to match his or her period of authorized stay as a V nonimmigrant").

[158] "NSC Processing Guidelines" (June 9, 2000), AILA Doc. No. 00060909.

[159] For a discussion of extensions of B status, see below. For a general discussion on requesting extensions of stay, see Volume 1: Chapter Two, "Basic Nonimmigrant Concepts."

[160] INA §274A(h)(3); 8 CFR §§274a.12(c)(17)(i)–(ii); 274a.14(a)(1)(i); and 274a.2(b)(1)(vii).

Copyright © 2017. American Immigration Lawyers Association. All rights reserved.

authorization.[161] The employee's employment authorization is entirely derived from the validity of the EAD.[162] Filing a timely B-1 extension should, however, be evidence that the employee has continued to maintain lawful immigration status.[163] Alternatively, a faster process may be for the employee to travel abroad and return to the United States in order to obtain an additional period of authorized stay, but the employee must still file an EAD application after admission.[164]

Although the B-1 extension and the EAD renewal application should be filed together,[165] reports indicate that the EAD applications have been previously denied because the adjudicating officer believes that the underlying B-1 status (the initial B-1 status as indicated on the I-94 card) has expired.[166] This processing issue arises because USCIS does not adjudicate the B-1 extension and EAD renewal application together.[167] Previously, the applications were adjudicated together, but this is no longer the case.[168] However, adjudicators "do check the computer system to verify that a domestic worker is still in status,"[169] and USCIS Product Lines have coordinated processes for concurrent adjudication.[170] The practitioner is advised to "attach to each application a duplicate copy (marked as 'copy') of the other application and supporting documents."[171] The practitioner is also advised to provide details on how the employee does not intend to abandon his or her foreign residence in the supporting documents for the B-1 extension.[172] In the event that the EAD renewal application is denied for this reason, a practitioner may file a Motion to Reopen.[173]

---

[161] 8 CFR §274a.12(b)(20). While the regulations were amended in 2016 to extend this benefit to additional classes of foreign nationals, USCIS specifically declined to include B-1 domestics. 81 Fed. Reg. 2068 (Jan. 15, 2015), AILA Doc. No. 16011402.

[162] 8 CFR §§274a.12(c)(17)(i) and (ii).

[163] 8 CFR §§214.1(c)(2) and (4). For a detailed discussion on requesting extensions of stay in the event that the underlying status expired before receipt of the request for extension, see Volume 1: Chapter Two, "Basic Nonimmigrant Concepts."

[164] INA §274A(h)(3); 8 CFR §§274a.12(c)(17)(i) and (ii).

[165] "VSC Liaison Minutes" (Apr. 6, 2000), AILA Doc. No. 00040671.

[166] "AILA/TSC Liaison Minutes" (July 14, 2004), AILA Doc. No. 04073062.

[167] AILA/TSC Liaison Meeting Minutes" (Nov. 7, 2005), AILA Doc. No. 05112875.

[168] Cf. "VSC Update" (May 28, 1998), AILA Doc. No. 98052871 (stating "[g]enerally we ask that the contractor keep all riding cases together … [where] the 539 would go to the Business Product Line for adjudication and then be sent, with the 765, to the Resident Product Line for their action").

[169] "AILA/TSC Liaison Minutes" (July 14, 2004), AILA Doc. No. 04073062.

[170] "VSC Liaison Minutes" (Apr. 6, 2000), AILA Doc. No. 00040671.

[171] "AILA/TSC Liaison Meeting Minutes" (Nov. 7, 2005), AILA Doc. No. 05112875.

[172] Id.

[173] "AILA/TSC Liaison Minutes" (July 14, 2004), AILA Doc. No. 04073062. For a further discussion of Motions to Reopen, see Volume 1: Chapter Two, "Basic Nonimmigrant Concepts."

Copyright © 2017. American Immigration Lawyers Association. All rights reserved.

During the pendency of the subsequent B-1 extension and EAD application, the employee may wind up engaging in unauthorized employment for the time period between expiration of the first EAD and approval of the subsequent EAD.[174] Consequently, the employer may be in violation of U.S. immigration laws and may be subject to civil and criminal penalties.[175] B-1 extensions have been known to take as long as six months to be adjudicated.[176] USCIS may approve an EAD renewal application with a start date that is the day after the date of expiration of the previous EAD in order to preserve continued employment authorization, even if the previous EAD expired before the date of issuance of the renewal EAD.[177] Unfortunately, the guidance specifically addresses EADs for applicants for adjustment of status and states that "[i]t is important to keep the period of employment on the EAD continuous for these [adjustment of status] applicants."[178] Nevertheless, the document also notes how certain individuals, such as domestic and personal employees, must apply for an EAD in order to obtain employment authorization.[179]

If the EAD renewal application is processed after reference to the B-1 extension application, such that the adjudicator of the EAD renewal application notices the need to address a potential break in employment authorization, it seems that issuance of the renewal EAD in this situation should also benefit from USCIS consideration. However, given the frequent delays in processing of EAD renewal applications,[180] and the fact that the USCIS guidance does not apply specifically to the situation of EADs for domestic or personal employees, the practitioner is advised to file the EAD renewal application as soon as possible.

It is possible to file an EAD renewal application up to 180 days in advance of the date of expiration of the current EAD.[181] This is a change from the prior practice of allowing EAD renewal applications no more than 120 days before the expiration of the current EAD, and is a result of the final regulation implemented on January 17, 2017, entitled "Retention of EB–1, EB–2, and EB–3 Immigrant Workers and Program Improvements Affecting High-Skilled Nonimmigrant Workers."[182] EAD

---

[174] 8 CFR §274a.2(b)(1)(vii).

[175] INA §§274A(a)(1)–(2); 8 CFR §274a.3 ("employer who continues the employment of an employee hired after Nov. 6, 1986, knowing that the employee is or has become an unauthorized alien with respect to that employment, is in violation" of U.S. immigration laws); 8 CFR §274a.14(a)(1)(i); INA §§274A(e)(5) and (f).

[176] *See., e.g.,* "California Service Center Processing Time Reports" http://www.aila.org/infonet/ processing-time-reports/csc, (updated monthly).

[177] "USCIS's SOPs for I-765 Processing" (undated; posted Sept. 7, 2007), AILA Doc. No. 07090761.

[178] *Id.*

[179] *Id.*

[180] "AILA Liaison/SCOPS Q&As" (Sept. 17, 2008), AILA Doc. No. 08092369.

[181] USCIS, "Employment Authorization Document" (updated Feb. 1, 2107), https://www.uscis.gov/ green-card/green-card-processes-and-procedures/employment-authorization-document.

[182] 81 Fed. Reg. 82398, 82455 (Jan. 17, 2017).

Copyright © 2017. American Immigration Lawyers Association. All rights reserved.

renewal applications filed before 180 days before expiration of the current EAD will either be treated as an application for a replacement EAD card, or will be denied.[183] If the B-1 extension and the EAD renewal application are approved, then the documents will most likely have expiration dates that are six months from the date of application, because this is the maximum extension permitted to domestic and personal employees in B-1 status.[184] For an employee whose services are demanded for more than one year, such as for a U.S. citizen on temporary assignment in the United States, these breaks in employment authorization may prove problematic. The practitioner is advised to contact clients regarding upcoming expiration dates and to encourage filing of extensions and EAD renewal applications as soon as possible. This may entail communicating the need to file the second extension and EAD renewal application immediately upon receipt of the first B-1 extension and EAD renewal or while the first extension remains pending.[185]

The practitioner should inform the client that the employer should maintain lawful immigration status in order to continue employing the personal or domestic worker by filing extension applications of his or her own,[186] and that the employee would be ineligible for this B-1 visa classification if the employer obtains permanent residence.[187] The practitioner is also advised to keep a tally of the potential dates of unauthorized employment by the employee and remind clients of the consequences of engaging in unauthorized employment, as discussed above.

The exception to the rule of unauthorized employment by the employee and potential liability for the employer is called the "receipt rule."[188] In the event that the document evidencing employment authorization is "lost, stolen, or damaged," an employee may present a receipt evidencing application of a replacement document and then must present the "replacement document within 90 days of the hire or, in the case of re-verification, the date employment authorization expires." It is notable, however, that the receipt rule applies only to replacement documents, and only in the situation of replacement because the original document was lost, stolen or damaged. The receipt rule does not apply to situations where an employee has applied for a

---

[183] "USCIS Liaison Update on EAD Extension Applications" (Feb. 14, 2008), AILA Doc. No. 08021468.

[184] 8 CFR §214.2(b)(1); "VSC Liaison Minutes" (Apr. 6, 2000), AILA Doc. No. 00040671.

[185] "VSC Practice Pointer: VSC Provides Guidance on Changing to and Extending B-1/B-2 Status" (Mar. 10, 2009), AILA Doc. No. 09031064.

[186] 9 FAM 402.2-5(D)(3).

[187] 9 FAM 402.2-5(D)(4).

[188] 8 CFR §274a.2(b)(1)(vi). Note that the "receipt rule" does not apply in these situations; it is only mentioned in the event that a client questions whether it would apply.

Copyright © 2017. American Immigration Lawyers Association. All rights reserved.

renewal of employment authorization, and an employee does not have employment authorization while the renewal application is pending with USCIS.[189]

The employee will not be able to apply for an SSN until he or she has an EAD.[190] Withholding of taxes may be delayed until the employee obtains an SSN, and taxes that were not previously withheld may have to be paid at a later date. Finally, if the employee has difficulty in establishing his or her nonimmigrant intent, as is frequently the case with au pairs or personal and domestic employees who are young, unmarried, and without their own families, a practitioner can discuss requesting a single use B-1 visa with limited duration or the posting of a bond, both discussed below.

2. Specific Situations

Certain situations are subject to additional scrutiny by consular officers. These B-1 visa applications should be supplemented with as much information as possible to avoid an erroneous denial.

a. Building and Construction-Related Activities

The Department of Homeland Security (DHS) and DOS categorically consider the performance of building or construction activities to be "local employment or labor for hire." Foreign nationals who seek B-1 visas to undertake these construction activities are ineligible for B-1 visas and status.[191] As stated by legacy INS, the "purpose of the rule is to insure that United States construction workers will not be denied access to construction jobs."[192]

The client should be advised of this prohibition. Then, in the event that a foreign national appropriately seeks a B-1 visa to observe work being performed to discuss specifications, as well as plan goals, and discuss progress in achieving the objectives, as discussed below,[193] the supporting documents should address this issue in a satisfactory manner by clarifying that the visa applicant will not perform any "'hands-on' construction work of a skilled or unskilled nature."[194]

One exception to the prohibition against performance of hands-on work by B-1 visitors is for those "otherwise qualified as B-1 nonimmigrants [who] may be issued

---

[189] Legacy INS, M. Cronin, "Standard Employment Authorization: Prohibition on Local Variations: Use of Receipts: Timely Adjudication: Interim Employment Authorization" (Mar. 10, 1998), AILA Doc. No. 98031091.

[190] 20 CFR §422.105; Social Security Administration, Immigration, "Visa Classifications that Allow You to Work in the U.S.," http://ssa.gov/immigration/visa.htm; see also "SSA POMS on Employment Authorization for Non-Immigrants" (July 5, 2013), AILA Doc. No. 13101142.

[191] 22 CFR §41.31(b)(1); 8 CFR §214.2(b)(5); 51 Fed. Reg. 44266 (Dec. 9, 1986).

[192] 51 Fed. Reg. 44266 (Dec. 9, 1986).

[193] "DOS on B-1s for Construction Work" (May 24, 2001), AILA Doc. No. 01053002.

[194] 51 Fed. Reg. 44266 (Dec. 9, 1986).

Copyright © 2017. American Immigration Lawyers Association. All rights reserved.

visas and may enter for the purpose of supervision or training of others engaged in building or construction work, but not for the purpose of actually performing any such building or construction work themselves."[195]

This exception was developed following the injunction in *International Union of Bricklayers v. Meese*,[196] which prohibited the admission of foreign nationals in B-1 status to install, service, or repair foreign-built equipment, and the subsequent outcry from U.S. industries, which complained of potential "losses of investment and lay-offs of American workers" and from foreign governments, who "viewed this new restriction as a constraint on trade and hinted at reciprocal actions."[197] The ultimate resolution prohibited issuance of B-1 visas and admission in B-1 status to foreign nationals who would engage in building or construction work, whether at the plant or onsite, but permitted the admission of B-1 nonimmigrants who would only supervise or train others performing building or construction work.[198]

DOS guidance states that the following activities are considered impermissible building or construction work:

- "The installation, maintenance, and repair of:
  - "Utility services;
  - "Any part of the fabric of any building or structure; and
  - "Installation of machinery or equipment to be an integral part of a building or structure; or
- "Work normally performed by laborers:
  - "Millwrights;
  - "Heat and frost insulators;
  - "Bricklayers;
  - "Carpenters and joiners;
  - "Electrical workers;
  - "Operating engineers (including heady equipment operators);
  - "Elevator constructors;
  - "Sheet metal workers;
  - "Teamsters;
  - "Boilermakers;

---

[195] 8 CFR §214.2(b)(5); *see also* 9 FAM 402-2.5(E)(1).
[196] 616 F. Supp. 1387 (N.D. Cal. 1985).
[197] 51 Fed. Reg. 44266 (Dec. 9, 1986).
[198] 51 Fed. Reg. 44266 (Dec. 9, 1986).

Copyright © 2017. American Immigration Lawyers Association. All rights reserved.

- – "Residential, commercial, or industrial painters (including the application of all surface coatings, no matter how applied);
- – "Bridge, structural, and ornamental ironworkers;
- – "Plumbers and pipefitters;
- – "Roofers;
- – "Plasterers;
- – "Cement masons; or
- ▪ "Work involving installation of:
  - – "Assembly lines;
  - – "Conveyor belts and systems;
  - – "Overhead cranes, heating, cooling, and ventilation or exhaust systems;
  - – "Elevators and escalators;
  - – "Boilers and turbines;
  - – "The dismantling or demolition of commercial or industrial equipment or machinery if the equipment or machinery is an integral part of a building or structure, whether onsite or in-plant; or
- ▪ "Site preparation work and services installation (*e.g.*, electricity, gas, water) and connection of such services to commercial or industrial equipment or machinery if the equipment or machinery is to be an integral part of a building or structure."[199]

The same DOS guidance addresses a few additional situations where use of the B-1 visa would be inappropriate and impermissible:

- ▪ Where foreign nationals will perform masonry and steelwork;

- ▪ Where foreign nationals will build "ornamental structures forming part of religious temples";

- ▪ Where foreign national "volunteers … will perform building and construction work for charitable organizations";[200] and

---

[199] "DOS on B-1s for Construction Work" (May 24, 2001), AILA Doc. No. 01053002.

[200] This prohibition would seem to prohibit use of the B-1 nonimmigrant category by foreign national volunteers participating in a "Habitat for Humanity"–type program or participating in rebuilding efforts, whether religious or humanitarian, following a catastrophe such as Hurricane Katrina.

Copyright © 2017. American Immigration Lawyers Association. All rights reserved.

- Where foreign nationals, who possess "unique skills," such as that of a master stonemason, will perform building and construction work.

In the event that an individual seeks to visit the United States to supervise or train others, who will, in turn, perform building or construction work, the support statement for the B-1 visa application should clearly state that the visa applicant will only provide supervision or training of the building or construction work. It is also advisable for the statement to proactively note that the visa applicant will not engage in any hands-on building or construction work, as the omission of this statement, combined with the trigger word of "construction," may result in the erroneous denial of the visa application. It would be unfortunate if the consular officer noticed the term "construction" in the support statement, mistakenly believed that the visa applicant would engage in building or construction work, and then denied the visa application because there was no affirmation that the visa applicant's duties would be limited to supervision and/or training. This would be an erroneous denial; but, as discussed in Volume 1: Chapter Two, "Basic Nonimmigrant Concepts," there is no review of a visa denial by the DOS, and a previous visa denial may have a negative impact on subsequent visa applications.

If applicable, an explanation of the visa applicant's managerial role abroad may be helpful in demonstrating that the visa applicant will not engage in hands-on building or construction work while in the United States. The rationale behind this approach is that, if the visa applicant does not perform skilled or unskilled labor abroad, but only supervises such labor or provides training on the labor abroad, then he or she may be less likely to deny a U.S. worker's access to building or construction jobs,[201] because a construction manager is a different occupational classification from a construction worker.[202] This approach is similar to the multinational manager immigrant visa petition, discussed in Volume 2: Chapter Three, "Immigrant Visa Petitions," in that a manager abroad is likely to perform primarily managerial duties in the United States.

Conversely, a visa applicant who is a professional or a skilled construction laborer abroad, or a visa applicant who has had no previous managerial, supervisory, or training experience abroad, may encounter difficulty in demonstrating that he or she will only supervise or train building or construction workers in the United States. One strategy to strengthen such a visa application is to provide concrete details on how the worker's experience with the foreign employer qualifies him or her to provide

---

[201] 51 Fed. Reg. 44266 (Dec. 9, 1986).

[202] Compare O*NET job descriptions for "Construction Managers," http://www.onetonline.org/link/summary/11-9021.00 and "First-Line Supervisors/Managers of Construction Trades and Extraction Workers," http://online.onetcenter.org/link/summary/47-1011.00?redir=47-1011.01, with O*NET job descriptions for "Construction Laborers," http://online.onetcenter.org/link/summary/47-2061.00 and "Construction Carpenters," http://online.onetcenter.org/link/summary/47-2031.01.

Copyright © 2017. American Immigration Lawyers Association. All rights reserved.

supervision or training to U.S. building or construction laborers. The aim is to connect the specific background of the visa applicant to the project in the United States in such a way as to demonstrate how the professional or skilled duties of the foreign employment are necessary to supervise and/or provide training on the construction activities in the United States.

For example, the building and construction may be performed pursuant to new methodologies that have been developed and perfected by the foreign employer or by construction firms in the particular foreign country. Alternatively, the U.S. construction project may be at the behest of the foreign company that employs the visa applicant, such as if the U.S. client contracted with the foreign company for a specific type of building or construction that cannot be managed or supervised by employees of a U.S. company.

Indeed, the visa applications for supervisors or trainers of building and construction workers should all benefit from an explanation of the details of the construction project, the necessity of an employee of a foreign company to supervise or provide training on the building or construction, and the qualification of the visa applicant to provide such supervision and training. As discussed above, these details should also provide information on the driving motivation for the U.S. visit.

b. Commercial and Industrial Activities

A foreign national may obtain a B-1 visa to perform hands-on work in the United States, as long as the hands-on work will be limited to the installation, service, or repair of commercial or industrial equipment or machinery that was purchased from a company located outside the United States.[203] The B-1 visitor may also train U.S. workers on how to perform such services, but, in all instances, "the contract of sale must specifically require the seller to provide such services or training and the visa applicant must possess specialized knowledge essential to the seller's contractual obligation to perform the services or training and must receive no remuneration from a U.S. source."[204] Other guidance states the additional requirement that the B-1 visit must take place within one year of the purchase of the equipment or machinery,[205] and allows for "the entry of service personnel coming to perform warranty work after installation of machinery purchased from a foreign company."[206] Although warranty work may well be included in the performance of service or repairs to equipment or machinery pursuant to a contractual obligation, it is helpful to have this explicit reference.

---

[203] 9 FAM 402.2-5(E)(1).

[204] *Id.*

[205] OI 214.2, "Special requirements for admission, extension, and maintenance of status"; 51 Fed. Reg. 44266 (Dec. 9, 1986).

[206] 51 Fed. Reg. 44266 (Dec. 9, 1986).

Copyright © 2017. American Immigration Lawyers Association. All rights reserved.

As discussed above, there previously was an injunction prohibiting the admission of B-1 visitors to install, service, or repair foreign-built equipment, as these activities were considered to be "labor for hire."[207] The injunction was subsequently lifted, however, pursuant to an agreement between the parties to the litigation, and legacy INS promulgated a new regulation which sought to balance the objectives of protecting U.S. workers and of avoiding restrictions on international trade.[208] Indeed, during the comment period for the new regulation, U.S. industries protested against potential "losses of investment and lay-offs of American workers," and foreign governments objected to the "constraint on trade and hinted at reciprocal actions."[209] The new regulation clearly prohibits B-1 visitors from providing hands-on construction or building work and reinstates the previously permissible admission of B-1 visitors to install, service, or repair equipment or machinery purchased from abroad.[210]

The FAM guidance does not offer a definition of "specialized knowledge" in the context of these B-1 commercial or industrial workers. In general, "specialized knowledge" is considered to be "special knowledge of the company product and its application in international markets"[211] or "an advanced level of knowledge of processes and procedures of the company."[212] This is interpreted by USCIS to mean knowledge that is "distinct or uncommon" as compared to the industry, or "greatly developed or further along in progress, complexity and understanding than that generally found within the employer."[213] For this type of B-1 visa application, "specialized knowledge" frequently entails an in-depth knowledge of the equipment or machinery, such that a person without such knowledge would be unable to install, service, or repair the equipment or machinery or would be unable to provide training on how to perform these activities. For a detailed discussion of the interpretation of the term "specialized knowledge" in the context of L petitions, where "specialized knowledge" is one of three critical eligibility requirements, see Volume 1: Chapter Eleven, "L-1 Visas and Status."

Appropriate evidence for this visa application includes the following:

- Copy of the dated contract of sale of the commercial or industrial equipment or machinery between the foreign seller and the U.S. buyer, stating the seller's

---

[207] 51 Fed. Reg. 44266 (Dec. 9, 1986); *International Union of Bricklayers v. Meese,* 616 F. Supp. 1387 (N.D. Cal. 1985). The case involved B-1 visitors who came to the United States to install a processing system onsite pursuant to a contractual obligation, because "it was not possible to premanufacture the entire system in West Germany."

[208] 51 Fed. Reg. 44266 (Dec. 9, 1986).

[209] *Id.*

[210] *Id.*

[211] INA §214(c)(2)(B).

[212] *Id.*

[213] USCIS, "L-1B Adjudications Policy," PM-602-0111 (Aug. 17, 2015), AILA Doc. No. 15081801.

Copyright © 2017. American Immigration Lawyers Association. All rights reserved.

obligation to provide installation, service, or repair of the purchased equipment or machinery or stating the seller's obligation to provide training on the installation, service, or repair;

- Copy of the foreign seller's certificates of incorporation or other documents evidencing the seller's status as a foreign company;

- Descriptions of the equipment or machinery purchased and their purpose;

- Evidence of the B-1 visitor's employment by the foreign seller;

- Statement from the foreign seller, including the following:
  - Confirmation that the B-1 visitor will receive no remuneration from a U.S. source;
  - Confirmation that the B-1 visitor will receive only remuneration or salary from the foreign seller during his or stay in the United States;
  - Explanation of the B-1 visitor's specialized knowledge;
  - Explanation of how this knowledge is essential to the seller's contractual obligation; and
  - Explanation of how this knowledge will be applied to install, service, or repair the equipment or machinery, or explanation of how this knowledge will be applied to train U.S. workers on the necessary installation, service, or repair; and

- Evidence of the B-1 visitor's educational qualifications, professional experience, or technical expertise, such as copies of diplomas, résumés, and other professional or vocational certificates.

For this subset, there is no explicit prohibition on payment or reimbursement for expenses incidental to the B-1 visitor's stay by a U.S. entity. Nevertheless, given the keen attention paid to this subset of the B-1 visa category by American unions and industries, risk-averse clients may wish to ensure that all expenses are paid from abroad.

c. Payment of Expenses from a U.S. Source

As discussed above, salary, wage, and other remuneration to the foreign national may not be paid from the United States, and "chargeback" situations, where the foreign firm is ultimately reimbursed by the U.S. company, constitute impermissible income from a U.S. source.[214] However, a U.S. company may provide an expense account or reimbursement for expenses that are incidental to the visit, such as for those costs associated with travel, meals, lodging, laundry, and other basic

---

[214] *See also Matter of G–*, 6 I&N Dec. 255 (BIA 1954). Although this case addressed B-1 status, as opposed to B-1 in lieu of H-1 or H-3 status, the BIA held that the "work which he does in the United States provides the entire source of his income," even though his salary was entirely paid by a foreign firm.

Copyright © 2017. American Immigration Lawyers Association. All rights reserved.

services.[215] The "incidental expenses may not exceed the actual reasonable expenses" incurred.[216] The reimbursement of expenses for costs incurred may not be "a disguised form of direct remuneration."[217]

d. The B Visa Applicant Is the Beneficiary of an Immigrant Visa Petition

As discussed in detail above, every B visa applicant is presumed to be an intending immigrant and is, therefore, subject to inquiry regarding nonimmigrant intent. Failure to establish nonimmigrant intent to the satisfaction of the consular officer results in visa denial. One of the facts considered by the consular officer is whether the visa applicant has taken any steps toward U.S. permanent residence, such as being the beneficiary of an immigrant visa petition. This information is gathered from Form DS-160, Nonimmigrant Visa Application.[218] An immigrant visa petition is a petition filed by a sponsoring U.S. company, U.S. citizen, or U.S. permanent resident to request an immigrant visa number for the foreign national beneficiary.[219]

Practitioners are advised to carefully counsel B-1 visa applicants in this situation. Although the FAM states that INA §214(b) "does not impose a separate standard on immigrant intent,"[220] and that the relevant requirement for the B visa category is whether the visa applicant has a residence abroad,[221] experience has shown that these visa applications are frequently denied because the consular officer doubted that the foreign national intended to maintain his or her foreign residence,[222] or visit the United States for "a period of specifically limited duration."[223] Establishing satisfaction of these two B visa eligibility requirements can be difficult if the applicant is the beneficiary of an immigrant visa petition. Establishing the applicant's credibility is critical.

Without other information, the consular officer may (and frequently does) presume that the visa applicant is attempting to arrive in the United States by the fastest means necessary and will permanently remain in the country, thereby overstaying and falling into unlawful immigration status. Moreover, taking such steps toward U.S. permanent residence is frequently considered to be evidence that the

---

[215] 9 FAM 402.205(F)(1).

[216] Id.

[217] Legacy INS, P. Virtue, "Classification of Visiting University Lecturers" (Aug. 20, 1993), 1 INS and DOJ Legal Opinions §93-61 (citing legacy OI 214.2(b), citing Matter of Hall, 18 I&N Dec. 203 (BIA 1982)).

[218] Form DS-160, https://ceac.state.gov/genniv/.

[219] For a detailed discussion of the immigrant visa petition, see Volume 2: Chapter Three, "The Immigrant Visa Petition."

[220] 9 FAM 401.1-3(E).

[221] 9 FAM 401.1-3(F)(1).

[222] 9 FAM 401.1-3(E) and (F)(1).

[223] 9 FAM 402.2-5(F)(1).

Copyright © 2017. American Immigration Lawyers Association. All rights reserved.

foreign national intends to abandon his or her foreign residence, since, after all, immigration does usually entail making a new home in a new place.

To overcome this misunderstanding, the visa applicant should present documents that clearly evidence the brief nature of the U.S. trip and for the appropriate B purpose, as well as his or her intent to maintain the foreign residence and return to the country of residence at the end of the visit. [224] The visa applicant should be able to concisely articulate these points during the visa interview; the practitioner may wish to prepare clients through the use of mock interviews.

For example, the visa applicant may be the unmarried son of a U.S. citizen and the beneficiary of an immigrant visa petition filed by his parent. Immigrant visa retrogression, which is when demand for a certain immigrant visa category outstrips the supply from the immigrant visa quotas, for such a petition may be more than seven years (and, for Mexican citizens, 21 years).[225] If the son applies for a B-1 visa to attend a professional conference in the United States, then, because an immigrant visa petition was filed, the consular officer may presume that the visa applicant intends to overstay his B-1 status and remain in the United States permanently.

To prevail over this erroneous assumption, the visa applicant should demonstrate how the purpose of his U.S. trip is to attend the professional conference, how the U.S. trip has a specific and limited duration (the time period of his attendance at the conference), how he will continue to maintain his foreign residence while visiting the United States, and how he will return to his foreign residence after the conference. This approach is akin to carving out a window of time, during which the U.S. visit will occur, to direct the focus of the consular officer, in the larger picture of the visa applicant's life and career. Additional helpful evidence may include an explanation of how attendance at this professional conference is necessary for his employment abroad and/or advantageous to his career in his home country. It is possible to also explain that attendance at the conference will be valuable for his overall career path, including his ultimate career plans for once he properly immigrates to the United States, but care should be taken to present these details in such a way that emphasizes the long-term career plans extending several years in the future (which is most likely when he will be able to immigrate to the United States) and contrasts the short-term plans for the U.S. visit. Similarly, the visa applicant could mention how he would not overstay in the United States because he knows he is eligible to lawfully immigrate to the country in the future. However, the practitioner may wish to discuss this strategy at length with the client;

---

[224] *See* U.S. Consulate in Santo Domingo, Dominican Republic, http://santodomingo.usembassy.gov/ atc-110523.html (updated May 23, 2011).

[225] DOS Visa Bulletin, https://www.travel.state.gov, and search for "Visa Bulletin." For a detailed discussion of immigrant visa retrogression, see Volume 2: Chapter Four, "Consular Processing, Adjustment of Status, and Permanent Residence Issues."

Copyright © 2017. American Immigration Lawyers Association. All rights reserved.

volunteering this information during the interview may backfire, as the consular officer may believe that the statements are made to merely deflect attention and that the opposite of the statements is the visa applicant's true intent.

It may be possible for an individual who has applied for an immigrant visa at a U.S. consulate abroad to obtain a B visa, but experience has shown that these B visa applications have even higher rates of denial. The immigrant visa application, which is made by a foreign national to a U.S. consulate abroad, and the immigrant visa interview at the U.S. consulate are the penultimate steps in obtaining U.S. permanent residence. The final step is to seek admission to the United States with the immigrant visa.[226] Because an immigrant visa application may be made only when an immigrant visa number is available, these individuals are typically closer to obtaining U.S. permanent residence, unlike beneficiaries of immigrant visa petitions, who may have to wait years before an immigrant visa number becomes available. B visa applicants who have already applied for immigrant visas are frequently directed to wait until the immigrant visa is issued. An exception may be made, however, for brief emergency travel to the United States.[227] Given that the legacy INS guidance specifically addresses emergency travel as a nonimmigrant by a U.S. lawful permanent resident and stipulates that the permanent residence need not be surrendered upon admission in nonimmigrant status, it seems that an exception may also be made for an individual who has applied for but not yet received an immigrant visa.[228]

e. The B Visa Applicant Has Family Members Who Are U.S. Citizens or Lawful Permanent Residents or Who Hold Other Nonimmigrant Status

A B visa applicant with immediate family members who are U.S. citizens or lawful permanent residents or who hold other nonimmigrant status should also be prepared to present additional evidence of nonimmigrant intent and the foreign residence. The consular officer may presume that the B visa applicant seeks to join his or her family member and remain in the United States beyond the period of authorized stay. Here, too, credibility of the applicant's claim will be at issue. This information is gathered from Form DS-160, Nonimmigrant Visa Application.[229] The strategy and helpful documents for such visa applications are described above in connection with B visa applications by individuals who are beneficiaries of immigrant visa petitions. The main difference is that this visa applicant should not be waiting to lawfully immigrate to the United States, since an immigrant visa petition has not been filed.

---

[226] For a detailed discussion of immigrant visa applications, see Volume 2: Chapter Four, "Consular Processing, Adjustment of Status, and Permanent Residence Issues."

[227] 14-1 (Legacy) INS Inspector's Field Manual 15.4, Ch. 15, "Requirements and Procedures for Nonimmigrant Classes."

[228] *Id.*

[229] DOS, "Form DS-160," https://ceac.state.gov/genniv/.

Copyright © 2017. American Immigration Lawyers Association. All rights reserved.

In addition, the visa applicant should be prepared to discuss whether an immigrant visa petition will be filed on his or her behalf by the citizen or permanent resident relative, as the consular officer may ask whether the B visa applicant has the intent to ultimately adjust status to that of a permanent resident.[230] In response, the B visa applicant should confirm his or her maintenance of a residence abroad and the lack of intent to abandon that residence.[231]

If the purpose of the U.S. trip is to visit with the citizen, permanent resident, or nonimmigrant relative(s), then this may also be emphasized, together with evidence establishing that the visit is truly for pleasure and in the nature of a vacation. For example, the B visa applicant may provide evidence of how his or her allotted vacation time from work will be used for this trip. Other helpful evidence includes explanations of a family event, such as a reunion, wedding, birthday party, baptism, bar or bat mitzvah, or other religious event, or funeral. The practitioner may wish to prepare the client for these questions through mock interviews.

Finally, if the purpose of the trip is to accompany or join the immediate nonimmigrant family member, then the foreign national should apply for a B-2 visa as an accompanying family member, as discussed below. If the B-2 visa application is made after the principal foreign national's visa application or admission to the United States, the practitioner may wish to advise the client on how to explain and document the reason(s) for the delay.

f. Business or Tourist Trips While a Nonimmigrant Petition Is Pending

A foreign national may wish to travel to the United States as a business visitor or tourist while a separate nonimmigrant visa petition, in which the foreign national is the beneficiary, is pending with USCIS. In general, these business or tourist visits are permissible, but the foreign national should be prepared to answer questions regarding his or her nonimmigrant intent and present supporting documents, such as itineraries, conference programs, or statements from the foreign employer and U.S. company in the case of B-1 in lieu of H-1 or H-3 visitors. As with foreign nationals who are beneficiaries of immigrant visa petitions, discussed above, the key is to emphasize the proper business or tourist purpose of the trip, including the specific plans and limited duration of the trip.

g. B Visa Application by an HIV-Positive Individual

Until 2010, being positive with the human immunodeficiency virus (HIV) was considered to be a ground of inadmissibility, and an HIV-positive foreign national who sought to visit the United States was required to apply for a waiver of the ground of inadmissibility. Effective January 4, 2010, however, HIV was removed from the

---

[230] 9 FAM 401.1-3(D).

[231] 9 FAM 401.1-3(E) and (F)(1).

Copyright © 2017. American Immigration Lawyers Association. All rights reserved.

list of communicable diseases.[232] Therefore individuals "will no longer be inadmissible ... based solely on the ground they are infected with HIV, and they will not be required to undergo HIV testing" for visa purposes. Further, applicants who are HIV-positive will no longer require waiver processing by the Department of Homeland Security."[233] A foreign national who was denied a B visa because of HIV-positive status may reapply.[234] For further discussion of this topic, see Volume 1: Chapter Two, "Basic Nonimmigrant Concepts," and Volume 2: Chapter Four, "Consular Processing, Adjustment of Status, and Permanent Residence Issues."

h. Chinese Nationals and EVUS

In November 2016, CBP began requiring that Chinese nationals who hold 10-year B visas enroll in the Electronic Visa Update System (EVUS). CBP describes the EVUS program as "designed to enhance border security in accordance with the bilateral arrangement with China to issue 10-year validity tourist and business visas."[235]

The requirement applies to all land, air, and sea travel. The individual must go online and complete biographic information.[236] At the time of this writing, there is no fee, but CBP "anticipates" that a fee will be implemented in the future,[237] and had at one point mentioned a fee of $150.[238] Both visitors obtaining new visas and those already holding 10-year visas must enroll, and cannot travel to the United States in B status until they enroll. Those already holding visas do not need to obtain a new visa. Enrollment is valid for two years or until the individual's passport expires, whichever comes first. The individual will at that point have to update the information in EVUS before traveling again to the United States.[239]

Visitors with B visas with shorter validity periods do not need to enroll in EVUS. Travelers from Hong Kong, Macau, or Taiwan with 10-year visas must enroll if they hold a Peoples Republic of China (PRC) passport. If, however, they hold another travel document, such as a Hong Kong SAR, Macau SAR, or Taiwan passport,

---

[232] 74 Fed. Reg. 56547 (Nov. 2, 2009).

[233] DOS, "Effective January 4, 2010 HIV Infection is Removed from CDC List of Communicable Diseases of Public Health Signficance" (Dec. 15, 2009), https://travel.state.gov/content/visas/en/news/effective-january-4--2010-hiv-infection-is-removed-from-the-cdc-.html.

[234] *Id.*

[235] "CBP Announces the Electronic Visa Update System" (Mar. 15, 2016), AILA Doc. No. 16031612.

[236] CBP, https://www.EVUS.gov.

[237] "CBP Now Requires EVUS Enrollments for Chinese National 10-Year Visa Holders" (Nov. 29, 2016), AILA Doc. No. 16112902.

[238] "AILA/U.S. CBP Office of Field Operations Meeting" (Apr. 6, 2016), AILA Doc. No. 16052700, item 14.

[239] CBP, "Electronic Visa Update System (EVUS) Frequently Asked Questions" (Feb. 26, 2016), AILA Doc. No. 16031612; https://www.cbp.gov/travel/international-visitors/electronic-visa-update-system-evus/frequently-asked-questions.

Copyright © 2017. American Immigration Lawyers Association. All rights reserved.

enrollment is not required. An individual who already qualified for a 10-year B visa by virtue of being a landed immigrant in Canada must enroll if he or she travels on a PRC passport.[240]

"Once enrollment information is submitted, a response is provided within 20 minutes. Response is either: enrolled, unsuccessful enrollment, pending, or DOS has revoked the visa and requires another application. Grounds for EVUS refusal include derogatory information learned subsequent to visa issuance, DOS revocation of a visa, or a lost or stolen passport. Visas are provisionally revoked pending successful EVUS enrollment."[241]

CBP "expects that this requirement may be applied to additional countries in the future."[242]

C. B Status for Canadian and Mexican Nationals

Pursuant to the North American Free Trade Agreement (NAFTA) Treaty, Canadian and Mexican nationals may engage in specific business activities that may not be considered "business" for nationals of other countries.[243] A NAFTA business visitor does not need to obtain employment authorization,[244] but he or she must be a "business person," which is defined as a Canadian or Mexican national "who is engaged in trade in goods, the provision of services or the conduct of investment activities."[245] As discussed in Volume 1: Chapter Two, "Basic Nonimmigrant Concepts," Canadian nationals are visa exempt, so they do not need to apply for B-1 visas at U.S. consulates abroad, whereas Mexican nationals who do not have Border Crossing Cards, as discussed below, need to apply for B visas. Although Canadian nationals may not be issued an I-94 card for a business or pleasure trip to the United States, a "Canadian citizen B-1 who requests documentation may be issued an arrival/departure record, Form I-94, in order to facilitate reentry and to reduce any uneasiness he or she may feel about working in the United States as a B-1 without documentation."[246] Note that Canadian and Mexican nationals must still hold valid nonimmigrant intent pursuant to INA §214(b) and must satisfy all of the other requirements for B-1 status, as discussed above, including source of remuneration abroad,[247] and other requirements for admission in nonimmigrant status.[248]

---

[240] *Id.*

[241] "Minutes from AILA/CBO Field Operations Liaison Meeting" (Nov. 4, 2016), AILA Doc. No. 17010304.

[242] *Id.*

[243] NAFTA Implementation Act, Pub. L. No. 103-182, 107 Stat. 2057.

[244] North American Free Trade Agreement, U.S.–Can.–Mex. (Dec. 17, 1992), 32 I.L.M. 289 (entered into force Jan. 1, 1994), Chap. 16, Annex 1603.

[245] North American Free Trade Agreement, U.S.–Can.–Mex. (Dec. 17, 1992), 32 I.L.M. 289 (entered into force Jan. 1, 1994), Article 1608.

[246] 16-1 OI Section 214.2, "Special requirements for admission, extension, and maintenance of status."

[247] 8 CFR §214.2(b)(4).

Copyright © 2017. American Immigration Lawyers Association. All rights reserved.

As with other B-1 visitors, performance of these activities must result in no income from a U.S. source, although the Canadian or Mexican national may receive an expense allowance or reimbursement.[249] Business visitors who seek B-1 admission pursuant to NAFTA must also present the following evidence:

- Evidence of Canadian or Mexican citizenship;

- Documents confirming that the foreign national is a "business person," as defined above;

- Documents describing the purpose of the U.S. visit; and

- "[E]vidence demonstrating that the proposed business activity is international in scope and that the business person is not seeking to enter the local labor market." The following evidence in turn may be presented to satisfy this requirement:

  – Evidence confirming that "the primary source of remuneration for the proposed business activity" is outside the United States; and

  – Evidence confirming that the "business person's principal place of business and the actual place of accrual of profits, at least predominantly, remain outside" the United States.[250]

Although the language of the NAFTA Treaty permits the acceptance of "an oral declaration" regarding "the principal place of business and the actual place of accrual of profits,"[251] the practitioner is advised to prepare a statement from the foreign national's employer and counsel the foreign national to present the executed statement when applying for admission. Affirmatively presenting such a statement may satisfy the need for further proof, if it should be required,[252] and save the time and expense of another application for admission. Supplementary evidence could be in the form of incorporation documents for the foreign enterprise, lease or property title for the premises of the place of business, paychecks issued from the foreign enterprise, and receipts or accounts receivable from sources outside the United States.

The practitioner should counsel against use of the B-1 category under NAFTA if the foreign national is the beneficiary of an immigrant visa petition. In addition to the

---

[248] 8 CFR §214.2(b)(4).

[249] 9 FAM 402.2-5(F)(1).

[250] North American Free Trade Agreement, U.S.–Can.–Mex. (Dec. 17, 1992), 32 I.L.M. 289 (entered into force Jan. 1, 1994), Chap. 16, Annex 1603.

[251] *Id.*

[252] *Id.*

Copyright © 2017. American Immigration Lawyers Association. All rights reserved.

immigrant intent concerns for B-1 visitors discussed above, the language of the NAFTA Treaty allows a foreign national to be granted "temporary entry," which is defined as "entry without the intent to establish permanent residence."[253] Legacy INS rejected application of the concept of "dual intent" to TN entries under NAFTA, noting that dual intent is "clearly inconsistent" with the aims of the NAFTA Treaty,[254] so it is highly likely that a foreign national who is pursuing permanent residence may be denied B-1 admission for failing to demonstrate purely nonimmigrant intent.

Because these provisions were negotiated pursuant to a free trade agreement with Canada and Mexico, the foreign enterprises, companies, and entities must be either Canadian or Mexican.[255] Therefore, all of the foreign enterprises discussed in this section must be Canadian or Mexican enterprises.[256] There is no explicit prohibition, however, on a Canadian national providing these services on behalf of a Mexican enterprise or vice versa. In addition, despite the similarities between the H-1B and TN nonimmigrant classifications, there is no "B-1 in lieu of TN" subset, because use of the B-1 category is for "foreign jobs that might temporarily require work in the United States incident to an international transaction, not [for] U.S. jobs."[257]

The following section discusses the permitted "business" activities, in which a Canadian or Mexican national may engage while holding B-1 status.[258] The categories were designed to represent "a complete business cycle,"[259] from start to finish. Many of the stipulated terms remain undefined in the NAFTA Treaty and guidance from DHS, DOS, and legacy INS, so the section will also suggest resources to consult for appropriate definitions. Appropriate evidence to document eligibility for these subsets may include copies of educational documents, résumés, and job descriptions from the foreign employer.

---

[253] North American Free Trade Agreement, U.S.–Can.–Mex. (Dec. 17, 1992), 32 I.L.M. 289 (entered into force Jan. 1, 1994), Chap. 16, Article 1608.

[254] 63 Fed. Reg. 1331 (Jan. 9, 1998); "INS Final Rule on Entry Under NAFTA" (Jan. 9, 1998), AILA Doc. No. 98010960.

[255] 8 CFR §214.2(b)(4); *see also* legacy INS, J. Bednarz, "CO 214b-C, CO 1815-C" (May 17, 1994), 71 Interp. Rel. 1247 (Sept. 12, 1994).

[256] For ease and brevity, throughout this section, these enterprises are termed "foreign enterprises" rather than "Canadian or Mexican enterprises."

[257] Legacy INS, Y. La Fleur, "File No. HQ 1815-C" (Dec. 21, 1995), *reproduced in* 73 *Interp. Rel.* 91 (Jan. 16, 1996).

[258] 8 CFR §214.2(b)(4); North American Free Trade Agreement, U.S.–Can.–Mex. (Dec. 17, 1992), 32 I.L.M. 289 (entered into force Jan. 1, 1994), Appendix 1603.A.1.

[259] 1 (Legacy) INS Inspector's Field Manual, Ch. 15, "NAFTA Admissions," 14-1 *INS Manuals* 15.5.

Copyright © 2017. American Immigration Lawyers Association. All rights reserved.

1. Research and Design

A foreign national who is a technical, scientific, or statistical researcher may conduct independent research or research on behalf of his or her foreign employer.[260] Given the absence of a clear definition of these terms, the practitioner may consider the interpretation of "independent research," as discussed above, and the common sense meanings of "technical," "scientific," "statistical," "researcher," and "research." The support statement detailing the purpose of the U.S. visit should explain how the proposed business activities are independent research or research on behalf of a foreign employer.

2. Growth, Manufacture, and Production

a. Harvester Owners

A harvester owner who will supervise a harvesting crew, who, in turn, has been "admitted under applicable law," may enter pursuant to NAFTA, as long as the harvesting will be of agricultural crops, including grain, fiber, fruit, and vegetables.[261] The foreign national should have evidence confirming ownership of the foreign harvesting enterprise, such as a certificate of incorporation and/or ledgers documenting ownership and control of stock. Although neither the language of the NAFTA Treaty nor the implementing regulation defines admission under applicable law, legacy INS interpreted this provision as referring to foreign nationals who have obtained H-2A status,[262] to perform agricultural labor or services.[263] There is no other employment-based nonimmigrant classification that would permit U.S. employment as a harvester.[264]

The harvesting crew could be comprised of U.S. workers, but employment of U.S. workers may make it difficult to demonstrate that the foreign national satisfies the requirements for B-1 admission under the NAFTA Treaty, as described above. For example, supervising a harvesting crew of U.S. workers could be interpreted as seeking to enter the U.S. labor market, and such a foreign national may need to present additional evidence to confirm that the principal place of business and source of remuneration is outside the United States and that the accrual of profits is at least predominantly outside the United States, as discussed above. The practitioner may also wish to consider the BIA's analysis in *Matter of M–*,[265] which

---

[260] 8 CFR §214.2(b)(4)(i)(A).

[261] 8 CFR §214.2(b)(4)(i)(B)(1).

[262] 1 OIs, 16-1 OI Section 214.2, "Special requirements for admission, extension, and maintenance of status."

[263] INA §101(a)(15)(H)(ii)(A); 8 CFR §214.2(h)(1)(ii)(C).

[264] The TN classification for nationals of Canada and Mexico is limited to occupations which are considered professional, and a harvester is not a professional occupation. *See, e.g.,* O*NET, "Summary Report for Farmworkers and Laborers, Crop," http://online.onetcenter.org/link/summary/45-2092.02.

[265] *Matter of M–*, 6 I&N Dec. 533 (BIA 1955).

Copyright © 2017. American Immigration Lawyers Association. All rights reserved.

entailed denial of B-1 status to foreign nationals who sold Christmas trees in the United States, as noted above.

The practitioner should counsel the client that the foreign national may only supervise the work of the harvesting crew; the supervisor should not engage in any harvesting work him– or herself. It seems highly likely that harvesting work would be considered hands-on work and local labor for hire, as discussed above. It also seems likely that the concerns and prohibitions applicable to construction and building managers and supervisors would apply to harvesting supervisors. The practitioner may wish to affirmatively confirm in the support statement that the supervisor will engage in no hands-on harvesting work and will only supervise the harvesting crew who will perform such harvesting work.

In addition to the documents detailed above, the foreign national should present evidence of his or her ownership of the harvesting operation, as discussed above. The foreign national should also be prepared to submit evidence that his or her harvesting crew has approval to perform H-2A duties, whether in the form of USCIS approval notices and/or H-2A visas.

b. Purchasing and Production Managers

A manager of purchasing and production activities may be admitted in B-1 status pursuant to NAFTA if he or she will conduct commercial transactions for a foreign enterprise.[266] This provision may not add anything different from the standard B-1 duties entailing business visitors who will engage in commercial transactions. General job descriptions for purchasing and production managers have been provided by the Department of Labor (DOL).[267] For a discussion of what constitutes "commercial transactions," see above.

The practitioner should note that a purchasing manager may be eligible for B-1 status under NAFTA pursuant to either this section or to the section on sales, where a buyer may purchase for a foreign enterprise, as discussed below. As a general rule, the practitioner may wish to counsel the client to request the foreign national's admission under this section where the purchasing manager will conduct the broader scope of "commercial transactions" rather than the narrower range of activities that are considered purchasing or buying, as discussed below.

---

[266] 8 CFR §214.2(b)(4)(i)(B)(2).

[267] O*NET, "Summary Report for Purchasing Managers," http://www.onetonline.org/link/summary/11-3061.00, and "Summary Report for Industrial Production Managers," http://www.onetonline.org/link/summary/11-3051.00.

Copyright © 2017. American Immigration Lawyers Association. All rights reserved.

3. Marketing

a. Market Researchers and Analysts

Market researchers and analysts are eligible for B-1 status under NAFTA, whether the research or analysis will be independent or on behalf of a foreign enterprise.[268] General job descriptions for market researchers and analysts have been provided by DOL.[269] For a discussion of interpreting the term "independent research," see above. In addition to the documents detailed above, it may be helpful to provide documents describing the research to be conducted in the United States and explaining how the research may be helpful to the foreign national or entity.

b. Trade Fair and Promotional Personnel

Foreign nationals who are trade fair and promotional personnel attending a trade convention may be admitted as B-1 under NAFTA.[270] Given that these individuals are listed under the "Marketing" section, it seems that the foreign nationals should engage in activities to market products and/or services at a trade fair or convention. Moreover, it seems likely that these individuals should not engage in hands-on building or construction of the trade booths and equipment, as with foreign national employees of international fairs and expositions,[271] as discussed above. General job descriptions for these occupations are provided by DOL.[272]

In general, trade fair and trade conventions allow companies to market, display, and demonstrate new products and services to an audience of representatives from the industry and/or the public. One example of a trade fair is the annual Consumer Electronics Show, which is sponsored by the Consumer Electronics Association.[273] The NAFTA subset is broader than the B-1 subset provided by the FAM for foreign national employees of international fairs and expositions,[274] because the fair or convention need not be international, although the business activity must be international in scope. The NAFTA subset is narrower than the FAM provision, however, because the fair or convention must be a trade event and because the

---

[268] 8 CFR §214.2(b)(4)(i)(C)(1).

[269] O*NET, "Summary Report for Market Research Analyst," http://online.onetcenter.org/link/summary/19-3021.00 and "Summary Report for Survey Researchers," http://online.onetcenter.org/link/summary/19-3022.00. Note that the Department of Labor (DOL) does not provide separate job descriptions for market researchers and market analysts.

[270] 8 CFR §214.2(b)(4)(i)(C)(2).

[271] 9 FAM 402.2-5(E)(7).

[272] O*NET, "Summary Report for Marketing Managers," http://www.onetonline.org/link/summary/11-2021.00, "Summary Report for Advertising and Promotions Managers," http://online.onetcenter.org/link/summary/11-2011.00, "Summary report for Demonstrators and Product Promoters," http://online.onetcenter.org/link/summary/41-9011.00, "Summary Report for Meeting and Convention Planners," http://online.onetcenter.org/link/summary/13-1121.00.

[273] Consumer Electronics Show, http://www.cesweb.org/default.asp.

[274] 9 FAM 402.2-5(E)(7).

Copyright © 2017. American Immigration Lawyers Association. All rights reserved.

foreign national must be "trade fair or promotional personnel" rather than merely an employee. The practitioner should consider these points when advising the client on the appropriate subset under which to request B-1 admission or visa.

4. Sales

a. Sales Representatives and Agents

Sales representatives and agents, who will take orders or negotiate contracts for goods or services for a foreign enterprise, are eligible for B-1 status pursuant to NAFTA, as long as they will not deliver the goods or provide services.[275] General job descriptions for sales representatives and agents have been provided by DOL.[276] Notably, this B-1 subset under NAFTA seems to mirror the guidance on how appropriate business activities include taking orders, as analyzed in *Matter of Hira*,[277] as discussed above, and on how negotiating contracts is an appropriate B-1 business activity, as discussed above. The sale may be made to an individual or entity end-user.[278]

Nevertheless, admission as a B-1 visitor under NAFTA may afford the foreign national more flexibility. NAFTA specifically allows sales representatives and agents to take orders and negotiate contracts, whereas the standard B-1 subset from the FAM may require a showing that the foreign national has the authority to take orders and/or negotiate contracts on behalf of the foreign enterprise.

B-1 visitors under NAFTA are not precluded from delivering goods in certain circumstances, as discussed below. However, in those cases, the distribution is accomplished by "transportation operators" and not by sales representatives and agents. The practitioner should advise the client against attempting to cobble the two separate provisions together, as the regulation specifically prohibits sales representatives and agents from delivering goods. Legacy INS guidance indicates, however, that this preclusion applies only to the same foreign national selling and

---

[275] 8 CFR §214.2(b)(4)(i)(D)(1).

[276] O*NET, "Summary Report for Sales Managers," http://www.onetonline.org/link/summary/11-2022.00, "Summary Report for Advertising Sales Agents," http://www.onetonline.org/link/summary/41-3011.00, "Summary Report for Insurance Sales Agents, http://online.onetcenter.org/link/summary/41-3021.00, "Summary Report for Sales Agents, Securities and Commodities," http://online.onetcenter.org/link/summary/41-3031.01, "Summary Report for Sales Agents, Financial Services," http://online.onetcenter.org/link/summary/41-3031.02, "Summary Report for Sales Representatives, Wholesale and Manufacturing, Technical and Scientific Products," http://online.onetcenter.org/link/summary/41-4011.00, "Summary Report for Sales Representatives, Except Technical and Scientific Products," http://www.onetonline.org/link/summary/41-4012.00, and "Summary Report for Sales Engineers," http://www.onetonline.org/link/summary/41-9031.00.

[277] *Matter of Hira*, 11 I&N Dec. 824 (BIA 1965, 1966; AG 1966).

[278] 16-1 OI Section 214.2, "Special requirements for admission, extension, and maintenance of status."

Copyright © 2017. American Immigration Lawyers Association. All rights reserved.

delivering the goods on the same trip. The foreign national may make a subsequent trip to deliver the goods.[279]

The prohibition on providing services in the United States is analyzed in *Matter of Neill*,[280] as noted above. In short, a foreign national may perform business activities that are a necessary incident to international trade or commerce, as discussed above. A foreign national may not, however, provide services, except for certain limited circumstances discussed above, because providing services, whether skilled, unskilled, or professional, is considered to be "labor for hire" in competition with U.S. workers,[281] and, therefore, precluded by the U.S. immigration laws.[282]

Foreign nationals seeking B-1 admission under NAFTA pursuant to this subset may submit evidence of the orders to be taken or the contracts to be negotiated. The practitioner is advised to include in the statement from the foreign employer that the foreign national will not deliver goods or provide services.

b. Buyers

In addition, buyers who will purchase for a foreign enterprise may be admitted in B-1 status under NAFTA.[283] General job descriptions of buyers have been provided by DOL; the practitioner should note that the job descriptions specifically state that purchasing agents may engage in the negotiation of contracts pursuant to the purchases.[284]

As noted above, a purchasing manager may be eligible for B-1 admission pursuant to NAFTA either as a buyer under this section or as a purchasing manager who will conduct "commercial transactions" on behalf of a foreign enterprise, as discussed above. The practitioner should consider which section is more applicable to the situation at hand. The activities that are considered "purchasing" are limited to actual sales from the farm, manufacturer, or supplier,[285] whereas "commercial transactions" may also include "marketing, distribution, advertisement, negotiation, procurement, transmission, or transportation of goods or services."[286] However, if a foreign

---

[279] *Id.*

[280] 15 I&N Dec. 331 (BIA 1975).

[281] *Matter of Neill*, 15 I&N Dec. 331 (BIA 1975).

[282] INA §101(a)(15)(B).

[283] 8 CFR §214.2(b)(4)(i)(D)(2).

[284] O*NET, "Summary Report for Purchasing Managers," http://www.onetonline.org/link/summary/11-3061.00, "Summary Report for Purchasing Agents and Buyers, Farm Products," http://online.onetcenter.org/link/summary/13-1021.00, and "Summary Report for Wholesale and Retail Buyers, Except Farm Products," http://www.onetonline.org/link/summary/13-1022.00.

[285] *The American Heritage Dictionary of the English Language*, 4th Ed., Houghton Mifflin Company, 2004, http://dictionary.reference.com/browse/purchase.

[286] OI Section 214.2, "Special requirements for admission, extension, and maintenance of status."

Copyright © 2017. American Immigration Lawyers Association. All rights reserved.

national is a buyer, but not a manager, either of function or personnel,[287] then it seems that he or she would not qualify for admission as a purchasing manager who will conduct commercial transactions, in which case application for B-1 admission under NAFTA as a buyer would be more appropriate.

Foreign nationals who seek B-1 admission under NAFTA pursuant to this provision may provide evidence of the goods to be purchased. The statement from the foreign employer may confirm that the goods will be purchased for a foreign enterprise.

5. Distribution

a. Transportation Operators

A Canadian or Mexican national may also engage in certain distribution and/or delivery activities. The range of permitted and forbidden activities arose from BIA case law.[288] A Canadian or Mexican national must be a "transportation operator," and U.S. duties must fall within one of the following categories:

- Transportation of goods or passengers to the United States from Canada or Mexico; or

- Loading and transporting goods or passengers from the United States to Canada or Mexico, with no unloading in the United States.[289]

A "transportation operator" is "a natural person, other than a tour bus operator, including relief personnel accompanying or following to join, necessary for the operation of a vehicle for the duration of a trip,"[290] or the "operator of a transportation vehicle."[291] In general, foreign nationals may engage in the transportation of goods and passengers in the stream of international commerce, which entails a point of origin or destination in Canada or Mexico.[292] For this subset in particular, legacy INS guidance emphasized the purpose of preventing "[p]urely domestic service or solicitation, in competition with United States operators."[293] It is likely that transportation operators

---

[287] For a discussion of the interpretations of function managers and personnel managers under U.S. immigration law, see Volume 1: Chapter Eleven, "L-1 Visas and Status."

[288] *Matter of Camilleri*, 17 I&N Dec. 441 (BIA 1980) and *Matter of Cote*, 17 I&N Dec. 336 (BIA 1980).

[289] 8 CFR §214.2(b)(4)(i)(E)(1).

[290] 1 NAFTA Handbook, 14-1 INS Manuals Annex 1603 (Nov. 1999). *See also,* 16-1 OI Section 214.2, "Special requirements for admission, extension, and maintenance of status" (providing truck driver as an example of a transportation operator).

[291] Legacy INS, M. Pearson, "Tour Bus Operators and Other Transportation Operators Applying for Admission as B-1 Visitors, for Business" (July 2, 1998), AILA Doc. No. 06081766.

[292] Legacy INS, G. Rees III, "Business Visitor (B-1) Issues Related to North American Free Trade Agreement (NAFTA) Negotiations" (May 29, 1992), 70 Interp. Rel. 1653 (Dec. 13, 1993), and 1 INS and DOJ Legal Opinions §92-28.

[293] 8 CFR §214.2(b)(4)(i)(E)(1).

Copyright © 2017. American Immigration Lawyers Association. All rights reserved.

will carry goods more often than passengers, as many activities relating to the transportation of passengers will fall under the provisions for tourism personnel and tour bus operators, discussed below. Two examples of transportation operators who will carry passengers and who are not considered tourism personnel or tour bus operators are taxi drivers and passenger-van operators. These foreign nationals "may enter the United States to pick up passengers for delivery to Canada pursuant to an oral or written contract for services; however, no intermediate loading and delivery of passengers within the United States is permissible."[294]

Transportation operators may not make deliveries in the United States, unless "all goods or passengers to be delivered were loaded" abroad.[295] Transportation operators also may not load goods or passengers in the United States, unless "all goods or passengers to be loaded will be delivered" in Canada or Mexico."[296] Any goods or passengers loaded in the United States must be transported to Canada or Mexico,[297] as the loading should be a "necessary incident" of international commerce.[298]

What is not permitted is "ordinary cabotage," which is also termed as "point-to-point loading and delivering,"[299] and which is "carrying goods or passengers picked up at one point in the United States and dropped off at another point in the United States."[300] The transportation operator may not perform any "intermediate loading and unloading or delivery" in the United States, even if the delivery would make economic sense because it is "on the way."[301] Even if the goods transported originated from Canada or Mexico, the focus of the inquiry is not on whether the "overall nature of the transportation" is international or on whether the transportation is a "continuation of an international transaction"; the regulation instead considers the act of transportation, such that a foreign national may not load and deliver in the United States.[302] As stated by CBP guidance:

---

[294] OI Section 214.2, "Special requirements for admission, extension, and maintenance of status."

[295] 8 CFR §214.2(b)(4)(i)(E)(1).

[296] *Id.*

[297] Legacy INS, P. Virtue, "Admissibility of Canadian Log Loaders" (Oct. 26, 1993), 1 INS and DOJ Legal Opinions §93-86.

[298] Legacy INS, M. Pearson, "Tour Bus Operators and Other Transportation Operators Applying for Admission as B-1 Visitors, for Business" (July 2, 1998), AILA Doc. No. 06081766; *see also* CBP, "How Do I Enter the United States as a Commercial Truck Driver?" (Feb. 28, 2003), https://www.cbp.gov/border-security/ports-entry/cargo-security/carriers/land-carriers/how. For a discussion of interpretations of the term "incident," see above.

[299] Legacy INS, G. Rees III, "Business Visitor (B-1) Issues Related to North American Free Trade Agreement (NAFTA) Negotiations" (May 29, 1992), 70 Interp. Rel. 1653 (Dec. 13, 1993).

[300] Legacy INS, M. Pearson, "Tour Bus Operators and Other Transportation Operators Applying for Admission as B-1 Visitors, for Business" (July 2, 1998), AILA Doc. No. 06081766

[301] CBP, "How Do I Enter the United States as a Commercial Truck Driver?" (Feb. 28, 2003), https://www.cbp.gov/border-security/ports-entry/cargo-security/carriers/land-carriers/how.

[302] *Id.*

Copyright © 2017. American Immigration Lawyers Association. All rights reserved.

"Cargo that has its origin and final destination within the United States generally moves in the stream of domestic, rather that international commerce. The mere fact that goods originate from a foreign source does not make such goods 'foreign' for purposes of immigration laws. The goods must remain in the international stream of commerce—once they have come to rest they assume a domestic character.... The entry of the driver must be for the purpose of an international movement of goods."[303]

However, as long as the purpose of the transportation remains international, the duration of the driving and the status of the foreign national as a "relay driver" are not pertinent.[304] Therefore, a "relay driver" is eligible for B-1 admission under NAFTA, even if his or her "portion of the driving is to be performed solely within the United States," as long as the "points of origin and/or destination are outside the United States," because the driving in the United States is "merely the domestic portion of an international trip."[305] Indeed, the relay driver may be admitted even if he or she is not accompanied by the transportation vehicle.[306]

In the event that the foreign national driver is permitted to operate only within a specified geological area, whether by the Interstate Commerce Commission or by another agency, then B-1 admission under NAFTA and performance of the business activities must also be limited to the specified geographical area.[307] The legacy INS guidance likened these conditions on admission to the conditions on admission applied to United Nations diplomats of "governments not recognized by the United States."[308]

The rules regarding transporting tractors and trailers are similar to those regarding transporting goods, and the loading, unloading, and pick up of trailers in the United States may be likened to loading, unloading, and delivering goods in the United States. A foreign national truck driver may "deadhead" by taking an empty trailer from one U.S. location to another U.S. location only if the trailer is "either the one the driver came in with or the one he or she is departing with"; he or she may not "haul an empty trailer from one location to drop it off at another location."[309] The

---

[303] *Id.*

[304] Legacy INS, G. Rees III, "Business Visitor (B-1) Issues Related to North American Free Trade Agreement (NAFTA) Negotiations" (May 29, 1992), 70 Interp. Rel. 1653 (Dec. 13, 1993).

[305] *Id.*

[306] *Id.*

[307] Legacy INS, G. Rees III, "Regulating Entry of Mexican Truck Drivers into U.S." (July 1, 1992), 1 INS and DOJ Legal Opinions §92-30.

[308] *Id.*

[309] CBP, "How Do I Enter the United States as a Commercial Truck Driver?" (Feb. 28, 2003), www.cbp.gov/border-security/ports-entry/cargo-security/carriers/land-carriers/how.

Copyright © 2017. American Immigration Lawyers Association. All rights reserved.

foreign national driver may enter the United States with an empty tractor in order to "pick up" an empty trailer and deliver the empty trailer to Canada or Mexico."[310]

A foreign national truck driver may enter the United States with an empty tractor to "pick up a loaded trailer" or to pick up goods "previously brought from Canada or Mexico and left at the port-of-entry or a Customs warehouse or lot for government inspection or entry processing by a government agency."[311] The driver of the empty tractor need not have transported the goods from Canada or Mexico to the United States, but this exception applies only "when the goods have been held for federal inspection by a government agency"; the exception does not apply "to goods that have already cleared inspection."[312] The driver may also unload a trailer in one U.S. location, "drive empty" to another U.S. location, and pick up a loaded trailer from the second location to deliver it to Canada or Mexico.[313]

There is no specific time limit on the amount of time the drivers may remain in the United States, other than "the time necessary to accomplish the purpose of admission" (*i.e.*, carry out the delivery of goods).[314]

Tour guides and tour bus drivers are allowed to meet and travel with passengers in the United States, as discussed below, but this activity is specifically permitted by the regulations and is "not analogous to the point-to-point delivery of goods in the United States."

Foreign national transportation operators may submit evidence of qualifying for this subset, such as contracts detailing the goods to be transported and documents describing the need for the transportation from abroad to the United States or vice versa. The practitioner may wish to include affirmative statements to confirm that the transportation operator will not engage in any impermissible activities, such as point-to-point hauling, as described above.

b. Customs Brokers

In addition, Canadian customs brokers are eligible for B-1 admission under NAFTA, as long as they will perform "brokerage duties associated with the export of goods from the United States to or through Canada."[315] It is important to note that, following negotiations for the NAFTA Treaty, Mexico opted against allowing the temporary entry of customs brokers into the signatory countries. Therefore, Mexican nationals do not have the protection of the NAFTA Treaty when seeking admission as

---

[310] *Id.*

[311] *Id.*

[312] *Id.*

[313] *Id.*

[314] "AILA National Liaison Meeting with U.S. Customs and Border Protection Office of Field Operations" (Oct. 8, 2015), AILA Doc. No. 16031104, item 11.

[315] 8 CFR §214.2(b)(4)(i)(E)(2).

Copyright © 2017. American Immigration Lawyers Association. All rights reserved.

customs brokers, although this should not preclude B-1 admission to the United States if the Mexican national customs broker meets the requirements for B-1 admission in general.[316] Therefore, if the client should wish for a Mexican national customs broker to seek admission in B-1 status, then the practitioner should work with the client to ensure that the Mexican national is eligible for B-1 admission pursuant to one of the FAM provisions discussed above and below.

The practitioner should also note that the language of the regulation differs from legacy INS guidance, which addressed NAFTA's predecessor, the Free Trade Agreement (FTA) with Canada, and which indicated that the custom brokerage duties could involve the export of goods from the United States or Canada to or through Canada or the United States.[317] Although legacy INS guidance indicates that the brokerage activities should involve exportation of goods from the United States "into or through Canada," and although the same legacy INS guidance indicates that a foreign national may be admitted to the United States to engage in export and import of goods,[318] risk-averse clients may wish to limit the activities of B-1 customs brokers to those involving export of goods from the United States and to or through Canada.

Customs brokers may "advise at processes, such as NAFTA verifications (determinations whether goods are entitled to NAFTA treatment for purposes of customs assessment)."[319] Although there is not an exact match for a "customs broker" job description, DOL has provided related job descriptions.[320] The practitioner may

---

[316] Legacy INS, G. Rees III, "Business Visitor (B-1) Issues Related to North American Free Trade Agreement (NAFTA) Negotiations" (May 29, 1992), 70 Interp. Rel. 1653 (Dec. 13, 1993).

[317] *Id.*

[318] *Id.* Boos and R. Pauw, "Reasserting the Right to Representation in Immigration Matters Arising at Ports of Entry" (Apr. 1, 2004), 9-7 Bender's Immigr. Bull. 1 (2004).

[318] DOT definition, 186.117-018 Customs Broker (financial), http://www.oalj.dol.gov/PUBLIC/DOT/REFERENCES/DOTALPHA.HTM (scroll down to "customs broker") and O*NET, "Summary Report for Cargo and Freight Agents," http://online.onetcenter.org/link/summary/43-5011.00. The practitioner should note that the DOT definitions does not have a helpful corresponding O*NET job code. O*NET Crosswalk, http://online.onetcenter.org/crosswalk/DOT?s=186.117-018&g=Go, and O*NET, "Summary Report for Business Operations Specialists, All Other," http://online.onetcenter.org/link/summary/13-1199.99. For a detailed discussion of the O*NET job codes and use of the Crosswalk tool, see Volume 2: Chapter Two, "Labor Certification Applications."

[318] CBP, "Becoming a Customs Broker," https://www.cbp.gov/trade/programs-administration/customs-brokers/becoming-customs-broker.

[318] 1 (Legacy) INS

[319] G. Boos and R. Pauw, "Reasserting the Right to Representation in Immigration Matters Arising at Ports of Entry" (Apr. 1, 2004), 9-7 Bender's Immigr. Bull. 1 (2004).

[320] DOT definition, 186.117-018 Customs Broker (financial), http://www.oalj.dol.gov/PUBLIC/DOT/REFERENCES/DOTALPHA.HTM (scroll down to "customs broker") and O*NET, "Summary Report for Cargo and Freight Agents," http://online.onetcenter.org/link/summary/43-5011.00. The practitioner should note that the DOT definitions does not have a helpful corresponding O*NET job code. O*NET Crosswalk, http://online.onetcenter.org/crosswalk/DOT?s=186.117-018&g=Go, and O*NET, "Summary Report for Business Operations Specialists, All Other,"

Cont'd

Copyright © 2017. American Immigration Lawyers Association. All rights reserved.

find it helpful to consider these job descriptions when evaluating whether B-1 admission under NAFTA would be appropriate, as well as guidance from CBP regarding the job duties of customs brokers in general, although the CBP guidance addresses U.S. customs brokers.[321]

Similarly, legacy INS guidance indicates that customs brokers may "provid[e] consulting services regarding the facilitation of the import or export of goods."[322] Unfortunately, no corresponding statement is made in the regulations,[323] so the practitioner may wish to discuss the nature of the foreign national's proposed job duties and counsel against use of the B-1 classification under NAFTA for a customs broker who will solely provide such consulting services.

In addition to the standard documents for B-1 visitors under NAFTA, discussed above, Canadian national customs brokers may present documents detailing the goods to be exported from the United States to or through Canada.

6. After-Sales Service

Foreign nationals who are installers, repair and maintenance personnel, and supervisors, and who possess "specialized knowledge essential to the seller's contractual obligation," may be admitted in B-1 status under NAFTA if they will perform services or train workers to perform services, pursuant to a warranty or other service contract that is incidental to the sale of commercial or industrial equipment or machinery.[324] The equipment or machinery must have been purchased from a Canadian or Mexican enterprise, must have been manufactured outside the United States,[325] and must not be of U.S. origin.[326] The services or training may be provided throughout the "life of the warranty or service agreement."[327] The life of the warranty or service agreement, in turn, "may include a renewable service contract,"[328] if "the language concerning the life of a renewable service contract must have been included in clear and definitive terms in the original contract at the point of sale."[329]

---

http://online.onetcenter.org/link/summary/13-1199.99. For a detailed discussion of the O*NET job codes and use of the Crosswalk tool, see Volume 2: Chapter Two, "Labor Certification Applications."

[321] CBP, "Becoming a Customs Broker," https://www.cbp.gov/trade/programs-administration/customs-brokers/becoming-customs-broker.

[322] 1 (Legacy) INS Inspector's Field Manual, Ch. 15, "NAFTA Admissions," 14-1 INS Manuals 15.5.

[323] 8 CFR §214.2(b)(4)(i)(E).

[324] 8 CFR §214.2(b)(4)(i)(F).

[325] Id.

[326] OI Section 214.2, "Special requirements for admission, extension, and maintenance of status."

[327] 8 CFR §214.2(b)(4)(i)(F).

[328] OI Section 214.2, "Special requirements for admission, extension, and maintenance of status."

[329] 1 (Legacy) INS Inspector's Field Manual, Ch. 15, "NAFTA Admissions," 14-1 INS Manuals 15.5.

Copyright © 2017. American Immigration Lawyers Association. All rights reserved.

For a discussion of the history of and issues surrounding B-1 admission for these foreign nationals, as well as appropriate evidence, see above. Notably, however, this subset under NAFTA differs from the standard permissible B-1 activities in several ways. First, the services and training may be provided for the duration of the warranty or service agreement, without the one-year limitation placed on nationals of countries other than Canada and Mexico.[330] Second, computer software is included in the category of commercial and industrial equipment or machinery.[331] Third, the after-sales service and training may be provided by a third party, rather than only the seller, as long as "the third party agreement was contracted at the time of sale."[332]

It is also possible that the U.S. entity, which will receive the after-sales service, need not be the original purchaser, based on legacy INS guidance that addressed the FTA between the United States and Canada.[333] Equipment or machinery that was leased by the original purchaser to another U.S. entity may be serviced, "as long as such equipment or machinery remains under ownership of the original purchaser and the warranty or service agreement is still in effect."[334] There can, however, be no after-sales service of "industrial equipment or machinery, or computer software leased from enterprises outside the United States";[335] the service must be pursuant to a warranty or service agreement incident to sale.[336]

DOL has provided template job descriptions for the relevant occupations.[337] Canadian and Mexican nationals seeking B-1 admission under NAFTA for this subset may submit the contract of sale, evidence of the warranty or service agreement, and

---

[330] *Cf.* 8 CFR §214.2(b)(4)(i)(F) and OI Section 214.2, "Special requirements for admission, extension, and maintenance of status."

[331] *Cf.* 8 CFR §214.2(b)(4)(i)(F) and 9 FAM 402.2(E)(1).

[332] 8 CFR §214.2(b)(4)(i)(F). *Cf.* 9 FAM 402.2(E)(1).

[333] OI Section 214.2, "Special requirements for admission, extension, and maintenance of status."

[334] *Id.*

[335] *Id.*

[336] Legacy INS, J. Bednarz, "CO 214b-C, CO 1815-C" (May 17, 1994), 71 Interp. Rel. 1247 (Sept. 12, 1994).

[337] O*NET, "Summary Report for First-Line Supervisors/Managers of Mechanics, Installers, and Repairers," http://online.onetcenter.org/link/summary/49-1011.00, "Summary for Industrial Machinery Mechanics," http://online.onetcenter.org/link/summary/49-9041.00, "Summary Report for Medical Equipment Repairers," http://online.onetcenter.org/link/summary/49-9062.00, "Summary Report for Telecommunications Equipment Installers and Repairers, Except Line Installers," http://online.onetcenter.org/link/summary/49-2022.03, "Summary Report for Electrical and Electronics Installers and Repairers, Transportation Equipment," http://online.onetcenter.org/link/summary/49-2093.00, "Summary Report for Electronic Equipment Installers and Repairers, Motor Vehicles," http://www.onetonline.org/link/summary/49-2096.00, "Summary Report for Security and Fire Alarm Systems Installers," http://online.onetcenter.org/link/summary/49-2098.00, "Summary Report for Control and Valve Installers and Repairers, Except Mechanical Door," http://online.onetcenter.org/link/summary/49-9012.00, and "Summary Report for Telecommunications Line Installers and Repairers," http://online.onetcenter.org/link/summary/49-9052.00.

Copyright © 2017. American Immigration Lawyers Association. All rights reserved.

evidence of the third-party warranty or service agreement, if applicable. As with other foreign nationals who will perform after-sales service or training, the practitioner is also advised to include a confirmation in the support statement that the foreign national visitor will not engage in any hands-on building or construction work, whether onsite or at the manufacturing plant, as discussed above.

7. General Service

This phase of the business cycle is comprised of many smaller categories, which are discussed individually.

a. Professionals

As discussed above, there is no "B-1 in lieu of TN" classification,[338] and so there will be no such annotation on a visa or I-94 card. Nevertheless, Canadian and Mexican national professionals may engage in "a business activity at a professional level" in one of the professions detailed in Appendix 1603.D.1 of the NAFTA Treaty.[339] This is the list of TN professions, and the practitioner may wish to advise the foreign national to have evidence that he or she meets the educational and/or licensure requirements stipulated in the appendix. For a detailed discussion of the TN nonimmigrant classification, see Volume 1: Chapter Fourteen, "TN Visas and Status." As with other B-1 visitors, there can be no U.S.-sourced remuneration other than expense allowance or reimbursement.[340] As a practical matter, practitioners should consider whether entry as a B-1 visitor is preferable to entry on a TN, as entry on a TN will be for a longer period of time and will allow for U.S. remuneration.

b. Commercial Transactions

Management and supervisory personnel, as well as financial services personnel, may be admitted to engage in commercial transactions for an enterprise located in Canada or Mexico.[341] It does not seem that this provision grants additional flexibility to Canadian and Mexican nationals, as engaging in commercial transactions are standard permissible B-1 activities. For a discussion of what constitutes a "commercial transaction," see above. It remains unclear whether a "function manager" would qualify for this admission, as discussed above. Only insurers, bankers, and investment brokers are named as financial services personnel,[342] so reference to template job descriptions provided by DOL may prove helpful in determining whether the foreign national qualifies.[343] In the event that a foreign

---

[338] Legacy INS, Y. La Fleur, "File No. HQ 1815-C" (Dec. 21, 1995), 73 Interp. Rel. 91 (Jan. 16, 1996).

[339] 8 CFR §214.2(b)(4)(i)(G)(1).

[340] 1 (Legacy) INS Inspector's Field Manual, Ch. 15, "NAFTA Admissions," 14-1 INS Manuals 15.5.

[341] 8 CFR §214.2(b)(4)(i)(G)(2) and (3).

[342] 8 CFR §214.2(b)(4)(i)(G)(3).

[343] O*NET, "Summary Report for Insurance Underwriters," http://www.onetonline.org/link/summary/13-2053.00, "Summary Report for Insurance Sales Agents," http://www.onetonline.org/
Cont'd

Copyright © 2017. American Immigration Lawyers Association. All rights reserved.

national is not an insurer, banker, or investment broker, then the practitioner may explore whether the foreign national would be admissible as a manager, supervisor, or professional. The foreign national applicant for B-1 status under NAFTA may submit evidence of the commercial transaction, as well as evidence of the objective of the Canadian or Mexican entity in undertaking the commercial transaction.

c. Public Relations and Advertising Personnel

Public relations and advertising personnel may be admitted to consult with business associates and attend or participate in conventions.[344] DOL has provided general job descriptions for these occupations.[345] It does not seem that this subset provides any additional flexibility to Canadian and Mexican nationals. DOS guidance clearly allows foreign nationals to use the B-1 visa classification to consult with business associates, as well as to attend and participate in conventions, and they need not be public relations or advertising personnel to do so.[346] In addition, there will likely be an overlap between the job duties of public relations and advertising personnel and of trade fair and promotional personnel,[347] such that a foreign national may be eligible for admission in both subsets. It may be that the provision was added at the request of Canada or Mexico or to clearly indicate that public relations and advertising personnel are eligible for B-1 status to perform activities related to this later stage of the business cycle at conventions that are not trade shows. The foreign national B-1 applicant under NAFTA may present evidence explaining the business meetings and discussions and the relevant conventions to be attended.

d. Tourism Personnel

Tourism personnel may be admitted to attend or participate in a convention, as well as to conduct a tour that began in Canada or Mexico.[348] The requirements of tourism personnel are similar to the requirements of transportation operators, discussed above. First, there must be a foreign point of origin and/or destination, and the tour must

---

link/summary/41-3021.00, "Summary Report for Sales Agents, Securities and Commodities," http://online.onetcenter.org/link/summary/41-3031.01, and "Summary Report for Sales Agents, Financial Services," http://online.onetcenter.org/link/summary/41-3031.02.

[344] 8 CFR §214.2(b)(4)(i)(G)(4).

[345] O*NET, "Summary Report for Public Relations and Fundraising Managers," http://www.onetonline.org/link/summary/11-2031.00, "Summary Report for Public Relations Specialists," http://online.onetcenter.org/link/summary/27-3031.00, "Summary Report for Advertising and Promotions Managers," http://www.onetonline.org/link/summary/11-2011.00, and "Summary Report for Advertising Sales Agents," http://online.onetcenter.org/link/summary/41-3011.00.

[346] 9 FAM 41.31 N8.

[347] O*NET, "Summary Report for Advertising and Promotions Managers," http://www.onet online.org/link/summary/11-2011.00.

[348] 8 CFR §214.2(b)(4)(i)(G)(5).

Copyright © 2017. American Immigration Lawyers Association. All rights reserved.

involve international commerce by "tak[ing] place primarily in a foreign country,"[349] and by crossing an international boundary.[350] If the tour began in the United States, then it "must terminate in foreign territory, and a significant portion of the tour must be conducted in foreign territory."[351] It is permissible for tourism personnel to conduct tours that start in the United States, travel into Canada or Mexico, return to the United States, and then return abroad.[352] Second, in this specific situation, there may be "deadheading," where the tourism personnel are likened to the transportation operator or crew and where the vehicle of transportation is likened to the goods or trailer of goods. Therefore, if the tour began in the United States, "an operator may enter the United States with an empty conveyance and a tour guide may enter on his or her own and join the conveyance."[353] Whether the tour operator or tour driver entered with the vehicle or separately, the "tour operator or tour driver must remain with the tour group throughout the course of the tour."[354] Upon the conclusion of an individual tour, the tour operator and tour driver may, however, remain in the United States for subsequent tour groups until "the conclusion of the touring season," as requiring "the drivers and tour guides to travel to and from the United States with each tour would only decrease [the tour operators'] efficiency, without increasing the international nature of its commerce."[355]

Only tour and travel agents, tour guides, and tour operators are named as tourism personnel,[356] so reference to the DOL template job descriptions may be helpful.[357] Legacy INS guidance indicates that fishing guides, who bring fishermen to U.S. shores, are considered tourism personnel.[358] Tourism personnel seeking B-1 admission under NAFTA may present itineraries for the tour and agendas or programs for the convention.

---

[349] Legacy INS, M. Pearson, "Tour Bus Operators and Other Transportation Operators Applying for Admission as B-1 Visitors, for Business" (July 2, 1998), AILA Doc. No. 06081766

[350] OI Section 214.2, "Special requirements for admission, extension, and maintenance of status."

[351] 8 CFR §214.2(b)(4)(i)(G)(5).

[352] Legacy INS, M. Pearson, "Tour Bus Operators and Other Transportation Operators Applying for Admission as B-1 Visitors, for Business" (July 2, 1998), AILA Doc. No. 06081766.

[353] 8 CFR §214.2(b)(4)(i)(G)(5).

[354] OI Section 214.2, "Special requirements for admission, extension, and maintenance of status."

[355] Legacy INS, P. Virtue, "Tour Guides Admissible as B-1 Business Visitor" (Oct. 22, 1993), 1 INS and DOJ Legal Opinions §93-83.

[356] 8 CFR §214.2(b)(4)(i)(G)(5).

[357] O*NET, "Summary Report for Tour Guides and Escorts," http://www.onetonline.org/link/summary/39-7011.00?redir=39-6021.00, "Summary Report for Travel Guides," http://www.onetonline.org/link/summary/39-7012.00?redir=39-6022.00, and "Summary Report for Travel Agents," http://www.onetonline.org/link/summary/41-3041.00.

[358] Legacy INS, G. Rees III, "Canadian Fishing Guides Entering U.S. Under U.S.-Canada Free-Trade Agreement" (Apr. 1, 1992), 1 INS and DOJ Legal Opinions §92-17.

Copyright © 2017. American Immigration Lawyers Association. All rights reserved.

e. Tour Bus Operators

Although tour bus operators may be considered transportation operators and tourism personnel,[359] there is a separate provision,[360] perhaps to clearly explain that the overlap of duties between transportation operators and tourism personnel is permissible. A tour bus operator is defined as "a natural person, including relief personnel accompanying or following to join, necessary for the operation of a tour bus for the duration of a trip."[361] The employer of the tour bus operator need not be incorporated in Canada or Mexico.[362]

The practitioner should discuss with the client the cross-applicability of the requirement of transportation operators,[363] such as the requirement that tourism personnel "must remain with the tour group throughout the course of the tour,"[364] and the cross-applicability of the guidance regarding "relay drivers" who are transportation operators.[365] Despite the fact that tour bus operators are addressed separately from tourism personnel, it seems safest to counsel clients that, after joining the tour, the tour bus operator should remain with the tour.[366] A risk-averse client may wish to ensure that tour bus operators remain with the bus throughout the U.S. tour and not serve in "relays." Conversely, as discussed above, the provisions for transportation operators and tour bus operators were not designed to function in isolation of each other.[367] Therefore, it may be possible for a tour bus operator to be eligible for B-1 admission under NAFTA even if his or her activities will "be performed solely within the United States," because the U.S. activities are "merely the domestic portion of an international trip."[368] For a further discussion of relay

---

[359] Legacy INS, M. Pearson, "Tour Bus Operators and Other Transportation Operators Applying for Admission as B-1 Visitors, for Business" (July 2, 1998), AILA Doc. No. 06081766 (noting that the regulations for transportation operators and tour bus operators were "not written so as to operate in isolation of each other").

[360] 8 CFR §214.2(b)(4)(i)(G)(6).

[361] 1 NAFTA Handbook, 14-1 (Legacy) INS Manuals Annex 1603 (Nov. 1999).

[362] Legacy INS, P. Virtue, "Tour Guides Admissible as B-1 Business Visitor" (Oct. 22, 1993), 1 INS and DOJ Legal Opinions §93-83.

[363] Legacy INS, P. Virtue, "Tour Guides Admissible as B-1 Business Visitor" (Oct. 22, 1993), 1 INS and DOJ Legal Opinions §93-83 (stating the reasoning of cases involving the transportation of goods should apply "with equal force to international tourism"). The cases referenced were *Matter of Duckett*, 19 I&N Dec. 493 (BIA 1987), *Matter of Camilleri*, 17 I&N Dec. 441 (BIA 1980), and *Matter of Cote*, 17 I&N Dec. 336 (BIA 1980).

[364] OI Section 214.2, "Special requirements for admission, extension, and maintenance of status."

[365] Legacy INS, G. Rees III, "Business Visitor (B-1) Issues Related to North American Free Trade Agreement (NAFTA) Negotiations" (May 29, 1992), 70 Interp. Rel. 1653 (Dec. 13, 1993).

[366] OI Section 214.2, "Special requirements for admission, extension, and maintenance of status."

[367] Legacy INS, M. Pearson, "Tour Bus Operators and Other Transportation Operators Applying for Admission as B-1 Visitors, for Business" (July 2, 1998), AILA Doc. No. 06081766.

[368] Legacy INS, G. Rees III, "Business Visitor (B-1) Issues Related to North American Free Trade Agreement (NAFTA) Negotiations" (May 29, 1992), 70 Interp. Rel. 1653 (Dec. 13, 1993).

Copyright © 2017. American Immigration Lawyers Association. All rights reserved.

drivers, see above. The practitioner should encourage the client to assess the appetite for risk by raising the absence of explicit guidance and exploring the potential cross-applicability of other guidance.

When seeking B-1 admission under NAFTA, tour bus operators may present itineraries for the U.S. tour, in addition to the other evidence for B-1 visitors under NAFTA, as described above.

(1) Admission with Passengers on U.S. Tours That Begin and End in Canada or Mexico

First, tour bus operators may be admitted to the United States with "a group of passengers on a bus tour that has begun in, and will return" to, Canada or Mexico.[369] These activities may be the most straightforward demonstration of "international commerce," because the tour itself would represent an international stream and path of travel.[370] Nevertheless, the practitioner is advised against relying upon the international nature of the tour to the detriment of confirming compliance with the standard requirements for B-1 admission under NAFTA.

For example, although there is no specific language in the regulation requiring that tours that start and end in Canada or Mexico must also take place predominantly outside the United States, unlike the provision for tour bus operators who will meet a group of passengers, discussed below, the practitioner should counsel the client that the tour must take place predominantly in a foreign territory.[371] As another example, even if the same group of passengers will travel from Canada or Mexico to the United States and end their tour in Canada or Mexico, the tour bus may not pick up additional passengers in the United States and discharge those new passengers at another U.S. location.[372] This prohibition applies whether the picking up is for travel that is on the way from the United States or from Canada or Mexico.[373]

(2) Admission with Passengers Unloaded in the United States

A tour bus operator may also be admitted with a group of bus tour passengers, who will disembark in the United States, as long as the tour bus operator will

---

[369] 8 CFR §214.2(b)(4)(i)(G)(6)(i).

[370] Legacy INS, G. Rees III, "Business Visitor (B-1) Issues Related to North American Free Trade Agreement (NAFTA) Negotiations" (May 29, 1992), 70 Interp. Rel. 1653 (Dec. 13, 1993); CBP, "How Do I Enter the United States as a Commercial Truck Driver?" (Feb. 28, 2003), https://www.cbp.gov/border-security/ports-entry/cargo-security/carriers/land-carriers/how.

[371] Legacy INS, M. Pearson, "Tour Bus Operators and Other Transportation Operators Applying for Admission as B-1 Visitors, for Business" (July 2, 1998), AILA Doc. No. 06081766 (stating "[w]here time spent in Canada or Mexico is so minimal that the tour actually does not involve international commerce, however, the B-1 is not an acceptable classification for the transportation/tour bus operator").

[372] Legacy INS, M. Pearson, "Tour Bus Operators and Other Transportation Operators Applying for Admission as B-1 Visitors, for Business" (July 2, 1998), AILA Doc. No. 06081766.

[373] *Id.*

Copyright © 2017. American Immigration Lawyers Association. All rights reserved.

"return[] with no passengers" or "will reload[] with the group for transportation" to Canada or Mexico.[374] This provision seems to allow a tour bus operator admission for a tour that starts in Canada or Mexico and ends in the United States. The tour bus operator may then return to Canada or Mexico with an empty tour bus or with the group of passengers who will ultimately alight in Canada or Mexico. The return abroad with an empty tour bus may be likened to returning abroad with an empty trailer, as discussed above.

At first blush, the regulatory language regarding return with passengers who will be transported to Canada or Mexico seems to describe the same situation as tour bus operators who will accompany a tour that begins and ends in Canada or Mexico, as discussed above. It is possible that this provision differs from the provision allowing tour bus operators to accompany a tour that starts and ends in the United States by allowing the tour bus operator to be accompanied by different groups of passengers for entry and departure from the United States, but there is no specific guidance allowing for this activity. It is also possible that the provision is intended to address tour buses that begin tours in Canada, travel through the United States, and then conclude in Mexico, or tour buses that begin tours in Mexico, travel through the United States, and then conclude in Canada.[375] Because of the lack of clear-cut guidance on this issue, the practitioner should discuss the provisions with the client to determine the appropriate strategy.

There is no specific regulatory language requiring that the overall tour be international in nature, but the practitioner is advised to discuss this point with the client, as discussed above.

(3) Admission to Meet Passengers in the United States

Finally, a tour bus operator may be admitted to "meet a group of passengers on a bus tour that will end, and the predominant portion of which will take place" in Canada or Mexico.[376] This provision is similar to the guidance that allows a foreign national to "deadhead" and join a tour that is bound for Canada or Mexico, as discussed above. This provision is also unique in that it is the only regulation that specifically requires that the bulk of the tour be conducted in Canada or Mexico.

f. Translators and Interpreters

Translators or interpreters may be admitted to the United States in order to perform translating or interpretation services as employees of a Canadian or Mexican

---

[374] 8 CFR §214.2(b)(4)(i)(G)(6)(iii).

[375] *Cf.* Legacy INS, G. Rees III, "Business Visitor (B-1) Issues Related to North American Free Trade Agreement (NAFTA) Negotiations" (May 29, 1992), Interp. Rel. 1653 (Dec. 13, 1993) (discussing a transportation operator who loaded goods in Canada, delivered goods in the United States, and then picked up goods in Mexico for delivery to Canada).

[376] 8 CFR §214.2(b)(4)(i)(G)(6)(ii).

Copyright © 2017. American Immigration Lawyers Association. All rights reserved.

enterprise.[377] The practitioner should note that the translation services should be on behalf of the foreign national's foreign employer; performing translation and interpretation activities on behalf of a U.S. entity would require U.S. employment authorization. Additional details on the job duties of translators and interpreters are provided by DOL.[378] The foreign national may present evidence of his or her translation and/or interpretation ability, such as professional certifications, as well as evidence of employment with a Canadian or Mexican enterprise and evidence of the need for such translation and/or interpretation services.

8. Border Crossing Cards

Mexican citizens may apply for Border Crossing Cards (BCC), which are also known as "laser visas."[379] Canadian citizens may apply for BCCs if they require waivers of inadmissibility.[380] A BCC application is made at a U.S. consulate in Mexico or Canada, with similar procedures as a B visa application.[381]

A BCC is issued as Form DSP-150 for Mexican citizens,[382] and as Form I-185 for Canadian citizens.[383] A BCC may be valid for up to 10 years.[384] When seeking admission as a business or pleasure visitor from either Canada or Mexico at a land port-of-entry or a sea port-of-entry if "arriving by pleasure vessel or ferry,"[385] the Mexican citizen should present the BCC, which should have a biometric identifier.[386] The biometric information on the BCC must match the foreign national's "appropriate biometric characteristic" in order for admission to be granted.[387] A passport is not required as long as the BCC has a biometric identifier.[388] A passport must be presented, however, if the foreign national seeks admission from a country that is not Canada or Mexico,[389] or a country that is not Canada if the foreign national

---

[377] 8 CFR §214.2(b)(4)(i)(G)(7).

[378] O*NET, "Summary Report of Interpreters and Translators," http://www.onetonline.org/link/summary/27-3091.00.

[379] GAO Report, "Border Security: State Department is Taking Steps to Meet Projected Surge in Demand for Visas and Passports in Mexico" (July 2008), AILA Doc. No. 08072573.

[380] 8 CFR §212.6(b)(1). For a further discussion of waivers of inadmissibility, see Volume 1: Chapter Two, "Basic Nonimmigrant Concepts."

[381] 8 CFR §212.6(a). See also U.S. Embassy in Mexico City, https://mx.usembassy.gov/visas/other-categories/how-to-apply/.

[382] 8 CFR §§212.6(a) and (b).

[383] 8 CFR §212.6(b)(1).

[384] DOS, "Mexico Reciprocity Schedule," https://travel.state.gov/content/visas/en/fees/reciprocity-by-country/MX.html.

[385] 22 CFR §41.2(g)(1).

[386] 8 CFR §212.1(c)(2)(i); 22 CFR §41.32(a)(4).

[387] 8 CFR §212.1(c)(3).

[388] 8 CFR §212.6(a).

[389] 8 CFR §212.6(b)(2)(iii)(A).

Copyright © 2017. American Immigration Lawyers Association. All rights reserved.

"has been in a country other than the United States or Canada since leaving Mexico."[390] In the latter two situations, the foreign national will also be issued an I-94 card,[391] following payment of the required fee if entering by land.[392]

If entering by sea or air, the individual will receive a stamp in the passport, and the I-94 will be recorded electronically.[393] If the individual does not have a passport, he or she will be sent to secondary inspection, and a paper will be I-94 issued.[394] Practitioners should advise clients who receive the passport stamp rather than the paper I-94 to check their I-94s on the online look-up[395] to ensure that it is correct and that the expiration date of their status is noted. If they leave the United States and re-enter during the admission period, they may be re-admitted on their previous I-94, with the same expiration date, if the officer believes that there is still time to accomplish the purpose of the initial entry.[396] Thus, the I-94 needs to be checked after every entry.

If the Mexican citizen will remain within 25 miles of the U.S.-Mexico border for a period of 30 days or less, then an I-94 card is not necessary.[397] The 25-mile radius is extended to 75 miles for Mexican citizens who are admitted at the following ports-of-entry in Arizona: "Sasabe, Nogales, Mariposa, Naco, or Douglas."[398] As stated by CBP:

"The time limits for BCC holders to remain in the border area without an I-94 have been expanded to promote commerce and development along the border, to make it easier for families living on both sides of the border to visit for longer periods, and to increase administrative efficiency by eliminating the I-94 in these circumstances."[399]

CBP has been rolling out Radio Frequency Identification (RFID) technology access at ports of entry "to further enhance and streamline border crossing for Border Crossing Card holders."[400]

---

[390] 8 CFR §212.6(b)(2)(iii)(B).

[391] 8 CFR §212.6(b)(2)(iii).

[392] 8 CFR §286.9(b)(3).

[393] 78 Fed. Reg. 18457 (Mar. 27, 2013). *See also* CBP Fact Sheet, "I-94 Automation" (Nov. 2015), https://www.cbp.gov/sites/default/files/assets/documents/2016-Mar/i-94-automation-fact-sheet.pdf.

[394] *Id.*

[395] CBP, "I-94 Website," https://i94.cbp.dhs.gov/I94/#/home#section.

[396] "AILA/U.S.CBP Office of Field Operations Meeting" (Apr. 6, 2016), AILA Doc. No. 16052700.

[397] 8 CFR §235.1(h)(1)(iii)(A).

[398] 8 CFR §235.1(h)(1)(v)(A).

[399] CBP, J. Ahern, "Change in Regulation for Border Crossing Cards," (Aug. 9, 2004), AILA Doc. No. 05040467.

[400] "CBP to Implement RFID at Texas Border Crossings" (July 28, 2008), AILA Doc. No. 08072861. For a detailed discussion of RFID technology, see Volume 1: Chapter Two, "Basic Nonimmigrant Concepts."

Copyright © 2017. American Immigration Lawyers Association. All rights reserved.

D. Pleasure Visits

This section addresses the B-2 visa classification, which allows foreign nationals to visit the United States for pleasure as opposed to the business visits discussed above. In a broad sense, visits for pleasure may include visits to engage in activities that are unrelated to any profession or vocation and that are for personal enjoyment and satisfaction. A more narrow definition includes only "tourism, amusement, visits with friends or relatives, rest, medical treatment, and activities of a fraternal, social, or service nature,"[401] where the social events may be "conventions, conferences, or convocation[s]."[402]

The interpretation of "pleasure" visits under U.S. immigration law most likely falls between these two ends of the spectrum and relates to "personal" activities. However, as a practical matter, because the reason for the U.S. visit drives the visa application, experience has shown that the latter interpretation is more frequently applied because of guidance stating that the B-2 visa category should not be "a catch-all category for all who wish to come to the United States temporarily for whatever purpose."[403] The following documents may be appropriate to present during the B-2 visa application:

- Itineraries, purchase receipts, and brochures of tourist activities and/or tourist packages;

- Letter of invitation from the family member(s) or friend(s) residing in the United States;

- Invitations to family, social, fraternal, or service events;

- Programs, agendas, or press releases of social, fraternal, or service conventions, conferences, or convocations;

- For B-2 visits to receive medical treatment:

  - "Medical diagnosis from a local physician," explaining the nature of the ailment and the reason the applicant requires treatment in the United States;

  - Letter from a physician or medical facility in the United States, expressing a willingness to treat this specific ailment and detailing the projected length and cost of treatment (including doctors' fees, hospitalization fees, and all medical-related expenses);

---

[401] 22 CFR §41.31(b)(2); 9 FAM 402.2-4(A).

[402] 9 FAM 402.2-4(A)(3); legacy INS, P. Virtue, "Classification of Visiting University Lecturers" (Aug. 20, 1993), 1 INS and DOJ Legal Opinions §93-61 (citing legacy OI 214.2(b)).

[403] Matter of Healy and Goodchild, 17 I&N Dec. 22 (BIA 1979).

Copyright © 2017. American Immigration Lawyers Association. All rights reserved.

- "Statement of financial responsibility from the individuals or an organization that will pay for the patient's transportation, medical and living expenses,"[404] as well evidence of the ability to pay the medical expenses, "often in the form of bank or other statements of income/savings or certified copies of income tax returns."[405]

The following discussion focuses on the typical use of the B-2 visa and on use of the B-2 visa as it relates to dependent spouses or children who will accompany a foreign national who holds another business-related nonimmigrant status. Most importantly, nonimmigrants in B-2 status are absolutely prohibited from engaging in employment while in the United States.[406] Although legacy INS guidance indicates that "[t]here is no fixed maximum period of stay for aliens in B-2 classification,"[407] it may be difficult to obtain B-2 extensions for more than one or two years. Exceptions may be made for foreign nationals receiving medical treatment and for B-2 visitors who accompany foreign nationals in other employment-related nonimmigrant status, in part because the situation of the principal foreign national is also considered. However, even then, each of the eligibility requirements for B-2 status, including nonimmigrant intent, will be evaluated with each extension application.[408] Additional discussion of requirements for B-2 extensions is below.

In most cases, the client will have a clear description of his or her reason(s) for visiting the United States, and/or clear personal relationships with people residing in the United States. In these situations, explaining the reason for the U.S. visit will also be clear-cut: to visit Yosemite National Park, for example, or to read the immigration entries at Ellis Island, or to attend the wedding of a relative, or to meet newborn grandchildren.

Unfortunately, not all proposed visits have such straightforward reasons. For these more challenging cases, it is critical to carefully review and discuss the client's goals and objectives for the U.S. visit. It would be more difficult to persuade a consular officer that an individual, who has no family or friends in the United States and who

---

[404] DOS, "Visitor Visa," https://travel.state.gov/content/visas/en/visit/visitor.html (scroll down to expand section titled "Travel for Medical Treatment").

[405] *Id.*

[406] 8 CFR §214.1(e); legacy INS, P. Virtue, "Classification of Visiting University Lecturers" (Aug. 20, 1993), 1 INS and DOJ Legal Opinions §93-61 (citing OI 214.2(b)).

[407] Legacy INS, T. Aleinikoff, "Classification for Alien Employees of IASCO" (Apr. 7, 1994), 1 INS and DOJ Legal Opinions 94-20.

[408] Legacy INS, T. Aleinikoff, "Classification for Alien Employees of IASCO" (Apr. 7, 1994), 1 INS and DOJ Legal Opinions 94-20 (stating that "[t]he fact that, at the time of initial admission, [B-2 visitors] may intend to seek extensions on nonimmigrant stay in order to remain with the D-1 alien for the duration of his or her three-year renewable contract, should not, in and of itself, preclude a finding that the alien's intent is to remain in this country temporarily. On the other hand, this factor, as well as other relevant factors, may be taken into consideration each time the family member applies for a new extension of stay").

Copyright © 2017. American Immigration Lawyers Association. All rights reserved.

is not involved in cattle ranching as an occupation, wishes to visit the cattle ranches of New Mexico, than it would be to explain that such an individual wishes to visit the Statue of Liberty and Niagara Falls. Nevertheless, it is possible for an individual to obtain a B visa for the former, if such a visa application provided concrete details on the rationale behind the visit. Examples of such an explanation include: a deceased family member of the individual had resided in New Mexico for a time and had established a cattle ranch that is now owned by another family; the individual resides in a country that refuses imports of corn-fed beef and wishes to taste fresh corn-fed beef; or the individual enjoys English literature as a hobby and wishes to visit the D.H. Lawrence Ranch, where the writer's ashes are buried, as well as other ranches in the proximity.

Exploring the client's professional and personal background may provide additional helpful details, even if the focus of the visa application is shifted from pleasure to business. For example, if such an individual was a cattle farmer in his home country, and he wished to visit New Mexico to discuss with ranch owners certain cattle ranching techniques that are performed only in New Mexico and observe their application, then the individual's activities would qualify as business, and he could obtain a B-1 visa. However, if the motivation for the visit is that of pleasure, as opposed to business, then it may be advisable to delineate how the visit is for pleasure and not for business.

Similarly, although a foreign national may "give a brief, impromptu speech" while in B-2 status, it is inappropriate for a foreign national to seek B-2 status if he or she intends to engage in other activities that are not for pleasure while in the United States.[409] If discussions with the client reveal that the purpose of the U.S. visit is not primarily for pleasure or one of the limited exceptions discussed below, then the practitioner may wish to explore other visa classifications that are more appropriate to the trip's objective.

1. Common Law Spouses, Same Sex Partners, Extended Family Members, and Other Household Members of Foreign Nationals in Other Nonimmigrant Status

If a foreign national will accompany another "principal" foreign national, who will hold nonimmigrant status, to the United States, but the first foreign national is not eligible for derivative nonimmigrant status as a dependent spouse or child of the principal foreign national, then the first foreign national may be eligible for a B-2 visa and status.[410] A B-2 visa application may be made by a cohabitating partner,

---

[409] Legacy INS, P. Virtue, "Classification of Visiting University Lecturers" (Aug. 20, 1993), 1 INS and DOJ Legal Opinions §93-61 (citing OI 214.2(b)),

[410] 9 FAM 402.2-4(B)(5); DOS, "B-2 Classification Appropriate for Cohabitating Partners" (July 11, 2001), AILA Doc. No. 01071131; 6 Bender's Immig. Bull. 744; USCIS, "Changes to B-2 Status and Extensions of B-2 Status for Cohabiting Partners and Other Nonimmigrant Household Members" (Aug. 17, 2011), AILA Doc. No. 11082673.

Copyright © 2017. American Immigration Lawyers Association. All rights reserved.

common law spouse, same-sex partner, extended family member, or another household member, and the relevant concerns for each of these individuals are discussed in more detail below.

The individuals may accompany principal foreign nationals in several nonimmigrant statuses, including E, H, I, L, F, J, M, A, G, and NATO. Even if the principal foreign national is not subject to the INA §214(b) presumption of immigrant intent, such as an H or L nonimmigrant, the B-2 visa applicant is nevertheless not exempt from the presumption of immigrant intent and the requirement to demonstrate a foreign residence.[411] This remains the case even though the B-2 visa applicant's sole intent for relocation is to accompany the principal foreign national.[412] Therefore, consular officers "should examine the B-2 applicant's ties abroad and the likelihood that he or she would stay in the U.S. illegally after the 'principal' alien departs."[413] Factors considered by the consular officer include visa applicants' "current circumstances and their prospects in their home countries upon return, as well as the strength of their relationship with the 'principal' alien and the 'principal' alien's own ties abroad."[414]

On a positive note, however, extended stays for more than one year and even up to four years in B-2 status may qualify as "temporary," and DOS acknowledged that B-2 extensions may be required.[415] Notably, the DOS cable stated, "The fact that the cohabiting partner may be living in the U.S. for an extended period is not a bar to B-2 classification," as long as the period of stay is "consistent with the stated purpose of the trip."[416] When evaluating whether the U.S. visit(s) will be temporary, the DOS cable directs consular officers to consider whether the length of the U.S. stay is consistent with the purpose of the trip, which would be to accompany the principal foreign national, which, in turn, is "considered travel for pleasure, within the meaning of INA §101(a)(15)(b)."[417] The DOS cable also instructs consular officers to "focus on whether the stay has some finite limit" and states that "posts should not focus on the absolute length of the stay."[418] As a practical matter, the inquiry should first turn on whether the B visa applicant's intent and motivation is to accompany the principal foreign national to the United States and then on whether the B visa applicant will

---

[411] Notes from London Liaison Meeting (Jan. 7, 1999), AILA Doc. No. 99012958.

[412] DOS, "B-2 Classification Appropriate for Cohabiting Partners" (July 11, 2001), AILA Doc. No. 01071131; 6 Bender's Immigr. Bull. 744.

[413] *Id.*

[414] *Id.*

[415] *Id.*

[416] *Id.*

[417] *Id.*

[418] *Id.*

Copyright © 2017. American Immigration Lawyers Association. All rights reserved.

also depart the United States with the principal foreign national.[419] In consonance, the ultimate aggregate stay of the B-2 visa applicant should be dictated by the total authorized stay of the principal foreign national, so that the B-2 visa applicant may accompany the principal foreign national "on a two-year work assignment or [on] a four-year degree program."[420]

Although much of the language of the DOS cable refers to "cohabiting partners," which include "both opposite and same-sex partners," the provisions should apply to extended family members and other household members because the DOS cable affirmatively notes the cross-applicability of the FAM guidance: "Although the examples in the FAM Note involve relatives, the same logic applies to cohabiting partners."[421] In addition, the FAM revision was not limited solely to cohabiting partners; the FAM was "amended to expressly refer to cohabiting partners (and other household members who may not qualify for derivative status)."[422]

In addition to the standard evidence for a B visa application, the following documents should be presented at the visa interview:

- Original or copy of the principal foreign national's nonimmigrant status, such as visa and/or Form I-797 approval notice from USCIS (U.S. consulates differ in accepting or requiring originals or accepting copies of documents; the practitioner should check the website of the consulate to confirm whether the original is required);

- Original or copy of the biographic page of the principal foreign national's passport;

- Evidence of the B-2 visa applicant's relationship with the principal foreign national, such as registration of the common-law marriage, registration of the same-sex partnership or marriage (if same sex-marriage is recognized in the home country), birth certificate of the principal foreign national or birth certificates of children-in-common, documents evidencing the financial dependence of the B-2 visa applicant, and documents evidencing the need for the B-2 visa applicant to reside with the principal foreign national;

---

[419] *Id.*

[420] *Id.*

[421] *Id.*

[422] *Id.*

Copyright © 2017. American Immigration Lawyers Association. All rights reserved.

- Pay stubs or other evidence of the principal foreign national's salary or remuneration; and

- Statement from the B-2 visa applicant explaining his or her purpose of travel, confirming that the accompanying family member will not work in the United States, and confirming that he or she will not remain in the United States without lawful immigration status. This statement may be supplemented from a statement from the principal foreign national's employer or school if the employer or school is willing to provide such a statement. An employer statement may also confirm the principal foreign national's salary to demonstrate financial support of the accompanying family member. If a statement from the employer or school is not available, a statement from the principal foreign national, confirming that the accompanying family member will not work in the United States and confirming financial support, should be provided.

The FAM guidance states that a foreign national who qualifies for derivative status but for whom it is "inconvenient or impossible to apply for the proper H-4, L-2, F-2 or other derivative visa," may apply for a B-2 visa.[423] As a practical matter, however, the practitioner may realize that the B-2 visa may not be the most appropriate visa, for the following reasons:[424]

- The period of B-2 admission is typically six months (or one year on occasion);

- Frequent B-2 extensions, with the supporting evidence establishing nonimmigrant intent and foreign residence abroad, may need to be filed with USCIS;[425]

- USCIS adjudication of these B-2 extensions is typically lengthy,[426] which may impose stress on the foreign national, in addition to the concern that the B-2 extension may not be approved;

---

[423] 9 FAM 402.2-4(B)(5).

[424] This analysis should not apply to individuals for whom, for whatever reason, it is "impossible" to apply for a derivative visa.

[425] DOS, "B-2 Classification Appropriate for Cohabitating Partners" (July 11, 2001), AILA Doc. No. 01071131; 6 Bender's Immigr. Bull. 744. *See also,* USCIS, "Changes to B-2 Status and Extensions of B-2 Status for Cohabiting Partners and Other Nonimmigrant Household Members" (Aug. 17, 2011), AILA Doc. No. 11082673.

[426] *See., e.g.,* California Service Center Processing Time Reports, http://www.aila.org/infonet/processing-time-reports/csc.

Copyright © 2017. American Immigration Lawyers Association. All rights reserved.

- The USCIS processing delays in adjudicating these extensions may necessitate filing subsequent B-2 extension immediately after approval of the previous B-2 extension or even while a previously filed B-2 extension remains pending with USCIS;

- Although an individual may depart the United States and seek re-admission in B-2 status, such an application for re-admission may also cause stress to the foreign national, who may worry about being denied admission to the United States; and

- The foreign national may not wish to pay the costs of B-2 extensions (the filing fee is currently $370) and/or international flights.

- In contrast, the derivative visa typically has the following benefits:

  – With a nonimmigrant visa in his or her passport, the foreign national should be admitted to the United States for a period longer than the period typically granted to B-2 visa holders (typically six months and one year on occasion), which would remove the need to file extension applications with USCIS and the resulting processing delays of obtaining approval of the extensions;

  – A longer visa validity period should allow the foreign national to travel internationally, without being questioned at length at each application for admission on why the B-2 visitor wishes to remain in the United States for longer than six months or one year;

  – The visa category (either H or L) may be exempt from the INA §214(b) presumption of immigrant intent, which means that the visa applicant would not be required to demonstrate maintenance of a foreign residence in order to qualify for the visa; and

  – Even with a required reciprocity fee for a derivative visa, which may be up to $240,[427] the total costs of the derivative visa application and maintenance of nonimmigrant status should be significantly less than costs of the B-2 visa application and subsequent extensions.

In short, although it may be inconvenient to gather the documents necessary to apply for the derivative visa, the practitioner should explore with the client whether the derivative visa application can be made instead of a B-2 visa application, as the short-term inconvenience of applying for a derivative visa may be far outweighed by

---

[427] DOS, "Cameroon Reciprocity Schedule," https://travel.state.gov/content/visas/en/fees/reciprocity-by-country/CM.html. For a discussion of the visa reciprocity fee, see Volume 1: Chapter Two, "Basic Nonimmigrant Concepts."

Copyright © 2017. American Immigration Lawyers Association. All rights reserved.

the long-term inconvenience of the B-2 visa and status. The financial reasons, combined with the continuing steps necessary to maintain lawful B-2 status for an extended period of time, should be persuasive. It may be that documents evidencing the familial relationship, such as birth, marriage, and adoption certificates, are difficult to obtain,[428] but the practitioner may wish to encourage clients to gather the documents or acceptable alternative documents. This approach may have the additional benefit of establishing familial relationships in the future, such as if the foreign national ultimately decides to pursue permanent residence.[429] Another type of application that may benefit from a practitioner's strategy and guidance is the derivative visa for a common-law spouse, as discussed below, and in Volume 1: Chapter Two, "Basic Nonimmigrant Concepts."

Consular officers are directed to annotate the B-2 visa "to indicate the purpose and length of stay in [these] cases, as that will increase the likelihood that the inspector grants the maximum possible admission period on initial entry."[430] The practitioner is advised to request such a visa annotation in the statement from the B-2 visa applicant, the statement from the principal foreign national's employer or school, and/or the statement from the principal foreign national.

Following issuance of the B-2 visa for the accompanying family member, he or she should make an application for admission to the United States at a port of entry. Ideally, the entire family should travel and seek U.S. admission together, because then the B-2 visa holder will actually be "accompanying" the principal foreign national. Travel together should also serve as evidence of the family unit and allow the immigration inspector to consider the B-2 visa holder's U.S. visit in the context of the principal foreign national's stay in the United States. In the event that the accompanying family member will not travel with the principal foreign national, the B-2 visa holder should have copies of all of the documents submitted for the B-2 visa application, as well as documentation of the principal foreign national's immigration status in the United States.

In an exception to the typical B-2 admission of six months, an accompanying family member may be admitted to the United States for one year.[431] In addition to the documents detailed below, the practitioner may also advise the client to carry the

---

[428] *See, e.g.*, DOS, "India Reciprocity Schedule," https://travel.state.gov/content/visas/en/fees/reciprocity-by-country/IN.html.

[429] For a discussion of the documents that must be filed in order for a foreign national to obtain permanent residence, see Volume 2: Chapter Four, "Consular Processing, Adjustment of Status, and Permanent Residence Issues."

[430] DOS, "B-2 Classification Appropriate for Cohabiting Partners" (July 11, 2001), AILA Doc. No. 01071131; 6 Bender's Immigr. Bull. 744. *See also* FAM 402.2-6(B).

[431] Legacy INS, J. Bednarz (Mar. 30, 1994), 71 Interp. Rel. 993 (Aug. 1, 1994); DOS, "B-2 Classification Appropriate for Cohabiting Partners" (July 11, 2001), AILA Doc. No. 01071131; 6 Bender's Immigr. Bull. 744.

Copyright © 2017. American Immigration Lawyers Association. All rights reserved.

DOS cable when traveling and to present it to the immigration inspector if the foreign national encounters difficulties obtaining a one-year admission. Of those documents, the practitioner should also note that legacy INS guidance on admission of these B-2 visitors indicates that B-2 admission is appropriate for a "dependent" of a principal family member.[432] Although, as a practical matter, the accompanying family member must be a dependent in the United States because he or she is forbidden from engaging in employment in B-2 status, he or she may not have been a dependent while residing abroad. In such a situation, the practitioner should urge the B-2 visa holder to obtain a statement from the principal foreign national's employer or school, as discussed above.

In many cases, the accompanying family member will need to request extensions of B-2 status from USCIS. DOS guidance provides that "there is no absolute limit on the maximum length of stay available in B-2 status." As discussed above, a visa annotation may also "facilitate subsequent extensions."[433] B extensions are discussed in detail below. Finally, the practitioner may wish to explore with the client if travel under the VWP may be a better strategy. This may be the case, for example, if the accompanying family member's visit to the United States will be brief and not for the duration of the principal's U.S. assignment.

a. Cohabitating Partners

A cohabitating partner may be a domestic or same-sex partner, common-law spouse, concubine, or an individual who has a romantic relationship of long duration with the principal foreign national. DOS guidance indicates that the length of the relationship may be considered when evaluating whether the accompanying foreign national has a residence abroad, such that a B-2 visa application by an individual who has only "recently entered into a relationship with the principal" may have a higher chance of denial.[434] The consular officer may be unpersuaded that the principal foreign national will provide complete financial support for a new boyfriend or girlfriend, which, in turn, could result in the B-2 visa holder engaging in unlawful U.S. employment. Alternatively, the consular officer may not believe that the relationship will last for the duration of the principal foreign national's stay in the United States, which, in turn, could result in the B-2 visa holder failing to depart the United States with the principal foreign national.

Importantly, however, DOS guidance states that the B-2 visa is available "for both opposite and same-sex partners."[435] For spouses of the same sex, the U.S. Supreme

---

[432] 14-1 (Legacy) INS Inspector's Field Manual 15.4, Ch. 15, "Requirements and Procedures for Nonimmigrant Classes."

[433] DOS, "B-2 Classification Appropriate for Cohabitating Partners" (July 11, 2001), AILA Doc. No. 01071131; 6 Bender's Immigr. Bull. 744.

[434] Id.

[435] Id.

Copyright © 2017. American Immigration Lawyers Association. All rights reserved.

Court's invalidation[436] of the Defense of Marriage Act[437] means that many spouses can now obtain other nonimmigrant derivative visas, and need not rely on the B-2 visa. However, the need for a B-2 may remain for some couples, either because they simply are not married or because they reside in jurisdictions where their marriage would still be considered illegal or where severe societal sanctions make marriage a difficult or even dangerous proposition.

Consular officers located in countries where homosexuality is illegal may be less than receptive to these visa applications and may suggest that the visa applicant apply instead for refugee status.[438] For these visa applications, the practitioner may wish to advise the client to present the DOS cable, with the relevant sentence on availability of the B-2 visa to same-sex partners highlighted and the page tabbed. The practitioner should advise the client to emphasize his or her intent to return to the home country following the principal foreign national's U.S. stay, as consideration of application for refugee status may be interpreted as an intent to immigrate to the United States and may, therefore, result in visa denial under INA §214(b).

Depending on the laws of the home country, a common-law relationship may be recognized. If common-law marriage bestows the same rights and obligations as a license-based legal marriage in the jurisdiction where it was celebrated and where the visa application will be made, then the common-law spouse should be eligible for a derivative visa instead of the B-2 "accompanying" visa.[439] As noted above, in these situations, the derivative visa should be much more advantageous than the B-2 visa, and the practitioner should explore with the client whether the common-law spouse may establish eligibility for a derivative visa. As a practical matter, however, if the common-law spouse does not have documentation evidencing the common-law marriage, the consular officer may conclude that the common-law spouse has not met his or her burden of proof to establish the marriage relationship. For a discussion of the requirements for a common-law marriage to be deemed valid for immigration purposes and of the issues relating to derivative visa applications by common-law spouses, see Volume 1: Chapter Two, "Basic Nonimmigrant Concepts."

If common-law marriage is recognized in the home country, but does not bestow the same rights and impose the same obligations of a traditional legal marriage or does not satisfy the conditions imposed for immigration purposes, then use of the B-2 visa is appropriate because the accompanying foreign national would not be eligible for a derivative visa. If the home country does not recognize common-law marriage, then the accompanying foreign national would submit a B-2 visa application as a

---

[436] *U.S. v. Windsor*, 133 S.Ct. 2675 (2013); *Obergefell v. Hodges*, 135 S.Ct. 2584 (2015).

[437] The Defense of Marriage Act (DOMA), Pub. L. No. 104-199, 110 Stat. 2419, 1 USC §7; 28 USC §1738C.

[438] For general information on refugee applications, *see* USCIS, "Refugees," https://www.uscis.gov/humanitarian/refugees-asylum/refugees.

[439] 9 FAM 102.3-1.

Copyright © 2017. American Immigration Lawyers Association. All rights reserved.

general "cohabitating partner," an individual who has a long-term romantic relationship with the principal foreign national. For purposes of a visa application, it is irrelevant whether the proposed state of U.S. residence recognizes common-law marriage, because the focus of the inquiry is on whether common-law marriage is recognized by the jurisdiction where the marriage was celebrated and where the visa application will be made.[440]

The laws of the home country may also recognize concubinage;[441] however, because concubinage does not confer the same rights and duties as legal or common-law marriage, a concubine is not eligible for a derivative visa.

The following documents may serve as evidence of the relationship between the accompanying and principal foreign nationals:

- Registration of common-law marriage, domestic partnership, civil union, or marriage, or concubine agreement;

- Evidence that the accompanying and principal foreign nationals have entered into a common-law marriage by satisfying the requirements of common-law marriage in the home country, if applicable;

- Birth and/or adoption certificates of children-in-common; and

- Evidence of the long-term duration of the relationship, such as property titles, mortgage contracts, or lease agreements to establish cohabitation, bank statements, utility bills, and/or credit card statements to establish commingling of funds, and photographs.

One embassy states that a government certificate "confirming that [the principal foreign national and domestic partner] are members of the same household" is necessary.[442]

b. Extended Family Members and Other Household Members

As only spouses and children are eligible for derivative visas, other family members, such as parents, grandparents, aunts and uncles, nieces and nephews, and cousins of the principal foreign national, may apply for B-2 visas. Other household members may include wards or foster children.[443] USCIS defines a "household

---

[440] *Adams v. Howerton*, 673 F.2d 1036 (9th Cir. 1982), *cert. denied*, 458 U.S. 1111 (1982); *Matter of Jose Lamas-Soto* (A70 178 883) (BIA 1995), *reprinted in* 15 *Immig. Rptr.* B1-191 (Feb. 28, 1996).

[441] *Rosales v. Battle*, 113 Cal. App. 4th 1178 (CA Ct. of Ap., 4th App. Dist., Div. 1. 2003).

[442] "AILA Liaison Questions for U.S. Embassy, Rome" (Jan. 2010), AILA Doc. No. 10031064.

[443] The practitioner should confirm whether the laws of the home country forbid a foster child from departing the home country.

Copyright © 2017. American Immigration Lawyers Association. All rights reserved.

member" as someone who "regularly resides in the same dwelling as the principal nonimmigrant and with whom the principal nonimmigrant maintains the type of relationship and care as one normally would expect between nuclear family members."[444]

The practitioner should note that some consulates forbid employment of a family member as a nanny or caretaker, as discussion above, so the extended family may be eligible only for a B-2 visa. The practitioner should counsel the client on the absolute prohibition of employment while in B-2 status, but it may be difficult to assess if there is some intermittent care of a child taking place as part of the family dynamic.

In contrast to cohabiting partners, who are considered to travel as part of the family unit, experience has shown that extended family members may need to present supplementary evidence of long-term residence in the household of the principal foreign national, of financial dependence on the principal foreign national, and/or of the reason why the accompaniment is necessary.[445] The extended family member or household member may be unable to care for him– or herself, for example, or may be ineligible for state-provided care. Alternatively, the cost of outside care through a private program may be prohibitive for the principal foreign national. Whatever the reason, the B-2 visa applicant should present evidence explaining why he or she may not remain in the home country for the duration of the principal foreign national's U.S. stay.

The following documents may be appropriate for these B-2 visa applications:

- Birth certificates, family registers, or other official records evidencing the familial relationship between the accompanying and principal foreign nationals;

- Official document awarding physical and legal custody of the accompanying foreign national in the case of wards and foster children;

- Evidence of long-term residence in the household of the principal foreign national. If independent evidence is unavailable, this point may be addressed in the statements from the B-2 visa applicant, principal foreign national, and/or the principal foreign national's employer or school;

---

[444] USCIS, "Changes to B-2 Status and Extensions of B-2 Status for Cohabiting Partners and Other Nonimmigrant Household Members" (Aug. 17, 2011), AILA Doc. No. 11082673.

[445] 9 FAM 402.2-4(B)(5). The fact that the only example provided in the FAM guidance is an "elderly parent[]" seems to indicate that the extended family member should be dependent on the principal foreign national. *See also* "AILA Liaison Questions for U.S. Embassy, Rome" (Jan. 2010), AILA Doc. No. 10031064, stating that a government certificate "confirming that [the principal foreign national and domestic partner] are members of the same household" is necessary).

Copyright © 2017. American Immigration Lawyers Association. All rights reserved.

- Evidence of financial dependence upon the principal foreign national, such as power of attorney for financial matters. This point also may be addressed in the statement(s); and

- Evidence of why the B-2 visa applicant may not remain in the home country for the duration of the principal foreign national's U.S. stay, such as doctor's letters, documents evidencing medical conditions that require close supervision and care, unavailability of other care arrangements, and high cost of other care arrangements.

2. Amateur Entertainers and Athletes

Amateur entertainers and athletes are eligible for B-2 status because they are "by definition, not a member of any of the profession[s] associated with that activity."[446] It is for this reason that they are not eligible for B-1 status; pursuit of the activity in the United States is not pursuant to business or vocation, but for pleasure in that the activity is more akin to the "social event" of a convention, conference, or convocation.[447] Specifically, the FAM states the following:

"An amateur is someone who normally performs without remuneration (other than an allotment for expenses). A performer who is normally compensated for performing cannot qualify for a B-2 visa based on this note even if the performer does not make a living at performing, or agrees to perform in the United States without compensation. Thus, an amateur (or group of amateurs) who will not be paid for performances and will perform in a social and/or charitable context or as a competitor in a talent show, contest or athletic event is eligible for B-2 classification, even if the incidental expenses associated with the visit are reimbursed."

An amateur entertainer or athlete may present the following evidence:

- Evidence of the U.S. performance or event, such as programs, press releases, agendas, or website print-outs;

- Evidence that the B-2 visa applicant is an amateur and not a professional entertainer or athlete, such as a letter confirming employment in a field or industry that is not entertainment or sports, pay stubs, résumé, educational documents, and professional or vocational certificates in a field or industry that is not entertainment or sports;

---

[446] 9 FAM 402.2-4(A)(7).
[447] 9 FAM 402.2-4(A)(3).

Copyright © 2017. American Immigration Lawyers Association. All rights reserved.

- Evidence that the visa applicant is not normally compensated for performing and only receives expense reimbursement, such as contracts or agreements for performance, documents explaining that the performances do not result in revenues for the coordinating organization (such as charity events), and documents describing the absence of payment or monetary winnings of previous performances (such as for talent competitions where the winner receives only a showcase); and

- Evidence of the social or charitable nature of the performance or event.

Many of these conditions may be confirmed in a statement from the coordinating organization that will present the performance. The organization may also confirm reimbursement of expenses in this statement.

For a discussion of professional entertainers and athletes, see below. For a discussion of amateur hockey players, see below.

3. Attending School in B-2 Status

Use of the B visa category is clearly prohibited if the primary purpose of the U.S. visit is to engage in study or to attend school.[448] It is also impermissible to attend school while awaiting F-1 change of status.[449] This section addresses certain potential exceptions to the rule. The practitioner is advised, however, to inform the client of the general prohibition from the immigration regulations and encourage application for a more appropriate visa classification for the reasons discussed above, as USCIS may reject legacy INS and DOS guidance in the face of the regulation.

Legacy INS and DOS guidance indicate that it is permissible for a visitor to attend school in B-2 status, as long as the "primary purpose to come to the United States is to accompany the principal,"[450] if the primary purpose is tourism, but there will be an "incidental" short course of study,[451] or if the school's program is recreational or avocational and if the B-2 visitor's purpose in enrolling is recreational or avocational.[452] Nevertheless, the practitioner is advised to carefully consider the circumstances surrounding the visit and carefully counsel the client on whether it

---

[448] INA §101(a)(15)(B); *Matter of Healy and Goodchild*, 17 I&N Dec. 22 (BIA 1979).

[449] USCIS, "SOPs for I-539 Processing" (Mar. 1, 2003), AILA Doc. No. 07090760.

[450] 9 FAM 402.1-3. *See also* Legacy INS, T. Aleinikoff, "Classification for Alien Employees of IASCO" (Apr. 7, 1994), 1 INS and DOJ Legal Opinions 94-20; legacy INS, M. Creppy, "Documentation and Registration of Nonimmigrant Students" (Sept. 21, 1993), 1 INS and DOJ Legal Opinions 93-74; 1 (Legacy) INS Exam. Handbook, Part VI, 15-1.

[451] 9 FAM 402.2-4(A)(6); DOS, "Student and Exchange Visitor Visa Update" (Apr. 1, 2010), AILA Doc. No. 10051363.

[452] 9 FAM 402.2-4(B)(9).

Copyright © 2017. American Immigration Lawyers Association. All rights reserved.

would be more appropriate to apply for a derivative visa or an F-1 visa, or to have the dependent children remain in the home country until the derivative visa or F-1 visa is issued.[453] For all of these exceptions, the practitioner should also confirm with the local school or educational program whether enrollment by a B-2 visitor is permitted, as local school districts may have differing interpretations of residence.

For the first exception, most nonimmigrants who accompany principal foreign nationals should be eligible for derivative visas, and these visas are frequently much more advantageous, as discussed above. This exception may be most applicable to a family member, typically a child, who will accompany a principal B-1 foreign national, such as a B-1 in lieu of H-1 professional. Despite the FAM and legacy INS guidance allowing such accompanying dependents to attend school in B-2 status, the plain language of the statute's title "[e]nrollment in a course of study prohibited" indicates that B-2 visitors should not enroll in school.[454] In the context of F-1 international students, the "course of study" must be full time,[455] but legacy INS has used the terms "course of study" and "full course of study" interchangeably.[456] Therefore, as a practical matter, drawing a distinction between a "course of study" and a "full course of study" may be difficult for a dependent child who will attend elementary, middle, or high school for between six and nine hours each school day.

Experience has shown that, where the primary purpose is to accompany the principal foreign national and where the intent to attend school is disclosed, B-2 visa applications by children tend to be considered most favorably, because most societies consider it natural that children should attend school. In the case of spouses who will attend school in the United States, the practitioner may wish to supplement the visa application with information on how the enrollment will be an incidental course of study or will be recreational or avocational in purpose, as discussed below. In addition, as a practical matter, the B-2 visa application may be less than well received if the principal foreign national's B-1 visit will only be a few weeks or a month; however, the B-1 principal foreign national may submit evidence showing that there is no alternative care arrangement for even the short term of the U.S. visit.

If, however, the B-2 visitor later decides to pursue a dedicated course of study, then an application for F-1 change of status must be filed.[457] These change of status applications tend to be closely scrutinized,[458] especially if the initial B-2 visa had no

---

[453] 9 FAM 401.2-5(C). *See also* 8 CFR §214.2(b)(7).

[454] 8 CFR §214.2(b)(7).

[455] INA §101(a)(15)(F); 8 CFR §214.2(f)(6).

[456] 14-1 INS Manuals Scope, "Twelve Case Law Summaries" (citing *Arctic Catering, Inc. v. Thornburgh*, 769 F. Supp. 1167 (D. Colo. 1991)).

[457] 67 Fed. Reg. 18061 (Apr. 12, 2002); "CSC Written Answers to AILA Liaison Questions" (Aug. 7, 2002), AILA Doc. No. 02080842.

[458] The rule was promulgated in part to address the negative publicity about how two of the 9/11 hijackers attended flight training programs while in B-2 status and while awaiting their F-1 change of status petitions to

Cont'd

Copyright © 2017. American Immigration Lawyers Association. All rights reserved.

annotation as to prospective F-1 status.[459] USCIS may question whether the B-2 visitor committed visa fraud when applying for the initial B-2 visa or applying for admission to the United States in B-2 status,[460] and/or USCIS may question whether the B-2 visitor violated the terms of B-2 status by attending school without authorization.[461] For these reasons, the practitioner is advised to explore with the client whether the attendance at school will truly not be the primary reason for the B-2 visitor's U.S. stay and whether the B-2 visitor may ultimately wish to pursue education in the United States.

In addition, for the second exception, it seems difficult to determine what would qualify as study that is "incidental" to a tourist visit. On the one hand, DOS guidance indicates that consular officers "need to make some findings as to what actually goes on in the[] courses."[462] Therefore, classroom instruction "coupled with social and other activities" with the general aim of "exposing high school students to a variety of subjects they might be interested in pursuing at the higher educational level rather than at providing students with any substantive academic instruction" may be permissible.[463] DOS cautioned:

> "The fact that the courses are offered by an academic institution should cause [the consular officer] to look into the activity more closely, but it should not preclude B-2 classification of the activity if circumstances warrant it. Don't forget to annotate those visas, 'STUDY INCIDENTAL TO VISIT – Form I-20 NOT REQUIRED.'"[464]

However, legacy INS indicated that use of the B visa would be improper for a foreign national who wished to study for a licensing examination in the United States, although the B visa was appropriate for the foreign national to enter the United States to take the examination.[465] This legacy INS guidance seems to contradict the common-sense interpretation, where studying for an examination would be incidental to the purpose of taking the examination. In practice, some period of stay prior to the exam seems to be permitted by CBP officers as incidental to the exam process. Other legacy INS guidance indicates that attendance in "[i]solated, casual, short-term classes, such as a single English language or crafts class" may be permissible for B-2

---

be approved. 67 Fed. Reg. 18061 (Apr. 21, 2002); "INS to Speed Tracking of Foreign Students," 7 Bender's Immigr. Bull. 656 (June 1, 2002).

[459] 9 FAM 402.2-4(A)(6) and 402.5-5(R)(2).

[460] INA §212(a)(6)(C).

[461] 9 FAM 402.1-5(C).

[462] DOS, "Student and Exchange Visitor Visa Update" (Apr. 1, 2010), AILA Doc. No. 10051363.

[463] Id.

[464] Id.

[465] Legacy INS, L. Weinig (Dec. 1, 1988), 66 Interp. Rel. 539 (May 15, 1989).

Copyright © 2017. American Immigration Lawyers Association. All rights reserved.

visitors,[466] but it remains unclear whether attendance at an elementary, middle, or high school would continue to be considered "incidental." Given the absence of clear USCIS guidance on this point, the practitioner may wish to emphasize the "short" duration of the course of study in the supporting documents and carefully advise the client on how to explain that the course of U.S. study will be "short."

For the third exception, there does not seem to be any specific guidance on what types of educational programs qualify as "recreational" or "avocational." The DOS guidance only states, "When the nature of a school's program makes determining its character difficult, officers should consult the appropriate DHS office in determining the alien's proper classification."[467] "Recreational" is defined as relating to "a pastime, diversion, exercise, or other resource affording relaxation and enjoyment."[468] "Avocational" is defined as relating to "an activity taken up in addition to one's regular work or profession, usually for enjoyment; a hobby."[469] A common-sense interpretation of the terms includes classes providing instruction on hobbies, such as cooking, art, or athletics, provided that the B-2 visitor earns no income from the hobbies and is not a professional in the field or the class, and that the courses are not for degree programs. In the absence of agency guidance on what constitutes a recreational or avocational study, the practitioner is advised to provide supporting evidence that addresses the dictionary definitions and the common-sense interpretations.

E. Additional Permissible Uses of the B Visa Category

There are certain select situations in which the B visa may appropriately be sought, even though it may seem that the activities would not qualify as "business" or "pleasure." The following provides a brief discussion of the qualifying activities and the evidence that such a B visa applicant should present as the reason for his or her U.S. visit. Although the situations may be unique, these B visa applicants must satisfy all other requirements, including nonimmigrant intent, specific duration of the U.S. trip, and possession of funds to cover the trip's expenses.

1. Visiting University Lecturers and Honoraria Payments

A visiting university lecturer is eligible for a B-1 visa and status either to participate or speak at a scientific, educational, professional, or business convention,

---

[466] Legacy INS, J. Williams "Commuter Part-time Students Residing in Contiguous Territory" (May 22, 2002), AILA Doc. No. 02060531; 7 Bender's Immigr. Bull. 820 (July 1, 2002).

[467] 9 FAM 402.5-5(P)(1). *See also* 9 FAM 402.3-4(B)(9).

[468] Random House Unabridged Dictionary, http://dictionary.reference.com/browse/recreational.

[469] *The American Heritage Dictionary of the English Language*, 4th Ed. Houghton Mifflin Co. (2004), http://dictionary.reference.com/browse/avocational.

Copyright © 2017. American Immigration Lawyers Association. All rights reserved.

conference, or seminar; to direct "cultural events sponsored by the university";[470] or to perform guest teaching.[471] The B-1 visa applicant may wish to provide the following documents:

- Program, agenda, and/or press releases for the convention, conference, or seminar;

- Invitation to speak or participate to visa applicant;

- Other evidence of the visa applicant's role, if it is not stated on the program or agenda;

- Evidence of the visa applicant's professional background and qualifications, such as résumé and/or educational documents;

- Evidence of the visa applicant's previous speaking engagements at other conferences, if applicable; and

- Evidence of the visa applicant's employment abroad.

If the foreign national will "receive an honorarium or other fee for services rendered, it must be determined that such is reimbursement for an incidental expense and not direct remuneration,"[472] and that the foreign national will not gain a monetary or material profit for his or her participation.[473] "Honorarium" is defined as a "fee offered" for professional services and an "honorary payment, usually in recognition of services for which it is not usual or not lawful to assign a fixed business price."[474] In addition, the following conditions must be met:[475]

- The academic activities for which the B-1 visitor receives an honorarium payment must "last no longer than nine days at any single institution or organization";

---

[470] Legacy INS, P. Virtue, "Classification of Visiting University Lecturers" (Aug. 20, 1993), 1 INS and DOJ Legal Opinions §93-61 (citing OI 214.2(b) that this involvement in cultural events should be differentiated from the cultural programs sponsored by a foreign country, as noted in 9 FAM 402.2-5(F)(4) and discussed below. Congress codified as INA §212(q), and set standards for, the ability to accept honoraria while present in B status, as part of the American Competitiveness and Workforce Improvement Act of 1998 (ACWIA)).

[471] 9 FAM 402.2-5(F)(2).

[472] Legacy INS, P. Virtue, "Classification of Visiting University Lecturers" (Aug. 20, 1993), 1 INS and DOJ Legal Opinions §93-61 (citing OI 214.2(b) (internal citation and insertion marks omitted)).

[473] *Id.*

[474] *Webster's Revised Unabridged Dictionary* (1998), http://dictionary.reference.com/browse/ honorarium.

[475] 9 FAM 402.2-5(F)(2).

Copyright © 2017. American Immigration Lawyers Association. All rights reserved.

- The payment is made by either of the following types of institution or organization:
  - "[A]n institution of higher education (as defined in section 101(a) of the Higher Education Act of 1965), or a related or affiliated nonprofit entity; or
  - [A] nonprofit research organization or a government research organization";[476]
- "The honorarium is for services conducted for the benefit of the institution or entity";[477] and

- The B-1 visitor "has not accepted such payment or expenses from more than five institutions or organizations over the last six months."

The determination of whether the visitor will gain a monetary or material profit is made on a case-by-case basis, using a "common-sense test" that considers the following factors:

- "Standards of living to which the applicant is accustomed"; and

- The "relative cost of living expenses in the United States."[478]

Under the "common-sense test," reimbursement for incidental expenses would be limited to payments to the business visitor that "will make him or her whole for attending the academic function or event [and] they may not exceed actual reasonable expenses the alien will incur in traveling to and from the event, together with living expenses the alien reasonably can be expected to incur for meals, lodging, laundry, and other basic services."[479]

In addition, what constitutes a "reasonable" travel or living expense is also determined on a case-by-case basis, with consideration to the following factors:

- "Flight availability;

- Seasonal price fluctuations;

---

[476] Legacy INS, M. Pearson, "Academic Honorarium for Visiting B Nonimmigrant Aliens" (Nov. 30, 1999), AILA Doc. No. 99121778. Although the terms "related or affiliated nonprofit entity" and "government research organization" are not defined in the context of B-1 visitors, the terms have been defined in the context of H-1B petitions. See Volume 1: Chapter Seven, "H-1B Visas and Status."

[477] 9 FAM 402.2-5(F)(2).

[478] Legacy INS, P. Virtue, "Classification of Visiting University Lecturers" (Aug. 20, 1993), 1 INS and DOJ Legal Opinions §93-61 (citing OI 214.2(b)).

[479] Legacy INS, P. Virtue, "Classification of Visiting University Lecturers" (Aug. 20, 1993), 1 INS and DOJ Legal Opinions §93-61 (citing OI 214.2(b)); *See also* 9 FAM 402.2-5(F)(1).

Copyright © 2017. American Immigration Lawyers Association. All rights reserved.

- Average cost of living in the locality visited;

- Availability of lodging;

- Duration of participation in the activity for which the alien will be reimbursed"; and

- "[A]ny other relevant factors."[480]

This guidance, and especially the inclusion of "any other relevant factors," indicates an understanding of "real-world" costs associated with speaking or attending conferences or other events, as well as an understanding that business trips are not necessarily fungible in terms of expenses. These lecturers and program participants should have evidence of the financial and academic arrangements to present at the visa interview and when applying for admission to the United States. It also may be helpful to provide documents evidencing how a particular visitor has incurred higher costs than usual, whether because of a late invitation, costs of living in the city to be visited, or length of the stay in the United States. Although legacy INS guidance directs immigration officers to admit these B-1 visitors without restriction and without requiring documentary evidence, the practitioner may wish to counsel clients to carry these important documents.

The practitioner should also note that "payment above and beyond that of the expenses that such persons will actually incur in providing services to the institution" will preclude use of the B-1 visa, even if the university or institution finds such payment necessary in order to attract the speaker or attendant.[481] In addition, use of the B-2 visa classification for this purpose may result in the foreign national's being deemed as having "violated the terms of their nonimmigrant status" and in the university or institution being deemed to "have violated section 274(a)(1)(A) of the Act by unlawfully 'hiring' and employing 'unauthorized aliens.'"[482] In such situations where payment exceeds the actual expenses incurred, the B-1 nonimmigrant category is inappropriate and the university or institution "must instead ensure that the alien is classified in another suitable nonimmigrant category."[483] The practitioner is reminded that honoraria payments, in addition to reimbursement for expenses, are proper only for those B-1 visitors who will engage in "usual academic

---

[480] Legacy INS, P. Virtue, "Classification of Visiting University Lecturers" (Aug. 20, 1993), 1 INS and DOJ Legal Opinions §93-61 (citing OI 214.2(b)).

[481] *Id.*

[482] Legacy INS, P. Virtue, "Classification of Visiting University Lecturers" (Aug. 20, 1993), 1 INS and DOJ Legal Opinions §93-61.

[483] Legacy INS, P. Virtue, "Classification of Visiting University Lecturers" (Aug. 20, 1993), 1 INS and DOJ Legal Opinions §93-61 (citing OI 214.2(b)).

Copyright © 2017. American Immigration Lawyers Association. All rights reserved.

activities."[484] Most other B-1 visitors are eligible to receive only reimbursement for expenses.[485] For a discussion of the J-1 visa category as a potential alternative to the B-1 visiting lecturer, see Volume 1: Chapter Nine, "H-3 Visas and Status" and Volume 1: Chapter Ten, "J-1 Visas and Status."

2. Religious, Charitable, and Missionary Activities

Although the "R" visa classification exists for religious workers,[486] certain individuals may obtain B-1 visas to engage in religious, charitable, and missionary activities.[487] DOS has underscored that a foreign national may be eligible for a B-1 visa even with the intent to remain in the United States for a year or more.[488] In addition, because "many cases involving religious workers generate substantial public or congressional interest," consulates were encouraged "to consider requesting an advisory opinion, or sending information cables to the Department in cases where a refusal might generate a response from the sponsoring religious organization."[489]

Ministers of religion may obtain B-1 visas if they meet the following requirements:

- They will engage in an evangelical tour in the United States;

- They "do not plan to take an appointment with any one church"; and

- They "will be supported by offerings contributed at each evangelical meeting."[490]

Although the final factor seems to be phrased as a requirement, it seems that the FAM merely allows for support from offerings made in the United States; it seems unlikely that the B-1 visa will be denied if the evangelical minister will not receive any offerings from the United States. In addition, it is notable that these evangelical ministers may accept monetary offerings made in the United States, even though in other situations this would most likely be deemed U.S. income.

These individuals are the only ones in this subset of the B-1 visa category who do not have the explicit prohibition on receiving U.S. income,[491] and they may be able to

---

[484] INA §212(q); 9 FAM 402.2-5(F)(2).

[485] 9 FAM 402.2-5(F)(1).

[486] INA §101(a)(15)(R).

[487] "DOS Cable Discusses Option of B-1 Visa for Religious Missionaries" (updated Feb. 17, 2009), AILA Doc. No. 09021363.

[488] *Id.*

[489] *Id.*

[490] 9 FAM 402.2-5(C)(1).

[491] *See* 9 FAM 402.2-5(C)(1)(a)(2) and (3), and 402.2-5(C)(2).

Copyright © 2017. American Immigration Lawyers Association. All rights reserved.

obtain SSNs.[492] Appropriate evidence may include programs, press releases, tour itinerary, lease agreements for arena or auditorium space, letters from churches confirming the presentations on the tour, and a statement from the evangelical minister describing his or her planned activities and confirming that he or she will not take any appointment with a U.S. church. The issued visa should be annotated to indicate that the foreign national will engage in evangelical activities.[493]

Non-evangelical ministers are eligible for B-1 status also, as long as they satisfy the following requirements:

- They are ministers of religion who will temporarily exchange pulpits with U.S. counterparts;

- They "will continue to be reimbursed by the foreign church"; and

- They "will draw no salary from the host church in the U.S."[494]

For evidence, the visa applicant may present certificates or other documents confirming his or her status as a minister, letters from the U.S. counterparts confirming the temporary exchange of pulpits, a statement from his or her foreign church confirming payment of reimbursement and/or salary from that source, bank or other financial statements to demonstrate how the minister will support himself or herself while in the United States, and a statement from the minister describing his or her planned activities. Given the general prohibition on B-1 visitors earning U.S.-sourced income,[495] these ministers also should not receive U.S. offerings or donations. Similarly, as discussed above, it seems that a "chargeback" situation, where the payment of minister's salary is reimbursed by the U.S. host church to the foreign church, is also prohibited. Finally, in contrast to other B-1 categories, where a U.S. host may pay or offer reimbursement for the trip's expenses, the plain language of the FAM guidance seems to prohibit payment or reimbursement of expenses by the U.S. host source.

Missionaries may also obtain B-1 visas. Missionary work includes "religious instruction, aid to the elderly or needy, [and] proselytizing," but it does not entail "ordinary administrative work" or "ordinary labor for hire."[496] The requirements for missionaries seeking B-1 visas are:

- They are ordained or un-ordained members of religious denominations;

---

[492] 9 FAM 402.2-5(H). *Cf.* SSA, "Section RM 00203.500 Employment Authorization for Nonimmigrants" (Oct. 17, 2007), https://secure.ssa.gov/poms.nsf/lnx/0110211420.

[493] 9 FAM 403.9-5(C).

[494] 9 FAM 402.2-5(C)(1)(a)(2).

[495] 9 FAM 402.2-5(F)(1).

[496] 9 FAM 402.2-5(C)(1)(a)(3).

Copyright © 2017. American Immigration Lawyers Association. All rights reserved.

- The sole purpose of their trip is to perform missionary work on behalf of the denomination;

- Their missionary work will not "involve any selling of articles or the solicitation or acceptance of donations"; and

- They "will receive no salary or remuneration from U.S. sources other than an allowance or other reimbursement for expenses incidental to the temporary stay."[497]

Notably, the language of the FAM and the title of this guidance in particular use the term "missionary work," which gives the impression that the B-1 visitor may engage in employment. However, neither the Social Security Administration (SSA) nor USCIS make any indication that a missionary is eligible for an Employment Authorization Document (EAD) or employment incident to status. The FAM also does not include missionaries in the list of B visitors who may obtain SSNs.[498] It seems that B-1 missionaries are similar to B-1 in lieu of H-1 professionals or B-1 in lieu of H-3 trainees, where an exception permits the visitor to engage in employment-type activities, as long as there is no income from a U.S. source, even though those activities would otherwise be deemed employment regardless of the source of income.[499] Evidence may include bank or other financial statements to demonstrate how the volunteer will support himself or herself while in the United States; a letter from the visa applicant's church confirming his or her membership in a religious denomination and confirming his or her missionary work in the United States; and a statement from the visa applicant confirming that the sole purpose of the trip is to perform missionary work, confirming that the work will not involve sales or solicitation or acceptance of donations, confirming the absence of a U.S. source of income, and describing the plans of the trip.

Where an individual is unable to qualify for R status, but he or she intends to participate in a voluntary service program of a religious organization (and "even if he or she intends to stay a year or more in the United States"), he or she may obtain a B-1 visa.[500] Although the FAM guidance does not explicitly link the performance of voluntary services for a religious organization with the voluntary service program of a religious organization, legacy INS guidance seems to indicate that the voluntary

---

[497] *Id.*

[498] 9 FAM 402.2-5(H).

[499] For a further discussion of what constitutes employment under U.S. immigration law, see Volume 1: Chapter Two, "Basic Nonimmigrant Concepts."

[500] 9 FAM 402.2-5(C)(1)(b) and (C)(2).

Copyright © 2017. American Immigration Lawyers Association. All rights reserved.

services must be performed pursuant to a voluntary service program.[501] A "voluntary service program" is "an organized project conducted by a recognized religious or nonprofit charitable organization to assist the poor or the needy or to further a religious or charitable cause" and benefit U.S. local communities.[502] The host organization bears the burden to establish that the program is eligible and that it does not "involve the selling of articles and/or the solicitation and acceptance of donations."[503] The following requirements also apply:

- The visa applicant must be a member of, "and have a commitment to, a particular recognized religious or nonprofit charitable organization";[504]

- The visa applicant will receive no U.S.-sourced salary or remuneration, other than an allowance or reimbursement for expenses;

- The visa applicant must present to the consular officer a written statement, provided by the sponsoring organization, with the following information:
  - The visa applicant's name, date of birth, and place of birth;
  - The visa applicant's foreign permanent residence abroad;
  - Name and address of the initial U.S. destination where the visitor will volunteer;
  - The anticipated length of the visa applicant's volunteer assignment.

- The visa applicant must present this written statement to the immigration officer at the port of entry when seeking admission to the United States.[505]

This subset is unusual because the FAM guidance stipulates requirements not only for the visa application, but also for the foreign national's application for admission to the United States. The volunteer may submit brochures, press releases, and website print-outs describing the program; copies of the organization's existence as a religious or nonprofit charitable organization, such as the 501(c)(3) IRS tax letter; a letter from the organization confirming the visa applicant's membership; evidence of the visa applicant's participation in similar volunteer programs offered by the organization, whether in the home country or in third countries; bank or other financial statements to demonstrate how the volunteer will support himself or herself while in the United States; and the required statement from the organization. It is

---

[501] *See* 15-1 *(Legacy)* INS Examinations Handbook, Part VI, "Nonimmigrants"; 14-1 (Legacy) INS Inspector's Field Manual 15.4, Ch. 15, "Requirements and Procedures for Nonimmigrant Classes."

[502] 9 FAM 402.2-5(C)(2).

[503] *Id.*

[504] Note, however, that legacy INS guidance indicates that the program must be "conducted by a recognized religious body." 15-1 Legacy INS Examinations Handbook, Part VI, "Nonimmigrants."

[505] 9 FAM 402.2-5(C)(2).

Copyright © 2017. American Immigration Lawyers Association. All rights reserved.

advisable that the required statement also confirm that the volunteer will receive no U.S.-sourced income and confirm that the program will not entail sales or solicitation or acceptance of donations.

3. Employment with an International Fair or Exposition Exhibitor

Certain individuals involved in international fairs or expositions are eligible for B-1 status. The following documents may serve as supporting evidence of eligibility for the visa:

- Documents evidencing the international fair or exposition, such as programs, agendas, flyers, or press releases;

- Documents evidencing the foreign employer's participation at the international fair or exposition; and

- Documents evidencing the foreign national's role and participation in the international fair or exposition.[506]

The FAM notes that, with "an appropriate note from [the foreign] government" and other proper documentation, the following individuals qualify for an "A" visa, rather than a B:[507]

- A representative of a foreign government "in a planning or supervisory capacity"; and/or

- An immediate staff member of a planning or supervisory representative of a foreign government.[508]

In addition, the practitioner should note that this FAM guidance indicates that such individuals may "plan, construct, dismantle, maintain, or be employed in connection with [these] exhibits,"[509] but other FAM guidance indicates that B-1 visitors may not engage in any hands-on construction or building work,[510] as discussed above. Although additional DOS guidance indicates that the prohibition on building or construction work may be limited to buildings and structures,[511] the practitioner should explore with the client whether the B-1 visitor associated with the international fair or exposition will engage in any hands-on construction work. If the

---

[506] 9 FAM 402.2-5(E)(7).

[507] Cf. 9 FAM 402.3-5 (no mention of A classification in connection with international fairs or expositions).

[508] 9 FAM 402.2-5(E)(7)(1).

[509] 9 FAM 402.2-5(E)(7).

[510] 9 FAM 402.2-5(E)(1).

[511] DOS, "B-1 Visas and Building/Construction Work" (May 24, 2001), AILA Doc. No. 01053002.

Copyright © 2017. American Immigration Lawyers Association. All rights reserved.

B-1 visitor will not perform any hands-on construction work, then the practitioner may wish to avoid confusion and erroneous denial of the visa application by explicitly stating this fact in the supporting documents for the visa application. If the B-1 visitor will perform construction at the international fair or exposition, then the practitioner may wish to explain how these construction activities do not run afoul of the purpose of the prohibition or how the prohibition should not apply to the situation. The practitioner may also wish to advise the client that the B-1 visa may ultimately be denied if the consular officer concludes that the activity performed will be prohibited construction work.

4. Professional Entertainers

In certain limited situations, professional entertainers may use the B-1 visa category to provide services instead of the "P" visa classification. Professional entertainers are defined as "member[s] of the entertainment profession," and include "not only performing artists such as stage and movie actors, musicians, singers and dancers, but also other personnel such as technicians, electricians, make-up specialists, film crew members coming to the United States to produce films, etc."[512] Professional entertainers may perform or participate in the following types of programs and submit the following evidence:

- Participation in a cultural program:
  - Evidence of the cultural program, such as programs, press releases, website print-outs, and flyers;
  - Evidence that the cultural program is sponsored by the foreign country, such as funding from a governmental office, department, or ministry;
  - Evidence that the cultural program will be performed "before a nonpaying audience"; and
  - Evidence that "[a]ll expenses, including per diem, will be paid by the member's government," such as a statement from the sending country's government.[513]

- Participation in an international competition:
  - Evidence of the competition, such as programs, press releases, website print-outs, and flyers; and
  - Evidence that there will be "no remuneration other than a prize (monetary or otherwise) and expenses."[514]

- Still photography:

---

[512] 9 FAM 402.2-5(F)(3).

[513] 9 FAM 402.2-5(F)(4).

[514] 9 FAM 402.2-5(F)(5).

Copyright © 2017. American Immigration Lawyers Association. All rights reserved.

- Documents discussing the still photography to be taken in the United States, such as a contract with purchasing publication or other media, travel itinerary, and statement from the B-1 visa applicant describing his or her plans; and

- Evidence that the B-1 visitor will receive no income from a U.S. source.[515]

- Recordings by musicians:

  - Evidence that the visa applicant is a musician;

  - Evidence that the visa applicant will visit the United States to "utilize recording facilities for recording purposes only";

  - Evidence that the recording will not be distributed or sold in the United States; and

  - Evidence that "[n]o public performances will be given," such as a statement from the visa applicant.[516]

- Creation of art:

  - Evidence that the visa applicant is an artist, such as a painter or sculptor;

  - Evidence that the visa applicant is not under contract with a U.S. employer; and

  - Evidence that the visa applicant "does not intend to regularly sell such art-work in the United States."[517]

Practitioners should note that all B-1 nonimmigrants are prohibited from engaging in hands-on building or construction work, as discussed above. It seems that electricians and technicians may be "professional entertainers" coming to theUnited States under this category, but may also fall within the DOS list of prohibited occupations for B-1 visitors.[518] In the event that a client wishes to utilize the services of a technician or electrician in B-1 status, the practitioner is advised to discuss the situation in detail with the client to explore whether the proposed duties of the technician or electrician will entail hands-on building or construction work. Strategies are discussed above. The practitioner is reminded to prepare clients for the possibility that the B-1 visa application could be denied.

5. Other Situations-Subsets of the B-1 and B-2 Classifications

In the following summary, the subsets of the B-1 visa are stated, followed by evidence that could be submitted to document satisfaction of the requirements. Experience has shown that some of this evidence, such as statements of intent and

---

[515] 9 FAM 402.2-5(F)(6).

[516] 9 FAM 402.2-5(F)(7).

[517] 9 FAM 402.2-5(F)(10).

[518] DOS, "B-1 Visas and Building/Construction Work" (May 24, 2001), AILA Doc. No. 01053002.

Copyright © 2017. American Immigration Lawyers Association. All rights reserved.

confirmation of an absence or lack, may be in the form of statements from the visa applicant, the visa applicant's employer, and the visa applicant's host or sponsor in the United States.

- Member of Board of Directors of a U.S. corporation: [519]
  - Evidence of the visa applicant's membership on the Board, such as an annual report, press releases, and website print-outs; and
  - Agenda for the Board meeting, or other documents describing the "other functions resulting from membership on the board";
- Professional athlete:[520]
  - Athletic competition with the primary source of income being abroad:
    - Programs, press releases, or other documents detailing the athletic competition;
    - Evidence of payment of awards from abroad, such as that the overall athletic sponsor is not based in the United States, or evidence that only prize money will be paid from the United States;
    - Evidence of the foreign national's participation in the athletic competition;
  - For athletes or team members of a foreign-based team:
    - Evidence that both the athlete and the team have a principal place of business or activity abroad;
    - Evidence that the income of the team and the salaries of the players are principally accrued in a foreign country; and
    - Evidence that the team is "a member of an international sports league or [that] the sporting activities involved have an international dimension";
  - For amateur hockey players who are asked to join a professional team for brief try-outs: [521]
    - Copy of the memorandum of agreement signed by the visa applicant and by a National Hockey League (NHL) parent team; or
    - If the agreement is not available, letter from the NHL team stating that an agreement has been signed; and
    - Letter from the NHL team "giving the details of the try-outs"
  - Participation in horse race: [522]

---

[519] 9 FAM 402.2-5(C)(3).

[520] 9 FAM 402.2-5(C)(4).

[521] 9 FAM 402.2-5(C)(4)(c).

Copyright © 2017. American Immigration Lawyers Association. All rights reserved.

- Evidence of the visa applicant's vocation as a jockey, sulky driver, trainer, or groomer of horses;

- Evidence of the horse race, such as brochures, programs, press releases, and website print-outs; and

- Evidence of the visa applicant's employment relationship with a foreign employer, such as a contract or previous pay stubs;

- Foreign airline employee:[523]

  – Employment contracts;

  – Documents establishing the executive, supervisory, or "highly technical" capacity of the foreign national's job duties;

  – Documents showing incorporation of the airline abroad;

  – International flight patterns (whether of passengers or freight) and/or manifests of flights previously undertaken by the airline and/or the employee; and

  – Documents evidencing absence of a treaty of friendship, commerce, and navigation between the United States and the country of the foreign national's citizenship, or copy of the foreign national's biographic passport page to evidence citizenship with a different country than that of the airline;[524] or

  – Alternatively, in the event that foreign national employees of a foreign airline will enter the United States in order to "join aircraft" if they are not admissible as a crewman and if they are not "transiting" the United States, the employees may present a "letter from the headquarters branch of the foreign airline verifying their employment and the official nature of their duties in the United States."[525]

- Yacht crewmembers:

  – Evidence that the yacht is privately owned; and

---

[522] 9 FAM 402.2-5(C)(8). Note that it is no longer a requirement that the employee have the same nationality as his or her employer. DOS, "INA 101(a)(15)(B) Horse Race Activities" (Sept. 2005), http://travel.state.gov/visa/laws/telegrams/telegrams_2775.html.

[523] 9 FAM 402.2-5(E)(2). These visas may be annotated to indicate the employer airline. 9 FAM 403.9-5(C)(a).

[524] 9 FAM 402.2-5(E)(2)(a).

[525] 9 FAM 402.2-5(E)(2)(b).

Copyright © 2017. American Immigration Lawyers Association. All rights reserved.

- – Evidence that the yacht will sail from a foreign home port and cruise in U.S. waters for more than 29 days, such as itineraries or charts of intended passage;[526]
- Coasting officers:
  - – Evidence that the officer of a foreign vessel has been granted home leave while the vessel is in U.S. ports;
  - – Evidence that the visa applicant will serve as the coasting officer to replace the officer granted home leave, while the vessel travels in and out of U.S. ports;
  - – Evidence that the officer granted home leave will return in time to depart U.S. waters with the vessel;
  - – Evidence that the vessel will not remain in U.S. waters for more than 29 days, such as itineraries or charts of intended passage;[527]
- Outer Continental Shelf operators:
  - – Letter from U.S. Coast Guard exempting the vessel or individual from the citizenship or permanent residence requirement, describing the particular purpose of the foreign national's visit, and describing the particular activities to be performed; and
  - – Evidence that the visa applicant meets the professional requirements stipulated in the letter from the U.S. Coast Guard;
- Clerkship at a U.S. medical school:
  - – Documents establishing the existence of the U.S. medical school; and
  - – The absence of payment from the U.S. medical school for any type of training, clerkship, or services provided by the foreign national;[528]
- Medical doctors:
  - – Documents establishing the visa applicant's profession as a medical doctor;
  - – Documents describing the observation of U.S. medical practices and consultations with colleagues on the latest techniques;
  - – Evidence that there will be no U.S.-sourced remuneration; and
  - – Evidence that the visitor will not engage in any patient care;[529]

---

[526] 9 FAM 402.2-5(C)(5); 9 FAM 402.8-7

[527] 9 FAM 402.2-5(C)(6); 9 FAM 402.8-5.

[528] 9 FAM 402.2-5(E)(3)(b).

[529] 9 FAM 402.2-5(F)(8).

Copyright © 2017. American Immigration Lawyers Association. All rights reserved.

- Participation in a program to furnish technical information and assistance pursuant to the Foreign Assistance Act of 1961:[530]
  - Documents evidencing the visa applicant's technical profession;
  - Documents evidencing the visa applicant's participation in a program pursuant to the Foreign Assistance Act of 1961; and
  - Documents describing the type of technical information or assistance to be provided;
- Training program for a Peace Corps volunteer:
  - Documents evidencing the Peace Corps program; and
  - Documents evidencing the foreign national's participation in the Peace Corps program;[531]
- Internship with the United Nations Institute for Training and Research:
  - Documents evidencing the internship program;
  - Documents evidencing that the participant is not an employee of a foreign government; and
  - Documents evidencing the foreign national's participation in the internship program, preferably with mention of the absence of remuneration.[532]

This summary states the subsets of the B-2 visa, followed by evidence that could be submitted to document satisfaction of the requirements.

- Dependents of a foreign national "member of any branch of the U.S. armed forces temporarily assigned for duty in the United States":
  - Evidence of the principal foreign national's membership in a branch of the U.S. armed forces;
  - Evidence of the principal foreign national's temporary assignment for duty in the United States; and
  - Evidence of the familial relationship between the principal foreign national service member and the B-2 visa applicant.[533]
- Dependents of foreign national crewmembers:
  - Evidence of the principal foreign national's employment as a crewmember;

---

[530] 9 FAM 402.2-5(E)(4); 75 Stat. 424, *also available at* https://www.usaid.gov/ads/policy/faa.

[531] 9 FAM 402.2-5(E)(5).

[532] 9 FAM 402.2-5(E)(6).

[533] 9 FAM 402.2-4(B)(8), which states that the "possibility of adjustment of status need not necessitate a 'denial of visa' under INA 212(d)(5)," and mandates that a 214(b) refusal be referred to DHS for parole consideration.

Copyright © 2017. American Immigration Lawyers Association. All rights reserved.

- Evidence of the principal foreign national's temporary assignment as a crewmember in the United States; and

- Evidence of the familial relationship between the principal foreign national crewmember and the B-2 visa applicant;[534]

• Foreign national parents of F-1 students under the age of 18:

- Evidence of the F-1 status of the child(ren); and

- Evidence of the parental relationship between the child(ren) and the parent(s), such as birth certificates, adoption certificates, or, in the case of stepchildren, marriage certificates.[535]

III. Process

With the exception of foreign nationals who qualify for the VWP, as discussed below, and Canadian nationals, as discussed above, foreign nationals should apply for B visas at the U.S. consulate in the country of citizenship or residence. It is possible to apply for a B visa in a third country, but "it may be more difficult to qualify for the visa outside the country of permanent residence."[536] Petition approval from USCIS is unnecessary and unavailable. The visa applicant should follow the visa appointment process detailed in Volume 1: Chapter Two, "Basic Nonimmigrant Concepts." In addition to the documents detailed in specific B visa subsets above, the following documents should be presented at the B visa interview:

• Form DS-160, Nonimmigrant Visa Application, completed online, printed (with bar code), as discussed in Volume 1: Chapter Two, "Basic Nonimmigrant Concepts";

• Document(s) detailing the reason for the visa applicant's visit to the United States, as discussed below;

• Documents evidencing the visa applicant's permanent residence in a foreign country, as discussed below;

• Documents evidencing the visa applicant's ties to his or her foreign residence, as discussed below; and

• Documents evidencing that the visa applicant has sufficient funds for the expenses of his or her visit.

---

[534] 9 FAM 402.2-4(A)(5); 9 FAM 402.1-4(F). *See also* Legacy INS, T. Aleinikoff, "Classification for Alien Employees of IASCO" (Apr. 7, 1994), 1 INS and DOJ Legal Opinions 94-20.

[535] Legacy INS, Y. LaFleur (June 6, 1996), 73 Interp. Rel. 970 (July 22, 1996).

[536] DOS, "Visitor Visa," https://travel.state.gov/content/visas/en/visit/visitor.html.

Copyright © 2017. American Immigration Lawyers Association. All rights reserved.

A. The Visa Interview

An applicant for a B-1 or B-2 visa must demonstrate that he or she is qualified to be issued the visa by demonstrating that he or she satisfies the following criteria:

- The visa applicant has a residence in a foreign country and he or she has no intent to abandon this residence;

- The visa applicant intends to visit the United States for a specific and limited period of time; and

- The visa applicant seeks admission to the United States to engage in appropriate and permissible business or pleasure activities.[537]

The following sections discuss strategies on types of evidence to gather and present to the U.S. consulate. Many of the suggestions are drawn from experience and anecdotal evidence, in large part because of the absence of guidance from USCIS, legacy INS, and DOS and because of the lack of review of visa denial decisions by consular officers.

1. Foreign Residence

As with most other nonimmigrant visa (NIV) categories, a B visa applicant is subject to the INA §214(b) restriction, so the consular officer must presume that the visa applicant intends to immigrate to the United States until he or she is presented with sufficient evidence to rebut this presumption.[538] In order for the visa to be issued, the visa applicant must overcome the presumption, and this process essentially entails a two-part demonstration:

- The visa applicant has a residence in a foreign country; and

- The visa applicant does not intend to abandon this residence.

For the first part, "residence" is defined as "the place of general abode or the principal, actual dwelling place in fact."[539] Copies of property titles or deeds, rental agreements or leases, or other evidence of a physical residence (whether the B visa applicant is named on the documents or not) may be presented to document the foreign residence.

It is not necessary that the visa applicant maintain an independent household; a B visa applicant may "customarily reside[] in the household of another, [and] that

---

[537] 9 FAM 302.1-2(A).

[538] 9 FAM 402.2-2(B).

[539] 9 FAM 402.1-2(C).

Copyright © 2017. American Immigration Lawyers Association. All rights reserved.

household is the residence in fact."[540] In addition, the B visa applicant need not maintain a residence in the country of his or her citizenship or he or she may not even have a residence in the country of citizenship. Rather, he or she may intend to establish a permanent residence in a third country, and this should not preclude him or her from obtaining a B visa.[541] The applicant should be prepared to document legal residence in a third country. Similarly, "suspicion" that a foreign national will desire to establish residence in the United States, because of the "more favorable living conditions" compared to the home country or the third country of present or intended residence, should not be a ground to deny the visa.[542]

However, evidence of ownership of property is typically stronger than leases or rental agreements, because property ownership may also demonstrate ties to the home country. Although the leases or rental agreements do not need to be extremely lengthy, a lease of extremely short duration or a rental agreement that will expire during the visa applicant's proposed visit to the United States will be less helpful in demonstrating the continued maintenance of the foreign residence. In addition, the consular officer may consider the value of the property owned, so that title to a country cottage may be accorded less weight than title to a condominium in a metropolitan area. Finally, for clients who reside in a home where the title or lease is in the name of another family member, it may be helpful to provide the title or lease, together with evidence of the family relationship. Submission of wills or other documents indicating that the visa applicant will inherit the property at some point in the future are typically less helpful, as this tends to document the mere potential of owning property at some point in the future.

For the second part, the goal is to establish that the visa applicant has long-standing and strong ties to the home country such that the foreign residence will not be abandoned. Good evidence of such ties includes letters confirming employment in the home country, property titles or leases, and title or deed for ownership of a business. Evidence of "meaningful financial connections," such as bank account statements, tax returns, or utility bills, may also be submitted.[543] Evidence of community involvement or participation in business organizations is also acceptable. For evidence of family ties, birth certificates for children, marriage certificates for spouses, and photographs may be presented. If any family member or dependent has a medical condition that requires continued care by the visa applicant, then hospital records and letters from doctors may be presented. Note, however, that in this situation, and especially if the U.S. visit is for pleasure, the visa applicant should be

---

[540] *Id.*

[541] 9 FAM 402.1-2(C)(c).

[542] 9 FAM 402.1-2(C)(d).

[543] Legacy INS, T. Aleinikoff, "Classification for Alien Employees of IASCO" (Apr. 7, 1994), 1 INS and DOJ Legal Opinions 94-20.

Copyright © 2017. American Immigration Lawyers Association. All rights reserved.

prepared to explain how the U.S. visit will not negatively impact the dependent's care. One approach is to emphasize the short duration of the U.S. visit, where only temporary care is available in the visa applicant's absence. The consular officer is forbidden from resolving a "doubtful case" in the applicant's favor based on the offer to "leave a child, spouse, or other dependent abroad."[544]

2. Specific and Limited Duration of the U.S. Visit

The visa applicant must demonstrate that he or she intends to visit the United States for a specific and limited time.[545] The length of the trip must be consistent with the purpose of the trip, and the applicant "must establish with reasonable certainty that departure from the United States will take place upon completion of the temporary visit."[546] However, the focus of the evaluation is not "the absolute length of the stay, but on whether the stay has some finite limit," such that the stay will be temporary.[547] The DOS considers "temporary" to mean "a limited period of stay," and a stay of more than one year does not necessarily entail a lack of temporariness, as long as the consular officer is "satisfied that the intended stay actually has a time limitation and is not indefinite in nature."[548]

The inquiry by the consular officer goes in part to addressing the INA §214(b) restriction, as failure to demonstrate the set duration of the visit will indicate the applicant's intent to immigrate to and reside permanently in the United States. However, the limited duration of the U.S. visit is also a substantive requirement, as the B visa category should not be used for a "potentially limitless visit."[549] The B visa is for brief visits and not for extended stays, except as discussed above. The documents that explain the reason and nature of the U.S. visit should include information on the specific and limited duration of the visit.

For example, a foreign national who seeks to visit the United States to speak at a professional conference should submit agendas or schedules for the conference, as well as the conference invitation. A foreign national who seeks to visit the United States to attend the wedding of a friend or family member should submit the wedding invitation and schedule of events. Recurring reasons for U.S. visits should not prohibit issuance of the B visa, as long as the visa applicant can demonstrate that the individual trips will be of limited duration.[550]

---

[544] 9 FAM 402.2-2(B).

[545] *Id.*

[546] 9 FAM 402.2-2(D)(b).

[547] 9 FAM 402.2-2(D)(d).

[548] 9 FAM 402.2-2(D)(a).

[549] *Matter of Lawrence*, 15 I&N Dec. 418 (BIA 1975).

[550] *Matter of G–P–*, 4 I&N Dec. 217 (BIA 1950); *Matter of Cortez-Vasquez*, 10 I&N Dec. 544 (BIA 1964).

Copyright © 2017. American Immigration Lawyers Association. All rights reserved.

3. Sufficient Funds for the U.S. Visit

As discussed above, the interviewing consular officer will inquire about the foreign national's financial ability to remain in the United States without engaging in unlawful employment in the United States,[551] and a B visa applicant must demonstrate possession of funds to cover these expenses at the time the visa application is made.[552] Financial support may be provided by the B visa applicant's foreign employer in the form of salary or remuneration, or by a U.S. company, as long as the U.S. company provides only reimbursement for expenses incurred as a result of the U.S. visit.[553]

If, however, the B visa applicant does not have sufficient funds to cover the costs of his or her U.S. visit, an affidavit of support may be filed by a sponsoring relative, friend, or other interested party who resides in the United States on Form I-134, as discussed in Volume 1: Chapter Two, "Basic Nonimmigrant Concepts."[554] However, while the State Department indicates that "if you cannot cover all the costs for your trip, you may show evidence that another person will cover some or all costs," it also states that an "Affidavit of Support is not needed to apply for a nonimmigrant tourist visa. If you do choose to bring a[n] ... Affidavit of Support to your interview, please remember that it is not one of the factors that we use in determining whether to issue or deny a nonimmigrant tourist visa."[555]

4. Appropriate Business or Pleasure Activities

As discussed above, the inquiry by the consular officer frequently focuses on the reason for the U.S. visit to evaluate whether the visa applicant has "specific and realistic plans for the entire period of the contemplated visit."[556] For B visa applications, the proposed U.S. activities must be legal,[557] and the principal purpose of the trip must be either business or pleasure and must fall within one of the categories discussed above.[558]

B. Visa Issuance

Foreign nationals with strong B visa applications may receive visas valid for multiple entries for up to 10 years, as long as the reciprocity schedules permit.[559] B visas with indefinite validity (so-called "Burroughs visas") are no longer issued. As

---

[551] 9 FAM 402.2-2(B), 402.2-2(E), 402.2-5(A).

[552] 22 CFR §41.31(a)(3); 9 FAM 402.2-2(E).

[553] 9 FAM 402.2-5(F)(1).

[554] USCIS, "Form I-134, Affidavit of Support," https://www.uscis.gov/files/form/I-134.pdf.

[555] DOS, "Visitor Visa," https://travel.state.gov/content/visas/en/visit/visitor.html.

[556] 9 FAM 402.2-2(D)(c).

[557] 9 FAM 402.2-2(E).

[558] 9 FAM 402.1-3.

[559] 9 FAM 403.9-4(B).

Copyright © 2017. American Immigration Lawyers Association. All rights reserved.

of April 1, 2004, all foreign nationals with such visas were required to apply for a new B visa.[560] Consular officers are directed to issue visas with the maximum validity period and for multiple entry[561] based on the foreign policy to avoid objections from foreign governments that the United States "is not according reciprocal treatment to its nationals" and to avoid retaliation in the form of "more stringent visa validities and number of entries on U.S. travelers to that country."[562] Limited validity periods or limited entries also increase the workloads at U.S. consulates.[563] Nevertheless, DOS may limit visa validity or place additional conditions on the visa's use, as discussed below.

1. Special Considerations for B Visa Applications

A consular officer may limit the duration of the visa and/or the number of entries for which the visa may be used in certain circumstances, such as when "current circumstances meet the requirements for visa issuance but may not continue to do so in the long term,"[564] or "when the applicant's bona fides in the immediate near term are not in question, but the stability of the applicant's longer-term ties to his or her residence abroad are in doubt."[565] The limitation is separate from any limitation caused by the reciprocity schedules.

The DOS has provided direction to consular officers regarding the potential absence of evidence of long-term ties to a home country specifically for F-1 and J-1 visa applicants.[566] The DOS rationale is that F-1 and J-1 visa applicants are typically young, and the F-1 and J-1 programs may be the vehicles for exploring career and life options. However, this guidance applies only to F-1 and J-1 visa applicants, and does not apply to B visa applicants.[567] Therefore, younger B visa applicants may find themselves at a disadvantage.

For these applicants, as well as for other applicants who may have difficulty in clearly demonstrating the existence of long-term ties to the home country, as discussed above, it may be prudent to request issuance of a single entry visa that is valid for just enough time to cover the date of intended travel. In these cases, the consular officer may feel more comfortable in issuing the visa because it seems to limit the time period during which the visa may be used or abused. Then, following use of the initial B visa and return to the home country before expiration of the period

---

[560] DOS "About Visas—The Basics," https://travel.state.gov/content/visas/en/general/frequently-asked-questions/about-visas-the-basics.html, questions under "Visa Validity."

[561] 9 FAM 403.9-4(C).

[562] 9 FAM 403.9-4(B).

[563] 9 FAM 403.9-4(C).

[564] 9 FAM 403.9-4(B).

[565] 9 FAM 403.9-4(C).

[566] DOS, "Students and Immigrant Intent" (Sept. 28, 2005), AILA Doc. No. 05110115.

[567] *Id.*

Copyright © 2017. American Immigration Lawyers Association. All rights reserved.

of authorized stay, the client may apply for another B visa for a subsequent trip to the United States. There are additional steps in this process, but it may be easier for the client to obtain the initial B visa, and then appropriate use of the initial B visa should be helpful for subsequent visa applications, as the applicant will have a positive history of complying with U.S. immigration laws.

Another strategy for these cases is to draw attention to the visa applicant's previous returns to the home country after travel to other foreign countries, if applicable. The visits may have been made for pleasure and/or business. The support statement(s) may state this fact. Previous passports and/or copies of the entry and exit stamps from the foreign countries may also be presented for the consular file. The consular officer should already have in his or her possession the valid passport as part of the B visa application.

2. Bond for B Visas

Alternatively, in a "borderline case,"[568] if the consular officer is unconvinced that the B visitor will depart the United States, the B visa applicant may be required to post a bond with the Secretary of Homeland Security "in a sufficient sum to ensure that at the end of the temporary visit ... the alien will depart from the United States."[569] As a practical matter, availability of this approach is rare, as the administrative steps are "cumbersome," DHS offices are "reluctant" to receive the bonds, use of bonds may give rise to the erroneous public perception that the consular officer accepted a bribe, a foreign national may be willing to forfeit the amount of the bond in favor of the economic opportunities in the United States,[570] and the DOS must approve the bond requirement.[571] The mechanics of posting a bond are multi-layered and include, in short:

- The consular officer must provide written notification, including the visa applicant's personal information and amount of the bond, to the visa applicant;

- The consular officer must instruct that the consular's written notification be provided to DHS;

- Payment may be in cash, U.S. treasury notes or bonds, or an international or domestic postal money order;

---

[568] 22 CFR §41.11(b)(2).

[569] 22 CFR §41.31(a)(1).

[570] 9 FAM 401.1-4(B)(a); 403.10-4(D)(1)(a).

[571] 9 FAM 401.1-4(B)(b); 403.10-4(D)(1)(b).

Copyright © 2017. American Immigration Lawyers Association. All rights reserved.

- The visa applicant, a representative of an approved U.S. surety company, or a friend, relative, or other interested person may execute the Form I-352, Immigration Bond;[572] and

- The bond is forfeited only if the foreign national violates the terms of his or her nonimmigrant status in the United States.[573]

A B visa issued pursuant to the posting of a bond will be annotated,[574] and the visa will be limited to "one entry, valid for six months" to "enable DHS to cancel bonds upon request without communicating with the visa-issuing post."[575]

3. Double Entry Visas

Even when the reciprocity schedule of the foreign national's country of citizenship limits the validity of the B visa to a single entry, consular officers may issue a visa valid for two entries when the individual needs to enter the United States more than once, without returning home, during the course of a trip.[576] In order for the double entry visa to be issued, the foreign national "must, on each occasion, be seeking admission for the same principal purpose, and the visa may not be valid for more than two applications for admission."[577] The foreign national must also pay double the reciprocity fee, but the visa application fee is not to be doubled.[578] One situation where such a double entry visa may be issued is where the foreign national will travel on a cruise line, with multiple stops at foreign and U.S. ports.

4. Visa Denial

If the visa is denied, then the practitioner may request further review, depending on whether the consulate permits it.[579] It may also be possible to request an Advisory Opinion from DOS regarding issues of law; consular determinations of fact may not be reviewed.[580] As discussed in Volume 1: Chapter Two, "Basic Nonimmigrant Concepts," there is generally no formal or appellate review of visa denials.

---

[572] 9 FAM 401.1-4(I); 403.10-4(D)(2). *See also* 22 CFR §22.1; 9 FAM 401.1-4(D)-(G).

[573] 9 FAM 401.1-4(G).

[574] 9 FAM 403.9(H)(d).

[575] 9 FAM 41.112 N7.1; 401.1-4(H).

[576] 9 FAM 403.9-4(D)(b)

[577] *Id.*

[578] *Id.*

[579] "DOs and DON'Ts for Attorneys Representing Visa Applicants (and for Consular Officers, Too!)" (Feb. 6, 2012), AILA Doc. No. 08121964.

[580] "Report of the AILA/Visa Office Liaison Meeting on 3/7/02" (Mar. 14, 2002), AILA Doc. No. 02031472; "DOS VO Inquiry Procedures" (Dec. 19, 2008), AILA Doc. No. 08121971; "DOs and DON'Ts for Attorneys Representing Visa Applicants (and for Consular Officers, Too!)" (Feb. 6, 2012), AILA Doc. No. 08121964.

Copyright © 2017. American Immigration Lawyers Association. All rights reserved.

Alternatively, the foreign national may apply again;[581] however, as a practical matter, a subsequent visa application should not be made unless there has been a significant change in circumstances, such that the foreign national is better able to present evidence of his or her nonimmigrant intent, residence abroad, and/or eligibility for the B visa.[582] As stated by DOS, "In the absence of new evidence, consular officers are not obliged to re-examine such cases."[583] However, given how short visa interviews are, often little more than two minutes, sometimes a reapplication on the same facts and circumstances, more carefully presented, can prove successful.

A foreign national may wish to wait for a sufficient period of time before making a subsequent B visa application after a previous B visa denial. In this situation, the practitioner should discuss the visa application and prepare the supporting documents necessary for a "first-time" visa application and then strategize approaches to explain the previous B visa denial and how circumstances have changed since that time. The passage of time may have brought about a significant change in a visa applicant's living situation.

For example, a woman whose B visa application was denied five years ago may now be eligible for a B visa. Five years ago, she freshly graduated from high school and applied for a visa to accompany a family to the United States as a nanny. That visa application was denied because the young woman did not present compelling evidence of her foreign residence and because she did not have strong ties to her home country. Today, however, she is the successful business owner of a nanny recruiting agency in her home country, she is active in a professional organization for female business owners, and she has purchased her own home. A subsequent visa application made pursuant to these facts would be more likely to be approved. If the woman presents evidence of an ongoing need to attend business meetings and discussions regarding the recruitment of nannies for U.S. citizens who will be sent on assignment to her home country, then she may be eligible for a general "business" visa, instead of a visa that is specifically for a domestic worker. Discussion of these new facts should be made in the supporting documents, and the practitioner may wish to use mock interviews to prepare the client on how to answer the consular officer's questions regarding the previous visa denial. For example, it would be helpful for the woman to point out that, after the B visa denial, she focused on her career in her home country and is now a successful businesswoman. It would be less helpful for the visa applicant to volunteer that she has always wanted to get to the United States, as this may be interpreted as a long-standing desire of five years to immigrate to the United States.

---

[581] DOS, "Visa Denials," https://travel.state.gov/content/visas/en/general/denials.html.

[582] Id.

[583] DOS, "Visitor Visa," https://travel.state.gov/content/visas/en/visit/visitor.html.

Copyright © 2017. American Immigration Lawyers Association. All rights reserved.

In addition, if the foreign national received a previous B-2 visa denial, but the subsequent visa application is for the B-1 category, or vice versa, then this point may be helpful in differentiating between the two applications and in establishing how the foreign national's circumstances have changed. For example, the previous visa application may have been made for a pleasure trip to visit relatives in the United States, but the subsequent visa application is being prepared for participation in a professional conference. Highlighting the foreign national's standing as a professional in his or her home country would serve as evidence of his or her ties to that country, as discussed above.

The passage of time is not an absolute requirement, but the practitioner is advised to explore the changes in the foreign national's situation carefully to ensure that a subsequent visa application would not be a waste of time and money in the form of legal fees and the nonimmigrant visa application fee.[584] Because a previous visa denial must be disclosed on all subsequent nonimmigrant visa applications,[585] and because the consular officer may consider such a previous visa denial to be "negative history," the practitioner should prepare as strong of an initial B visa application as possible.

C. Admission to the United States and Maintenance of B Status

Upon issuance of the visa, the foreign national may seek admission to the United States at a port of entry, and the foreign national should present his or her passport with the issued visa, as well as the supporting documents that were submitted for the B visa interview.

Following admission to the United States, the foreign national should have in his or her passport a completed Form I-94, which provides the expiration date of his or her status, as discussed in Volume 1: Chapter Two, "Basic Nonimmigrant Concepts." As discussed above, B visitors in general may be admitted for up to one year. B-1 visitors are admitted "for a period of time which is fair and reasonable for completion of the purpose of the trip," and B-2 visitors are typically admitted for six months.[586] The practitioner should be aware, however, of a previous attempt to limit the typical and maximum terms of admission in B status and the availability of B extensions.[587]

During his or her period of authorized stay, the foreign national may then engage in permissible activities, such as attending business meetings and discussions, touring the United States, and visiting family. If the foreign national needs to remain in the United States beyond the date indicated on the I-94 card, then an extension

---

[584] DOS, "Visa Denials," https://travel.state.gov/content/visas/en/general/denials.html.

[585] Form DS-160, Nonimmigrant Visa Application, https://travel.state.gov/content/visas/en/forms/ds-160--online-nonimmigrant-visa-application.html (posing the question "have you ever been refused a U.S. visa?").

[586] OI Section 214.2, "Special requirements for admission, extension, and maintenance of status"; 14-1 (Legacy) INS Inspector's Field Manual 15.4, Ch. 15, "Nonimmigrants and Border Crossers."

[587] 67 Fed. Reg. 18065 (Apr. 12, 2002).

Copyright © 2017. American Immigration Lawyers Association. All rights reserved.

application must be filed.[588] In general, applicants requesting extension of B status should submit evidence confirming that they continue to meet the eligibility requirements for B status, including residence abroad and possession of sufficient funds.[589] The application must be physically received by USCIS by the date of B status expiration stated on the I-94 card,[590] although exceptions to the timely filing requirement are available. If the B extension application is not approved before the requested end date of the extension application, then the practitioner should "interfile a new I-539."[591] For a detailed discussion of extension applications, see Volume 1: Chapter Two, "Basic Nonimmigrant Concepts."

D. Change of Status from B

A foreign national may request change of status from B to another nonimmigrant status, such as L, H-1, or F-1. Change of status is available only to those who continuously maintained the previous nonimmigrant status.[592] Violation of the terms and conditions, such as unauthorized employment while in B status, is considered to be failure to maintain valid nonimmigrant status.[593] In addition, there are potential fraud and misrepresentation concerns with requesting a change of status if there has been unauthorized employment or if the request is made shortly after admission in B status.[594] As discussed above, seeking F-1 change of status soon after admission may result in USCIS scrutiny regarding the foreign national's intent and of statements made when applying for the visa and admission. Experience has shown that change of status from B-2 may be particularly difficult because the foreign national should demonstrate how the purpose of the U.S. visit shifted from pleasure and tourism.[595] For example, if the visa classification sought is employment-based, then the foreign national should establish that the visit was not undertaken for the improper purpose of obtaining an employment offer in the United States.

Similarly, applying for adjustment of status while in B status is likely to result in an inquiry regarding potential misrepresentations, with an increased likelihood of

---

[588] *See also* "USCIS's SOPs for I-539 Processing" (undated, posted Sept. 7, 2007), AILA Doc. No. 07090760.

[589] "CSC Liaison Minutes for 3/26/03" (Apr. 4, 2003), AILA Doc. No. 03040442.

[590] *See also* "USCIS's SOPs for I-539 Processing" (undated, posted Sept. 7, 2007), AILA Doc. No. 07090760.

[591] "VSC Practice Pointer: VSC Provides Guidance on Changing to and Extending B-1/B-2 Status" (Mar. 10, 2009), AILA Doc. No. 09031064.

[592] 8 CFR §§248.1(a) and (b).

[593] 8 CFR §214.1(e). *See also* "USCIS's SOPs for I-539 Processing" (undated, posted Sept. 7, 2007), AILA Doc. No. 07090760.

[594] *See also* "USCIS's SOPs for I-539 Processing" (undated, posted Sept. 7, 2007), AILA Doc. No. 07090760.

[595] *Id.*

Copyright © 2017. American Immigration Lawyers Association. All rights reserved.

such an inquiry the shorter the period of time between admission and application to adjust status.

Strategies and issues relating to change of status petitions are discussed in more detail in Volume 1: Chapter Two, "Basic Nonimmigrant Concepts." For further discussion of the accrual of unauthorized employment, its impact on subsequent petitions, and strategies to address accrual of unauthorized employment, see Volume 1: Chapter Two, "Basic Nonimmigrant Concepts," and Volume 2: Chapter One, "Basic Immigrant Visa Concepts."

If change of status is requested, however, the expiration date of the foreign national's B status should be calendared. Ideally, the change of status petition will be approved before the beneficiary's B status expires, and premium processing may make this scenario possible. The practitioner may wish to advise clients on the intricacies of situations where the initial status expires before the change of status petition is approved. As discussed in Volume 1: Chapter Two, "Basic Nonimmigrant Concepts," a timely filed request for change of status will extend the beneficiary's period of authorized stay, such that the transferee should not accrue unlawful presence during pendency of the change of status petition, but USCIS takes the view that a change of status petition will not extend the beneficiary's immigration status.[596]

However, if the change of status petition is ultimately denied because the beneficiary engaged in unauthorized employment or because the petition is deemed frivolous, then all of the time that the foreign national remained in the United States after expiration of his or her initial grant of admission will be considered unlawful presence.[597] Due to lengthy processing times, it is possible for a foreign national to accrue 180 days of unlawful presence while awaiting adjudication of a change of status petition. Premium processing of the change of status petition may be requested to address this issue. Accrual of more than 180 days of unlawful presence will trigger the three-year bar to re-entry to the United States upon departure from the United States. Accrual of more than 365 days of unlawful presence will trigger the 10-year ban to re-entry to the United States upon departure from the United States. For a detailed discussion of the three-year and 10-year bars, see Volume 1: Chapter Two, "Basic Nonimmigrant Concepts," and Volume 2: Chapter One, "Basic Immigrant Visa Concepts."

---

[596] USCIS, "Consolidation of Guidance Concerning Unlawful Presence for Purposes of Sections 212(a)(9)(B)(i) and 212(a)(9)(C)(i)(I) of the Act" (May 6, 2009), AILA Doc. No. 09051468, p. 37. ("However, the filing of a request for EOS or COS does not put an individual into valid and authorized nonimmigrant status, *i.e.,* he or she is not in authorized status. Therefore, if an individual has filed an initial application for EOS or COS and subsequently files additional (untimely) requests for EOS or COS, the subsequently filed request will not stop the individual from accruing unlawful presence, if the initial request is denied").

[597] *Id.*

Copyright © 2017. American Immigration Lawyers Association. All rights reserved.

A request for extension of B status may be filed, but the practitioner should be aware that USCIS may question the validity of the B extension request and whether a legitimate B purpose is being served or fulfilled.[598] The B extension application should "include return tickets, proof of residence abroad, and financial support in the United States" to document the foreign national's continued ability to support the U.S. visit.[599] If this strategy is pursued, then following expiration of the initial nonimmigrant status, the change of status petition should be updated with the receipt notice for the timely filed extension request to evidence that the beneficiary has not failed to maintain lawful immigration status.[600] The practitioner should also follow up with the client to request copies of visas and I-94 cards to ensure that the information is correct, and calendar the expiration dates and monitor the B status, as discussed in Volume 1: Chapter Two, "Basic Nonimmigrant Concepts."

IV. The Visa Waiver Program (VWP)

As noted above, the VWP allows nationals of certain approved countries to apply for admission to the United States even without a B visa.[601] A foreign national may apply for VWP admission in order to transit through the United States.[602] A foreign national crewmember is eligible for VWP admission to transit through the United States, as long as he or she has a letter stating that he or she will join a vessel docked in the United States,[603] or as long as he or she is an air crewmember who will enter as a passenger or non-working crewmember on board a regular flight or positioning aircraft solely for the purpose of joining the working crew of an outbound flight.[604] A foreign national who was previously removed after being determined to be deportable may not use the VWP.[605]

A. Requirements and Interpretations

A VWP participant must meet the following requirements:

---

[598] AILA-VSC Conference Call Minutes (Mar. 5, 2008), AILA Doc. No. 08031331.

[599] "CSC Liaison Minutes for 3/26/03" (Apr. 4, 2003), AILA Doc. No. 03040442.

[600] "AILA-VSC Conference Call Minutes" (Mar. 5, 2008), AILA Doc. No. 08031331. Note that it is not current USCIS policy to apply the "last action rule," as discussed in Volume 1: Chapter Two, "Basic Nonimmigrant Concepts."

[601] INA §217(a); 8 CFR §§217.1 and 217.2. For a general overview of the VWP, *see* Congressional Research Service publication, A. Siskin, "Visa Waiver Program" (updated Dec. 11, 2015), https://www.fas.org/sgp/crs/homesec/RL32221.pdf, and GAO publication, "Visa Waiver Program" (Sept. 2008), AILA Doc. No. 08091569.

[602] 8 CFR §217.2(d). *See also* 9 FAM 201.1-4(C)(b)(3).

[603] 1 (Legacy) INS Inspector's Field Manual, Ch. 15, 14-1 INS Manuals 15.7 "Visa Waiver Pilot Program (VWPP)."

[604] 1 (Legacy) INS Inspector's Field Manual, Ch. 15, 14-1 INS Manuals 15.7 "Visa Waiver Pilot Program (VWPP)"; Legacy INS, G. Rees III, "Business Visitor (B-1) Issues Related to North American Free Trade Agreement (NAFTA) Negotiations" (May 29, 1992), 70 Interp. Rel. 1653 (Dec. 13, 1993).

[605] 8 CFR §217.2(b)(2).

Copyright © 2017. American Immigration Lawyers Association. All rights reserved.

- The purpose of the U.S. visit is to engage in permissible business or tourist activities pursuant to INA §101(a)(15)(B) and related guidance, as discussed above;[606]

- The foreign national is a national or citizen of a VWP program country, as discussed below;[607]

- The foreign national seeks a period of admission of no more than 90 days;[608]

- The foreign national has a machine readable, electronic passport;[609]

- The foreign national has enrolled in the ESTA, as discussed below;[610]

- The foreign national presents a "completed, signed Form I-94W, Nonimmigrant Visa Waiver Arrival/Departure Form";[611]

- Manner of travel:
  - If arriving by air, the airline is an approved carrier,[612] and the foreign national has a round-trip airline ticket indicating departure from the United States to a foreign non-contiguous territory or country, unless the foreign national is a national, citizen, or resident of a contiguous territory or country;[613]
  - If arriving by sea, the foreign national has a round-trip ticket indicating departure from the United States to a foreign non-contiguous territory or country, unless the foreign national is a national, citizen, or resident of a contiguous territory or country;[614] or

---

[606] INA §217(a)(1); 9 FAM 402.2-1.

[607] INA §217(a)(2).

[608] INA §217(a)(1).

[609] INA §217(a)(3).

[610] INA §217(a)(11).

[611] 8 CFR §217.2(b)(1). However, "CBP now gathers travelers' arrival/departure information automatically from their electronic travel records," and thus only individuals entering by land need to physically complete and present the I-94W. CBP, "Arrival/Departure Forms: I-94 and I-94W," https://www.cbp.gov/travel/international-visitors/i-94-instructions.

[612] 8 CFR §217.2(a).

[613] INA §217(a)(8).

[614] *Id.*

Copyright © 2017. American Immigration Lawyers Association. All rights reserved.

- – If arriving by land, the foreign national presents evidence to the immigration inspector at the port of entry of "financial solvency and a domicile abroad to which the applicant intends to return";[615]

- ▪ The foreign national does not pose a threat to the welfare, health, safety, or security of the United States (these threats constitute grounds of inadmissibility pursuant to INA §212(a));[616]

- ▪ The foreign national is not a national of Iraq, Syria, Iran, Sudan,[617] Somalia, Libya, Yemen,[618] or other country that DHS might designate as a state sponsor of terrorism, as discussed below;

- ▪ On or after March 1, 2011, the foreign national has not been present in Iraq, Syria, Iran, Sudan,[619] Somalia, Libya, Yemen,[620] or other countries that DHS might designate, with certain exceptions and waivers,[621] as discussed below;

- ▪ The foreign national has not previously violated the terms and conditions of any previous admission to the United States under the VWP;[622] and

- ▪ The foreign national waives his or her right "to review or appeal" the immigration inspector's determination of admissibility and his or her right "to

---

[615] 8 CFR §217.2(c)(2).

[616] INA §217(a)(6).

[617] INA §217(a)(12)(A)(ii), designating Iraq and Syria, as well as other countries determined as state sponsors of terrorism (which currently includes Iran, Sudan, and Syria—see DOS, "State Sponsors of Terrorism, https://www.state.gov/j/ct/list/c14151.htm), and authorizing the Secretary of Homeland Security to designate other countries for such limitations.

[618] Press Release "DHS Announces Further Travel Restrictions for the Visa Waiver Program" (Feb. 18, 2016), AILA Doc. No. 16021804, https://www.dhs.gov/news/2016/02/18/dhs-announces-further-travel-restrictions-visa-waiver-program. See also 81 Fed. Reg. 39680 (June 17, 2016), adding related categories of records to ESTA.

[619] INA §217(a)(12)(A)(ii), designating Iraq and Syria, as well as other countries determined as state sponsors of terrorism (which currently includes Iran, Sudan, and Syria—see DOS, "State Sponsors of Terrorism, https://www.state.gov/j/ct/list/c14151.htm), and authorizing the Secretary of Homeland Security to designate other countries for such limitations.

[620] Press Release "DHS Announces Further Travel Restrictions for the Visa Waiver Program" (Feb. 18, 2016), AILA Doc. No. 16021804, https://www.dhs.gov/news/2016/02/18/dhs-announces-further-travel-restrictions-visa-waiver-program. See also 81 Fed. Reg. 39680 (June 17, 2016), adding related questions categories of records to ESTA.

[621] INA §217(a)(12)(B) and (C).

[622] INA §217(a)(7).

Copyright © 2017. American Immigration Lawyers Association. All rights reserved.

contest, other than on the basis of an application for asylum, any action for removal."[623]

1. VWP Countries

Nationals of the following countries are eligible for the VWP program: [624]

Andorra	France	Lithuania	Singapore
Australia	Germany	Luxembourg	Slovakia
Austria	Greece	Malta	Slovenia
Belgium	Hungary	Monaco	South Korea
Brunei	Iceland	The Netherlands	Spain
Chile	Ireland	New Zealand	Sweden
Czech Republic	Italy	Norway	Switzerland
Denmark	Japan	Portugal	Taiwan
Estonia	Latvia	San Marino	United Kingdom
Finland	Liechtenstein		

With respect to nationals and citizens of the United Kingdom, the VWP is available only to those individuals who are "British citizens who have the unrestricted right of permanent abode in the United Kingdom, which is specified as England, Scotland, Wales, Northern Ireland, the Channel Islands, and the Isle of Man.[625] "British overseas citizens, British dependent territories' citizens, or citizens of British Commonwealth countries" may not use the VWP and must apply for B visas.[626]

Taiwan is included only with regard to individuals who "have unrestricted right of permanent abode on Taiwan and are in possession of an electronic passport bearing a personal identification (household registration) number."[627] Taiwan was added as a VWP country in 2012.[628] Chile is the most recent addition, in 2014.[629]

Other relatively recent additions to the VWP countries—the Czech Republic, Estonia, Hungary, Latvia, Lithuania, Malta, Slovakia, and South Korea—joined the VWP as part of a "Road Map Initiative."[630] This program sought to extend VWP

---

[623] INA §217(b).

[624] DOS, "Visa Waiver," https://travel.state.gov/content/visas/en/visit/visa-waiver-program.html.

[625] 8 CFR §217.2(a).

[626] *Id.*

[627] *Id.*

[628] 77 Fed. Reg. 64409 (Oct. 22, 2012).

[629] 79 Fed. Reg. 17852 (Mar. 31, 2014).

[630] GAO, "Visa Waiver Program" (Sept. 2008), AILA Doc. No. 08091569.

Copyright © 2017. American Immigration Lawyers Association. All rights reserved.

participation to countries that agreed to share law enforcement information with the United States in order to prevent and combat crime,[631] and it may have derived in part from the role of the countries as "U.S. partners in the war in Iraq" and from the countries' "high expectations that they will join the program due to their close economic, political, and military ties to the United States."[632]

Of this set of VWP countries, Hungary, Latvia, Lithuania, and Slovakia had nonimmigrant visa refusal rates of more than 10 percent, and the Czech Republic, Estonia, and South Korea had nonimmigrant visa refusal rates of between three percent and 10 percent.[633] Congress authorized the shift in the focus of the requirements to participate in the VWP, including allowing consideration of cooperation with counterterrorism activities, sharing of information from law enforcement agencies, and allowing consideration of "sustained reduction rate of refusals for nonimmigrant visas" in place of complete compliance with nonimmigrant visa refusal rate.[634]

Congress also allowed the requirement that the country have a nonimmigrant visa refusal rate of less than three percent[635] to be waived by the DHS Secretary, to a maximum of 10 percent, upon certification that:

- An air exit system to verify the departure of at least 97 percent of foreign nationals from U.S. airports is "in place" by July 1, 2009; and

- "An electronic travel authorization system is in place and fully operational."[636]

However, a departure verification system meeting the statutory criteria was not in place in time (and, in fact, as of this writing, still is not in place),[637] and thus DHS's ability to waive compliance with the three percent requirement was suspended.[638] A proposed rule, which would have airlines and sea vessels collect biometrics from exiting foreign nationals, was issued,[639] but has never been finalized. Members of

---

[631] Michael Chertoff, Robert Kalinak, Mark Filip, "Electronic Visa Application Begins for Visa Waiver Countries," 9 Foreign Policy Bulletin 1 (Mar. 2009).

[632] GAO, "Visa Waiver Program" (Sept. 2008), AILA Doc. No. 08091569.

[633] Id.

[634] Implementing Recommendations of the 9/11 Commission Act of 2007, Pub. L. No. 110-53 (Aug. 3, 2007).

[635] INA §217(c)(2).

[636] Id.

[637] For a critique of DHS's efforts to establish a biometric exit verification system, see GAO Report, "Actions Needed by DHS to Address Long-Standing Challenges in Planning for a Biometric Exit System" (Jan. 20, 2016), AILA Doc. No. 07062866.

[638] GAO, "Homeland Security: Key US-VISIT Components at Varying Stages of Completion, but Integrated and Reliable Schedule Needed," (Nov. 19, 2009), AILA Doc. No. 09111968.

[639] 73 Fed. Reg. 22065 (Apr. 24, 2008).

Copyright © 2017. American Immigration Lawyers Association. All rights reserved.

Congress and "other stakeholders" expressed concerns with this approach, and the airline industry in particular commented strong opposition, because the industry "believes [collecting biometrics] is a public sector function."[640] Indeed, even responsibility for data collection, which was previously required of individual carriers, has been transferred to the Transportation Security Administration.[641]

2. Admission Period of 90 Days

VWP participants are admitted to the United States for 90 days, unless the foreign national's passport will expire within that time, in which case the foreign national will be admitted until the date of passport expiration.[642] Note that a foreign national seeking admission to the United States must have a passport that is valid for at least six months beyond the period of intended stay, unless the visitor is a national or citizen of a country on the DOS list for which the six-month passport validity requirement is waived.[643] Admitted business visitors receive passport stamps with the "WB" notation, and admitted tourist visitors receive stamps with the "WT" notation.[644] Paper Forms I-94W are issued at land ports of entry, and they should be valid for multiple entries.[645] Entrants by air and sea receive only the passport stamps,[646] and must retrieve their I-94Ws electronically to review them.[647]

The practitioner should note that, because VWP participants have not undergone the inquiry of a visa interview at a U.S. consulate, immigration inspectors at the port of entry may focus "additional attention" on the foreign national's admissibility and the authenticity of documents presented.[648] Indeed, immigration inspectors may closely scrutinize VWP participants for two reasons. First, "immigration inspectors have stated that terrorists and criminals believe[] they would receive less scrutiny during the immigration inspection process if they applied for admission into the United States

---

[640] GAO, "Visa Waiver Program" (Sept. 2008), AILA Doc. No. 08091569.

[641] "Secure Flight Final Rule," 73 Fed. Reg. 64017 (Oct. 28, 2008).

[642] 1 (Legacy) INS Inspector's Field Manual, Ch. 15, 14-1 INS Manuals 15.7 "Visa Waiver Pilot Program (VWPP)."

[643] 1 (Legacy) INS Inspector's Field Manual, Ch. 15, 14-1 INS Manuals 15.7 "Visa Waiver Pilot Program (VWPP)." For a discussion of which countries are on the list, see Volume 1: Chapter Two, "Basic Nonimmigrant Concepts."

[644] 1 (Legacy) INS Inspector's Field Manual, Ch. 15, 14-1 INS Manuals 15.7 "Visa Waiver Pilot Program (VWPP)." This chapter draws no distinction between business and tourist visitors under the VWP and refers to all admissions as VWP admissions.

[645] Id..

[646] CBP, "Arrival/Departure Forms: I-94 and I-94W," https://www.cbp.gov/travel/international-visitors/i-94-instructions.

[647] CBP, "I-94 Website," https://i94.cbp.dhs.gov/I94/#/home#section.

[648] 1 (Legacy) INS Inspector's Field Manual, Ch. 15, 14-1 INS Manuals 15.7 "Visa Waiver Pilot Program (VWPP)."

Copyright © 2017. American Immigration Lawyers Association. All rights reserved.

under the VWP."[649] Second, "in September 2007, the director of National Intelligence testified that Al Qaeda is recruiting Europeans because most of them do not require a visa to enter the United States."[650] After terrorist attacks in European cities, these concerns became acute, leading to passage of the Visa Waiver Program Improvement and Terrorist Travel Prevention Act of 2015,"[651] discussed in greater detail below.

Except for those applying for asylum, it is generally not possible to change status to another nonimmigrant classification.[652] It is also generally not possible to apply to adjust status to that of a permanent resident.[653] The first exception is for an immediate relative, which is defined as a spouse, parent (of a citizen over age 21), or child of a U.S. citizen,[654] who can apply to adjust status even after the 90-day period of admission, provided he or she is not under a removal order.[655] The second exception is for applicants for asylum in the United States, who upon being granted asylum, may ultimately apply to adjust status.[656]

A person who overstays the 90-day period of admission is not subject to automatic visa voidance under INA §222(g),[657] but such an individual would become ineligible to participate in the VWP for future admissions.[658]

The one exception is if the foreign national had a "brief, prior overstay" of the VWP admission. The foreign national may be granted a discretionary waiver of the visa requirement and "one-time parole" into the United States, unless he or she "poses a threat for terrorism, criminality or is likely to become an economic migrant."[659] The overstay should have been "short and inadvertent or for reasons beyond the applicant's control,"; the parole will be "granted on a case-by-case basis," and foreign nationals granted the one-time parole "will be informed of their status as

---

[649] A. Siskin, "Visa Waiver Program" (updated Oct. 18, 2004), http://fpc.state.gov/documents/organization/32808.pdf (citing DOJ report, Office of Inspector General Report I-2002-002 "Follow-Up Report on the Visa Waiver Program" (Dec. 2001)).

[650] GAO publication, "Visa Waiver Program" (Sept. 2008), AILA Doc. No. 08091569.

[651] Pub. L. No. 114-113 (2015).

[652] INA §248(a)(4). The two exceptions are change of nonimmigrant status to T or U. For details on the requirements of these nonimmigrant statuses, see INA §§101(a)(15)(T) and (U), respectively.

[653] INA §245(c)(4).

[654] INA §201(b)(2)(A)(i).

[655] USCIS, "Adjudication of Adjustment of Status Applications for Individuals Admitted to the United States Under the Visa Waiver Program," PM-602-0093 (Nov. 14, 2103), AILA Doc. No. 13111840.

[656] INA §209.

[657] 9 FAM 302.9-10B)(1)(b).

[658] INA §217(a)(7).

[659] CBP, "U.S. Customs and Border Protection Commissioner Broadens Authority, Directs More Leeway for Admitting No Risk Visitors to the United States" (Aug. 12, 2004), AILA Doc. No. 04081370. *See also* "AILA National Liaison Meeting with U.S. Customs and Border Protection Office of Field Operations" (Oct. 8, 2015), AILA Doc. No. 16031104, item 23.

Copyright © 2017. American Immigration Lawyers Association. All rights reserved.

a Visa Waiver overstay and the need to obtain a visa for any future visits to the U.S."[660]

A VWP participant may remain in the United States for an additional 30 days if "an emergency prevents [him or her] from departing from the United States within his or her period of authorized stay" and if USCIS "grant[s] a period of satisfactory departure."[661] If the foreign national departs the United States within the additional 30-day period, then he or she will not be deemed to have overstayed for purposes of using the VWP program in the future.[662]

USCIS, legacy INS, and DOS guidance on what constitutes an "emergency" for purposes of the additional 30 days remains scant. Legacy INS guidance states that the additional 30-day period is "for emergent cases only" and provides the example of when a foreign national "become[s] ill and cannot depart the U.S. within the[] 90-day period of admission."[663] An "emergency" may involve "exigent circumstances," but the term "exigent circumstances" is also not defined for purposes of B or VWP admission or for purposes of the grant of an additional 30 days of authorized stay.[664] The INA allows the attorney general to waive compliance with a requirement for P status if the foreign national should nevertheless be considered eligible for P status "because of illness or unanticipated and exigent circumstances."[665] Similarly, DOS guidance indicates that humanitarian parole should be provided as "a last option for persons who … [h]ave urgent humanitarian reasons to travel to the United States."[666]

On the basis of the standards articulated in the guidance, it seems likely that medical treatment constitutes an "emergency" or "exigent circumstances." Indeed, experience has shown that VWP visitors have been granted an additional 30-day period of authorized only for individuals requiring emergency medical treatment, although this does not rule out other reasons, such as the unexpected death of a family member. Given the high standards of the assorted guidance, business situations may not qualify as emergencies, even if there would be a significant loss of income.[667]

---

[660] *Id.*

[661] 8 CFR §217.3(a).

[662] *Id.*

[663] 1 (Legacy) INS Inspector's Field Manual, Ch. 15, 14-1 INS Manuals 15.7 "Visa Waiver Pilot Program (VWPP)."

[664] The sole DOS definition of "exigent circumstances" relates to U.S. passport applications on behalf of minors: "'Exigent circumstances' are defined as time-sensitive circumstances in which the inability of the minor to obtain a passport would jeopardize the health and safety or welfare of the minor or would result in the minor being separated from the rest of his or her traveling party." 22 CFR §51.28; 72 Fed. Reg. 64930 (Nov. 11, 2007).

[665] INA §214(c)(4)(B)(iii)(II).

[666] 9 FAM 202.3-3(B)(1). The other two requirements are that the individual is "otherwise ineligible for a visa" and "[c]annot benefit from a waiver." *Id.*

[667] *Cf.* "AILA Practice Pointer: Submitting an Expedite Request" (Feb. 8, 2012), AILA Doc. No. 08022567.

Copyright © 2017. American Immigration Lawyers Association. All rights reserved.

The procedure for requesting the additional 30 days of authorized stay also remains unclear, as there is no guidance on how to make such a request. Both CBP and USCIS have indicated willingness to entertain such a request,[668] but specifics as to process have been lacking. In the absence of such guidance, the practitioner is advised to assist the client by calling the USCIS National Customer Service Center,[669] by writing to USCIS, and by accompanying the foreign national to an INFOPASS appointment with the local USCIS office[670] or to a visit to a CBP office in a nearby international airport. Anecdotal evidence indicates that a request made in writing may result in a favorable resolution. The practitioner should consider, however, that there is no clear guidance indicating that such a request may be directly made to the USCIS Service Center with jurisdiction over the foreign national's temporary residence in the United States, and that USCIS is frequently slow to respond to inquiries. It is hoped that these requests will fall under the expedite criteria provided by USCIS Service Centers,[671] despite the absence of guidance from USCIS or legacy INS that is directly on point. It is also hoped that USCIS adjudicators will process these requests within the requested additional 30-day period. However, because none of these hopes are supported by USCIS or legacy INS guidance, the practitioner is advised to cover all the bases by launching a tri-fold request for assistance. It is hoped that, with the tri-fold attack, the client (whether the foreign national or a representative) will be able to explain the situation to a receptive USCIS officer, who will in turn arrange approval of the additional 30-day period of stay.

The language of the regulation indicates that the request must be approved by USCIS and the foreign national must depart within the 30-day period in order to be eligible for subsequent use of the VWP.[672] USCIS guidance indicates that there are no extensions of VWP status.[673] The language of the regulation also terms the USCIS approval of the additional 30-day period as "a grant [of] a period of satisfactory departure," rather than an extension per se, which indicates that, for purposes of continued VWP eligibility, it seems insufficient to merely file the request with USCIS and depart the United States within the 30-day period.[674] Therefore, it is

---

[668] USCIS, "Can I extend my stay if I came to the U.S. under the Visa Waiver Program (VWP)?" https://my.uscis.gov/helpcenter/article/2754, indicating that the local USCIS Director can grant 30 days' satisfactory departure; See also "AILA/CBP Liaison Practice Alert: Managing Departure Compliance with the Icelandic Volcano" (Apr. 21, 2010), AILA Doc. No. 1004219, indicating that VWP admittees stuck in the United States because of flight cancellations due to a volcanic eruption can seek relief at either a CBP airport office or at USCIS.

[669] USCIS, https://www.uscis.gov/about-us/contact-us/national-customer-service-center.

[670] USCIS, https://www.infopass.uscis.gov.

[671] "AILA Practice Pointer: Submitting an Expedite Request" (Feb. 8, 2012), AILA Doc. No. 08022567.

[672] 8 CFR §217.3(a).

[673] See USCIS's SOPs for I-539 Processing, AILA Doc. No. 07090760.

[674] 8 CFR §217.3(a).

Copyright © 2017. American Immigration Lawyers Association. All rights reserved.

recommended that the foreign national and/or the practitioner follow up by calling the USCIS National Customer Service Center and by attending an INFOPASS appointment, as discussed above.

With all of the efforts to secure the additional 30-day period of authorized stay, the foreign national and the practitioner should present all relevant documents detailing the emergency. The foreign national must be in status and within the 90-day period of admission when the request is made.[675] Experience has shown that approval of the request is provided in writing, and the document may be helpful to the foreign national if he or she should apply for VWP admission at a later date.

Immigration laws previously permitted a foreign national admitted under the VWP to be granted voluntary departure valid for a period longer than the statutorily provided 120 days.[676] (A grant of voluntary departure allows a foreign national to depart from the United States at his or her own expense in lieu of being subject to removal proceedings,[677] and voluntary departure from the United States may be more beneficial to a foreign national who wishes to seek U.S. admission at a later date. For example, a foreign national who departs voluntarily after accruing unlawful status for more than 180 days but less than one year is inadmissible to the United States for three years,[678] rather than the five- or 10-year period of inadmissibility for a foreign national who was ordered removed.[679]) The exception, which was valid only from October 2000 through September 2003, allowed a VWP visitor to remain in the United States beyond the initial 90-day grant of admission and potentially beyond the standard 120-day period of voluntary departure in order to continue "to receive medical treatment from a physician associated with a health care facility,"[680] or to accompany and remain with a family member who was receiving such medical treatment.[681]

In addition, a foreign national may travel to a foreign contiguous territory or adjacent island during the validity period of his or her VWP admission. The foreign national may then be re-admitted to the United States for the balance of the initial VWP validity period, even if the second trip to the United States was not on an approved carrier.[682] Canada and Mexico are the two foreign contiguous territories,

---

[675] 1 (Legacy) INS Inspector's Field Manual, Ch. 15, 14-1 INS Manuals 15.7 "Visa Waiver Pilot Program (VWPP)."

[676] INA §240B(a)(2)(A).

[677] INA §240B(a)(1).

[678] INA §212(a)(9)(B)(i)(I).

[679] INA §§212(a)(9)(A)(i) and (ii).

[680] INA §240B(a)(2)(B)(i).

[681] INA §240B(a)(2)(B)(ii).

[682] 8 CFR §217.3(b).

Copyright © 2017. American Immigration Lawyers Association. All rights reserved.

and the list of "adjacent islands" is provided by CBP.[683] If the second trip was on an approved carrier, the foreign national may be granted a new 90-day period of admission, but the immigration inspector is directed to consider "the potential for fraud in certain cases of repeated entries."[684]

3. Machine-Readable Electronic Passport

On December 18, 2015, Congress included in an omnibus spending bill the "Visa Waiver Program Improvement and Terrorist Travel Prevention Act."[685] Among the changes in this legislation was the requirement that, as of April 1, 2016, governments in countries participating in the VWP certify that they issue to their citizens electronic passports that are fraud resistant and contain biographic and biometric information.[686] It also commands that, as of October 1, 2016, they certify that they require these electronic passports (e-passports) for entry into their countries, [687] except for travel within the European Union's Schengen Zone.[688]

As a result of this legislation, the foreign national now must have a machine-readable, e-passport that "is tamper-resistant," "incorporates document authentication identifiers," "is fraud-resistant," "contains relevant biographic and biometric information," and "otherwise satisfies the internationally accepted standard[s]" for machine readability and electronic passports.[689]

An e-passport "contains the security feature of an electronic chip, which holds all of a passenger's [biographic information] including name, date of birth and other biographical information."[690] DOS describes the e-passport as "an enhanced secure passport with an embedded electronic chip. The chip can be scanned to match the identity of the traveler to the passport. E-Passports are issued by the proper passport issuing authority and must be in compliance with standards set by the International Civil Aviation Organization (ICAO). You can readily identify an e-Passport, because it has a unique international symbol on the cover."[691]

---

[683] CBP, "Travel Reentry" https://www.ice.gov/sevis/travel#wcm-survey-target-id. Scroll down to question "Which islands are defined as 'adjacent islands?'"

[684] 1 (Legacy) INS Inspector's Field Manual, Ch. 15, 14-1 INS Manuals 15.7 "Visa Waiver Pilot Program (VWPP)."

[685] Pub. L. No. 114-113 (2015).

[686] INA §217(c)(2)(B)(i).

[687] INA §217(c)(2)(B)(ii).

[688] European Commission, Migration and Home Affairs, "Schengen Area" (Jan. 7, 2013), http://ec.europa.eu/dgs/home-affairs/what-we-do/policies/borders-and-visas/schengen/index_en.htm.

[689] INA §217(a)(3).

[690] DHS, "Statement by Secretary Jeh C. Johnson on Strengthening Travel Security with E-Passports" (Apr. 1, 2016), AILA Doc. No. 16040532.

[691] DOS, "Visa Waiver Program," https://travel.state.gov/content/visas/en/visit/visa-waiver-program.html. The site contains an image of the international symbol for an e-passport.

Copyright © 2017. American Immigration Lawyers Association. All rights reserved.

Infants and children must have individual machine readable passports; they may not be listed as dependents on the passport of a parent.[692] Because machine readable passports "typically have biodata for only one traveler in the machine-readable zone, families traveling together, with infant(s) or child(ren) with passport information on the passports of the parents, may be denied admission, "if the biodata for only one traveler is machine-readable."[693]

Those who do not hold a machine-readable e-passport must obtain a visa to enter the United States.[694]

4. Enrollment in the Electronic System for Travel Authorization (ESTA)

DHS has established ESTA, which requires a VWP traveler to register online for authorization to participate in the VWP.[695] As of January 12, 2009, ESTA is mandatory for air and sea travel,[696] where all VWP travelers must "receive travel authorization through ESTA prior to boarding a conveyance destined for an air or sea port of entry in the United States."[697] ESTA is not required of VWP travelers who will seek admission at a land port of entry.[698] A VWP traveler must register with ESTA even if he or she will only transit through the United States by air: "In the address field of the application, write 'In Transit.'"[699] In addition, although "ESTA is not needed for a land entry (*i.e.*, U.K. citizen with Canadian landed immigrant status who is entering the United States from Canada), ESTA is required if a person flies from the United States to a foreign destination, and then back to the United States before returning to Canada."[700] ESTA registration is also required for travel to Puerto Rico and the U.S. Virgin Islands.[701]

DHS believes that ESTA will identify travelers who are ineligible for the VWP, such that these travelers will not board U.S.-bound carriers, in an effort to increase security of U.S. borders, reduce delays in applications for admission made at U.S. ports of entry, and reduce the costs borne by carriers who must transport foreign nationals deemed ineligible for VWP admission.[702] DHS also indicates that ESTA

---

[692] *Id.*

[693] DOS, "MRP Required for All VWP Travelers" (July 15, 2003), AILA Doc. No. 03070110.

[694] DOS, "Visa Waiver Program," https://travel.state.gov/content/visas/en/visit/visa-waiver-program.html.

[695] 80 Fed. Reg. 32267 (June 8, 2015); *see also* 73 Fed. Reg. 32440 (June 9, 2008); 8 CFR §9217.5.

[696] 73 Fed. Reg. 67354 (Nov. 13, 2008).

[697] 80 Fed. Reg. 32267 (June 8, 2015), p, 32269.

[698] CBP, https://help.cbp.gov/app/answers/detail/a_id/1094/kw/who%20must%20apply%20for%20esta.

[699] CBP, "Frequently Asked Questions about the Visa Waiver Program (WP) and the Electronic System for Travel Authorization (ESTA)" (ESTA FAQ) (Mar. 16, 2016), AILA Doc. No. 16031614.

[700] "AILA National CBP Liaison Committee Meeting Liaison Agenda" (Mar. 25, 2010), AILA Doc. No. 10072870.

[701] CBP, https://help.cbp.gov/app/answers/detail/a_id/1094/kw/who%20must%20apply%20for%20esta.

[702] 73 Fed. Reg. 32440 (June 9, 2008).

Copyright © 2017. American Immigration Lawyers Association. All rights reserved.

participation may prevent "significant delays" for a foreign national who is unaware that he or she is inadmissible to the United States.[703]

However, it is critical to note that, in essence, ESTA approval provides information that the foreign national is not inadmissible to the United States, but it does not provide affirmative confirmation that a foreign national is admissible. Specifically, DHS is careful to state the following:

"[A]n authorization to travel to the United States under ESTA is not a determination that the alien ultimately is admissible to the United States. That determination is made by a CBP Officer only after an applicant for admission is inspected by the CBP officer at a U.S. port of entry. In addition, ESTA is not a visa or a process that acts in lieu of any visa issuance determination made by the Department of State. Travel authorization under ESTA allows a VWP participant to travel to the United States, and does not confer admissibility to the United States. ESTA, therefore, allows DHS to identify potential grounds of ineligibility for admission before the VWP traveler embarks on a carrier destined for the United States... an approved travel authorization only allows an alien to board a conveyance for travel to a U.S. port of entry and does not restrict, limit, or otherwise affect the authority of CBP to determine an alien's admissibility to the United States during inspection at a port of entry."[704]

DHS views the ESTA program as a shift to automate the Form I-94W "with the ultimate goal of replacing it, not duplicating it."[705] Indeed, the requirement to complete the paper Form I-94W was eliminated for VWP travelers arriving in the United States at air or sea ports of entry on or after June 29, 2010.[706]

Previous DHS guidance stated that foreign nationals who were denied U.S. visas or denied U.S. admission, whether the application was made pursuant to the VWP or not, were ineligible to apply for ESTA approval.[707] However, a later iteration of the FAQ portion of that guidance omits those statements.[708]

Although legacy INS guidance indicated that refusal of VWP admission did not preclude a foreign national from applying for VWP admission on another occasion because the refusal was not deemed removal under the U.S. immigration laws,[709]

---

[703] *Id.*

[704] 73 Fed. Reg. 32440 (June 9, 2008). *See also* INA 217(h)(3).

[705] 80 Fed. Reg. 32267, 32275 (June 8, 2015).

[706] *Id.*

[707] DHS Fact Sheet and FAQ, "Electronic System for Travel Authorization (ESTA)," AILA Doc. No. 08060380 (June 3, 2008).

[708] ESTA FAQ (Mar. 16, 2016), AILA Doc. No. 16031614.

[709] 1 (Legacy) INS Inspector's Field Manual, Ch. 15, 14-1 INS Manuals 15.7 "Visa Waiver Pilot Program (VWPP)."

Copyright © 2017. American Immigration Lawyers Association. All rights reserved.

CBP appears to regard such a refusal as a probable roadblock to approval, stating "[I]f you were previously denied a visa, or previously refused entry to the United States, or previously removed from the U.S., your ESTA application will most likely be denied."[710]

One rationale for this approach is that an individual previously refused admission will be denied admission upon a subsequent application; but this analysis presumes that the foreign national was refused admission because he or she was subject to an ongoing ground of inadmissibility, and it ignores the possibility that the foreign national failed to comply with a technical requirement, such as having a round-trip ticket.

One route to overcome an ESTA refusal is DHS's Traveler Redress Inquiry System (TRIP).[711] While generally used for correction of errors in the government's records, such as a wrong departure date from a previous entry, the TRIP website does indicate that it can be used for "situations where travelers believe they have been unfairly or incorrectly delayed."[712]

It also appears that CBP and DOS "have had different understandings of the meaning and legal effect of the terms 'refusal' and 'denial' when INA §221(g) notice is used to refuse a visa application."[713] As discussed in Volume 1: Chapter Two, "Basic Nonimmigrant Concepts," administrative processing under INA §221(g) may occur for a number of reasons and may result in a visa refusal. The ESTA application only asks if the foreign national has been denied a visa, and CBP takes the position that a visa refusal is the same as a visa denial.[714] CBP indicated the intent to "work[] closely with DOS on ESTA issues, including 221(g)" and to "work[] on 'framing' the 221(g) question on the ESTA site,"[715] but the online ESTA application does not yet reflect a change.

Similarly, it is hoped that having a visa cancelled without prejudice will not preclude a foreign national from receiving ESTA approval. At this time, it remains unclear whether a visa that was "cancelled without prejudice" would result in further inquiry into the application following an "Authorization Pending" response or in an

---

[710] CBP, "Previously denied a visa or immigration benefit" (updated Nov. 10, 2015), https://help.cbp.gov/app/answers/detail/a_id/1097/related/1/~/esta-application-denied.

[711] CBP, "Why was I (or my friend, relative, etc.) denied entry to the U.S.?" https://help.cbp.gov/app/answers/detail/a_id/757. *See also* "AILA National Liaison Meeting with U.S. Customs and Border Protection Office of Field Operations" (Oct. 8, 2015), AILA Doc. No. 16031104, item 23(f).

[712] DHS, "TRIP: One-Stop Travelers' Redress Process," https://www.dhs.gov/one-stop-travelers-redress-process.

[713] "AILA National CBP Liaison Committee Meeting Liaison Agenda" (Mar. 25, 2010), AILA Doc. No. 10072870.

[714] *Id.*

[715] *Id.*

Copyright © 2017. American Immigration Lawyers Association. All rights reserved.

automatic ESTA denial. This is because the ESTA application form asks whether the foreign national has had a U.S. visa cancelled,[716] but no other CBP or DHS guidance indicates that those with cancelled visas are ineligible for ESTA approval.

ESTA approval is valid for a maximum of two years, and foreign nationals may use the same valid ESTA approval for multiple U.S. trips.[717] A foreign national must obtain a new ESTA approval if any of the following events occurs:

- The foreign national "is issued a new passport";

- The foreign national has a name change;

- The foreign national has a gender change;

- The foreign national changes the country of citizenship or nationality; or

- The foreign national's circumstances change, such that there is a change in any answer to the inadmissibility questions."[718]

If the foreign national's passport will expire in the coming six months, then ESTA approval will not be granted.[719] If the foreign national's passport will expire in less than two years, then the ESTA approval will be valid for a shorter period of time.[720] If the VWP traveler is a national of a country which has signed an agreement where passports may be used for return of the bearer for six months after the passport's expiration date, as discussed in Volume 1: Chapter Two, "Basic Nonimmigrant Concepts," then the ESTA approval will be valid until the passport's date of expiration.[721] If the VWP traveler is a national of a country that has not signed such an agreement, then the ESTA approval will be valid for the date that is six months before the passport's expiration.[722] If the client anticipates a U.S. trip in the final six months of the validity of the passport, then the practitioner may wish to advise the foreign national to obtain a new or renewed passport before applying for ESTA approval. If the client has more than one passport, the passport that was used on the ESTA application must be used for the travel.[723]

---

[716] ESTA application, https://esta.cbp.dhs.gov, posing the question "Have you ever been denied a U.S. visa or entry into the U.S. or had a U.S. visa canceled?"

[717] 8 CFR §215.5(d)(1) and (f)(1); 73 Fed. Reg. 32440 (June 9, 2008).

[718] 8 CFR §215.5(e).

[719] 8 CFR §215.5(d)(2).

[720] Id.

[721] Id.

[722] Id.

[723] ESTA FAQ (Mar. 16, 2016), AILA Doc. No. 16031614.

Copyright © 2017. American Immigration Lawyers Association. All rights reserved.

CBP retains the discretion to revoke the ESTA approval at any time and for any reason.[724] There is no recourse to judicial review if a foreign national is denied ESTA approval.[725]

DHS recommends, but does not require, that a traveler seek ESTA approval at least 72 hours before the carrier's departure, so that resources may be devoted to assisting last minute and emergency travelers.[726] Foreign nationals need not have specific U.S. travel plans in order to apply for ESTA approval; foreign nationals are encouraged to apply as soon as they begin to plan a U.S. trip because travel details may be updated after ESTA approval.[727]

The application form is available online[728] in 13 additional foreign languages.[729] Initially, there was no ESTA application fee,[730] but now a fee of $14 is required:

"[This] is the sum of two amounts: a $10 travel promotion fee for an approved ESTA statutorily set by the Travel Promotion Act and a $4 operational fee for the use of ESTA as set by the Secretary of Homeland Security to ensure recovery of the full costs of providing and administering the ESTA system."[731]

DHS regulations seem to indicate that the travel promotion fee sunset on September 30, 2015,[732] but Congress in 2014 extended the fee until September 30, 2020.[733] The operational fee "does not include a sunset provision but will be reassessed on a regular basis to ensure it is set at a level to fully recover ESTA operating costs."[734] Changes to the operational fee should be published as a rulemaking.[735] The operational fee is incurred "upon initial application" for ESTA authorization, and the travel promotion fee is due "only if [the foreign national] receives travel authorization."[736] A foreign national should not need to pay the fee

---

[724] INA §217(h)(3)(C)(i); 8 CFR §215.5(f)(4).

[725] INA §217(h)(3)(C)(iv); 8 CFR §215.5(f)(3).

[726] 73 Fed. Reg. 32440 (June 9, 2008); GAO publication, "Visa Waiver Program" (Sept. 2008), AILA Doc. No. 08091569; CBP, "ESTA FAQ" (Mar. 16, 2016), AILA Doc. No. 16031614.

[727] "ESTA FAQ" (Mar. 16, 2016), AILA Doc. No. 16031614.

[728] "ESTA application," https://esta.cbp.dhs.gov.

[729] DHS Press Release, "ESTA Web site available in 13 additional languages for U.S.-bound travelers from visa waiver countries" (Oct. 15, 2008), https://www.dhs.gov/xnews/releases/pr_1224103683923.shtm.

[730] INA §217(h)(3)(B); 73 Fed. Reg. 32440 (June 9, 2008).

[731] 73 Fed. Reg. 32440 (June 9, 2008).

[732] 8 CFR §215.5(h)(1).

[733] Travel Promotion, Enhancement, and Modernization Act §5, Pub. L. No. 113-235, 128 Stat. 2130 (2014).

[734] 73 Fed. Reg. 32440 (June 9, 2008).

[735] Id.

[736] Id.

Copyright © 2017. American Immigration Lawyers Association. All rights reserved.

with each visit to the United States "during the authorization period."[737] Information may be updated during the two-year authorization period without payment of the fees again, but a new authorization is required, and thus the fees need to be remitted, if the foreign national obtains a new passport, or if there is change in name, gender, country of citizenship, or circumstances underlying the individual's "yes" or "no" responses.[738]

The fees should be paid by credit or debit card (MasterCard, Visa, American Express, or Discover)[739] "when applying for or renewing an ESTA."[740] In addition: "Payment arrangements may be made through a third-party, such as a travel agent, since the name on the credit card does not have to match the name of the traveler. The ESTA application will not be submitted for processing until all payment information is received."[741]

After the foreign national submits a completed ESTA application online, the application will be compared against law enforcement databases.[742] The ESTA response, which may be approval, denial, or pending, is generally provided quickly.[743] If the foreign national receives an "Authorization Pending" response, he or she should check the website within 72 hours for a final response.[744] CBP notes, however, that "[i]n most cases, a response is received within seconds of submitting an application."[745]

It is a good idea to print out the ESTA application response in order to maintain a record of the ESTA application number. The number is not necessary in order to board the airplane or sea vessel, but it is helpful when checking the status of the ESTA application, though the website does provide a look-up mechanism if the individual does not have his or her number.[746]

Mistyped contact or travel information may be corrected or updated at a later date, and the practitioner may wish to advise the client to do so, "as it may reduce the number of questions" asked of the foreign national upon arrival in the United

---

[737] *Id.*

[738] "ESTA FAQ" (Mar. 16, 2016), AILA Doc. No. 16031614.

[739] 75 Fed. Reg. 47701 (Aug. 9, 2010). *See also* ESTA FAQ (Mar. 16, 2016), AILA Doc. No. 16031614.

[740] CBP, "DHS, CBP Remind Travelers ESTA Fee to Begin" (Sep. 7, 2010), AILA Doc. No. 10090961; "ESTA FAQ" (Mar. 16, 2016), AILA Doc. No. 16031614.

[741] *Id.*

[742] "ESTA FAQ" (Mar. 16, 2016), AILA Doc. No. 16031614.

[743] *Id.*

[744] *Id.*

[745] *Id.*

[746] ESTA application, "Retrieve Individual Application," https://esta.cbp.dhs.gov/esta/application.html?execution=e1s1.

Copyright © 2017. American Immigration Lawyers Association. All rights reserved.

States.[747] Unfortunately, errors in entering biometric or passport information may not be corrected by updating an existing profile; the foreign national must reapply, with the old application "automatically ... voided" upon submission of a new application.[748] In order to reapply, it is necessary to close the user's browser, then reopen it. If that doesn't work, "click on the 'Ask a Question' button on the right side of the screen, and submit the original application number, if [the user has] it; the full name; passport number; date of birth of the applicant; contact phone number (including country code), as well as a description of what was entered incorrectly."[749] CBP will then review the application, and notify with next steps.

Finally, CBP instructs that if the applicant "misunderstood the question, or thought something in [his or her] background was a reason to be denied and found out later that it was not, we advise you to contact us so we can review your answer. You should send us an email ... explaining why you selected 'yes' to that question, and asking for clarification on next steps. Emails are sent using "the "Email us your Question" button on the webpage.[750] CBP also notes that "[r]eapplying with false information for the purposes of qualifying for an ESTA could make you permanently ineligible for travel to the U.S."[751] CBP also offers the option of calling its Information Center at 1-877-227-5511.[752]

If the foreign national is denied ESTA approval, then he or she will need to apply for a B visa in order to travel to the United States.[753] A foreign national may not reapply for ESTA approval unless circumstances have changed, but can try to contact CBP as discussed above to try to correct an error on the application.[754] DHS indicates that "due to security/privacy laws, U.S. Customs and Border Protection cannot tell you the reason for your denial of ESTA authorization."[755]

If a foreign national wishes to contest the ESTA denial, he or she may file an inquiry with DHS Travel Redress Inquiry Program (TRIP),[756] but DHS cautions such an inquiry may not resolve the issue that caused the ESTA application to be

---

[747] CBP, "I made a mistake on my ESTA application," http://help.cbp.gov (click "Find an Answer, Ask a Question" and insert the page's title).

[748] *Id.*

[749] *Id.*

[750] *Id.*

[751] CBP, "ESTA application was denied," http://help.cbp.gov (click "Find an Answer, Ask a Question" and insert the page's title).

[752] "ESTA FAQ" (Mar. 16, 2016), AILA Doc. No. 16031614.

[753] 73 Fed. Reg. 32440 (June 9, 2008).

[754] "ESTA FAQ" (Mar. 16, 2016), AILA Doc. No. 16031614.

[755] CBP, "ESTA application was denied," http://help.cbp.gov (click "Find an Answer, Ask a Question" and insert the page's title).

[756] DHS, "Traveler Redress Inquiry Program (DHS TRIP)," https://www.dhs.gov/trip.

Copyright © 2017. American Immigration Lawyers Association. All rights reserved.

denied.[757] This would be the case, for example, if the foreign national was ineligible to use the VWP and/or inadmissible. Because the ESTA program is administered by CBP, inquiries made to DOS or a U.S. consulate on the reasons for ESTA denial would most likely be unsuccessful.[758]

The foreign national's application data will remain on the ESTA system for as long as the ESTA approval is valid.[759] After that time, DHS will maintain the information for one more year and then "will archive the information for 12 years to allow retrieval of the information for law enforcement, national security, or investigatory purposes."[760] With respect to the safety and security of the ESTA website, DHS states that "[i]nformation submitted by applicants through the ESTA website is subject to the same strict privacy provisions and controls that have been established for similar traveler screening. Access to such information is limited to those with a professional need to know. The website is operated by the U.S. government and employs technology to prevent unauthorized access to the information entered and viewed. Information is protected and governed by U.S. laws and regulations, including but not limited to the Federal Information Security Management Act."[761]

DHS has exempted[762] certain portions of ESTA data from the Privacy Act:[763]

- An individual must not receive his or her record upon request because the record could "reveal any investigative interest," "compromise ongoing efforts to investigate a violation of U.S. law, including investigations of a known or suspected terrorist," and "permit the record subject to take measures to impede the investigation";

- CBP must not be required to undertake reasonable efforts to notify an individual when his or her record is made public by virtue of legal process, because such individual notice requirements "would pose an impossible administrative burden on DHS and other agencies and could alert the subjects of counterterrorism or law enforcement investigations to the fact of those investigations when not previously known; and

---

[757] "ESTA FAQ" (Mar. 16, 2016), AILA Doc. No. 16031614.

[758] *Id.*

[759] *Id.*

[760] *Id.*

[761] *Id.*

[762] 74 Fed. Reg. 45070 (Aug. 31, 2009).

[763] 5 USC §552a.

Copyright © 2017. American Immigration Lawyers Association. All rights reserved.

- The availability of civil remedies to individuals is precluded.[764]

The ESTA program may address the concerns of VWP abuse expressed by immigration inspectors and other stakeholders, as discussed above, because the existence of a security risk and/or law enforcement reason for a foreign national's inadmissibility would preclude him or her from boarding a U.S.-bound carrier.[765] Concerns have been expressed that mandatory ESTA registration for VWP travelers will result in an increased workload at U.S. consulates, as foreign nationals would apply for B visas, which may have validity of up to 10 years, instead of registering with ESTA every two years, or even more frequently in the case of name changes.[766] Foreign nationals whose ESTA applications are rejected, a rough estimation of which is between one and three percent, would also be forced to apply for B visas.[767] In addition, there is a concern that the ESTA program limits the VWP only to nationals of developed countries who have easy access to the Internet and would effectively bar foreign nationals who do not have access to the Internet from engaging in visa-free travel. In response, DHS indicated that the ESTA application need not be made by the foreign national, but may be made by a representative, such as a travel agent, or by the airline;[768] however, it remains to be seen whether these accommodations are proving sufficient to ensure full availability of the VWP.

5. Manner of Travel

a. Travel by Air and Sea

If the foreign national will travel to the United States by air or sea, he or she must have a round-trip ticket "that will transport the traveler out of the United States to any other foreign port or place."[769] The destination country stated on the ticket must not be a "contiguous territory or an adjacent island," unless the foreign national is "a resident of the country of destination."[770] The "contiguous territory" and "adjacent island" countries are as discussed above. A round-trip ticket is defined as follows:

"[A]ny return trip transportation ticket in the name of an arriving Visa Waiver Pilot Program applicant on a participating carrier valid for at least 1 year, electronic ticket record, airline employee passes indicating return passage, individual vouchers for return passage, group vouchers for return passage for charter flights, and military travel orders which include military dependents for

---

[764] 74 Fed. Reg. 45070 (Aug. 31, 2009).

[765] *Id.*

[766] GAO, "Visa Waiver Program" (Sept. 2008), AILA Doc. No. 08091569; "AILA's Comment on CBP's Interim Rule to Implement ESTA for Visa Waiver Participants" Aug. 8, 2008), AILA Doc. No. 08081365.

[767] GAO, "Visa Waiver Program" (Sept. 2008), AILA Doc. No. 08091569.

[768] "ESTA FAQ" (Mar. 16, 2016), AILA Doc. No. 16031614.

[769] 8 CFR §217.2(c)(1).

[770] *Id.*

Copyright © 2017. American Immigration Lawyers Association. All rights reserved.

return to duty stations outside the United States on U.S. military flights. A period of validity of 1 year need not be reflected on the ticket itself, provided that the carrier agrees that it will honor the return portion of the ticket at any time."[771]

Although the regulation indicates that the round trip ticket must be valid for at least one year, as a practical matter, presentation of a ticket with a departure date that is more than 90 days in the future may result in denial of admission to the United States. The immigration inspector may determine that the foreign national is not eligible for admission under the VWP,[772] because the foreign national is not "seeking entry as a tourist for 90 days or less."[773] The practitioner should advise the client that the ticket should have a departure date that is less than 90 days from the date of proposed admission to the United States.

The round-trip ticket requirement may be waived "under regulations" by the Secretary of Homeland Security,[774] or it may be waived if the foreign national will arrive in the United States on limited types of civil aircraft,[775] or on limited types of noncommercial aircraft owned and operated by a domestic corporation conducting operations.[776] As a practical matter, however, use of these waivers is not encouraged. Either the waiver must be obtained ahead of the foreign national's travel to the United States, which would entail processing time that may rival the processing time of a B visa application, or, if the waiver is sought at the time of applying for admission at the U.S. port of entry, the foreign national must risk being denied U.S. admission.

The regulations do not provide for a waiver specifically for individuals who do not meet the VWP requirements. Thus, a waiver would need to be under the "unforeseen emergency" provisions for waiver of visa requirements, utilizing Form I-193,[777] or the individual would need to be paroled into the United States.[778] Experience has shown, however, that CBP inspectors are not particularly generous with granting waivers or parole in these circumstances.

In addition, the airline of the foreign national's travel must be an approved carrier, which signed an agreement with the Secretary of Homeland Security,[779] to guarantee the return transportation of inadmissible or removable foreign nationals, among other

---

[771] 8 CFR §217.2(a). *See also* 9 FAM 201.1-4(C)(e).

[772] 8 CFR §217.4(a)(1).

[773] INA §217(a)(1).

[774] INA §217(a)(8).

[775] INA §§217(a)(8) and 217(e)(3). For a list of the qualifying civil aircraft, see 14 CFR §135.25.

[776] INA §§217(a)(8) and 217(e)(3). For a list of the noncommercial aircraft, see 14 CFR §91.501.

[777] 8 CFR 212.1(g). *See also* 9 FAM 201.1.-6(F).

[778] INA §212(d)(5)(A). *See also* "AILA National Liaison Meeting with U.S. Customs and Border Protection Office of Field Operations" (Oct. 8, 2015), item 23. Although the discussion relates to VWP applicants for admission with previous overstays, the process should apply with respect to other grounds of ineligibility.

[779] INA §217(e); 8 CFR §217.6(a).

Copyright © 2017. American Immigration Lawyers Association. All rights reserved.

conditions.[780] "Carrier" is defined as an "owner, charterer, lessee, or authorized agent of any commercial vessel or commercial aircraft engaged in transporting passengers to the United States from a foreign place."[781]

In general, private aircraft, yachts, or other sea vessels do not qualify as carriers because they are not "commercial," and passengers on private aircraft, yachts, or other sea vessels may not use the VWP.[782] The exceptions are for certain specific types of civil aircraft and noncommercial aircraft owned and operated by a domestic corporation conducting operations, as discussed above.[783] The civil and noncommercial aircraft may be required to post a bond,[784] and the aircraft must sign the carrier agreement, which acknowledges the aircraft's responsibility to transport inadmissible or deportable foreign nationals out of the United States, with the Secretary of Homeland Security.[785] Private aircraft carrying nonimmigrants must meet certain requirements relating to passenger arrival and departure information.[786]

Ferries are sea vessels, but a foreign national who travels to the United States on a ferry may be considered either under the provisions for arrival by land or under the provisions for arrival by sea. Foreign nationals traveling for a short duration with ferry companies with the primary purpose of providing transportation as "a continuation of the highway from one side of the water to the other and ... as a service normally attributed to a bridge or tunnel" are considered in the same way as those seeking admission at a land port of entry.[787] These foreign nationals are subject to the requirements of applying for admission after arriving by land, as discussed below. In contrast, foreign nationals traveling for a longer duration, sometimes up to 12 to 15 hours, on ferry operations that "go beyond a quick trip ... are more like vessel operations."[788] These ferry operations must be signatories to the carrier agreement, and foreign nationals who seek VWP admission after arriving on a non-signatory carrier are subject to denial of admission, although in "unforeseen

---

[780] 9 FAM 201.1-4(C)(e). For a list of signatory carriers, *see* CBP, https://www.cbp.gov/document/report/signatory-visa-waiver-program-vwp-carriers.

[781] 8 CFR §217.2(a).

[782] 1 (Legacy) INS Inspector's Field Manual, Ch. 15, 14-1 INS Manuals 15.7 "Visa Waiver Pilot Program (VWPP)."

[783] INA §§217(a)(8) and 217(e)(3). For a list of the qualifying aircraft, *see* 14 CFR §§135.25 and 91.501.

[784] INA §217(a)(5).

[785] INA §217(e).

[786] 8 CFR §231.3, 10 CFR §122.22. *See also* CBP, "Private Aircraft Reporting Requirements for Arriving or Departing United States," https://www.cbp.gov/travel/travel-industry-personnel/apis/private-aircraft.

[787] 1 (Legacy) INS Inspector's Field Manual, Ch. 15, 14-1 INS Manuals 15.7 "Visa Waiver Pilot Program (VWPP)."

[788] *Id.*

Copyright © 2017. American Immigration Lawyers Association. All rights reserved.

emergencies," the foreign national may be paroled into the United States following issuance of a waiver pursuant to INA §212(d)(4),[789] as discussed above.

The carrier must electronically transmit to CBP, before the carrier's departure, its passenger arrival manifest data for the foreign national's arrival in and departure from the United States.[790] The passenger data includes name, date of birth, gender, country issuing the travel document, U.S. destination, entry date, and departure date.[791] The civil and noncommercial aircraft must provide this information, as well as information "necessary for the identification of any alien passenger being transported and for the enforcement of the immigration laws," and this information must be electronically transmitted no later than one hour before the flight's arrival at the port of entry.[792]

If the individual arrived by air or sea, but departs by land or via a private conveyance, the departure is unlikely to be recorded by CBP, and thus it is recommended that the process for reporting the departure after the fact to CBP, discussed below, be followed.

b. Arrival by Land

If the foreign national will make an application for admission at a land port of entry, then the return trip ticket is not necessary.[793] The foreign national must, however, present evidence of "financial solvency and a domicile abroad to which the applicant intends to return."[794] This evidence should be very similar to the evidence of sufficient funds and foreign residence abroad for B visa applicants, as discussed above. The foreign national must also pay a fee for the Form I-94W, Nonimmigrant Visa Waiver Arrival/Departure Form.[795] The fee is currently $6.[796]

It is important to surrender the I-94W to CBP, if departing by land or private conveyance, to ensure that CBP has a record of the timely departure.[797]

---

[789] 1 (Legacy) INS Inspector's Field Manual, Ch. 15, 14-1 INS Manuals 15.7 "Visa Waiver Pilot Program (VWPP)." For a discussion of how parole into the United States differs from admission to the United States, *see* Volume 1: Chapter Two, "Basic Nonimmigrant Concepts."

[790] INA §§217(h)(1)(B)(i) and (ii); 8 CFR §217.7(a).

[791] GAO, "Visa Waiver Program" (Sept. 2008), AILA Doc. No. 08091569.

[792] INA §217(a)(10).

[793] 8 CFR §217.2(c)(2).

[794] *Id.*

[795] *Id.*

[796] 8 CFR §103.7(b)(1)(ii)(E).

[797] CBP, "Arrival/Departure Forms: I-94 and I-94W," https://www.cbp.gov/travel/international-visitors/i-94-instructions. *See also* CBP, "I still have my I-94," https://help.cbp.gov/app/answers/detail/a_id/752.

Copyright © 2017. American Immigration Lawyers Association. All rights reserved.

c. Reporting a Departure After the Fact

If a visa waiver nonimmigrant's departure from the United States is not recorded with CBP, it is critical to resolve the situation before the foreign national attempts to apply for VWP admission at a later date, because overstaying a previous VWP admission makes a person ineligible for subsequent VWP admission.[798] This failure to record can occur if someone who entered through a land port does not surrender the I-94W upon departure. If the departure is by commercial air or sea carrier, CBP indicates that it can obtain confirmation of the departure independently, and no further action is needed on the individual's part.[799] However, if an individual who entered by land does not return the Form I-94W CBP upon departure from the United States by land or private conveyance, then it is necessary to resolve the situation.

Although CBP does not explicitly address this situation, it would appear that if the individual entered via air or sea, but departed via land or private conveyance, the departure also likely was not recorded.

To resolve the problem after the person has departed, correspondence should be sent to CBP, via its contractor, to explain and document the situation. The correspondence should be accompanied by the I-94W, if one was issued, as well as documentation of the departure and the individual's presence outside the United States, such as copies of boarding passes if an airplane was boarded in a contiguous country, passport entry stamps into another country (also include the biographic page and all non-blank pages of the passport), dated records showing presence in another country, such as credit card receipts, pay slips, school records, etc. The individual should be sure to carry a copy of the correspondence and documentation on his or her next entry into the United States, in case issues are raised at that time.[800]

If the individual was not issued a paper I-94W, CBP's look-up system should be used to get the I-94 number and should be included with the correspondence.[801]

The correspondence and documentation should be sent to CBP's contractor at:

> Coleman Data Solutions
>
> Box 7965
>
> Akron, OH 44306
>
> Attn: NIDPS (I-94)

If using a courier service, the following address should be used:

> Coleman Data Solutions

---

[798] INA §217(a)(7).

[799] CBP, "I still have my I-94," https://help.cbp.gov/app/answers/detail/a_id/752.

[800] Id.

[801] CBP, "I-94 Website," https://i94.cbp.dhs.gov/I94/#/home#section_

Copyright © 2017. American Immigration Lawyers Association. All rights reserved.

> 3043 Sanitarium Rd., Suite 2
>
> Akron, OH 44312
>
> Attn: NIDPS (I-94)[802]

6. "Countries of Concern"

a. Visa Waiver Program Improvement and Terrorist Travel Prevention Act Overview

The "Visa Waiver Program Improvement and Terrorist Travel Prevention Act,"[803] discussed earlier in the context of e-passport requirements, also prohibits use of the VWP by anyone who is a national of—or on or after March 1, 2011, has traveled to—certain designated countries.[804]

The legislation specifically named Iraq and Syria as affected countries, as well as those countries whose governments have been designated as having "repeatedly provided support of acts of international terrorism."[805] Thus, Iran and Sudan were immediately added to the list by virtue of this provision (Syria, which was specified in the legislation, also was already designated as a state sponsor of terrorism).[806]

The legislation also empowered the Secretary of Homeland Security to designate other countries or areas of concern.[807] Since then, Somalia, Libya, and Yemen[808] have been added to the list by DHS, for a total of seven affected countries as of this writing.

Shortly before the enactment of this legislation, CBP had added or amended 21 questions in ESTA to "improve[] the Department's ability to screen potential VWP travelers while more accurately identifying those who pose a security risk."[809] After the legislation, CBP added more questions to ESTA in order to elicit information needed to determine whether an individual might be impacted by the new restrictions. Those questions include whether the person has traveled to, or been present in, any of the designated countries since March 1, 2011, has been issued a passport or travel

---

[802] CBP, "I still have my I-94," https://help.cbp.gov/app/answers/detail/a_id/752.

[803] Pub. L. No. 114-113 (2015).

[804] INA §217(a)(12).

[805] Id.

[806] See DOS, "State Sponsors of Terrorism," http://www.state.gov/j/ct/list/c14151.htm.

[807] INA §217(a)(12).

[808] Press Release "DHS Announces Further Travel Restrictions for the Visa Waiver Program" (Feb. 18, 2016), AILA Doc. No. 16021804, https://www.dhs.gov/news/2016/02/18/dhs-announces-further-travel-restrictions-visa-waiver-program. See also 81 Fed. Reg. 39680 (June 17, 2016), adding related categories of records to ESTA.

[809] 79 Fed. Reg. 73096 (Dec. 9, 2014).

Copyright © 2017. American Immigration Lawyers Association. All rights reserved.

document by any other country, is now a citizen or national of any other country, or has ever been a citizen or national of another country.[810] An affirmative answer to any will generate additional questions on ESTA.[811]

Persons who are affected by these changes, and hold an ESTA approval that predates the provisions' implementation with respect to the country in question, are urged to verify their ESTA status on the website prior to making a travel reservation and prior to travel to ensure that their approval has not been revoked.[812]

While CBP has stated that it "is engaging in extensive outreach,"[813] it has not specifically stated that it will be contacting individuals whose authorization is revoked to inform them of the fact.

If a person's ESTA approval has been revoked, or if a new ESTA has been denied, that individual must apply for a B-1/B-2 visa before entering the United States. (Exceptions and waivers exist for certain people who have traveled to one of the designated countries, as discussed under "Travel to Countries of Concern" below, but their applicability is decided as part of the ESTA process.) If the individual immediately needs a visa "for urgent business, medical, or humanitarian travel to the United States, U.S. Embassies and Consulates stand ready to handle applications on an expedited basis."[814] CBP has recommended that the individual retain a copy of the ESTA denial or revocation, in case it is requested to schedule an appointment.[815]

b. Nationals of Affected Countries

None of the countries designated for the restrictions are, or ever have been, part of the VWP. However, some individuals may be considered dual nationals of both the visa waiver country and one of the designated countries, and thus fall under the visa waiver restriction relating to nationals of those countries.

The legislation uses the term "national" and not "citizen," though the two terms are often used interchangeably. The INA defines "national" as "a person owing permanent allegiance to a state,"[816] and enumerates four circumstances in which a person would be a national but not a citizen of the United States.[817] But the INA does

---

[810] CBP, "Visa Waiver Program Improvement and Terrorist Travel Prevention Act Frequently Asked Questions" (June 19, 2017), AILA Doc. No. 16012200. Also at https://www.cbp.gov/travel/international-visitors/visa-waiver-program/visa-waiver-program-improvement-and-terrorist-travel-prevention-act-faq.

[811] Id.

[812] Id. To verify status, go to https://esta.cbp.dhs.gov.

[813] Id.

[814] DOS, "Visa Waiver Program," https://travel.state.gov/content/visas/en/visit/visa-waiver-program.html.

[815] CBP, "Visa Waiver Program Improvement and Terrorist Travel Prevention Act Frequently Asked Questions" (June 19, 2017), AILA Doc. No. 16012200. Also at https://www.cbp.gov/travel/international-visitors/visa-waiver-program/visa-waiver-program-improvement-and-terrorist-travel-prevention-act-faq.

[816] INA §101(a)(21).

[817] INA §308.

Copyright © 2017. American Immigration Lawyers Association. All rights reserved.

not specifically define the term "citizen." DOS, however, indicates that "dual nationality is the simultaneous possession of two citizenships."[818] Most of the pronouncements issued by DHS on the subject of the VWP bans use the two terms interchangeably.

Whether a person is a dual national of a VWP country and a country subject to the nationality restriction is at best a cloudy question. DHS has indicated that it "will make nationality determinations in accordance with U.S. legal standards and practices, not merely by reference to the laws and practices of foreign governments."[819] As U.S. legal standards on dual nationality relate primarily, if not exclusively, to situations in which the United States is one of the nationalities, it is not clear how those standards will be applied.

CBP had indicated that it will look at each application on a "case-by-case basis," using the answers to the questions it has added to ESTA for this purpose, in order to "analyze all relevant factors, including whether the individual holds a passport for one of the designated countries and when they last traveled there." It further noted that, even if an individual answers "yes" to whether he or she is a citizen of a designated country, "that will not result in an automatic ESTA denial. CBP will look at whether the person appears to be a nominal citizen, in which case ESTA may still be approved."[820] However, DHS has stated that any current ESTA authorization will be revoked for someone who has previously indicated that he or she holds dual nationality with a designated country.[821]

c. Travel to Countries of Concern

As indicated above, individuals who have been present in any of the designated countries on or after March 1, 2011, are unable to use the VWP.[822] There are, however, exceptions to and waivers of this restriction.

The restrictions do not apply to those who DHS determines were in one of the designated countries as part of military service in the armed forces of their VWP country and those who were there to carry out "official duties as a full time employee of the government of a program country."[823] CBP recommends that those who fall

---

[818] 7 FAM 081(a).

[819] CBP, "Visa Waiver Program Improvement and Terrorist Travel Prevention Act Frequently Asked Questions" (June 19, 2017), AILA Doc. No. 16012200. Also at https://www.cbp.gov/travel/international-visitors/visa-waiver-program/visa-waiver-program-improvement-and-terrorist-travel-prevention-act-faq.

[820] "AILA/U.S. CBP Office of Field Operations Meeting" (Apr. 6, 2016), AILA Doc. No. 16052700, item 11a.

[821] DHS and DOS, "United States Begins Implementation of Changes to the Visa Waiver Program" (Jan. 1, 2016). AILA Doc. No. 16012131.

[822] INA §217(a)(12).

[823] INA §217(a)(12)(B).

Copyright © 2017. American Immigration Lawyers Association. All rights reserved.

under this exception bring with them documentation of the military or official government service to the port of entry in case questions arise.[824]

In addition, the Secretary of Homeland Security is authorized to waive application of the travel restriction upon determination that the waiver "is in the law enforcement or national security interests of the United States."[825] CBP has indicated that waivers will be granted on a case-by-case basis, and that categories of persons who may be eligible include:

- Individuals who have traveled to Iran, Iraq, Sudan, or Syria on behalf of international organizations, regional organizations, or sub-national governments on official duty;

- Individuals who have traveled to Iran, Iraq, Sudan, or Syria on behalf of a humanitarian nongovernmental organization (NGO);

- Individuals who have traveled to Iran, Iraq, Sudan, or Syria as a journalist for reporting purposes;

- Individuals who traveled to Iran for legitimate business-related purposes following the conclusion of the Joint Comprehensive Plan of Action (July 14, 2015); and

- Individuals who have traveled to Iraq for legitimate business-related purposes.[826]

Individuals cannot initiate a process for obtaining a waiver. Instead, the waiver is an opaque element of the ESTA process: "If an applicant answers a question that triggers a possible ESTA ineligibility ground, they will automatically be asked questions to determine whether they are eligible for a waiver. If the waiver is granted, the applicant will not be notified that a waiver was approved; they will simply be notified that their ESTA was approved."[827] Presumably, if the waiver was denied, the ESTA will be denied, and the individual will need to apply for a B visa to enter the

---

[824] CBP, "Visa Waiver Program Improvement and Terrorist Travel Prevention Act Frequently Asked Questions" (June 19, 2017), AILA Doc. No. 16012200. Also at https://www.cbp.gov/travel/international-visitors/visa-waiver-program/visa-waiver-program-improvement-and-terrorist-travel-prevention-act-faq.

[825] INA §217(a)(12)(C).

[826] CBP, "Visa Waiver Program Improvement and Terrorist Travel Prevention Act Frequently Asked Questions" (June 19, 2017), AILA Doc. No. 16012200. Also at https://www.cbp.gov/travel/international-visitors/visa-waiver-program/visa-waiver-program-improvement-and-terrorist-travel-prevention-act-faq. *See also* DHS and DOS, "United States Begins Implementation of Changes to the Visa Waiver Program" (Jan. 1, 2016). AILA Doc. No. 16012131.

[827] "AILA/U.S. CBP Office of Field Operations Meeting" (Apr. 6, 2016), AILA Doc. No. 16052700, item 13.

Copyright © 2017. American Immigration Lawyers Association. All rights reserved.

United States. Practitioners report that waivers are not being granted generally despite announcements to the contrary.

It should be noted that the exceptions and waivers apply only to the travel provisions, and not to the provisions regarding nationality. There are no exceptions or waivers for them—only the ambiguity of whether one is considered a national of an affected country.

d. Ban on Entry

A March 2017 Executive Order suspends entry into the United States of nationals of six of the seven countries discussed above as subject to the restrictions on VWP (Iraq is excepted).[828] The order states that the suspension is for 90 days, but before nationals of the six countries can resume entering the United States , an assessment of each country must be conducted by the DHS Secretary, Secretary of State, and the Director of National Intelligence. The order requires the Secretary of State to request additional information from each country, and if the country does not provide the additional information, or the DHS Secretary does not certify that the country has a plan to provide that information, certain categories of nationals of those countries are to be included in a presidential proclamation prohibiting entry. The Secretary of State, Attorney General, or DHS Secretary can at any time recommend that additional countries be added to or taken off the list. Lawful permanent residents are excepted from this version of the order, as are individuals issued who were visas prior to the effective date of the order or who were admitted or paroled into the United States prior to the date of the order.[829]

This order supersedes an earlier Executive Order[830] that had been enjoined by multiple courts.[831] However, the March 2017 order also was enjoined.[832] At the time of this writing, the injunctions are still in effect and are being appealed by the government.

7. Threats to the Welfare, Health, Safety, or Security of the United States

A foreign national may not use the VWP if he or she poses a threat to the welfare, health, safety, or security of the United States.[833] As a practical matter, the analysis of whether an individual poses such a threat is conducted pursuant to considering the

---

[828] Exec. Order No. 13780, 82 Fed. Reg. 13209 (Mar. 9, 2017), AILA Doc. No. 17030604.

[829] Id.

[830] Exec. Order No. 13769, 82 Fed. Reg. 13769 (Feb. 1, 2017), AILA Doc. No. 17012560.

[831] E.g., State of Washington, No. C17-0141JLR (W.D.Wash. 2017). See "President Trump's Executive Actions on Immigration," AILA Doc. No. 16113030, for ongoing updates on the orders, their status, and the federal court challenges to them.

[832] E.g., State of Hawaii v. Trump, CV. No. 17-00050 DKW-KSC (D.Haw. 2017). See "President Trump's Executive Actions on Immigration," AILA Doc. No. 16113030, for ongoing updates on the orders, their status, and the federal court challenges to them.

[833] INA §217(a)(6).

Copyright © 2017. American Immigration Lawyers Association. All rights reserved.

individual's inadmissibility under the grounds enumerated in INA §212(a).[834] CBP checks an automated electronic database that contains information provided by DHS and DOS, including photographs and previous determinations of inadmissibility,[835] but CBP should not rely exclusively on the system check. A foreign national who discloses to the immigration inspector an intent to engage in terrorist activities, for example, would be deemed inadmissible and denied admission, even if such a ground of inadmissibility was not revealed by the system check.

When seeking admission to the United States, the foreign national should present documents evidencing the reason for his or her visit to the country and documents evidencing return abroad following completion of the visit.

8. Previous Violation of the Terms and Conditions of Previous VWP Admission

A foreign national who previously violated the terms and conditions of any previous VWP admission may not use the VWP for a subsequent application for admission, but must apply for a B visa at a U.S. consulate abroad.[836] Such violations would include remaining in the United States beyond the 90-day period of admission and unauthorized employment.[837] However, CBP has indicated that "[d]elays beyond the traveler's control, such as cancelled or delayed flights, medical emergencies requiring a doctor's care, etc., are not considered unauthorized overstays, however, you will need to bring proof of the cause of your overstay next time you travel to the U.S. in order for it to be forgiven. For airline delays, ask the airline for a letter affirming the delay or a copy of your cancelled boarding pass."[838]

Note, however, that the automatic visa voidance provision of INA §222(g) does not apply to a foreign national who overstayed after being admitted under the VWP.[839]

9. Waivers of Rights

An individual who makes an application for VWP admission waives the right to review or appeal a determination of inadmissibility and the right to contest any action for removal.[840] The one exception is that the foreign national may make an application for asylum.[841] If a foreign national is deemed to be inadmissible or

---

[834] INA §217(a)(9). For a discussion of the grounds of inadmissibility, *see* Volume 1: Chapter Two, "Basic Nonimmigrant Concepts."

[835] INA §217(h)(2).

[836] INA §217(a)(7).

[837] 9 FAM 201.1-4(C).

[838] CBP, "I still have my I-94," https://help.cbp.gov/app/answers/detail/a_id/752.

[839] 9 FAM 302.9-10B)(1)(b).

[840] INA §217(b); 9 FAM 201.1-4(C).

[841] INA §217(b); 8 CFR §217.4(a)(1). The federal court of appeals may have jurisdiction to review denials of asylum applications by VWP participants. *Nreka v. U.S. Att'y General* (11th Cir. 2005), AILA Doc. No. 05061561; *Shehu v. Att'y General* (3d Cir. 2007), AILA Doc. No. 07041867.

Copyright © 2017. American Immigration Lawyers Association. All rights reserved.

ineligible for admission, or if he or she possesses and presents fraudulent or counterfeit travel documents,[842] then he or she will be denied admission and will be removed from the United States.[843] Denial of admission under these circumstances will not, however, be considered removal for other immigration law purposes,[844] and a foreign national who was denied VWP admission is not barred from seeking VWP admission on a subsequent trip.[845] Not all foreign nationals who are removable are removed, however. To continue the example above, the foreign national who professed the intent to engage in terrorist activities may not be removed immediately, but he or she may be paroled into the United States in the custody of federal, state, or local law enforcement for investigation of any previous terrorist activities and/or criminal prosecution or punishment.[846]

The practitioner should note that being inadmissible is not identical to being ineligible for admission. An individual is inadmissible when CBP (or DOS, in the context of visa applications) determines that one of the grounds of inadmissibility stated in INA §212(a) applies to the foreign national. Conversely, an individual may be ineligible for admission for a variety of reasons that are not stated in INA §212(a). For example, the individual may not have the proper business or tourist purpose for the U.S. visit. A VWP applicant for admission at a land port of entry may lack sufficient evidence of his or her financial solvency, or he or she may lack a machine readable passport or a round-trip ticket. However, because being denied VWP admission may disrupt a foreign national's business or tourist plans, the practitioner should ensure that the client meets each of the requirements for VWP admission and has the necessary supporting evidence.

If, however, the foreign national is denied U.S. admission because he or she is deemed inadmissible for one of the reasons enumerated in INA §212(a), the foreign national must apply for a B visa at a U.S. consulate abroad.[847] There is "no other means of administrative or judicial review of such a denial, and no court or person otherwise shall have jurisdiction to consider any claim attacking the validity of such a denial."[848]

---

[842] Note that in the context of asylum applications, a foreign national is not inadmissible for fraud or misrepresentation if the foreign national did not present or intend to use fraudulent documents in order to gain entry to the United States and if the foreign national immediately makes an asylum application. *Matter of D–L– and A–M–*, 20 I&N Dec. 409 (BIA 1991).

[843] 8 CFR §217.4(a)(1).

[844] 8 CFR §217.4(a)(3).

[845] 1 (Legacy) INS Inspector's Field Manual, Ch. 15, 14-1 INS Manuals 15.7 "Visa Waiver Pilot Program (VWPP)."

[846] 8 CFR §217.4(a)(2).

[847] INA §217(g).

[848] *Id.*

Copyright © 2017. American Immigration Lawyers Association. All rights reserved.

In addition, if the foreign national is admitted, deemed deportable,[849] and removed from the United States, then this removal will constitute removal for other purposes of the immigration laws,[850] such that the foreign national may not use the VWP program at a later date, must apply for a visa at a U.S. consulate abroad, and must apply for a waiver if seeking to visit the United States during the 10 years following the removal.[851] If the foreign national is deemed deportable, he or she may not contest his or her deportability before an immigration judge, except that he or she may apply for asylum,[852] at which point he or she will be placed in proceedings before an immigration judge.[853] It is generally not possible, however, to seek to adjust status as an immediate relative while in asylum-only immigration court proceedings,[854] even if the application to adjust status was filed before the administrative order of removal.[855] However, there is a split among circuits as to whether, if the government fails to prove that the individual did indeed waive his or her right to a hearing, the court has jurisdiction over a petition for review.[856]

B. Strategy: B Visa vs. VWP

Despite the new requirements for VWP participation, the lure and ease of visa-free travel cannot be denied. Nevertheless, the practitioner should counsel against use of the VWP in certain situations, because VWP admission may cause more problems down the road. The practitioner is advised that foreign nationals who will engage in employment-type activities while in B-1 status, such as domestic or personal employees and B-1 in lieu of H-1 professionals or H-3 trainees, should affirmatively apply for B-1 visas, as then they should be most protected against charges of unauthorized employment. In general, foreign nationals who will engage in activities that are not clearly demarcated as standard business or pleasure activities should apply for B visas, as discussed below.

---

[849] The grounds of deportability and removal are enumerated in INA §237. The practitioner should note that the grounds of deportability are not identical to the grounds of inadmissibility. *Cf.* INA §212(a).

[850] 8 CFR §217.4(b)(2).

[851] 1 (Legacy) INS Inspector's Field Manual, Ch. 15, 14-1 INS Manuals 15.7 "Visa Waiver Pilot Program (VWPP)." A foreign national who was removed is subject to a 10-year bar until he or she may seek admission to the United States. INA §212(a)(9)(A)(ii)(I).

[852] 8 CFR §§217.4(b)(1) and 1208.2(c)(1).

[853] 8 CFR §1208.2(b).

[854] *Zine v. Mukasey* (8th Cir. 2006), AILA Doc. No. 08040268.

[855] *Ferry v. Gonzales* (10th Cir. 2006), AILA Doc. No. 07012313.

[856] *See Galuzzo v. Holder,* 633 F.3d 111 (2d Cir. 2011), holding that, where the government submitted no explicit evidence of a waiver of rights, the court will not presume by the fact that the petitioner entered under the VWP. *But see Bradley v. Attorney General,* 603 F.3d 235 (3d Cir. 2010), which rejected the *Galuzzo* reasoning and concluded that it could reasonably be presumed from the VWP entry that the right to review had been waived.

Copyright © 2017. American Immigration Lawyers Association. All rights reserved.

The objectives of the VWP have been clearly articulated as "eliminating unnecessary barriers to travel, stimulating the tourism industry, and permitting the Department of State to focus consular resources in other areas."[857] Given these objectives, plus the indication that employment following VWP admission is impermissible[858] and a lack of clear guidance from DOS, DHS, or legacy INS indicating that a foreign national may use the VWP for employment as a domestic or personal employee, a B-1 in lieu of H-1 professional or H-3 trainee, an airline employee, or an evangelical minister, the practitioner is advised to counsel against use of the VWP for employment that would otherwise be permissible under the B-1 visa category. In addition, as a practical matter, the VWP admission period of 90 days may be insufficient for the foreign national to complete the proposed U.S. activities, and repeated applications for VWP admission may result in increased scrutiny, as the immigration inspector may question whether the purpose of the U.S. visits are truly for business.[859]

In contrast, USCIS instructions and/or the FAM clearly indicate that foreign nationals may engage in employment in B-1 status as domestic or personal employees,[860] B-1 in lieu of H-1 professionals or H-3 trainees,[861] airline employees,[862] and evangelical ministers.[863] The FAM also notes that domestic or personal employees, airline employees, and evangelical ministers are eligible to apply for SSNs.[864]

In counseling clients on the need for B visa applications, the practitioner should consider the safeguards afforded by the B visa application process. As stated by the DHS Office of Inspector General (OIG), "[t]he visa is more than a mere stamp in a passport. It is the end result of a rigorous screening process the bearer must undergo before travel."[865] First, the information gathered by the U.S. consulates on Form DS-160 is substantially more comprehensive than the information gathered for the

---

[857] DOS, "Visa Waiver Program," https://travel.state.gov/content/visas/en/visit/visa-waiver-program.html.

[858] *Id.*

[859] 1 (Legacy) INS Inspector's Field Manual, Ch. 15, 14-1 INS Manuals 15.7 "Visa Waiver Pilot Program (VWPP)."

[860] 9 FAM 402.2-5(D); USCIS Instructions for I-765, Application for Employment Authorization, https://www.uscis.gov/files/form/I-765instr.pdf.

[861] 9 FAM 402.2-5(F).

[862] 9 FAM 402.2-5(E)(2); USCIS Instructions for I-765, Application for Employment Authorization, https://uscis.gov.files/form/ I-765instr.pdf.

[863] 9 FAM 402.2-5(C)(1).

[864] 9 FAM 402.2-5(H).

[865] DHS Office of Inspector General, "An Evaluation of the Security Implications of the Visa Waiver Program" (Apr. 2004), https://www.oig.dhs.gov/assets/Mgmt/OIG_SecurityImpVisaWaiverProgEval_Apr04.pdf.

Copyright © 2017. American Immigration Lawyers Association. All rights reserved.

VWP,[866] even with the new questions added to ESTA. Consular officers consider this information about the foreign national and the purpose of the U.S. visit when evaluating whether to issue the visa.[867] Although visa interviews may be quick, B visa applicants must pass security clearances from a number of databases.[868] These security clearance databases are different from and in addition to the security clearance databases checked by immigration inspectors at the port of entry.[869] As such, the visa issuance process should provide an additional layer of protection and comfort to both the foreign national and the immigration inspector at the port of entry.[870]

If DHS determines that a VWP foreign national has violated the terms of his or her admission, such as by engaging in unauthorized employment, then the foreign national cannot contest the removal, except to claim asylum, as discussed above. Following such a removal, the foreign national would be ineligible to use the VWP for any future U.S. visit,[871] and would be deemed inadmissible and require a waiver in addition to a U.S. visa in order to be admitted to the United States.[872] It may be particularly important for B-1 in lieu of H-1 or H-3 visitors to obtain B visas, rather than use the VWP program, because of the repeated expressions of the governmental desire to eliminate the B-1 in lieu of H-1 or H-3 provision altogether.[873]

The practitioner should note that additional resources may be devoted to ensuring VWP integrity in the future. Reports indicate that additional DHS resources will be devoted to enforcing the 90-day period of admission for VWP travelers and to removing violators. For example, "ICE has received funding to establish a Visa Waiver Enforcement Program within the Compliance Enforcement Unit to investigate the additional leads from [U.S. Visitor and Immigrant Status Indicator Technology] US-VISIT."[874] Alternatively, there has been discussion to place overall

---

[866] Cf. Forms DS-160, https://travel.state.gov/content/visas/en/forms/ds-160--online-nonimmigrant-visa-application.html, and ESTA, https://www.cbp.gov/travel/international-visitors/esta.

[867] For a discussion of the visa interview process in general, see Volume 1: Chapter Two, "Basic Nonimmigrant Concepts." For a discussion of the visa interview process vis-à-vis an application for admission under the VWP, see DHS OIG Report "An Evaluation of the Security Implications of the Visa Waiver Program" (Apr. 2004),https://www.oig.dhs.gov/assets/Mgmt/OIG_SecurityImpVisaWaiverProgEval_Apr04.pdf

[868] Congressional Research Service publication, A. Siskin, "Visa Waiver Program" (updated Dec. 11, 2015), https://www.fas.org/sgp/crs/homesec/RL32221.pdf.

[869] Id.

[870] 73 Fed. Reg. 32440 (June 9, 2008).

[871] INA §217(a)(7).

[872] INA §212(a)(9)(A).

[873] 58 Fed. Reg. 58982 (Nov. 5, 1993); 58 Fed. Reg. 40024 (July 26, 1993).

[874] GAO publication, "Visa Waiver Program" (Sept. 2008), AILA Doc. No. 08091569. For a discussion of US-VISIT, see Volume 1: Chapter Two, "Basic Nonimmigrant Concepts."

Copyright © 2017. American Immigration Lawyers Association. All rights reserved.

responsibility for managing and administering the VWP with ICE.[875] In addition, officials from the US-VISIT office have the capability of confirming whether VWP entrants do not have lawful immigration status and could provide this information to the Visa Waiver Program Office.[876] Consular officers abroad may conduct validation studies to determine the percentage of foreign nationals who overstay in the United States following admission with nonimmigrant visas, and this data could be used to evaluate whether a country should remain a VWP participant.[877]

C. Refusal of VWP Admission

In the event that a foreign national is refused VWP admission, whether it is because of ineligibility for the VWP program or because of inadmissibility, he or she will be transported back to the country of departure at the carrier's expense.[878] It remains to be seen whether mandatory ESTA participation is resulting in admission denials exclusively on grounds of inadmissibility that are revealed during inspection by an immigration officer, as ESTA is designed to prohibit foreign nationals from using the VWP if they are ineligible or inadmissible. Prior to mandatory ESTA participation, there was a procedure for refusal of VWP admission, and it is hoped that this procedure will remain in place.

Previously, the immigration inspector was directed to "ensure that refusals are handled fairly and are thoroughly documented, because, as a practical matter, the inspecting offer's decision is final."[879] In the event of refusal of admission, the foreign national was entitled to a copy of his or her sworn statement, which established the grounds of inadmissibility.[880] Review of this document may be helpful to cure any defects if the foreign national wishes to make another application for admission at a later date.

As discussed above, refusal of VWP admission is not considered to be removal under the U.S. immigration laws; it is likened to a foreign national with a nonimmigrant visa withdrawing his or her application for admission pursuant to Form I-275, Withdrawal of Application/Consular Notification.[881] Inadmissible applicants for admission under VWP are not subject to expedited removal, unless the immigration inspector determines that the VWP traveler is not a national of a

---

[875] DHS OIG Report "An Evaluation of the Security Implications of the Visa Waiver Program" (Apr. 2004), https://www.oig.dhs.gov/assets/Mgmt/OIG_SecurityImpVisaWaiverProgEval_Apr04.pdf.

[876] GAO publication, "Visa Waiver Program" (Sept. 2008), AILA Doc. No. 08091569.

[877] Id.

[878] 73 Fed. Reg. 32440 (June 9, 2008).

[879] 1 (Legacy) INS Inspector's Field Manual, Ch. 15, 14-1 INS Manuals 15.7 "Visa Waiver Pilot Program (VWPP)."

[880] Id.

[881] 1 (Legacy) INS Inspector's Field Manual, Ch. 15, 14-1 INS Manuals 15.7 "Visa Waiver Pilot Program (VWPP)." See also 9 FAM 403.10-2(B)(2).

Copyright © 2017. American Immigration Lawyers Association. All rights reserved.

qualifying VWP country.[882] In short, expedited removal, the provisions of which are discussed in INA §238(a), apply to these VWP travelers because an individual who presents fraudulent evidence of nationality or citizenship of a VWP country is considered to be an aggravated felon.[883] In all other situations of refusal of VWP admission, the foreign national would be processed for return transportation abroad, would have a record created within CBP databases, and would not be placed in removal proceedings for being inadmissible.[884]

---

[882] *Id.*

[883] INA §101(a)(43)(P). For a further discussion on expedited removal, see Volume 1: Chapter Two, "Basic Nonimmigrant Concepts."

[884] 1 (Legacy) INS Inspector's Field Manual, Ch. 15, 14-1 INS Manuals 15.7 "Visa Waiver Pilot Program (VWPP)."

Copyright © 2017. American Immigration Lawyers Association. All rights reserved.

CHAPTER FOUR
E-1 AND E-2 VISAS AND STATUS

I. Executive Summary

The "E" visa category allows foreign nationals who are citizens of countries with which the United States has certain types of treaties to engage in activities as a treaty trader, as a treaty investor, or as an employee of a qualifying E visa entity. Treaty traders engage in substantial international trade of goods, services, or technology between the treaty country and the United States. Treaty investors direct and develop a business in which the investor has either already invested or is in the process of investing. E employees should be executives, supervisors, or essential. E status may be valid for up to two years, and E visas are issued for up to five years. The foreign national may apply for new E visas or E extensions as long as he or she continues to engage in appropriate treaty activities through the E visa entity. Dependent spouses and minor children of E nonimmigrants also obtain E status, and dependent spouses are eligible to apply for employment authorization.

A. Checklist of Requirements

- Appropriate treaty between the United States and the country of the trader or investor's nationality.

- Trader: substantial international trade of goods, services, or technology. principally between the United States and the treaty country.

- Investor: direction and development of an investment enterprise, where the investment is real (at risk of loss, irrevocably committed, and possessed and controlled by the investor), substantial, and bona fide.

- Employees: executive, supervisory, or essential.

B. Documents Necessary to Prepare E-1 Petition

- Evidence of nationality of the E enterprise.

- Evidence of substantial trade for E-1 applicants OR

- evidence of investment for E-2 applicants.

- Information on ownership of the E entity.

- Job description for E visa applicant.

- Basic information about the company, including a strong five-year business plan in certain circumstances.

- Basic biographic information about the E visa applicant and his or her family, if applicable.

- Copies of biographic pages of passports of E visa applicant and his or her family, if applicable, including marriage and/or birth certificates to evidence qualifying relationship.

315

Copyright © 2017. American Immigration Lawyers Association. All rights reserved.

C. Checklist of Questions to Ask the Client

- What is the volume of trade or the amount of investment?
- Has the E enterprise been established?
- Is the E enterprise publicly owned or privately held?
- What will be the nature of the foreign national's role at the E business?
- What was the nature of his or her role at the foreign company, if applicable? (Can explore numerous roles, if applicable.)
- Will the foreign national provide services to a related corporate entity or pursuant to a contract between the E enterprise and a U.S. entity?
- Will the E enterprise be a joint venture?
- Is there a labor dispute or other work stoppage at the worksite?
- Will the E-2 enterprise hire employees?
- Does the enterprise have a business plan or financial statement prepared?

II. Requirements and Definitions

The E visa classification allows foreign nationals to visit and reside in the United States "in pursuance of the provisions of a treaty of commerce and navigation" between the United States and the foreign national's country of citizenship or nationality.[1] There are two subsets of E visa classification: the E-1 is for "Treaty Traders," and the E-2 is for "Treaty Investors."[2] The Department of State (DOS) directs consular officers to consider the "spirit" of the "treaties which were entered into, at least in part, to enhance or facilitate economic and commercial interaction between the United States and the treaty country."[3] Although there are similarities between the E-1 and E-2 visa categories, such as the requirement of a treaty or law governing trader and investor activities between the United States and the foreign country, the E-1 and E-2 are not identical. The practitioner is advised to consider the individual requirements, as discussed in the sections below.

Dependent spouses and children also hold the same E-1 and E-2 status, respectively,[4] regardless of their nationality.[5] Dependent spouses are eligible to apply for employment authorization, as discussed below.

A. Treaty Between the United States and the Foreign Country

First and foremost, there must be a "treaty of commerce and navigation" between the United States and the country of the foreign national's nationality.[6] Qualifying

---

[1] Immigration and Nationality Act (INA) §101(a)(15)(E).

[2] 9 Foreign Affairs Manual (FAM) 402.9-2.

[3] 9 FAM 402.9-2.

[4] INA §101(a)(15)(E); 8 CFR §214.2(e)(4).

[5] 8 Code of Federal Regulations (CFR) §214.2(e)(4); Adjudicator's Field Manual (AFM) 34.2(a) and 34.3(a).

Copyright © 2017. American Immigration Lawyers Association. All rights reserved.

treaties "include treaties of Friendship, Commerce and Navigation and Bilateral Investment Treaties."[7] DOS noted that the treaties were negotiated and entered into for the purpose of "develop[ing] international commercial trade."[8] In the absence of a treaty, a statute may be in effect to "accord[] treaty visa privileges ... by specific legislation,"[9] such as for Jordan, Chile, and Singapore,[10] or "to extend that same privilege" as is accorded by a qualifying treaty.[11]

DOS has provided a list of the treaty countries:[12]

E-1 Treaty Countries	E-2 Treaty Countries
	Albania
Argentina	Argentina
	Armenia
Australia	Australia
Austria	Austria
	Azerbaijan
	Bahrain
	Bangladesh
Belgium	Belgium
Bolivia	Bolivia (*see below for limitation)
Bosnia and Herzegovina	Bosnia and Herzegovina
Brunei	
	Bulgaria
	Cameroon

[6] INA §101(a)(15)(E).
[7] 9 FAM 402.9-4(A).
[8] 9 FAM 41.51 N4.3.
[9] Id.
[10] Pub. L. No. 107-43, §301 (Sept. 28, 2001); Pub. L. No. 108-77, §401 (Sept. 3, 2003); Pub. L. No. 108-78, §401 (Sept. 3, 2003), respectively.
[11] 9 FAM 402.9-4(A).
[12] 9 FAM 402.9-10.

Copyright © 2017. American Immigration Lawyers Association. All rights reserved.

E-1 Treaty Countries	E-2 Treaty Countries
Canada	Canada
Chile	Chile
China (Taiwan)	China (Taiwan)
Colombia	Colombia
	Congo (Brazzaville)
	Congo (Kinshasa)
Costa Rica	Costa Rica
Croatia	Croatia
	Czech Republic
Denmark	Denmark
	Ecuador
	Egypt
Estonia	Estonia
Ethiopia	Ethiopia
Finland	Finland
France	France
	Georgia
Germany	Germany
Greece	
	Grenada
Honduras	Honduras
Iran	Iran
Ireland	Ireland
Israel	
Italy	Italy
	Jamaica

Copyright © 2017. American Immigration Lawyers Association. All rights reserved.

E-1 Treaty Countries	E-2 Treaty Countries
Japan	Japan
Jordan	Jordan
	Kazakhstan
Korea (South)	Korea (South)
	Kyrgyzstan
Latvia	Latvia
Liberia	Liberia
	Lithuania
Luxembourg	Luxembourg
Macedonia	Macedonia
Mexico	Mexico
	Moldova
	Mongolia
Montenegro	Montenegro
	Morocco
Netherlands	Netherlands
Norway	Norway
Oman	Oman
Pakistan	Pakistan
	Panama
Paraguay	Paraguay
Philippines	Philippines
Poland	Poland
	Romania
	Senegal
Serbia	Serbia

Copyright © 2017. American Immigration Lawyers Association. All rights reserved.

E-1 Treaty Countries	E-2 Treaty Countries
Singapore	Singapore
	Solvak Republic
Slovenia	Slovenia
Spain	Spain
	Sri Lanka
Suriname	Suriname
Sweden	Sweden
Switzerland	Switzerland
Thailand	Thailand
Togo	Togo
	Trinidad and Tobago
	Tunisia
Turkey	Turkey
	Ukraine
United Kingdom	United Kingdom
Yugoslavia	Yugoslavia

* "Bolivian nationals with qualifying investments in place in the United States by June 10, 2012 continue to be entitled to E-2 classification until June 10, 2022. The only nationals of Bolivia (other than those qualifying for derivative status based on a familial relationship to an E-2 principal alien) who may qualify for E-2 visas at this time are those applicants who are coming to the United States to engage in E-2 activity in furtherance of covered investments established or acquired prior to June 10, 2012."[13]

In addition, Australian nationals may be eligible for the E-3 visa. This visa is discussed in detail in Volume 1: Chapter Five, "E-3 Visas and Status."

The practitioner is reminded that an individual country may be a party to a treaty only for E-1 or E-2 activities rather than both trader and investor activities.[14]

---

[13] *Id.*

[14] AFM 34.2(a) and 34.3(a).

Copyright © 2017. American Immigration Lawyers Association. All rights reserved.

In addition, if the United States imposes an embargo or other economic sanctions on a foreign country, then the trader or investor treaty may be rendered inoperable.[15] It should not be assumed, however, that both trade and investment activities are precluded; a foreign national may be permitted to engage in E-1 activities even if E-2 activities are forbidden.[16]

B. Nationality

The treaty trader or investor must hold the nationality of the treaty country, as "determined by the authorities of the foreign state of which the alien is a national."[17] If the treaty trader or investor is a business or an employing entity, then nationality "is determined by the nationality of the individual owners of that business,"[18] where "ownership must be traced as best as is practicable to the individuals who are ultimately its owners."[19] At least 50 percent of the business must be owned by nationals of the treaty country,[20] and "shares of a corporation or other business organization owned by permanent resident aliens cannot be considered in determining majority ownership by nationals of the treaty country to qualify the company for bringing in alien employees" in E status.[21] For E-2 treaty investors, ownership is intertwined with control, as discussed below. For purposes of brevity, this chapter will refer primarily to nationality, since this is the term used in the statute, regulations, and other guidance.

For a small or privately held company, establishing ownership and nationality may be straightforward. In contrast, entities with larger corporate structures should gather and present evidence of the ultimate ownership and nationality of at least 50 percent of the parent corporation.[22] Similarly, it may be more difficult to demonstrate the nationality of a publicly traded corporation, as the "nationality of the owners of the stock" will be considered,[23] even if the stock is publicly traded.[24] And if "a business in turn owns another business, then nationality of ownership must be traced to the

---

[15] 60 Fed. Reg. 24757 (May 9, 1995); *Matter of [name not provided]*, WAC 02 110 53910 (AAO July 14, 2006), http://bit.ly/jul06d7.

[16] Department of State (DOS), 98 State 128375 (July 8, 1999), 76 Interpreter Releases 1124 (July 26, 1999).

[17] 8 CFR §214.2(e)(7). *See also* AFM 34.2(a) and 34.3(a).

[18] 9 FAM 402.9-4(B).

[19] 8 CFR §214.2(e)(7).

[20] 9 FAM 402.9-4(B); AFM 34.2(a) and 34.3(a); *Matter of N–S–*, 7 I&N Dec. 426 (D.D. 1957).

[21] 9 FAM 402.9-7(A).

[22] 9 FAM 402.9-4(B) (noting that "in modern business structures and layered relationships, [consular officers] will have to rely heavily on the evidence presented to adjudicate whether the business entity in question possesses the requisite nationality").

[23] 9 FAM 402.9-4(B).

[24] 9 FAM 41.51 N3.2 ("In the case of a multinational corporation whose stock is exchanged in more than one country, then the applicant must satisfy [the consular officer], by the best evidence available, that the business meets the nationality requirement").

Copyright © 2017. American Immigration Lawyers Association. All rights reserved.

point of reaching the 50 percent rule with respect to the parent organization."[25] The "country of incorporation is irrelevant to the nationality requirement for E visa purposes,"[26] because the focus of the inquiry is the ownership nationality.[27]

If the "corporation is sold exclusively on a stock exchange in the country of incorporation, one can presume that the nationality of the corporation is that of the location of the exchange,"[28] and the foreign national should "still provide the best evidence available to support such a presumption."[29] For larger companies and corporations "whose stock is exchanged in more than one country, then the applicant must satisfy [the consular officer], by the best evidence available, that the business meets the nationality requirement."[30] DOS guidance notes potential "complex corporate structures in these cases" and recommends that consular officers request advisory opinions when necessary.[31] Despite a request for updated Foreign Affairs Manual (FAM) guidance or DOS instruction to U.S. consulates to accept Officer's Certificates confirming ownership for large multinational corporations that are publicly traded "with millions of outstanding shares," in place of "voluminous shareholder records," DOS stated a "prefer[ence] to allow the consular officer to evaluate the evidence and determine if it satisfies the nationality requirement."[32]

Appropriate evidence of ownership and nationality include:

- Articles of Incorporation for corporations;

- Articles of Organization for limited liability companies (LLCs);

- "[C]ertificate of ownership issued by the commercial section of a foreign embassy";

- "[R]eports from a certified personal accountant";[33]

- Share certificates;

- Operating agreement;

---

[25] 9 FAM 402.9-4(B).

[26] Id.

[27] "AILA Liaison Questions for U.S. Embassy, Rome" (Jan. 2010), AILA Doc. No. 10031064 ("Companies that are applying for an E visa should be advised that just because a company is incorporated in Italy this does not mean the company fulfills the nationality requirement of 9 FAM [402.9-4(B)] as in complicated corporate structures where the company is sold on the international market, lawyers need to demonstrate that at least fifty percent of the company is Italian owned").

[28] 9 FAM 402.9-4(B).

[29] Id.

[30] Id.

[31] Id.

[32] "Q&As from March 2007 AILA Liaison/DOS Meeting" (Mar. 2007), AILA Doc. No. 07041668.

[33] Instructions for Form I-129, Petition for a Nonimmigrant Worker, E Supplement, https://www.uscis.gov/sites/default/files/files/form/i-129instr.pdf ("personal" is likely an error and "public" was the intended term).

Copyright © 2017. American Immigration Lawyers Association. All rights reserved.

- An organizational chart displaying "the full ownership structure," including legal evidence of the chain of ownership, such as if there are intermediary corporate entities;
- A copy of the most recent Annual Report, if the company is publicly owned and traded, listing the stock exchanges where company stock is traded;
- Copies of the biographic pages of the passports of the owners combined with evidence of their percentage of ownership;[34]
- Copies of stock exchange listings;
- "An affidavit signed by the appropriate corporate official asserting that the company is traded exclusively on the [treaty country's] Stock Exchange;
- "A copy of the most recent trading information on the stock";[35]
- Documents relating to a merger, acquisition, spin-off, or other corporate event;
- Officer's Certificate or affidavit, or statement from the company's accountant; and
- Blanket L certification, if applicable.

In almost all cases, the E business must "have only one qualifying nationality," which must also be held by the "owner and all E visa employees of the company."[36] The one exception is if the "enterprise is owned and controlled equally (50/50) by nationals of two treaty countries," as a joint venture, in which case "employees of either nationality may obtain E visas to work for that company,"[37] as discussed below. In addition, individual treaties, such as the treaty between the United States and the United Kingdom, may extend the treaty to certain territories or possessions,[38] or may require that the foreign national hold nationality and domicile in the treaty country, such that the foreign national must "reside[] actually and permanently in a given place, and ha[ve] his domicile there,"[39] for both E-1 and E-2 visa applications.[40] A consular officer from the U.S. Embassy in London "indicated that his unit uses a 'reasonable human standard' in applying the treaty requirement" of

---

[34] U.S. Embassy in Honduras, "Treaty Trader and Treaty Investor Visas," http://www.ustraveldocs.com/hn/hn-niv-typee.asp; DOS, "Form DS-156E: Nonimmigrant Treaty Trader/Investor Application Instructions," https://www.state.gov/documents/organization/217452.pdf.

[35] U.S. Embassy in London, "Treaty Investor Visa," https://uk.usembassy.gov/visas/treaty-trader-or-treaty-investor/treaty-investor-e-2/.

[36] 9 FAM 402.9-4(B).

[37] *Id.*

[38] 9 FAM 402.9-10, footnotes (the treaty with France extends to Martinique, Guadeloupe, French Guiana, and Reunion of France).

[39] *Id.*, footnote 10.

[40] "AILA Rome District Chapter Updates from U.S. Embassy, London" (Oct. 17, 2008), AILA Doc. No. 08102850.

Copyright © 2017. American Immigration Lawyers Association. All rights reserved.

residence and domicile, although this may be "waived for a person currently in the U.S. in E or other long-term nonimmigrant visa status."[41]

If the owner or owners have dual nationality, then the individual(s) must select the nationality to be assigned to the E entity, which must in turn be held by the trader, investor, and/or employees.[42] If a dual national "possesses a passport for each country of nationality," then the individual "may have a visa issued in each passport, provided the visas are of different classification."[43] For example, a foreign national may have a B visitor visa in the passport of one country and also an E visa in the passport of another country, as long as the E visa is "issued in the passport of the treaty country,"[44] because all individuals must "hold themselves as nationals of that country for all E visa purposes involving that company, regardless of whether they also possess the nationality of another E visa country."[45] Employees of E enterprises must also hold the nationality of the E business, as discussed below,

In summary, only one nationality may predominate.[46] If the foreign national has the nationalities of a treaty country and the United States, then E-2 status for an employee is inappropriate if the owner of the E-2 enterprise claimed U.S. citizenship for the purpose of establishing and operating the business, because the owner is ineligible for E-2 status and therefore may not be the employer of an E-2 employee.[47] Similarly, a foreign national may not enter the United States based on his or her nationality of one country that is not a treaty country and then seek E-2 status based on nationality of another country that is a treaty country:

"It is hereby found that, in the case of a dual national alien nonimmigrant, the nationality claimed or established by him at the time of his entry into the United States must be regarded... as his sole or operative nationality for the duration of his temporary stay in the U.S."[48]

C. Intent to Depart the U.S. upon Termination of Status

A foreign national seeking E status must seek temporary entry, which should be distinguished from the "temporary entry" of foreign nationals seeking admission

---

[41.] *Id.*

[42] 9 FAM 402.9-4(B).

[43] 9 FAM 403.9-2(C).

[44] *Id.*

[45] 9 FAM 402.9-4(B).

[46] *Matter of Ognibene*, 18 I&N Dec. 425 (Reg'l Comm'r 1983); *Matter of Damioli*, 17 I&N Dec. 303 (Comm'r 1980).

[47] *Matter of Damioli*, 17 I&N Dec. 303 (Comm'r 1980) (stating "the very existence of the business upon which the applicant seeks treaty investor status would not be possible unless its owner were a citizen of the United States..." and that it is improper for the owner to "secure benefits from one Government agency by claiming to be a United States citizen, and simultaneously secure other benefits from a second Government agency by claiming to be an Italian citizen").

[48] *Matter of Ognibene*, 18 I&N Dec. 425 (Reg'l Comm'r 1983).

Copyright © 2017. American Immigration Lawyers Association. All rights reserved.

pursuant to the NAFTA Treaty,[49] from the requirement for maintenance of a residence abroad required of other nonimmigrants,[50] and from the explicit dual intent permitted of H and L nonimmigrants.[51] The foreign national's "expression of an unequivocal intent to return [abroad] when the E status ends is normally sufficient, in the absence of specific indications of evidence that the alien's intent is to the contrary."[52] Importantly, unlike other nonimmigrant visa classifications, the E visa applicant is not required to demonstrate the intent to remain in the United States "for a specific temporary period of time" or to demonstrate maintenance of a foreign residence.[53] The foreign national may "sell his or her residence and move all household effects to the United States,"[54] but he or she must also "indicate the intent to depart the U.S. upon termination of status, ceasing business operations or sale of business."[55]

In the event that there are "objective indications" of an intent to remain in the United States beyond the period of authorized stay, an "inquiry is justified to assess the applicant's true intent."[56] It is important to note, however, that E-2 status was granted to a foreign national who had a U.S. citizen spouse and children.[57] An E-2 extension was also granted to a foreign national who stated that he had traveled to the United States "to immigrate to U.S.A. and go into business [sic]," because this statement was deemed to express a "desire to remain" in the United States which should not "negate his intent to depart upon termination of his temporary status."[58] Despite the holding and dicta of this case, the practitioner should advise the client against such expressions, as they may be deemed "objective indications" and result in questioning of nonimmigrant intent. The foreign national in the second case also possessed income and property abroad, which the court construed "to show his intent to return there if he must."[59]

Supplementary evidence of the intent to depart may include the following:

- Title, deed, or mortgage of residence or other property in the home country;
- Bank or credit card statements from the home country;

---

[49] For a discussion of the "temporary entry" of the NAFTA Treaty, see Volume 1: Chapter Eleven, "L-1 Visas and Nonimmigrant Status."

[50] 9 FAM 402.9-4(C).

[51] INA §214(h); 8 CFR §214.2(*l*)(16); 9 FAM 402.12-15.

[52] 9 FAM 402.9-4(C).

[53] *Id.*

[54] *Id.*

[55] 1 U.S. Customs and Border Protection (CBP) Inspector's Field Manual (IFM) ch. 15: Nonimmigrants and Border Crossers, 14-1 Agency Manuals 15.5.

[56] 9 FAM 402.9-4(C).

[57] *Matter of [name not provided]*, EAC 95 173 50884 (AAU Aug. 12, 1999), 21 Immig. Rptr. B2-1.

[58] *Lauvik v. INS*, 910 F.2d 658 (9th Cir. 1990).

[59] *Id.*

Copyright © 2017. American Immigration Lawyers Association. All rights reserved.

- Professional or personal plans for the time period following completion of the E assignment, such as admission to a professional or educational program abroad;

- Evidence demonstrating the continued residence of family members in the home country;

- A copy of the current lease for a residence in the home country;

- Copies of recent paystubs for the E visa applicant;

- "[T]he most recent school transcript for each child between the ages of 5 and 18 inclusive"; and

- "Signed statement of intent to depart the U.S. upon termination of status."[60]

It may also be permissible for an E visa applicant to "be a beneficiary of an immigrant visa petition" and nevertheless "satisfy [the consular officer] that his and/or her intent is to depart the United States upon termination of status, and not stay in the United States to adjust status or otherwise remain in the United States regardless of legality of status."[61] Unfortunately, the citation offered by the FAM guidance relates to L visa applicants,[62] who may have dual intent,[63] but dual intent is not explicitly permitted for those in E status.[64] DOS guidance formerly stated that "an application for initial admission, change of status, or extension of stay in E classification may not be denied solely on the basis of an approved request for permanent labor certification or a filed or approved immigrant visa preference petition,"[65] but this statement has since been deleted.[66] Experience has shown, however, that foreign nationals may be able to hold E status for long periods of time, even 10 or 15 years, as long as the other requirements are satisfied.

Legacy Immigration and Naturalization Service (INS) guidance also stated:

"E nonimmigrants have long been able to extend their stay indefinitely in the United States in order to pursue their treaty-based activities and to return to E classification, should an application for adjustment of status be denied.

"Based on the language contained in the statute and the supporting regulations, an E-1 [or] E-2 … nonimmigrant alien (and any of such person's derivatives) may maintain status or obtain an extension of temporary stay while, at the same time,

---

[60] U.S. Embassy in London, "Interview Documents for Employees of E-1 and E-2 Businesses," https://uk.usembassy.gov/visas/treaty-trader-or-treaty-investor/documents-required-interview-employees-e-1-e-2-investor-businesses/.

[61] 9 FAM 402.9-4(C).

[62] *Id.* (citing 9 FAM 402.12-14(B)).

[63] INA §214(h); 8 CFR §214.2(*l*)(16); 9 FAM 402.12-14(B).

[64] Legacy INS, J. Bednarz (Oct. 1, 1993), 70 Interpreter Releases 1444–45 (Nov. 1, 1993) (commenting that the doctrine of dual intent has been applied to E nonimmigrants in the past and that the proposed regulation would codify this practice) (internal citation omitted).

[65] Former 9 FAM 41.51 N15.

[66] Current 9 FAM 402.9-4(C).

Copyright © 2017. American Immigration Lawyers Association. All rights reserved.

pursuing an application for adjustment of status. Therefore, an application for an extension of stay that is timely filed on behalf of an E-1 [or] E-2 ... nonimmigrant alien may be approved in spite of the alien's pending application for adjustment of status. Note that ... E nonimmigrants must continue to observe the requirements of their nonimmigrant status, including limiting employment to the designated employer."[67]

D. E-1 Treaty Traders

As stated by U.S. Citizenship and Immigration Services (USCIS) guidance: "The enterprise (company, corporation, etc.) must be engaged principally and substantially in trade between the U.S. and the treaty country."[68] Specifically, E-1 treaty traders may be admitted "solely to carry on substantial trade, including trade in services or trade in technology, principally between the United States and the foreign state of which he is a national."[69] When adjudicating an E-1 visa application, consular officers are directed to confirm that:

- "The requisite treaty exists," as discussed above;

- "The individual and/or business possesses the nationality of the treaty country," as discussed above;

- "The activities constitute trade," as discussed below;

- Such trade is "substantial," as discussed below;

- Such trade is "principally between the United States and the treaty country," as discussed below;

- The visa applicant, "if an employee, is destined to an executive/supervisory position or possesses skills essential to the firm's operations in the United States," as discussed below; and

- The visa applicant "intends to depart the United States when the E-1 status terminates," as discussed above.[70]

In addition to being "the actual owner of a qualifying enterprise," an E-1 nonimmigrant may be "an employee of such enterprise working in an executive or supervisory capacity or in a capacity which requires special qualifications essential to the operation of the enterprise," as long the foreign national has "the same nationality as the principal employer,"[71] as discussed below [in the section titled "Employees of E-1 and E-2 Entities"].

---

[67] Legacy INS, P. Virtue, "Considerations for Adjustment of Status (HQ 70/6.2.5, 70/6.2.9, 70/6.2612, 70/23.1, 120/17.2)" (Aug. 5, 1997), AILA Doc. No. 97080580. See below in this chapter for a discussion of moonlighting by a foreign national who holds E status and who has applied to adjust status.

[68] AFM 34.2(a). The terms "principally" and "substantially" are discussed in below.

[69] INA §101(a)(15)(E)(i).

[70] 9 FAM 402.9-5(A).

[71] AFM 34.2(a).

Copyright © 2017. American Immigration Lawyers Association. All rights reserved.

1. E-1 Trade Activities

As stated by DOS, "[t]here must been an actual exchange, in a meaningful sense, of qualifying commodities such as goods, moneys, or services to create transactions considered trade."[72] DOS guidance provides a three-prong test for determining what constitutes trade:

- "Trade must constitute an exchange;
- "Trade must be international in scope; and
- "Trade must involve qualifying activities."[73]

Documentation suggested by various governmental sources over the years as appropriate evidence of the trade includes:[74]

- Negotiated contracts;
- Bills of lading or invoices to indicate that the goods or services moved from one country to another;
- Customs clearances, warehouse receipts, [and] sales receipts;
- Letter of credit;
- Trade brochures;
- Insurance papers, documenting commodities imported;
- Carrier inventories;
- Correspondence showing trading activities;
- Purchase orders;
- Orders for goods shipped or awaiting shipment;
- Spreadsheet detailing "every qualifying transaction of international trade between the treaty countries during the last calendar year" and stating the date, the invoice number, and the dollar value of the transaction;
- Copies of airbills, shipping receipts, or shipping invoices to demonstrate transfer of the goods or services between the two countries;
- Calculations of the total international trade undertaken by the treaty investor business;

---

[72] 9 FAM 402.9-5(B).

[73] Id.

[74] See, e.g., Matter of Seto, 11 I&N Dec. 290 (Reg'l Comm'r 1965); U.S. Embassy in Honduras, "Treaty Traders and Treaty Investors," http://www.ustraveldocs.com/hn/hn-niv-typee.asp# applicationdocse1; DOS, "Form DS-156E: Nonimmigrant Treaty Trader/Investor Application," https://www.state.gov/documents/organization/217452.pdf; U.S. Embassy and Consulates in Italy, "E-1 First-Time Application Requirements," https://it.usembassy.gov/visas/niv/e/e1/; U.S. Consulate in Islamabad, "Treaty Traders and Treaty Investors Visas," http://www.ustraveldocs.com/pk/pk-niv-typee.asp#applicationdocse2.

Copyright © 2017. American Immigration Lawyers Association. All rights reserved.

- Financial statements;
- Copy of the most recent U.S. tax return filed with the Internal Revenue Service (IRS);
- Copy of the business plan;
- Copies of confidentiality agreements with clients or customers;
- Copies of consultancy agreements; and
- Copies of documents discussing projects, processes, or technologies in development and/or in patent review.

a. Exchange of Goods, Services, or Business Activities

In order to qualify as trade, the exchange must be "actual," "meaningful," and for consideration.[75] A foreign national "cannot qualify for E-1 status for the purpose of searching for a trading relationship."[76] Rather: "Trade between the treaty country and the United States must already be in progress on behalf of the individual or firm to entitle one to treaty trader classification."[77] In particular, trade entails an "exchange" of "commodities" between the two countries that in turn "create transactions":[78]

"Trade is the existing international exchange of items of trade for consideration between the United States and the treaty country. Existing trade includes successfully negotiated contracts binding upon the parties which call for the immediate exchange of items of trade.... This exchange must be traceable and identifiable. Title to the trade item must pass from one treaty party to the other."[79]

Existing trade, however, "does not include transactions merely in the state of negotiation without the existence of a current actual volume of trade."[80] For a discussion of items that may be traded, see below. It is also unclear whether the manufacture of goods in a non-treaty country would disqualify the trade from being between the treaty country and the United States. On the one hand, if title passes from the treaty country to the United States, then the requirement would be satisfied. But on the other hand, if a consular officer considers the origin of the goods, then the E visa application may be denied. The practitioner is advised to research the website of the U.S. consulate to determine and/or contact the U.S. consulate to inquire whether such an approach would be acceptable.

---

[75] 9 FAM 402.9-5(B).

[76] *Id.*

[77] *Id.*

[78] *Id.*

[79] 8 CFR §214.2(e)(9). *Accord* 9 FAM 402.9-5(B).

[80] *Matter of Seto*, 11 I&N Dec. 290 (Reg'l Comm'r 1965).

Copyright © 2017. American Immigration Lawyers Association. All rights reserved.

b. International Scope of Trade Activities

Because the objective of the treaties "is to develop international commercial trade between the two countries," the trade activities must be international in scope.[81] Therefore, "[d]omestic trade or the development of domestic markets without international exchange does not constitute trade."[82] Instead, the exchange of goods, services, or business activities must flow between the United States and the treaty country.[83]

c. Qualifying Trade Activities

Items that may be traded "include but are not limited to goods, services, international banking, insurance, monies, transportation, communications, data processing, advertising, accounting, design and engineering, management consulting, tourism, technology and its transfer, and some news-gathering activities,"[84] as well as "tourism and other intangible items with intrinsic value."[85]

"Goods" are defined as "tangible commodities or merchandise having extrinsic value."[86] "Services" are defined as "legitimate economic activities which provide other than tangible goods."[87] Notably, DOS acknowledged: "In the rapidly changing business climate with an increasing trend toward service industries, many more services, whether listed below or not, might benefit from E-1 visa classification.... Essentially, any service item commonly traded in international commerce would qualify."[88] The important requirement is that "the provision of that service by an enterprise must be the purpose of that business and, most importantly, must itself be the saleable commodity which the enterprise sells to clients."[89]

It is insufficient, however, to merely deposit "proceeds from services performed in the United States … in a bank account in a treaty country," as this "does not necessarily indicate that meaningful exchange has occurred if the proceeds do not support any business activity in the treaty country."[90]

---

[81] 9 FAM 402.9-5(B).

[82] 8 CFR §214.2(e)(9).

[83] 9 FAM 402.9-5(B).

[84] 8 CFR §214.2(e)(9). The practitioner is reminded that I status is available to representatives of "foreign press, radio, film, or other foreign information media." INA §101(a)(15)(E)(i); see also 8 CFR §214.2(i).

[85] AFM 34.2(f).

[86] 8 CFR §214.2(e)(9).

[87] Id.

[88] 9 FAM 402.9-5(B).

[89] Id.

[90] 9 FAM 402.9-5(B).

Copyright © 2017. American Immigration Lawyers Association. All rights reserved.

2. The Trade Is Substantial

The E-1 visa classification is inappropriate for trade that entails only "a single transaction, regardless of how protracted or monetarily valuable the transaction."[91] Rather, "[s]ubstantial trade is an amount of trade sufficient to ensure a continuous flow of international trade items between the United States and the treaty country," through "numerous transactions over time."[92] Stated another way: "Substantial trade does not necessarily refer to the monetary value of the transactions but rather to the volume of trade."[93]

DOS guidance directs consular officers to "focus primarily on the volume of trade conducted but … also consider the monetary value of the transactions as well."[94] Although "the number of transactions and the value of each transaction will vary, greater weight should be accorded to cases involving more numerous transactions of larger value."[95]

Still, the available guidance acknowledges that an E-1 entity may be a "smaller business:"[96]

"The smaller businessman should not be excluded if demonstrating a pattern of transactions of value. Thus, proof of numerous transactions, although each may be relatively small in value, might establish the requisite continuing course of international trade. *Income derived from the international trade which is sufficient to support the treaty trader and family should be considered favorably when assessing the substantiality of trade in a particular case.*"[97]

The fact that DOS guidance accepts that an E-1 business may only provide income to support the foreign national and his or her family distinguishes the E-1 visa classification from the E-2 classification, where it is insufficient for a business to support only the foreign national and his or her family, as discussed below. In addition, the adjudicator may consider "any conditions" in the foreign national's country "which may affect the alien's ability to carry on such substantial trade."[98]

---

[91] 8 CFR §214.2(e)(10).

[92] *Id.*; 9 FAM 402.9-5(C) ("The word 'substantial' is intended to describe the flow of the goods or services that are being exchanged between the treaty countries. The trade must be a continuous flow that should involve numerous transactions over time."); "AILA Liaison Questions for U.S. Embassy, Rome" (Jan. 2010), AILA Doc. No. 10031064.

[93] *Matter of Seto*, 11 I&N Dec. 290 (Reg'l Comm'r 1965).

[94] 9 FAM 402.9-5(C).

[95] 8 CFR §214.2(e)(10); 9 FAM 402.9-5(C).

[96] 8 CFR §214.2(e)(10).

[97] 9 FAM 402.9-5(C) (emphasis added).

[98] 8 CFR §214.2(e)(1)(i).

Copyright © 2017. American Immigration Lawyers Association. All rights reserved.

3. The Trade is Principally Between the United States and the Treaty Country

As stated by the regulations, "[p]rincipal trade between the United States and the treaty country exists when over 50 percent of the volume of international trade of the treaty trader is conducted between the United States and the treaty country."[99] The trade must be "conducted by the legal 'person' who is the treaty trader," which may be "an individual, a partnership, a joint venture, a corporation (whether a parent or subsidiary corporation), etc."[100] A subsidiary is considered "a separate legal person/entity," whereas "a branch is not considered to be a separate legal person or trader but part and parcel of another entity."[101] In order to determine the trade conducted by a branch, the consular officer "should look to the trade conducted by the entity of which it is a part, usually a foreign-based business (individual, corporation, etc.)."[102]

Whatever the remainder of the trade conducted by the foreign national or the E-1 entity, it "may be international trade with other countries or domestic trade,"[103] but experience has shown that consular officers are typically most concerned with confirming that the amount of trade conducted between the United States and the treaty country is at least 50 percent of all worldwide international trade, without including the amount of any domestic trade. In addition, if the E-1 trader satisfies this principal trade requirement, then "the duties of an employee need not be similarly apportioned to qualify for an E-1 visa," as long as the qualifying trade was not conducted by a branch office.[104] For a further discussion of eligibility requirements for E-1 employees, see below.

Appropriate evidence of the trade between the United States and the treaty country include "U.S. customs invoices and/or purchase receipts" as well as a "certified public accountant letter detailing percentage breakdown of company trade."[105]

E. E-2 Treaty Investors

An E-2 treaty investor may be admitted to the United States "solely to develop and direct the operations of an enterprise in which he has invested, or of an enterprise in which he is actively in the process of investing, a substantial amount of capital."[106] The U.S. enterprise must be bona fide.[107] Each of these requirements is discussed in

---

[99] 8 CFR §214.2(e)(11).

[100] 9 FAM 402.9-5(D).

[101] Id.

[102] Id.

[103] Id.

[104] Id.

[105] U.S. Embassy in Seoul, "Treaty Traders and Treaty Investors Visas," http://www.ustraveldocs.com/kr/kr-niv-typee.asp#applicationdocse1.

[106] INA §101(a)(15)(E)(ii).

[107] 8 CFR §214.2(e)(2)(i).

Copyright © 2017. American Immigration Lawyers Association. All rights reserved.

turn, with the distinction between making an actual investment and being in the active process of investing,[108] discussed below. When adjudicating an E-2 visa application, consular officers are directed to confirm that:

- "The requisite treaty exists," as discussed above;

- "The individual and/or business possess the nationality of the treaty country," as discussed above;

- The visa applicant "has invested or is actively in the process of investing";

- The enterprise "is a real and operating commercial enterprise";

- The visa applicant's "investment is substantial";

- The visa applicant's investment "is more than a marginal one solely for earning a living";

- The visa applicant "is in a position to 'develop and direct' the enterprise";

- The visa applicant who is an employee "is destined to an executive/ supervisory position or possesses skills essential to the firm's operations in the United States," as discussed below; and

- The visa applicant "intends to depart the United States when the E-2 status terminates," as discussed above.[109]

Stated simply, the investment must be for "a commercial enterprise, thus it must be for profit."[110] For this reason: "E-2 investor status shall not, therefore, be extended to non-profit organizations."[111] In addition, an E-2 visa may be issued to a physician who will invest in a medical practice.[112] If the physician will engage in direct patient care, then health care certification must be obtained.[113]

1. The Investment Must Be Real

The E-2 treaty investor must have already invested or be "actively in the process of investing" capital for a U.S. enterprise.[114] The regulations define investment as "the treaty investor's placing of capital, including funds and other assets (which have not been obtained, directly or indirectly, through criminal activity), at risk in the commercial sense with the objective of generating a profit."[115] The following are also requirements:

---

[108] 9 FAM 402.9-6(B)..

[109] 9 FAM 402.9-6(A).

[110] 9 FAM 402.9-6(C).

[111] 9 FAM 402.9-6(B).

[112] U.S. Consul (Toronto), J. Schlosser, (Jan. 25, 1993), AILA Doc. No. 94080490.

[113] *Cf. Id.* For a discussion of health care certification, see Volume 1: Chapter Seven, "H-1B Visas and Status."

[114] 8 CFR §214.2(e)(2)(i); *Matter of Khan*, 16 I&N Dec. 138 (BIA 1977).

[115] 8 CFR §214.2(e)(12).

Copyright © 2017. American Immigration Lawyers Association. All rights reserved.

- The investor must possess and control the funds;

- The investor must put the investment capital at risk; and

- The investor must irrevocably commit the capital to the E-2 enterprise.[116]

DOS has stated the following regarding the scrutiny of the investment, and the practitioner may wish to convey the sentiments to clients who question the need for extensive evidence of the investment: "The rules regarding the amount of funds committed to the commercial enterprise and the character of the funds, primarily personal or loans based on personal collateral, are intended to weed out risky undertakings and to ensure that the investor is unquestionably committed to the success of the business."[117]

Similarly, one embassy states: "It is important to provide proof of actual purchases and/or signed contracts and leases related to the enterprise, not just wire transfers to a U.S. account."[118] As noted by one consular officer:

"[T]he most problematic aspect of E-2 visa processing is the manner in which applicants document the underlying investment transaction. Applicants are urged to carefully document every step in the investment chain, from how they initially took possession and control of the capital assets, all the way to the financial arrangement by which these funds have been committed to the E-2 enterprise."[119]

Documentation suggested by various DOS and USCIS sources over the years as appropriate evidence of the investment includes:[120]

- A complete money trail of the funds invested, including:

  - "Documentation of the original source of the funds (sale of property, inheritance, loans, earnings, sale of business, etc.);

  - "Movement of these funds to a U.S. account; and

---

[116] 9 FAM 41.51 402.9-6(B).

[117] 9 FAM 402.9-6(D).

[118] U.S. Embassy and Consulates in France, "Nonimmigrant Visas: Treaty Traders and Investor Required Formats," https://fr.usembassy.gov/visas/nonimmigrant-visas/treaty-trader-investor/. *See also Matter of Khan,* 16 I&N Dec. 138 (BIA 1977).

[119] "AILA Rome District Chapter Updates from U.S. Embassy, London" (Oct. 17, 2008), AILA Doc. No. 08102850.

[120] See, e.g., U.S. Embassy and Consulates in Italy, "E-2 First-Time Application Requirements," https://it.usembassy.gov/visas/niv/e/e2/; U.S. Embassy & Consulates in the United Kingdom, "Treaty Investor (E-2)," https://uk.usembassy.gov/visas/treaty-trader-or-treaty-investor/treaty-investor-e-2/; U.S. Embassy and Consulates in France, "Nonimmigrant Visas: Treaty Traders and Investor Required Formats," https://fr.usembassy.gov/visas/nonimmigrant-visas/treaty-trader-investor/; U.S. Embassy in Honduras, "Treaty Traders and Treaty Investors Visas," http://www.ustraveldocs.com/hn/hn-niv-typee.asp; U.S. Consulate in Islamabad, "Treaty Traders and Treaty Investors Visas," http://www.ustraveldocs.com/pk/pk-niv-typee.asp#applicationdocse2; DOS, "Form DS-156E: Nonimmigrant Treaty Trader/Investor Application," https://www.state.gov/documents/organization/217452.pdf; Instructions for Form I-129, Petition for a Nonimmigrant Worker, E Supplement, https://www.uscis.gov/files/form/i-129instr.pdf.

Copyright © 2017. American Immigration Lawyers Association. All rights reserved.

- – "Use of these funds for qualifying business expenses," including "invoices, cancelled checks, and bank statements showing matching debits," with the figures highlighted;
- Copies of partnership agreements (with a statement on proportionate ownership);
- Insurance appraisals;
- Net worth statements from CPAs;
- Advertising invoices;
- Bank records, financial statements, personally secured loans, savings, and promissory notes;
- Shares, titles, contracts, receipts, and licenses;
- A signed, dated, valid purchase agreement;
- A binding escrow agreement … that explicitly confirms how the money will be distributed if the visa is issued, what will happen if the visa is not issued, and is signed and dated by all parties;
- Articles of incorporation or partnership agreement;
- Signed, dated, valid lease for business premises, including evidence of payments;
- Evidence of any other funds spent to acquire and set up the business;
- Evidence of purchase of inventory and/or equipment for the enterprise;
- Copies of any relevant contracts for the E enterprise;
- Organizational or staffing charts, or payroll records or IRS Form 941 for the E enterprise;
- Catalogs, sales literature, [and] news articles";
- Signed and dated franchise agreement, as well as evidence of payment of the franchise fee;
- Copies of debits from bank accounts, checks, and business invoices;
- Copies of any necessary and/or relevant local, state and/or federal licenses;
- Monthly bank statements for the current calendar year;
- Copies of the business's U.S. tax returns filed with the IRS for the previous three years, including all statements and schedules;
- Copies of Forms W-2 and/or 1099s for the previous two tax years;
- Profit and loss statements for the current and previous calendar years;
- A business plan that analyzes the local market and competition and gives a five-year projection of profit and loss, as supported by external sources;
- A breakdown of start-up costs necessary for the business to become operational;

Copyright © 2017. American Immigration Lawyers Association. All rights reserved.

- Copies of confidentiality agreements with clients or customers;
- Copies of consultancy agreements;
- Copies of documents discussing projects, processes, or technologies in development and/or in copyright/patent review; and
- Statements from independent reviewers within the field attesting to the value of the copyright or patent

a. Possession and Control of the Funds or Assets

As stated by the regulations: "The treaty investor must be in possession of and have control over the capital invested or being invested."[121] Possession of the funds may be demonstrated by bank statements and bank transfers with the foreign national named as the owner, or by bequeath or inheritance documents, or contest or lottery awards with the foreign national named as the beneficiary.[122] The source of the capital should be "lawful."[123] For such "legitimate means" of earning or receipt of funds, "the proper employment of the funds may constitute an E-2 investment."[124] DOS has acknowledged that E-2 visa applications have been delayed by difficulty in "identifying the source of funding" for "small, family-owned businesses with modest levels of investments."[125]

The foreign national or foreign corporation must also establish ownership of at least 50 percent of the E-2 enterprise,[126] in order to direct and develop the enterprise, as discussed below, because "otherwise, other individuals who do have the controlling interest are in a position to dictate how the enterprise is to be developed and directed."[127] In the event that control of the capital results from possession of the capital, such as if the funds were earned or were bequeathed or awarded solely to the foreign national, then the foreign national must have "unrestricted use" of the funds invested,[128] and he or she must have control over the use of the investment funds to direct and develop the enterprise,[129] as discussed below. Unsecured personal loans should be considered to be under the possession and control of the investor,[130] but older guidance indicated that "the required element of possession does not apply

---

[121] 8 CFR §214.2(e)(12).

[122] *Matter of Lee*, 15 I&N Dec. 187 (Reg'l Comm'r 1975).

[123] "AILA Liaison Report from the CSC Stakeholder Meeting" (Oct. 27, 2010), AILA Doc. No. 10112462; "CSC Stakeholders Meeting" (Apr. 28, 2010), AILA Doc. No. 10062988 (USCIS "is concerned about funds being obtained via a lawful means").

[124] 9 FAM 402.9-6(B).

[125] "Q&As from March 2007 AILA Liaison/DOS Meeting" (Mar. 2007), AILA Doc. No. 07041668.

[126] 9 FAM 402.9-6(F); *Matter of Lee*, 15 I&N Dec. 187 (Reg'l Comm'r 1975).

[127] *Matter of Lee*, 15 I&N Dec. 187 (Reg'l Comm'r 1975).

[128] *Matter of Csonka*, 17 I&N Dec. 254 (Reg'l Comm'r 1978).

[129] *Matter of Kung*, 17 I&N Dec. 260 (Comm'r 1970); *Matter of Lee*, 15 I&N Dec. 187 (Reg'l Comm'r 1975).

[130] "AILA Liaison Report from the CSC Stakeholder Meeting" (Oct. 27, 2010), AILA Doc. No. 10112462.

Copyright © 2017. American Immigration Lawyers Association. All rights reserved.

unless the unsecured loan is paid" and that payment of a loan to a business instead of directly to the foreign national would also be insufficient.[131]

The practitioner should note two points. First, merely inheriting a business "does not constitute an investment" for purposes of E-2 visa eligibility.[132] Second, it is not a requirement "that the source of the funds be outside the United States."[133] However, if the source of the capital is within the United States, the practitioner is advised to demonstrate how the foreign national, rather than an individual or entity in the United States, has full possession and control.[134]

Other forms of financial transactions, property ownership, or property rights may also be considered to be investments.[135] If the E-2 treaty investor has already spent funds to purchase goods or equipment for the proposed U.S. enterprise, then the amount spent "may be calculated in the investment total."[136] In addition, the "value of the goods or equipment transferred to the United States (such as factory machinery shipped to the United States to start or enlarge a plant) may be considered an investment."[137] Equipment given as a gift to the U.S. company should be considered to be possessed and controlled by the investor who is the sole owner of the company.[138] But in order for any goods, equipment, or machinery to be considered an investment, the foreign national must establish that any usage "will be put, or [is] being put, to use in an ongoing commercial enterprise," specifically "for investment and not personal purposes."[139]

Similarly, DOS guidance states the following regarding the inclusion of intangible property in the calculation of assets or investment capital:

"Rights to intangible or intellectual property may also be considered capital assets to the extent to which their value can reasonably be determined. Where no market value is available for a copyright or patent, the value of current publishing or manufacturing contracts generated by the asset may be used. If none exist, the opinions of experts in the particular field in question may be submitted for consideration and acceptance."[140]

---

[131] "CSC Stakeholders Meeting" (Apr. 28, 2010), AILA Doc. No. 10062988.

[132] 9 FAM 402.9-6(B).

[133] *Id.*; "CSC Stakeholders Meeting" (Apr. 28, 2010), AILA Doc. No. 10062988.

[134] *Matter of Lee*, 15 I&N Dec. 187 (Reg'l Comm'r 1975).

[135] 9 FAM 402.9-6(B).

[136] *Id.*

[137] *Id.*

[138] *All Bright Sanitation of Colorado, Inc. v. USCIS*, Case No. 10-cv-2180-SCOLA (S.D.Fla. 2012), AILA Doc. No. 12091851.

[139] *Id.*

[140] *Id.*

Copyright © 2017. American Immigration Lawyers Association. All rights reserved.

Finally, the investment total may include payment of rents or leases of property or equipment, but an important point to note is that the valuation will be of the actual amount paid on a monthly basis rather than an annual basis.[141] The rationale is that "the market value of the leased equipment is not representative of the investment and neither is the annual rental cost."[142] This is because the E-2 treaty investor does not own the equipment or the property and therefore cannot claim the market value to be his or her investment of capital.[143] Instead, the adjudicator will consider the monthly payment of rent or leasing since this should be the actual amount of investment and since some portion of the payments may derive from capital earned from the business rather than exclusively from the investment.[144] The one exception is if the rent or lease payments are paid in advance, rather than from the proceeds of the business, in which case the actual amount paid should be included in the investment total.[145]

b. Risk of Investment

The E-2 treaty investor must put the investment capital at risk.[146] As stated by DOS guidance:

> "The concept of investment connotes the placing of funds or other capital assets at risk, in the commercial sense, in the hope of generating a financial return.... If the funds are not subject to partial or total loss if business fortunes reverse, then it is not an 'investment' in the sense intended by [the statute].... In short, at risk funds in the E-2 context would include only funds in which personal assets are involved, such as personal funds, other unencumbered assets, a mortgage with the alien's personal dwelling used as collateral, or some similar personal liability. A reasonable amount of cash, held in a business bank account or similar fund to be used for routine business operations, may be counted as investment funds."[147]

Clearly appropriate investment capital includes "the investor's unsecured personal business capital or capital secured by personal assets."[148] But "[o]nly indebtedness collateralized by the alien's own personal assets, such as a second mortgage on a home or unsecured loans, such as a loan on the alien's personal signature may be included, since the alien risks the funds in the event of business

---

[141] Id.

[142] Id.

[143] Id.

[144] Id.

[145] Id.

[146] 8 CFR §214.2(e)(12).

[147] 9 FAM 402.9-6(B).

[148] 8 CFR §214.2(e)(12); "AILA Liaison Report from the CSC Stakeholder Meeting" (Oct. 27, 2010), AILA Doc. No. 10112462.

Copyright © 2017. American Immigration Lawyers Association. All rights reserved.

failure."[149] Any evidence presented should demonstrate the investor's "financial ability to make the ... investment."[150]

However, capital arising from indebtedness secured by the business assets, such as "mortgage debt or commercial loans secured by the assets of the enterprise cannot count toward the investment, as there is no requisite element of risk."[151] This is the case especially when the foreign national pledges the proposed E-2 business as collateral, because all of the "funds from the resulting loan or mortgage are not at risk, even if some personal assets are also used as collateral."[152] In addition, an investment of funds obtained through loans guaranteed by an individual other than the E-2 treaty investor are insufficient, even if there is an agreement between the guarantor and the proposed E-2 treaty investor.[153]

c. Irrevocable Commitment of the Capital

In order to qualify for an E-2 visa or status, the foreign national must demonstrate that the capital has been irrevocably committed to the proposed E-2 business;[154] the investment must not be "speculative" or unsubstantiated.[155] For enterprises where the funds have already been devoted to the U.S. business, appropriate evidence may include bank statements or transfers. The regulations also acknowledge that use of an escrow account may "also extend personal liability protection to the treaty investor in the event the application for E classification is denied."[156]

In contrast, if the capital has not been provided to the U.S. enterprise, then the foreign national must establish that he or she is "in the process of investing," such that he or she has "reached an irrevocable point to qualify."[157] It may be helpful to view this "irrevocable point" as the stage of undertaking every step necessary to set up the U.S. business except for actually providing the capital, as the foreign national "must be close to the start of actual business operations, not simply in the stage of signing contracts (which may be broken) or scouting for suitable locations and property."[158] In fact, one circuit court has noted that signing a contract may not represent irrevocable

---

[149] 9 FAM 402.9-6(B).

[150] *Matter of Lee*, 15 I&N Dec. 187 (Reg'l Comm'r 1975).

[151] 9 FAM 402.9-6(B); *Matter of Ognibene*, 18 I&N Dec. 425 (Reg'l Comm'r 1983). *But see All Bright Sanitation of Colorado, Inc. v. USCIS*, Case No. 10-cv-2180-SCOLA (S.D.Fla. 2012), AILA Doc. No. 12091851 (finding that USCIS should have given "reasonable consideration" to investor's personal guaranty given on loans to, and secured by assets of, the business).

[152] 9 FAM 402.9-6(B).

[153] *Matter of Csonka*, 17 I&N Dec. 254 (Reg'l Comm'r 1978).

[154] 8 CFR §214.2(e)(12).

[155] *Matter of Lee*, 15 I&N Dec. 187 (Reg'l Comm'r 1975).

[156] 8 CFR §214.2(e)(12).

[157] 9 FAM 402.9-6(B).

[158] *Id. Cf. Matter of Khan*, 16 I&N Dec. 138 (BIA 1977) ("For example, evidence establishing that an investor claimant is 'actively in the process of investing,' could consist of copies of contracts showing that he is legally committed to making certain expenditures, or similar items").

Copyright © 2017. American Immigration Lawyers Association. All rights reserved.

commitment, because a contract allows only for a party to sue for damages or specific performance if the contract is breached or broken, but "[r]esolution of the lawsuit could take years, therefore [the plaintiff] would not be close to the start of actual operations."[159] DOS guidance provides the following example:

> "[A] purchase or sale of a business which qualifies for E-2 status in every respect may be conditioned upon the issuance of the visa. Despite the condition, this would constitute a solid commitment if the assets to be used for the purchase are held in escrow for release or transfer only on the condition being met."[160]

The foreign national bears "the burden of establishing such irrevocable commitment."[161] When determining whether the foreign national has demonstrated the commitment, the adjudicator should reject as insufficient the "[m]ere intent to invest, or possession of uncommitted funds in a bank account, or even prospective investment arrangements entailing no present commitment."[162] Because merely having "funds deposited in an idle bank account cannot be considered part of an investment,"[163] the practitioner is advised to present substantiating evidence of the commitment, such as "lease contracts, how the money would be invested,"[164] or purchase of necessary equipment or goods for the E-2 business.[165] Similarly, purchasing multiple inventory items "by itself, does not show that [a foreign national] is 'actively in the process of investing.'"[166]

2. The Investment Must Be Substantial

The investment of capital or assets must be "a substantial amount ... as distinct from a relatively small amount of capital ... solely for the purpose of earning a living."[167] DOS has stated:

> "The purpose of the requirement is to ensure to a reasonable extent that the business invested in is not speculative, but is, or soon will be a successful enterprise.... Consequently, [the consular officer] must view the proportionate amount of funds invested, as evidenced by the proportionality test, in light of the nature of the business and the projected success of the business."[168]

---

[159] *Han v. Hendricks*, 949 F.2d 399 (9th Cir. 1991).

[160] 9 FAM 402.9-6(B).

[161] 8 CFR §214.2(e)(12).

[162] 9 FAM 402.9-6(B).

[163] *Matter of Chung*, 15 I&N Dec. 681 (Reg'l Comm'r 1976).

[164] *Id.*

[165] 9 FAM 402.9-6(B).

[166] *Matter of Khan*, 16 I&N Dec. 138 (BIA 1977).

[167] 8 CFR §214.2(e)(2)(i); AFM 34.3(a) ("The E-2 enterprise (company, corporation, etc.) must involve the investment of a substantial amount of capital, rather than a marginal investment solely for the purpose of earning a living for the investor").

[168] 9 FAM 402.9-6(D).

Copyright © 2017. American Immigration Lawyers Association. All rights reserved.

The "proportionality test" focuses on comparing the amount of qualifying invested funds vis-à-vis "the cost of an established business or, if a newly created business, the cost of establishing a business."[169] The amount of the investment must be sufficient to demonstrate the investor's commitment to the enterprise:[170]

- By purchasing an appropriate proportion of "an established enterprise" or by applying funds to "creat[e] the type of enterprise under consideration";

- By ensuring the "successful operation" of the E-2 entity through the commitment of the funds; and

- By being "[o]f a magnitude to support the likelihood that the treaty investor will successfully develop and direct the enterprise."[171]

Importantly, DOS guidance states: "No set dollar figure constitutes a minimum amount of investment to be considered 'substantial' for E-2 visa purposes."[172] Instead, the inquiry considers the proportion between the two figures:[173] the "amount of the funds or assets actually invested" and the value of the business,[174] with the evaluation "best … understood as a sort of inverted sliding scale."[175] For E-2 visa applicants who have made an investment that equals or exceeds the value of the business, then this "investment is substantial," even for "small business of $100,000 or less."[176] In addition, a smaller business that is a joint venture may also qualify as an E-2 enterprise,[177] as discussed below.

DOS acknowledges, however, that the "vast majority of cases involve lesser percentages,"[178] which in turn results in the following caveat: "Generally, the lower the cost of the enterprise, the higher, proportionately, the investment must be to be considered a substantial amount of capital."[179] Although there "are no bright line percentages that exist in order for an investment to be considered substantial," the adjudicator will weigh the nature of the business against the amount of investment made:[180]

---

[169] *Id.*

[170] *Id.*

[171] 9 FAM 402.9-6(D). *See also* 8 CFR §214.2(e)(14).

[172] 9 FAM 402.9-6(D).

[173] *Id.*

[174] *Id.*

[175] 9 FAM 402.9-6(D). *See also* 1 CBP IFM ch. 15: Nonimmigrants and Border Crossers, 14-1 Agency Manuals 15.5.

[176] 9 FAM 402.9-6(D).

[177] *See generally* 9 FAM 402.9-6(F).

[178] 9 FAM 402.9-6(D).

[179] 8 CFR §214.2(e)(14)(iii); 9 FAM 402.9-6(D).

[180] *Matter of Chung*, 15 I&N Dec. 681 (Reg'l Comm'r 1976); 9 FAM 402.9-6(D).

Copyright © 2017. American Immigration Lawyers Association. All rights reserved.

"The value (cost) of the business is clearly dependent on the nature of the enterprise. Any manufacturing business, such as an automobile manufacturer, might easily cost many millions of dollars to either purchase or establish and operate. At the extreme opposite pole, the cost to purchase an on-going commercial enterprise or to establish a service business, such as a consulting firm, may be relatively low. As long as all the other requirements for E-2 status are met, the cost of the business per se is not independently relevant or determinative of qualification for E-2 status."[181]

If the investor purchased an existing business, then the cost is "generally, its purchase price, which is normally considered to be the fair market value."[182] If the investor will set up a new business, then the value is "the actual cost needed to establish such a business to the point of being operational,"[183] which may also be the "total start up costs."[184] In calculating this cost, the adjudicator may consider the purchase price of "necessary assets" already procured and other "cost figures for additional assets needed to run the business,"[185] such as:

- "Invoices or contracts for substantial purchases of equipment and inventory;
- "[A]ppraisals of the market value of land, buildings, equipment, and machinery;
- "[A]ccouting audits; and
- "[R]ecords required by various governmental authorities."[186]

DOS has indicated that "small, family-owned businesses with modest levels of investments" may face closer scrutiny.[187] The consular officer may question the amounts stated in these documents and may request additional evidence "to help establish what would be a reasonable amount," such as "letters from chambers of commerce or statistics from trade associations."[188] But "[u]nverified and unaudited financial statements based exclusively on information supplied by an applicant normally are insufficient to establish the nature and status of an enterprise."[189] The evidence should also remain consistent regarding the value of the investment and the

---

[181] 9 FAM 402.9-6(D).

[182] Id.

[183] Id.

[184] DOS, "Form DS-156E: Nonimmigrant Treaty Trader/Investor Application," https://www.state.gov/documents/organization/217452.pdf.

[185] 9 FAM 402.9-6(D).

[186] Id.

[187] "Q&As from Mar. 2007 AILA Liaison/DOS Meeting" (Mar. 2007), AILA Doc. No. 07041668.

[188] 9 FAM 402.9-6(D).

[189] Id.

Copyright © 2017. American Immigration Lawyers Association. All rights reserved.

value of the business, as discrepancies in these amounts may result in denial of the E-2 visa.[190]

Investment in a "marginal enterprise" is insufficient for E-2 classification, as stated by DOS guidance and the regulations:

"A marginal enterprise is an enterprise that does not have the present or future capacity to generate more than enough income to provide a minimal living for the treaty investor and his or her family. An enterprise that does not have the capacity to generate such income but that has a present or future capacity to make a significant economic contribution is not a marginal enterprise."[191]

Evidence of the income to be earned should be submitted if possible,[192] as well as evidence of the "significant economic contribution," if available: "The projected future capacity should generally be realizable within five years from the date the alien commences normal business activity of the enterprise."[193] If the E-2 enterprise is already viable and provides revenue for the investor foreign corporation, then evidence of the business's success and/or growth should be presented.[194] One embassy notes that "the history of a business" is also considered: "For example, in the case of renewal of E-2 registration, if the business has only recently suffered financially but in the past was very successful this is a much better case than a business that has never gotten off the ground."[195] Another embassy stated the following regarding real estate enterprises:

"When dealing with real estate companies that reflect a loss on income taxes, the Visa Section will consider the fact that depreciation of an asset would not necessarily be indicative of the enterprise's income, which is particularly true of assets like real property which are subject to market changes (especially during time of economic crisis). However, if even discounting depreciation, the business is still operating at or near a loss, and not generating sufficient income to support more than the applicant, the investor would not be eligible for an E visa."[196]

The expansion of job opportunities for U.S. workers is another factor,[197] but the E-2 entity should clearly demonstrate how the number of full-time employees has

---

[190] *Matter of Lee*, 15 I&N Dec. 187 (Reg'l Comm'r 1975).

[191] 9 FAM 402.9-6(E); 8 CFR §214.2(e)(15).

[192] *Matter of Lee*, 15 I&N Dec. 187 (Reg'l Comm'r 1975).

[193] 9 FAM 402.9-6(E); 8 CFR §214.2(e)(15).

[194] *Matter of Walsh and Pollard*, 20 I&N Dec. 60 (BIA 1988).

[195] "AILA Liaison Questions for U.S. Embassy, London" (Oct. 13, 2010), AILA Doc. No. 10110960.

[196] "AILA Liaison Questions for U.S. Embassy, Rome" (Jan. 2010), AILA Doc. No. 10031064.

[197] "AILA Liaison Questions for U.S. Embassy, London" (Oct. 13, 2010), AILA Doc. No. 10110960; "AILA Liaison Questions for U.S. Embassy, Rome" (Jan. 2010), AILA Doc. No. 10031064 ("An investment generally will qualify as more than marginal if it will expand U.S. job opportunities."); "AILA Liaison/DOS Q&As" (Oct. 24, 2007), AILA Doc. No. 07112732. The final document states: "This requirement, however, would only be satisfied by creating jobs for qualified U.S. workers." It is unclear what is meant by
Cont'd

Copyright © 2017. American Immigration Lawyers Association. All rights reserved.

increased following the foreign national's investment.[198] For evidence of this factor, "normally the consular officer should only look to I-9 filings" and not copies of U.S. passports or permanent resident cards,[199] or "payroll records" may be considered.[200] The employment of part-time or seasonal workers by the E-2 enterprise or evidence of net loss of income would most likely be deemed insufficient as a "significant economic contribution."[201] In addition, one circuit court stated:

> "Even though [the foreign national's business] produced certain economic advantages to the economy of the United States through the employment of American workers and purchase of American goods, these economic advantages alone will not make his investment 'substantial.' Every investment produces certain benefits to an economy by generating economic activity."[202]

One embassy has cautioned: "The visa applicant may not overcome the 'marginality requirement' by having substantial income from other sources, such that he need not rely on the investment enterprise to provide basic living expenses."[203] But older cases, indicate that submitting evidence of other sources of income,[204] or substantial "reserve funds," may be sufficient to overcome the determination that the enterprise is marginal,[205] as do the instructions for the Form DS-156E.[206] In evaluating whether the reserve funds are substantial, the focus may be on the proportion of the reserve funds to the overall investment.[207]

One Administrative Appeals Unit (AAU, now known as AAO) case denied E-2 status to a foreign national who owned $16,500 of a business valued at approximately $20,000, based on former FAM guidance, which stated:

> "A newly-created business, *e.g.*, a consulting firm, might only need $50,000 investment to be set up and to become fully operational. As this cost figure is

---

"qualified," but the response addressed verification of employment eligibility on Form I-9. For a discussion of Form I-9, see *AILA's Guide to Worksite Enforcement and Corporate Compliance Handbook* (AILA 2008).

[198] *Matter of [name not provided]*, LIN 93 143 50157 (AAU Oct. 26, 1993), 12 Immig. Rptr. B2-87 (citing former 9 FAM 41.51 N9.3).

[199] "AILA Liaison/DOS Q&As" (Oct. 24, 2007), AILA Doc. No. 07112732.

[200] DOS, "Form DS-156E: Nonimmigrant Treaty Trader/Investor Application," https://www.state.gov/documents/organization/217452.pdf

[201] *Matter of [name not provided]*, LIN 93 143 50157 (AAU Oct. 26, 1993), 12 Immig. Rptr. B2-87 (citing former 9 FAM 41.51 N9.3).

[202] *Kim v. INS*, 586 F.2d 713 (9th Cir. 1978).

[203] "AILA Liaison Questions for U.S. Embassy, Rome" (Jan. 2010), AILA Doc. No. 10031064.

[204] *Lauvik v. INS*, 910 F.2d 658 (9th Cir. 1990).

[205] *Matter of Kung*, 17 I&N Dec. 260 (Comm'r 1970).

[206] DOS, "Form DS-156E: Nonimmigrant Treaty Trader/Investor Application," https://www.state.gov/documents/organization/217452.pdf (listing "personal tax records" and "evidence of other personal assets and income" as "evidence that the enterprise is not marginal").

[207] *Matter of Kung*, 17 I&N Dec. 260 (Comm'r 1970). In this case, the foreign national invested $53,000 in an enterprise and also had $46,000 in reserve funds.

Copyright © 2017. American Immigration Lawyers Association. All rights reserved.

relatively low, a higher percentage of investment is anticipated. An investment approaching 90–100% would easily meet the test.

"A business costing $100,000 might require an investment of 75–100% to meet the test.

"A small business costing $500,000 would demand generally upwards of a 60% investment, with a $375,000 investment clearly meeting the test.

"In the case of a million dollar business, a lesser percentage might be needed, but 50–60% investment would qualify.

"A business requiring $10 million to purchase or establish would require a much lower percentage. A $3 million investment might suffice in view of the sheer magnitude of the dollar amount invested.

"An investment of $10,000,000 in a $100 million business would qualify based on the sheer magnitude of the investment itself."[208]

Although these figures and percentages of investment are no longer stated in the FAM, they are provided here as potential benchmarks to consider when advising a client on the amount of investment necessary for an E-2 enterprise, as consular officers may nevertheless have been trained on the former guidance, even as it cautions that the proportionality test "is not a simple arithmetic exercise."[209] The practitioner should also note that, in this case, the E-2 visa applicant owned more than 50 percent of the E-2 enterprise, but the visa was denied because the investment amount was deemed to be neither substantial nor proportional to the value of the business.[210]

3. The U.S. Enterprise Must Be Bona Fide

The proposed E-2 enterprise must be a bona fide business and "must be a real and active commercial or entrepreneurial undertaking, producing some service or commodity,"[211] which operates for the purpose of earning a profit.[212] The business must also comply with "applicable legal requirements for doing business in the particular jurisdiction in the United States."[213]

As noted above, the E-2 entity may not be a "marginal enterprise" that exists solely to provide the foreign national and his or her family with merely "a living."[214] In addition, the business "cannot be a paper organization or an idle speculative

---

[208] *Matter of [name not provided]*, LIN 93 143 50157 (AAU Oct. 26, 1993), 12 Immig. Rptr. B2-87 (citing former 9 FAM 41.51 N9.3).

[209] *Id.*

[210] *Id.*

[211] 9 FAM 402.9-6(C).

[212] 8 CFR §214.2(e)(13).

[213] *Id.*

[214] 8 CFR §214.2(e)(2)(i).

Copyright © 2017. American Immigration Lawyers Association. All rights reserved.

investment held for potential appreciation in value, such as undeveloped land or stocks held by an investor without the intent to direct the enterprise."[215]

One embassy requires "[p]roof that the enterprise is currently running or will open its doors imminently" and accepts as evidence "Business licenses, Special permits (food, alcohol, health, etc.), Photos of enterprise, Utility bills (electrical, water, etc.), Bank statements, Sales contracts and invoices."[216]

4. The Foreign National Will Have Executive or Supervisory Duties in the United States

The E-2 visa applicant must also establish that he or she "does or will develop and direct the investment enterprise," whether as an investor or as the owner of the E-2 enterprise who seeks U.S. admission as an employee of the E-2 entity.[217] Importantly, however, "[t]he test of 'develop and direct' applies only to the investor(s), not to the individual employees."[218] The executive or supervisory scope of the visa applicant's activities may be demonstrated by providing the following evidence:

- Control over the enterprise based on ownership of at least 50 percent of the E-2 business;
- "[O]perational control through a managerial position or other corporate device"; or
- "[B]y other means,"[219] as discussed below.

Ownership of at least 50 percent of the E-2 entity is especially important for visa applications by investors; without such ownership, it is likely that the adjudicator will presume that "other individuals who do have the controlling interest ... [will] dictate how the enterprise is to be developed and directed."[220] The majority ownership and control is especially important if the foreign national will be an employee of the E-2 enterprise or of a foreign parent corporation,[221] as discussed below. In some situations, it may be difficult to demonstrate that one individual or entity will direct and develop the E-2 enterprise, because "treaty country ownership may be too diffuse," in which case the owners must establish and show the following:

- "Show that together they own 50 percent of the U.S. enterprise"; and

---

[215] 9 FAM 402.9-6(C).

[216] U.S. Embassy in Seoul, "Treaty Traders and Treaty Investors Visas," http://www.ustraveldocs.com/kr/kr-niv-typee.asp#e2qualifications (formatting deleted).

[217] 8 CFR §214.2(e)(16); 8 CFR §214.2(e)(2)(ii).

[218] 9 FAM 402.9-6(G).

[219] 8 CFR §214.2(e)(16).

[220] *Matter of Lee*, 15 I&N Dec. 187 (Reg'l Comm'r 1975).

[221] 9 FAM 402.9-6(F).

Copyright © 2017. American Immigration Lawyers Association. All rights reserved.

- "[D]emonstrate, that at least collectively, they have the ability to develop and direct the U.S. enterprise."[222]

Importantly, the E-2 visa applicant's duties "must be principally and primarily, as opposed to incidentally or collaterally, executive or supervisory in nature," and must "provide the employee ultimate control and responsibility for the enterprise's overall operation or a major component thereof."[223] An executive position should entail "great authority to determine the policy of, and the direction for, the enterprise,"[224] whereas a supervisory position should involve "responsibility for a significant proportion of an enterprise's operations and does not generally involve the direct supervision of low-level employees."[225] To evaluate whether the activities are appropriately executive or supervisory, the adjudicator may consider whether the foreign national has the following attributes:[226]

- Previous experience or skills as an executive or supervisor;
- "[A] salary and position title commensurate with executive or supervisory employment";
- "[R]ecognition or indicia of the position as one of authority and responsibility in the overall organizational structure," such as demonstrated by an organizational chart; and
- Discretionary authority to make senior-level decisions, "direct[] and manage[e] business operations, [and] supervis[e] other professional and supervisory personnel."[227]

DOS has acknowledged that "small, family-owned businesses with modest levels of investments" may face difficulty in establishing the E-2 visa applicant's executive or supervisory duties.[228] If the foreign national will engage in hands-on "routine work usually performed by a staff employee," then these activities must be "of an incidental nature."[229] In one case, a circuit court stated that an E-2 investor "may perform some menial tasks without negating his treaty investor status if he primarily acts to direct, manage, and protect his investment," if the foreign national "compete[s] with other entrepreneurs, but [does] not compete in the job market for skilled or unskilled labor."[230] The practitioner should note, however, that the circuit

---

[222] *Id.*

[223] 8 CFR §214.2(e)(17). For a discussion of "primarily" executive or managerial duties, see Volume1: Chapter Eleven, "L-1 Visas and Status."

[224] 8 CFR §214.2(e)(17)(i).

[225] 8 CFR §214.2(e)(17)(ii).

[226] 8 CFR §214.2(e)(17).

[227] 8 CFR §214.2(e)(17)(iii).

[228] "Q&As from March 2007 AILA Liaison/DOS Meeting" (Mar. 2007), AILA Doc. No. 07041668.

[229] 8 CFR §214.2(e)(17)(iii).

[230] *Lauvik v. INS*, 910 F.2d 658 (9th Cir. 1990).

Copyright © 2017. American Immigration Lawyers Association. All rights reserved.

court relied on Board of Immigration Appeals (BIA) cases that addressed the investor activities in the context of applying for permanent residence.[231]

In the event that the E-2 enterprise is a franchise, direction and development may be established if the investor will have authority to hire and fire employees, determine pay scales, and establish the hours of business.[232] Other potentially restrictive factors may nevertheless be overcome by demonstrating the decision-making ability of the investor, such as the authority to set retail prices and control profit margins even if the products sold must be approved by the franchiser, the authority to purchase necessary goods and materials on the open market even if the usage of the goods is mandated by the franchise agreement, and the authority to select advertising efforts even if the percentage of gross sales that must be committed to local advertising is set forth in the franchise agreement.[233]

F. Managing Client Expectations: Increased Scrutiny for Certain Situations

Certain facts may trigger increased scrutiny by the adjudicator, and it may be helpful to manage client expectations and to prepare the client by discussing these situations in greater detail.

1. Joint Ventures

Joint ventures may qualify as E entities, but the practitioner should gather and submit evidence of ownership and control. As noted above, at least 50 percent of the enterprise must be owned by a citizen of the treaty country. Ownership of 50 percent is typically deemed to be a controlling interest in the E entity, as long as the enterprise is established as a joint venture or equal partnership and as long as both parties "each retain full management rights and responsibilities."[234] DOS calls this "arrangement" by the term "Negative Control," where "each of the two parties possess[] equal responsibilities [and] ... each have the capacity of making decisions that are binding on the other party."[235] For joint ventures and partnerships, however, there must be no more than two partners, because "an equal partnership with more than two partners would not give any of the parties control based on ownership, as the element of control would be too remote even under the negative control theory."[236]

As discussed above, E-2 treaty investor applications are specifically required to demonstrate the 50 percent ownership and, by the language of the statute, that the E-2 visa applicant will "through ownership or by other means, develop[] and direct[] the

---

[231] *Matter of Ruangswang*, 16 I&N Dec. 76 (BIA 1976); *Matter of Ahmad*, 15 I&N Dec. 81 (BIA 1974); *Matter of Ko*, 14 I&N Dec. 349 (BIA 1973).

[232] *Matter of Kung*, 17 I&N Dec. 260 (Comm'r 1970).

[233] *Id.*

[234] 9 FAM 402.9-6(F).

[235] *Id.*

[236] *Id.*

Copyright © 2017. American Immigration Lawyers Association. All rights reserved.

activities of the enterprise."[237] DOS guidance states that the "type of enterprise being sought will determine how this requirement is applied,"[238] but also acknowledges that "[m]odern business practices constantly introduce new business structures," which makes it "difficult to list all the qualifying structures."[239] An "investor (individual or business)" who demonstrates "control of the business through managerial control" and who demonstrates that he or she "is developing and directing the business," should be issued an E-2 visa.[240]

2. Employees of E-1 and E-2 Entities

The E-1 and E-2 visa categories are not limited to treaty traders and investors; an employee of a qualifying entity may also apply for E-1 or E-2 status, as long as he or she has the same nationality as the E employer.[241] The E employer may not be a permanent resident of the United States, and any ownership interest of a permanent resident may not be counted.[242] The E employer must be either:

- A foreign national who holds E-1 or E-2 status in the United States or who "would be classifiable" as an E-1 treaty trader or E-2 treaty investor if the foreign national resides outside the United States;[243] or

- An entity that is owned at least 50 percent by foreign nationals who hold E-1 or E-2 status in the United States or who "would be classifiable" as E-1 treaty traders or E-2 treaty investors if the foreign nationals reside outside the United States.[244]

The owner of a company seeking to send an employee must demonstrate that he, she, or it (*i.e.*, a corporation) "develops and directs the enterprise."[245] The development and direction of the E-2 enterprise can be established in the following situations:

---

[237] *Id.*

[238] *Id.*

[239] *Id.*

[240] *Id.*

[241] 8 CFR §214.2(e)(3); AFM 34.2(a) ("An E-1 alien may be … or an employee of such enterprise working in an executive or supervisory capacity or in a capacity which requires special qualifications essential to the operation of the enterprise. Such employees must have the same nationality as the principal employer."); AFM 34.3(a) ("An E-2 alien may be the actual owner of a qualifying enterprise or an employee of such enterprise working in an executive or supervisory capacity or in a capacity which requires special qualifications essential to the operation of the enterprise. Such employees must have the same nationality as the principal employer").

[242] 9 FAM 402.9-7(A); AFM 34.2(f) and 34.3(f).

[243] 8 CFR §214.2(e)(3)(i).

[244] 8 CFR §214.2(e)(3)(ii); AFM 34.2(f).

[245] 9 FAM 402.9-6(F).

Copyright © 2017. American Immigration Lawyers Association. All rights reserved.

- If a foreign national will apply for an E-2 visa as a personal employee of the E-2 investor or as an employee of the E-2 business, then the owner must personally develop and direct the business; or

- If a foreign parent company owns at least 50 percent of the E-2 enterprise, then the foreign parent company, rather than an individual, must develop and direct the enterprise, regardless of whether the foreign national will be an employee of the parent corporation or of the E-2 enterprise.[246]

As discussed above, in situations in which ownership is "diffuse" and difficult to establish, collective ownership and authority to develop and direct the E-2 must be demonstrated. In these situations, the E-2 visa applicant may not apply as the investor or as an employee of the owner; instead, the foreign national "must be shown to be an employee of the U.S. enterprise coming to the United States to fulfill the duties of an executive, supervisor, or essentially skilled employee."[247]

For E visa applications by persons other than an individual E-2 investor, the employee's U.S. assignment must entail executive or supervisory duties or duties of "a lesser capacity" that involve "special qualifications that make the alien's services essential to the efficient operation of the enterprise."[248] Legacy INS guidance notes the similarity between the E and L nonimmigrant visa classifications: "The employment must be in a managerial capacity or one which requires special technical knowledge." This employment is not unlike the type of employment which would qualify for an L-1 visa. As stated by USCIS guidance: "Discussions found in various precedent decisions pertaining to L-1 classification are helpful in deciding E-1 cases as well."[249]

a. Executive or Supervisory Duties

As discussed above, executive or supervisory duties involve broad managerial responsibility and authority over "a large portion of a firm's operations," and the adjudicator should consider the following factors in addition to the duties of E-2 treaty investors:[250]

- The job title and duties for the proposed U.S. assignment, as well as the role's remuneration and position in the organizational hierarchy;

- The extent of the visa applicant's "ultimate control and responsibility for the firm's overall operations or a major component thereof"; and

---

[246] *Id.*

[247] 9 FAM 402.9-6(F).

[248] 8 CFR §214.2(e)(3).

[249] AFM 34.2(f); 1 legacy INS AFM, 14-1 Agency Manuals 34.2.

[250] 9 FAM 402.9-7(B).

Copyright © 2017. American Immigration Lawyers Association. All rights reserved.

- The number of employees to be managed or supervised, as well as the educational, experience, and "skill level[]" of the subordinate employees.[251]

The visa applicant should demonstrate that the executive and/or supervisory duties are "a principal and primary function and not an incidental or collateral function" of the assignment; E classification is inappropriate if the assignment "chiefly involves routine work and secondarily entails supervision of low-level employees."[252] There is no bright line test to determine the weight of the individual factors:

"For example, the position title of 'vice president' or 'manager' might be of use in assessing the supervisory nature of a position if the applicant were coming to a major operation having numerous employees. However, if the applicant were coming to a small two-person office, such a title in and of itself would be of little significance."[253]

E-2 status was denied in the following situations because the duties were not primarily executive or supervisory:

- Two foreign nationals who lacked experience as managers and who had experience only as entertainers were to train and supervise other employees on ethnic entertainment and on the preparation and service of ethnic foods;[254] and

- A foreign national would merely provide training to subordinate employees while also performing some hands-on work because these activities entailed only "a modest supervisory role."[255]

b. Essential Duties

If the foreign national will not be an executive or supervisor, then the United States role must entail "special qualifications that make the alien's services essential to the efficient operation of the enterprise."[256] "Special qualifications" are defined as "those skills and/or aptitudes that an employee in a lesser capacity brings to a position or role that are essential to the successful or efficient operation of the treaty enterprise."[257] The inquiry basically entails a two-prong test:

"The employee must, therefore, possess specialized skills and, similarly, such skills must be needed by the enterprise. The burden of proof to establish that the

---

[251] *Id.*

[252] *Id.*

[253] *Id.*

[254] *Matter of Kobayashi and Doi*, 10 I&N Dec. 425 (Dep. Assoc. Comm'r 1963).

[255] *Matter of Udagawa*, 14 I&N Dec. 578 (BIA 1974).

[256] 8 CFR §214.2(e)(3).

[257] 8 CFR §214.2(e)(18).

Copyright © 2017. American Immigration Lawyers Association. All rights reserved.

applicant has special qualifications essential to the effectiveness of the firm's United States operations is on the company and the applicant."[258]

Just as there is no bright line test to establish an employee's executive or supervisory duties, "[t]he determination of whether an employee is an 'essential employee' in this context requires the exercise of judgment."[259] A foreign national's unique knowledge or experience may be deemed essential if they are necessary in order for the E-2 enterprise to satisfy contractual obligations,[260] but mere knowledge of a foreign language and culture does not, by itself, meet the special qualifications requirement."[261] The relevant factors to determine whether skills are "essential" include the following:

- The extent of the foreign national's "proven expertise … in the area of operations involved,"[262] as well as the "uniqueness of the specific skills";[263]

- The interrelationship between "the skill or knowledge" and the E entity's "specific processes or applications,"[264] including the "function" of the proposed assignment;[265]

- The level or duration of "experience and training necessary to achieve such skill(s)," including any previous training or experience with the E business, as discussed below;

- "The salary such special expertise can command";

- The existence of the necessary skills or qualifications held by U.S. workers,[266] as discussed below; and

- The anticipated duration of need for the essential skills, as discussed below.

The practitioner should provide as much evidence of the factors as possible. In one case, the E petition was denied based on an absence of documents discussing the job duties and the foreign national's education and experience.[267] Individual U.S. consulates may have additional requirements; one embassy requests "evidence that employee has essential skills that the enterprise urgently needs, as well as the

---

[258] 9 FAM 402.9-7(C).

[259] Id.

[260] Matter of Walsh and Pollard, 20 I&N Dec. 60 (BIA 1988).

[261] 8 CFR §214.2(e)(18)(i). See also Matter of Konishi, 11 I&N Dec. 815 (Reg'l Comm'r 1966). Cf. Matter of N–S–, 7 I&N Dec. 426 (D.D. 1957) (stating that the foreign national's "Japanese background and his ability to speak the Japanese and English languages are special qualifications which make his services essential to the efficient operations of the employer's enterprise").

[262] 8 CFR §214.2(e)(18)(i).

[263] 9 FAM 402.9-7(C).

[264] 8 CFR §214.2(e)(18)(i).

[265] 9 FAM 402.9-7(C).

[266] 8 CFR §214.2(e)(18)(i). See also 9 FAM 402.9-7(C).

[267] Matter of Konishi, 11 I&N Dec. 815 (Reg'l Comm'r 1966).

Copyright © 2017. American Immigration Lawyers Association. All rights reserved.

projected duration of this essentiality."[268] The "Apply for a U.S. Visa" webpages used by a number of consulates suggest copies of "relevant diplomas, job training certificates, or letters from previous employers."[269] USCIS also suggests "operators' manuals."[270]

In evaluating the essential nature of the visa applicant's proposed duties, the adjudicator should consider all relevant factors,[271] bearing in mind that "the E classification is intended for specialists and not for ordinary skilled workers."[272] U.S. Customs and Border Protection (CBP) guidance also states: "The essential employee must possess special skills including skills which are unique to the operations in the U.S. Such employees are highly and specially trained."[273] The practitioner may note that being "highly and specially trained" seems similar to the "specialized knowledge" requirement for L-1B status. As stated by USCIS guidance, the standard for an essential employee is "somewhat lower than the L-1 'specialized knowledge' qualifications."[274] Nevertheless, an individual consulate may request "[a]n explanation as to why the enterprise was unable to find a qualified U.S. citizen or Legal Permanent Resident to fill the position."[275]

The practitioner should also note that the regulations and DOS guidance seem to intertwine the final two factors, existence of necessary skills held by U.S. workers and duration of assignment, such that there is a balancing test:

> "The question of duration of need will cause variances among the kinds of skills involved…. The availability of U.S. workers provides another factor in assessing the degree of specialization the applicant possesses and the essentiality of this skilled worker to the successful operation of the business. This consideration is not a labor certification test, but a measure of the degree of specialization of the skills in question and the need for such."[276]

Similarly, the regulations state:

---

[268] U.S. Embassy and Consulates in Germany, "Treaty Investor E2, https://de.usembassy.gov/visas/treaty-investor-e-2/.

[269] *E.g.,* U.S. Embassy in Manila, "Treaty Traders and Treaty Investors," http://www.ustraveldocs.com/ph/TTISOVisas.html; U.S. Mission in Czech Republic, "Treaty Traders and Treaty Investors," http://www.ustraveldocs.com/cz/cz-niv-typee.asp.

[270] Instructions for Form I-129, Petition for a Nonimmigrant Worker, E Supplement, https://www.uscis.gov/files/form/i-129instr.pdf.

[271] 8 CFR §214.2(e)(18)(ii).

[272] 9 FAM 402.9-7(C).

[273] 1 CBP IFM ch. 15: Nonimmigrants and Border Crossers, 14-1 Agency Manuals 15.5.

[274] AFM 34.2(f); 1 legacy INS AFM, 14-1 Agency Manuals 34.2.

[275] U.S. Embassy and Consulates in Germany, "Treaty Investor E2," https://de.usembassy.gov/visas/treaty-investor-e-2/.

[276] 9 FAM 402.9-7(C).

Copyright © 2017. American Immigration Lawyers Association. All rights reserved.

"A skill that is essential at one point in time may become commonplace at a later date. Skills that are needed to start up an enterprise may no longer be essential after initial operations are complete and running smoothly. Some skills are essential only in the short-term for the training of locally hired employees."[277]

Therefore, for shorter-term E employees, it may be sufficient to explain how the special or essential skills are necessary for the business's operations, such as if the employee's services are needed to set up the E entity and/or train U.S. workers on methodologies not available in the U.S. workforce.[278] A short-term assignment is interpreted as "one or two years ... when the purpose of the employee(s) relate to start-up operations (of either the business or a new activity by the business) or to training and supervision of technicians employed in manufacturing, maintenance and repair functions."[279] In one case, E-2 status was granted to a foreign national who had knowledge of a specific type of ethnic cooking, where qualified "chefs [were] scarce in the United States and ... the applicant's employer ha[d] been searching for such a chef for several years," and where the foreign national was to train other employees for a period of one year and then return abroad.[280] But E-2 status would most likely be denied if qualified workers could not be located due to the employer's "unwillingness adequately to compensate those available American workers."[281]

As noted above, "'[e]ssential' employees possess skills which differentiate them from ordinarily skilled laborers," but "[i]n some cases, ordinarily skilled workers can qualify as essential employees, and almost always this involves workers needed for start-up or training purposes."[282] Specifically, DOS guidance states:

"A new business or an established business expanding into a new field in the United States might need employees who are ordinarily skilled workers for a short period of time. Such employees derive their essentiality from their familiarity with the overseas operations rather than the nature of their skills. The specialization of skills lies in the knowledge of the peculiarities of the operation of the employer's enterprise rather than in the rote skill held by the applicant."[283]

The practitioner should be aware that if an employee's E visa application states that the foreign national is an "ordinarily skilled" worker who will train U.S. workers, then the adjudicator may require that the E-2 enterprise have a training program for U.S. workers to ultimately replace the E-2 employee,[284] or that the foreign national

---

[277] 8 CFR §214.2(e)(18)(ii).

[278] 9 FAM 402.9-7(C) (providing the example of "a TV technician coming to train U.S. workers in new TV technology not generally available in the U.S. market").

[279] 9 FAM 402.9-7(C).

[280] *Matter of Nago*, 16 I&N Dec. 446 (BIA 1978).

[281] *Matter of Udagawa*, 14 I&N Dec. 578 (BIA 1974).

[282] 9 FAM 402.9-7(C).

[283] *Id.*

[284] *Matter of [name not provided]*, EAC 92 256 50312 (AAU Apr. 23, 1993), 12 Immig. Rptr. B2-79.

Copyright © 2017. American Immigration Lawyers Association. All rights reserved.

have gained previous training or experience with a foreign entity with a corporate relationship with the E entity in the United States.[285] Although there is generally "no requirement that an 'essential' employee have any previous employment with the enterprise in question," the guidance seems to refer to the E entity in the United States,[286] and any such previous training or employment should be irrelevant since the E entity in the United States is the enterprise that requires the foreign national's services.[287] If the foreign national has "familiarity with the overseas operations ... [and] knowledge of the peculiarities of the operation of the employer's enterprise," then that familiarity and knowledge should have been gained with a foreign employer with a corporate relationship with the U.S. enterprise: "The only time when such previous employment is a factor is when the needed skills can only be obtained by that employment. The focus of essentiality is on the business needs for the essential skills and of the alien's possession of such."[288]

In addition, the consular officer may "set a time frame within which the business must replace such foreign workers with locally hired employees."[289] Subsequent visa applications by the foreign national may result in closer scrutiny, especially regarding the hiring of U.S. workers within the stipulated period of time and regarding the reason why the "ordinarily skilled" employee's services continue to be required.[290] The adjudicator may also consider whether other foreign nationals previously held E-2 status in order to train U.S. workers, based on the rationale that "the continued use of foreign workers may function as a means of securing adequate help at less than the prevailing United States wage standards for jobs of comparable complexity."[291] The regulations state:

> "With limited exceptions, it is presumed that employees of treaty enterprises with special qualifications who are responsible for start-up operations should be able to complete their objectives within 2 years. Absent special circumstances, therefore, such employees will not be eligible to obtain an extension of stay."[292]

Similarly, legacy INS guidance states:

> "When granting an extension of stay to [an essential employee], or a change of status to that of a treaty trader, the employing firm shall be advised that the action

---

[285] 8 CFR §214.2(e)(18)(i); *Matter of [name not provided]*, EAC 92 256 50312 (AAU Apr. 23, 1993), 12 Immig. Rptr. B2-79.

[286] 9 FAM 402.9-7(C).

[287] *Id.* (stating that "[f]irms may need skills to operate their business, even though they don't have employees with such skills currently on their employment rolls").

[288] *Id.* In certain respects, this analysis is similar to the inquiry for specialized knowledge employees seeking L-1B status, as discussed in Volume 1: Chapter Eleven, "L-1 Visas and Status."

[289] 9 FAM 402.9-7(C).

[290] *See generally Id.*

[291] *Matter of Udagawa*, 14 I&N Dec. 578 (BIA 1974).

[292] 8 CFR §214.2(e)(20)(ii).

Copyright © 2017. American Immigration Lawyers Association. All rights reserved.

has been taken with the understanding that the employer will utilize U.S. citizens or permanent resident aliens, as such persons become available to make the repairs or to be trained. When the employing firm has been so notified, the alien's Form I-[129] should be annotated to so indicate. If the alien should subsequently apply for a further extension of stay, the adjudicator shall determine what steps the firm has taken to train or employ resident U.S. workers to perform the specialty work. The extension should not be granted if it appears the firm has failed to make serious efforts to comply with the notification."[293]

In contrast, if the E employee's services are truly "essential for the efficient operations of the treaty enterprise for the long-term, the training of United States workers (for) (as) replacement workers is not required."[294] Long-term need may be "a need for the skill(s) on an on-going basis," such as if "the employee(s) will be engaged in functions such as continuous development of product improvement, quality control, or provision of a service otherwise unavailable."[295] Even though "[s]ome skills may be essential for as long as the business is operating,"[296] DOS guidance acknowledges the closer scrutiny: "Long-term employment presents a different issue, in that what is highly specialized and unique today might not be in a few years. It is anticipated that such changes would more likely occur in industries of rapid development, such as any computer-related industry."[297] The practitioner is strongly encouraged to provide additional evidence for a longer E assignment:

> "Under certain circumstances, an applicant may be able to establish his or her essentiality to the treaty enterprise for a longer period of time, such as, in connection with activities in the areas of product improvement, quality control, or the provision of a service not yet generally available in the United States. Where the treaty enterprise's need for the applicant's special qualifications, and therefore, the applicant's essentiality, is time-limited, Service officers may request that the applicant provide evidence of the period for which skills will be needed and a reasonable projected date for completion of start-up or replacement of the essential skilled workers."[298]

Whether the need for the E employee's services is short- or long-term, the adjudicating officer should "make a judgment as to whether the employee is essential for the efficient operation of enterprise for an indefinite period or for a shorter period."[299] The visa applicant also bears the burden to demonstrate the projected

---

[293] AFM 34.2(f); 1 legacy INS AFM, 14-1 Agency Manuals 34.2. The guidance references the Form I-539, but this should not apply, since the Form I-129 is now used for E petitions.

[294] 9 FAM 402.9-7(C).

[295] *Id.*

[296] *Id.*

[297] 9 FAM 402.9-7(C).

[298] 8 CFR §214.2(e)(18)(ii).

[299] 9 FAM 402.9-7(C).

Copyright © 2017. American Immigration Lawyers Association. All rights reserved.

duration of the need for the essential skills,[300] and also "must prove that he or she possesses these skills, by demonstrating the requisite training and/or experience."[301] The practitioner may also wish to provide evidence or statements from "chambers of commerce, labor organizations, industry trade sources, or state employment services as to the unavailability of U.S. workers in the skill areas concerned."[302] These documents may be particularly important and/or helpful if the foreign national has been previously been issued an E visa or granted E status, because "the consular officer should monitor [whether the skills remain 'highly specialized and unique'] at the time of any application for reissuance," and because the foreign national who engages in a longer-term assignment "bears the burden of establishing that his or her specialized skills are still needed and that the applicant still possesses such skills."[303]

If the proposed salary or remuneration to the essential employee seems low to the practitioner, then it is likely that it will seem low to the adjudicator. In such a situation, the practitioner may wish to review the prevailing wage, as calculated by the Foreign Labor Certification Data Center Online Wage Library, available at *www.flcdatacenter.com*, by selecting the FLC Wage Search Wizard, the state of intended employment from the drop-down menu, the county of intended employment, and the job code from the drop-down list (or searching by keyword). A print-out of the prevailing wage may be supplied to demonstrate that the proposed remuneration meets or exceeds the wages paid to U.S. workers in comparable positions.[304]

3. Substantive Changes of E Status Eligibility and Employment with a Related Corporate Entity

If there is a "substantive change" in the terms and conditions of E status or eligibility, then the substantive change must be approved by USCIS through the approval of an amended E petition or by DOS through issuance of a new E visa and re-admission to the United States.[305] Events that are considered "substantive changes" generally entail "a fundamental change in the employing entity's basic characteristics" and include mergers, acquisitions, or "sale of the division" where the E nonimmigrant is employed.[306] The new petition or visa application should include "evidence of continued eligibility for E classification in the new capacity."[307] The foreign national "is not authorized to begin the new employment until the application is approved"[308]

---

[300] *Id.*

[301] *Id.*

[302] *Id.*

[303] *Id.*

[304] For a discussion of how to calculate the level of the prevailing wage, see Volume 1: Chapter Six, "The Labor Condition Application."

[305] 8 CFR §214.2(e)(8)(iii).

[306] 8 CFR §214.2(e)(8)(iii).

[307] *Id.*

[308] 8 CFR §214.2(e)(8)(vi).

Copyright © 2017. American Immigration Lawyers Association. All rights reserved.

through issuance of a new Form I-797; changing E employers without prior approval "will constitute a failure to maintain status."[309] If the foreign national departs the United States, then he or she may be re-admitted after presenting the new Form I-797 and an unexpired E visa.[310] But as discussed below, [in the section titled "E Visa Application vs. Change of Status Petition"], it is preferable for the foreign national to apply for a new E visa and seek readmission rather than wait for USCIS approval of a petition.

The regulations allow E nonimmigrants to "perform work for the parent treaty organization or enterprise, or any subsidiary of the parent organization or enterprise."[311] Such work "will not be deemed to constitute a substantive change in the terms and conditions of the underlying E treaty employment," as long as the foreign national presented the following evidence with the E visa application or change of status petition:[312]

- The name of the enterprise and any subsidiaries "where the work will be performed";

- Proof of the necessary corporate relationship between the parent and subsidiary entities;

- Proof that the "subsidiary independently qualifies as a treaty organization or enterprise";[313]

- If the foreign national is an employee of an E enterprise, then evidence of how the assignment "requires executive, supervisory, or essential skills";[314] and

- Evidence of how the "work is consistent with the terms and conditions of the activity forming the basis of the classification."[315]

For non-substantive changes in E employment or eligibility, neither prior approval nor an amended E petition or visa application needs to be filed.[316] Prior approval is also "not required if corporate changes occur which do not affect the previously approved employment relationship, or are otherwise non-substantive."[317] If the client is risk-averse, then it is possible to "facilitate admission" by taking one of the following actions:

---

[309] 8 CFR §214.2(e)(8)(vii).

[310] 8 CFR §214.2(e)(8)(vi).

[311] 8 CFR §214.2(e)(8)(ii); AFM 34.2(a) and 34.3(a).

[312] 8 CFR §214.2(e)(8)(ii).

[313] 8 CFR §214.2(e)(8)(ii)(A).

[314] 8 CFR §214.2(e)(8)(ii)(B).

[315] 8 CFR §214.2(e)(8)(ii)(C).

[316] 8 CFR §214.2(e)(8)(iv).

[317] Id.

Copyright © 2017. American Immigration Lawyers Association. All rights reserved.

- "Present a letter from the treaty-qualifying company through which the alien attained E classification explaining the nature of the change";[318]

- File a new E petition with USCIS, "with fee, and a complete description of the change";[319] or

- Apply for a new E visa at a U.S. consulate abroad.[320]

Importantly, the practitioner may wish to advise the client that a foreign national "who does not elect one of the three options ... is not precluded from demonstrating to the satisfaction of the immigration officer at the port-of-entry in some other manner, his or her admissibility" as an E nonimmigrant.[321] In addition, if the foreign national will be employed by a subsidiary, then "the subsidiary is required to comply with" the regulations regarding control of the employment of foreign nationals.[322]

It is possible to request advice from USCIS on "whether a change is substantive" by filing an amended E petition, "with fee, and a complete description of the change."[323] If there are multiple employees who will be impacted by "a merger or other corporate restructuring," the request may also be made on a single amended petition, "attaching a list of the related receipt numbers for the employees involved and an explanation of the change or changes," to inquire whether subsequent individual petitions must be filed.[324] Like all E-1 and E-2 petitions to USCIS, the request should be filed with the California Service Center (CSC).[325]

4. E Employees Will Perform Activities Pursuant to a Contract Between a U.S. Entity and Either Foreign Corporation or an E-2 Entity

As noted above, an E-2 entity may be established in order to perform on a contract for services or goods with a U.S. business.[326] The existence of such a contract, however, should not be construed to entail the creation of a "job shop," which is interpreted as "involv[ing] the providing of workers needed by an employer to perform pre-designated duties."[327] Although a job shop may supply qualified workers on an as-needed basis to a client, DOS guidance states that establishment of an E-2 enterprise in order to perform pursuant to a contract does not "in any way facilitate

---

[318] 8 CFR §214.2(e)(8)(iv)(A).

[319] 8 CFR §214.2(e)(8)(iv)(B).

[320] 8 CFR §214.2(e)(8)(iv)(C).

[321] *Id.*

[322] 8 CFR §214.2(e)(8)(vii).

[323] 8 CFR §214.2(e)(8)(v).

[324] *Id.*

[325] USCIS, "Direct Filing Addresses for Form I-129, Petition for a Nonimmigrant Worker," https://www.uscis.gov/i-129-addresses.

[326] *Matter of Walsh and Pollard*, 20 I&N Dec. 60 (BIA 1988).

[327] 9 FAM 402.9-6(G).

Copyright © 2017. American Immigration Lawyers Association. All rights reserved.

the creation of job shops under the E-2 visa classification."[328] This is because the E-2 employees would not fill existing positions within the U.S. business but would provide "services which the U.S. business did not have the capacity to perform,"[329] based on a "project-oriented commodity."[330]

DOS guidance also states: "The fact that the [performing] entity might prepare the design anywhere, even on the sites of contracting business, does not alter the nature of the transaction."[331] Nevertheless, because of increased scrutiny of L-1B nonimmigrants who are sent to third-party sites, the practitioner may wish to supplement the visa application or petition with a copy of the contract and evidence of why the receiving business is unable to perform the contracted services, such as if the receiving company is engaged in different business activities or lacks regular employees who are qualified to perform the contracted services.[332]

5. Impact of Labor Disputes on Canadian and Mexican Transferees

A Canadian or Mexican citizen may not be admitted in E status if the "Secretary of Labor certifies or otherwise informs the Commissioner that a strike or other labor dispute involving a work stoppage of workers is in progress at the place where the alien is or intends to be employed,"[333] and if the admission of the Canadian or Mexican citizen would "adversely affect either:"[334]

- "The settlement of any labor dispute that is in progress at the place or intended place of employment, or
- "The employment of any person who is involved in such dispute."[335]

The practitioner should note that the strike or labor dispute must be certified by the Secretary of Labor; otherwise, the Canadian or Mexican citizen should be admitted.[336] The United States must consider and apply the "strikebreaker" provision when the E petition is adjudicated, if applicable; when the foreign national applies for an E visa; and when the foreign national applies for admission to the United States at

---

[328] Id.

[329] Id.

[330] Id.

[331] Id.

[332] Id. ("Since the distinction might be clouded in some circumstances, [the consular officer] should exercise care in adjudicating such cases and not hesitate to submit any questionable cases for an advisory opinion").

[333] 8 CFR §214.2(e)(22)(i)(A).

[334] 8 CFR §214.2(e)(22)(i)(B).

[335] Id.

[336] 8 CFR §214.2(e)(22)(iv).

Copyright © 2017. American Immigration Lawyers Association. All rights reserved.

a port of entry.[337] The certification or notification from the Secretary of Labor "may include the locations and occupations affected by the strike."[338]

If E admission or visa is denied because of a certified labor dispute, the foreign national must be notified in writing of the reasons, and the foreign national's home country government must also be notified.[339] A foreign national holding E status "shall not be deemed to be failing to maintain his or her status solely on account of past, present, or future participation in a strike or other labor dispute involving a work stoppage of workers," whether the strike or labor dispute is certified by the Secretary of Labor or not.[340] However, the following conditions apply:

- The foreign national "shall remain subject to all applicable provisions of the Act and regulations applicable to all other E nonimmigrants";[341] and

- The E status "is not modified or extended in any way by virtue of [the] participation in a strike or other labor dispute involving a work stoppage of workers."[342]

Therefore, "participation by an E nonimmigrant alien in a strike or other labor dispute involving a work stoppage of workers will not constitute a ground for deportation," but the foreign national should not violate E status or remain in the United States after E status has expired, because these actions should "subject [the foreign national] to deportation."[343] For a further discussion of the intent of the strikebreaker provision, see Volume 1: Chapter Eleven, "L-1 Visas and Status."

III. Process

In seeking E status, a foreign national may apply directly for an E visa at a consulate abroad; it is not necessary to file a petition with USCIS before the visa application.[344] DOS guidance directs consular officers "to be flexible, fair, and uniform in adjudicating E visa applications," although they may request additional evidence of eligibility.[345]

If the foreign national is within the United States, a petition may be filed to request E change of status.[346] Both approaches are discussed below.

---

[337] Legacy INS, J. Puleo, "NAFTA Implementation of Strikebreaker Provisions" (Oct. 17, 1994), AILA Doc. No. 94101780.

[338] *Id.*

[339] *Id.*; NAFTA Implementation Cable 003, 1 NAFTA Handbook (Nov. 1999), 14-1 legacy INS Manuals Scope.

[340] 8 CFR §214.2(e)(22)(ii).

[341] 8 CFR §214.2(e)(22)(ii)(A).

[342] 8 CFR §214.2(e)(22)(ii)(B).

[343] 8 CFR §214.2(e)(22)(iii).

[344] 1 legacy INS AFM, 14-1 Agency Manuals 34.3; AFM 34.2(b) and 34.3(b).

[345] 9 FAM 402.9-2.

[346] AFM 34.2(b); 1 legacy INS AFM, 14-1 Agency Manuals 34.2.

Copyright © 2017. American Immigration Lawyers Association. All rights reserved.

A. Preparing the E Visa Application or Petition

The following documents must be prepared and submitted regardless of which process is selected:

- Form G-28;
- Evidence that the foreign national holds the nationality of the treaty country, in the form of the passport or copy of the biographic page of the passport;
- Evidence that the E enterprise satisfies the requirements for E-1 or E-2 status;
- Evidence of the business activities of the E enterprise, if any;
- Evidence of the scope of employment activities;
- Evidence of the ownership of the E enterprise;[347]
- U.S. company support statement;
- Evidence that the foreign national's stay in the United States will be "temporary," which may be in the form of an affidavit or statement from the foreign national, if this is required by the individual U.S. consulate, as discussed below.

DOS suggests the following for answers to questions on a form: "If an enterprise is not fully operational, estimates and projections should be made concerning the potential income, job creation, volume of sales, etc."[348]

1. Form G-28

For E visa applications, the foreign national is the "applicant." For E change of status petitions, the U.S. company is the "petitioner" and the foreign national is the "beneficiary" of the E petition. The addresses for the U.S. company and the foreign national should be provided. If there is limited time to prepare and file the petition before the U.S. assignment is to begin, such as if the forms are emailed to and printed by the client, this form may be printed on plain white paper. However, as discussed in Volume 1: Chapter Two, "Basic Nonimmigrant Concepts," the Form G-28 should be printed on blue paper whenever possible, in order to avoid processing delays.[349]

2. U.S. Company Support Statement

The support statement from the U.S. employer should connect the E enterprise's activities with the need for the foreign national's services. For this reason, it is critical to provide the government official with the information necessary to adjudicate the petition for approval and to state important details, as discussed above, in the support statement.

---

[347] 1 legacy INS AFM, 14-1 Agency Manuals 34.3; AFM 34.2(b) and 34.3(b).

[348] DOS, "Form DS-156E: Nonimmigrant Treaty Trader/Investor Application," https://www.state.gov/documents/organization/217452.pdf. Although the guidance specifically relates to the Form DS-156E, the principle should be the same for the USCIS forms as well.

[349] "VSC Practice Pointer: G-28s" (Sept. 4, 2008), AILA Doc. No. 08090469.

Copyright © 2017. American Immigration Lawyers Association. All rights reserved.

The statement should be on the U.S. company's letterhead and signed by a representative of the U.S. company. One format of a support statement is as follows:

- Introduction;

- Information about the employer;

- Discussion of the E business's activities, project, or reason for need of the foreign national's services for the U.S. assignment;

- Discussion of the duties of the U.S. assignment;

- Discussion of the foreign national's educational and experience background; and

- Thank you and conclusion.

The most critical parts of the support statement are the paragraphs that address the need for the foreign national's services and the daily job duties. Therefore, the support statement should provide details on the project(s) or initiative(s) that gave rise to the assignment and how the job duties will contribute to the successful completion of the employer's objectives. The conclusion paragraph may contain the necessary information on the length of the U.S. assignment as the anticipated length of stay, as this is relevant particularly for essential employee assignments and the amount of remuneration for the services.

B. E Visa Application vs. E Change of Status Petition

The main advantage of the E visa application is convenience. If the foreign national is outside the United States or is in the United States but has plans to visit his or her home country, perhaps to wrap up personal affairs before beginning the E assignment, then this approach is most appropriate. In addition, if the foreign national anticipates any travel at all outside the United States, he or she must apply for an E visa abroad in order to return, and the U.S. consulate usually will require the full set of E registration documents even if USCIS approved an E change of status petition,[350] as discussed below. Further, experience has shown that U.S. consulates may apply a stricter de novo standard when adjudicating E visa applications than those considered by USCIS. Thus, a client may find him– or herself in the untenable situation of having established and run a business in the United States for some time, but then being unable to return to the United States to continue to operate the E business should the E visa application be denied or delayed.

USCIS processing times for E petitions can vary,[351] and a visa application may take a similar amount of time, depending on the next available visa appointment and

---

[350] U.S. Embassy and Consulates in the United Kingdom, "Treaty Trader or Treaty Investor/Change of Status," https://uk.usembassy.gov/visas/treaty-trader-or-treaty-investor/change-of-status/.

[351] "USCIS Processing Time Information." https://egov.uscis.gov/cris/processTimesDisplay.do. Select "CSC-California Service Center in the drop-down box for "Service Center."

Copyright © 2017. American Immigration Lawyers Association. All rights reserved.

processing time for visa issuance at the individual U.S. consulate.[352] Nevertheless, the processing time may be longer for visa applications, based on high demand during a season,[353] whether it is an initial application or a renewal,[354] or the intricacies of reviewing the company's E registration documents,[355] as discussed above. In addition, depending on staffing at any given time, some U.S. consulates can become known for long processing times.

If the foreign national initially entered the United States under the Visa Waiver Program (VWP), then he or she must apply for an E visa abroad, because one cannot change status from VWP. The disadvantages of the E visa application are the cost of airfare for the foreign national and his or her dependent family members, if applicable, and the possibility that visa issuance may be delayed by the E registration procedure or by administrative processing, as discussed in Volume 1: Chapter Two, "Basic Nonimmigrant Concepts."

In contrast, filing an E change of status petition with USCIS has the benefits of saving the costs of international airfare and allowing the E dependent spouse to concurrently file an employment authorization document (EAD) application. This concurrent filing would be an alternative to filing the EAD application after the principal E foreign national has obtained E status. Nevertheless, the practitioner should consider that the timing of the concurrent filing may take longer than applying for the EAD after admission in E status. This is because the EAD application may not be approved until USCIS confirms that the principal foreign national holds valid E status,[356] and adjudication of the principal's E change of status petition may take several months. The drawbacks of filing an E change of status petition are the absence of employment authorization until the E petition is approved by USCIS, the need to monitor the immigration status of foreign national(s) and file extension(s) if necessary, and the potential increased scrutiny of the E business and its employees. The E Supplement form requests the number of foreign national employees in E, L, and H status, as well as the number of employees in executive or managerial roles and the number of positions that require "special qualifications," all regardless of nationality.[357] In addition, an E-2 change of status petition may be denied if it is

---

[352] DOS, "Visa Appointment & Processing Wait Times," https://travel.state.gov/content/visas/en/general/wait-times.html/.

[353] "Q&As from March 2007 AILA Liaison/DOS Meeting" (Mar. 2007), AILA Doc. No. 07041668 (stating that "fluctuations in demand for E visa appointments cause variations in applicant waiting time").

[354] "U.S. Consulate in Toronto Updates Document Submission Processes for E Visa Applicants" (Feb. 10, 2014), AILA Doc. No. 14021442.

[355] *Id.* (noting that "posts that deal with processing small investment cases, especially those involving new companies, are often required to spend more time processing each case").

[356] "Service Center Operations Teleconference" (Dec. 16, 2003), AILA Doc. No. 03121710.

[357] Form I-129, Petition for a Nonimmigrant Worker, E Supplement, https://www.uscis.gov/files/form/i-129.pdf.

Copyright © 2017. American Immigration Lawyers Association. All rights reserved.

submitted soon after the foreign national enters the United States in B-2 visitor for pleasure status.[358]

1. Request for Change of Status

A foreign national is eligible for change of status only if he or she continuously maintained the previous nonimmigrant status.[359] Violation of the terms and conditions, such as unauthorized employment while in B status, is considered to be failure to maintain valid nonimmigrant status.[360] In addition, there are potential fraud and misrepresentation concerns with requesting a change of status if there has been unauthorized employment. Strategies and issues relating to change of status petitions are discussed in more detail in Volume 1: Chapter Two, "Basic Nonimmigrant Concepts." For further discussion of the accrual of unauthorized employment, its impact on subsequent petitions, and strategies to address accrual of unauthorized employment, see Volume 1: Chapter Two, "Basic Nonimmigrant Concepts."

If change of status is requested, however, the expiration date of the foreign national's B status should be calendared. Ideally, the E change of status petition will be approved before the beneficiary's B status expires, and premium processing may be requested to maximize the likelihood of timely approval. The practitioner may wish to advise the client on the intricacies of situations in which the initial status expires before the change of status petition is approved. As discussed in Volume 1: Chapter Two, "Basic Nonimmigrant Concepts," a timely filed request for change of status will extend the beneficiary's period of authorized stay, such that the foreign national should not accrue unlawful presence during pendency of the change of status petition, but the government takes the view that a change of status petition will not serve to maintain the beneficiary's immigration status.[361] If the change of status petition is approved, then the foreign national will be accorded a new period of authorized stay retroactive to the date the initial immigration status expired, and he or she would accrue no unlawful presence.[362]

However, if the change of status petition is ultimately denied because the beneficiary engaged in unauthorized employment or because the petition is deemed frivolous, then all of the time that the foreign national remained in the United States

---

[358] *Patel v. Minnix*, 663 F.2d 1042 (11th Cir. 1981) (denying E-2 status where foreign national purchased a business 15 days after entering the country in B-2 status and requested E-2 change of status 32 days after admission, and provided only unsubstantiated affidavits from the applicant and the applicant's brother regarding his intent to visit the United States as a visitor).

[359] 8 CFR §248.1(a) and (b).

[360] 8 CFR §214.1(e). *See also* "USCIS SOPs for I-539 Processing," AILA Doc. No. 07090760.

[361] Legacy INS, J. Podolny, "Interpretation of 'Period of Stay Authorized by the Attorney General' in determining 'unlawful presence' under INA section 212(a)(9)(B)(ii)" (Mar. 27, 2003), AILA Doc. No. 03042140.

[362] Legacy INS, M. Pearson, "Period of stay authorized by the Attorney General after 120-day tolling period for purposes of section 212(a)(9)(B) of the Immigration and Nationality Act (the Act). (AD 00-07)" (Mar. 3, 2000), AILA Doc. No. 00030774.

Copyright © 2017. American Immigration Lawyers Association. All rights reserved.

after expiration of his or her initial grant of admission will be considered unlawful presence.[363] Due to sometimes lengthy processing times, it is possible for a foreign national to accrue 180 days of unlawful presence while awaiting adjudication of a change of status petition. Accrual of more than 180 days of unlawful presence will trigger the three-year bar to re-entry to the United States upon departure from the United States Accrual of more than 365 days of unlawful presence will trigger the 10-year ban to re-entry to the United States upon departure from the United States. For a detailed discussion of the three– and 10-year bars, see Volume 1: Chapter Two, "Basic Nonimmigrant Concepts," and Volume 2: Chapter One, "Basic Immigrant Visa Concepts."

A request for extension of B status may be filed, but the practitioner should be aware that USCIS may question the validity of a B extension request and whether a legitimate B purpose is being served or fulfilled.[364] Nevertheless, if this strategy is pursued, then following expiration of the initial nonimmigrant status, the change of status petition should be updated with the receipt notice for the timely filed extension request, to evidence that the beneficiary has not failed to maintain lawful immigration status.[365]

2. Canadian and Mexican Citizens

The NAFTA Treaty is the applicable treaty for Canadian and Mexican citizens.[366] Unlike other nonimmigrant visa classifications, as discussed in Volume 1: Chapter Two, "Basic Nonimmigrant Concepts," Canadian citizens are required to have valid E visas in order to enter the United States in E status.[367] If a Canadian citizen is granted E-2 change of status by USCIS, then he or she must nevertheless apply for an E visa in order to seek re-admission to the United States.[368] Because Canadian citizens require E visas, the concerns regarding temporary entry pursuant to the NAFTA Treaty for L-1 nonimmigrants should not apply.[369] As discussed above, it is also critical to note that E admission may be denied if the E visa holder's admission

---

[363] *Id.*

[364] "AILA-VSC Conference Call Minutes" (Mar. 5, 2008), AILA Doc. No. 08031331.

[365] *Id.* Note that it is not current USCIS policy to apply the "last action rule," as discussed in Volume 1: Chapter Two, Basic Nonimmigrant Concepts.

[366] North American Free Trade Agreement, U.S.–Can.–Mex. (Dec. 17, 1992), 32 I.L.M. 289 (entered into force Jan. 1, 1994), Chap. 16; 1 CBP IFM ch. 15: Nonimmigrants and Border Crossers, 14-1 Agency Manuals 15.5.

[367] 8 CFR §214.1(*l*); legacy INS Operations Instruction (OI) 248.8; NAFTA Implementation Cable 007, 1 NAFTA Handbook (Nov. 1999), 14-1 legacy INS Manuals Scope; "INS Issues Cable on NAFTA Implementation" (Dec. 8, 1993), AILA Doc. No. 94010780.

[368] OI 248.8.

[369] For a discussion of the potential issues surrounding L-1 admission as "temporary entry" under NAFTA, see Volume 1: Chapter Eleven, "L-1 Visas and Status."

Copyright © 2017. American Immigration Lawyers Association. All rights reserved.

to the United States would "adversely affect" the resolution of a labor dispute or the employment of an individual involved in a labor dispute.[370]

Unfortunately, Mexican citizens applying for E visas may no longer obtain visas valid for up to two years by paying the reciprocity fee of $100 for each year of visa validity.[371] Instead, there now is no reciprocity fee, but the reciprocity schedule limits the duration of an E visa to 12 months.[372]

C. E Registration and Visa Application at a U.S. Consulate

The practitioner should consult the website of the individual U.S. embassy or consulate for the most recent information on visa application procedures. Because E entities typically need to be registered with the U.S. consulate in the treaty country, visa applications may generally not be made by third country nationals, although certain consulates accept applications from foreign nationals who physically reside in the third country.[373] For example, the U.S. Embassy in London "posts its instructions regarding the format and filing of E visa applications on its web site" and will accept E visa applications by third country nationals, as discussed in Volume 1: Chapter Two, "Basic Nonimmigrant Concepts," "but will want to know why the applicant is not applying in his or her home country."[374]

The supporting documents for the E visa application, whether for the entity's registration and/or the foreign national's visa application, "should be submitted in a binder with a table of contents and tabs."[375] Most individual U.S. consulates are very particular about how the documents are organized, presented, and submitted.[376] Therefore, it is essential that the practitioner consult the consulate's website when preparing for the E visa application.

---

[370] 8 CFR §214.2(e)(22)(i)(B).

[371] DOS, "Mexico Reciprocity Schedule," https://travel.state.gov/content/visas/en/fees/reciprocity-by-country/MX.html. *Cf.* former DOS website, "Mexico Reciprocity Schedule," formerly http://travel.state.gov/visa/frvi/reciprocity/reciprocity_3622.html#B (link no longer works).

[372] DOS, "Mexico Reciprocity Schedule," https://travel.state.gov/content/visas/en/fees/reciprocity-by-country/MX.html.

[373] *See, e.g.*, "AILA Liaison Questions for U.S. Embassy, London" (Oct. 13, 2010), AILA Doc. No. 10110960; "AILA Liaison Q&As with U.S. Embassy, Athens" (Jan. 19, 2011), AILA Doc. No. 11030728.

[374] AILA Liaison Questions for U.S. Embassy, London" (Oct. 13, 2010), AILA Doc. No. 10110960.

[375] DOS, "Form DS-156E: Nonimmigrant Treaty Trader/Investor Application," https://www.state.gov/documents/organization/217452.pdf.

[376] *See, e.g.*, U.S. Embassy in Honduras, "Treaty Traders and Treaty Investors Visas," http://www.ustraveldocs.com/hn/hn-niv-typee.asp; U.S. Consulate in Islamabad, "Treaty Traders and Treaty Investors Visas," http://www.ustraveldocs.com/pk/pk-niv-typee.asp#applicationdocse2; U.S. Embassy and Consulates in Italy, "E-2 First-Time Application Requirements," https://it.usembassy.gov/visas/niv/e/e2/; U.S. Embassy & Consulates in the United Kingdom, "Treaty Investor (E-2)," https://uk.usembassy.gov/visas/treaty-trader-or-treaty-investor/treaty-investor-e-2/; U.S. Embassy and Consulates in France, "Nonimmigrant Visas: Treaty Traders and Investor Required Formats," https://fr.usembassy.gov/visas/nonimmigrant-visas/treaty-trader-investor/.

Copyright © 2017. American Immigration Lawyers Association. All rights reserved.

The issued visa should be annotated with the name of the U.S. employer. The issued visa may or may not be valid for the full duration of the reciprocity period. As stated by one embassy:

> "[W]hether or not to issue for that length of time is solely the judgment of the consular officer deciding the case. In London, we typically issue the first E-1 or E-2 for two years. We do so because most of the businesses we see are relatively small and small businesses are volatile and often do not succeed. If we renew an E-1 or E-2 visa, we generally do so for the maximum five years although not always. In the case of large companies with high turnover and employing many Americans, we sometimes issue the first visas for five years."[377]

1. E Registration

First-time E visa applications should typically be accompanied by documents to register the E enterprise with the U.S. consulate.[378] As stated by DOS: "Evaluation of a company for Treaty Trader or Treaty Investor status is not a separate adjudication but is the first step in the adjudication of an E-1 or E-2 application."[379] Similarly, one embassy states:

> "The first step in applying for a Treaty Trader or a Treaty Investor visa is to establish the qualification of the company or operation in the U.S. This process is known as registration. All companies seeking E visas for their owners or employees must be registered with the U.S. Embassy…[or Consulate]…."[380]

It may be necessary to schedule a separate appointment with the U.S. consulate to submit the E registration documents.[381] The E visa application process may be delayed for a few weeks, because many U.S. consulates require additional time to review the E registration documents before scheduling a personal interview with the visa applicant.[382] For a discussion of E visa renewals after the enterprise has been registered with the U.S. consulate, see below.

---

[377] U.S. Embassy & Consulates in the United Kingdom, "Treaty Investor/Length of Visa," https://uk.usembassy.gov/visas/treaty-trader-or-treaty-investor/length-of-visa/.

[378] *See, e.g.*, U.S. Embassy and Consulates in Japan, "Treaty Traders and Investors Visas," https://jp.usembassy.gov/visas/nonimmigrant-visas/e1-e2-visas/apply-step-1/.

[379] "Q&As from March 2007 AILA Liaison/DOS Meeting" (Mar. 2007), AILA Doc. No. 07041668.

[380] U.S. Embassy and Consulates in Japan, "Treaty Traders and Investors Visas," https://jp.usembassy.gov/visas/nonimmigrant-visas/e1-e2-visas/apply-step-1/.

[381] U.S. Embassy in Honduras, "Treaty Traders and Treaty Investors Visas," http://www.ustraveldocs.com/hn/hn-niv-typee.asp.

[382] *See, e.g.*, "AILA Liaison Questions for US Embassy, Rome" (Jan. 2010), AILA Doc. No. 10031064; "AILA Liaison Questions for US Embassy, Rome" (Jan. 2010), AILA Doc. No. 10031064; U.S. Embassy in Honduras, "Treaty Traders and Treaty Investors Visas," http://www.ustraveldocs.com/hn/hn-niv-typee.asp.

Copyright © 2017. American Immigration Lawyers Association. All rights reserved.

2. E Visa Application

In addition to the documents discussed above and in Volume 1: Chapter Two, "Basic Nonimmigrant Concepts," Form DS-160 must be completed and submitted for each applicant. In addition, Form DS-156E, Nonimmigrant Treaty Trader/Investor Application, must be submitted for all E-1 Treaty Trader applications, and for E-2 Treaty Investor applications involving employees (executive, manager, or essential). The DOS website indicates that DS-156E is not required for the investor,[383] but experience has shown that virtually all consular posts require this form for investors as well. The practitioner should check the website of the individual U.S. consulate and confirm that the E visa application includes all requested documents, in the order and format requested.[384] For example, the U.S. consulate may require a cover letter describing the E enterprise and the foreign national; a letter from the proposed employer describing the employee's assignment and qualifications, as well as the enterprise's business activities; and a copy of the visa applicant's résumé.[385] The practitioner is advised to strongly encourage the client and/or foreign national to present a detailed business plan: "The E Visa Officer relies heavily on the applicant's business plan which should explain in detail the investor's credentials and plan to develop the business to determine how well the business will do in the U.S."[386] Finally, the practitioner should respond to consular inquiries promptly: "E visa cases are the cases that involve the most interaction between Post and attorneys. Prompt responses from attorneys will allow Post to process these cases as quickly as possible."[387]

The visa for a dependent, including one who is stateless or who is a national of a non-treaty country, should be issued according to the reciprocity schedule of the principal E nonimmigrant.[388] If the dependent's nationality is that of another treaty country, then he or she should be issued an E visa according to the reciprocity

---

[383] DOS, "DS-160: Frequently Asked Questions," https://travel.state.gov/content/visas/en/forms/ds-160--online-nonimmigrant-visa-application/frequently-asked-questions.html.

[384] "AILA Liaison Questions for U.S. Embassy, Rome" (Jan. 2010), AILA Doc. No. 10031064 ("We encourage E visa applicants to submit their applications in a binder divided into sections clearly separated by lettered or numbered tabs, in order to ensure efficient and effective processing (a clear explanation is provided on our website). Applications not complying with this format will be accepted but may experience additional processing delays").

[385] U.S. Embassy and Consulates in Pakistan, "Treaty Traders and Treaty Investors," http://www.ustraveldocs.com/pk/pk-niv-typee.asp.

[386] "AILA Liaison Questions for US Embassy, London" (Oct. 13, 2010), AILA Doc. No. 10110960.

[387] "AILA Liaison Questions for US Embassy, Rome" (Jan. 2010), AILA Doc. No. 10031064.

[388] DOS, "Reciprocity Schedule—Visa Category Footnote 2," https://travel.state.gov/content/visas/en/fees/reciprocity-by-country/KS.html. This is part of the DOS interactive portal, Reciprocity and Civil Documents by Country. Footnote 2 appears for any E country for which E-1 or E-2 is entered in the drop-down box.

Copyright © 2017. American Immigration Lawyers Association. All rights reserved.

schedule of his or her nationality, even if the principal nonimmigrant's nationality has a more favorable reciprocity schedule.[389]

3. Form DS-156E

The Form DS-156E is the basis for the E visa application. If the E enterprise has already been registered with the U.S. consulate, as discussed above, then it may be necessary only to complete Part III for the individual visa applicant;,[390] but the practitioner should confirm that documents to update Parts I and II have been provided recently according to any particular processing requests of the individual U.S. consulate.[391]

a. Part I

Information about the E business should be provided: name, type of entity, contact information, date of establishment or incorporation in the United States, and type of business activities, including a description of the goods and/or services. If the business is a start up, then the lease address that was used for registering the business in the United States may be provided. The practitioner may wish to also provide the names and contact information for any affiliated and/or subsidiary companies of the U.S. enterprise. If there are more than a few affiliate and subsidiary companies, the other company information may be attached as a separate document to the Form DS-156E, with "Please see attached list of companies" stated in #3. Evidence of the business's date of establishment or incorporation in the United States should also be attached to the Form DS-156E. The description of the business activities may be the same introductory language in the support statement.

If there is a foreign parent corporation, then contact information for that parent should be provided. In the case of an E-2 registration for an individual investor where there is no foreign parent business, "N/A" may be stated in the address, telephone number, and fax number fields. The names and nationality of the foreign entity or foreign individual owner(s) of the U.S. business should be provided, as discussed above.

The information about the financial statement in #9 should match the information on the financial statement. For larger companies with publicly available financial information, it may be simpler to state "See attached financial documents" where asked for specific figures, and then to tab the relevant pages where the applicable figures are highlighted for the reviewing officer. For smaller clients, the figures and other requested information should be provided. If the E enterprise is a start-up business, then

---

[389] "AILA Liaison/DOS Meeting Minutes" (Nov. 5, 2008), AILA Doc. No. 09022660.

[390] DOS, "Form DS-156E: Nonimmigrant Treaty Trader/Investor Application," https://www.state.gov/documents/organization/217452.pdf ("All first-time applicants seeking Treaty Trader or Treaty Investor status must complete Parts I and II. Parts I and II must be updated periodically. All individual applicants must complete Part III").

[391] *Id. See also* U.S. Embassy in Honduras, "Treaty Traders and Treaty Investors," http://www.ustraveldocs.com/hn/hn-niv-typee.asp#applicationdocse1.

Copyright © 2017. American Immigration Lawyers Association. All rights reserved.

the financial information may be projected or estimated figures, based on anticipated sales, signed contracts, or other accounts receivable; but there should be a note that the figures are projected figures, and supporting documents should be provided.

Information for #10 should be provided only for E-1 entities and should be supported by the documents discussed above. The "optional" number of transactions may be stated as "multiple" or "numerous."

Questions #11 through 13 should be answered for E-2 entities only and should be supported by the documents discussed above. If values of the initial investment are unavailable, such as if the entity is part of a larger corporate family that publishes an annual report and/or investor certificates, or if the entity has been in business for some time, then only the information on the cumulative investment may be provided, using the most recent annual report, investor certificates, balance sheet, or current financial statements. Conversely, for an E-2 investor start-up company, the initial investment figures should be provided.

b. Part II

Information about the personnel of the E enterprise should be provided and supplemented by a staffing or organizational chart. For larger clients, it may be permissible to leave #14 blank and include a detailed response in #15, but #14 should be completed in full for smaller companies or if the U.S. consulate specifically requires the information.

c. Part III

Part III should be completed only if there is an E-1 or E-2 visa application for an individual attached to the E registration application. If the entity will submit only a stand-alone registration application, then "N/A" may be indicated for #16 through 25, although the practitioner should confirm that the U.S. consulate will accept this application for E registration without an individual visa application.

The following information should be provided about the E visa applicant: name, type of role to be held with the E enterprise, duties of current position, name and contact information for the current employer, history of employment with the current employer, education and experience details, description of the proposed E duties, salary and other compensation, and the name and relevant information about the employee being replaced by the E visa applicant, if applicable. If the foreign national has many years of experience, then it may be acceptable to state "Please see attached résumé" for #22 and to attach the résumé.

When discussing the E visa applicant's current position and proposed role in the United States, it is important to note that the language should be consistent, especially if the current position has provided training, qualification, or relevant experience for the E assignment. As discussed above, the previous experience is a relevant factor in determining whether the foreign national is a qualified executive, supervisor, or essential employee. And for essential employee visa applications, it is critical to connect how the foreign national will apply the same essential skills in the United

Copyright © 2017. American Immigration Lawyers Association. All rights reserved.

States that he or she gained and/or applied in the previous position, especially if the previous position was with a company in the corporate family.

Finally, the form should be executed by a responsible officer, and the practitioner may provide his or her own contact information for #27.

D. Admission to the United States

When seeking admission to the United States, the foreign national should present his or her passport with the E visa. Due to the visa reciprocity schedules,[392] as discussed in Volume 1: Chapter Two, "Basic Nonimmigrant Concepts," an E nonimmigrant may receive a visa valid for a period shorter than two years. However, the individual generally should be admitted for two years upon each entry as long as the visa is valid,[393] except that the period of admission cannot be more than six months beyond the expiration date of the passport itself.[394] However, when the individual already has an unexpired I-94 and is entering through a land port, the inspector usually will not issue a new two-year I-94 unless the person asks to go to secondary inspection to request one, in which case he or she should have a letter from counsel explaining the need.[395]

In November 2016, DHS extended a rule that had long applied to H-1Bs to make E-1 and E-2 nonimmigrants eligible for a 10-day grace period added to the beginning and end of the validity period of the authorized stay.[396] Employment is not authorized during this period—it is strictly a consideration to allow the nonimmigrant to make preparations for starting life in the United States and for departing or changing status.[397] It should be noted that DHS has long required in the H-1B context that the grace period be specified by CBP on the I-94 to be effective.[398] The final rule regarding Es is silent on this point, but presumably the same qualification would apply. Experience with H-1Bs has shown that the grace period is rarely added to the I-94, unless the nonimmigrant insists upon it at entry, so it should not be presumed. It would be important to check a beneficiary's I-94 record for the period of admission to see if the grace period was added and, if it was, to ensure that he or she understands that employment during that period is prohibited.

---

[392] "Reciprocity and Civil Documents by Country," https://travel.state.gov/content/visas/en/fees/reciprocity-by-country.html.

[393] 8 CFR §214.2(e)(19)(i). *See also* 22 CFR §41.112(a) ("The period of validity of a nonimmigrant visa is the period during which the alien may use it in making application for admission. The period of visa validity has no relation to the period of time the immigration authorities at a port of entry may authorize the alien to stay in the United States").

[394] 8 CFR §214.2(e)(19)(iii).

[395] "AILA National Liaison Meeting with U.S. Customs and Border Protection Office of Field Operations" (Oct. 8, 2015), AILA Doc. No. 16031104.

[396] 81 Fed. Reg. 82398 (Nov. 18, 2016).

[397] *Id.*

[398] Inspector's Field Manual, 15(h)(1).

Copyright © 2017. American Immigration Lawyers Association. All rights reserved.

As discussed in Volume 1: Chapter Two, "Basic Nonimmigrant Concepts," a physical I-94 card is no longer issued for entries other than by land, so it would be wise to check the CBP website once the individual has entered to obtain the I-94 number and ensure that all family members were admitted in the proper category and for the proper amount of time.[399] Good follow-up should include requesting copies of visas and passport stamps, as well as I-94 cards for those who entered by land, to ensure that all the information is correct, and calendaring the expiration dates to monitor the individuals' status. This is particularly important for dependents in the E-1/E-2 context, since it is not uncommon for the principal to travel internationally much more often than the dependents. Because of the two-year admission regulation, the principal's admission may be extended frequently through entry, but the dependents' admissions may stay unchanged, and thus be different from the principal's.

Once admitted to the United States, the treaty trader or investor "may engage only in employment which is consistent with the terms and conditions of his or her status and the activity forming the basis for the E treaty status."[400]

E. E Change of Status Petition Filed with USCIS

If the client wishes to file a change of status petition with USCIS, then the practitioner should advise that the foreign national may not "perform productive labor or actively participate in the management of the business prior to receiving a grant of E-2 status."[401] E petitions "may be approved for a period of up to two years."[402] In addition to the documents discussed above, the E change of status petition should include the following:

- Form I-129;
- E Supplement;
- Form I-907, if applicable;
- Copy of passport biographic page of passport; and
- Copy of I-94 card to evidence lawful immigration status.

After preparing the E petition, it should be filed in duplicate with the USCIS Service Center designated by USCIS,[403] which at the time of this writing is the California Service Center. Practitioners may also find it helpful to write the following in large block letters across the side of the Form I-129: "DUPLICATE PETITION; PLEASE FORWARD TO KCC."

---

[399] CBP, "I-94 Website," https://i94.cbp.dhs.gov/I94/#/home.

[400] 8 CFR §214.2(e)(8)(i).

[401] OI 214.2. Although the legacy INS guidance refers only to E-2 status, it is highly unlikely that a foreign national could engage in productive labor prior to approval of an E-1 change of status petition.

[402] AFM 34.2(c); 1 legacy INS AFM, 14-1 Agency Manuals 34.2.

[403] USCIS, "Direct Filing Addresses for Form I-129, Petition for a Nonimmigrant Worker," https://www.uscis.gov/i-129-addresses.

Copyright © 2017. American Immigration Lawyers Association. All rights reserved.

The second set of original documents should be forwarded to the U.S. consulate where the foreign national will later apply for an E visa as supplementary evidence for the Petition Information Management Service (PIMS), as discussed in Volume 1: Chapter Two, "Basic Nonimmigrant Concepts."[404] Following approval of a petition, USCIS forwards approval notification to the Kentucky Consular Center (KCC), which in turn creates an electronic record to confirm the petition approval,[405] so that the information becomes available to a consular officer to verify the petition approval.[406] Although duplicate original documents are not required, preparing and providing them may facilitate the foreign national's visa application in the future.[407]

E status is available to H and L nonimmigrants who have exhausted the maximum period in H or L status.[408] There is no appeal from the denial of an E petition.[409]

1. Form I-129

Part 1: Information on the U.S. company, including name, address, contact person, contact person's telephone number and email address, and Federal Employer Identification Number (FEIN), should be provided.

Part 2: For most E petitions, "New employment" should be checked and change of status requested.

Parts 3 and 4: Information about the beneficiary, including name, alternate names, date of birth, country of birth and country of nationality, and passport information, should be provided.

If the foreign national is present in the United States when the petition is filed, then the I-94 card information should be provided, even if the foreign national will depart the United States during pendency of the E petition. In this case, consular notification should be requested in Part 2; however, to avoid the situation of being subjected to USCIS processing times while the foreign national is abroad and able to apply for an E visa, the practitioner should strategize with the client ahead of time to arrange for an initial E visa application rather than apply for change of status, as discussed above.

An individual must have a passport that is valid for at least six months from the petition's expiration date; otherwise, he or she is inadmissible and ineligible for nonimmigrant status.[410] If the individual does not have such a passport, then the

---

[404] DOS, "Accessing NIV Petition Information Via the CCD" (Nov. 2007), AILA Doc. No. 08040331; "PIMS Processing Update" (Mar. 21, 2008), AILA Doc. No. 08032132.

[405] DOS, "PIMS Update," AILA Doc. No. 08081564; "PIMS Processing Update" (Mar. 21, 2008), AILA Doc. No. 08032132.

[406] DOS, "Accessing NIV Petition Information Via the CCD" (Nov. 25, 2007), AILA Doc. No. 07112560.

[407] "PIMS Processing Update" (Mar. 21, 2008), AILA Doc. No. 08032132.

[408] 8 CFR §214.2(h)(13)(iii)(A).

[409] AFM 34.2(d) and 34.3(d). *Matter of L-O-, Inc.*, ID# 108962 (AAO, Jan. 13, 2017).

[410] INA §212(a)(7)(B)(i). The exceptions to this rule in INA §212(a)(d)(4) are discussed in Volume 1: Chapter Two, "Basic Nonimmigrant Concepts."

Copyright © 2017. American Immigration Lawyers Association. All rights reserved.

following options are available: either delay filing the E petition until he or she obtains a renewed passport, or file the E petition, have the foreign national apply for a renewed passport in the interim, wait for a Request for Evidence (RFE), and then submit a photocopy of the biographic page of the renewed passport once it is available. For nationals of countries where passport renewal takes months, the second strategy can prevent the petition from being significantly delayed. If the client is willing to pay an additional $1,225 fee to USCIS, the delay caused by the RFE, which might also be several months, can be addressed by requesting premium processing when submitting the documentation of the renewed passport. But the practitioner should discuss with the client ahead of time whether an E visa application is the better strategy, as discussed above, especially if the foreign national must return to his or her home country to obtain a new passport.

Parts 5 through 8: Information about the job title, worksite, itinerary, compensation, employment dates, and general information about the petitioner should be provided. The petitioner's representative and the practitioner should sign the form. Note that Part 6, regarding export control, does not apply to E categories.

Part 9: This section may be used to provide additional details or explanation of answers.

2. E Supplement

The E Supplement requests information similar to that requested on Form DS-156E, which is discussed above. In the introduction section, information about the petitioner, foreign national, visa classification, and treaty country should be provided.

Section 1: If the petition is for an E-2 individual investor, the answers for each of the questions in Section 1 should be "N/A." If the foreign national will be employed by a foreign entity and requires E status for U.S. employment authorization, as discussed in Volume 1: Chapter Two, "Basic Nonimmigrant Concepts," then information on the foreign employer should be provided. If there is no foreign employer, then information on the U.S. employer may be provided: name, number of employees, address, type of goods or services provided, and details about the foreign national's assignment. The practitioner may wish to append each of the answers with "(U.S.)" to clarify that the responses refer to U.S. activities. If the visa applicant is not employed by a related foreign entity or by a U.S. company, then the "N/A" may be stated in the "Employee's Position" blank. If information on the "Employee's Position" will be provided, then it may be attached as an addendum to the form and "See addendum" should be stated in the box, or it may be provided in the support statement and "See company statement" should be stated to refer the reviewing officer to the duty description in the support statement.

Section 2: If the foreign national will be employed by a U.S. entity, then information about the E business should be provided: relationship to the foreign entity, if applicable, date of establishment or incorporation in the United States, nationality of ownership, assets, net worth, and annual income. If the petition is for an E-2 individual investor or the business relationship is not listed (such as privately owned, start-up,

Copyright © 2017. American Immigration Lawyers Association. All rights reserved.

etc.), then "N/A" should be typed beside the options of #1, and the true business type should be stated. If the business is a start-up, then the lease address that was used for registering the business in the United States may be provided. Evidence of the business's date of establishment or incorporation in the United States should also be attached. The names and nationality of the foreign entity or foreign individual owner(s) of the U.S. business should be clear, as discussed above. If the E enterprise is a start-up business, then the figures may be projected, based on anticipated sales, signed contracts, or other accounts receivable, but there should be a note that the figures are projected figures and supporting documents should be provided.

As noted above, there are similarities between E and L status, and certain foreign nationals may be eligible for both nonimmigrant classifications. Perhaps because of this fact, and perhaps because the L-1B nonimmigrant visa category has come under increased scrutiny of late, the E Supplement requests information on employees of the E enterprise that hold E or L status.[411] Information on E and L employees, as well as information on managerial, executive, and specialized knowledge employees, regardless of nationality, should be provided and should be supplemented by a staffing or organizational chart where possible.

The job description of #8 may be attached as an addendum to the form and "See addendum" should be stated in the box, or it may be provided in the support statement and "See company statement" should be stated. When discussing the E visa applicant's current proposed role in the United States, it is important to note that the language should be consistent with the support statement, especially regarding any discussion of any experience necessary for the E assignment that was gained through previous employment or training with a related entity abroad. As discussed above, the previous experience is a relevant factor in determining whether the foreign national is a qualified executive, supervisor, or essential employee. And for petitions on behalf of essential employees, it is critical to connect how the foreign national will apply the same essential skills in the United States that he or she gained and/or applied in the previous position, especially if the previous position was with a company in the corporate family.[412]

Section 3: This section should be completed only for E-1 entities and should be supported by the documents discussed above.

Section 4: This section should be completed only for E-2 entities and should be supported by the documents discussed above. If values of the initial investment are unavailable, such as if entity is part of a larger corporate family that publishes an annual report and/or investor certificates, or if the entity has been in business for some time, then only the information on the cumulative investment may be provided,

---

[411] For a discussion of the increased scrutiny of L-1B petitions, see Volume 1: Chapter Eleven, "L-1 Visas and Status."

[412] For a discussion of how to connect the U.S. job duties with any previous experience gained abroad, see discussion above.

Copyright © 2017. American Immigration Lawyers Association. All rights reserved.

using the most recent annual report, investor certificates, balance sheet, or current financial statements. Conversely, for an E-2 investor start-up company, the initial investment figures should be provided.

3. Form I-907

If the client wishes to have a response (approval, denial or RFE) within 15 calendar days, then the client may pay USCIS an additional $1225 for premium processing. This request may be filed concurrently with the E petition, or the attorney or client may request premium processing after the petition has been filed by submitting Form I-907 with the petition's receipt notice, as discussed in Volume 1: Chapter Two, "Basic Nonimmigrant Concepts."

IV. Additional Follow-Up

After a foreign national has obtained E status, the practitioner should follow up to request copies of the I-94 cards and the visas, to ensure that all the information is correct, and to calendar the expiration dates to monitor the foreign national's status, as discussed in Volume 1: Chapter Two, "Basic Nonimmigrant Concepts."

It is particularly important to note that although an E principal may have frequent international travel, which would result in recurring admission for two years, E dependents may have less international travel, which would cause members of the family unit to have different dates of status expiration. The practitioner is advised to monitor the expiration of E status for these dependents and to remind the client of the need to extend the E status of dependents.

A. EADs for E Spouses

Spouses of E treaty traders and investors are eligible to apply for employment authorization documents (EADs).[413] The statutory provision does not, however, extend to dependent children in E status.[414] An E spouse may wish to obtain an EAD solely in order to apply for a Social Security number (SSN).

The following documents should be prepared and filed:

- Form G-28;
- Form I-765;
- Statement from U.S. company, confirming the E employment of the principal foreign national and/or paystubs evidencing current employment;
- Copy of the principal nonimmigrant's E visa and I-94;
- Copy of biographic page of passport of the E spouse;
- Copy of spouse's E visa and I-94; and

---

[413] 9 FAM 41.51 N18; AFM 34.2(a) and 34.3(a).

[414] INA §214(e)(6); USCIS, M. Yates, "Guidance on Employment Authorization for E and L Nonimmigrant Spouses and for Determinations on the Requisite Employment Abroad for L Blanket Petitions" (Feb. 28, 2002), AILA Doc. No. 02022832.

Copyright © 2017. American Immigration Lawyers Association. All rights reserved.

- Copy of marriage certificate.

The EAD application may be filed concurrently with an E change of status petition,[415] but these applications must be filed with the California Service Center (CSC).[416] Otherwise, the EAD application should be filed with the either the Phoenix or the Dallas Lockbox, depending on where is the applicant's place of residence.[417] Upon issuance of the EAD, the E spouse may be employed by any employer.[418] An EAD renewal application may also be filed concurrently with the dependent spouse's E extension application, as discussed below.

Although legacy INS guidance indicates that E dependent spouses and children "will not be deemed to have violated status" if they engage in unauthorized employment and that "so long as the principal E nonimmigrant is maintaining status, no action will be taken to require their departure,"[419] the practitioner is not advised to rely upon this guidance, as it predates the availability of EADs to E spouses.

B. E Visa Renewals

Once the company has been registered with the U.S. consulate, as discussed above, visa renewal applications may be made by the treaty trader, investor, or employee on a streamlined basis. This is because "[p]osts with a high volume of repeat applications from employees of the same company have developed systems for rolling over company information from one application to another in order to save time."[420] But some individual visa applications may nevertheless experience the same processing times as initial E visa applications. Individual consulates may have additional requirements regarding the scope of the registration. For example, one embassy requires that an E-2 business with multiple applications each year maintain the registration by submitting financial statements or tax returns with one application each year.[421] For a general rule, DOS recommends: "While there is no specific regulation, best practices from posts suggest it would be reasonable for 'E' visa companies for update 'registration' files at post every year."[422]

---

[415] 71 Fed. Reg. 29662 (May 23, 2006).

[416] USCIS, "Direct Filing Addresses for Form I-129, Petition for a Nonimmigrant Worker," https://www.uscis.gov/i-129-addresses.

[417] USCIS, "Direct Filing Addresses for Form I-765, Application for Employment Authorization," https://www.uscis.gov/i-765-addresses.

[418] USCIS, M. Yates, "Guidance on Employment Authorization for E and L Nonimmigrant Spouses and for Determinations on the Requisite Employment Abroad for L Blanket Petitions" (Feb. 28, 2002), AILA Doc. No. 02022832.

[419] 1 NAFTA Handbook (Nov. 1999), 14-1 Agency Manuals Scope, Sec. 3 "E-1 and E-2 Nonimmigrant Pursuant to NAFTA."

[420] "Q&As from March 2007 AILA Liaison/DOS Meeting" (Mar. 2007), AILA Doc. No. 07041668.

[421] U.S. Embassy and Consulates in Japan, "Treaty Traders and Treaty Investors Visas," https://jp.usembassy.gov/visas/nonimmigrant-visas/e1-e2-visas/apply-step-2/.

[422] "AILA Liaison/DOS Meeting Minutes" (Oct. 22, 2009), AILA Doc. No. 10020230. *But see* U.S. Embassy and Consulates in Japan, "Treaty Traders and Treaty Investors Visas," *Cont'd*

Copyright © 2017. American Immigration Lawyers Association. All rights reserved.

Employees of registered companies may be able to schedule visa appointments without awaiting review of the E enterprise documents, but they may be required to submit other documentation, such as "the first two pages of U.S. corporate tax returns."[423] But, as with initial E visa applications, the practitioner should check the website of the U.S. consulate to confirm that the E visa application documents are organized in the manner required.[424]

An E visa renewal application may need to provide the following:

- Financial, corporate, tax, and employment documents to update the information required for the initial E visa application, as discussed above;

- Updated "spreadsheet listing every qualifying transaction of international trade between the treaty countries during the last calendar year ... includ[ing] the date, the invoice number, and the dollar value of the transaction [and] [s]how[ing] in a prominent place the total number and value of these transactions";

- Independent evidence of the transactions, such as copies of invoices, air bills or shipping invoices, and tax returns;

- Evidence of and an explanation for "any changes of ownership since last issuance";

- Updated evidence regarding any new investment(s) in the E-2 business;

- Evidence of purchase of additional businesses, if applicable, in the form of purchase agreements and closing documents;

- Proof of regular payments towards any promissory notes, if applicable;

- Proof that the funds placed in escrow prior to issuance of the E-2 visa were disbursed to the E-2 business's seller, in the form of "all closing documents and direct evidence (cancelled checks and corresponding debits from bank statements)"; and

- Job titles and immigration status of any subordinate employees.

C. E Extensions

In order to establish eligibility for an E extension, the request should include evidence that the foreign national:

---

http://www.ustraveldocs.com/jp/jp-niv-typee.asp#CompanyRegDuration ("Qualified companies will remain on the registry as long as the companies keep their status as E visa qualified companies, and there is at least 1 employee holding a current E Visa. Registered companies are no longer required to send DS-156E and financial documents annually to the Embassy/Consulate").

[423] U.S. Embassy and Consulates in Italy, "Vetted Company Applications," https://it.usembassy.gov/visas/niv/e/vetted/

[424] U.S. Embassy and Consulates in Japan, "Treaty Traders and Investors Visas," https://jp.usembassy.gov/visas/nonimmigrant-visas/e1-e2-visas/apply-step-1/.

Copyright © 2017. American Immigration Lawyers Association. All rights reserved.

- "Has at all times maintained the terms and conditions of his or her E nonimmigrant classification;

- "Was physically present in the United States at the time of filing the application for extension of stay; and

- "Has not abandoned his or her extension request."[425]

Engaging in other employment (in addition to the E activities) that does not relate to the E business has been determined to be a violation of status.[426] An E extension filed with USCIS may be approved in "two-year increments."[427] The regulations state that "there is no specified number of extensions of stay that a treaty trader or treaty investor may be granted," as long as the foreign national continues to have the intent to depart the United States upon the expiration of status and as long as the need for the essential employee's services was not short term, as discussed above.[428] If a foreign national has been granted multiple extensions, however, the practitioner may wish to discuss the temporary intent requirement, as discussed above. Although reports indicate that extension periods have been limited to one year, USCIS responded that there has been no policy change.[429]

An extension request for the principal is filed on Form I-129, and requests for dependents are filed on Form I-539. If the principal is filing alone or if the principal's and dependents' applications are filed concurrently, they should go to the California Service Center.[430] If only the dependents are filing for extension, the I-539 should be sent to the Dallas Lockbox.[431] If the spouse is filing to extend an employment authorization document concurrently with the I-539, both applications should be sent in one package to the Dallas Lockbox.[432] As mentioned above, if solely an extension of the employment authorization is being sought, and not an extension of status, it should go to either the Phoenix Lockbox or the Dallas Lockbox, depending on the place of residence.[433] The practitioner should re-check the USCIS website frequently with respect to this information, as USCIS periodically changes the places of filing.

---

[425] 1 NAFTA Handbook (Nov. 1999), 14-1 Agency Manuals Scope, Sec. 3 "E-1 and E-2 Nonimmigrant Pursuant to NAFTA."

[426] *Matter of Laigo*, 15 I&N Dec. 65 (BIA 1974).

[427] 1 legacy INS AFM, 14-1 Agency Manuals 34.2.

[428] 8 CFR §214.2(e)(20)(iii).

[429] "CSC & AILA Working Group Meeting Agenda" (Jan. 28, 2009), AILA Doc. No. 09012968.

[430] USCIS, "Direct Filing Addresses for Form I-129, Petition for a Nonimmigrant Worker," https://www.uscis.gov/i-129-addresses.

[431] USCIS, "Direct Filing Addresses for Form I-539, Application to Extend/Change Nonimmigrant Status," https://www.uscis.gov/i-539-addresses.

[432] *Id.*; USCIS, "Direct Filing Addresses for Form I-765, Application for Employment Authorization," https://www.uscis.gov/i-765-addresses.

[433] USCIS, "Direct Filing Addresses for Form I-765, Application for Employment Authorization," https://www.uscis.gov/i-765-addresses.

Copyright © 2017. American Immigration Lawyers Association. All rights reserved.

A timely filed E-1 or E-1 extension should provide continued employment authorization for the principal for 240 days after the date the initial E status expires.[434] But if the current E status and visa will expire in the near future, then the practitioner may wish to counsel the client to travel abroad and apply for a new E visa.

D. Change in Duties or Ownership

As discussed above, in the event of a change in duties or ownership of the E enterprise, the practitioner may request an advisory opinion on whether an amended petition must be filed if any of these events occurs.[435] The adjudicator should "either recommend the filing of another application, or prepare a new I-797 reflecting the non-substantive changes."[436] It seems that E status should not be automatically revoked if there is a substantive change, but there should be an inquiry into continuing eligibility for E status.[437]

E. If Employment Ceases

E nonimmigrants whose employment ends prior to the expiration of their authorized stay are able to remain in the United States lawfully for the shorter of 60 days or when the existing validity period ends.[438] This can be used only once during each "authorized validity period." The purpose is to allow the beneficiary to wind up affairs or to seek other employment and request a change of status if needed and eligible.[439] The individual is not able to work during this period, unless otherwise authorized.[440] The rulemaking that put in place this grace period was silent as to what would be an "authorized validity period" in the E context, but presumably it means any given two-year period of admission, or the validity period of the approved USCIS petition, whichever is in effect for the individual at the time.

F. Sponsoring an E Nonimmigrant for Permanent Residence

1. Impact of Owner or Majority Shareholder Pursuing Permanent Residence on Other E Employees

If the owner or majority shareholder of an E business obtains permanent residence, then this will likely impact whether foreign nationals are eligible for E status as employees. As noted above, a U.S. permanent resident may not be an E employer, and any ownership interest in the E entity by a permanent resident may

---

[434] 8 CFR §274a.12(b)(20).

[435] AFM 34.2(e).

[436] AFM 34.2(e) and 34.3(e); 1 legacy INS AFM, 14-1 *Agency Manuals* 34.3.

[437] Legacy INS, R. Scully, "Validity of Certain Nonimmigrant Visas" (Aug. 15, 1996), http://www.ailalink.org (search for "Scully" and "LaFleur").

[438] 8 CFR §214.1(*l*)(ii).

[439] 80 Fed. Reg. 81900, 81923 (Dec. 31, 2015)..

[440] *Id.*

Copyright © 2017. American Immigration Lawyers Association. All rights reserved.

not be counted towards the majority ownership requirement.[441] This remains the case even if the owner or majority shareholder has commuter permanent resident status and resides outside the United States.[442] If the owner or majority shareholder nevertheless wishes to pursue permanent residence or if there are no foreign national employees in E status, then the path to permanent residence may entail a Form I-526, Immigrant Petition by an Alien Entrepreneur. If the foreign national was an executive or manager at a foreign parent, affiliate, or subsidiary for at least one year within the immediate three years preceding the E assignment, then the path to permanent residence may entail a Form I-140, Immigrant Petition for Alien Worker, as a multinational manager.[443]

For an E employee who does not qualify under these two categories, a labor certification application may be required.[444] The practitioner should be aware, however, that the Department of Labor (DOL) is likely to audit the application, because of concerns of influence and/or control over the U.S. business by the foreign national:

> "Where an alien for whom labor certification is sought has an ownership interest in, or some other special relationship with, the sponsoring employer, the employer must demonstrate that a bona fide job opportunity exists for qualified U.S. applicants and that, if hired, the alien will not be self employed. Because confusion exists regarding the meaning of these regulations in 'investor' cases, we elected to revisit the issue en banc."[445]

If DOL determines that the job opportunity was not truly available to U.S. worker applicants because the job essentially entails self-employment, then the labor certification application will be denied:[446] "'Employment' means permanent full-time work by an employee for an employer other than oneself. For purposes of this definition an investor is not an employee."[447] Specifically, the Board of Alien Labor Certification Appeals (BALCA) held: "[I]f the alien or close family members have a substantial ownership interest in the sponsoring employer, the burden is on the employer to establish that employment of the alien is not tantamount to self-employment, and therefore [is] a per se bar to labor certification."[448]

---

[441] 9 FAM 41.51 N14.1.

[442] DOS, E. Odom correspondence (Aug. 18, 1994), 71 Interpreter Releases 1378 (Oct. 7, 1994).

[443] For a discussion of these immigrant petitions, see Volume 2: Chapter Three, "The Immigrant Visa Petition."

[444] For a discussion of this process, see Volume 2: Chapter Two, "The Labor Certification Application."

[445] *Matter of Modular Container Systems, Inc.*, 1989-INA-228 (BALCA 1991) (en banc) (internal citations omitted).

[446] *Id.*

[447] 20 CFR §656.3.

[448] *Matter of Modular Container Systems, Inc.*, 1989-INA-228 (BALCA 1991) (en banc).

Copyright © 2017. American Immigration Lawyers Association. All rights reserved.

DOL may audit or deny the labor certification even where the foreign national is an employee rather than an owner or shareholder,[449] simply based on the fact that the beneficiary holds an E visa, because the "visa application stresses the importance of the Alien to the Employer's success,"[450] even where no U.S. worker applicants respond to the recruitment efforts.[451] DOL may also audit the application if there are concerns that the foreign national has a familial relationship with an owner, shareholder, or officer,[452] although this should result first in an audit rather than an outright denial:

> "We did not hold nor did we mean to imply ... that a close family relationship between the alien and the person having the hiring authority, standing alone, establishes, that the job opportunity is not bona fide or available to U.S. workers. Such a relationship does require that this aspect of the application be given greater attention."[453]

Even though an individual and a business may have separate legal identities, such as for corporate or taxation purposes, "[c]orporate status does not remove the alien, as part owner ... from control over who is hired and fired."[454] The BIA rejected the principle that a business and its shareholders are separate to the extent that the relationship should be "beyond scrutiny save in cases of fraud:"[455]

> "In matters affecting the public interest, we are not bound to find fraud or sham in order to look behind the corporation to determine the validity of its actions. Public interest and policy considerations override the immunity given the stockholders under the corporate entity.... Although a corporation and its shareholders are deemed separate entities for most purposes, the corporate form may be disregarded in the interests of justice where it is used to defeat an overriding public policy.... Labor certification is a matter of important public concern, which requires attention to substance rather than form."[456]

BALCA acknowledged that many E-2 businesses "will have difficulty overcoming this regulatory proscription, [but] we hold that the sponsoring employer

---

[449] *Matter of Driessen Aircraft Interior Systems*, 1993-INA-82 (BALCA 1995) (labor certification initially denied by the Certifying Officer (CO)).

[450] *Matter of Barrio Fiesta Restaurant*, 2000-INA-309 (BALCA Mar. 14, 2001).

[451] *Matter of Rimaco, Inc.*, 89-INA-362 (BALCA 1990).

[452] *Matter of Rainbow Imports, Inc.*, 88-INA-289 (BALCA 1988) (stating that the "CO had reason to believe, based on the alien's status as President of a corporation with an almost identical name as the Employer's and engaged in the same line of business, that the alien may have exercised influence or control over the Employer's business").

[453] *Matter of Paris Bakery Corp.*, 1988-INA-337 (BALCA 1990) (en banc) (citing *Matter of Young Seal of America, Inc.*, 1988-INA-121 (BALCA 1989) (en banc)).

[454] *Matter of Modular Container Systems, Inc.*, 1989-INA-228 (BALCA 1991) (en banc) (citing the decision of the CO).

[455] *Matter of Edelweiss Manufacturing Co., Inc.*, 87-INA-562 (BIA 1988) (en banc).

[456] *Id.*

Copyright © 2017. American Immigration Lawyers Association. All rights reserved.

can overcome it if it can establish genuine independence and vitality not dependent on the alien's financial contribution or other contribution indicating self-employment."[457] The mere facts of hiring and firing authority or that the foreign national "has such a dominant role in, or close personal relationship with, the sponsoring employer's business … [do] not establish the lack of a bona fide job opportunity per se."[458]

Instead, BALCA decided that a totality of the circumstances test should be applied. First, "the business cannot have been established for the sole purpose of obtaining certification for the alien, *i.e.*, a sham."[459] Second, factors to be considered "include, but are not limited to, whether the alien:"

- "[I]s in the position to control or influence hiring decisions regarding the job for which labor certification is sought;

- "[I]s related to the corporate directors, officers, or employees;

- " [W]as an incorporator or founder of the company;

- " [H]as an ownership interest in the company;

- " [I]s involved in the management of the company;

- " [I]s on the board of directors;

- " [I]s one of a small number of employees;

- " [H]as qualifications for the job that are identical to specialized or unusual job duties and requirements stated in the application; and

- " [I]s so inseparable from the sponsoring employer because of his or her pervasive presence and personal attributes that the employer would be unlikely to continue in operation without the alien."[460]

---

[457] *Matter of Modular Container Systems, Inc.*, 1989-INA-228 (BALCA 1991) (*en banc*).

[458] *Id.*

[459] *Id.*

[460] *Id. See also Matter of ATI Consultores*, 2007-INA-00064 (BALCA Feb. 11, 2008); *Matter of Barrio Fiesta Restaurant*, 2000-INA-309 (BALCA Mar. 14, 2001); *Matter of Amger Corp.*, 87-INA-545 (BALCA 1987); *Matter of Rainbow Imports, Inc.*, 88-INA-289 (BALCA 1988); *Matter of Keyjoy Trading Co.*, 87-INA-592 (BALCA 1987); *Matter of Malone & Asso.*, 1990-INA-360 (BALCA 1991) (en banc); *Matter of Young Seal of America, Inc.*, 1988-INA-121 (BALCA 1989) (en banc) (deemed unlikely that a wife would hire a U.S. worker in place of her husband); *Matter of Shehrazade, Inc.*, 1988-INA-170 (BALCA 1988) (beneficiary of labor certification application owned 48 percent of the business and the remaining 52 percent was owned by the beneficiary's wife and children); *Matter of Paris Bakery Corp.*, 1988-INA-337 (BALCA 1990) (en banc) (fraternal relationship between employer-owner and beneficiary of labor certification deemed irrelevant where the job opportunity represented an expansion of personnel and where there were "not even arguably qualified U.S. applicants"); *Matter of Lignomat USA, Ltd.*, 1988-INA-276 (BALCA 1989) (en banc) (beneficiary of labor certification application deemed inseparable from the employer because he and his wife owned 49 percent of the business and were officers of the corporation, he was the president, and he developed technology which the employer sought to market); *Matter of B.F. Hope Construction Inc.*, 1989-INA-162 (BALCA 1990); *Matter of Ocean Paradise of Hawaii*, 1989-INA-188 (BALCA 1989); *Matter of GHR Atlanta Realty, Inc.*, 1989-INA-123 (BALCA 1990) (beneficiary of labor certification was a director
Cont'd

Copyright © 2017. American Immigration Lawyers Association. All rights reserved.

The employer-applicant may not claim the lack of authority for personnel decisions by appointing or retaining another individual to conduct the recruitment and interviews if the appointed or retained individual is in turn an employee of the company and therefore an employee of the owner or majority shareholder.[461] DOL may also consider whether the foreign national has "a significant financial interest in the corporation," even if he or she does not have any ownership interest, such as if the foreign national is "a major creditor of the corporation and own[s] debentures."[462] In addition, the absence of majority ownership does not automatically mean the job opportunity was bona fide and available to U.S. workers; in one case, BALCA denied labor certification where the foreign national owned only 10 percent of the business but also had control over the business as a director, manager, and the first individual to organize the company in the United States.[463] Further, DOL may inquire into any ownership interest or managerial or executive responsibility before the labor certification was filed,[464] as a resignation from an executive office alone does not constitute "a legitimate relinquishment of authority and control."[465]

2. Moonlighting Under EAD

In addition, if the E nonimmigrant obtains an EAD after filing the application to adjust status, it remains unclear whether the foreign national may "moonlight" with an employer who is not the E entity without losing E status.[466] Legacy INS guidance stated:

"E nonimmigrants must continue to observe the requirements of their nonimmigrant status, including limiting employment to the designated employer....

"An E-1 [or] E-2 ... nonimmigrant who has filed an application for adjustment of status may choose between working pursuant to their continued nonimmigrant employment authorization [as an E nonimmigrant] ... or filing form I-765 for employment authorization as an adjustment applicant.... E-1 [or] E-2 ... adjustment applicants choosing to apply for an [EAD] ... may continue to work under their unexpired nonimmigrant employment authorization, while waiting for adjudication and receipt of the EAD. After receiving the EAD, the alien may work for any employer desired and is not subject to E ... restrictions. However, such an

---

and the only employee of the business although not a shareholder); *Matter of Kica Inc.*, 1988-INA-169 (BALCA 1988); *Matter of Medical Equipment Designs*, 1987-INA-673 (BALCA 1988); *Matter of Bulk Farms Inc.*, 1989-INA-51 (BALCA 1990).

[461] *Matter of Malone & Assoc.*, 1990-INA-360 (BALCA 1991) (en banc).

[462] *Matter of Rainbow Imports, Inc.*, 88-INA-289 (BALCA 1988).

[463] *Matter of Keyjoy Trading Co.*, 87-INA-592 (BALCA 1987).

[464] *Matter of Rainbow Imports, Inc.*, 88-INA-289 (BALCA 1988); *Matter of Lignomat USA, Ltd.*, 1988-INA-276 (BALCA 1989) (en banc); *Matter of B.F. Hope Construction Inc.*, 1989-INA-162 (BALCA 1990).

[465] *Matter of B.F. Hope Construction Inc.*, 1989-INA-162 (BALCA 1990).

[466] "AILA/USCIS Q&As" (Apr. 2, 2008), AILA Doc. No. 08040235.

Copyright © 2017. American Immigration Lawyers Association. All rights reserved.

alien would lose his or her E-1 [or] E-2 ... nonimmigrant status by working in open-market employment."[467]

Subsequent legacy INS guidance stated that a foreign national would "violate his/her nonimmigrant status if s/he uses the EAD to leave the employer listed on the approved 1-129 petition and engage in employment for a separate employer."[468] At least one interpretation distinguishes between a "separate" employer and an "additional" employer.[469] Unfortunately, the legacy INS guidance specifically addressed the H and L nonimmigrants, following promulgation of the interim final rule that allows H and L nonimmigrants two options for employment authorization (the EAD or the underlying H or L nonimmigrant status). In addition, the guidance specifically stated the agency's desire to "consider[] expanding the 'dual intent' concept to cover long term nonimmigrants, in E ... visa classification[], who are visiting this country as traders [and] investors,"[470] which could be construed as indicating that the guidance does not apply to E nonimmigrants. Upon a request for clarification and confirmation that E nonimmigrants who have applied to adjust status may "moonlight" with an additional employer, USCIS responded that it would "take this matter under advisement."[471] Therefore, the practitioner should discuss the risks in detail with the client and/or foreign national.

Although USCIS was requested to promulgate regulations to allow foreign nationals in E status who have filed applications to adjust status to travel without advance paroles and without being considered to have abandoned the underlying nonimmigrant E status, USCIS indicated that this regulation was not a priority.[472] Risk-averse clients and/or foreign nationals may therefore wish to avoid filing E visa applications or petitions after an immigrant visa petition has been filed. The practitioner should also discuss the impact of international travel by the foreign national, as related DOS guidance states that an E visa applicant must "demonstrate that he or she does not intend to remain or work permanently in the United States"[473] when applying for admission.

Finally, if the application to adjust status is denied, then the foreign national should be able to return to E status and "will only be subject to removal proceedings

---

[467] Legacy INS, P. Virtue, "Considerations for Adjustment of Status (HQ 70/6.2.5, 70/6.2.9, 70/6.2612, 70/23.1, 120/17.2)" (Aug. 5, 1997), AILA Doc. No. 97080580.

[468] Legacy INS, M. Cronin, "AFM Update: Revision of March 14, 2000 Dual Intent Memorandum (HQADJ 70/ 2.8.6, 2.8.12, 10.18)" (May 16, 2000), AILA Doc. No. 00052603.

[469] "AILA/USCIS Q&As" (Apr. 2, 2008), AILA Doc. No. 08040235.

[470] 64 Fed. Reg. 28209 (June 1, 1999).

[471] "AILA/USCIS Q&As" (Apr. 2, 2008), AILA Doc. No. 08040235.

[472] *Id.*

[473] 9 FAM 402.9-8.

Copyright © 2017. American Immigration Lawyers Association. All rights reserved.

if he or she is not otherwise qualified to continue to maintain E ... nonimmigrant status in the United States," although the EAD would be terminated.[474]

---

[474] Legacy INS, P. Virtue, "Considerations for Adjustment of Status (HQ 70/6.2.5, 70/6.2.9, 70/6.2612, 70/23.1, 120/17.2)" (Aug. 5, 1997), AILA Doc. No. 97080580.

Copyright © 2017. American Immigration Lawyers Association. All rights reserved.

CHAPTER FIVE

E-3 VISAS AND STATUS

I. Executive Summary

The E-3 nonimmigrant classification is for Australian citizens who will perform professional "specialty occupation" assignments in the United States. E-3 status may be valid for up to two years and may be renewed indefinitely. The foreign national may apply for an E-3 visa at a U.S. consulate abroad or request a change of status or change of employer from U.S. Citizenship and Immigration Services (USCIS). Either process requires a labor condition application (LCA) from the Department of Labor (DOL). Dependent spouses and children of E-3 professionals hold E-3D status. E-3D spouses are eligible for employment authorization documents. An extension of E-3 status may be filed with USCIS, or the foreign national may apply for a new period of E-3 status at a U.S. consulate abroad. There is an ample annual numerical limitation of 10,500 E-3 visa numbers, which has never come close to being reached. E-3 extensions with the same employer and E-3D dependents are not counted toward the quota.

A. Checklist of Requirements

- Citizen or national of Australia.
- Professional assignment in the United States.
- Bachelor's degree or equivalent experience.
- Professional license, if required for the assignment by federal, state, or local law.

B. Documents Necessary to Prepare the Petition

- U.S. job description.
- Copies of the foreign national's educational degrees, including transcripts.
- Copies of the foreign national's professional licenses, if applicable.
- Foreign national's experience letters, if applicable.
- Copy of foreign national's detailed résumé.
- Basic information about the company.
- Copy of biographic page(s) of passport(s) of the foreign national and any dependent spouse and children.

C. Checklist of Questions to Ask the Client

- Will the U.S. assignment be a professional specialty occupation assignment?
- Does the foreign national possess at least a bachelor's degree in the specialty field or in a related field?
- How many years of progressively more responsible and professional experience does the foreign national possess?

Copyright © 2017. American Immigration Lawyers Association. All rights reserved.

- Does the foreign national have dependent family members who are not citizens of Australia?

- Is the foreign national a beneficiary of an immigrant visa petition or labor certification application?

II. Introduction

The E-3 visa classification was created by the REAL ID Act of 2005.[1] Although foreign nationals who hold this status are considered "treaty aliens" pursuant to the E nonimmigrant category, the E-3 more resembles the H-1B classification,[2] as "the E-3 visa is not limited to employment that is directly related to international trade and investment."[3] Despite the similarities, however, the practitioner should avoid viewing the E-3 and H-1B visa classifications as identical.

E-3s have an annual numerical limitation of 10,500,[4] but "[o]nly E-3 principals who are initially being issued E-3 visas *for the first time*, or who are otherwise initially obtaining E-3 status," are counted toward this cap.[5] E-3D dependents are not subject to the quota.[6] The statute indicates that the quota applies only to "initial applications submitted for aliens described in section 101(a)(15)(E)(iii)."[7] However, the Department of State (DOS) takes the position that, to be excluded from the quota, the E-3 must be for the same employer for which the initial E-3 was issued, stating in guidance that "returning E-3 principals who are being issued new E-3 visas *for continuing employment with the original employer*, are exempt from the annual numerical limit."[8]

DOS also takes the position that, to avoid being subject to the numerical limitation, an E-3 applying for a new visa after expiration of the prior visa or status must establish "that there has been uninterrupted continuity of employment," defined as the applicant having "worked, and continues to work, for the U.S.-based employer who submitted the original labor condition application (LCA) and offer of employment."[9]

---

[1] REAL ID Act of 2005, Pub. L. No. 109-13, div. B, 119 Stat. 231, 302–23.

[2] 70 Fed. Reg. 52292 (Sept. 2, 2005). For a discussion of E-1 and E-2 status, see Volume 1: Chapter Four, "E-1 and E-2 Visas and Status." For a discussion of the H-1B category, see Volume 1: Chapter Seven, "H-1B Visas and Status."

[3] 9 Foreign Affairs Manual (FAM) 402.9-8(A).

[4] Immigration and Nationality Act (INA) §214(g).

[5] 9 FAM 402.9-8(I) (emphasis in original).

[6] INA §214(g)(C); 9 FAM 402.9-8(A) and 402.9-9.

[7] INA §214(g).

[8] 9 FAM 402.9-8(I) (emphasis in original).

[9] 9 FAM 402.9-8(I).

Copyright © 2017. American Immigration Lawyers Association. All rights reserved.

Unused E-3 visa numbers "do not carry over to the next fiscal year."[10] DOS tracks usage of the visa numbers used by the U.S. consulates and by USCIS, so if it appears that the quota will be exhausted, DOS "will instruct posts to cease E-3 issuances for that fiscal year."[11]

It seems unlikely, however, that the cap will be reached; DOL indicated that only 2,600 E-3 labor condition applications were filed in fiscal year 2006,[12] and DOS stated that approximately 1,150 E-3 numbers were used between October 1, 2006, and April 20, 2007.[13] While no government agency has released data more recently, a news report from Australia quoted the U.S. Charge D'Affaires as saying that "only 3,000" E-3s had been issued, presumably referring to fiscal year 2015.[14] As indicated by DOS: "If it did appear to be likely that the limit would be reached, [DOS] would post the numbers in the visa bulletin."[15]

The practitioner should discuss with the client early on whether to file an E-3 visa application at a U.S. consulate or to file the E-3 change of status petition if the individual is in the United States. Premium processing is not available for this petition,[16] and processing times may be lengthy, as discussed below. For a discussion of the strategizing between filing an E-3 visa application at a U.S. consulate versus filing an E-3 change of status petition with USCIS, see below.

The E-3 is not appropriate for fashion models of distinguished merit and ability,[17] although such models may be eligible for H-1B status.[18] It is permissible to work part-time while holding E-3 status, but the foreign national should be able to demonstrate that he or she will earn enough U.S. income and/or has sufficient financial assets to avoid becoming a public charge.[19] For a discussion of the standards of likelihood of becoming a public charge, see Volume 2: Chapter Four, "Consular Processing, Adjustment of Status, and Permanent Residence Issues." A foreign national who is

---

[10] *Id.*

[11] *Id.*

[12] 73 Fed. Reg. 19943 (Apr. 11, 2008).

[13] "Update from AILA-DOS Liaison Committee on E-3 Visa Issuance" (May 23, 2006), AILA Doc. No 06072362.

[14] News.com.au, "It's easier to get a US visa than you think" (Dec. 15, 2016), http://bit.ly/E3story.

[15] *Id.*

[16] "Vermont Service Center (VSC) Practice Pointer: File E-3s and H-1B1s Early!" (updated Sept. 11, 2008), AILA Doc. No. 08090865; *see also* USCIS, "How Do I Use the Premium Processing Service?" https://www.uscis.gov/premiumprocessing.

[17] 20 Code of Federal Regulations (CFR) §655.700(d).

[18] INA §101(a)(15)(H)(i)(b).

[19] 9 FAM 402.9-8(J).

Copyright © 2017. American Immigration Lawyers Association. All rights reserved.

subject to the two-year foreign residence requirement is eligible for E-3 status, although the foreign residence requirement is not waived by obtaining E-3 status.[20]

Dependent spouses and children of foreign nationals in E-3 status may obtain E-3D status by presenting "reasonable evidence" of the relationship, such as a certified copy of a marriage or birth certificate.[21] However, the certified copies are "not mandatory if [the consular officer is] otherwise satisfied that the necessary relationship actually exists."[22] Dependents need not hold Australian citizenship, and foreign nationals with other citizenships should receive the same reciprocity considerations as the principal—the same visa validity, number of entries, and reciprocity fee, if any.[23] At this time, E-3s receive multiple entry visas valid for 24 months, and there is no reciprocity fee.[24]

III. Requirements and Interpretations

The eligibility requirements for an E-3 assignment are as follows:

- The assignment must be for a professional "specialty occupation" and must require at least a bachelor's degree or its equivalent;[25]
- The foreign national must meet the professional qualifications of the job duties through a bachelor's degree, the equivalent, and/or license;[26]
- The foreign national must be a national of Australia;[27]
- The U.S. employer must obtain a certified labor condition application from DOL;[28] and
- The foreign national must have the intent to depart the United States upon "termination of status."[29]

A. Professional "Specialty Occupation" Assignment in the United States

The foreign national must have an employment offer for an assignment that entails a professional "specialty occupation," which is defined as "an occupation that

---

[20] "Visa Office Clarifies E-3 Visa Eligibility of Aliens Subject to INA §212(e)" (May 18, 2006), AILA Doc. No. 06051861; "DOS Answers to AILA Questions" (Oct. 20, 2005), AILA Doc. No. 05112874. For a discussion of the two-year foreign residence requirement, see Volume 1: Chapter Ten, "J-1 Visas and Status."

[21] 9 FAM 402.9-9.

[22] Id.

[23] Id.

[24] DOS, "Australia Reciprocity Schedule," https://travel.state.gov/content/visas/en/fees/reciprocity-by-country/AS.html.

[25] 22 CFR §41.51(c)(1)(ii).

[26] 22 CFR §§41.51(c)(1)(ii) and (iv).

[27] INA §101(a)(15)(e)(iii).

[28] 22 CFR §41.51(c)(1)(iii).

[29] 9 FAM 402.9-8(G).

Copyright © 2017. American Immigration Lawyers Association. All rights reserved.

requires theoretical and practical application of a body of highly specialized knowledge, and attainment of a bachelor's or higher degree in the specific specialty (or its equivalent) as a minimum for entry into the occupation in the United States."[30] In evaluating whether the assignment qualifies as a specialty occupation, DOS follows the "applicable standards and criteria determined" for H-1B occupations by the Department of Homeland Security (DHS) and the legacy Immigration and Naturalization Service (INS).[31] The Foreign Affairs Manual (FAM) guidance indicates that qualification as a specialty occupation "will often come down to a judgment call by the adjudicating consular officer,"[32] after the consular officer reviews the nature of the job duties and the foreign national's qualifications, as discussed below.

The "definition of a specialty occupation for the E-3 visa program is the same as it is for the H-1B visa program."[33] For a further discussion of specialty occupations, see Volume 1: Chapter Seven, "H-1B Visas and Status." As noted in that chapter, it is not sufficient for the foreign national to hold a bachelor's degree; the job must also require such a degree.

B. Qualification as a Professional

1. Educational Qualifications

The foreign national must "meet the general academic and occupational requirements for" the proposed E-3 assignment:[34] "Generally, a specialty occupation is one that cannot be performed without a bachelor's degree or higher (or its equivalent) in a specific field of study or a narrow range of fields of study."[35]

2. Equivalence to a University Degree Through Professional Experience

If the foreign national did not earn at least a bachelor's degree or the foreign equivalent degree, he or she may nevertheless hold the equivalent to a bachelor's degree through progressively more responsible professional experience.[36] For a detailed discussion of these equivalencies, see Volume 1: Chapter Seven, "H-1B Visas and Status."

---

[30] INA §214(i)(1); 20 CFR §655.715.

[31] 9 FAM 402.9-8(D).

[32] 9 FAM 402.9-8(E).

[33] 73 Fed. Reg. 19943 (Apr. 11, 2008).

[34] 9 FAM 402.9-8(B).

[35] U.S. Customs and Border Protection (CBP), M. Hrinyak, "New Nonimmigrant Visa Classification: E-3" (Sept. 19, 2005), AILA Doc. No. 06040712.

[36] 9 FAM 402.9-8(B); 8 CFR §§214.2(h)(4)(iii)(C)(4) and (D).

Copyright © 2017. American Immigration Lawyers Association. All rights reserved.

3. Evidence of Licensure

If the foreign national will perform a professional assignment in a role for which licensure is required, then evidence of licensure or "official permission to perform the specialty occupation" must be presented.[37] For a discussion of professions for which licensure is typically required, see Volume 1: Chapter Seven, "H-1B Visas and Status."

It may be possible to obtain an E-3 visa or E-3 status without evidence of licensure: "[W]here such license or other official permission is not required immediately, an alien must demonstrate that he or she will obtain such licensure or permission within a reasonable period of time following admission to the United States."[38] But the foreign national must then present evidence of satisfying the requirements to apply for the licensure or take the licensure examination.[39]

C. Australian Citizenship

The foreign national must present evidence of being an Australian national.[40] As a practical matter, this evidence must be in the form of an Australian passport for those foreign nationals who apply for E-3 visas at U.S. consulates abroad, since the visa will be issued in the passport. For foreign nationals who apply for E-3 extensions, change of status, or change of employer petitions with USCIS, the evidence may be a copy of the biographic page of the valid Australian passport.

D. Certified Labor Condition Application

The E-3 visa application or petition should include a certified LCA[41] that was filed and approved electronically,[42] except for very limited circumstances, as discussed in Volume 1: Chapter Six, "The Labor Condition Application." The employer must attest to the following conditions:

- Absence of a "strike or lockout in the course of a labor dispute in the occupational classification at the worksite";

- Provision of working conditions for the foreign national "that will not adversely affect working conditions for similarly employed workers";

- Notification of the filing of an LCA to the employees' bargaining representative for the position or, in the absence of a bargaining representative, notification to

---

[37] 9 FAM 402.9-8(H); *see also* USCIS, M. Aytes, "Processing Guidelines for E-3 Australian Specialty Occupation Workers and Employment Authorization for E-3 Dependent Spouses" (Dec. 15, 2005), AILA Doc. No. 05121590.

[38] 9 FAM 402.9-8(A) and (H).

[39] 9 FAM 402.9-8(H).

[40] INA §101(a)(15)(e)(iii).

[41] 20 CFR §655.700; 9 FAM 402.9-8(B) and 402.9-8(C).

[42] 20 CFR §655.720(a).

Copyright © 2017. American Immigration Lawyers Association. All rights reserved.

all employees in the affected position "by a physical posting in a conspicuous location at the worksite or other means such as electronic notification"; and

- Payment, throughout the period of authorized employment, of at least "the actual wage level paid to other employees with similar experience and qualifications for the specific employment in question, or the prevailing wage level for the occupational classification in the area of intended employment, whichever is greater (based on the best information available at the time of filing the attestation)."[43]

Therefore, LCA preparation for an E-3 nonimmigrant will entail researching the prevailing wage for the assignment, preparing the actual wage memorandum, preparing the physical posting notice, arranging for posting of the notice at the worksite, and informing the client of the obligations of an LCA. For a detailed discussion of these documents and proper maintenance of the public access file, see Volume 1: Chapter Six, "The Labor Condition Application."

The LCA conditions and preparation requirements are the same for H-1B and E-3 nonimmigrants, with the following exceptions:

- The LCA application must state the E-3 visa classification; a foreign national may not present an LCA that was approved for the H-1B visa classification;[44]

- The maximum period for which an E-3 LCA may be approved is two years from the employment start date stated on the application;[45]

- The additional attestation requirements of willful H-1B program abusers or H-1B dependent employers are not demanded of E-3 employers;[46]

- The special provisions for short-term placement of H-1B workers do not apply to E-3 nonimmigrants;[47]

- The E-3 employer attests to compliance with the LCA program by "submitting a signed and completed LCA" and "reaffirms its acceptance of all of the attestation obligations by transmitting the certified labor attestation to the nonimmigrant, the Department of State, and/or the USCIS according to the procedures of those agencies";[48] and

---

[43] 73 Fed. Reg. 19943 (Apr. 11, 2008).

[44] 20 CFR §655.730(c)(5); 9 FAM 402.9-8(M).

[45] 20 CFR §655.750(a); 73 Fed. Reg. 19943 (Apr. 11, 2008).

[46] 20 CFR §§655.700(d), 655.730(c)(4)(vii), and 655.730(d)(5).

[47] 20 CFR §655.735.

[48] 73 Fed. Reg. 19943 (Apr. 11, 2008).

Copyright © 2017. American Immigration Lawyers Association. All rights reserved.

- Any "person, firm, contractor, or other association or organization in the United States that files an LCA with the Department of Labor on behalf of the [E-3] nonimmigrant is deemed to be the employer of that nonimmigrant."[49]

It is important to note that the following enforcement provisions for E-3 LCAs apply, just as they apply to H-1B and H-1B1 LCAs:

- DOL may "receive, investigate, and make determinations on complaints filed by any aggrieved person or organization regarding the failure of an employer to meet the terms of its attestations";

- "DOL is also authorized to conduct random investigations for a period of up to five years of any employer found by DOL to have committed a willful failure to meet a required attestation or to have made a willful misrepresentation of a material fact in an attestation"; and

- "Penalties for failure to meet conditions of the E-3 labor attestations are the same as those under the H-1B1 program."[50]

E. Intent to Depart the United States upon Termination of Status

A foreign national seeking E-3 status must seek temporary entry under the same standard as for E-1 and E-2 treaty investors and traders.[51] The foreign national's "expression of an unequivocal intent to return when the E-3 status ends is normally sufficient, in the absence of specific evidence that the alien's intent is to the contrary."[52] Importantly, unlike other nonimmigrant visa classifications, the E-3 visa applicant is not required to demonstrate the intent to remain in the United States "for a specific temporary period of time" or to demonstrate maintenance of a foreign residence; the foreign national may "sell his or her residence and move all household effects to the United States."[53]

It is also permissible for an E-3 visa applicant to "be a beneficiary of an immigrant visa (IV) petition filed on his or her behalf."[54] Similarly, USCIS guidance states: "An application for initial admission, change of status, or extension of stay in E-3 classification, however, may not be denied *solely* on the basis of an approved request for permanent labor certification or a filed or approved immigrant visa preference petition."[55] Although USCIS was requested to promulgate regulations to allow foreign

---

[49] *Id.*

[50] *Id.* (citing INA §212(t)(3)(E)).

[51] 9 FAM 402.9-8(G).

[52] *Id.*

[53] *Id.*

[54] *Id.*

[55] USCIS, M. Aytes, "Processing Guidelines for E-3 Australian Specialty Occupation Workers and Employment Authorization for E-3 Dependent Spouses" (Dec. 15, 2005), AILA Doc. No. 05121590 (emphasis added).

Copyright © 2017. American Immigration Lawyers Association. All rights reserved.

nationals in E status who have filed applications to adjust status to travel without advance paroles and without being considered to have abandoned the underlying nonimmigrant E status, USCIS indicated that this regulation was not a priority.[56]

IV. Process

In seeking E-3 status, a foreign national may apply directly for an E-3 visa at a U.S. consulate abroad; it is not necessary to file a petition with USCIS before the visa application.[57] If the foreign national is within the United States, a petition may be filed to request E-3 change of status. Both approaches are discussed below. The issued E-3 visa and E-3 approval notice may not exceed the validity period of the labor condition application.[58]

A. Preparing the E-3 Visa Application or Petition

The following documents must be prepared and submitted regardless of which process is selected:

- U.S. company support statement;
- Evidence of professional qualifications, such as certified copies of the foreign degree and credentials evaluation, a certified copy of the U.S. degree, experience letters, or a certified copy of professional license; and
- Copy of approved labor condition application.

1. U.S. Company Support Statement

The most important document is the support statement from the U.S. employer. This is especially true for E-3 visa applications, as the consular officer will not have general information about the company from the Form I-129. For this reason, it is critical to provide the government official with the information necessary to adjudicate the petition for approval and to state the following on the support statement:

- Description of "the specialty occupation to be engaged in";
- Anticipated length of the assignment; and
- "Arrangements for remuneration."[59]

The statement should be on the U.S. company's letterhead and signed by a representative of the U.S. company. One format of a support statement is as follows:

- Introduction;

---

[56] AILA/USCIS Q&As (Apr. 2, 2008), AILA Doc. No. 08040235.

[57] 9 FAM 402.9-8(C). *See also* U.S. Embassy & Consulates in Australia, http://www. ustraveldocs.com/au/au-niv-typee3.asp.

[58] 9 FAM 402.9-8(L).

[59] USCIS, M. Aytes, "Processing Guidelines for E-3 Australian Specialty Occupation Workers and Employment Authorization for E-3 Dependent Spouses" (Dec. 15, 2005), AILA Doc. No. 05121590.

Copyright © 2017. American Immigration Lawyers Association. All rights reserved.

- Information about the petitioner;
- Discussion of the project or reason for need of the foreign national's professional services for the U.S. assignment;
- Discussion of the duties of the U.S. assignment;
- Discussion of the foreign national's educational and experience background; and
- Thank you and conclusion.

The most critical parts of the support statement are the paragraphs that address the need for the foreign national's professional services and the daily job duties. The adjudicator generally will focus on this centerpiece first; only after being satisfied that there is a professional assignment will the adjudicator consider whether the foreign national possesses the appropriate professional credentials. Therefore, the support statement should provide details on the project(s) or initiative(s) that gave rise to the assignment and how the job duties will contribute to the successful completion of the employer's objectives.

The conclusion paragraph may contain the necessary information on the length of the U.S. assignment as the "anticipated length of stay,"[60] the amount of remuneration for the professional services, and a statement confirming compliance with the LCA obligations.

2. The Labor Condition Application

For a detailed analysis of how to prepare the labor condition application and the related public access file documents, see Volume 1: Chapter Six, "The Labor Condition Application." This section will focus on the aspects of E-3 LCAs that differ from the requirements of H-1B LCAs. When preparing the electronic LCA on the ETA Form 9035E, all sections should be completed, except for Section I, which is only for H-1B LCAs.

The original DOS rule stated: "At the time of visa application, the visa applicant must present the consular officer with the original or copy of the approved LCA. However, if the applicant cannot provide the original, the consular officer, at his or her discretion, may accept a certified copy of the approval."[61] But the practitioner should note that the rule stated that the foreign national must submit "to a consular officer a copy of the labor condition application signed by the employer and approved by the Department of Labor";[62] and an original certified LCA that is signed by the employer must be maintained in the public access file.[63] The U.S. Consulate in Australia has indicated, and experience has shown, that a copy of the approved LCA

---

[60] *Id.*

[61] 70 Fed. Reg. 52292 (Sept. 6, 2005).

[62] 22 CFR §41.51(c)(1)(iii).

[63] 20 CFR §655.760(a)(1).

Copyright © 2017. American Immigration Lawyers Association. All rights reserved.

is sufficient for the visa application,[64] but risk-averse clients may wish to provide the foreign national with a copy of the LCA that is stamped as a certified copy by the attorney of record, particularly if applying at a post outside of Australia.

This DOS guidance should not apply to USCIS, and experience has shown that a copy of the approved LCA is acceptable for an H-1B petition. Therefore, it seems unlikely that the E-3 change of status petition would be denied or result in a Request for Evidence (RFE) for failure to include a copy of the LCA that is stamped as a certified copy by the attorney of record, but risk-averse clients may wish to submit this document.

B. E-3 Visa Application vs. E-3 Change of Status Petition

The advantages of the E-3 visa application are convenience and a faster processing time. E-3 petitions are all filed at USCIS's Vermont Service Center,[65] and processing times have varied from 30 days to nearly six months since that office first started reporting the times in 2016.[66] On the other hand, a visa application may take significantly less time, often just a few days, depending on the next available visa appointment and processing time for visa issuance at the individual U.S. Consulate.[67] If the foreign national is already outside the United States or has plans to visit his or her home country, perhaps to wrap up personal affairs before beginning the E-3 assignment, then this approach may be most appropriate. These advantages would also apply to E-3 extensions, which may be processed as E-3 visa renewal applications, as discussed below. In addition, if the foreign national initially entered the United States under the Visa Waiver Program (VWP), then he or she must apply for an E-3 visa abroad, as he or she is not eligible for E-3 change of status from VWP. The disadvantages of the E-3 visa application are the cost of airfare for the foreign national and his or her dependent family members, if applicable, and the possibility that visa issuance may be delayed by administrative processing, as discussed in Volume 1: Chapter Two, "Basic Nonimmigrant Concepts."

In contrast, filing an E-3 change of status petition with USCIS has the benefits of saving the costs of international airfare and allowing the E-3 dependent spouse to concurrently file an employment authorization document (EAD) application. This concurrent filing would be an alternative to filing the EAD application after the principal E-3 foreign national has obtained E-3 status. Nevertheless, the practitioner

---

[64] U.S. Embassy and Consulates in Australia, http://www.ustraveldocs.com/au/au-niv-typee3.asp.

[65] "Direct Filing Addresses for Form I-129, Petition for a Nonimmigrant Worker," https://www.uscis.gov/i-129-addresses.

[66] See, e.g., "Vermont Service Center Processing Time Report" as of Nov. 11, 2107, AILA Doc. No. 17011205, showing a processing time of approximately 30 days, and the Report as of Sept. 30, 2016, AILA Doc. No. 16111703, showing a time of nearly six months.

[67] DOS, "Visa Appointment and Processing Wait Times," https://travel.state.gov/content/visas/en/general/wait-times.html.

Copyright © 2017. American Immigration Lawyers Association. All rights reserved.

should consider that the timing of the concurrent filing may take longer than applying for the EAD after admission in E-3D status. This is because the EAD application may not be approved until USCIS confirms that the principal foreign national holds valid E-3 status,[68] and adjudication of the principal's E-3 change of status petition may take several months. A drawback of filing an E-3 change of status petition is the absence of employment authorization until the E-3 petition is approved by USCIS.

A foreign national is eligible for change of status only if he or she continuously maintained the previous nonimmigrant status.[69] Violation of the terms and conditions, such as unauthorized employment while in B status, is considered a failure to maintain valid nonimmigrant status.[70] In addition, there are potential fraud and misrepresentation concerns with requesting a change of status if there has been unauthorized employment. Strategies and issues relating to change of status petitions, as well as further discussion of the accrual of unauthorized employment, its impact on subsequent petitions, and strategies to address accrual of unauthorized employment, are discussed in more detail in Volume 1: Chapter Two, "Basic Nonimmigrant Concepts."

If change of status is requested, the expiration date of the foreign national's B status should be calendared. Ideally, the E-3 change of status petition will be approved before the beneficiary's B status expires, but premium processing is not available for E-3 petitions. The practitioner may wish to advise the client on the intricacies of situations where the initial status expires before the change of status petition is approved. As discussed in Volume 1: Chapter Two, "Basic Nonimmigrant Concepts," a timely filed request for change of status will extend the beneficiary's period of authorized stay, such that the foreign national should not accrue unlawful presence during pendency of the change of status petition, but the government takes the view that a change of status petition will not serve to maintain the beneficiary's immigration status, although it is viewed as a period of stay authorized by the Secretary of Homeland Security.[71]

If the change of status petition is ultimately denied because the beneficiary engaged in unauthorized employment or because the petition is deemed frivolous, then all of the time that the foreign national remained in the United States after expiration of his or her initial grant of admission will be considered unlawful presence.[72] Due to sometimes lengthy processing times, it is possible for a foreign

---

[68] USCIS, M. Aytes, "Processing Guidelines for E-3 Australian Specialty Occupation Workers and Employment Authorization for E-3 Dependent Spouses" (Dec. 15, 2005), AILA Doc. No. 05121590.

[69] 8 CFR §248.1(a) and (b).

[70] 8 CFR §214.1(e). *See also* "USCIS's Standard Operating Procedures (SOPs) for I-539 Processing" (undated, posted Sept. 7, 2007), AILA Doc. No. 07090760.

[71] USCIS, "Consolidation of Guidance Concerning Unlawful Presence for Purposes of Sections 212(a)(9)(B)(i) and 212(a)(9)(C)(i)(I) of the Act" (May 6, 2009), AILA Doc. No. 09051468, pp. 37-38.

[72] *Id.*

Copyright © 2017. American Immigration Lawyers Association. All rights reserved.

national to accrue 180 days of unlawful presence while awaiting adjudication of a change of status petition. Accrual of more than 180 days of unlawful presence will trigger the three-year bar to re-entry to the United States upon departure from the United States. Accrual of more than 365 days of unlawful presence will trigger the 10-year ban to re-entry to the United States upon departure from the United States. For a detailed discussion of the three– and 10-year bars, see Volume 1: Chapter Two, "Basic Nonimmigrant Concepts," and Volume 2: Chapter One, "Basic Immigrant Visa Concepts."

A request for extension of B status may be filed, but practitioners should be aware that USCIS may question the validity of the B extension request and whether a legitimate B purpose is being served or fulfilled.[73] Nevertheless, if this strategy is pursued, then following expiration of the initial nonimmigrant status, the change of status petition should be updated with the receipt notice for the timely filed extension request, to evidence that the beneficiary has not failed to maintain lawful immigration status.[74]

C. E-3 Visa Application at a U.S. Consulate

In addition to the documents discussed above and in Volume 1: Chapter Two, "Basic Nonimmigrant Concepts," the E-3 visa application should include the Australian passport to evidence Australian citizenship. It is likely that the U.S. consulates in Australia have the most experience with E-3 visa applications, but consular officers in third countries may refer to the regulations and the FAM.[75] In practice, consular officers at the U.S. consulates in Canada and Europe regularly process E-3 applications. As always, the practitioner should confirm that the particular U.S. consulate will process visa applications by third country nationals.

The FAM directs consular officers to undertake the following analysis to determine if E-3 visa classification is appropriate:

> "You must determine whether the job itself falls within the definition of 'specialty occupation,' and also examine the alien's qualifications, including his or her education and experience. You should consider the available offer of employment and the information obtained during the interview, and then on the basis of this information, make a reasoned evaluation whether or not the offer of employment is for a 'specialty occupation.' Then you must be sure that the applicant has the required degree, or equivalency of experience and education, to adequately perform the stipulated job duties."[76]

---

[73] "AILA-VSC Liaison Conference Call Minutes" (Mar. 5, 2008), AILA Doc. No. 08031331.

[74] *Id.* Note that it is not current USCIS policy to apply the "last action rule," as discussed in Volume 1: Chapter Two, "Basic Nonimmigrant Concepts."

[75] U.S. Embassy and Consulates in Australia, http://www.ustraveldocs.com/au/au-niv-typee3.asp.

[76] 9 FAM 402.9-8(E) (italics omitted).

Copyright © 2017. American Immigration Lawyers Association. All rights reserved.

Consular officers may request assistance from the DOS Visa Office if there are concerns that the foreign national and/or position do not qualify for E-3 visa classification, and from the Kentucky Consular Center (KCC) if there are concerns about the employer information.[77]

There currently is no reciprocity fee for the E-3 visa.[78] The issued visa should be annotated with the name of the U.S. employer, as well as the certification date and case number of the LCA.[79]

D. Admission to the United States

When seeking admission to the United States, the foreign national should present his or her passport, with the E-3 visa. It is also recommended that the foreign national carry a copy of the approved LCA. The foreign national should be admitted until the end date of the LCA.

In November 2016, DHS extended a rule that had long applied to H-1Bs to make E-3 nonimmigrants eligible for a 10-day grace period added to the beginning and end of the validity period of the authorized stay.[80] Employment is not authorized during this period—it is strictly a consideration to allow the nonimmigrant to make preparations for starting life in the United States and for departing or changing status.[81] It should be noted that DHS has long required in the H-1B context that the grace period be specified by CBP on the I-94 to be effective.[82] The final rule regarding E-3s is silent on this point, but presumably the same qualification would apply. Experience with H-1Bs has shown that the grace period is rarely added to the I-94, unless the nonimmigrant insists upon it at entry, so it should not be presumed. It would be important to check a beneficiary's I-94 record for the period of admission to see if the grace period was added and, if it was, to ensure that he or she understands that employment during that period is prohibited.

As discussed in Volume 1: Chapter Two, "Basic Nonimmigrant Concepts," a physical I-94 card is no longer issued for entries other than by land, so it would be wise to check the CBP website once the individual has entered to obtain the I-94 number and ensure that all family members were admitted in the proper category and for the proper amount of time.[83] Good follow-up should include requesting copies of visas and passport stamps, as well as I-94 cards for those who entered by land, to ensure that all

---

[77] 9 FAM 402.9-8(F).

[78] 9 FAM 402.9-8(L).

[79] Id.

[80] 81 Fed. Reg. 82398 (Nov. 18, 2016).

[81] Id.

[82] Inspector's Field Manual, 15(h)(1).

[83] CBP, "I-94 Website," https://i94.cbp.dhs.gov/I94/#/home.

Copyright © 2017. American Immigration Lawyers Association. All rights reserved.

the information is correct, and calendaring the expiration dates to monitor the individuals' status.

E. E-3 Change of Status Petition Filed with USCIS

In addition to the documents discussed above, the E-3 change of status petition should include the following:

- Form G-28;
- Form I-129;
- Copy of the biographic page of Australian passport to evidence Australian citizenship;
- Copy of I-94 card to evidence lawful immigration status; and
- Filing fee.

All E-3 petitions, including extensions, must be filed with the Vermont Service Center, regardless of the place of employment.[84] E-3 petitions should not include the E Supplement to Form I-129, as this form is applicable only to E-1 and E-2 extensions.[85] Neither should the H Supplement or Free Trade Agreement Supplement be submitted, as discussed below. The practitioner is also advised to "clearly and boldly note[] on the front of the I-129 Petition that this is for E-3 classification."[86] Despite the similarities with the H-1B visa classification, the additional H-1B fees do not apply to E-3 petitions.[87]

Given that USCIS has many years of experience in adjudicating H-1B petitions,[88] which are similar in many ways to E-3 petitions, as discussed above, USCIS generally will adjudicate E-3 petitions without significant problems. Indeed, during the time since enactment of the statute, there have been very few reports of recurring issues in E-3 adjudication.

1. Form G-28

The U.S. company is the "petitioner" and the foreign national is the "beneficiary" of an E-3 petition. The addresses for the U.S. company and the foreign national should be provided. If there is limited time to prepare and file the petition before the U.S. assignment is to begin, such as if the forms are emailed to and printed by the client, this form may be printed on plain white paper. However, as discussed in Volume 1: Chapter

---

[84] "Direct Filing Addresses for Form I-129, Petition for a Nonimmigrant Worker," https://www.uscis.gov/i-129-addresses.

[85] "Filing E-3 Applications at VSC" (Feb. 17, 2006), AILA Doc. No. 06021711.

[86] *Id.*

[87] USCIS, M. Aytes, "Processing Guidelines for E-3 Australian Specialty Occupation Workers and Employment Authorization for E-3 Dependent Spouses" (Dec. 15, 2005), AILA Doc. No. 05121590.

[88] 9 FAM 402.9-8(F).

Copyright © 2017. American Immigration Lawyers Association. All rights reserved.

Two, "Basic Nonimmigrant Concepts," the Forms G-28 should be printed on blue paper whenever possible, in order to avoid processing delays.[89]

2. Form I-129

Part 1: Information on the U.S. company, including name, address, contact person, contact person's telephone number and email address, and Federal Employer Identification Number (FEIN), should be provided.

Part 2: For initial E-3 petitions, "New employment" should be checked, and "change of status" should be requested.

Parts 3 and 4: Information about the beneficiary, including name, alternate names, date of birth, country of birth and country of nationality, and passport information, should be provided.

Australian nationals are exempt from the rule that an individual must have a passport that is valid for at least six months from the petition's expiration date.[90] Thus, an Australian beneficiary must have a passport valid until the petition's expiration date, otherwise he or she is inadmissible and ineligible for nonimmigrant status.[91] If the foreign national does not have such a passport, then the following options are available: either delay filing the E-3 petition until he or she obtains a renewed passport, or file the E-3 petition, have the foreign national apply for a renewed passport in the interim, wait for an RFE, and then submit a photocopy of the biographic page of the renewed passport once it is available. But because Australian passport renewal should take only a few weeks,[92] it seems advisable to wait until the foreign national has a valid passport, as the RFE may delay final adjudication of the E-3 petition for much longer than a few weeks, premium processing is not available, and the foreign national may accrue 180 days of unlawful presence.

If the foreign national is present in the United States on a business trip when the petition is filed, then the I-94 card information should be provided, even if the foreign national will depart the United States during pendency of the E-3 petition. In this case, consular notification should be requested in Part 2, as discussed above; however, to avoid the situation of being subjected to USCIS processing times while the foreign national is abroad and to be able to apply for an E-3 visa, the practitioner should strategize with the client ahead of time to arrange for an initial E-3 visa application.

---

[89] VSC Practice Pointer: G-28s (Sept. 4, 2008), AILA Doc. No. 08090469.

[90] CBP, "Six-Month Club Update" (updated Jan. 6, 2017), https://www.cbp.gov/document/bulletins/six-month-club-update.

[91] INA §212(a)(7)(B)(i). The exceptions to this rule in INA §212(a)(d)(4) are discussed in Volume 1: Chapter Two, "Basic Nonimmigrant Concepts."

[92] Embassy of Australia, "Passports FAQs," http://www.usa.embassy.gov.au/whwh/PassportsFAQ.html.

Copyright © 2017. American Immigration Lawyers Association. All rights reserved.

Parts 5 through 7: Information about the title, job description, location, compensation, and general information about the petitioner should be provided. The form should be signed by the petitioner's representative and the practitioner.

Note that Part 6, regarding export control, does not apply to E categories.

V. Additional Follow-up

After a foreign national has obtained E-3 status, the practitioner should follow up to request copies of the I-94 cards and the visas, to ensure that all the information is correct, and to calendar the expiration dates to monitor the foreign national's status, as discussed in Volume 1: Chapter Two, "Basic Nonimmigrant Concepts."

A. E-3 Extensions

As discussed above, foreign nationals who obtain E-3 extensions are not counted toward the numerical limitation, as long as "there has been uninterrupted continuity of employment," which "means that the applicant has worked, and continues to work, for the U.S.-based employer who submitted the original labor condition application (LCA) and offer of employment."[93] DOS calls these foreign nationals "returning E-3 principals" and states that the new visas will have the code "'E-3R' (with the 'R' representing the status of 'returning')."[94]

As stated by USCIS guidance: "Extensions of stay may be granted indefinitely.... As there is no limit on the total length of stay for an E-3 alien in the legislation, there is no specified number of extensions a qualifying E-3 Specialty Occupation Worker may be granted."[95] If a foreign national has been granted multiple extensions, however, the practitioner should discuss the temporary intent requirement, as discussed above.

When filing an E-3 extension, in Part 2, Question 5, the box for "Extend the stay of the person(s) since they now hold this status" should be checked.[96] Neither of the boxes relating to a Free Trade Agreement should be checked.[97] Further, the Free Trade Agreement Supplement should not be submitted with the E-3 extension, as this form is for TNs and H-1B1s.[98]

---

[93] 9 FAM 402.9-8(I).

[94] *Id.*

[95] USCIS, M. Aytes, "Processing Guidelines for E-3 Australian Specialty Occupation Workers and Employment Authorization for E-3 Dependent Spouses" (Dec. 15, 2005), AILA Doc. No. 05121590.

[96] "AILA/VSC Practice Pointer: VSC Clarifies E-3 Extension Protocols" (Dec. 14, 2009), AILA Doc. No. 09121460.

[97] *Id.*

[98] *Id.*

Copyright © 2017. American Immigration Lawyers Association. All rights reserved.

As of January 2016, a timely filed extension will provide an additional 240 days of employment authorization with the petitioning employer, during pendency of the E-3 extension filing and after expiration of the current E-3 status.[99]

B. Change in Work Location

As discussed in Volume 1: Chapter Six: "The Labor Condition Application," when an employee is moved to a different area of intended employment, a new LCA needs to be filed.[100] DOS has indicated that the new LCA does not have to be submitted to the consular post until a subsequent E-3 visa application is filed.[101]

With respect to USCIS, the issue is more complicated. DHS/USCIS has never promulgated a regulation on the E-3 category, leaving guidance to be extrapolated from the rules and case law surrounding a hybrid of H-1Bs and E-1s/E-2s. In 2015, a precedent Administrative Appeals Office (AAO) decision reversed years of informal guidance and held in *Matter of Simeio Solutions, LLC* that a change in the place of employment for an H-1B, such that a new LCA is required, is a material change and thus requires filing of an amended petition with USCIS.[102] Subsequent guidance issued by USCIS spoke only to H-1Bs, and did not address other categories, such as the E-3, that also require LCAs.[103]

One might argue that, because the E-3 is a consular-based application system, *Simeio* does not apply, at least to those who obtained their status by visa and not by change or extension of status through USCIS. After all, there is no petition to amend. The fact that DOS, the visa-issuing authority, does not require that the LCA be submitted to it until time to renew the visa would seem to bolster the argument.

However, USCIS does have regulations on the E-1/E-2 categories, which also involve nonimmigrants who often obtained their status through the visa process and have no petition to amend. USCIS notes that DHS has a hand in determining the "terms and conditions of the E treaty status at the time of admission,"[104] and that prior "approval must be obtained where there will be a substantive change in the terms or conditions of E status."[105] It goes on to require that either a new I-129 be filed or the individual obtain a new visa and apply for admission to the United States.[106] It makes

---

[99] 8 CFR §274a.12(b)(25); 81 Fed. Reg. 2068 (Jan. 15, 2016).

[100] 20 CFR §655.735(g).

[101] "AILA/Department of State Liaison Meeting" (Oct. 6, 2016), AILA Doc. No. 16100705.

[102] *Matter of Simeio Solutions, LLC* 26 I&N Dec. 542 (AAO 2015), AILA Doc. No. 15040969.

[103] "USCIS Final Guidance on When to File an Amended or New H-1B Petition After *Matter of Simeio Solutions, LLC*," PM-602-0120 (July 21, 2015), AILA Doc. No. 15072105.

[104] 8 CFR §214.2(e)(8)(i).

[105] 8 CFR §214.2(e)(8)(iii).

[106] *Id.*

Copyright © 2017. American Immigration Lawyers Association. All rights reserved.

no distinction in the application of its requirement between status obtained by DOS visa issuance and status obtained by USCIS petition.

The regulation also states, however, that "[p]rior approval is not required, and there is no need to file a new Form I-129, if there is no substantive, or fundamental, change in terms and conditions of the alien's employment that would affect the alien's eligibility for E classification."[107] As discussed in Volume 1: Chapter Four, "E-1 and E-2 Visas and Status," in most instances a mere change of work location would not be considered a substantive change for an E-1 or E-2. However, unlike the E-3, those categories do not require an LCA, whose attestations are tied to the area of employment.

Thus, while it is conceivable that USCIS could view *Simeio* as applying to the E-3 category, in practice there have been no reports of this occurring. In the absence of any guidance, it does not appear that an employer would need to file a petition with USCIS or apply for a new visa when there has been a change in job location that requires a new LCA but no fundamental change in job duties.

C. E-3 Change of Employer Petitions

The E-3 change of employer petition should contain the same documents as the E-3 extension petition. The practitioner should advise the clients of the advantages and disadvantages of filing a change of employer petition over making a new E-3 visa application at a U.S. consulate abroad. The considerations are the same as the strategy of deciding between an E-3 visa application and an E-3 change of status petition, discussed above. E-3 change of employer petitions are, however, counted against the numerical limitation again.[108]

D. If Employment Ceases

E-3 nonimmigrants whose employment ends prior to the expiration of their authorized stay are able to remain in the United States lawfully for the shorter of 60 days or when the existing validity period ends.[109] This can be used only once during each "authorized validity period." The purpose is to allow the beneficiary to wind up affairs or to seek other employment and request a change of status if needed and eligible.[110] The individual is not able to work during this period, unless otherwise authorized[111] The rulemaking that put in place this grace period was silent as to what would be an "authorized validity period" in the E context, but presumably it means any

---

[107] 8 CFR §214.2(e)(8)(iv).

[108] USCIS, M. Aytes, "Processing Guidelines for E-3 Australian Specialty Occupation Workers and Employment Authorization for E-3 Dependent Spouses" (Dec. 15, 2005), AILA Doc. No. 05121590.

[109] 8 CFR §214.1(*l*)(ii).

[110] 80 Fed. Reg. 81900, 81923 (Dec. 31, 2015).

[111] *Id.*

Copyright © 2017. American Immigration Lawyers Association. All rights reserved.

given period of admission, or the validity period of the approved USCIS petition, whichever is in effect for the individual at the time.

E. EADs for E-3D Spouses

Spouses of E-3 professionals are eligible to apply for employment authorization.[112] The statutory provision does not, however, extend to dependent children in E-3D status.[113] An E-3 spouse may wish to obtain an EAD solely in order to apply for a Social Security number (SSN).

The following documents should be prepared and filed:

- Form G-28;
- Form I-765;
- Statement from U.S. company, confirming the E-3 employment of the principal foreign national;
- Copy of the principal E-3 nonimmigrant's E-3 visa;
- Copy of biographic page of passport of the E-3S spouse;
- Copy of E-3D visa and I-94 card; and
- Copy of marriage certificate of E-3 professional and spouse.

The EAD application may be filed concurrently with an E-3 change of status petition, but these applications must be filed with VSC.[114] Otherwise, the EAD application should be filed with the either the Phoenix or the Dallas Lockbox, depending on where the applicant's place of residence is.[115] Upon issuance of the EAD, the E-3D spouse may be employed by any employer;[116] he or she need not be employed in a specialty occupation.[117]

---

[112] 9 FAM 402.9-9.

[113] INA §214(e)(6); USCIS, W. Yates, "Guidance on Employment Authorization for E and L Nonimmigrant Spouses, and for Determinations on the Requisite Employment Abroad for L Blanket Petitions" (Feb. 22, 2002), AILA Doc. No. 02022832.

[114] USCIS, M. Aytes, "Processing Guidelines for E-3 Australian Specialty Occupation Workers and Employment Authorization for E-3 Dependent Spouses" (Dec. 15, 2005), AILA Doc. No. 05121590 (posted Dec. 15, 2005).

[115] USCIS, "Direct Filing Addresses for Form I-765, Application for Employment Authorization," https://www.uscis.gov/i-765-addresses.

[116] USCIS, W. Yates, "Guidance on Employment Authorization for E and L Nonimmigrant Spouses, and for Determinations on the Requisite Employment Abroad for L Blanket Petitions" (Feb. 22, 2002), AILA Doc. No. 02022832.

[117] 70 Fed. Reg. 52292 (Sept. 2, 2005).

Copyright © 2017. American Immigration Lawyers Association. All rights reserved.

CHAPTER SIX

THE LABOR CONDITION APPLICATION

I. Executive Summary

The labor condition application (LCA) is the first step in the H-1B specialty occupation,[1] H-1B1 Singapore/Chile Free Trade,[2] and E-3 Australian specialty occupation worker[3] nonimmigrant processes.[4] Not to be confused with the labor certification application discussed in Volume 2: Chapter Two, "The Labor Certification Application," the LCA is attestation-based, meaning that the employer makes certain promises to the government—in this case the Department of Labor (DOL)—but does not submit any documentation to support those promises. Instead, the employer is required to keep supporting documentation on file, which is to be available for "public examination."[5] This file is often referred to as the public access file.

In these attestations, the employer promises that:

- It will pay the required wage: the higher of the prevailing wage and the actual wage;

- It will provide working conditions for the nonimmigrant that will not adversely affect working conditions of workers similarly employed;

- There is not a strike or lockout in the occupational field at the place of employment; and

- It has provided notice of the filing of the LCA to the applicable union representative, or if there is no such representative, has provided notice of the filing through posting in the workplace or electronic notification to employees in the occupational classification.[6]

If the employer is considered H-1B dependent[7] or is a "willful violator,"[8] additional attestations are required in the H-1B context:[9]

---

[1] Immigration and Nationality Act (INA) §101(a)(15)(H)(i)(b), regarding specialty occupation workers, requires a Labor Condition Application (LCA) as described in INA §212(n)(1).

[2] INA §101(a)(15)(H)(i)(b)(1), regarding nonimmigrants under the Singapore or Chile Free Trade Agreements, requires an LCA as described in INA §212(t).

[3] INA §101(a)(15)(E)(iii), regarding Australian specialty occupation workers, requires an LCA as described in INA §212(t).

[4] An LCA was also previously required for TN status for Mexican nationals. That provision sunset on Jan. 1, 2004, and was never renewed. *See* 69 Fed. Reg. 11287 (Mar. 10, 2004).

[5] INA §§212(n)(1) and (t)(2)(A). The statute states only that the contents of the public file must include the LCA and "such accompanying documents as are necessary." The Department of Labor's (DOL) regulation, discussed in detail throughout this chapter, fills in the details on what documents it regards as "necessary."

[6] INA §§212(n)(1)(A)–(D) and (t)(1)(A) through (D). 20 Code of Federal Regulations (CFR) §655.730(d).

[7] As defined in INA §212(n)(3).

[8] As defined in 20 CFR §655.736(f).

Copyright © 2017. American Immigration Lawyers Association. All rights reserved.

- The employer did not and will not displace a U.S. worker within a period of 90 days before and 90 days after the filing of the H-1B petition (or 90-day/90-day "look" period").

- The H-1B nonimmigrant will not be placed at a third-party worksite where there are indicia of employment by the other employer, unless the petitioner has inquired whether there has been or will be a displacement of a U.S. worker during those 90-day periods and has no knowledge of such a displacement.

- The employer has taken good faith steps to recruit U.S. workers for the position and has offered the job to any U.S. worker who applied and is at least as qualified as the H-1B.[10]

If the H-1B nonimmigrant is considered "exempt"—i.e., is paid at least $60,000 per year or holds a master's degree or higher (or its equivalent) in a specialty related to the intended occupation[11]—the three additional attestations are not required.[12]

DOL administers the labor condition application process, with the Employment and Training Administration (ETA) being "responsible for receiving and certifying labor condition applications."[13] In addition, the "ETA is also responsible for compiling and maintaining a list of LCAs and makes such list available for public examination" in Washington, D.C.[14] The Wage and Hour Division of the Employment Standards Administration (ESA) within DOL bears responsibility "for investigating and determining an employer's misrepresentation in or failure to comply with LCAs in the employment of H-1B nonimmigrants."[15]

II. Required Wage Attestation

Employers are required to pay nonimmigrants in the H-1B, H-1B1, and E-3 categories the higher of the prevailing wage for the occupational classification in the area of employment, or the actual wage—the amount paid by that employer to "all other individuals with similar experience and qualifications for the specific employment in question."[16] This is the first attestation on the Form ETA-9035 Labor Condition Application.

---

[9] The H-1B1 and E-3 LCA provisions, while nearly identical to the H-1B provisions in many respects, do not contain special provisions for "dependent" employers or for "willful violators."

[10] INA §212(n)(1)(E) through (G).

[11] INA §212(n)(3)(B).

[12] INA §212(n)(1)(E)(ii). But be careful when you see the term "exempt" used in the H-1B context. It could, as here, be referring to exemption from the dependent attestations. It also could refer to exemption from the additional fees for H-1Bs, or exemption from the H-1B quota, both of which are discussed in Volume 1: Chapter Seven, "H-1B Visas and Status."

[13] 20 CFR §655.705(a).

[14] 20 CFR §655.705(a)(1).

[15] 20 CFR §§655.705(a)(2), 710(a), and 805.

[16] INA §§212(n)(1)(A) and (t)(1)(A).

Copyright © 2017. American Immigration Lawyers Association. All rights reserved.

A. Prevailing Wage

1. A Working Definition

Despite its importance to the three nonimmigrant categories that require an LCA, and to the nonimmigrant and permanent processes that require a labor certification application, nowhere in the statute or regulations is there a concise definition of prevailing wage. Nevertheless, the pages upon pages of regulation and guidance that govern prevailing wage can be narrowed down to this working definition: the competitive wage offered by other employers in the area of intended employment for the occupation, with an equivalent level of preparedness.

2. When to Determine the Prevailing Wage

The Immigration and Nationality Act (INA) declares that the required wage is to be "based on the best information available *as of the time of filing the application*."[17] At least with respect to the prevailing wage, DOL's regulation carries forward this statutory formulation, indicating that the prevailing wage must be "determined as of the time of filing the application."[18] This means that it is not be necessary to update the prevailing wage during the validity period of the LCA.[19]

3. How to Determine the Prevailing Wage

The process of fulfilling the required wage attestation includes identifying, documenting, and stating on the LCA the prevailing wage. So, the first step becomes determining the prevailing wage.

No specific methodology is required to establish the prevailing wage,[20] but the regulation sets out a list of potential sources for prevailing wages and the criteria by which those sources might qualify. It also sets forth something of a continuum, with the implication that some sources, much like Orwell's animals, are "more equal than others."[21]

Functionally speaking, the collective bargaining agreement is treated as first-ranked.[22] While nothing in the regulation states explicitly that the union/employer wage rate must govern if there is one, it is implied by the structure of the regulation, which indicates that if "the job opportunity is in an occupation which is not covered by [the collective bargaining provision], the prevailing wage shall be"[23] determined according to a formula discussed below. Also, DOL's guidance on determining prevailing wage declares the collective bargaining agreement as determinative if one

---

[17] INA §§212(n)(1)(A)(i) and (t)(1)(A)(i) (emphasis added).

[18] 20 CFR §655.731(a)(2).

[19] Under 20 CFR §655.750(a), an LCA can be valid for up to three years.

[20] 20 CFR §655.731(a)(2).

[21] G. Orwell, *Animal Farm*.

[22] 20 CFR §655.731(a)(2)(i).

[23] 20 CFR §655.731(a)(2)(ii).

Copyright © 2017. American Immigration Lawyers Association. All rights reserved.

is provided.[24] Thus, it would seem that the figure in a union contract would be the prevailing wage, if the employer has such an agreement with a rate applicable to the occupation.

The regulation indicates that, other than in the union contract context, the prevailing wage is the arithmetic mean of the wages of similarly employed workers. It lists an "order of priority" of prevailing wage sources that are the "most accurate and reliable."[25] First among these is the government determination, followed by the independent authoritative source (generally, a published wage survey), and, last, "another legitimate source of wage information."[26]

a. Government Determination

Requests for a government prevailing wage determination (PWD) must be submitted to the National Prevailing Wage Center (NPWC) at the National Processing Center (NPC) of DOL's Office of Foreign Labor Certification (OFLC) on ETA Form 9141.[27] PWD requests can be submitted electronically, through the iCert portal at *http://icert.doleta.gov*,[28] or by mail or overnight service to:

U.S Dept. of Labor, Employment and Training Administration
Office of Foreign Labor Certification
National Prevailing Wage Center
200 Constitution Ave. NW
Room N-5311
Washington, D.C. 20210.[29]

The methodology used by the NPWC to determine the prevailing wage is discussed below in the section titled "OES Wages."

A government determination operates as a safe harbor: "In all situations where the employer obtains the PWD from the NPC, the Department will deem that PWD as correct as to the amount of the wage."[30] The NPWC determination is a safe harbor

---

[24] DOL, "Prevailing Wage Determination Guidance" (Nov. 2009) AILA Doc. No. 10010468, p. 5. ("If the NPWHC determines the job opportunity is covered by a collective bargaining agreement… as evidenced by information provided by the employer, that wage rate shall be controlling.")

[25] *Id.*

[26] *Id.*

[27] Since the inception of the LCA, an employer could obtain a PWD from state departments of labor, known generically as State Workforce Agencies (SWAs). Then, in Dec. 2008, DOL issued a regulation to phase in "federalization" of the prevailing wage process, shifting the function from the SWAs to the National Processing Center (NPC) as of Jan. 1, 2010. 73 Fed. Reg. 78019 (Dec. 19, 2008).

[28] DOL, "Frequently Asked Questions (FAQs) on National Prevailing Wage and Helpdesk Center" (Mar. 2010), *AILA* Doc. No. 10032662.

[29] 81 Fed. Reg. 5485 (Feb. 2, 2016).

[30] 20 CFR §655.731(a)(2)(ii)(A)(3).

Copyright © 2017. American Immigration Lawyers Association. All rights reserved.

only with respect to the amount of the prevailing wage.[31] It is still possible for DOL to contest the accuracy of the underlying information.[32]

The practicality of the government PWD is questionable. As of the time of this writing, it is taking three to four months to obtain a determination, and DOL has indicated that it is unlikely to be able to reduce the processing time below an average of 80 to 90 days,[33] a time frame that is not useable for many H-1B, H-1B1, or E-3 requests. While it is possible to request a wage determination, proceed before receiving it, and still utilize the PWD as a safe harbor, there are pitfalls, as discussed immediately below.

(1) Using Alternative Source While Awaiting Government Determination

An employer can take advantage of the safe harbor of the government determination without having to wait the time it takes to actually obtain the PWD, if the employer has some flexibility with respect to the wage. The regulation allows an employer to rely for the filing of the LCA on one of the other prevailing wage sources in the continuum. Then, if a higher wage is later received from the government, the employer can rely on that later information if, within 30 days of receipt of the determination, it retroactively compensates the H-1B nonimmigrant for the difference.[34]

What happens if the employer uses another prevailing wage source while waiting for the PWD, then gets a determination that is higher than it is willing to pay? Can the employer continue to use the other source? The regulation states that "in all situations" where a government PWD is obtained "the Department will deem that PWD as correct."[35] This language is written in connection with the safe harbor, but "in all situations" could be read to also refer to an enforcement action. Thus, it is possible that the presence of a higher prevailing wage determination obtained with respect to the LCA[36] could be used as an adverse factor if the prevailing wage in the other source is ever challenged.

What is clear is that, if a PWD is obtained prior to filing the LCA, but the employer disagrees with the determination, it should not use that determination on the LCA. Once a prevailing wage determination is used on an LCA, the employer is

---

[31] *Id.*

[32] DOL, "FAQs on *Prevailing Wage Determinations for Nonagricultural Programs*" (Aug. 1, 2005), AILA Doc. No. 05081067, Part I, question 2: "Wage and Hour will not challenge the validity of the prevailing wage as long as *it was applied properly (i.e., correct geographic area, occupation, and skill level)*" (emphasis added). While this FAQ is no longer on the DOL website, the implicit caution is still worth noting.

[33] "Minutes from DOL PERM/H-1B Stakeholder Meeting" (Mar. 7, 2017), AILA Doc. No. 17031303.

[34] 20 CFR §655.731(a)(2)(ii)(A)(2).

[35] 20 CFR §655.731(a)(2)(ii)(A)(3).

[36] At least one Administrative Law Judge (ALJ) has found that a PWD obtained in connection with a permanent labor certification, filed two months after the LCA, could not be used to show that the alternative source used on the LCA was inaccurate, but noted that the employer had never requested a PWD for the H-1B petition. *Baiju v. Fifth Avenue Committee*, 2009-LCA-00045 (ALJ Mar. 8, 2010), AILA Doc. No. 10040835.

Copyright © 2017. American Immigration Lawyers Association. All rights reserved.

deemed to have accepted it and cannot contest it.[37] However, if an employer wishes to contest the PWD, it can use another source while the contest is ongoing[38] and then later use the process discussed above to rely on the safe harbor.

What the employer absolutely should not do is indicate on the LCA that it is using a government PWD without having the determination in hand. "The employer may not use iCERT tracking numbers and wage rates requested on the ETA 9141, in lieu of an actual final NPWC prevailing wage determination. Listing an NPWG-issued prevailing wage on an LCA operates as an endorsement of that wage and forecloses the employer's ability to appeal the PWD after filing the LCA.... If the employer wishes to qualify for the 'safe harbor' ... the employer must request a PWD from the NPWC and file an LCA during the prevailing wage validity period specified on the ETA Form 9141."[39]

(2) Government Determination Based on Employer-Provided Survey

It is possible to provide input to the government to help it arrive at an appropriate prevailing wage in the first place.[40] Most of the guidance on this subject is written primarily for the permanent labor certification process, but an employer wanting the safe harbor of a PWD may provide input in the LCA context as well.[41]

If the employer provides information that the position is covered by a collective bargaining agreement (or if the government finds it to be covered), then the government will use the wage from that agreement as its determination.[42] Otherwise, if the employer provides a survey that meets the criteria discussed below, the government is supposed to use the wage rate from that survey. If there is no collective bargaining agreement or employer-provided survey, it uses the Occupational Employment Statistics (OES) survey,[43] discussed in the next section. If the employer does not provide a survey, the government must use the OES wage. It cannot, on its own initiative, utilize a private survey.[44]

The criteria for acceptance of an employer-provided survey are:[45]

- The data must have been collected within 24 months of the publication date or, if it is an employer-conducted survey, within 24 months of submission to the NPWC;

---

[37] 20 CFR §655.731(a)(2)(ii)(A)(1).

[38] 20 CFR §655.731(a)(2)(ii)(A)(2) (stating "[i]f the employer is unable to wait for ... the CO and/or the BALCA to issue a decision ... the employer may rely on other legitimate sources").

[39] DOL, "FAQs on H-1B, H-1B1, and E-3 Programs Round 1" (Feb. 17, 2011), AILA Doc. No. 11021867.

[40] DOL, "Prevailing Wage Determination Guidance" (Nov. 2009), AILA Doc. No. 10010468.

[41] "DOL Updates FAQs on Prevailing Wage Program" (Feb. 6, 2013), AILA Doc. No. 13022844.

[42] Id.

[43] Id.

[44] See DOL, "ETA Remand Notification" (Feb. 12, 2009), AILA Doc. No. 09021838.

[45] All items in this list are derived from DOL, "Prevailing Wage Determination Guidance" (Nov. 2009), AILA Doc. No. 10010468, Appendix F, unless noted otherwise.

Copyright © 2017. American Immigration Lawyers Association. All rights reserved.

- A published survey must have been published within 24 months of submission and must be the most recent edition;

- The data must represent similar jobs within normal commuting distance of the address of the job. However, some flexibility is allowed with respect to geographic scope of the survey. If the employer can establish that there were not enough comparable workers in the area of intended employment to provide a representative sample, a broader geographic reach can be used;

- The survey's job description must match the job description in the employer's request. The two documents "should not have differences that would place the job in a different occupation," and the job description should not require "extra or unusual duties, skills, or conditions of employment."[46] If the survey does not include the unusual items in its description of the position, "the survey should have multi-tiered wages" so that the NPWC can use its methodology discussed below and "increase the wage level by one level for each restrictive or atypical requirement."[47] Also, if the employer's job description combines duties from more than one position in the survey, "and the survey documentation does not provide a method for the assignment of wages in such circumstances," the survey will be rejected;[48]

- The data must have been collected across industries that employ people in that occupation (in other words, it cannot be limited to the industry in which the employer operates if the occupation occurs in other industries). DOL's "suggested survey methodology" states that data should come from "at least three employers and at least 30 employees. Results for 30 workers is the minimum acceptable sample; for most occupations there should be wage data for many more workers";

- The survey should provide a weighted average for workers in the occupational classification in the area of intended employment. A median can be used if the survey provides only a median and not a weighted average; and

- The survey must show a statistically valid methodology.

When submitting a survey for acceptance, DOL requires information regarding the methodology used in the survey,[49] and requires the following specific information if it is not already contained in the survey itself:[50]

- Name of the survey;

---

[46] "DOL Updates FAQs on Prevailing Wage Program" (Feb. 6, 2013), AILA Doc. No. 13022844.

[47] *Id.*

[48] *Id.* See Volume 2: Chapter Two, "The Labor Certification Application" for a discussion of combination of duties and the impact on prevailing wages.

[49] 20 CFR §656.40(g)(2).

[50] 74 Fed. Reg. 63796 (Dec. 4, 2009).

Copyright © 2017. American Immigration Lawyers Association. All rights reserved.

- Publication schedule for the survey, including the publication date of the submitted survey, the date of the previous version of the survey, and the date of the next release of the survey (actual or anticipated);

- When the data was collected;

- Description of the job duties or activities used in the survey;

- How the universe of surveyed positions is defined;

- How the sample size was determined;

- How the participants were selected;

- The number of employers surveyed for the occupation in the area;

- The number of wage value responses (employees) for the occupation in the area;

- A list of employer participants or explanation of how the cross-industry nature of the survey was maintained;

- How the presented wage was determined and if it is mean or median;

- Any other appropriate information on the survey's methodology; and

- The area covered by the survey or relevant portion and an explanation of any expansion of the area beyond normal commuting distance.

Note the absence of the requirement that the survey contain the four wage levels discussed in the section titled "OES Wages" below. This is because the statute requires four levels only of governmental surveys.[51] Surveys provided by employers are not required to present multiple levels,[52] except in the situation discussed above in which the employer's position includes "non-normal" requirements not included in the survey's description, in which case multiple levels are needed to enable the NPWC to increase the wage level for each such requirement.[53]

An employer also can elect to use a wage rate under the Davis-Bacon or McNamara-O'Hara Service Contract Act (SCA), and these will be treated in much the same way as employer-provided surveys,[54] although the detailed information about the survey listed above does not have to be submitted.[55]

---

[51] INA §212(p)(4).

[52] DOL, " Prevailing Wage Determination Guidance" (Nov. 2009), AILA Doc. No. 10010468.

[53] "DOL Updates FAQs on Prevailing Wage Program" (Feb. 6, 2013), AILA Doc. No. 13022844.

[54] *Id.* Prior to 2005, when the PERM regulation changed the prevailing wage scheme for both permanent and temporary programs, the prevailing wage for any job that was listed in either of those Acts had to be the wage under the Act, regardless of whether the employer was actually subject to the Act. *See* 20 CFR §656.40(a)(1) (2004). Once the PERM regulation took effect, Davis-Bacon and SCA wages became optional sources. 69 Fed. Reg. 77325 (Dec. 27, 2004) at 77365–66; 20 CFR §656.40(b)(4). Interestingly, H-2B regulations prohibit the use of Davis-Bacon and SCA wages to determine prevailing wage for temporary labor certifications. 20 CFR §655.10(d).

[55] 74 Fed. Reg. 63796 (Dec. 4, 2009).

Copyright © 2017. American Immigration Lawyers Association. All rights reserved.

(3) Contesting a PWD

A PWD is contested first by requesting, within 30 days of the determination's issuance, review by the NPC that issued the determination. The redetermination request can be made directly through the iCert system, but the system provides a very limited amount of space in which to explain why the determination is incorrect. If the wage determination is upheld following the redetermination request, the employer can then seek Center Director Review, where a more detailed explanation of the challenge to the determination can be made in a detailed letter or other written material. The director of the NPWC reviews the request "solely on the basis upon which the PWD was made," and either affirms or modifies. If not satisfied by the determination, an employer then can seek Board of Alien Labor Certification Appeals (BALCA) review of the decision by submitting a request to the NPWC director who rendered the decision, who in turn forwards it to BALCA.[56] This process also is used when the prevailing wage is at issue in a complaint or investigation.[57]

In practice, this is a lengthy process. Each step of the redetermination process with the NPWC takes approximately as long as a new prevailing wage request, so going through the initial determination, redetermination request, and Center Director review can take nearly nine months.[58] As a result, in many instances the employer will not be able to wait long enough before proceeding with the filing to effectively contest the wage, and the practitioner should warn the employer of these practical concerns when deciding whether to request a wage determination as part of the LCA process.

b. Independent Authoritative Source

Next in DOL's ranking is the independent authoritative source, which is presumed by the language of the regulation to be a published survey.[59] Such a survey may be used "in lieu of an NPC PWD."[60] While this language does not provide the safe harbor of the government determination, it appears to give the independent authoritative source strong credibility, particularly when contrasted with the language used with respect to the "other legitimate source," discussed below.

To qualify as an "independent authoritative source," a survey must:[61]

- Be published in a book, newspaper, periodical, loose-leaf service, newsletter, or "other similar medium" no earlier than 24 months before the LCA is filed. At the time this part of the regulation was last amended, in 2000, online wage surveys were not as common as they are today, and thus likely did not merit specific

---

[56] 20 CFR §656.41.

[57] 20 CFR §655.731(d)(2).

[58] "Minutes from DOL Stakeholder Meeting" (May 24, 2016), AILA Doc. No. 16062232.

[59] 20 CFR §655.731(a)(2)(ii)(B).

[60] *Id.*

[61] 20 CFR §655.731(b)(3)(iii)(B).

Copyright © 2017. American Immigration Lawyers Association. All rights reserved.

mention. There is no reason to think that a wage survey published online would not be considered an "other similar medium";

- Be based on data collected within the 24 months before publication of the survey;

- Be the latest published finding by that source for the occupation in the geographic area; and

- Reflect a weighted average or median wage paid to those similarly employed in the area of intended employment. The regulation states the median option as useable if the survey does not provide a weighted average, leading to the conclusion that, if the survey provides both a weighted average and a median, the weighted average should be used.

Apart from these criteria, the regulation does not specify a methodology other than that the employer "shall base the prevailing wage on the best information available...."[62] The guidance issued by DOL on the subject of methodology primarily relates to the prevailing wage process for permanent labor certification, but also encompasses nonimmigrant programs with respect to government determinations. However, the permanent program regulations are incorporated into the nonimmigrant program regulations only with respect to government determinations.[63] Otherwise, the nonimmigrant program regulations stand on their own. Thus, the detailed guidance memos issued by DOL, including the 2009 guidance and its Appendix F discussed above, generally apply only to surveys that are being used to obtain SWA determinations and not to those being used as an independent authoritative source.

A number of companies publish surveys that will meet the criteria of the regulation. In addition, many trade and professional associations and local business groups provide surveys that could meet these criteria. Usually, the employer is familiar with surveys commonly used in its field or area, and can direct the practitioner to the best sources, though the practitioner must investigate to ensure that the survey does indeed meet all the requirements. While DOL's OFLC "does not maintain and/or endorse a list of acceptable wage source survey instruments,"[64] it has pointed out that it maintains a web page with disclosure data from certified LCAs that shows its wage source entries,[65] and also provides a list of examples of "commonly used prevailing wage surveys."[66]

It is important when completing the labor condition application, ETA Form 9035/9035E, that the survey used be named with as much clarity as possible in the limited amount of space provided on the iCert form. Too often, DOL has rejected an

---

[62] 20 CFR §655.731(a)(2).

[63] 20 CFR §655.731(a)(2)(ii)(A).

[64] DOL, "FAQs for H-1B, H-1B1, and E-3 Programs" (July 31, 2015), AILA Doc. No. 15080502.

[65] DOL, "H-1B Program Data," http://www.flcdatacenter.com/CaseH1B.aspx.

[66] DOL, "FAQs for H-1B, H-1B1, and E-3 Programs" (July 31, 2015), AILA Doc. No. 15080502. The list can be found at DOL, "ETA 9035CP - Instructions for the 9035 & 9035E Appendix II: Sample of Acceptable Wage Survey Sources," http://bit.ly/9035CPsurveylist.

Copyright © 2017. American Immigration Lawyers Association. All rights reserved.

application because it did not recognize the survey. "[T]he information provided by the employer must be sufficient to ensure that both the survey company name and the survey title are obviously identifiable."[67] If an abbreviation is used, as it often must be, enough information should be shown to identify the survey company and the survey title. It is not necessary to include the year of the survey in the title, as there is a separate space on the form for that.[68] "Other" should be checked for "Prevailing Wage Source."[69]

c. Other Legitimate Source

Third in the DOL ranking, use of "another legitimate source" shifts the burden of showing the legitimacy of the wage to the employer: "the employer will be required to demonstrate the legitimacy of the wage in the event of an investigation."[70] Because the criteria for this type of source are somewhat vague, and because of its lowest ranking in the continuum, use of the "other legitimate source" offers the most risk of challenge to the wage determination itself.

The criteria for other legitimate sources are similar to those for the independent authoritative source. The primary difference is that it need not be a published survey, and the regulation does not specifically dictate how old the data can be. These types of sources must:

- Reflect a weighted average or median wage paid to those similarly employed in the area of intended employment. The regulation states the median option is useable if the source does not provide a weighted average, which leads to the conclusion that, if the source provides both a weighted average and a median, the weighted average should be used;

- Be "based on the most recent and accurate information available"; and

- Be "reasonable and consistent with recognized standards and principles...."[71]

As a matter of practice, these "other" sources are frequently studies commissioned by the employer or a group to which the employer belongs. Indeed, DOL assumes that this category refers to a "custom-made survey."[72] They are most useful when there is no wage survey that meets the criteria for an independent authoritative source, or when an existing survey is too broad or too narrow in terms of the occupational category or area of intended employment.

No other criteria are specified in the regulation, and, as discussed above with respect to independent authoritative sources, the guidance for prevailing wages under Program Electronic Review Management (PERM) is not incorporated by reference to

---

[67] Id.

[68] Id.

[69] Id.

[70] 20 CFR §655.731(a)(2)(ii)(C).

[71] 20 CFR §655.731(b)(3)(iii)(B).

[72] DOL, "FAQs for H-1B, H-1B1, and E-3 Programs" (July 31, 2015), AILA Doc. No. 15080502.

Copyright © 2017. American Immigration Lawyers Association. All rights reserved.

the nonimmigrant context with respect to other legitimate sources. Nonetheless, in an employer-conducted survey, an employer might want to consider using the criteria and suggested methodology in Appendix F of the 2009 Policy Guidance.[73]

DOL instructs that, when using custom-made survey, "Other" should be checked for "Prevailing Wage Source," and the source specified should be the name of the company that conducted the survey followed by the words "Custom Survey."[74] In practice, however, this is at best problematic. It is common to see LCAs denied where the wage source does not match a wage survey already recognized by the DOL system. As a result, an employer seeking to use an employer-conducted survey often will have no choice but to seek a prevailing wage determination to be able to utilize such a survey.

(1) OES Wages

The DOL's Bureau of Labor Statistics maintains and annually updates the OES wage library, which estimates wages paid in various areas of the country for some 800 occupations.[75] Interestingly, DOL seems to regard an OES wage as an "other legitimate source," rather than the higher-ranked "independent authoritative source."[76] As OES data is updated annually, is published online, and is the required default source for a government determination, this is a distinction without a difference. In many cases, even where a private wage survey is submitted to DOL as part of a prevailing wage determination request, the prevailing wage will nevertheless be based upon OES, because DOL will determine that the wage survey is not the best match to the job opportunity.

The INA was amended in 2004[77] to require that any governmental survey DOL makes available to employers or uses to make its own determinations must provide at least four wage levels based on experience, education and level of supervision.[78] If the survey has only two levels, the statute provides a mathematical formula for extrapolating four levels from two.[79] Thus, the OES wage library and NPC determinations operate on a four-level system, with the method for placement within levels being dictated by DOL guidance and FAQs.[80]

---

[73] DOL, "Prevailing Wage Determination Guidance" (Nov. 2009), AILA Doc. No. 10010468.

[74] DOL, "FAQs for H-1B, H-1B1, and E-3 Programs" (July 31, 2015), AILA Doc. No. 15080502.

[75] DOL, "Occupational Employment Statistics," http://www.bls.gov/oes/.

[76] DOL, "FAQs for H-1B, H-1B1, and E-3 Programs" (July 31, 2015), AILA Doc. No. 15080502 ("...A wage rate produced by another legitimate source of information, including the Bureau of Labor Statistics Occupational Employment Statistics Survey (OES) data available through the iCERT Portal System and the FLC Data Center").

[77] L-1 Visa and H-1B Visa Reform Act, enacted as Title IV of the Consolidated Appropriations Act for Fiscal Year 2005, Pub. L. No. 108-447, §423.

[78] INA §212(p)(4).

[79] Id. Don't worry—lawyers are not required to do math. The OES survey provides the results so you don't have to calculate them.

[80] DOL, "Prevailing Wage Determination Guidance" (Nov. 2009), AILA Doc. No. 10010468. See also DOL, "FAQs for H-1B, H-1B1, and E-3 Programs" (July 31, 2015), AILA Doc. No. 15080502, and DOL, "FAQs
Cont'd

Copyright © 2017. American Immigration Lawyers Association. All rights reserved.

Most guidance that has been issued on OES wage levels has been oriented to the permanent labor certification context, but has application to the LCA process as well. The guidance assumes that the OES survey is being used by the government to provide a determination, but in most cases the practitioner will look up the OES wage and state it on the LCA. The prevailing wage may be calculated from the Foreign Labor Certification Data Center Online Wage Library, available at *www.flcdatacenter.com*, by selecting the FLC Wage Search Wizard, the state of intended employment from the drop-down menu, the county of intended employment, and the job code from the drop-down list (or searching by keyword). The job description should be reviewed to ensure it is a good match to the job duties of the proposed nonimmigrant role.

The guidance on how to determine the level of the position uses a point system.[81] The employer using the OES wage library is expected to use the same approach. DOL cautions that this process is not intended to be "automated"[82] or "automatically" applied.[83] Instead, the level "depends on full consideration of the experience, education, and skill required by the employer as indicators of the complexity of the job duties, the level of judgment required, and the amount of supervision involved."[84]

The four wage levels are defined by these factors. See Figure A-B below for how they break down.[85]

Figure A-B

LEVEL	SKILLS, EDUCATION, EXPERIENCE	COMPLEXITY OF DUTIES	JUDGMENT	SUPERVISION
I (Entry)	Beginners	Only basic understanding of occupation. Higher level work only for training and development purposes	Receives specific instructions	Works under close supervision

on FLC Data Center" (undated, posted June 29, 2006), *AILA* Doc. No. 06062961 (hereinafter, "Data Center FAQ").

[81] DOL, "Prevailing Wage Determination Guidance" (Nov. 2009), AILA Doc. No. 10010468.

[82] *Id.*

[83] *Id.*

[84] *Id.*

[85] The chart is based on the factors delineated in Appendix A of the November 2009 Guidance.

Copyright © 2017. American Immigration Lawyers Association. All rights reserved.

LEVEL	SKILLS, EDUCATION, EXPERIENCE	COMPLEXITY OF DUTIES	JUDGMENT	SUPERVISION
II (Qualified)	Requirements for education or experience are generally described in O*NET	Moderately complex. Attained good understanding of occupation through education or experience	Limited	Not specified
III (Experienced)	Requires education or experience at higher O*NET ranges	Attained sound understanding of occupation through education or experience	Requires exercise of judgment	May have supervisory authority or coordinate the activities of others
IV (Fully Competent)	Advanced skills	Diversified knowledge to solve complex problems	Independent evaluation, selection, modification, and application of techniques	Receives only technical guidance. Often has supervisory or management responsibility

In order to classify positions into this grid, DOL instructs that all positions start at 1, then adds points for additional factors based on comparing the employer's job requirements with the general requirements in the O*NET.[86] If no additional factors are added, the wage level is I. Additional factors can take the level up to IV. The level corresponds to the number of points, up to four. The tally can be more than four, but the level will stop at the highest: IV.

DOL has published a worksheet for determining the level.[87] The factors for which points can be added to the initial "1" in the worksheet are experience, education, special skills, and supervisory duties. They are each calculated as follows:[88]

---

[86] DOL, "Prevailing Wage Determination Guidance" (Nov. 2009), AILA Doc. No. 10010468, Appendix A.

[87] *Id.*

[88] *Id.*

Copyright © 2017. American Immigration Lawyers Association. All rights reserved.

1. **Experience**. Start with identifying the job in the O*NET occupational code classification, then identify the overall experience delineated for that occupation by the Specific Vocational Preparation (SVP) system in the O*NET.[89] Then compare that experience amount to the experience required by the employer. For occupations with an O*NET Job Zone of 1, if the employer's requirements match the O*NET SVP, no points are added. If the employer's requirements fall into an SVP of 2, add one point; an SVP of 3, add two points; and an SVP of 4, add three points. For all other Job Zones, no points are added if the employer's experience requirements are at or below the bottom of the SVP range. If the experience requirements are in the low end of the range, add one point. If they are in the high end of the range, add two points. If they are above the range, add three.

2. **Education**. For professional occupations as identified in Appendix A of the preamble to the PERM regulation,[90] Appendix D of the May 9, 2005, Policy Guidance provides a list of the usual education and training. If the employer requirement is less than or equal to the Appendix D amount, no points are added. If the requirement is more by one category (*e.g.*, Appendix D says bachelor's degree, but employer requires a master's) one point is added. If it is more by two categories (*e.g.*, Appendix D requires a bachelor's, but the employer requires a doctoral degree), two points are added. For nonprofessional occupations,[91] use the education level for what is "most of these occupations" or "the occupations usually require" in the O*NET Job Zone. Add one or two points, respectively, if the employer requires one or two levels above the Job Zone educational indication. Experience and education are treated separately for these purposes, but if education is considered as an equivalent to experience, the requirement should be counted only once, in the experience category.[92]

3. **Special skills**. Employer requirements are to be examined to see if they should raise the level. If the skills are not listed in the O*NET, they may still not merit an additional point if they are generally encompassed by the position description. However, if they indicate a higher level of skill, then a point may be in order. License requirements would merit a point only if the requirement indicates that skills above entry level are required. If the license is needed to perform the occupation at the entry level (such as an attorney or teacher), no point should be added. If, however, the license indicates a level of independent judgment, a point might be added. However, DOL emphasizes that if a substantial amount of experience, education or training is needed to get the license, a point should be added only under Experience, Education, or Skills, not under every category. A language requirement may or may not trigger the addition of a point. Ordinarily, it

---

[89] *See* DOL, "Prevailing Wage Determination Guidance" (Nov. 2009), AILA Doc. No. 10010468, Appendix E, for an outline of the meaning of each SVP category. *See also* the discussion of O*NET and SVP in Volume 2: Chapter Two, "The Labor Certification Application."

[90] 69 Fed. Reg. 77325, 77377 (Dec. 27, 2004).

[91] Most of the nonprofessional occupations will not qualify for H-1B, H-1B1, or E-3.

[92] *See Matter of Reed Elsevier, Inc.*, 2008-PER-00201 (BALCA Apr. 13, 2009), *AILA* Doc. No. 09051572.

Copyright © 2017. American Immigration Lawyers Association. All rights reserved.

would be considered a special skill meriting a point, but not if the language skill is intrinsic to the position (such as a teacher of the language or translator), or if the language does not sufficiently increase the seniority or complexity of the position (such as a specialty cook). It should be noted that, in practice, in most cases DOL views a travel requirement as a special skill requiring the addition of a point to the prevailing wage level.

4. **Supervisory duties**. If there is a supervision requirement, a point is added unless the supervision is a customary duty for the O*NET occupation. Once all the points are assigned, they are added together to arrive at the wage level. However, even at this juncture, DOL emphasizes that judgment exercised, complexity of duties, independence of judgment, and amount of supervision must be evaluated and judgment applied to arrive at the appropriate level. Again, the system is not to be utilized automatically.

(2) Special Case for Prevailing Wages: §212(p)(1) Entities

For many years, case law held that academic and nonprofit institutions could obtain prevailing wages by comparison to other similar entities, rather than to industries at large.[93] However, in 1994, BALCA reversed that approach and held that such institutions must compare prevailing wages across all industries.[94] Thus, for example, mathematics professors would be compared to mathematicians in private industry. This created a crisis for academia, which was eventually resolved legislatively in 1998 in the American Competitiveness and Workforce Improvement Act (ACWIA).[95]

Under ACWIA, institutions of higher education as defined in the Higher Education Act of 1965, related or affiliated nonprofits, and nonprofit or governmental research organizations were authorized to take into account only employees at such institutions and organizations in the area of intended employment. Consistent with this statute, BALCA has held that employer-provided wage surveys for employers covered by ACWIA need not sample employers from the various industries covered by ACWIA and that surveys sampling only other institutions of higher education are acceptable for a higher education employer.[96]

The DOL regulation defines institutions of higher education as those "in any state" that:

- Admit only secondary school graduates or the equivalent;
- Are legally authorized to provide post-secondary education;
- Award a bachelor's degree or provide a two-year program acceptable for full credit toward a bachelor's degree;

---

[93] *See Matter of Tuskegee University*, 87 INA 561 (BALCA Feb. 23, 1988) (en banc).

[94] *Matter of Hathaway Children's Services*, 91 INA 388 (BALCA Feb. 4, 1994).

[95] Pub. L. No. 105-277. INA§212(p)(1).

[96] *Matter of University of Michigan*, 2015 PWD 00006 (BALCA Nov. 18, 2015).

Copyright © 2017. American Immigration Lawyers Association. All rights reserved.

- Are public or nonprofit; and

- Are nationally accredited or have been granted pre-accredited status and are on their way to meeting accreditation standards in a reasonable time.[97]

A related or affiliated nonprofit entity must satisfy one of the following criteria:[98]

- Be "connected or associated with an institution of higher education, through shared ownership or control by the same board or federation";

- Be "operated by an institution of higher education"; or

- Be "attached to an institution of higher education as a member, branch, cooperative, or subsidiary."

The connection also can be via an oversight body "with authority to direct the members of" both entities, an agreement "requiring a position to have decision making authority in both entities," or "shared responsibility for conducting the qualifying activity."[99] An example of the latter would be a medical school and hospital that jointly established curricula for medical residents and fellows.[100] Even at that, "the number of cross-designated employees in relation to the total number of employees in the particular program is a relevant factor in establishing affiliation": the larger the proportion within the overall workforce in the occupation of employees "cross-designated" between the institution of higher learning and the requesting employer, the more likely affiliation is to be found.[101]

It is important to note that USCIS has a somewhat different definition of "related or affiliated" in connection with the ACWIA exemptions from the H-1B cap and the ACWIA fee. See Volume 1: Chapter Seven, "H-1B Visas and Status," for a discussion of the USCIS definition. This difference at times can lead to an entity qualifying under ACWIA for one set of rules and not qualifying under the other. DOL has stated that it "is willing to speak with USCIS to try to harmonize the difference in regulatory definitions but noted that there may still be different determinations due to the difference in regulatory definitions."[102]

A nonprofit research organization or a government research organization is defined as a nonprofit primarily engaged in basic or applied research, or a U.S. government entity with a primary mission of promotion or performance of basic or applied research.[103] The regulation contemplates science as the subject of the

---

[97] 20 CFR §656.40(e)(1)(i). While this provision is structured as part of the PERM regulation, the nonimmigrant regulation incorporates the definition at 20 CFR §655.731(a)(2)(vii).

[98] 20 CFR §656.40(e)(1)(ii).

[99] "DOL Updates FAQs on Prevailing Wage Program" (June 21, 2012), AILA Doc. No. 12062154, item 8.

[100] Id.

[101] Id.

[102] "Minutes from DOL PERM/H-1B Stakeholder Meeting" (Dec. 6, 2016), AILA Doc. No. 16122301.

[103] 20 CFR §656.40(e)(1)(iii).

Copyright © 2017. American Immigration Lawyers Association. All rights reserved.

research, and includes social sciences in the scope.[104] It is not sufficient that research be merely one mission of the entity; it must be the primary mission.[105]

To be a nonprofit for these purposes, the entity must have received IRS approval as a tax-exempt organization relating to research or educational purposes. It must also qualify under Internal Revenue Code (IRC) section 501(c)(3), (c)(4), or (c)(6).[106]

DOL has set up within iCert's Online Wage Library an ACWIA database to meet these provisions.[107] It can be used by the government for a determination, or an employer can access it for use as an alternative source (presumably, like the OES wage, an "other legitimate source"). The ACWIA database should be used for all occupations at a covered institution, not just the academic or research-related jobs.[108] If no ACWIA wage is available for the occupation, the "wages for the closest occupation where an ACWIA Higher Education wage is available" should be used.[109]

If a PWD is being sought from the government, it is highly advisable to highlight on the ETA Form 9141 that the employer is eligible for an ACWIA wage: "On the ETA Form 9141 item D.a.6 (Job Duties), after the description of job duties, include the following statement surrounded by asterisks: '***This employer is an institution of higher education or a research entity under 20 CFR 656.40(e).***'"[110]

d. Area of Intended Employment

In reaching the prevailing wage, three elements must be examined: the employer's job description, including the requirements for the position (the considerations for which are discussed above); similarly employed individuals (discussed in the next section); and area of intended employment.[111] To arrive at a prevailing wage, one must compare the employer's job description and requirements to the jobs of similarly employed individuals within the same area of intended employment.

Area of intended employment is the area within "normal commuting distance" of the address where the nonimmigrant will work.[112] Rather than an automatic

---

[104] *Id.*

[105] *Admin'r, Wage & Hour Division v. Dallas VA Medical Center*, 01-077, 081 (ARB, Oct. 3, 2003) (Veterans Affairs hospital that engages in research as part of its provision of services to patients, and receives two to five percent of its funding for research purposes, is primarily engaged in medical care, not research.).

[106] 20 CFR §656.40(e)(2).

[107] DOL, "Welcome to the iCERT Visa Portal System," https://icert.doleta.gov/.

[108] DOL, "FAQs on *Prevailing Wage Determinations for Nonagricultural Programs*" (Aug. 1, 2005), AILA Doc. No. 05081067. Although this FAQ no longer appears on the DOL website, this is still a valid reading of INA §212(p)(1), which refers to "employees" of such institutions without limitation.

[109] DOL, "OFLC Frequently Asked Questions and Answers" (Mar. 15, 2011), https://www. foreignlaborcert.doleta.gov/faqsanswers.cfm. Scroll down to "Prevailing Wage (PERM, H-2B, H-1B, H-1B1 and E-3)," select the drop-down menu for "Alternate Wage Sources," and select question 5.

[110] DOL, "OFLC Frequently Asked Questions and Answers" (Mar. 15, 2011), https://www. foreignlaborcert.doleta.gov/faqsanswers.cfm. Scroll down to "Prevailing Wage (PERM, H-2B, H-1B, H-1B1 and E-3)," select the drop-down menu for "Alternate Wage Sources," and select question 4.

[111] *See* "Prevailing Wage Determination Guidance" (Nov. 2009), AILA Doc. No. 10010468.

[112] INA §§212(n)(4)(A) and (t)(4)(A); 20 CFR §655.715.

Copyright © 2017. American Immigration Lawyers Association. All rights reserved.

mathematical formula, the regulation looks at the overall factual situation of the locality.[113] Metropolitan Statistical Areas (MSAs)[114] provide some definition for what might fall within normal commuting distance. If the place of employment is within an MSA or a Primary Metropolitan Statistical Area (PMSA),[115] any place within the MSA or PMSA is automatically considered within normal commuting distance of the place of employment. However, locations within a Consolidated Metropolitan Statistical Area (CMSA) are not viewed as within normal commuting distance just because they are within the CMSA—some may not be within normal commuting distance.

Conversely, just because a location is outside of an MSA or PMSA or even CMSA, it may still be within normal commuting distance of a location that is inside the MSA, PMSA, or CMSA.[116] However, if a survey is being used that includes data from outside the MSA, or a party is trying to prove in a prevailing wage dispute that such data is valid, it is advisable to marshal evidence that the scope is within normal commuting distance. An article in the local newspaper,[117] documentation from area chambers of commerce, or documentation from a municipality regarding the scope of the commuting distance may be available with a simple online search. The existence of a commuter train that connects the two areas could be intrinsic evidence of the commuting distance, as could carpool-matching websites. Some imagination may be necessary to find the evidence, but in the age of the Internet, it often is there.

If there are no comparable positions within the area of intended employment, the regulation allows the employer to look outside the area of intended employment.[118] However, the geographic scope should not be expanded any further than is necessary to achieve a reasonable sampling.[119]

---

[113] 20 CFR §655.715.

[114] MSAs are defined by the Office of Management and Budget. *See* OMB Bulletin No. 15-01, "Revised Delineations of Metropolitan Statistical Areas, Micropolitan Statistical Areas, and Combined Statistical Areas, and Guidance on Uses of the Delineations of These Areas" (July 15. 2015), https://obamawhitehouse.archives.gov/sites/default/files/omb/bulletins/2015/15-01.pdf.

[115] PMSAs and CMSAs are now considered obsolete terms. OMB, "Update of Statistical Area Definitions and Guidance on Their Usage," (Feb. 22, 2005), Bulletin 05-02, https://obamawhitehouse.archives.gov/omb/bulletins_fy05_b05-02, but DOL continues to use them: "The terminology CMSAs and PMSAs are being replaced by…OMB; however, ETA will continue to recognize the use of these…concepts as well as their replacements." DOL, "Prevailing Wage Determination Guidance" (Nov. 2009) AILA Doc. No. 10010468.

[116] 20 CFR §655.715.

[117] *See* "Washington's Road to Outward Growth," *Washington Post* (Aug. 4, 2004), p. A1.

[118] 20 CFR §655.731(a)(2)(iii)(B).

[119] DOL, L. Jacobs-Simmons, "Availability and Use of Occupational Employment Statistics Survey Data for Alien Labor Certification Prevailing Wage Purposes," GAL 1-00 (May 16, 2000), *AILA* Doc. No. 00052301, Attachment A, Question 11. Although this memo pre-dates the current PERM system, it is still cited in current guidance. *See* DOL, "Prevailing Wage Determination Guidance" (Nov. 2009), AILA Doc. No. 10010468.

Copyright © 2017. American Immigration Lawyers Association. All rights reserved.

e. Similarly Employed

This element of the prevailing wage comparison looks at "substantially comparable jobs in the occupational classification…."[120] In classifying occupations for comparison, DOL generally looks to the Standard Occupation Classification (SOC), which appears as a seven-digit code in the OES. These, in turn, are cross-referenced to the O*NET classification system in DOL's online wage library. The O*NET is often more detailed than the SOC, in that it includes more detailed definitions for positions and provides information on experience and training requirements.[121]

However, if use of the occupational classification does not produce a representative sampling, jobs within the area of intended employment requiring "a substantially similar level of skills" can be utilized for comparison.[122] If there are no substantially comparable jobs in the area of intended employment, comparison with employers outside the area of intended employment is allowed.[123]

4. Stating the Wage

Once the prevailing wage has been obtained, it must be stated on the LCA, as must the wage offered to the beneficiary. The offered wage may be stated as a range, but the bottom of the range can be no lower than the prevailing wage.[124] The prevailing wage needs to be stated in accordance with the wage structure for the position—in other words, if the position is to be paid hourly, an hourly wage should be stated; if based on an annual wage, an annual wage stated. However, if the position is part time, the wage must always be stated as hourly.[125] If the prevailing wage determination was expressed in some other form, the employer can convert to the appropriate expression of the wage on the basis that there are 2,080 work hours in a year. Thus, a prevailing wage determination that was expressed as an hourly rate can be converted to an annual rate by multiplying by 2,080, and a determination expressed as an annual rate can be made hourly by dividing by 2,080.[126]

5. Documentation of the Prevailing Wage

The public access file should include documentation of the prevailing wage determination. The documentation need not be the specific wage data—a general description of the source and methodology is all that is required for the public file—but the underlying wage data must be retained and made available to DOL in an

---

[120] 20 CFR §655.731(a)(2)(iii).

[121] DOL, "FAQs on FLC Data Center" (undated) *AILA* Doc. No. 06062961.

[122] DOL does not indicate what would or would not constitute a representative sampling. "Prevailing Wage Determination Guidance" (Nov. 2009), AILA Doc. No. 10010468 at Appendix F "suggests" a sampling of at least three employers and at least 30 workers.

[123] 20 CFR §655.731(a)(2)(iii)(A) and (B).

[124] 20 CFR §655.731(a)(2)(v).

[125] DOL, "FAQs on H-1B, H-1B1, and E-3 Programs Round 1" (Feb. 17, 2011), AILA Doc. No. 11021867, p. 12.

[126] 20 CFR §655.731(a)(2)(vi).

Copyright © 2017. American Immigration Lawyers Association. All rights reserved.

investigation.[127] However, where a government determination or published survey was used, often the document itself is the best documentation for the public file, and the easiest to provide.

The underlying documentation may consist of:

- The government determination;
- A copy of the wage survey;
- The Davis-Bacon or Service Contract Act determination; or
- The relevant excerpt from the union contract.[128]

B. Actual Wage

Actual wage is the amount paid by the employer to its own employees who have experience and qualifications similar to the H-1B nonimmigrant's "for the specific employment in question at the place of employment."[129] "Specific employment" means the "set of duties and responsibilities performed or to be performed by the ... nonimmigrant"—in other words, those with the same job duties as the nonimmigrant's. "Place of employment" is "the worksite or physical location where the work actually is performed."[130]

Thus, to determine the actual wage, the employer must look at its other employees in the same location where the nonimmigrant will work, and identify the individuals or the class of individuals performing the same duties as the nonimmigrant. That universe is then further narrowed to those with similar experience and qualifications to the nonimmigrant's. In making this evaluation, the employer may consider such factors as "experience, qualifications, education, job responsibility and function, specialized knowledge, and other legitimate business factors." "Legitimate business factors" are defined as attributes that "it is reasonable to conclude are necessary because they conform to recognized principles or can be demonstrated by accepted rules and standards."[131]

In making these comparisons, job title alone may not be dispositive.[132] Instead, the regulation anticipates examination of the responsibility and function of the job rather than its title. Thus, an employee could be considered comparable even if the job titles are different, provided the major tasks of the two jobs are substantially the same. For example, a process engineer and a chemist who both test chemical processes for a factory might be considered to have comparable jobs for actual wage purposes.

Conversely, two employees with the same job title may not be at all comparable if the major tasks of the job are not substantially the same. An example would be two

---

[127] 20 CFR §655.760(a)(4).

[128] 20 CFR §655.731(b)(3).

[129] INA §§212(n)(1)(A)(i)(I) and (t)(1)(A)(i)(I); 20 CFR §655.715.

[130] 20 CFR §655.715.

[131] 20 CFR §655.731(a)(1).

[132] 57 Fed. Reg. 1316, 1319 (Jan. 13, 1992).

Copyright © 2017. American Immigration Lawyers Association. All rights reserved.

process engineers at the same factory where one tests chemical processes and the other deals with automated work flows.

So what happens if there are no other comparable employees? Then, the actual wage is the amount paid to the nonimmigrant.[133] But what is meant by "amount paid to" the nonimmigrant? It is not the amount contractually agreed to between the employer and the nonimmigrant. [134] Nor is it the amount indicated on the LCA. DOL administrative decisions have found it to be the amount that the employer paid in fact to the nonimmigrant, notwithstanding what was stated on the LCA.[135] Where no wages were ever paid, and no comparable workers exist, generally the prevailing wage is used as the actual wage.[136]

On the other hand, what happens if there are multiple employees who are considered comparable, and they all receive different wages? After all, only H-1B, E-3, and H-1B1 nonimmigrants are required to be paid the higher of the prevailing or actual wage—there is no such requirement for U.S. employees or other nonimmigrant employees.[137] The employer should not use an average of wages paid to arrive at the actual wage.[138] Instead, the employer needs to show how the wage set for the nonimmigrant relates to the wages paid to the comparable employees—in other words, the employer must consider what factors it takes into account in setting wages and how the nonimmigrant fits into those factors.[139]

---

[133] 20 CFR §655.731(a)(1).

[134] *See Galal v. Z&A Infotek Corp.*, 2008-LCA-00010 (ALJ, May 13, 2008), AILA Doc. No. 08072469 (stating that DOL's "enforcement power is limited to the terms contained within the LCA, and does not extend to enforce private contractual agreements, such as the terms or subsequent changes in terms, of an offer letter").

[135] *E.g., Admin'r, Wage & Hour Div. v. Efficiency3 Corp.*, 15-005, 2014-LCA-7 (ARB Aug. 4, 2016) (In a case in which there were no other comparable workers, "[t]he actual wage was $46,000 per year because that was what Efficiency3 paid Mr. Liu from the time he began work under the H-1B visa."); *Mao v. Nasser*, 2005-LCA-36 (ALJ May 26, 2006), *aff'd* 06-121 (ARB Nov. 26, 2008), AILA Doc. No. 08072962, citing *Admin'r, Wage & Hour Div. v. Novinvest, LLC*, 2002-LCA-24 (ALJ Jan. 21, 2003). In *Mao*, an employer that for a period consistently paid a salary higher than the LCA amount, then later reverted to a lesser amount, was required to pay the higher amount as the actual wage.

[136] *Chellandurai v. Infinite Solutions, Inc.*, 03-072 (ARB Apr. 26, 2006), AILA Doc. No. 08080765 (DOL relied on the prevailing wage to award back pay where no wages were ever paid, and thus no actual wage rate was ever established).

[137] An earlier iteration of DOL's regulation did indeed require that employers have an objective wage system that seemed to require that employers adhere to at least the actual wage for all employees, regardless of immigration status. 20 CFR Subpart H, Appendix A (1993). This, along with a number of other provisions of that regulation, was struck down by the U.S. District Court for the District of Columbia in *National Ass'n of Manufacturers v. Dept. of Labor*, Civ. No. 95-0175 (D.D.C. July 22, 1996), AILA Doc. No. 96010359.

[138] 20 CFR §655.715.

[139] 20 CFR §655.731(b)(2). *See also DOL v. Kutty*, 03-022 (ARB May 31, 2005), AILA Doc. No. 08072576, *aff'd Kutty v. U.S. Dep't of Labor*, 764 F.3d 540 (6th Cir. 2014). (not all 17 H-1B nonimmigrant doctors had the same qualifications or specialties, and thus they were not all entitled to the same wage).

Copyright © 2017. American Immigration Lawyers Association. All rights reserved.

1. Changes in the Actual Wage

Although the INA states that both elements of the required wage—prevailing wage and actual wage—are to be established "as of the time of filing the application,"[140] DOL's regulation applies this timing only to the prevailing wage.[141] For actual wage, the regulation requires that, where the employer's pay system provides for adjustments during the period of the LCA, those adjustments are to be made to the nonimmigrant's pay,[142] thus requiring a subsequent review of what is the actual wage and whether the nonimmigrant is receiving it. In addition, if the employer's wage system changes during the LCA validity period, the employer is required by the regulation to retain documentation of the change in the system and show that the nonimmigrant is still earning the higher of the prevailing wage or the actual wage under the changed system.[143] Further, if there are no comparable workers, and thus the beneficiary's wage is the actual wage, if that employee's pay increases during the course of the employment, the actual wage thus also increases, and cannot then be reduced, because the increased amount has established a new actual wage.[144]

2. Documenting Establishment of the Actual Wage

In addition to the prevailing wage documentation, employers are required to retain documentation in their LCA files showing how they established the actual wage. That documentation needs to show how the wage for the nonimmigrant relates to the wages of the employees determined to be comparable using the analysis discussed above.[145] The documentation in the public access file need not refer to the amounts of the wages themselves, but should be as clear an explanation as possible of the system used to set the wages paid to the nonimmigrant and comparable workers, including how wage adjustments are determined.[146] Generally, this requirement can be met with a memo to file setting out the factors that are considered in setting wages, such as levels of experience, credit for education, additional managerial or supervisory responsibility, special skills or background meriting special pay consideration, as well as other less objective factors that can influence pay, such as reputation in the field.

While the explanation of the system used to establish the actual wage, including a summary of the system for pay increases, must be in the public access file, documentation comparing wages to other workers need only be provided to DOL in an investigation.[147]

---

[140] INA §§212(n)(1)(A)(i) and (t)(1)(A)(i).

[141] 20 CFR §655.731(a)(2).

[142] 20 CFR §655.731(a)(1).

[143] 20 CFR §655.731(b)(2).

[144] *Admin'r, Wage & Hour Div. v. Efficiency3 Corp.*, 15-005, 2014-LCA-7 (ARB Aug. 4, 2016).

[145] *Id.*

[146] 20 CFR §655.760(a)(3).

[147] *Id.*

Copyright © 2017. American Immigration Lawyers Association. All rights reserved.

C. Benefits

Under the statutory scheme, it is a violation of the required wage provisions to fail to offer benefits to the nonimmigrant "on the same basis, and in accordance with the same criteria, as the employer offers to United States workers."[148] This provision overlaps with the second attestation element, requiring provision of working conditions that will not adversely affect the working conditions of those similarly employed. In fact, the regulation's recitation of the working conditions attestation contains the same language as is contained in the statute with respect to provision of benefits to meet the required wage attestation.[149]

What are considered to be benefits? Reason would say anything that the employer would hold out to potential employees as compensation beyond regular wages. And, indeed, the regulation points specifically to benefits "provided as compensation for services" and gives as examples a typical menu of employer-offered benefits: bonuses, stock options, paid leave, insurance, and retirement plans.[150]

What is meant by "on the same basis, and in accordance with the same criteria"? Eligibility requirements cannot be stricter for the nonimmigrant than they are for U.S. workers who are similarly employed. An "apples-to-apples" comparison is needed, such as comparing full-time workers to full-time workers, and part-time to part-time. DOL does caution in its regulation that nonimmigrants should not be denied benefits as temporary employees by virtue of their nonimmigrant status. It is acceptable under the regulation to offer nonimmigrants greater benefits, but care must be taken not to run afoul of anti-discrimination laws in so doing.[151]

The nonimmigrant does not, however, have to choose to receive the same benefits as the employer's U.S. workers, as long as the same benefits package is at least offered.[152] Thus, a nonimmigrant may opt to receive cash in lieu of a particular benefit.[153] Also, if the employer is part of a multinational entity, and the nonimmigrant is in the United States for 90 consecutive calendar days or less, the nonimmigrant can stay on the benefits program for the home country, provided reciprocal treatment is offered for U.S. workers temporarily stationed abroad. However, if there is a pattern of the nonimmigrant continually leaving the United States just shy of the 90-day cutoff then returning, this exception cannot be used.[154]

The nonimmigrant also can be kept on the home country's benefits plan even if he is in the United States longer than the 90 days, provided:

---

[148] INA §§212(n)(2)(C)(viii) and (t)(3)(C)(viii).

[149] 20 CFR §655.730(d)(2). *Compare with* INA §§212(n)(2)(C)(viii) and (t)(3)(C)(viii).

[150] 20 CFR §655.731(c)(3).

[151] 20 CFR §655.731(c)(3)(i).

[152] *Mao v. Nasser*, 2005-LCA-36 (ALJ May 26, 2008), *aff'd* 06-121 (ARB Nov. 26, 2008), AILA Doc. No. 08072962, p.20.

[153] 20 CFR §655.731(c)(3)(ii).

[154] 20 CFR §655.731(c)(3)(iii)(B).

Copyright © 2017. American Immigration Lawyers Association. All rights reserved.

- The nonimmigrant continues to be employed in the home country with the employer or "a corporate affiliate" (presumably, because of the use of the adjective "corporate" this is not intended to have the same meaning as an L-1 "affiliate," but instead is meant to signal a related company);

- The home country benefits are equivalent to "or equitably comparable to" the U.S. benefits;

- The nonimmigrant is actually enrolled in the home country plan;

- Reciprocal treatment is offered to U.S. workers stationed abroad;

- If health benefits are offered to U.S. workers, the same plan is offered to the nonimmigrants if the home country health benefits otherwise would not provide the same coverage as the United States plan for medical treatment in the United States; and

- The nonimmigrant is offered those U.S. benefits that are paid directly to the worker, such as paid leave.[155]

D. Documenting Payment of Wages

While not required to be kept in the public access file, documentation of the fact that the required wages were paid—in other words, payroll records—must be retained for DOL inspection in the case of an investigation. In practice, these are often reviewed not only in the course of a DOL Wage and Hour investigation relating to the LCA, but also in a routine site visit conducted by the Department of Homeland Security's (DHS) Fraud Detection and National Security Directorate.

Similarly, payroll records for other employees in the specific employment in question at the place of employment also must be retained and shown to DOL in an investigation to document satisfaction of the actual wage requirement.[156] Note that the payroll documentation requirement does not include reference to experience and qualifications. It refers only to the specific employment in question and the place of employment. This means that the documentation must be kept and provided not only for all the employees who were found comparable for actual wage purposes, but for those with similar duties at the same worksite who do not necessarily have the same experience and qualifications. The wage information must be kept to cover the period from submission of the LCA and continuing throughout the period of employment of the nonimmigrant, and must be kept for three years from the date of creation unless they are the subject of an investigation, in which case they must be kept through the period of the investigation.[157]

---

[155] 20 CFR §655.731(c)(3)(iii)(C).

[156] 20 CFR §655.731(b)(1).

[157] 20 CFR §655.760(c).

Copyright © 2017. American Immigration Lawyers Association. All rights reserved.

The payroll records must include names, home addresses, occupations, rate of pay, hours worked each day and week if non-salaried or part-time, additions and deductions from pay, and total amount paid each pay period.[158]

In addition, to satisfy the benefits element of the required wage, documentation of the benefits offered to the nonimmigrant must be kept and shown to DOL on request. This includes a copy of benefit descriptions/employee handbooks; a copy of benefit plans and any rules for differentiating benefits among employees; evidence of the benefits actually provided, including what was actually selected or declined, by both U.S. and nonimmigrant workers; and, where a nonimmigrant is provided with home country benefits, evidence of the benefits provided before and after the nonimmigrant came to the United States.[159]

E. When the Required Wage Must Be Paid

DOL requires that the required wage be paid to the nonimmigrant worker "cash in hand, free and clear, when due":[160]

- *Cash in hand.* This means that the required amount must actually be paid to the nonimmigrant as cash wages. To qualify as cash wages, the payments must be shown on the employer's payroll[161] and reported to the Internal Revenue Service (IRS) (with appropriate withholdings for taxes and payments for the Federal Insurance Contributions Act (FICA)) as earnings,[162] and payments must be reported and documented as the employee's earnings with employee and employer taxes paid to all other appropriate governmental entities. FICA payments are not required if the nonimmigrant is a citizen of a country that has a totalization agreement with the United States and the documentation shows that all appropriate reports have been filed and taxes paid in the employee's home country. Future bonuses and similar compensation may be credited toward satisfying the required wage if payment of these is not conditional on an event or circumstance such as attainment of a certain level of sales.[163]

- *Free and clear.* No unauthorized deductions from the nonimmigrant's wages may be made.[164] Authorized and unauthorized deductions are discussed in greater detail later in this chapter.

---

[158] 20 CFR §655.731(b)(1).

[159] 20 CFR §655.731(b)(1)(viii).

[160] 20 CFR §655.731(c)(1) and (2).

[161] *Admin'r, Wage & Hour Division v. Avenue Dental Care*, 07-101 (ARB Jan. 7, 2010), AILA Doc. No. 10070930, stating that draws paid under a business agreement, and not shown in payroll records, are not H-1B wages.

[162] *Admin'r, Wage & Hour Division v. Itek Consulting, Inc.*, 2008-LCA-00046 (ALJ May 6, 2009), AILA Doc. No. 09051463. Paychecks showing payment of required wage were rejected as evidence where wages reported to the IRS showed a lesser amount.

[163] 20 CFR §655.731(c)(2).

[164] 20 CFR §655.731(c)(1). *See also* 20 CFR §655.731(c)(9).

Copyright © 2017. American Immigration Lawyers Association. All rights reserved.

- *When due.* DOL's regulation specifies the pattern by which nonimmigrant workers covered by LCAs must be paid. Salaried employees must be paid in prorated installments no less often than monthly. There are two exceptions to this rule: (1) The salary can be supplemented by other non-discretionary payments to meet the required wage (the example given is a quarterly bonus), in which case the employer's documentation must show the commitment to make the payments, that the obligation was met for prior pay periods, and that upon payment the required wage will be met for each current or future pay period; and (2) Educational institutions with an established practice of paying those in the same occupational classification an annual salary over a compressed period of less than 12 months may continue to do so, provided the nonimmigrant agrees to the payment schedule prior to starting work and the practice would not "otherwise" cause the nonimmigrant to violate status.[165]

F. Prohibition Against "Benching"

The practice commonly referred to as "benching" occurs when an employee is taken out of active employment status and is not paid, or is paid less than a full salary—in other words, "put on the bench." Concerns about this practice led Congress to enact in ACWIA a prohibition against its use for H-1Bs,[166] which later was applied to the other LCA-subject nonimmigrant categories when they were added.[167] Under the statutory formulation, it is a violation of the wage obligation to fail to pay the required wage to a full-time employee who is subject to an LCA and who has been placed in nonproductive status due to a decision by the employer (such as because of insufficient business volume)[168] or because of a lack of license or permit. With respect to a part-time employee subject to an LCA, failure to pay the required wage for the number of hours designated on the I-129 petition in the same circumstances would be a violation.[169] If a range of hours is shown on the I-129, the employer is required to pay at least the average number of hours worked by the nonimmigrant, provided that average is within the range. If the average number of hours is below the bottom of the range, payment for the minimum number of hours in the range is required.[170]

This obligation begins when the nonimmigrant "enters into employment."[171] Entry into employment occurs when the individual first makes himself available for work

---

[165] INA §§212(n)(2)(C)(vii)(V) and (t)(3)(C)(vii)(V); 20 CFR §655.731(c)(4).

[166] American Competitiveness and Workforce Improvement Act of 1998 (ACWIA), Pub. L. No. 105-277 §413.

[167] Enacted as INA §212(t)(3)(C)(vii).

[168] *See, e.g., Admin'r, Wage & Hour Division v. Help Foundation of Omaha, Inc.,* 07-008 (ARB Dec. 31, 2008), AILA Doc. No. 09011570 (posted Jan. 15, 2009).

[169] INA §§212(n)(2)(C)(vii) and 212(t)(3)(C)(vii). 20 CFR §655.731(c)(7)(i).

[170] 20 CFR §655.731(c)(7)(i).

[171] INA §§212(n)(2)(C)(vii)(III) and (t)(3)(C)(vii)(III). 20 CFR §655.731(c)(6).

Copyright © 2017. American Immigration Lawyers Association. All rights reserved.

or comes under the control of the employer.[172] Awaiting an assignment, meeting with a customer, or studying for a licensing examination are all considered to be actions rendering an individual under the control of an employer or available for work.[173]

Regardless of whether the nonimmigrant has entered into employment, the obligation to begin paying the required wage takes effect in any event as of 30 days after a nonimmigrant is first admitted to the United States under the petition, or, if the nonimmigrant is present in the United States on the date the petition is approved, 60 days after the nonimmigrant becomes eligible to work.[174] A nonimmigrant present in the United States when the petition is approved is considered to have become eligible for work either on the date of need stated on the approved petition, or the date of "adjustment" of the individual's status, whichever date is later.[175]

It is important to note how the 30–/60-day rule is formulated in juxtaposition to the "entry into employment" rule. Essentially, if the nonimmigrant makes him– or herself available for employment before the 30 or 60 days run, even if the employer is not yet ready, the employer must begin paying the nonimmigrant or risk the consequences of violating the no-benching rule.[176]

Under the American Competitiveness in the 21st Century Act of 2000 (AC21),[177] a nonimmigrant who was previously provided H-1B status is authorized to accept new employment upon the filing of a new petition. An early DOL administrative appeal decision indicated that the no-benching obligation can be triggered for a new employer by the *filing* of an H-1B petition requesting change of employer, if the nonimmigrant has made him– or herself available for work at that point.[178] However, a later decision by the same administrative appellate body indicated that the benching provision should be triggered only if the beneficiary had worked under AC21 portability:

"On its face, this portability provision merely 'authorizes' an H-1B worker to accept employment if he qualifies to do so...; it does not address the employer's payment obligations during the portability period.... [T]he portability provisions

---

[172] 20 CFR §655.731(c)(6)(i).

[173] *Id. See also Vojtisek-Lom v. Clean Air Technologies Int'l Inc.*, 2006-LCA-00009 (ALJ June 18, 2007), AILA Doc. No. 0872564.

[174] INA §§212(n)(2)(C)(vii)(III) and (t)(3)(C)(vii)(III). 20 CFR §655.731(c)(6)(ii).

[175] 20 CFR §655.731(c)(6)(ii). *See also Rajan v. Int'l Business Solutions, Ltd.*, 03-104 (ARB Aug. 14, 2004), AILA Doc. No. 08080666. "Adjustment" here does not refer to the change from nonimmigrant status to permanent residence discussed in Volume 2: Chapter Four, "Consular Processing, Adjustment of Status, and Permanent Residence Issues." Instead, it refers to a change from one nonimmigrant status to another and perhaps also to amendments such as a change of employer.

[176] INA §§212(n)(2)(C)(vii)(III) and (t)(3)(C)(vii)(III) apply the 30– and 60-day rules only where the nonimmigrant has "not yet entered into employment."

[177] Pub. L. No. 106-313.

[178] *Chellandurai v. Infinite Solutions, Inc.*, No. 03-072 (ARB Apr. 26, 2006), AILA Doc. No. 08080765 (employer never "found work for" the nonimmigrant, and was found liable for back pay starting from the date the H-1B petition was filed, when the nonimmigrant made herself available for work); *Mao v. Nasser*, 2005-LCA-36 (ALJ, May 26, 2006), AILA Doc. No. 08072962.

Copyright © 2017. American Immigration Lawyers Association. All rights reserved.

permit the H-1B employer and the H-1B employee to decide whether to work together while the H-1B petition is pending approval by USCIS. Consequently, in the absence of mandatory employment provisions, we find that it is the H-1B employee's burden to prove that he qualifies…to work for a new employer during a portability phase *and* that he engaged in compensable activities for such employer."[179]

What may have made a difference in the two decisions is the degree to which the beneficiary was available for work. In the earlier case, the nonimmigrant had moved to the employer's location upon filing of the petition, and thus was clearly available for work. Also, she never actually started working, because the employer never found an assignment for her. In the later case, it was disputed whether the beneficiary was still working for his prior employer during the portability period, although the DOL's Administrative Review Board (ARB) noted that an H-1B beneficiary is authorized to work for both during this period, and the beneficiary did indeed enter into work for the petitioner after the petition was approved.

E-3s and H-1B1s are not eligible for AC21 portability, so they would not be subject to this concern.[180]

An exception to the obligation to pay during nonproductive periods is when the nonimmigrant becomes nonproductive for non-work related factors, such as a voluntary request for leave or circumstances rendering the individual unable to work.[181] These factors must be unrelated to employment and at the nonimmigrant's "voluntary request and convenience," or must "render the nonimmigrant unable to work." Examples of circumstances that would not be considered benching are surgery and recovery,[182] touring the United States, caring for a sick relative, maternity leave, or an automobile accident which temporarily incapacitates the nonimmigrant.[183] On the other hand, lack of assigned work, lack of a license,[184] or lack of a Social Security number[185] are considered work-related factors, and a failure to pay wages in these situations would be regarded as prohibited benching.

Payment obligations cease where there has been a "bona fide termination of the employment relationship." Rather than define this term, the DOL regulation passively states that "DHS regulations require the employer to notify the DHS that the

---

[179] *Gupta v. Compunnel Software Group, Inc.*, 12-049, 2011-LCA-45 (ARB May 29, 2014).

[180] Pub. L. No. 106-313.

[181] INA §§212(n)(2)(C)(vii)(IV) and (t)(3)(C)(vii)(IV). 20 CFR §655.731(c)(7)(ii).

[182] *See Vojtisek-Lom v. Clean Air Technologies Int'l Inc.*, 2006-LCA-00009 (ALJ June 18, 2007), AILA Doc. No. 08072564 and *Rajan v. Int'l Business Solutions, Ltd.*, 03-104 (ARB Aug. 14, 2004), AILA Doc. No. 08080666.

[183] 20 CFR §655.731(c)(7)(ii).

[184] 20 CFR §655.731(c)(7)(i).

[185] *Admin'r, Wage & Hour Division v. Itek Consulting, Inc.*, 2008-LCA-00046 (ALJ May 6, 2009), AILA Doc. No. 09051463; *Admin'r, Wage & Hour Division v. University of Miami, Miller School of Medicine*, 10-90, 93, 2009-LCA-26 (Dec. 20, 2011).

Copyright © 2017. American Immigration Lawyers Association. All rights reserved.

employment relationship has been terminated so that the petition is canceled (8 CFR §214.2(h)(11)), and require the employer to provide the employee with payment for transportation home under certain circumstances (8 CFR §214.2(h)(4)(iii)(E))."[186]

Administrative appeal decisions have found that to show a bona fide termination, an employer should "demonstrate that it: (1) expressly terminated the employment relationship with the H-1B worker; (2) notified USCIS of the termination so that the petition could be cancelled; and (3) provided the worker with the reasonable cost of return transportation to his or her home country."[187] If the employer notifies DHS of a termination, but behaves in a way that suggests an ongoing employment relationship, DOL may conclude that a bona fide termination has not occurred.[188] The notification to DHS does not necessarily have to come from the employer—the beneficiary's notice to the agency may suffice.[189] Notification to DOL does not suffice.[190]

Even if the employer did not effect a bona fide termination for compensation obligation purposes, the statute of limitations period for filing a complaint, discussed later in this chapter, may begin to run if the nonimmigrant is given final and definitive notice of the termination of employment, regardless of whether DHS was notified.[191]

G. Deductions from Wages

Any unauthorized deduction from wages would be considered non-payment of the wage amount, and could subject the employer to back pay awards, plus civil damages and debarment if the non-payment is willful.[192] The regulation is structured so as to indicate that the only deductions from pay that are allowed are the ones that are specifically authorized by the regulation. Those authorized deductions are:

- Those that are required by law, such as taxes and Social Security;[193]

---

[186] 20 CFR §655.731(c)(7)(ii).

[187] *DeDios v. Medical Dynamic Systems, Inc.*, 2013-LCA-9 (May 17, 2016), AILA Doc. No. 16052512, citing *Amtel Group of Florida, Inc. v. Yongmahapakorn*, 04-087 (ARB Sept. 26, 2006), AILA Doc. No. 06102310. *See also Admin'r, Wage & Hour Division v. Pegasus Consulting Group, Inc.*, 03-032 (ARB June 30, 2005), AILA Doc. No. 05070562.

[188] *See, e.g., Innawalli v. American Information Technology Corp.*, 2004-LCA-13 (ARB Sept. 29, 2006), AILA Doc. No. 08080672 (after notifying INS of termination, company continued to market beneficiary's expertise to clients) and *Mao v. Nasser*, 2005-LCA-36 (ALJ May 26, 2006), AILA Doc. No. 08072962 (agreement to grant personal leave, taken together with failure to notify DHS, evidences an ongoing employment relationship).

[189] *Vojtisek-Lom v. Clean Air Technologies Int'l Inc.*, 2006-LCA-00009 (ALJ June 18, 2007), AILA Doc. No. 0872564 (*posted* July 25, 2008).

[190] *Admin'r, Wage & Hour Division v. Help Foundation of Omaha, Inc.*, 07-008 (ARB Dec. 31, 2008), AILA Doc. No. 09011570.

[191] *Ndiaye v. CVS Store No. 6081*, 05-024 (ARB May 9, 2007), AILA Doc. No. 08080762.

[192] 20 CFR §655.731(c)(11).

[193] 20 CFR §655.731(c)(9)(i).

Copyright © 2017. American Immigration Lawyers Association. All rights reserved.

- Those that are authorized by union agreement or that are "reasonable and customary in the occupation and/or area of employment."[194] Any such deduction must meet four additional criteria:

  - It may not recoup the employer's business expense. Costs associated with the LCA and H-1B, such as attorney's fees, are explicitly treated as such a business expense.

  - It must have been revealed prior to the start of employment.

  - If it was a condition of employment, it must have been clearly identified as such.

  - It cannot be charged only against nonimmigrants—if there are U.S. workers, they must also be subject to the deduction.

- Deductions that may not fall into either of the above categories, if they meet five specific criteria:[195]

  - The deduction is in accordance with a voluntary written authorization from the employee. Mere acceptance of a job with this condition, even if stated in writing, is not enough.

  - The deduction is principally for the benefit of the employee. Food and housing would be such benefit, provided the employee is not on travel status (see discussion of temporary changes of worksite later in this chapter), or the arrangement is not principally for the convenience of the employer.

  - The deduction is not a recoupment of the employer's business expense. Items like equipment, transportation that is part of the employment, and attorneys' fees and other costs associated with the employer's functions in the LCA/petitioning process would be considered such a recoupment.

  - The amount does not exceed the lower of the actual cost or the fair market value.

  - The amount does not exceed garnishment limits in Consumer Credit Protection Act and its regulations (generally, 25 percent of disposable earnings).

In addition to direct deductions from wages, DOL prohibits imposition of the employer's business expenses on the nonimmigrant employee "even if the matter is not shown in the employer's payroll records as a deduction."[196] Thus, the amount does not have to be actually taken from pay to be considered a deduction. The

---

[194] 20 CFR §655.731(c)(9)(ii).

[195] 20 CFR §655.731(c)(9)(iii). *See also Admin'r, Wage & Hour Div. v. Prism Enterprises of Central Florida*, 01-080 (ARB Nov. 25, 2003), AILA Doc. No. 08080667 ($30,000 paid by the beneficiary as an "opportunity cost" under a written agreement not a deduction from wages).

[196] 20 CFR §655.731(c)(12).

Copyright © 2017. American Immigration Lawyers Association. All rights reserved.

employer can merely require, or even allow, the nonimmigrant employee to pay the expense in order for it to be considered an unauthorized deduction.[197]

DOL's regulation seems to hold as automatically suspect deductions that are made for repayment of loans or wage advances, placing the burden onto the employer of showing the legitimacy and purpose of the loan or advance and that any such deductions for repayment meet all five criteria of the third category of deductions above.[198]

Although the regulatory section on deductions seems to read as though there is an absolute prohibition on what DOL terms imposition of the employer's business expenses, the prohibition is within the context of a discussion of meeting the required wage. Thus, it would seem that these deductions would be disallowed only to the extent that they do not decrease the nonimmigrant's wages below the required wage. DOL, in the preamble to the interim final regulation on the subject, confirmed this reading:

> "An H-1B employer is prohibited from imposing its business expenses on the H-1B worker—including attorney fees and other expenses associated with the filing of an LCA and H-1B petition—only to the extent that the assessment would reduce the H-1B worker's pay below the required wage, *i.e.*, the higher of the prevailing wage and the actual wage."[199]

As a practical matter, this distinction between an absolute prohibition on deductions and a prohibition only against reducing the wage below the required wage may be irrelevant in many cases. Because the required wage is the higher of the actual or the prevailing wage, and because if there are no comparable employees for actual wage purposes, the actual wage is what is paid to the nonimmigrant, and the result is a prohibition against any reduction of the nonimmigrant's wage when there are no comparable employees for actual wage purposes.[200]

There is considerable question as to the legitimacy of the prohibition against payment of attorney fees by the beneficiary,[201] particularly given the need by the individual for representation of his or her interests and the fact that the individual is the primary party in interest of the entire process. Nevertheless, DOL has held firm in

---

[197] 65 Fed. Reg. 80109, 80199 (Dec. 20, 2000): "An employer cannot avoid its wage requirements by paying an employee a check at the required wage and then accepting a prohibited payment from a worker either directly, or indirectly through the worker's payment of an expense which is the employer's responsibility."

[198] 20 CFR §655.731(c)(13).

[199] 65 Fed. Reg. 80109, 80199 (Dec. 20, 2000). *See also Admin'r, Wage & Hour Div. v. Woodmen of the World Life Insurance Society*, 2016-LCA18 (ALJ Oct. 26, 2016), AILA Doc. No. 16103105.

[200] *Admin'r, Wage & Hour Div. v. Woodmen of the World Life Insurance Society*, 2016-LCA18 (ALJ Oct. 26, 2016), AILA Doc. No. 16103105. While not reaching the question of whether there were other comparable employees, the ALJ presumed throughout the decision that the actual wage would be the amount paid to the nonimmigrant if there were no comparable employees, and would be based on the wages of three other employees if in fact they were comparable. However, the case was decided on other grounds.

[201] *See, e.g.*, "Comment of the American Immigration Lawyers Association to the Interim Final Rule Regarding the H-1B Program," AILA Doc. No. 01051407.

Copyright © 2017. American Immigration Lawyers Association. All rights reserved.

its position, and has since imposed it on the permanent labor certification,[202] H-2A,[203] and H-2B[204] processes.

A Federal circuit court has upheld the extension of the prohibition to expenses that might ordinarily be considered the individual nonimmigrant's expense, i.e., the costs for obtaining a waiver of the J-1 home residency requirement.[205] However, the court left the door open as to whether other sets of facts would produce the same result, instead finding the employees' payment of the costs inappropriate where:

> "[A]ll but one of the doctors, who happened to have a green card, were nonimmigrant physicians hired under contracts that made their employment contingent on their receipt of both an H-1B visa and a J-1 waiver. In addition, as the ARB [Administrative Review Board] observed, the record supports that in most cases, either Kutty or his in-house attorney pressured the physicians to hire HealthIMPACT, which apparently had some relationship to Kutty, to process their applications for the J-1 waivers. Under these facts, the ARB's conclusion that the Administrator did not err in including the physicians' J-1 waiver application costs as a business expense is adequately supported."[206]

The court stated, however:

> "We note that we understand the ARB's decision on the J-1 waiver expenses to be based on the facts of this case and the propriety of the remedy based on those facts, and not a determination that the Administrator has the discretion to treat J-1 waiver expenses as business expenses of the employer in every case, regardless of the facts. We will not assume that the ARB would so decide, and leave that question to a case in which it is properly presented."[207]

These prohibitions against payment of the expenses of the nonimmigrant process are an invention of DOL, and are not part of the statute, with one exception. Congress did prohibit requiring the beneficiary to pay the $1500/$750 "training fee" either directly or through a reimbursement scheme.[208] Violation of this statutory prohibition can result in a $1,000 penalty and an ordered return of the money to the nonimmigrant under the statutory scheme. However, the regulation expands this penalty to also provide for other possible civil penalties, including debarment, in cases of willful violation.[209]

---

[202] 72 Fed. Reg. 27903 (May 17, 2007).

[203] 20 CFR §655.135(j).

[204] 20 CFR §655.22(j).

[205] *Kutty v. U.S. Dep't of Labor*, 764 F.3d 540 (6th Cir. 2014), AILA Doc. No. 14082040.

[206] *Id.*

[207] *Id.*

[208] INA §212(n)(2)(C)(vi)(II). The "fraud fee" added as INA §214(c)(12) by the Consolidated Appropriations Act of 2005, Pub. L. No. 108-447, is not included in the specific prohibition against payment by the beneficiary, but the provision does specify that DHS "shall impose ... *on an employer*" the $500 fee. (emphasis added).

[209] 20 CFR §655.731(c)(12).

Copyright © 2017. American Immigration Lawyers Association. All rights reserved.

It is unclear whether these restrictions on the beneficiary paying for costs also apply to USCIS's premium processing fee. Frequently, premium processing is pursued at the insistence of the beneficiary, and thus could be considered the individual nonimmigrant's expense. USCIS will accept the premium processing fee from the beneficiary[210] even though it will not accept the "training fee," discussed above, from the beneficiary, thus seeming to indicate an acceptance that the beneficiary can pay this fee.[211]

DOL has come out both ways on this issue. On one hand, it has found that the premium processing fee, along with attorney's fees and the cost of a credentials evaluation, was "in relation to [the nonimmigrant's] H-1B application process and H-1B program functions," and thus an employer expense that could not be passed to the beneficiary.[212] On the other hand, where the employer had objected to paying the premium processing fee, and premium processing was requested at the nonimmigrant's behest, the expense was found not to be an employer expense.[213] The decisions that found the employer liable for the premium processing fee did not explore the question of whether the premium processing request was the choice of the employer or the employee, so that factual issue may be what is pivotal to the question of whether the employee can pay the premium processing fee.

Interestingly, in a case involving the intersection between charging a penalty for cessation of employment, discussed immediately below, and the limitation against having a nonimmigrant pay attorney's fees, a DOL administrative law judge (ALJ) found that deduction of attorney's fees from a nonimmigrant's final paycheck was acceptable. In this case, the parties had entered into a repayment agreement, whereby the nonimmigrant would reimburse the employer for attorneys' fees should he leave employment early, by means of deduction of the amount from any outstanding vacation pay due in the final check. Because the amount was deducted from accumulated vacation pay, and not regular salary, and because the employer had an identical agreement with U.S. worker employees with respect to tuition reimbursement, the ALJ found that the nonimmigrant was treated the same as U.S. workers, and that this was not an improper deduction from pay.[214]

H. Penalties for Ceasing Employment

Employers are prohibited from requiring a nonimmigrant covered by an LCA to pay a penalty for ceasing employment prior to an agreed-upon date unless DOL finds

---

[210] USCIS Vermont Service Center, "VSC Helpful Filing Tips" (Aug. 12, 2009), AILA Doc. No. 09112363, p.12.

[211] *Id.*, p.7.

[212] *DeDios v. Medical Dynamic Systems, Inc.*, 2013-LCA-9 (May 17, 2016), AILA Doc. No. 16052512. *See also Komakula v. Aqua Information Systems, Inc.*, 2015-LCA-14 (ALJ Mar. 9, 2016).

[213] *Brambhatt v. Temple Group, Inc.*, 2013-LCA-21 (Dec. 6, 2013). *See also Admin'r, Wage & Hour Div. v. Woodmen of the World Life Insurance Society*, 2016-LCA18 (ALJ Oct. 26, 2016), AILA Doc. No. 16103105.

[214] *Admin'r, Wage & Hour Div. v. Woodmen of the World Life Insurance Society*, 2016-LCA18 (ALJ Oct. 26, 2016), AILA Doc. No. 16103105.

Copyright © 2017. American Immigration Lawyers Association. All rights reserved.

that the amount constitutes liquidated damages under relevant state law.[215] For the amount to be considered liquidated damages, DOL requires that it meet the five criteria for deductions from wages for the third category discussed above,[216] and that it conform to the applicable state law for liquidated damages. With respect to the latter point, the DOL regulation, referencing §356, comment (b), of the Restatement (Second) of Contracts among other authorities, attempts to provide an outline of what liquidated damage laws generally hold, noting that they usually:

- Are amounts "fixed or stipulated by the parties at the inception" of the employment agreement;

- Are "reasonable approximations or estimates of the anticipated or actual damage caused to one party by the other party's breach of the contract";

- Take into account the respective power and relationship of the parties, so that fraud or oppression by one party results in the amount being considered a prohibited penalty rather than liquidated damages; and

- Require that the stipulated amount take into account whether the breach is total or partial—in other words, account for the percentage of the agreed duration of employment that was completed.[217]

DOL also cautions that it will take into account actions by the employer that may have led to early cessation of employment, such as failure to comply with LCA obligations or constructive discharge under the general body of employment law, and reminds employers that the training fee can never be included in the liquidated damages.[218]

DOL ALJs and the ARB have consistently looked to state law, as required in the regulation, to determine if a penalty constitutes liquidated damages. Thus, a $15,000 penalty for early cessation of employment in an employment agreement was found to be appropriate under New Jersey law where that amount was to cover certain visa-related expenses but also approximated the employer's lost profits for the three weeks that was the required notice period in the agreement (the employee had resigned without notice).[219] The ALJ noted that New Jersey law closely approximates the Restatement referenced in the regulation, and indicated:

"[The Restatement] states that a fixed amount is reasonable 'to the extent that it approximates the actual loss that has resulted from the particular breach, and also is reasonable to the extent it approximates the loss anticipated at the time of the making of the contract, even though it may not approximate the actual loss that might have been anticipated under other possible breaches.'

---

[215] INA §§212(n)(2)(C)(vi) and 212(t)(3)(C)(vi)(I).
[216] 20 CFR §§655.731(c)(10)(i)(B) and 655.731(c)(9)(iii). Text accompanying note 193.
[217] 20 CFR §655.731(c)(10)(i)(C).
[218] Id.
[219] Malik v. Knack Systems LLC, 2013-LCA-17 (ALJ Feb. 14, 2014).

Copyright © 2017. American Immigration Lawyers Association. All rights reserved.

"Regarding the difficulty of proof of loss, the Restatement's comment states that the greater the difficulty either of proving that loss has occurred or establishing the amount with requisite certainty, the easier it is to show that the amount fixed is reasonable. The comment goes on to state that if the difficulty of proof of loss is great, then considerable latitude is allowed in the approximation of anticipated or actual harm; but if the difficulty of proof of loss is slight, less latitude is allowed. The comment also indicates that, if it is clear that no loss at all has occurred, a provision fixing a substantial sum as damages is unenforceable."[220]

An ALJ similarly looked to the Restatement in conjunction with Missouri law, and found that an employment agreement with graduated damages, depending on the length of employment before resignation, was a "'reasonable forecast' of the harm caused by an H-1B employee's early termination of employment" and the harm was "a type that is difficult to ascertain." Thus, the early termination clause was found enforceable.[221]

In another case, an ALJ applied similar criteria under Georgia law, namely that "1) the injury caused by the breach is difficult or impossible to accurately estimate, 2) the parties intended to provide for damages rather than a penalty, and 3) the stipulated sum is a reasonable pre-estimate of the probable loss." The ALJ noted that the employer provided no information as to how it arrived at its $5,000 figure for damages, and thus did not satisfy Georgia law for comprising liquidated damages.[222]

I. Job for Which Required Wage Must Be Paid

What happens if the nonimmigrant winds up performing a job different from the one represented on the LCA? DOL's regulation dictates that the employer's required wage obligation is based on the occupation identified on the LCA, and not on the job the nonimmigrant actually performs.[223] This is the case even if the job actually performed has a higher wage requirement than the one on the LCA.[224] Of course, from a practical standpoint, a material change in the job duties would necessitate an amended H-1B petition to be filed with USCIS, thus resulting in the employer's obtaining an LCA for the new position with the appropriate wage obligation. See Volume 1: Chapter Seven, "H-1B Visas and Status" for a discussion of when an amended petition is required.

---

[220] Id., citing Restatement (Second) Contracts §356 (comment b), as well as state case law.

[221] Admin'r, Wage & Hour Div. v. Greater Missouri Medical Pro-Care Providers, Inc., 2008-LCA-26 (ALJ Oct. 18, 2011). Rev'd on other grounds, Greater Missouri Medical Pro-Care Providers, Inc. v. Perez, 812 F.3d 1132 (8th Cir, 2015).

[222] Admin'r, Wage & Hour Div. v. Novinvest, LLC, 2002-LCA-24 (ALJ Jan. 21, 2003), aff'd ARB 03-060 (July 30, 2004) (internal citations omitted).

[223] 20 CFR §655.731(c)(8).

[224] Amtel Group of Florida, Inc. v. Yongmahapakorn, 2004-LCA-006 (ARB Sept. 26, 2006), AILA Doc. No. 06102310.

Copyright © 2017. American Immigration Lawyers Association. All rights reserved.

III. Working Conditions Attestation

The second LCA attestation is that the employer "will provide working conditions for such a nonimmigrant that will not adversely affect the working conditions of workers similarly employed."[225] This has long been an attestation in search of a purpose. Because benefits have been treated since the enactment of ACWIA as part of the required wage attestation, as discussed above, it has been a puzzlement as to what exactly this attestation is meant to govern. The DOL regulation circles back around to benefits:

> "The employer will provide working conditions for such nonimmigrants that will not adversely affect the working conditions of workers similarly employed (including benefits in the nature of working conditions, which are to be offered to the nonimmigrants on the same basis and in accordance with the same criteria as the employer offers such benefits to U.S. workers)."[226]

However, some other elements also are noted: "Working conditions include matters such as hours, shifts, vacation periods, and benefits such as seniority-based preferences for training programs and work schedules."[227]

DOL indicates that this attestation would be satisfied "when the employer affords working conditions to its H-1B nonimmigrant employees on the same basis and in accordance with the same criteria as it affords to its U.S. worker employees who are similarly employed, and without adverse effect upon the working conditions of such U.S. worker employees."[228] No specific documentation on this attestation is required to be kept in the public access file, but in an enforcement action, the employer would be required to "produce documentation to show that it has afforded its H-1B nonimmigrant employees working conditions on the same basis and in accordance with the same criteria as it affords its U.S. worker employees who are similarly employed."[229] It is unlikely that any documentation on this point would be actually required unless the working conditions attestation is specifically brought into issue under the individual facts underlying the investigation.

IV. Strike or Lockout Attestation

The regulation affirms that the LCA "requirement shall be satisfied when the employer signs the [LCA] attesting that, as of the date the application is filed, the employer is not involved in a strike, lockout, or work stoppage in the course of a labor dispute in the occupational classification in the area of intended employment."[230] The term "strike" is defined as "a labor dispute wherein employees engage in a concerted stoppage of work (including stoppage by reason of the

---

[225] INA §§212(n)(1)(A)(ii) and 212(t)(1)(A)(ii).

[226] 20 CFR §655.730(d)(2).

[227] 20 CFR §655.732(a).

[228] *Id.*

[229] 20 CFR §655.732(b).

[230] 20 CFR §655.733(a).

Copyright © 2017. American Immigration Lawyers Association. All rights reserved.

expiration of a collective-bargaining agreement) or engage in any concerted slowdown or other concerted interruption of operation."[231] The term "lockout" is defined as "a labor dispute involving a work stoppage, wherein an employer withholds work from its employees in order to gain a concession from them."[232]

Importantly, the regulation specifies that the pertinent labor disputes "relate only" to the H-1B employer's employees who work in the same occupational classification and "at the place of employment" as that "named" on the LCA.[233] The statute defines the term "area of employment" as "the area within normal commuting distance of the worksite or physical location where the work of the H-1B nonimmigrant is or will be performed."[234] In addition, if any "worksite or location is within a Metropolitan Statistical Area, any place within such area is deemed to be within the area of employment."[235] For further discussion of this term, see Volume 2: Chapter Two, "The Labor Certification Application."

Unfortunately, it remains unclear whether "the place of employment" means the "area of intended employment."[236] The regulation uses the term "place of employment" when discussing the impact of a labor dispute.[237] However, if there are multiple worksites within the "area of intended employment," then the more risk-averse client may wish to delay filing the LCA until there is no labor dispute in the area of intended employment. This approach is supported by the use of the term "place(s) of employment" to explain the term "worksite."[238]

If, after the LCA is certified, there is a labor dispute "in the same occupational classification as the H-1B nonimmigrant … at the place of employment during the validity of the labor condition application," then the employer must "within three days of the occurrence of the strike or lockout … submit to [DOL's] ETA, by U.S. mail, facsimile (FAX), or private carrier, written notice of the strike or lockout."[239] The employer is also prohibited from utilizing an H-1B nonimmigrant to replace any employees involved in a labor dispute:

> "Further, the employer shall not place, assign, lease, or otherwise contract out an H–1B nonimmigrant, during the entire period of the labor condition application's validity, to any place of employment where there is a strike or lockout in the course of a labor dispute in the same occupational classification as the H–1B

---

[231] 20 CFR §655.715.

[232] *Id.*

[233] 20 CFR §655.733(a).

[234] INA §212(n)(4)(A); 20 CFR §655.715.

[235] INA §212(n)(4)(A).

[236] Although the DOL regulations cite to the DHS regulations, the cross-referenced rules do not address this issue. 20 CFR §655.733(a) (citing 8 CFR §214.2(h)(17)).

[237] 20 CFR §655.733(a).

[238] *Id.* (discussing short-term placement of H-1B nonimmigrants at new worksite(s)).

[239] 20 CFR §655.733(a)(1) (section titled "Strike or lockout subsequent to certification of labor condition application").

Copyright © 2017. American Immigration Lawyers Association. All rights reserved.

nonimmigrant. Finally, the employer shall not use the labor condition application in support of any petition filings for H-1B nonimmigrants to work in such occupational classification at such place of employment until ETA determines that the strike or lockout has ended."[240]

After the employer notifies DOL of the labor dispute, DOL "shall examine the documentation, and may consult with the union at the employer's place of business or other appropriate entities."[241] DOL may also inform DHS of the labor dispute in progress,[242] which may result in H-1B petition denial, H-1B petition suspension, and/or denial of H-1B admission to a foreign national. For further discussion of DHS's response to labor disputes arising after an H-1B petition has been approved, see below. However, the employer is not required to "develop nor maintain documentation to substantiate the statement" that there is no labor dispute in progress, but:

"In the case of an investigation, however, the employer has the burden of proof to show that there was no strike or lockout in the course of a labor dispute for the occupational classification in which an H–1B nonimmigrant is employed, either at the time the application was filed or during the validity period of the LCA."[243]

No documentation need be retained with respect to the strike or lockout attestation, but in an investigation, DOL places the burden on the employer of showing that there was no applicable strike or lockout at the time the LCA was filed or during the LCA's validity.[244]

V. Notice Attestation

The fourth attestation requires that the employer provide notice to the bargaining representative of its employees in the occupational classification and area of employment covered by the LCA. If, as is usually the case with occupations subject to an LCA, there is no bargaining representative, the employer is required to provide notice "of filing in the occupational classification through such methods as physical posting in conspicuous locations at the place of employment or electronic notification to employees in the occupational classification for which … nonimmigrants are sought."[245]

The notice, in whichever form it is provided, must be made on, or within 30 days before, the date of filing of the LCA.[246] The information required to be on the notice is:

- The number of nonimmigrants the employer is seeking to hire;

---

[240] 20 CFR §655.733(a)(1).

[241] *Id.*

[242] 20 CFR §655.733(a)(2).

[243] 20 CFR §655.733(b).

[244] 20 CFR §655.733(b).

[245] INA §§212(n)(1)(C) and 212(t)(1)(C).

[246] 20 CFR §655.734(a)(1).

Copyright © 2017. American Immigration Lawyers Association. All rights reserved.

- The occupational classification in which the nonimmigrant(s) will be employed;

- The wages offered (a salary range is acceptable, as long as the bottom of the range meets the required wage);[247]

- The location(s) at which the nonimmigrant(s) will be employed; and

- The statement: "Complaints alleging misrepresentation of material facts in the labor condition application and/or failure to comply with the terms of the labor condition application may be filed with any office of the Wage and Hour Division of the United States Department of Labor."

The LCA contains all of this information, so it is acceptable to post copies of the LCA if the employer so prefers.

In addition, if the LCA is for an H-1B and is subject to the H-1B dependent or willful violator provisions (discussed below) and the H-1B petition is not being used only for nonimmigrants exempt from those requirements, the notice must also set forth the non-displacement and recruitment obligations, and must contain this additional language:

"Complaints alleging failure to offer employment to an equally or better qualified U.S. applicant or an employer's misrepresentation regarding such offers of employment may be filed with the Department of Justice, Civil Rights Division, Office of Special Counsel for Immigration-Related Unfair Employment Practices, 950 Pennsylvania Avenue, NW., Washington, DC 20530, Telephone: 1 (800) 255-8155 (employers), 1 (800) 255-7688 (employees); web address: www.usdoj.gov/crt/osc."[248]

This language also is on the LCA, minus the telephone number and web address, so employers subject to the dependent attestation may use the form for posting, though it would be advisable to add the telephone and web information to be certain of full compliance.

Notice for other than the collective bargaining situation can be either in hard form or electronic. The use of the plural "locations" is taken to mean that hard form postings, if used, must appear in at least two locations at the place or places where the nonimmigrant will be employed.

The DOL regulation requires two conspicuous postings at all places of employment, even if a place is not the employer's own site. DOL takes the view that, if the third party refuses to cooperate with the posting, the petitioner should not place

---

[247] While the regulation does not explicitly authorize a range on the notice, the fact that 20 CFR §655.731(a)(2)(vi) allows use of a range for prevailing wage purposes supports the conclusion that a range is acceptable on the notice.

[248] 20 CFR §655.734(a)(1)(ii). Note that this DOJ office is now called the "Immigrant and Employee Rights Section." https://www.justice.gov/crt/immigrant-and-employee-rights-section. However, the url on the notice language is still valid as of the time of this writing, as it redirects the user to the page with the new name.

Copyright © 2017. American Immigration Lawyers Association. All rights reserved.

the nonimmigrant at that site.[249] A petitioner can be sanctioned with fines and debarment for a substantial or willful failure to comply with posting requirements.[250] The regulatory definition of "willful" is a "knowing failure" or "reckless disregard" as to whether the conduct was in violation of the relevant INA provisions or regulations.[251] The regulation contains no definition of substantial, but at least one ALJ has defined it as "compliance with the essential requirements."[252] Failing to post at third-party sites has been found by DOL to be a substantial failure, resulting in fines and debarment,[253] but at least one court has found it not to be a willful violation where the employer was under the mistaken impression that an effort to post was all that was required, had carefully documented its efforts to post, and had corrected its practices once it was made aware that actual posting was necessary.[254] See the section below on short-term placements regarding when a third-party site is considered a place of employment.

The reference to two locations for the posting means two locations *at each site*, not one posting at each of the different sites.[255] The locations must be where workers in the same occupational classification can easily see them (proximity to wage and hour or Occupational Safety and Health Administration (OSHA) notices is suggested), and must be of sufficient size and visibility to be easily read. The notices must remain posted for 10 calendar days.[256]

An employer may, instead of using hard-copy notice, provide the notice electronically. It must go to all workers in the same occupational classification at each place of employment where the nonimmigrant will be employed. It is important to note that "both employees of the H-1B employer and employees of another person or entity which owns or operates the place of employment" are included in the category of "employees in the occupational classification … for which H-1B nonimmigrants are sought" who must be notified of the filing of an LCA.[257] Therefore, these individuals who also work "at each place of employment where any H–1B nonimmigrant will be employed" must also be notified,[258] although, as a

---

[249] *Admin'r, Wage & Hour Div. v. Core Education and Consulting Solutions, Inc.*, 2013-LCA-25 (ALJ Nov. 25, 2014).

[250] 20 CFR §655.805(b), referencing 20 CFR §655.805(a)(5).

[251] 20 CFR §655.805(c), citing *McLaughlin v. Richland Shoe Co.*, 486 U.S. 128 (1988) and *Trans World Airlines v. Thurston*, 469 U.S. 111 (1985).

[252] *Admin'r, Wage & Hour Div. v. Core Education and Consulting Solutions, Inc.*, 2013-LCA-25 (ALJ Nov. 25, 2014).

[253] *Id.*

[254] *CAMO Technologies, Inc. v. Solis*, No. 12-cv-6050-WJM-MF (D.N.J. 2013).

[255] *Santiglia v. Sun Microsystems, Inc.*, No. 03-076 (ARB July 29, 2005), AILA Doc. No. 05080367. The employer's practice of posting one copy at the worksite and another at corporate headquarters was found to be a violation of the rule, but was neither willful nor a substantial failure to comply, and thus no penalties were imposed.

[256] 20 CFR §655.734(a)(1)(ii)(A).

[257] 20 CFR §655.734(a)(1)(ii)(B).

[258] *Id.*

Copyright © 2017. American Immigration Lawyers Association. All rights reserved.

practical matter, an H-1B petitioner may find it difficult to electronically notify individuals who are not directly employed by the H-1B employer. This is especially difficult since DOL regulations require that "[n]otification shall be readily available to the affected employees."[259]

The information must be kept available for 10 days, unless individual direct notice (*i.e.*, by email) is provided, in which case it need only occur once during the required 30-day period. The means that the employer ordinarily uses to notify employees of job openings may be used, or the employer may use email or an electronic newsletter. If the employees who are required to receive notice do not have access to passive electronic means at their workplace, email or another passive means that they do have access to should be used. If they do not have electronic access as a practical matter, the hard-copy posting discussed above must be used, or individual copies must be sent to the employees.[260]

In addition to the notices to the other employees, the employer must provide a copy of the signed and certified LCA to the nonimmigrant, no later than the date that the individual reports to work. If the nonimmigrant so requests, a copy of the ETA-9035CP cover pages also must be provided.[261]

If a nonimmigrant is moved to a worksite within the same area of intended employment listed on the LCA that was not contemplated at the time of filing, a new LCA is not required, but postings that comply with the above requirements must be made at the new site before the nonimmigrant begins work there.[262]

To document compliance with this attestation, the employer must place in the public access file a copy of the dated notice and name and address of the collective bargaining representative or, if there is no such representative, a copy of the notice that was posted or circulated with a notation as to the dates when, and locations where, the notice was posted.[263] While the regulation does not address how to document compliance with the requirement that the employer provide a copy of the LCA to the nonimmigrant, the practitioner may wish to provide the client with a confirmation of receipt for the foreign national to sign.

VI. Dependents and Willful Violators

Employers of H-1Bs that are considered "H-1B dependent" or "willful violators" are subject to additional attestations,[264] described below. These provisions do not apply to H-1B1s or E-3s.

These provisions did apply to employers that were recipients of the Troubled Assets Relief Program (TARP) or certain Federal Reserve Act funding[265] and that

---

[259] *Id.*

[260] *Id.*

[261] 20 CFR §655.734(a)(2).

[262] 20 CFR §655.734(a)(2).

[263] 20 CFR §655.734(b).

[264] INA §212(n)(1)(E) through (G).

Copyright © 2017. American Immigration Lawyers Association. All rights reserved.

were hiring a new employee in H-1B status, regardless of whether the employer was H-1B dependent or a willful violator.[266] That provision sunset on February 17, 2011, and thus no longer applies.

A. Determining Who Is Dependent

An H-1B dependent employer is one that:

- Has 25 or fewer full-time equivalent (FTE) employees in the United States (including both U.S. workers and H-1Bs[267]) and employs more than seven H-1Bs; or

- Has 26 to 50 FTE employees in the United States and employs more than 12 H-1Bs; or

- Has 51 or more FTE employees in the United States and at least 15 percent of them are H-1Bs.[268]

For purposes of calculating the overall number of employees in these equations, an FTE is one who works 40 or more hours per week, unless the employer can show that fewer than 40 hours, down to a minimum of 35 hours per week, is the norm in its regular course of business. Each full-time employee counts as one FTE, even if the employee routinely works more than 40 hours.[269] If the employer has part-time employees, the count of those employees must be aggregated by one of two methods:

- Each employee working part-time is counted as one-half of an FTE, with the total rounded to the next highest whole number; or

- The number of hours worked by all part-time employees in the last pay period (or over the previous quarter if the last payroll is not representative, or by a reasonable approximation if hours of work records are not kept[270]) is totaled, then divided by the number of hours per week that constitute full-time employment. Then, the quotient is rounded to the nearest whole number.[271]

So, if an employer has 22 full-time employees and seven part-time employees, under the first method it would be considered to have 26 FTEs, since every two part-timers count as one FTE, and the "extra" part-timer is rounded up to count as another, so that seven part-timers equal four FTEs. As a result, the employer using this calculation would be considered dependent if it employs more than 12 H-1Bs, since it falls into the second category above.

---

[265] Funding under Title I of the Emergency Economic Stabilization Act of 2008, Pub. L. No. 110-343, or §13 of the Federal Reserve Act.

[266] Section 1611 of the American Recovery and Reinvestment Act of 2009.

[267] 20 CFR §655.736(a)(1).

[268] INA §212(n)(3).

[269] 20 CFR §655.736(a)(2)(iii)(A).

[270] 20 CFR §655.736(a)(2)(iii)(B).

[271] Id.

Copyright © 2017. American Immigration Lawyers Association. All rights reserved.

If the same employer were to use the second method of calculation, and the seven part-timers worked, respectively, 8, 12, 15, 17, 20, 22, and 25 hours in the last pay period,[272] the total number of hours worked would be 119. Assuming a 40-hour work week, 119 is divided by 40 to arrive at 2.975, rounded to the nearest whole number of three, which is then added to the 22 full-timers for a total of 25 FTEs. Thus, by this calculation, the employer would be dependent if it employs more than seven H-1Bs, since it falls into the first category above.

Only persons "employed by the employer"[273] are considered FTEs. Thus, bona fide consultants and contractors are not included in the definition, and DOL will accept the employer's designation as such. However, DOL will look to consistency of treatment, so the employer will need to have treated the person as a non-employee for such purposes as FICA and the Fair Labor Standards Act (FLSA).[274]

The formula above cannot be used to determine the number of H-1Bs in the calculation. Instead, each H-1B must be counted toward this part of the equation, regardless of whether the nonimmigrant is full-time or part-time.[275] However, any H-1Bs that are part-time are counted as part-time in the portion of the calculation that arrives at the overall number of FTEs.

If an employer is plainly not H-1B dependent, there is no requirement that it perform the calculation above.[276] However, if there is any doubt, the employer may use a "snap shot" test. Employers of 50 or fewer employees, both full-time and part-time, do not need to do a full calculation if they have 25 or fewer employees and seven or fewer H-1Bs, or 26 to 50 employees and 12 or fewer H-1Bs employed on either a full-time or part-time basis. Larger employers (51 or more employees) divide the number of H-1Bs (full– and part-time) by the number of full-time employees (including H-1Bs and U.S. workers). If the quotient is 0.15 or more, the employer must either accept and attest that it is dependent or perform the full calculation.

So, if an employer has 60 full-time employees, 10 part-time employees, and 12 H-1B employees, it would divide 12 by 60 (the part-time employees are ignored for this purpose), for a result of 0.2. Since 0.2 is larger than 0.15, the employer would need to

---

[272] Oddly, the regulation indicates that the number of hours worked by all part-timers *in the pay period* is to be divided by the number of hours *per week* that constitute full-time employment (*id.*), rather than dividing into the number of hours worked *in a week* during the pay period. Since many employers' pay periods are longer than one week, this would produce an absurd result in practice. In fact, the illustrative calculation in the regulation, at 20 CFR §655.736(a)(2)(iv), seems to anticipate a week's worth of hours divided by a week's worth of regular full-time hours. The preamble language when this formula was proposed also seems to anticipate a one-week/one-week formulation: "The number of FTEs in the workforce would then be determined by aggregating the average hours of the part-time workers, dividing that total by the standard for a full-time schedule, and adding the resulting number to the number of full-time workers in the workforce." 64 Fed. Reg. 628, 633 (Jan. 5, 1999).

[273] *See* 20 CFR §655.715. The regulatory definition looks to the common law, emphasizing the employer's right to "control the means and manner in which the work is performed."

[274] 20 CFR §655.736(a)(2)(i).

[275] 65 Fed. Reg. 80109, 80126 (Dec. 12, 2000).

[276] 20 CFR §655.736(c)(1).

Copyright © 2017. American Immigration Lawyers Association. All rights reserved.

perform the full calculation. (Using Method 1 for the full calculation, the employer would indeed be dependent, since it would have 65 FTEs, and more than 15 percent of its workforce would be H-1Bs.) However, if an employer had 85 full-time employees, 10 part-time employees, and 12 H-1B employees, it would divide 12 by 85, for a result of 0.14, and thus would not be required to make the full calculation.

1. Single Employer Rule

Multiple entities "within a controlled group of corporations"[277] that are treated as a single employer under the IRC[278] are treated as a single employer for purposes of determining H-1B dependency. The relationships between companies are gauged under the IRC, rather than ordinary immigration definitions of parent/subsidiary or affiliate. Thus, a parent/subsidiary controlled group is one where at least 80 percent of the stock, either by voting rights or value, of each subsidiary is owned by one or more of the other companies in the group and the common parent owns at least 80 percent of at least one of the companies.[279]

A brother/sister controlled group is where five or fewer individuals, estates, or trusts own more than 50 percent of the stock of each company, either by voting rights or value, but only to the extent that such stock ownership is identical with respect to each such corporation.[280] A combined controlled group is three or more corporations, each of which is a member of a parent/subsidiary or brother/sister controlled group and one of which is a parent/subsidiary controlled group that is also included in a brother/sister controlled group.[281]

The above single employers can be corporations, sole proprietorships, partnerships, estates, or trusts.[282] Affiliated service groups (service organizations, such as in health care, law firms, or accounting firms) are also single employers for dependency purposes where either a second organization regularly performs services for the first organization, or a significant portion of the second organization's business is the performance of services for the first organization and 10 percent or more of the interest in the second organization is held by highly compensated employees of the first organization.[283]

2. Documenting Dependency Status

If an employer's status as H-1B dependent or non-H-1B dependent is readily apparent or borderline under the "snap shot" test discussed above under "Determining

---

[277] 20 CFR §655.736(b).

[278] 26 USC §414(b), (c), (m), or (o), as per INA §212(n)(3)(C)(ii).

[279] 20 CFR §655.736(b)(1)(i) and 26 USC §1563(a)(1).

[280] The DOL regulation at 20 CFR §655.736(b)(1)(ii) indicates that the ownership percentage for brother/sister group is 80 percent, but it also states that the relationships are controlled by the definitions at 26 USC §1563(a), which at subparagraph (ii) states that the controlling percentage is 50 percent.

[281] 20 CFR §655.736(b)(1)(iii) and 26 USC §1563(a)(3).

[282] 20 CFR §655.736(b)(2) and 26 CFR §1.414(c)–2(b)(2).

[283] 20 CFR §655.736(b)(3) and 26 USC §414(m).

Copyright © 2017. American Immigration Lawyers Association. All rights reserved.

Who Is Dependent," or if the employer has attested that it is H-1B dependent, all that is needed in the public access file to document that status is a copy of the LCA (which will reflect the dependency status).[284]

If the employer had to perform a full calculation, rather than the snap shot test, to determine that it is not dependent, it must also retain a dated copy of the calculation, although that calculation is not required to be part of the public access file.[285]

If a "single employer" definition is used, a list of all entities included in the single employer calculation must be included in the public access file.[286] Also, if the single employer definition is used, documentation of either type of calculation (snap shot or full) must be retained in the event of an investigation.[287]

3. Changes in Dependency Status

If an employer's dependency status changes because of a change in the ratio of H-1B employees to its total workforce, the employer is not required to file new LCAs unless it seeks to hire a new H-1B or extend the status of an existing H-1B. If the employer has moved from non-dependent to dependent, the dependent attestations take effect only if a new LCA is required. If the employer has moved from dependent to non-dependent, it must perform a full calculation of its status—the snap shot test will not suffice—and retain a copy of that calculation in case of investigation. In the dependent to non-dependent situation, the employer has the choice of filing new LCAs for its new H-1B hires and H-1B extensions, or using existing certified LCAs if available. If the employer follows the latter route, it will remain bound by the dependent attestations.[288]

If an employer experiences a change in corporate structure and wishes to file a new LCA, new H-1B petition, or H-1B extension, the "new" entity must re-determine its dependency status, following the same rules discussed previously.[289] However, a change in corporate structure has no impact on the existing H-1Bs, unless and until an extension of status is sought,[290] as long as the new entity assumes the liabilities of the LCA, as discussed below, in "Changes in Corporate Structure."

B. Identifying Willful Violators

An employer that is found by DOL during the five years preceding the filing of the LCA to have willfully failed to comply with one of its attestations, or to have misrepresented a material fact, is subject to the same additional attestations as the H-1B dependent employer.[291] Similarly, an employer that is subject to the additional

---

[284] 20 CFR §655.736(d)(1)–(3).

[285] 20 CFR §655.736(d)(4).

[286] 20 CFR §§655.736(d)(7) and 655.760(a).

[287] 20 CFR §655.736(d)(7).

[288] 20 CFR §655.736(d)(5).

[289] 20 CFR §655.736(d)(6).

[290] 20 CFR §655.730(e)(3).

[291] INA §§212(n)(1)(E)(ii) and (n)(2)(C), and 20 CFR §655.736(f).

Copyright © 2017. American Immigration Lawyers Association. All rights reserved.

attestations and is found during the past five years by DOJ to have failed to offer the job that is the subject of an H-1B LCA to a U.S. worker who is equally or better qualified for the job, is subject to the additional attestations.[292]

"Willful failure" is defined as a "knowing failure" or "reckless disregard" as to whether the conduct was in violation of the relevant INA provisions or regulations.[293]

C. Exempt H-1Bs

The additional attestations do not apply if the LCA covers only "exempt" H-1Bs.[294] To be exempt, the H-1B must either receive wages equal to at least $60,000 per year, or must hold a master's degree or higher (or its foreign equivalent) in a specialty related to the intended occupation.[295]

This exemption does not mean that the employer is across-the-board exempt from the dependency/willful violator provisions—it must still mark on the form that it is dependent or a willful violator. It only means that, for the LCA underlying that particular individual's H-1B petition, it is not necessary to make or comply with the three additional attestations for dependent/willful violator employers.[296] The dependency/willful violator exemption should not be confused with other exemptions related to H-1B status, such as exemptions from the numeric quota or from the additional filing fees.

To qualify under the wage alternative, the H-1B must actually receive $60,000 during the calendar year, and bonuses and similar compensation can be included if they are paid "cash in hand, free and clear, when due" and payment is assured, at least up to the $60,000 amount.[297] The standards applicable to meeting the required wage also apply to meeting the $60,000 wage requirement.[298]

A part-time H-1B employee whose pay for the hours worked does not amount to $60,000 per year cannot qualify for the exemption on the salary basis, even if the wage would reach $60,000 when calculated out to full time. However, if the H-1B starts or stops employment part way through the year, the wages received can be pro rated if the employee receives the pro rata share of the $60,000 for the period of actual employment. So, if an H-1B resigns after three months, that employee must have received at least $15,000, or ¼ of the $60,000 required for the year.[299]

---

[292] INA §§212(n)(1)(E)(ii) and (n)(2)(5), and 20 CFR §655.736(f). Yes, this provision seems redundant—why re-subject an employer already subject to the attestations? However, it could prove important for an employer that has ceased to be dependent or could extend a willful violator's period of being subject to the additional attestations.

[293] 20 CFR §655.805(c), citing *McLaughlin v. Richland Shoe Co.*, 486 U.S. 128 (1988) and *Trans World Airlines v. Thurston*, 469 U.S. 111 (1985).

[294] INA §212(n)(1)(E)(ii).

[295] INA §212(n)(3)(B).

[296] 20 CFR §655.736(g)(3).

[297] 20 CFR §655.737(c).

[298] *Id.*

[299] *Id.*

Copyright © 2017. American Immigration Lawyers Association. All rights reserved.

To qualify under the master's alternative, a foreign degree must be equivalent to a master's or higher under the U.S. educational system and must be from an institution accredited or recognized under the law of the country in which it was issued, according to DOL's reading of the statute. Equivalency on the basis of experience is not accepted. Employers are required to prove the nonimmigrant's receipt of the degree, that the degree was in the necessary specialty, and the equivalence of the degree, "upon the request of the DHS or the [DOL]."[300] To qualify as being in a specialty related to the intended employment, the degree must be in "a specialty which is generally accepted in the industry or occupation as an appropriate or necessary credential or skill for …the employment in question."[301]

DOL has delegated to DHS the determination of whether a particular H-1B qualifies as exempt. In an investigation, DOL will consider the DHS determination dispositive unless it was based on false information.[302]

The employer is required to keep in the public access file a list of H-1B employees whose petitions are supported by an LCA claiming the exemption.[303]

If the employer designates "exempt" on the LCA, but is found to have used the LCA for a non-exempt H-1B, it can be penalized in an enforcement action for failing to comply with the additional attestations. If the employer is dependent or a willful violator, and does not designate "exempt" on the LCA, it will be held to the additional attestations even if the H-1B would have been eligible.[304]

D. The Additional Attestations

In addition to the standard attestations already discussed in this chapter, H-1B dependent employers and willful violators that are hiring H-1Bs must make three more attestations:

- The employer did not and will not displace a U.S. worker within a period 90 days before and 90 days after the filing of the H-1B petition;

- The H-1B nonimmigrant will not be placed at a third-party worksite where there are indicia of employment by the other employer, unless the petitioner has inquired whether there has been or will be a displacement of a U.S. worker during those 90-day periods and has no knowledge of such a displacement; and

- The employer has taken good faith steps to recruit U.S. workers for the position and has offered the job to any U.S. worker who applied and is at least as qualified as the H-1B.[305]

---

[300] 20 CFR §655.737(d)(1).

[301] 20 CFR §655.737(d)(2).

[302] 20 CFR §655.737(e).

[303] Id.

[304] 20 CFR §655.737(e)(2) and (3).

[305] INA §212(n)(1)(E) through (G).

Copyright © 2017. American Immigration Lawyers Association. All rights reserved.

1. The Non-Displacement Attestation

The employer must attest that it did not and will not displace a U.S. worker within a period 90 days before and 90 days after the filing of the H-1B petition.[306]

A U.S. worker is considered by DOL to be a citizen or national of the United States, a lawful permanent resident, a refugee or asylee, or an immigrant otherwise authorized by the INA or DHS to be employed in the United States.[307] The DOL regulation does not define immigrant, so presumably it carries its INA meaning, which is, fundamentally, every alien in the United States except a nonimmigrant.[308] Thus, any foreign national authorized to work who is not a nonimmigrant is treated as a U.S. worker for non-displacement purposes. This would include a number of categories not considered U.S. workers in other contexts, such as those in Temporary Protected Status (TPS), asylum applicants, adjustment of status applicants, etc.

Displacement is considered to have occurred if the employer lays off a U.S. worker from a job that is essentially the equivalent of one for which the H-1B is sought.[309] An essentially equivalent position is one that involves essentially the same responsibilities, was held by a U.S. worker with substantially equivalent qualifications and experience, and is located in the same area of employment.[310]

a. Definition of Layoff

A layoff occurs when there is a loss of employment, other than for performance-based reasons, cause, voluntary departure or retirement, violation of workplace rules, or expiration of a contract or grant (unless entered into to avoid these provisions).[311] Voluntary departure is not considered to have occurred if the situation amounts to constructive discharge.[312] Expiration of a contract does not occur if, at the time, there is work available on another contract such as in a staffing company situation.[313]

The layoff of a U.S. worker can be negated if the worker is offered a similar employment opportunity with the same employer at equivalent or higher compensation.[314] The offer must be bona fide and not arranged with the expectation and intent that the U.S. worker will refuse it, and must provide similar authority, opportunity for advancement, tenure, and work scheduling. Comparisons of compensation between the two jobs must take into account both wage and non-wage

---

[306] INA §212(n)(1)(E)(i).

[307] 20 CFR §655.715.

[308] INA §101(a)(15).

[309] INA §212(n)(4)(B).

[310] INA §212(n)(4)(A).

[311] INA §212(n)(4)(D).

[312] 20 CFR §655.738(a)(1)(ii).

[313] 20 CFR §655.738(a)(1)(iii).

[314] INA §212(n)(4)(D).

Copyright © 2017. American Immigration Lawyers Association. All rights reserved.

remuneration, as well as cost of living differentials for geographic relocations and relocation expenses.[315]

b. Essentially Equivalent Position

Evaluation of whether the position from which the U.S. worker has been laid off is "essentially equivalent" to a position offered to an H-1B nonimmigrant may, "where appropriate," be based on a one-on-one comparison (individual employee to individual employee) or on a broader focus (*e.g.*, an entire department is laid off, then its functions staffed with H-1Bs). The same duties and responsibilities must be involved. The DOL regulation focuses on "core elements and competencies," noting broad arenas like supervisory duties or engineering duties. "Peripheral, non-essential duties that could be tailored" are to be discarded under the regulatory scheme.[316] What is not clear is the status of essential but specific duties, such as particular skill in engineering that is critical to the job.

The qualifications of the H-1B and the laid off worker must be substantially equivalent. Only experience and qualifications that are directly relevant to the performance requirements of the job can be considered, and the comparisons need not be identical: DOL views 10 years of experience as substantially equivalent to 15 years.[317]

The third element of "essentially equivalent" is that the jobs must be located in the same area of intended employment. This is defined for these purposes as within normal commuting distance. If both jobs are within the same MSA or PMSA, they are deemed in the same area of employment.[318]

c. Documenting the Non-Displacement Attestation

The employer is required to retain all records it creates or receives regarding the circumstances under which any U.S. workers left its employ during the 90-day/90-day "look" period before/after filing of an H-1B petition, if those U.S. workers were in the same area and occupation as the H-1B worker. This includes any notices of termination, as well as the employee's name, last known address, title and job description, documentation regarding experience and qualifications, principal assignments, evaluations, and all documents concerning the employee's departure.[319]

2. The Secondary Non-Displacement Attestation

A subject employer placing an H-1B employee with another employer, where the H-1B will perform duties at the second employer's site and where there are indicia of employment by the second employer, is required to inquire of the second employer whether it has displaced or will displace U.S. workers within a period of 90 days

---

[315] 20 CFR §655.738(b)(iv).

[316] 20 CFR §655.738(b)(2)(i).

[317] 20 CFR §655.738(b)(2)(ii).

[318] 20 CFR §655.738(b)(2)(iii).

[319] 20 CFR §655.738(e)(1).

Copyright © 2017. American Immigration Lawyers Association. All rights reserved.

before to 90 days after the date of the placement.[320] It is irrelevant whether the second employer is itself an H-1B dependent or willful violator.[321] If the H-1B is placed with another company that in turn places the H-1B with a third employer, the duty to inquire extends to the third employer as well; the fact that the petitioning employer does not know the third employer does not relieve it of the duty to make inquiry.[322] The standards for what constitutes an indirect displacement are the same as for a direct displacement as discussed in the previous section of this chapter.[323]

Even if the required inquiry is made, the employer placing the H-1B has absolute liability if the secondary employer in fact displaces a U.S. worker during the applicable time frame.[324] While such a displacement could result in civil fines for the placing employer, that employer would not be subject to debarment unless it knew or had reason to know of the displacement at the time of the placement of the H-1B or unless it had previously been sanctioned for a previous placement with the same secondary employer.[325] The civil fine for the placing employer can be up to $1,000 per violation for the absolute liability without knowledge, and up to $35,000 per violation where the failure was willful.[326]

However, if the employer filing the LCA fails to make the displacement inquiry of the employer where the H-1B is placed, it can be subjected to a one-year debarment regardless of whether the failure was substantial or willful.[327]

The INA and regulation impose no penalty on the secondary employer.

To be considered to have indicia of an employment relationship, the relationship need not fully constitute "employment." Instead, DOL will weigh a number of factors, including whether:

- The second employer has the right to control when, where and how the H-1B does the job. This is the most important of the criteria.

- The second employer furnishes the tools and equipment.

---

[320] INA §212(n)(2)(F).

[321] *Id.*

[322] *Cyberworld Enterprise Technologies v. Administrator*, No. 04-049 (ARB May 24, 2006), affirming and adopting the decision of the Administrative Law Judge, No. 2003-LCA-17 (ALJ Dec. 23, 2003), both decisions at AILA Doc. No. 08080764.

[323] 20 CFR §655.738.

[324] INA §212(n)(2)(E) and 20 CFR §655.738(d).

[325] INA §212(n)(2)(E)(i) and (ii).

[326] INA §212(n)(2)(C). Subparagraph (ii) imposes a fine of up to $5,000 per violation for a willful violation of the non-displacement rule. Subparagraph (iii) imposes fines of up to $35,000 per violation where, in the course of a willful failure to meet an attestation's condition or a willful misrepresentation of material fact, a U.S. worker is displaced. This provision applies whether the employer is subject to the dependent/willful violator/TARP-funded attestations or not.

[327] INA §212(n)(2)(c)(i) and *Cyberworld Enterprise Technologies*, No. 04-049 (ARB May 24, 2006), affirming and adopting the decision of the Administrative Law Judge, No. 2003-LCA-17 (ALJ Dec. 23, 2003), both decisions at AILA Doc. No. 08080764.

Copyright © 2017. American Immigration Lawyers Association. All rights reserved.

- The work is performed on the premises of the second employer. In addition to being a possible indicator of an employment relationship, this is the second prong of the test of whether secondary employment in fact exists.

- There is a continuing relationship between the H-1B and the second employer.

- The second employer has the right to assign additional work.

- The second employer sets the work hours and duration of the job.

- The work is part of the second employer's ordinary business.

- The second employer is itself a business.

- The second employer can discharge the H-1B from providing services.[328]

The general purpose of these provisions was to target "job shops," as there had been publicity that some job shops had placed H-1Bs at client sites to do U.S. workers' jobs after the client's U.S. workers had been laid off. However, the provisions are not limited to these staffing firms, and can touch all manner of contracted services.[329]

To discharge its obligation under the secondary displacement attestation, the employer is required to make an actual inquiry of the second employer and to have no knowledge of any displacement or intended displacement of a similarly employed U.S. worker by the second employer within the period 90 days before and 90 days after the date of placement. The inquiry must encompass a "reasonable effort to enquire" and can be by such methods as obtaining a written assurance from the second employer, obtaining an oral assurance and preparing a memo to file recording that assurance, or including a non-displacement clause in the contract with the second employer.[330] The employer must retain whichever type of record it used in order to document its satisfaction of the secondary displacement attestation.[331]

The requirement that the employer have no knowledge of a displacement or intended displacement includes not only actual knowledge, but imputed knowledge "where there is information which indicates that U.S. workers have been or will be displaced...." Thus, if there had been publicity about the second employer's lay-off before placement of the H-1B, the H-1B employer would be expected to re-contact the second employer for additional assurances.[332] This would help to alleviate the chance of debarment or fines at the willfulness level should the second employer have actually displaced a U.S. worker, but as discussed above, would still not eliminate the chance of a fine of up to $1,000 per worker should the secondary employer have actually displaced U.S. workers during the 90-day/90-day window period.

---

[328] 20 CFR §655.738(d)(2)(ii).

[329] 20 CFR §655.738(d)(3).

[330] 20 CFR §655.738(d)(5)(i).

[331] 20 CFR §655.738(e)(2).

[332] 20 CFR §655.738(d)(5)(ii).

Copyright © 2017. American Immigration Lawyers Association. All rights reserved.

3. Recruitment of U.S. Workers Attestation

The third extra attestation is that the employer has taken good faith steps to recruit U.S. workers for the job for which the H-1B is sought, using standard industry-wide procedures and offering compensation at least as great as that required to be offered to the H-1B. The employer also must attest that it has offered the job to any U.S. worker who applied who is equally or better qualified than the H-1B.[333]

Recruitment must follow industry standards, with "industry" defined as "the set of employers which primarily compete for the same type of workers."[334] So, for example, a hospital would follow the standards of the health care industry, a computer company the information technology industry, and so on. Staffing firms should use the standards of the industry in which they will place the personnel.[335]

Notwithstanding a statement that "an employer is not required to utilize any particular number or type of recruitment methods,"[336] DOL requires that the recruitment include both internal (the employer's own personnel, which must include both current and former employees) and external (the workforce at large) methods, and "at least some active recruitment."[337] Advertising in publications and on the internet is considered passive recruitment. Active recruitment can be internal or external, and includes such actions as providing training to incumbent workers, outreach to trade and professional organizations, job fairs, use of placement services or headhunters, or other proactive steps to get information into the hands of potential candidates.[338]

The recruitment must be in good faith, which means that the process should offer "fair opportunities" to U.S. workers "without skewing the … process against U.S. workers or in favor of H-1B nonimmigrants." The screening process cannot treat U.S. workers differently from H-1B workers, and cannot prefer incumbent F-1 students on practical training.[339]

The INA cautions that "nothing in [the recruitment provisions] shall be construed to prohibit an employer from using legitimate selection criteria that are normal or customary to the type of job involved, so long as such criteria are not applied in a discriminatory manner."[340] A discriminatory manner would include use of screening criteria prohibited by an applicable discrimination law, or application of selection criteria in a "disparate manner"—be it between H-1B workers and U.S. workers or between jobs where H-1Bs are involved and jobs where they are not.[341]

---

[333] INA §212(n)(1)(G).

[334] 20 CFR §655.739(b).

[335] Id.

[336] 20 CFR §655.739(e).

[337] Id.

[338] 20 CFR §655.739(d).

[339] 20 CFR §655.739(h).

[340] INA §212(n)(1)(G).

[341] 20 CFR §655.739(g).

Copyright © 2017. American Immigration Lawyers Association. All rights reserved.

DOL requires that legitimate selection criteria: (1) be legally cognizable and not violate any law; (2) have a nexus to the job's duties and responsibilities; and (3) be necessary and appropriate based on the standards of the industry rather than on the preferences of the employer.[342]

The compensation offered in the recruitment effort does not necessarily have to be as high as the compensation offered to the H-1B. It only must be as high as the required wage—the higher of the prevailing or the actual wage—as previously discussed in this chapter.[343] However, it should be kept in mind that, where there are no comparable employees, the actual wage is the amount paid to the H-1B, thus de facto requiring that the wage offered be at least as high as that offered to the H-1B in such a circumstance.

The recruitment attestation is not required for the LCA for any nonimmigrant who would qualify for the employment-based, first preference category (alien of extraordinary ability, outstanding researcher or professor, or multi-national manager or executive).[344] It is not clear how one would demonstrate that the nonimmigrant would qualify for the first preference, in that no process is provided. As a practical matter, it would be highly unusual for the issue to come up in the context of an alien of extraordinary ability or a multi-national manager or executive, since the individual is likely to hold an O-1 or L-1, respectively, and not need an LCA. For an outstanding researcher or professor, using this exception would be highly risky, as without an actual adjudication of qualification, the nonimmigrant's qualification for the exception could be called into question.

Employers subject to this attestation are required to offer the job to any U.S. worker who applies who is equally or better qualified than the H-1B.[345] As previously noted, in the LCA context a U.S. worker is considered to be a citizen or national of the United States, a lawful permanent resident, a refugee or asylee, or an immigrant otherwise authorized by the INA or DHS to be employed in the United States.[346] The last item on that list appears to include all aliens who are not nonimmigrants and are authorized to work.[347]

To document this attestation, the public access file should contain materials summarizing the recruitment methods used and the time frame in which the recruitment took place, and can be either copies of the relevant documents or a memo to file.[348]

---

[342] 20 CFR §655.739(f).

[343] 20 CFR §655.739.

[344] INA §212(n)(1)(G)(ii), referencing INA §203(b)(1)(A), (B), and (C).

[345] 20 CFR §655.739(j).

[346] 20 CFR §655.715.

[347] INA §101(a)(15).

[348] 20 CFR §655.739(i)(4).

Copyright © 2017. American Immigration Lawyers Association. All rights reserved.

In addition, the employer must maintain documentation in the case of an investigation, to include recruiting methods used, places and dates of recruitments, and compensation terms. This can be copies of the documents themselves, or a memo to file.[349] In addition, the employer must retain documentation received or prepared regarding the treatment of applicants, such as application forms, interview records, records of job offers, applicant responses, etc.[350]

The enforcement procedures for this attestation differ from those for other elements of the LCA process, discussed later in this chapter. If an investigation is initiated by a complaint by "an aggrieved individual who has submitted a résumé or otherwise applied in a reasonable manner for the job that is the subject of the condition," which relates to offering employment to any equally or better qualified U.S. worker.[351] As with other procedures, the "Attorney General shall establish a process for the receipt, initial review, and disposition in accordance with this paragraph of complaints respecting an employer's failure to meet the condition ... or a petitioner's misrepresentation of material facts with respect to such condition."[352] Similarly, the complaint must have been "filed not later than 12 months after the date of the failure or misrepresentation, respectively."[353] Such complaints go to the Immigrant and Employee Rights Section (formerly known as the Office of Special Counsel for Immigration-Related Unfair Employment Practices) within the Department of Justice.[354]

The practitioner should note that arbitration is required, as opposed to an investigation and hearing. However, the provisions "shall not be construed to limit or affect the authority of the Secretary or the Attorney General with respect to any other violation."[355] If the attorney general determines that "there is reasonable cause to believe that such a failure or misrepresentation described in such complaint has occurred, the Attorney General shall initiate binding arbitration proceedings by requesting the Federal Mediation and Conciliation Service to appoint an arbitrator from the roster of arbitrators maintained by such Service."[356] The selection of the arbitrator and the rules of procedure for the arbitration proceedings should follow the rules and procedure of the Federal Mediation and Conciliation Service, with the Attorney General paying the arbitrator's fees and expenses.[357]

---

[349] 20 CFR §655.739(i)(1).

[350] 20 CFR §655.739(i)(2).

[351] INA §§212(n)(5)(A) and (B) (citing INA §212(n)(1)(G)(i)(II)).

[352] INA §212(n)(5)(B).

[353] Id.

[354] 20 CFR §655.734(a)(1)(ii). The Justice Department has never developed regulations to administer this provision, nor does its website specify how complaints for such violations are to be filed. Presumably, the process would be the same as for complaints alleging discrimination based on citizenship status, described at https://www.justice.gov/crt/filing-charge.

[355] INA §212(n)(5)(A).

[356] INA §212(n)(5)(C).

[357] Id.

Copyright © 2017. American Immigration Lawyers Association. All rights reserved.

In this procedure, "arbitrator shall make findings respecting whether a failure or misrepresentation" transpired.[358] Specifically:

"If the arbitrator concludes that failure or misrepresentation was willful, the arbitrator shall make a finding to that effect. The arbitrator may not find such a failure or misrepresentation (or that such a failure or misrepresentation was willful) unless the complainant demonstrates such a failure or misrepresentation (or its willful character) by clear and convincing evidence. The arbitrator shall transmit the findings in the form of a written opinion to the parties to the arbitration and the attorney general. Such findings shall be final and conclusive, and, except as provided in this subparagraph, no official or court of the United States shall have power or jurisdiction to review any such findings."[359]

The arbitrator's findings may be reviewed, reversed, and/or modified only to the extent and "only on the same bases as an award of an arbitrator may be vacated or modified under section 10 or 11 of title 9, United States Code."[360] As stated by statute:

"With respect to the findings of an arbitrator, a court may review only the actions of the Attorney General [in reviewing, reversing, or modifying the arbitrator's findings]… and may set aside such actions only on the grounds described in subparagraph (A), (B), or (C) of section 706(a)(2) of title 5, United States Code. Notwithstanding any other provision of law, such judicial review may only be brought in an appropriate United States court of appeals."[361]

Failure to offer employment to an equally or better qualified U.S. worker and/or misrepresentation of a material fact regarding this factor may result in "administrative remedies (including civil monetary penalties in an amount not to exceed $1,000 per violation or $5,000 per violation in the case of a willful failure or misrepresentation) as the Attorney General determines to be appropriate."[362] USCIS may not approve immigrant visa or H-1B petitions filed by the employer for one year, if the employer is found to have violated the condition.[363] If the employer made a "willful failure or willful misrepresentation," then these petitions may not be approved for two years.[364] The one exception is if the Attorney General reverses or modifies the arbitrator's finding.[365]

---

[358] INA §212(n)(5)(D)(i).
[359] Id.
[360] INA §212(n)(5)(D)(ii).
[361] INA §212(n)(5)(D)(iii).
[362] INA §212(n)(5)(E).
[363] INA §212(n)(5)(E)(ii).
[364] Id.
[365] INA §212(n)(5)(E).

Copyright © 2017. American Immigration Lawyers Association. All rights reserved.

VII. Other Issues

A. Changes in Corporate Structure

When an H-1B employer is restructured, whether by merger, acquisition, spin-off, or other reorganization, a new petition is not required if the new entity succeeds to the original employer's interests and obligations and if the conditions of employment remain the same.[366]

The same is true of the underlying LCA, provided certain steps are taken. An "authorized representative" of the new entity must prepare a sworn statement that expressly assumes all "obligations, liabilities, and undertakings" connected to any still-effective LCAs of the original entity. That statement must explicitly agree to abide by DOL's regulations, maintain a copy of the statement in the public access file, and make the required documentation available to any member of the public or the DOL upon request.[367] The required documentation must be added to the public access file, and must be a document that includes:

- A list of each affected LCA and its date of certification;

- A description of the new entity's actual wage system;

- The Federal Employer Identification Number (FEIN) of the new entity; and

- The authorized representative's sworn statement.[368]

The new entity must obtain new LCAs for any new H-1B petitions—it may not use remaining space on multiple-opening LCAs from the original entity.[369]

As a practical matter, the immigration attorney often is not made aware of a restructure until after the fact, and thus may not be in a position to ensure compliance before the deal is closed. The preamble to DOL's regulation indicates that the new entity must agree to assume the predecessor's obligations and liabilities "prior to the continued employment of the H-1B nonimmigrant."[370] Some have read this to require that the sworn statement be prepared prior to the ongoing employment by the new entity, and thus prior to the restructure.[371] However, the regulatory language itself is silent on the timing issue, and the preamble language looks only for the entity's agreement to assume the H-1B obligations and liabilities, not the sworn statement itself, prior to the restructure. The preamble does indicate that the agreement to assume the liabilities must be documented with a memo in the public access file, but does not explicitly require that the memo be prepared prior to the closing of the deal.[372]

---

[366] INA §214(c)(10).

[367] 20 CFR §655.730(e)(1)(iv).

[368] 20 CFR §655.730(e)(1).

[369] 20 CFR §655.730(e)(2).

[370] 65 Fed. Reg. 80110, 80112 (Dec. 20, 2000).

[371] "USCIS Letter from E. Hernandez to M. Schoonover" (June 7, 2001), AILA Doc. No. 01062832.

[372] 20 CFR §655.730(e)(1).

Copyright © 2017. American Immigration Lawyers Association. All rights reserved.

In many corporate changes, the documentation of the deal itself will include an assumption of obligations and liabilities, and thus the agreement to assume them might be demonstrable prior to the ongoing employment by the new entity. If, however, there is no such assumption in the deal's documentation, it would be important to have the sworn statement prior to the closing of the deal. If there is documentation of such an assumption, it would be less dangerous to prepare the sworn statement after the fact, though all haste should be made to ensure that the required documentation is in the public access file immediately. It may be worthwhile to consider whether to file new LCAs in this circumstance, but that approach may raise its own issues. If the deal already has closed and the nonimmigrants are continuing in their employment, the filing of new LCAs may be viewed as conceding that new LCAs were needed, and the failure to do so earlier could be viewed as a violation in and of itself.

Whatever approach is taken, it is critical that the succeeding employer abide by the terms of whatever LCA is in place.

By its terms, this corporate change provision applies only to H-1Bs. There are no explicit rules on this subject with respect to H-1B1s or E-3s, so presumably new LCAs and petitions would be required for those status types.

B. Short-Term Placements

The rules governing short-term placement of workers are strictly a creature of regulation, and are not contained in the INA. The DOL regulation starts from the premise that an H-1B cannot work at a site not on the LCA unless a new LCA is filed. Thus, its tenor is that its "short-term placement" rule is a way to provide flexibility to employers whose personnel may spend short times at sites other than their permanent places of employment.[373]

That being said, the regulation contemplates that some assignments would not be considered worksites, and thus would not be subject to the "short-term placement" rule. The locations of employee development activities, such as trainings and seminars, would be not considered worksites unless the nonimmigrant is an instructor who regularly performs such duties at such locations.[374]

Also, itinerant workers—those for whom the nature of the job is such that they frequently change location with little time spent at any one place—would not be going to new worksites for purposes of LCA requirements if: (1) either the normal duties of the occupation require frequent travel from place to place, or the duties require that the nonimmigrant spend most time at one place but occasionally go for short periods to other locations; (2) the presence at the "away" location is casual and short-term (it can be recurring but cannot exceed five consecutive workdays for a visit by a frequent traveler or 10 consecutive workdays for a visit by a worker who spends most time at one location); and (3) the nonimmigrant is not performing work

---

[373] 20 CFR §655.735(a).

[374] 20 CFR §655.715, definition of "Place of employment."

Copyright © 2017. American Immigration Lawyers Association. All rights reserved.

in an occupation in which workers are on strike or in a lockout at the location. In all such situations, the employer is required to reimburse for travel expenses.[375]

If the assignment is to a place that is considered a worksite, the employer must instead either obtain an LCA for the assignment or utilize the short-term placement rule.[376] Under the short-term placement rule, an employer may assign an H-1B to an area of employment not listed on its LCA for up to 30 workdays per either calendar year or fiscal year, if certain conditions discussed below are met. The assignment can be for up to 60 workdays in a year if other additional conditions, detailed below, are met.[377]

To qualify for the 30-day rule, the employer must be in compliance with its LCA for the area of employment listed, and cannot place the individual at a site where there is a strike or lockout in the same occupational classification as the H-1B's. For every day the H-1B is there, the required wage for the permanent worksite must be paid, and actual costs of lodging, travel, meals, and incidentals must be paid for both workdays and non-workdays.[378]

If the placement runs in the 30– to 60-day range, the employer must also ensure that the H-1B continues to maintain an office at the permanent worksite, spend a "substantial amount of time" during the year at that site, and maintain a residence in the area of the permanent site and not at the temporary site.[379]

The short-term placement rule looks not at worksites per se, but at the area of employment. So, if an H-1B is placed at one site in a given MSA for 60 days, he or she cannot then be placed at a different site within commuting distance in the same year. Also, the employer cannot rotate multiple H-1Bs in and out of one area such that the employer has a continuous presence there.[380]

If the employer has an LCA for a particular area for the occupational classification, it cannot use the short-term placement rule for that area. Also, the H-1B's initial placement cannot be under the short-term rule.[381]

If an H-1B reaches the maximum number of workdays in a given area, the employer must either file and obtain DOL certification of a new LCA (in which case no other short-term assignments can be made in that area), or terminate the assignment.[382]

---

[375] *Id.*

[376] 20 CFR §655.735. As discussed in Volume 1: Chapter Seven, "H-1B Visa and Status," if an LCA is required, then a new or amended H-1B petition is required. *Matter of Simeio Solutions, LLC*, 26 I&N Dec. 542 (AAO 2015), AILA Doc. No. 15040969.

[377] 20 CFR §655.735(c) and (d).

[378] 20 CFR §655.735(b).

[379] 20 CFR §655.735(c). *See also* the indictment in *United States v. Vision Systems Group, Inc.* (S.D. Iowa Jan. 22, 2009), AILA Doc. No. 09021362, in which the failure to abide by these requirements was cited as a factor in an alleged criminal conspiracy to fraudulently use Iowa as a place of employment instead of Pennsylvania.

[380] 20 CFR §655.735(e).

[381] *Id.*

Copyright © 2017. American Immigration Lawyers Association. All rights reserved.

The rules regarding short-term placements at worksites apply only to H-1Bs—the regulation explicitly excludes E-3s and H-1B1s from their application.[382] As the exclusion was added to the regulation in 2008 without explanation or comment, it is not clear whether this means that E-3s and H-1B1s can be given short-term assignments without complying with the conditions of the rule, or that DOL intended to prohibit all short-term assignments for them. However, the provisions dictating when a placement is not considered to be a worksite do apply to E-3s and H-1B1s.[384]

C. Displacement in the Course of a Willful Violation

In addition to the non-displacement provisions applicable to H-1B dependent employers, all employers of H-1B, H-1B1, and E-3 nonimmigrants can be sanctioned for having displaced a U.S. worker if the displacement occurs during a period 90 days before or 90 days after the filing of the nonimmigrant petition in the event of a willful failure to meet an attestation condition or a willful misrepresentation.[385] This provision applies whether the employer is H-1B dependent or not. Sanctions here are particularly severe—up to $35,000 per violation and debarment for at least three years.[386]

D. Retaliation

Employers are prohibited from retaliating or otherwise discriminating against an employee (including former employee and applicant for employment) because that person has informed the employer or any other person of information he or she reasonably believes shows a violation of the LCA rules or because the employee cooperates or tries to cooperate in an investigation.[387] Sanctions for this violation include fines of up to $5,000 per violation and at least three years' debarment.[388] Reinstatement to the same or a substantially equivalent position can be ordered[389] or, where reinstatement is not a viable option, back pay and benefits can be awarded.[390]

A nonimmigrant who files a complaint alleging a violation of the retaliation provision may stay in the United States for a period up to the maximum period allowed for such a nonimmigrant, provided he or she is otherwise eligible to stay and work in the United States.[391] Thus, "if credible documentary evidence is provided in support of a petition seeking an extension of H-1B stay in or change of status to

---

[382] 20 CFR §655.735(f).

[383] 20 CFR §655.735. This exclusion had not been in the proposed rule amending the LCA provisions to include E-3s or H-1B1s, but was included in the final rule without comment. *See* final regulation at 73 Fed. Reg. 19943 (Apr. 11, 2008), and proposed regulation at 72 Fed. Reg. 1650 (Jan. 12, 2007).

[384] 20 CFR §§655.700(c)(3) and (4), and (d)(1).

[385] INA §§212(n)(2)(c)(iii) and (t)(3)(c)(iii).

[386] 20 CFR §§655.810(b)(3) and 810(d)(3).

[387] INA §§212(n)(2)(C)(iv) and (t)(3)(C)(iv), and 20 CFR §655.801(a) and (b).

[388] INA §§212(n)(2)(C)(iii) and (t)(3)(C)(iii).

[389] *Talukdar v. Dept. of Veterans Affairs*, 04-100 (Jan. 31, 2007), AILA Doc. No. 08080664.

[390] *Huang v. Ultimo Software Solutions, Inc.*, 2008-LCA-00011 (ALJ Dec. 17, 2008), AILA Doc. No. 09030360.

[391] INA §§212(n)(2)(C)(v) and (t)(3)(C)(v), and 20 CFR §655.801(c).

Copyright © 2017. American Immigration Lawyers Association. All rights reserved.

another classification that the beneficiary faced" such retaliation, adjudicators may consider any related loss of status as an "extraordinary circumstance" under 8 CFR §214.1(c)(4) or §248.1(b), justifying a favorable exercise of discretion.[392] A copy of the complaint filed by the beneficiary, along with corroborative documentation that such a complaint has resulted in the retaliatory action, should be filed in support of the exercise of discretion.[393]

In the absence of direct evidence, retaliation can be proven through establishment of a prima facie case, showing that: (1) the employer is governed by the INA; (2) the complainant engaged in protected activity; (3) an adverse employment action was taken; and (4) a nexus exists between the protected activity and the adverse action. If offering a prima facie case, the complainant bears the burden of demonstrating by a preponderance of the evidence that adverse action was taken against him or her because of protected activity. The employer can rebut by articulating a legitimate, nondiscriminatory, non-pretextual reason for the adverse employment action.[394]

VIII. Process and Filing

LCAs must be filed electronically unless the employer has permission from DOL to file by mail. That permission is granted upon written request[395] only if a physical disability or lack of Internet access prevents an employer from filing electronically. There is no specific form for the request, but it must be accompanied by documentation that the Internet cannot be accessed from the employer's location, such as showing that no Internet Service Provider (ISP) serves the area, or by such documentation of disability as a physician's statement or invoices for relevant medical devices. If permission to file by mail is granted, it is valid for one year.[396]

Electronic filing is through the DOL's iCert portal, at *http://icert.doleta.gov/*. Under the iCert system, the user sets up a main account and multiple sub-accounts, through which LCAs, prevailing wage determination requests, and H-2A and H-2B petitions are filed.[397]

One LCA may be used for multiple unnamed beneficiaries, which means that an LCA may be valid for more than one beneficiary. Then, in the event that "all of the beneficiaries covered by [a] labor condition application have not been identified at the time a petition is filed, ... petitions for newly identified beneficiaries may be filed at

---

[392] 8 CFR §214.2(h)(20).

[393] USCIS, D. Neufeld, "Supplemental Guidance Relating to Processing Forms I-140 Employment-Based Immigrant Petitions and I-129 H-1B Petitions, and Form I-485 Adjustment Applications Affected by the American Competitiveness in the Twenty-First Century Act of 2000 (AC21) (Public Law 106-313), as amended, and the American Competitiveness and Workforce Improvement Act of 1998 (ACWIA), Title IV of Div. C. of Public Law 105-277" (May 30, 2008), *AILA* Doc. No. 08060560, p.8.

[394] *See Vojtisek-Lom v. Clean Air Technologies Int'l Inc.*, 2006-LCA-00009 (ALJ June 18, 2007), AILA Doc. No. 0872564, p.27, citing *Kahn v. U.S. Sec'y of Labor*, 64 F.3d 271 (7th Cir. 1995).

[395] Requests for permission to file by mail, as well as the filings themselves, should be sent to the address on DOL's website, https://www.foreignlaborcert.doleta.gov/preh1bform.cfm.

[396] 20 CFR §655.720.

[397] 74 Fed. Reg. 17545 (Apr. 15, 2009).

Copyright © 2017. American Immigration Lawyers Association. All rights reserved.

any time during the validity of the labor condition application using photocopies of the same application."[398] The subsequently filed petitions "must refer by file number to all previously approved petitions for that labor condition application."[399] As a practical matter, this may be done with an addendum to the labor condition application, which should state the case number of the labor condition application and the receipt numbers for the petitions which relied upon the labor condition application. The practitioner may also provide the names of the other beneficiaries. If the nonimmigrant will work at multiple locations, then the LCA must state the worksites and provide the relevant prevailing wages.

However, substitution of beneficiaries of the labor condition application is not permitted: "When petitions have been approved for the total number of workers specified in the labor condition application, substitution of aliens against previously approved openings shall not be made. A new labor condition application shall be required."[400] Specifically, "once a slot on the LCA has been used for a specific alien, that slot cannot be used for another alien even if the original alien leaves the job permanently before the LCA has expired."[401]

The LCA can be filed no earlier than six months before the start date shown on the LCA. DOL can then take up to seven business days to process the LCA, which it can refuse to certify if the LCA is incomplete or obviously inaccurate.[402] If the LCA is certified, it is returned to the employer for filing with the nonimmigrant petition or visa application.[403] In practice, this delivery is done by email. The email contains a link to the certified LCA, and the LCA can then be printed by clicking on the link. The certified LCA can also be obtained directly by logging into the iCert account. If DOL refuses to certify, the LCA is returned by email to the employer with an explanation of the reason. The employer can re-submit, but the re-submission will be treated as a new application.[404]

The LCA can be valid for up to three years for an H-1B or initial H-1B1, and up to two years for an E-3 or extension H-1B1, all with the start date no earlier than the date the application is certified.[405]

If the LCA is being filed in anticipation of the April 1 opening of H-1B quota-subject filing opportunities with October 1 start dates, then particular attention should be paid to the employment start dates of the LCA and the H-1B petition. It is not advisable to wait to file the LCA on April 1 with an employment start date of October 1, as there would be insufficient time for DOL to process and certify the LCA to allow

---

[398] 8 CFR §214.2(h)(4)(i)(B)(3).

[399] *Id.*; USCIS Adjudicator's Field Manual (AFM) 31.3(b).

[400] 8 CFR §214.2(h)(4)(i)(B)(4).

[401] AFM 31.3(b).

[402] INA §212(n)(1)(G) and 20 CFR §§655.730(b) and 655.740(a)(2).

[403] 20 CFR §655.740(a)(1).

[404] 20 CFR §655.740(a)(3).

[405] 20 CFR §655.750(a).

Copyright © 2017. American Immigration Lawyers Association. All rights reserved.

for submission of the H-1B petition on the first date H-1B filings are accepted. This problem may be alleviated by requesting an earlier start date on the LCA, such as the date six months from the date the LCA is filed. October 1 must be stated as the employment start date on the H-1B petition, but the H-1B employment end date must fall within the validity period of the LCA. This will necessarily result in an H-1B validity period that is shorter than three years.

For example, the LCA start date may be stated as September 15, with an expiration on September 14 three years later. The H-1B petition would have an employment start date of October 1, so it would fall within the new fiscal year, but the H-1B employment end date would be no later than September 14 (rather than September 30) three years later. This would enable the filing of the LCA on March 15. However, experience has shown that the iCert system sometimes has technical problems during the two to three weeks prior to April 1, due undoubtedly to the high volume of use. Thus, it may be advisable to start filing even earlier, with a corresponding earlier start date.

As noted in Volume 1: Chapter Seven, "H-1B Visas and Status," requesting an employment period of more than exactly three years will result in denial of the H-1B petition. Although this approach would result in an H-1B employment period that is short of the maximum H-1B validity period, the employer and foreign national will benefit from the opportunity of filing as of the first date that numeric quota-subject H-1B filings are accepted.

An LCA can be filed for more than one position, but only within the same occupation.[406] In addition, an LCA can be filed for multiple places of employment. However, the same LCA cannot be used for different statuses—separate LCAs must be filed for H-1Bs, H-1B1s and E-3s.[407] Full-time and part-time positions also must not be combined on one LCA.[408]

If an employer wishes to minimize potential liability under a certified LCA that is not being used, it can withdraw the application by writing to the DOL. For the LCA to be withdrawn, no nonimmigrant can be employed under it, and an investigation by DOL cannot have been commenced. If it turns out that a nonimmigrant is employed under the LCA, and there is no superseding LCA, the employer will be held to the attestations on the LCA.[409]

A. Registering for and Using the iCert System

An iCert account is necessary in order to file a PWD request and file the LCA with the NPC. Registration for an account should be performed online at *http://icert.doleta.gov*. The practitioner should note that any field in the iCert system

---

[406] 20 CFR §655.730(c)(5) and *Santiglia v. Sun Microsystems, Inc.*, 03-076 (ARB, July 29, 2005), AILA Doc. No. 05080367, pp.6–7: "though an employer must file a separate LCA for each *occupation* for which it seeks H-1B workers, the LCA may cover more than one intended position within that occupation." (emphasis in original).

[407] 20 CFR §655.730(c)(5).

[408] 20 CFR §655.730(c)(6).

[409] 20 CFR §655.750(b).

Copyright © 2017. American Immigration Lawyers Association. All rights reserved.

where an asterisk appears is a required field. Failure to provide the required information will result in an error being generated, though the user will be prompted. If the question does not apply, "N/A" should be selected or typed; the question or field should not be left blank.

To register, information concerning the practitioner, who is the requestor, should be provided in the "Your Login Information" section. The online system will request entry of a secret question and answer, in the event account or password information later should need to be retrieved. In order to submit a prevailing wage request, under "Select Visa Programs," the checkboxes for LCA and/or prevailing wage services should be selected.

Information concerning the company with whom the attorney/agent is affiliated should be provided in the "Your Company Information" section. The FEIN of the practitioner's law firm or business should also be provided. Once the account has been created, an email with a temporary password will be sent to the registered user's email address to confirm the creation of an account. At the first visit, with the email address used as the log-in identification, the system should prompt a password change. Users are required to change their passwords periodically to maintain access to the iCert account. DOL sends an email to the account holder when the password change is required. Once the account is created, the system allows multiple people to be logged into the account simultaneously, so multiple paralegals can access an attorney's account at the same time.

The iCert system is frequently "slow due to high demand," and at times the system is down.[410] Sometimes iCert is unavailable as DOL updates the system,[411] adds enhancements,[412] or performs routine maintenance.[413] Issues with LCAs on iCert may be explained in an email to *LCA.Chicago@dol.gov*.[414] Technical issues with the system should be addressed via email to *oflc.portal@dol.gov*.[415]

B. The Prevailing Wage Determination Request (PWDR), ETA Form 9141

In preparing an LCA, an employer can identify the prevailing wage in two ways, as discussed earlier in this chapter. The practitioner may submit a prevailing wage request to the NPWC or identify the prevailing wage through an alternative source, usually by either using the OES or an acceptable alternative wage survey. If the practitioner plans to use an alternative source, the LCA may be filed without submitting a PWDR.

---

[410] *E.g.*, "PERM Has Been Restored" (Updated Dec. 10, 2010), AILA Doc. No. 10101531; "Notes from USDOL Open Forum" (July 1, 2010), AILA Doc. No. 10072067.

[411] "PERM Has Been Restored" (Updated Dec. 10, 2010), AILA Doc. No. 10101531.

[412] "Minutes from DOL Stakeholders Meeting" (Oct. 28, 2010), AILA Doc. No. 10111762.

[413] "Information from DOL Regarding Electronic Submission of Prevailing Wage Requests" (Jan. 14, 2010), AILA Doc. No. 10011460.

[414] "Important Department of Labor Email Addresses" (updated June 29, 2010), AILA Doc. No. 09012860.

[415] DOL, "OFLC E-mail Help Desks" (updated Feb. 4, 2014), https://www.foreignlaborcert. doleta.gov/pdf/oflcHelpDesks.pdf

Copyright © 2017. American Immigration Lawyers Association. All rights reserved.

To request a new prevailing wage determination, the practitioner must first be registered for iCert as discussed above. He or she then should "click the Begin New ETA Form 9141 button from the Portfolio summary or My Cases screen."[416] The system has occasional technical issues and a timeout feature. Therefore, while completing the online form, it is strongly recommended that the application be saved often. A help feature provides additional information for each question, accessible through the question mark icon after each question. The practitioner should note:

"All fields on the ETA Form 9141 must be completed prior to submitting a request for a PWD via iCERT. When a request is processed, if any fields are missing the request is returned to the requestor and is voided in iCERT. The requestor should complete a new ETA Form 9141 and submit it via iCERT."[417]

For additional discussion of the PWD form, see Volume 1: Chapter Eight, "H-2B Visas and Status" and DOL guidance.[418]

1. Parts A Through C

The visa category for which the prevailing wage determination is being filed should be selected: E-3 Australian, H-1B, H-1B1 Chile, H-1B1 Singapore, H-2B, or PERM. The practitioner's point of contact information is also requested, but this information should auto-populate in this section if the employer has used this form before.

The information in Part C should reflect the employer's headquarters location and not the location where the foreign national will work, if these locations differ. The iCert system should save the employer's information from previously submitted PWDRs, allowing selection of an employer using a look-up feature instead of re-typing the information with each request. The employer's North American Industry Classification System (NAICS) should also be selected.[419]

2. Part D

This part asks questions to identify the appropriate source of the wage information, namely whether the employer is covered by ACWIA, whether the position is covered by a collective bargaining agreement, or whether the employer requests consideration of Davis-Bacon or McNamara Service Contract Act wages. It also asks if the employer is requesting consideration of a wage survey and, if so, the name and date of the survey

3. Part E

---

[416] DOL, "iCERT Prevailing Wage System External User Guide for the Office of Foreign Labor Certification" (June 2013), at 4, https://icert.doleta.gov/library/user_guides/iCERT_Prevailing_Wage_External_User_Guide.pdf.

[417] DOL, "National Prevailing Wage and Helpdesk Center Prevailing Wage Frequently Asked Questions" (Mar. 2010), AILA Doc. No. 10032662.

[418] DOL, "iCERT Prevailing Wage Quick Start Guide for External Users," AILA Doc. No. 10011460.

[419] See Volume 1, Chapter 8, "H-2B Visas and Status," for an explanation of this code.

Copyright © 2017. American Immigration Lawyers Association. All rights reserved.

Details regarding the position should be provided, including the SOC (O*NET/OES) code and occupation title. The "suggested" SOC code and occupation title for #2 and #2a may be identified from the Foreign Labor Certification Data Center Online Wage Library, available at *www.flcdatacenter.com*, by selecting the FLC Wage Search Wizard, the state of intended employment from the drop-down menu, the county of intended employment, and the job code from the drop-down list (or searching by keyword). Alternatively, the iCert portal provides a prevailing wage search function,[420] but the practitioner may prefer the Foreign Labor Certification Data Center Online Wage Library since it also offers a hyperlink to the template job description.[421] As stated by DOL, "The number on the left is the SOC code and the title to the right is the Occupation Title."[422] The job description of the SOC code should be reviewed to ensure it is a good match to the position's job duties, as discussed above. Once the SOC code is selected, the SOC occupation title should auto-populate.

Additional information should also be provided, concerning the number of hours worked per week, the hourly work schedule, job title of the supervisor, supervisory duties of the position, the position job duties, and any travel and/or conditions that would affect the rate of pay. The minimum requirements for the position should also be stated, regarding the minimum education, field(s) of study, and necessary amount of training and experience, which in turn should be stated in months rather than years. Special requirements, such as skills, licenses, certificates, and/or certification, should also be provided. The form provides character limits in many of the fields, but Section E.a.5 of the ETA Form 9141 is a free text field where the full job description is placed. It is permissible to refer to Section E.a.5 in fields where there is not sufficient space to include a full answer, and then provide a full list of job duties and job requirements in that field. If the employer wants the PWD expressed as an hourly wage, "Request Hourly Wage" should be stated in the Job Duties block, though DOL notes that it will not issue the determination in hourly terms if the OES survey does not provide a wage on that basis.[423]

The practitioner should include in Section C any and all location(s) where the foreign national will work, including additional locations where the foreign national may work within the MSA.

Once all required fields have been completed, the system should search the form to determine whether any questions or fields are empty. At the end of the online form, the system should provide a list of deficiencies, if any, that should be corrected before proceeding. When the form is submitted, a processing case number will be assigned

---

[420] DOL, "Welcome to the iCert Visa Portal System," https://icert.doleta.gov/.

[421] DOL, Foreign Labor Certification Data Center Online Wage Library, http://www.flcdatacenter.com.

[422] "FAQs on H-2B Final Rule: Round One" (Apr. 20, 2009), AILA Doc. No 09042066.

[423] "DOL Updates FAQs on Prevailing Wage Program" (June 21, 2012), AILA Doc. No. 12062154.

Copyright © 2017. American Immigration Lawyers Association. All rights reserved.

and can be used to track the progress of the application. The case number should also be referenced in any future communication with DOL concerning the application.

C. Preparing the LCA[424]

DOL requires that the employer or the attorney/agent respond to attestations concerning the retention, maintenance, posting, accuracy, and distribution of the LCA. Therefore, in order to draft and submit an LCA on the iCert system, the practitioner must attest to the statements listed on the ETA Form 9035.

1. Completing the ETA Form 9035 – Parts A and B

The type of visa classification for which the LCA is required should be stated: H-1B, H-1B1 Chile, H-1B1 Singapore, or E-3. This information should exactly match to the information entered on the H-1B petition, Form I-129 at Part 2, #2(a–f). Additional information should also be provided concerning the job, including the SOC (O*NET/OES) code, occupation title, full– or part-time nature of the employment, and period of intended employment, stated in mm/dd/yyyy format.

The number of positions being requested for LCA certification should also be stated. This number should be the total of the number of positions provided in the "Basis for the visa classification supported by this application" question. For example, if the employer requests one LCA for three "New employment" jobs and two "Change in employer" jobs, then five should be the number stated for the "Total Worker Positions Being Requested for Certification" question.

2. Completing the ETA Form 9035 – Parts C Through F

Details about the employer's legal name, trade name, address, FEIN, and NAICS code should be provided in this section. Contact information for the employer's representative, or point of contact, should also be stated. This information should be different than the attorney/agent information provided, unless the attorney or agent is an employee of the company. The practitioner's information is also required on the form, including contact information and bar information, although this information should auto-populate.

The rate of pay may be stated as a wage, salary, or salary range, but the rate of pay, including the bottom of any range, must equal or exceed the prevailing wage as determined by the NPWC or as identified in OES or an alternate wage survey. The practitioner should then indicate whether the rate of pay is per hour, week, biweekly, month, or year.

3. Completing the ETA Form 9035 – Part G

Details concerning the proposed employment and prevailing wage information should be provided in this section. The worksite of the employment, which should match the location of the PWD, should be entered. The practitioner should note that the location should be stated as a physical address and not a P.O. box.

---

[424] DOL, "Form ETA-9035," https://www.foreignlaborcert.doleta.gov/pdf/ETA_Form_9035_2009_Revised.pdf. The same attestations are required on the online version of the form.

Copyright © 2017. American Immigration Lawyers Association. All rights reserved.

Information about the agency that issued the prevailing wage determination should be provided. If the prevailing wage is from OES or an alternate wage survey, then "N/A" should be entered for Questions 7 and 7a and may be entered for Question 8. Alternatively, the appropriate wage level may be selected for Question 8 if OES information is used. If the practitioner obtained a PWD from the NPC, then the appropriate information, including the tracking number and wage level, should be stated, and "NPC" entered for Question 7.

The prevailing wage as determined by the NPC or OES should then be entered, as well as the timeframe for the rate of pay. The appropriate source for the prevailing wage information, such as OES, CBA, DBA, or SCA, should be provided, as well as the source's year of publication or execution. "Other" should be selected if the prevailing wage is from an employer-provided independent source.

The full name of the OES salary survey should be provided if the prevailing wage was pulled directly from the OES and was not stated in a PWD issued by the NPC. The source should be stated as "OFLC Online Data Center." A recent enhancement to the ETA Form 9035 in iCert provides a drop-down menu allowing this precise title for the OES survey to be inserted automatically. For a source other than the OES and a PWD issued by an SWA or NPC, the name of the source should be provided. Unfortunately, the field allows only a limited number of characters. As noted in the discussion regarding wage surveys earlier in this chapter, the survey used must be named with as much clarity as possible in this space. "[T]he information provided by the employer must be sufficient to ensure that both the survey company name and the survey title are obviously identifiable."[425] If an abbreviation is used, as it often must be, enough information should be shown to identify the survey company and the survey title. It is not necessary to include the year of the survey in the title, as there is a separate space on the form for that.[426] "Other" should be checked for "Prevailing Wage Source."[427]

While DOL's Office of Foreign Labor Certification (OFLC) "does not maintain and/or endorse a list of acceptable wage source survey instruments,"[428] it has pointed out that it maintains a webpage with disclosure data from certified LCAs that shows its wage source entries,[429] and also provides a list of examples of "commonly used prevailing wage surveys."[430]

---

[425] DOL, "FAQs for H-1B, H-1B1, and E-3 Programs" (July 31, 2015), AILA Doc. No. 15080502.
[426] Id.
[427] Id.
[428] Id.
[429] DOL, "H-1B Program Data," http://www.flcdatacenter.com/CaseH1B.aspx.
[430] DOL, "FAQs for H-1B, H-1B1, and E-3 Programs" (July 31, 2015), AILA Doc. No. 15080502. The list can be found at DOL, "ETA 9035CP - Instructions for the 9035 & 9035E Appendix II: Sample of Acceptable Wage Survey Sources," http://bit.ly/9035CPsurveylist.

Copyright © 2017. American Immigration Lawyers Association. All rights reserved.

The same steps should be performed for any additional worksite(s), which would require the filing of a separate prevailing wage determination or wage survey analysis.

4. Completing the ETA Form 9035 – Parts H and I

For Part H, additional attestations are necessary. These address payment of the higher of the prevailing wage and the actual wage; benefits; working conditions; the absence of a "strike, lockout of work stoppage in the named occupation at the place of employment"; notification to the bargaining representative or to workers that "has been or will be provided in the named occupation at the place of employment"; and provision of a copy of the LCA "to each nonimmigrant worker employed pursuant to the application."

Part I applies only to LCAs for H-1B petitions. The appropriate box should be checked in subsection 1 to indicate whether the employer is H-1B dependent and/or a willful violator of the LCA program and, if yes, whether the LCA will be used only for H-1B beneficiaries who are exempt from the additional requirements. If either Question 1 or 2 is answered in the affirmative, and Question 3 is answered in the negative, the additional attestations should be made concerning displacement and hiring of U.S. workers in subsection 2. For detailed discussion of these issues and subsequent responsibilities, see above.

5. Completing the ETA Form 9035 – Parts J through N

Part J should indicate where the LCA will be maintained: either at the employer's principal place of business or at the place of employment. Stated another way, for Part J, the options are either the headquarters or the worksite location.

In Part K, the employer's representative should also declare, "on behalf of the employer," that the information in the LCA is "true and accurate" and make the required attestations. These include having read the LCA form's instructions, complying with the applicable regulations and form instructions, and "agree[ing] to make this application, supporting documentation, and other records available to officials of [DOL] upon request during any investigation under the [INA]." The practitioner should note that the form also states how "[m]aking fraudulent representations on this Form can lead to civil or criminal action under 18 USC §1001, 18 USC §1546, or other provisions of law." The declaration requires entry of the employer's designated signatory's full name and title. This individual will also be responsible for signing the certified LCA.

Part L should be completed, by providing name and contact information, only if the LCA was prepared by any individual other than the attorney/agent or the employer's representative. The practitioner should note that Part M is absent on the online version of the form because it is where DOL certifies an approved LCA. Part N addresses the LCA complaint procedure and informs how "any resulting [LCA] certification *must* be signed *immediately upon receipt* from the Department of Labor before it can be submitted to USCIS for further processing."

Copyright © 2017. American Immigration Lawyers Association. All rights reserved.

D. Filing the LCA and Certification

Once all required fields have been completed, the system will search the form to determine whether any questions or fields are empty or if any answers will result in automatic denial of the application. If any deficiencies are detected, the system will provide a list of items that should be corrected before proceeding. When the form is submitted, a processing case number is assigned and can be used to track the progress of the application. The case number should also be referenced in any future communication with DOL concerning the application.

One recurring issue is the need to verify the employer's FEIN:[431]

"DOL uses a live database for employer FEIN verifications on LCA and PERM cases. DOL does not use Dunn and Bradstreet. The database is updated quarterly so newer companies may not be included. Also, the database focuses on business so some public employers are not included. A verification request can be made in advance of the [LCA] submission and turn around on those requests and typically 48 hours."[432]

"[DOL] does quarterly updates of its FEIN records that are linked to the iCERT system, and if an employer is newly registered, or has changed its FEIN, the record does not automatically get updated with DOL. DOL is building the FEIN list as they get evidence that additional FEINs are valid."[433]

Therefore, the practitioner is strongly advised to request verification of the employer's FEIN before filing the LCA. To determine whether the FEIN is already verified in the DOL system, the LCA can be completed on the iCert system, and the system will produce a warning if the FEIN is not in the database. If no warning appears, there is no need to request FEIN verification. Verification often is needed, however, for a company that has a "recently issued FEIN," or has experienced a corporate name change,[434] as well as newer and public employers. As indicated by DOL: "Suitable evidence of FEIN issuance includes a copy of government correspondence showing the FEIN number and company name."[435] Requesting FEIN verification before filing the LCA is a much better strategy than the alternative, which requires receiving an LCA denial and then filing a new LCA "once the FEIN has been validated."[436]

Once submitted, DOL should process the LCA and issue a determination within seven business days. DOL notifies the practitioner via email when the determination

---

[431] "Notes from USDOL Open Forum" (July 1, 2010), AILA Doc. No. 10072067 ("DOL processes FEIN verifications within 48 hours. Verification requests are accepted in advance of LCA filings").

[432] "Notes from USDOL Open Forum" (July 1, 2010), AILA Doc. No. 10072067; "Minutes from DOL Stakeholders Meeting" (Oct. 28, 2010), AILA Doc. No. 10111762 ("DOL gets approximately 165 requests for FEIN verification daily. It takes approximately 48 hours to verify an FEIN").

[433] "Notes from DOL Stakeholders Meeting" (July 31, 2009), AILA Doc. No. 09080760.

[434] Id.

[435] Id.

[436] Id. ("DOL will not reopen LCAs previously denied for lack of a valid FEIN").

Copyright © 2017. American Immigration Lawyers Association. All rights reserved.

has been made, or the practitioner can simply access iCert to check the status of the LCA. The certified LCA should be available on the iCert website system for retrieval and printing. As noted above, the approved LCA should be signed *"immediately upon receipt."*[437]

DOL "tr[ies] to provide all bases for rejection in its initial denial to avoid creating duplicate work for DOL."[438] Common reasons for denial include "FEIN not recognized, private wage survey not recognized, wage level not included, and prevailing wage issues."[439]

An LCA may be withdrawn online by logging into the iCert system, selecting the certified LCA, and following the instructions to withdraw the LCA online. Alternatively, the LCA can be withdrawn by emailing *LCA.Chicago@dol.gov*, with "Certified LCA Withdraw Request" in the subject line, a copy of the LCA as an attachment, and the LCA case number and the reason for the withdrawal in the body of the email.[440]

IX. Recordkeeping Requirements

Employers are required by statute to retain for public inspection a copy of each LCA filed and "such accompanying documents as are necessary."[441] DOL's regulation details what it views as such "necessary" documents, as well as documentation that it requires employers to keep, albeit not in the public access file, in case of an investigation. Information regarding development of each of these types of documentation is provided in the discussions of the respective attestation elements earlier in this chapter.

A. The Public Access File

Within one working day after the filing of the LCA, the employer must make available for public inspection at its principal place of business or at the place of employment the following documentation:[442]

- A copy of the certified LCA. Electronically filed LCAs should be printed out and signed by the employer.

- Documentation of the wage rate to be paid to the nonimmigrant. A wage range, rather than the specific wage paid to the individual nonimmigrant, should satisfy this requirement.[443]

---

[437] DOL, "Form ETA-9035," https://www.foreignlaborcert.doleta.gov/pdf/ETA_Form_9035_2009_Revised.pdf (emphasis in original).

[438] "Notes from DOL Stakeholders Telephone Conference" (June 22, 2010), AILA Doc. No. 10062462; "Notes from DOL Stakeholders Meeting" (July 31, 2009), AILA Doc. No. 09080760.

[439] "Minutes from DOL Stakeholders Meeting" (Oct. 28, 2010), AILA Doc. No. 10111762; "Notes from USDOL Open Forum" (July 1, 2010), AILA Doc. No. 10072067.

[440] "Important Department of Labor E-mail Addresses (Updated June 29, 2010)," AILA Doc. No. 09012860.

[441] INA §212(n)(1)(G).

[442] 20 CFR §655.760(a).

Copyright © 2017. American Immigration Lawyers Association. All rights reserved.

- An explanation of the actual wage system, in such forms as a memo or a copy of the employer's pay system or pay scales. The actual amounts of the wages of the nonimmigrant and comparable employees need not be named in the public documentation, but the explanation of the system used to set the wages and adjustments to wages should be provided.[444]

- Documentation of the prevailing wage. This can be a general description of the source and methodology used, or can be the actual determination or source.

- A copy of the dated posting or notification to the union. This should include the name and address of the collective bargaining representative or, if there is no such representative, a notation as to the dates when, and locations where, the notice was posted.[445]

- A summary of the benefits offered to comparable U.S. workers and a statement explaining any differentiation of benefits.

- If the employer uses the "single employer" definition in making its determination as to H-1B dependency, a list of the entities included as part of the single employer.

If the employer is H-1B dependent or a willful violator, the public access file also must include:[446]

- A summary of the recruitment methods used, and time frames of the recruitment, or copies of the "pertinent documents," if the LCA is not for an exempt H-1B.

- If only exempt H-1Bs are employed under the LCA, a list of the individuals so employed.

If there has been a change in corporate structure, the following documentation also is required for the public access file:[447]

- A sworn statement by a responsible official of the new entity that it accepts all responsibilities under the predecessor's LCAs.

- A list of each affected LCA and its date of certification.

- A description of the actual wage system of the new entity.

- The new entity's FEIN.

The public access file must be retained at the employer's principal place of business in the United States or at the place of employment. The public access file,

---

[443] *Santiglia v. Sun Microsystems, Inc.,* 03-076 (ARB, July 29, 2005), AILA Doc. No. 05080367, p.11, upholding the ALJ's finding that "while the wage rate to be paid a H-1B worker hired under an LCA must be made part of the public access records, there is no right of public access to the specific wage being paid a specific worker under the LCA."

[444] 20 CFR §655.731(b)(2).

[445] 20 CFR §655.734(b).

[446] 20 CFR §655.760(a)(9) and (10).

[447] 20 CFR §655.760(a)(7).

Copyright © 2017. American Immigration Lawyers Association. All rights reserved.

including the signed LCA itself, can be maintained in hard copy, or it can be maintained entirely electronically.[448] The public access file records must be kept for one year beyond the last date on which an H-1B was employed under the LCA. If no one was ever employed under the LCA, the file must be kept for one year from the date the LCA expired or was withdrawn.[449]

B. Non-Public Records That Must Be Maintained

In addition to the public access file, the DOL regulation requires that employers retain other documentation in case of an investigation. This non-public information is largely what would be considered by most employers to be sensitive competitive information or information that would be regarded as private with respect to the individual employee(s):

- To the extent that the public access file does not contain this documentation (for instance, if it contains only a general description of the source and methodology as allowed by the regulation), the employer must retain the underlying documentation of the prevailing wage; namely, the SWA determination, a copy of the wage survey, the Davis-Bacon or SCA determination, or the relevant excerpt from the union contract.[450]

- If the nonimmigrant's salary is supplemented by other non-discretionary payments to meet the required wage, the employer's documentation must show the commitment to make the payments that the obligation was met for prior pay periods, and that upon payment the required wage will be met for each current or future pay period.[451]

- For actual wage, the employer is required to retain documentation showing how the wage set for the nonimmigrant relates to the wages paid to other comparable employees. While the explanation of the system used to establish the actual wage, including a summary of the system for pay increases, must be in the public access file, documentation comparing wages to other workers need only be provided to DOL in an investigation.[452] The regulation specifies that this requirement is in addition to the payroll data requirement, but is more specific than the general description of the actual wage system required for the public access file. A memo showing what comparisons were made and how differentiations were made should satisfy this provision.

- If the employer's wage system changes during the LCA validity period, the employer is required by the regulation to retain documentation of the change in

---

[448] "Minutes from DOL PERM/H-1B Stakeholder Meeting" (Mar. 7, 2017), AILA Doc. No. 17031303.

[449] 20 CFR §655.760(c).

[450] 20 CFR §§655.760(a)(4) and 655.731(b)(3).

[451] 20 CFR §655.731(c)(4).

[452] 20 CFR §655.760(a)(3).

Copyright © 2017. American Immigration Lawyers Association. All rights reserved.

the system and show that the nonimmigrant is still earning the higher of the prevailing wage or the actual wage under the changed system.[453]

- Payroll records regarding the nonimmigrant and all other employees in the specific employment in question at the place of employment must be retained and shown to DOL in an investigation to document satisfaction of the actual wage requirement.[454] The payroll records must include names, home addresses, occupations, rate of pay, hours worked each day and week if non-salaried or part-time, additions and deductions from pay, and total amount paid each pay period.[455] Payroll records must be kept at the employer's principal place of business in the United States or at the place of employment for three years from the date of creation of the record, except that if an enforcement action is commenced, they must be retained until the proceeding is completed.[456]

- To satisfy the benefits element of the required wage, documentation of the benefits offered to the nonimmigrant must be kept and shown to DOL on request. This includes a copy of benefit descriptions/employee handbooks; a copy of benefit plans and any rules for differentiating benefits among employees; evidence of the benefits actually provided, including what was actually selected or declined, by both U.S. and nonimmigrant workers; and, where a nonimmigrant is provided with home country benefits, evidence of the benefits provided before and after the nonimmigrant went to the United States.[457]

- Employers that had to perform a full calculation to determine that they were not H-1B dependent must also retain a dated copy of the calculation.[458] If a "single employer" definition was used, documentation of whatever calculation was used (snap shot or full) must be retained in the event of an investigation.[459] If the employer moved from dependent to non-dependent, it must retain a copy of the calculation used to reach that conclusion.[460]

- Employers subject to the additional attestations by virtue of being H-1B dependent or willful violators are required to retain additional backup documentation of compliance with those additional attestations:

  - For the non-displacement attestation: all records created or received regarding the circumstances under which any U.S. workers in the same area and same occupation as any H-1Bs hired left their employ during the 90-day/90-day "look" period. This includes any notices of termination, as well

---

[453] 20 CFR §655.731(b)(2).

[454] 20 CFR §655.731(b)(1).

[455] *Id.*

[456] 20 CFR §655.760(c).

[457] 20 CFR §655.731(b)(1)(viii).

[458] 20 CFR §655.736(d)(4).

[459] 20 CFR §655.736(d)(7).

[460] 20 CFR §655.736(d)(5).

Copyright © 2017. American Immigration Lawyers Association. All rights reserved.

as the employee's name, last known address, title and job description, documentation regarding experience and qualifications, principal assignments, evaluations, and all documents concerning the employee's departure.[461]

- For the secondary non-displacement attestation: whatever type of record the employer used to document its efforts at making the inquiry and obtaining the needed assurances.[462]

- For the recruitment attestation: recruiting methods used, places and dates of recruitment, and compensation terms. This can be copies of the documents themselves, or a memo to file.[463] In addition, the employer must retain documentation received or prepared regarding the treatment of applicants, such as application forms, interview records, records of job offers, applicant responses, etc.[464]

Other than payroll records, the regulation is not specific as to how long this documentation must be retained. Because the documentation largely expands upon what is required in the public access file, it could be presumed that the retention requirements are the same as for those files: one year beyond the last date on which an H-1B is employed under the LCA.[465]

X. Enforcement

As well-stated by a DOL ALJ, "[f]our things can initiate an investigation and enforcement proceedings against an H-1B employer:

1. "an investigation following receipt of a complaint filed by an aggrieved person or organization, pursuant to [INA §212(n)(2)(A)];

2. "a random investigation of an employer, if that employer has been found a willful violator within the past five years, pursuant to [INA §212 (n)(2)(F)];

3. "an investigation after the Secretary of Labor personally certified, pursuant to [INA §212 (n)(2)(G)(i)], that there is reasonable cause to believe an employer is not in compliance with the INA; and

4. "an investigation pursuant to [INA §212 (n)(2)(G)(ii)], where the Secretary received specific and credible information from a source likely to have knowledge of an employer's practices that an employer has committed a willful failure, a pattern of practice of failures, or a substantial failure that affects multiple employees with respect to certain subsections of [INA §212(n)(1)]."[466]

---

[461] 20 CFR §655.738(e)(1).

[462] 20 CFR §655.738(e)(2).

[463] 20 CFR §655.739(i)(1).

[464] 20 CFR §655.739(i)(2).

[465] 20 CFR §655.760(c).

[466] *Admin'r, Wage and Hour Div. v. Volt Management Corp.*, 2012-LCA-44 (ALJ June 16, 2106), AILA Doc. No. 16062136.

Copyright © 2017. American Immigration Lawyers Association. All rights reserved.

A. Complaint by Aggrieved Party

An aggrieved party can be a person or an entity. The party's operations or interests must have been adversely affected by the alleged violation. Workers, both U.S. and nonimmigrant, whose job or pay was affected, union representatives, competitors, and government agencies with impacted programs are all potentially aggrieved parties.[467]

Complaints by aggrieved parties regarding violations of the LCA provisions (except related to failure by an H-1B dependent employer to offer a job to an equally or better qualified U.S. worker) are filed with the Administrator, Wage and Hour Division, of the Employment Security Administration (ESA) of the DOL[468] at any local Wage and Hour office.[469] Note that this is a different division than the Employment and Training Administration (ETA), of which OFLC is a part. Essentially, OFLC is responsible for processing and administration of the LCA program and the Wage and Hour Division is responsible for enforcement.

Complaints regarding failure by an H-1B dependent employer to offer a job to an equally or better qualified U.S. worker are filed with the Department of Justice's Immigrant and Employee Rights Section, formerly known as the Office of Special Counsel for Immigration-Related Unfair Employment Practices.[470]

Complaints filed with Wage and Hour do not require any particular form, but should provide sufficient facts to determine if there is reasonable cause to believe a violation has occurred. Wage and Hour has 10 days to determine whether a complaint by an aggrieved party presents reasonable cause to warrant an investigation. If it decides that investigation is not warranted, it notifies the complainant, who may submit a new complaint but otherwise has no right to an appeal or hearing. If Wage and Hour determines that an investigation is warranted, it accepts the complaint for filing, and a written determination is supposed to be issued within 30 calendar days thereafter. Extensions of this investigative time are available with the consent of the employer and complainant, or if additional time is needed to get information for reasons outside of Wage and Hour's control.[471] However, the 30-day deadline is not considered jurisdictional, and thus the failure of Wage and Hour to meet the timeframe has no practical effect.[472]

The employer has no right of appeal or hearing from the determination that an investigation is warranted.[473]

---

[467] 20 CFR §655.715.

[468] 20 CFR §655.710(a).

[469] 20 CFR §655.806(a)(6).

[470] 20 CFR §655.710(b).

[471] 20 CFR §655.806(a).

[472] *Cyberworld Enterprise Technologies Inc. v. Administrator*, 04-049 (ARB May 24, 2006), AILA Doc. No. 08080764; *Admin'r, Wage & Hour Division v. Synergy Systems, Inc.*, 04-076 (ARB June 30, 2006), AILA Doc. No. 06071071, citing *Brock v. Pierce County*, 476 U.S. 253 (1986).

[473] 20 CFR §655.806(a)(3).

Copyright © 2017. American Immigration Lawyers Association. All rights reserved.

A federal appeals court has held that DOL cannot expand an aggrieved party investigation beyond what is properly part of the complaint, rejecting the position that "reasonable cause to investigate any single violation alleged by an aggrieved party 'establishes a reasonable cause to investigate the employer' and every action the employer has taken with respect to the H-1B program and its H-1B employees."[474] The court went on to state:

> "Rather than authorize an open-ended investigation of the employer and its general compliance without regard to the actual allegations in the aggrieved-party complaint, [INA §212(n)(2)(A)] expressly ties the Secretary's initial investigatory authority to the complaint and those specific allegations 'respecting [an employer's alleged] failure to meet a condition specified in an [LCA] or [an employer's] misrepresentation of material facts in such an [LCA]' for which the Secretary finds 'reasonable cause to believe' the employer committed the alleged violation."[475]

At least one ALJ has specifically relied upon this case's reasoning in finding that Wage and Hour did not have the authority to investigate the treatment of 80 employees based on the complaint of one employee. Noting that the case before him arose in a different circuit from *Greater Missouri Medical Pro-Care Providers, Inc. v. Perez*, the ALJ nevertheless adopted the reasoning and found that "the INA text doesn't permit a comprehensive investigation of an H-1B employer when the Secretary has received no more than a single complaint from an aggrieved employee. Comprehensive investigation is reserved to an employer found guilty of a willful violation in the past … or done in the course of a general compliance review of an employer…."[476]

B. Random Investigations

Wage and Hour is authorized to conduct random investigations of an employer for five years after a finding by DOL that that employer willfully violated an attestation or willfully misrepresented a material fact. Random investigations also can occur for five years after a finding by DOJ that an H-1B dependent employer willfully failed to offer employment to an equally or better qualified U.S. worker. These investigations can occur at any time in the five years, and do not require a reason to believe a violation has occurred.[477]

C. Specific, Credible Information and Secretary-Certified Reasonable Cause

This investigation authority exists under statute only for H-1Bs. There is no parallel statutory provision for H-1B1s or E-3s.

---

[474] *Greater Missouri Medical Pro-Care Providers, Inc. v. Perez*, 812 F.3d 1132 (8th Cir, 2015). DOL had conducted a wide-ranging investigation of the employer's LCA practices triggered by one employee's complaint involving primarily conduct outside the statute of limitations, discussed below.

[475] *Id.*

[476] *Admin'r, Wage and Hour Div. v. Volt Management Corp.*, 2012-LCA-44 (ALJ June 16, 2106), AILA Doc. No. 16062136.

[477] INA §212(n)(2)(F); 20 CFR §655.808.

Copyright © 2017. American Immigration Lawyers Association. All rights reserved.

The violations about which non-aggrieved parties can submit information are limited to willful violations of provisions related to misrepresentations of material facts, failure to pay required wages, failure to provide required working conditions, violation of the strike/lockout provisions, displacement of U.S. workers by H-1B dependent employers, failure by an H-1B dependent employer to make appropriate inquiries of third-party worksites, or failure of an H-1B dependent employer to recruit in good faith.[478]

An employee of DOL can provide information under this provision only if it was obtained in the course of a lawful investigation and the information does not include any documents submitted by the employer to DOL or DHS in the course of obtaining the H-1B.[479] As discussed above, a court has found that this does not mean that DOL can expand an investigation triggered by a single aggrieved party complaint to a full investigation of the employer, but the court did leave open the possibility that this provision could be used by DOL if information about one of the types of violations allowed to be investigated under this provision is properly uncovered in the course of an aggrieved party investigation.[480]

The non-aggrieved party is not required to submit any particular form (though one may be provided), but the information provided must include the person's identity and relationship to the employer, other information indicating the basis for the knowledge, and a description of the possible violation in sufficient detail for Wage and Hour to determine if reasonable cause to believe a willful violation has occurred.[481] The person submitting the information may be interviewed and advised that his or her identity will be kept confidential.[482]

Wage and Hour must promptly notify the employer of the information once it confirms that the person likely possessed relevant knowledge, that specific credible information of a violation described above was provided, and that there is reasonable cause to believe that either the violation was willful, the employer has engaged in a pattern and practice of violations, or the employer has committed substantial violations that affect multiple employees. This notification is not required if DOL determines that disclosure might interfere with the employer's compliance. If the employer is notified, it must be given sufficient detail to enable a response, which must be submitted within 10 days.[483]

Once the employer responds, Wage and Hour must then determine if the allegations should be referred to the Secretary of Labor. If it is so referred, in order for an investigation to be commenced, the Secretary must personally (this cannot be delegated) certify that the information provides reasonable cause to believe a relevant

---

[478] INA §212(n)(2)(G)(ii) and 20 CFR §655.807(a).

[479] 20 CFR §655.807(e).

[480] *Greater Missouri Medical Pro-Care Providers, Inc. v. Perez*, 812 F.3d 1132 (8th Cir, 2015).

[481] 20 CFR §655.807(a).

[482] 20 CFR §655.807(b).

[483] 20 CFR §655.807(d) and (f).

Copyright © 2017. American Immigration Lawyers Association. All rights reserved.

violation has occurred; that the violation is willful, part of a pattern and practice, or substantial and affecting multiple employees; and that all other requirements of this process have been met.[484] There is no hearing from a decision to initiate or not initiate an investigation, but once an investigation is certified, it is to be conducted and a written determination issued within 30 days. Extensions of this investigative time are available with the consent of the employer, or if additional time is needed to get information for reasons outside of Wage and Hour's control.[485]

D. If Prevailing Wage Violations Are at Issue

If prevailing wage is at issue from any of the investigative triggers, Wage and Hour can look at whether the employer has the required documentation and whether the documentation supports the wage attestation. Lack of documentation can be a violation in and of itself. In addition, if there is no documentation or if Wage and Hour has reason to believe, based on significant evidence, that the prevailing wage from an independent authoritative source or another legitimate source varies substantially from the prevailing wage or that the other legitimate source does not conform to regulatory criteria, it can seek a prevailing wage determination from ETA. In such a case, the 30 days for investigation can be suspended while the determination is pending.[486]

The employer can challenge a prevailing wage determination in the course of an investigation by filing a request for review with BALCA within 30 days of receipt of the determination.[487] If the employer does not challenge the determination, it is deemed accepted.[488] If the employer does challenge the prevailing wage determination, the 30-day investigation period is suspended until that process is completed.[489]

Administrative law judges (ALJs) are not allowed to determine the validity of a wage determination or examine the basis for the determination. If, in the course of the ALJ hearing discussed below, the ALJ determines that the Wage and Hour request to the ETA was not warranted, the matter is to be remanded to Wage and Hour for further proceedings. If there is no such remand, the ALJ must accept the ETA determination or the final determination obtained through the challenge process above.[490]

E. Good Faith Compliance

Generally, "a person or entity is considered to have complied with the requirements..., notwithstanding a technical or procedural failure to meet such

---

[484] 20 CFR §655.807(h).

[485] 20 CFR §655.807(h) and (i).

[486] 20 CFR §655.731(d)(1).

[487] 20 CFR §§655.731(d)(2) and 656.41(e).

[488] 20 CFR §655.731(d)(2)(ii).

[489] 20 CFR §§655.731(d)(2)(i), 806(a)(4), and 807(j). Interestingly, subsection 731 refers to a "final ruling" and 806 and 807 refer to "completion of such complaint process." Thus, it is unclear what impact a request for judicial review would have on the investigative timetable.

[490] 20 CFR §655.840(c).

Copyright © 2017. American Immigration Lawyers Association. All rights reserved.

requirements, if there was a good faith attempt to comply with the requirements."[491]
If an investigation reveals that the prevailing wage requirement was violated, no fine
or penalty should be imposed "if the person or entity can establish that the manner in
which the prevailing wage was calculated was consistent with recognized industry
standards and practices."[492]

However, an employer cannot use the good faith exception if:

- The "basis for the failure" was "explained" by DOL "or another enforcement
  agency";

- The "person or entity has been provided a period of not less than 10 business
  days (beginning after the date of the explanation) within which to correct the
  failure"; and

- The failure was not "voluntarily" rectified within the allotted time period.[493]

The good faith provision similarly does not apply, "to a person or entity that has
engaged in or is engaging in a pattern or practice of willful violations."[494] Further,
these enforcement measures should not "be construed as superseding or preempting
any other enforcement-related authority under" the INA or "any other Act."[495]

F. Statute of Limitations

In investigations triggered either by an aggrieved party's complaint or information
from a non-aggrieved party, the complaint must be filed or information submitted no
later than 12 months after the latest date the alleged violations were committed. Thus,
the date on which the employer failed to fulfill a condition or the date on which the
misrepresentation was last demonstrated would begin the running of the limitation
period. If a complaint is timely filed, DOL can reach back to earlier violations to
assess a remedy (such as back wages dating to a period more than one year before the
complaint was filed).[496] However, discrete violations that occurred more than 12
months before the complaint is filed "are not actionable."[497] If a violation is
continuing, such as failing to pay a nonimmigrant the required wage while an
employment relationship is ongoing, the limitations period does not begin to run until
the violation ceases.[498]

---

[491] INA §212(n)(2)(H)(i).

[492] INA §212(n)(2)(H)(iii).

[493] INA §212(n)(2)(H)(ii).

[494] INA §212(n)(2)(H)(iv).

[495] INA §212(n)(2)(I).

[496] 20 CFR §§655.806(a)(5) and 807(c).

[497] *Greater Missouri Medical Pro-Care Providers, Inc. v. Perez*, 812 F.3d 1132 (8th Cir, 2015). The
complaint included allegations of improper deductions from wages, benching, and early termination penalty.
However, only the early termination penalty had occurred within the 12 months, so only that allegation was
found actionable.

[498] *Gupta v. Jain Software Consulting, Inc.*, 05-008 (ARB Mar. 30, 2007), AILA Doc. No. 08080661
(Despite notification to INS of supposed termination of employment, the record was not clear whether notice
had been given to the nonimmigrant or return transportation payment provided, and thus termination may not
Cont'd

Copyright © 2017. American Immigration Lawyers Association. All rights reserved.

Administrative bodies have discretion to accept filings outside the limitations period where the respondent has actively misled the complainant regarding his or her right to file a petition, the complainant has been prevented from exercising his or her rights in some extraordinary way, or the complainant has in fact raised the precise claim in issue but did so in the wrong forum.[499]

G. Determinations and Hearings

A determination issued under any of the types of investigation must be served personally or by certified mail on the employer, complainant, and "other known interested parties," and filed with DOL's Chief ALJ along with a copy of the complaint. Where certified mail is not accepted by the party, DOL can use regular mail. The determination must be written, and must include the reasons for the determination, any remedies assessed, and the reasons for the remedies. The parties must be informed that they can request a hearing; the request must be received by the Chief ALJ within 15 calendar days of the date of the determination.[500]

If a timely request for a hearing is made in writing to the Chief ALJ, the determination is inoperative until the process is completed. The request must be dated, typed or legibly written, specify the issues giving rise to the request, state the reasons the determination is believed to be in error, include the address where the party wants to receive communications, and be signed. If Wage and Hour's determination is that there is no violation, the complainant or "other interested party" may request the hearing, and thus become the prosecuting party, and Wage and Hour may appear as amicus or intervenor. If the determination is that there is a violation, the employer may request the hearing, and Wage and Hour is the prosecuting party.[501]

The hearing request can be filed by fax, in person, by certified or regular mail, or by courier. If faxed, an original signed version must be submitted within 10 days.[502] A copy of the request must be sent to the Wage and Hour official who issued the determination, the Solicitor of Labor representative identified on the determination, and all known interested parties.[503] Pleadings and documents can be served by regular mail to the last known address of the party, though the ALJ may order an alternative

---

have occurred and violation may have been ongoing). *Compare to Ndiaye v. CVS Store No. 6081*, 05-024 (ARB May 9, 2007), AILA Doc. No. 08080762 (DHS not notified but nonimmigrant was given definitive notification of termination, and thus the 12-month limitation period had begun to run).

[499] *Admin'r, Wage & Hour Division v. Wings Digital Corp.*, 05-090 (ARB July 22, 2005), AILA Doc. No. 05072663. *But see Admin'r, Wage & Hour Division v. Board of Trustees of Indiana University*, 05-106 (ARB Aug. 31, 2005), AILA Doc. No. 08080766 (posted Aug. 7, 2008) (noting that these three elements are not exclusive and other factors could possibly justify tolling the limitations period). See also *Ndiaye v. CVS Store No. 6081*, 05-024 (ARB May 9, 2007), AILA Doc. No. 08080762 (a filing for unemployment compensation did not raise the precise claim in issue).

[500] 20 CFR §655.815.

[501] 20 CFR §655.820.

[502] 20 CFR §655.820(e).

[503] 20 CFR §655.820(f).

Copyright © 2017. American Immigration Lawyers Association. All rights reserved.

form of service. Two copies are to be served on Wage and Hour's attorney and one copy on the Solicitor. Time periods begin the day following the action and include the last day of the period, unless it falls on a weekend or federal holiday, in which case the next business day is included.[504] An interested party who fails to meet the 15-day deadline for requesting a hearing may nevertheless participate by consent of the ALJ as amicus curiae or as an intervenor.[505]

The Chief ALJ assigns the case, and the ALJ then has seven calendar days to notify the parties of the time and place of the hearing. At least 14 days' notice must be given, but the hearing must be no more than 60 days after the date of the determination. Any requests for postponement must be for compelling reasons and with the consent of all parties. A schedule for prehearing briefs can be designated, but no post-hearing briefs will be allowed except as specifically requested by the ALJ.[506] DOL's Rules of Practice and Procedure for Administrative Hearings Before the Office of Administrative Law Judges (other than Subpart B)[507] apply in these proceedings, except that any oral or documentary evidence can be received, and the ALJ can exclude any evidence that is immaterial, irrelevant, or repetitive.[508]

The ALJ is required to issue a decision within 60 days of the hearing. The decision must state the findings and conclusions, the reasons for them, and an appropriate order on each material issue in the record.[509]

H. Appeals

Any interested party can request review of the ALJ's decision within 30 days by petition to the Administrative Review Board (ARB). Like the request for hearing, the request for review must be dated, typed or legibly written, specify the issues in the ALJ's decision giving rise to the request, state the reasons the decision is believed to be in error, include the address where the party wants to receive communications, be signed, and include copies of the ALJ's decision and order along with any other record documents that would assist the ARB in determining if a review is in order.[510] Unlike with service of pleadings in an ALJ proceeding, if the end of the 30-day period falls on a weekend or holiday, the due date is *not* considered to be the next business day.[511]

The ARB must serve on all parties its decision whether it will review the ALJ's decision within 30 calendar days of its receipt of the petition for review. The ALJ

---

[504] 20 CFR §655.830.

[505] 20 CFR §655.820(d),

[506] 20 CFR §655.835.

[507] 29 CFR part 18.

[508] 20 CFR §655.825.

[509] 20 CFR §655.840(a) and (b).

[510] 20 CFR §655.845(a) and (b).

[511] *Admin'r, Wage & Hour Division v. Board of Trustees of Indiana University*, 05-106 (ARB Aug. 31, 2005), AILA Doc. No. 08080766.

Copyright © 2017. American Immigration Lawyers Association. All rights reserved.

has 15 days after the ARB's notice to forward the record. If the ARB does decide to review the decision, it must notify the parties what issues will be reviewed, the form of submissions it will require, and the time frames for the submissions. Copies of all submissions must be served on all parties, and must be received at the ARB by the due date. The ARB must issue its decision within 180 days of the notice of intent to review.[512]

I. Remedies

The civil remedies that can be ordered, depending on the type of degree of violation, include fines, back pay and reimbursement, debarment, and other appropriate administrative remedies. Also, as discussed above, the employer can be subjected to random investigations for five years,[513] The exact remedies for each type and degree of violation are charted in Figure X-Y below.

Fines can range from up to $1,000 per violation to up to $35,000 per violation. The base and maximum fines can be adjusted at least every four years in accordance with a cost of living formula. The adjustment amounts are published in the Federal Register.[514] As of the time of this writing, the adjusted amounts of the fines range from $1,811 to $51,588.[515] These adjusted amounts are reflected in Figure X-Y below.

In addition to the rules reflected in Figure X-Y, DOL may take into account in determining fine amounts such other factors as previous history of violations, number of workers affected, gravity of the violation, the employer's good faith efforts to comply, the employer's explanation of the situation, the employer's commitment to future compliance, and the extent to which the employer gained financially from the violation.[516]

Back pay and reimbursement of fringe benefits are determined by looking at the difference between the amount that should have been paid and the amount actually paid.[517] Interest on back pay may be awarded, generally at the interest rate charged on the underpayment of federal income taxes.[518] However, the doctrine of sovereign immunity precludes the award of back pay by employers that are federal agencies, such as Veterans Affairs hospitals.[519]

---

[512] 20 CFR §655.845(c) through (h).

[513] 20 CFR §655.808.

[514] 20 CFR §655.810(g).

[515] 82 Fed. Reg. 5373 (Jan. 18, 2107).

[516] 20 CFR §655.810(c).

[517] 20 CFR §655.810(a).

[518] *Amtel Group of Florida, Inc. v. Yongmahapakorn*, 04-087 (ARB Sept. 26, 2006), AILA Doc. No. 06102310, and *Admin'r, Wage & Hour Division v. Help Foundation of Omaha, Inc.*, 07-008 (ARB Dec. 31, 2008), AILA Doc. No. 09011570.

[519] DOJ Office of Legal Counsel, "Payment of Back Wages to Alien Physicians Hired under H-1B Visa Program" (Feb. 11, 2008), AILA Doc. No. 0902268.

Copyright © 2017. American Immigration Lawyers Association. All rights reserved.

If the employer is found to have improperly required payment of a penalty for ceasing employment or payment of the training fee, those amounts can be ordered reimbursed. If the employee cannot be located, the reimbursement would go to the U.S. Treasury.[520]

Debarment is the disqualification from approval of all nonimmigrant petitions under INA §214 and immigrant petitions under INA section 204 filed by the employer. When a remedy of debarment is found, DOL notifies DHS of the debarment and its length, which can range from one year to three years or more, depending on the nature of the violation as noted in Figure X-Y below.[521] The notification to DHS is made upon the earliest of when Wage and Hour determines there is a basis for finding a violation and no timely request for a hearing has been made, when an ALJ finds a violation and no request for ARB review is made, when the ARB declines to entertain an appeal of an adverse determination, or when the ARB reverses an ALJ holding of no violation.[522] Debarment also includes the invalidation of the LCA.[523] USCIS will apply the debarment to petitions filed by the employer prior to the start of the debarment period, if it actually adjudicates the petition during the debarment period.[524]

Other appropriate administrative remedies can include reinstatement of employment, back pay to displaced employees, or other equitable remedies.[525]

In most cases, willfulness of a violation either triggers the imposition of a remedy or increases the intensity of the penalty. "Willful" is defined as a "knowing failure" or "reckless disregard" as to whether the conduct was in violation of the relevant INA provisions or regulations.[526] Awareness of an obligation and then failing to meet the obligation can indicate willfulness,[527] as can developing false records to attempt to negate a violation.[528]

Figure X-Y

Violation/ Standard	Applies to	Penalty	Statutory/ Regulatory Section

---

[520] 20 CFR §655.810(e).

[521] 20 CFR §655.810(d).

[522] 20 CFR §655.855(b).

[523] 20 CFR §655.855(d).

[524] *Matter of [name not provided]*, SRC 08 059 52164 (AAO Mar. 3, 2009), AILA Doc. No. 10101864.

[525] 20 CFR §655.810(e)(2).

[526] 20 CFR §655.805(c), citing *McLaughlin v. Richland Shoe Co.*, 486 U.S. 128 (1988) and *Trans World Airlines v. Thurston*, 469 U.S. 111 (1985).

[527] *Admin'r, Wage & Hour Division v. Pegasus Consulting Group, Inc.*, 03-032 (June 30, 2005), AILA Doc. No. 05070562.

[528] *Admin'r, Wage & Hour Division v. Help Foundation of Omaha, Inc.*, 07-008 (ARB Dec. 31, 2008), AILA Doc. No. 09011570.

Copyright © 2017. American Immigration Lawyers Association. All rights reserved.

Violation/ Standard	Applies to	Penalty	Statutory/ Regulatory Section
Failure to pay required wage and benefits	H-1B, H-1B1, E-3	Back pay and benefits	INA §§212(n)(2)(D) and §212(t)(3)(D); 20 CFR §655.810(a)
Willful failure to pay required wage	H-1B, H-1B1, E-3	- Back pay - Up to $7,370 fine per violation - Debarment of at least two years - Other appropriate administrative remedies - Subject to random investigations for up to five years - Invalidation of LCA	INA §§212(n)(2)(C)(ii), (D), and (F), and 212(t)(3)(C)(ii), (D), and (E); 20 CFR §§655.750(c), 808, 810(b)(2)(i), and 810(d)(2)
Willful failure to provide working conditions that will not adversely affect similarly employed	H-1B, H-1B1, E-3	-Up to $7,370 fine per violation -Debarment of at least two years -Other appropriate administrative remedies -Subject to random investigations for up to five years -Invalidation of LCA	INA §§212(n)(2)(C)(ii) and (F) and 212(t)(3)(C)(ii) & (E); 20 CFR §§655.750(c), 808, 810(b)(2)(i), and 810(d)(2)
Failure to comply with the strike/lockout attestation	H-1B, H-1B1, E-3	-Fines up to $1,811 per violation -Debarment of at least one year -Other appropriate administrative remedies -Invalidation of LCA	INA §§212(n)(2)(C)(i) and 212(t)(3)(C)(i); 20 CFR§§655.750(c), 810(b)(1)(i), and 810(d)(1)

Copyright © 2017. American Immigration Lawyers Association. All rights reserved.

Violation/ Standard	Applies to	Penalty	Statutory/ Regulatory Section
Willful failure to comply with the strike/lockout attestation	H-1B, H-1B1, E-3	Up to $7,370 fine per violation -Debarment of at least two years -Other appropriate administrative remedies -Subject to random investigations for up to five years -Invalidation of LCA	INA §§212(n)(2)(C)(ii) and (F) and 212(t)(3)(C)(ii) and (E); 20 CFR §§655.750(c), 808, 810(b)(2)(i), and 810(d)(2)
Substantial failure to meet notice/posting requirement	H-1B, H-1B1, E-3	-Fines up to $1,811 per violation -Debarment of at least one year -Other appropriate administrative remedies -Invalidation of LCA	INA §§212(n)(2)(C)(i) and 212(t)(3)(C)(i); 20 CFR §§655.750(c), 810(b)(1)(ii), and 810(d)(1)
Willful failure to meet notice/posting requirement	H-1B, H-1B1, E-3	Up to $7,370 fine per violation -Debarment of at least two years -Other appropriate administrative remedies -Subject to random investigations for up to five years -Invalidation of LCA	INA §§212(n)(2)(C)(ii) and (F) and 212(t)(3)(C)(ii) and (E); 20 CFR §§655.750(c), 810(b)(2)(i), and 810(d)(2)

Copyright © 2017. American Immigration Lawyers Association. All rights reserved.

Violation/ Standard	Applies to	Penalty	Statutory/ Regulatory Section
Willful failure to provide access to public file	H-1B, H-1B1, E-3	Up to $7,370 fine per violation -Debarment of at least two years -Other appropriate administrative remedies -Subject to random investigations for up to five years	INA §§212(n)(2)(C)(ii) and (F) and 212(t)(3)(C)(ii) and (E); 20 CFR §§655.808
Failure to provide access to files that results in impeding investigation or ability to complain	H-1B, H-1B1, E-3	-Fines up to $1,811 per violation -Debarment of at least one year -Other appropriate administrative remedies	20 CFR §§655.808, 810(b)(1)(vi), and 810(d)(1)
Substantial failure to provide required LCA information	H-1B, H-1B1, E-3	-Fines up to $1,811 per violation -Debarment of at least one year -Other appropriate administrative remedies	INA §§212(n)(2)(C)(i) and 212(t)(3)(C)(i); 20 CFR §§655.810(b)(1)(ii) and 810(d)(1)
Willful failure to provide required LCA information	H-1B, H-1B1, E-3	Up to $7,370 fine per violation -Debarment of at least two years -Other appropriate administrative remedies -Subject to random investigations for up to five years	INA §§212(n)(2)(C)(ii) and (F) and 212(t)(3)(C)(ii) and (E); 20 CFR §§655.808, 810(b)(2)(i), and 810(d)(2)

Copyright © 2017. American Immigration Lawyers Association. All rights reserved.

Violation/ Standard	Applies to	Penalty	Statutory/ Regulatory Section
Misrepresentation of material fact in an LCA	H-1B, H-1B1, E-3	-Fines up to $1,811 per violation -Debarment of at least one year -Other appropriate administrative remedies -Invalidation of LCA	INA §§212(n)(2)(C)(i) and 212(t)(3)(C)(i); 20 CFR §§655.750(c), 810(b)(1)(iii), and 810(d)(1)
Willful misrepresentation of material fact	H-1B, H-1B1, E-3	-Up to $7,370 fine per violation -Debarment of at least two years -Other appropriate administrative remedies -Subject to random investigations for up to five years -Invalidation of LCA -Criminal penalties of up to $10,000 and/or five years imprisonment for knowing and willful submission of false statements	INA §§212(n)(2)(C)(ii) and (F) and 212(t)(3)(C)(ii) and (E); 18 USC 1001, 1546; 20 CFR §§655.808, 810(b)(2)(ii), and 810(d)(2)
Retaliation	H-1B, H-1B1, E-3	-Up to $7,370 fine per violation -Debarment of at least two years -Other appropriate administrative remedies -Subject to random investigations for up to five years	INA §§212(n)(2)(C)(ii) and (F) and 212(t)(3)(C)(ii) and (E); 20 CFR §§655.808, 810(b)(2)(iii), and 810(d)(2)

Copyright © 2017. American Immigration Lawyers Association. All rights reserved.

Violation/ Standard	Applies to	Penalty	Statutory/ Regulatory Section
Displacement of U.S. worker in the course of a willful failure to meet a condition of an attestation or a willful misrepresentation of material fact	H-1B, H-1B1, E-3	-Up to $51,588 fine per violation -Debarment of at least two years -Other appropriate administrative remedies	INA §§212(n)(2)(C)(iii) and 212(t)(3)(C)(iii); 20 CFR §§655.810(b)(3) and 810(d)(3)
Requiring payment of a penalty for ceasing employment	H-1B, H-1B1, E-3	-$1,811 fine per violation -Return of payment to the nonimmigrant	INA §§212(n)(2)(C)(vi) and 212(t)(3)(C)(vi); 20 CFR §655.810(b)(1)(iv)
Requiring payment or reimbursement of training fee	H-1B	-$1,811 fine per violation -Return of payment to the nonimmigrant	INA §212(n)(2)(C)(vi); 20 CFR §655.810(b)(1)(v)
H-1B dependent employer's displacement of U.S. worker	H-1B	-Fines up to $1,811 per violation -Debarment of at least one year -Other appropriate administrative remedies	INA §212(n)(2)(C)(i); 20 CFR §§655.810(b)(1)(i) and 810(d)(1)
H-1B dependent employer's willful displacement of U.S. worker	H-1B	-Fines up to $7,370 per violation -Debarment of at least two years -Other appropriate administrative remedies	INA §212(n)(2) (F); 20 CFR §§655.808, 810(b)(2)(i), and 810(d)(2)

Copyright © 2017. American Immigration Lawyers Association. All rights reserved.

Violation/ Standard	Applies to	Penalty	Statutory/ Regulatory Section
H-1B dependent employer's placement of nonimmigrant at third-party worksite that displaces U.S. worker	H-1B	-Fines up to $1,811 per violation -Debarment of at least one year -Other appropriate administrative remedies	INA §212(n)(2)(C)(i); 20 CFR §§655.810(b)(1)(i) and 810(d)(1)
H-1B dependent employer's failure to make displacement inquiry	H-1B	-Up to $7,370 fine per violation -Debarment of at least two years -Other appropriate administrative remedies -Subject to random investigations for up to five years	INA §212(n)(2)(F); 20 CFR §§655.808, 810(b)(2)(i), and 810(d)(2)
H-1B dependent employer's placement of nonimmigrant at third-party worksite where employer knew or should have known of displacement of U.S. worker or where employer had previously been sanctioned regarding same third party	H-1B	-Fines up to $51,588 per violation -Debarment of one to three years or more -Other appropriate administrative remedies	INA §212(n)(E); 20 CFR §§655.810(b)(3) and 810(d)(3)

Copyright © 2017. American Immigration Lawyers Association. All rights reserved.

Violation/ Standard	Applies to	Penalty	Statutory/ Regulatory Section
Substantial failure by H-1B dependent employer to conduct good faith recruitment	H-1B	-Fines up to $1,811 per violation -Debarment of at least one year -Other appropriate administrative remedies	INA §212(n)(2)(C)(i); 20 CFR §§655.810(b)(1)(ii) and 810(d)(1)
Willful failure by H-1B dependent employer to conduct good faith recruitment	H-1B	-Up to $7,370 fine per violation -Debarment of at least two years -Other appropriate administrative remedies -Subject to random investigations for up to five years	INA §§212(n)(2)(C)(ii) and (F); 20 CFR §§655.808, 810(b)(2)(i) and 810(d)(2)
Willful failure by H-1B dependent employer to offer the job to an equally or better qualified U.S. worker	H-1B	-Up to $7,370 fine per violation -Debarment of at least two years -Other appropriate administrative remedies -Subject to random investigations for up to five years	INA §§212(n)(2)(C)(ii) and (F); 20 CFR §§655.808, 810(b)(2)(i), and 810(d)(2)

Copyright © 2017. American Immigration Lawyers Association. All rights reserved.

CHAPTER SEVEN

H-1B VISAS AND STATUS

I. Executive Summary

The H-1B classification allows foreign nationals to accept professional assignments with U.S. employers, after the employer has obtained an approved labor condition application (LCA) from the Department of Labor (DOL). "H-1B dependent" employers have additional obligations. There is an annual numerical limitation of 65,000 for H-1B status, with an additional 20,000 H-1B visas for foreign nationals holding U.S. advanced degrees. An H-1B petition may be valid for up to three years. A foreign national may change H-1B employers. The nonimmigrant may simultaneously pursue permanent residence while holding H-1B status. Recapture of H-1B time is also available. H-1B petitions may be extended for an additional period of up to three years, to a maximum of six years in H-1B status. Limited exceptions allow for continued H-1B extensions until the foreign national obtains permanent residence. Dependent spouses and children of H-1B nonimmigrants hold H-4 status.

A. Checklist of Requirements

- Professional assignment
- Beneficiary qualifies for the specialty occupation
- H-1B visa number available for an initial petition
- Employer attestations on a labor condition application
- Valid employment relationship
- Additional filing fees
- No labor dispute in progress at the worksite for the occupation

B. Documents Necessary to Prepare the Petition

- Job description, including employment period and job requirements, if any
- Copies of the foreign national's educational and/or experience credentials, including transcripts
- Copy of the foreign national's résumé
- Basic information about the company
- Copy of biographic page(s) of passport(s) of the foreign national and any dependent spouse and children

C. Checklist of Questions to Ask the Client

- Does the job qualify as a profession and/or specialty occupation, or require licensure?
- Does the beneficiary have at least a four-year bachelor's degree? Alternatively, does he or she qualify for the job through a combination of education, experience, and/or training?

Copyright © 2017. American Immigration Lawyers Association. All rights reserved.

- Is the employer an educational or nonprofit organization?

- Is the petitioner an H-1B dependent employer?

- Does the petitioner know of other H-1B petition(s) that may be filed by other employers on behalf of the beneficiary during cap season?

- Was the beneficiary previously awarded an H-1B visa number and/or did he or she previously hold H-1B status?

- Will the employer agree to and abide by the labor condition application attestations?

- Did the employer comply with the requirement to post notice of the labor condition application at the proposed worksite, even if it is a third-party worksite?

- Will the job involve temporary or permanent placement at a third-party worksite?

- Will the petitioner have the right to control the beneficiary?

- Is the petitioner an agent?

- Will there be multiple worksites or employers?

- Is there a labor dispute at the worksite of the proposed H-1B assignment?

- Is the foreign national a beneficiary of a labor certification application or immigrant visa petition?

II. Requirements and Interpretations

The statute defines H-1B status as being available to a foreign national who will temporarily "perform services … in a specialty occupation,"[1] as long as "the Secretary of Labor determines and certifies to the Attorney General that the intending employer has filed with the [DOL] Secretary" a labor condition application,[2] as discussed below. This definition replaced the previous standard of distinguished merit or ability,[3] in 1990,[4] through the enactment of the Immigration Act of 1990 (IMMACT90), although the former standard applies to fashion models. The H-1B services may not entail agricultural labor pursuant to H-2A status or activities appropriate to O or P status.[5] As explained by U.S. Citizenship and Immigration Services (USCIS):

"The Immigration Act of 1952 established a new nonimmigrant class of temporary workers. In these provisions, Congress sought to grant the Attorney General sufficient authority to admit temporarily certain alien workers, industrial,

---

[1] Immigration and Nationality Act (INA) §101(a)(15)(H)(i)(b); 8 Code of Federal Regulations (CFR) §214.2(h)(1)(i).

[2] INA §101(a)(15)(H)(i)(b); 8 CFR §214.2(h)(1)(ii)(B)(1).

[3] Immigration Act of 1990 (IMMACT 90), Pub. L. No. 101-649, §205(c), 104 Stat. 4978 (Nov. 29, 1990). For background on the previous standard, see 55 Fed. Reg. 2606 (Jan. 26, 1990); Matter of Shaw, 11 I&N Dec. 277 (D.D. 1965).

[4] Adjudicator's Field Manual (AFM) 31.1(b).

[5] INA §101(a)(15)(H)(i)(b); 8 CFR §214.2(h)(1)(ii)(B)(1).

Copyright © 2017. American Immigration Lawyers Association. All rights reserved.

agricultural, or otherwise, for the purpose of alleviating labor shortages as they exist or may develop in certain areas or certain branches of American productive enterprises, particularly in periods of intensified production.... Prior to 1989, there were three H nonimmigrant worker classifications. The H-1 category included all 'persons of distinguished merit and ability' which was generously interpreted to include all persons engaged in occupations which required a bachelor's degree or equivalent."[6]

USCIS acknowledged that the regulations and other guidance on H-1B petitions "are detailed and somewhat complex, because the requirements of the statute itself are complex."[7] Numerous statutory and regulatory amendments and additions have resulted in what appears to be a constantly shifting landscape. This chapter seeks to provide a comprehensive overview of the issues and potentially applicable strategies, including those utilized under previous standards. Therefore, although USCIS guidance directs adjudicators against "rely[ing] on pre-IMMACT precedent case law for guidance on specialty occupations,"[8] this chapter discusses these older precedent cases because they still have value for background.

This chapter will not, however, discuss in detail H-1B status for fashion models and individuals providing services for Department of Defense (DOD) projects. A fashion model may also obtain H-1B status, either by having "distinguished merit or ability,"[9] or by "meet[ing] the requirements for the [specialty] occupation,"[10] relating to licensure, completion of a degree, or possession of "experience in the specialty equivalent to the completion of such degree, and recognition of expertise in the specialty through progressively responsible positions relating to the specialty."[11] H-1B status is also available for individuals who will perform "services relating to a Department of Defense (DOD) cooperative research and development project or coproduction project."[12]

As stated by regulation: "The employer must file a petition with the Service for review of the services or training and for determination of the alien's eligibility for classification as a temporary employee or trainee, before the alien may apply for a visa or seek admission to the United States."[13] The H-1B petition is filed on Form I-129,[14] as discussed below. An H-1B petition "shall be made and approved before

---

[6] AFM 31.1(b).

[7] AFM 31.2(a).

[8] AFM 31.3(a).

[9] INA §101(a)(15)(H)(i)(b); Miscellaneous and Technical Immigration and Naturalization Amendments of 1991 (MTINA), Pub. L. No. 102-232, §207(b) 105 Stat. 1733 (Dec. 12, 1991); 8 CFR §§214.2(h)(1)(i) and 214.2(h)(1)(ii)(B)(3).

[10] INA §101(a)(15)(H)(i)(b) (citing INA §214(i)(2)).

[11] INA §214(i)(2).

[12] 8 CFR §214.2(h)(1)(i). *See also* 8 CFR §§214.2(h)(1)(ii)(B)(2), 214.2(h)(4)(i)(A)(2), and 214.2(h)(4)(i)(A)(3).

[13] 8 CFR §214.2(h)(1)(i).

[14] 8 CFR §214.2(h)(2)(i)(A).

Copyright © 2017. American Immigration Lawyers Association. All rights reserved.

the visa is granted," but "approval of such a petition shall not, of itself, be construed as establishing that the alien is a nonimmigrant."[15] The statute provides that the "question of importing any alien as a nonimmigrant" in H-1B status "in any specific case or specific cases shall be determined by the Attorney General, after consultation with appropriate agencies of the Government, upon petition of the importing employer."[16]

An H-1B petition must name only a single beneficiary.[17] A foreign national may hold H-1B status for up to six years,[18] with certain key exceptions, as discussed below. USCIS has indicated separate requests must be made for H-1B status and Temporary Protected Status (TPS): "TPS is not granted in conjunction with H-1B.... If the individual would like to hold TPS and H-1B status, he or she may do so, but the individual will need to comply with the terms and conditions for each status."[19] The requirements of H-2 status should not be applied to H-1 status.[20] The dependent spouse and children of an H-1B nonimmigrant may obtain H-4 nonimmigrant status.[21]

Pursuant to Free Trade Agreements,[22] H-1B1 status is available to citizens of Chile and Singapore[23] who will engage in specialty occupations.[24] A labor condition application must be certified by DOL to the Department of Homeland Security (DHS) and the Department of State (DOS).[25] An initial H-1B1 petition may be approved for up to one year and may be extended,[26] as discussed below. Also as discussed below, an H-1B1 petition does not need to be filed with USCIS; the foreign national may apply for an H-1B1 visa at a U.S. consulate abroad.[27]

---

[15] INA §214(c)(1).

[16] *Id.*

[17] 8 CFR §§214.2(h)(2)(ii) (the regulation does not state that multiple beneficiaries may be named on a single H-1B petition) and 214.2(h)(2)(iii).

[18] INA §214(g)(4).

[19] USCIS, "Q & A Stakeholder Conference" (Sept. 20, 2010 and updated Oct. 19, 2010), AILA Doc. No. 10101471. This document has an extended discussion of the interrelationship of TPS and H-1B status.

[20] *Matter of Essex Cryogenics Industries, Inc.*, 14 I&N Dec. 196 (Dep. Assoc. Comm'r 1972).

[21] 8 CFR §214.2(h)(9)(iv); 9 Foreign Affairs Manual (FAM) 402.10-14(A) (dependents of H-1B nonimmigrants may obtain H-4 status).

[22] INA §§214(g)(8)(A) and 101(a)(15)(H)(i)(b)(1) (citing INA §214(g)(8)(A)); United States–Chile Free Trade Agreement Implementation Act, Pub. L. No. 108-77, §402 (Sept. 3, 2003); United States–Singapore Free Trade Agreement Implementation Act, Pub. L. No. 108-78, §402 (Sept. 3, 2003).

[23] INA §214(g)(8)(A); United States–Chile Free Trade Agreement Implementation Act, Pub. L. No. 108-77, §402 (Sept. 3, 2003); United States–Singapore Free Trade Agreement Implementation Act, Pub. L. No. 108-78, §402 (Sept. 3, 2003).

[24] INA §101(a)(15)(H)(i)(b)(1).

[25] *Id.*

[26] INA §214(g)(8)(C).

[27] 9 FAM 402.10-5(C); 69 Fed. Reg. 68221 (Nov. 23, 2004) (noting that the "[d]eterminations of specialty occupation and of nonimmigrant qualifications" are made by Department of State (DOS) and/or USCIS).

Copyright © 2017. American Immigration Lawyers Association. All rights reserved.

A. Profession and Specialty Occupation

In the list of "nonimmigrant aliens," the statute defines the H-1B visa classification as available for a foreign national who will "perform services … in a specialty occupation."[28] First and foremost, the practitioner should confirm that both the job and the beneficiary qualify when exploring whether H-1B status is appropriate, as discussed in further detail in the following sections.

The term specialty occupation "was created by the Immigration Act of 1990 (IMMACT), although its definition was taken from prior case law which related to 'professional' occupations which qualified for pre-IMMACT H-1 status."[29] In creating the term, Congress deemed a specialty occupation to be one "that requires theoretical and practical application of a body of highly specialized knowledge, and "attainment of a bachelor's or higher degree in the specific specialty (or its equivalent) as a minimum for entry into the occupation in the United States."[30]

The regulations expand on this to define specialty occupation as one "which requires theoretical and practical application of a body of highly specialized knowledge in fields of human endeavor including, but not limited to, architecture, engineering, mathematics, physical sciences, social sciences, medicine and health, education, business specialties, accounting, law, theology, and the arts, and which requires the attainment of a bachelor's degree or higher in a specific specialty, or its equivalent, as a minimum for entry into the occupation in the United States." This definition aligns with the definition of "profession," below, thus often making the inquiry of whether an occupation is "specialty" to be whether it is a profession.

1. Profession

The statute defines "profession" as including "but not limited to architects, engineers, lawyers, physicians, surgeons, and teachers in elementary or secondary schools, colleges, academies, or seminaries."[31] By way of background, the term "profession" formerly has been described as:

"[C]ontemplat[ing] knowledge or learning, not merely skill, of an advanced type in a given field gained by a prolonged course of specialized instruction and study of at least baccalaureate level, which is a realistic prerequisite to entry into the particular field of endeavor."[32]

"[R]equir[ing] a standard and at least baccalaureate level of university education for practice, in which that education is used and applied, and which requires

---

[28] INA §101(a)(15)(H)(1)(b).

[29] AFM 31.3(a)(1).

[30] INA §§214(i)(1) and (3); Immigration Act of 1990, Pub. L. No. 101-649, §205(c), 104 Stat. 4978 (Nov. 29, 1990). (Internal paragraph numbering omitted.)

[31] INA §101(a)(32).

[32] *Matter of Sea. Inc.*, 19 I&N Dec. 817 (Comm'r 1988) (citing former INA §101(a)(32) and *Matter of Ling*, 13 I&N Dec. 35 (Reg'l Comm'r 1968)).

Copyright © 2017. American Immigration Lawyers Association. All rights reserved.

extensive autonomous application of individual professional knowledge to particular fact situations."[33]

"[E]ncompass[ing] constantly expanding areas of activity consistent with the greater knowledge and specialized training a highly industrialized society demands. In addition to various scientific fields, highly specialized activities in business administration, finance, management, and the like require training gained only by an extended course of specialized instruction and study of at least the baccalaureate level. The term 'profession' originally contemplated only theology, law and medicine. However, as applications of science and learning were extended to other areas of human endeavor, other vocations were included in that term, which implies professed attainments in special knowledge as distinguished from mere skill."[34]

Legacy INS also noted in a precedent decision the following interpretation stated by the U.S. Supreme Court: "The word implies professed attainments in special knowledge, as distinguished from mere skill, a practical dealing with affairs, as distinguished from mere study or investigation; and an application of such knowledge to uses for others, as a vocation, as distinguished from its pursuit for its own purposes."[35] In general, H-1B status is appropriate for an individual who:

"Will perform services in a specialty occupation which requires theoretical and practical application of a body of highly specialized knowledge and attainment of a baccalaureate or higher degree or its equivalent as a minimum requirement for entry into the occupation in the United States, and who is qualified to perform services in the specialty occupation because he or she has attained a baccalaureate or higher degree or its equivalent in the specialty occupation."[36]

Importantly, the list of "the vocations included in the term 'profession' in our modern highly industrialized society are constantly expanding, consistent with the greater knowledge and specialized training that such a society demands."[37]

Specifically:

"The Service also recognizes that some occupations may be in transition from nonprofessional to professional status. In these transitional occupations, it may be possible for some employers to establish the professional nature of positions by demonstrating that they have consistently required the higher standard of a

---

[33] *Matter of Portugues Do Atlantico Information Bureau, Inc.*, 19 I&N Dec. 194 (Comm'r 1984).

[34] *Matter of Sun*, 12 I&N Dec. 535 (D.D. 1966).

[35] *Matter of Caron International, Inc.*, 19 I&N Dec. 791 (Comm'r 1988) (citing *U.S. v. Laws*, 63 U.S. 258 (1896)).

[36] 8 CFR §214.2(h)(4)(i)(A)(1).

[37] *Matter of Caron International, Inc.*, 19 I&N Dec. 791 (Comm'r 1988) (quoting *Matter of Shin*, 11 I&N Dec. 686 (D.D. 1966)).

Copyright © 2017. American Immigration Lawyers Association. All rights reserved.

specific baccalaureate or advanced degree for the more complex positions within their organizations."[38]

"The occupations included in the professions are not limited to these few groups [listed above], and, in fact, the overall number and specific occupations which fall within this definition are constantly changing due to technological advances and due to changes in labor practices."[39]

The "transition" of an occupation may be driven by "the ever-increasing need for more sophisticated and specialized expertise,"[40] and/or "material and substantial changes in the requirements for qualification and registry in th[e] field."[41] A petitioner may be able to establish that the job requirements for an occupation have changed by submitting a DOL job description,[42] discussed below, a statement from a relevant professional association, documents from other employers within the industry, articles, affidavits,[43] and/or printouts from job postings of other employers. It may be necessary to distinguish the specialty occupation from other, related fields.[44]

As noted below, "business specialties" are included in the list of fields of specialty occupations. However, it seems that the general field of business management may not qualify as a profession, even though it may fall within the category of "transitional occupations":[45]

"In fact, general managerial occupations such as those of vice-president are normally *not* considered to be professional endeavors requiring specific academic

---

[38] *Matter of Caron International, Inc.*, 19 I&N Dec. 791 (Comm'r 1988).

[39] *Matter of Michael Hertz Associates*, 19 I&N Dec. 558 (Comm'r 1988) (overruling *Matter of Huckenbeck*, 3 I&N Dec. 118 (Reg'l Comm'r 1969)).

[40] *Matter of Villanueva*, 13 I&N Dec. 733 (Dep. Asso. Comm'r 1971) (overruling *Matter of Ancheta*, 12 I&N Dec. 785 (Reg'l Comm'r 1968)).

[41] *Matter of Villanueva*, 13 I&N Dec. 733 (Dep. Asso. Comm'r 1971) (overruling *Matter of Ancheta*, 12 I&N Dec. 785 (Reg'l Comm'r 1968)); *Matter of Panganiban*, 13 I&N Dec. 581 (Dep. Asso. Comm'r 1970); *Matter of Reyes*, 13 I&N Dec. 406 (Reg'l Comm'r 1969) (overruling *Matter of Cruz*, 13 I&N Dec. 61 (Reg'l Comm'r 1968)); *Matter of Perez*, 12 I&N Dec. 701 (D.D. 1968). *Cf. Matter of [name not provided]*, WAC 02 220 54035 (AAO Feb. 3, 2006), http://bit.ly/feb064d ("While a bachelor's degree in a construction-related specialty may be increasingly favored by large companies, it is not an industry standard for entry into the occupation").

[42] *Cf. Matter of [name not provided]*, WAC 02 220 54035 (AAO Feb. 3, 2006), http://bit.ly/feb064d (reliance on Occupational Outlook Handbook (OOH) to determine that there has been no change in qualifications).

[43] *Matter of Michael Hertz Associates*, 19 I&N Dec. 558 (Comm'r 1988) (overruling *Matter of Huckenbeck*, 3 I&N Dec. 118 (Reg'l Comm'r 1969)); *Matter of Desai*, 17 I&N Dec. 569 (Reg'l Comm'r 1980) (statements from professional association, industry professionals, and the director of an educational program); *Matter of Essex Cryogenics Industries, Inc.*, 14 I&N Dec. 196 (Dep. Asso. Comm'r 1972) (statement from professional association with corroboration from the "accrediting authority for educational programs" of the field); *Matter of Panganiban*, 13 I&N Dec. 581 (Dep. Assoc. Comm'r 1970) (overruling *Matter of Asuncion*, 11 I&N Dec. 660 (Reg'l Comm'r 1966) (OOH job description)).

[44] *Matter of Villanueva*, 13 I&N Dec. 733 (Dep. Assoc. Comm'r 1971) (medical record librarians have different job requirements and duties from medical record technicians) (overruling *Matter of Ancheta*, 12 I&N Dec. 785 (Reg'l Comm'r 1968)).

[45] *Matter of Caron International, Inc.*, 19 I&N Dec. 791 (Comm'r 1988).

Copyright © 2017. American Immigration Lawyers Association. All rights reserved.

degrees. A manager is not considered to be a member of the professions unless he or she is qualified for, and intends to work in, a professional occupation requiring the attainment of such a degree.... While the recent edition of the *Occupational Outlook Handbook* [OOH] reflects that higher education is becoming increasingly prevalent among managers and executives, it does not establish that at least a baccalaureate-level degree in a specific major or even a narrow range of majors is required for all or most occupations within this broad field."[46]

"'Business administration' is a broad field, a field which contains various occupations and/or professions, all of which are related to the world of business but each requiring a different academic preparation and experience peculiar to its needs. The [OOH], also published by the Department of Labor, shows that business administration is a general term and includes various occupations such as accountant, advertising workers, industrial traffic manager, marketing research workers, personnel workers, and purchasing agents; thus, including both professional and nonprofessional activities. Careful review of the discussion of these occupations shows that while all are related to the world of business, each has its own emphasis on the academic training and experience required for qualification in that occupation. It is evident that while a person may have a degree in business administration, such degree may qualify him for some but not all of the occupations included in the broad field of business administration.... Therefore, a petitioner with a business administration degree must clearly establish a particular area and occupation in the field of business administration in which he is engaged or plans to be engaged and must also establish that he meets the special academic and experience requirements of that designated activity, as a prerequisite to a determination as to professional status."[47]

For discussion of an alternative strategy for business occupations, see below. The practitioner should also note that a job is not considered a profession merely because the beneficiary has earned a degree: "The attainment of an undergraduate degree is a material requisite to qualifying only where such degree is a minimum and realistic prerequisite for entry into a profession."[48]

2. Specialty Occupation

As noted above, for H-1B and H-1B1 petitions, the term "specialty occupation" is defined as an occupation that requires the following:

- The "theoretical and practical application of a body of highly specialized knowledge"; and

---

[46] *Id.* (emphasis in original).

[47] *Matter of Ling*, 13 I&N Dec. 35 (Reg'l Comm'r 1968); *Matter of [name not provided]* LIN 04 257 51922 (AAO Feb. 10, 2005), http://bit.ly/feb057d.

[48] *Matter of General Atomic Co.*, 17 I&N Dec. 532 (Comm'r 1980) (internal citation omitted).

Copyright © 2017. American Immigration Lawyers Association. All rights reserved.

- The "attainment of a bachelor's or higher degree in the specific specialty (or its equivalent) as a minimum for entry into the occupation in the United States."[49]

The appropriate "fields of human endeavor" for specialty occupations may include, but are "not limited to, architecture, engineering, mathematics, physical sciences, social sciences, medicine and health, education, business specialties, accounting, law, theology, and the arts."[50] The practitioner should note that this list is similar to the list of professions, although teaching is on the list of professions, but not on the list of fields of human endeavor. For discussion of H-1B status for nurses, see below.

The regulations provide further guidance on the requirements of a specialty occupation, where "the position must meet one of the following criteria," discussed in more detail in the following sections:

- "A baccalaureate or higher degree or its equivalent is normally the minimum requirement for entry into the particular position;
- "The degree requirement is common to the industry in parallel positions among similar organizations or, in the alternative, an employer may show that its particular position is so complex or unique that it can be performed only by an individual with a degree;
- "The employer normally requires a degree or its equivalent for the position; or
- "The nature of the specific duties [is] so specialized and complex that knowledge required to perform the duties is usually associated with the attainment of a baccalaureate or higher degree."[51]

In recent years, USCIS has taken the position that, rather than being a delineation of how one can prove that the occupation meets the definition of specialty occupation, this recitation of possible criteria is a separate requirement unto itself: "Pursuant to 8 C.F.R. §214.2(h)(4)(iii)(A), to qualify as a specialty occupation, the position must also meet one of the following criteria...."[52]

The Administrative Appeals Office (AAO) has defended this position by maintaining that "the criteria stated in 8 C.F.R. §214.2(h)(4)(iii)(A) should logically be read as being necessary but not necessarily sufficient to meet the statutory and regulatory definition of specialty occupation. To otherwise interpret this section as stating the necessary and sufficient conditions for meeting the definition of specialty occupation would result in particular positions meeting a condition under 8 C.F.R.

---

[49] INA §§214(i)(1) and (3); Immigration Act of 1990, Pub. L. No. 101-649, §205(c), 104 Stat. 4978 (Nov. 29, 1990).

[50] 8 CFR §214.2(h)(4)(ii).

[51] 8 CFR §214.2(h)(4)(iii)(A).

[52] *E.g., Matter of [name and case number not provided]* (AAO Apr. 7, 2014), AILA Doc. No. 15041361; *Matter of [name not provided]*, WAC 10 008 50309 (AAO, Apr. 7, 2011), *http://bit.ly/apr112d. See also* "AILA Memorandum to USCIS Interprets H-1B 'Specialty Occupation'" (Apr. 4, 2012), AILA Doc. No. 12040451.

Copyright © 2017. American Immigration Lawyers Association. All rights reserved.

§214.2(h)(4)(iii)(A) but not the statutory or regulatory definition."[53] Thus, the practitioner will need to ensure that documentation and arguments are submitted supporting both the definition and at least one of the criteria.

The H-1B petition must include "[d]ocumentation, certifications, affidavits, declarations, degrees, diplomas, writings, reviews, or any other required evidence sufficient to establish … that the services the beneficiary is to perform are in a specialty occupation."[54] This evidence may include "[c]opies of any written contracts between the petitioner and beneficiary, or a summary of the terms of the oral agreement under which the beneficiary will be employed, if there is no written contract."[55]

The adjudicator should "[c]onsider all the information provided by the petitioner in making [the] decision as to whether or not the position qualifies as a specialty occupation."[56] USCIS guidance notes when evaluating whether the job qualifies as a specialty occupation, "approval or denial often comes down to a judgment call by the adjudicating officer."

Obtaining an approved "labor condition application in an occupational classification does not constitute a determination by that agency that the occupation in question is a specialty occupation."[57] Rather, USCIS "shall determine if the application involves a specialty occupation … [and] shall also determine whether the particular alien for whom H-1B classification is sought qualifies to perform services in the specialty occupation."[58] For further discussion of the LCA, see Volume 1: Chapter Six, "The Labor Condition Application."

For citizens of Chile seeking H-1B1 status, "additional occupations that qualify as specialty occupations are Disaster Relief Claims Adjuster, Management Consultant, Agricultural Manager, and Physical Therapist."[59] For citizens of Singapore seeking H-1B1 status, "additional occupations that qualify as specialty occupations are Disaster Relief Claims Adjuster and Management Consultant."[60] For discussion of alternative qualifications for these occupations, see below.

---

[53] *Matter of [name and case number not provided]* (AAO Apr. 7, 2014), AILA Doc. No. 15041361.

[54] 8 CFR §214.2(h)(4)(iv)(A). *See also Matter of Doultsions*, 12 I&N Dec. 153 (D.D. 1967) (statement from an accounting professor regarding the field of accountancy).

[55] 8 CFR §214.2(h)(4)(iv)(B).

[56] USCIS, "I-129 H-1B Standard Operating Procedures" (undated, posted July 26, 2007), AILA Doc. No. 07072668.

[57] 8 CFR §214.2(h)(4)(i)(B)(2); AFM 31.3(b).

[58] 8 CFR §214.2(h)(4)(i)(B)(2). *See also* 20 CFR §655.715 ("Determinations of specialty occupation and of nonimmigrant qualifications for the H-1B and H-1B1 programs are not made by the Department of Labor, but by the Department of State and/or United States Citizenship and Immigration Services (USCIS) of the Department of Homeland Security in accordance with the procedures of those agencies for processing visas, petitions, extensions of stay, or requests for change of nonimmigrant status for H-1B or H-1B1 nonimmigrants").

[59] 20 CFR §655.715.

[60] *Id.*

Copyright © 2017. American Immigration Lawyers Association. All rights reserved.

a. A Degree Is Normally a Minimum Requirement for the Occupation

Stated simply, the H-1B classification requires that the occupation itself normally require at least a bachelor's degree, based on the duties to be performed:

"Consideration of a claim to such eligibility [for H-1B status] first focuses on the tasks, demands, duties, and actual requirements of the position in question…. A petitioner must establish that the position realistically requires knowledge, both theoretical and applied, which is almost exclusively obtained through studies at an institution of higher learning. The depth of knowledge and length of studies required are best typified by a degree granted by such institution at the baccalaureate level."[61]

Also, it "is not sufficient to simply establish that a bachelor's degree or higher degree is a minimum for entry into the occupation, the position must require a degree in a specific specialty."[62] Legacy INS noted its "interpretation over the years" required that the degree be "awarded for academic study in a specific discipline or narrow range of disciplines,"[63] and this is confirmed by the AAO: "[USCIS] consistently interprets the term 'degree'… to mean not just any baccalaureate or higher degree, but one in a specific specialty that is directly related to the proffered position."[64] Legacy INS stated in a precedent decision:

"It must be demonstrated that the position requires a precise and specific course of study which relates directly and closely to the position in question. Since there must be a close corollary between the required specialized studies and the position, the requirement of a degree of generalized title, such as business administration or liberal arts, without further specification, does not establish eligibility. The mere requirement of a college degree for the sake of general education, or to obtain what an employer perceives to be a higher caliber employee, also does not establish eligibility."[65]

AAO has taken the view that, while it is not necessarily the case that a particular specialty requires only one specific area of study, there must be a close correlation between the area of study and the field of the occupation:

---

[61] *Matter of Michael Hertz Associates*, 19 I&N Dec. 558 (Comm'r 1988).

[62] USCIS, "I-129 H-1B Standard Operating Procedures" (undated, posted July 26, 2007), AILA Doc. No. 07072668 (citing INA §214(i)(1)); *Fred 26 Importers, Inc. v. USCIS*, 445 F. Supp. 2d 1174 (C.D. Cal. 2006) (USCIS and AAO denial).

[63] 55 Fed. Reg. 2606 (Jan. 26, 1990); *Matter of Caron International, Inc.*, 19 I&N Dec. 791 (Comm'r 1988) (internal citations omitted). *But see Residential Finance Corp. v. USCIS*, 839 F. Supp. 2d 985 (S.D. Ohio 2012), AILA Doc No. 12031265.

[64] *See, e.g., Matter of [name not provided]* WAC 07 137 52988 (AAO June 3, 2008), http://bit.ly/jun082d (denial where, inter alia, the OOH "indicates that a wide variety of courses will prepare a person to perform the duties of a market research analyst"); *Matter of [name not provided]* EAC 06 216 52028 (AAO Sept. 8, 2006), http://bit.ly/sep066d (USCIS denial).

[65] *Matter of Michael Hertz Associates*, 19 I&N Dec. 558 (Comm'r 1988).

Copyright © 2017. American Immigration Lawyers Association. All rights reserved.

"In general, provided the specialties are closely related, e.g., chemistry and biochemistry, a minimum of a bachelor's or higher degree in more than one specialty is recognized as satisfying the "degree in the specific specialty (or its equivalent)" requirement.... In such a case, the required 'body of highly specialized knowledge' would essentially be the same. Since there must be a close correlation between the required 'body of highly specialized knowledge' and the position, however, a minimum entry requirement of a degree in two disparate fields, such as philosophy and engineering, would not meet the statutory requirement that the degree be 'in the specific specialty (or its equivalent),' unless the petitioner establishes how each field is directly related to the duties and responsibilities of the particular position such that the required 'body of highly specialized knowledge' is essentially an amalgamation of these different specialties.... In other words, while the statutory 'the' and the regulatory 'a' both denote a singular 'specialty,' the AAO does not so narrowly interpret these provisions to exclude positions from qualifying as specialty occupations if they permit, as a minimum entry requirement, degrees in more than one closely related specialty.... This also includes even seemingly disparate specialties providing, again, the evidence of record establishes how each acceptable, specific field of study is directly related to the duties and responsibilities of the particular position."[66]

At the very least, the H-1B petition should include "a *detailed* description of the job duties to be performed," ideally in "non-technical terminology," since the adjudicator may request this information in a Request for Evidence (RFE),[67] and this would delay processing. As explained by AAO, a "generic" job description is not helpful:

"The duties described neither relate specific work that the beneficiary would perform, elucidate concrete business matters of this particular petitioner that would be the focus of that work, nor exemplify how performance of that work upon those matters would require the theoretical and practical application of at least a bachelor's level of a highly specialized body of knowledge. Consequently, because the proposed duties are limited to generic terms that do not relate what they involve in actual performance to this specific petitioner's particular business matters, the petitioner has not provided sufficient information to satisfy any of the specialty occupation criteria."[68]

A detailed job description is particularly important if the beneficiary will provide services for a client or customer of the petitioner, because, as discussed below, third-party placements are closely scrutinized. In one case, AAO observed that the absence

---

[66] *Matter of [name and case number not provided]* (AAO Apr. 7, 2014), AILA Doc. No. 15041361 (denied on other, multiple grounds).

[67] USCIS, "I-129 H-1B Standard Operating Procedures" (undated, posted July 26, 2007), AILA Doc. No. 07072668 (emphasis in original).

[68] *Matter of [name not provided]* WAC 07 137 52988 (AAO June 3, 2008), http://bit.ly/jun082d. *See also Matter of [name not provided]* WAC 07 151 50781 (AAO June 3, 2008), http://bit.ly/jun081d2; *Matter of [name not provided]* LIN 04 257 51922 (AAO Feb. 10, 2005), http://bit.ly/feb057d.

Copyright © 2017. American Immigration Lawyers Association. All rights reserved.

of specificity regarding the beneficiary's "particular work to be done for either client" made it "impossible for [USCIS] to determine whether the actual performance requirements of the proffered position support the petitioner's claim that the position is a specialty occupation."[69]

(1) DOL Job Description

The practitioner may also wish to include DOL job descriptions because USCIS guidance encourages adjudicators to consider them:

"There are numerous references available (such as the DOL's Occupational Outlook Handbook) to describe specific vocational preparation for various occupations."[70]

"A good reference for determining if a position meets specialty occupation criteria is the Department of Labor's Occupational Outlook Handbook (OOH). The OOH outlines the duties normally performed by an occupation, and its basic educational and experience requirements."[71]

"Factors considered by the AAO when determining this criterion include whether the Department of Labor's *Occupational Outlook Handbook (Handbook)*, on which the AAO routinely relies for the educational requirements of particular occupations, reports that the industry requires a degree."[72]

"The AAO recognizes the [OOH] as an authoritative source on the duties and educational requirements of a wide variety of occupations."[73]

AAO also noted that consultation with the OOH is appropriate even if the occupation is not specifically discussed in the OOH:

"A petitioner's assignment of a job title that is not included among the occupational titles described in the [OOH] does not preclude the possibility that the [OOH] would have information relevant to the underlying duties. The director was correct to concentrate on the proposed duties rather than the job title...."[74]

---

[69] *Matter of [name not provided]* WAC 03 232 53697 (AAO Feb. 3, 2006), http://bit.ly/feb064d.

[70] AFM 31.3(g). The OOH can be found at http://www.bls.gov/oco/.

[71] USCIS, "I-129 H-1B Standard Operating Procedures" (undated, posted July 26, 2007), AILA Doc. No. 07072668. *See also Matter of De Vera*, 13 I&N Dec. 340 (D.D. 1969) ("The views of the United States Department of Labor in setting the minimum educational requirements for dieticians ... as professional and kindred, must be given considerable weight"); *Matter of Doultsions*, 12 I&N Dec. 153 (D.D. 1967) (reliance on OOH to classify an occupation as professional); *Matter of Roldan*, 11 I&N Dec. 869 (D.D. 1966) (reliance on Dictionary of Occupational Titles (DOT) and OOH to classify an occupation as professional); *Matter of [name not provided]* WAC 07 137 52988 (AAO June 3, 2008), http://bit.ly/jun082d. *Cf. Matter of [name not provided]* WAC 02 220 54035 (AAO Feb. 3, 2006), http://bit.ly/feb064d. (reliance on OOH to determine that there has been no change in qualifications).

[72] *Matter of [name not provided]* EAC 06 136 50756 (AAO Nov. 13, 2007), http://bit.ly/nov074d (emphasis in original); *Matter of [name not provided]* EAC 06 216 52028 (AAO Sept. 8, 2006), http://bit.ly/sep066d.

[73] *Matter of [name not provided]* LIN 04 257 51922 (AAO Feb. 10, 2005), http://bit.ly/feb057d.

[74] *Id.*

Copyright © 2017. American Immigration Lawyers Association. All rights reserved.

USCIS adjudicators have been known to take the position that a job is not in a specialty occupation if the OOH indicates multiple fields of study for the occupation. However, several courts have rejected this approach, finding that it impermissibly narrows the statutory language and that the regulations do not restrict qualifying occupations to those for which there is only a single, specifically tailored degree program.[75] USCIS has also somewhat repudiated this approach, noting that the cases in question were taken to the district courts without first having appealed to the AAO.[76]

Also, issues can arise if the OOH recitation of possible fields of study includes a generalized degree. Thus, a court upheld USCIS's denial of an H-1B for a deputy controller with a finance degree where the OOH description for the field included business administration, seen as a "general field of study," and thus rendering the occupation not truly specialized.[77]

An alternative to the OOH is DOL's O*NET system online,[78] which "contains comprehensive information on job requirements and worker competencies" and "captures changes in the work place in terms that reflect the latest research in the field of job analysis."[79] Reliance upon a template job description provided by O*NET information is advantageous because O*NET's SOC Codes are also stated on the LCA, as discussed in Volume 1: Chapter Six, "The Labor Condition Application," and USCIS is more likely to accept an occupational classification that has been accepted by DOL. To that end, in preparing the LCA, it is important to consider the occupational classification being listed, as USCIS can look at that classification to question whether the job requires at least a bachelor's degree. In the alternative, the petitioner may wish to submit information from DOL's Dictionary of Occupational Titles (DOT),[80] which, in turn, relies upon calculations of Specific Vocational Preparation (SVP), although the SVP should not be used "as the sole determining

---

[75] *Residential Finance Corp. v. USCIS*, 839 F. Supp. 2d 985 (S.D. Ohio 2012), AILA Doc No. 12031265; *Raj and Co. v. USCIS*, Case No. C14-123RSM (W.D. Washington, 2015), AILA Doc No. 15022300; *Warren Chiropractic & Rehab Clinic v USCIS*, 2015 WL 732428 (C.D. California, 2015) AILA Doc. No. 15011542.

[76] "AILA/USCIS HQ Liaison Q&As" (Apr. 16, 2015), AILA Doc. No. 15042032.

[77] *Irish Help at Home LLC v. Melville*, No. 13-cv-00943MEJ (N.D.Cal. 2015), AILA Doc. No. 15030664, aff'd No.15-15830 (9th Cir. 2017).

[78] "O*NET Online," http://online.onetcenter.org.

[79] USCIS, "I-129 H-1B Standard Operating Procedures" (undated, posted July 26, 2007), AILA Doc. No. 07072668. *See also Matter of Wissen, Inc.*, 2009-PER-00405 (BALCA Apr. 15, 2010) ("The O*Net is a database containing information on hundreds of standardized and occupation-specific descriptors.") (internal footnotes and citations omitted).

[80] *Matter of Sea. Inc.*, 19 I&N Dec. 817 (Comm'r 1988). *Cf. Matter of Caron International, Inc.*, 19 I&N Dec. 791 (Comm'r 1988) (stating that "a reference in the DOT is not enough to establish the professional nature of an occupation"); *Matter of Wu*, 12 I&N Dec. 459 (D.D. 1967) (reliance on DOT to classify an occupation as professional); *Matter of Sun*, 12 I&N Dec. 535 (D.D. 1966) (same); *Matter of Rabbani*, 12 I&N Dec. 15 (D.D. 1966) (same); *Matter of Shin*, 11 I&N Dec. 686 (D.D. 1966) (same); *Matter of Roldan*, 11 I&N Dec. 869 (D.D. 1966) (reliance on DOT and OOH to classify an occupation as professional). The DOT can be found at http://www.occupationalinfo.org/.

Copyright © 2017. American Immigration Lawyers Association. All rights reserved.

factor in assessing whether or not a position qualifies as a specialty occupation."[81] For further discussion of the OOH, O*NET, and DOT and SVP, see Volume 2: Chapter Two, "The Labor Certification Application."

Whichever DOL resource is used to classify the occupation, the job description should "accurately reflect[] the job duties to be performed."[82] The DOL job description may in fact indicate that a master's degree rather than a bachelor's degree is the common requirement for entry into the profession.[83] However, the practitioner is also strongly advised against allowing a petitioner to submit a job description that merely "repeat[s] portions of the generalized descriptions found" in the OOH because the petitioner should "detail[] the actual work to be performed for this position rather than describing the occupation."[84] Details are key to demonstrate "the duties attached to specific employment."[85] As the Vermont Service Center (VSC) indicated:

> "While a petitioner may provide a generic job description normally associated with a position, the information should also be presented in a manner that provides a clear understanding of the services to be provided, rather than a recitation of the O*NET or Occupational Outlook Handbook."[86]

(2) Focus on Job Duties

USCIS guidance directs adjudicators to "[l]ook at each case individually" and to avoid "the habit of classifying based only on the job title."[87] The practitioner is strongly advised to take the same approach:

---

[81] USCIS, "I-129 H-1B Standard Operating Procedures" (undated, posted July 26, 2007), AILA Doc. No. 07072668. *See also Matter of [name not provided]* EAC 06 136 50756 (AAO Nov. 13, 2007), http://bit.ly/nov074d ("However, the AAO does not consider the DOT to be a persuasive source of information as to whether a job requires the attainment of a baccalaureate or higher degree (or its equivalent) in a specific specialty. DOT provides only general information regarding the tasks and work activities associated with a particular occupation, as well as the education, training, and experience required to perform the duties of that occupation. It does not describe how those years are to be divided among training, formal education, and experience and it does not specify the particular type of degree, if any, that a position would require."); *Matter of [name not provided]* LIN 04 257 51922 (AAO Feb. 10, 2005), http://bit.ly/feb057d.

[82] USCIS, "I-129 H-1B Standard Operating Procedures" (undated, posted July 26, 2007), AILA Doc. No. 07072668.

[83] *Matter of Shin*, 11 I&N Dec. 686 (D.D. 1966).

[84] *Matter of [name not provided]* WAC 07 137 52988 (AAO June 3, 2008), http://bit.ly/jun082d; *Matter of [name not provided]* WAC 02 220 54035 (AAO Feb. 3, 2006), http://bit.ly/feb064d. ("Though the petitioner recites some of the [OOH's] language on industrial engineers in its list of the job duties, no specific information is provided about the tasks the beneficiary performs on a daily basis").

[85] *Matter of [name not provided]* WAC 07 137 52988 (AAO June 3, 2008), http://bit.ly/jun082d; *Matter of [name not provided]* WAC 02 220 54035 (AAO Feb. 3, 2006), http://bit.ly/feb064d.

[86] AILA Liaison/VSC Meeting Minutes, (Jan. 21, 2009), AILA Doc. No. 09012768.

[87] USCIS, "I-129 H-1B Standard Operating Procedures" (undated, posted July 26, 2007), AILA Doc. No. 07072668; *Matter of [name not provided]* WAC 02 220 54035 (AAO Feb. 3, 2006), http://bit.ly/feb064d ("In determining the nature of a particular position and whether it qualifies as a specialty occupation, the duties actually performed are determinative, not the title of the position. The petitioner must establish that a specialty degree is required by the performance demands of the position").

Copyright © 2017. American Immigration Lawyers Association. All rights reserved.

"[I]t is important to note that occupations are rapidly evolving and job titles themselves are often meaningless. In order to correctly adjudicate a case, it is · necessary to consider all the facts surrounding the petition: the beneficiary's education and work experience, the nature of the petitioner's business, industry practice, and salary (both offered to the beneficiary and typical for the industry). It is important not to be so influenced by a single factor, such as the job title or salary, that other indicators are overlooked."[88]

"To determine whether a particular job qualifies as a specialty occupation, [USCIS] does not simply rely on a position's title. The specific duties of the proffered position, combined with the nature of the petitioning entity's business operations, are factors to be considered. [USCIS] must examine the ultimate employment of the alien, and determine whether the position qualifies as a specialty occupation."[89]

In one case, the AAO indicated that, based on the proposed job duties, a job that "is generally associated with a specialty occupation" may not necessarily be a specialty occupation with a particular petitioner.[90] The H-1B petition was filed for an accountant, and the AAO noted that a bookkeeping job, which does not qualify as a specialty occupation, may require knowledge of accounting principles:

"[T]he performance of duties requiring accounting knowledge does not establish the proffered position as that of an accountant. The question is not whether the petitioner's position requires knowledge of accounting principles, which it does, but rather whether it is one that normally requires the level of accounting knowledge that is signified by at least a bachelor's degree, or its equivalent, in accounting."[91]

Similarly, AAO drew a distinction between an engineer and a construction manager:

"[T]he decisive question is not whether the petitioner's position requires knowledge of engineering principles, but whether the position is one that normally requires the level of engineering knowledge that is acquired through the completion of a bachelor's degree, or its equivalent, in engineering. The AAO's review of the duties of the proffered position finds they do not establish that the engineering knowledge required of the beneficiary would be on a par with that possessed by an engineer.

---

[88] AFM 31.3(g).

[89] *Matter of [name not provided]* WAC 07 137 52988 (AAO June 3, 2008), http://bit.ly/jun082d (internal citation omitted).

[90] *Matter of [name not provided]* EAC 06 136 50756 (AAO Nov. 13, 2007), http://bit.ly/nov074d (USCIS denial). *See also Matter of [name not provided]* WAC 04 228 53792 (AAO Mar. 21, 2006), http://bit.ly/mar065d2 (USCIS denial reversed by AAO) ("It is noted that not all food service manager positions may be considered specialty occupations. Each position must be evaluated based on the nature and complexity of the actual duties").

[91] *Matter of [name not provided]* EAC 06 136 50756 (AAO Nov. 13, 2007), http://bit.ly/nov074d.

Copyright © 2017. American Immigration Lawyers Association. All rights reserved.

"The duties to be performed by the beneficiary do not reflect the breadth and complexity of engineering employment. Instead, this position, with responsibility for overseeing the stonework to be performed by the petitioner under its construction contracts, appears to combine the employment of a construction manager with that of an engineering technician or drafter, jobs that require some knowledge of engineering but are not performed by engineers."[92]

USCIS and/or the AAO may also request and consider samples of work produced by an employee who formerly held the job.[93] In one case, the AAO discussed this evidence in the context of this first criterion of whether the degree is the normal requirement for entry into the position, rather than when evaluating the criterion of whether the employer normally requires a degree,[94] discussed below. This may be because work product can reveal the job duties.

(3) Petitioner's Size and Industry

The petitioner's size is a relevant inquiry because the "complexity of the duties in relation to the petitioner's business must be analyzed."[95] In the case involving the accountant/bookkeeper, the AAO stated:

"While the size of a petitioner's business is normally not a factor in determining the nature of a proffered position, both level of income and organizational structure are appropriately reviewed when a petitioner seeks to employ an H-IB worker as an accountant. It is reasonable to assume that the size of an employer's business has an 'impact on the duties of a particular position.... In matters where a petitioner's business is relatively small, the AAO reviews the record for evidence that its operations, are, nevertheless, of sufficient complexity to indicate that it would employ the beneficiary in an accounting position requiring a level of financial knowledge that may be obtained only through a baccalaureate degree in accounting or its equivalent."[96]

Similarly, USCIS, inter alia, "asserted that as a one-person business, the beneficiary would be responsible for administrative and clerical duties, which are not

---

[92] *Matter of [name not provided]* WAC 03 100 50458 (AAO Aug. 25, 2005), http://bit.ly/aug0536d.

[93] *Matter of [name not provided]* WAC 07 137 52988 (AAO June 3, 2008), http://bit.ly/jun082d; *Matter of [name not provided]* EAC [redacted] (AAO Feb. 23, 2006), AILA Doc. No. 08041470.

[94] *Matter of [name not provided]* WAC 07 137 52988 (AAO June 3, 2008), http://bit.ly/jun082d.

[95] *Matter of [name not provided]* WAC 07 137 52988 (AAO June 3, 2008), http://bit.ly/jun082d (internal citation omitted); *Fred 26 Importers, Inc. v. USCIS*, 445 F. Supp. 2d 1174 (C.D. Cal. 2006) ("The CSC Director noted that a human resources manager in a large company often qualifies as a specialty occupation because the nature of the manager's duties in a larger company necessitates a degree in human resources or a related field."); *Matter of [name not provided]* LIN 04 184 51951 (AAO Feb. 3, 2006), http://bit.ly/feb065d.

[96] *Matter of [name not provided]* EAC 06 136 50756 (AAO Nov. 13, 2007), http://bit.ly/nov074d (internal citation omitted). *See also Matter of [name not provided]* WAC 04 054 50130 (AAO Feb. 3, 2006), http://bit.ly/feb061d2 ("By failing to provide a copy of its license to operate its medical services business and the tax information requested in the RFE [Request for Evidence], the petitioner prevented the director from accurately assessing whether the beneficiary would be employed by the petitioner in an occupation requiring the services of a medical researcher with at least a bachelor's degree, or its equivalent, in a specific specialty."); *Matter of [name not provided]* WAC 03 262 52383 (AAO Feb. 3, 2006), http://bit.ly/feb068d.

Copyright © 2017. American Immigration Lawyers Association. All rights reserved.

specialty occupations," although this ground of denial was reversed by the AAO.[97] In another case, AAO noted that "proposed duties that related exclusively to the operation of the retail store for which a location has not yet been obtained are not a basis for approval of the petition."[98] In a sense, this analysis is similar to the requirement that an L-1A nonimmigrant employed by a smaller company primarily engage in managerial or executive activities, as discussed in Volume 1: Chapter Eleven, L Visas and Status.

To avoid denial on these grounds, the practitioner may wish to submit evidence of other individuals who will perform the administrative tasks, perhaps on a part-time basis, and/or explain how the other duties "are deminimus and merely incidental to the professional responsibilities."[99] Because of the closer scrutiny of smaller employers,[100] discussed below, the practitioner is strongly encouraged to include proof of the number of employees,[101] such as federal tax returns, Forms W-2, or state unemployment tax records.

A smaller employer may be able to demonstrate a need for the beneficiary's services in a specialty occupation by explaining the business's growth or expansion.[102] Appropriate evidence of "a pattern of growth in the petitioner's revenues or business operations" includes copies of tax returns for the years preceding the filing of the H-1B petition, financial audits, sales projections, "debt repayment schedules, loan applications, correspondence, or a business plan related to the acquisition of additional" businesses.[103] For further discussion of plans for business growth or expansion, see Volume 2: Chapter Two, "The Labor Certification Application." Alternatively, the initial H-1B petition could be for part-time employment, with an amended petition filed later "when the level of work justifies the upgrade."[104]

The petitioner's industry may also be considered vis-à-vis the described job duties. For example, in upholding the revocation of an H-1B petition filed on behalf of an industrial engineer, the AAO noted: "The petitioner is not in the business of

[97] *Matter of [name not provided]* EAC [*redacted*] (AAO Feb. 23, 2006), AILA Doc. No. 08041470 ("Despite the fact that the beneficiary may also be engaged in some administrative tasks as a sole proprietor, most of the duties of the position include those of a graphic designer, which the [OOH] indicates could not be performed without the training and education that are included in a bachelor's degree in graphic design").

[98] *Matter of [name not provided]* WAC 04 043 51523 (AAO Feb. 3, 2006), http://bit.ly/feb063d.

[99] "AILA/VSC Liaison Practice Pointer: Responding to 'Small Company' RFEs" (Oct. 26, 2009), AILA Doc. No. 09102667.

[100] *Matter of [name not provided]* EAC [*redacted*] (AAO Feb. 23, 2006), AILA Doc. No. 08041470 (USCIS denial).

[101] *Matter of [name not provided]* EAC 06 136 50756 (AAO Nov. 13, 2007), http://bit.ly/nov074d.

[102] *Id.*

[103] *Id.*

[104] "AILA/VSC Liaison Practice Pointer: Responding to 'Small Company' RFEs" (Oct. 26, 2009), AILA Doc. No. 09102667.

Copyright © 2017. American Immigration Lawyers Association. All rights reserved.

manufacturing or production; it is a construction and remodeling company."[105] The intimation seemed to be that a construction company would more likely require the services of a construction manager rather than an industrial engineer.[106] For further discussion of the petitioner's business purpose, see below.

b. *A Degree Is Normally Required in the Industry or by the Employer, and/or the Job Duties Are Specialized and Complex*

As a practical matter, the final three criteria listed above may be considered true alternatives to the primary criterion,[107] based on how the regulations are worded,[108] especially for occupations "in transition," as noted above:

"For a job to be considered within the professions, it is not enough that a petitioner desires to employ a person with a degree. The degree requirement must be an industry standard in parallel positions among similar firms and institutions. In addition, it must be shown the employer normally imposes this requirement."[109]

"An analysis of [eligibility] includes not only the actual requirements specified by the petitioner but also those required by the specific industry in question, to determine, in part, the validity of the petitioner's requirements."[110]

Experience has shown that when an RFE is issued, it typically requests evidence regarding all four types of criteria, and the practitioner is strongly encouraged to make alternative arguments for each criterion when responding to the RFE.[111]

Evidence that a degree in the specialty is commonly required by other employers in the same industry, such as "job announcements, industry letters,"[112] or "Internet job postings" should include "meaningful descriptions of the positions."[113] Other evidence includes "surveys, studies, or other publications,"[114] or a statement from a university professor,[115] but "one letter does not constitute an industry standard."[116] A

---

[105] *Matter of [name not provided]*, WAC 03 055 52649 (AAO Oct. 2, 2006). http://bit.ly/oct061d2.

[106] *Id.*

[107] *Matter of [name not provided]* LIN 04 257 51922 (AAO Feb. 10, 2005), http://bit.ly/feb057d ("Also, the petitioner has not satisfied either of the alternative prongs of 8 C.F.R. §214.2(h)(4)(iii)(A)(2)").

[108] 8 CFR §214.2(h)(4)(iii)(A).

[109] *Matter of Caron International, Inc.*, 19 I&N Dec. 791 (Comm'r 1988).

[110] *Matter of Michael Hertz Associates*, 19 I&N Dec. 558 (Comm'r 1988).

[111] *Matter of [name not provided]* WAC 07 137 52988 (AAO June 3, 2008), http://bit.ly/jun082d (consideration of all four criteria by both USCIS and AAO).

[112] *Matter of [name not provided]* EAC 06 136 50756 (AAO Nov. 13, 2007), http://bit.ly/nov074d; *Matter of [name not provided]* LIN 04 184 51951 (AAO Feb. 3, 2006), http://bit.ly/feb065d.

[113] *Matter of [name not provided]* WAC 07 137 52988 (AAO June 3, 2008), http://bit.ly/jun082d.

[114] *Matter of [name not provided]* WAC 03 100 50458 (AAO Aug. 25, 2005), http://bit.ly/aug0536d.

[115] *Matter of [name not provided]* WAC 04 228 53792 (AAO Mar. 21, 2006), http://bit.ly/mar065d2. *Cf. Matter of [name not provided]* LIN 04 257 51922 (AAO Feb. 10, 2005), http://bit.ly/feb057d ("The AAO does not assign expert weight to the professor's conclusion that the proffered position is a specialty occupation. The record does not establish the professor as an expert on the requirements for qualifying a position as a specialty occupation. There is no evidence that the professor has specialized knowledge of the

Cont'd

Copyright © 2017. American Immigration Lawyers Association. All rights reserved.

statement, such as from a university professor, should explain how the job duties require the particular education, rather than simply stating the conclusion that the job is a specialty occupation. In other words, the statement should address what would be within the writer's knowledge. If the advertisements are not from entities in the same industry, then it may possible to demonstrate that the degree requirement is typical "among similar organizations" through parity in size, revenues, or number of employees,[117] although the practitioner is strongly advised to submit postings from industry employers if possible. The AAO rejected job announcements as insufficient, however, where they "corroborate[d] the information in the [OOH] that a broad range of degrees is acceptable for entry into the position."[118]

When reviewing an employer's historical degree requirement, "the critical element is not the title of the position or the employer's self-imposed standards, but whether the position actually requires the theoretical and practical application of a body of highly specialized knowledge" and a degree.[119] Appropriate evidence may include documents discussing "past recruiting and hiring practices with regard to the proffered position or other similarly situated employees."[120] The petitioner may submit affidavits from previous employees, but all of the information should be corroborated, such as copies of degrees, descriptions of job duties, and employment records.[121] As stated by the AAO:

> "The AAO reviews the petitioner's past employment practices as well as the histories, including names and dates of employment, of those employees with degrees who previously held the position, and copies of those employees' diplomas to aid in determining the third criterion. To interpret the regulations any other way would lead to absurd results: if [US]CIS were limited to reviewing a petitioner's self-imposed employment requirements, then any alien with a bachelor's degree could be brought into the United States to perform a menial, non-professional, or an otherwise non-specialty occupation, so long as the employer required all such employees to have baccalaureate or higher degrees."[122]

---

relevant statutes, regulations, case law, and precedent decisions, or that he has been recognized as an authority in this area").

[116] *Matter of [name not provided]* WAC 03 262 52383 (AAO Feb. 3, 2006), http://bit.ly/feb066d.

[117] *Matter of [name not provided]* WAC 07 137 52988 (AAO June 3, 2008), http://bit.ly/jun082d ("Neither do these listings indicate that the businesses publishing the advertisements are similar to the petitioner in size, number of employees, or level of revenue"); *Matter of [name not provided]* WAC 02 255 53547 (AAO Feb. 3, 2006), http://bit.ly/feb067d.

[118] *Matter of [name not provided]* LIN 04 184 51951 (AAO Feb. 3, 2006), http://bit.ly/feb065d.

[119] *Matter of [name not provided]* WAC 07 137 52988 (AAO June 3, 2008), http://bit.ly/jun082d; *Matter of [name not provided]* WAC 07 151 50781 (AAO June 3, 2008), http://bit.ly/jun081d; *Matter of [name not provided]* LIN 04 184 51951 (AAO Feb. 3, 2006), http://bit.ly/feb065d.

[120] *Matter of [name not provided]* WAC 07 151 50781 (AAO June 3, 2008), http://bit.ly/jun081d.

[121] *Matter of [name not provided]* WAC 03 262 52383 (AAO Feb. 3, 2006), http://bit.ly/feb066d.

[122] *Matter of [name not provided]* WAC 07 137 52988 (AAO June 3, 2008http://bit.ly/jun082d; *Matter of [name not provided]* WAC 07 151 50781 (AAO June 3, 2008), http://bit.ly/jun081d; *Matter of [name not provided]* WAC 03 100 50458 (AAO Aug. 25, 2005), http://bit.ly/aug0536d.

Copyright © 2017. American Immigration Lawyers Association. All rights reserved.

The practitioner should also confirm that the employer "normally" requires an individual with the appropriate degree. In one case, legacy INS noted that the previous incumbent had qualified through his experience rather than through his bachelor's degree and that "the position can be performed successfully by an experienced person whose education and training are not equal to a baccalaureate degree in a specialized area."[123] In another case, the AAO noted that "the employer's acceptance of a variety of liberal arts degrees, rather than requiring a human resources background is further indication that it does not require a degree in a specific specialty and that the position, therefore, is not a specialty occupation."[124] Also, if the petitioner will place the beneficiary at a third-party worksite, then USCIS may require evidence that "the entities ultimately employing the proposed beneficiaries require a bachelor's degree for all employees in that position" because "the degree requirement should not originate with the employment agency that brought the beneficiaries to the United States for employment with the agency's clients."[125]

Based on an analysis of the specialized and complex job duties, the AAO reversed USCIS's denial in one case filed by a highly regarded and "world renowned" restaurant operation.[126] Noting that the beneficiary would also be a member of the petitioner's management team, all members of which hold bachelor's degrees or the equivalent, the AAO stated:

> "The [OOH] provides valuable information about a wide range of occupations in the nation's economy. That information however, is not all inclusive. It provides a general composite description of jobs and cannot reasonably be expected to reflect all work situations in specific establishments or localities. It is therefore, necessary, to consider the nature of the petitioner's operations and the specific duties of the proffered position when determining whether the job is a specialty occupation. Here, the petitioner is a large specialty restaurant with a complex operational and delivery structure. The duties of the proffered position are more complex than those described in the Handbook for a typical chef's position. Thus, the petitioner's requirement of a bachelor's degree is a reasonable requirement. The petitioner has established that the nature of the specific duties is so specialized and complex that knowledge required to perform the duties is usually associated with the attainment of a baccalaureate or higher degree."[127]

In another case, a district court reversed denial, stating that "AAO provided no basis for its decision" but "merely reiterated the criterion and then stated that the position does not meet the requirement" and neglected to discuss statements provided by

---

[123] *Matter of Caron International, Inc.*, 19 I&N Dec. 791 (Comm'r 1988).

[124] *Matter of [name not provided]* LIN 04 184 51951 (AAO Feb. 3, 2006), http://bit.ly/feb065d.

[125] *Matter of [name not provided]* WAC 03 232 53697 (AAO Feb. 3, 2006), http://bit.ly/feb063d.

[126] *Matter of [name not provided]* EAC 03 143 51185 (AAO Jan. 28, 2005), http://bit.ly/jan0514d.

[127] *Id.*

Copyright © 2017. American Immigration Lawyers Association. All rights reserved.

university professors.[128] A petitioner may be able to demonstrate that the job requires an individual with a bachelor's degree because it "represent[s] a combination of jobs that would require the beneficiary to have a unique set of skills beyond those of" an individual without a degree.[129] For further discussion of a combination of jobs, see Volume 2: Chapter Two, "The Labor Certification Application."

It should be noted that a job is not deemed a specialty occupation merely because it requires managing other managers; the petition must demonstrate that "the proposed duties involve significant supervision or quality review over the work of professional employees so as to make the holding of professional credentials mandatory."[130]

USCIS may also differentiate between positions that are entry level and those at more advanced levels. Guidance indicating that computer programming generally would not be considered a specialty occupation because the OOH indicates that individuals with only an associate's degree may enter the field, nevertheless noted that this fact "does not necessarily disqualify all positions in the computer programming occupation (viewed generally) from qualifying as positions in a specialty occupation."[131] Criticizing an earlier guidance issued by a Service Center director,[132] the later guidance stated that the earlier memo "does not properly explain or distinguish an entry-level position from that is, for example, more senior, complex, specialized, or unique."[133]

A footnote in that guidance confirms as policy a trend that had been noted in USCIS decisions in recent years:

"USCIS officers must also review the LCA to ensure the wage level designated by the petitioner corresponds to the proffered position. If a petitioner designates a position as a Level I, entry-level position, for example, such an assertion will likely contradict a claim that the proffered position is particularly complex, specialized, or unique compared to other positions *within the same occupation*."[134]

Indeed, the LCA is often brought into play on the substantive question of specialty occupation when the prevailing wage determination that underlies the LCA is for a position and/or level that suggests that the duties are not "specialized and complex":

---

[128] *Fred 26 Importers, Inc. v. USCIS*, 445 F. Supp. 2d 1174 (C.D. Cal. 2006).

[129] *Matter of [name not provided]* EAC 06 136 50756 (AAO Nov. 13, 2007), http://bit.ly/nov074d.

[130] *Matter of Caron International, Inc.*, 19 I&N Dec. 791 (Comm'r 1988); *Matter of [name not provided]* LIN 04 257 51922 (AAO Feb. 10, 2005), http://bit.ly/feb057d (stating that "the management of professionals is not necessarily an indication of a specialty occupation position").

[131] USCIS, "Rescission of the December 22, 2000 'Guidance memo on H1B computer related positions'" (Mar. 31, 2017), AILA Doc. No. 17040300.

[132] Legacy INS, T. Way, "Guidance memo on H1B computer related positions" (Dec. 22, 2000), AILA Doc. No. 01040603.

[133] USCIS, "Rescission of the December 22, 2000 'Guidance memo on H1B computer related positions'" (Mar. 31, 2017), AILA Doc. No. 17040300.

[134] *Id.*, footnote 6 (emphasis in original).

Copyright © 2017. American Immigration Lawyers Association. All rights reserved.

"[B]y attesting on the LCA that the proffered position is a Level I, entry-level position, the petitioner indicates that the job may only require 'a basic understanding of the occupation' expected of a 'worker in training' or an individual performing an 'internship.' As such, absent evidence to the contrary, this LCA is countervailing evidence against any claim by the petitioner that the proffered position or its duties are relatively complex and/or specialized as compared to others within the same occupation. In accordance with the relevant DOL explanatory information on wage levels, the selected wage rate indicates that the holder of the position would only be required to have a basic understanding of the occupation; would be expected to perform routine tasks that require limited, if any, exercise of judgment; would be closely supervised and have his or her work closely monitored and reviewed for accuracy; and would receive specific instructions on required tasks and expected results."[135]

That being said, a Level 1 prevailing wage is not an absolute bar to qualification as a specialty occupation:

"Nevertheless, it is important to note that a Level 1 wage-designation does not preclude a proffered position from classification as a specialty occupation. In certain occupations (doctors or lawyers, for example), such a position would still require a minimum of a bachelor's degree in a specific specialty, or its equivalent, for entry. Similarly, however, a Level IV wage-designation would not reflect that an occupation qualifies as a specialty occupation if that higher-level position does not have an entry requirement of at least a bachelor's degree in a specific specialty or its equivalent. That is, a position's wage level designation may be a consideration but is not a substitute for a determination of whether a proffered position meets the requirements of section 214(i)(1) of the Act."[136]

From this, it would seem that a position with a Level 1 prevailing wage would be difficult to qualify on the basis of either of the two criteria that require the position to be complex, but would be less of a factor where the criteria in question relate to whether the degree is the normal requirement. However, some of the decisions conflate the question of complexity with the overarching question of whether the position "requires theoretical and practical application of a body of highly specialized knowledge"—in other words, whether the position meets the definition of specialized knowledge.[137] Thus, under these analyses, a position in the lowest wage category that ordinarily requires a degree could still be found not to be a specialty occupation.

---

[135] *Matter of [name and case number not provided]* (AAO Apr. 7, 2014), AILA Doc. No. 15041361. *See also [Matter of name and case number not provided]* (AAO May 31, 2012), http://bit.ly/may1216d; *Health Carousel, LLC v. BCIS*, No. 1:130cv023 (S.D. Ohio 2014); *Matter of S-P-F-, Inc.*, ID# 15014 (AAO Dec. 14, 2015); *Matter of S-P-F-D-, Inc.*, ID# 17731 (AAO Aug. 18, 2016).

[136] *Matter of G-H-P-, Inc.*, ID# 152392 (AAO Dec. 21, 2106).

[137] *Matter of [name and case number not provided]* (AAO Apr. 7, 2014), AILA Doc. No. 15041361; *Health Carousel, LLC v. BCIS*, No. 1:130cv023 (S.D. Ohio 2014).

Copyright © 2017. American Immigration Lawyers Association. All rights reserved.

B. Qualifying for the Specialty Occupation

The practitioner should note that the mere fact that the H-1B job qualifies as a specialty occupation is insufficient to obtain H-1B status on behalf of the beneficiary:

"The facts of a beneficiary's background only come at issue after it is found that the position in which the petitioner intends to employ him falls within the professions. After that determination is made, attention turns to the qualifications of the beneficiary to determine if he meets the standards and requirements of the position."[138]

Therefore, the H-1B petition must also present "[e]vidence that the alien qualifies to perform services in the specialty occupation."[139] The statute states that an individual may qualify for H-1B status by possessing one of the following:

- "[F]ull state licensure to practice in the occupation, if such licensure is required to practice in the occupation," as discussed below;

- "[C]ompletion" of the baccalaureate or higher degree in the specialty that is required for the occupation; or

- Both:
    - "[E]xperience in the specialty equivalent to the completion of such degree"; and
    - "[R]ecognition of expertise in the specialty through progressively responsible positions relating to the specialty."[140]

The regulations expand upon the statute by stating that the beneficiary must possess one of the following qualifications:

- U.S. bachelor's degree or higher degree "required by the specialty occupation from an accredited college or university";

- "[F]oreign degree determined to be equivalent to a United States baccalaureate or higher degree required by the specialty occupation from an accredited college or university;

- "[A]n unrestricted state license, registration or certification which authorizes him or her to fully practice the specialty occupation and be immediately engaged in that specialty in the state of intended employment"; or

- Cumulative "education, specialized training, and/or progressively responsible experience that is equivalent to completion of a United States baccalaureate or higher degree in the specialty occupation, and have recognition of expertise in the specialty through progressively responsible positions directly related to the specialty."[141]

---

[138] *Matter of Michael Hertz Associates*, 19 I&N Dec. 558 (Comm'r 1988).

[139] 8 CFR §214.2(h)(4)(iii)(B)(3).

[140] INA §214(i)(2); Immigration Act of 1990, Pub. L. No. 101-649, §205(c), 104 Stat. 4978 (Nov. 29, 1990).

[141] 8 CFR §214.2(h)(4)(iii)(C).

Copyright © 2017. American Immigration Lawyers Association. All rights reserved.

The filed H-1B petition must include "[d]ocumentation, certifications, affidavits, declarations, degrees, diplomas, writings, reviews, or any other required evidence sufficient to establish that the beneficiary is qualified to perform services in a specialty occupation."[142] Educational documents, such as "[s]chool records, diplomas, degrees, affidavits, declarations, contracts, and similar documentation submitted[,] must reflect periods of attendance, courses of study, and similar pertinent data, [and must] be executed by the person in charge of the records of the educational or other institution, firm, or establishment where education or training was acquired."[143]

Equivalence to an advanced or master's degree requires a bachelor's degree "followed by at least five years of experience in the specialty."[144] If a doctoral degree is "required by a specialty," then the foreign national "must hold a Doctorate degree or its foreign equivalent."[145] Work experience equivalent to a baccalaureate degree in a three to one ratio of years of experience to education is discussed in detail below. For discussion of letters confirming completion of degree requirements in the context of H-1B change of status from F-1, see below.

Licensure, foreign degrees, and educational equivalencies are discussed below. When promulgating the previous version of the H-1B regulations, legacy INS declined to define the term "profession" as requiring "completion of a course of education..., culminating in a degree, where attainment of such degree or its equivalent is the minimum requirement for entry into the profession in the United States,"[146] because to do so "would mean that any field in which a college or university grants a degree would become a profession."[147] Legacy INS was "opposed to broadening the definition of profession" to explicitly include liberal arts degrees for the same reason, although an individual may qualify for a profession based on coursework,[148] as discussed below.

As discussed above, the field of the awarded degree should be related to the occupation.[149] For example, an individual with a degree in Actuarial Science should be qualified for the position of Actuary. The practitioner may find it helpful to confirm that the beneficiary's credentials meet the petitioner's job requirements, as the employer is unlikely to accept dissimilar fields of study. In some cases, the petitioner may accept degrees in a variety of related fields. In the previous example,

---

[142] 8 CFR §214.2(h)(4)(iv)(A).

[143] 8 CFR §214.2(h)(4)(iv)(A)(1).

[144] 8 CFR §214.2(h)(4)(iii)(D)(5).

[145] 8 CFR §214.2(h)(4)(iii)(D)(5); USCIS, "I-129 H-1B Standard Operating Procedures" (undated, posted July 26, 2007), AILA Doc. No. 07072668 ("There are no substitutions for a Ph.D.").

[146] 55 Fed. Reg. 2606 (Jan. 26, 1990). The phrase discussed is now stated in 8 CFR §214.2(h)(4)(ii).

[147] 55 Fed. Reg. 2606 (Jan. 26, 1990).

[148] Id.

[149] 8 CFR §214.2(h)(4)(ii) ("Specialty occupation means an occupation ... which requires the attainment of a bachelor's degree or higher in a specific specialty, or its equivalent, as a minimum for entry into the occupation in the United States"); INA §212(n)(3)(B) (master's degree); 8 CFR §214.2(h)(4)(iii)(D)(5) (degree equivalency); 8 CFR §214.2(f)(10) (employment through practical training).

Copyright © 2017. American Immigration Lawyers Association. All rights reserved.

other suitable degree fields may include Mathematics, Statistics, Economics, or Finance. The petitioner's industry may also be relevant. For example, the job of Engineer at a pharmaceutical manufacturer may accept a degree in Industrial, Chemical, Electrical, Civil, or Mechanical Engineering, depending on the specific duties of the job.

Alternatively, the beneficiary's university coursework may demonstrate qualification for the specialty occupation, as stated by USCIS guidance:

"When a beneficiary's degree is not directly related to the position occupation, evaluate the beneficiary's course work related to the occupation to determine his or her qualifications.

"For example, the beneficiary in an H-1B petition for an accountant has a degree in Business Administration. Generally, a degree in Business Administration will not satisfy the requirement that the beneficiary have a degree in a specialty because of the general, non-specific nature of the coursework required for this type of degree. The beneficiary may, however, have taken a significant number of accounting courses while obtaining the degree in Business Administration. These accounting courses may be sufficient to establish that the alien has the required education for H-1B status."[150]

Similarly, in response to a comment that "many American businesses prefer that recruited graduates for business positions have a liberal arts degree because that provides them with the intellectual insight and educational development together with the mental flexibility necessary for one to be successful in a business career," legacy INS stated:

"However, the Service recognizes that many of an individual's college-level courses, regardless of how broad the major field, will closely relate to the coursework required for a more specific baccalaureate degree program. When combined with appropriate experience, the holder of such a degree may be able to demonstrate membership in a specific profession."[151]

For example, a legacy Immigration and Naturalization Service (INS) precedent decision accepted that chiropractic is a professional occupation because the required coursework "consist[s] largely of advanced courses in the fields of biology and chemistry, both of which are recognized as professional fields."[152] Multiple anecdotal reports indicate that this approach remains generally effective for business and other fields. The practitioner is strongly encouraged to detail the relevant coursework in the H-1B support statement and to physically highlight the classes on the foreign national's transcript. However, discussion of coursework may prove unsuccessful if

---

[150] USCIS, "I-129 H-1B Standard Operating Procedures" (undated, posted July 26, 2007), AILA Doc. No. 07072668. *See also Matter of Caron International, Inc.*, 19 I&N Dec. 791 (Comm'r 1988); *Matter of Michael Hertz Associates*, 19 I&N Dec. 558 (Comm'r 1988); *Matter of Sun*, 12 I&N Dec. 535 (D.D. 1966) (mention of courses in the curriculum).

[151] 55 Fed. Reg. 2606 (Jan. 26, 1990).

[152] *Matter of Mcgowan*, 11 I&N Dec. 898 (D.D. 1966).

Copyright © 2017. American Immigration Lawyers Association. All rights reserved.

USCIS determines that the job offered is not a specialty occupation.[153] For discussion of equivalencies based on a combination of education and experience, see below.

1. Positions Requiring Licensure

The foreign national's professional licensure may be presented as evidence that the beneficiary qualifies for the specialty occupation.[154] When promulgating a previous version of the regulations, legacy INS explained that licensed individuals may "nevertheless [be] regarded as professionals," because they, "after passage of normal professional tests and requirements, are granted full state licenses (or registration or certification) to practice the profession."[155] For example, appellate bodies have stated:

> "The laws of the State of California quite clearly regulate the practice of Chiropractic on a professional level and a person meeting the educational requirements for licensure clearly possess the equivalent of at least a baccalaureate degree."[156]

> "Public primary and secondary teaching positions may be specialty occupations even where such positions do not require a bachelor's degree in a specific specialty, as long as state certification is also mandatory. The decision to certify teachers, and the determination of what requirements must be met for certification, are matters uniquely within the expertise and control of state governments. The essential inquiry is whether the state has granted, through a formal certification or licensure process of its choosing, an individual the right to teach students in its public schools."[157]

Although filing proof of current licensure should theoretically be sufficient, the practitioner is advised to submit evidence of both educational qualifications and valid licensure in order to avoid an RFE.

Evidence of full licensure may be required in addition to educational credentials:[158]

> "If an occupation requires a state or local license for an individual to fully perform the duties of the occupation, an alien ... seeking H classification in that occupation must have that license prior to approval of the petition to be found qualified to

---

[153] *Matter of [name not provided]* WAC 02 220 54035 (AAO Feb. 3, 2006), http://bit.ly/feb064d (discussion of coursework in mechanics, economics, mathematics, computer science, and material processing unhelpful where USCIS found that the job duties were more akin to a construction manager than an industrial engineer).

[154] 8 CFR §214.2(h)(4)(iii)(C)(3).

[155] 55 Fed. Reg. 2606 (Jan. 26, 1990).

[156] *Matter of Mcgowan*, 11 I&N Dec. 898 (D.D. 1966).

[157] *Matter of [name not provided]* EAC 06 216 52028 (AAO Sept. 8, 2006), http://bit.ly/sep066d.

[158] 8 CFR §214.2(h)(4)(v)(A).

Copyright © 2017. American Immigration Lawyers Association. All rights reserved.

enter the United States and immediately engage in employment in the occupation."[159]

"The petitioner must provide a certified copy of the alien's valid State license, certification, or registration to practice the profession…. When the alien has a temporary license, the approval period of the petition and/or extension of stay application cannot exceed the validity period of the temporary license."[160]

The practitioner should note that if the beneficiary holds only temporary licensure, then the validity period of the H-1B petition may be truncated: "Where licensure is required in any occupation, including registered nursing, the H petition may only be approved for a period of one year or for the period that the temporary license is valid, whichever is longer, unless the alien already has a permanent license to practice the occupation."[161] USCIS denied a petition where the beneficiary "would be hired under a 'conditional' certification," but the AAO reversed, stating: "Although the proffered position can be performed by a college graduate possessing only a 'probationary certificate' from the State of Texas, the record indicates that the duties of the proffered position, as well as the salary and benefits, are the same as those of a certified teacher."[162] For a discussion of the interrelationship between state licensure requirements and petition approval, see below. For discussion of the interrelationship of H-1B status and healthcare occupations, which may be cross-applicable to other industries, see below.

There are two exceptions to this rule, which are "examined on a case-by-case basis to determine if the beneficiary can be considered to be employed in a professional capacity."[163] First, evidence of temporary licensure may be sufficient, if it "is available and the alien is allowed to perform the duties of the occupation without a permanent license."[164] USCIS "shall examine the nature of the duties, the level at which the duties are performed, the degree of supervision received, and any limitations placed on the alien."[165] The H-1B petition may be approved as long "an analysis of the facts demonstrates that the alien under supervision is authorized to fully perform the duties of the occupation."[166]

The second exception applies if the state permits "an individual without licensure to fully practice the occupation under the supervision of licensed senior or supervisory personnel in that occupation," even if the occupation "generally

---

[159] Id.

[160] AFM 31.3(d) (citing 8 CFR §214.2(h)(v)).

[161] 8 CFR §214.2(h)(4)(v)(E); AFM 31.3(e) ("If the occupation is one which requires a license, the validity period for the approval cannot exceed the validity period of the license"). Not all nursing jobs qualify for H-1B status, however, as discussed in further detail below.

[162] Matter of [name not provided] EAC 06 216 52028 (AAO Sept. 8, 2006), http://bit.ly/sep066d.

[163] AFM 31.3(d).

[164] 8 CFR §214.2(h)(4)(v)(B).

[165] Id.

[166] Id.

Copyright © 2017. American Immigration Lawyers Association. All rights reserved.

require[s] licensure."[167] USCIS "shall examine the nature of the duties and the level at which they are performed, as well as evidence … as to the identity, physical location, and credentials of the individual(s) who will supervise the alien, and evidence that the petitioner is complying with state requirements."[168] The H-1B petition may be approved if "the facts demonstrate that the alien under supervision will fully perform the duties of the occupation."[169] In practice, this situation occurs frequently for individuals who are at the interim stage of awaiting issuance of the license, such as U.S. trained attorneys who have passed the bar exam, but are not yet admitted, among others. However, foreign attorneys who will only provide consulting services and who will not offer services as a lawyer should not be required to hold a license to practice law in a U.S. state.[170]

Presenting evidence of licensure for purposes of qualifying for the specialty occupation should be differentiated from applying for an H-1B visa. DOS guidance notes:

"The requirements for classification as an H-1B nonimmigrant professional may or may not include a license because states have different rules in this area. If a state permits aliens to enter the United States as a visitor to take a licensing exam, then USCIS will generally require a license before they will approve the H-1B petition. However, some states do not permit aliens to take licensing exams until they enter the United States in H-1B status and obtain a taxpayer identification number. Therefore, a visa must not be denied based solely on the fact that the applicant does not already hold a license to practice in the United States."[171]

An H-1B1 nonimmigrant should not be required to present a valid license to qualify for the specialty occupation:

"The H-1B1 category does not require possession of a relevant professional license as a condition to admission. H-1B1 professionals will be expected to comply with all applicable state and federal licensure requirements for engaging in their professions *following* their admission."[172]

"[H-1B1] admission and/or classification should not be denied based solely on the fact that the applicant does not already hold a license to practice in the United States."[173]

---

[167] 8 CFR §214.2(h)(4)(v)(C)(1).

[168] *Id.*

[169] *Id.*

[170] 55 Fed. Reg. 2606 (Jan. 26, 1990).

[171] 9 FAM 402.10-4(B).

[172] Customs and Border Protection (CBP), J. Ahern, "Free Trade Agreements with Chile and Singapore" (Apr. 19, 2004), AILA Doc. No. 05040166 (emphasis in original); USCIS, W. Yates, "Lifting of Numerical Cap on Mexican NAFTA Nonimmigrant Professionals (TN) and Free Trade Agreements with Chile and Singapore" (Jan. 8, 2004), AILA Doc. No. 04030361.

[173] 9 FAM 402.10-5(G).

Copyright © 2017. American Immigration Lawyers Association. All rights reserved.

a. State Requirements for Licensure vis-à-vis H-1B Eligibility Requirements

Two common issues arose in the past with jobs requiring state licensure and caused a foreign national to face a "Catch-22" due to the intersection of state prerequisites for licensure and the regulatory requirements:

- A state authority will not issue a license until the foreign national holds H-1B status, but USCIS in turn may not approve an H-1B petition until the beneficiary obtains the necessary license; and

- A state authority requires a license applicant "to present a social security number [SSN] that is valid for employment" but the foreign national is ineligible for such an SSN until he or she obtains H-1B status.[174]

USCIS guidance had offered "provisional" relief to address these situations, and in 2016 the relief was codified into regulations. Under the regulations, the H-1B petition may be approved for a validity period of up to one year, if the petitioner can show, "through evidence from the … licensing authority" that the only thing preventing issuance of the license is lack of a Social Security number, lack of employment authorization in the U.S., or failure to meet "a similar technical requirement."[175] The petitioner must present evidence that the individual is "fully qualified to receive the state or local license in all other respects," and has filed an application for the license under applicable rules, unless the sole reason for not filing is that same lack of Social Security number, work authorization, or other technical item.[176]

USCIS would not view such a requirement as completion of post-graduate training as a "similar technical requirement," noting that it will not "excuse substantive prerequisites for obtaining licensure."[177] However, individuals in this situation often will fall under the exception for persons under the supervision of other professionals, discussed above.

The pre-regulatory guidance noted that petition approval "does not constitute authorization by USCIS for the alien to engage in any activities requiring such licensure,"[178] but, in fact, "is merely a means to facilitate the state or local licensing authority's issuance of such a license to the alien, provided all other requirements are satisfied."[179] This would mean that the foreign national may perform licensed

---

[174] AFM 31.3(d). *See also* 80 Fed. Reg. 81900 (Dec. 31, 2015); USCIS, B. Velarde, "Requirements for H-1B Beneficiaries Seeking to Practice in a Health Care Occupation" (May 20, 2009), AILA Doc. No. 09052766; USCIS, D. Neufeld, "Adjudicators Field Manual Update: Chapter 31; Accepting and Adjudicating H-1B Petitions When a State License is not Available due to State Licensing Requirements Mandating Possession of a Valid Immigration Document as Evidence of Employment Authorization" (Mar. 21, 2008), AILA Doc. No. 08032432; Legacy INS, T. Cook, "Social Security Cards and the Adjudication of H-1B Petitions" (Nov. 20, 2001), AILA Doc. No. 01112131.

[175] 8 CFR §214.2(h)(4)(v)(C)(2).

[176] *Id.*

[177] 81 Fed. Reg. 82398, 82442 (Nov. 18, 2016).

[178] AFM 31.3(d).

[179] USCIS, B. Velarde, "Requirements for H-1B Beneficiaries Seeking to Practice in a Health Care Occupation" (May 20, 2009), AILA Doc. No. 09052766.

Copyright © 2017. American Immigration Lawyers Association. All rights reserved.

activities only after he or she actually obtains the necessary license. While the regulations did not include a similar proviso, the limitation nevertheless should apply if only to satisfy other rules regarding practice of a profession without proper authorization. While awaiting issuance of the license, the employer and employee may wish to look to the supervision exception discussed above.

The regulations require that the beneficiary have obtained the license in order to extend status after the initial approval period, or to obtain approval of any other subsequent H-1B petition,[180] with two exceptions. The first is a petition "seeking to employ the alien in a position requiring a different license," and the second is a petition under which the beneficiary will be employed in a different location that "does not require a state or local license to fully perform the duties of the occupation."[181] Although the regulations are silent on the point, presumably the former situation will require the same conditions, evidence, and time limitation as the initial petition in which the license was not yet obtained. Also presumably, the latter exception will be free of those limitations and requirements.

b. Healthcare Occupations

This section is intended to provide an overview of a select few of the typical issues for H-1B petitions on behalf of healthcare professionals. This chapter will not discuss in detail all of the issues common to these H-1B petitions, so the practitioner is strongly encouraged to consult other resources on behalf of medical and healthcare professionals,[182] which, as long as the job qualifies as a specialty occupation, include:

- Physicians;[183]

- Licensed Practical Nurses, Licensed Vocational Nurses, and Registered Nurses;

- Occupational Therapists;

- Physical Therapists;

- Speech-Language Pathologists and Audiologists;

- Medical Technologists (Clinical Laboratory Scientists);

- Physician Assistants; and

- Medical Technicians (Clinical Laboratory Technicians).[184]

---

[180] 8 CFR §214.2(h)(4)(v)(C)(3).

[181] Id.

[182] The practitioner should note that foreign nationals entering healthcare occupations often require a VisaScreen Certificate. For the requirements applying to physicians, see INA §212(j); 8 CFR §214.2(h)(4)(viii); AFM 31.3(a). For further background on non-physician healthcare occupations, see USCIS, B. Velarde, "Requirements for H-1B Beneficiaries Seeking to Practice in a Health Care Occupation" (May 20, 2009), AILA Doc. No. 09052766 (footnotes for other resources). For background on the employment relationship in the context of healthcare jobs, see "USCIS Implements H-1B and L-1 Fee Increase According to Public Law 111-230" (Aug. 19, 2010), AILA Doc. No. 10081920. For a detailed discussion of all of these issues, see Immigration Options for Physicians, (AILA 3d Ed. 2009), https://agora.aila.org/product/detail/71.

[183] 8 CFR §214.2(h)(4)(viii).

Copyright © 2017. American Immigration Lawyers Association. All rights reserved.

532   BUSINESS IMMIGRATION: LAW & PRACTICE, 2ND ED.

For these healthcare occupations, the "licensing board standards" of individual states may supersede the qualifications stated as necessary in the OOH.[185] Therefore: "If the petitioner provides documentary evidence that the beneficiary has a valid license to practice a health care occupation in the state in which the beneficiary will be employed, the adjudicator should not look beyond the license."[186] USCIS also notes that "most states require a license to be renewed periodically,"[187] regardless of whether the underlying license is unrestricted. So, in the event that "the beneficiary is in possession of an unrestricted license, the renewal date should not be considered when determining the validity period of the approval."[188] However, if the license is restricted, such as if it is valid for all activities "except for mandatory supervised practice," then it should be approved "for a period of one year, or the duration of the restricted license, whichever is longer."[189]

Licensure is not required of a physician who will primarily "teach or conduct research, or both, at or for a public or nonprofit private educational or research institution or agency" and will only provide direct patient care "that is incidental to his or her teaching and/or research."[190] Such a petition should "be adjudicated like a petition for an alien coming to perform services in a specialty occupation."[191]

A foreign medical school graduate may be granted H-1B status "if he or she has a full and unrestricted license to practice medicine in a foreign state or if he or she has graduated from medical school in either the United States or in a foreign state."[192] In order to "provide direct patient care," however, the beneficiary "must generally have a valid medical license in the state of intended employment," although "USCIS may grant a limited-validity petition in order to allow the beneficiary time to obtain a professional license,"[193] as discussed above. Alternatively, a foreign national "involved in a medical residency program" may be the beneficiary of an approved

---

[184] USCIS, B. Velarde, "Requirements for H-1B Beneficiaries Seeking to Practice in a Health Care Occupation" (May 20, 2009), AILA Doc. No. 09052766 (citing 8 CFR §212.15(c)).

[185] USCIS, B. Velarde, "Requirements for H-1B Beneficiaries Seeking to Practice in a Health Care Occupation" (May 20, 2009), AILA Doc. No. 09052766 ("Adjudicators should be mindful, however, that in certain instances, other authoritative sources exist that indicate whether the position in question qualifies as a specialty occupation (e.g., State licensing board standards). Thus, the OOH is not determinative in all cases").

[186] USCIS, B. Velarde, "Requirements for H-1B Beneficiaries Seeking to Practice in a Health Care Occupation" (May 20, 2009), AILA Doc. No. 09052766.

[187] Id.

[188] Id.

[189] Id.

[190] 9 FAM 402.10-4(B); AFM 31.3(a) ("If no patient care is involved, neither a license or authorization from the state needs to be submitted").

[191] AFM 31.3(a).

[192] 9 FAM 402.10-4(B).

[193] Id.

Copyright © 2017. American Immigration Lawyers Association. All rights reserved.

H-1B petition, "even though he or she does not yet have a full and unrestricted U.S. medical license."[194]

USCIS guidance, however, takes the position that "[m]ost registered nurse (RN) positions do not qualify as a specialty occupation because they do not normally require a U.S. bachelor's or higher degree in nursing (or its equivalent) as the minimum for entry into those particular positions."[195] All U.S. jurisdictions require a license for an RN, and in turn all such licensing requires graduation from an approved nursing program and passage of the National Council Licensure Examination (NCLEX) examination.[196] Nevertheless, such a license will not, in and of itself, suffice for H-1B qualification, since "no state requires a bachelor's degree in nursing for licensure" at this time.[197] The guidance notes that, according to the OOH, registered nurses may hold a bachelor's or associate's degree, or a diploma from a nursing program, and that the associate's degree is the most common. But it also acknowledges that bachelor's degrees are increasingly being pursued.[198]

However, the guidance also acknowledges that there may be "some situations …where the petitioner may be able to show that a nursing position qualifies as a specialty occupation," and that "[t]he private sector is increasingly showing a preference for more highly educated nurses."[199] While the guidance does not state that any particular category of nursing definitively qualifies as a specialty occupation, it does suggest three areas in which a nurse may qualify for H-1B status:

- Advanced Practice Registered Nurses (APRNs). While APRNs "typically perform many of the same duties as RNs," they also perform additional, often more advanced functions. Thus, APRN positions "will generally be specialty occupations due to the advanced level of education and training required for certification." Some APRN occupations that "may satisfy" H-1B requirements include Certified Nurse-Midwife, Certified Clinical Nurse Specialist, Certified Nurse Practitioner, and Certified Registered Nurse Anesthetist.[200] That being said, merely referencing the occupation will not be enough—the petitioner will need to submit evidence from the state's regulatory body to establish that the occupation normally requires a bachelor's degree.[201]

---

[194] *Id.*

[195] USCIS, "Adjudication of H-1B Petitions for Nursing Occupations," PM-602-0104 (Feb. 18, 2015), AILA Doc. No. 15030210.

[196] *Id.*

[197] *Id.*

[198] *Id.*

[199] *Id.*

[200] *Id.*

[201] "Practice Pointer: H-1B Petitions for Nurses" (Nov. 13, 2014), AILA Doc. No. 14110340. This practice advisory was based on an earlier version of the USCIS guidance, but its insights are equally applicable to the later version.

Copyright © 2017. American Immigration Lawyers Association. All rights reserved.

- American Nurses Credentialing Center (ANCC) Magnet Recognition Program. While the guidance does not explicitly state that healthcare organizations that have achieved magnet status offer positions that would qualify as specialty occupations, it does indicate that nursing at such facilities has "attained a number of high standards," and provides as an example that "100% of nurse managers of [individual units] must have at least a baccalaureate degree in nursing" to qualify for magnet status. It also notes that magnet entities must show plans to achieve a nursing workforce of 80 percent bachelor's degree education by 2020.[202] The guidance does not indicate the impact of magnet recognition given these indicators, but it seems likely a nurse manager at a facility with magnet recognition could qualify, while a general RN still would not qualify on that basis.

- Specialized positions. The USCIS guidance notes that "nurses' duties and titles often depend on where they work and the patients with whom they work," and that, depending on the facts, "some … RN positions may qualify as specialty occupations." It specifically points to addiction, cardiovascular, critical care, emergency room, genetics, neonatology, nephology, oncology, pediatric, peri-operative, and rehabilitation nurses, as well as nurses who "do not work directly with patients, but must still have an active registered nurse license."[203] With respect to the last grouping, it should be noted that the occupations for which degrees in other fields may be satisfactory according to the OOH or the employer likely will not qualify, as the other acceptable degrees could be found to indicate that the occupation is not a specialty.[204]

While USCIS gives great weight to the OOH, it acknowledges that that resource "is not always determinative," and states that other "authoritative and/or persuasive sources provided by the petitioner will also be considered."[205] In general, documentation suggested by USCIS includes evidence regarding: the nature of the petitioner's business, industry practices, details of duties within the business operations, advanced certification requirements, ANCC magnet status, clinical experience requirements, and wages relative to others in the occupation.[206] Practitioners may wish to consider including such evidence as the educational background of other nurses employed by the petitioner in similar positions, printouts of job advertisements for similar nursing positions with the petitioner or comparable

---

[202] USCIS, "Adjudication of H-1B Petitions for Nursing Occupations," PM-602-0104 (Feb. 18, 2015), AILA Doc. No. 15030210.

[203] Id.

[204] See, e.g., Matter of M-S-L-M- Corp., ID# 123137 (AAO Oct. 12, 2016) (a degree in any medical science acceptable for program director position); Matter of G-H-P-, Inc., ID# 152392 (AAO Dec. 21, 2106) (medical services manager); Matter of C-S-I-, LLC, ID# 124421 (AAO Nov. 29, 2016) (health operations manager).

[205] USCIS, "Adjudication of H-1B Petitions for Nursing Occupations," PM-602-0104 (Feb. 18, 2015), AILA Doc. No. 15030210.

[206] Id,

Copyright © 2017. American Immigration Lawyers Association. All rights reserved.

535

employers, marketing or promotional materials from the petitioner that highlight the advanced training and education of the petitioners nursing staff, industry articles about the need for bachelor's level education for certain nursing duties, or an expert opinion letter explaining why at least a bachelor's degree would be needed for the particular nursing position in question. As previously discussed, use of a Level 1 prevailing wage could undermine a "claim that the position is particularly complex, specialized, or unique compared to other positions within the same occupation."[207]

2. Credentials Evaluations of Foreign Degrees and Three-Year Bachelor's Degrees

As stated by USCIS guidance:

"The petitioner may establish from an authoritative source or from transcripts, certificates, or other such school records that the alien has college-level education. College-level training may have been acquired at a college or university or other academic institution which grants a degree, diploma, or certificate, such as a technical college."[208]

Foreign degrees should be accompanied by a credentials evaluation,[209] because petition approval is dependent upon the beneficiary having "foreign education equivalent to a United States degree."[210] The practitioner is not advised, however, to depend on the adjudicator's determination of the beneficiary's qualifications, but should attach a credentials evaluation. Such reliance may result in processing delays because of the need for an RFE.[211]

Credentials evaluations "are advisory only," such that no specific evaluators are endorsed or recommended.[212] USCIS guidance directs adjudicators to "[l]ook at transcripts and credentials to get a feel for whether a beneficiary qualifies for the position before looking at the credentials evaluation."[213] Then, if the credentials evaluation "is reasonably close" to the determination by the adjudicator, and "particularly if the evaluator's methodology makes sense," the adjudicator "can give

---

[207] *Matter of M-S-L-M- Corp.*, ID# 123137 (AAO Oct. 12, 2016), *See also Matter of G-H-P-, Inc.*, ID# 152392 (AAO Dec. 21, 2106).

[208] AFM 31.3(g).

[209] 55 Fed. Reg. 2606 (Jan. 26, 1990).

[210] USCIS, "I-129 H-1B Standard Operating Procedures" (undated, posted July 26, 2007), AILA Doc. No. 07072668.

[211] USCIS, "I-129 H-1B Standard Operating Procedures" (undated, posted July 26, 2007), AILA Doc. No. 07072668 ("If [the adjudicator is] unable to make a determination, [he or she should] send an RFE asking for an advisory evaluation of the beneficiary's education") (emphasis in original).

[212] USCIS, "I-129 H-1B Standard Operating Procedures" (undated, posted July 26, 2007), AILA Doc. No. 07072668 (emphasis in original); AFM 31.3(g) ("USCIS does not specifically recognize or accredit any sources of evaluations"); *Matter of Sea. Inc.*, 19 I&N Dec. 817 (Comm'r 1988). *See also Matter of Arjani*, 12 I&N Dec. 649 (Reg'l Comm'r 1967) (stating that "the advisory opinions of other governmental agencies regarding the applicant's qualifications are entitled to great weight but the ultimate decision concerning the beneficiary's qualifications rests with this Service").

[213] USCIS, "I-129 H-1B Standard Operating Procedures" (undated, posted July 26, 2007), AILA Doc. No. 07072668.

Copyright © 2017. American Immigration Lawyers Association. All rights reserved.

the evaluation a higher degree of credibility."[214] Indeed, experience has shown that USCIS increasingly relies upon specific third-party vendors for data and confirmation of educational credentials, with the American Association of Collegiate Registrars and Admissions Officers Electronic Database for Global Education (AACRAO EDGE) currently in favor.[215]

Although the following provisions are placed in a section titled "Equivalence to completion of a college degree" and seem to address experience equivalencies as opposed to foreign degree equivalencies,[216] they are relevant[217] because experience has shown that these factors are considered by USCIS adjudicators when reviewing the equivalency of foreign degrees. The regulations state that the "level of knowledge, competence, and practice in the specialty occupation" should "be determined by" at least one of the following criteria:

- "An evaluation" from a specific type of educational official;[218]

- A credentials evaluation of education prepared "by a reliable credentials evaluation service which specializes in evaluating foreign educational credentials";[219]

- "The results of recognized college-level equivalency examinations or special credit programs, such as the College Level Examination Program (CLEP), or Program on Noncollegiate Sponsored Instruction (PONSI)."[220]

---

[214] USCIS, "I-129 H-1B Standard Operating Procedures" (undated, posted July 26, 2007), AILA Doc. No. 07072668. *Matter of Caron International, Inc.*, 19 I&N Dec. 791 (Comm'r 1988) ("This Service may, in its discretion, use as advisory opinions statements from universities, professional organizations, or other sources submitted in evidence as expert testimony. Nevertheless, since the Service is responsible for making the final determination regarding a beneficiary's eligibility for the benefit sought, where an opinion is not in accord with other information or is in any way questionable, the Service is not required to accept or may give less weight to that evidence").

[215] *See* USCIS, Letter to Rep. Joseph Crowley (Mar. 13, 2014), AILA Doc. No. 14121240 (stating "USCIS considers all opinions rendered by an educational credentials evaluator(s) in conjunction with a review of the foreign worker's relevant educational credentials. In the course of adjudication, USCIS may refer to other available credible resource material regarding the equivalency of the educational credentials to college degrees obtained in the United States, such as AACRAO EDGE database").

[216] 8 CFR §214.2(h)(4)(iii)(D). *See also* USCIS, "I-129 H-1B Standard Operating Procedures" (undated, posted July 26, 2007), AILA Doc. No. 07072668 (relevant discussion placed in a section titled "Degree Equivalencies").

[217] AFM 31.3(g) states: "One of the most common situations an adjudicator will encounter is an H-1B petition filed for an alien in specialty occupation where the alien lacks a U.S. bachelor's degree." The practitioner should note that the distinction seems to focus on U.S. bachelor's degrees and other types of qualifications.

[218] 8 CFR §214.2(h)(4)(iii)(D)(1); USCIS, "I-129 H-1B Standard Operating Procedures" (undated, posted July 26, 2007), AILA Doc. No. 07072668.

[219] 8 CFR §214.2(h)(4)(iii)(D)(3); USCIS, "I-129 H-1B Standard Operating Procedures" (undated, posted July 26, 2007), AILA Doc. No. 07072668. For this provision, the guidance specifically references credentials evaluations of foreign education.

[220] 8 CFR §214.2(h)(4)(iii)(D)(2); USCIS, "I-129 H-1B Standard Operating Procedures" (undated, posted July 26, 2007), AILA Doc. No. 07072668.

Copyright © 2017. American Immigration Lawyers Association. All rights reserved.

- Recognition from a professional association; or

- USCIS determination.[221]

Specifically, the H-1B petition can include a statement from "an official who has authority to grant college-level credit for training and/or experience in the specialty at an accredited college or university."[222] Such a credentials evaluation "should be given considerable weight in determining eligibility."[223] Importantly, the particular college or university must have "a program for granting such credit based on an individual's training and/or work experience,"[224] and the individual "must be formally involved with" the program in order "to have the required authority and expertise to make such evaluations."[225] The credentials evaluation may be provided in the individual's personal or official capacity,[226] and "USCIS does not require the alien to be enrolled in a program for college credit at the university in order to accept the evaluation of such an expert."[227]

In practice, any credentials evaluation should include a biography of the evaluator to confirm that the evaluator has the appropriate professional qualifications to issue credentials evaluations.[228] This conservative approach is supported by USCIS guidance,[229] which confirms that "foreign educational degree evaluations can be of assistance if they are thorough, well documented and specific in reaching an equivalency determination."[230] Further, the credentials evaluation should:

- "Consider formal education only, not practical experience;

- "State if the collegiate training was post-secondary education, (*i.e.*, whether the applicant completed the U.S. equivalent of high school before entering college);

- "Provide a detailed explanation of the material evaluated rather than a simple concluding statement; and

---

[221] 8 CFR §§214.2(h)(4)(iii)(D)(4)-(5); USCIS, "I-129 H-1B Standard Operating Procedures" (undated, posted July 26, 2007), AILA Doc. No. 07072668. The final two criteria are discussed below.

[222] 8 CFR §214.2(h)(4)(iii)(D)(1); AFM 31.3(g); USCIS, "I-129 H-1B Standard Operating Procedures" (undated, posted July 26, 2007), AILA Doc. No. 07072668.

[223] AFM 31.3(g).

[224] 8 CFR §214.2(h)(4)(iii)(D)(1); USCIS, "I-129 H-1B Standard Operating Procedures" (undated, posted July 26, 2007), AILA Doc. No. 07072668.

[225] AFM 31.3(g).

[226] AFM 31.3(g) ("The evaluation may be done in the official's name as an individual, or as an authorized representative of the college or university").

[227] AFM 31.3(g).

[228] 8 CFR §214.2(h)(4)(ii); 55 Fed. Reg. 2606 (Jan. 26, 1990). The practitioner should note that the regulations do not specifically term this type of determination to be a credentials evaluation. *See also* USCIS, "I-129 H-1B Standard Operating Procedures" (undated, posted July 26, 2007), AILA Doc. No. 07072668 (stating that the evaluation should "[b]riefly state the qualifications and experience of the evaluator providing the opinion").

[229] USCIS, "I-129 H-1B Standard Operating Procedures" (undated, posted July 26, 2007), AILA Doc. No. 07072668.

[230] AFM 31.3(g).

Copyright © 2017. American Immigration Lawyers Association. All rights reserved.

- "Briefly state the qualifications and experience of the evaluator providing the opinion."[231]

The practitioner should carefully review the credentials evaluation to confirm that the beneficiary qualifies, on the basis of education alone, for H-1B classification. USCIS guidance states:

"Just because the degree says it is a bachelor's degree does not necessarily mean that it is equivalent to a United States bachelor's degree.

"For example, India has both three– and four-year bachelor's degrees. Generally, the three-year degrees are equivalent to three years of undergraduate coursework at a U.S. institution of higher learning. The four-year degrees from India can usually be considered equivalent to a U.S. bachelor's degree."[232]

Therefore, the adjudicator will evaluate whether the beneficiary completed coursework for which he or she would be awarded a four-year degree in the United States: "It may be useful to compare the beneficiary's age at completion and the duration of the course of study, with the average age of graduates of United States institutions offering similar programs as a factor in determining equivalency of education."[233] However, substance should be elevated over form, such that the total years of attendance at school are less important than the courses completed, and the adjudicator should not "penalize a beneficiary who earns four-year degree in three years."[234] A beneficiary may qualify for H-1B status through a foreign degree that is equivalent to two years of baccalaureate study in the United States combined with two years of graduate coursework, even if he or she does not earn the higher degree.[235] For further discussion of credentials evaluations in the context of experience or training as equivalence to a degree, see below.

3. Experience and Training Equivalent to a Degree

The regulations detail that "equivalence to completion of a United States baccalaureate or higher degree shall mean achievement of a level of knowledge, competence, and practice in the specialty occupation that has been determined to be equal to that of an individual who has a baccalaureate or higher degree in the specialty."[236] When promulgating a previous version of the regulations, legacy INS explained that individuals without university degrees may "nevertheless [be] regarded as professionals" if they, "by virtue of a combination of academic training and

---

[231] USCIS, "I-129 H-1B Standard Operating Procedures" (undated, posted July 26, 2007), AILA Doc. No. 07072668 (citing 8 CFR §214.2(h)(4)(iii)(D)(3)).

[232] USCIS, "I-129 H-1B Standard Operating Procedures" (undated, posted July 26, 2007), AILA Doc. No. 07072668 (emphasis in original).

[233] AFM 31.3(g).

[234] USCIS, "I-129 H-1B Standard Operating Procedures" (undated, posted July 26, 2007), AILA Doc. No. 07072668. *Cf. Matter of Rabbani*, 12 I&N Dec. 15 (D.D. 1966) (foreign doctoral degree earned in six years deemed equivalent to a U.S. bachelor's degree).

[235] *Matter of Arjani*, 12 I&N Dec. 649 (Reg'l Comm'r 1967).

[236] 8 CFR §214.2(h)(4)(iii)(D).

Copyright © 2017. American Immigration Lawyers Association. All rights reserved.

professional experience are, in fact, lawfully practicing at a professional level."[237] For example, "it is recognized that in a few areas of the professions it is not always possible to obtain the usual formal education," and the foreign national may lack a degree because the home country did not offer degree programs in the field.[238] As another example, the AAO determined in the context of a petition for a teacher "that the combination of a bachelor's degree and specialized training resulting in state certification constitutes the equivalent of a bachelor's degree in a specific specialty."[239]

Despite language in the regulations that equivalence to completion of a degree can be "determined by" the results of an equivalency examination,[240] USCIS takes the position that the examination results are not enough, in and of themselves. Instead, it states that a college or university official must find the results applicable:

> "Results of recognized college-level equivalency examinations or special credit programs, such as the College Level Examination Program (CLEP), or Program on Noncollegiate Sponsored Instruction (PONSI) must be translated into college credits by an authoritative source in the particular program or by an authorized official from an accredited college or university, such as the registrar, in order for the results to be applied towards the degree requirement."[241]

As an alternative to CLEP or PONSI results or a credentials evaluation,[242] the necessary "level of knowledge, competence, and practice in the specialty occupation" may be demonstrated by "[e]vidence of certification or registration from a nationally-recognized professional association or society for the specialty."[243] The regulations state that the association or society should be "known to grant certification or registration to persons in the occupational specialty who have achieved a certain level of competence in the specialty."[244] Similarly, a legacy INS precedent decision noted that the association should be "professional, as opposed to a trade organization, or that membership in this organization requires at least a specific academic degree or its equivalent."[245] However, USCIS guidance further specifies that "[m]embership in a

---

[237] 55 Fed. Reg. 2606 (Jan. 26, 1990).

[238] *Matter of Yaakov*, 13 I&N Dec. 203 (Reg'l Comm'r 1969).

[239] *Matter of [name not provided]* EAC 06 216 52028 (AAO Sept. 8, 2006), http://bit.ly/sep066d.

[240] 8 CFR §214.2(h)(4)(iii)(D)(3).

[241] AFM 31.3(g).

[242] 8 CFR §214.2(h)(4)(iii)(D)(3); USCIS, "I-129 H-1B Standard Operating Procedures" (undated, posted July 26, 2007), AILA Doc. No. 07072668.

[243] 8 CFR §214.2(h)(4)(iii)(D)(4); USCIS, "I-129 H-1B Standard Operating Procedures" (undated, posted July 26, 2007), AILA Doc. No. 07072668.

[244] 8 CFR §214.2(h)(4)(iii)(D)(4); USCIS, "I-129 H-1B Standard Operating Procedures" (undated, posted July 26, 2007), AILA Doc. No. 07072668. *Accord Matter of Sea. Inc.*, 19 I&N Dec. 817 (Comm'r 1988); *Matter of Caron International, Inc.*, 19 I&N Dec. 791 (Comm'r 1988).

[245] *Matter of Caron International, Inc.*, 19 I&N Dec. 791 (Comm'r 1988). *See also Matter of Arjani*, 12 I&N Dec. 649 (Reg'l Comm'r 1967) (membership in a professional organization following examination and "a minimum of five years practical accountancy experience" correlated to "a status similar to a Certified Public Accountant in the United States").

Copyright © 2017. American Immigration Lawyers Association. All rights reserved.

professional association, *per se*, is insufficient evidence of equivalency."[246] For a detailed discussion of membership in a professional association, see Volume 1: Chapter Twelve, "O Visas and Status" and Volume 2: Chapter Three, : "The Immigrant Visa Petition.".

Alternatively, a beneficiary may qualify for H-1B status even without a baccalaureate degree if USCIS determines in a two-part analysis "that the equivalent of a degree required by the specialty occupation has been acquired,"[247] as discussed below. A foreign national may qualify for H-1B status through a combination of education, training, and work experience,[248] even though he or she may not qualify for the Employment-Based Second Preference (EB-2) classification, as discussed in Volume 2: Chapter Three, "The Immigrant Visa Petition." If the foreign national received education abroad, then it may be necessary to have two separate credentials evaluations: one for the foreign education and another for work experience.[249] Even though a credentials evaluation of the experience may be given little weight,[250] the practitioner is encouraged to submit one in the interests of preserving the record. In addition, the discussion of the beneficiary's experience may demonstrate how he or she "is more fully developed as a professional ... than a recent graduate would be."[251]

The foreign national may have gained educational training outside of an academic institution, such as "through an apprenticeship program, employee-sponsored training courses, vocational training schools, or other commercial training facilities."[252] The H-1B petition should include copies of training certificates, which, in turn, must state the start and end dates of the training, as well as "an outline or summary of the curriculum," in addition to the credentials evaluation.[253] A very early Notice of

---

[246] AFM 31.3(g).

[247] 8 CFR §214.2(h)(4)(iii)(D)(5); USCIS, "I-129 H-1B Standard Operating Procedures" (undated, posted July 26, 2007), AILA Doc. No. 07072668.

[248] 8 CFR §214.2(h)(4)(iii)(C)(4); AFM 31.3(a) ("An alien may qualify for a specialty occupation by virtue of formal education, experience, or a combination of both"); *Matter of Caron International, Inc.*, 19 I&N Dec. 791 (Comm'r 1988) (stating that "substantial academic course work in a professional field combined with professional experience and achievement may be considered equivalent to a bachelor's degree") (internal citation omitted).

[249] USCIS, "I-129 H-1B Standard Operating Procedures" (undated, posted July 26, 2007), AILA Doc. No. 07072668. The document discusses credentials evaluations of foreign education in a section titled "Degree Equivalence," but the rest of the guidance focuses on experience equivalencies as opposed to the equivalency of foreign education.

[250] *Matter of Portugues Do Atlantico Information Bureau, Inc.*, 19 I&N Dec. 194 (Comm'r 1984) ("Credential evaluation services do not evaluate experience because experience is not education and does not result in attainment of academic credentials"). *See also Matter of Sea. Inc.*, 19 I&N Dec. 817 (Comm'r 1988) (credentials evaluation of college-level education only); *Matter of [name not provided]* LIN 04 257 51922 (AAO Feb. 10, 2005), http://bit.ly/feb057d.

[251] *Matter of Yaakov*, 13 I&N Dec. 203 (Reg'l Comm'r 1969).

[252] AFM 31.3(g); 55 Fed. Reg. 2606 (Jan. 26, 1990) ("in-house training, industry courses, and apprenticeships" noted in legacy INS's discussion of comments to NPRM [Notice of Proposed Rulemaking] but neither accepted nor rejected).

[253] AFM 31.3(g).

Copyright © 2017. American Immigration Lawyers Association. All rights reserved.

Proposed Rulemaking (NPRM) required all H-1B beneficiaries to "have completed at least two years of college-level training appropriate to the profession," but this requirement thankfully was not included in the final rule.[254]

a. Professional Experience

First, the foreign national must have "a combination of education, specialized training, and/or work experience in areas related to the specialty."[255] USCIS applies a three to one ratio when evaluating equivalence to a bachelor's degree, where "three years of specialized training and/or work experience must be demonstrated for each year of college-level training the alien lacks."[256] As described in a precedent legacy INS decision: "Case law also accommodates those rare instances where individuals attain professional standing through directed experience and specialized noninstitutional instruction, as in 'reading' law, where such a program is recognized by appropriate professional bodies as a form of preparation for practice of that profession."[257] Stated another way, the beneficiary may have gained "knowledge through the medium of intensive work, instruction and study in that activity under the direction and guidance of members of that profession."[258]

Because the "most critical aspect of this type of adjudication is deciding whether the *quality* of experience is at high enough level to qualify as 'professional,'"[259] the H-1B petition "must … clearly demonstrate[]" the following facts:

- The foreign national's "training and/or work experience included the theoretical and practical application of specialized knowledge required by the specialty occupation";

- The foreign national's "experience was gained while working with peers, supervisors, or subordinates who have a degree or its equivalent in the specialty occupation"; and

- The foreign national "has recognition of expertise in the specialty,"[260] as discussed below.

As a practical matter, H-1B educational equivalencies often rely upon experience letters, which detail the type of experience gained and the length of employment, from the beneficiary's former and/or current employers. The statements should serve two purposes: to confirm the beneficiary's experience in fact and provide a testament

---

[254] 55 Fed. Reg. 2606 (Jan. 26, 1990).

[255] 8 CFR §214.2(h)(4)(iii)(D)(5).

[256] *Id. See also* 55 Fed. Reg. 2606 (Jan. 26, 1990) ("In addition to the trend of court decisions, representatives of business interests have maintained that it is a common practice among modern businesses to equate education, specialized training, and/or experience to college-level training required for a profession").

[257] *Matter of Portugues Do Atlantico Information Bureau, Inc.*, 19 I&N Dec. 194 (Comm'r 1984) (citing *Matter of Shin*, 11 I&N Dec. 686 (D.D. 1966)).

[258] *Matter of Shin*, 11 I&N Dec. 686 (D.D. 1966).

[259] AFM 31.3(g).

[260] 8 CFR §214.2(h)(4)(iii)(D)(5).

Copyright © 2017. American Immigration Lawyers Association. All rights reserved.

to the beneficiary's status as professional.[261] Therefore, the practitioner should work with the client and/or beneficiary to ensure that the experience letters clearly explain how the experience gained was professional: "Experience is generally documented through letters from past employers and may be so lacking in specificity as to make the qualitative determination difficult or impossible…. Foreign educational credentials, licenses and other forms of documentation are easier to evaluate than experience."[262] For both of these types of documents, the regulations state:

> "Affidavits or declarations made under penalty of perjury submitted by present or former employers or recognized authorities certifying as to the recognition and expertise of the beneficiary shall specifically describe the beneficiary's recognition and ability in factual terms and must set forth the expertise of the affiant and the manner in which the affiant acquired such information."[263]

Importantly, the beneficiary's experience should "show[] a progression to more responsible duties."[264] Also, the petitioner should "demonstrate [how] the beneficiary's employment has conveyed to him the theoretical and practical application of specialized knowledge required at the professional level of an occupation."[265] The available guidance "do[es] not stand for the proposition that longevity in a particular nonprofessional occupation demonstrates a professional level of ability or merit on the part of the incumbent."[266]

USCIS guidance notes that credentials evaluations of only experience have "*little weight.*"[267] As stated by the AAO: "[USCIS] has the obligation to gauge the accuracy, reliability, and adequacy of the factual foundation of such conclusions, on the basis of the information from which they were developed."[268] Nevertheless, in practice, it is often helpful to include such a credentials evaluation, as it may highlight relevant work experience. USCIS guidance has noted that such evaluations "can be of assistance if they are thorough, well documented and specific in reaching an equivalency determination."[269] Statements from recognized authorities may also be submitted, as discussed below.

An evaluation from a university or college official who has authority to grant college-level credit based on experience or training may be used to demonstrate that the individual has achieved the equivalent of a degree through experience.[270] The

---

[261] *Matter of Yaakov*, 13 I&N Dec. 203 (Reg'l Comm'r 1969) (statements offered confirmed both points).

[262] AFM 31.3(g).

[263] 8 CFR §214.2(h)(4)(iv)(A)(*2*).

[264] *Matter of Sea. Inc.*, 19 I&N Dec. 817 (Comm'r 1988).

[265] *Matter of Caron International, Inc.*, 19 I&N Dec. 791 (Comm'r 1988); *Matter of [name not provided]* LIN 04 257 51922 (AAO Feb. 10, 2005), http://bit.ly/feb057d.

[266] *Matter of Portugues Do Atlantico Information Bureau, Inc.*, 19 I&N Dec. 194 (Comm'r 1984).

[267] AFM 31.3(g)(3) (emphasis in original).

[268] *Matter of [name not provided]* LIN 04 257 51922 (AAO Feb. 10, 2005), http://bit.ly/feb057d.

[269] AFM 31.3(g)(3).

[270] 8 CFR §214.2(h)(4)(iii)(D)(1).

Copyright © 2017. American Immigration Lawyers Association. All rights reserved.

entity of which the evaluator is an official must have a program for granting credit based on training and/or work experience,[271] but the beneficiary need not be enrolled in a program at that college.[272] However, "the official must be formally involved with the college or university's official program for granting credit based on training and/ or experience," and can be "in the official's name as an individual, or as an authorized representative of the college or university."[273] The guidance notes that "[a]ny such evaluation should be given considerable weight in determining eligibility,"[274] but experience has shown some resistance on the part of adjudicators to crediting such evaluations.[275]

b. Recognition in the Specialty Occupation

The beneficiary may qualify by demonstrating that he or she has "achieved recognition of expertise in the specialty occupation as a result of such training and experience."[276] Fortunately, it should no longer be necessary that the beneficiary earned "national or international acclaim and recognition."[277] This fact must be "evidenced by at least one type of documentation such as" one of the following:

- "Recognition of expertise in the specialty occupation by at least two recognized authorities in the same specialty occupation;

- "Membership in a recognized foreign or United States association or society in the specialty occupation;

- "Published material by or about the alien in professional publications, trade journals, books, or major newspapers;

- "Licensure or registration to practice the specialty occupation in a foreign country; or

- "Achievements which a recognized authority has determined to be significant contributions to the field of the specialty occupation."[278]

The regulations define the term "recognized authority" as "a person or an organization with expertise in a particular field, special skills or knowledge in that field, and the expertise to render the type of opinion requested."[279] The statement from the recognized authority must state the following:

---

[271] *Id.*

[272] AFM 31.3(g)(3).

[273] *Id.*

[274] *Id.*

[275] *See* "AILA/USCIS HQ Liaison Q&As" (Apr. 16, 2015), AILA Doc. No. 15042032, item 20; Brief accompanying *Matter of [name and case number not provided]* (AAO Sept. 4, 2013), AILA Doc. No. 13091743; "AILA/SCOPS Liaison Q&As" (Mar. 17, 2010), AILA Doc. No. 10032360, item 6.

[276] 8 CFR §214.2(h)(4)(iii)(D)(5).

[277] 55 Fed. Reg. 2606 (Jan. 26, 1990) (citing former 8 CFR §214.2(h)(3)(iv)(B)(*1*)). For further discussion of international or national acclaim or recognition, see Volume 1: Chapter Twelve, "O Visas and Status."

[278] 8 CFR §214.2(h)(4)(iii)(D)(5).

[279] 8 CFR §214.2(h)(4)(ii).

Copyright © 2017. American Immigration Lawyers Association. All rights reserved.

- "The writer's qualifications as an expert;
- "The writer's experience giving such opinions, citing specific instances where past opinions have been accepted as authoritative and by whom;
- "How the conclusions were reached; and
- "The basis for the conclusions supported by copies or citations of any research material used."[280]

USCIS guidance also states:

"An association which grants certification or registration in the profession should have an accrediting body which has standards for the profession, and which issues an official document to applicants verifying that they have been awarded professional credentials in the profession. The standards of the organization should be reviewed to ensure that bachelor's degree or higher, or its equivalent, is required for membership."[281]

For further discussion of membership in professional associations, published material about a beneficiary, and significant contributions, see Volume 1: Chapter Twelve, "O Visas and Status" and Volume 2: Chapter Three, "The Immigrant Visa Petition."

C. Numerical Limitation

There is a quota on the number of available H-1B visas of 65,000 in each fiscal year,[282] plus an additional annual quota of 20,000 for beneficiaries who have "earned a master's or higher degree from a United States institution of higher education."[283] In the early 2000s, the 65,000 cap was raised to over 100,000 visas per year, but automatically reverted to 65,000 after fiscal year 2003;[284] further efforts to increase the quota have been unsuccessful. During the years of highest demand, the cap was hit within the first few days that H-B petitions could be filed,[285] resulting in a black-out period during which no new H-1B visa numbers were available for 18 months. This has continued to be the case in recent years, with the H-1B cap being reached effectively on the first day of filing for each of the last five fiscal years.[286] Typically, demand for H-1B visas far exceeds the available supply, as explained by USCIS:

---

[280] *Id.*; 55 Fed. Reg. 2606 (Jan. 26, 1990). *See also* USCIS, "I-129 H-1B Standard Operating Procedures" (undated, posted July 26, 2007), AILA Doc. No. 07072668 (stating that the evaluation should "[b]riefly state the qualifications and experience of the evaluator providing the opinion"). Although this guidance specifically references credentials evaluations of foreign education, the principle should remain the same.

[281] AFM 31.3(g); *Matter of Sea. Inc.*, 19 I&N Dec. 817 (Comm'r 1988).

[282] INA §214(g)(1)(A)(vii); 8 CFR §214.2(h)(8)(i)(A).

[283] INA §214(g)(5)(C).

[284] INA §§214(g)(1)(A)(iii)–(vi); American Competitiveness in the Twenty-First Century Act of 2000 (AC21), Pub. L. No. 106-313, §102(a) (Oct. 17, 2000).

[285] "H-1B Cap Count History" (updated Apr. 13, 2016), AILA Doc. No. 15120404.

[286] *See* American Immigration Council, "The H-1B Program: A Primer on the Program and Its Impact on Jobs, Wages, and the Economy" (Apr. 1, 2016), https://www.americanimmigrationcouncil.org/research/h1b-visa-program-fact-sheet.

Copyright © 2017. American Immigration Lawyers Association. All rights reserved.

"...[T]he H–1B category is now oversubscribed to such a degree that USCIS' final receipt date for petitions is now announced even before the start of the fiscal year for which the petitions are being submitted and, in the absence of an expansion of the 65,000 cap by Congress, this state of affairs will likely continue indefinitely."[287]

As stated by regulation: "Each alien issued a visa or otherwise provided nonimmigrant status under sections 101(a)(15)(H)(i)(b) ... of the Act shall be counted for purposes of any applicable numerical limit, unless otherwise exempt from such numerical limit."[288] Therefore, the practitioner may find it helpful to view the H-1B visa number as being assigned to an H-1B nonimmigrant even though the foreign national was the beneficiary of the petition and not the petitioner.[289] By statute, a beneficiary should be counted toward the H-1B cap only once during a six period:

"Any alien who has already been counted, within the 6 years prior to the approval of a petition..., toward the numerical limitations ... shall not again be counted toward those limitations unless the alien would be eligible for a full 6 years of authorized admission at the time the petition is filed. Where multiple petitions are approved for 1 alien, that alien shall be counted only once."[290]

A beneficiary seeking to recapture time spent outside the United States (discussed later in this chapter) is not subject to the cap "whether or not the alien has been physically outside the United States for 1 year or more and would otherwise be eligible for a new period of admission.... An H-1B petitioner may either seek such recapture on behalf of the alien or seek a new period of admission on behalf of the alien under section 214(g)(1) of the Act."[291] If the latter route is chosen, the beneficiary becomes subject to the cap again.

H-1B petition extensions and H-1B status extensions do not count toward the quota,[292] and neither do requests for concurrent H-1B employment or to "change the terms of current employment."[293]

Similarly, H-4 dependents do not require H-1B visa numbers.[294] Statutorily, H-1B visas for beneficiaries who have "earned a master's or higher degree from a United

---

[287] 73 Fed. Reg. 18944 (Apr. 8, 2008) ("The race to meet the filing date of each fiscal year has become a ritual for H-1B petitioners and USCIS expects the 65,000 and 20,000 maximums to be met easily every year").

[288] 8 CFR §214.2(h)(8)(ii)(A).

[289] 73 Fed. Reg. 15389 (Mar. 25, 2008) ("H-1B cap numbers are allotted per alien, and not per petition" and "[b]y statute, USCIS may only allot one cap number per alien beneficiary, regardless of the number of petitions that were filed on the alien's behalf"). For discussion of the prohibition on filing multiple H-1B petitions on behalf of a single beneficiary, see below.

[290] INA §214(g)(7); American Competitiveness in the Twenty-First Century Act of 2000 (AC21), Pub. L. No. 106-313, §103 (Oct. 17, 2000).

[291] 8 CFR §214.2(h)(13)(iii)(C)(2).

[292] 8 CFR §214.2(h)(8)(ii)(A).

[293] 73 Fed. Reg. 15389 (Mar. 25, 2008) (citing INA §214(g)(2) and 8 CFR §214.2(h)(8)(ii)(A)).

Copyright © 2017. American Immigration Lawyers Association. All rights reserved.

States institution of higher education," defined below, are exempt from the regular cap, but there is a separate annual quota of 20,000 for these H-1B visas.[295] As discussed below, after the separate 20,000 limitation is exhausted, individuals with U.S. master's degrees are counted against the regular cap. Petitions subject to the cap should be clearly identified, as discussed below.

The H-1B quota also "is reduced by the amount of the annual numerical limitations" of H-1B1 petitions.[296] However, if the H-1B1 cap "has not been exhausted at the end of a given fiscal year, the Secretary of Homeland Security shall adjust upwards the numerical limitation" of available H-1B visas "for that fiscal year by the amount remaining in the numerical limitation" of H-1B1 visas.[297] In other words, if the H-1B1 cap is not depleted, then any remaining balance of H-1B1 numbers is added to the number of available H-1B visas: "At the end of each fiscal year, unused H-1B1 numbers will be returned to that year's total global numerical limit and will be made available to H-1B aliens during the first 45 days of the new fiscal year."[298] USCIS further indicated that the unused H-1B1 visa numbers from the current fiscal year would be added to the H-1B visa numbers of the next fiscal year, "based either on projected H-1B1 usage to the end of [the current fiscal year], or on actual determined usage during that year, depending on when the cap is hit."[299]

The statute also provides that beneficiaries "shall be issued visas (or otherwise provided nonimmigrant status) in the order in which petitions are filed for such visas or status."[300] In the event that a beneficiary obtains an H-1B visa or status and has been "counted against the numerical limitations," but "is found to have been issued such visa or otherwise provided such status by fraud or willfully misrepresenting a material fact and such visa or nonimmigrant status is revoked, then one number shall be restored to the total number of aliens who may be issued visas or otherwise provided such status under the numerical limitations … in the fiscal year in which the petition is revoked, regardless of the fiscal year in which the petition was approved."[301] However, it seems that the H-1B visa number of a petition revoked for reasons other than fraud or willful misrepresentation will not be restored to the cap in

---

[294] 8 CFR §214.2(h)(8)(ii)(A); INA §214(g)(2) (stating that the quota "shall only apply to principal aliens and not to the spouses or children of such aliens").

[295] INA §214(g)(5)(C); 70 Fed. Reg. 23775 (May 5, 2005) ("Although there is no direct legislative history for this provision, it has the purpose of expanding the availability of needed professional workers for employers in the United States").

[296] INA §214(g)(8)(B)(iv).

[297] Id.

[298] 9 FAM 402.20-5(B); INA §214(g)(8)(B)(iv) (stating that H-1B visas "may be issued pursuant to such adjustment within the first 45 days of the next fiscal year to aliens who had applied for such visas during the fiscal year for which the adjustment was made").

[299] USCIS, "USCIS National Stakeholder Meeting" (Jan. 26, 2010), AILA Doc. No. 10012963.

[300] INA §214(g)(3).

[301] Id.

Copyright © 2017. American Immigration Lawyers Association. All rights reserved.

the fiscal year during which it was revoked, if the petition was approved in a previous fiscal year.[302]

Similarly, an H-1B visa number may be recaptured if the beneficiary does not apply for U.S. admission pursuant to the approved H-1B petition. The petitioner is directed to "notify the Service Center Director who approved the petition that the number(s) has not been used," the H-1B "petition shall be revoked," and "USCIS will take into account the unused number during the appropriate fiscal year."[303] A consular officer "should not be concerned about the availability of visa numbers for beneficiaries of approved petitions, nor should [he or she] inform DHS when H visa applications in affected categories are abandoned or denied."[304]

H-1B1 petitions are also subject to "annual numerical limitations on approvals of initial applications by aliens for admission":[305] 1,400 for citizens of Chile, and 5,400 for citizens of Singapore.[306] The H-1B1 caps "shall only apply to principal aliens and not to the spouses or children of such aliens."[307] An H-1B1 extension should count against the numerical limitation if it is filed on behalf of a foreign national "who has obtained 5 or more consecutive prior extensions."[308] In short, as stated by the Foreign Affairs Manual (FAM): "Initial applications for H-1B1 classification, as well as the sixth and all subsequent extensions of stay, are counted against the H-1B1 annual numerical limitations."[309] USCIS is responsible for the H-1B1 numerical count, but DOS provides "periodic" updates to USCIS on the number of H-1B1 visas issued."[310]

1. Filing Procedure and Lottery System

In most years, only petitions filed during the first five business days of April stand any chance of being accepted for filing, and even at that, often only a fraction of those cases actually are accepted. This is because the earliest that an H-1B petition will be accepted by USCIS is "6 months before the date of actual need for the beneficiary's services."[311] This means that, since USCIS's fiscal year runs from October 1 through September 30, an H-1B petition will be accepted no earlier than April 1 of any year.

---

[302] 69 Fed. Reg. 8675 (Feb. 25, 2004) (no restoration of H-1B visa numbers revoked in FY2004 for petitions approved in previous fiscal years); 65 Fed. Reg. 15178 (Mar. 21, 2000) ("The Service will subtract revocations of any H-1B petitions for new employment from the total H-1B count in the fiscal year for which the new employment was approved").

[303] 8 CFR §214.2(h)(8)(ii)(C).

[304] 9 FAM 402.10-10(A).

[305] INA §214(g)(8)(B)(i).

[306] INA §214(g)(8)(B)(ii); 9 FAM 402.10-5(B).

[307] INA §214(g)(8)(B)(iii); 9 FAM 402.10-5(B).

[308] INA §214(g)(8)(D).

[309] 9 FAM 402.10-5(B); USCIS, W. Yates, "Lifting of Numerical Cap on Mexican NAFTA Nonimmigrant Professionals ("TN") and Free Trade Agreements with Chile and Singapore" (Jan. 8, 2004), AILA Doc. No. 04030361.

[310] 9 FAM 402.10-5(B).

[311] 8 CFR §214.2(h)(9)(i)(B).

Copyright © 2017. American Immigration Lawyers Association. All rights reserved.

April 1 thus becomes the start of "cap season," during which USCIS follows a set procedure from April 1 until the caps are reached. For both the regular H-1B cap and the advanced degree cap, "USCIS will make numbers available to petitions in the order in which the petitions are filed," in a First-In, First-Out (FIFO) procedure.[312]

Next, "USCIS will monitor the number of petitions (including the number of beneficiaries requested when necessary) received and will notify the public of the date that USCIS has received the necessary number of petitions (the 'final receipt date')."[313] The practitioner should note that this "final receipt date" is not necessarily the same date that "the news is published."[314] Throughout this process, there is an "unavoidable use of projection and estimation in cap management," because of the challenge of "[p]icking the number of petitions necessary for the cap to be reached":[315]

"USCIS will make projections of the number of petitions necessary to achieve the numerical limit of approvals, taking into account historical data related to approvals, denials, revocations, and other relevant factors."[316]

"USCIS cannot wait until the petitions received have been adjudicated to make this decision, because during the time the adjudications are being completed and an exact count obtained, the cap would be exceeded by these petitions already received and unnecessarily processed. Petitioners whose petitions were received and initially processed after the point at which the cap would be found to have been reached would have gained an unrealistic expectation of having a chance at an H-1B number, and either such petitioners would lose significant filing fees without substantive adjudication or USCIS would expend unnecessary resources on initially processing such petitions and fees and then returning those petitions and refunding the fees.... The specific factors and rates may vary from year to year and will be applied in USCIS' discretion with assistance of the DHS Office of Statistics."[317]

Then, if the H-1B cap is exhausted, or "hit," USCIS uses a lottery system to determine which H-1B petitions received on the final receipt date may be allocated an H-1B visa number: "When necessary to ensure the fair and orderly allocation of [H-1B visa] numbers..., USCIS may randomly select from among the petitions received on the final receipt date the remaining number of petitions deemed necessary to generate the numerical limit of approvals."[318] The "lottery winning" H-1B petitions are selected "via computer-generated selection as validated by the Office of

---

[312] 8 CFR §214.2(h)(8)(ii)(B).

[313] Id.; 70 Fed. Reg. 23775 (May 5, 2005).

[314] 8 CFR §214.2(h)(8)(ii)(B) ("The day the news is published will not control the final receipt date").

[315] 70 Fed. Reg. 23775 (May 5, 2005).

[316] 8 CFR §214.2(h)(8)(ii)(B).

[317] 70 Fed. Reg. 23775 (May 5, 2005).

[318] 8 CFR §214.2(h)(8)(ii)(B).

Copyright © 2017. American Immigration Lawyers Association. All rights reserved.

Immigration Statistics."[319] At least one court has upheld USCIS's lottery system, finding it "reasonable" and a "logical" way to address the problems created by the cap.[320]

Since 2008, the lottery includes petitions filed during the first five business days after April 1 of any year if the H-1B cap is hit on any of those days, "conducting the random selection among the petitions" requesting an advanced degree H-1B visa numbers first, in the following situation:

> "If the final receipt date is any of the first five business days on which petitions subject to the applicable numerical limit may be received (*i.e.*, if the numerical limit is reached on any one of the first five business days that filings can be made), USCIS will randomly apply all of the numbers among the petitions received on any of those five business days."[321]

"[O]n the first available filing day for fiscal year (FY) 2008, USCIS received H-1B petitions totaling nearly twice the 65,000 cap," causing "logistical problems" for USCIS, mail couriers, and H-1B petitioners.[322] USCIS indicated "understand[ing] that petitioners anticipate the cap being reached on the first day for future fiscal years" and, therefore, "feel pressured to file petitions on that day for fear of being excluded from the random selection process."[323] The rule sought to address USCIS's "significant logistical difficulties" when "handl[ing] such a large number of filings being made on the same day."[324] USCIS stated that the five-business-day period "is sufficient to account for a wider range of mail delivery times offered by the various mail delivery providers available to the public."[325]

Another 2008 change was to require lottery selection of advanced degree petitions before petitions filed under the regular H-1B cap to allow certain advanced degree petitions "to have another opportunity to be selected for an H-1B number in the second random selection process."[326] An H-1B petition that should be counted toward the advanced degree cap may nevertheless be placed in the queue for the regular H-1B cap, as long as the regular cap has not been hit, in the following situations:

- The advanced degree quota has been hit and the petition was not selected by the lottery for the advanced degree quota; or

---

[319] *Id.*

[320] *Walker Macy LLC v. USCIS*, No. 3:16-cv-00995-SI (D. Or. 2017), AILA Doc. No. 17032001.

[321] *Id.*

[322] 73 Fed. Reg. 15389 (Mar. 25, 2008). Anecdotal evidence reports that two FedEx planes full of mostly H-1B petitions were received on April 2, 2008.

[323] 73 Fed. Reg. 15389 (Mar. 25, 2008).

[324] *Id.*

[325] *Id.*

[326] *Id.*

Copyright © 2017. American Immigration Lawyers Association. All rights reserved.

- The advanced degree quota has been hit and the petition was filed after the final receipt date for the advanced degree cap.[327]

Similarly, the need to run the lottery may result in delays of petitions requesting premium processing, since a petition "cannot be processed until after the random selection has been completed."[328] Therefore, the "premium processing 15-day adjudication period (processing deadline) will not begin until such time as USCIS has completed the random selection process."[329] For the fiscal year 2017 cap season, when the cap was hit during the first five days of filing, premium processing was resumed on May 12.[330] For the fiscal year 2018 season, USCIS announced in advance that it would suspend premium processing for all H-1Bs, as of April 3, the first business day of the cap season, and that the "suspension my last up to 6 months." The reason given was to enable USCIS to catch up on its H-1B backlog.[331] See Volume 1: Chapter Two, "Basic Nonimmigrant Concepts," for a discussion of premium processing.

If the regular H-1B cap has been exhausted, then a petition that qualifies for the advanced degree cap will also be rejected.[332] Similarly, if a filed H-1B petition that indicated exemption from any H-1B quota is later "determined by USCIS after the final receipt date to be subject to the numerical limit, [then it] will be denied and filing fees will not be returned or refunded."[333]

> "USCIS has determined that denial of these petitions is appropriate because USCIS must adjudicate them in order to make a determination on whether the alien beneficiary is subject to the numerical cap. USCIS only rejects filings before an adjudication takes place. Because USCIS must adjudicate these petitions, it will not return the petition and refund the filing fee."[334]

Any H-1B petition that was received on the final receipt date and was not selected in the lottery "will be rejected."[335] The same is true for any H-1B petition received after the final receipt date.[336] Any cap-subject H-1B petitions filed after the quota has been exhausted should be rejected, as should the filing fee, and "returned with a notice that

---

[327] 8 CFR §214.2(h)(8)(ii)(B); 73 Fed. Reg. 15389 (Mar. 25, 2008) ("With respect to the 20,000 cap, USCIS will count any non-selected or subsequently filed H-1B petitions towards the 65,000 cap").

[328] USCIS, "USCIS Announces Interim Rule on H-1B Visas" (Mar. 19, 2008), AILA Doc. No. 08190340 (select "USCIS Fact Sheet: Changes to the FY2009 H-1B Program").

[329] Id.

[330] "USCIS Announces that FY2017 H-1B Cap Premium Processing to Begin May 12" (Apr. 22, 2016), AILA Doc. No. 16042231.

[331] "USCIS Will Temporarily Suspend Premium Processing for All H-1B Petitions" (Mar. 3, 2017), AILA Doc. No. 17030335.

[332] 8 CFR §214.2(h)(8)(ii)(B).

[333] 8 CFR §§214.2(h)(8)(ii)(B) and (D).

[334] 73 Fed. Reg. 15389 (Mar. 25, 2008) (citing 8 CFR 103.2(a)(7)); 8 CFR §§214.2(h)(8)(ii)(B) and (D).

[335] 8 CFR §214.2(h)(8)(ii)(B).

[336] Id.

Copyright © 2017. American Immigration Lawyers Association. All rights reserved.

numbers are unavailable for the particular nonimmigrant classification until the beginning of the next fiscal year."[337] If USCIS implements "special instructions" for administering H-1B cap cases, then the adjudicator should "[f]ollow that guidance."[338]

In 2010, USCIS proposed a rule to establish "an electronic registration program for petitions subject to numerical limitations," beginning with H-1B petitions "because the demand for H-1B specialty occupation workers generally exceeds the numerical limitation" and later extended to "other nonimmigrant classifications ... as needed."[339] This regulation was never finalized, and has since been removed from DHS's regulatory agenda,[340] indicating that the effort has been abandoned. However, in April 2017, the President signed an Executive Order instructing the Department of Justice (DOJ), DHS, and DOL to "as soon as practicable, suggest reforms to help ensure that H-1B visas are awarded to the most-skilled or highest-paid petition beneficiaries."[341] Press reports surrounding the order suggested that one idea behind it would be to "change the lottery system for awarding H-1B visas, giving extra preference to the highest-paying jobs," a proposal "which has drawn bipartisan support from Congress."[342]

2. Prohibition of Multiple Petitions on Behalf of a Single Beneficiary

Importantly, however, the regulations state that an "employer may not file, in the same fiscal year, more than one H-1B petition on behalf of the same alien," if the foreign national must be allotted an H-1B visa number under the regular quota or under the separate H-1B cap for individuals with master's degrees or higher degrees from U.S. institutions.[343] If an employer does so, then the multiple H-1B petitions will be denied,[344] and the filing fees will not be refunded.[345] Although "USCIS recognize[d] that, by statute, multiple filings of H-1B petitions are contemplated" and that an employer may "have a legitimate business need to file two or more separate H-1B petitions on behalf of the same alien," it believed that allowing multiple filings on behalf of a single beneficiary "would undermine the purpose of the H-1B

---

[337] 8 CFR §214.2(h)(8)(ii)(D).

[338] USCIS, "I-129 H-1B Standard Operating Procedures" (undated, posted July 26, 2007), AILA Doc. No. 07072668 (emphasis in original).

[339] 75 Fed. Reg. 21806 (Apr. 26, 2010).

[340] Office of Management and Budget (OMB), "Agency Rule List-Fall 2016," http://bit.ly/DHSregagenda. The rulemaking, which had a registrant identification number (RIN) of 1615-AB71, is not on the list.

[341] Exec. Order No. 13788, "Buy American and Hire American" (Apr. 18, 2017), AILA Doc. No. 17041899.

[342] G. Thrush, N. Wingfield, V. Goel, "Trump Signs Order That Could Lead to Curbs on Foreign Workers," Apr. 18, 2017, N. Y. Times, https://www.nytimes.com/2017/04/18/us/politics/executive-order-hire-buy-american-h1b-visa-trump.html.

[343] 8 CFR §214.2(h)(2)(i)(G).

[344] Id.

[345] USCIS, "USCIS Announces Interim Rule on H-1B Visas" (Mar. 19, 2008), AILA Doc. No. 08190340 (select "USCIS FAQs: Interim Rule on H-1B Visas").

Copyright © 2017. American Immigration Lawyers Association. All rights reserved.

numerical cap since multiple filings can result in the misallocation of the total available cap numbers."[346]

This prohibition came about after "USCIS found approximately 500 instances" where an employer filed more than one H-1B petition on behalf of a single beneficiary, "in what appears to have been an attempt to increase the chances of being selected in the random selection process."[347] The rule sought to stipulate the "adverse consequences … [to] a petitioner that seeks to exploit the system through filing multiple petitions" and to provide for a more "fair and orderly administration of the cap."[348] USCIS indicated concern that allowing multiple petitions on behalf of a single beneficiary would give an "unfair advantage" to those employers, cause "unnecessary adjudications" and, therefore, slow adjudication times, and result in the potential issuance of "more than one receipt number to the same beneficiary," which would inhibit USCIS's ability to "achieve an accurate projection of the number of petitions needed to generate the required number of approvals to reach the cap."[349]

In the event that an H-1B petition is denied by USCIS, "on a basis other than fraud or misrepresentation, the employer may file a subsequent H-1B petition on behalf of the same alien in the same fiscal year, provided that the numerical limitation has not been reached or if the filing qualifies as exempt from the numerical limitation."[350] The regulations provide that this subsequent filing is the only way that more than one H-1B petition may be filed by an employer on behalf of a single beneficiary in the same fiscal year: "Otherwise, filing more than one H-1B petition by an employer on behalf of the same alien in the same fiscal year will result in the denial or revocation of all such petitions."[351]

Importantly, the "preclusion applies even if the petitions are not duplicative,"[352] so an employer also should not file an H-1B petition under the regular cap and an additional petition under the master's degree cap.[353] Even though the argument could be made that the petitions should be distinguished because the job requirements differ, it is most likely that both petitions will be denied.[354] Further, USCIS noted that

---

[346] 73 Fed. Reg. 15389 (Mar. 25, 2008) (citing INA §214(g)(7)).

[347] 73 Fed. Reg. 15389 (Mar. 25, 2008).

[348] *Id.*

[349] *Id.*

[350] 8 CFR §214.2(h)(2)(i)(G).

[351] *Id.*

[352] 73 Fed. Reg. 15389 (Mar. 25, 2008).

[353] *Id.* ("The same problem holds true if employers of aliens subject to the master's degree exemption seek to increase the chances of obtaining an H-1B number by filing concurrent petitions for the same aliens under both the master's degree exemption and the 65,000 cap. In its administration of the 65,000 and 20,000 caps, USCIS must remove any potential for unfairness and ensure that the H-1B petitions filed on behalf of aliens subject to either or both caps have an equal chance of being selected").

[354] 8 CFR §214.2(h)(2)(i)(G). When explaining the regulatory preclusion in the context of different job offers, although not specifically while discussing requirements of educational qualifications, USCIS also noted that

Cont'd

Copyright © 2017. American Immigration Lawyers Association. All rights reserved.

comparison of multiple petitions with differing requirements requires an evaluation of substance, but the lottery process was designed to be random and "not intended to be a decision on the merits."[355]

USCIS also indicated that, if a beneficiary will truly perform "materially distinct employment positions," then the petitioner could "file an amended petition or a petition for concurrent employment to reflect the different nature of the duties that are associated with the beneficiary's second employment position," after the beneficiary is awarded an H-1B visa number: "Since the alien would have already been counted against the cap, such amended or additional petition would not be affected by the prohibition on multiple petition filings."[356] In the event that the multiple filings are identified after one or more of the H-1B petitions are approved, then "USCIS may revoke all such petitions."[357]

However, multiple filings by companies in the same corporate family may be allowed: "This rule does not, however, preclude related employers from filing petitions on behalf of the same alien. USCIS recognizes that an employer and one or more related entities ... may extend the same alien two or more job offers for distinct positions."[358] The final rule provided the permissible example of multiple subsidiaries of a "Fortune 500" parent company, where although "the subsidiaries are ultimately related to the parent company through corporate ownership," each petitioning subsidiary has its own Federal Employer Identification Number (FEIN) and "has a legitimate business need to hire such alien for a position within that subsidiaries' corporate structure."[359] What is forbidden is an employer "filing a petition to facilitate the alien's hiring by a different, although related, subsidiary" and "the unscrupulous employer that establishes or uses shell subsidiaries or affiliates to file additional petitions on behalf of the same alien in order to increase the alien's chances of being allotted an H-1B number."[360]

USCIS should inquire, through an RFE, a Notice of Intent to Deny (NOID), or a Notice of Intent to Revoke (NOIR), whether "related entities (such as a parent company, subsidiary, or affiliate) ... have a legitimate business need to file more than one H-1B petition on behalf of the same alien" who must be assigned an H-1B visa number under the regular cap or under the master's cap.[361] As stated by regulation:

"employers could file multiple petitions on behalf of the same alien under the guise that the petitions are based on different job offers, when the employment positions are in fact the same or only very slightly different." 73 Fed. Reg. 15389 (Mar. 25, 2008).

[355] 73 Fed. Reg. 15389 (Mar. 25, 2008). USCIS also unfavorably viewed the "significant expenditure of limited USCIS adjudicative resources" to make such determinations.

[356] 73 Fed. Reg. 15389 (Mar. 25, 2008) (citing INA §214(g)(7)).

[357] 8 CFR §214.2(h)(2)(i)(G); 73 Fed. Reg. 15389 (Mar. 25, 2008).

[358] 73 Fed. Reg. 15389 (Mar. 25, 2008).

[359] Id.

[360] Id.

[361] 8 CFR §214.2(h)(2)(i)(G).

Copyright © 2017. American Immigration Lawyers Association. All rights reserved.

"If any of the related entities fail to demonstrate a legitimate business need to file an H-1B petition on behalf of the same alien, all petitions filed on that alien's behalf by the related entities will be denied or revoked."[362] The petitioner bears the burden to demonstrate the legitimate business need for petitions filed by related entities.[363]

USCIS did make allowance one year for a second filing amid reports of problems at a major delivery service that may have destroyed or prevented the delivery of petition packages at the beginning of the five-day period of the cap season. USCIS allowed for a second petition, as long as it was delivered before the end of the five days or before the cap was reached, if that date was later than the fifth day, under these conditions:

> "If a petitioner filed an FY16 H-1B cap petition in a timely manner, but received notification from the delivery service that suggests that there may be a delay or damage to the package, the petitioner may file a second H-1B petition with a new fee payment and ...[a]n explanation why a second petition is being filed, with supporting evidence, such as the notice from the delivery service; and ...[a] request to withdraw the first petition filed for the FY16 H-1B cap. Petitioners who do not include these items will be considered to have submitted duplicate filings.... [I]f the petitioner submits a second H-1B petition and withdraws the first, USCIS will not adjudicate the withdrawn petition and will return it to the petitioner regardless of whether the petition has already been receipted."[364]

3. Exemption for Certain Employees of Educational and Nonprofit Institutions

a. Qualifying Entities

A beneficiary is not subject to the H-1B cap, however, if he or she "is employed (or has received an offer of employment)" at any of the following institutions:

- An "institution of higher education";
- A nonprofit entity related to or affiliated with an institution of higher education;
- A "nonprofit research organization"; or
- A "governmental research organization."[365]

(1) Institution of Higher Education

The term "institution of higher education" is, in turn, defined as "an educational institution in any State that" meets the following conditions:

- "[A]dmits as regular students only persons having a certificate of graduation from a school providing secondary education, or the recognized equivalent of such a certificate;

---

[362] Id.

[363] 73 Fed. Reg. 15389 (Mar. 25, 2008).

[364] "Delivery Service Error Guidance for FY16 H-1B Cap Filings" (Apr. 6, 2015), AILA Doc. No. 15040661.

[365] INA §214(g)(5) (citing 20 USC §1001(a)); H-1B Visa Reform Act of 2004, Pub. L. No. 108-447, §425; American Competitiveness in the Twenty-First Century Act of 2000 (AC21), Pub. L. No. 106-313, §103 (Oct. 17, 2000).

Copyright © 2017. American Immigration Lawyers Association. All rights reserved.

- "[I]s legally authorized within such State to provide a program of education beyond secondary education;

- "[P]rovides an educational program for which the institution awards a bachelor's degree or provides not less than a 2-year program that is acceptable for full credit toward such a degree;

- "[I]s a public or other nonprofit institution; and

- "[I]s accredited by a nationally recognized accrediting agency or association, or if not so accredited, is an institution that has been granted preaccreditation status by such an agency or association that has been recognized by the Secretary for the granting of preaccreditation status, and the Secretary has determined that there is satisfactory assurance that the institution will meet the accreditation standards of such an agency or association within a reasonable time."[366]

This definition does not include for-profit institutions of higher education, and thus such entities are subject to the cap.[367]

The AAO discussed the legislative history that brought about the exemption for institutions of higher education:

"The principal reason for the ... exemption is that by virtue of what they are doing, people working in universities are necessarily immediately contributing to educating Americans. The more highly qualified educators in specialty occupations we have in this country, the more Americans we will have ready to take positions in these fields upon completion of their education. Additionally, U.S. universities are on a different hiring cycle from other employers. The H-1B cap has hit them hard because they often do not hire until numbers have been used up; and because of the academic calendar, they cannot wait until October 1, the new fiscal year, to start a class."[368]

(2) Related to or Affiliated with Institution of Higher Learning

A nonprofit entity is one that is tax exempt under section 501(c)(3), (4), or (6) of the Internal Revenue Code (IRC), and "has been approved as a tax exempt organization for research or educational purposes by the Internal Revenue Service."[369] A nonprofit entity is "related to or affiliated with" an institution of higher learning if one of the following applies:

- The two entities have shared ownership or control "by the same board or federation";

- The nonprofit is operated by the higher education institution;

---

[366] 20 USC §1001(a), in accordance with 8 CFR §214.2(h)(8)(ii)(F)(1).

[367] 80 Fed. Reg. 81900, 81919 (Dec. 31, 2015).

[368] *Matter of [name not provided]* WAC 09 059 50704 (AAO Oct. 5, 2010), AILA Doc. No. 10121432 (citing Sen. Rep. No. 106-260 (Apr. 1, 2000)).

[369] 8 CFR §214.2(h)(19)(iv). This definition for purposes of the ACWIA fee, discussed below, is incorporated for purposes of the cap exemption by 8 CFR §241.2(h)(8)(ii)(F)(3).

Copyright © 2017. American Immigration Lawyers Association. All rights reserved.

- The nonprofit is "attached to" a higher education institution as a "member, branch, cooperative, or subsidiary"; or

- The nonprofit has "entered into a formal written affiliation agreement" with the higher education institution that "establishes an active working relationship between" the two entities "for the purposes of research or education, and a fundamental activity of the nonprofit entity is to directly contribute to the research or education mission of the institution of higher education."[370]

A 2016 regulation addressing cap exemptions, among other issues, codified much of existing guidance on the topic, but made some changes on specific issues, the standards for "related or affiliated" being perhaps foremost among them.[371] Previous guidance included only the first three of the above criteria.[372] The 2016 regulation added the fourth, noting in the preamble to the proposed rule that the prior definition "does not sufficiently account for the nature and scope of common, bona fide affiliations between nonprofit entities and institutions of higher education."[373]

An example given by USCIS of the fourth criterion is the Veterans Affairs (VA) hospital that would be considered affiliated with a medical school based on a "contract or agreement ... for the training or education of health personnel."[374] USCIS goes on to acknowledge that "such bona fide affiliation contracts or agreements are common in the private sector as well."[375] It may be that situations that would have been found to be subject to the cap prior to the 2016 regulations now would be found to be cap exempt. For example, a school system that had an arrangement with a university for assignment of student teachers previously qualified only with respect to individuals employed in a specific program jointly managed by the school system and the university; other personnel employed by the school did not fall under the exemption.[376] However, now, if the school meets the definition of nonprofit (public schools might be 501(c)(3) entities[377]), the two entities have a formal agreement that establishes an active working relationship, and the school's contribution to the university's educational mission is found to be a "fundamental activity" of the school, the school could be considered cap exempt.

---

[370] 8 CFR §214.2(h)(8)(ii)(F)(2).

[371] 80 Fed. Reg. 81900 (Dec. 31, 2015) (proposed rule), and 81 Fed. Reg. 82398 (Nov. 18, 2016) (final rule).

[372] USCIS, M. Aytes, "Guidance Regarding Eligibility for Exemption from the H-1B Cap Based on §103 of the American Competitiveness in the Twenty-First Century Act of 2000 (AC21) (Public Law 106-313)" (June 6, 2006), AILA Doc. No. 06060861.

[373] 80 Fed. Reg. 81900, 81919 (Dec. 31, 2015).

[374] *Id.*, citing 38 USC 7423(d)(1).

[375] 80 Fed. Reg. 81900, 81919 (Dec. 31, 2015).

[376] *Matter of [name not provided]* EAC 06 216 52028 (AAO Sept. 8, 2006), http://bit.ly/sep066d.

[377] Internal Revenue Service, "Section 501(c)(3) Organizations," https://www.irs.gov/publications/p557/ch03.html.

Copyright © 2017. American Immigration Lawyers Association. All rights reserved.

The key issues here would be what is an "affiliation agreement" and what constitutes a "fundamental activity." The fact that the preambles to both the proposed and the final rule did not attempt to define or explain "affiliation agreement" in any manner, other than to point to the requirements in the regulatory section for "active working relationship" and "fundamental activity," would indicate that those clauses are meant to define affiliation agreement.[378] Thus, no other meanings should be read into the use of the word "affiliation" before "agreement."

With respect to "fundamental activity," it is important to note that the proposed rule initially used the term "primary purpose" instead.[379] It was changed to "fundamental activity" in the final rule to make it "clearer that nonprofit entities may qualify for the cap and fee exemptions even if they are engaged in more than one fundamental activity, any one of which may directly contribute to the research or education mission of a qualifying college or university."[380] Thus, while a school system would have as a fundamental activity the education of children, training of future teachers would also be fundamental, even if it is not a primary purpose, and certainly would directly contribute to the education mission of the university.

Another situation previously found not to be cap exempt was an arrangement whereby students in a college's nursing program served clinical rotations at a nonprofit hospital. The AAO denied a petition by that hospital for a medical technologist, finding that because the two entities were separately operated and controlled, and the hospital provided only "space and opportunities for observation" and did not have "an active role" in the college's program.[381] It is unclear whether this petitioner would now be found cap exempt, as the regulations require an "active working relationship" which may not differ from "an active role."

It is important to note that the cap exemption attaches to the petitioner, not the beneficiary: "[I]f the petitioner is an exempt employer, *i.e.*, an institution of higher education *or a related or affiliated nonprofit entity*, then there is no legal requirement that the beneficiary participate in a particular program.... [T]he on-site employment by an institution of higher education or a related or affiliated nonprofit entity is sufficient in itself to meet the plain statutory requirements."[382] Thus, a beneficiary directly employed *by* the related or affiliated entity need not be employed in the particular operation that is the subject of the affiliation agreement. If, however, the beneficiary is only employed at the related or affiliated entity, the additional criteria discussed below under "Employed at" must be considered.

(3) Nonprofit Research Organization

---

[378] 80 Fed. Reg. 81900 (Dec. 31, 2015) (proposed rule), and 81 Fed. Reg. 82398 (Nov. 18, 2016) (final rule).

[379] 80 Fed. Reg. 81900 (Dec. 31, 2015), proposed §214.2(h)(8)(ii)(F)(2).

[380] 81 Fed. Reg. 82398, 82444 (Nov. 18, 2016).

[381] *Matter of [name not provided]* WAC 09 059 50704 (AAO Oct. 5, 2010), AILA Doc. No. 10121432.

[382] *Matter of [name not provided]* WAC 09 059 50704 (AAO Oct. 5, 2010), AILA Doc. No. 10121432 (emphasis added).

Copyright © 2017. American Immigration Lawyers Association. All rights reserved.

As stated above, a nonprofit entity is one that is tax exempt under section 501(c)(3), (4), or (6) of the IRC, and "has been approved as a tax exempt organization for research or educational purposes by the Internal Revenue Service.[383] A nonprofit research organization is defined as "an organization that is primarily engaged in basic research and/or applied research." These types of research in turn are defined respectively as "general research to gain more comprehensive knowledge or understanding of the subject under study, without specific applications in mind," and "research to gain knowledge or understanding to determine the means by which a specific, recognized need may be met."[384]

(4) Governmental Research Organization

A governmental research organization "is a federal, state, or local entity whose primary mission is the performance or promotion of basic research and/or applied research."[385] Basic and applied research for such organizations have the same definitions as for nonprofit entities, above.[386]

Prior to 2016, the regulatory definition of governmental was limited to the Federal government.[387] However, in a rulemaking to make "program improvements affecting high-skilled nonimmigrant workers,"[388] USCIS accepted a commenter's argument that, because the "g" in the term "governmental" was not capitalized in the statute, the intent of Congress was to encompass state and local entities.[389]

b. "Employed at"

As indicated above, "any H-1B nonimmigrant worker would be exempt if employed directly" by any of the four types of entities exempted,[390] so the beneficiary's job duties for direct employment need not be related to the qualifying institution's mission. However, the statute provides the exemption from the cap for beneficiaries "employed at" a qualifying entity. This means that a petition can, under the conditions discussed below, be exempt from the cap even if it is not filed by the qualifying institution itself:

> "Congress deemed certain institutions worthy of an H-1B cap exemption because of the direct benefits they provide to the United States. Congressional intent was to exempt from the H-1B cap certain alien workers who could provide direct contributions to the United States through their work on behalf of institutions of

---

[383] 8 CFR §214.2(h)(19)(iv). This definition for purposes of the ACWIA fee, discussed below, is incorporated for purposes of the cap exemption by 8 CFR §241.2(h)(8)(ii)(F)(3).

[384] 8 CFR §214.2(h)(19)(iii)(C). This definition for purposes of the ACWIA fee, discussed below, is incorporated for purposes of the cap exemption by 8 CFR §241.2(h)(8)(ii)(F)(3).

[385] *Id.*

[386] *Id.*

[387] Former 8 CFR §214.2(h)(19)(iii)(C) (2015).

[388] 80 Fed. Reg. 81900 (Dec. 31, 2015) (proposed rule), and 81 Fed. Reg. 82398 (Nov. 18, 2016) (final rule).

[389] 81 Fed. Reg. 82398, 82446-7 (Nov. 18, 2016).

[390] 80 Fed. Reg. 81900, 81918 (Dec. 31, 2015).

Copyright © 2017. American Immigration Lawyers Association. All rights reserved.

higher education and related nonprofit entities, or nonprofit research organizations, or governmental research organizations. In effect, this statutory measure ensures that qualifying institutions have access to a continuous supply of H-1B workers without numerical limitation.

"Congress chose to exempt from the numerical limitations… aliens who are employed 'at' a qualifying institution, which is a broader category than aliens employed 'by' a qualifying institution. This broader category may allow certain aliens who are not employed directly by a qualifying institution to be treated as cap exempt when needed to further the essential purposes of the qualifying institution."[391]

Thus, if a petition is filed by an entity that is not one of the four types eligible for exemption, but the "beneficiary will spend the majority of his or her work time at a qualifying…entity," the petition may still be exempt from the cap, provided the job duties "directly and predominately further the essential purpose, mission, objectives, or functions of the qualifying…entity."[392] In other words, the petitioner must show a "nexus between the work performed by the H-1B" and the purpose or functioning of the qualifying entity.[393]

"[C]ompanies that have contracts with qualifying federal agencies (or other qualifying institutions) which require the placement of professionals on-site at the particular agency" are seen in USCIS guidance as fulfilling the "employed at" scenario.[394] Similarly, physicians employed in private practice who perform their job duties at an exempt non-profit hospital affiliated with a university often fall under the "employed at" exception. Examples provided in USCIS guidance indicate consideration of the following factors, which should not be mutually exclusive:[395]

- Whether the petitioner and qualifying institution have a formal affiliation, such as a "cooperative relationship";

- Whether the beneficiary's work will be for the benefit of the qualifying institution rather than the petitioner;

- Whether the beneficiary's work is related to the qualifying institution's purpose or reason for existence;

---

[391] AFM 31.3(g)(13)(A)(i).

[392] 8 CFR §214.2(h)(8)(ii)(F)(*4*).

[393] 80 Fed. Reg. 81900, 81918-9 (Dec. 31, 2015).

[394] AFM 31.3(g)(13)(A)(i). ("The H-1B employees generally perform work directly related to the purposes of the particular qualifying federal agency or entity and thus may qualify for an exemption to the H-1B cap"). This guidance was written before the 2016 regulations were promulgated, but USCIS noted that the rulemaking "codifies…longstanding policy interpretations" with respect to cap exemptions, except where "clarifications" are made. 81 Fed. Reg. 82398, 82443 et. seq. (Nov. 18, 2016).

[395] AFM 31.3(g)(13)(A)(ii). The illustrative examples will not be discussed or reproduced, but the practitioner is strongly encouraged to read them.

Copyright © 2017. American Immigration Lawyers Association. All rights reserved.

- Whether the beneficiary will physically work at the qualifying institution for a majority of his or her time (a required element in all "employed at" situations);

- Whether the beneficiary's duties "would or could otherwise be performed by employees of the qualifying institution"; and/or

- Whether the beneficiary was previously employed by the qualifying institution in the same capacity as that anticipated for the petitioner.

c. When Cap-Exempt Employment Ends

A beneficiary, who has "not previously been counted toward the numerical limitations" because he or she obtained H-1B status pursuant to employment with an exempt employer, and later "ceases to be employed" by the cap-exempt employer, "shall ... be counted toward those limitations the first time the alien is employed by an employer other than" a cap-exempt employer.[396] The operative term is "ceases to be employed"" a beneficiary who works concurrently for an exempt and a non-exempt employer will not be counted toward the cap, as long as the "beneficiary is employed in valid H-1B status under a cap exemption…, the beneficiary's employment with the cap-exempt employer is expected to continue…, and the beneficiary can reasonably and concurrently perform the work described in each employer's respective positions."[397]

USCIS guidance indicates that:

"Documentary evidence, such as a current letter of employment or a recent pay stub, should be provided in support of such a concurrent employment petition at the time that it is filed with USCIS in order to confirm that the H 1B alien beneficiary is still employed in a cap-exempt position."[398]

However, if the employment that is the subject of the cap exemption ends, "the alien who is concurrently employed in a cap-subject position becomes subject to the numerical limitations…unless the alien was previously counted with respect to the 6-year period of authorization to which the petition applies or another exemption applies."[399] Once such a beneficiary becomes subject to the numerical limitations, "USCIS may revoke the cap-subject petition."[400]

Needless to say, if employment of a beneficiary in a cap-exempt position ends, and the individual is not the subject of another cap-exempt petition, he or she will

---

[396] INA §214(g)(6); American Competitiveness in the Twenty-First Century Act of 2000, Pub. L. No. 106-313, §103 (Oct. 17, 2000); 9 FAM 402.10-10(A) ("Such aliens will be counted if they move from such a position to one which is within the ceiling applicability").

[397] 8 CFR §214.2(h)(8)(ii)(F)(6). The word "positions" is likely an error, and "petitions" was the intended term.

[398] AFM 31.3(g)(13)(D).

[399] 8 CFR §214.2(h)(8)(ii)(F)(6)(ii).

[400] Id.

Copyright © 2017. American Immigration Lawyers Association. All rights reserved.

become subject to the cap unless previously counted in the past six years,[401] as discussed in the next section. Consequently, when preparing an H-1B change of employer petition, the practitioner should carefully assess prior H-1B approval notices to determine whether the H-1B beneficiary was counted against the H-1B quota, and should seek copies of prior H-1B petitions if necessary to determine whether a cap exemption was applied. For further discussion of H-1B portability petitions from cap-exempt to non-cap-exempt employers, see below.

4. Previous H-1B Visa Number Issuance

As noted above, a foreign national should be counted toward the H-1B cap only once during a six-year period,[402] and as noted below, a foreign national may hold H-1B status for a total of six years.[403] Based on the interrelationship of these statutory provisions, a beneficiary, who previously held H-1B status for less than a total of six years after being counted toward an H-1B cap and is eligible for a new H-1B visa number after remaining outside the United States for one year, should not require a new H-1B visa number, but is eligible for the remaining balance of H-1B time.[404] In short, such a beneficiary may either request a new H-1B visa number or seek readmission "for the 'remainder' of the initial six-year admission period without being subject to the H-1B cap."[405]

USCIS guidance uses the term "remainder time" to describe "the full six-year period of admission minus the period of time that the alien previously spent in the United States in valid H-1B status."[406] The beneficiary bears the burden of proof to establish previous H-1B status and physical presence outside the United States for at least one year.[407] Appropriate evidence includes copies of Form I-797 approval notices, visa stamps, and I-94 cards,[408] as well as the evidence described above.

During years of high demand for H-1B visa numbers, where the cap may be exhausted during the first week of filing, the availability of remainder time means that qualifying H-1B workers may be hired during the black-out period. The practitioner should note that foreign nationals who were cap-exempt during their previous H-1B status are not eligible for this relief.[409]

Alternatively, a petitioner may wish to request a new H-1B visa number on behalf of a foreign national if the beneficiary previously held H-1B status for more than

---

[401] 8 CFR §214.2(h)(8)(ii)(F)(5).

[402] INA §214(g)(7); American Competitiveness in the Twenty-First Century Act of 2000, Pub. L. No. 106-313, §103 (Oct. 17, 2000).

[403] INA §214(g)(4).

[404] AFM 31.3(g)(15).

[405] *Id.*

[406] *Id.*

[407] *Id.*

[408] *Id.*

[409] *Id.* ("If the alien was not previously counted against the H-1B numerical limitations (*i.e.*, because cap-exempt), the alien will be counted against the H-1B cap unless he or she is eligible for another exemption").

Copyright © 2017. American Immigration Lawyers Association. All rights reserved.

three or four years. Factors to be considered include whether the petitioner seeks to employ the foreign national for longer than the remainder time, the availability of H-B visa numbers, the projected length of time to sponsor the foreign national residence, the availability of AC21 extensions, and the availability of other paths to permanent residence, such as family based immigration and the Diversity Visa Lottery.

D. Labor Condition Application

In order to file an H-1B petition, the employer must first obtain from DOL an approved "labor condition application in the occupational specialty in which the alien(s) will be employed."[410] Generally, LCA requirements are identical for H-1B and H-1B1 petitions;[411] deviations include the attestation requirements applying to H-1B dependent employers and willful violators.[412] The labor condition application is discussed in detail in Volume 1: Chapter Six, "The Labor Condition Application."

H-1B dependent employers are subject to a number of additional requirements. Determination of what constitutes an H-1B dependent employer, and what additional requirements are attached to such employers, also are discussed in Chapter Six.

E. H-1B Employment Relationship, Termination of the Relationship, and Return Transportation Obligation

An H-1B petition must be filed by a U.S. employer,[413] or agent. The regulations define the term "United States employer" as "a person, firm, corporation, contractor, or other association, or organization in the United States," which, in turn, meets the following conditions:

- "Engages a person to work within the United States;

- "Has an employer-employee relationship with respect to employees…, as indicated by the fact that it may hire, pay, fire, supervise, or otherwise control the work of any such employee; and

- "Has an Internal Revenue Service Tax identification number."[414]

A particular focus in USCIS adjudications is on the employment relationship between the petitioner and the beneficiary.[415] USCIS guidance updated in 2006 noted

---

[410] 8 CFR §§214.2(h)(4)(i)(B)(*1*) and 214.2(h)(4)(iii)(B)(*1*) (the H-1B petition must include a "certification from the Secretary of Labor that the petitioner has filed a labor condition application with the Secretary"); 20 CFR §655.700(a)(3) and (b); INA §212(n)(1).

[411] 69 Fed. Reg. 68221 (Nov. 23, 2004) ("This rule amends the subpart headings, applicability section, and other sections of the Department of Labor regulations pertaining to employers seeking the temporary entry on H-1B visas of nonimmigrant aliens in specialty occupations… to extend the same procedures, with limited exceptions based upon statutory requirements, to temporary entry and employment on H–1B1 visas").

[412] 69 Fed. Reg. 68221 (Nov. 23, 2004) (internal citations omitted).

[413] USCIS, "I-129 H-1B Standard Operating Procedures" (undated, posted July 26, 2007), AILA Doc. No. 07072668. AFM 31.2(b)(2) ("Although the statute requires the employer to file an H petition… [a] U.S. employer or an agent where appropriate may file the petition").

[414] 8 CFR §214.2(h)(4)(ii).

Copyright © 2017. American Immigration Lawyers Association. All rights reserved.

how a "technical" employer was "therefore a petitioning employer."[416] Similarly, DOL regulations state that "the person, firm, contractor, or other association or organization in the United States that files a[n H-1B] petition with [USCIS] on behalf of the nonimmigrant is deemed to be the employer of that nonimmigrant."[417] For H-1B1 status, a "person, firm, contractor, or other association or organization in the United States that files an LCA with [DOL] on behalf of the nonimmigrant is deemed to be the employer of that nonimmigrant."[418] However, language from January 2010 sets forth additional criteria to be considered by the adjudicator,[419] as discussed in detail below.

Importantly, however, the inquiry should focus on the employment relationship. It "does not empower [the adjudicator] to question the employer's ability to pay the wage stated in the petition."[420] The adjudicator may consider, however, if "there is an actual job offer."[421] In addition, a small business employer may be questioned on the need for the beneficiary's services and/or the employer's financial assets.[422] For discussion of these issues. see below.

DOS guidance states that a foreign national "may be classified H-1B whether the position to be temporarily occupied is permanent or temporary in nature."[423] To evidence the term of the H-1B assignment, the H-1B petition may include "[c]opies of any written contracts between the petitioner and beneficiary, or a summary of the terms of the oral agreement under which the beneficiary will be employed, if there is no written contract."[424]

---

[415] AFM 31.3(g)(16); USCIS, "Determining Employer-Employee Relationship for Adjudication of H-1B Petitions, Including Third-Party Site Placements" (Jan. 8, 2010), AILA Doc. No. 10011363.

[416] AFM 31.3(g): H-1B Classification and Documentary Requirements. *See also Matter of Ord*, 18 I&N Dec. 285 (Reg'l Comm'r 1982) ("It is clear by the terms and conditions of the beneficiary's employment contract that he is actually an employee of the petitioning firm notwithstanding that his services are to be rendered for a firm which contracts with the petitioner for them").

[417] 20 CFR §655.715.

[418] *Id.*

[419] AFM 31.3(g)(16); USCIS, "Determining Employer-Employee Relationship for Adjudication of H-1B Petitions, Including Third-Party Site Placements" (Jan. 8, 2010), AILA Doc. No. 10011363.

[420] USCIS, "I-129 H-1B Standard Operating Procedures" (undated, posted July 26, 2007), AILA Doc. No. 07072668.

[421] *Id.*

[422] AFM 31.3(g)(5).

[423] 9 FAM 402.10-4(G). *Cf. Matter of Ord*, 18 I&N Dec. 285 (Reg'l Comm'r 1982) (discussing the former requirements of temporary employment and maintenance of a residence abroad and stating that the "petitioner's 'need' for a permanent employee is not relevant to the H-1 classification, but, nonetheless, the employer is required to demonstrate that it is his intention to employ the specific beneficiary being petitioned for, for only a temporary period").

[424] 8 CFR §214.2(h)(4)(iv)(B).

Copyright © 2017. American Immigration Lawyers Association. All rights reserved.

Part-time and concurrent employment in H-1B status is permitted,[425] unlike with labor certification applications and immigrant visa petitions, as discussed in Volume 2: Chapters Two and Three, "The Labor Certification Application" and "The Immigrant Visa Petition," respectively. If the beneficiary will switch from full-time to part-time employment, then an amended petition is necessary,[426] as discussed below. USCIS guidance does not specify a set number of hours required for part-time employment, and the hours may be stated as a range.[427] The beneficiary's income from the part-time employment should be "at least a living wage or the petition should be accompanied by proof that the beneficiary has sufficient means to support himself or herself."[428]

If the foreign national obtains H-1B status and subsequently "is dismissed from employment by the employer before the end of the period of authorized admission, the employer shall be liable for the reasonable costs of return transportation of the alien abroad,"[429] to the alien's last place of residence abroad.[430] This requirement does not apply if the alien voluntarily terminates the employment.[431] Notably, the "provision applies to any employer whose offer of employment became the basis for the alien obtaining or continuing H-1B status," [432] which means that H-1B employers who file extension petitions may be responsible for these costs, as well as initial H-1B petitioners. A foreign national may notify the Service Center that adjudicated the underlying H-1B petition "in writing," in the event that he or she "believes that the employer has not complied with this provision."[433] This "complaint will be retained in the file relating to the petition."[434] For further discussion of the return transportation obligation, see Volume 1: Chapters Eight, "H-2B Visas and Status" and Volume 1: Chapter Twelve, "O Visas and Status.".

1. Right to Control

DOL regulations indicate that the existence of an employment relationship should be "determined under the common law, "under which the key determinant is the putative employer's right to control the means and manner in which the work is performed."[435] USCIS agrees that the "employer-employee relationship hinges on the

---

[425] USCIS, "I-129 H-1B Standard Operating Procedures" (undated, posted July 26, 2007), AILA Doc. No. 07072668; AFM 31.2(b).

[426] "AILA/VSC Practice Pointer: Strategic Use of the Part Time H-1B" (Nov. 19, 2009), AILA Doc. No. 09111960.

[427] Id.

[428] Id.

[429] INA §214(c)(5)(A); 9 FAM 402.10-13(C).

[430] 8 CFR §214.2(h)(4)(iii)(E); 9 FAM 402.10-16.

[431] Id.

[432] 8 CFR §214.2(h)(4)(iii)(E).

[433] Id.

[434] Id.

[435] 20 CFR §655.715.

Copyright © 2017. American Immigration Lawyers Association. All rights reserved.

right to control the beneficiary."[436] However, a USCIS memorandum formulates specific criteria of the employer's right to control and, therefore, of a valid employment relationship because "[e]ngaging a person to work in the United States is more than merely paying the wage or placing that person on the payroll."[437] To explain the rationale for its requirements, USCIS noted the need to ensure that the LCA covers all work locations and indicated closer scrutiny of third-party placements:

"The lack of guidance clearly defining what constitutes a valid employer-employee relationship as required by 8 CFR 214.2(h)(4)(ii) has raised problems, in particular, with independent contractors, self-employed beneficiaries, and beneficiaries placed at third-party worksites. The placement of the beneficiary/employee at a work site that is not operated by the petitioner/employer (third-party placement), which is common in some industries, generally makes it more difficult to assess whether the requisite employer-employee relationship exists and will continue to exist.

"While some third-party placement arrangements meet the employer-employee relationship criteria, there are instances where the employer and beneficiary do not maintain such a relationship. Petitioner control over the beneficiary must be established when the beneficiary is placed into another employer's business, and expected to become a part of that business's regular operations. The requisite control may not exist in certain instances when the petitioner's business is to provide its employees to fill vacancies in businesses that contract with the petitioner for personnel needs. Such placements are likely to require close review in order to determine if the required relationship exists."[438]

There is strong evidence suggesting that the target of this policy change is IT consulting companies.[439] Indeed, years before the policy was stated in guidance, USCIS denied a petition for failure to provide the requested "contractual agreements between the petitioner and the companies for which the beneficiary will be providing consulting services and copies of the statements of work, work orders and any other documents and appendices."[440] Also, three IT consulting firms filed a lawsuit shortly after issuance of the guidance, requesting a preliminary injunction of the application

---

[436] AFM 31.3(g)(16). Treatment of the employment relationship in the context of healthcare jobs may be different. "USCIS Implements H-1B and L-1 Fee Increase According to Public Law 111-230" (Aug. 19, 2010), AILA Doc. No. 10081920.

[437] AFM 31.3(g)(16); USCIS, "Determining Employer-Employee Relationship for Adjudication of H-1B Petitions, Including Third-Party Site Placements" (Jan. 8, 2010), AILA Doc. No. 10011363.

[438] USCIS, "Determining Employer-Employee Relationship for Adjudication of H-1B Petitions, Including Third-Party Site Placements" (Jan. 8, 2010), AILA Doc. No. 10011363. *See also Matter of [name not provided]* WAC 03 232 53697 (AAO Feb. 3, 2006), http://bit.ly/feb063d. This decision predates the USCIS guidance on the right to control, but, nevertheless, may indicate an adjudicative policy by USCIS.

[439] "Q & A Stakeholder Conference" (Sept. 20, 2010 and updated Oct. 19, 2010), AILA Doc. No. 10101471.

[440] *Matter of [name not provided]* WAC 03 232 53697 (AAO Feb. 3, 2006), http://bit.ly/feb063d.

Copyright © 2017. American Immigration Lawyers Association. All rights reserved.

of the USCIS memorandum.[441] The plaintiffs asserted that the memorandum "establishes a different standard" from the "right to control test" required by the regulatory definition of a U.S. employer "and therefore constitutes a new, binding rule," which, in turn, should be "invalidated" because it "was not issued in accordance with the [Administrative Procedure Act] APA's procedures for agency rulemaking."[442] However, the Court noted that the memorandum "both on its face and in its application, leaves USCIS adjudicators considerable discretion in applying the eleven factors," so it was not binding.[443] Further acknowledged was the absence of the "P" designation, which characterizes policy memoranda that are binding on USCIS adjudicators,[444] as discussed in Volume 1: Chapter One, "Introduction." Therefore, the Court held "that the Memorandum establishes interpretive guidelines for the implementation of the Regulation" and concluded that the memorandum was subject to neither judicial review nor the notice and comment procedure of the APA.[445] The suit was dismissed with prejudice.[446]

The practitioner should note that the right to control is distinguished from "actual control," such that a petitioner "may have the right to control the beneficiary's job-related duties and yet not exercise actual control over each function performed by that beneficiary."[447] To "determine whether the petitioner has the right to control over when, where, and how the beneficiary performs the job," USCIS will evaluate the following factors, stated in the form of questions:

- "Does the petitioner supervise the beneficiary and is such supervision off-site or on-site?

- "If the supervision is off-site, how does the petitioner maintain such supervision, *i.e.*, weekly calls, reporting back to main office routinely, or site visits by the petitioner?

- "Does the petitioner have the right to control the work of the beneficiary on a day-to-day basis if such control is required?

- "Does the petitioner provide the tools or instrumentalities needed for the beneficiary to perform the duties of employment?

- "Does the petitioner hire, pay, and have the ability to fire the beneficiary?

---

[441] *Broadgate, Inc. v. USCIS*, No. 09-cv-1423 (D.C. Dist. Aug. 10, 2010), AILA Doc. No. 10060830; "Suit Challenging Employer-Employee/Third-Party Placement Memo" (updated Aug. 16, 2010), AILA Doc. No. 10060830.

[442] *Broadgate, Inc. v. USCIS*, No. 09-cv-1423 (D.C. Dist. Aug. 10, 2010), AILA Doc. No. 10060830.

[443] *Id.* ("[T]here is no evidence that it either binds USCIS adjudicators or requires a different outcome for third-party employers like Plaintiffs than the Regulation does. In fact, in addition to emphasizing that no single factor among the eleven is dispositive, the Memorandum instructs USCIS adjudicators to look to the totality of the circumstances in each case to determine whether there is an employer-employee relationship").

[444] *Broadgate, Inc. v. USCIS*, No. 09-cv-1423 (D.C. Dist. Aug. 10, 2010), AILA Doc. No. 10060830.

[445] *Id.*

[446] *Id.*

[447] AFM 31.3(g)(16).

Copyright © 2017. American Immigration Lawyers Association. All rights reserved.

- "Does the petitioner evaluate the work-product of the beneficiary, *i.e.*, progress/performance reviews?

- "Does the petitioner claim the beneficiary for tax purposes?

- "Does the petitioner provide the beneficiary any type of employee benefits?

- "Does the beneficiary use proprietary information of the petitioner in order to perform the duties of employment?

- "Does the beneficiary produce an end-product that is directly linked to the petitioner's line of business?

- "Does the petitioner have the ability to control the manner and means in which the work product of the beneficiary is accomplished?"[448]

Even though DOL regulations indicate that the overall employment relationship should be evaluated,[449] USCIS guidance focuses on the right to control:

"The common law is flexible about how these factors [stated above] are to be weighed. The petitioner will have met the relationship test, if, in the totality of the circumstances, a petitioner is able to present evidence to establish its right to control the beneficiary's employment. In assessing the requisite degree of control, the officer should be mindful of the nature of the petitioner's business and the type of work of the beneficiary. The petitioner must also be able to establish that the right to control the beneficiary's work will continue to exist throughout the duration of the beneficiary's employment term with the petitioner."[450]

The examples provided in USCIS guidance indicate that the length of the beneficiary's placement off-site is not necessarily dispositive and illustrate the other factors that may be favorably considered:

- The beneficiary will provide services at a location that is owned or leased by the petitioner;

- The beneficiary will report on a regular and frequent basis to the petitioner, at a "centralized office";

- The petitioner will set the beneficiary's work schedule, which is the "when, where, and how" of the beneficiary's work, as noted above;

- The petitioner will review the beneficiary's work product, either in the form of progress or performance reviews, as noted above, or before it is submitted to the off-site client or customer;

---

[448] *Id.*

[449] 20 CFR §655.715 ("Under the common law, no shorthand formula or magic phrase can be applied to find the answer. All of the incidents of the relationship must be assessed and weighed with no one factor being decisive") (internal citation omitted and internal formatting removed).

[450] AFM 31.3(g)(16).

Copyright © 2017. American Immigration Lawyers Association. All rights reserved.

- The beneficiary will apply the petitioner's established policies and/or practices or utilize the petitioner's systems, even if these are not considered "proprietary information";

- The petitioner will pay for "food and lodging costs" while the beneficiary is placed off-site, and reimbursement for transportation costs, though not mentioned, may be relevant;

- The beneficiary "has an assigned office space" at the petitioner's worksite; and/or

- There is a contract detailing the services to be provided and the manner in which they will be provided between the petitioner and the off-site client or customer.[451]

A shortage of qualified workers in the industry may be another favorable factor.[452] It also seems highly likely that the number of nonimmigrants employed by the petitioner may be considered,[453] based on the increased scrutiny of "job shops" and consulting firms, discussed above. USCIS has indicated that the contract between the petitioner and the off-site client or customer may also evidence the existence of "a specialty occupation... at the third-party worksite."[454] In addition to the converse of the advantageous factors stated above, the following considerations will most likely be viewed as establishing the absence of a valid employment relationship:

- Self-employment of the beneficiary, such that the "beneficiary cannot be fired by the petitioning company," as discussed below;

- The beneficiary will be an independent contractor rather than an employee of the petitioner;

- The contract between the petitioner and the off-site client or customer does not detail the beneficiary's "specific position[]" and/or the positions "are staffed on an as-needed basis"; and

- The beneficiary will report to an employee of the off-site client or customer.[455]

USCIS guidance is careful to "acknowledge[] that a sole stockholder of a corporation can be employed by that corporation as the corporation is a separate legal entity from its owners and even its sole owner,"[456] but takes the position that the corporate existence of a petitioner does not absolve the petitioner of the need to

---

[451] *Id.* For discussion of established policies and practices, the practitioner may wish to refer to discussion of "specialized knowledge" in the context of L-1B petitions, as discussed in Volume 1: Chapter Eleven, "L-1 Visas and Status."

[452] *Matter of Ord*, 18 I&N Dec. 285 (Reg'l Comm'r 1982).

[453] *Matter of Ord*, 18 I&N Dec. 285 (Reg'l Comm'r 1982) ("job shop" employer).

[454] USCIS, A. Mayorkas, (Nov. 10, 2009), AILA Doc. No. 09120161.

[455] 31.3(g)(16).

[456] *Id.* (citing *Matter of Aphrodite*, 17 I&N Dec. 530 (BIA 1980)). This case is discussed in Volume 1: Chapter Eleven, "L-1 Visas and Status."

Copyright © 2017. American Immigration Lawyers Association. All rights reserved.

establish that the beneficiary will be a "bona fide 'employee.'"[457] To USCIS, the issue seems to be whether the petitioner as an "outside entity… can exercise control over the beneficiary" for the benefit of the petitioner, which may be permissible,[458] as opposed to the beneficiary controlling his or her work without regard to the company's needs, which is prohibited. Therefore, although "a petitioner may employ and seek H-1B classification for a beneficiary who happens to have a significant ownership interest in a petitioner, this does not automatically mean that the beneficiary is a bona fide employee."[459] USCIS's interpretation has been criticized as improperly piercing the corporate veil, but it remains a concern for practitioners who represent smaller businesses.

2. Evidence of the Employment Relationship

Absent or inadequate evidence of the employment relationship may result in denial "for failure of the employer to satisfy the requirements of being a United States employer."[460] Generally, the H-1B petition "should provide sufficient detail that the employer and beneficiary are engaged in a valid employer-employee relationship," with emphasis on:

- The petitioner's "ability to hire, fire and supervise the beneficiary;"

- The petitioner's supervision over "the overall direction of the beneficiary's work"; and

- Continued existence of the right to control the beneficiary "throughout the duration of the requested H-1B validity period."[461]

As stated by USCIS guidance: "The petitioner can demonstrate an employer-employee relationship by providing a combination of the following or similar types of evidence";

- "A complete itinerary of services or engagements that specifies the dates of each service or engagement, the names and addresses of the actual employers, and the names and addresses of the establishment, venues, or locations where the services will be performed for the period of time requested;

- "Copy of signed Employment Agreement between the petitioner and beneficiary detailing the terms and conditions of employment;

- "Copy of an employment offer letter that clearly describes the nature of the employer-employee relationship and the services to be performed by the beneficiary;

---

[457] AFM 31.3(g)(16) ("However, an H-1B beneficiary/employee who owns a majority of the sponsoring entity and who reports to no one but him or herself may not be able to establish that a valid employment relationship exists in that the beneficiary, who is also the petitioner, cannot establish the requisite 'control.") (fn 4) (internal citation omitted).

[458] AFM 31.3(g)(16).

[459] Id.

[460] Id. (citing 8 CFR §§214.2(h)(9)(i) and (h)(4)(ii)).

[461] AFM 31.3(g)(16) (citing 8 CFR §214.2(h)(4)(ii)).

Copyright © 2017. American Immigration Lawyers Association. All rights reserved.

- "Copy of relevant portions of valid contracts between the petitioner and a client (in which the petitioner has entered into a business agreement for which the petitioner's employees will be utilized) that establishes that while the petitioner's employees are placed at the third-party worksite, the petitioner will continue to have the right to control its employees;

- "Copies of signed contractual agreements, statements of work, work orders, service agreements, and letters between the petitioner and the authorized officials of the ultimate end-client companies where the work will actually be performed by the beneficiary, which provide information such as a detailed description of the duties the beneficiary will perform, the qualifications that are required to perform the job duties, salary or wages paid, hours worked, benefits, a brief description of who will supervise the beneficiary and their duties, and any other related evidence;

- "Copy of position description or any other documentation that describes the skills required to perform the job offered, the source of the instrumentalities and tools needed to perform the job, the product to be developed or the service to be provided, the location where the beneficiary will perform the duties, the duration of the relationship between the petitioner and beneficiary, whether the petitioner has the right to assign additional duties, the extent of petitioner's discretion over when and how long the beneficiary will work, the method of payment, the petitioner's role in paying and hiring assistants to be utilized by the beneficiary, whether the work to be performed is part of the regular business of the petitioner, the provision of employee benefits, and the tax treatment of the beneficiary in relation to the petitioner;

- "A description of the performance review process; and/or

- "Copy of petitioner's organizational chart, demonstrating beneficiary's supervisory chain."[462]

USCIS acknowledges that the petitioner may submit "similarly probative documents" if the above-listed evidence is unavailable, whether for the H-1B petition or in response to an RFE.[463] Despite the previous emphasis on confirmation statement from the off-site client or customer, discussed above, VSC stated:

"Sufficient information from an end client can be a strong piece of evidence to establish the existence of work for the beneficiary and the petitioner's right to control the beneficiary's employment, however it is not the only evidence that is relied upon at the VSC.... While end client letters may provide important and unique insight into assessing an employer-employee relationship such as describing the employment relationship between the beneficiary and the end client, the ultimate work performed by the beneficiary, and the duration of the end

---

[462] AFM 31.3(g)(16).

[463] "USCIS Issues Guidance Memorandum on Establishing the 'Employee Employer Relationship' in H-1B Petitions" (Jan. 13, 2009), AILA Doc. No. 10011331.

Copyright © 2017. American Immigration Lawyers Association. All rights reserved.

client work, end client letters are only one type of documentary evidence to be considered."[464]

This flexibility is a welcome accommodation to petitioners with employees placed at organizations with "a policy that prohibits them from confirming the existence of contract employees."[465] Other acceptable evidence includes "a copy of the contract or contracts that relate to the end client employment, the related work order(s), invoices, or a statement from the end client addressing their policy on confirming contract worker status."[466] However, as with recapturing H-1B time, the validity period of an approved petition depends on the evidence presented: "When an employer-employee relationship is established in a third party employment situation, USCIS grants an approval period to cover the amount of time for which the third party work assignment is established."[467] For further discussion of this issue, see below.

An RFE should be issued "in cases where the petitioner has failed to establish that a valid employer-employee relationship exists and will continue to exist throughout the duration of the beneficiary's employment term with the employer,[468] as discussed below. An explanation of how the submitted documents demonstrate the employment relationship or "address the deficiency(ies) raised in the RFE" should be provided.[469] The validity period of an approved H-1B petition may be truncated if the evidence demonstrates the employment control for only a portion of the requested employment period.[470] H-1B petitions with multiple worksites must include a full itinerary, as discussed below. For discussion of appropriate evidence of the employment relationship for an H-1B petition filed by an agent, see below. Evidence for H-1B extensions requests is discussed below.

F. Technical Considerations

The following sections address technical considerations for filing H-1B petitions.

1. Agent-Petitioners

As specifically stated by USCIS guidance: "The procedure where each employer must file a separate petition in order for the alien to work part-time for multiple employers does not apply in petitions filed by agents."[471] The agent may be "the actual employer of the beneficiary, the representative of both the employer and the beneficiary, or, a person or entity authorized by the employer to act for, or in place of,

---

[464] "Q & A Stakeholder Conference" (Sept. 20, 2010 and updated Oct. 19, 2010), AILA Doc. No. 10101471.

[465] *Id.*

[466] "*Id.*

[467] *Id.* Although the guidance specifically addresses H-1B extensions, the principle should remain the same.

[468] AFM 31.3(g)(16). The guidance specifically addresses RFEs regarding the employment relationship, but the principle should remain the same.

[469] "USCIS Issues Guidance Memorandum on Establishing the 'Employee Employer Relationship' in H-1B Petitions" (Jan. 13, 2009), AILA Doc. No. 10011331.

[470] *Id.*

[471] AFM 31.2(b)(3).

Copyright © 2017. American Immigration Lawyers Association. All rights reserved.

the employer as its agent."[472] DHS regulations indicate that an agent may be a "person or company in business as an agent."[473] When promulgating H-1B regulations, legacy INS provided the somewhat circular explanation that this "means that the service which the person or business provides in the normal course of doing business is that of an agent."[474]

An agent may file an H-1B petition on behalf of "multiple employers as the representative of both the employers and the beneficiary or beneficiaries," as long as "the supporting documentation includes a complete itinerary of services or engagements."[475] However, only confirmed dates of employment should be stated in the itinerary.[476] Copies of contracts should not be necessary, but they may be requested: "The itinerary of firm engagements provided by the agent is acceptable in lieu of signed contracts, unless the adjudicator has reason to believe the statements are not true and correct."[477] The exception is if "the agent, such as a modeling agency, is functioning as the employer, [then] a contract between the agency and the alien, guaranteeing the wages and conditions of employment, must accompany the petition."[478] In this case, the agent-petitioner must "provide an itinerary of definite employment and information on any other services planned for the period of time requested" to USCIS.[479] The following requirements apply:

> "The itinerary shall specify the dates of each service or engagement, the names and addresses of the actual employers, and the names and addresses of the establishment, venues, or locations where the services will be performed. In questionable cases, a contract between the employers and the beneficiary or beneficiaries may be required. The burden is on the agent to explain the terms and conditions of the employment and to provide any required documentation."[480]

Alternatively, an established agent may be authorized to file the petition by "workers who are traditionally self-employed," or by "workers who use agents to arrange short-term employment on their behalf with numerous employers."[481] In response to criticism that this provision would jeopardize the relationship between the agent and nonimmigrant, legacy INS noted that allowing agents to file on behalf of individuals who are typically self-employed "allowed for more efficient coordination of engagement" and that this practice does not appear to have "been abused."[482]

---

[472] 8 CFR §214.2(h)(2)(i)(F).

[473] 8 CFR §214.2(h)(2)(i)(F)(2).

[474] 55 Fed. Reg. 2606 (Jan. 26, 1990) (citing former 8 CFR §214.2(h)(2)(i)(F)).

[475] 8 CFR §214.2(h)(2)(i)(F)(2).

[476] AFM 31.2(b)(5) ("Speculative employment should not be included in an itinerary").

[477] AFM 31.2(b)(5).

[478] AFM 31.2(b)(5); 8 CFR §214.2(h)(2)(i)(F)(1). See also 55 Fed. Reg. 2606 (Jan. 26, 1990).

[479] 8 CFR §214.2(h)(2)(i)(F)(1).

[480] 8 CFR §214.2(h)(2)(i)(F)(2).

[481] 8 CFR §214.2(h)(2)(i)(F).

[482] 55 Fed. Reg. 2606 (Jan. 26, 1990).

Copyright © 2017. American Immigration Lawyers Association. All rights reserved.

Indeed, approval of an H-1B petition filed by an agent on behalf of the "actual employer" of "one who is traditionally self-employed or who uses agents to arrange short-term employment on their behalf with numerous employers" requires evidence that the end-employer has a "valid employer-employee relationship with the beneficiary."[483] This means that the client or customer, rather than the agent-petitioner, must have the right to control the beneficiary, as evidenced by the terms of the contract between the agent and the beneficiary.[484] USCIS guidance provides the example of the agent of a fashion model,[485] which is a separate H-1B category, the guidance should be cross-applicable. For further discussion of the right to control, see above.

Although the regulations permit an established agent to file a petition on behalf of a foreign employer who does not have U.S. operations,[486] and require that the foreign employer comply with employment verification requirements,[487] these provisions contradict the general rule that an H-1B petition must be filed by a U.S. employer.[488] The regulatory discussion of petitions filed by foreign employers should apply only to the H-2 classifications.[489] For further discussion of agent-petitioners, see Volume 1: Chapter Twelve, "O Visas and Status."

2. "Emergent Situations," Multiple Worksites, and Multiple Employers

As detailed below, the place where the H-1B petition should be filed is governed by factors such as whether it is cap-subject, cap-exempt, an extension without change, employment located in Guam, an H-1B1, etc.[490] If there will be multiple worksites, and more than one USCIS service center accepts the type of H-1B filing, then the H-1B petition should be filed with the service center with jurisdiction over the petitioner's headquarters and should include "an itinerary with the dates and locations of the services."[491] USCIS guidance further requires a petitioner to "submit a complete itinerary of services or engagements that specifies the dates of each service or engagement, the names and addresses of the actual employers, and the names and addresses of the establishment, venues, or locations where the services will be

---

[483] USCIS, "I-129 H-1B Standard Operating Procedures" (undated, posted July 26, 2007), AILA Doc. No. 07072668.

[484] Id.

[485] AFM 31.2(b)(5).

[486] 8 CFR §214.2(h)(2)(i)(F).

[487] 8 CFR §214.2(h)(2)(i)(F)(3) (citing INA §274a and 8 CFR §274a).

[488] 8 CFR §214.2(h)(4)(ii) read in conjunction with 8 CFR §214.2(h)(2)(i)(A); USCIS, "I-129 H-1B Standard Operating Procedures" (undated, posted July 26, 2007), AILA Doc. No. 07072668.

[489] 8 CFR §214.2(h)(2)(i)(F) does not specify any particular H classification and 8 CFR §214.2(h)(2)(i)(F)(3) states that a "person or company in business as an agent may file the H petition...."

[490] USCIS, "Direct Filing Addresses for Form I-129, Petition for a Nonimmigrant Worker, https://www.uscis.gov/i-129-addresses.

[491] 8 CFR §214.2(h)(2)(i)(B) (stating that the "address that the petitioner specifies as its location on the Form I-129 shall be where the petitioner is located for purposes of this paragraph"); 9 FAM 402.10-17(A) ("A labor contractor or consultant petitioning for H-1B workers to work at multiple client sites must provide a detailed itinerary of those sites at the time the petition is filed"); AFM 31.2(b)(3) (requiring "a detailed itinerary").

Copyright © 2017. American Immigration Lawyers Association. All rights reserved.

performed for the period of time requested."[492] This language is drawn from a regulation applying to agent-petitioners,[493] perhaps because USCIS believes that H-1B petitions with multiple worksites are "usually filed by an agent who is representing numerous employers in various locations, or by one employer which has work to be performed by the beneficiary in more than one location."[494] For discussion of agent-petitioners, see above.

The detailed information "assists USCIS in determining that the petitioner has concrete plans in place for a particular beneficiary, that the beneficiary is performing duties in a specialty occupation, and that the beneficiary is not being "benched" without pay between assignments."[495] Also, as discussed in Volume 1: Chapter Six, "The Labor Condition Application," the approved LCA should identify and include the prevailing wages for multiple worksites.

Similarly, if there will be multiple H-1B employers, then "each employer must file a separate petition,"[496] unless the petition is filed by an established agent.[497] A single beneficiary may concurrently provide services to multiple employers, provided each employer files and has approved a petition on the beneficiary's behalf.[498]

3. Additional Fees

Certain additional fees are required for H-1B petitions above and beyond the usual filing fees. Also, "insufficient payment" of these fees will cause the H-1B petition to receive the "filing date the date the fee deficiency is corrected, as long as the cap has not been met."[499] If the date for the corrected filing is after the cap has been reached, the filing will be rejected.[500] USCIS prefers that the fees be paid in separate remittances.[501]

The first fee, which is called the "ACWIA fee,"[502] pursuant to the Amercan Competitiveness and Workforce Improvement Act of 1998 (ACWIA), applies to any employer that is not "a primary or secondary education institution, an institution of

---

[492] USCIS, "Determining Employer-Employee Relationship for Adjudication of H-1B Petitions, Including Third-Party Site Placements" (Jan. 8, 2010), AILA Doc. No. 10011363 (citing 8 CFR §214.2(h)(2)(i)(B)).

[493] 8 CFR §214.2(h)(2)(i)(F)(2).

[494] AFM 31.2(b)(3) (citing 8 CFR §214.2(h)(2)(i)(B)).

[495] USCIS, "Determining Employer-Employee Relationship for Adjudication of H-1B Petitions, Including Third-Party Site Placements" (Jan. 8, 2010), AILA Doc. No. 10011363 (citing 8 CFR §214.2(h)(2)(i)(B)).

[496] 8 CFR §214.2(h)(2)(i)(C).

[497] AFM 31.2(b)(3); 9 FAM 402.10-10(C).

[498] 8 CFR §214.2(h)(2)(i)(H).

[499] USCIS, "Optional Processing Worksheet for FY 2010 H-1B Filings," AILA Doc. No. 09032070.

[500] Id.

[501] USCIS, "Questions and Answers: USCIS to Accept H-1B Petitions for FY 2010 Beginning April 1, 2009" (Mar. 20, 2009), AILA Doc. No. 09032365.

[502] USCIS, "Form M-735, Optional Processing Worksheet for H-1B Filings" (Mar. 13, 2017), http://www.uscis.gov/files/form/m-735.pdf.

Copyright © 2017. American Immigration Lawyers Association. All rights reserved.

higher education…, a nonprofit entity related to or affiliated with any such institution, a nonprofit entity which engages in established curriculum-related clinical training of students registered at any such institution, a nonprofit research organization, or a governmental research organization."[503] For further discussion of these entities, see below and Volume 1: Chapter Six, The Labor Condition Application. The ACWIA fee is required in the following situations:

- When filing a petition that will "initially" grant the beneficiary H-1B status;
- When filing a petition that will extend H-1B status, "unless the employer previously has obtained an extension" on behalf of the beneficiary; and
- When filing an H-1B change of employer petition.[504]

The ACWIA fee is $1,500 for employers with at least 26 employees and $750 for employers with 25 or fewer employees.[505] The employee count should include "full-time equivalent employees who are employed in the United States," as "determined by including any affiliate or subsidiary of such employer."[506]

The ACWIA fee may be included in a single check or money order with the H-1B petition filing fee or in two separate checks or money orders, but payment of the filing and ACWIA fees "must be made at the same time to constitute a single remittance."[507] In addition, the ACWIA fee must be in a remittance from either the U.S. employer or its representative.[508] It may not be, for example, a check from the beneficiary's bank account. This fee may not be waived.[509]

An employer must not "require" an H-1B beneficiary "to reimburse, or otherwise compensate, the employer for part or all of the cost of such fee" and must not "otherwise to accept such reimbursement or compensation from such an alien."[510] The penalties are as follows:

"If the Secretary finds, after notice and opportunity for a hearing, that an employer has committed [such a] violation…, the Secretary may impose a civil monetary penalty of $1,000 for each such violation and issue an administrative order requiring the return to the nonimmigrant of any amount paid in violation of this

[503] INA §214(c)(9)(A) (citing 20 USC §1001(a)); 8 CFR §214.2(h)(19)(iii).

[504] INA §214(c)(9)(A); 8 CFR §214.2(h)(19)(i).

[505] INA §214(c)(9)(B); H-1B Visa Reform Act of 2004, Pub. L. No. 108-447, §422.

[506] INA §214(c)(9)(B). See Volume 1: Chapter 6, "The Labor Condition Application," for a discussion of the definition of a full-time equivalent employee.

[507] 8 CFR §214.2(h)(19)(ii); 70 Fed. Reg. 23775 (May 5, 2005). The regulations call this fee a "filing fee," but the text refers to the additional fee required of all employers who are not exempt. It is referenced here as the ACWIA fee to avoid confusion with the actual filing fee.

[508] 8 CFR §214.2(h)(19)(ii). The regulations call this fee a "filing fee," but the text refers to the additional fee required of all employers who are not exempt. It is referenced here as the ACWIA fee to avoid confusion with the actual filing fee.

[509] USCIS, "I-129 H-1B Standard Operating Procedures" (undated, posted July 26, 2007), AILA Doc. No. 07072668.

[510] INA §212(n)(2)(C)(vi)(II).

Copyright © 2017. American Immigration Lawyers Association. All rights reserved.

clause, or, if the nonimmigrant cannot be located, requiring payment of any such amount to the general fund of the Treasury."[511]

Specifically, the foreign national is prohibited from paying "any part" of the ACWIA fee, "whether directly or indirectly, voluntarily or involuntarily," and an employer must not reduce or deduct from the employee's wages "for purposes of a rebate of any part of this fee."[512] In the event that the employee pays the employer liquidated damages for early termination of the employment relationship, then "such liquidated damages shall not include any part of the $1,000 filing fee."[513] Payment of the ACWIA fee by a third party and reimbursement to the third party by the beneficiary is also prohibited, and "the employer shall be considered to be in violation of this prohibition since the employer would in such circumstances have been spared the expense of the fee which the H-1B nonimmigrant paid."[514]

Proceeds from the ACWIA fee are deposited in the "H-1B Nonimmigrant Petitioner Account,"[515] and are to be used for certain job training, scholarship, and grant programs,[516] for administrative costs for H-1B petitions and employment-based immigrant visa petitions,[517] and for backlog reduction of labor condition applications and investigations of labor condition applications.[518]

The fee of either $1,500 or $750, depending on the number of employees,[519] as discussed above, may also be imposed on non-exempt employers who file initial H-1B1 petitions and for "every second extension."[520] The additional fee may be imposed by "the Secretary of Homeland Security or the Secretary of State, as appropriate,"[521] although currently no additional fee is required of H-1B1 employers for applications made at consulates,[522] although it is charged to petitioners filing the

---

[511] INA §212(n)(2)(C)(vi)(III). *See also* 20 CFR §655.810(b)(1). Because of periodic adjustments to penalties due to inflation, the penalty as of 2017 is $1,811. 82 Fed. Reg. 5373, 5380 (Jan. 18, 2017).

[512] 20 CFR §655.731(c)(10)(ii).

[513] 20 CFR §655.731(c)(10)(ii). For further discussion of liquidated damages, see Volume 1: Chapter Six, "The Labor Condition Application."

[514] 20 CFR §655.731(c)(10)(ii).

[515] INA §286(s)(1).

[516] INA §§286(s)(2)-(4); H-1B Visa Reform Act of 2004, Pub. L. No. 108-447, §§428–429.

[517] INA §286(s)(5); American Competitiveness in the Twenty-First Century Act of 2000, Pub. L. No. 106-313, §113(a) (Oct. 17, 2000).

[518] INA §286(s)(6).

[519] INA §§214(c)(11)(A) and (B) (citing INA §214(c)(9)).

[520] INA §214(c)(11)(A) (citing INA §§212(t) and 214(g)(8)(C)). *See also* USCIS, "H and L Filing Fees for Form I-129, Petition for a Nonimmigrant Worker," https://www.uscis.gov/forms/h-and-l-filing-fees-form-i-129-petition-nonimmigrant-worker.

[521] INA §214(c)(11)(A).

[522] U.S. Consulate in Singapore, "Apply for a U.S. Visa," http://www.ustraveldocs.com/sg/sg-niv-visafeeinfo.asp. The site includes no reference to this fee. 70 Fed. Reg. 23775 (May 5, 2005) ("USCIS notes that the $500 Fraud Prevention and Detection Fee is not required for Chileans and Singaporeans entering the United States under the Free Trade Agreements").

Copyright © 2017. American Immigration Lawyers Association. All rights reserved.

I-129 form with USCIS.[523] A change of status from H-1B to H-1B1,vor vice versa, requires the ACWIA fee unless the petitioner is exempt.[524] Any such fees should be deposited in the H-1B Nonimmigrant Petitioner Account,[525] as discussed above.

A second additional H-1B fee is called the "fraud prevention and detection fee,"[526] or the "fraud fee,"[527] for short. This fee of $500[528] is imposed on initial and change of employer H-1B petitions,[529] and must apply only to principal aliens and not to the spouses or children who are accompanying or following to join such principal aliens.[530] It is not imposed on H-1B1 petitioners.[531] This fee should be in a separate check or money order from the filing fee and ACWIA fee, if applicable.[532] The monies from this fee are deposited in a Fraud Prevention and Detection Account,[533] with one-third of each of the funds to be used as follows:

- By DOS "for programs and activities at United States embassies and consulates abroad" in order "to prevent and detect visa fraud" by H-1B visa applicants and to "assist DHS in carrying out the fraud prevention and detection programs and activities";

- By DHS "for programs and activities to prevent and detect fraud" in H-1B petitions; and

- By DOL "for enforcement programs and activities" related to labor condition applications.[534]

Finally, a $4,000 fee is required of H-1B petitioners who employ at least 50 employees in the United States, more than 50 percent of whom "are in H-1B, L-1A, or L-1B nonimmigrant status."[535] Set to expire on September 30, 2025,[536] the

---

[523] USCIS, "H and L Filing Fees for Form I-129, Petition for a Nonimmigrant Worker," https://www.uscis.gov/forms/h-and-l-filing-fees-form-i-129-petition-nonimmigrant-worker.

[524] Id.

[525] INA §286(s)(1).

[526] INA §214(c)(12)(A).

[527] USCIS, "Form M-735, Optional Processing Worksheet for H-1B Filings" (Mar. 13, 2017), http://www.uscis.gov/files/form/m-735.pdf.

[528] INA §214(c)(12)(C).

[529] INA §214(c)(12)(A); H-1B Visa Reform Act of 2004, Pub. L. No. 108-447, §426.

[530] INA §214(c)(12)(D).

[531] USCIS, "H and L Filing Fees for Form I-129, Petition for a Nonimmigrant Worker," https://www.uscis.gov/forms/h-and-l-filing-fees-form-i-129-petition-nonimmigrant-worker.

[532] 70 Fed. Reg. 23775 (May 5, 2005) ("Those petitioners who must pay the $500 fraud prevention and detection fee must pay with a check or money order that is separate from the additional ACWIA application fees of $1,500 (or $750) and the $185 petition filing fees").

[533] INA §286(v)(1); H-1B Visa Reform Act of 2004, Pub. L. No. 108-447, §426.

[534] INA §286(v)(2); H-1B Visa Reform Act of 2004, Pub. L. No. 108-447, §426. The funds are also to be used to prevent and detect fraud in H-2 and L visa applicants and petitions.

[535] AFM 31.1(b) (citing Pub. L. No. 111-230 (Aug. 13, 2010)). As of this writing, the AFM still shows the old fee of $2,000, which was increased to $4,000 by the Consolidated Appropriations Act, 2016, Pub. L. No. 114-113 (Dec. 18, 2015).

Copyright © 2017. American Immigration Lawyers Association. All rights reserved.

fee is required for petitions requesting initial H-1B status or H-1B change of employer.[537] Like the fraud fee, it is not imposed on H-1B1 petitioners, but can be imposed when an H-1B1 nonimmigrant changes status to H-1B for a petitioner subject to the fee.[538] For purposes of the additional fee, the term "employer" has the same definition as a "United States employer,"[539] as discussed above. Therefore, because this analysis differs from the standard to determine H-1B dependency, it is possible that a petitioner may be subject to the additional fee, even though it is not considered an H-1B dependent employer.[540] However, a successor-in-interest should not be required to pay the fee, as the petition "will be treated as an extension petition."[541]

H-4 dependents will not be counted, and neither should L-2 nonimmigrants with employment authorization.[542] Both full-time and part-time employees "will count towards the calculation of whether an employer is subject to the new fee."[543] Similarly, the focus is on the percentage of H-1B and L-1 employees, so these employees will be counted even if their wages are paid through foreign payroll.[544]

The fee should be paid in a separate remittance, so "USCIS will be able to more quickly issue a refund, if it is later determined that the increased fee was not required."[545] The beneficiary should not pay this fee.[546] Before development of the current H-1B Data Collection and Filing Fee Exemption Supplement, USCIS advised petitioners to submit either the fee or evidence that the fee was not required,[547] in the form of:

---

[536] Consolidated Appropriations Act, 2016, Pub. L. No. 114-113 (Dec. 18, 2015).

[537] USCIS, "USCIS Implements H-1B and L-1 Fee Increase According to Public Law 111-230" (Aug. 19, 2010), AILA Doc. No. 10081920.

[538] USCIS, "H and L Filing Fees for Form I-129, Petition for a Nonimmigrant Worker," https://www.uscis.gov/forms/h-and-l-filing-fees-form-i-129-petition-nonimmigrant-worker.

[539] USCIS, "USCIS Implements H-1B and L-1 Fee Increase According to P.L. 111-230" (Oct. 7, 2010), AILA Doc. No. 10100767 (citing 8 CFR §214.2(h)(4)(ii)).

[540] "AILA Liaison Practice Tip: Determining Applicability of P.L. 111-230 Fees" (Dec. 8, 2010), AILA Doc. No. 10120861.

[541] USCIS, "Implementation of Provisions of Public Law 111-230 Instituting Increased Fees for Certain H-1B and L-1 Petitions and Applications," PM-602-0009.1 (Jan. 18, 2011), AILA Doc. No. 10100771.

[542] "USCIS Implements H-1B and L-1 Fee Increase According to P.L. 111-230" (Oct. 7, 2010), AILA Doc. No. 10100767 ("Only H-1B, L-1A, and L-1B employees are counted towards the 50% calculation").

[543] AFM 31.3(h).

[544] AFM 31.3(h); USCIS, "USCIS Implements H-1B and L-1 Fee Increase According to P.L. 111-230" (Oct. 7, 2010), AILA Doc. No. 10100767.

[545] USCIS, "Teleconference: Implementing Public Law 111-230" (Sept. 1, 2010), AILA Doc. No. 10090367; "USCIS Implements H-1B and L-1 Fee Increase According to P.L. 111-230" (Oct. 7, 2010), AILA Doc. No. 10100767.

[546] "USCIS Implements H-1B and L-1 Fee Increase According to P.L. 111-230" (Oct. 7, 2010), AILA Doc. No. 10100767.

[547] "USCIS Implements H-1B and L-1 Fee Increase According to Public Law 111-230" (Aug. 19, 2010), AILA Doc. No. 10081920.

Copyright © 2017. American Immigration Lawyers Association. All rights reserved.

- A cover letter noting "whether or not the fee is required in bold capital letters";[548]
- A "certification" statement on the cover letter;[549] and/or
- An addendum on the Form I-129 "if the petitioner has more than 50 employees … to state affirmatively whether the petitioner is or is not subject to the new fee rules,"[550] which did not need to be signed.[551]

However, USCIS later suggested that it "is not enough for the attestation to say the petitioner is exempt,"[552] and it seems that this "attestation" is the Supplement. USCIS then indicated that a statement from the attorney would be acceptable, as long as it "explains why the petitioner is exempt" and is accompanied by a valid Form G-28, Notice of Entry of Appearance as Attorney or Accredited Representative.[553]

It should be noted that an "RFE may be required even if such evidence is submitted, if questions remain."[554] The notation in capital letters may be placed below the cap information, discussed above. USCIS has not to date provided a list of evidence that would conclusively demonstrate the inapplicability of the fee, although it seems highly likely that USCIS will review the number of H-1B and L-1 petitions filed by the employer. The risk-averse client may wish to also include copies of Forms W-2s,[555] Forms I-797, annual reports, payroll statements, and/or a certified statement from an officer of the company. For discussion of RFEs for failure to pay the additional fee, see below.

a. Exemption from the ACWIA Fee for Certain Employers

The regulations note that four types of organizations are exempt from the ACWIA fee:

- Institutions of higher education;

---

[548] USCIS, "Teleconference: Implementing Public Law 111-230" (Sept. 1, 2010), AILA Doc. No. 10090367; "USCIS Implements H-1B and L-1 Fee Increase According to Public Law 111-230" (Aug. 19, 2010), AILA Doc. No. 10081920.

[549] "AILA/USCIS Liaison Practice Pointer: Understanding the New H & L Fee Imposed by Public Law 111-230," AILA Doc. No. 10082633. A sample certification would be: "[Name of employer] has over [insert total U.S. employees] in the United States, of whom fewer than [insert number or percent] are H-1B or L nonimmigrants. As such, [name of employer] is not subject to the additional fees required under P.L. 111-230."

[550] "AILA–SCOPS Q&A" (Aug. 25, 2010), AILA Doc. No. 10090230.

[551] "Q&A Stakeholder Conference" (Sept. 20, 2010, and updated Oct. 19, 2010), AILA Doc. No. 10101471.

[552] *Id.*

[553] *Id.*

[554] "USCIS Implements H-1B and L-1 Fee Increase According to Public Law 111-230" (Aug. 19, 2010), AILA Doc. No. 10081920.

[555] "Q&A Stakeholder Conference" (Sept. 20, 2010, and updated Oct. 19, 2010), AILA Doc. No. 10101471. Although Forms W-2 are acceptable specifically in the context of H-1B extensions, the principle should remain the same.

Copyright © 2017. American Immigration Lawyers Association. All rights reserved.

- Nonprofit organizations that are affiliated with or related to institutions of higher education;

- Nonprofit research organizations; and

- Governmental research organizations. [556]

The term "institution of higher education" is, in turn, defined as "an educational institution in any State that" meets the following conditions:

- "[A]dmits as regular students only persons having a certificate of graduation from a school providing secondary education, or the recognized equivalent of such a certificate;

- "[I]s legally authorized within such State to provide a program of education beyond secondary education;

- "[P]rovides an educational program for which the institution awards a bachelor's degree or provides not less than a 2-year program that is acceptable for full credit toward such a degree;

- "[I]s a public or other nonprofit institution; and

- "[I]s accredited by a nationally recognized accrediting agency or association, or if not so accredited, is an institution that has been granted preaccreditation status by such an agency or association that has been recognized by the Secretary for the granting of preaccreditation status, and the Secretary has determined that there is satisfactory assurance that the institution will meet the accreditation standards of such an agency or association within a reasonable time."[557]

A nonprofit entity is one that is tax exempt under section 501(c)(3), (4), or (6) of the IRC, and "has been approved as a tax exempt organization for research or educational purposes by the Internal Revenue Service."[558] A nonprofit entity is "related to or affiliated with" an institution of higher learning if one of the following applies:

- The two entities have shared ownership or control "by the same board or federation";

- The nonprofit is operated by the higher education institution;

- The nonprofit is "attached to" a higher education institution as a "member, branch, cooperative, or subsidiary"; or

- The nonprofit has "entered into a formal written affiliation agreement" with the higher education institution that "establishes an active working relationship between" the two entities "for the purposes of research or education, and a fundamental activity of the nonprofit entity is to directly

---

[556] 8 CFR §214.2(h)(19)(iii).

[557] Higher Education Act of 1965 §101(a), in accordance with 8 CFR §214.2(h)(19)(iii)(A).

[558] 8 CFR §214.2(h)(19)(iv).

Copyright © 2017. American Immigration Lawyers Association. All rights reserved.

contribute to the research or education mission of the institution of higher education."[559]

The fourth criterion for "related or affiliated" was added in a rulemaking finalized in 2016,[560] noting in the preamble to the proposed rule that the prior definition "does not sufficiently account for the nature and scope of common, bona fide affiliations between nonprofit entities and institutions of higher education.[561] See the section earlier in this chapter on exemptions from the numerical limitations for a more detailed discussion of the kinds of petitioners affected by this change.

As stated above, a nonprofit entity is one that is tax exempt under section 501(c)(3), (4), or (6) of the IRC, and "has been approved as a tax exempt organization for research or educational purposes by the Internal Revenue Service."[562] A nonprofit research organization is defined as "an organization that is primarily engaged in basic research and/or applied research." These types of research in turn are defined respectively as "general research to gain more comprehensive knowledge or understanding of the subject under study, without specific applications in mind," and "research to gain knowledge or understanding to determine the means by which a specific, recognized need may be met."[563]

A governmental research organization "is a federal, state, or local entity whose primary mission is the performance or promotion of basic research and/or applied research."[564] Basic and applied research for such organizations have the same definitions as for nonprofit entities, above.[565]

Prior to 2016, the regulatory definition of governmental was limited to the federal government.[566] However, in a rulemaking to make "program improvements affecting high-skilled nonimmigrant workers,"[567] USCIS accepted a commenter's argument that, because the "g" in the term "governmental" was not capitalized in the statute, the intent of Congress was to encompass state and local entities.[568]

b. Exemption from the ACWIA Fee in Certain Situations

As discussed above, the ACWIA fee must be paid, except if the petitioner has obtained at least one H-1B extension on behalf of the beneficiary. This means that the "second and subsequent" H-1B extensions will not require the fee, "regardless of when the first extension of stay was filed or whether the … fee was paid on the initial

---

[559] 8 CFR §214.2(h)(19)(iii).

[560] 80 Fed. Reg. 81900 (Dec. 31, 2015) (proposed rule), and 81 Fed. Reg. 82398 (Nov. 18, 2016) (final rule).

[561] 80 Fed. Reg. 81900, 81919 (Dec. 31, 2015).

[562] 8 CFR §214.2(h)(19)(iv).

[563] 8 CFR §214.2(h)(19)(iii)(C).

[564] *Id.*

[565] *Id.*

[566] Former 8 CFR §214.2(h)(19)(iii)(C) (2015).

[567] 80 Fed. Reg. 81900 (Dec. 31, 2015) (proposed rule), and 81 Fed. Reg. 82398 (Nov. 18, 2016) (final rule).

[568] 81 Fed. Reg. 82398, 82446-7 (Nov. 18, 2016).

Copyright © 2017. American Immigration Lawyers Association. All rights reserved.

petition or the first extension of stay."[569] The ACWIA fee is also unnecessary in the following situations:

- When filing "an amended H-1B petition that does not contain any requests for an extension of stay"; and

- When filing "an H-1B petition filed for the sole purpose of correcting a Service error."[570]

The H-1B petition must submit a statement describing why the ACWIA fee is not required to evidence that the petition is exempt "for one of the reasons described" above.[571] A nonprofit research organization must submit evidence of its tax-exempt status under IRC section 501(c)(3), (4), or (6).[572] The practitioner is strongly encouraged to include any other available supporting documents. For example, if the filing is necessary because USCIS erroneously truncated the validity period by what appeared to be the foreign national's passport expiration, then attention should be drawn to the error and to the previously submitted Form I-129 and the passport page showing extended validity.

G. Impact of Labor Disputes

An employer may not use the H-1B category to employ foreign nationals in the United States if the Secretary of Labor certifies or otherwise informs the Attorney General that "a strike or other labor dispute involving a work stoppage of workers is in progress in the occupation and at the place where the beneficiary is to be employed."[573] For definitions of the terms "strike" and "lockout," see above. If such a labor dispute is in progress and "the employment ... of the beneficiary would adversely affect the wages and working conditions of U.S. citizens and lawful resident workers," then the H petition "shall be denied."[574] If an H-1B petition has been approved already, but the foreign national "has not yet entered the United States, or has entered the United States but not yet commenced employment," then the petition approval "is automatically suspended, and the application for admission on the basis of the petition shall be denied."[575]

---

[569] 8 CFR §214.2(h)(19)(v)(C). The regulations call this fee a "filing fee," but the text refers to the additional fee required of all employers who are not exempt. It is referenced here as the ACWIA fee to avoid confusion with the actual filing fee.

[570] 8 CFR §§214.2(h)(19)(v)(A) and (B). The regulations call this fee a "filing fee," but the text refers to the additional fee required of all employers who are not exempt. It is referenced here as the ACWIA fee to avoid confusion with the actual filing fee.

[571] 8 CFR §214.2(h)(19)(vii)(B).

[572] Id.

[573] 8 CFR §214.2(h)(17)(i).

[574] Id.

[575] 8 CFR §214.2(h)(17)(i)(B).

Copyright © 2017. American Immigration Lawyers Association. All rights reserved.

USCIS adjudicators should be kept apprised of "current strike information."[576] USCIS may also inform the U.S. consulate, or port of entry to which cable notification of petition approval was sent, to respectively request "deferral of visa issuance, or revocation of the visa if already issued" or "action to place the alien in removal proceedings, permit withdrawal or defer inspection, as appropriate."[577]

The practitioner should note that the strike or labor dispute must be certified by the Secretary of Labor:[578] "If there is a strike or other labor dispute involving a work stoppage of workers in progress, but such strike or other labor dispute is not certified..., the Commissioner shall not deny a petition or suspend an approved petition."[579] Labor disputes also impact the employment of F-1 students with Optional Practical Training (OPT), as discussed below:

"Any employment authorization, whether or not part of an academic program, is automatically suspended upon certification ... that a strike or other labor dispute involving a work stoppage of workers is in progress in the occupation at the place of employment. As used in this paragraph, 'place of employment' means the facility or facilities where a labor dispute exists. The employer is prohibited from transferring F-1 students working at other facilities to the facility where the work stoppage is occurring."[580]

Moreover, a foreign national who engages in authorized H-1B employment and subsequently participates in the strike or labor dispute "shall not be deemed to be failing to maintain his or her status solely on account of past, present, or future participation in a strike or other labor dispute involving a work stoppage of workers," regardless of whether the strike or labor dispute has been certified by DOL.[581] The foreign national does, however, remain "subject to the following terms and conditions":

- The foreign national must comply with the terms and conditions of H-1B status stated in the statutes and regulations "in the same manner as all other H nonimmigrants";

- The foreign national's H-1B "status and authorized period of stay ... is not modified or extended in any way by virtue of his or her participation in a strike or other labor dispute involving a work stoppage of workers"; and

- The foreign national "will be subject to deportation" if he or she "violates his or her status or who remains in the United States after his or her authorized

---

[576] USCIS, "I-129 H-1B Standard Operating Procedures" (undated, posted July 26, 2007), AILA Doc. No. 07072668.

[577] AFM. 31.8.

[578] 8 CFR §214.2(h)(17)(i).

[579] 8 CFR §214.2(h)(17)(ii).

[580] 8 CFR §214.2(f)(14).

[581] 8 CFR §214.2(h)(17)(iii). Background on the rationale for these provisions was offered by legacy INS. 55 Fed. Reg. 2606 (Jan. 26, 1990) (internal citation omitted).

Copyright © 2017. American Immigration Lawyers Association. All rights reserved.

period of stay has expired," even though participation in a strike or labor dispute "will not constitute a ground for deportation."[582]

H. Exemption from Nonimmigrant Intent Requirement

By statute, the fact that a foreign national in H-1B status is the beneficiary of an immigrant visa petition "or has otherwise sought permanent residence in the United States shall not constitute evidence of an intention to abandon a foreign residence for purposes of obtaining a visa as a nonimmigrant ... or otherwise obtaining or maintaining the status of a nonimmigrant."[583] In 1970, Congress rescinded the requirement that the H-1 nonimmigrant "must be coming to a temporary position," although "both the petitioner and the beneficiary must intend that the employment be for a temporary period of time."[584] Then, in 1990, the condition that an H-1B nonimmigrant maintain a foreign residence was eliminated.[585]

An H-4 dependent also need not establish the maintenance of a residence abroad.[586] The foreign national must, however, have "obtained [H-1B] change of status ... before the alien's most recent departure from the United States"[587] in order for the exemption to apply during the visa application process, although this requirement should not pertain to a foreign national applying for an H-1B visa pursuant to consular notification.

In short, a foreign national may simultaneously pursue permanent residence while holding H-1B status. As stated by regulation:

> "The approval of a permanent labor certification or the filing of a preference petition for an alien shall not be a basis for denying an ... H-1B petition or a request to extend such a petition, or the alien's admission, change of status, or extension of stay. The alien may legitimately come to the United States for a temporary period as an ... H-1B nonimmigrant and depart voluntarily at the end of his or her authorized stay and, at the same time, lawfully seek to become a permanent resident of the United States."[588]

Therefore, an H-1B nonimmigrant may be a beneficiary of a labor certification application and/or immigrant visa petition without jeopardizing his or her ability to obtain H-1B extensions, visas, or admission to the United States.

---

[582] 8 CFR §214.2(h)(17)(iii).

[583] INA §214(h).

[584] AFM 31.1(b). The requirement was eliminated under the previous H-1 standard of "distinguished merit and ability."

[585] Immigration Act of 1990, Pub. L. No. 101-649, §205(e), 104 Stat. 4978 (Nov. 29, 1990). The section is titled "Removal of Foreign Residence Requirement for H-1 Nonimmigrants."

[586] 9 FAM 402.10-14(A).

[587] INA §214(h).

[588] 8 CFR §214.2(h)(16)(i).

Copyright © 2017. American Immigration Lawyers Association. All rights reserved.

Although H-1B1 nonimmigrants are not specifically included in these provisions,[589] the "temporary entry" standard is less stringent than the nonimmigrant intent required of B, H-2B, H-3, and J-1 nonimmigrants. The term "temporary entry" means "an entry into the United States without the intent to establish permanent residence."[590] The FAM provides the following direction to consular officers:

"You must be satisfied that the alien's proposed stay is temporary. A temporary period has a reasonable, finite end that does not equate to permanent residence. The circumstances surrounding an application should clearly and convincingly indicate that the alien's temporary work assignment in the United States will end predictably and that the alien will depart upon completion of the assignment. An intent to immigrate in the future, which is in no way connected to the proposed immediate trip, need not in itself result in a finding that the immediate trip is not temporary. An extended stay, even in terms of years, may be temporary, as long as there is no immediate intent to immigrate."[591]

This guidance is similar to DHS and DOS regulations on the temporary entry of TN nonimmigrants, as discussed in Volume 1: Chapter Fourteen, "TN Visas and Status." The main difference is that that the final two sentences explicitly state that neither an intent to immigrate nor extended periods of stay in H-1B status negate the temporary entry of H-1B1 nonimmigrants.[592] DOS guidance states that "a letter or contract of employment should be evidence that the employment is being offered on a temporary basis."[593]

When evaluating how long a foreign national may hold H-1B1 status, however, the standard is likely similar to the temporary entry of E-1 and E-2 nonimmigrants: "H-1B1 nonimmigrant professionals are admitted for a one-year period renewable indefinitely, provided the alien is able to demonstrate that he or she does not intend to remain or work permanently in the United States."[594] As discussed in Volume 1: Chapter Four, "E-1 and E-2 Visas and Status," a future intent to immigrate should be differentiated from a present intent to hold nonimmigrant status.

Also, it should be noted that the statute provides that nonimmigrant intent must be demonstrated at the time the foreign national applies for a visa at the consulate abroad and at the time of admission.[595] It does not, by the statutory terms, apply to a change of status or extension of stay request in the United States. Thus, experience has

---

[589] CBP, J. Ahern, "Free Trade Agreements with Chile and Singapore" (Apr. 19, 2004), AILA Doc. No. 05040166; USCIS, W. Yates, "Lifting of Numerical Cap on Mexican NAFTA Nonimmigrant Professionals ("TN") and Free Trade Agreements with Chile and Singapore" (Jan. 8, 2004), AILA Doc. No. 04030361.

[590] 9 FAM 402.10-5(F).

[591] *Id.*

[592] *Cf.* 8 CFR §214.6(b); 22 CFR §41.59(c).

[593] 9 FAM 402.10-5(F).

[594] 9 FAM 402.10-5(H); CBP, J. Ahern, "Free Trade Agreements with Chile and Singapore" (Apr. 19, 2004), AILA Doc. No. 05040166.

[595] INA §214(b).

Copyright © 2017. American Immigration Lawyers Association. All rights reserved.

shown that USCIS generally does not address nonimmigrant intent in adjudicating change or extension petitions to categories such as H-1B1. For further discussion of these issues, see Volume 1: Chapter Fourteen, "TN Visas and Status," and Volume 1: Chapter Four, "E-1 and E-2 Visas and Status."

I. H-4 Dependents

The H-4 dependent spouse and children of an H-1B nonimmigrant "are entitled to H nonimmigrant classification, subject to the same period of admission and limitations as the beneficiary, if they are accompanying or following to join the beneficiary in the United States."[596] In particular, "[b]rief periods of time when the principal alien is outside the United States (*e.g.*, on business) do not affect dependent status."[597] This is also true even if the principal H-1B nonimmigrant "is working pursuant to portability benefits,"[598] as discussed below. The practitioner should discuss with the client and/or beneficiary whether H-4 extensions should be filed concurrently with the H-1B portability petition, as this may be unnecessary if dependents will have valid H-4 status until they travel abroad and apply for new H-4 visas. One factor to consider is whether the dependents will apply for visas in their home country, as discussed in Volume 1: Chapter Two, "Basic Nonimmigrant Concepts." Also, it is important to track the dependents' authorized periods of stay, in addition to the H-1B principal's, to ensure that a difference in expiration dates does not cause them to fall out of status.

The authorized period of stay of H-4 dependents may be controlled or limited by USCIS, U.S. Customs and Border Protection (CBP), and/or DOS:

"USCIS may limit, deny or revoke on notice any stay for an H-4 dependent that is not primarily intended for the purpose of being with the principal worker in the United States, and a spouse or child may be required to show that his requested stay is not intended to evade the normal requirements of the nonimmigrant classification that otherwise would apply when the principal alien is absent from the United States.

"USCIS (as well as port inspectors and consular officers) may adjudicate applications for dependent stays in order to prevent an H-1B alien from using only occasional work visits to the United States in order to 'park' the family members in the United States for extended periods while the principal alien is normally absent.[599]

"If it appears that the dependent is not using or is not intending to use H-4 status primarily to accompany or follow to join the principal H-1B alien, such as a

---

[596] 8 CFR §214.2(h)(9)(iv); 9 FAM 402.10-14(A); AFM 31.2(d) ("Normal rules for maintenance of derivative status still apply such that the spouse or dependent may remain in the United States only for the purpose of unity with the principal worker").

[597] AFM 31.9.

[598] AFM 31.3(g)(11).

[599] AFM 31.2(d)(2).

Copyright © 2017. American Immigration Lawyers Association. All rights reserved.

situation in which the principal only is physically present or intends to be physically present in the United States for a small proportion of his or her period of H-1B admission and the dependents are using H-4 status to evade the limitations on or eligibility rules of the nonimmigrant options that otherwise would be available, then the H-4 extension of stay may be denied, limited or revoked on notice giving the H-4 the opportunity to provide evidence of the intention primarily to accompany the principal."[600]

"Note, an H-1B or L-1 worker who appropriately brings his or her family to the United States may from time to time be stationed temporarily outside the United States while leaving the family in the United States for purposes of continuity in schooling or similar arrangements."[601]

As noted below, physical presence in H-4 status is not counted toward the six-year time limitation of H-1B status.[602] However, if the principal nonimmigrant is granted H-1B recapture time, "then his or her H-4 dependents, if seeking extension of stay, should be given an extension of stay up to the new expiration of the H-1B alien's stay."[603] If the H-4 dependent seeks a change of status to H-1B, then "upon the switch, the new 'principal alien' would be subject to the H-1B cap if not independently exempt."[604] As discussed in Volume 1: Chapter Two, "Basic Nonimmigrant Concepts," change of status is generally available only if the foreign national properly maintained nonimmigrant status.[605] USCIS may also decide "whether the H-4 alien complied with the requirements of accompanying or joining the H-1B alien."[606]

H-4 dependents "may attend school and may individually be eligible for student status."[607] In many if not most cases, H-4 dependents may not "accept employment unless he or she is the beneficiary of an approved petition filed on his or her behalf and has been granted a nonimmigrant classification authorizing his or her

---

[600] AFM 31.3(g)(9)(B).

[601] USCIS, M. Aytes, "Guidance on Determining Periods of Admission for Aliens Previously in H-4 or L-2 Status; Aliens Applying for Additional Periods of Admission beyond the H-1B Six Year Maximum; and Aliens Who Have Not Exhausted the Six-Year Maximum But Who Have Been Absent from the United States for Over One Year" (Dec. 5, 2006), AILA Doc. No. 06122063, p. 3.

[602] 9 FAM 402.10-12.

[603] AFM 31.3(g)(9)(B) ("The status of an H-4 dependent of an H-1B nonimmigrant is subject to the same period of admission and limitations as the principal alien").

[604] USCIS, M. Aytes, "Guidance on Determining Periods of Admission for Aliens Previously in H-4 or L-2 Status; Aliens Applying for Additional Periods of Admission beyond the H-1B Six Year Maximum; and Aliens Who Have Not Exhausted the Six-Year Maximum But Who Have Been Absent from the United States for Over One Year" (Dec. 5, 2006), AILA Doc. No. 06122063, p. 3.

[605] Id.

[606] Id.

[607] AFM 31.9.

Copyright © 2017. American Immigration Lawyers Association. All rights reserved.

employment."[608] However, in 2015, USCIS amended its regulations to allow work authorization for H-4 spouses if the H-1B principal:

- Is the beneficiary of an approved Form I-140, Immigrant Petition for Alien Worker, or

- Is the subject of an extension of stay beyond the six-year limit under AC21 section 106(a) and (b), discussed below. Such an extension would be based on being the beneficiary of either a labor certification application or immigrant visa petition that was filed 365 days or more prior, and that has not been denied (or an adjustment of status or immigrant visa petition based on it has not been decided).[609]

To obtain an employment authorization document (EAD) in these circumstances, the spouse must submit Form I-765, Application for Employment Authorization, "accompanied by documentary evidence establishing eligibility."[610] This should include:

- A copy of the marriage license;

- A copy of the approval notice of the spouse's Form I-140, if the basis of eligibility is that the spouse is the beneficiary of an approved immigrant petition;

- A copy of the documentation showing that the labor certification application or petition was filed at least 365 days ago, if AC21 section 106 is the basis of eligibility, along with evidence such as I-797 approval notices and I-94s showing that the principal's H-1B status has been extended beyond six years;

- Proof that the H-1B and H-4 are currently in status, such as an approved I-797 approval notice or current I-94;

- A government-issued photo identification for the H-4 spouse, such as a copy of the biometric page of the passport;

- Several recent paystubs for the H-1B spouse, or an employment confirmation letter from the H-1B spouse's employer, to show continued employment in H-1B status; and

- Two 2x2 inch passportstyle color photographs of the H-4 spouse.[611]

If the EAD application is being filed concurrently with an I-129 petition for the principal's H-1B status and an I-539 application for the spouse's H-4 status, it should

---

[608] 8 CFR §214.2(h)(9)(iv); 9 FAM 402.10-14(c) (stating that H-4 status does not confer employment authorization incident to status, and that dependents are not authorized to accept employment "unless they qualify independently for a classification in which employment is, or can be, authorized").

[609] 8 CFR §214(h)(9)(iv).

[610] *Id.*

[611] USCIS, "Employment Authorization for Certain H-4 Dependent Spouses" (May 20, 2015), AILA Doc. No. 15052001, https://www.uscis.gov/working-united-states/temporary-workers/employment-authorization-certain-h-4-dependent-spouses. USCIS, "FAQs: Employment Authorization for Certain H-4 Dependent Spouses" (Feb. 2, 2017), AILA Doc. No. 15052062). *See also* 8 CFR §214(h)(9)(iv).

Copyright © 2017. American Immigration Lawyers Association. All rights reserved.

be filed where the I-129 is required to be filed, which, as discussed above, can vary depending on the circumstances.[612] If it is being filed just with an I-539 application to extend or change the dependent's status, or filed as a standalone without either an I-129 or I-539, it should be filed at either the Dallas Lockbox, if the principal's most recent approval notice number had an EAC or LIN prefix, or the Phoenix Lockbox, if the principal's most recent approval notice had a WAC prefix.[613]

The rulemaking that put in place this employment authorization provision was challenged in federal court, with the district court denying preliminary relief on the basis that the plaintiff failed to show irreparable harm.[614] At the time of this writing, the motion for preliminary injunction is on appeal to the circuit court, and the government had filed a motion requesting proceedings to be held in abeyance while it "reconsider(s) whether to revise the H-4 rule through notice-and-comment rulemaking."[615]

III. Common Issues

The following sections address interpretations and strategies for common situations and issues. Certain facts may trigger increased scrutiny by USCIS, and it may be helpful to manage client expectations and to prepare the client for RFEs by discussing these situations in greater detail.

A. Interrelationship Between F-1 and H-1B Status

This section will primarily discuss issues specific to H-1B petitions requesting change of status from F-1 on behalf of the beneficiary[616] because change of status from F-1 to H-1B is very common. Although F-1 international students should maintain nonimmigrant intent, the interrelationship between F-1 and H-1B status has evolved such that transitioning from a nonimmigrant student to a nonimmigrant worker is, in practice, common.

The foreign national beneficiary must maintain lawful F-1 status when the H-1B change of status petition is filed.[617] Unlike other nonimmigrant classifications, under which a foreign national is admitted for a period of time stated on the I-94 card, an F-1 nonimmigrant is generally "admitted for duration of status" (D/S), which "is defined as the time during which an F-1 student is pursuing a full course of study at

---

[612] USCIS, "Direct Filing Addresses for Form I-129, Petition for a Nonimmigrant Worker," https://www.uscis.gov/i-129-addresses. Filing addresses and locations change periodically, so it is important to check the USCIS website prior to filing.

[613] USCIS, "Direct Filing Addresses for Form I-765, Application for Employment Authorization," https://www.uscis.gov/i-765-addresses; USCIS, "Direct Filing Addresses for Form I-539," Application to Extend/Change Nonimmigrant Status," https://www.uscis.gov/i-539-addresses.

[614] *Save Jobs USA v. DHS*, No. 15-cv-615 (TSC) (D.D.C. 2015).

[615] *Save Jobs USA v. DHS*, No. 16-5287 (D.C. Cir.), "Defendant-Appellee's Motion to Hold Proceedings in Abeyance for Six Months (Apr. 3, 2017), AILA Doc. No. 15052675.

[616] For general guidance on F-1 nonimmigrant status, see 8 CFR §214.2(f).

[617] For discussion of maintaining lawful status for purposes of requesting change of status, see Volume 1: Chapter Two, "Basic Nonimmigrant Concepts."

Copyright © 2017. American Immigration Lawyers Association. All rights reserved.

an educational institution approved by the Service for attendance by foreign students, or engaging in authorized practical training following completion of studies."[618] Further discussion of D/S for students engaging in practical training is below. The term "full course of study" is, in turn, described as "leading to the attainment of a specific educational or professional objective."[619] Admission for D/S means that the foreign national need not "apply for extension of stay as long as the student is maintaining status and making normal progress toward completion of his or her educational objective."[620] Further, an "F-1 student who continues from one educational level to another is considered to be maintaining status, provided that the transition to the new educational level is accomplished according to transfer procedures" that are discussed in the regulations.[621]

In the event that the beneficiary has completed the requirements, but has not yet been formally awarded the degree, then the petition may include "a copy of the beneficiary's final transcript" or a statement "from the Registrar confirming that all of the degree requirements have been met."[622] Alternatively, the letter may "be signed by the person in charge of the educational records where the degree will be awarded," if the college or university "does not have a Registrar."[623] Experience has shown that the practitioner should be "wary of letters prepared by unauthorized employees at the school stating that the student has completed all requirements toward a degree, when in fact there are still examinations or papers to be completed" after the date the petition is to be submitted.[624]

Both F-1 and J-1 nonimmigrants may receive signing bonuses "before the validity date of the H-1B petition," because a "signing bonus does not represent a salary or reimbursement for services rendered and, as a result, may be accepted by the alien."[625] For discussion of change of status from J-1 to H-1B status,[626] see Volume 1: Chapter Ten, "J-1 Visas and Status."

If the H-1B petition is approved, but the change of status request is denied, then consular notification should be provided, even if the Form I-824, Application for Action on an Approved Application or Petition, is not filed.[627] Petitions filed

---

[618] 8 CFR §214.2(f)(5)(i). For explanation of the exception for "border commuter students," see 8 CFR §214.2(f)(18).

[619] 8 CFR §214.2(f)(6)(i). This section details the various types of educational programs which qualify as full courses of study.

[620] 8 CFR §214.2(f)(7)(i).

[621] 8 CFR §214.2(f)(5)(ii) (citing 8 CFR §214.2(f)(8)).

[622] USCIS, "Questions and Answers: USCIS to Accept H-1B Petitions for FY 2010 Beginning April 1, 2009" (Mar. 20, 2009), AILA Doc. No. 09032365.

[623] Id.

[624] "FY2018 H-1B Filing Tips and Resources" (Mar. 15, 2017), AILA Doc. No. 17031535.

[625] 65 Fed. Reg. 15178 (Mar. 21, 2000).

[626] 9 FAM 402.10-9(D); 22 CFR §41.53(f).

[627] USCIS, "I-129 H-1B Standard Operating Procedures" (undated, posted July 26, 2007), AILA Doc. No. 07072668.

Copyright © 2017. American Immigration Lawyers Association. All rights reserved.

requesting a change of status with an I-824 may be questioned, absent a reasonable explanation such as the potential for the beneficiary being outside the United States prior to adjudication.

1. Practical Training

Practical training allows a student to gain hands-on experience at a workplace to apply the theoretical principals learned during the educational program.[628] Therefore, employment authorization is granted for "a position that is directly related to [the student's] major area of study."[629] For discussion of the impact of labor disputes on employment pursuant to practical training, see above. Generally, an F-1 student may obtain employment authorization to pursue "practical training" after completing one academic year of study: "A student may be authorized 12 months of practical training, and becomes eligible for another 12 months of practical training when he or she changes to a higher educational level."[630] As discussed below, students in science, technology, engineering, or mathematics (STEM) fields are eligible for lengthier periods of practical training. The Form I-20 provided by the foreign national to the practitioner should reflect the grant of practical training.[631] An F-1 student enrolled "in [an] English language training program [is] ineligible for practical training."[632]

The two types of practical training should be differentiated. Essentially, an F-1 nonimmigrant may engage in Curricular Practical Training (CPT) while still attending school, whereas Optional Practical Training (OPT) is generally, although not necessarily, available after the student has completed the degree program.[633] In practice, most H-1B beneficiaries will have employment authorization pursuant to OPT and will be employed by the petitioner pursuant to OPT when the H-1B petition is filed.[634] The practitioner should note that both types of practical training are aggregated when calculating the total length of a student's employment

---

[628] ICE, "Student and Exchange Visitor Program and Designated School Officials of SEVP-Certified Schools with F-1 Students Eligible for or Pursuing Post-Completion Optional Practical Training" (Apr. 23, 2010), AILA Doc. No. 10042761 (superseding ICE, "Updates to Post-Completion Optional Practical Training" (Apr. 24, 2008), AILA Doc. No. 09040761). This document provides very good background on practical training in general.

[629] 8 CFR §214.2(f)(10).

[630] Id.

[631] 8 CFR §214.2(f)(1)(iii) (stating that "schools must issue a SEVIS Form I-20 to any current student requiring a reportable action (e.g., extension of status, practical training, and requests for employment authorization")).

[632] 8 CFR §214.2(f)(10).

[633] OPT may be used while the student is attending school. 8 CFR §214.2(f)(11)(i)(B)(1) ("Students may file a Form I-765 for pre-completion OPT up to 90 days before being enrolled for one full academic year, provided that the period of employment will not start prior to the completion of the full academic year").

[634] 73 Fed. Reg. 18944 (Apr. 8, 2008) ("Many employers who hire F-1 students under the OPT program eventually file a petition on the students' behalf for classification as an H-1B worker in a specialty occupation. If the student is maintaining his or her F-1 nonimmigrant status, the employer may also include a request to have the student's nonimmigrant status changed to H-1B").

Copyright © 2017. American Immigration Lawyers Association. All rights reserved.

authorization:[635] "If the student has not used any pre-completion OPT, then the student's post-completion OPT period could be up to 12 months."[636] For example, if the student obtained full-time CPT for seven months, then he or she would be eligible for a maximum of five months of OPT.

CPT "is defined to be alternative work/study, internship, cooperative education, or any other type of required internship or practicum that is offered by sponsoring employers through cooperative agreements with the school" and should be in the form of a "program that is an integral part of an established curriculum."[637] A graduate student may participate in CPT without having completed an academic year of study if the graduate program "require[s] immediate participation in curricular practical training."[638] The part-time or full-time employment authorization is documented in the Form I-20 endorsed by the school official.[639]

In contrast, OPT may be understood as free market employment, as long as the job is related to the student's educational program. The regulations reiterate that the OPT must be "directly related to the student's major area of study."[640] This may be demonstrated by a job description, as well as evidence of holding the position, "proof of the duration of that position, the job title, [and] contact information for the student's supervisor or manager."[641] Further: "If it is not clear from the job description that the work is related to the student's degree, Student and Exchange Visitor Program (SEVP) highly recommends that the student obtain a signed letter from the employer's hiring official, supervisor, or manager stating how the student's degree is related to the work performed."[642] An F-1 student may obtain OPT employment authorization during the following time periods:

- "During the student's annual vacation and at other times when school is not in session, if the student is currently enrolled, and is eligible for registration and intends to register for the next term or session;

- "While school is in session, provided that practical training does not exceed 20 hours a week while school is in session"; or

- After completing the educational program.[643]

---

[635] 8 CFR §214.2(f)(10)(i) ("Students who have received one year or more of full-time curricular practical training are ineligible for post-completion academic training").

[636] 73 Fed. Reg. 18944, 18946 (Apr. 8, 2008).

[637] 8 CFR §214.2(f)(10)(i).

[638] *Id.*

[639] 8 CFR §214.2(f)(10) ("A student may begin curricular practical training only after receiving his or her Form I-20 with the DSO endorsement") and 8 CFR §214.2(f)(10)(i)(B). *See also, generally*, 8 CFR §§214.2(f)(10)(i)(A) and (B).

[640] 8 CFR §214.2(f)(10)(ii)(A).

[641] ICE, "Policy Guidance 1004-03—Update to Optional Practical Training" (Apr. 23, 2010), AILA Doc. No. 10042761.

[642] *Id*

[643] 8 CFR §§214.2(f)(10)(ii)(A)(*1*)–(*3*).

Copyright © 2017. American Immigration Lawyers Association. All rights reserved.

If the student pursued a baccalaureate, graduate, or doctoral degree, then OPT is available once he or she has completed "all course requirements for the degree (excluding thesis or equivalent)."[644] Specifically: "Continued enrollment, for the school's administrative purposes, after all requirements for the degree have been met does not preclude eligibility for optional practical training."[645] OPT employment authorization "is automatically terminated when the student transfers to another school or begins study at another educational level."[646]

As noted above, F-1 nonimmigrants are admitted for duration of status. The regulations state:

"For a student with approved post-completion OPT, the duration of status is defined as the period beginning when the student's application for OPT was properly filed and pending approval, including the authorized period of post-completion OPT, and ending 60 days after the OPT employment authorization expires."[647]

Therefore, an F-1 student should have valid immigration status in the following circumstances:

- After he or she has completed an educational program, as long as an application for OPT has been properly filed and is pending approval;
- While he or she properly engages in OPT;
- For 60 days after the end date of the OPT employment authorization.

The F-1 student must apply to USCIS for employment authorization and "may not begin optional practical training until the date indicated on his or her employment authorization document, Form I-766."[648] An F-1 student may request OPT by filing Form I-765, Application for Employment Authorization, with USCIS as early as "90 days prior to his or her program end-date and no later than 60 days after his or her program end-date."[649] The Form I-765 must be filed "within 30 days of the date the DSO [Designated School Official] enters the recommendation for OPT into his or her SEVIS record,"[650] which, in turn, may not occur until after the school official has "ensure[d] that the student is eligible for the given type and period of OPT and that the student is aware of his or her responsibilities for maintaining status while on OPT."[651] In addition, the school official "must provide the student with a signed,

---

[644] 8 CFR §214.2(f)(10)(ii)(A)(3).

[645] Id.

[646] 8 CFR §214.2(f)(10)(ii)(B).

[647] 8 CFR §214.2(f)(10)(ii)(D).

[648] 8 CFR §214.2(f)(10)(ii)(A). For details on the procedure for applying for OPT, see 8 CFR §214.2(f)(11).

[649] 8 CFR §214.2(f)(11)(i)(B)(2). Previously, F-1 students were required to "apply for post-completion OPT prior to completing their course requirements," but this is no longer the case. 73 Fed. Reg. 18944, 18949-50 (Apr. 8, 2008).

[650] 8 CFR §214.2(f)(11)(i)(B)(2).

[651] 8 CFR §214.2(f)(11)(ii)(A).

Copyright © 2017. American Immigration Lawyers Association. All rights reserved.

dated Form I-20 indicating that OPT has been recommended."[652] USCIS should adjudicate the Form I-765 according to "the DSO's recommendation and other eligibility considerations,"[653] and provide notification of any reason(s) for denial,[654] which is not appealable.[655]

The requested start date of the OPT employment authorization must not be "more than 60 days after the student's program end date."[656] The F-1 student must not engage in employment before the approved OPT start date, which should be either "the date requested or the date the employment authorization is adjudicated, whichever is later."[657] OPT employment authorization "ends at the conclusion of the remaining time period of post-completion OPT eligibility,"[658] although extension is possible for certain students in STEM fields, as discussed below. While remaining in the United States pursuant to OPT employment, the F-1 nonimmigrant must "report any change of name or address, or interruption of such employment to the DSO for the duration of the optional practical training," and the school official should in turn update the Student and Exchange Visitor Information System (SEVIS) record with any changes "for the duration of the time that training is authorized."[659]

Importantly, an F-1 student should avoid periods of unemployment: "During post-completion OPT, F-1 status is dependent upon employment. Students may not accrue an aggregate of more than 90 days of unemployment during any post-completion OPT carried out under the initial post-completion OPT authorization."[660] As previously explained by USCIS:

"As status during OPT is based on the premise that the F-1 student is working, there must be a limit on unemployment, just as the F-1 student's period in school is based on the premise that he is actually pursuing a full-time course of study, and there are limits on how often the student can reduce his course load. An F-1 student who drops out of school or does not pursue a fulltime course of study loses status; an F-1 student with OPT who is unemployed for a significant period should similarly put his status in jeopardy.... In addition to clarifying the student's status,

---

[652] 8 CFR §214.2(f)(11)(ii)(C). Failure to file the I-765 with a properly dated DSO recommendation can result in loss of OPT.

[653] 8 CFR §214.2(f)(11)(iii).

[654] 8 CFR §214.2(f)(11)(iii)(B).

[655] 8 CFR §214.2(f)(11)(iii)(C).

[656] 8 CFR §214.2(f)(11)(i)(D).

[657] 8 CFR §§214.2(f)(11)(i)(D) and (f)(11)(iii)(A). The exception for STEM students is discussed below.

[658] 8 CFR §214.2(f)(11)(iii)(A).

[659] 8 CFR §214.2(f)(12)(i). For general guidance on reporting requirements and procedures, see 8 CFR §214.2(f)(17).

[660] 8 CFR §214.2(f)(10)(ii)(E). STEM students may have up to 150 days of unemployment, as discussed below.

Copyright © 2017. American Immigration Lawyers Association. All rights reserved.

this measure allows time for job searches or a break when switching employers."[661]

A student "who splits OPT time between two degrees at the same level" is eligible for an OPT unemployment period for each degree: "For each new period of post-completion OPT, the student will have the full 90-day period of unemployment."[662] In aggregating the unemployment period, every day in the OPT validity period that the student lacks "qualifying employment" is counted "as a day of unemployment."[663] A previous exclusion from the calculation for "periods of up to 10 days between the end of one job and the beginning of the next job" was removed in 2010.[664] As long as the foreign national holds qualifying employment, time spent in international travel, such as "during a period of leave authorized by an employer or traveling as part of his or her employment," should not count toward the unemployment day period.[665] A student may accrue a day of unemployment even while outside the United States, if he or she travels abroad "while unemployed" during the OPT validity period.[666]

Another critical consideration is that the F-1 student "must complete all practical training within a 14-month period following the completion of study."[667] This means that, in order for an F-1 student to have and use twelve months of OPT employment authorization, the employment authorization must be valid no later than exactly two months after the student completed the educational program. The one exception applies to students who will obtain a degree in a STEM field,[668] as discussed below. As noted above, if the student goes on to a higher level of education, he or she can be eligible for a second 12-month period of OPT.[669]

---

[661] 73 Fed. Reg. 18944, 18950 (Apr. 8, 2008).

[662] ICE, "Policy Guidance 1004-03—Update to Optional Practical Training" (Apr. 23, 2010), https://www.ice.gov/doclib/sevis/pdf/opt_policy_guidance_042010.pdf.

[663] Id.

[664] Id.

[665] Id.

[666] Id.

[667] 8 CFR §214.2(f)(10)(ii)(A)(3).

[668] Id.

[669] 8 CFR §214.2(f)(10).

Copyright © 2017. American Immigration Lawyers Association. All rights reserved.

OPT should also be distinguished from on-campus employment,[670] from employment authorization to engage in an internship with an international organization,[671] and from employment authorization granted pursuant to emergent circumstances,[672] such as severe economic hardship.[673]

a. "Cap-Gap" Relief

Certain F-1 students may now remain employed in the United States after expiration of the post-completion OPT period. Previously, H-1B beneficiaries often "would have a gap in authorized stay and employment ... commonly referred to as the 'cap-gap'" between the OPT expiration date and the earliest available H-1B petition start date of October 1.[674] As explained by USCIS:

"An F-1 student in a cap-gap situation would have to leave the United States and return at the time his or her H-1B status becomes effective at the beginning of the next fiscal year. This gap creates a hardship to a number of students and provides a disincentive to remaining in the United States for employment. The cap-gap therefore creates a recruiting obstacle for U.S. employers interested in obtaining F-1 students for employment and submitting H-1B petitions on their behalf. Moreover, when the student is already working for a U.S. company on OPT and has to leave the United States, frequently for several months, during the cap-gap period, the employer suffers a major disruption."[675]

The previous system required USCIS to publish notice in the Federal Register of any cap-gap relief,[676] in each fiscal year, and OPT employment authorization was not extended.[677] Although the F-1 nonimmigrant had an additional period of authorized stay during the "60-day departure preparation period," he or she could not engage in employment after the OPT expiration.[678] However, now a beneficiary of an H-1B change of status petition may be considered to have lawful status and continued employment authorization through the start of the new fiscal year pursuant to the previously granted OPT, even if the foreign national did not earn a STEM degree: "The duration of status, and any [OPT] employment authorization..., of an F-1 student who is the beneficiary of an H-1B petition and request for change of status shall be automatically extended until October 1 of the fiscal year for which such H-1B visa is being requested," provided the petition is timely filed and requests a

---

[670] For a general discussion of on-campus employment, *see* 8 CFR §214.2(f)(9)(i).

[671] 8 CFR §214.2(f)(9)(iii).

[672] 8 CFR §214.2(f)(9)(ii)(A).

[673] For discussion of employment authorization due to severe economic hardship, *see* 8 CFR §§214.2(f)(9)(ii)(D)–(F).

[674] 73 Fed. Reg. 18944 (Apr. 8, 2008).

[675] *Id.*

[676] *Id.*; 65 Fed. Reg. 15178 (Mar. 21, 2000).

[677] 65 Fed. Reg. 15178 (Mar. 21, 2000).

[678] 73 Fed. Reg. 18944 (Apr. 8, 2008).

Copyright © 2017. American Immigration Lawyers Association. All rights reserved.

start date of October 1 of the upcoming fiscal year.[679] DHS has noted that "the Cap-Gap provision applies only to the beneficiaries of H–1B petitions that are subject to the annual numerical cap."[680]

Importantly, the student's OPT employment authorization is also extended, as long as the OPT was valid when the H-1B change of status petition was filed.[681] U.S. Immigration and Customs Enforcement (ICE) indicates that "[b]ecause the cap-gap extension is automatic, the updated Form I-20 is not required for a student to continue working," although the document could "serve[] as proof of continued employment authorization."[682]

Conversely, both USCIS and ICE take the position that employment is not authorized during the cap-gap period in the absence of an EAD valid at the time of filing the H-1B petition, and that the cap-gap relief does not extend employment authorization.[683] Specifically, if the foreign national completed OPT and was in the 60-day grace period, then F-1 status would be extended, but not employment authorization, because "the cap gap does not serve to reinstate or retroactively grant employment authorization."[684] However, at least this approach means that the student should not be deemed to have failed to maintain lawful status by being unemployed during the cap-gap period.[685]

---

[679] 8 CFR §214.2(f)(5)(vi)(A) (citing 8 CFR §§274a.12(c)(3)(i)(B) and (C)). *See also* 73 Fed. Reg. 18944 (Apr. 8, 2008).

[680] 81 Fed. Reg. 13040, 13101 (Mar. 11, 2016).

[681] *Id.;* USCIS, "Supplemental Questions & Answers: Extension of Optional Training Program for Qualified Students" (May 23, 2008, AILA Doc. No. 08052760 ("In order for a student to have employment authorization during the cap gap extension, the student must be in an approved period of post-completion OPT on the eligibility date"); ICE, "Student and Exchange Visitor Program and Designated School Officials of SEVP-Certified Schools with F-1 Students Eligible for or Pursuing Post-Completion Optional Practical Training" (Apr. 23, 2010), AILA Doc. No. 10042761 (superseding ICE, "Updates to Post-Completion Optional Practical Training" (Apr. 24, 2008), AILA Doc. No. 09040761).

[682] ICE, "Fact Sheet: Information for Employers on the Cap-Gap Extension of Optional Practical Training" (Mar. 2009), AILA Doc. No. 09033161 ("If you employ an F-1 nonimmigrant student on post-completion optional practical training (OPT) and that student is the beneficiary of a pending or approved H-1B petition, the student may be able to continue working beyond the expiration date on his or her employment authorization document (EAD)").

[683] USCIS, "Extension of Post-Completion Optional Practical Training (OPT) and F-1 Status for Eligible Students under the H-1B Cap-Gap Regulations" (updated May 10, 2016), http://bit.ly/CapGapUSCIS; ICE, "Students: Determining STEM OPT Extension Eligibility," https://studyinthestates.dhs.gov/students-determining-stem-opt-extension-eligibility.

[684] USCIS, "Extension of Post-Completion Optional Practical Training (OPT) and F-1 Status for Eligible Students under the H-1B Cap-Gap Regulations" (updated May 10, 2016), http://bit.ly/CapGapUSCIS. *See also* ICE, "Students: Determining STEM OPT Extension Eligibility," https://studyinthestates.dhs.gov/students-determining-stem-opt-extension-eligibility.

[685] USCIS, "Extension of Post-Completion Optional Practical Training (OPT) and F-1 Status for Eligible Students under the H-1B Cap-Gap Regulations" (updated May 10, 2016), http://bit.ly/CapGapUSCIS.

Copyright © 2017. American Immigration Lawyers Association. All rights reserved.

This cap-gap relief is available without separate notification in the Federal Register, regardless of whether "the H-1B cap is likely to be reached prior to the end of the current fiscal year."[686] The following requirements must be met:

- The H-1B petition must have been "timely filed";[687]
- The H-1B petition must request a start date of "October 1 of the following fiscal year";[688] and
- The beneficiary did not "violate[] the terms and conditions of his or her nonimmigrant status,"[689] as discussed in Volume 1: Chapter Two, "Basic Nonimmigrant Concepts."

To obtain proof of work authorization during this period of automatic authorization, the foreign national will need provide to the DSO proof of the timely submission of the H-1B petition to obtain a new Form I-20 valid until June 1.[690] Then, if the petition is accepted for filing, the student will need to go back to the DSO with the filing receipt to obtain an updated I-120 form to show authorization to October 1. "Because the Cap-Gap extension is automatic, the updated Form I-120 is not required … it merely serves as proof of the extension of OPT employment authorization."[691]

The "automatic extension" of lawful nonimmigrant status "also applies to the duration of status of any F-2 dependent aliens."[692] If USCIS processing times for H-1B petitions considerably slows down, USCIS has, in the past, "prioritize[d] the adjudication of H-1B change of status cases for F-1 cap-gap students who are otherwise prohibited from continuing employment after September 30."[693]

The practitioner should note that this "automatic extension of an F-1 student's duration of status and employment authorization … shall immediately terminate upon the rejection, denial, or revocation of the H-1B petition filed on such F-1 student's behalf,"[694] as well as upon H-1B petition withdrawal.[695] Starting "on the date that the rejection, denial, or revocation letter is post marked," the foreign national should enter the 60-day grace period.[696] Alternatively, an eligible student may apply for a

---

[686] 73 Fed. Reg. 18944 (Apr. 8, 2008).

[687] 8 CFR §214.2(f)(5)(vi)(A)(1).

[688] 8 CFR §214.2(f)(5)(vi)(A)(2).

[689] 8 CFR §214.2(f)(5)(vi)(C) (citing 8 CFR §248).

[690] USCIS, "Extension of Post-Completion Optional Practical Training (OPT) and F-1 Status for Eligible Students under the H-1B Cap-Gap Regulations" (updated May 10, 2016), http://bit.ly/CapGapUSCIS.

[691] Id.

[692] 8 CFR §214.2(f)(5)(vi)(D).

[693] "USCIS Advises AILA on Priority Adjudication of H-1B Cap-Subject Cases" (updated Sept. 29, 2010), AILA Doc. No. 10092338.

[694] 8 CFR §214.2(f)(5)(vi)(B).

[695] USCIS, "Extension of Post-Completion Optional Practical Training (OPT) and F-1 Status for Eligible Students under the H-1B Cap-Gap Regulations" (updated May 10, 2016), http://bit.ly/CapGapUSCIS.

[696] Id.

Copyright © 2017. American Immigration Lawyers Association. All rights reserved.

STEM extension, discussed below, during the cap-gap extension period,[697] though the "application may not be made once the cap-gap extension period is terminated *(e.g.,* rejection, denial, or revocation of the H-1B petition), and the student enters the 60-day departure preparation period."[698]

However, "the 60-day grace period does not apply to an F-1 student whose accompanying change of status request is denied due to discovery of a status violation," though the practitioner should note that "[s]uch a student in any event is not eligible for the automatic cap gap extension."[699] Also, if "the H-1B petition is denied or revoked based on fraud, misrepresentation, or a status violation, the student is ineligible for the 60-day grace period and is required to leave the United States immediately."[700]

If a student has an approved change of status to H-1B, but loses his or her job before the petition's effective date, the student can continue in OPT under an existing, unexpired EAD, and will remain in F-1 status. It will be important to ensure that the employer submits a withdrawal of the petition to USCIS before the effective date of the change of status, to avoid having the H-1B status take effect and thus the student lose F-1 status. The student should provide the DSO with a copy of the USCIS acknowledgement of the withdrawal and revocation of the petition, so that the DSO can request a "fix" in SEVIS to prevent that system from showing the student as ceasing F-1 status on the H-1B petition's start date. "If USCIS does not receive the withdrawal request prior to the H-1B petition change of status effective date, then the student will need to stop working, file Form I-539, Application to Extend/Change Nonimmigrant Status, to request reinstatement, and wait until the reinstatement request is approved, before resuming employment.... If the student had to file Form I-539 to request reinstatement to F-1 student status, the student may not work or attend classes until the reinstatement is approved."[701]

Thus, if the H-1B revocation occurs before October 1, the student may continue working past October 1 while the data fix remains pending, provided the new employment is appropriate to the OPT field, the OPT period is still valid, and the DSO has requested the SEVIS fix. If the H-1B revocation occurs on or after October 1, the student will need to stop working immediately, apply for reinstatement, and wait until the reinstatement request is approved before resuming employment. In any event, the student would have the standard 60-day grace period to prepare for and depart the United States, unless the H-1B petition was revoked because of fraud or violation of status.[702]

b. International Travel During OPT

---

[697] *Id.*
[698] *Id.*
[699] *Id.*
[700] *Id.*
[701] *Id*
[702] *Id.*

Copyright © 2017. American Immigration Lawyers Association. All rights reserved.

A student engaging in "post-completion practical training" may be readmitted to the United States "to resume employment after a period of temporary absence," upon presenting the "EAD ... in combination with an I-20 ID endorsed for reentry by the DSO within the last six months."[703] The foreign national must also present a valid F-1 visa,[704] unless exempt from the visa requirement, as discussed in Volume 1: Chapter Two, "Basic Nonimmigrant Concepts." Unfortunately, it remains unclear whether the student must seek readmission in order to resume employment with the same employer. In a previous section, the regulations allow a student engaging in pre-completion OPT and with a valid EAD to "resume employment only if the student is readmitted to attend the same school which granted the employment authorization,"[705] so it is possible that a similar approach is taken to post-completion OPT.

A student who has obtained cap-gap relief should be readmitted to the United States in F-1 status if the change of status to H-1B has been approved, readmission is sought before the H-1B period of employment begins, and the student is "otherwise admissible."[706] As a practical matter, the student generally must have a valid F-1 visa stamp to be able to travel during the cap-gap period, as it may be problematic to obtain a new F-1 visa stamp from a U.S. consulate abroad with an approved H-1B petition. It is also very important that the student does not depart the United States while the H-1B change of status petition is still pending, as doing so will result in an abandonment of the change of status request and thus the cap-gap relief.

c. 24-Month OPT Extension for STEM Degree Students

In April 2008, DHS issued an interim final regulation to permit students in certain STEM fields to obtain OPT employment authorization for a total of 29 months—12 months plus an extension up to 17 months.[707] Although this rule was vacated in 2014 for lack of notice and comment,[708] the vacatur was stayed in 2015 to allow DHS time to conduct such notice and comment.[709] DHS then proposed a regulation, which it finalized in 2016, that expanded the potential OPT employment authorization period to a total of 36 months—12 months plus an extension of up to 24 months—and added some further conditions to the use of the extended OPT.[710] After promulgation of this final rule, the court dismissed the challenge to the rulemaking.[711]

---

[703] 8 CFR §214.2(f)(13)(ii); "Q&A Stakeholder Conference" (Sept. 20, 2010, and updated Oct. 19, 2010), AILA Doc. No. 10101471.

[704] *Id.*

[705] 8 CFR §214.2(f)(13)(i).

[706] USCIS, "Extension of Post-Completion Optional Practical Training (OPT) and F-1 Status for Eligible Students under the H-1B Cap-Gap Regulations" (updated May 10, 2016), http://bit.ly/CapGapUSCIS.

[707] 73 Fed. Reg. 18944 (Apr. 8, 2008); 8 CFR §214.2(f)(10)(ii)(C).

[708] *Washington Alliance of Technology Workers v. DHS*, 74 F. Supp. 3d 247 (D.D.C. 2014).

[709] *Washington Alliance of Technology Workers v. DHS*, 156 F. Supp. 3d 123 (D.D.C. 2015).

[710] 81 Fed, Reg. 13040 (Mar. 11, 2016); 8 CFR §214.2(f)(10)(ii)(C).

[711] *Washington Alliance of Technology Workers v. DHS*, No. 16-1170 (RBW) (D.D.C. Apr. 19, 2017).

Copyright © 2017. American Immigration Lawyers Association. All rights reserved.

As explained by USCIS at the time of the 2008 rulemaking:

"The inability of U.S. employers, in particular in the fields of science, technology, engineering and mathematics, to obtain H-1B status for highly skilled foreign students and foreign nonimmigrant workers has adversely affected the ability of U.S. employers to recruit and retain skilled workers and creates a competitive disadvantage for U.S. companies."[712]

The STEM OPT time is considered a "24-month extension,"[713] and is in addition to the usual 12 months of OPT following completion of all course requirements. A "thesis or equivalent" does not need to be completed prior to beginning OPT.[714] The employment must be for at least 20 hours per week to qualify.[715] The employer and student must have an employer-employee relationship, and volunteer work does not satisfy the employment requirements for OPT.[716]

Specifically, "a qualified student may apply for an extension of OPT while in a valid period of post-completion OPT," as long as certain requirements, discussed below, are satisfied. Upon completion of course requirements for a higher-level degree, the student may similarly "apply for a second 24-month extension of OPT while in a valid period of post-completion OPT."[717] However, "[i]n no event may a student be authorized for more than two lifetime STEM OPT extensions."[718] Students with 17-month extensions under the prior regulation generally were able to obtain another seven months under transitional rules, provided the conditions discussed below regarding 24-month extensions were met.[719] However, regardless of whether a student obtained an additional seven months or not, an extended OPT under the old rules counts as one OPT extension toward the lifetime limit of two STEM OPT extensions.[720]

A STEM field is one "included in the Department of Education's Classification of Instructional Programs taxonomy within the two-digit series … containing engineering, biological sciences, mathematics, and physical sciences, or a related field."[721] Related fields generally include those "involving research, innovation, or development of new technologies using engineering, mathematics, computer science,

---

[712] 73 Fed. Reg. 18944 (Apr. 8, 2008).

[713] 8 CFR §214.2(f)(10)(ii)(C) (titled "24-month extension of post-completion OPT for students with a science, technology, engineering, or mathematics (STEM) degree"); 8 CFR §214.2(f)(11)(iii)(A).

[714] 8 CFR §214.2(f)(10)(ii)(C); 81 Fed. Reg. 13040, 13072-3 (Mar. 11, 2016).

[715] 8 CFR §214.2(f)(10)(ii)(C)(8).

[716] 81 Fed. Reg. 13040 (Mar. 11, 2016).

[717] 8 CFR §214.2(f)(10)(ii)(C).

[718] *Id.*

[719] 8 CFR §214.16.

[720] 8 CFR §214.2(f)(10)(ii)(C).

[721] 8 CFR §214.2(f)(10)(ii)(C)(*2*)(i).

Copyright © 2017. American Immigration Lawyers Association. All rights reserved.

or natural sciences (including physical, biological, and agricultural sciences)."[722] The full and current list of qualifying degree fields is available online.[723]

As with standard OPT, the school official must recommend the grant of employment authorization. However, before recommending a 24-month OPT extension, the DSO must certify that the degree "being used to qualify that student…, as shown in SEVIS or official transcripts, is a bachelor's, master's, or doctorate degree with a degree code that is contained within a category on the current STEM Designated Degree Program List."[724] In addition, the school official "must ensure that the student is eligible for the given type and period of OPT and that the student is aware of his or her responsibilities for maintaining status while on OPT,"[725] as discussed below.

The STEM OPT can be based on a degree earned prior to the degree forming the basis for the current OPT, provided the prior degree:

- Was in a field that is on the STEM-qualified list at the time the DSO recommends the student for the 24-month extension;

- Was conferred "from a U.S. educational institution that is accredited and SEVP-certified at the time" the DSO recommends the student for the 24-month extension; and

- Was conferred no more than 10 years prior to the date the DSO recommends the student for the 24-month extension.[726]

All criteria for the prior degree must have been met for the STEM field to apply to the OPT for the more recent degree. This means that the exception mentioned above, whereby a "thesis or equivalent" is not required, does not apply to prior degrees.[727]

Like the requirement for a STEM OPT following the immediate degree, the employment in the OPT must be "directly related" to the STEM field for the prior degree. While DHS offers no definition for "directly related" in this context, the final rule's preamble does contemplate the common situation of a student who has earned an MBA after an earlier science or engineering degree:

"DHS also notes that the rule does expand the availability of STEM OPT extensions to certain STEM students with advanced degrees in non-STEM fields. Under the rule, a student who earns a STEM degree and then goes on to earn a non-STEM advanced degree, such as a Master of Business Administration

[722] Id.

[723] ICE, "STEM Designated Degree Program List" (May 10, 2016), AILA Doc. No. 16060702, https://www.ice.gov/sites/default/files/documents/Document/2016/stem-list.pdf.

[724] 8 CFR §214.2(f)(11)(ii)(A).

[725] Id.

[726] 8 CFR §214.2(f)(10)(ii)(C)(3).

[727] 81 Fed. Reg. 13040, 13073 (Mar. 11, 2016).

Copyright © 2017. American Immigration Lawyers Association. All rights reserved.

(MBA), may apply for a STEM OPT extension following the MBA so long as the practical training opportunity is directly related to the prior STEM degree."[728]

While this statement does not explicitly bless the situation where, for example, a student with a bachelor's degree in engineering followed by an MBA takes an OPT position involving business management of an engineering operation, the same rulemaking's preamble acknowledges in a different context that individuals in business positions can be engaged in STEM-related work:

> "A 2013 analysis from the Census Bureau found that more than one out of five U.S. STEM graduates who were not employed in a core STEM field were working in a managerial or business position utilizing quantitative skills developed through their STEM studies and often directly related to their degree."[729]

Before the DSO can recommend a 24-month extension, the student must complete, and have his or her employer complete, Form I-983, as discussed below.[730] As with the standard OPT, once the DSO recommends the OPT extension, he or she must give to the student a signed and dated Form I-20 indicating the recommendation. The student, in turn, submits the I-20 to USCIS along with a Form I-765 application for employment authorization "up to 90 days prior to the expiration date" of the current OPT EAD.[731] The EAD application must be filed within 60 days of when the DSO enters the recommendation for the OPT extension into SEVIS.[732] The EAD validity for the extension period "begins on the day after the expiration of the initial post-completion OPT employment authorization and ends 24 months thereafter, regardless of the date the actual extension is approved."[733] Employment authorization is automatically extended for up to 180 days if the Form I-765 requesting a STEM OPT extension was filed prior to the expiration of the prior EAD.[734] The automatic extension ends upon grant or denial of the EAD application.[735] An EAD denial is not appealable.[736]

During the STEM OPT, the student must report to the DSO for entry into SEVIS any change in legal name, residential or mailing address, employer name, employer address, or loss of employment within 10 days of the change.[737] In addition, the student must submit to the DSO a "validation report" confirming that this information has not changed every six months starting on the date the 24-month extension

---

[728] 81 Fed. Reg. 13040, 13074 (Mar. 11, 2016).

[729] 81 Fed. Reg. 13040, 13053 (Mar. 11, 2016).

[730] 8 CFR §214.2(f)(10)(ii)(C)(7)(i).

[731] 8 CFR §214.2(f)(11)(i)(C).

[732] *Id.*

[733] 8 CFR §214.2(f)(11)(iii)(A).

[734] 8 CFR §274a.12(b)(6)(iv).

[735] *Id.*

[736] 8 CFR §214.2(f)(11)(iii)(C).

[737] 8 CFR §214.2(f)(12)(ii)(A).

Copyright © 2017. American Immigration Lawyers Association. All rights reserved.

begins.[738] Further, the student is required to submit, "within 12 months of the approved starting date" on the EAD granted in connection with the 24-month OPT extension application, an initial self-evaluation of his or her progress toward the training goals discussed below.[739] A final evaluation also must be submitted within 10 days of the conclusion of the employment or reporting period. The employer must sign each self-evaluation "to attest to its accuracy."[740]

Employers of students granted STEM OPT must also comply with certain requirements. First, the employer must be enrolled in E-Verify. Registration with USCIS's E-Verify program may be established by providing "a valid E-Verify company identification number,"[741] to be placed on the Form I-765,[742] as discussed below. Alternatively, if a designated agent "perform[s] the E-Verify queries" on behalf of the employer, then "a valid E-Verify client company identification number" may be provided.[743]

Second, the employer must sign Form I-983, Training Plan for STEM OPT Students,[744] whereby it certifies that it:

- Will report within five business days to the DSO any termination or departure of the student prior to the end of the authorized OPT period. The student is considered to have departed if he or she leaves the employer or fails to report without the employer's consent for five consecutive business days;[745]

- Will adhere to the training plan on the form, as discussed below;[746]

- Has "sufficient resources and personnel available and is prepared to provide adequate training" at the location of the OPT;[747]

- Will not use the student to replace a U.S. worker, be it full– or part-time, temporary or permanent;[748]

---

[738] 8 CFR §214.2(f)(12)(ii)(B).

[739] 8 CFR §214.2(f)(10)(iii)(C)(9)(i).

[740] Id.

[741] 8 CFR §214.2(f)(10)(ii)(C)(5). The regulation refers to "a participant in good standing with E-Verify, as determined by USCIS," which is not defined either by regulation or in the "E-Verify User Manual" (Aug. 1, 2016), AILA Doc. No. 16110301.

[742] USCIS, "Form I-765, Application for Employment Authorization" (exp. Feb. 28, 2019), https://www.uscis.gov/i-765.

[743] 8 CFR §214.2(f)(10)(ii)(C)(5).

[744] ICE, "Form I-983, Training Plan for STEM OPT Students" (exp. Mar. 31, 2019), https://www.ice.gov/sites/default/files/documents/Document/2016/i983.pdf.

[745] 8 CFR §214.2(f)(10)(ii)(C)(6).

[746] 8 CFR §214.2(f)(10)(ii)(C)(7)(i).

[747] 8 CFR §214.2(f)(10)(ii)(C)(10)(i).

[748] 8 CFR §214.2(f)(10)(ii)(C)(10)(ii).

Copyright © 2017. American Immigration Lawyers Association. All rights reserved.

- Ensure that the "opportunity assists the student in reaching" the training goals[749] and that the position is directly related to the qualifying STEM degree;[750]

- Will provide terms and conditions, including duties, hours, and compensation, that are commensurate with those provided to its "similarly situated U.S. workers in the area of employment," and, if it does not employ and has not recently employed more than two such workers, it will provide terms and conditions commensurate with "similarly situated" U.S. workers—*i.e.*, workers with similar duties, supervision, responsibility, education, experience, and skills—in the area of employment;[751] and

- Will notify the DSO of any material changes, via a modified Form I-983, such as a change in the employer's FEIN, a reduction in compensation "not tied to a reduction in hours," any "significant decrease in hours per week," a decrease in hours below the minimum requirement of 20, and "any change or deviation that renders an employer attestation inaccurate or renders inaccurate the information in the Form I-983 … on the nature, purpose, oversight or assessment" of the OPT.[752]

The training plan must be described on the Form I-983, and incorporate the goals for the training, including "specific knowledge, skills, or techniques that will be imparted."[753] The plan should explain how the goals will be achieved, describe the performance evaluation process and the methods for supervision and oversight, and reveal how the training directly relates to the qualifying STEM degree.[754] Employers may rely on their existing programs to meet the evaluation and supervision requirements,[755] and "employers may use their existing training programs for STEM OPT students, so long as the existing training program meets" the requirements of the regulation.[756]

DHS reserves the right to conduct an employer site visit, upon 48 hours' notice, to ensure that it "possesses and maintains the ability and resources to provide structured and guided work-based learning experiences" as described on the Form I-983. No notice is provided if the visit "is triggered by a complaint or other evidence of noncompliance."[757]

---

[749] 8 CFR §214.2(f)(10)(ii)(C)(*10*)(*iii*).

[750] ICE, "Form I-983, Training Plan for STEM OPT Students" (exp. Mar. 31, 2019), https://www.ice.gov/sites/default/files/documents/Document/2016/i983.pdf.

[751] 8 CFR §214.2(f)(10)(ii)(C)(*8*).

[752] 8 CFR §214.2(f)(10)(ii)(C)(*9*)(*ii*).

[753] 8 CFR §214.2(f)(10)(ii)(C)(*7*)(*ii*).

[754] 8 CFR §214.2(f)(10)(ii)(C)(*7*)(*ii*) and (*iii*).

[755] 8 CFR §214.2(f)(10)(ii)(C)(*7*)(*ii*).

[756] 81 Fed. Reg. 13040, 13090 (Mar. 11, 2016).

[757] 8 CFR §214.2(f)(10)(ii)(C)(*11*).

Copyright © 2017. American Immigration Lawyers Association. All rights reserved.

If the student changes employers, a new Form I-983 must be completed with the new employer and submitted to the DSO within 10 days of starting the new employment.[758]

As with regular OPT, long periods of unemployment should be avoided to the extent possible, as a STEM student "granted a 24-month OPT extension ... may not accrue an aggregate of more than 150 days of unemployment during a total OPT period, including any post-completion OPT period ... and any subsequent 24-month extension period."[759] STEM OPT "is automatically terminated" if the student enters a new educational program or transfers schools.[760] For further discussion of this issue, see above.

2. Strategies If the H-1B Petition Is Rejected or Denied

When the demand for H-1B visa numbers is high, which occurs most years,[761] it is possible and sometimes highly likely, that an individual H-1B petition will not be approved, whether on the merits or because it was not selected during the lottery, as discussed above. A denied H-1B petition may be appealed, although the denial of a change of status request is not appealable, as discussed in Volume 1: Chapter Two, "Basic Nonimmigrant Concepts."

However, the practitioner should take care to caution the client and/or the beneficiary that USCIS's use of a lottery system to select H-1B petitions that will be awarded H-1B visa numbers means that an H-1B petition may be unsuccessful at random. The most deserving beneficiary may learn that the H-1B petition filed on his or her behalf was not approved for reasons outside the merits of the petition. In these situations, the practitioner may wish to discuss the following strategies:

- The foreign national may depart the United States;
- The foreign national may enroll in a higher degree educational program;
- The foreign national may request change of status to another nonimmigrant classification, as discussed in Volume 1: Chapter Two, "Basic Nonimmigrant Concepts";[762] or
- If eligible, the foreign national may request a STEM OPT extension, as discussed above, as long as the STEM extension is requested before "the cap-gap extension period is terminated (e.g., rejection, denial, or revocation of the

---

[758] 8 CFR §214.2(f)(10)(ii)(C)(7)(*iv*).

[759] 8 CFR §214.2(f)(10)(ii)(E).

[760] 8 CFR §214.2(f)(10)(ii)(B).

[761] "H-1B Cap Count History" (Apr. 13, 2016), AILA Doc. No. 15120404.

[762] 73 Fed. Reg. 18944 (Apr. 8, 2008) ("Once an F–1 student has completed his or her course of study, and any authorized practical training following completion of studies, the student must either transfer to another SEVP-certified school to continue studies, change to a different nonimmigrant status, otherwise legally extend their period of authorized stay in the United States, or leave the United States" (citing 8 CFR §214.2(f)(5)(iv))).

Copyright © 2017. American Immigration Lawyers Association. All rights reserved.

H-1B petition), and the student enters the 60-day departure preparation period."[763]

After exhausting any OPT time available upon completing the F-1 course of study, an F-1 nonimmigrant is "allowed an additional 60-day period to prepare for departure from the United States."[764] The following is an example sequence of events set during a fiscal year with high demand for H-1B visa numbers:[765]

- May 1, 2015: the F-1 nonimmigrant completes his or her educational program;

- May 2, 2015 through May 1, 2016: the F-1 nonimmigrant engages in OPT;

- April 1, 2016: the employer files an H-1B petition on behalf of the beneficiary;[766]

- May 6, 2016: the H-1B petition is rejected in the lottery;[767] and

- July 5, 2016: the foreign national departs the United States.[768]

The regulations do not prohibit an employer from filing an H-1B petition on behalf of a foreign national before the beneficiary has been employed by the petitioner. Therefore, unlike H-1B change of employer petitions, discussed below, there is no regulatory requirement that the beneficiary of an H-1B change of status petition be employed by the petitioner when the H-1B petition is filed. Therefore, an F-1 student could be the beneficiary of an H-1B petition, even if he or she is still attending school, as long as the beneficiary has completed all requirements toward a qualifying degree at the time of filing.

However, the practitioner should note that the H-1B petition must include evidence that the beneficiary qualifies for the specialty occupation through possession of at least a bachelor's degree in a field that is related to the profession, as discussed above. In addition, as a practical matter, this situation is not common since many employers seem to prefer seeing how an individual fits with the organization and/or the foreign national's work product/ethic. An employer that is proactive in filing H-1B petitions and that chooses to take the risk of filing an H-1B petition with a school letter may encounter the following sequence of events:[769]

---

[763] USCIS, "Questions and Answers: Extension of Post Completion Practical Training and F-1 Status for Eligible Students under the Cap Gap Regulations" (Apr. 1, 2009), AILA Doc. No. 09040236.

[764] 8 CFR §214.2(f)(5)(iv).

[765] If demand for H-1B visa numbers is not high, then the employer should not need to file an H-1B petition during the first available week of the fiscal year, as discussed above.

[766] This example is based on the assumption that the petitioner is proactive and files the H-1B petition on the first allowable day, as discussed above.

[767] Experience has shown that notification of H-1B petitions rejected in the lottery is provided between two and eight weeks after the one-week receipt period; this date allows exactly four weeks for the notification.

[768] This date is exactly 60 days after the H-1B petition rejection date and, therefore, the last day of the 60-day departure period.

[769] This example assumes the same facts as the previous example.

Copyright © 2017. American Immigration Lawyers Association. All rights reserved.

- April 1, 2015: the employer files an H-1B petition on behalf of the beneficiary;

- May 1, 2015: the F-1 nonimmigrant completes his or her educational program;

- May 2, 2015 through May 1, 2016: the F-1 nonimmigrant engages in OPT;

- May 6, 2016: the employer receives notification that the H-1B petition was not selected in the lottery through return of the unselected H-1B petition; and

- June 30, 2016: the foreign national departs the United States.

Alternatively, the F-1 nonimmigrant may transfer to a higher degree program during the 60-day grace period.[770] As noted above, a foreign national who properly transfers educational institutions should be considered to be maintaining F-1 status.[771] The chief caveats, however, are that:

"[A]n F-1 student is not permitted to remain in the United States when transferring between schools or programs unless the student will begin classes at the transfer school or program within 5 months of transferring out of the current school or within 5 months of the program completion date on his or her current Form I-20, whichever is earlier. In the case of an F-1 student authorized to engage in post-completion optional practical training (OPT), the student must be able resume classes within 5 months of transferring out of the school that recommended OPT or the date the OPT authorization ends, whichever is earlier."[772]

Therefore, if the H-1B change of status petition was denied more than five months after the beneficiary's OPT expired, then the foreign national is ineligible to transfer schools or programs.[773] Further, a beneficiary who did not "pursu[e] a full course of study at the school he or she was last authorized to attend is ineligible for school transfer and must apply for reinstatement … or, in the alternative, may depart the country and return as an initial entry in a new F-1 nonimmigrant status."[774] Unfortunately, although the regulations permit a student to register for "a reduced course load in the student's final term, semester, or session if fewer courses are needed to complete the course of study," they seem to indicate that such a reduced course load during the final term does not qualify as a full course of study:

---

[770] 8 CFR §214.2(f)(5)(iv) (stating that an "F-1 student who has completed a course of study and any authorized practical training following completion of studies will be allowed an additional 60-day period … to transfer" schools and/or programs) (citing 8 CFR §214.2(f)(8)). General transfer requirements are discussed in 8 CFR §§214.2(f)(8)(ii) and (iii).

[771] 8 CFR §214.2(f)(5)(ii) (citing 8 CFR §214.2(f)(8)). General transfer requirements are discussed in 8 CFR §§214.2(f)(8)(ii) and (iii).

[772] 8 CFR §214.2(f)(8)(i).

[773] 8 CFR §214.2(f)(8)(i) read in conjunction with 8 CFR §214.2(f)(5)(ii) (terming a "[c]hange in educational levels" as a transfer).

[774] 8 CFR §214.2(f)(8)(i). For discussion of reinstatement procedures, see 8 CFR §214.2(f)(16).

Copyright © 2017. American Immigration Lawyers Association. All rights reserved.

"If the student is not required to take any additional courses to satisfy the requirements for completion, but continues to be enrolled for administrative purposes, the student is considered to have completed the course of study and must take action to maintain status. Such action may include application for change of status or departure from the United States."[775]

B. H-1B Portability

A change of employer petition (COE) may be filed on behalf of a foreign national who already holds H-1B status in the United States:

"If the alien is in the United States and seeks to change employers, the prospective new employer must file a petition on Form I-129 requesting classification and an extension of the alien's stay in the United States. If the new petition is approved, the extension of stay may be granted for the validity of the approved petition."[776]

Similarly, a petition for concurrent employment may be filed for "new employment with an additional employer in the same nonimmigrant classification the beneficiary currently holds while the beneficiary will continue working for his or her current employer in the same classification."[777]

Although a foreign national typically may not begin working until an H-1B petition is approved by USCIS, the general rule does not apply if he or she was "previously ... provided [H-1B] status" and seeks to work for a new H-1B employer.[778] H-1B status may be ported, which means that a foreign national "who was previously issued a visa or otherwise provided [H-1B] nonimmigrant status ... is authorized to accept new employment upon the filing by the prospective employer of a new petition on behalf of such nonimmigrant."[779] The beneficiary of the new H-1B petition will continue to have valid employment authorization to work for the new petitioner, including a concurrent petitioner, "until the new petition is adjudicated," although the employment authorization will terminate in the event that "the new petition is denied."[780] The following conditions must be satisfied:

- The foreign national "has been lawfully admitted into the United States";

- The foreign national is the beneficiary of "a nonfrivolous petition for new employment" that is filed "before the date of expiration of the period of stay authorized by the Attorney General"; and

---

[775] 8 CFR §214.2(f)(6)(iii)(C).

[776] 8 CFR §214.2(h)(2)(i)(D).

[777] USCIS, "Instructions for Petition for Nonimmigrant Worker" (exp. Dec. 31, 2018), https://www.uscis.gov/sites/default/files/files/form/i-129instr.pdf.

[778] INA §214(n)(1).

[779] INA §214(n)(1); American Competitiveness in the Twenty-First Century Act of 2000, Pub. L. No. 106-313 (AC21), §105(a) (Oct. 17, 2000).

[780] Id.; See also 8 CFR§214.2(h)(2)(i)(H)(2).

Copyright © 2017. American Immigration Lawyers Association. All rights reserved.

- The foreign national did not engage in any unauthorized employment after being lawfully admitted to the United States and before the new H-1B petition is filed.[781]

Essentially, the beneficiary may either await USCIS approval of the H-1B COE or concurrent petition or may port his or her H-1B employment authorization[782] and begin working for the new H-1B employer with proof of filing. In practice, rather than wait several months for petition approval, many foreign nationals port their H-1B employment authorization after the concurrent or COE petition is filed.

USCIS regulations add the proviso that authorization to start the new or concurrent employment begins upon filing of the non-frivolous petition or "as of the requested start date, *whichever is later.*"[783] Thus, it is important when seeking to start the new employment immediately that the petition and the underlying LCA request a start date that is no later than the date of filing.

The proof of filing may be in the form of the Form I-797 receipt notice from USCIS or the delivery confirmation. Generally, the Form I-797 is more authoritative evidence that USCIS received the petition, but it does take up to several weeks to be delivered. Although use of the delivery confirmation is not foreclosed by any available guidance, the more risk-averse client may wish to wait for the Form I-797. This is because "while proof of delivery by Federal Express confirms that the petition has been delivered to USCIS, it does NOT guarantee that the petition has been accepted for processing."[784] Alternatively, urgent business reasons may necessitate use of the delivery confirmation, which is typically available on the day of delivery.

In 2016, USCIS issued regulations that addressed a number of subjects regarding high-skilled workers, including many issues that had arisen over the years with respect to AC21.[785] While previous guidance had indicated that portability does not require "that the alien currently be in H-1B status as long as he or she is in a 'period of stay authorized by the Attorney General,'"[786] USCIS in its 2016 rulemaking insisted that it had not taken such a position.[787] Instead, it indicated that "to be

---

[781] INA §214(n)(1); AC21 §105; 8 CFR§214.2(h)(2)(i)(H)(*1*).

[782] 8 CFR §214.2(h)(2)(i)(D) ("Except as provided by 8 CFR 274a.12(b)(21) or section 214(n) of the Act, 8 U.S.C. 1184(n), the alien is not authorized to begin the employment with the new petitioner until the petition is approved").

[783] 8 CFR §214.2(2)(i)(H) (emphasis added).

[784] "AILA/VSC Liaison Committee Practice Pointer: Clarification on Revocation of H-1B Status and Non-immigrant Status" (Feb. 19, 2009), AILA Doc. No. 09021960 (emphasis in original).

[785] 81 Fed. Reg. 82398 (Nov. 18, 2016).

[786] USCIS, W. Yates, "Interim Guidance for Processing Form I-140 Employment-Based Immigrant Petitions and Form I-485 and H-1B Petitions Affected by the American Competitiveness in the Twenty-First Century Act of 2000 (AC21) (Public Law 106-313)" (May 12, 2005), AILA Doc. No. 05051810.

[787] 81 Fed. Reg. 82398, 82440 (Nov. 18, 2016). "USCIS has long interpreted INA 214(n) as allowing only those nonimmigrants who are currently in H-1B status, or in a period of authorized stay as a result of a timely filed H-1B extension petition, to begin employment upon the filing by prospective employers of new H-1B portability petitions on the nonimmigrants' behalf.", citing USCIS, M. Aytes,

Cont'd

Copyright © 2017. American Immigration Lawyers Association. All rights reserved.

eligible for H-1B portability the new H-1B petition must have been filed while the foreign worker is in H-1B status or is in a period of authorized stay based on a timely filed H-1B extension petition,"[788] and that "H-1B portability does not apply to a nonimmigrant who is in a valid status other than H-1B."[789]

As discussed in Volume 1: Chapter Two, "Basic Nonimmigrant Concepts," the foreign national bears the burden of proof to establish admissibility.[790] H-1B portability extension requests, like all H-1B extension requests, "must conform to the limits on the alien's temporary stay," which means that the foreign national may be accorded no more than six total years of physical presence in the United States in H-1B status,[791] except as discussed later in this chapter. After approval of an H-1B change of employer petition, the beneficiary does not need a new visa annotated with the name of the new H-1B employer. A foreign national may apply for U.S. admission with the H-1B visa issued pursuant to the previous H-1B employment.[792] The beneficiary "must present the new Form I-797, Notice of Action, evidencing the approval of the change of employer in addition to the visa."[793]

a. Porting While the Beneficiary Is Unemployed

Prior to the 2016 regulations, it was ambiguous at best whether an H-1B nonimmigrant whose employment had ceased prior to the filing of the new petition could begin the new employment upon filing.[794] The 2016 regulations added a grace period, discussed in more detail later in this chapter, enabling an H-1B nonimmigrant whose employment ends prior to the expiration of the current authorized stay to remain in the United States lawfully for the shorter of 60 days or when his or her existing validity period ends.

The new regulatory grace period seems to have addressed this ambiguity, albeit not overtly. Neither the regulatory provisions themselves, nor the preambles to the proposed or final rules, directly addresses the question of whether an H-1B in the 60-

---

"Interim guidance for processing I–140 employment-based immigrant petitions and I–485 and H–1B petitions affected by the American Competitiveness in the Twenty-First Century Act (AC21) (Public Law 106–313)'' (Dec. 27, 2005), AILA Doc. No. 06092763. The cited memo gives the example of the period of stay resulting from a timely extension application, but goes on to say "In other words, porting under INA §214 does not require that the alien currently be in H-1B status as long as he or she is in a 'period of stay authorized by the Attorney General.'"

[788] 81 Fed. Reg. 82398, 82439 (Nov. 18, 2016).

[789] 81 Fed. Reg. 82398, 82440. (Nov. 18, 2016).

[790] USCIS, M. Pearson, "Interim Guidance for Processing H-1B Applicants for Admission as Affected by the American Competitiveness in the Twenty-first Century Act of 2000, Public Law 106-313" (Jan. 19, 2001), AILA Doc. No. 01020802.

[791] 8 CFR §214.2(h)(2)(i)(D).

[792] 9 FAM 402.10-11(C).

[793] Id.

[794] "AILA/VSC Liaison Committee Practice Pointer: VSC Liaison Committee Discusses the VSC's Clarification of Revocation of H-1B Status and Non-immigrant Status" (Feb. 20, 2009), AILA Doc. No. 09022076.

Copyright © 2017. American Immigration Lawyers Association. All rights reserved.

day grace period can take advantage of portability. The preambles to both the proposed and final rules repeat multiple times that "the alien may not work" during the grace period,[795] though never in the context of the portability provision. The regulatory provision itself also uses that language, but contains the caveat "[u]nless authorized under 8 CFR 274a.12."[796] That section, in turn, states that "[i]n the case of a nonimmigrant with H-1B status, employment authorization will automatically continue upon the filing of a qualifying petition under [the portability provision] until such petition is adjudicated."[797]

The issue then turns on whether a nonimmigrant in the 60-day grace period is someone "with H-1B status." Again, the rulemaking does not overtly state that nonimmigrants in the grace period continue to hold their status, instead stating that they "shall not be considered to have failed to maintain nonimmigrant status solely on the basis of a cessation of the employment on which the alien's classification was based."[798] But, since there is no other status they would have during that period, it seems that the nonimmigrant status would continue for the grace period's duration. Moreover, the time spent by the foreign national in the grace period very likely would be counted against his or her maximum six-year stay in H-1B status, lending further support to the position that he or she is in H-1B status during the grace period.

If the interplay between those two sections does not confirm that portability applies during the grace period, the conditions of portability should do so. As noted above, the nonimmigrant must have been admitted in, or otherwise provided, H-1B status. The person in the grace period would meet that condition. The new petition must have been filed before the "nonimmigrant's period of stay authorized by the Secretary of Homeland Security expires." The grace period keeps the nonimmigrant within an authorized period of stay, so that condition is met. Finally, the individual must not have been employed without authorization "from the time of the last admission through the filing of the petition for new employment." If the individual waits until the filing of the new petition to begin the new employment, then being in a grace period arguably will not cause him or her to run afoul of this condition.

Thus, it would seem that a person in the grace period should be able to take advantage of the portability provisions. That is not to say that a particularly strict adjudicator might not find the individual to have worked without authorization after the filing of the petition, but that would not negate the ability to work under portability, though it may require the individual to leave the United States to obtain a new visa and re-enter in order to be authorized to continue working after the petition is adjudicated, since the work authorization under portability ceases upon adjudication.[799] In light of this ambiguity, those individuals in this scenario for whom traveling to consular

---

[795] 80 Fed. Reg. 81900 (Dec. 31, 2015) (proposed rule); 81 Fed. Reg. 82398 (Nov. 18, 2016) (final rule).

[796] 8 CFR §214.1(*l*)(2).

[797] 8 CFR §274a.12(b)(9).

[798] 8 CFR §214.1(*l*)(2).

[799] 8 CFR §274a.12(b)(9).

Copyright © 2017. American Immigration Lawyers Association. All rights reserved.

process presents a problem and those who are risk averse may wish not to work under portability and instead wait for petition approval,

b. "Bridging" Petitions

USCIS allows an H-1B nonimmigrant "who has changed employment based on an H-1B portability petition ... [to] again change employment based on the filing of a new H-1B portability petition, even if the former H-1B portability petition remains pending."[800] This is generally referred to as "bridging." During this bridging between one portability petition and the next, the individual "shall be considered to be in a period of stay authorized by the Secretary of Homeland Security" for purposes of portability eligibility.[801] However, if any filing in the string of portability filings is denied, the bridge is broken, and successive extension of stay requests "cannot be approved ... unless the beneficiary's previously approved period of H-1B status remains valid."[802]

Thus, "[a]pproval of any subsequent H-1B portability petition ... would effectively be dependent on the approval of any prior H-1B portability petition if the individual's ... I-94 ... has expired and the prior portability petitions remain pending at the time the subsequent portability petition is filed."[803] Stated conversely, "[a]s long as the petitioner can demonstrate that the beneficiary remained in valid and unexpired H-1B nonimmigrant status when a successive portability petition was filed, the timely filed petition and associated extension of stay request should not be denied simply because of a denial or withdrawal of the preceding portability petition."[804]

If a portability petition in the string is denied, the individual should be able to resume work under a previously approved H-1B petition if the petition is still valid and the beneficiary has maintained H-1B status or "been in a period of authorized stay and has not been employed ... without authorization"[805]—in other words, has been properly working under portability.

c. Portability from Cap-Exempt to Cap-Subject Employer

USCIS indicated in the explanatory section of the 2016 regulation that, for a beneficiary moving from a cap-exempt to a cap-subject position, "cap-subject employment may not begin prior to October 1 of the fiscal year for which [a] cap-subject petition is approved."[806] Thus, "the H-1B nonimmigrant worker would not be eligible to begin working upon the timely filing of a nonfrivolous petition" under the portability provisions.[807] This regulatory language is something of a shift from prior

---

[800] 80 Fed. Reg. 81900, 81917 (Dec. 31, 2015).

[801] 8 CFR §214.2(h)(2)(i)(H)(3)(i).

[802] 8 CFR §214.2(h)(2)(i)(H)(3)(ii).

[803] 80 Fed. Reg. 81900, 81917 (Dec. 31, 2015).

[804] 81 Fed. Reg. 82398, 82441. (Nov. 18, 2016).

[805] 8 CFR §214.2(h)(2)(i)(H)(3)(iii).

[806] 81 Fed. Reg. 82398, 82441. (Nov. 18, 2016).

[807] Id.

Copyright © 2017. American Immigration Lawyers Association. All rights reserved.

informal guidance on this issue, which seemed to indicate that a foreign national was able to port his or her H-1B status from a cap-exempt employer to an employer subject to the H-1B quota during a black-out period when new H-1B visa numbers are unavailable.[808] The new regulatory language, however, makes it clear that this is not permissible.

d. International Travel During Pendency of the H-1B Portability Petition

International travel during the pendency of the H-1B portability petition is possible in some circumstances. USCIS noted in the 2016 rulemaking that, if the original H-1B petition has expired or is otherwise no longer valid when the foreign national seeks admission to the United States, "the beneficiary must present evidence that USCIS has approved a new H-1B petition to be admitted."[809] Thus, international travel during a period in which the foreign national is working under portability but the prior H-1B period has expired is not possible.

However, if the original H-1B petition has not expired, the beneficiary "may be admissible" if he or she presents "a valid passport and visa (unless visa exempt) … [and] a copy of the previously issued Form I-94 or Form I-797 approval notice (evidencing the petition's validity dates), and a Form I-797 receipt notice" for the portability petition showing that the petition was timely filed.[810] Thus, the practitioner should advise the client and/or foreign national that the beneficiary should not travel internationally if H-1B bridge petitions have been filed where the original status has expired.

As discussed in Volume 1: Chapter Two, "Basic Nonimmigrant Concepts," the foreign national bears the burden of proof to establish admissibility,[811] and the "inspecting officer at the port of entry will make the ultimate determination as to whether the applicant is admissible."[812]

As long as the above-stated conditions are satisfied, the foreign national should be admitted "to the validity date of the previously approved petition, plus 10 days."[813]

---

[808] "USCIS Letter on H-1B Portability from Cap Exempt to Cap Subject" (May 23, 2007), AILA Doc. No. 07052563. |

[809] 81 Fed. Reg. 82398, 82440 (Nov. 18, 2016).

[810] 81 Fed. Reg. 82398, 82440-1 (Nov. 18, 2016). *See also* 9 FAM 402.10-11(B) (section titled "H-1B Aliens May Travel Abroad While Change of Employer Pending"); USCIS, M. Pearson, "Initial Guidance for Processing H-1B Petitions as Affected by the 'American Competitiveness in the Twenty-First Century Act' (Public Law 106-313) and Related Legislation (Public Law 106-311) and (Public Law 106-396)" (Jan 19, 2001), AILA Doc. No. 01062031.

[811] USCIS, M. Pearson, "Interim Guidance for Processing H-1B Applicants for Admission as Affected by the American Competitiveness in the Twenty-first Century Act of 2000, Public Law 106-313" (Jan. 19, 2001), AILA Doc. No. 01020802.

[812] 81 Fed. Reg. 82398, 82441 (Nov. 18, 2016).

[813] USCIS, M. Pearson, "Initial Guidance for Processing H-1B Petitions as Affected by the 'American Competitiveness in the Twenty-First Century Act' (Public Law 106-313) and Related Legislation (Public Law 106-311) and (Public Law 106-396)" (Jan. 19, 2001), AILA Doc. No. 01062031.

Copyright © 2017. American Immigration Lawyers Association. All rights reserved.

An H-4 dependent may be admitted while the H-1B portability petition is pending by showing the same evidence relating to the principal nonimmigrant.[814]

C. Compliance Programs

1. Fraud Detection and National Security (FDNS)

When signing Form I-129, the petitioner agrees that "any supporting evidence submitted may be verified by USCIS through any means determined appropriate by USCIS, including but not limited to, on-site compliance reviews."[815] Thus, USCIS will, from time to time, conduct unannounced site visits, also known as site inspections, of the H-1B petitioner.[816] As explained by USCIS:

> "USCIS started the Administrative Site Visit and Verification Program in July 2009 as an additional way to verify information in certain visa petitions. Under this program, Fraud Detection and National Security (FDNS) officers make unannounced visits to collect information as part of a compliance review."[817]

> "We also commenced operation of the Administrative Site Visit and Verification Program (ASVVP) in July of this year to determine whether the location of employment actually exists and if a beneficiary is employed at the location specified, performing the duties as described, and paid the salary as identified in the petition."[818]

Generally, with respect to H-1B petitions, "FDNS conducts site visits on randomly selected petitioners after USCIS adjudicates their petitions."[819] However, in 2017, USCIS announced that it would "take a more targeted approach" and focus on:

- "Cases where USCIS cannot validate the employer's basic business information through commercially available data;
- "H-1B dependent employers...; and
- "Employers petitioning for H-1B workers who work off-site at another company or organization's location."[820]

---

[814] *Id.*

[815] USCIS, "Form I-129, Petition for a Nonimmigrant Worker" (exp. Dec. 31, 2018), https://www.uscis.gov/i-129.

[816] "AILA Liaison/FDNS Meeting Minutes" (June 7, 2010), AILA Doc. No. 10060862.

[817] USCIS, "Administrative Site Visit and Verification Program" (updated Oct. 30, 2014), https://www.uscis.gov/about-us/directorates-and-program-offices/fraud-detection-and-national-security/administrative-site-visit-and-verification-program; USCIS, "Compliance Review Report: Job Aid for Employment (H1B)-Based" (Dec. 5, 2008), AILA Doc. No. 10030561 (use of the term "Site Inspectors").

[818] "USCIS Letter to Senator Grassley on H-1B Fraud Prevention and Detection" (Nov. 10, 2009), AILA Doc. No. 09120161.

[819] USCIS, "Administrative Site Visit and Verification Program" (updated Oct. 30, 2014), https://www.uscis.gov/about-us/directorates-and-program-offices/fraud-detection-and-national-security/administrative-site-visit-and-verification-program.

[820] USCIS, "Putting American Workers First: USCIS Announces Further Measures to Detect H-1B Visa Fraud and Abuse" (Apr. 3, 2017), AILA Doc. No. 17040332.

Copyright © 2017. American Immigration Lawyers Association. All rights reserved.

A focus of the visits to H-1B dependent employers was announced to be whether they are "evading their obligation to make a good faith effort to recruit U.S. workers."[821] USCIS indicated, however, that it will continue its "random and unannounced visits nationwide."[822]

The site inspectors are provided with the names of the petitioner and beneficiary, worksite address from Part 5 on Form I-129, and beneficiary's occupation, job duties, and salary, as well as the petitioner's hours of operation and number of employees, if this information is "included in the file."[823] They "do not make decisions on immigration benefit petitions or applications";[824] reports indicate that they are often contractors who should follow written protocols.[825] In addition, while many site visits are conducted with an in-person visit, experience has shown that FDNS also periodically conducts the inquiry with a petitioner via email, and asks for verification of working conditions, job duties, and copies of relevant documents such as payroll records.

Site inspectors should perform the following actions:

- "Verify the information submitted with the petition, including supporting documentation submitted by the petitioner, based on a checklist prepared by USCIS;

- "Verify the existence of a petitioning entity;

- "Take digital photographs;

- "Review documents; and/or

- "Speak with organizational representatives to confirm the beneficiary's work location, employment workspace, hours, salary and duties."[826]

The practitioner may wish to review the site visit checklist.[827] It is particularly noteworthy that the document directs the termination of the site visit if the petitioner requests an attorney's presence, but "the attorney is not immediately available."[828]

---

[821] *Id.* H-1B dependent employers are discussed in Volume 1: Chapter Six, "The Labor Condition Application."

[822] *Id.*

[823] "AILA Liaison/FDNS Meeting Minutes" (June 7, 2010), AILA Doc. No. 10060862.

[824] USCIS, "Administrative Site Visit and Verification Program" (updated Oct. 30, 2014), https://www.uscis.gov/about-us/directorates-and-program-offices/fraud-detection-and-national-security/administrative-site-visit-and-verification-program.

[825] "AILA Liaison/FDNS Meeting Minutes" (June 7, 2010), AILA Doc. No. 10060862.

[826] USCIS, "Administrative Site Visit and Verification Program" (updated Oct. 30, 2014), https://www.uscis.gov/about-us/directorates-and-program-offices/fraud-detection-and-national-security/administrative-site-visit-and-verification-program.

[827] USCIS, "Compliance Review Report: Job Aid for Employment (H1B)-Based" (Dec. 5, 2008), AILA Doc. No. 10030561. A previous version of the checklist is at AILA Doc. No. 09101461.

[828] USCIS, "Compliance Review Report: Job Aid for Employment (H1B)-Based" (Dec. 5, 2008), AILA Doc. No. 10030561.

Copyright © 2017. American Immigration Lawyers Association. All rights reserved.

Also commendable is USCIS's emphasis on "officer safety" and sensitivity to diversity issues.[829] The checklist illustrates the foci of the site visit:

- Confirmation that the worksite "facility visually appear[s] to be that of the organization," through signage or corroboration from "neighboring business and/or residents," photographs, and the Site Inspector's notes on the appearance of the business;

- Interaction with "an organizational representative" or confirmation of appropriate business activities from "neighboring business and/or residents," as well as notes on the individual(s) interviewed;

- Confirmation of "the presence of a legitimate organization," through a site tour and details on the type of business, number of employees, number of full-time and part-time H-1B employees, numbers of employees working onsite and offsite, number of employees holding nonimmigrant status, number of lawful permanent resident (LPR) employees, and the length of "time the organization has been in business";

- Confirmation that the H-1B petition and beneficiary were known to the petitioner, including details on "hours of duty, salary and job duties," as well as length of the beneficiary's employment and the type of petition filed "(immigrant visa or nonimmigrant visa)," and verification that "the petitioner had authority to file the petition on behalf of the employer," which presumably applies to agent-petitioners or is a typographical error;

- Confirmation that the beneficiary is currently "working for the organization," through review of "recent pay stubs, business cards, [and] employee ID" or information on the beneficiary's employment that is not with the petitioner;

- Identification of the beneficiary through "work or government issued identification";

- Interaction with the beneficiary to confirm the details of his or her employment, including job title, job duties, work schedule, wages, and work location, as well as educational qualifications and whether he or she "paid for the USCIS filing costs of the I-129 petition and if the organization deducted the filing costs [from] the beneficiary's paycheck";

- Confirmation of payment of wages pursuant to the H-1B petition, through review of W-2 or paystub; and

- Recommendation for "further inquiry."[830]

In the event that the signatory of the H-1B petition is unavailable, the site inspector should request to "speak with a knowledgeable management representative, and to annotate the name/position of the person interviewed on the site inspection

---

[829] *Id.*

[830] *Id.*

Copyright © 2017. American Immigration Lawyers Association. All rights reserved.

report."[831] Then, if "knowledgeable personnel are not available, an effort will be made to obtain the information through other means, such as by telephone, e-mail, or perhaps a site visit by an FDNS officer."[832] If a third-party client has temporarily transferred the beneficiary to a different worksite with the same entity, then the site inspector should request the new address and include it in the report, although the contractor "cannot proceed to a second location."[833] A USCIS officer should decide "what follow-up action is taken."[834]

In response to a question about cooperation by the petitioner, USCIS indicated: "Voluntary participation in the site visit helps to ensure the Compliance Review process is completed quickly and efficiently. If petitioners/beneficiaries choose not to participate in the site visit, the case will be reviewed by USCIS to determine what, if any, follow-up action should be taken."[835] If the beneficiary is employed at a third-party worksite and the "third party end user will not cooperate with the contractor," then the site inspector "will annotate the reason in the report and submit it to USCIS," which "will review the report and determine what, if any, follow-up action is taken."[836]

A site visit is "considered *Verified* when no derogatory or questionable information exists" and "*Not Verified* where there is insufficient information on which to conclude with confidence that the petition is bona [] fide."[837] In the latter situation, the case may be referred:

- To FDNS if there are "indicators of fraud and/or technical noncompliance" which "are insufficient to support a denial or notice of intent to deny or revoke (NOID/NOIR)"; and

- To Adjudications if there is "sufficient evidence of fraud and/or technical noncompliance."[838]

After the site visit, the findings will be documented in a "Compliance Review Report," which becomes part of the record.[839] If the information stated on the petition cannot be verified by FDNS or is "inconsistent with the facts recorded from the site visit," then the ISO may either "request additional evidence from the petitioner or initiate denial or revocation proceedings."[840] USCIS also indicated: "FDNS provides

---

[831] "AILA Liaison/FDNS Meeting Minutes" (June 7, 2010), AILA Doc. No. 10060862.

[832] *Id.*

[833] *Id.*

[834] *Id.*

[835] *Id.*

[836] *Id.*

[837] *Id.* (emphasis in original).

[838] *Id.*

[839] USCIS, "Administrative Site Visit and Verification Program" (updated Oct. 30, 2014), https://www.uscis.gov/about-us/directorates-and-program-offices/fraud-detection-and-national-security/administrative-site-visit-and-verification-program.

[840] *Id.*; "USCIS Letter to Senator Grassley on H-1B Fraud Prevention and Detection" (Nov. 10, 2009), AILA Doc. No. 09120161.

Copyright © 2017. American Immigration Lawyers Association. All rights reserved.

Adjudications with a written report of fact-based findings" but "does not make recommendations to Adjudications."[841] The petitioner and/or practitioner should be provided "an opportunity to review and address the information" before the underlying petition is denied or revoked by USCIS "based on information obtained during a site inspection."[842] If the report contains indicators of fraud, USCIS will then assess "whether further investigation is warranted," and may refer the case to ICE.[843] The impact to current and pending nonimmigrant and immigrant visa petitions of a referral to ICE depends "on the individual facts and significance of the fraud and available evidence."[844]

Immigration attorneys have noted some items that seem to be common "red flags" for Site Investigators:

- "The beneficiary's salary in pay statements does not match the amount stated in the petition.
- "Reported income on the beneficiary's Form 1040 does not match the beneficiary's salary, or the beneficiary reports as 'self-employed.'
- "The address of the beneficiary's work location in the petition is not an actual work site.
- "Virtual offices or empty offices without equipment are listed as the beneficiary's place of employment,
- "The beneficiary lacks a work email or work phone number."[845]

The ASVVP program is the most talked about, but not the only, anti-fraud tool. FDNS lists among its functions:

- "Performance of fraud assessments – FDNS officers engage in fraud assessments (including Benefit Fraud and Compliance Assessments) to determine the types and volumes of fraud in certain immigration benefits programs;
- "Compliance Reviews – Systematic reviews of certain types of applications or petitions to ensure the integrity of the immigration benefits system, and
- "Targeted site visits – Inquiries conducted in cases where fraud is suspected."[846]

---

[841] "AILA Liaison/FDNS Meeting Minutes" (June 7, 2010), AILA Doc. No. 10060862.

[842] USCIS, "Fraud Detection and National Security Directorate" (updated Nov. 18, 2011), https://www.uscis.gov/about-us/directorates-and-program-offices/fraud-detection-and-national-security/fraud-detection-and-national-security-directorate.

[843] USCIS, "Administrative Site Visit and Verification Program" (updated Oct. 30, 2014), https://www.uscis.gov/about-us/directorates-and-program-offices/fraud-detection-and-national-security/administrative-site-visit-and-verification-program.

[844] "AILA Liaison/FDNS Meeting Minutes" (June 7, 2010), AILA Doc. No. 10060862.

[845] "Practice Pointer: H-1B and L-1 FDNS Site Visits" (July 26, 2016), AILA Doc. No. 16072604. This document, prepared by AILA's Vermont Service Center (VSC) Liaison Committee, contains a description of a typical site visit, and provides some helpful pointers on advising clients regarding site visits.

Copyright © 2017. American Immigration Lawyers Association. All rights reserved.

The practitioner may wish to review USCIS's internal "actionable fraud referral" worksheet.[847] As discussed above, these programs are funded by the Fraud Prevention and Detection Account. On the front end, USCIS has a program, the Verification Initiative for Business Enterprises (VIBE), which "provide[s] adjudicators with a tool to accurately verify the financial viability and current level of business operations for employment-based petitions,"[848] as discussed in Volume 1: Chapter Two, "Basic Nonimmigrant Concepts."

FDNS officers may also access social networking websites to conduct an "unannounced cyber 'site-visit' on petitioners and beneficiaries."[849] A USCIS document explains: "This social networking gives FDNS an opportunity to reveal fraud by browsing these sites to see if petitioners and beneficiaries are in a valid relationship or are attempting to deceive [USCIS] about their relationship."[850]

The USCIS adjudicator is charged to "[b]e familiar with the latest visa fraud trends, possible detection points, and current investigation information," to address "upon other signs of suspect documentation, reasons to suspect involvement of a dummy corporation, etc.,"[851] even though these concerns are not properly within FDNS jurisdiction. In addition, the Form I-129 was revised to require further attestations from the petitioner, including:

- "Placement of the beneficiary off-site during the period of employment will be in compliance with the statutory and regulatory requirements of the H-IB nonimmigrant classification"; and

- Confirmation that the petitioner will pay the beneficiary "the prevailing rate of pay at any offsite location."[852]

USCIS stated that an attestation that the "beneficiary has been advised of the offsite placement and accepts the terms of the H-IB employment, including the job location and possible relocation" and inclusion of the "work itinerary" would also be

---

[846] USCIS, "Fraud Detection and National Security Directorate" (updated Nov. 18, 2011), https://www.uscis.gov/about-us/directorates-and-program-offices/fraud-detection-and-national-security/fraud-detection-and-national-security-directorate.

[847] USCIS, "H-1B Petition Fraud Referral Sheet" (Aug. 27, 2008), http://www.aila.org/File/Related/12052147aa.pdf.

[848] "USCIS Letter to Senator Grassley on H-1B Fraud Prevention and Detection" (Nov. 10, 2009), AILA Doc. No. 09120161.

[849] USCIS, "Social Networking Sites and Their Importance to FDNS," AILA Doc. No. 10101473 (typographical error corrected).

[850] Id.

[851] USCIS, "I-129 H-1B Standard Operating Procedures" (undated, posted July 26, 2007), AILA Doc. No. 07072668.

[852] "USCIS Letter to Senator Grassley on H-1B Fraud Prevention and Detection" (Nov. 10, 2009), AILA Doc. No. 09120161; USCIS, "Form I-129, Petition for a Nonimmigrant Worker" (exp. Dec. 31, 2018), https://www.uscis.gov/i-129, which now refers to "the higher of the prevailing or actual wage at any and all off-site locations."

Copyright © 2017. American Immigration Lawyers Association. All rights reserved.

required,[853] but the current iteration of the form does not specifically request these attestations.[854] The practitioner should know that the requirement of a valid employment relationship between the petitioner and beneficiary is also viewed by USCIS as an anti-fraud tool. For example, the right to control analysis is closely intertwined with an emphasis on third-party placements,[855] and essentially requires an itinerary.[856]

2. Petition Verification by DOS

The Kentucky Consular Center (KCC) of DOS also has a Fraud Prevention Unit (FPU), which "research[es] approval of the [H-1B] petition" following inquiries from consular officers,[857] and which receives and monitors reports of potential labor law violations.[858] The first of the DOS reviews is performed by the KCC when USCIS's database lacks information about a petitioner in order "to create a base petitioner record as part of the Petition Information Management Service (PIMS) report for all first time petitioners."[859] KCC may verify the petitioner's information through "review of the company website, company contact information, and use of Google earth to confirm that an office exists in an appropriate physical location," in addition to other activities.[860] After "the base petitioner record is complete, the KCC will not normally re-verify the petitioner information for two years."[861]

The FPU also implemented a program to confirm, "on a random basis ... factual aspects related to the beneficiaries and their proposed U.S. employment."[862] This is typically done with an "unannounced" telephone call to the petitioner and "should be anticipated to occur shortly after the petition is transferred to the KCC from" USCIS.[863] Only 15 contractors "have been authorized by the DOS to conduct these telephonic beneficiary reviews with petitioners,"[864] the list of whom is available.[865]

---

[853] "USCIS Letter to Senator Grassley on H-1B Fraud Prevention and Detection" (Nov. 10, 2009), AILA Doc. No. 09120161.

[854] USCIS, "Form I-129, Petition for a Nonimmigrant Worker" (exp. Dec. 31, 2018), https://www.uscis.gov/i-129.

[855] "USCIS Letter to Senator Grassley on H-1B Fraud Prevention and Detection" (Nov. 10, 2009), AILA Doc. No. 09120161.

[856] USCIS, D. Neufeld, "Determining Employer-Employee Relationship for Adjudication of H-1B Petitions, Including Third-Party Site Placements" (Jan. 8, 2010), AILA Doc. No. 10011363.

[857] 9 FAM 402.10-9(A).

[858] 9 FAM 402.10-17.

[859] "AILA/DOS Liaison Practice Pointer: Kentucky Consular Center Audit of Nonimmigrant Visa Petitions, Including Unannounced Telephonic Contact of Employers" (Aug. 26, 2010), AILA Doc. No. 10082634.

[860] Id.

[861] Id.

[862] Id.

[863] Id.

[864] Id.

[865] "KCC Audit of Nonimmigrant Visa Petitions" (Aug. 26, 2010), AILA Doc. No. 10082634.

Copyright © 2017. American Immigration Lawyers Association. All rights reserved.

The contractor "may request to speak to an authorized official" to inquire about the following facts:

- Confirmation that "the petitioner, in fact, submitted the petition";
- Date of the petitioner's incorporation;
- Physical location of the petitioner;
- Petitioner's number of employees;
- Names of the shareholders of the petitioner;
- "Location of Attorney of Record; and
- "General information regarding the petitioner's operations and business plan."[866]

As a practical matter, a petitioner that is ready for an H-1B site visit should, in turn, be ready for a telephone call with a KCC contractor,[867] since the site visit is more likely more involved. The practitioner should review the discussion of preparing a client for an FDNS site visit above and assist the client in taking similar anticipatory actions. A few points relate specifically to KCC verifications:

- The petitioner should verify that the KCC set of documents "is a complete and accurate copy of the original petition that was reviewed by the employer";[868]
- KCC telephonic contact may "occur shortly after the approval of the Petition, but prior to the visa issuance" and "even after visa issuance"; and
- The petitioner should "be advised to request the name of the KCC contractor" and to confirm his or her credentials before "providing any information," and the practitioner may corroborate the contractor's identity with the KCC by calling (606) 526-7500.[869]

Then:

"Once the review is completed, the findings of the beneficiary review are normally finalized within two days and available to consular officers. Consular officers are instructed to review the report, question the beneficiary regarding any discrepancies, and request that the KCC correct any information if a finding was in error. If the discrepancies were not in error, the consular officer will provide additional information to the KCC to update their report to include any additional

---

[866] "AILA/DOS Liaison Practice Pointer: Kentucky Consular Center Audit of Nonimmigrant Visa Petitions, Including Unannounced Telephonic Contact of Employers," AILA Doc. No. 10082634.

[867] Id.

[868] Id. The KCC set of documents should include the forms, LCA, employer support statement, petitioner's tax documents, beneficiary's educational and experience documents, affidavits, and itineraries.

[869] Id.; "KCC Audit of Nonimmigrant Visa Petitions" (Aug. 26, 2010), AILA Doc. No. 10082634.

Copyright © 2017. American Immigration Lawyers Association. All rights reserved.

incriminating evidence discovered during the course of the nonimmigrant visa interview."[870]

IV. Process

This section will address the particulars of preparing and filing an H-1B petition. For discussion of how to complete the prevailing wage determination request form, see Volume 2: Chapter Two, "The Labor Certification Application." For discussion of how to complete the LCA, see Volume 1: Chapter Six, "The Labor Condition Application."

A. H-1B Petition

The H-1B petition should be filed in duplicate, with original signatures on one set of documents, and the duplicate being a complete photocopy of the petition, including supporting documents.[871] The USCIS Service Center at which it should be filed depends upon a number of factors, including whether the petitioner is cap-exempt or cap-subject, whether the petition is an extension request without change, whether the petition is for an H-1B1, and where the place of employment is located. USCIS changes the designated Service Centers from time to time, so it is important to monitor the agency's website to ensure the proper address.[872] For those types of filings, such as cap-subject H-1Bs, for which more than one Service Center is listed, the petition should be filed at the one having jurisdiction over the place of employment. However, if the beneficiary will work in more than one location, the Service Center having jurisdiction over the company's "primary office" should be used, even if the multiple locations are all within the same state.[873] Although USCIS may forward a "misfiled" case to the correct Service Center, it is not required to do so, and "the Service will not forward Premium Processing and H-1 cap subject that are sent to the wrong location."[874] In practice, H-1B petitions filed at the wrong location are rejected by the USCIS mailroom and returned to the employer or the practitioner, and are not forwarded internally by USCIS. In addition, the practitioner should not rely on USCIS forwarding because it will affect the receipt date: "Cases are forwarded un-receipted with checks attached and un-cashed."[875]

Importantly, an H-1B "petition may not be filed or approved earlier than 6 months before the date of actual need for the beneficiary's services."[876] Because USCIS

---

[870] "AILA/DOS Liaison Practice Pointer: Kentucky Consular Center Audit of Nonimmigrant Visa Petitions, Including Unannounced Telephonic Contact of Employers," AILA Doc. No. 10082634.

[871] TSC Liaison Minutes (Aug. 13, 2000), AILA Doc. No. 00090703; "CSC Quarterly Stakeholder Newsletter" (3d Qtr. 2017), AILA Doc. No. 17040432 (failure to file in duplicate may result in processing delays abroad).

[872] USCIS, "Direct Filing Addresses for Form I-129, Petition for a Nonimmigrant Worker," https://www.uscis.gov/i-129-addresses.

[873] *Id.*

[874] "September 2010 SCOPS Agenda Questions" (Sept. 2010), AILA Doc. No. 10100868.

[875] *Id. See also* "AILA-SCOPS Q&A" (Aug. 25, 2010), AILA Doc. No. 10090230.

[876] 8 CFR §214.2(h)(9)(i)(B).

Copyright © 2017. American Immigration Lawyers Association. All rights reserved.

"shall consider all the evidence submitted and such other evidence as he or she may independently require to assist his or her adjudication,"[877] the practitioner is strongly encouraged to submit as much pertinent evidence as possible. Reference to USCIS's processing checklist may be helpful, and if "one or more of the required fees are returned due to insufficient payment, the H-1B petition will NOT retain the original filing date."[878] USCIS prefers separate checks for each fee, "stapled to the bottom right corner of the top document."[879] An H-1B petition must be filed on behalf of visa-exempt Canadian citizens.[880] For a discussion of TN status in lieu of H-1B status,[881] see Volume 1: Chapter Fourteen, "TN Visas and Status."

The petition should indicate whether it is subject to the numerical limitation. In addition to marking the Form I-129, as discussed below, the practitioner may include a brightly colored sheet with the applicable statement in capital letters:

- SUBJECT TO H-1B REGULAR CAP;
- SUBJECT TO H-1B MASTER'S CAP;
- SUBJECT TO CHILE/SINGAPORE H-1B1 CAP;
- NOT SUBJECT TO CAP (EXTENSION/CHANGE OF EMPLOYER/ REMAINDER TIME).

As discussed in Volume 1: Chapter Two, "Basic Nonimmigrant Concepts," petitions should be filed for delivery either by the United States Postal Service (USPS) or by a private courier that is bonded, such as DHL, Federal Express, and UPS.[882] USCIS does not accept personal delivery of H-1B petitions.[883] However, the practitioner is advised to use regular mail[884] only if mailing the package before or on the first filing day:

> "USCIS does not consider the package received or timely filed until it is actually *on-site at the Service Center*. The service centers pick up correspondence delivered to the P.O. Box at one or more scheduled times during the day. Therefore, while customers may file applications by USPS at the P.O. Box,

---

[877] 8 CFR §214.2(h)(9)(i).

[878] USCIS, "Optional Processing Worksheet for FY 2010 H-1B Filings," AILA Doc. No. 09032070; USCIS, "Questions and Answers: USCIS to Accept H-1B Petitions for FY 2010 Beginning April 1, 2009" (Mar. 20, 2009), AILA Doc. No. 09032365.

[879] USCIS, "Questions and Answers: USCIS to Accept H-1B Petitions for FY 2010 Beginning April 1, 2009" (Mar. 20, 2009), AILA Doc. No. 09032365; USCIS, "Optional Checklist of Form I-129 H-1B Filing" (Mar. 3, 2017), https://www.uscis.gov/sites/default/files/files/form/m-735.pdf.

[880] 9 FAM 402.10-8(F).

[881] 9 FAM 402.10-8(E).

[882] USCIS, "Questions and Answers #1: H-1B Petition Mailing During Cap Season" (Mar. 27, 2008), AILA Doc. No. 08032869 (emphasis in original).

[883] 70 Fed. Reg. 23775 (May 5, 2005) (stating that H-1B "petitions may not be personally delivered to the applicable USCIS Service Center"); USCIS, "Questions and Answers #1: H-1B Petition Mailing During Cap Season" (Mar. 27, 2008), AILA Doc. No. 08032869.

[884] USPS's Express Mail may be used to ship to courier addresses as well.

Copyright © 2017. American Immigration Lawyers Association. All rights reserved.

delivery to that P.O. Box does not ensure that the filing will be picked up by the USCIS the same day it is placed in the P.O. Box by the USPS, and thus, will not be considered timely filed."[885]

All deliveries involve a certain amount of unforeseeable risk, so it is important to plan accordingly and to make every effort to file as early as allowable.[886] Note, however, that "no advantage will be gained by the particular time of day a filing is received."[887] In 2008, USCIS accepted "deliveries from couriers until 7 p.m., local time" on the last day of the filing period and until 5:00 pm on the other four days.[888] USCIS also stated that if, upon the closing of the Service Center office on the final filing day, "there are still trucks attempting to deliver packages, the Service Centers will work out a process to get those packages into the system."[889]

The practitioner may use a single package to mail multiple H-1B petitions to USCIS, but should "place individual petitions into separate envelopes within the package."[890] Assuming all of the petitions in the single package are appropriately sent to the same address, the individual envelopes "should be marked with the following labels to reference the type of petition":

- "Masters Premium
- "Masters
- "Regular Premium
- "Regular
- "Chile/Singapore."[891]

This section discusses the documents of the H-1B petition. USCIS has stated its "preferred order of documents," as follows:

- Form I-907, if applicable
- Form G-28
- Form I-129
- Supplement H
- Form I-129W

---

[885] USCIS, "Questions and Answers #1: H-1B Petition Mailing During Cap Season" (Mar. 27, 2008), AILA Doc. No. 08032869 (emphasis in original).

[886] *E.g.,* "Members Report FedEx Scanning Troubles at CSC" (Apr. 3, 2013), AILA Doc. No. 13040540.

[887] 70 Fed. Reg. 23775 (May 5, 2005). Although the guidance specifically relates to the former system, the principle should remain the same.

[888] USCIS, "Questions and Answers #1: H-1B Petition Mailing During Cap Season" (Mar. 27, 2008), AILA Doc. No. 08032869.

[889] *Id.* (emphasis in original).

[890] USCIS, "Questions and Answers: USCIS to Accept H-1B Petitions for FY 2010 Beginning April 1, 2009" (Mar. 20, 2009), AILA Doc. No. 09032365.

[891] *Id.*

Copyright © 2017. American Immigration Lawyers Association. All rights reserved.

- ▪ Table of Contents, with the following documents tabbed:
  - – Evidence of the foreign national's lawful immigration status, if applicable, and a copy of the biographic page of the passport
  - – Approved LCA
  - – Support statement from U.S. company
  - – Attorney's cover letter
  - – "Other supporting documentation," which may include evidence that the foreign national meets the minimum requirements for the job opening as stated on the temporary labor certification, as discussed above, if applicable
- ▪ Duplicate copy of the H-1B petition.[892]

The practitioner should not be alarmed if the USCIS receipt notice is issued from a Service Center to which the H-1B petition was not mailed:

"In order to fully utilize its data entry and initial processing capacity, USCIS may choose to distribute filings received at one service center to other service centers for data entry. In the event that USCIS exercises this option, petitioners may receive receipt notices or other correspondence from a service center other than the one to which their H-1B petition was mailed."[893]

1. Form G-28

The U.S. company is the "petitioner" and the foreign national is the "beneficiary" of an H-1B petition. The U.S. company representative should sign this form. If there is limited time to prepare and file the petition before the U.S. assignment is to begin, such as if the forms are emailed to and printed by the client, this form may be printed on plain white paper. However, as discussed in Volume 1: Chapter Two, "Basic Nonimmigrant Concepts," the Forms G-28 should be printed on blue paper whenever possible, in order to assist the USCIS mailroom in identifying the Form G-28.[894]

2. Form I-907

If the client wishes a response (approval, denial, or RFE) within 15 calendar days, then the client may pay USCIS an additional $1,225 for premium processing. This request may be filed concurrently with the H-1B petition, or the attorney or the client may request premium processing after the petition has been filed, by submitting Form I-907, Request for Premium Processing Service, with the petition's receipt notice, as discussed in Volume 1: Chapter Two, "Basic Nonimmigrant Concepts."

---

[892] USCIS, "Questions and Answers: USCIS to Accept H-1B Petitions for FY 2010 Beginning April 1, 2009" (Mar. 20, 2009), AILA Doc. No. 09032365.

[893] USCIS, "USCIS Announces Interim Rule on H-1B Visas" (Mar. 19, 2008), AILA Doc. No. 08190340 (select "USCIS Fact Sheet: Changes to the FY2009 H-1B Program"); "AILA-SCOPS Q&A" (Aug. 25, 2010), AILA Doc. No. 10090230.

[894] "Practice Pointer: Getting USCIS to Recognize the G-28" (June 3, 2015), AILA Doc. No. 08090469.

Copyright © 2017. American Immigration Lawyers Association. All rights reserved.

3. Form I-129

For H-1B petitions subject to the cap, the Form I-129, Petition for a Nonimmigrant Worker, should bear a statement to that effect. USCIS directs petitioners: "Clearly label all H-1B cap cases *in red ink* on the top margin of Form I-129. Use the following codes":

- "Regular Cap (65,000 regular cap cases, not including Chile/Singapore cap cases)
- "C/S Cap (Chile/Singapore H-1B1s)
- "U.S. Masters (20,000 cap for beneficiaries with U.S. Masters or higher degrees)."[895]

The second set of documents may be filed and should be "[c]learly identify[ied] … as a COPY, so that it is not mistaken for a duplicate filing."[896] The practitioner may also find it helpful to write the following in large block letters across the side of the Form I-129: "DUPLICATE PETITION; PLEASE FORWARD TO KCC." The duplicate copy of the petition will be forwarded to the U.S. consulate where the beneficiary will apply for an H-1B visa as supplementary evidence for the PIMS, as discussed in Volume 1: Chapter Two, "Basic Nonimmigrant Concepts."[897] Following approval of an H-1B petition, USCIS forwards approval notification to the KCC, which in turn creates an electronic record to confirm the petition approval. If a duplicate set of documents is filed with USCIS, then USCIS will forward these documents to the KCC for scanning and entry into the PIMS database.[898] Although duplicate original documents are not required, preparing and providing them may facilitate the beneficiary's visa application in the future,[899] as "USCIS will not make [a] second copy if one is not provided."[900]

Part 1: Information on the U.S. company, including name, address, contact person, contact person's telephone number, email address, and FEIN, should be provided.

Part 2: For most H-1B petitions, "New employment" should be checked. As discussed in Volume 1: Chapter Two, "Basic Nonimmigrant Concepts," if consular notification is requested under "Requested Action," then USCIS should notify the

---

[895] USCIS, "Questions and Answers: USCIS to Accept H-1B Petitions for FY 2010 Beginning April 1, 2009" (Mar. 20, 2009), AILA Doc. No. 09032365 (emphasis in original). USCIS, "Fiscal Year (FY) 2018 Cap Season" (updated Apr. 7, 2017), http://bit.ly/fy2018Hcap.

[896] *Id.* (emphasis in original).

[897] "DOS Practice Pointer: PIMS" (Nov. 16, 2010), AILA Doc. No. 11061060; PIMS Processing Update, AILA Doc. No. 08032132.

[898] DOS, "Accessing NIV Petition Information Via the CCD" (Nov. 25, 2007), AILA Doc. No. 7112560.

[899] PIMS Processing Update, AILA Doc. No. 08032132.

[900] USCIS, "Questions and Answers: USCIS to Accept H-1B Petitions for FY 2010 Beginning April 1, 2009" (Mar. 20, 2009), AILA Doc. No. 09032365.

Copyright © 2017. American Immigration Lawyers Association. All rights reserved.

KCC, and the consulate abroad should then be able to confirm petition approval when the foreign national applies for an H-1B visa.

Change of status may be requested as long as the beneficiary has maintained nonimmigrant status and has engaged in no unauthorized employment. In addition, the expiration date of the foreign national's current status should be calendared, so that a request to extend status may be timely filed. Ideally, the H-1B change of status petition will be approved before the beneficiary's underlying status expires, and premium processing may make this scenario possible if it is available at the time.[901] The practitioner may wish to advise clients on the intricacies of situations where the initial status expires before the change of status petition is approved, as discussed in Volume 1: Chapter Two, "Basic Nonimmigrant Concepts." For more information on the eligibility requirements for change of status, on accrual of unlawful presence, and on filing an extension while a change of status petition is pending, see Volume 1: Chapter Two, "Basic Nonimmigrant Concepts."

As discussed in Volume 1: Chapter Two, "Basic Nonimmigrant Concepts," a timely filed request for change of status will extend the beneficiary's period of authorized stay, such that the beneficiary should not accrue unlawful presence during pendency of the change of status petition, but USCIS takes the view that filing a change of status petition will not extend the beneficiary's nonimmigrant status.[902] If the change of status petition is approved, then the foreign national will be accorded a new period of authorized stay retroactive to the date the initial immigration status expired and the beneficiary would accrue no unlawful presence.[903]

However, if the change of status petition is ultimately denied because the beneficiary engaged in unauthorized employment or because the petition is deemed frivolous, then all of the time that the foreign national remained in the United States after expiration of the initial grant of admission will be considered unlawful presence.[904] If the petition is denied because it was not timely filed, unlawful presence begins to accrue when the I-94 expires, and if it is denied "for cause"—*i.e.*, a reason other than unauthorized employment, fraud, or untimeliness, unlawful presence begins the day after the request is denied.[905] Due to lengthy processing

---

[901] USCIS has been known to suspend premium processing for H-1Bs or sub-groups of H-1Bs for temporary periods. *See* "USCIS Will Temporarily Suspend Premium Processing for All H-1B Petitions" (Mar. 3, 2017), AILA Doc. No. 17030335; "USCIS Temporarily Suspends Premium Processing for Extension of Stay H-1B Petitions" (May 22, 2015), AILA Doc. No. 15051970.

[902] USCIS, "Consolidation of Guidance Concerning Unlawful Presence for Purposes of Sections 212(a)(9)(B)(i) and 212(a)(9)(C)(i)(I) of the Act" (May 6, 2009), AILA Doc. No. 09051468, p. 37. ("However, the filing of a request for EOS or COS does not put an individual into valid and authorized nonimmigrant status, i.e. he or she is not in authorized status. Therefore, if an individual has filed an initial application for EOS or COS and subsequently files additional (untimely) requests for EOS or COS, the subsequently filed request will not stop the individual from accruing unlawful presence, if the initial request is denied").

[903] *Id.* at 36.

[904] *Id.*

[905] *Id.* at 36-37.

Copyright © 2017. American Immigration Lawyers Association. All rights reserved.

times, it is possible for a foreign national to accrue 180 days of unlawful presence while awaiting adjudication of a change of status petition. Premium processing of the H-1B petition may be requested, when available, to address this issue. Accrual of more than 180 days of unlawful presence will trigger the three-year bar to re-entry to the United States upon departure from the United States. Accrual of more than 365 days of unlawful presence will trigger the 10-year ban to re-entry to the United States upon departure from the United States. For a detailed discussion of the three– and 10-year bars, see Volume 1: Chapter Two, "Basic Nonimmigrant Concepts," and Volume 2: Chapter One, "Basic Immigrant Visa Concepts."

Parts 3 and 4: Information about the beneficiary, including name, alternate names, date of birth, country of birth, country of birth and country of nationality, and passport information, should be provided.

An individual must have a passport that is valid for at least six months from the petition's expiration date. Otherwise, he or she is inadmissible and ineligible for nonimmigrant status.[906] If the foreign national does not have such a passport, then the following options are available: either delay filing the H-1B petition until he or she obtains a renewed passport, or file the H-1B petition with a notation that the passport will be renewed, have the foreign national apply for a renewed passport in the interim, wait for an RFE if one is issued, and then submit a photocopy of the biographic page of the renewed passport once it is available. For nationals of countries where passport renewal takes months, the second strategy can prevent the petition from being significantly delayed. If the client is willing to pay an additional $1,225 fee to USCIS, the delay caused by the RFE, which might also be several months, can be addressed by requesting premium processing when submitting the documentation of the renewed passport, if premium processing is available at the time.

If the foreign national is present in the United States when the petition is filed, then the I-94 card information should be provided, even if the foreign national will depart the United States during pendency of the H-1B petition. In this case, consular notification should be requested in Part 2, as discussed above

Parts 5 through 7: Information about the job title, description of proposed job duties, location, compensation, and general information about the petitioner should be provided. The job title, worksite address, wages offered, and end date of the employment period must match those stated on the labor condition application.

The information in this section should be complete, and any worksite different from the company headquarters should be explained and corroborated. As the Vermont Service Center (VSC) indicated:

"A petitioner should complete all blocks in Part 5 of the petition with accurate information. The petitioner's description of its business should be accurate....

---

[906] INA §212(a)(7)(B)(i). The exceptions to this rule in INA §212(a)(4) are discussed in Volume 1: Chapter Two, "Basic Nonimmigrant Concepts."

Copyright © 2017. American Immigration Lawyers Association. All rights reserved.

Also important is that the petitioner address whether the beneficiary will provide his or her services to the petitioner or to another entity. Often Part 5 of the I-129 petition provides a job address different from the petitioner's address, yet there is no information provided such as the name of the business that is associated with the job address. If the alien will provide services for or work at a different business, please document this arrangement."[907]

The "LCA Case Number" is the case number assigned to the labor condition application by DOL. The form should be signed by the petitioner's representative and the practitioner. Signature in an incorrect location will result in an RFE "because the attestation is improper."[908]

Part 6: See the discussion in Volume 1: Chapter Two, "Basic Nonimmigrant Concepts," on export control requirements.

4. H Supplement

Only the introduction section and Section 1 of this form needs to be completed. In Section 1, the answers to Questions 1 and 2 should be very similar to the information provided on the support statement. Alternatively, the petitioner may state: "Please see attached statement."

5. Data Collection and Filing Fee Exemption Supplement

This form, which replaces the Form I-129W, must be filed with all H-1B petitions. It is used to determine applicability of the ACWIA filing fee and whether the petitioner is cap exempt, and to "collect additional information about the H-1B employer and beneficiary."[909]

Section 1. Question 1, items a and b of this section ask whether the petitioner is H-1B dependent or determined to be a willful violator, thus triggering additional requirements as part of the labor condition application. Item c and its subparts should be "not applicable" if the answer was "no" to item a and b, but given that there is no "not applicable" option and leaving the items blank could result in rejection of the filing in the mail room, it is appropriate to simply answer those questions "yes" or "no" based upon the facts of the case even though the answers are irrelevant. Item d goes to the issue of whether the petitioner must pay the extra $4,000 fee discussed earlier in this chapter.

Questions 2, 3, and 4 are for USCIS's statistical purposes, but of course should match the information provided on the I-129 and H supplement.

Section 2. As discussed earlier in this chapter, the ACWIA fee is $1,500 for non-exempt employers with at least 26 employees and $750 for employers with 25 or

---

[907] "AILA Liaison/VSC Meeting Minutes" (Jan. 21, 2009), AILA Doc. No. 09012768.

[908] USCIS, "I-129 H-1B Standard Operating Procedures" (undated, posted July 26, 2007), AILA Doc. No. 07072668.

[909] USCIS, "Instructions for Petition for Nonimmigrant Worker" (exp. Dec. 31, 2018), https://www.uscis.gov/sites/default/files/files/form/i-129instr.pdf.

Copyright © 2017. American Immigration Lawyers Association. All rights reserved.

fewer employees.[910] This section is to determine if the petitioner is exempt from that fee and, if not, the amount of the fee. If an employer is claiming exemption from this fee, documentation that it meets one of the exemptions should be submitted: For nonprofit research organizations, evidence of the qualifying tax exempt status must be provided; and "[a]ll other employers claiming an exemption must submit a statement describing why the organization or entity is exempt."[911]

Section 3. If requesting exemption from the regular cap, then item 1 should indicate that the beneficiary earned a master's degree or higher degree from a U.S. institution. The practitioner should mark the box matching the foreign national's highest level of formal education, and not the box for the "equivalency he or she has attained as a result of training and/or experience."[912] The information in item 2 regarding the U.S. university need only be provided if a U.S. master's degree is being claimed.

If claiming an exemption from the cap, the appropriate box should be checked, and the documentation discussed earlier in this chapter with respect to cap exemptions should be submitted.

Section 4. This section asks if the beneficiary will be assigned to "off-site" locations during the period of employment, and asks the employer to attest that it will comply with all requirements during those assignments and will pay the higher of the actual or prevailing wage at the locations. See Volume 1: Chapter Six, "The Labor Condition Application," for a discussion of the required wage.

6. Support Statement

The petitioner's support statement should summarize the job duties and the beneficiary's qualifications. The statement should be on the U.S. company's letterhead and signed by a representative of the U.S. company. One format of a support statement is as follows:

- Introduction;
- Information about the petitioner;
- Discussion of the job duties and requirements;
- Discussion of the foreign national's educational and experience background; and
- Thank you and conclusion.

The final paragraph may contain the necessary information about the amount of remuneration and confirmation that the petitioner will comply with the terms of the labor condition application during the beneficiary's H-1B employment.

---

[910] INA §214(c)(9)(B); H-1B Visa Reform Act of 2004, Pub. L. No. 108-447, §422.

[911] 8 CFR §214.2(h)(19)(vi)(A).

[912] USCIS, "I-129 H-1B Standard Operating Procedures" (undated, posted July 26, 2007), AILA Doc. No. 07072668.

Copyright © 2017. American Immigration Lawyers Association. All rights reserved.

B. RFEs

This section provides background on RFEs of H-1B petitions and discusses a few common reasons for an RFE. Generally, an RFE indicates that "USCIS believes that the petitioner has failed to establish eligibility for the benefit sought."[913] When reviewing an H-1B petition, the USCIS adjudicator may refer to the "RFE checklist."[914] USCIS guidance directs adjudicators:

"Such RFEs, however, must specifically state what is at issue … and be *tailored* to request specific illustrative types of evidence from the petitioner that goes directly to what USCIS deems as deficient. Officers should first carefully review all the evidence provided with the H-1B petition to determine which required elements have not been sufficiently established by the petitioner.

"The RFE should neither mandate that a specific type of evidence be provided, unless provided for by regulations (*e.g.*, an itinerary of service dates and locations), nor should it request information that has already been provided in the petition. Officers should state what element the petitioner has failed to establish and provide examples of documentation that could be provided to establish H-1B eligibility."[915]

As discussed above, a common reason for an RFE is to confirm that the petitioner has a bona fide professional job in the business. RFEs may be issued for "H-1B petitions filed by small businesses for aliens with professional skills not normally associated with persons employed in such a business."[916] USCIS guidance also states: "Often, such petitions are filed by a relative or family friend as an accommodation to the beneficiary."[917] The concern seems to be that the beneficiary "will be employed in a lesser capacity or he or she will seek other employment immediately upon arrival."[918] The petitioner bears the burden of proof to "demonstrate the need for such an employee," and the petition may be denied for failure "to demonstrate that the beneficiary will be employed in a qualifying specialty occupation."[919] Therefore, the petition should include evidence of the new project or initiative that gave rise to the "legitimate need" for the beneficiary's services.[920] For example, an enterprise that owns two restaurants may seek to hire a management analyst as part of a plan to open

---

[913] AFM 31.3(g). The guidance specifically addresses RFEs regarding the employment relationship, but the principle should remain the same.

[914] USCIS, "I-129 H-1B Standard Operating Procedures" (undated, posted July 26, 2007), AILA Doc. No. 07072668. ("A checklist which can be used to track the area which require further documentation to establish that a petition meets approval criteria").

[915] AFM 31.3(g) (emphasis in original). The guidance specifically addresses RFEs regarding the employment relationship, but the principle should remain the same.

[916] AFM 31.3(g) (stating the example of "a petition for an accountant filed by an auto repair business or restaurant").

[917] AFM 31.3(g).

[918] *Id.*

[919] *Id.*

[920] *See* 24 AILA's Immigration Law Today 12 (Sept./Oct. 2005), by Romulo E. Guevara.

Copyright © 2017. American Immigration Lawyers Association. All rights reserved.

a new restaurant. As a practical matter, the requested validity period of the H-1B petition should not be longer than the planned activities or project.

Similarly, even though it "is not necessary that complete financial data be submitted with every H-1B petition," an RFE may request financial documents from a small business petitioner.[921] The focus of the inquiry is again on whether the H-1B petition is "an accommodation to a relative or friend who will seek other employment," although another factor may be whether there is "an agreement to work for lower wages."[922] Specifically:

> "[I]f in the discretion of the adjudicating officer the financial condition of the petitioner is so questionable as to call into question whether the petitioner really intends to employ the alien as claimed, evidence of financial ability may be requested. This is because the financial standing of the petitioner, when taken in consideration with other factors, may be indication that the petition is an accommodation and not a valid job offer. Other factors that may be examined include, but are not limited to, the nature of the petitioner's business, the relationship between the beneficiary and the owners/officers of the petitioning entity, and the petitioner's immigration history."[923]

The adjudicator may wish to evaluate whether the job offered is "speculative in nature" by inquiring whether the petitioner has "sufficient H-1B caliber work to justify the position(s) identified in th[e] petition."[924] USCIS defines "speculative employment" as the opposite of "anticipated employment," which, in turn, is defined as: "The establishment of a position(s) by a petitioner based on *sound business projections* (contrast with speculative employment). Sound business projections will demonstrate that the petitioner has a sound basis for anticipating that it will have sufficient work to justify the position(s)."[925] In contrast, the AAO, in one case, seemed to agree that an H-1B petition should not be denied solely based on the speculative nature of the employment: "Counsel asserts that the director improperly raised the concept of speculative employment, which the AAO has previously determined is not a sound basis for denying a petition."[926] Although it remains unclear whether "speculative employment" is a valid ground for denial, the practitioner is advised to discuss the issue with the client, as it seems likely that USCIS will follow its own guidance over an unpublished AAO decision. However, adjudicators are also cautioned:

---

[921] *Id.*

[922] *Id.*

[923] *Id.*

[924] USCIS, "I-129 H-1B Standard Operating Procedures" (undated, posted July 26, 2007), AILA Doc. No. 07072668; *Matter of [name not provided]* EAC *[redacted]* (AAO Feb. 23, 2006), AILA Doc. No. 08041470 (*posted* Apr. 14, 2008).

[925] USCIS, "I-129 H-1B Standard Operating Procedures" (undated, posted July 26, 2007), AILA Doc. No. 07072668 (emphasis in original).

[926] *Matter of [name not provided]* EAC *[redacted]* (AAO Feb. 23, 2006), AILA Doc. No. 08041470. No citation for the principle was stated in the AAO decision.

Copyright © 2017. American Immigration Lawyers Association. All rights reserved.

"Use discretion in determining whether the petitioner has met the burden of establishing that it has an actual employment opportunity for the alien. Requests for contracts and/or other types of documentation should be made only in those cases where you can articulate a specific need for such documentation."[927]

For example, USCIS requested evidence "regarding the structure of the petitioner's organization" where the beneficiary owned the petitioner-entity and later determined that a petitioner, as a newly established company with the beneficiary as the only employee, did not have the "clientele established, work contracts in place and expectations of the position defined."[928] Although the AAO reversed in 2006,[929] the practitioner should discuss with the client whether the petitioner has the right to control the beneficiary, as discussed earlier in this chapter.

In summary, the RFE should "address[] the issues for which [the adjudicator] will deny the case if no response is received."[930] However, the USCIS adjudicator should "not issue RFEs, denials, or intent correspondence based solely on non-H criteria,"[931] such as those applying to other nonimmigrant classifications or immigrant visa petitions. A NOIR should be issued "when the Service becomes aware that" any of the following circumstances have occurred:

- The "beneficiary is no longer employed by the petitioner";

- The "statement of facts contained in a petition was not true and correct";

- The "petitioner violated terms and conditions of the approved petition";

- The petitioner violated the statutory or regulatory requirements; or

- Approval of the petition violated the regulations or involved gross error.[932]

An RFE may be issued if the required fee was not paid,[933] although the petition may be rejected outright, as discussed in Volume 1: Chapter Two, "Basic Nonimmigrant Concepts." Alternatively, "if the adjudicator cannot determine whether the fee applies, the adjudicator should issue an RFE to the petitioner soliciting the additional fee or a statement or other evidence that the fee does not

---

[927] USCIS, "I-129 H-1B Standard Operating Procedures" (undated, posted July 26, 2007), AILA Doc. No. 07072668.

[928] *Matter of [name not provided]* EAC *[redacted]* (AAO Feb. 23, 2006), AILA Doc. No. 08041470. *See also* "AILA Liaison/VSC Meeting Minutes" (Jan. 21, 2009), AILA Doc. No. 09012768.

[929] *Matter of [name not provided]* EAC *[redacted]* (AAO Feb. 23, 2006), AILA Doc. No. 08041470 ("Despite the fact that the beneficiary may also be engaged in some administrative tasks as a sole proprietor, most of the duties of the position include those of a graphic designer, which the [OOH] indicates could not be performed without the training and education that are included in a bachelor's degree in graphic design").

[930] USCIS, "I-129 H-1B Standard Operating Procedures" (undated, posted July 26, 2007), AILA Doc. No. 07072668.

[931] *Id.*

[932] USCIS, "I-129 H-1B Standard Operating Procedures" (undated, posted July 26, 2007), AILA Doc. No. 07072668 (citing 8 CFR §214.2(h)(4)) (internal typographical error corrected).

[933] AFM 31.3(h).

Copyright © 2017. American Immigration Lawyers Association. All rights reserved.

apply."[934] The response period should be a maximum of 30 days if the additional fee is the only reason for the RFE, but in the event that "the RFE addresses other deficiencies that would normally allow for more time to respond, then the RFE may provide more than 30 days."[935]

Failure to respond to the RFE will result in denial of the petition, and the filing fees will not be refunded.[936] The petition will also be denied, with no refund of the filing fees, if the petitioner "provides evidence that it is subject to the additional fee, but fails to submit the additional fee with the response."[937] The USCIS adjudicator should refer the petition to the Center Fraud Detection Office when "there is information or documentation to substantiate that the petitioner has inaccurately presented material facts in the petition and supporting documentation to avoid paying the additional fee."[938] In addition: "If the petitioner responds to the RFE and indicates that it is not subject to the fee, but there are discrepancies that indicate otherwise, further clarifying information may be requested, or in certain cases, a notice of intent to deny (NOID) may be issued."[939] Similarly, a NOID requesting the fee may be issued if "an adjudicator encounters an H-1B petition that was receipted without the additional fee and determines that the fee was required."[940]

Response to a NOIR must be submitted within 30 days, and a failure to respond or an inadequate response will result in a revocation.[941] For a detailed discussion of RFEs, NOIDs, and NOIRs, see Volume 1: Chapter Two, "Basic Nonimmigrant Concepts."

C. Approval Notice and Petition Validity

Approval of an H-1B petition is made on Form I-797, Notice of Action,[942] for "a visa petition, an extension of a visa petition, or an alien's extension of stay."[943] As stated by regulation: "The approval notice shall include the beneficiary's(ies') name(s) and classification and the petition's period of validity."[944] The approval notice should not name any beneficiaries holding status that is not H status.[945] The

---

[934] *Id.*

[935] *Id.*

[936] *Id.*

[937] *Id.*

[938] *Id.*

[939] *Id.*

[940] *Id.*

[941] USCIS, "I-129 H-1B Standard Operating Procedures" (undated, posted July 26, 2007), AILA Doc. No. 07072668 (citing 8 CFR §214.2(h)(11)(iii)).

[942] 8 CFR §214.2(h)(9)(i).

[943] 8 CFR §214.2(h)(18); 9 FAM 402.10-8(C).

[944] 8 CFR §214.2(h)(9)(i)(A).

[945] *Id.*

Copyright © 2017. American Immigration Lawyers Association. All rights reserved.

petitioner should note that an H-1B petition filed in order for the beneficiary to perform "multiple services may be approved in whole or in part."[946]

An approved H-1B petition may be valid "for a period of up to three years but may not exceed the validity period of the labor condition application."[947] The H-1B validity period is assigned according to the following rules:

- The start and end dates should be the same as the dates requested on the petition, if the petition is approved before the requested start date;

- The start date should be the date of approval and the end date should be the date requested by the petitioner, if the petition is approved after the start date that was requested on the petition;[948] and

- The start date should be the LCA start date,[949] if the LCA validity period begins after the petitioner's requested start date in the future.

The end date of the petition validity period may also be truncated by the end date of the relevant LCA or by "other Service policy,"[950] such as the beneficiary's eligibility for H time under the time limitation.[951] If change of status and/or extension of stay are not requested, then notification of petition approval should be provided to the U.S. consulate or port of entry,[952] stated on the Form I-129.

D. Denial, Revocation, and Appeals

If the H-1B petition is denied, then the "petitioner shall be notified of the reasons for the denial and of the right to appeal the denial of the petition."[953] Specifically: "The petition will be denied if it is determined that the statements on the petition were inaccurate, fraudulent, or misrepresented a material fact."[954] The practitioner should note that although a "petition denied in whole or in part may be appealed,"[955] there "is no appeal from a decision to deny an extension of stay to the alien."[956] For further discussion of denied petitions, see Volume 1: Chapter Two, "Basic Nonimmigrant Concepts."

---

[946] Id.

[947] 8 CFR §214.2(h)(9)(iii)(A)(1); 9 FAM 402.10-8(D); AFM 31.3(b).

[948] 8 CFR §§214.2(h)(9)(ii)(A) and (B).

[949] USCIS, "I-129 H-1B Standard Operating Procedures" (undated, posted July 26, 2007), AILA Doc. No. 07072668.

[950] 8 CFR §§214.2(h)(9)(ii)(A), (B), and (C) (citing 8 CFR §214.2(h)(9)(iii) ("If the period of services or training requested by the petitioner exceeds the limit specified in paragraph (H)(9)(iii) of this section, the petition shall be approved only up to the limit specified in that paragraph")); USCIS, "I-129 H-1B Standard Operating Procedures" (undated, posted July 26, 2007), AILA Doc. No. 07072668.

[951] USCIS, "I-129 H-1B Standard Operating Procedures" (undated, posted July 26, 2007), AILA Doc. No. 07072668.

[952] AFM 31.3(f).

[953] 8 CFR §214.2(h)(10)(ii).

[954] Id.

[955] 8 CFR §214.2(h)(12)(i).

[956] 8 CFR §214.2(h)(10)(ii).

Copyright © 2017. American Immigration Lawyers Association. All rights reserved.

As stated by regulation, USCIS "may revoke a petition at any time, even after the expiration of the petition."[957] An approved H-1B petition "is immediately and automatically revoked" in the following circumstances:

- The "petitioner goes out of business";
- The petitioner "files a written withdrawal of the petition"; or
- DOL "revokes the labor certification upon which the petition is based."[958]

An H-1B petition may also be revoked upon notice.[959] USCIS should issue a NOIR "in relevant part" if it is determined that any of the following have occurred:

- The foreign national "is no longer employed by the petitioner in the capacity specified in the petition;
- "The statement of facts contained in the petition … was not true and correct, inaccurate, fraudulent, or misrepresented a material fact;
- "The petitioner violated terms and conditions of the approved petition;
- "The petitioner violated [the] requirements of" the applicable statutes or regulations; or
- "The H-1B petition violated the regulations or involved gross error."[960]

As discussed above, approved H-1B petitions may be revoked if USCIS later discovers that the employer filed multiple cap petitions on behalf of the same beneficiary.[961] USCIS will not refund any filing fees for a revoked petition.[962]

The NOIR "shall contain a detailed statement of the grounds for the revocation and the time period allowed for the petitioner's rebuttal."[963] The regulations provide that the petitioner may file rebuttal evidence "within 30 days of receipt of the notice," and USCIS "shall consider all relevant evidence presented in deciding whether to revoke the petition in whole or in part."[964] In the event that only part of the H-1B petition is revoked, then "the remainder of the petition shall remain approved and a revised approval notice shall be sent to the petitioner with the revocation notice."[965] An H-1B petition that was "revoked on notice in whole or in part may be appealed," but "[a]utomatic revocations may not be appealed."[966] The AAO upheld the

---

[957] 8 CFR §214.2(h)(11)(i)(B).

[958] 8 CFR §214.2(h)(11)(ii). "Revokes the labor certification" may refer only to H-2A and H-2B petitions, which require temporary labor certifications. However, it is possible that USCIS could take the position that an LCA approved by DOL was "certified" by that agency, and thus considered a labor certification.

[959] 8 CFR §214.2(h)(11)(iii).

[960] 8 CFR §214.2(h)(11)(iii)(A).

[961] 8 CFR §214.2(h)(2)(i)(G); 73 Fed. Reg. 15389 (Mar. 25, 2008).

[962] 69 Fed. Reg. 8675 (Feb. 25, 2004).

[963] 8 CFR §214.2(h)(11)(iii)(B).

[964] Id.

[965] Id.

[966] 8 CFR §214.2(h)(12)(ii).

Copyright © 2017. American Immigration Lawyers Association. All rights reserved.

revocation of an H-1B petition where it was determined that the beneficiary provided services as a construction manager, which is not a specialty occupation, instead of as an industrial engineer as claimed on the petition.[967]

E. Visa Application

Upon approval of the H-1B petition, USCIS will send the attorney or representative an approval notice and the company representative will receive a courtesy copy. With the approval notice, the foreign national may make an appointment to apply for an H-1B visa at a U.S. consulate abroad.[968] If the foreign national's previous visa has expired or "will have expired before the date of his or her intended return," but the H-1B petition remains valid, then he or she also "may use a copy of Form I-797 to apply for a new or revalidated visa during the validity period of the petition."[969]

Consular officers are instructed not to require Form I-797 as evidence of petition approval. Instead, "[a]ll petition approvals must be verified through the PIMS or through the PCQS."[970] Nevertheless, the I-797 is needed to make the visa interview appointment, and it is generally preferable for the foreign national to present the original approval notice instead of the courtesy copy or a copy. Providing detailed instructions on how to apply for an H-1B visa, including a certified copy of the H-1B petition, is frequently very helpful to the client and the employee. If the H-1B petition has not yet been approved, then the foreign national should not apply for a visa.

Following approval of the H-1B petition, the foreign national, and his or her dependent spouse and family members, if applicable, may apply for H visas at a U.S. consulate abroad. In addition to the general visa application documents discussed in Volume 1: Chapter Two, "Basic Nonimmigrant Concepts," the following documents should be presented, and individual consulates frequently have additional requirements:

- Original Form I-797 approval notice from USCIS;
- Statement from the petitioner confirming that the foreign national continues to perform the H-1B assignment, if the foreign national obtained change of status from another nonimmigrant category;
- Certified copy of the H-1B petition, to be presented only if specifically requested; and
- Evidence of the visa applicant's qualifications.

Because an H-1B petition must be approved by USCIS in order for a foreign national to apply for an H-1B visa, and because the "DHS regulations governing adjudication of H petitions are complex," consular officers have been directed to

---

[967] *Matter of [name not provided]* WAC 02 220 54035 (AAO Feb. 3, 2006), bit.ly/feb064d.

[968] 9 FAM 402.10-8(C).

[969] 8 CFR §214.2(h)(18).

[970] 9 FAM 402.10-9(B). PCQS stands for Person Centric Query Service.

Copyright © 2017. American Immigration Lawyers Association. All rights reserved.

"rely on the expertise of DHS, specifically USCIS, in this area."[971] This means that the consular officer should not readjudicate the H-1B petition, as the H-1B petition approval "is prima facie evidence that the requirements for H classification which are examined in the petition process have been met," although in the interview "questions may arise as to the beneficiaries' eligibility." Where "evidence which was not available to USCIS" emerges, the consular officer "may request any additional evidence which bears a reasonable relationship to this issue. Disagreement with USCIS interpretation of the law or the facts, however, is not sufficient reason to ask USCIS to reconsider its approval of the petition."[972] As discussed above, the consular officer's "evaluation of an applicant's eligibility for an H-1B visa shall not focus on the issue of immigrant intent."[973]

Certain U.S. consulates may issue H-1B visas well in advance of the assignment start date in order to manage a "possible flood of applicants" seeking visas in September,[974] although the visa application may not be made until 90 days before the employment start date.[975] Visas issued earlier than 10 days before the employment start date will be annotated with the following statement: "not valid until (ten days prior to petition validity date)."[976]

H-1B visas may also be issued for periods shorter than the petition validity or authorized period of stay, such as "on the basis of reciprocity or the terms of a waiver of a ground of ineligibility," and such visas should be properly annotated.[977] In such situations, H-1B visas may be "reissue[d] … any number of times within the period allowable," and the reciprocity fees should be collected with "each reissuance."[978] For a discussion of reciprocity schedules, see below and Volume 1: Chapter Two, "Basic Nonimmigrant Concepts."

A foreign national may also obtain an H-1B visa valid through the end of an existing H-1B petition, as well as "any extensions" and/or through the end of a subsequent H-1B petition, as long as the beneficiary has not changed H-1B employers and has had "no gap in authorized status."[979] For example, if the initial H-1B petition was approved through December 31, 2017, and a second H-1B petition with the same employer was approved from January 1, 2018, through December 31, 2019, then an H-1B visa may be issued, valid from September 1, 2017, through

---

[971] 9 FAM 402.10-7(A).

[972] 9 FAM 402.10-7(B).

[973] 9 FAM 402.10-9(C).

[974] "DOS Cable Encourages Issuance of H-1B and H-2B Visas with Deferred Validity Dates" (Apr. 2, 2004), AILA Doc. No. 04040862.

[975] 9 FAM 402.10-11.

[976] "DOS Cable Encourages Issuance of H-1B and H-2B Visas with Deferred Validity Dates" (Apr. 2, 2004), AILA Doc. No. 04040862; 9 FAM 402.10-11.

[977] 9 FAM 402.10-11(D).

[978] 9 FAM 402.10-11(F).

[979] 9 FAM 402.10-11.

Copyright © 2017. American Immigration Lawyers Association. All rights reserved.

December 31, 2019. In this situation, the beneficiary "does not have to wait until 10 days before the start date of the second petition to re-enter the United States."[980] For discussion of H-1B visa applications pursuant to H-1B portability, see above.

If an H-4 dependent applies for a visa "to follow to join a principal alien already in the United States, [the consular officer] must be satisfied that the principal alien is maintaining H status before issuing the visa."[981] For this reason, the practitioner is encouraged to prepare a statement confirming the principal's continued H-1B employment. The consular officer may also consult PIMS or request information from the KCC's Fraud Prevention Unit.[982]

1. H-1B1 Visa Applications

An employer need not file an H-1B1 petition with USCIS: "Instead, an employee will [or may] present evidence for classification directly to [a consular officer] at the time of visa application."[983] The following documents must be submitted, each of which are discussed in further detail below:

- Approved LCA, "clearly annotated as 'H-1B1 Chile' or 'H-1B1 Singapore;'"[984]
- Statement offering employment from the employer;[985]
- Evidence of educational and occupational qualifications;
- Evidence of the temporary stay; and
- Evidence of payment of all applicable fees.[986]

DOS guidance notes:

"[T]he requirements for … H-1B1 … do not include licensure. Licensure to practice a given profession in the United States is a post-entry requirement subject to enforcement by the appropriate state or other sub-federal authority. Proof of licensure to practice in a given profession in the United States may be offered along with a job offer letter, or other documentation in support of an application for an H-1B1 visa. However, admission and or classification must not be denied based solely on the fact that the applicant does not already hold a license to practice in the United States." [987]

---

[980] Id.

[981] 9 FAM 402.10-14(B).

[982] Id.

[983] 9 FAM 402.10-5(C); CBP, J. Ahern, "Free Trade Agreements with Chile and Singapore" (Apr. 19, 2004), AILA Doc. No. 05040166; USCIS, W. Yates, "Lifting of Numerical Cap on Mexican NAFTA Nonimmigrant Professionals (TN) and Free Trade Agreements with Chile and Singapore" (Jan. 8, 2004), AILA Doc. No. 04030361.

[984] 9 FAM 402.10-5(D) and (H).

[985] DOS, "H-1B1 Temporary Entry of Nonimmigrant Professionals" (Mar. 2004), AILA Doc. No. 04033165.

[986] 9 FAM 402.10-5(H).

[987] 9 FAM 402.10-5(G).

Copyright © 2017. American Immigration Lawyers Association. All rights reserved.

As with H-1B petitions, "the visa validity period is limited to that of the underlying ... LCA."[988] The U.S. embassy websites for both Singapore and Chile indicate that H-1B1 visas are multiple entry and valid for a maximum of 18 months.[989]

The documents for an H-1B1 change of status petition are similar.[990] For discussion of the advantages of a visa application over a change of status application, see Volume 1: Chapter Five, "E-3 Visas and Status" and Volume 1: Chapter Fourteen, "TN Visas and Status."

As discussed above, the definition of the term "specialty occupation" for H-1B1 visa applications "is presently identical to the regulatory definition for H-1Bs."[991] The visa applicant should provide evidence that he or she "meet[s] the general academic and occupational requirements for the position pursuant to the definition cited,"[992] such as copies of educational documents, license, and certifications. Alternative credentials are acceptable for certain occupations, although evidence of a bachelor's degree or higher degree may be submitted:[993]

Chilean citizens	Singaporean citizens
Disaster Relief Claims Adjuster	Disaster Relief Claims Adjuster
Management Consultant	Management Consultant
Agricultural Managers	
Physical Therapists	

Disaster Relief Claims Adjusters and Management Consultants must have a degree, "even if in an unrelated discipline," in which case they may present evidence of "3 years of experience in a field or specialty related to the consulting agreement" in addition to the unrelated degree.[994] Guidance regarding qualifying for these professions in the context of TN status, as discussed in Volume 1: Chapter Fourteen, "TN Visas and Status," may be helpful for the practitioner, since TN status is available pursuant to a treaty like H-1B1 status. Chilean Agricultural Managers and

---

[988] DOS, "H-1B1 Temporary Entry of Nonimmigrant Workers" (Mar. 11, 2004), AILA Doc. No. 04033165.

[989] U.S. Embassy in Singapore, "Apply for a U.S. Visa in Singapore," http://www.ustraveldocs.com/sg/sg-niv-typeh1b1.asp; U.S. Embassy in Chile, "Labor Visas under the Free Trade Agreement (H-1B1), https://cl.usembassy.gov/visas/visas-de-trabajo-bajo-el-tratado-de-libre-comercio-h-1b1/.

[990] USCIS, W. Yates, "Lifting of Numerical Cap on Mexican NAFTA Nonimmigrant Professionals ("TN") and Free Trade Agreements with Chile and Singapore" (Jan. 8, 2004), AILA Doc. No. 04030361.

[991] 9 FAM 402.10-5(E).

[992] 9 FAM 402.10-5(H).

[993] 9 FAM 402.10-5(E).

[994] *Id.*

Copyright © 2017. American Immigration Lawyers Association. All rights reserved.

Physical Therapists may submit evidence of "a combination of a post-secondary certificate in the specialty and three years' experience in lieu of the standard degree requirements."[995]

For a discussion of the "temporary entry" of H-1B1 nonimmigrants, see above. As with other nonimmigrant visa applications, the visa applicant must present evidence of payment of the Machine Readable Visa fee.[996] As discussed above, there is currently no additional fee required of H-1B1 employers.[997]

2. Information on Worker Rights

DOS guidance indicates that cards stating "legal protections for H-1B workers" are available and "are a simple and effective way to get the word out to each beneficiary."[998]

In addition to information on U.S. labor laws, H-1B visa applicants should be informed of their "legal rights under federal immigration, labor, and employment laws," including "the illegality of slavery, peonage, trafficking in persons, sexual assault, extortion, blackmail, and worker exploitation in the United States."[999] Therefore, during the visa interview, the consular officer "must confirm that a pamphlet … prepared by [DOS] detailing this information has been received, read, and understood by the applicant."[1000] The pamphlet includes "a discussion of procedural issues, legal rights, and available legal resources" about the following topics:

- The process of applying for a nonimmigrant visa;
- The portability of H-1B status;
- "The legal rights of employment or education-based NIV holders under Federal immigration, labor, and employment laws";
- "The illegality of slavery, peonage, trafficking in persons, sexual assault, extortion, blackmail, and worker exploitation in the United States";
- "The legal rights of immigrant victims of trafficking in persons and worker exploitation," including:
  - "The right of access to immigrant and labor rights groups;
  - "The right to seek redress in U.S. courts;
  - "The right to report abuse without retaliation;

---

[995] *Id.*

[996] 9 FAM 402.10-5(H).

[997] USCIS, "H and L Filing Fees for Form I-129, Petition for a Nonimmigrant Worker," https://www.uscis.gov/forms/h-and-l-filing-fees-form-i-129-petition-nonimmigrant-worker.

[998] 9 FAM 402.10-17(D). A pdf of the card can be found at https://www.dol.gov/whd/FLSAEmployeeCard/H1BEnglish.pdf.

[999] 9 FAM 402.10-9(E).

[1000] *Id.*

Copyright © 2017. American Immigration Lawyers Association. All rights reserved.

- – "The right of the nonimmigrant not to relinquish possession of his or her passport to his or her employer;

- – "The requirement of an employment contract between the employer and the nonimmigrant; and

- – "An explanation of the rights and protections included in the mandatory employment contract"; and

■ "Information about nongovernmental organizations that provide services for victims of trafficking in persons and worker exploitation," including details about:

- – "Anti-trafficking in persons telephone hotlines operated by the Federal Government;

- – "The Operation Rescue and Restore hotline; and

- – "A general description of the types of victims' services available for individuals subject to trafficking in persons or worker exploitation."[1001]

Even if "the pamphlet was not received, read, or understood," the consular officer must "provide a copy [of the pamphlet] to the applicant and orally disclose in a language that the alien understands, and offer to answer any questions that the alien may have regarding information contained in the pamphlet as well as information described below regarding legal rights, U.S. law, and victim services."[1002] The oral explanation "should include" the following information:

■ "The legal rights of employment-based nonimmigrants under Federal immigration, labor, and employment laws;

■ "The illegality of slavery, peonage, trafficking in persons, sexual assault, extortion, blackmail, and worker exploitation in the United States; and

■ "The legal rights of immigrant victims of trafficking in persons, worker exploitation, and other related crimes, including:

- – "The right of access to immigrant and labor rights groups;

- – "The right to seek redress in U.S. courts; and

- – "The right to report abuse without retaliation; and

■ "The availability of services for victims of human trafficking and worker exploitation in the United States, including victim services complaint hotlines."[1003]

3. DOS Reporting of Violations to DOL

DOS may report certain violations of "labor law" to DOL, although DOS does not actually bear responsibility for enforcing compliance with the LCA program.[1004]

[1001] 9 FAM 402.3-9(C)(1).

[1002] 9 FAM 402.3-9(C)(2).

[1003] *Id.*

Copyright © 2017. American Immigration Lawyers Association. All rights reserved.

Even if a violation is reported to DOL, an H-1B visa would nevertheless most likely be issued.[1005]

DOS may only report violations, on behalf of nonimmigrants who have been physically present in the United States and improperly employed by the petitioner in H-1B status, that occurred in the United States within the immediate preceding 12 months, because DOL has authority to investigate only these violations,[1006] as discussed in Volume 1: Chapter Six, "The Labor Condition Application." DOS guidance notes that it "is difficult to show that a violation occurred within the last 12 months."[1007] However, DOL may be able to "file a labor complaint up until the end of the current calendar year," in the event that "the applicant provides tax documents for the preceding calendar year and these show evidence of significant underpayment of wages without explanation," such as "illness, return to country of origin for a portion of the year,"[1008] or another appropriate reason.

Alternatively, the violation may be "ongoing," such as if information stated on the petitioner's tax documents varies widely from information provided on the H-1B petition and/or in the KCC's data system.[1009] DOS guidance offers the example of great divergence in the number of employees for whom "unemployment and social security taxes were paid" as contrasted with headcount stated on the Form I-129 "and the number of petitions for that employer for which still valid visas have been issued."[1010] The FAM cautions: "While there may be an explanation for this, such a large discrepancy implies there may be no employer/employee relationship between the petitioner and the petitioned-for aliens or that the aliens are not being appropriately compensated, a situation calling for a labor violation complaint."[1011] The following potential violations should be reported to DOL:

- Failure to pay the higher of the prevailing or actual wage, as discussed in Volume 1: Chapter Six, "The Labor Condition Application";

- Payment of petition and/or fraud fees by the beneficiary;

- Benching of the employee, which may be evidenced by the beneficiary "report[ing] wages on Form IRS-1099-C, Cancellation of Debt, identifying

---

[1004] 9 FAM 402.10-17 (stating that the consular officer's "primary responsibility in visa adjudication is to carry out the requirements of U.S. immigration law" as opposed to compliance). For details on how a consular may report potential violations, *see* 9 FAM 402.10-17(B).

[1005] 9 FAM 402.10-17 ("In most of these situations, [the consular officer] likely would still issue a visa").

[1006] 9 FAM 402.10-17(A).

[1007] *Id.*

[1008] *Id.*

[1009] *Id.*

[1010] *Id.* ("For example, the petitioner's quarterly tax documents may show that unemployment and social security taxes were paid for 10 employees, which is the same number the employer reports on the Form I-129. A CCD review may show 50 visa applications in the CCD for that petitioner, however, and that 30 of those visas are still valid").

[1011] 9 FAM 402.10-17(A).

Copyright © 2017. American Immigration Lawyers Association. All rights reserved.

themselves as independent contractors, not on a W-2 as would be the case for a true employee"; and

- "Systematic LCA Violations, Including Off-Site Work," because LCAs "are made for a specific location, and temporary workers are supposed to be living and working in that location," except for LCAs indicating multiple worksites, as discussed in Volume 1: Chapter Six, "The Labor Condition Application."[1012]

F. Admission to the United States

A foreign national may seek H-1B admission up to 10 days before the start date of the petition and may remain in the United States for 10 days after expiration of the petition if the I-94 card lists an expiration date incorporating this additional 10-day period, although the "beneficiary may not work except during the validity period of the petition."[1013] As discussed below, H-1B nonimmigrants are subject to a time limitation on H-1B status, with certain exceptions.

When seeking admission to the United States, the foreign national should present his or her passport, with the H-1B visa and the H-1B petition approval notice from USCIS. The Form I-797 should be presented with each application for admission: "The copy of Form I-797 shall be retained by the beneficiary and presented during the validity of the petition when re-entering the United States to resume the same employment with the same petitioner."[1014]

As discussed in Volume 1: Chapter Two, "Basic Nonimmigrant Concepts," Canadian citizens do not require visas in order to enter the United States.[1015] Canadian nationals may apply for admission with the H-1B approval notice and Canadian passport at the port of entry.[1016] For a more in-depth discussion of applications for admission in nonimmigrant status by Canadian citizens, see Volume 1: Chapter Two, "Basic Nonimmigrant Concepts."

If entering by land, the foreign national will be issued an I-94 card. If entering by sea or air, the individual will receive a stamp in the passport, and the I-94 will be recorded electronically.[1017] Practitioners should advise clients who receive the passport stamp rather than the paper I-94 to check their I-94s on the online look-up[1018] to ensure that it is correct and that the expiration date of their status is noted.

[1012] *Id.*

[1013] 8 CFR §214.2(h)(13)(i)(A).

[1014] *Id.*

[1015] 8 CFR §212.1(a).

[1016] 9 FAM 402.10-8(F).

[1017] 78 Fed. Reg. 18457 (Mar. 27, 2013). *See also* CBP Fact Sheet, "I-94 Automation" (Nov. 2015), https://www.cbp.gov/sites/default/files/assets/documents/2016-Mar/i-94-automation-fact-sheet.pdf.

[1018] CBP, "I-94 Website," https://i94.cbp.dhs.gov/I94/#/home.

Copyright © 2017. American Immigration Lawyers Association. All rights reserved.

Due to the visa reciprocity schedules,[1019] as discussed in Volume 1: "Chapter Two, Basic Nonimmigrant Concepts," a foreign national may receive a visa valid for a shorter time period than the H-1B petition, but the expiration of H-1B status should match the end date of the H-1B petition and not the end date of the H-1B visa.

For example, Chinese citizens are eligible for H visas valid for no longer than 12 months.[1020] Therefore, even though the underlying H-1B petition was approved for three years, a Chinese citizen will be able to obtain an H visa that is valid for only 12 months from the date of visa issuance. The Petition Expiration Date (PED) provided in the lower right corner of the visa should, however, match the dates of validity of the H-1B petition as stated on the Form I-797 approval notice. For applicants for admission with visas valid for a shorter period of time than the H-1B petition, practitioners may wish to reiterate the need to present the original Form I-797 approval notice to ensure that the period of authorized stay stated on the passport stamp and I-94 record matches the dates of the petition validity. Practitioners may also wish to contact petitioners with these employees well in advance of the visa expiration date to strategize subsequent applications for visas, so the foreign nationals may travel internationally and re-enter the United States during the remaining time of petition validity.

The spouse and children of an H-1B nonimmigrant may also use a B visa when seeking admission to the United States if the "planned period of stay is to be brief," or "if the spouse or child already has a valid B-2 visa and it would be inconvenient or impossible for him or her to apply for an H-4 visa."[1021] The practitioner should carefully discuss this approach with the client and the foreign national, however, because the dependent will also need to "overcome INA 214(b)."[1022] In addition, the dependents should make no misrepresentation when seeking admission in B-2 status at the port of entry. In particular, the practitioner may wish to have the dependents gather evidence of the brief stay, such as round-trip airfare, enrollment or admission in educational programs in the home country or elsewhere abroad, evidence of continued employment abroad, or other evidence of the reasons why the dependents will not remain in the United States for an extended period of time.

For all foreign nationals, good follow-up should include requesting copies of visas and obtaining a copy of the I-94 to ensure that all the information is correct, and calendaring the expiration dates to monitor the foreign national's status, as discussed below.

[1019] DOS, "Reciprocity and Civil Documents by Country," https://travel.state.gov/content/visas/en/fees/reciprocity-by-country.html.

[1020] DOS, "China Reciprocity Schedule," https://travel.state.gov/content/visas/en/fees/reciprocity-by-country/CH.html.

[1021] 9 FAM 402.10-14(D).

[1022] *Id.*

Copyright © 2017. American Immigration Lawyers Association. All rights reserved.

V. Additional Follow-up

A. Amended Petitions

An amended H-1B petition is required to "immediately notify" USCIS[1023] of "any material changes in the terms and conditions of employment … or the alien's eligibility as specified in the original approved petition."[1024] An amended petition is defined by USCIS guidance as a "petition involving a material change in the terms and conditions of employment that *does not* involve a change of classification or an extension of stay beyond that which was previously authorized,"[1025] and is necessary "when the petitioner continues to employ the beneficiary."[1026] However, if the petitioner no longer has an employment relationship with the beneficiary, then "the petitioner shall send a letter explaining the change(s) to the director who approved the petition."[1027]

The amended H-1B petition should be filed, with the filing fee, at either the California Service Center or the Vermont Service Center, depending upon the place of employment,[1028] and "must be accompanied by a current or new Department of Labor determination," which is "a new labor condition application."[1029] The practitioner should also submit "evidence addressing the change which necessitated the filing of the amended petition."[1030] USCIS guidance states that "[b]ecause the amended petition supplements the original petition, documentation does not have to be duplicated in the amended petition."[1031] Nevertheless, the prudent practitioner should include evidence of eligibility for the H-1B classification, as discussed below.

An amended H-1B petition is required in the following circumstances:

- "When a beneficiary is transferred from one employer to another, the filing of a new petition ensures that the new employer is liable for the alien's return transportation abroad and that the employer files a labor condition application.

- "A change of the alien's duties from one specialty occupation to another.

- "When a beneficiary is transferred from a firm to another firm within the same organization, and the new firm becomes the beneficiary's employer. The mere transfer of the beneficiary to another work site, in the same occupation, does not require the filing of an amended petition provided the initial petitioner remains

---

[1023] 8 CFR §214.2(h)(11)(i)(A).

[1024] 8 CFR §214.2(h)(2)(i)(E); AFM 31.2(e).

[1025] USCIS, "I-129 H-1B Standard Operating Procedures" (undated, posted July 26, 2007), AILA Doc. No. 07072668 (emphasis in original).

[1026] 8 CFR §214.2(h)(11)(i)(A).

[1027] *Id.*

[1028] USCIS, "Direct Filing Addresses for Form I-129, Petition for a Nonimmigrant Worker," https://www.uscis.gov/i-129-addresses. USCIS changes filing locations from time to time, so the practitioner should monitor this webpage to stay aware of the current filing address.

[1029] 8 CFR §214.2(h)(2)(i)(E).

[1030] AFM 31.2(b)(4).

[1031] *Id.*

Copyright © 2017. American Immigration Lawyers Association. All rights reserved.

the alien's employer and, provided further, the supporting labor condition application remains valid.

- "When the beneficiary's employer merges with another firm to create a third entity which will subsequently employ the beneficiary. *This circumstance is distinguished from a change in ownership.*"[1032]

It is important to note that this guidance pre-dates *Matter of Simeio Solutions, LLC*,[1033] and thus the third bullet, while technically correct with respect to changes in worksite because of the "supporting labor condition application remains valid" clause, requires deeper examination. *Simeio*, and that deeper examination, is discussed in detail below under the section titled "Change in Worksite."

In addition, an amended petition is most likely necessary if the beneficiary switches from full-time to part-time employment.[1034] Although USCIS did not explicitly say as much, when asked about the need for an amended petition if the reduced hours are a result of return to work after temporary medical disability and/or if the H-1B petition stated the remuneration in hourly wages as opposed to "a set salary," USCIS only responded: "An amended petition is required whenever there is a material change in the terms and conditions of employment."[1035]

1. Corporate Reorganization

As stated by statute:

"An amended H-1B petition shall not be required where the petitioning employer is involved in a corporate restructuring, including but not limited to a merger, acquisition, or consolidation, where a new corporate entity succeeds to the interests and obligations of the original petitioning employer and where the terms and conditions of employment remain the same but for the identity of the petitioner."[1036]

Although legacy INS indicated the intent to issue regulations to "define the eligible forms of corporate restructuring, and the type of evidence required, including the manner in which that evidence should be submitted for extension of stay requests by the new corporate entity,"[1037] no such regulations have been promulgated to date. In the event of a corporate reorganization, "the previous approval and previously issued approval notice remain valid" and "the Service will not issue amended

---

[1032] AFM 31.2(e).

[1033] 26 I&N Dec. 542 (AAO 2015), AILA Doc. No. 15040969.

[1034] "AILA/VSC Practice Pointer: Strategic Use of the Part Time H-1B," AILA Doc. No. 09111960; 8 CFR §214.2(h)(2)(i)(E).

[1035] "Q & A Stakeholder Conference" (Sept. 20, 2010 and updated Oct. 19, 2010), AILA Doc. No. 10101471.

[1036] INA §214(c)(10); 9 FAM 402.10-8(D).

[1037] USCIS, M. Pearson, "Initial Guidance for Processing H-1B Petitions as Affected by the 'American Competitiveness in the Twenty-First Century Act' (Public Law 106-313) and Related Legislation (Public Law 106-311) and (Public Law 106-396)" (Jan. 19, 2001), AILA Doc. No. 01062031.

Copyright © 2017. American Immigration Lawyers Association. All rights reserved.

approval notices bearing the new company name."[1038] If the petitioner desires an amended approval notice, then "the appropriate procedure for obtaining a new approval notice will continue to be through the filing of an amended Form I-129 with fee."[1039] A beneficiary may be readmitted to the United States following the corporate reorganization as long as:

- He or she "is otherwise admissible";

- He or she presents a valid passport and visa, unless exempt from these requirements; and

- He or she "presents a letter from the new corporate entity stating that":

  – The "new corporate entity has succeeded to the interests and obligations of the original H-1B petitioning employer"; and

  – The "terms and conditions of employment of the H-1B nonimmigrant remain the same."[1040]

The following is a list of other situations in which an amended H-1B petition is not required:

- "When a beneficiary is transferred from one branch of a firm to another branch of the same firm. A branch of a firm is not considered to be a separate entity from its parent company.

- "If the petitioner changes its name. The petitioner should advise USCIS of the name change if and when it files to extend the alien's stay.

- "Changes in the ownership structure of the petitioning entity. It is understood that the new owner(s) of the firm assumes the previous owner's liabilities which would include the assertions the prior owner made on the labor condition application."[1041]

The employer should not file an amended petition "merely as an avenue to advise USCIS of minor changes in the conditions of employment or the beneficiary's eligibility."[1042] Instead, the petitioner "should advise USCIS of these minor, immaterial changes when extensions of the beneficiary's stay are filed."[1043] However, see the discussion immediately below with respect to what might be considered a material change requiring an amended petition.

2. Change in Worksite

As discussed in Volume 1: Chapter Six, "The Labor Condition Application," a new labor condition application is required if the beneficiary will work at a new

---

[1038] *Id.* Although the statements were made by legacy INS, the principle should remain the same for USCIS.

[1039] *Id.*

[1040] *Id.*

[1041] AFM 31.2(e).

[1042] *Id.*

[1043] *Id.*

Copyright © 2017. American Immigration Lawyers Association. All rights reserved.

worksite. Over the years, the question of whether an amended petition is required when a new LCA is needed, or when an existing LCA covers the employee's move to the new worksite, has been muddled at best, although informal guidance did tend to indicate that where there was an existing LCA, a posting at the new site would be all that was required.[1044] However, a 2015 precedent decision, *Matter of Simeio Solutions, LLC*,[1045] and subsequent USCIS guidance addressed the issue, and reversed much of the informal guidance.

Matter of Simeio held that a change in the place of employment that requires an LCA for that location not previously tied to that beneficiary is a material change, requiring the filing of an amended H-1B petition.[1046] USCIS guidance based on the *Simeio* decision states that "a petitioner must file an amended or new H-1B petition if the H-1B employee is changing his or her place of employment to a geographical area requiring a corresponding LCA to be certified to USCIS, even if a new LCA is already certified by the U.S. Department of Labor and posted at the new work location."[1047]

USCIS views this as a situation to which portability applies, and thus "the H-1B employee can immediately begin work at the new place of employment" once the amended petition is filed, "provided the requirements of section 212(n) of the INA are otherwise satisfied."[1048] DOS also states that a request for a visa for a beneficiary whose amended petition has been filed but not yet adjudicated "should be processed to conclusion based on the receipt notice."[1049]

USCIS specified three circumstances in which an amended or new petition is not needed:

- A different location within the same area of intended employment, since "there are no changes in the terms and conditions of employment that might affect eligibility of H-1B classification." However, the original LCA must still be posted in the new location in accordance with DOL regulations;

- Short-term placements of up to 30 or 60 days, depending on the circumstances, as described in DOL rules and in Volume 1: Chapter Six, "The Labor Condition Application"; and

- The beneficiary is going to a non-worksite location for such activities as employee development or a conference, little time will be spent at the

---

[1044] *See* American Immigration Lawyers Association/American Immigration Council, "*Matter of Simeio Solutions* and Subsequent USCIS Guidance on Amended H-1B Petitions" (June 26, 2015), AILA Doc. No. 15062668, tracing the history of informal correspondence on the subject.

[1045] *Matter of Simeio Solutions, LLC*, 26 I&N Dec. 542 (AAO 2015), AILA Doc. No. 15040969.

[1046] *Id.*

[1047] "USCIS Final Guidance on When to File an Amended or New H-1B Petition After *Matter of Simeio Solutions, LLC*," PM-602-0120 (July 21, 2015), AILA Doc. No. 15072105.

[1048] *Id.*

[1049] DOS, "New Guidance on H-1B Adjudications Involving Changes in Places of Employment" (Nov. 30, 2015), AILA Doc. No. 15122110.

Copyright © 2017. American Immigration Lawyers Association. All rights reserved.

location, or the job is "peripatetic in nature" and the visits are casual and short term "(*i.e.*, not exceeding 5 consecutive workdays for any one visit by a peripatetic worker or 10 consecutive workdays for ... a worker who spends most work time at one location)."[1050]

In other words, an amended petition is not needed where a new or separate LCA is not needed. See Volume 1: Chapter Six, "The Labor Condition Application" for a discussion of these circumstances.

While USCIS denied that *Simeio* is a departure from the past, it portrayed the case and the guidance as "clarify[ying]."[1051] USCIS thus declared that, if an H-1B employee moved to a *new* area of employment prior to publication of *Simeio*, USCIS would "generally not pursue new adverse actions (e.g., denials or revocations)" based only on a failure to file an amended petition.[1052] However, it "will preserve adverse actions already commenced or completed prior to July 21, 2015 [the date of the guidance memo] and will preserve new adverse actions if other violations are determined to have occurred."[1053] The guidance also put in place a "safe harbor" period, until January 15, 2016, during which filings would be considered timely for changes that occurred prior to *Simeio*. Any moves to a new place of employment not covered by these transitional rules "will be out of compliance ... and thus subject to adverse action.[1054]

If the amended petition is denied, and the original petition is still valid, the beneficiary can return to the original place of employment. A petitioner can file multiple, successive amended petitions, which will be treated in the same way as "bridging" petitions in the portability context, [1055] discussed earlier in this chapter. As mentioned above, a request for a visa for a beneficiary whose amended petition has been filed but not yet adjudicated "should be processed to conclusion based on the receipt notice."[1056] DOS consular officers "are not expected to verify the LCA or place of employment," but if an officer becomes aware of a discrepancy, he or she should verity that "the petitioner has taken the appropriate steps."[1057]

B. If Employment Ceases

As discussed above in the context of portability while the beneficiary is unemployed, H-1B and H-1B1 nonimmigrants whose employment ends prior to the expiration of their authorized stay are able to remain in the United States lawfully for

---

[1050] "USCIS Final Guidance on When to File an Amended or New H-1B Petition After *Matter of Simeio Solutions, LLC*," PM-602-0120 (July 21, 2015), AILA Doc. No. 15072105.

[1051] *Id.*

[1052] *Id.*

[1053] *Id.*

[1054] *Id.*

[1055] *Id.*

[1056] DOS, "New Guidance on H-1B Adjudications Involving Changes in Places of Employment" (Nov. 30, 2015), AILA Doc. No. 15122110.

[1057] *Id.*

Copyright © 2017. American Immigration Lawyers Association. All rights reserved.

the shorter of 60 days or when the existing validity period ends.[1058] This can be used only once during each "authorized validity period," and cannot be aggregated,[1059] *i.e.*, the grace period cannot be used for 20 days and then, later in the same validity period, another 40 days. The purpose is to allow the beneficiary to wind up affairs or to seek other employment and request a change of status if needed and eligible.[1060] The individual is not able to work during this period, unless otherwise authorized.[1061]

The rulemaking that put in place this grace period was silent as to what would be an "authorized validity period" in the H-1B context, but presumably it means the validity period of the approved USCIS petition that is in effect for the individual at the time. Thus, if the nonimmigrant finds a new employer that files an H-1B petition with a request for extension of stay, the period of validity of the approval of that new petition should start a new validity period where the 60-day grace period would again be available.

C. H-1B Time Limitations

H-1B status may be held for a maximum of six years,[1062] except as discussed below. Therefore:

"When an alien in an H classification has spent the maximum allowable period of stay in the United States, a new petition under sections 101(a)(15)(H) or (L) of the Act may not be approved unless that alien has resided and been physically present outside the United States, except for brief trips for business or pleasure, for the time limit imposed on the particular H classification. Brief trips to the United States for business or pleasure during the required time abroad are not interruptive, but do not count towards fulfillment of the required time abroad.... The petitioner shall provide information about the alien's employment, place of residence, and the dates and purposes of any trips to the United States during the period that the alien was required to reside abroad."[1063]

Essentially, if a foreign national has held H-1B status for six years and does not qualify for any exception, then he or she is ineligible for H or L status: "At the end of the six-year period, such alien must either seek permanent resident status or depart the United States."[1064] A new petition will not be approved on behalf of the beneficiary until he or she "has resided and been physically present outside" the

---

[1058] 8 CFR §214.1(*l*)(2).

[1059] 81 Fed. Reg. 82398, 82438 (Nov. 18, 2016).

[1060] 80 Fed. Reg. 81900, 81923 (Dec. 31, 2015).

[1061] *Id.*

[1062] INA §214(g)(4); 8 CFR §214.2(h)(15)(ii)(B)(*1*) ("The alien's total period of stay may not exceed six years"). Before 1989, there "was no maximum time limit on the total period of stay or number of extensions that could be approved for an H-1, although in practice an H-1 requesting an extension beyond five years was generally denied as an 'intending immigrant.'" AFM 31.1(b).

[1063] 8 CFR §214.2(h)(13)(i)(B); *Matter of Safetran*, 20 I&N Dec. 49 (Comm'r 1989).

[1064] 73 Fed. Reg. 15389 (Mar. 25, 2008) (citing 8 CFR §214.2(h)(13)(iii)(A)).

Copyright © 2017. American Immigration Lawyers Association. All rights reserved.

United States[1065] for one year.[1066] This includes an H-1B extension.[1067] DOS FAM guidance previously stated that "[p]eriods when the alien fails to maintain status shall be counted towards the applicable limit; an alien may not circumvent the limit by violating his or her status."[1068] The current version of the FAM no longer contains this statement, but there is no reason other than its omission to believe that DOS has abandoned this position. The practitioner should also note that time spent in L status also counts toward the six-year limitation on H-1B status:

> "An H-1B alien in a specialty occupation or an alien of distinguished merit and ability who has spent six years in the United States under section 101(a)(15)(H) and/or (L) of the Act may not seek extension, change status, or be readmitted to the United States under section 101(a)(15)(H) or (L) of the Act unless the alien has resided and been physically present outside the United States, except for brief trips for business or pleasure, for the immediate prior year."[1069]

If the foreign national travels to the United States as a tourist or as a business visitor during the required one year of residence abroad, those trips will not break the continuity of the one-year period. Therefore, the foreign national should not be required to have remained outside the United States for one year since his or her most recent departure from the United States, if that date is after the last date that the foreign national held H status. However, the foreign national must have been physically present outside the United States for the number of days that he or she was present within the United States in addition to the one year. For example, if the foreign national last held H status on December 31, 2010, and made one business trip to the United States for a period of ten days, then an H-1B petition may not be filed until January 11, 2012, at the earliest. Evidence of residence outside the United States includes copies of mortgages, copies of rental agreements, employment confirmation letters, and is similar to evidence of physical presence outside the United States, as discussed below.

However, physical presence outside the United States during brief trips also "does not count toward fulfillment of the required time abroad."[1070] USCIS guidance cautions:

> "The maximum time limit in an H classification and the requirement to reside abroad upon expiration of this period cannot be avoided by leaving the United States before the expiration of the maximum time limit and re-entering within a short period of time under a new petition. In such cases, the approval period of the new petition shall be consistent with and count towards the maximum time limit on an alien's temporary stay.

[1065] 8 CFR §214.2(h)(13)(i)(B).

[1066] 8 CFR §214.2(h)(13)(iii)(A).

[1067] 8 CFR §214.2(h)(15)(i) ("When the total period of stay in an H classification has been reached, no further extensions may be granted").

[1068] Former 9 FAM 41.53 N13.

[1069] 8 CFR §214.2(h)(13)(iii)(A).

[1070] 9 FAM 402.10-13.

Copyright © 2017. American Immigration Lawyers Association. All rights reserved.

"A new [six-year] period of authorized stay may begin only when the alien has resided outside the United States for a period required by the classification, or when the alien qualifies for an exemption from limits on the maximum period of stay...."[1071]

For discussion of H-1B time recapture, see below. Fortunately, physical presence in H-4 status "does not count against the maximum allowable period of stay available to a principal H-1B alien."[1072] As stated by USCIS guidance:

"Limitations on the duration of time spent in H-1B nonimmigrant status refer only to the principal alien worker in H-1B status and do not apply independently to the principal worker's spouse and children.... Thus, an alien who was previously an H-4 and subsequently becomes an H-1B principal will be entitled to a maximum period of stay. Conversely, an H-1B principal who subsequently converts H-4 status may remain in the derivative status for as long as the principal alien spouse maintains that principal status."[1073]

"Further, from a policy perspective, this interpretation promotes family unity by affording each qualified spouse the opportunity to spend six-years in H-1B status while allowing the other spouse to remain as an H-4 dependent and without undermining the Congressional intent to limit a principal alien's ability to work in a specialty occupation for six-year maximum period."[1074]

For further discussion on changing status from H-4 to H-1B, see above. The other exception to the six-year time limitation is if:

- The foreign national "did not reside continually in the United States and [his or her] employment in the United States was seasonal or intermittent or was for an aggregate of 6 months or less per year"; and

- The foreign national "reside[s] abroad and regularly commute to the United States to engage in part-time employment."[1075]

The petitioner and the beneficiary "must provide clear and convincing proof that the alien qualifies for such an exception," such as through "arrival and departure records, copies of tax returns, and records of employment abroad."[1076] This exception "will not apply if the principal alien's dependents have been living continuously in the United States in H-4 status."[1077]

[1071] AFM 31.2(d).

[1072] 9 FAM 402.10-12.

[1073] AFM 31.2(d).

[1074] USCIS, M. Aytes, "Guidance on Determining Periods of Admission for Aliens Previously in H-4 or L-2 Status; Aliens Applying for Additional Periods of Admission beyond the H-1B Six Year Maximum; and Aliens Who Have Not Exhausted the Six-Year Maximum But Who Have Been Absent from the United States for Over One Year" (Dec. 5, 2006), AILA Doc. No. 06122063.

[1075] 8 CFR §214.2(h)(13)(v); 9 FAM 402.10-13(C).

[1076] *Id.*

[1077] 9 FAM 402.10-13(C).

Copyright © 2017. American Immigration Lawyers Association. All rights reserved.

The following sections address common approaches to employ an H-1B worker for longer than six years. The practitioner should note that the strategies are not mutually exclusive; a beneficiary may be able to obtain an AC21 extension after holding H-1B status for longer than six calendar years and vice versa.

1. AC21 Exemptions from Time Limitations for Beneficiaries Sponsored for Permanent Residence

Pursuant to AC21, foreign nationals may hold H-1B status for more than six cumulative years as long as certain conditions are met.[1078] As noted by USCIS guidance: "Congress provided exemptions from maximum stay rules for certain H-1B aliens who were being sponsored by employers for permanent residence and were subject to long delays either for government processing or for visa numbers."[1079] A qualifying foreign national may obtain H-1B extensions beyond six years, as discussed below.

The employer and/or foreign national bear the burden of proof to demonstrate the beneficiary's "eligibility for any additional periods of stay in H-1B status beyond the six year maximum, including evidence of job requirements, alien credentials, labor condition application approval, previous H-1B status, pending labor certification or immigrant petition, and unavailability of immigrant visa number, and admissibility or maintenance of nonimmigrant status."[1080]

a. Extensions for Lengthy Adjudications

The first exception from the six-year time limitation is available if "365 days or more have elapsed since":

- A nonfrivolous labor certification application was filed on behalf of the foreign national, if labor certification is required; or

- A nonfrivolous employment-based immigrant visa petition was filed.[1081]

An eligible foreign national may obtain extensions in one-year increments "until such time as a final decision is made on the alien's lawful permanent residence,"[1082] *i.e.*, until the immigrant visa application or adjustment of status application is decided or "administratively or otherwise close[d]."[1083] If the labor certification application was approved, then it must remain unrevoked and unexpired, and if the immigrant petition was approved, it must remain unrevoked.[1084] Since a 2016 regulation change,

---

[1078] AFM 31.2(d).

[1079] *Id.*

[1080] AFM 31.2(d).

[1081] 8 CFR §214.2(h)(13)(iii)(D); American Competitiveness in the Twenty-First Century Act of 2000, Pub. L. No. 106-313, §106(a) (Oct. 17, 2000). The statutory section is titled "Exemption from Limitation" (all capitals removed).

[1082] American Competitiveness in the Twenty-First Century Act of 2000, Pub. L. No. 106-313, §106(b) (Oct. 17, 2000).

[1083] 8 CFR §214.2(h)(13)(iii)(D)(2).

[1084] *Id.*

Copyright © 2017. American Immigration Lawyers Association. All rights reserved.

effective in 2017, an employer's withdrawal of an immigrant petition usually does not result in revocation of the petition.[1085] See Volume 2: Chapter Three, "The Immigrant Visa Petition" for a discussion of these 2016 changes on revocations of immigrant petitions. As discussed below, a labor certification application on appeal may be used as the basis for an AC21 extension.

For subsequent H-1B extensions beyond the seventh year, the labor certification application or immigrant petition "need not be the same as that used to qualify for the initial" extension beyond the sixth year,[1086] but the time that elapsed from the filing of one application or petition cannot be aggregated with the time elapsed since the filing of "another such application or petition" to meet the 365-day requirement.[1087]

Importantly, if the beneficiary "fails to file an adjustment of status application or apply for an immigrant visa within 1 year of an immigrant visa being authorized for issuance based on her or her preference category and country of chargeability," he or she will cease to be eligible for this exception to the six-year limit.[1088] However, if the one year is interrupted by a retrogression in visa availability, as discussed in Volume 2: Chapter One, "Basic Immigrant Visa Concepts," a new one-year period will start when the visa numbers again become available.[1089] Also, "USCIS may excuse a failure to file in its discretion if the alien establishes that the failure to apply was due to circumstances beyond his or her control."[1090] Thus, it will be essential for the practitioner, the petitioner, and the beneficiary to keep a careful eye on immigrant visa availability dates to ensure that the ability to stay in H-1B status is not accidently lost.

This restriction has the potential to be problematic, particularly where the H-1B beneficiary has changed employers and is required to go through the labor certification and I-140 immigrant petition process with a new employer. Depending upon processing times, it may well take more than one year to get to the point where the underlying labor certification application and I-140 immigrant petition with the new employer are complete such that the individual can apply for adjustment of status. It is unknown if this will be viewed by USCIS as "circumstances beyond [the H-1B beneficiary's] control."

The beneficiary need not necessarily be in H-1B status at the time the petition involving this exception to the six-year limit is filed.[1091] He or she can be seeking a change from another status, as long as the individual previously held H-1B status and is otherwise eligible. In addition, the beneficiary need not be in the United States at the time the petition is filed, again provided he or she previously held H-1B status

---

[1085] 8 CFR §205.1(a)(3)(iii)(C) and (D).

[1086] 8 CFR §214.2(h)(13)(iii)(D)(7).

[1087] 8 CFR §214.2(h)(13)(iii)(D)(8).

[1088] 8 CFR §214.2(h)(13)(iii)(D)(10).

[1089] Id.

[1090] Id.

[1091] 8 CFR §214.2(h)(13)(iii)(D)(1); 80 Fed. Reg. 81900, 81914 (Dec. 31, 2015).

Copyright © 2017. American Immigration Lawyers Association. All rights reserved.

and is otherwise eligible.[1092] Further, the petitioner need not be the same company that filed the qualifying labor certification application or immigrant petition.[1093]

Only principal beneficiaries may use this exception to the six-year limit. USCIS takes the position that, while derivative beneficiaries can extend H-4 status along with the principal's extension of H-1B status, the derivative cannot extend his or her own H-1B based on a labor certification application or immigrant petition filed on behalf of that individual's spouse.[1094]

The practitioner should take into account timing considerations of the filed labor certification application or immigrant visa petition vis-à-vis the requested start date of the AC21 extension. A beneficiary who has already exhausted six years of H-1B status should be "eligible for an extension of H-1B status beyond the 6th year as long as the qualifying labor certification application or I-140 petition has been pending for at least 365 days prior to the alien's requested start date on the petition seeking the extension."[1095] The extension beyond the sixth year under AC21 section 106 can be requested up to six months before "the requested H-1B start date."[1096] Plus, the petition may be filed before the required 365 days have elapsed, provided the 365 days will have run prior to the date that that period of admission under the exemption will take effect.[1097] The extension request may "include any time remaining within the general six-year period including, for example, periods ... for which 'recapture' of H-1B remainder time is sought," provided the approval period does not exceed three years or the LCA validity period.[1098]

b. Extensions Due to Impact of Immigrant Quota Backlogs

The second exception applies to a foreign national who is the beneficiary of an approved EB-1, EB-2, and/or EB-3 immigrant visa petition and "is eligible to be granted that status [as an LPR] but for application of the per country limitations applicable to immigrants under those paragraphs."[1099] The beneficiary may obtain H-1B extensions in three-year increments[1100] "until the alien's application for adjustment of status has been processed and a decision made thereon."[1101]

Although the statute refers to "per country limitations," this exception is also available to those caught in the worldwide immigrant quota backlog:

[1092] Id.

[1093] 8 CFR §214.2(h)(13)(iii)(D)(6).

[1094] 8 CFR §214.2(h)(13)(iii)(D)(9); 80 Fed. Reg. 81900, 81914 (Dec. 31, 2015).

[1095] "AILA Liaison/VSC Meeting Minutes" (Jan. 21, 2009), AILA Doc. No. 09012768.

[1096] 8 CFR §214.2(h)(13)(iii)(D)(5).

[1097] Id.

[1098] 80 Fed. Reg. 81900, 81915 (Dec. 31, 2015).

[1099] American Competitiveness in the Twenty-First Century Act of 2000, Pub. L. No. 106-313, §104(c) (Oct. 17, 2000); 8 CFR §214.2(h)(13)(iii)(E).

[1100] 8 CFR §214.2(h)(13)(iii)(E)(1).

[1101] American Competitiveness in the Twenty-First Century Act of 2000, Pub. L. No. 106-313, §104(c) (Oct. 17, 2000).

Copyright © 2017. American Immigration Lawyers Association. All rights reserved.

"The reference to 'per country limitations' in section 104(c) invokes chargeability: The determination as to which country's numerical limits the beneficiary's visa will be 'charged to'' or counted against.... For purposes of section 104(c), when reviewing the relevant Visa Bulletin chart, there is no difference between nationals of countries who are identified separately on the Visa Bulletin because their applicable per-country limitation has been exceeded (*i.e.*, nationals of India, China, or Mexico), and nationals of those countries who are grouped under the 'All Chargeability' column, as long as the priority date has not been reached for the particular beneficiary in question."[1102]

Similarly, although the heading for the statutory section refers to "one-time protection,"[1103] USCIS notes that "the statutory text makes clear that the exemption remains available until the beneficiary has an EB-1, EB-2, or EB-3 immigrant visa immediately available to him or her."[1104] As long as the immigrant visa number is unavailable when the H-1B extension is filed, the beneficiary should receive a three-year extension,[1105] even if the immigrant visa number becomes available when the petition is adjudicated.[1106]

Thus, multiple extensions can be obtained under this provision, until a final decision is made on the adjustment of status or immigrant visa application or a final decision to revoke the petition.[1107] Since a 2016 USCIS rulemaking, an employer's withdrawal of an immigrant petition usually does not result in revocation of the petition.[1108] See Volume 2: Chapter Three, "The Immigrant Visa Petition "for a discussion of these 2016 changes on revocations of immigrant petitions.

The petitioner need not be the same company that filed the immigrant petition.[1109] The beneficiary need not necessarily be in H-1B status at the time the petition involving this exception to the six-year limit is filed.[1110] He or she can be seeking a change from another status, as long as the individual previously held H-1B status and is otherwise eligible. Thus, a foreign national holding O-1 status after gaining international recognition of his or her career achievements may nevertheless be eligible

---

[1102] 81 Fed. Reg. 82398. 82452 (Nov. 18, 2016).

[1103] American Competitiveness in the Twenty-First Century Act of 2000, Pub. L. No. 106-313, §104(c) (Oct. 17, 2000).

[1104] 81 Fed. Reg. 82398, 82451 (Nov. 18, 2016).

[1105] 8 CFR §214.2(h)(13)(iii)(E).

[1106] 81 Fed. Reg. 82398, 82451 (Nov. 18, 2016); "AILA Liaison/VSC Meeting Minutes" (Jan. 21, 2009), AILA Doc. No. 09012768.

[1107] 8 CFR §214.2(h)(13)(iii)(E)(*2*).

[1108] 8 CFR §205.1(a)(3)(iii)(C) and (D).

[1109] 8 CFR §214.2(h)(13)(iii)((E)(*4*).

[1110] 8 CFR §214.2(h)(13)(iii)(E)(*3*); 80 Fed. Reg. 81900, 81913 (Dec. 31, 2015).

Copyright © 2017. American Immigration Lawyers Association. All rights reserved.

for AC21 relief, if he or she previously held H-1B status, although a request for change of status to H-1B should be made.[1111]

In addition, the beneficiary need not be in the United States at the time the petition is filed, again provided he or she previously held H-1B status and is otherwise eligible.[1112] In other words, a foreign national who resides abroad may be the beneficiary of an H-1B petition approved, under AC21, for consular notification instead of extension of status.[1113] For example, USCIS may approve an H-1B petition that was filed on March 2, 2017, on behalf of a beneficiary who departed the United States on December 31, 2016, after physical presence in H-1B status for six years, if the immigrant visa petition began pending with USCIS on March 1, 2016.

Only principal beneficiaries may use this exception to the six-year limit. USCIS takes the position that, while derivative beneficiaries can extend H-4 status along with the principal's extension of H-1B status, a derivative cannot extend his or her own H-1B based on an immigrant petition filed on behalf of that individual's spouse.[1114]

With respect to timing, a petition utilizing this exception may be "within 6 months of the requested H-1B start date. The petitioner may request any time remaining to the beneficiary under the maximum period of admission … along with the exemption request, but in no case may the H-1B approval period exceed" the three-year validity limit or the LCA validity.[1115]

c. Appeal of Labor Certification Application and Immigrant Visa Petition for AC21 Extension

As discussed in Volume 2: Chapter Two, "The Labor Certification Application," denial or revocation of a labor certification application may be appealed within 30 days.[1116] Importantly:

> "USCIS will not consider a DOL decision [on a labor certification application] to be final until either the time for appeal has run and no appeal has been filed or, if an appeal is taken, the date a decision is issued by BALCA [Board of Alien Labor Certification Appeals].

[1111] AFM 31.2(d) ("The alien may obtain such additional periods of H-1B admission through a petition to change status from another nonimmigrant classification….")

[1112] 8 CFR §214.2(h)(13)(iii)(E)(*3*); 80 Fed. Reg. 81900, 81913 (Dec. 31, 2015).

[1113] USCIS, M. Aytes, "Guidance on Determining Periods of Admission for Aliens Previously in H-4 or L-2 Status; Aliens Applying for Additional Periods of Admission beyond the H-1B Six Year Maximum; and Aliens Who Have Not Exhausted the Six-Year Maximum But Who Have Been Absent from the United States for Over One Year" (Dec. 5, 2006), AILA Doc. No. 06122063 ("Further, in examining eligibility for the 7th year extension, USCIS will focus on whether the alien is eligible for an additional period of admission in H-1B status, rather than whether the alien is currently in H-1B status that is about to expire and seeking an extension of that status in the United States pursuant to 8 CFR 214.1(c)").

[1114] 8 CFR §214.2(h)(13)(iii)(E)(*6*); 80 Fed. Reg. 81900, 81913 (Dec. 31, 2015).

[1115] 8 CFR §214.2(h)(13)(iii)(E)(*5*).

[1116] 20 CFR §656.26(a).

Copyright © 2017. American Immigration Lawyers Association. All rights reserved.

"Therefore, the labor certification will still be considered 'pending' while the denial or revocation of the labor certification application may be appealed, or while the appeal is actually pending, for the purposes of determining if an H-1B nonimmigrant is eligible for extension of stay."[1117]

Reports indicate, however, that if an appeal, or a Request for Review or Request for Reconsideration, is filed, DOL may not "consistently update[] the case status system to reflect that the case is still pending."[1118] USCIS has indicated that "copies of email correspondence or affidavits from counsel or the employer that a request for review/reconsideration or appeal on a denied labor certification has been filed with DOL" should be accepted, and "adjudicators have been asked to elevate these cases to the attention of a senior adjudicator."[1119] For a detailed discussion of appeal of labor certification applications, see Volume 2: Chapter Two, "The Labor Certification Application."

A denial of an immigrant visa petition is not considered "final" for purposes of qualifying for an AC21 extension if it "may be reversed on direct appeal or certification to the Administrative Appeals Office (AAO)."[1120]

2. Recapture of H-1B Time

In 2016, USCIS codified into regulation its long-standing interpretation that only days of physical presence in the United States in H-1B status are counted toward the time limitation.[1121] "Time spent physically outside the United States exceeding 24 hours by an alien during the validity of an H-1B petition ... shall not be considered for purposes of calculating the alien's total period authorized admission."[1122] The time outside the United States does not need to be meaningfully interruptive of the beneficiary's stay, nor does it matter what the reason for the absence(s) was.[1123] There is "no time limitation on recapturing the remainder of of the initial 6-year period ... [but] the remainder of any time granted pursuant to an AC21 extension cannot be recaptured."[1124]

As explained by the AAO:

"The plain language of the status and the regulations indicate[] that the six-year period accrues only during periods when the alien is lawfully admitted and physically present in the United States.... [T]he AAO determines that the time the

---

[1117] AFM 31.3(g)(8).

[1118] "Q&A Stakeholder Conference" (Sept. 20, 2010 and updated Oct. 19, 2010), AILA Doc. No. 10101471.

[1119] Id.

[1120] USCIS, W. Yates, "Interim Guidance for Processing Form I-140 Employment-Based Immigrant Petitions and Form I-485 and H-1B Petitions Affected by the American Competitiveness in the Twenty-First Century Act of 2000 (AC21) (Public Law 106-313)" (May 12, 2005), AILA Doc. No. 05051810.

[1121] 81 Fed. Reg. 82398 (Nov. 18, 2016), amending 8 CFR §214.2(h)(13)(iii)(C).

[1122] 8 CFR §214.2(h)(13)(iii)(C).

[1123] Id.

[1124] 81 Fed. Reg. 82398, 82449 (Nov. 18, 2016).

Copyright © 2017. American Immigration Lawyers Association. All rights reserved.

beneficiary spends in the United States after lawful admission in H-1B status is the time that counts toward the maximum six-year period of authorized stay. The beneficiary in this case was admitted to the United States in H-1B status each time he returned from outside the country. When he was outside the United States he was not in any status for U.S. immigration purposes. Thus, the beneficiary interrupted his period of H-1B status when he departed the country, and renewed his period of H-1B status each time he was readmitted in the United States."[1125]

This means that a foreign national's final date in H-1B status should be factored in all trips outside the United States;[1126] and "upon requesting an extension, the H-1B nonimmigrant can request that full days spent outside the United States during the period of petition validity be recaptured and added back to his or her total maximum period of stay."[1127] For example, if a beneficiary first obtained H-1B status on January 1, 2011, and vacationed in France twice for two weeks each, then the sixth year anniversary should be January 28, 2017, if the individual spent part of the first and last day of each vacation in the United States.

"It is the petitioner's burden to request and demonstrate the specific amount of time for recapture."[1128] Appropriate evidence of physical presence abroad includes I-94 records, exit and entry stamps in the passport, airplane tickets,[1129] "frequent flyer miles,"[1130] boarding passes, and visas, as well as proof of purchases abroad, although ideally these receipts should not resemble Internet print-outs. In particular, the practitioner should note that "the DHS electronic system on entries and exits is not always accurate."[1131] In practice, however, USCIS will almost always approve at least as much recapture time as indicated by the DHS electronic entry and departure history record available on the CBP's I-94 website.[1132]

The regulations specifically mention,[1133] and the practitioner is strongly encouraged to present, a chart listing the travel dates and locations, and referencing the accompanying evidence. The evidence should be arranged in the same order as on the chart:

"Copies of passport stamps or Form I-94 arrival-departure records, without an accompanying statement or chart of dates the beneficiary spent outside the

---

[1125] *Matter of IT Ascent, Inc.*, Adopted Decision 06-0001 (AAO Sept. 2, 2005), AILA Doc. No. 05102760 (internal citation omitted).

[1126] 9 FAM 402.10-13 ("All time spent outside of the United States is, generally, subtracted and thus does not count towards the maximum allowable period of stay in H-1B or L visa status").

[1127] AFM 31.3(g).

[1128] 8 CFR §214.2(h)(13)(iii)(C)(*i*).

[1129] *Id.*

[1130] "AILA/VSC Practice Pointer: Proof for Recapture of Unused H-1B Visa Validity" (Oct. 2, 2009), AILA Doc. No. 09100210.

[1131] *Id.*

[1132] CBP, "I-94 Website," https://i94.cbp.dhs.gov/I94/#/home.

[1133] 8 CFR §214.2(h)(13)(iii)(C)(*i*).

Copyright © 2017. American Immigration Lawyers Association. All rights reserved.

country, could be subject to error in interpretation, might not be considered probative, and may be rejected. Similarly, a statement of dates spent outside of the country must be accompanied by consistent, clear and corroborating proof of departures from and reentries into the United States."[1134]

USCIS guidance acknowledges that such a format "eases review of the accompanying documentation," but emphasizes that "independent documentary evidence" is required.[1135] Each period of physical presence abroad should be considered discretely:

> "The fact that the burden may not be met for some claimed periods, or has been met for some claimed periods, has no bearing on the remaining claimed periods. Any periods of time for which the burden has been met may be added to the eligible period of admission upon approval of the application for extension of status. An alien may not be granted an extension of stay for periods of time that are not supported by independent documentary evidence. A Request for Evidence should not be sent to the petitioner for any claimed periods unsupported by evidence."[1136]

If independent evidence is not offered for all of the requested recapture time, then "the approval notice should be issued for the period of time for which eligibility has been demonstrated."[1137]

Importantly, time spent in the United States in statuses other than H-1B or L-1 can be recaptured. While USCIS did not codify this interpretation into regulations, it acknowledged in the rulemaking that:

> "The 'remainder' period of the initial 6-year admission period is that full admission period minus any time that the H-1B nonimmigrant worker previously spent in the United States in valid H-1B or L status. This policy allows time spent in any other nonimmigrant status ... to be 'recapturable.' This final rule does not impose any additional limitations on this policy."[1138]

D. Extensions

An H-1B extension should also be filed on Form I-129 to "extend the validity of the original petition."[1139] Importantly: "A request for a petition extension may be filed only if the validity of the original petition has not expired."[1140] An extension of status

---

[1134] *Matter of IT Ascent, Inc.*, Adopted Decision 06-0001 (AAO Sept. 2, 2005), AILA Doc. No. 05102760 (internal citations omitted).

[1135] AFM 31.3(g).

[1136] *Id.* (emphasis in original).

[1137] AFM 31.3(g) ("In some instances, the alien may not be granted the entire period of time requested because the evidence submitted does not establish eligibility for the entire period of stay requested").

[1138] 81 Fed. Reg. 82398, 82449 (Nov. 18, 2016), citing USCIS, M. Aytes, "Procedures for Calculating Maximum Period of Stay Regarding the Limitations on Admission for H-1B and L-1 Nonimmigrants (AFM Update AD 05-21)" (Oct. 21, 2005), AILA Doc. No. 05110363.

[1139] 8 CFR §§214.2(h)(14) and (h)(15)(i).

[1140] 8 CFR §214.2(h)(14).

Copyright © 2017. American Immigration Lawyers Association. All rights reserved.

must be requested on the form,[1141] and the foreign national "must be physically present in the United States at the time of the filing of the extension of stay."[1142] As stated by regulation: "If the alien is required to leave the United States for business or personal reasons while the extension requests are pending, the petitioner may request the director to cable notification of approval of the petition extension to the consular office abroad where the alien will apply for a visa."[1143]

Although the regulations state in one place that "[s]upporting evidence is not required unless requested by the director,"[1144] another provision states that "A petitioner seeking the services of an ... H-1B [or] H-1B1 ... nonimmigrant beyond the period previously granted, must apply ... with the initial evidence specified in §214.2, and in accordance with the form instructions.[1145] Yet another regulatory section indicates that the form should be "accompanied by the documents described for the particular classification,"[1146] which for H-1B nonimmigrants is "either a new or a photocopy of the prior certification from the Department of Labor that the petitioner continues to have on file a labor condition application valid for the period of time requested for the occupation."[1147]

As discussed in Volume 1: Chapter Two, "Basic Nonimmigrant Concepts," previous approval of an H-1B petition does not guarantee approval of an extension.[1148] Specifically:

"Evidence of prior approvals as a form of documentation on a subsequent new petition cannot serve as the basis for future eligibility. Knowledge of prior approval of an H petition can be helpful to USCIS when considered along with other evidence eligibility. A prior approval, however, does not obligate USCIS to approve a subsequent petition or relieve the petitioner of providing sufficient documentation to establish current eligibility."[1149]

The practitioner is strongly advised to include as much evidence as possible of continued eligibility in the H-1B extension. H-1B extensions can be "costly to petitioners, and shortened validity periods can lead to a number of consequences, such as the expiration of driver's licenses tied to I-94 validity for H-1B beneficiaries and their dependents."[1150] An H-1B extension may be approved "for a period of up to three years."[1151] After the foreign national has been physically present in the United

---

[1141] 8 CFR §214.2(h)(15)(i) ("The petitioner must also request a petition extension").

[1142] 8 CFR §214.2(h)(15)(i).

[1143] *Id.*

[1144] 8 CFR §214.2(h)(14).

[1145] 8 CFR §214.1(c)(1).

[1146] 8 CFR §214.2(h)(15)(i).

[1147] 8 CFR §214.2(h)(15)(ii)(B)(*1*).

[1148] 55 Fed. Reg. 2606 (Jan. 26, 1990).

[1149] AFM 31.2(c).

[1150] "Q&A Stakeholder Conference" (Sept. 20, 2010, and updated Oct. 19, 2010), AILA Doc. No. 10101471.

[1151] 8 CFR §214.2(h)(15)(ii)(B)(*1*).

Copyright © 2017. American Immigration Lawyers Association. All rights reserved.

States in H-1B status for the maximum six years, no further extensions are permitted,[1152] except as discussed below. The validity period of the approved extension may be "back-date[d] ... to the day after the beneficiary's status expires to eliminate gaps," as long as the extension request was made by the same employer for whom the previous H-1B petition was approved.[1153] In this situation, the adjudicator should "treat petitions filed as a result of a merger or acquisition as though filed by the original employer."[1154] The validity period should not be back-dated if a different petitioner requested the extension,[1155] such as in the case of an H-1B portability petition requesting an extension of status. USCIS guidance also directs adjudicators to consider nunc pro tunc extensions, which are discussed in Volume 1: Chapter Two, "Basic Nonimmigrant Concepts": "A gap between the expiration of the beneficiary's existing status and either the requested from date or the LCA from date does not automatically require that you deny the EOS [Extension of Stay]. Look at the evidence provided to determine if the reason for the gap is excusable."[1156]

The practitioner should note that "[e]ven though the requests to extend the petition and the alien's stay are combined on the petition, the director shall make a separate determination on each,"[1157] as discussed in Volume 1: Chapter Two, "Basic Nonimmigrant Concepts." If the H-1B petition and extension request are approved, then the "dates of extension shall be the same for the petition and the beneficiary's extension of stay."[1158] If the H-1B petition is approved, but the extension request is denied, then consular notification should be provided, even if the Form I-824 is not filed.[1159] Regardless of whether an extension of stay or consular notification is granted, the foreign national may use the approval notice to make an appointment to apply for a new H-1B visa. The consular officer should "access the details of approved NIV petitions using the PIMS Petition Report in the Consular Consolidated Database (CCD), under the Nonimmigrant Visa tab. If no record of the petition is found in PIMS, [the officer] may use the Person Centric Query Service (PCQS), via the CCD, to verify that the petition has been approved."[1160]

[1152] 9 FAM 402.10-13; 73 Fed. Reg. 15389 (Mar. 25, 2008) (citing INA §214(g)(4) and 8 CFR §214.2(h)(13)(iii)(A)) (stating that an "extension only may only be granted for a period of time such that the total period of the temporary worker's admission does not exceed six years").

[1153] USCIS, "I-129 H-1B Standard Operating Procedures" (undated, posted July 26, 2007), AILA Doc. No. 07072668.

[1154] *Id.* It is useful to note that this recognition of the surviving employer as the "original" employer also should result in the surviving employer being treated as the original employer for purposes of the fraud fee and training fee, discussed above.

[1155] *Id.*

[1156] *Id.*

[1157] 8 CFR §214.2(h)(15)(i).

[1158] *Id.*; 9 FAM 402.10-12.

[1159] USCIS, "I-129 H-1B Standard Operating Procedures" (undated, posted July 26, 2007), AILA Doc. No. 07072668.

[1160] 9 FAM 402.10-9(A).

Copyright © 2017. American Immigration Lawyers Association. All rights reserved.

Evidence of the ongoing and continuing right to control the beneficiary's work must also be submitted. In addition to the evidence listed above, proof that the petitioner "maintained a valid employer-employee relationship with the beneficiary throughout the initial H-1B status approval period" may be in the form of the following documents:

- "Copies of the beneficiary's pay records (leave and earnings statements, and pay stubs, etc.) for the period of the previously approved H-1B status;

- "Copies of the beneficiary's payroll summaries and/or Form W-2s, evidencing wages paid to the beneficiary during the period of previously approved H-1B status;

- "Copy of Time Sheets during the period of previously approved H-1B status;

- "Copy of prior years' work schedules;

- "Documentary examples of work product created or produced by the beneficiary for the past H-1B validity period (*i.e.*, copies of: business plans, reports, presentations, evaluations, recommendations, critical reviews, promotional materials, designs, blueprints, newspaper articles, web-site text, news copy, photographs of prototypes, etc.)," which "must clearly substantiate the author and date created";

- "Copy of dated performance review(s); and/or

- "Copy of any employment history records, including but not limited to, documentation showing date of hire, dates of job changes, *i.e.*, promotions, demotions, transfers, layoffs, and pay changes with effective dates."[1161]

This evidence is required "to increase H-1B program compliance and curtail violations."[1162] The validity period of an H-1B extension may be only one year if a third-party placement "is documented for less than one year."[1163] Although not "routine," USCIS may request proof of all work performed by the beneficiary "if compliance issues arose during the previous H-1B approval period."[1164] In addition, "[p]ast employment history may not be used to establish future employment."[1165] Similarly, eligibility for a three-year extension, based on the per-country limits for immigrant visa numbers, "does not guarantee that the petition will be approved for a full three years." Evidence of the continuing employment relationship must be submitted.[1166]

[1161] AFM 31.3(g).

[1162] *Id.*

[1163] "Q & A Stakeholder Conference" (Sept. 20, 2010 and updated Oct. 19, 2010), AILA Doc. No. 10101471.

[1164] *Id.*

[1165] *Id.*

[1166] "AILA/VSC Liaison Practice Pointer: AC21 §104(c): 3 Year Extension-Must Document Need for Three Years" (May 10, 2010), AILA Doc. No. 10051072.

Copyright © 2017. American Immigration Lawyers Association. All rights reserved.

USCIS may also conduct "pre– or post-adjudication compliance review site visits for either initial or extension petitions,"[1167] as discussed above. Therefore, an H-1B extension may be denied if "USCIS determines, while adjudicating the extension petition, that the petitioner failed to maintain a valid employer-employee relationship with the beneficiary throughout the initial approval period, or violated any other terms of its prior H-1B petition."[1168] The exception, available "solely on a case-by-case basis," is if "there is a compelling reason to approve the new petition," such as if "the petitioner is able to demonstrate that it did not meet all the terms and conditions through no fault of its own."[1169] USCIS declined, however, to "provide a list of examples."[1170]

Filing a timely H-1B extension provides the foreign national with an additional 240 days of employment authorization beyond the expiration date of the underlying H-1B petition. The foreign national is "authorized to continue employment with the same employer for a period not to exceed 240 days beginning on the date of the expiration of the authorized period of stay," although the "authorization shall be subject to any conditions and limitations noted on the initial authorization."[1171] Nevertheless, filing early is strongly recommended, as discussed in Volume 1: Chapter Two, "Basic Nonimmigrant Concepts." In addition, if USCIS "adjudicates the application prior to the expiration of this 240 day period and denies the application for extension of stay, the employment authorization under this paragraph shall automatically terminate upon notification of the denial decision."[1172]

In 2016, USCIS expanded the 240-day rule to apply to H-1B1s as well.[1173] H-1B1 extensions may be granted "only in 1-year increments,"[1174] and there is no statutory time limitation.[1175] In addition:

"After every second extension, the next following extension shall not be granted unless the Secretary of Labor had determined and certified to the Secretary of Homeland Security and the Secretary of State that the intending employer has filed with the Secretary of Labor an attestation [pursuant to a filed labor condition

---

[1167] AFM 31.3(g).

[1168] Id.; "USCIS Issues Guidance Memorandum on Establishing the 'Employee Employer Relationship' in H-1B Petitions" (Jan. 13, 2009), AILA Doc. No. 10011331.

[1169] AFM 31.3(g); "USCIS Issues Guidance Memorandum on Establishing the 'Employee Employer Relationship' in H-1B Petitions" (Jan. 13, 2009), AILA Doc. No. 10011331.

[1170] "Q&A Stakeholder Conference" (Sept. 20, 2010 and updated Oct. 19, 2010), AILA Doc. No. 10101471.

[1171] 8 CFR §274a.12(b)(20).

[1172] Id.

[1173] 81 Fed. Reg. 2068 (Jan. 15, 2016), amending 8 CFR §245a.12(b)(20).

[1174] INA §214(g)(8)(C).

[1175] 9 FAM 402.10-5(F) ("H-1B1 nonimmigrant professionals are admitted for a one-year period renewable indefinitely, provided the alien is able to demonstrate that he or she does not intend to remain or work permanently in the United States").

Copyright © 2017. American Immigration Lawyers Association. All rights reserved.

application] under section 212(t)(1) for the purpose of permitting the nonimmigrant to obtain such extension."[1176]

E. Sponsoring an H-1B Worker for Permanent Residence

Departure from the United States after an application to adjust status has been filed "shall not be deemed an abandonment of the application," as long as the foreign national is not in proceedings.[1177] The foreign national must "remain[] eligible for H ... status" and possess a valid H visa, if a visa is required.[1178] The H-1B principal must be returning to "resume employment with the same employer for whom he or she had previously been authorized to work as an H-1 ... nonimmigrant."[1179] When an H-4 dependent seeks U.S. admission, the H-1B principal must be "maintaining H-1 ... status" and the H-4 dependent must "remain[] otherwise eligible for H-4 ... status."[1180] As discussed in Volume 2: Chapter Four, "Consular Processing, Adjustment of Status," and Permanent Residence Issues, foreign nationals in H-1B and H-4 status no longer need to present the receipt for the adjustment of status application.[1181]

In addition, after applying for adjustment of status, foreign nationals in H-1B and H-4 may travel internationally and re-enter the United States by presenting valid H visas; they do not necessarily need to apply for advance parole documents.

The H-1B and H-4 dependents may be eligible for employment authorization in "compelling circumstances"[1182] once the immigrant visa petition is approved. The circumstances required to qualify are discussed in Volume 2: Chapter Three, "The Immigrant Visa Petition." As noted there, the availability of this option is so limited, and the pitfalls surrounding it so severe, that it is rarely useful.

For a discussion of Adjustment of Status (AOS) portability,[1183] see Volume 2: Chapter Four, "Consular Processing, Adjustment of Status, and Permanent Residence Issues."

F. H-1B Petition Withdrawals

A petitioner may request withdrawal of an H-1B petition by sending a written request to the "Service Center where the petition is pending or was filed and approved."[1184] As a general matter, a petitioner should withdraw an H-1B petition after termination of the nonimmigrant's employment "to avoid monetary

---

[1176] INA §214(g)(8)(C).

[1177] 8 CFR §245.2(a)(4)(ii)(C).

[1178] Id.

[1179] Id.

[1180] Id.

[1181] Cf. 8 CFR §1245.2(a)(4)(ii)(C). It appears that this section of the regulations was not updated with 8 CFR §245.2(a)(4)(ii)(C), which makes no mention of the receipt requirement.

[1182] 8 CFR §204.5(p).

[1183] 9 FAM 402.10-11(E).

[1184] 69 Fed. Reg. 8675 (Feb. 25, 2004).

Copyright © 2017. American Immigration Lawyers Association. All rights reserved.

penalties,"[1185] and the anti-benching provisions discussed in Volume 1: Chapter Six: "The Labor Condition Application."

The letter should be "signed by the petitioner or an authorized representative and include the filing receipt number and the names of both the petitioner and beneficiary."[1186] USCIS should process the withdrawal request in the same fashion as an automatic revocation, "except that withdrawal cannot be retracted."[1187] The following conditions must be met:

- The "beneficiary has not been admitted to the U.S."; or

- The approved petition did grant request change of status; and

- The requested start date of an H-1B extension "has not passed."[1188]

If the above-mentioned criteria are not satisfied, petition withdrawal may "be automatically revoked without first sending" a NOIR.[1189] This is also the procedure if the petitioner requests withdrawal of the H-1B petition after the beneficiary has terminated his or her employment.[1190] An H-1B petition may also be withdrawn after the foreign national has obtained permanent resident status, although there is no guidance from USCIS or DOL indicating any requirement to do so. Because the H-1B beneficiary would no longer hold H-1B status after becoming a permanent resident, it would not appear that the H-1B wage obligation would continue, and thus would not need to be terminated through withdrawal of the petition.

A request for withdrawal of an unadjudicated H-1B should be processed by USCIS as a denial.[1191] USCIS takes the position that "upon revocation of the petition, the beneficiary's H-1B status terminates as of the date the employment ceased ... or the date the petition was revoked, whichever is later."[1192] The filing fee should not be refunded if an H-1B petition is withdrawn.[1193]

[1185] "AILA/VSC Liaison Committee Practice Pointer: VSC Liaison Committee Discusses the VSC's Clarification of Revocation of H-1B Status and Non-immigrant Status" (Feb. 20, 2009), AILA Doc. No. 09022076.

[1186] 69 Fed. Reg. 8675 (Feb. 25, 2004).

[1187] USCIS, "I-129 H-1B Standard Operating Procedures" (undated, posted July 26, 2007), AILA Doc. No. 07072668.

[1188] Id. (citing 8 CFR §103.2(b)(6)) (formatting corrected).

[1189] Id. (citing 8 CFR §214.2(h)(11)(ii)).

[1190] Id.

[1191] Id.

[1192] "AILA Liaison/VSC Meeting Minutes" (Jan. 21, 2009), AILA Doc. No. 09012768 (internal citation omitted).

[1193] 65 Fed. Reg. 15178 (Mar. 21, 2000).

Copyright © 2017. American Immigration Lawyers Association. All rights reserved.

CHAPTER EIGHT

H-2B VISAS AND STATUS

I. Executive Summary

The H-2B classification allows foreign nationals who are citizens of certain named countries, with limited exceptions, to accept temporary non-agricultural employment in the United States, after the employer has obtained temporary labor certification by establishing that there were no willing, able, and qualified U.S. workers available during the period of recruitment. The foreign national must also demonstrate nonimmigrant intent through the maintenance of a foreign residence. There is an annual numerical limitation of 66,000 for H-2B visas. Under the rules, an H-2B petition may be valid for up to one year for seasonal, intermittent, and peakload needs, and up to three years for one-time need. However, the reality can differ. Also under the rules, H-2B petitions may be extended for periods of up to one year, to a maximum of three years in H-2B status in some circumstances, but again, the reality can differ. To be eligible for a period of H-2B status beyond the limit, a foreign national must remain physically present outside the United States for at least three months. Recapture of H-2B time is not available. Dependent spouses and children of H-2B nonimmigrants hold H-4 status.

A. Checklist of Requirements

- ETA 9141 Prevailing Wage Determination from the Department of Labor
- Certified ETA 9142 temporary labor certification for non-agricultural employment with Appendix B State Workforce Agency (SWA) job order including employer's assurances and obligations
- Temporary need based on one-time occurrence or seasonal, peakload, or intermittent need
- H-2B visa number available
- Offer of full-time employment
- Citizen of country designated on H-2B Countries List

B. Documents Necessary to Prepare the Petition

- Job description, including duties, offered salary, offered hours, employment period and job requirements, and whether on-the-job training is available
- Copies of the foreign national's academic credentials (résumé, degrees including transcripts, and/or employment history, where applicable)
- Basic information about the company
- Copy of biographic page(s) of passport(s) of the foreign national and any dependent spouse and children
- Evidence of temporary need

Copyright © 2017. American Immigration Lawyers Association. All rights reserved.

C. Checklist of Questions to Ask the Client

- Is the employment full time?
- Is the basis for the temporary need a one-time occurrence, or a seasonal, peakload, or intermittent need?
- What are the start and end dates of need?
- Will there be any non-legally required deductions (*i.e.*, housing, uniforms, grocery cards, etc.)?
- Will there be multiple worksites, beneficiaries, or employers?
- Have all of the workers been identified?
- Did or will the employer use foreign recruiters/agents to find H-2B workers?
- Is there a labor dispute at the worksite of the proposed H-2B assignment?
- Will the foreign national maintain a foreign residence for the duration of H-2B assignment?
- Is the foreign national a beneficiary of an immigrant visa petition or labor certification application?

II. Evolution of the Current State of the Law

Recent years have seen a difficult and checkered path to the current state of the law relating to H-2Bs. In 2008, the U.S. Department of Labor (DOL) promulgated regulations to "re-engineer[] the application filing and review process," and "enhance[] the integrity of the H-2B program."[1] While acknowledging that Congress had conferred authority for enforcement of H-2B program requirements on the Department of Homeland Security (DHS), DOL asserted that "recent discussions between DHS and the Department have yielded an agreement for the delegation of H-2B enforcement authority from DHS to the Department."[2]

In 2012, DOL re-thought some of its changes, and issued new regulations to address perceived issues such as "expansion of opportunities for U.S. workers, evidence of violations of program requirements, some rising to a criminal level, need for better worker protections, and a lack of understanding of program obligations."[3] Those regulations were quickly challenged in court by employers, and were enjoined three days after they were to take effect.[4] The court found that DHS did not have the authority to delegate these duties to DOL, and thus the 2012 regulations were issued without authority and were invalid.

---

[1] 73 Fed. Reg. 78020 (Dec. 19, 2008). At the same time, DHS published a separate rule with the stated goal of "facilitating a timely flow of legal workers while ensuring the integrity of the program," 73 Fed. Reg. 78104 (Dec. 19, 2008).

[2] *Id.*

[3] 77 Fed. Reg. 10038 (Feb. 21, 2012).

[4] *Bayou Lawn & Landscape Services v. Sec'y of Labor*, No. 3:12-cv-183 (N.D. Fla. Apr. 26, 2012), AILA Doc. No. 12042740 (issuing preliminary injunction), *aff'd* 713 F.3d 1080 (11th Cir. 2013), AILA Doc. No. 13040244.

Copyright © 2017. American Immigration Lawyers Association. All rights reserved.

Given that this left DOL operating under the 2008 regulations which, as noted above, it had stated were issued under delegated authority, it was inevitable that those regulations also would be challenged. Indeed, this time it was a worker challenging the rules, on the basis that his prospective job opportunities were adversely affected by the rules' generosity to employers. His lawsuit wound up before the same judge who enjoined the 2012 regulations, and that judge issued a temporary restraining order vacating the 2008 regulations.[5]

This left H-2Bs in something of a legal abyss. DOL issued a notice stating that it would no longer accept or process prevailing wage determination requests or labor certification applications in the H-2B program while it considered its options.[6] U.S. Citizenship and Immigration Services (USCIS) likewise stopped adjudicating or accepting H-2B petitions.[7] DOL sought, unopposed, and received a stay of the order to resume operation of the H-2B program, promising to work with DHS to issue a joint interim final rule "as soon as possible."[8]

With this stay, DOL and USCIS resumed processing, and on April 29, 2015, the two agencies jointly promulgated the interim final rule that is currently in effect,[9] along with a final rule on prevailing wage methodology.[10] It should be noted that the court had never invalidated the DHS rulemaking, and thus much of what was promulgated in 2008 by that agency remains in effect, albeit amended by the 2015 joint rulemaking.

That was not to be the end of it. Congress, in December 2015, included in appropriations legislation some provisions to limit or alter certain provisions of the interim final rule and of the prevailing wage rule.[11] As a result, DOL issued guidance to address the legislation.[12] However, as discussed below, DOL takes the position that those mandates were valid only for the fiscal year covered by the appropriations bill.

---

[5] *Perez v. Perez*, 3:14-cv-682 (N.D. Fla. Mar. 4, 2015), AILA Doc. No. 15030562. In the meantime, the judge had issued a permanent injunction against the 2012 regulations, *Bayou Lawn & Landscape Services v. Sec'y of Labor*, No. 3:12-cv-183 (N.D. Fla. Dec. 18, 2014), AILA Doc. No. 14121942.

[6] "DOL Can No Longer Accept or Process Requests for H-2B PWDs or Applications Due to District Court Decision" (Mar. 4, 2015), AILA Doc. No. 15030563.

[7] "USCIS Suspends Adjudication of H-2B Petitions Following Court Order" (Mar. 9, 2015), AILA Doc. No. 15030904.

[8] *Perez v. Perez*, 3:14-cv-682, "Defendant's Unopposed Motion for Limited Relief from the Vacatur Order and Judgment" (Mar. 16, 2015), and Order granting motion (Mar. 18, 2015), AILA Doc. No. 15030562.

[9] 80 Fed. Reg. 24042 (Apr. 29, 2015).

[10] 80 Fed. Reg. 24146 (Apr. 29, 2015).

[11] 2016 Consolidated Appropriations Act, Pub. L. No. 114-113 (2015), Div. H, Title I and Div. F, Title V, AILA Doc. No. 15121601

[12] DOL, "Emergency Guidance, Implementation of 2016 DOL Appropriations Act" (Jan. 5, 2016), AILA Doc. No. 15123000.

Copyright © 2017. American Immigration Lawyers Association. All rights reserved.

Then, again in May 2017, Congress passed the Consolidated Appropriations Act of 2017,[13] which expanded the H-2B quota for fiscal year 2017 by "not more than the highest number of H-2B nonimmigrants who participated in the H-2B returning worker program in any fiscal year in which returning workers were exempt from such numerical limitation The."[14]

III. Requirements and Interpretations

Overview

H-2B classification allows foreign nationals to provide "temporary or seasonal" services or labor,[15] provided such employment does not displace U.S. workers "available to perform such services or labor" and as long as the H-2B employment will not adversely affect the wages and working conditions of U.S. workers.[16]

The Office of the Chief Administrative Hearing Officer (OCAHO) at the U.S. Department of Justice (DOJ) noted that U.S. workers "are given a preference over foreign workers for jobs that become available within this country."[17] But, as stated by DHS, "The H-2B temporary nonimmigrant program often is a place of last resort for U.S. employers who cannot find sufficient U.S. workers," despite the "additional burdens on the employer."[18] DOL has stated: "Foreign workers hired through the H-2B temporary worker program tend to be low-skilled workers, often the most vulnerable to exploitation. Top occupations for which ETA [the Employment and Training Administration] issues labor certifications include landscapers, laborers, hotel cleaners and housekeepers, cooks, and construction workers."[19]

The temporary job may be professional, skilled, or unskilled.[20] There must be a seasonal, peak load, intermittent, or one-time need for the temporary services or labor,[21] as discussed below. The employer or agent must obtain temporary labor certification from DOL before being able to file the H-2B petition with USCIS,[22] as

---

[13] 2017 Consolidated Appropriations Act, Pub. L. No. 115-31 (2017), Div. H, Title I and Div. F, Title V, AILA Doc. No. 17050367. (As of this writing, DHS has yet to implement the procedures and rules to allow for filing of H-2B petitions under the expanded cap).

[14] Id.

[15] 8 Code of Federal Regulations (CFR) §§214.2(h)(1)(ii)(D); See also Immigration and Nationality Act (INA) §101(a)(15)(H)(ii)(B).

[16] 8 CFR §214.2(h)(6)(i).

[17] Mid-Atlantic Regional Organizing Coalition v. Heritage Landscape Services, LLC, 10 OCAHO 1134 (OCAHO June 17, 2010), AILA Doc. No. 10090264 (internal citation omitted).

[18] 73 Fed. Reg. 78104 (Dec. 19, 2008).

[19] "US Department of Labor: Fall Regulatory Agenda 2009 Fact Sheet" (Dec. 7, 2009), AILA Doc. No. 09120730.

[20] Legacy Immigration and Naturalization Service (INS) Memorandum, P. Virtue, "Classification of Visiting University Lecturers" (Aug. 20, 1993), 1 INS and DOJ Legal Opinions §93-61.

[21] 8 CFR §214.2(h)(6)(ii)(B).

[22] 8 CFR §§214.2(h)(6)(iii), (h)(1)(ii)(D), and (h)(2)(i)(A).

Copyright © 2017. American Immigration Lawyers Association. All rights reserved.

discussed below. The start date of the H-2B petition must match the date of need stipulated on the labor certification application.[23]

An approved H-2B petition is valid through the expiration date of the approved temporary labor certification,[24] which in theory can be valid for up to one year for three of the types of need,[25] and for up to three years if the petitioner successfully demonstrates a one-time need for temporary services,[26] as discussed below. (Labor certifications for employment in the U.S. Virgin Islands can be valid only for 45 days, and only for entertainers and athletes.[27])

However, DOL takes the position that "[w]ith the exception of a one-time occurrence need which can last up to 3 years, temporary need will not be approved for longer than 9 months."[28] DOL currently allows employers to request up to 10 months[29] even though Congress indicated in its appropriations legislation for 2016 and 2017 that temporary need could be defined as up to one year,[30] as discussed in detail below.

With respect to a one-time occurrence, while DHS regulations seem to allow for three-year validity,[31] DOL regulations are not specific as to the length of validity of an initial temporary labor certification,[32] other than to limit to three years the overall period, with extensions, in which such a nonimmigrant can hold H-2B status.[33] Otherwise, DOL "will instruct the employer on any additional recruitment requirements."[34] Initial experience under these particular regulations is that DOL limits the validity of the labor certification to one year. Since USCIS will not approve

---

[23] 8 CFR §214.2(h)(6)(iv)(D).

[24] 8 CFR §214.2(h)(9)(iii)(B); 9 Foreign Affairs Manual (FAM) 402.10-8(D).

[25] The 2017 Consolidated Appropriations Act, Pub. L. No. 115-31 (2017), Div. H, Title I and Div. F, Title V, AILA Doc. No. 17050367 states that "the definition of 'temporary need' shall be that provided in 8 CFR 214.2(h)(6)(ii)(B)," which in turn states that the period of need generally will be "limited to one year or less," except in the case of a one-time event.

[26] 8 CFR §214.2(h)(6)(ii)(B); 20 CFR §655.55; 8 CFR §214.2(h)(9)(iii)(B); "DOL, "2015 H-2B Interim Final Rule FAQs, Round 1," https://www.foreignlaborcert.doleta.gov/pdf/H-2B_2015_IFR_FAQs_Round1.pdf.

[27] 8 CFR §214.2(h)(6)(iv)(C).

[28] DOL, "H-2B Temporary Non-agricultural Program," https://www.foreignlaborcert.doleta.gov/2015_H-2B_IFR.cfm.

[29] "Minutes from DOL H-2 Stakeholder Meeting" (Feb. 23, 2016), AILA Doc. No. 16052535.

[30] 2016 Consolidated Appropriations Act, Pub. L. No. 114-113 (2015), §113, AILA Doc. No. 15121601; 2017 Consolidated Appropriations Act, Pub. L. No. 115-31 (2017), Div. H, Title I and Div. F, Title V, AILA Doc. No. 17050367.

[31] 8 CFR §214.2(h)(6)(ii)(B).

[32] 20 CFR §655.55(a).

[33] 20 CFR §655.60.

[34] 8 CFR §655.15(g).

Copyright © 2017. American Immigration Lawyers Association. All rights reserved.

a petition for a period longer than the validity of the temporary labor certification,[35] the net effect is that one-time occurrence H-2Bs are granted in one-year increments.

The validity of the temporary labor certification can be extended only due to factors beyond the employer's control, and will not be extended for longer than a time amounting to a total work period of nine months for seasonal, peak load, or intermittent need and three years for a one-time occurrence.[36] The H-2B petition may be extended only for the validity period of the labor certification.[37] A foreign national may hold H-2B status for a maximum of three years,[38] although certain periods of time spent outside the United States interrupt the accrual of H-2B time,[39] as discussed toward the end of this chapter. An H-2B nonimmigrant who has spent more than three years in the United States in any H or L status must remain physically outside the United States for three months to be eligible for H-2B status again.[40]

In the 2015 joint rule, DOL "bifurcates the current application process into a registration phase, which addresses the employer's temporary need, and an application phase, which addresses the labor market test."[41] As discussed in detail later in this chapter, employers must first submit to DOL a registration, the stated purpose of which is to establish that the employer's need is temporary.[42] Once the registration is approved, the employer then can submit temporary labor certification applications under that registration for up to three years.[43] This process was not immediately effective. Instead, DOL "will announce in the Federal Register a separate transition period for the registration process, and until that time, will continue to adjudicate temporary need during the processing of applications."[44] As of this writing, no announcement has yet been forthcoming.

Graduates of foreign medical schools are ineligible for H-2B classification to provide services "as members of the medical profession."[45] In contrast, H-2B status may be appropriate for employees of U.S. "exhibitors or employers at international fairs or expositions held in the United States."[46]

---

[35] 8 CFR §214.2(h)(9)(iii)(B).

[36] 20 CFR §655.60.

[37] 8 CFR §214.2(h)(9)(iii)(B); 9 FAM 402.10-12. *See also* 8 CFR §214.2(h)(15)(B)(C), stating that an H-2B extension may be granted "for the validity of the labor certification or for a period of up to one year."

[38] 8 CFR §214.2(h)(13)(iv).

[39] 8 CFR §214.2(h)(13)(v).

[40] 8 CFR §214.2(h)(13)(iv).

[41] 80 Fed. Reg. 24042 (Apr. 29, 2015).

[42] *Id.*

[43] 20 CFR §655.12(a).

[44] 20 CFR §655.11(j).

[45] 8 CFR §214.2(h)(1)(ii)(D).

[46] 9 FAM 402.10-10(E).

Copyright © 2017. American Immigration Lawyers Association. All rights reserved.

DHS has delegated certain enforcement activities of the H-2B program to DOL, where DOL may impose fines or debarment from the H-2B program.[47] In turn, following exhaustion of administrative remedies with DOL, DHS may deny any petition for any H (other than H-1B1), L, O, or P-1 status filed by that employer for a period of one to five years, depending on the severity of the employer's violation.[48]

B. Temporary Services or Labor

To qualify for H-2B classification, the services or labor must be temporary, "which is generally defined as a period of duration of one year, but could be for a specific one-time need of up to 3 years."[49] This removes an earlier requirement that "extraordinary circumstances" must be proven before an H-2B petition based on a one-time need with employment dates of longer than one year may be approved,[50] as discussed below.

USCIS defines a "temporary" job as one in which "the need for the employee will end in the near, definable future,"[51] and as "any job in which the petitioner's need for the duties to be performed by the employee(s) is temporary, whether or not the underlying job can be described as permanent or temporary."[52] The practitioner should note that the term "temporary" is stated twice in the statute,[53] although the "legislative history of the statute is silent about the expected duration of 'temporary' work."[54] For this inquiry, the focus is on the petitioner's need for the services;[55] the standard shifted from examining whether the job itself was permanent.[56] Specifically, the commissioner rejected the principle that a labor shortage in the occupation meant that the job offer was for permanent employment.[57] Legacy Immigration and Naturalization Service (INS) guidance notes the balance between the petitioner's need and the nature of the job duties: "This policy does not make the H-2B

---

[47] INA §214(c)(14)(B); 8 CFR §214.2(h)(6)(ix); 20 CFR §73; 80 Fed. Reg. 24042 (Apr. 29, 2015).

[48] 8 CFR §214.1(k).

[49] 8 CFR §214.2(h)(6)(ii)(B). *See also* 2017 Consolidated Appropriations Act, Pub. L. No. 115-31 (2017), Div. H, Title I and Div. F, Title V, AILA Doc. No. 17050367.

[50] 80 Fed. Reg. 24042 (Apr. 29, 2015).

[51] 8 CFR §214.2(h)(6)(ii)(B).

[52] 8 CFR §214.2(h)(6)(ii)(A).

[53] INA §101(a)(15)(H)(ii)(B); *Matter of Contopoulos*, 10 I&N Dec. 654 (Reg'l Comm'r 1964).

[54] Opinion of the Office of Legal Counsel, J. Elwood, "Meaning of 'Temporary' Work Under 8 U.S.C. §1101(a)(15)(H)(ii)(B)" (Dec. 18, 2008), AILA Doc. No. 09022664.

[55] *Matter of Artee Corp.*, 18 I&N Dec. 366 (Comm'r 1982). *See also* 73 Fed. Reg. 78120 (Dec. 19, 2008).

[56] *Wilson v. Smith*, 587 F. Supp. 470 (D.D.C. 1984) (comparing *Matter of Artee Corp.*, 18 I&N Dec. 366 (Comm'r 1982) and *Matter of Contopoulos*, 10 I&N Dec. 654 (Reg'l Comm'r 1964)). *Accord Matter of General Dynamics Corp.*, 13 I&N Dec. 23 (Reg'l Comm'r 1968) and Opinion of the Office of Legal Counsel, J. Elwood, "Meaning of 'Temporary' Work Under 8 U.S.C. §1101(a)(15)(H)(ii)(B)" (Dec. 18, 2008), AILA Doc. No. 09022664.

[57] *Matter of Artee Corp.*, 18 I&N Dec. 366.

Copyright © 2017. American Immigration Lawyers Association. All rights reserved.

classification indiscriminately available to any employer since, in most cases, the nature of the employer's need usually coincides with the nature of the job."[58]

The practitioner should note that one part of the Foreign Affairs Manual (FAM) guidance, stating that the H-2B nonimmigrant's "position" must be "temporary in nature," may be misleading.[59] Other FAM guidance, however, is correct; a foreign national "may not be classified as … H-2B for the purpose of occupying a permanent or indefinite position."[60] In addition, if the petitioner's need and the nature of the job offered are both permanent, then the H-2B classification is inappropriate: "The test of the true nature of the temporary need for the position lies in examination of the temporary need of the temporary help service, not its customers.… It is the nature of the need for the duties to be performed which determines the temporariness of the position."[61] A prior exception to this rule involved sheepherders, with the FAM noting that "consular officers may process applications for visas received from sheepherders who are the beneficiaries of H-2B petitions even if they are coming to occupy positions which are permanent or continuing in nature."[62] The Department of State (DOS) still takes that position with respect to sheepherders, but now indicates that H-2A is the appropriate category for them.[63]

It will in most cases be inappropriate to temporarily fill permanent positions, such as university chairs, professors, or lecturers, with H-2B workers, although an H-2B job opportunity may be professional, skilled, or unskilled.[64] Similarly, H-2B classification is unavailable for foreign nationals "employed on board 'cruises to nowhere,'" to conduct gambling in waters outside U.S. and foreign territory, as this activity is prohibited by U.S. law and therefore there is no U.S. labor market.[65]

The first consideration may be the length of the H-2B assignment. DHS regulations state: "Generally, that period of time will be limited to one year or less,"[66] although the need involved in a one-time event could last up to three years, as discussed below. In contrast, DOL takes the position that "[w]ith the exception of a one-time occurrence need which can last up to 3 years, temporary need will not be

---

[58] Legacy INS Operations Instruction (OI) 214.2.

[59] 9 FAM 402.10-4(G).

[60] *Id.*

[61] *Matter of M–S–H–*, 8 I&N Dec. 460 (Asst. Comm'r 1960).

[62] Former 9 FAM 41.53 N22.

[63] 9 FAM 402.10-4(G). The H-2A category is not covered in this book.

[64] Legacy Immigration and Naturalization Service (INS), P. Virtue, "Classification of Visiting University Lecturers" (Aug. 20, 1993), 1 INS and DOJ Legal Opinions §93-61.

[65] Legacy INS, P. Virtue, "Alien Crewmen and Casino Operator Classification" (Jan. 11, 1991), 1 INS and DOJ Legal Opinions §91-4.

[66] 8 CFR §214.2(h)(6)(ii)(B). *See also Matter of [name not provided]*, EAC 94 254 51543 (AAU May 1, 1995), 14 Immig. Rptr. B2-216.

Copyright © 2017. American Immigration Lawyers Association. All rights reserved.

approved for longer than 9 months."[67] Even though Congress indicated in its appropriations legislation for 2016 and 2017 that USCIS's definition of temporary need is to be used,[68] DOL allows only 10 months, noting that it "believes that this is consistent with the DHS requirement. DHS regulations state that, other than a one-time occurrence ... 'temporary' can be *up to* one year.... DOL believes it is appropriate to question whether there really is a temporary need for anything beyond 10 months despite the language in the Appropriations Bill."[69]

DOL's findings regarding temporary need are said to be advisory only, and USCIS may reach a different conclusion on the issue.[70] However, in fact, USCIS will not approve a longer period than the period on the labor certification.[71] Also, as a practical matter, it means only that the employer has two chances for denial on the basis of temporariness—one at DOL and one at USCIS—and no chance for USCIS to approve if DOL denied. If DOL denies the temporary labor certification, the employer cannot file a petition with USCIS,[72] and thus USCIS never has the opportunity to consider the temporariness issue in those cases.[73]

In adjudicating the petition, USCIS looks to:

- "What duties the workers will perform, as specified in the petition;

- "Whether the employer needs the number of temporary workers requested to perform those duties; and

- "Whether the need extends throughout the employment period requested."[74]

Factors that USICS may consider in this inquiry include:[75]

---

[67] DOL, "H-2B Temporary Non-agricultural Program," https://www.foreignlaborcert.doleta.gov/2015_H-2B_IFR.cfm. *See also Vito Volpe Landscaping, et. al.*, 91 INA 300, (BALCA Sept. 29, 1994) (en banc).

[68] 2016 Consolidated Appropriations Act, Pub.L.No. 114-113 (2015), §113, AILA Doc. No. 15121601; 2017 Consolidated Appropriations Act, Pub. L. No. 115-31 (2017), §113, AILA Doc. No. 17050367 (both stating that "the definition of 'temporary need' shall be that provided in 8 CFR 214.2(h)(6)(ii)(B)," which in turn states that the period of need generally will be "limited to one year or less" except in the case of a one-time event).

[69] "Minutes from DOL H-2 Stakeholder Meeting" (Feb. 23, 2016), AILA Doc. No. 16052535 (emphasis added). The reference to "10 months" appears to be a vestige of the 2008 regulation. The 10-month limitation was changed to nine months in the 2015 regulation, 80 Fed. Reg. 24042, 24055 (Apr. 29, 2015).

[70] 8 CFR §214.2(h)(6)(iii)(A); "Minutes from DOL H-2 Stakeholder Meeting" (Sept. 12, 2016), AILA Doc. No. 16102430.

[71] 8 CFR §214.2(h)(9)(iii)(B) ("the approval of the petition ... shall be valid for the period of the approved labor certification").

[72] 8 CFR §214.2(h)(6)(iii)(C); USCIS, "Guidance on 'Temporary Need' in H-2B Positions" (Apr. 13, 2016), AILA Doc. No. 16100501.

[73] USCIS, "Guidance on 'Temporary Need' in H-2B Positions" (Apr. 13, 2016), AILA Doc. No. 16100501 ("at the time DOL adjudicates a [temporary labor certification], it may not have the same information that we have at the time we examine the Form I-129").

[74] USCIS, "Guidance on 'Temporary Need' in H-2B Positions" (Apr. 13, 2016), AILA Doc. No. 16100501.

[75] *Id.*

Copyright © 2017. American Immigration Lawyers Association. All rights reserved.

- Whether the employer employs on a permanent basis others who perform the same duties. If faced with a situation in which H-2B nonimmigrants will work in the same occupation as permanent employees, the practitioner may wish to submit payroll records or other documentation such as job descriptions or employee agreements that differentiate the H-2Bs' jobs from the permanent employees' jobs.

- Particularly with respect to seasonal workers, as discussed below, whether there are periods in which H-2B workers are not needed to perform the job duties. In this regard, USCIS notes that H-2Bs cannot be used to cover for vacationing permanent workers.

- Whether the employer filed more than one H-2B petition for the same job duties in one year. The practitioner may wish to submit documentation to show that the separate petitions cover separate seasons, looking to the factors discussed below regarding seasonal work. Alternatively, or in addition, one may document that the different petitions reflect different job duties. For the latter, USCIS will look to the Standard Occupational Classification (SOC) codes for the different positions, or to the tools used and the tasks performed. If job duties are the same, USCIS will look at the overall time cycle to determine if the petitions reflect a permanent, year-round need.

- If different but related business entities submit petitions, USCIS will look to the separateness of the companies. "Adjudicators will use internal system databases to examine petitioners' relationships with other petitioners and their filing history."[76] If it believes that related entities are, together, trying to fill a permanent, year-round need, a Request for Evidence (RFE) and ultimate denial could result.

In determining whether the petitioner's need is temporary, the adjudicator may consider the nature of the entity's business. For example, H-2B petitions on behalf of musicians and vocalists were denied because the petitioner's business as a bar, restaurant, and night club meant that "the organization constantly needs singers and musicians in order to operate."[77] In general, temporary staffing or employment agencies face difficulty in establishing temporary need, because the nature of the business indicates an ongoing need for temporary workers:[78]

"The business of a temporary help service is to meet the temporary needs of its clients. To do this they must have a *permanent* cadre of employees available to refer to their customers for the jobs for which there is frequently or generally a demand. By the very nature of this arrangement, it is obvious that a temporary

---

[76] *Id.*

[77] *Matter of [name not provided]*, EAC 94 254 51543 (AAU May 1, 1995), 14 Immig. Rptr. B2-216. Note that the petitions were denied even though H-2B petitions on behalf of the same beneficiaries had previously been approved.

[78] *Matter of Smith*, 12 I&N Dec. 772 (D.D. 1968); *Matter of Artee Corp.*, 18 I&N Dec. 366 (Comm'r 1982).

Copyright © 2017. American Immigration Lawyers Association. All rights reserved.

help service will maintain on its payroll, more or less continuously the types of skilled employee most in demand."[79]

Another factor considered by USCIS is the number of requested workers:

"As it is within USCIS scope to evaluate whether there is an actual need for the work itself and whether there is a genuine job offer, adjudications officers are advised to evaluate an H-2B petitioner's actual need for the number of employees requested and to issue an RFE in cases where there is doubt as to the need for the number of H-2B workers requested."[80]

A temporary staffing agency may be successful in petitioning for an H-2B worker if the job offered requires "skill for which the company has a non-recurring demand or infrequent demand."[81] Temporary labor certification applications filed by job contractors face similar difficulties and have additional requirements,[82] as discussed below.

However, the adjudicator should not consider the beneficiary's intent when evaluating whether the job offered is temporary, although this factor is relevant in determining whether the foreign national has the proper nonimmigrant intent.

The petitioner must also demonstrate that the need for H-2B services is temporary because it is "a one-time occurrence, a seasonal need, a peakload need, or an intermittent need."[83] As stated in the legislative history, the H-2 classification enables the temporary admission of "certain alien workers, industrial, agricultural, or otherwise, for the purpose of alleviating labor shortages as they exist or develop in certain areas or certain branches of American productive enterprise, particularly in periods of intensified production."[84]

1. Process and Documentation to Show Temporary Need

At the time of this writing, the method to show temporary need to DOL is in a state of transition. Prior to the litigation discussed at the beginning of this chapter, evidence of the temporary need and how such need is based on a one-time occurrence, or a need that is seasonal, peakload, or intermittent, had to be submitted to DOL with the labor certification application and retained by the employer for three years after the temporary labor certification was decided or withdrawn.[85] The requirement for record retention has survived, but guidance issued after the 2015 joint

---

[79] *Matter of Artee Corp.*, 18 I&N Dec. 366 (emphasis in original).

[80] Adjudicator's Field Manual (AFM) 31.5(k)(2).

[81] *Matter of Artee Corp.*, 18 I&N Dec. 366.

[82] "H-2B Temporary Labor Certification Process Stakeholder Briefing" (Sept. 2009), AILA Doc. No. 09092568.

[83] 8 CFR §214.2(h)(6)(ii)(B).

[84] *Matter of Contopoulos*, 10 I&N Dec. 654 (Reg'l Comm'r 1964) (citing H.R. Rep. No. 82-1365, 82d Congress, 2d Session, discussing HR 5678).

[85] 73 Fed. Reg. 78020 (Dec. 19, 2008).

Copyright © 2017. American Immigration Lawyers Association. All rights reserved.

regulation indicates that employers should no longer submit the documentation to the Department of Labor.

Instead, the employer should complete Section B "Temporary Need Information," Field 9 "Statement of Temporary Need" on the Form ETA-9142B[86] to "clearly explain the nature of the employer's business or operations, why the job opportunity and number of workers being requested for certification reflect a temporary need, and how the request ... meets one of the four DHS regulatory standards of temporary need." [87] Appendix B, attesting to the employer's temporary need, also needs to be signed by the attorney or agent and by the employer, under penalty of perjury.[88]

The employer is then required to retain the documentation and produce it if DOL issues a Notice of Deficiency (NOD). To determine whether a NOD will be issued, DOL will look at the employer's recent filing history for inconsistencies, to assess whether the nature of the need has changed or is unclear, or to see if "other employer information about the nature of its need requires further explanation."[89] While DOL states that "issuance of prior certifications to the employer does not preclude the CO [Certifying Officer] from issuing a NOD,"[90] it also indicates that disclosure of the underlying information on the form may suffice "particularly where the employer's temporary need has been demonstrated in earlier applications certified or the work is clearly tied to a temporary, seasonal cycle."[91] The implication of this is that employers new to the H-2B program are more likely to receive a NOD.

That implication also would be consistent with the change to which DOL is transitioning: an employer registration system.[92] That system, detailed further later in this chapter, is not yet in place, but the practitioner should monitor the DOL[93] and AILA[94] websites for relevant announcements of its implementation.

Although, as previously discussed, the 2008 regulations were invalidated by the court, they contained some guidance as to what documents were to be provided with

---

[86] DOL, "H-2B Application for Employment Certification" (exp. Dec. 31, 2018), https://www.foreignlaborcert.doleta.gov/pdf/ETA_Form_9142B.pdf.

[87] DOL, "H-2B Temporary Nonimmigrant Visa Program/Announcement of Procedural Change to Streamline the H-2B Process for Non-Agricultural Employers: Submission of Documentation Demonstrating 'Temporary Need'" (Sept. 1, 2016), http://bit.ly/h2btempdoc.

[88] DOL, "H-2B Application for Employment Certification Appendix B" (exp. Dec. 31, 2018), http://bit.ly/h2bAppB.

[89] DOL, "H-2B Temporary Nonimmigrant Visa Program/Announcement of Procedural Change to Streamline the H-2B Process for Non-Agricultural Employers: Submission of Documentation Demonstrating 'Temporary Need'" (Sept. 1, 2016), http://bit.ly/h2btempdoc.

[90] Id.

[91] "DOL Announces Procedural Change in Submitting Temporary Need Documentation" (Sept. 1, 2016), AILA Doc. No. 16090262.

[92] 80 Fed. Reg. 24042 (Apr. 29, 2015); 8 CFR §655.11.

[93] DOL, "H-2B Temporary Non-agricultural Program," https://www.foreignlaborcert.doleta.gov/2015_H-2B_IFR.cfm.

[94] American Immigration Lawyers Association, http://www.aila.org.

Copyright © 2017. American Immigration Lawyers Association. All rights reserved.

respect to temporariness. While that provision did not survive to the 2015 joint regulation, its guidance is still useful. Thus, the practitioner may want to include this information in its statement on the form:

- "A description of the employer's business history and activities (*i.e.*, primary products or services) and schedule of operations throughout the year;

- "An explanation regarding why the nature of the employer's job opportunity and number of foreign workers being requested for certification reflect a temporary need;

- "An explanation regarding how the request for temporary labor certification" is a one-time occurrence, seasonal, peakload, or intermittent need; and

- "If applicable, a statement justifying any increase or decrease in the number of H-2B positions being requested for certification from the previous year."[95]

The final piece of suggested information is included because DOL has acknowledged "that conventional evidence such as payroll information may not be sufficient to demonstrate a one-time or intermittent need, or seasonal or peakload need in cases in which the employer's need has changed significantly from the previous year."[96] As such, a statement may explain the reasons for any change in the number of H-2B workers requested. The practitioner is advised to explore other types of evidence that are available and relevant,[97] such those discussed below.

The 2008 regulation and its related guidance also contain some useful suggestions for retained documentation. It is advisable that that documentation include a majority of the following documents, which should "have dates of service that correspond to the period of need":[98]

- "[S]ummarized monthly payroll records for a minimum of one previous calendar year that identify, for each month and separately for full-time permanent and temporary employment in the requested occupation, the total number of workers employed, the total hours worked";[99]

- "Annualized and/or multi-year work contracts or work agreements,"[100] invoices, or client letters of intent, with a clear statement of the specific end date of the project or contract;[101] or

- "Other evidence that demonstrates how the job opportunity exists and "is temporary in nature."[102]

---

[95] 73 Fed. Reg. 78020 (Dec. 19, 2008); former 8 CFR §655.21 (2009).
[96] *Id.*
[97] *Id.*
[98] "H-2B FAQs—Round II," https://www.foreignlaborcert.doleta.gov/pdf/H-2B_2015_IFR_FAQs_Round2.pdf.
[99] 73 Fed. Reg. 78020 (Dec. 19, 2008).
[100] 72 Fed. Reg. 38621 (July 13, 2007).
[101] 73 Fed. Reg. 78020 (Dec. 19, 2008).

Copyright © 2017. American Immigration Lawyers Association. All rights reserved.

DOL has indicated that each petition and the supporting evidence are evaluated on a case-by-case basis, with the most important factor being whether the evidence "contain[s] the basic indicators of a true temporary need."[103] The necessary number of payroll records, invoices, contracts, or client letters of intent is the number "to adequately demonstrate the temporary need," but DOL also noted that for most applications, "a sample set of work contracts or invoices can demonstrate the need for the requested months and employees."[104] The evidence may also include "any other documents that are appropriate for [the] industry, such as hotel occupancy and staffing reports, in order to draw a complete picture."[105]

Although this outdated DOL guidance states that employers may use a combination of documents from the list above,[106] the practitioner may wish to advise the client to retain as many documents as may be gathered, particularly if the employer is relatively new to the H-2B program or if questions about the new applications can be anticipated.

If the employer is newly established and does not possess the majority of these documents, then old but still useful guidance suggests "newspaper articles, promotional articles, and official Visitor's Bureau's documents" may be retained.[107] An employer, whose business opening was delayed because H-2B workers could not begin work until after the date of need, and who files an H-2B petition in a subsequent year, is "encouraged to indicate that its previous year's workers arrived late due to NPC [National Processing Center] delays in processing cases on its temporary needs statement."[108]

Once the temporary labor certification application is approved, the same issues must again be addressed with USCIS, which requires submission of a Statement of Need "describing in detail the temporary situation or conditions," stating which of the four types of need is involved, and indicating, for other than a one-time occurrence, "whether the situation or conditions are expected to be recurrent."[109] USCIS may, however, determine that the type of need is different from the one certified by DOL (for example, USCIS may find that a certification for a seasonal worker in fact involves a peak load worker), but can still approve the petition on the basis of the "correct" need.[110] In addition, USCIS guidance indicates that, "if the beneficiary will

---

[102] *Id.*

[103] "H-2B FAQs—Round II," https://www.foreignlaborcert.doleta.gov/pdf/H-2B_2015_IFR_FAQs_Round2.pdf.

[104] *Id.*

[105] *Id.*

[106] *Id.*

[107] "Frequently Asked Questions: H-2B Processing" (July 18, 2007), AILA Doc. No. 07071871.

[108] *Id.*

[109] 8 CFR §214.2(h)(6)(vi)(D).

[110] USCIS, "Guidance on 'Temporary Need' in H-2B Positions" (Apr. 13, 2016), AILA Doc. No. 16100501.

Copyright © 2017. American Immigration Lawyers Association. All rights reserved.

be performing services in more than one location, then an itinerary with the dates and locations" must be submitted.[111]

For the most part, the statement used on the DOL form should also be useable for the USCIS Statement of Need. USCIS indicates that, if that statement is sufficiently detailed, and "there is no articulable basis to doubt its credibility," supporting documentation would not be needed.[112]

2. The Four Types of Temporary Need

a. One-time Occurrence

H-2B classification may be appropriate if the petitioner will require temporary services for a single event or project:

> "The petitioner must establish that it has not employed workers to perform the services or labor in the past and that it will not need workers to perform the services or labor in the future, or that it has an employment situation that is otherwise permanent, but a temporary event of short duration has created the need for a temporary worker."[113]

An individual can hold H-2B status for a one-time occurrence for a maximum of three years.[114] While DHS regulations seem to allow petition approvals to be valid for the full three years,[115] DOL regulations are not specific as to the length of validity of an initial temporary labor certification for a one-time occurrence,[116] other than to limit to three years the overall period, with extensions, in which a such a nonimmigrant can hold H-2B status.[117] DOL's FAQs seem to suggest that the Department may approve a labor certification for up to three years.[118] However, its regulations state that DOL "will instruct the employer on any additional recruitment requirements with respect to the continuing validity of the labor market test or offered wage obligation."[119] In practice, DOL will approve a one-time need labor certification for one year, noting that the temporary need has been demonstrated for three years, but that another labor test will be required after one year. Since USCIS will not approve a petition for a period longer than the validity of the temporary labor

---

[111] USCIS, "H-2B Clarifying Guidance on 'Statement of Need'" (Sept. 13, 2016), AILA Doc. No. 16100502.

[112] *Id.*

[113] 8 CFR §214.2(h)(6)(ii)(B)(1).

[114] 8 CFR §214.2(h)(6)(ii)(B); 20 CFR §655.55; 8 CFR §214.2(h)(9)(iii)(B).

[115] 8 CFR §214.2(h)(6)(ii)(B).

[116] 20 CFR §655.55(a).

[117] 20 CFR §655.60.

[118] DOL, "2015 H-2B Interim Final Rule FAQs, Round 1," https://www.foreignlaborcert.doleta.gov/pdf/H-2B_2015_IFR_FAQs_Round1.pdf (stating that "an employer's temporary need justified on a one-time occurrence basis can be approved for up to 3 years").

[119] 8 CFR §655.15(g).

Copyright © 2017. American Immigration Lawyers Association. All rights reserved.

certification,[120] the net effect is that one-time occurrence H-2Bs are granted in one-year increments.

DOL indicated in its 2008 rulemaking that DOL and DHS had a "long-established definition of one-time occurrence which encompasses both unique non-recurring situations but also any 'temporary event of a short duration [that] has created the need for a temporary worker.'"[121] The practitioner is strongly encouraged to provide evidence of the one-time need, such as "contracts showing the need for the one-time services, letters of intent from clients, news reports, event announcements, and similar documentation."[122]

Approved H-2B petitions for this subcategory have included the following:

- A production manager for a new technology being introduced to U.S. operations was approved for a one-time occurrence where his duties involved setting up and training personnel, rather than managing on an ongoing basis, and where the company was able to show that it had had a similar situation in its U.K. operations, and the temporary employee completed his project in a little over a year.[123]

- An artisan was granted H-2B status to continue to engrave and install religious artifacts in a temple being built by the petitioner.[124]

- Fifteen electricians were permitted to fulfill the petitioner's contractual obligation valued at $2.5 million. The petitioner took steps to license itself in the United States solely for one contract. The Administrative Appeals Unit (AAU) cautioned that if the petitioner remained an electrical contractor "beyond a limited and brief period of time" and continued to require the services of electricians, then the need might be considered permanent and subsequent H-2B petitions would not be approved.[125]

In contrast, an H-2B petition filed on behalf of a bilingual secretary and personal assistant was denied, despite the petitioner's statement that the worker's services would be needed only for one year, while an executive from Japan performed a "temporary assignment to set up a Japanese customer division."[126] The denial may have been based on the generic nature of the job duties provided,[127] so the

---

[120] 8 CFR §214.2(h)(9)(iii)(B).

[121] 73 Fed. Reg. 78020 (Dec. 19, 2008).

[122] "H-2B FAQs—Round II" (Dec. 16, 2007), AILA Doc. No. 07121661.

[123] *Matter of [name not provided]*, EAC 93 043 53371 (AAU July 12. 2006), http://bit.ly/jul061d4.

[124] *Matter of [name not provided]*, EAC 93 090 52290 (AAU June 23, 1993), 12 Immig. Rptr. B2-10. This case is also discussed below, because an H-2B extension was granted.

[125] *Matter of [name not provided]*, AGA N 8018 (AAU June 20, 1986), 4 Immig. Rptr. B2-4.

[126] *Matter of [name not provided]*, EAC 90 187 00314 (AAU Mar. 18, 1992), 10 Immig. Rptr. B2-93.

[127] *Id.* (stating "petitioner's need for the duties of the offered position such as answering telephones, preparing memos, etc., is so basic to the operation of the organization, that the need would continue beyond the departure of the beneficiary").

Copyright © 2017. American Immigration Lawyers Association. All rights reserved.

practitioner may wish to strengthen such a petition by emphasizing the necessary foreign-language skills, by highlighting the need for the executive's return abroad after his own one-year assignment, and by explaining why the duties must be performed in the United States and could not be undertaken by an employee of the foreign parent company. The practitioner should also note that a foreign-language requirement may result in increased scrutiny and delays when seeking temporary labor certification, as discussed below.

There is significant case history of H-2B petitions filed on behalf of domestic staff, including nannies, child care workers, and housekeepers. In general, unsuccessful petitions feature job descriptions with duties needed on a permanent or long-term basis.[128] For example, petitions describing the following situations were denied:

- The H-2B worker's child care services are necessary until the children become of elementary or nursery school age.[129]

- The H-2B worker's services as a companion or an aide to an invalid are needed only temporarily because the invalid will either "probably pass away or be hospitalized."[130] Notably, "because of the sympathetic factors present," the AAU did remand the case to legacy INS to gather "medical opinion or testimony which would cause the decision of the director to be reversed."[131]

- The need for a housekeeper is not temporary, even though the petitioner stated that, because of pain caused by a medical condition, she would reduce her work hours upon the requested end date of the H-2B petition.[132] The home attendant duties to care for the petitioner's daughter, who also had a medical condition, were insufficient to overcome the "ongoing" need for "general housekeeping and cooking duties."[133]

- The petitioner desired the H-2B worker's child care and domestic services for 17 years.[134]

In contrast, H-2B petitions for domestic staff have been approved for the following situations:

- The petitioner needed two housekeepers while recovering from major surgery because his wife maintained the family business and traveled frequently. The petitioner submitted a letter from a doctor explaining the medical condition and

---

[128] *Matter of [name not provided]*, HHW N 5989 (AAU Nov. 10, 1987), 5 Immig. Rptr. B2-68.

[129] *Id. Cf. Wilson v. Smith*, 587 F. Supp. 470 (D.D.C. 1984) (approving H-2B petition for child care worker despite period of need requested until child turned three years old because the "fact that plaintiffs cannot specify a date on which their need for the duties of a live-in employee will cease does not rob that need of its 'temporary' character").

[130] *Matter of [name not provided]*, WAC 88 050 0048 (AAU Apr. 11, 1989), 7 Immig. Rptr. B2-103.

[131] *Id.*

[132] *Matter of [name not provided]*, EAC 94 022 50211 (AAU May 18, 1994), 13 Immig. Rptr. B2-32.

[133] *Id.*

[134] *Matter of [name not provided]*, WAC 92 181 51334 (AAU Apr. 19, 1993), 11 Immig. Rptr. B2-62.

Copyright © 2017. American Immigration Lawyers Association. All rights reserved.

stating that the petitioner should make a full recovery by the requested end date of the H-2B petition.[135]

- The H-2B worker's services are necessary until the oldest child becomes 18 years old.[136]

The 2015 rulemaking expressed particular concerns about two industries in the context of one-time occurrences: job contractors and construction. With respect to job contractors, a subject discussed in detail later in this chapter, the regulation states that the contractor must demonstrate its own temporary need, not that of its clients.[137] With respect to construction, the preamble to the rulemaking notes:

> "The Departments do not intend for the 3-year accommodation of special projects to provide a specific exemption for industries like construction in which many of an employer's projects or contracts may prove a permanent rather than a temporary need. Therefore, we will closely review all assertions of temporary need on the basis of a one-time occurrence to ensure that the use of this category is limited to those circumstances where the employer has a non-recurring need which exceeds the 9-month limitation. For example, an employer who has a construction contract that exceeds 9 months may not use the program under a one-time occurrence if it has previously filed an *Application for Temporary Employment Certification* identifying a one-time occurrence and the prior *Application for Temporary Employment Certification* requested H-2B workers to perform the same services or labor in the same occupation."[138]

b. Seasonal Need

Seasonal need entails services or labor that "is traditionally tied to a season of the year by an event or pattern and is of a recurring nature."[139] Need is considered seasonal if the business "completely shuts down" for a season.[140] Seasonal need may also arise from "a predictable cyclical budget constraint or a holiday season."[141] The employer must state the off-season, which is "the period(s) of time during each year in which it does not need the services or labor"; and off-season periods of unemployment that are "unpredictable or subject to change or … considered a vacation period for the petitioner's permanent employees" are unacceptable.[142]

---

[135] *Matter of [name] not provided]*, LIN 94 039 50139 (AAU June 10, 1994), 13 Immig. Rptr. B2-119.

[136] *Matter of [name not provided]*, WAS N 30088 (AAU Dec. 24, 1985), 3 Immig. Rptr. B2-52.

[137] 20 CFR §655.6(c).

[138] 80 Fed. Reg. 24042 (Apr. 29, 2015).

[139] 8 CFR §214.2(h)(6)(ii)(B)(2).

[140] "Frequently Asked Questions: H-2B Processing" (July 18, 2007), AILA Doc. No. 07071871.

[141] "H-2B FAQs—Round II," www.foreignlaborcert.doleta.gov/faqsanswers.cfm#h2b36.

[142] 8 CFR §214.2(h)(6)(ii)(B)(2); "H-2B Temporary Labor Certification Process Stakeholder Briefing" (Sept. 2009), AILA Doc. No. 09092568.

Copyright © 2017. American Immigration Lawyers Association. All rights reserved.

In many cases, the seasonal need is tied to the physical seasons.[143] This was the case for musicians who would perform and provide "a unique cultural experience" during the summer and fall seasons.[144] Examples of seasonal need provided by USCIS include:

- "Dining staff at Cape Cod resorts for the summer season;
- "Ski instructors for ski resorts in the Rocky Mountains; and
- "Summer lifeguards in the coastal regions."[145]

To substantiate the temporary seasonal need, the employer should gather evidence of the recurring nature of the employment, such as payroll records, work agreements, contracts, and client letters of intent. The practitioner should note that DOL cautions against relying on documents that describe a "'season' in general terms," such as "hotel occupancy rates, weather charts, [or] newspaper accounts," because "in the Department's experience, such generalized statements fail to link a season to a specific position sought to be filled by the employer."[146]

The practitioner should note that the broader definition of "seasonal" provided by the Migrant and Seasonal Agricultural Worker Protection Act (MSPA) most likely does not apply to general seasonal H-2B workers, as the definition was imposed by federal court decisions specifically for tree planting and related reforestation occupations, as discussed below.

c. Peakload Need

Peakload need covers situations in which the petitioner must "supplement" regular, permanent staff who ordinarily provide the services or labor with temporary workers "due to a seasonal or short-term demand."[147] The petitioner should demonstrate "that the temporary additions to staff will not become a part of the petitioner's regular operation."[148] USCIS provided the following example: "A toy manufacturing company makes a product that has suddenly surpassed all sales predictions and expectations. It may be able to demonstrate that it has a peakload need for assembly-line workers to meet its unprecedented production demands for the Christmas season."[149]

When requesting H-2B classification based on a peakload need, it is important to explain why the temporary worker's services are required in addition to the services

---

[143] 73 Fed. Reg. 78020 (Dec. 19, 2008). While the particular rule was enjoined, the discussion should still apply.

[144] *Matter of [name not provided]*, EAC 90 195 00722 (AAU Jan. 18, 1991), 9 Immig. Rptr. B2-13.

[145] AFM 31.5

[146] 73 Fed. Reg. 78020 (Dec. 19, 2008). While the particular rule was enjoined, the discussion should still apply.

[147] 8 CFR §214.2(h)(6)(ii)(B)(3).

[148] *Id.*; "H-2B Temporary Labor Certification Process Stakeholder Briefing" (Sept. 2009), AILA Doc. No. 09092568.

[149] AFM 31.5.

Copyright © 2017. American Immigration Lawyers Association. All rights reserved.

of the existing U.S. workforce.[150] Peakload and seasonal need are similar in that the need must be differentiated from the regular season or off-season need.[151] In one successful petition, the employer confirmed that H-2 workers would be employed only during the peak season because there were "ample American workers employed in these same fields to handle its off-season business."[152] In response, the AAU noted: "Prospectively, continued eligibility will be dependent on the facts of the petitioner's operation, its workforce, and occupancy patterns. As the resort continues to operate year-round, it can be anticipated that over the long term its 'peak-season,' for the purpose of H-2 eligibility, should decrease significantly."[153]

As another example, an H-2B approval was remanded where the employer failed to provide evidence that the effects of Hurricanes Katrina and Rita made the need for welders both temporary and peakload.[154] The petitioner submitted a letter of intent between the petitioner and a client, as well as a statement from the petitioner noting the client's temporary need.[155] The Administrative Appeals Office (AAO) noted that there was no direct evidence of the reason for the peakload need, the relationship between petitioner and its client, or of the employment to be offered to the H-2B beneficiaries.[156] The petitioner was granted the opportunity to provide additional evidence, including monthly payroll reports, monthly staffing tables with summaries of the number of welders employed as regular and temporary staff, quarterly tax returns, federal unemployment payments, and evidence of the "contractual commitment" between the petitioner and its client.[157]

d. Intermittent Need

To establish the existence of an intermittent need, the petitioner must demonstrate "that it has not employed permanent or full-time workers to perform the services or labor, but occasionally or intermittently needs temporary workers to perform services or labor for short periods."[158] USCIS's example of intermittent need is of a sports jersey manufacturer that "has a need for apparel workers when recurrent surges in production occur around major sporting events (such as the Super Bowl)."[159] An H-2B petition was approved on behalf of a foreign national actor, whose services were needed to reshoot movie scenes that had been previously filmed.[160] Another

---

[150] *Matter of [name not provided]*, CLT N 3900 (AAU May 5, 1986), 3 Immig. Rptr. B2-105.

[151] *Id.*

[152] *Id.*

[153] *Id.*

[154] *Matter of [name not provided]*, EAC 08 030 51332 (AAO June 19, 2008), http://bit.ly/jun081d3.

[155] *Id.*

[156] *Id.*

[157] *Id.*

[158] 8 CFR §214.2(h)(6)(ii)(B)(4).

[159] AFM 31.5.

[160] *Matter of [name not provided]*, WAC 92 237 51078 (AAU Aug. 13, 1992), 10 Immig. Rptr. B2-69.

Copyright © 2017. American Immigration Lawyers Association. All rights reserved.

H-2B petition was approved on behalf of foreign nationals who would "participate in musical performances" with a nonprofit educational organization.[161]

Another example of a successful H-2B petition based on intermittent need was approved on behalf of log loaders.[162] The petitioner explained that its U.S. customers made "sporadic and unpredictable requests ... to have logs picked up in U.S. waters" and that "other traditional modes of log transportation" were unavailable.[163] The petitioner employed no U.S. workers to perform these duties, and a training program for U.S. workers was unsuccessful "apparently due to the infrequency of trips necessary to develop the skills to safely and efficiently perform the duties."[164] In discussing how the employment offer lacked "guaranteed dates of employment," the AAU stated that "such a guarantee would be inconsistent with the regulations regarding a petitioner's occasional and intermittent need for temporary workers."[165]

C. Full-time Employment with Employer

The H-2B job offered must be full time, which for purposes of temporary labor certification employment, is defined as "35 or more hours per week."[166] The work week "must be a fixed and regular recurring period of 168 hours—seven consecutive 24-hour periods." It need not coincide with the calendar week but may begin on any day and at any hour of the day.[167]

The 2015 regulation imposes a requirement on H-2B and corresponding employees (described below under the section titled "Wage Requirements for H-2B Workers and Workers in Corresponding Employment") with respect to the number of hours offered, known as the "three-fourths guarantee." Under this provision, employment must be offered for "a total number of work hours equal to at least three-fourths of the workdays in each 12-week period (each 6-week period if the period of employment covered by the job order is less than 120 days)."[168] A workday means the number of hours per day stated on the job order.[169] The obligation begins the later of the first workday after the worker arrives at the place of employment or the advertised first date of need, and continues until the expiration date on the job order or any extensions.[170] The guaranteed number of hours for partial workweeks, due to

---

[161] *Matter of [name not provided]*, WAC 92 019 01395 (AAU Nov. 18, 1991), 9 Immig. Rptr. B2-96.

[162] *Matter of [name not provided]*, LIN 91 035 00494 (AAU Jan. 6, 1992), 9 Immig. Rptr. B2-117.

[163] *Id.*

[164] *Id.*

[165] *Id.* Note that the statement that a full-time employment offer is not required by statute or regulation is now incorrect, as the regulations do require a full-time employment offer.

[166] 20 CFR §655.5.

[167] 20 CFR §655.20(e).

[168] 20 CFR §655.20(f)(1).

[169] 20 CFR §655.20(f)(2).

[170] 20 CFR §655.20(f)(1) and (3).

Copyright © 2017. American Immigration Lawyers Association. All rights reserved.

the arrival date of the employee or the conclusion date of the job falling on other than the first and last day of the workweek, can be pro-rated.[171]

A worker may be offered more than the specified hours on a single workday, but the worker is not required to work for more than the number of hours specified in the job order for a workday. "The employer, however, may count all hours actually worked in calculating whether the guarantee has been met."[172] However, "[i]f during any 12-week period (6-week period if the period of employment covered by the job order is less than 120 days) during the period of the job order the employer affords the U.S. or H-2B worker less employment than that required under paragraph (f)(1) of this section, the employer must pay such worker the amount the worker would have earned had the worker, in fact, worked for the guaranteed number of days."[173]

DOL gives this explanation of how the guarantee works:

"An employer has not met the work guarantee if the employer has merely offered work on three-fourths of the workdays in a 12-week period (or 6-week period, as appropriate) if each workday did not consist of a full number of hours of work time as specified in the job order…. Any hours the worker fails to work, up to a maximum of the number of hours specified in the job order for a workday, when the worker has been offered an opportunity to work in accordance with paragraph (f)(1) of this section, and all hours of work actually performed (including voluntary work over 8 hours in a workday), may be counted by the employer in calculating whether each 12-week period (or 6-week period, as appropriate) of guaranteed employment has been met."[174]

The payroll records kept by the employer, and the pay statements given to the employee, must reflect the number of hours offered each day, broken out by hours worked in accordance with, and hours worked above, the number of hours required by the three-fourths guarantee.[175]

The appropriations legislation for fiscal years 2016 and 2017 prohibit DOL from using funds from those years to enforce the three-fourths guarantee.[176] DOL took the position that "the 2016 DOL Appropriations Act did not vacate [this] regulatory provision, and [it remains] in effect, thus imposing a legal duty on H-2B employers." DOL just did not enforce the three-fourths provision while under fiscal 2016 funding,[177] and presumably will do the same for fiscal 2017.

---

[171] 20 CFR §655.20(f)(4).

[172] 20 CFR §655.20(f)(7).

[173] Id.

[174] 20 CFR §655.20(f)(7) and (8).

[175] 20 CFR §655.20(f)(8) and (i).

[176] 2016 Consolidated Appropriations Act, Pub. L. No. 114-113 (2015), §113; 2017 Consolidated Appropriations Act, Pub. L. No. 115-31 (2017), §113, AILA Doc. No. 17050367.

[177] DOL, "Emergency Guidance, Implementation of 2016 DOL Appropriations Act" (Jan. 5, 2016), AILA Doc. No. 15123000.

Copyright © 2017. American Immigration Lawyers Association. All rights reserved.

Although the Immigration and Nationality Act (INA) does not define "employer" for purposes of H-2B classification,[178] DOL regulations define an employer as a "person, firm, corporation or other association or organization" that meets the following requirements:

- "Has a place of business (physical location) in the United States and a means by which it may be contacted;

- "Has an employer relationship with respect to H-2B employees or related U.S. workers under this part; and

- "Possesses, for purposes of the filing of an application, a valid Federal Employer Identification Number (FEIN)."[179]

In addition, there may be joint employment by at least two employers if each individual employer meets the requirements stated above and one of them is a job contractor.[180] For a discussion of how to prepare and file H-2B petitions on behalf of more than one employer, see below.

For purposes of the H-2B classification, an "employee" is defined "under the general common law," and the following factors are considered, although "[o]ther applicable factors should be considered and no one factor is dispositive":

- "The hiring party's right to control the manner and means by which the work is accomplished";

- The "skill required to perform the work";

- The "source of the instrumentalities and tools for accomplishing the work";

- The "location of the work";

- The "hiring party's discretion over when and how long to work"; and

- "[W]hether the work is part of the regular business of the hiring party."[181]

D. Numerical Limitation

Generally, the annual numerical limitation for H-2B visas is 66,000,[182] although there is no quota on the number of temporary labor certifications.[183] In response to complaints from employers' industries with seasonal and peakload needs in the spring and summer, Congress split the 66,000 quota, so that 33,000 H-2B visas are available in each half of the fiscal year.[184] Despite this effort by Congress to evenly

---

[178] *Matter of [name not provided]*, SRC 91 125 00585 (AAU July 17, 1991), 9 Immig. Rptr. B2-37.

[179] 20 CFR §655.5.

[180] *Id.*

[181] 20 CFR §655.5; "H-2B Temporary Labor Certification Process Stakeholder Briefing" (Sept. 2009), AILA Doc. No. 09092568.

[182] 8 CFR §§214.2(h)(8)(i)(C), (h)(8)(ii), and (h)(14); 9 FAM 402.10-4(B) and 9 FAM 402.10-9(D).

[183] 73 Fed. Reg. 78020 (Dec. 19, 2008).

[184] Pub. L. No. 109-13, 119 Stat. 320 (May 11, 2005).

Copyright © 2017. American Immigration Lawyers Association. All rights reserved.

distribute the 66,000 visas, employers whose temporary need falls later in the fiscal year can still be left with no H-2B numbers available.

Nevertheless, the H-2B visa classification remains highly oversubscribed; DHS has acknowledged that the "annual cap of 66,000 H-2B visas is reached earlier every year,"[185] where "all visas are typically allocated in the early weeks of availability."[186] In May 2017, Congress expanded the H-2B quota for fiscal year 2017 by "not more than the highest number of H-2B nonimmigrants who participated in the H-2B returning worker program in any fiscal year in which returning workers were exempt from such numerical limitation."[187] It appears that the highest number occurred in 2007, so the quota for fiscal 2017 should be 129,547.[188] As of this writing, no guidance has been issued with respect to the 2017 legislation, so it is unclear how the split between the two halves of the year will be handled.

Even with this one-year increase in the quota, oversubscription is expected to continue, and thus it is critical for employers to file their petitions as early as allowed under the regulations.

In 2009, USCIS "attribute[d] the number of H-2B filings being lower than they were at the same time last year, in part, to recent changes in the H-2B program concerning when an employer may file an H-2B petition with USCIS, and in part, due to the current economic downturn and the increased demand by U.S. workers for otherwise unfillable positions."[189] In response, USCIS reopened the H-2B petition filing period after the quota had been filled when DOS reported that 66,000 H-2B visas had not been issued:[190] "Due to the unexpectedly low visa issuance rate, USCIS is reopening the filing period, as a courtesy to the public, to allow employers to file petitions for qualified H-2B temporary foreign nonagricultural workers."[191] The filing period was similarly reopened in 2015 when it was found that "the number of actual H-2B visas issued by DOS is substantially less than the number of H-2B beneficiaries seeking consular notification listed on cap-subject H-2B petitions approved by USCIS."[192] It is hoped that the same consideration will be offered again in such circumstances.

---

[185] *Id.*

[186] 73 Fed. Reg. 78020 (Dec. 19, 2008).

[187] 2017 Consolidated Appropriations Act, Pub. L. No. 115-31 (2017), Div. H, Title I and Div. F, Title V, AILA Doc. No. 17050367.

[188] Congressional Research Service, A. Bruno, "The H-2B Visa and the Statutory Cap: In Brief" (Dec. 11, 2015), https://fas.org/sgp/crs/homesec/R44306.pdf.

[189] "SCOPS/AILA Call" (July 15, 2009), AILA Doc. No. 09071574.

[190] USCIS, "USCIS to Accept New H-2B Fiscal Year 2009 Petitions" (Aug. 6, 2009), AILA Doc. No. 09080665.

[191] USCIS, "Questions and Answers: USCIS Reopens Fiscal Year 2009 H-2B Filing Period" (Aug. 6, 2009), AILA Doc. No. 09080665.

[192] "USCIS to Reopen H-2B Cap for the Second Half of Fiscal Year 2015" (June 5, 2015), https://www.uscis.gov/news/alerts/uscis-reopen-h-2b-cap-second-half-fiscal-year-2015.

Copyright © 2017. American Immigration Lawyers Association. All rights reserved.

H-4 spouses and children are not counted against the cap.[193] Also, "H-2B workers who have previously been counted against the cap in the same fiscal year that the proposed employment begins will not be subject to the cap if the employer names the workers on the petition and indicates that they have already been counted."[194]

Another exception is that fish roe processors, fish roe technicians, and supervisors of fish roe processing are not subject to the quota.[195] USCIS indicated that the "filing should have a cover sheet or something obvious that clearly indicates it is not subject to the H-2B cap."[196] Finally, H-2B workers in the Commonwealth of the Northern Mariana Islands (CNMI) and Guam are not subject to the numerical limitation.[197]

In many years, certain "returning" H-2B nonimmigrants have been exempted from the quota, so foreign nationals who were physically present outside the United States and who had been awarded H-2B visa numbers in the immediate preceding three years were not counted against the cap. Such foreign nationals could "return" to the United States for temporary employment.[198] Unfortunately, Congress rarely renews this exemption without a sunset, and it is not at all unusual for the provision to sunset before Congress renews it. Anticipating renewal, USCIS will sometimes advise applicants to simply identify returning workers on petitions so that it can back them out of the quota count if and when the provision is renewed.[199] Congress did not renew the exemption for fiscal year 2017, but instead increased the quota for fiscal year 2017 to equal the highest number admitted in any year in which returning resident provisions were in place.[200] What Congress will do in succeeding years remains to be seen.

In any event, an H-2B nonimmigrant who has spent more than three years in the United States in any H or L status must remain physically outside the United States for three months to be eligible for H-2B status again.[201]

E. Wage Requirements for H-2B Workers and Workers in Corresponding Employment

The offered wage must equal or exceed the higher of the prevailing wage or the "highest wage required by any Federal, State or local law,"[202] which generally means

---

[193] 8 CFR §214.2(h)(8(ii)(A).

[194] "Cap Count for H-2B Nonimmigrants" (Mar. 17, 2017), AILA Doc. No. 16110861.

[195] Pub. L. No. 108-287, 118 Stat. 1014 (Aug. 5, 2004); AFM 31.5.

[196] "Nebraska Service Center Business Products Teleconference" (Jan. 25, 2005), AILA Doc. No. 05020162.

[197] USCIS, D. Neufeld, "Numerical Limitation Exemption for H Nonimmigrants Employed in the CNMI and Guam" (Jan. 29, 2010), AILA Doc. No. 10021162.

[198] 9 FAM 402.10-4(E); "Implementation of H-2B Legislation" (May 16, 2005), AILA Doc. No. 05051610; 2016 Consolidated Appropriations Act, Pub. L. No. 114-113 (2015), §565, AILA Doc. No. 15121601.

[199] USCIS, "H-2B Employers Should Continue to Identify 'Returning Workers' in Petitions for FY2017" (Sept. 13, 2016), AILA Doc. No. 16091401.

[200] 2017 Consolidated Appropriations Act, Pub. L. No. 115-31 (2017), Div. H, Title I and Div. F, Title V, AILA Doc. No. 17050367.

[201] 8 CFR §214.2(h)(13)(iv).

Copyright © 2017. American Immigration Lawyers Association. All rights reserved.

the applicable minimum wage. The wage must not be "based on commissions, bonuses, or other incentives, including paying on a piece-rate basis, unless the employer guarantees a wage earned every workweek that equals or exceeds the offered wage."[203] Any piece-rate pay must be shown to be no less than the normal rate paid by non-H-2B employers and must result in a rate at least equal to the offered wage. If, at the end of the workweek, the pay does not amount to at least the offered hourly wage, the employer must supplement the pay to reach that amount.[204]

Employees must be paid at least every two weeks or according to the "prevailing practice in the area of intended employment," whichever is more frequent.[205] Wages must be paid "free and clear," meaning that deductions from the worker's pay must be "authorized" and any not required by law must be disclosed in the job order.[206] Authorized deductions include those required by law, such as tax withholdings and garnishments, reasonable costs of room and board, and union dues. The wage requirements are not met if there are unauthorized deductions, including rebates, refunds, or "kickbacks" to the employer or a third party for the employer's benefit, that reduce the wage payment to below the offered wage. "Any deductions not disclosed in the job order are prohibited."[207]

The offered wage must be paid to the H-2B worker and to all workers in "corresponding employment,"[208] and employers must apply all conditions governing H-2B employment to its corresponding employees.[209] Corresponding employment is defined as "the employment of workers who are not H-2B workers by an employer that has a certified H-2B *Application for Temporary Employment Certification* when those workers are performing either substantially the same work included in the job order or substantially the same work performed by the H-2B workers." Excluded from the definition are two categories of more permanent incumbent employees:

Those continuously employed by the employer during the 52 weeks prior to the certified period of employment and "who have worked or been paid for at least 35 hours in at least 48 of the prior 52 workweeks" and "for an average of at least 35 hours per week over the prior 52 weeks," and

Those employees covered by a collective bargaining agreement or individual contract guaranteeing at least 35 hours per workweek and employment that is to continue at

---

[202] 20 CFR §§655.10(a) and 655.20(a).

[203] 20 CFR §655.20(a).

[204] 20 CFR §655.20(a)(4).

[205] 20 CFR §655.20(h).

[206] 20 CFR §655.20(b) and (c).

[207] 20 CFR §655.20(c).

[208] 20 CFR §§655.10(a) and 655.18(a)(1).

[209] 20 CFR §655.20.

Copyright © 2017. American Immigration Lawyers Association. All rights reserved.

least through the period on the job order, "except that the employee may be dismissed for cause."[210]

If the terms and working conditions of employment are substantially reduced by the employer during the period covered by the job order, the former group of incumbent employees would cease to be excluded from the definition.[211]

The appropriations legislation for fiscal years 2016 and 2017 prohibited DOL from using funds for those fiscal years to enforce the provisions on corresponding employment.[212] DOL took the position that "the 2016 DOL Appropriations Act did not vacate this regulatory provision, and it remains in effect, thus imposing a legal duty on H-2B employers." DOL just did not enforce the provision while under fiscal 2016 funding,[213] and presumably will do the same for fiscal year 2017. It did, however, continue to enforce the requirement that the employer offer "to U.S. workers no less than the same benefits, wages, and working conditions that the employer is offering, intends to offer, or will provide to H-2B workers."[214]

The employer must give to the worker, on or before each pay day, a statement that includes the worker's total earnings for each workweek in the pay period, the hourly or piece rate, hours offered during each workweek of the pay period (broken out by hours in accordance with, and above, the "three-fourths guarantee"), hours actually worked, an itemization of deductions, units produced daily if piece rates are used, the beginning and end dates of the pay period, and "the employer's name, address and FEIN."[215]

IV. Temporary Labor Certification

The temporary labor certification process is considered to protect U.S. workers "from adverse effect due to foreign competition for temporary jobs with U.S. employers."[216] As stated by regulation:

"This part and its subparts shall be construed to effectuate the purpose of the INA that U.S. workers rather than aliens be employed wherever possible. Where temporary alien workers are admitted, the terms and conditions of their employment must not result in a lowering of the terms and conditions of domestic

---

[210] 20 CFR §§655.5.

[211] *Id.*

[212] 2016 Consolidated Appropriations Act, Pub. L. No. 114-113 (2015), §113; 2017 Consolidated Appropriations Act, Pub. L. No. 115-31 (2017), §113, AILA Doc. No. 17050367.

[213] DOL, "2015 H-2B Interim Final Rule FAQs, Round 14" (Jan. 5, 2016), https://www.foreignlaborcert.doleta.gov/pdf/H-2B_2015_IFR_FAQ_Corresponding-Employment_2016_DOL_Appropriations_Act.pdf.

[214] 20 CFR §655.18(a)(1).

[215] 20 CFR §655.20(i)(2).

[216] 73 Fed. Reg. 78020 (Dec. 19, 2008).

Copyright © 2017. American Immigration Lawyers Association. All rights reserved.

workers similarly employed…, and the job benefits extended to any U.S. workers shall be at least those extended to the alien workers."[217]

It is no longer possible to file an H-2B petition without an approved temporary labor certification.[218] USCIS may no longer "delve into the merits of the sufficiency of the employer's market test," because DHS lacks "the expertise needed to make any labor market determinations, independent of those already made by DOL."[219] A previous attempt to eliminate the labor certification requirement was strongly opposed by commentators who expressed concern about decreased protection of U.S. workers and increased fraud; DHS withdrew the proposed rule.[220]

An addition from the 2008 regulation that was retained in the 2015 joint rulemaking, however, is an appeals process if DOL denies the temporary labor certification,[221] which was unavailable before,[222] as discussed below. But even if the denied temporary labor certification is appealed, the petitioner may not file an H-2B petition with USCIS, as there is no approved temporary labor certification.[223]

An employer may not file a temporary labor certification application if the job opportunity is available because of a strike or other work stoppage situation; the employer must attest that no such strike or lockout exists,[224] as discussed below. A strike is defined as "a labor dispute wherein employees engage in a concerted stoppage of work (including stoppage by reason of the expiration of a collective-bargaining agreement) or engage in any concerted slowdown or other concerted interruption of operations." DOL stated that the evaluation of "whether job opportunities are vacant because of a strike, lockout, or work stoppage" will be made "on an individualized, position-by-position basis."[225]

As discussed below, an employer, agent, or attorney may file a temporary labor certification application for multiple worksites as long as the worksites are in the same metropolitan statistical area (MSA): "As a general rule, an employer seeking to employ workers who will perform work at more than one location outside of a single area of intended employment are required to file a separate application for each area of intended employment, regardless of the number of workers named in the

---

[217] 20 CFR §655.0 (internal citations omitted) (citing *Elton Orchards, Inc. v. Brennan*, 508 F.2d 493, 500 (1st Cir. 1974); *Flecha v. Quiros*, 567 F.2d 1154 (1st Cir. 1977); *Williams v. Usery*, 531 F.2d 305 (5th Cir. 1976); *Florida Sugar Cane League, Inc. v. Usery*, 531 F.2d 299 (5th Cir. 1976)).

[218] 8 CFR §214.2(h)(6)(iii)(C).

[219] 73 Fed. Reg. 78104 (Dec. 19, 2008).

[220] 73 Fed. Reg. 49122 (Aug. 20, 2008).

[221] 20 CFR §655.53.

[222] *See, e.g., Matter of B&B Glass, Inc.*, 99-TLC-4 (Apr. 21, 1999), 1999 DOL TLC LEXIS 4; *Matter of Mustache Café*, 95-TLC-28 (Oct. 24, 1995), 1995 DOL TLC LEXIS 7.

[223] 8 CFR §214.2(h)(6)(iii)(C).

[224] 20 CFR §655.20(u).

[225] *Id.*

Copyright © 2017. American Immigration Lawyers Association. All rights reserved.

application."[226] An application for multiple beneficiaries may be filed "[a]s long as all H-2B workers will perform the same services or labor under the same terms and conditions, in the same occupation, in the same area of intended employment, and during the same period of employment."[227] However, employers in the seafood industry may, with certain limitations, bring in workers on a staggered basis at any time during the 120 days after the start date,[228] as explained in detail under the section titled "Seafood Workers" later in this chapter.

DOL regulations have, over the years, changed back and forth between requiring that the recruitment for the labor certification, including the SWA job order, take place before filing or after filing the temporary labor certification application. The current regulatory iteration requires that the recruitment take place after filing, except that the job order is to be submitted to the SWA "at the same time" as the filing of the labor certification application.[229]

As detailed below, employers seeking H-2B temporary labor certifications with dates of need on or after October 1, 2015,[230] must:

- Register within the timeframe of 150 to 120 days before the date of need, once the registration process is in effect. Before that, the issue of temporary need covered by the registration process is handled as part of the application;[231]

- Obtain a prevailing wage determination (PWD). This determination, which will have a validity period of between 90 and 365 days,[232] must be valid on the date the job order is posted.[233] DOL suggests seeking it as early as possible, up to one year before the date of need;[234]

- Concurrently submit a job order to the applicable State Workforce Agency and the temporary labor certification application, along with supporting documents and a copy of the SWA job order as filed, to the DOL's National Processing Center (NPC) in Chicago. Both must be filed within 90 to 75 calendar days prior to the needed start date.[235]

---

[226] DOL, "2015 H-2B Interim Final Rule FAQs, Round 17" (Oct. 4, 2016), AILA Doc. No. 16100430, https://www.foreignlaborcert.doleta.gov/pdf/Round-17_FAQs_Worksites-AIE.pdf.

[227] 20 CFR §655.15(e) and (f).

[228] 20 CFR§655.15(f).

[229] 20 CFR §655.16(a).

[230] For earlier dates of need involved in the transition to the current procedures, *see* 20 CFR §655.4.

[231] DOL, "H-2B Temporary Non-agricultural Program" (updated Oct. 4, 2016), https://www.foreign laborcert.doleta.gov/2015_H-2B_IFR.cfm.

[232] 20 CFR §655.10(h).

[233] 20 CFR §655.10(f)(2).

[234] DOL, "H-2B Temporary Non-agricultural Program" (updated Oct. 4, 2016), https://www.foreign laborcert.doleta.gov/2015_H-2B_IFR.cfm.

[235] *Id.*

Copyright © 2017. American Immigration Lawyers Association. All rights reserved.

The start date requested on the H-2B Form I-129 must match the date of need on the temporary labor certification, and this date of need is defined as "the first date the employer requires services of the H-2B workers as listed on the [application]."[236]

DOL allows the dates of need on the temporary labor certification to be changed in two situations. First, as previously mentioned, the employer may request changes to the period of employment for a period of 14 days, provided the overall period of employment does not exceed nine months except in the case of a one-time occurrence.[237] The request must be made in writing, and DOL will consider "whether the proposed amendments are sufficiently justified and must take into account the effects of the changes on the underlying labor market test for the job opportunity."[238] For example, employers filing in the first half of the fiscal year for a March 18 to 31 start date have been allowed to amend their applications if they requested a change in the start date of 14 or fewer days.[239]

Second, an extension of the period of employment may be requested due to "weather conditions or other factors beyond the control of the employer (which may include unforeseeable changes in market conditions), and must be supported in writing, with documentation showing why the extension is needed and that the need could not have been reasonably foreseen by the employer."[240] Extensions beyond the respective nine-month or three-year limits will not be granted "except in extraordinary circumstances."[241] A denial of such an extension can be appealed to the Board of Alien Labor Certification Appeals (BALCA).[242]

Neither a registration nor a temporary labor certification application may be transferred to another employer, unless that entity is a successor in interest.[243] Indicia of successorship include:

- Substantial continuity of the same business operations;
- Use of the same facilities;
- Continuity of the work force;
- Similarity of jobs and working conditions;
- Similarity of supervisory personnel;
- Whether the former management or owner retains a direct or indirect interest in the new enterprise;
- Similarity in machinery, equipment, and production methods;

[236] 20 CFR §655.5.
[237] 20 CFR §655.35(b).
[238] Id.
[239] "Minutes from DOL H-2 Stakeholder Meeting" (Mar. 7, 2017), AILA Doc. No. 17032836, item 12b.
[240] 20 CFR §655.60.
[241] Id.
[242] Id.
[243] 20 CFR §§655.12(b) and 655.55(b).

Copyright © 2017. American Immigration Lawyers Association. All rights reserved.

- Similarity of products and services; and
- The ability of the predecessor to provide relief.[244]

A. Qualifications and Requirements

The prevailing wage request, SWA job order, and temporary labor certification application steps all involve an articulation of the qualifications and requirements for the job, and the recruitment "must comply with the assurances applicable to job orders," as discussed below.[245]

Every qualification and requirement listed on the job order, and thus also on the application, "must be bona fide and consistent with the normal and accepted qualifications and requirements imposed by non-H-2B employers in the same occupation and area of intended employment."[246]

Qualification is defined as "a characteristic that is necessary to an individual's ability to perform the job," while requirement "means a term or condition of employment which a worker is required to accept in order to obtain the job."[247]

To determine whether a job requirement or qualification is "normal," DOL generally references the Occupational Information Network (O*NET) for specific occupations. "For other qualifications and requirements not addressed by the O*NET (*e.g.*, criminal background checks, licensing requirements, or drug tests), [DOL] relies on its own historical experience with case-by-case application review as well as information received from outside sources (*e.g.*, information on non-H-2B job requirements and qualifications available to the State Workforce Agency, other employers in the industry or occupation, or interest groups with knowledge of the industry or occupation) to identify job requirements and qualifications that do not appear consistent with the regulatory standard."[248]

Thus, for example, if an employer prefers six months of experience, but in that geographic area and occupation, three months are generally considered sufficient to do the job satisfactorily, the employer cannot require more than three months of experience, as that is what is minimally required for the workers to perform the job.[249]

B. Employer Registration

As previously discussed, DOL is transitioning to a system that "bifurcates the current application process into a registration phase, which addresses the employer's

---

[244] *Id.*

[245] 20 CFR §655.41(a).

[246] 20 CFR §655.20(e).

[247] *Id.*

[248] DOL, "2015 H-2B Interim Final Rule FAQs, Round 5," https://www.foreignlaborcert.doleta.gov/pdf/H-2B_2015_IFR_FAQs_Round5.pdf. The O*Net can be found at https://www.onetonline.org/.

[249] *Id.*

Copyright © 2017. American Immigration Lawyers Association. All rights reserved.

temporary need, and an application phase, which addresses the labor market test."[250] DOL explains the purpose behind this:

> "Separating the two processes will give OFLC the time to make a considered decision about temporary need without negatively impacting an employer's ability to have the workers it needs in place in a timely manner. In addition, we anticipate that many employers, with 3 years of registration validity, will benefit from a one-step process involving only the labor market test in their second and third years after registration, which will allow DOL to process these applications more efficiently. We conclude that enforcement alone cannot ensure program integrity; in the move from an attestation-based model to a compliance-based model, the bifurcation of application processing into registration and labor market test phases contributes to program integrity."[251]

This process was not immediately effective. Instead, DOL "will announce in the Federal Register a separate transition period for the registration process, and until that time, will continue to adjudicate temporary need during the processing of applications."[252] As of this writing, an announcement has not yet been made. The practitioner should monitor the DOL[253] and AILA[254] websites for relevant announcements of the transition and implementation.

Once the registration process is in place, employers will be required to first submit to DOL a registration, the purpose of which is to establish that the employer's need is temporary, and then the employer then can submit temporary labor certification applications under that registration for up to three years.[255] The registration process requires that the employer submit with the registration evidence documenting:

- The number of positions to be sought in the first year of registration;

- The time period in which the need is expected;

- That the need is temporary and non-agricultural;

- That the need "is justified as either a one-time occurrence, a seasonal need, a peakload need, or an intermittent need";

- If the employer is a job contractor, that its own need is seasonal or a one-time occurrence.[256]

DOL will review the registration application in accordance with the standards for temporary need, and determine if the job is non-agricultural, the number of positions

---

[250] 80 Fed. Reg. 24042 (Apr. 29, 2015).

[251] *Id.*

[252] 20 CFR §655.11(j).

[253] DOL, "H-2B Temporary Non-agricultural Program," https://www.foreignlaborcert.doleta.gov/2015_H-2B_IFR.cfm.

[254] American Immigration Lawyers Association, http://www.aila.org.

[255] 20 CFR §655.12(a).

[256] 20 CFR §655.11(a).

Copyright © 2017. American Immigration Lawyers Association. All rights reserved.

and time periods for them are justified, and the "request represents a bona fide job opportunity.[257] A Request for Information (RFI) is supposed to be issued "within 7 days" if the certifying officer determines that the registration cannot be approved. However, DOL has stated with respect to its regulatory seven-day deadline for NODs for temporary labor certification applications that if a NOD is not received in seven days, that doesn't mean that one is not coming.[258] There is no reason to think that the agency will respect its regulatory RFI deadline any more than it respects the one for NODs. The RFI should state why the registration cannot be approved and what information or documentation is needed "to correct the deficiencies." The employer will be given up to seven days to respond.[259] This deadline has teeth—the registration will be denied if DOL does not receive a timely response.[260]

If the registration is approved, the employer will be authorized for a period of up to three years to file temporary labor certification applications.[261] However, if the number of workers to be employed has increased by more than 20%, or 50% for employers requesting fewer 10 ten employees, if the dates of need have changed by more than 30 days total from the initial year, if the nature of the job has changed, or if the temporary nature of the need has materially changed, the employer must file for a new registration.[262]

If the registration is denied, the employer can request administrative review[263] by BALCA.[264]

C. Prevailing Wage

Like the H-2B program overall, as discussed early in this chapter, prevailing wage methodology applicable to H-2Bs has undergone considerable litigation and legislation in recent years.[265] At the time of this writing, prevailing wages are governed by a regulation issued in April 2015 jointly by DHS and DOL, but amending only DOL regulations.[266]

The employer must obtain a prevailing wage determination (PWD) from the National Prevailing Wage Center (NPWC)[267] on Form ETA-9141, the Prevailing Wage Determination Request (PWDR).[268] "Electronic filing is strongly

---

[257] 20 CFR §655.11(d).

[258] "Minutes from DOL H-2 Stakeholder Meeting" (Mar. 7. 2017), AILA Doc. No. 17032836.

[259] 20 CFR §655.11(g).

[260] 20 CFR §655.11(g)(4).

[261] 20 CFR §655.12.

[262] Id.

[263] 20 CFR §655.11(h)(2).

[264] 20 CFR §655.61.

[265] A good summary of this history until the regulation can be found in the preamble to DOL's and DHS's 2015 prevailing wage final rule, 80 Fed. Reg. 24146 (Apr. 29, 2015).

[266] 80 Fed. Reg. 24146 (Apr. 29, 2015), amending 20 CFR §655.10.

[267] 20 CFR §655.10(c).

[268] 20 CFR §655.5, definition of Prevailing Wage Determination (PWD).

Copyright © 2017. American Immigration Lawyers Association. All rights reserved.

recommended," and is done through DOL's iCert portal.[269] The PWDR also may be filed by mail.[270] The physical form is available as a document online,[271] together with instructions.[272]

"Area of intended employment" is defined as "the geographic area within normal commuting distance of the place (worksite address) of the job opportunity."[273] DOL does not stipulate a "rigid measure of distance" to calculate a "normal commuting distance or normal commuting area, because there may be widely varying factual circumstances among different areas (*e.g.*, average commuting times, barriers to reaching the worksite, quality of regional transportation network, etc.)."[274] Therefore, if the worksite is in a metropolitan statistical area, even a multistate MSA, such as the metropolitan New York City area, which includes parts of New York, New Jersey, and Connecticut, then any worksite in the MSA "is deemed to be within normal commuting distance."[275] In addition, the practitioner should not consider the physical MSA borders to be "controlling" when identifying the normal commuting distance or area. One example provided by DOL notes that "a location outside of an MSA may be within normal commuting distance of a location that is inside (*e.g.*, near the border of) the MSA."[276] For further discussion of MSAs, see Volume 2: Chapter Two, "The Labor Certification Application."

Under DOL's 2015 wage regulation, if the job is covered by an arms' length collective bargaining agreement (CBA), the wage set by the CBA is the prevailing wage.[277] If the wage is for a professional athlete, the wage set forth in the rules or regulations, if there are any, is the prevailing wage.[278] If there is no CBA or applicable rules for athletes, the prevailing wage is the arithmetic mean of the wages of workers similarly employed in the area of intended employment, using the DOL Bureau of Labor Statistics' (BLS) Occupational Employment Statistics (OES) Wage Data Survey.[279]

DOL's regulation uses the arithmetic mean for all wages for the occupation in determining prevailing wage in the H-2B context; it does not base its determinations

---

[269] DOL, "Welcome to the iCERT Visa Portal System," https://icert.doleta.gov/.

[270] "National Prevailing Wage and Helpdesk Center Prevailing Wage Frequently Asked Questions" (Mar. 2010), AILA Doc. No. 10032662.

[271] Department of Labor (DOL), "Application for Prevailing Wage Determination," https://www.foreignlaborcert.doleta.gov/pdf/ETA_Form_9141.pdf.

[272] DOL, "ETA Form 9141—General Instructions for the 9141," www.foreignlaborcert.doleta.gov/pdf/ETA_Form_9141_General_Instructions.pdf.

[273] 8 CFR §655.5.

[274] *Id.*

[275] *Id.*

[276] *Id.*

[277] 8 CFR §655.10(b)(1).

[278] 20 CFR §655.10(i).

[279] 8 CFR §655.10(b)(2); 80 Fed. Reg. 24146 (Apr. 29, 2015).

Copyright © 2017. American Immigration Lawyers Association. All rights reserved.

on different tiers for different levels of skill and experience.[280] This abandons a prior four-tier system, on the basis that "there are no significant skill-based wage differences in the occupations that predominate in the H-2B program, and to the extent such differences might exist, those differences are not captured by the existing four-tier wage structure."[281]

However, the 2016 and 2017 appropriations legislation define prevailing wage as "the greater of — (1) the actual wage level paid by the employer to other employees with similar experience and qualifications for such position in the same location; or (2) the prevailing wage level for the occupational classification of the position in the geographic area in which the H-2B nonimmigrant will be employed, based on the best information available at the time of filing the petition."[282]

To address the actual wage element of the Appropriations Act definition, DOL has indicated that, rather than requesting the employer to submit documentation of its actual wage, it will include in the PWD the requirement that the employer pay the higher of the "actual wage paid to employees of similar experience and qualifications" or the PWD issued by DOL.[283] While that framing of actual wage, borrowed from the H-1B context, refers to skill and experience levels, DOL continues to decline to use skill and experience levels for the prevailing wage, instead adhering to the single arithmetic mean approach.[284]

Under the regulation, if multiple worksites are involved within an area of intended employment, and there are different prevailing wages for the different sites, the prevailing wage is the highest among the sites.[285]

Davis-Bacon Act (DBA) and Service Contract Act (SCA) wages, once required when a wage determination under them existed in the area of intended employer, and later made optional for employers to use, are barred by the regulation from being used in determining prevailing wage.[286] If a government contractor required to pay those acts' wages requests a prevailing wage for an H-2B, the employer will still need to pay prevailing wage determined by DOL. The net effect of this is that the employer must pay the higher of the PWD for the H-2B or the DBA/SCA wage.[287]

As initially written, the 2015 DOL wage rule allowed the use of nongovernmental employer-provided surveys "only where the OES survey does not provide any data

---

[280] 80 Fed. Reg. 24146 (Apr. 29, 2015) (reciting the litigation and legislative history of how it reached this point).

[281] Id.

[282] 2016 Consolidated Appropriations Act, Pub. L. No. 114-113 (2015), §112; 2017 Consolidated Appropriations Act, Pub. L. No. 115-31 (2017), §112, AILA Doc. No. 17050367.

[283] DOL, "Effects of the 2016 Department of Labor Appropriations Act" (Dec. 29, 2105), http://bit.ly/AppropsPW.

[284] Id.

[285] 8 CFR §655.10(d).

[286] Id.

[287] Id., footnote 42.

Copyright © 2017. American Immigration Lawyers Association. All rights reserved.

for an occupation in a specific geographical location, or where the OES survey does not accurately represent the relevant job classification."[288] However, Congress pushed back on this provision, and instructed in the 2016 appropriations legislation that DOL accept private wage surveys even in instances in which OES survey data is available, unless the methodology and data in the survey "are not statistically supported."[289] This provision was repeated in the 2017 appropriations legislation.[290]

Accordingly, during the periods covered by the 2016 and 2017 Appropriations Act, an employer can "submit a 'statistically supported' private survey, including one that was privately conducted by an entity other than a state, even if it does not fit within one of the exceptions in 20 CFR [Code of Federal Regulations] 655.10(f)(1). However, an employer can not submit a private survey if there is an applicable CBA."[291]

After the end of FY2017, unless Congress acts again, an employer once again will not be able to provide a survey unless:

"The survey was independently conducted and issued by a state, including any state agency, state college, or state university";

The survey is for a geographic area where the OES does not collect data or provides an arithmetic mean "only at a national level for workers employed in" the Standard Occupational Code (SOC);

There is not an SOC in the system in which the position is included; or

The position is within an SOC "designated as an 'all other'" classification.[292]

The survey "must provide the arithmetic mean of the wages of all workers similarly employed in the area of intended employment." If the survey provides no mean but instead provides a median, then the median can be used for the area of employment.[293] The geographic area covered can be expanded beyond the area of intended employment only if it is necessary to ensure the requirement that the data cover at least 30 workers and at least three employers, and only if the expanded area includes only contiguous areas.[294] The survey must be based on the most current edition of the survey, and on "wages paid not more than 24 months before the date the survey is submitted."[295]

---

[288] 80 Fed. Reg. 24146 (Apr. 29, 2015), referring to its promulgation of 20 CFR §655.10(f).

[289] 2016 Consolidated Appropriations Act, Pub. L. No. 114-113 (2015), §112.

[290] 2017 Consolidated Appropriations Act, Pub. L. No. 115-31 (2017), §112, AILA Doc. No. 17050367.

[291] *Id. See* 20 CFR §655.10(f)(1), stating that a survey can be provided only "[i]f the job opportunity is not covered by a CBA, or by a professional sports league's rules or regulations"

[292] 20 CFR §655.10 (f)(1). See Volume 2: Chapter Two, "The Labor Certification Application," for an explanation of SOCs and the "all other" category.

[293] 20 CFR §655.10(f)(2).

[294] 20 CFR §655.10(f)(3) and (4)(ii).

[295] 20 CFR §655.10(f)(5).

Copyright © 2017. American Immigration Lawyers Association. All rights reserved.

To use a survey, the employer must complete and submit with the PWD request the Form ETA-9165.[296] The form requests such information as sample size, titles and job duties included in the survey, methodology used, and geographic area covered. It requires the employer to attest that the surveyor made a reasonable effort to contact all applicable employers; that the survey includes data from at least 30 employees and three employers; that the survey was conducted by a bona fide third party and not the employer or its agent, representative, or attorney; that the survey crossed industries that employ workers in the occupation; that the wage reported includes all types of pay; and that the survey included workers regardless of immigration status.[297]

If the NPC determines that the employer-provided survey is unacceptable, then the employer will be informed "in writing of the reasons the survey was not accepted."[298] The employer may seek review by filing a written request to the NPWC Director within seven business days from issuance of the denial.[299] If the employer disagrees with the Director's determination, it can request an appeal to BALCA within ten business days of the date the determination was issued. The appeal must be in writing to the NPWC that made the determination, and can include only information, documents, and arguments already in the record.[300]

DOL recommends that employers file PWD requests as early as possible and up to one year before the date of need, and "at least 60 days in advance of the date they intend to use it."[301] Once issued, the PWD must be valid for at least 90 days from the date of determination and must not be valid for longer than 365 days after the date of determination.[302] The prevailing wage determination must be valid on the date that the job order is submitted and the temporary labor certification is filed.[303] Finally, the employer must retain the PWD for three years from the later of the date of issuance or the date of final determination on the temporary labor certification application, and must submit it in the case of a NOD or to DOL if the application is audited or if there is a Wage and Hour Division (WHD) investigation, such as in a compliance or enforcement action.[304]

D. SWA Submission

The job order must be submitted to the SWA serving the area of intended employment "at the same time" the temporary labor certification application is

---

[296] DOL, "Employer-Provided Survey Attestations to Accompany H-2B Prevailing Wage Determination Request Based on a Non-OES Survey" (exp. Dec. 31, 2018), http://bit.ly/ETA9165.

[297] Id., 8 CFR §655.10(f)(4).

[298] 8 CFR §655.10(g).

[299] 8 CFR §655.13(a) and (b).

[300] 8 CFR §655.13(c).

[301] "DOL FAQs on Processing H-2B Prevailing Wage Determinations Under the 2015 H-2B Wage Final Rule" (Sept. 1, 2016), AILA Doc. No. 16091200.

[302] 20 CFR §655.10(h).

[303] 20 CFR §655.15(a).

[304] 20 CFR §655.10(j).

Copyright © 2017. American Immigration Lawyers Association. All rights reserved.

submitted, and the employer must advise the SWA that the order is in connection with an H-2B application.[305] "If the job opportunity is located in more than one State within the same area of intended employment, the employer may submit the job order to any one of the SWAs having jurisdiction over the anticipated worksites, but must identify the receiving SWA" to DOL with the submission of the labor certification application.[306]

The job order must comply with any requirements of the state to which the order is being submitted.[307] The order must offer to U.S. workers "no less than the same benefits, wages, and working conditions" that are offered to H-2B workers, and must not contain any restrictions or obligations not imposed on the H-2B.[308]

In addition, DOL requires that the job order contain extensive detail.[309] Specifically, the order must:

- Name the employer and provide contact information;
- State that the position is full time and temporary;
- Indicate the number of job openings;
- Describe the position "with sufficient information to apprise U.S. workers of the services or labor to be performed," including:
  - Duties;
  - Minimum education and experience required;
  - Work hours and days;
  - Anticipated start and end dates of the position;
- Indicate the geographic area of employment "with enough specificity to apprise applicants of any travel requirements and where applicants will likely have to reside…";
- State the offered wage or range of offered wages, ensuring that the offer equals or exceeds the higher of the prevailing wage or the federal, state, or local minimum wage;
- If overtime is available, indicate that fact and the amount to be paid for it;

---

[305] 20 CFR §655.16(a).

[306] Id.

[307] 20 CFR §655.16(b). These requirements generally can be found on each state's website. DOL has a link to the states on a page misleadingly labelled "National Federal Processing Centers," https://www.foreignlaborcert.doleta.gov/states_npc.cfm, but unfortunately the links there frequently do not work. One can also access the home pages of the SWA sites through the US Jobs website, https://us.jobs/state-workforce-agencies.asp, but the user will need to search the site to find the applicable information. AILA members can also find the information on that organization's "Resources by State" page, http://www.aila.org/infonet/state, by selecting the state from the map and "Job Order Placement Instructions."

[308] 20 CFR §655.16(b).

[309] The requirements included in these details, as well as the assurances in the prior paragraph, are largely an articulation of the "assurances and obligations" detailed in 20 CFR §655.20.

Copyright © 2017. American Immigration Lawyers Association. All rights reserved.

- If training will be provided, say so;

- State that the employer's standard for computing wages is a single work week;

- Indicate the frequency with which the worker will be paid, which "must be at least every 2 weeks or according to the prevailing practice in the area of intended employment, whichever is more frequent";

- "If the employer provides ... the option of board, lodging, or other facilities, including fringe benefits, or intends to assist workers to secure such lodging, disclose the provision and cost of the board, lodging, or other facilities, including fringe benefits to be provided";

- State that the employer will make all paycheck deductions required by law;

- Specify other paycheck deductions;

- Detail how "the worker will be provided with or reimbursed for transportation and subsistence from the place from which the worker has come to work for the employer, whether in the U.S. or abroad, to the place of employment, if the worker completes 50 percent of the period of employment covered by the job order. 'Subsistence' refers to 'meals and, if required, lodging costs incurred on the employer's behalf along the way.' [310]";

- State that the employer "will provide or pay for the worker's cost of return transportation and daily subsistence from the place of employment to the place from which the worker, disregarding intervening employment, departed to work for the employer, if the worker completes the certified period of employment or is dismissed from employment for any reason by the employer before the end of the period";

- If the employer will provide daily transportation to and from the worksite, say so;

- State that the employer will reimburse the H-2B worker within the first week for all visa, processing, border crossing, and other related fees;

- Indicate that the employer will provide, without charge or deposit, all tools, supplies, and equipment required for the job;

- Articulate the "three-fourths guarantee," discussed later in this chapter, whereby employment must be offered for "a total number of work hours equal to at least three-fourths of the workdays of each 12-week period, if the period of employment ... is 120 days or more days, or each 6-week period of employment ... is less than 120 days";

- Instruct applicants to inquire or apply to the nearest SWA office of the state in which the advertisement is appearing; and

---

[310] DOL, "2015 H-2B Interim Final Rule FAQs, Round 5," https://www.foreignlaborcert.doleta.gov/pdf/H-2B_2015_IFR_FAQs_Round5.pdf.

Copyright © 2017. American Immigration Lawyers Association. All rights reserved.

- Include the SWA contact information.[311]

The SWA must review the job order and notify DOL within six business days if the order does not comply with "applicable criteria."[312] The SWA is to post the job order "upon receipt of the Notice of Acceptance" from DOL.[313] Anecdotal reports indicate that experience has been at best mixed regarding some SWAs' timeliness in this regard,[314] but "[a]n NOA serves as an order to the state to activate the job order and the state should activate the job order immediately."[315]

The SWA also must, upon receipt of the Notice of Acceptance (NOA), "promptly place the job order in intrastate ... and interstate clearance by providing a copy of the job order to other states as directed by the CO."

The SWA must keep the job order active until the end of the recruitment period.[316] The regulations require the SWA to post the job order upon receipt of the Notice of Acceptance and to keep the job order posted until 21 days before the date of need. Because the employer is required to file its application no more than 90 calendar days and no less than 75 calendar days before the date of need, as discussed below, the net result in most cases is that the job order will be posted for at least 54 days.[317]

The SWA should refer to the employer only "individuals who have been apprised of all the material terms and conditions of employment and who are qualified and will be available."[318] This does not mean that the fact of a referral is dispositive of whether an applicant is qualified, but the fact of a SWA referral will increase scrutiny regarding that applicant:

> "The Departments do not presume that the judgment of the SWAs as to an applicant's qualifications is irrebuttable or a substitute for the employer's business judgment with respect to any candidate's suitability for employment. However, to the extent that the employer does not hire a SWA referral who was screened and assessed as qualified, the employer will have a heightened burden to demonstrate to DOL that the applicant was rejected only for lawful, job-related reasons."[319]

E. DOL Filing

The temporary labor certification application can be filed on the Form ETA-9142B through the DOL's iCert system,[320] or by mail or overnight courier to:[321]

---

[311] 20 CFR §655.18(b). DOL provides a suggested checklist for the SWA order at https://www.foreign laborcert.doleta.gov/pdf/H-2B_Job_Order_Checklist.pdf.

[312] 8 CFR §655.16(b).

[313] 8 CFR §655.16(d). Notice of Acceptance is discussed below.

[314] "Minutes from DOL H-2 Stakeholder Meeting" (May 24, 2016), AILA Doc. No. 16071500, item 32.

[315] "Minutes from DOL H-2 Stakeholder Meeting" (Mar. 7, 2017), AILA Doc. No. 17032836, item 2.

[316] 8 CFR §655.16(d).

[317] 80 Fed. Reg. 24042, 24061 (Apr. 29, 2015).

[318] 8 CFR §655.47.

[319] 80 Fed. Reg. 24042, 24079 (Apr. 29, 2015).

[320] DOL, "Welcome to the iCERT Visa Portal System," https://icert.doleta.gov/.

Copyright © 2017. American Immigration Lawyers Association. All rights reserved.

U.S. Department of Labor
Employment and Training Administration
Office of Foreign Labor Certification
Chicago National Processing Center
11 West Quincy Court
Chicago, IL 60604-2105
Attn: H-2B Application

If the application is filed by mail, it must contain the original signature of the employer and the attorney or agent, if there is one.[322] If filed electronically via iCert, the application is signed when the employer receives the approval.[323] The application must be accompanied by a copy of the job order that is being submitted concurrently to the SWA, a valid prevailing wage determination (as discussed later in this chapter), Appendix B, and copies of all contracts or agreements with agents or recruiters used in connection with the positions.[324]

Upon receipt, DOL reviews the application and job order for compliance,[325] and issues an NOD if the CO finds the application or job order is incomplete.[326] The CO must send the NOD "using methods to assure next day delivery, including electronic mail."[327] The NOD is required to state the reasons that the application or job order was not accepted,[328] and the employer must respond within 10 business days or the application will be denied.[329] The employer can respond either by submitting a modified application and job order, or by requesting review by BALCA.[330] If a modified application is submitted, the CO can either accept it or deny it. In the latter case, the employer can appeal to BALCA at that point.[331]

Once the CO receives the application and job order, the employer will be sent an NOA or NOD within seven business days of receipt of the application.[332] If a NOA is issued, DOL will issue the guidance regarding the recruitment process, including notifying the SWA, as described below. The CO also must, upon accepting the

---

[321] DOL, "H-2B Temporary Non-agricultural Program" (updated Oct. 4, 2016), https://www.foreign laborcert.doleta.gov/2015_H-2B_IFR.cfm.

[322] 20 CFR §655.15(d).

[323] *Id.*; 20 CFR §655.52.

[324] 20 CFR §655.15(a).

[325] 20 CFR §655.30(a).

[326] 20 CFR §655.31(a).

[327] 20 CFR §655.30(b).

[328] 20 CFR §655.31(b)(1).

[329] 20 CFR §655.31(b)(4).

[330] 20 CFR §655.31(b)(2) and (3).

[331] 20 CFR §655.32.

[332] 20 CFR §655.33.

Copyright © 2017. American Immigration Lawyers Association. All rights reserved.

application, place a copy of the job order on DOL's electronic job registry until the end of the recruitment period.[333]

The CO can, "irrespective of the decision to accept" the application, require modifications to the job order at any time before the final determination, if it is determined that the wages, benefits, and working conditions provisions are not being met. In that case, the employer must provide all workers recruited in connection with the application a copy of the modified job order "no later than the date the work commences, as approved by the CO."[334]

After the employer has filed an application, a request may be made to amend the registration (or, presumably, the application, during the transition period discussed above before the registration process takes effect) to increase the number of positions requested in the initial application by not more than 20 percent (50 percent for employers requesting less than 10 positions).[335] The employer may also request changes to the period of employment for a period of 14 days, provided the overall period of employment does not exceed nine months except in the case of a one-time occurrence.[336] Other amendments also can be requested, and the CO determines whether they "are sufficiently justified," taking into account "the effect of the changes on the underlying labor market test."[337]

All requests for amendments must be submitted in writing to the CO, who submits to the SWA any necessary changes to the job order, and updates the job registry.[338] Requests can be sent via email to *TLC.Chicago@dol.gov*, with the words "H-2B Amendment Request" contained in the subject line of the email. Those without internet access may fax the request to (312) 886-1688 (Attn.: H-2B Amendment Request), or mail it to the Chicago address above, Attn: H-2B Amendment Request.[339] All amendments must be made before the application is approved: "amendments after certification are not permitted."[340]

An employer may withdraw an application any time after it has been accepted but before it is adjudicated. The withdrawal must be in writing.[341] Documentation must nonetheless be retained for three years from the date of withdrawal.[342]

F. Recruitment

---

[333] 20 CFR §655.34. The registry can be found at DOL, "Welcome to the Labor Certification Registry," http://bit.ly/DOLregistry.

[334] 20 CFR §655.32(e).

[335] 20 CFR §655.35(a).

[336] 20 CFR §655.35(b).

[337] 20 CFR §655.35(c).

[338] 20 CFR §655.35.

[339] DOL, "2015 H-2B Interim Final Rule FAQs, Round 11" (Dec. 8, 2015), https://www.foreign laborcert.doleta.gov/pdf/H-2B_2015_IFR_FAQs_Round11.pdf.

[340] 20 CFR §655.35(d).

[341] 20 CFR §655.62.

[342] 20 CFR §655.56(b).

Copyright © 2017. American Immigration Lawyers Association. All rights reserved.

The employer must complete recruitment of U.S. workers within 14 calendar days of when the Notice of Acceptance of the labor certification application is issued.[343] However, "the employer must accept referrals and applications of all U.S. applicants until 21 days before the employer's start date of need."[344] Also, as noted below, if there is no bargaining representative, a posting must be made for 15 business days. Thus, the posting "must be started, but need not be completed, within the 14-day period after NOA is issued."[345]

The purpose of the recruitment is "to ensure that there are not qualified U.S. workers who will be available for the positions," and such workers can be rejected "only for lawful job-related reasons.[346] All recruitment must offer terms and conditions, and impose qualifications and requirements, no less favorable than being offered to or imposed on the H-2B workers.[347] The recruitment "must comply with the assurances applicable to job orders," as discussed above.[348]

1. U.S. Workers

The definition of "U.S. worker" includes the following individuals:

- U.S. citizens and nationals;

- U.S. lawful permanent residents;

- Refugees;

- Asylees; and

- "An individual who is not an unauthorized alien (as defined in … section 274a(h)(3) of the INA) with respect to the work in which the worker is engaging."[349] The cited section defines unauthorized alien as "not at that time either (A) an alien lawfully admitted for permanent residence, or (B) authorized to be so employed by [the INA or DHS].

The phrases "with respect to the work" and "authorized to be so employed" indicate that nonimmigrants authorized to work for specific employers, such as those in other H categories, L-1 principals, Ps, etc., would not be considered U.S. workers for these purposes, but that those with "open market" employment authorization documents (EADs), such as spouses of Ls and Es, adjustment of status applicants, DACA recipients, etc., would be considered U.S. workers. This definition is broader than the definition of a "protected individual" used by the Justice Department's

---

[343] 20 CFR §655.40(b).

[344] 20 CFR §655.20(t); "DOL, "2015 H-2B Interim Final Rule FAQs, Round 7," https://www.foreign laborcert.doleta.gov/pdf/H-2B_2015_IFR_FAQs_Round7.pdf.

[345] *Id.*

[346] 20 CFR §655.40(a).

[347] 20 CFR §§655.20(e) and 655.40(a).

[348] 20 CFR §655.41(a).

[349] 20 CFR §655.5.

Copyright © 2017. American Immigration Lawyers Association. All rights reserved.

Immigrant and Employee Rights Section (formerly known as the Office of Special Counsel for Unfair Immigration Related Employment Practices, or OSC).[350]

In any event, foreign nationals who are undocumented are not authorized for employment, and thus are not U.S. workers.

2. Advertising Requirements

Advertisements must be run on two separate days, one of which must be a Sunday, "in a newspaper of general circulation serving the area of intended employment and appropriate to the occupation and the workers likely to apply."[351] If the position is in a rural area where there is no newspaper with a Sunday edition, the employer must, in place of a Sunday advertisement, "advertise in the regularly published daily edition with the widest circulation in the area of intended employment."[352] The practitioner should note that this is the only exception to the requirement of running a Sunday advertisement.[353]

The two days may be consecutive, but are not required to be.[354] If the CO indicates that a foreign language newspaper is appropriate, the advertisement must be run in such a publication.[355]

The employer must direct applicants to apply to the SWA, rather than to the employer, although employer contact information must be provided.[356] SWAs are instructed by the regulations to "only refer for employment individuals who ... are qualified and will be available for employment."[357] As noted previously in the SWA job order discussion, this does not mean that the fact of a referral is dispositive of whether an applicant is qualified, but the fact of a SWA referral will increase scrutiny regarding that applicant.[358]

The following information must be included in the advertisements: [359]

- The name of the employer and its contact information;

- The geographic area of employment "with enough specificity to apprise applicants of any travel requirements and where applicants will likely have to reside to perform the services or labor";

- Job description "with sufficient information to apprise U.S. workers of the services or labor to be performed, including:

---

[350] 8 CFR §274B(a)(3).

[351] 20 CFR §655.42(a).

[352] 20 CFR §655.42(b).

[353] Id.

[354] 20 CFR §655.42(a).

[355] 20 CFR §655.41(b).

[356] Id.

[357] 20 CFR §655.47.

[358] 80 Fed. Reg. 24042, 24079 (Apr. 29, 2015).

[359] 20 CFR §655.17.

Copyright © 2017. American Immigration Lawyers Association. All rights reserved.

- "The duties
- "The minimum education and experience requirements; and
- "The work hours and days, and the anticipated start and end dates of the job opportunity";

- "A statement that the job opportunity is a temporary, full-time position, including the total number of job openings the employer intends to fill";

- A statement that overtime will be available, if applicable, and the rate for working such overtime;

- A statement that on-the-job training will be provided, if applicable;

- The offered wage or, "in the event that there are multiple wage offers," the range of wages, "each of which must equal or exceed the highest of the prevailing wage or" the applicable minimum wage;

- Any "board, lodging, or other facilities" offered or that the employer will assist the workers in finding;

- Deductions from pay not required by law, including applicable board, lodging, or "other facilities." These amounts must be "reasonable";

- A statement that "transportation and subsistence from the place where the worker has come to work for the employer to the place of employment and return transportation and subsistence" will be provided by the employer;

- "A statement that daily transportation to and from the worksite" will be provided, if applicable;

- A statement that tools, supplies, and equipment will be provided without charge, if applicable;

- A "statement summarizing the three-fourths guarantee"; namely, that employment must be offered for "a total number of work hours equal to at least three-fourths of the workdays of each 12-week period, if the period of employment ... is 120 days or more days, or each 6-week period of employment...is less than 120 days;[360] and

- A statement directing applicants to apply at the nearest SWA office in the state in which the advertisement appeared, and providing the SWA contact information including the job order number, if there is one.

Copies of the newspaper pages, including the dates of publication and a full copy of the advertisements, tearsheets of the pages, or "other proof of publication furnished by the newspaper containing the text of the printed advertisements and the dates of

---

[360] 20 CFR §655.20(f).

Copyright © 2017. American Immigration Lawyers Association. All rights reserved.

publication" must be maintained by the employer.[361] If the advertisement was in another language, an English translation also must be made and retained.[362]

3. Required Contacts and Postings

The employer is required to contact "by mail or other effective means" its former U.S. workers, "including those who have been laid off within 120 calendar days before the date of need," who were employed in the occupation at the place of employment during the previous year. Workers dismissed for cause or who abandoned the worksite need not be contacted. In the contact, the employer must "disclose the terms of the job order" and solicit the workers' return to the job. Documentation of these contacts must be maintained.[363]

If there is a bargaining representative for "any of the employer's employees in the occupation and area of intended employment," the employer must provide a copy of the temporary labor certification application and the job order to that representative, and maintain documentation that it was sent.[364]

If there is no bargaining representative, the employer must post the job availability for at least 15 consecutive business days "in at least 2 conspicuous locations at the place(s) of anticipated employment or in some other manner that provides reasonable notification to all employees in the job classification and are in which the work will be performed." Electronic posting, such as on an internal or external website that the employer maintains and uses for notices to employees about employment matters, is acceptable if it meets all other requirements. A copy of the notice, along with information regarding where and when it was posted, must be maintained.[365]

If the Notice of Acceptance so instructs, based on the appropriateness "to the occupation and area of intended employment," the employer must provide written notice to a community-based organization and maintain documentation that it was sent to the designated organization.[366]

4. Additional Recruitment

At the discretion of the CO, the employer may be required to conduct "additional reasonable recruitment where the CO has determined that there is a likelihood that U.S. workers who are qualified and will be available for the work."[367] Such a requirement is most likely to be made when the job is located in an "area of substantial unemployment,"[368] which is defined as "a contiguous area with a population of at least 10,000 in which there is an average unemployment rate equal to

---

[361] 20 CFR §655.41(d).
[362] Id.
[363] 20 CFR §655.43.
[364] 20 CFR §655.45(a).
[365] 20 CFR §655.45(b).
[366] 20 CFR §655.45(c).
[367] 20 CFR §655.46(a).
[368] Id.

Copyright © 2017. American Immigration Lawyers Association. All rights reserved.

or exceeding 6.5 percent for the 12 months preceding the determination of such areas made by the ETA."[369] However, the CO has the discretion to require additional recruitment in other areas as well.

If such additional recruitment is required, the CO will advise the employer of what efforts must be undertaken. The efforts can include such things as a posting on a web site; contact with community-based organizations, as discussed in the preceding section; contact with a career center, or advertisement in other publications. The CO is supposed to consider the cost of the additional recruitment and its likelihood of producing qualified and available U.S. workers.[370]

Documentation of the additional recruitment must be maintained.[371]

5. Recruitment Report

The employer must prepare, sign, and date the recruitment report, and submit it to the CO by the date specified in the Notice of Acceptance.[372] As previously noted, the employer must continue to accept referrals until 21 days before the date of need, and thus the employer must continue to update the recruitment report during that period.[373] However, the employer "is not required to submit the updated recruitment report to DOL, but is required to retain the report and make it available in the event of a post-certification audit, a WHD investigation, or upon request by the CO."[374]

The report must include the following documents and information:[375]

- List "[t]he name of each recruitment activity or source (*e.g.*, job order and the name of the newspaper)";

- Provide "the name and contact information of each U.S. worker who applied or was referred to the job opportunity up to the date of the preparation of the recruitment report, and the disposition of each worker's application";

- Clearly state, with respect to each U.S. worker applicant or referral, whether the job was offered and whether the individual accepted or declined;

- Provide "the lawful job-related reason(s) for not hiring" any U.S. workers who applied or were referred to the position and were not hired, if applicable;

- Confirm that former U.S. employees were contacted as required, and by what means;[376]

---

[369] 20 CFR §655.5.

[370] 20 CFR §655.46(b).

[371] 20 CFR §655.46(c).

[372] 20 CFR §655.48(a).

[373] 20 CFR §§655.20(t) and 655.48(b); "DOL, "2015 H-2B Interim Final Rule FAQs, Round 7," https://www.foreignlaborcert.doleta.gov/pdf/H-2B_2015_IFR_FAQs_Round7.pdf.

[374] 80 Fed. Reg. 24042, 24079 (Apr. 29, 2015).

[375] 20 CFR §655.48.

[376] *See also* 20 CFR §655.43.

Copyright © 2017. American Immigration Lawyers Association. All rights reserved.

- Information confirming that any bargaining representative was notified of the openings, the means used for the contact, and whether the organization referred qualified U.S. workers, including the number of workers referred, or whether the union was "non-responsive to the employer's requests."[377]

- If there was no bargaining representative, confirm that the posting was made;[378]

- If required by the CO to have contacted a community-based organization, information confirming that the contact was made, that the organization was notified of the openings, and the number of any workers referred or whether the organization was "non-responsive";[379] and

- Confirm that any additional recruitment required by the CO was conducted.

For a detailed discussion of lawful rejection of U.S. worker-applicants, see Volume 2: Chapter Two, "The Labor Certification Application." Specifically in the context of H-2B temporary labor certification applications, BALCA has noted that an individual may lack required experience even if he or she has been employed in a similar occupation.[380] In one case, the CO had denied the application based on the reasoning that a horse trainer was qualified for the position of a horse groomer, but BALCA reversed, stating: "Ultimately, while the two jobs may overlap somewhat based on their proximity to the horses, a trainer would not necessarily be experienced as a groom more than a groom is experienced as a trainer."[381] Similarly, "a horse trainer is a more experienced position, while a groom is an entry level position, but nothing in the [job] descriptions suggest that in order to become a trainer, a person need work as a groom."[382]

G. Emergency Applications

The CO can waive the time periods required for filing the temporary labor certification "for good and sufficient cause," provided "the CO has sufficient time to thoroughly test the domestic labor market."[383] The employer must otherwise meet the filing requirements. Once the registration process is operational, if the employer does not already have a registration, it must undergo that process,[384] but can submit the registration application less than the otherwise-required 120 days before the date of need.[385] Similarly, the temporary labor certification application can be submitted less than the otherwise-required 75 days in advance.[386]

---

[377] 20 CFR §655.45(a).

[378] *See also* 20 CFR §655.45(a).

[379] *See also* 20 CFR §655.45(c).

[380] *Matter of Margaret Pirovano*, 2010-TLN-00059 (BALCA Apr. 30, 2010), AILA Doc. No. 10050662.

[381] *Id.*

[382] *Id.*

[383] 20 CFR §655.17(a).

[384] 20 CFR §655.17(b).

[385] 80 Fed. Reg. 24042, 24061 (Apr. 29, 2015).

[386] *Id.*

Copyright © 2017. American Immigration Lawyers Association. All rights reserved.

The employer should submit the waiver request to the NPC, providing "detailed information describing the good and substantial cause" that necessitates the request. "Good and substantial cause may include, but is not limited to, the substantial loss of U.S. workers due to Acts of God, or a similar unforeseeable man-made catastrophic event (such as an oil spill or controlled flooding) that is wholly outside of the employer's control, unforeseeable changes in market conditions, or pandemic health issues. A denial of a previously submitted H-2B Registration ... does not constitute good and substantial cause." [387]

To facilitate the expedite, the employer also must submit a completed temporary labor certification application; a proposed job order that identifies the appropriate SWA; and, if the employer does not have a prevailing wage determination, it must submit a completed request for one.[388] If the CO grants the waiver request, a Notice of Acceptance will be issued and forwarded to the SWA along with the job order.[389] The CO may deny the request in a Final Determination either because the emergency was not justified, or because there is insufficient time to determine temporary need or ensure compliance with the certification requirements.[390]

An application filed under the emergency provision "is subject to the same recruitment activities, audit processes, and enforcement mechanisms as a non-emergency" application, but DOL "intends to subject emergency applications to a higher level of scrutiny than non-emergency applications in order to make certain that the provision is not subject to abuse."[391]

H. Other Requirements and Assurances

DOL regulations state that, as part of the temporary labor certification application, the employer must agree to abide by a list of "obligations and assurances"[392] regarding its H-2B workers and workers in corresponding employment.[393] When filing the temporary labor certification application on Form ETA-9142B, the employer must also file Appendix B to that form, in which the employer certifies knowledge of, and compliance with, the list of 26 conditions and requirements "applicable to H-2B workers and/or U.S. workers who are hired during the recruitment period for positions covered by this application, including any approved extension thereof." [394] The employer's representative also declares under penalty of

---

[387] 20 CFR §655.17(b).

[388] Id.

[389] 20 CFR §655.17(c).

[390] Id.

[391] 80 Fed. Reg. 24042, 24061 (Apr. 29, 2015).

[392] 20 CFR §655.20.

[393] Corresponding Employment is described above under the section titled "Wage Requirements for H-2B and Workers in Corresponding Employment."

[394] DOL, "H-2B Application for Employment Certification Appendix B" (exp. Dec. 31, 2018), http://bit.ly/h2bAppB.

Copyright © 2017. American Immigration Lawyers Association. All rights reserved.

perjury that he or she has reviewed the application and that "to the best of my knowledge the information contained therein is true and correct."[395]

If an employer has ceased doing business or cannot be located, a successor in interest may be held liable for the obligations of the violating employer.[396] Indicia of successorship include:

- Substantial continuity of the same business operations;
- Use of the same facilities;
- Continuity of the work force;
- Similarity of jobs and working conditions;
- Similarity of supervisory personnel;
- Whether the former management or owner retains a direct or indirect interest in the new enterprise;
- Similarity in machinery, equipment, and production methods;
- Similarity of products and services; and
- The ability of the predecessor to provide relief.[397]

DOL has provided a summary that comprises a useful checklist of the obligations, assurances, conditions, and requirements enumerated in 20 CFR §655.20 and on Appendix B:

"a. Payment of the offered wage, which equals or exceeds the highest of the prevailing wage or Federal, State or local minimum wage, free and clear at least every two weeks during the entire certified period of employment. Alternative payment arrangements such as piece-rate, commissions, or bonuses are only permissible if the employer guarantees a weekly wage that equals or exceeds the offered wage. Any piece-rate must be no less than the normal rate paid by non-H-2B employers in the same occupation and area of intended employment.

"b. Deductions from wages must be made if they are required by law; all other deductions must be specifically disclosed in the job order and may only include the reasonable cost or fair value of board, lodging, and facilities furnished; and deductions of amounts authorized to be paid to third persons for the worker's benefit through his/her voluntary assignment or deductions that are authorized through a collective bargaining agreement(s);

"c. Offer of full-time employment of at least 35 hours per week, with a single week being used for wage computation purposes;

---

[395] Id.

[396] 20 CFR §655.5.

[397] Id.

Copyright © 2017. American Immigration Lawyers Association. All rights reserved.

"d. Disclosure of job qualifications and requirements which must be bona fide and consistent with the normal and accepted job qualifications and requirements of non-H-2B employers in the occupation and area of intended employment;

"e. Offer to each worker employment for a total number of work hours equal to at least three-fourths of the workdays of each 12-week period (6-week period if the job order is less than 120 days), unless the certified period of employment is shortened by the contracting officer due to unforeseeable circumstances outside the employer's control;

"f. Payment or reimbursement of transportation and subsistence for workers to the place of employment after the worker completes 50 percent of the period of employment covered by the job order, if the employer has not previously reimbursed such costs;

"g. Payment of return transportation and subsistence [meals and, if required, lodging costs incurred on the employer's behalf along the way] if the worker completes the job order period or is dismissed early;

"h. Payment or reimbursement of visa, border crossing and related government mandated fees in the first workweek;

"i. Provision of all tools, supplies and equipment;

"j. Provision of accurate earnings statements to employees each pay period with all deductions and reimbursements clearly itemized and hours worked and hours offered listed;

"k. Requirement that employers provide workers with copies of the job order no later than the time at which the worker applies for the visa, if the worker is departing directly from his or her home country, and display a poster describing employee rights and protections in English and, if necessary and made available by the Department, another language common to a significant portion of the workers at the work site;

"l. Prohibition of retaliation (such as by intimidation, threats, coercion, blacklisting, discharge or other discrimination) against employees who complained against violations, including through filing or participating in legal actions or seeking assistance from third parties;

"m. Prohibition against: passing on of fees associated with the H-2B applications or employment, such as application/petition costs, attorney fees, recruitment fees or other related fees (and employers must contractually prohibit agents and recruiters from seeking or receiving such fees from employees);

"n. Prohibition against: treating H-2B workers more favorably than U.S. workers; discriminating in hiring based on race, color, national origin, age, sex, religion, disability or citizenship; and laying off U.S. workers within the 120-day period before the start date of work through the end of the period of certification;

Copyright © 2017. American Immigration Lawyers Association. All rights reserved.

"o. Prohibition against: placing workers into uncertified employment or geographic area; and using the H-2B program if there is a strike or lockout in the area of intended employment at the time of application;

"p. Compliance with recruitment requirements under 20 CFR 655.40-.46;

"q. Continuing to consider and hire all qualified U.S. workers who apply for the job opportunity until 21 days before the start date of need;

"r. Notifying DOL when a worker abandons the job or is terminated for cause (and DHS if the person is an H-2B worker);

"s. Complying with all applicable Federal, State, and local employment-related laws; and

"t. Disclosing the identity of all foreign labor recruiters and their employees as well as pertinent agreements related to the recruitment of foreign workers."[398]

Given the increased number of audits, employers are encouraged to prepare public access compliance files to demonstrate compliance with the obligations and requirements indicated above.

Most of these are discussed elsewhere in this chapter, under the applicable subjects. Others are addressed below:

1. Layoffs

The employer must "not lay off any similarly employed U.S. worker in the occupation that is the subject of" the temporary labor certification application in the area of intended employment within the period of 120 days before the date of need and the end of the certified period.[399] However, a layoff "for lawful, job-related reasons," such as lack of work or the end of a season, is permissible if all H-2B workers are laid off before any U.S. worker in corresponding employment.[400] "Layoff" is defined as "any involuntary separation of one or more U.S. employees without cause."[401] Thus, it appears that layoffs for the usual reasons are in fact permissible as long as all the H-2B nonimmigrants are dismissed before any U.S. workers who are in corresponding employment are laid off.

As previously discussed, corresponding employment is where the employee is "performing either substantially the same work included in the job order or substantially the same work performed by the H-2B workers," except for more permanent incumbent employees—namely, those who have been continuously employed by the H-2B employer during the 52 weeks prior to the date of need in the job order, who have worked or been paid for at least 35 hours in at least 48 of the prior 52 workweeks, and who have worked or been paid for an average of at least 35

---

[398] DOL, "2015 H-2B Interim Final Rule FAQs, Round 5," https://www.foreignlaborcert.doleta.gov/pdf/H-2B_2015_IFR_FAQs_Round5.pdf.

[399] 20 CFR §655.20(v).

[400] Id.

[401] 20 CFR §655.5.

Copyright © 2017. American Immigration Lawyers Association. All rights reserved.

hours per week over the prior 52 weeks, as demonstrated by the employer's payroll records (except that the employer may take credit for hours that were reduced by the employee's voluntarily choosing not to work due to personal reasons like illness or vacation), and whose terms and working conditions of employment have not been substantially reduced by the employer during the period of the job order. Also excluded are incumbent employees covered by a collective bargaining agreement or an individual employment contract that guarantees both an offer of at least 35 hours of work each workweek and continued employment with the H-2B employer at least through the period of the job order (except that the employee may be dismissed for cause).[402]

If the employer seeks H-2B workers in the next year, it must contact its former U.S. workers, "including those who have been laid off within 120 calendar days before the date of need (except those who were dismissed for cause or who abandoned the worksite)," whom it employed during the previous year in the occupation at the place of employment. The contact should be "by mail or other effective means," and should disclose the terms of the job order and solicit the former employees' return.[403]

2. Prohibitions on Fee Payments by H-2B Workers

DOL regulations prohibit H-2B beneficiaries from paying "the employer's attorneys' or agent fees, application and H-2B Petition fees, recruitment costs, or any fees attributed to obtaining the approved" temporary labor certification.[404] In addition, the employer is required to either pay for or reimburse the employee within the first workweek for all visa, border crossing, and other related government or other fees that the employee initially paid.[405] The employer is not responsible for passport costs "or other charges primarily for the benefit of the worker."[406]

DOL notes that "payment includes, but is not limited to, monetary payments, wage concessions (including deductions from wages, salary, or benefits), kickbacks, bribes, tributes, in kind payments, and free labor."[407] DOL regulations also require the employer to contractually forbid "any agent or recruiter whom the employer engages, directly or indirectly, in recruitment of H-2B workers to seek or receive payments or other compensation from prospective workers."[408] Petitioners and third parties may not seek reimbursement from H-2B beneficiaries for fees for recruitment, attorney assistance, or preparation of visa applications.[409]

---

[402] 20 CFR §§655.5.

[403] 20 CFR §655.20(w).

[404] 20 CFR §655.20(o).

[405] 20 CFR §655.20(j)(2).

[406] *Id.*

[407] 20 CFR §655.20(o).

[408] 20 CFR §655.20(p).

[409] 20 CFR §§655.20(o) and (p).

Copyright © 2017. American Immigration Lawyers Association. All rights reserved.

Similarly, under DHS regulations, a foreign national may not pay a "job placement fee or other compensation (either direct or indirect)" for an H-2B petition, whether that fee is paid to "a petitioner, agent, facilitator, recruiter, or similar employment service as a condition of an offer or condition of H-2B employment."[410] This prohibition is designed to "deter petition padding, visa selling, and human trafficking schemes that lead to the effective indenture of H-2B workers," to prevent "worker exploitation by unscrupulous employers, recruiters, or facilitators imposing costs on workers as a condition of selection for the offer of H-2B employment,"[411] and to avoid an adverse effect on "the wages and working conditions of U.S. workers by creating conditions akin to indentured servitude, driving down wages and working conditions for all workers, foreign and domestic."[412] The prohibition also seeks to avoid lowering the prevailing wage paid to the H-2B workers, "thereby ensuring the validity of the labor market test and compliance" with the statutory definition of the H-2B visa classification.[413] Abuse of H-2B workers has been documented, with some workers paying up to $80,000 to recruiters and other third parties.[414]

As discussed below, on the Form I-129, the petitioner must attest that there has been no prohibited fee payment and must answer questions about whether the beneficiary "paid a fee to anyone," whether a recruiting firm was used and/or paid, the amount of the payment, and the name of the recruiting firm.[415] USCIS guidance states that an adjudicator "will review the petitioner's answers to ensure that they are consistent with the petitioner's type of business."[416]

Such fee payment by a foreign national is grounds for denial or revocation of the H-2B petition.[417] If USCIS determines that such a fee was "collected," that there was "an agreement to collect such a fee," or that the petitioner knew or "reasonably" should have known when the H-2B petition was filed that the foreign national had paid or agreed to pay such a fee, even if it was to an "agent, facilitator, recruiter, or similar employment service," then the petitioner will be provided notice of the intent to deny or revoke.[418] Importantly, the standard is actual or constructive knowledge; DHS rejected a request to impose only the standard of actual knowledge:

"The employer is responsible for initiating the recruitment process and chooses whom it will use to obtain foreign labor. The U.S. employer has control over whether to use recruiters and the terms and conditions of any recruitment arrangement, including the costs of such services. The employer can comply with

---

[410] 8 CFR §214.2(h)(6)(i)(B).

[411] 73 Fed. Reg. 78020 (Dec. 19, 2008).

[412] 73 Fed. Reg. 78104 (Dec. 19, 2008).

[413] Id.

[414] Id.

[415] AFM 31.5(e)(5).

[416] Id.

[417] 8 CFR §214.2(h)(6)(i)(B).

[418] Id.

Copyright © 2017. American Immigration Lawyers Association. All rights reserved.

this requirement by making reasonable arrangements and inquiries as to whether its employees have paid or will be required to pay a fee…. And the employer will be in a position to require, as a condition of any such contract [with a recruiter], that the domestic recruiter and agent working in the worker's home country do not charge any fee of prospective alien workers."[419]

Therefore, the practitioner should advise clients to ask recruiters and other third parties about any fee payment arrangements, so that the employer may honestly attest that there have been no prohibited payments on the Form I-129, as discussed above. As noted by DHS, employers may need to "switch[] from one foreign labor recruiter to another until one is found that does not charge alien's [*sic*] fees."[420]

USCIS also stated that it "anticipates the possibility of using Requests for Evidence (RFEs) to certain petitioners."[421] Petitioners should be allowed 84 days to respond; if the petitioner submits a response in fewer than 84 days, then "USCIS will review the response upon receipt."[422] Failure to respond to the RFE will result in denial, without issuance of a Notice of Intent to Deny (NOID).[423] USCIS may also share information provided in an RFE response "with other federal agencies."[424]

The exceptions to the rule are if the petitioner demonstrates any of the following:

- The foreign national was reimbursed in full for the prohibited fees paid before the H-2B petition was filed;

- The petitioner terminated the payment agreement before the worker paid the fees and before the petition was filed; or

- The petitioner learns of the prohibited fee payment or payment agreement of a recruiter or agent after the petition is filed, and "notifies USCIS about the prohibited payments, or agreement to make such payments, within 2 work days of finding out about such payments or agreements."[425]

For the first exception, "evidence of reimbursement must be submitted."[426] A petitioner may establish that the fee was reimbursed by copies of receipts, signed contracts, or correspondence to the foreign national's last known address.[427] Other

---

[419] 73 Fed. Reg. 78104 (Dec. 19, 2008).

[420] *Id.*

[421] USCIS, "Talking Points and Executive Summary: Teleconference with H-2A Petitioners" (Aug. 2, 2010), AILA Doc. No. 10080473 ("While the [guidance] focused on prohibited fees with respect to the H-2A nonimmigrant agricultural worker classification, similar principles and rules apply to the H-2B nonimmigrant, non-agricultural classification"). *Cf. Castellanos-Contreras v. Decatur Hotels, LLC*, No. 07-30942 (E.D. La. July 21, 2009), AILA Doc. No. 09081468.

[422] *Id.*

[423] *Id.*

[424] *Id.*

[425] 8 CFR §214.2(h)(6)(i)(B)(4).

[426] AFM 31.5(e)(5).

[427] 73 Fed. Reg. 78104 (Dec. 19, 2008).

Copyright © 2017. American Immigration Lawyers Association. All rights reserved.

appropriate evidence may include copies of cancelled checks or money orders, or copies of the foreign national's bank statements.

If an H-2B petition is denied or revoked because of the prohibited fee payments made by the foreign national, then any subsequent H-2B petition filed by the same petitioner within one year of the denial or revocation must establish one of the following "as a condition of the approval of the later petition":

- The beneficiary who paid the prohibited fees for the denied or revoked H-2B petition was reimbursed; or

- The foreign national "cannot be located despite the petitioner's reasonable efforts."[428]

If the H-2B petition is denied or revoked, then the petitioner remains responsible for the return cost of transportation to the home country,[429] as discussed below, unless another H-2B petition filed by another petitioner is approved on behalf of the foreign national.[430] The foreign national's stay will remain authorized and he or she will not accrue unlawful presence for 30 days after the petition is revoked, to allow him or her to prepare for departure from the United States or to seek an extension of stay pursuant to an H-2B petition filed by a different petitioner.[431]

3. Recruiters

An employer using a recruiter must file with the temporary labor certification application[432] a copy of "all agreements with any agent or recruiter whom it engages or plans to engage in the recruitment of H-2B workers."[433] Any such agreements must contain a contractual prohibition against charging fees to the workers,[434] as discussed above. The identities and locations of "all persons and entities hired by or working for the recruiter or agent" and any "agents or employees of those persons and entities" must be provided as well.[435]

DOL maintains a publicly available list of recruiters compiled from these filings.[436] "The Department does not endorse or vouch for any foreign labor agent or recruiter included in the Foreign Labor Recruiter List, nor does inclusion on this list signify that the recruiter is in compliance with the H-2B program. The list is simply a

---

[428] 8 CFR §214.2(h)(6)(i)(D).

[429] 8 CFR §214.2(h)(6)(i)(C).

[430] Id.

[431] Id.

[432] 20 CFR §655.15(a).

[433] 20 CFR §655.9(a).

[434] Id.

[435] 20 CFR §§655.9(b) and 655.20(aa).

[436] 20 CFR §§655.9(c). The list can be accessed at https://www.foreignlaborcert.doleta.gov/Foreign_Labor_Recruiter_List.cfm.

Copyright © 2017. American Immigration Lawyers Association. All rights reserved.

list of current recruiters being used by employers in the H-2B program that are disclosed pursuant to the regulation to the Department."[437]

4. Transportation Costs

Once the employee has completed 50 percent of the period of employment covered by the job order, the employer must pay for transportation, including meals and lodging during travel, to the place of employment. If the employer is covered by the Fair Labor Standards Act (FLSA), then the reimbursement for transportation costs must be paid within the first week of employment.[438]

Amounts for transportation to the place of employment can be paid directly by the employer, advanced to the employee, or reimbursed to the worker for the reasonable costs that he or she incurred. The employer must advance "or otherwise provide" these costs to workers in corresponding employment who are traveling to the worksite if it is the prevailing practice of non-H-2B employers in the occupation in the area, or if the employer does so for "similarly situated" H-2B workers.[439]

The amount of transportation payments can be no less than, and is not required to be more than, "the most economical and reasonable common carrier charges."[440] The amounts for meals and lodging while traveling must be at least the amount allowed under the rules for what employers can charge to H-2A agricultural workers for meals.[441] Those amounts are announced on the DOL website.[442] When the employer is going to reimburse the employee, it must keep records of the costs incurred by the worker, the amount reimbursed, and the dates of the reimbursement.[443]

The employer also must provide or pay at the time of departure for the same expenses for return "to the place from which the worker, disregarding intervening employment, departed to work for the employer," if the worker completes the period of employment covered by the job order or if the worker is dismissed "for any reason" before that date, unless the worker has immediate subsequent H-2B employment.[444] "However, if separation from employment is due to voluntary abandonment by an H-2B worker or a corresponding worker, and the employer

---

[437] DOL, "2015 H-2B Interim Final Rule FAQs, Round 16," https://www.foreignlaborcert.doleta.gov/pdf/Round-16_Foreign_Labor_Recruiter.pdf.

[438] DOL, Wage and Hour Division, Fact Sheet #78F, "Inbound and Outbound Transportation Expenses, and Visa and Other Related Fees under the H-2B Program," https://www.dol.gov/whd/regs/compliance/whdfs78f.htm.

[439] 20 CFR §655.20(j)(1)(i).

[440] Id.

[441] 20 CFR §655.20(j)(1)(i), referencing 20 CFR §655.173.

[442] DOL, "Allowable Meal Charges and Reimbursements for Daily Subsistence," https://www.foreignlaborcert.doleta.gov/meal_travel_subsistence.cfm.

[443] 20 CFR §655.20(j)(1)(i).

[444] 20 CFR §655.20(j)(1)(ii). See also 8 CFR §214.2(h)(6)(vi)(E), the DHS regulation requiring the employer to pay for "the reasonable costs of return transportation of the alien abroad, if the alien is dismissed for any reason by the employer before the end of the period of authorized admission." The juxtaposition of the two agencies' requirements is discussed in the section below titled "Return Transportation Obligation."

Copyright © 2017. American Immigration Lawyers Association. All rights reserved.

provides appropriate notification specified under [20 CFR] §655.20(y), the employer is not responsible for providing or paying for return transportation and subsistence expenses of that worker."[445] If the subsequent employer has not agreed in the job order to pay for the transportation from the initial employer's worksite, the initial employer must pay for that transportation. If the subsequent employer has agreed in the job order to cover those costs, then the initial employer has no obligation in that regard.[446]

The employer must also comply with its obligations under the FLSA as it applies to the payment of transportation to the place of employment. If the employee's payment of transportation expenses brings his or her first week of wages below the minimum wage, the H-2B employer must reimburse the employee for transportation within the first week of employment.[447]

The employer is not required to pay for daily transportation from where the worker lives or from designated pick-up points to the worksite. But, if the employer does offer or provide daily transportation to H-2B workers, "the employer also must offer the benefit to U.S. workers and must disclose the benefit, and if applicable, any associated costs to the worker, including related deductions, in the job order and advertisements for the job opportunity."[448]

5. Tools, Equipment, Etc.

Tools, supplies and equipment needed to perform the job must be provided by the employer.[449] "This requirement does not prohibit employees from electing to use their own equipment, nor does it penalize employers whose employees voluntarily do so, so long as a bona fide offer of adequate, appropriate equipment has been made."[450]

This provision is part of DOL's overall application of FLSA, about which it has noted:

"[A] deduction for any cost that is primarily for the benefit of the employer is never reasonable and therefore never permitted under this interim final rule. Some examples of costs that DOL has long held to be primarily for the benefit of the employer are: Tools of the trade and other materials and services incidental to carrying on the employer's business; the cost of any construction by and for the employer; the cost of uniforms (whether purchased or rented) and of their laundering, where the nature of the business requires the employee to wear a

---

[445] 80 Fed. Reg. 24042 (Apr. 29, 2015).

[446] 20 CFR §655.20(j)(1)(ii).

[447] DOL, WHD, "Fact Sheet #78F: Inbound and Outbound Transportation Expenses, and Visa and Other Related Fees under the H-2B Program" (undated), https://www.dol.gov/whd/regs/compliance/whdfs78f.htm.

[448] DOL, "2015 H-2B Interim Final Rule FAQs, Round 5," https://www.foreignlaborcert.doleta.gov/pdf/H-2B_2015_IFR_FAQs_Round5.pdf. *See also* 20 CFR §655.18(b)(14).

[449] 20 CFR §655.20(k).

[450] 80 Fed. Reg. 24042 (Apr. 29, 2015).

Copyright © 2017. American Immigration Lawyers Association. All rights reserved.

uniform; and transportation charges where such transportation is an incident of and necessary to the employment."[451]

6. Placement of Workers

Employers must affirm that there is not a strike or lockout at any of its worksites within the area of intended employment.[452] H-2B workers employed under the temporary labor certification cannot be placed at a site outside the area of intended employment without a new application being certified.[453]

7. Worker Protections and Notifications

An employer may not intimidate, retaliate, or discriminate against "any person" who has filed a complaint or instituted a proceeding, testified or is about to testify, has consulted with an organization or attorney, or has asserted a right on behalf of anyone related to the nonimmigrant provisions of the law.[454]

Throughout the recruitment process, the position(s) must be open to any U.S. worker "regardless of race, color, national origin, age, sex, religion, disability, or citizenship."[455]

The employer must comply with all applicable federal, state, and local employment and related health and safety laws. This includes a prohibition against the employer or its agents or attorneys "knowingly holding, destroying, or confiscating workers' passports, visas, or other immigration documents."[456]

The employer must "post and maintain in a conspicuous locations at the place of employment"[457] a DOL poster[458] setting out the rights and protections for H-2B workers and workers in corresponding employment. The poster must be in English and "[t]o the extent necessary, the employer must request and post additional posters, as made available by the Department of Labor, in any language common to a significant portion of the workers if they are not fluent in English."[459] The posters currently are available only in English and Spanish.[460]

H-2B workers and workers in corresponding employment must be given a copy of the job order. The timing of when the worker must receive the job order copy is:

---

[451] Id.

[452] 20 CFR §655.20(u).

[453] 20 CFR §655.20(x).

[454] 20 CFR §655.20(n).

[455] 20 CFR §655.20(r).

[456] 20 CFR §655.20(z), citing 18 USC §1592(a).

[457] 20 CFR §655.20(m).

[458] DOL, "Employee Rights under the H-2B Program," *https://www.dol.gov/whd/posters/pdf/H2B-eng.pdf.* Information on ordering or downloading the poster can be found at https://www.dol.gov/whd/resources/posters.htm.

[459] 20 CFR §655.20(m).

[460] DOL, "Wage and Hour Division/H-2B," https://www.dol.gov/whd/immigration/h2b.htm.

Copyright © 2017. American Immigration Lawyers Association. All rights reserved.

- For H-2Bs outside the United States, no later than when the worker applies for the visa;

- For H-2Bs in the United States and changing employers, no later than the time the offer of employment is made; and

- For workers in corresponding employment, no later than the day the work commences.[461]

8. Cessation of Employment

If the employment ends prior to the end date on the job order because fulfillment of the job order has become impossible due to circumstances beyond the employer's control, such as fire, weather, other Act of God, or "similar unforeseeable man-made catastrophic event (such as an oil spill or controlled flooding)," the employer may terminate the job order with the approval of the CO. In that event, the employer must fulfill the three-fourths guarantee, discussed above, for the period from the later of the start date on the job order or the first workday after the employee arrived until the date of termination.[462]

In this circumstance, the employer is required to try to transfer the H-2B worker or worker in corresponding employment to other comparable employment acceptable to the worker and consistent with the immigration laws. If a transfer cannot be made, the employer must pay to return the worker to the place from which he or she came or to the worker's next certified H-2B employer, whichever the worker prefers.[463]

Under USCIS regulations, if the employer dismisses an H-2B worker before the end of the H-2B assignment, then the employer is responsible for providing the reasonable cost of transportation to the foreign national's last place of residence.[464] DOL regulations, as discussed above, provide a bit more detail and require a bit more.[465] The employer must either directly provide the return transportation or pay for it at the time of departure. Expenses include not just the transportation itself, but also any needed meals and lodging (referred to as subsistence) during the trip. The place to which the transportation must be covered is "the place from which the worker, disregarding intervening employment, departed to work for the employer," if the worker is dismissed "for any reason" before that date, unless the worker has immediate subsequent H-2B employment. DOL's return transportation rules apply to U.S. workers in corresponding employment as well as H-2B workers.

If an H-2B nonimmigrant's employment ends prior to the end date specified in the temporary labor certification application, the employer must notify DOL and DHS in writing within two days work days after the employment cessation. If the employee fails to report to work at the scheduled time for five consecutive work days without

---

[461] 20 CFR §655.20(*l*).

[462] 20 CFR §655.20(g).

[463] *Id.*

[464] 8 CFR §214.2(h)(6)(vi)(E).

[465] 20 CFR §655.20(j)(1)(ii).

Copyright © 2017. American Immigration Lawyers Association. All rights reserved.

the consent of the employer, that would be considered an "abandonment or abscondment."[466] "[I]if separation from employment is due to voluntary abandonment by an H-2B worker or a corresponding worker, and the employer provides appropriate notification … the employer is not responsible for providing or paying for return transportation and subsistence expenses of that worker."[467] Also, the three-fourths guarantee is considered to end in this circumstance with the last full 12-week or six-week period, as applicable, "preceding the worker's voluntary abandonment or termination for cause."[468]

I. Document Retention Requirements

All employers who file an H-2B registration and application for temporary labor certification[469] must retain certain documents for three years from the date of certification, denial, or withdrawal.[470] Documents connected to the registration must be retained in connection with all applications filed under it,[471] and thus may need to be retained for a longer period.

The following documents must be retained and provided to DOL or "other Federal agencies" in an audit or investigation:[472]

- The H-2B registration, job order, and a copy of the temporary labor certification application and original signed Appendix B. If the registration and/or application were electronically filed, a printed copy of each adjudicated application, "including any modifications, amendments or extensions," must be signed by the employer;

- Documentation substantiating temporary need that was not already submitted with the registration or, during the transition, the application;

- Recruitment documentation, namely:
  - Job order placement records. The current regulations do not specify what should comprise these records, but an earlier rulemaking asked for print-outs from the website where the job order was placed "showing the beginning and the ending date of the posting or a copy of the job order provided by the SWA with the dates of posting listed";[473]
  - Copies of the newspaper pages, including the dates of publication and a full copy of the advertisements, tearsheets of the pages, or "other proof of publication furnished by the newspaper containing the text of the printed

---

[466] 20 CFR §655.20(y).

[467] 80 Fed. Reg. 24042 (Apr. 29, 2015); 20 CFR §655.20(y).

[468] 20 CFR §655.20(y).

[469] 20 CFR §655.56(c).

[470] 20 CFR §655.56(b).

[471] *Id.*

[472] 20 CFR §655.56(c).

[473] 73 Fed. Reg. 78020 (Dec. 19, 2008).

Copyright © 2017. American Immigration Lawyers Association. All rights reserved.

advertisements and the dates of publication," along with an English translation if the advertisement was in another language;[474]

- Documentation "sufficient to prove" that the required contacts with former U.S. employees were made.[475] "This documentation may consist of a copy of a form letter sent to all former employees, along with evidence of its transmission (postage account, address list, etc.)." The documentation should also demonstrate that the U.S. worker was offered the job and either turned it down or was rejected for a lawful, job-related reason;[476]

- Evidence of contact with the bargaining representative, if there is one;

- If there is no bargaining representative, a copy of the posting of the job opportunity, noting where and when it was posted;[477]

- Documentation of any additional recruitment required by the CO. The CO should specify what must be maintained to satisfy this requirement;[478]

- A copy of the final recruitment report, along with copies of any résumés received and the applicants' contact information. This should include updates to the report to cover referrals until 21 days before the date of need, discussed above under "Recruitment," and the same documentation with respect to those later referrals;[479]

- Substantiation of the information submitted in the recruitment report, "such as evidence of nonapplicability of contact with former workers";

- Evidence of contact with U.S. worker applicants, including documentation that any rejections were for lawful, job-related reasons;

- Each worker's pay records. This includes the "nature, amount and location(s) of the work"; number of hours offered each day (broken out by hours in accordance with, and above, the "three-fourths guarantee"); hours actually worked each day; if applicable, the reasons why the employee worked less than the offered hours; the time the worker started and ended work each day; applicable piece rate and/or hourly rate of pay; earnings per pay period; the worker's home address; and reasons for all deductions from wages;[480]

- Records of reimbursement of transportation and subsistence costs, if applicable, as discussed above under "Travel Costs";

---

[474] 20 CFR §655.41(d).

[475] 20 CFR §655.43.

[476] 80 Fed. Reg. 24042, 24077 (Apr. 29, 2015).

[477] 20 CFR §655.45(c).

[478] 20 CFR §655.46(c).

[479] 80 Fed. Reg. 24042, 24079 (Apr. 29, 2015).

[480] 20 CFR §655.20(i)(1).

Copyright © 2017. American Immigration Lawyers Association. All rights reserved.

- Written contracts with agents or recruiters, along with the "list of identities and locations of persons hired by or working for the agent or recruiter" and those persons' agents and/or employees;

- The written notice that was provided to DOL informing it that an H-2B worker or worker in corresponding employment has separated from employment prior to the end of the period stated on the temporary labor certification application;

- The H-2B petition and all supporting documents; and

- Documentation substantiating any claim that incumbent workers are not included in corresponding employment, such as collective bargaining agreements, individual employment contracts, or payroll records.

J. Decision on the Temporary Labor Certification Application

The CO must inform the employer or the employer's attorney or agent in writing of the approval (by certification of the application) or denial of the temporary labor certification application.[481] The approval, which includes the certified application and a final determination letter, is to be sent "by means normally assuring next day delivery," including electronic mail.[482] A copy is sent to an attorney or agent, if there is one.[483]

An approved temporary labor certification is "valid only for the period as approved on the Application … [and] expires on the last day of authorized employment."[484] A certified application is also "valid only for the number of H-2B positions, the area of intended employment, the job classification and specific services or labor to be performed, and the employer specified," and temporary labor certification "may not be transferred from one employer to another," other than in the case of a successor in interest, discussed later in this chapter.[485] The employer should sign the certified application upon receipt, if the application was filed electronically, and retain a signed copy of the application as well as an original signed Appendix B.[486] Due to confusion as to what documentation must bear original signatures for USCIS filing, DOL and USCIS issued guidance regarding the submission of the ETA Form 9142B and Appendix B. The key is to complete the footer of the originally signed ETA 9142B and Appendix B in the file upon certification and have the employer sign the original certified Form ETA 9142B to file with a completed Appendix B.[487]

---

[481] 20 CFR §655.50(b).

[482] 20 CFR §655.52.

[483] *Id.*

[484] 20 CFR §655.55(a).

[485] *Id.*

[486] 20 CFR §655.52.

[487] USCIS, "H-2A and H-2B Signature Requirements for Electronically Filed Temporary Labor Certifications and the H Classification Supplement to Form I-129" (Feb. 21, 2013), http://bit.ly/H2Bsign.

Copyright © 2017. American Immigration Lawyers Association. All rights reserved.

A denied temporary labor certification application should be sent by next-day means, including email, and should include the reason(s) for the denial.[488] The determination letter should also provide "[n]otice of [the] opportunity to request administrative review" with BALCA.[489] If an appeal is not sought in accordance with regulatory procedures, the "the denial is final and the Department will not accept any appeal on that Application."[490]

DOL may also "issue a partial certification, reducing either the period of need, the number of H-2B workers, or both."[491] "The number of workers certified will be reduced by one for each U.S. worker who is qualified and who will be available at the time and place needed ... and who has not been rejected for lawful job-related reasons."[492] The final determination letter of a partial certification should explain why the reductions were made, inform the employer of the availability of appeal, and "address the availability of U.S. workers in the occupation," if applicable.[493] The letter should also notify the employer that if an appeal is not filed, then the partial certification is the final decision.[494]

If, after issuance of a partial certification and starting 21 calendar days before the date of need until the end of the certified period, any of the qualified U.S. workers are no longer available, the employer may request a new determination on the application. The request should be made by email "or other appropriate means" and include a signed statement confirming the unavailability and providing the names and contact information for the unavailable workers unless a notification of abandonment or termination of employment, discussed below, was provided. Upon such a request, the CO should "promptly ascertain" whether qualified replacement U.S. workers are available "or can reasonably expected to be present at the employer's establishment within 72 hours" from when the request was received. The CO should issue a decision within 72 hours of receipt of a complete request. This is not a one-time process; the employer can make subsequent requests based on subsequently arising facts.[495]

K. Appeals to BALCA

An employer may appeal the denial or partial approval of a temporary labor certification application by requesting review by BALCA within 10 calendar days of the date of denial.[496] The CO should simultaneously be sent a copy of the appeal

---

[488] 20 CFR §655.53.
[489] Id.
[490] Id. The procedures can be found at 20 CFR §655.61.
[491] 20 CFR §655.54.
[492] Id.
[493] Id.
[494] Id.
[495] 20 CFR §655.57.
[496] 20 CFR §655.61(a).

Copyright © 2017. American Immigration Lawyers Association. All rights reserved.

request.[497] A notification requiring assisted recruitment, as discussed below, may also be appealed in this manner,[498] as may a revocation of an approved certification.[499]

As previously discussed, prevailing wage determinations can also be appealed to BALCA. However, those appeals must be sent to the National Prevailing Wage Center, which in turn will prepare the appeal file and forward it to BALCA.[500]

The appeal request should include the following information:

- Statement of the grounds for the request for review;

- Identification of the denied application, such as by DOL case number, applicant, and foreign national beneficiary;

- Copy of the final determination; and

- Any briefs or other legal arguments.[501]

New issues should not be raised on appeal; the request "[m]ay contain only legal argument and such evidence as was actually submitted to the CO before the date the CO's determination was issued."[502]

After receipt of the request for review, DOL "will, within 7 business days, assemble and submit the Appeal File using means to ensure same day or overnight delivery, to the BALCA, the employer, and the Associate Solicitor for Employment and Training Legal Services, Office of the Solicitor, U.S. Department of Labor."[503] Counsel for DOL may file "a brief in support of the CO's decision" within seven business days of receiving the Appeal File, to be sent by "means to ensure same day or overnight delivery."[504]

An appeal may be decided by either "a single member or a three member panel of the BALCA," and "BALCA must review a denial of temporary labor certification only on the basis of the Appeal File, the request for review, and any legal briefs submitted."[505] BALCA's decision, which must be provided within the later of seven business days of the submission of the CO's brief or 10 business days after receipt of the appeal file using means to ensure same-day or overnight delivery,[506] will be affirmance of the DOL decision, reversal or modification of the CO's decision, or "[r]emand to the CO for further action."[507]

---

[497] Id.

[498] 20 CFR §655.71(d).

[499] 20 CFR §655.72(b).

[500] 20 CFR §655.13(c)(1).

[501] 20 CFR §655.61(a).

[502] Id.

[503] 20 CFR §655.61(b).

[504] 20 CFR §655.61(c).

[505] 20 CFR §655.61(d).

[506] 20 CFR §655.61(f).

[507] 20 CFR §655.61(e).

Copyright © 2017. American Immigration Lawyers Association. All rights reserved.

L. Enforcement and Sanctions

1. Post-Adjudication Audit

The post-adjudication audit is among the four processes that DOL characterizes as "integrity measures."[508] Applications denied or withdrawn after approval can be audited, in addition to applications that were certified.[509]

Selection of applications for post-adjudication audit is solely within the discretion of the CO.[510] Selection may be at random or because the case meets certain criteria.[511] If selected, the employer and its attorney or agent will receive a letter with the following information:[512]

- Specification of the documentation that must be submitted;

- Notification of the deadline for response, which must be no more than 30 days from the date of the audit letter's issuance; and

- Notification that failure to fully comply with the audit process may result in supervised recruitment for future filings for up to two years, revocation of the certification, and/or debarment from the H-2B and any other labor certification program, as discussed below.

DOL may request multiple additional requests for information and documentation from the employer throughout the course of the audit.[513]

DOL may in turn forward the "audit findings and underlying documentation to DHS, [DOL's Wage and Hour Division], or another appropriate enforcement agency."[514] DOL may also "refer any findings that an employer discouraged an eligible U.S. worker from applying, or failed to hire, discharged, or otherwise discriminated against an eligible U.S. worker" to DOJ's Immigrant and Employee Rights Section.[515]

2. Assisted Recruitment

The second of the four "integrity measures," assisted recruitment may be imposed for future temporary labor certification applications if the CO finds a violation in an audit or otherwise that does not rise to the level of requiring debarment.[516] DOL also anticipates use of this provision where, "due to either program inexperience or

---

[508] 80 Fed. Reg. 24042, 24081 (Apr. 29, 2015).

[509] *Id.*

[510] 20 CFR §655.70(a).

[511] 80 Fed. Reg. 24042, 24082 (Apr. 29, 2015).

[512] 20 CFR §655.70(b).

[513] 20 CFR §655.70(c).

[514] 20 CFR §655.70(d).

[515] *Id.*

[516] 20 CFR §655.71(a).

Copyright © 2017. American Immigration Lawyers Association. All rights reserved.

confusion," the employer has made mistakes "that indicate a need for further assistance from DOL."[517]

The employer and its agent or attorney is to be notified in writing if the CO is going to require assisted recruitment. The notice should indicate the period of imposition, which can be up to two years, and should state the reason(s) for the measure. It also should indicate that agreement to the assisted recruitment "will constitute [the conditions'] inclusion as bona fide conditions and terms" of a temporary labor certification application.[518]

Assisted recruitment can add to the usual recruitment obligations one or more further requirements, as the CO instructs:[519]

- At the time of filing a temporary labor certification, the employer may be required to submit a draft advertisement for the CO to review and approve;

- The CO may designate the sources for recruitment, including in what publication the advertisements are to be placed;

- The CO may extend the length of placement of the advertisement or the job order;

- The employer may be required to give the CO and SWA written notification when the advertising is placed;

- The employer may be required to provide proof of the publication of all advertisements;

- Proof of all SWA referrals may be required;

- Proof of contact with all referrals and past U.S. workers may be required;

- The employer may be required to provide additional documentation to verify it conducted the assisted recruitment; and/or

- The CO can require the employer to perform additional assisted recruitment.

An employer may appeal to BALCA the requirement for assisted recruitment.[520]

If the employer materially fails to comply with the ordered requirements, "the certification will be denied and the employer and/or its attorney or agent may be debarred."[521]

3. Revocation

Under this third "integrity measure," DOL may revoke an approved temporary labor certification if it finds:

---

[517] 80 Fed. Reg. 24042, 24082 (Apr. 29, 2015).

[518] 20 CFR §655.71(b).

[519] 20 CFR §655.71(c).

[520] 20 CFR §655.71(a).

[521] 20 CFR §655.71(d).

Copyright © 2017. American Immigration Lawyers Association. All rights reserved.

- Approval was not justified due to fraud or willful misrepresentation of a material fact in the application process.[522] Willful misrepresentation of a material fact is defined as when the party "knows a statement is false or that the conduct is in violation, or shows reckless disregard for the truthfulness of it representation or for whether its conduct satisfies the required conditions."[523]

- The employer "substantially failed to comply with any of the terms or conditions" of the application. This is defined as "a willful failure to comply that constitutes a significant deviation from the terms and conditions" of the application.[524]

- The employer did not cooperate with a DOL investigation, inspection, audit, or law enforcement function.[525]

- The employer failed to comply with a sanction or remedy imposed by DOL's Wage and Hour Division, or with an order of the Secretary of Labor with respect to the H-2B program.[526]

As stated in DOL's April 2015 final rule:

> "When an employer's certification is revoked, the revocation applies to that particular certification only; violations relating to a particular certification will not be imputed to an employer's other certifications in which there has been no finding of employer culpability. However, in some situations, DOL may revoke all of an employer's existing labor certifications where the underlying violation applies to all of the employer's certifications."[527]

The decision to revoke rests with the Administrator of the Office of Foreign Labor Certification (OFLC),[528] who then sends the employer and its attorney or agent a Notice of Revocation detailing the grounds for revocation and advising the employer of its right to rebut or appeal. The notice becomes final agency action if the employer does not rebut or appeal within 10 business days from the date the notice is issued.[529]

The OFLC Administrator is supposed to make a final determination on a timely rebuttal within 10 business days of receiving the rebuttal. If the Administrator confirms the revocation decision, the employer may appeal to BALCA at this point. If it does not, the decision becomes final.[530] The regulation is silent as to the time

---

[522] 20 CFR §655.72(a)(1).

[523] 20 CFR §655.73(d).

[524] 20 CFR §655.72(a)(2).

[525] 20 CFR §655.72(a)(3).

[526] 20 CFR §655.72(a)(4).

[527] 80 Fed. Reg. 24042, 24082 (Apr. 29, 2015).

[528] 20 CFR §655.72(a).

[529] 20 CFR §655.72(b)(1).

[530] 20 CFR §655.72(b)(2).

Copyright © 2017. American Immigration Lawyers Association. All rights reserved.

period for this appeal, but its preamble indicates that the deadline is 10 business days.[531]

Timely filing of a rebuttal or an appeal stays the revocation "pending outcome of those proceedings."[532]

If an application is revoked, DOL will send a copy of the final agency action to DHS and DOS.[533] Also, the employer remains responsible for the workers' inbound and outbound transportation expenses, payment of amounts due under the three-fourths guarantee, and any other wages or other items due to the workers.[534]

4. Debarment

The fourth "integrity measure" is the most severe—debarment. OFLC and WHD have concurrent jurisdiction to debar, and are to coordinate in the matter, but there will be a single proceeding.[535]

During the time an employer, attorney, or agent is debarred, which lasts for one to five years,[536] OFLC may not issue temporary labor certifications to the debarred employer or its successor in interest,[537] or to an employer represented by the debarred attorney or agent.[538] In determining whether an entity is a successor in interest for purposes of debarment, "the primary consideration will be the personal involvement of the firm's ownership, management, supervisors, and others associated with the firm in the violation(s) at issue."[539]

For employers, debarment may result when OFLC or WHD determines that the employer willfully misrepresented a material fact, or substantially failed to meet a term or condition, in its registration, prevailing wage determination request, or application for temporary labor certification. DOL regards a substantial failure as a willful failure that constitutes a "significant deviation" from the terms and conditions of the document.[540] Debarment also can result from a willful misrepresentation of a material fact to DOS in the visa process.[541]

Attorneys and agents may be debarred if that individual committed one of the above violations or participated in an employer's violation.[542] One situation DOL targets is where an employer has contractually banned the attorney or agent from

---

[531] 80 Fed. Reg. 24042, 24082 (Apr. 29, 2015).

[532] 20 CFR §655.72(b)(4).

[533] 20 CFR §655.72(b)(5).

[534] 20 CFR §655.72(c).

[535] 20 CFR §655.73(h). *See also* 29 CFR §503.21.

[536] 20 CFR §655.73(c).

[537] 20 CFR §655.73(a).

[538] 20 CFR §655.73(b).

[539] 20 CFR §655.5.

[540] 20 CFR §655.73(a); 29 CFR §503.19(a).

[541] 20 CFR §655.73(a)(3); 29 CFR §503.19(a)(3).

[542] 20 CFR §655.73(b); 29 CFR §503.24(b).

Copyright © 2017. American Immigration Lawyers Association. All rights reserved.

collecting prohibited fees, yet the attorney or agent independently charges the worker such fees. "In this situation, the employer will not be debarred for the independent violation of the agent or attorney because the employer has not committed any violation, provided the employer did not know or have reason to know of such independent violation." In that case, the attorney or agent alone will face debarment.[543]

Willful misrepresentation of a material fact is defined as when the party "knows a statement is false or that the conduct is in violation, or shows reckless disregard for the truthfulness of it representation or for whether its conduct satisfies the required conditions."[544] Factors that can help DOL to assess whether a violation is a "significant deviation" include:[545]

- Previous history of H-2B violations;
- The affected number of H-2B workers, workers in corresponding employment, and/or U.S. applicant(s) improperly rejected;
- The gravity of the violations;
- The extent of resulting financial gain to the violator;
- The extent of potential financial loss or injury to the worker; and
- Whether U.S. workers have been harmed.

It is worth noting the statement in the 2015 rule's preamble that "[t]he Departments do not intend to debar employers, attorneys, or agents who make minor, unintentional mistakes in complying with the program, but rather those who commit a willful misrepresentation of a material fact, or a substantial failure to meet the terms and conditions.... [J]ust because OFLC has the authority to debar a party for up to 5 years does not mean that would be the result for all debarment determinations, as OFLC retains the discretion to determine the appropriate period of debarment based on the severity of the violation."[546]

Violations that can result in debarment include the following:

- Failure to provide the required wages, benefits, or working conditions to H-2B or corresponding employment workers;
- Failure to offer the position to qualified U.S. worker applicants, other than for lawful job-related reasons;
- Failure to comply with recruitment obligations;
- Improper layoff or displacement of U.S. workers or workers in corresponding employment
- Failure to comply with sanctions or remedies;

[543] 80 Fed. Reg. 24042, 24084 (Apr. 29, 2015).
[544] 20 CFR §655.73(d); 29 CFR §503.19(b).
[545] 20 CFR §655.73(e); 29 CFR §503.19(c).
[546] 80 Fed. Reg. 24042, 24084 (Apr. 29, 2015).

Copyright © 2017. American Immigration Lawyers Association. All rights reserved.

- Failure to comply with a Notice of Deficiency;

- Failure to comply with an assisted recruitment process;

- Impeding an investigation or audit;

- Employing an H-2B worker outside the area of intended employment, in an activity not on the job order, or outside the validity period of the job order;

- Violating the provisions prohibiting payment of fees by the worker;

- Discriminatory hiring practices, including the job not being open to any qualified U.S. worker or rejecting U.S. workers for other than lawful job-related reasons;

- Any other act showing such flagrant disregard for the law that future compliance with program requirements cannot reasonably be expected

- Fraud in the registration, prevailing wage, temporary labor certification application, or H-2B petition process; or

- "Material misrepresentation of material fact during the registration or application process."[547]

An employer, attorney, or agent selected for debarment will receive a Notice of Debarment from OFLC, "which will state the reason for the debarment finding, including a detailed explanation of the grounds for and the duration of the debarment and inform the party … of its right to submit rebuttal evidence or request a debarment hearing."[548] The regulation governing OFLC-initiated debarment does not specify the means by which a debarment notice is to be served, but a debarment initiated by WHD must be issued by personal service or certified mail at the party's last known address, although the WHD "may exercise discretion to serve the determination by regular mail" if the employer refuses to accept the certified mail.[549]

If rebuttal evidence or a hearing request is not filed within 30 calendar days of the date the notice was issued by OFLC, the debarment takes effect at that time.[550] Submission of such evidence or request stays the debarment pending outcome of the process, including any appeal.[551]

The regulations governing WHD-initiated debarment do not allow for rebuttal submissions, only for a request for a hearing.[552] See the section below on "Enforcement of Obligations" for a discussion of the timing and procedures for a WHD-initiated debarment proceeding.

If rebuttal evidence is timely filed, OFLC should issue a final determination within 30 calendar days of its receipt. If the debarment decision holds, the party will

---

[547] 20 CFR §655.73(f); 29 CFR §503.24(a).

[548] 20 CFR §655.73(g)(1).

[549] 29 CFR §503.41.

[550] 20 CFR §655.73(g)(1).

[551] *Id.*

[552] 29 CFR §503.24(d).

Copyright © 2017. American Immigration Lawyers Association. All rights reserved.

be informed of the right to request a hearing, which request must be submitted within 30 calendar days from the date of that determination. If a timely hearing request is not submitted, the debarment takes effect at the end of the 30 days.[553]

A hearing request at either of the two stages above for an OFLC-initiated debarment must be sent within the allowed 30 calendar days to Chief ALJ, U.S. Department of Labor, 800 K St. NW, Suite 400-N, Washington, DC 20001-8002. A copy must be served on the Administrator, OFLC. The hearing is not before BALCA, but instead is before a non-BALCA ALJ, and is governed by 29 CFR, Part 18.[554] The Administrative Law Judge (ALJ) can affirm, reverse, or modify the debarment determination, within 60 calendar days of completion of the hearing,[555] and serve the decision on all parties "by means normally assuring next day delivery."[556]

Either party can appeal to the Administrative Review Board (ARB) by petitioning to it within 30 calendar days of the ALJ's decision and serving the petition on all parties.[557] The ARB can decide whether to accept the petition. If the ARB declines the petition or does not respond within 30 days, the ALJ's decision is the final agency action.[558]

Conversely, if the ARB grants the petition for review, then the ALJ's decision "shall be stayed unless and until the ARB issues an order affirming the decision."[559] The "Office of Administrative Law Judges will promptly forward a copy of the complete hearing record to the ARB."[560] The ARB bears responsibility for informing the parties of the following:

- "The issue or issues raised;
- "The form in which submissions shall be made (i.e., briefs, oral argument, etc.); and
- "The time within which such presentation shall be submitted."[561]

The ARB's decision must be issued "within 90 days from the notice granting the petition and served upon all parties and the ALJ."[562] Once all administrative remedies have been exhausted, the final decision to debar the employer, attorney, or agent will be shared among other federal agencies: "Copies of the final debarment decisions will be forwarded to DHS and DOS."[563]

---

[553] 20 CFR §655.73(g)(2).

[554] 20 CFR §655.73(g)(3).

[555] 20 CFR §655.73(g)(4); 29 CFR §503.50.

[556] 20 CFR §655.73(g)(4).

[557] 20 CFR §655.73(g)(5); 29 CFR §503.51.

[558] *Id.*

[559] 20 CFR §655.73(g)(5).

[560] *Id.*

[561] 20 CFR §655.73(g)(5); 29 CFR §503.53.

[562] 20 CFR §655.73(g)(5); 29 CFR §503.55.

[563] 20 CFR §655.73(h).

Copyright © 2017. American Immigration Lawyers Association. All rights reserved.

Additional details regarding the ARB process can be found in the "Enforcement of Obligations" section, below.

Debarred parties "will be disqualified from filing any labor certification applications or labor condition applications ... for the same period set forth in the final debarment decision."[564]

5. Enforcement of Obligations

In addition to OFLC's four "integrity measures, under the INA an employer can be fined, debarred, and subjected to other administrative penalties for failure to meet conditions or for willful misrepresentation of a material fact.[565] The statute grants this authority to DHS, which is in turn authorized to delegate some or all of it to DOL.[566] As a result, compliance with statutory and regulatory obligations applicable to the employment of H-2B workers and workers in corresponding employment is enforced by the WHD of DOL.[567]

WHD's enforcement provisions attach as of the date the temporary labor certification application is accepted for filing.[568] Representations on the H-2B registration, prevailing wage determination request, survey attestation on Form ETA-9165, labor certification application, Appendix B, and H-2B petition all comprise acknowledgement that the employer "knows and accepts the obligations of the program."[569]

The three types of violations for which WHD can impose penalties are: willful misrepresentation of a material fact on a registration, prevailing wage determination request, or temporary labor certification application; substantial failure to meet any of the terms and conditions of those documents; or misrepresentation of a material fact to the State Department during the visa application process.[570] A substantial failure is a willful failure that constitutes a "significant deviation" from the terms and conditions of the document.[571] Factors that can lead WHD to conclude that a violation is a "significant deviation" include:[572]

- Previous history of H-2B violations;

- The affected number of H-2B workers, workers in corresponding employment, and/or U.S. applicant(s) improperly rejected;

- The gravity of the violations;

---

[564] 20 CFR §655.73(i); 29 CFR §503.24(f).

[565] INA §214(c)(14)(A).

[566] INA §214(c)(14)(B).

[567] 29 CFR §§503.0, 503.1(c), and 503.7.

[568] 29 CFR §503.19(d).

[569] *Id.*

[570] 29 CFR §503.19(a).

[571] INA §214(c)(14)(D); 29 CFR §503.19(a).

[572] 29 CFR §503.19(c).

Copyright © 2017. American Immigration Lawyers Association. All rights reserved.

- The extent of resulting financial gain to the violator;
- The extent of potential financial loss or injury to the worker; and
- Whether U.S. workers have been harmed.

When WHD determines that any of the three types of violations has occurred it can, as appropriate, institute administrative proceedings to recover unpaid wages, prohibited recruitment fees, impermissible deductions from pay, or wages due from placing workers outside the area of intended employment or in the wrong occupation; assess civil money penalties; obtain relief for persons discriminated against; reinstate and "make whole" any U.S. worker improperly rejected, laid off or displaced; or seek debarment.[573] Debarment is discussed in its own section, above.

Back pay is not explicitly referenced here, but the provision does indicate that remedies "are not limited to" those listed, and the provisions regarding hearings before an ALJ for findings of these violations do discuss awards of back pay.[574]

WHD may impose civil monetary penalties "equal to the difference between the amount that should have been paid and the amount that actually was paid" or "the wages that would have been earned but for" the violation for each violation related to wages, impermissible deductions, prohibited fees or expenses, or impermissible layoffs or failures to hire. These penalties cannot exceed $13,135 per violation. WHD also may assess penalties "in an amount not to exceed [$13,135] per violation for any other" of the three types of violations.[575]

To establish the amount of the monetary penalty, "WHD will consider the type of violation committed and other relevant factors," with the largest amounts "reserved for willful failures to meet any of the conditions of [the application and petition] that involve harm to U.S. workers."[576] WHD may also consider the following factors:

- Whether the employer has a history of violations regarding the H-2B program;
- The number of affected "H-2B workers, workers in corresponding employment, or improperly rejected U.S. workers";
- "The gravity of the violation(s)";
- Good faith efforts to comply with the statutory and regulatory requirements of the H-2B program;
- Any explanations provided by the "person charged with the violation(s)";
- The employer's commitment to future compliance; and

---

[573] 29 CFR §503.20.

[574] 29 CFR §503.50(c).

[575] 29 CFR §503.23(a)-(d). While the regulation states that the penalty is $10,000, these penalties are subject to inflation adjustment, thus increasing them to $13,135 as of March 7, 2017. That amount will be adjusted each year. See "Wage and Hour Division/H-2B," https://www.dol.gov/whd/immigration/h2b.htm.

[576] 29 CFR §503.23(e).

Copyright © 2017. American Immigration Lawyers Association. All rights reserved.

- "The extent to which the violator achieved a financial gain due to the violation, or the potential financial loss or potential injury to the workers."[577]

"No person will interfere or refuse to cooperate with any employee of the Secretary who is exercising or attempting to exercise the Department's investigative or enforcement authority."[578] If WHD believes an employer has interfered or refused to cooperate, it "may make such information available to OFLC and may recommend that OFLC revoke the existing certification." Revocation is discussed in its own section, above. It also "may take such action as appropriate" where the failure to cooperate meets any of the three types of violations discussed above. "Appropriate" action can include debarment and/or civil penalties.[579]

WHD must provide written notification of its decision to assess a civil monetary penalty, debar, or impose other penalties by personal service or certified mail at the party's last known address, although the WHD "may exercise discretion to serve the determination by regular mail" if the employer refuses to accept the certified mail.[580]

This notice of determination must provide the following information:

- List the reason(s) for the determination;
- State the amount of any "monetary relief due," the amount of "any civil money penalty assessment" and/or other administrative remedies imposed, or "whether debarment is sought";
- Notify the employer that a hearing may be requested;
- Provide details on how to request a hearing, including the addresses of the ALJ and DOL counsel, as discussed below;
- Notify the employer that failure to request a hearing within 30 calendar days of the date of the determination will result in the WHD determination becoming "final and not appealable," as discussed below; and
- Inform the employer that DOL and DHS will be notified of the violation(s), if applicable.[581]

A timely written request for a hearing must be "received by the Chief ALJ ... no later than 30 calendar days after the date of the determination,"[582] with copies served on "the representative(s) of the Solicitor of Labor" and the WHD official who made the initial determination.[583] "The request may be filed in person, by facsimile transmission, by certified or regular mail, or by courier service."[584] If the request is

---

[577] *Id.*

[578] 29 CFR §503.25(a).

[579] 29 CFR §503.25(b).

[580] 29 CFR §503.41.

[581] 29 CFR §503.42.

[582] 29 CFR §503.43(c).

[583] 29 CFR §503.43(f).

[584] 29 CFR §503.43(d).

Copyright © 2017. American Immigration Lawyers Association. All rights reserved.

initially filed by facsimile, then the original request, with signature by the employer or authorized representative, must be filed within 25 days.[585]

If a party does not file a timely request for a hearing, then the employer may "participate in the proceedings only by consent of the ALJ."[586] A timely filed request for a hearing will make the WHD determination "inoperative unless and until the case is dismissed or the ALJ issues an order affirming the decision."[587] The WHD Administrator will be the plaintiff, and the employer the respondent, throughout the proceeding.[588]

There is no form to request a hearing, but the request should be dated, "typewritten or legibly written," and "signed by the party making the request or by an authorized representative of such employer."[589] The request should also provide the following information:

- Statement of "the issue or issues stated in the notice of determination giving rise to such request";

- Explanation of the "specific" reason(s) "why the employer believes such determination is in error"; and

- Address of the party or authorized representative where subsequent correspondence should be sent.[590]

The rules of practice for the hearing will generally follow the "Rules of Practice and Procedure for Administrative Hearings Before the Office of Administrative Law Judges," as given in 29 CFR part 18.[591] The exception is that the admission of oral and documentary evidence will not be governed by the Federal Rules of Evidence or the "Rules of Practice and Procedure for Administrative Hearings Before the Office of Administrative Law Judges."[592] Instead, "principles designed to ensure production of relevant and probative evidence will guide the admission of evidence," where "evidence which is immaterial, irrelevant, or unduly repetitive," may be excluded by the administrative law judge.[593]

Two copies of pleadings and documents must be served on the WHD Administrator, and one copy must be served to the attorney representing the Administrator as well as to the Associate Solicitor, Division of Fair Labor Standards.

---

[585] *Id.*

[586] 29 CFR §503.43(c).

[587] 29 CFR §503.43(a).

[588] *Id.*

[589] 29 CFR §503.43(b).

[590] *Id.*

[591] 29 CFR §503.44.

[592] *Id.*

[593] *Id.*

Copyright © 2017. American Immigration Lawyers Association. All rights reserved.

Pleadings may be served by regular mail, and service is complete upon mailing to the last known address.[594]

"Time will be computed beginning with the last day following service and includes the last day of the period unless" it is a weekend day or federal holiday, "in which case the time period includes the next business day."[595]

The regulations allow, at the discretion of the ALJ, for deferral of proceedings after their initiation but before receipt of evidence to permit time to negotiate a consent agreement. If an agreement is reached, the ALJ must rule on it within 30 days of its submission, accepting the agreement "if satisfied with its form and substance … by issuing a decision based upon the agreed findings."[596]

In any event, the ALJ's decision, which is to be issued within 60 days after the hearing's completion, will provide a "statement of the findings and conclusions, with reasons and basis therefore, upon each material issue presented on the record," as well as an order to "affirm, deny, reverse, or modify, in whole or in part," the WHD Administrator's determination, and a statement of the reasons for the order.[597]

If the ALJ decides that the award of back pay,[598] whether for wage violations or based upon an incorrect PWD, "was not warranted," then the matter will be remanded to the WHD Administrator "for further proceedings on the Administrator's determination."[599] The absence of "such determination and remand" by the ALJ means the acceptance "as final and accurate" of the PWD, whether provided initially or determined upon appeal.[600] Importantly, the ALJ will "[u]nder no circumstances … determine the validity of the wage determination or require submission into evidence or disclosure of source data or the names of establishments contacted in developing the survey which is the basis for the PWD."[601]

Any party may request review, "including judicial review," of the ALJ's decision.[602] The party must petition the ARB within 30 days of the ALJ's decision and order, with copies "served on all parties and on the ALJ."[603]

There is no ETA form for a request for a hearing, but the request should be dated, "typewritten or legibly written," and "signed by the party filing the petition or by an

---

[594] 29 CFR §503.45.

[595] 29 CFR §503.45(c).

[596] 29 CFR §503.49.

[597] 29 CFR §503.50.

[598] The penalty section at 29 CFR §503.23 does not explicitly provide for award of back pay for violations of H-2B provisions, but does indicate that remedies "are not limited to" the enumerated sanctions.

[599] 29 CFR §503.50(c).

[600] Id.

[601] Id.

[602] 29 CFR §503.51.

[603] Id.

Copyright © 2017. American Immigration Lawyers Association. All rights reserved.

authorized representative of such party."[604] The request should also provide the following information and documents:

- Statement of "the issue or issues stated in the ALJ decision and order giving rise to such petition";

- Explanation of the "specific" reason(s) "why the party petitioning for review believes such decision and order are in error";

- Address of the party or authorized representative where subsequent correspondence should be sent; and

- "Attach copies of the ALJ's decision and order, and any other record documents which would assist the ARB in determining whether review is warranted."[605]

If the ARB does not issue a notice accepting a petition for review within 30 days after receipt of a timely filed petition, "or within 30 days of the date of decision if no petition has been received," the ALJ's decision will be deemed the final agency action.[606]

If the ARB determines to review the ALJ decision, either by acceptance of a petition or on its own motion, notice will "be served upon the ALJ and upon all parties to the proceeding."[607] The following information will be provided in the ARB's notice:

- "The issue or issues to be reviewed;

- "The form in which submissions will be made (*e.g.*, briefs, oral argument); and

- "The time within which such presentation will be submitted."[608]

Upon receipt of the notification of the ARB's review, "the OALJ [Office of the Administrative Law Judge] will promptly forward a copy of the complete hearing record to the ARB."[609] Any documents submitted to ARB must be filed with two copies, with copies served on all other parties.[610] Documents must be received on or before the due date in order to be properly filed.[611] The ARB's final decision must "be issued within 90 days from the notice granting the petition," and served on the ALJ and all parties involved in the proceeding.[612]

---

[604] *Id.*

[605] *Id.*

[606] *Id.*

[607] *Id.*

[608] 29 CFR §503.53.

[609] 29 CFR §503.52.

[610] 29 CFR §503.54.

[611] *Id.*

[612] 29 CFR §503.55.

Copyright © 2017. American Immigration Lawyers Association. All rights reserved.

M. Role of Attorney or Agent in the Temporary Labor Certification Process

DOL regulations define agent as "a legal entity or person who is authorized to act on behalf of an employer for temporary non-agricultural labor certification purposes," as long as the agent does not qualify as an "employer, or a joint employer," and as long as the agent is not an "association[] or other organization[] of employers."[613] An attorney is "a member in good standing" of the highest court of a U.S. jurisdiction who is not under "suspension, debarment, expulsion, disbarment, or otherwise restricted from practice before any court, the Department, the Executive Office for Immigration review ... or DHS."[614]

Attorneys and agents are authorized to file H-2B registrations and temporary labor certification applications on behalf of an employer, but the employer is still required to sign those documents.[615] An agent, but not an attorney, also is required to file with the temporary labor certification application a copy of the agent agreement or other document granting representation authority, as well as a copy of the agent's registration under the Migrant and Seasonal Agricultural Protection Act, if one is required under that statute.[616]

As DOL's April 2015 final rule states:

"DOL will review the documents to make certain that there is evidence that a bona fide relationship exists between the agent and the employer and, where the agent is also engaged in recruitment, to ensure that the agreements include the language required at §655.20(p) prohibiting the payment of fees by the worker. DOL also reserves the right to further review the agreements in the course of an investigation or other integrity measure. A certification of an employer's application that includes such a submitted agreement in no way indicates a general approval of the agreement or the terms therein.... The interim final rule only requires the agent to provide sufficient documentation to clearly demonstrate the scope of the agency relationship."[617]

The practitioner should note that "some of an agent's or attorney's duties in representing an employer may put the agent or attorney in the role of the employer and be a basis for assigning liability for the employer's acts or omissions."[618] Specifically, regarding the attestations about compliance by the employer with the H-2B program obligations made on the temporary labor certification application form, DOL stated:

"Attorneys and agents undertake a significant duty in making such representations. They are, therefore, responsible for reasonable due diligence in

---

[613] 20 CFR §655.5.

[614] Id.

[615] 20 CFR §655.7.

[616] 20 CFR §655.8.

[617] 80 Fed. Reg. 24042, 24056 (Apr. 29, 2015).

[618] 73 Fed. Reg. 78020 (Dec. 19, 2008).

Copyright © 2017. American Immigration Lawyers Association. All rights reserved.

ensuring that employers understand their responsibilities under the program and are prepared to execute those obligations. Agents and attorneys do not themselves make the factual attestations and are not required to have personal knowledge that the attestations they submit are accurate. They are, however, required to inform the employers they represent of the employers' obligations under the program, including the employers' liability for making false attestations, and the prohibition on submitting applications containing attestations they know or should know are false. Failure to perform these responsibilities may render the agent or attorney personally liable for false attestations."[619]

In short, to minimize the risk of personal liability to the attorney, the practitioner should carefully discuss with the client the many details of employer obligations under the H-2B program, including the prohibition on making representations that are actually or constructively known to be false and the penalties and consequences of making such representations.

As discussed above under "Debarment," attorneys and agents may also be debarred from the H-2B temporary labor certification program.[620] DOL has noted that it does not "intend to make attorneys or agents strictly liable for debarrable offenses committed by their employer clients, nor ... intend to debar attorneys who obtain privileged information during the course of representation about their client's violations or whose clients disregard their legal advice and commit willful violations. DOL will be sensitive to the facts and circumstances in each particular instance when considering whether an attorney or agent has participated in an employer's violation; DOL will seek to debar only those attorneys or agents who work in collusion with their employer-clients to either willfully misrepresent material facts or willfully and substantially fail to comply with the regulations."[621]

III. H-2B Petition

As discussed above, before filing an H-2B petition with USCIS, an employer must first obtain from DOL a temporary labor certification,[622] which "shall be advice to the director on whether or not United States workers capable of performing the temporary services or labor are available and whether or not the alien's employment will adversely affect the wages and working conditions of similarly employed United States workers."[623] Despite USCIS's use of language portraying the labor certification as advisory only, and statements that USCIS may reach a different conclusion on issues involved in the application,[624] the fact is, if DOL denies the

---

[619] *Id.*

[620] 20 CFR §655.73(b); 29 CFR §503.24(b).

[621] 80 Fed. Reg. 24042, 24084 (Apr. 29, 2015).

[622] 8 CFR §214.2(h)(6)(iii)(C).

[623] 8 CFR §214.2(h)(6)(iii)(A).

[624] 8 CFR §214.2(h)(6)(iii)(A); "Minutes from DOL H-2 Stakeholder Meeting" (Sept. 12, 2016), AILA Doc. No. 16102430.

Copyright © 2017. American Immigration Lawyers Association. All rights reserved.

temporary labor certification, the employer cannot file a petition with USCIS.[625] Thus, USCIS never has the opportunity to review DOL's "advice" in those cases.[626] USCIS can, however, reverse a previous DOL finding on temporary need even if certified on the labor certification.[627]

The petitioner can be "a United States employer, a United States agent, or a foreign employer filing through a United States agent."[628] The petition must be filed at the USCIS office having jurisdiction over the place of intended employment,[629] as discussed below. The petition must state a start date that is the same as the date of need on the labor certification, but if an amended petition is being filed due to the unavailability of workers in the original request, a later start date can be used.[630] It should be noted that a somewhat different process applies to positions in Guam.[631]

A. Timing Considerations for Filing the H-2B Petition and the Temporary Labor Certification Application

As noted above, the start date of the H-2B petition must match the date of need stipulated on the labor certification application,[632] despite concerns expressed by employers "with seasonal needs beginning in later months" of each half of the fiscal year that "this change will effectively leave them 'shut out' of the H-2B visa program."[633] Although DHS acknowledged that the regulation "may have the effect of disadvantaging certain filers whose employment start date begins more than four months after the beginning of the first or second half of the fiscal year," DHS indicated that the regulation would prohibit petitioners from "competing unfairly … by using a fictitious employment start date."[634] DHS also believed that the requirement would better protect U.S. workers by giving them a set start date to consider for their own availability for temporary employment.[635]

Unlike other nonimmigrant petitions, which may be filed up to six months before the employer's date of need, an H-2B petition "may not be filed or approved more than 120 days before the date of the actual need" for the foreign national's service, as that

---

[625] 8 CFR §214.2(h)(6)(iii)(C); USCIS, "Guidance on 'Temporary Need' in H-2B Positions" (Apr. 13, 2016), AILA Doc. No. 16100501.

[626] USCIS, "Guidance on 'Temporary Need' in H-2B Positions" (Apr. 13, 2016), AILA Doc. No. 16100501 ("[A]t the time DOL adjudicates a [temporary labor certification], it may not have the same information that we have at the time we examine the Form I-129").

[627] 8 CFR §214.2(h)(6)(iii)(A)

[628] 8 CFR §214.2(h)(6)(iii)(B).

[629] 8 CFR §214.2(h)(6)(iii)(E).

[630] 8 CFR §214.2(h)(6)(iv)(D).

[631] 8 CFR §214.2(h)(6)(v).

[632] 8 CFR §214.2(h)(6)(iv)(D).

[633] 73 Fed. Reg. 78104 (Dec. 19, 2008).

[634] *Id.*

[635] *Id.*

Copyright © 2017. American Immigration Lawyers Association. All rights reserved.

date is stipulated on the labor certification application.[636] But the 120 days is deceptive, due to the operation of the DOL rules. The application for the temporary labor certification cannot be filed any earlier than 90 days before the date of need,[637] and after filing, DOL must review the application and issue a Notice of Acceptance (NOA).[638] After that, the employer must conduct the recruitment, which takes a minimum of 14 days.[639] Then, the application must be adjudicated. As of May 2017, DOL processing took an average of 52 days in cases with no deficiencies, and 72 days where deficiencies were found.[640] Thus, the reality is that the petition is usually not ready to be filed until between two weeks and one month before the actual date of need.

This reality should underscore the importance of beginning the temporary labor certification process as soon as possible in the required 90 to 75 days' time frame before the date of need, and of performing any preparatory activities prior to 90 days before the date of need, if at all possible. For example, the PWDR may be submitted earlier, because the NPC will accept a PWD as long as it is valid on the date that the job order is submitted and the temporary labor certification is filed.[641] The PWD must be valid for at least 90 days from the date of determination, and is valid for up to one year.[642] Thus, the timing for a PWDR should be governed by the current processing times for fulfillment of the request. In May 2017, the NPWC was taking 27 days on average.[643] Thus, to provide a margin of safety, a PWDR during a period of that processing time should be submitted no later than 45 days in advance of the filing date. Many practitioners file the PWDR for the coming year as soon as DOL issues new wages at the end of June. The practitioner could also contact the employer six to nine months before the H-2B petition may be filed to discuss whether the employer will have a need for H-2B workers, to examine the job duties and requirements, and to begin gathering evidence of the temporary need.

B. Multiple Worksites, Multiple Employers, Foreign Employers, and Agent-Petitioners

As discussed below, the H-2B petition should be filed with the USCIS Service Center with jurisdiction over the place of employment.[644] If there will be multiple worksites, however, then the H-2B petition should include "an itinerary with the

---

[636] 8 CFR §214.2(h)(9)(i)(B).

[637] 20 CFR §655.14(b).

[638] 20 CFR §655.32(b).

[639] 20 CFR §655.40(b).

[640] DOL, "Welcome to the iCERT Visa Portal System," https://icert.doleta.gov/. Select the Processing Times tab, then scroll down to H-2B Processing Activity. This processing time is calculated from the time of filing until the time the NOA is issued.

[641] 20 CFR §655.15(a).

[642] 20 CFR §655.10(h).

[643] DOL, "Welcome to the iCERT Visa Portal System," https://icert.doleta.gov/. Select the Processing Times tab, then scroll down to Average Number of Days to Issue Wage Determinations/ H-2B.

[644] "Direct Filing Addresses for Form I-129, Petition for a Nonimmigrant Worker," https://www.uscis.gov/i-129-addresses.

Copyright © 2017. American Immigration Lawyers Association. All rights reserved.

dates and locations of the services" and should be filed with the USCIS Service Center with jurisdiction over the petitioner's headquarters.[645] Unfortunately, there is at the time of this writing a lack of clarity as to what constitutes a worksite under the current rules. It should be noted, as discussed earlier in this chapter, that multiple worksites in different areas of intended employment require separate labor certifications: "As a general rule, an employer seeking to employ workers who will perform work at more than one location outside of a single area of intended employment are required to file a separate application for each area of intended employment, regardless of the number of workers named in the application." [646]

There is no USCIS definition of "employer" specific to H-2B petitions, but the DOL definition may be cross-applicable because an employer must file both a temporary labor certification and an H-2B petition to sponsor a foreign national for H-2B status.[647] For purposes of temporary labor certification, an "employer" is defined as a person or entity that meets the following qualifications:

"Has a place of business (physical location) in the U.S. and a means by which it may be contacted for employment;

"Has an employer relationship (such as the ability to hire, pay, fire, supervise or otherwise control the work of employees) with respect to H-2B employees or a worker in corresponding employment; and

"Possesses, for purposes of the filing an Application for Temporary Employment Certification a valid Federal Employer Identification Number (FEIN)."[648]

DOL has indicated that the U.S. physical location is necessary because U.S. workers "must be referred to a U.S. location for employment," and that the FEIN is required at the time the temporary labor certification is filed.[649]

If there will be multiple H-2B employers, then "each employer must file a separate petition"[650] with the USCIS Service Center with jurisdiction over the worksite location. However, two or more employers "will be considered to jointly employ" an H-2B worker if each employer meets the requirements for that employee.[651] This generally arises in the context of a job contractor, discussed in detail below. The one

---

[645] 8 CFR §214.2(h)(2)(i)(B).

[646] DOL, "2015 H-2B Interim Final Rule FAQs, Round 17" (Oct. 4, 2016), AILA Doc. No. 16100430, https://www.foreignlaborcert.doleta.gov/pdf/Round-17_FAQs_Worksites-AIE.pdf.

[647] Cf. 8 CFR §214.2(h)(4)(ii). The practitioner should note that the definition of U.S. employer for H-1B petitions should not have cross-applicability, because the H-2B regulations do not require that an H-2B employer be a U.S. employer.

[648] 20 CFR §655.5.

[649] 73 Fed. Reg. 78020 (Dec. 19, 2008).

[650] 8 CFR §214.2(h)(2)(i)(C); 9 FAM 402.10-10(C).

[651] 20 CFR §655.5.

Copyright © 2017. American Immigration Lawyers Association. All rights reserved.

exception to the requirement of separate petitions is that a U.S. agent may file a petition on behalf of multiple employers.[652]

A U.S. agent may file a petition when authorized by "workers who are traditionally self-employed," by "workers who use agents to arrange short-term employment on their behalf with numerous employers," or by a foreign employer who does not have U.S. operations.[653] An agent may be the actual employer, the representative of the employer and beneficiary (as in the multiple employer instance below), or "a person or entity authorized by the employer to act for, or in place of, the employer as its agent."[654] The practitioner should note that this definition of agent differs from the definition of agent provided by DOL, as discussed above.

When filing a petition on behalf of multiple employers, the agent files "as the representative of both the employers and the beneficiary or beneficiaries." The supporting documentation must include "a complete itinerary of services or engagements."[655] The following requirements apply:

"The itinerary shall specify the dates of each service or engagement, the names and addresses of the actual employers, and the names and addresses of the establishment, venues, or locations where the services will be performed. In questionable cases, a contract between the employers and the beneficiary or beneficiaries may be required. The burden is on the agent to explain the terms and conditions of the employment and to provide any required documentation."[656]

A foreign employer, which is defined as "any employer who is not amenable to service of process in the United States," is forbidden from directly filing an H-2B petition.[657] Thus, a foreign employer "must use the services of a United States agent to file a petition for an H-2B nonimmigrant."[658] The agent must in turn be authorized to file the H-2B petition and must be able "to accept service of process" in the United States on behalf of the foreign employer regarding issues of verification of identity and employment authorization.[659] The foreign employer should authorize the agent to exercise "hiring authority to consider United States workers for the job, to offer prevailing wages and working conditions, and to file the petition," which should "include a statement from the foreign employer granting authority to the United States representative to acts in its behalf."[660]

---

[652] 8 CFR §214.2(h)(2)(i)(F)(2); 9 FAM 402.10-10(C).

[653] 8 CFR §214.2(h)(2)(i)(F).

[654] 8 CFR §214.2(h)(2)(i)(F).

[655] 8 CFR §214.2(h)(2)(i)(F)(2).

[656] *Id.*

[657] 8 CFR §214.2(h)(6)(iii)(B).

[658] *Id.*

[659] *Id.*

[660] Legacy INS's Operations Instructions (OI) 214.2.

Copyright © 2017. American Immigration Lawyers Association. All rights reserved.

If the agent files the H-2B petition on behalf of a foreign employer, the foreign employer is nevertheless "responsible for complying with all of the employer sanctions provisions" regarding verifying the identity and employment authorization of workers in the United States.[661] In addition, if the agent will perform "the function of an employer," then the agent "must guarantee the wages and other terms and conditions of employment by contractual agreement with the beneficiary or beneficiaries of the petition ... [and] provide an itinerary of definite employment and information on any other services planned for the period of time requested" to USCIS.[662]

C. Multiple and Unnamed Beneficiaries and Substitution of Beneficiaries

It is permissible for an H-2B petition to be filed for multiple beneficiaries.[663] DOL in turn requires that a temporary labor certification application on behalf of multiple workers entail "the same service or labor on the same terms and conditions, in the same occupation, in the same area of intended employment, and during the same period of employment."[664] USCIS should use the definition of "area of intended employment" discussed above when determining whether an H-2B petition on behalf of multiple beneficiaries may be approved.[665] The practitioner should also note that it is not permissible to file a single H-2 petition on behalf of beneficiaries who will perform agricultural services and beneficiaries who will perform non-agricultural services, as the type of service would differ.[666]

Any H-2B beneficiaries who are physically present in the United States must be named on the H-2B petition, because these foreign nationals would obtain new or extended H-2B status without an interview by a consular officer or inspection by a CBP officer.[667] It should not be necessary to name beneficiaries who reside abroad, based on the language of the regulation, which states:

"Except as provided in this paragraph (h), all H-2A and H-2B petitions must include the name of each beneficiary who is currently in the United States, but need not name any beneficiary who is not currently in the United States. Unnamed beneficiaries must be shown on the petition by total number."[668]

Although beneficiaries need not be named if they are outside the country, "all H-2A and H-2B petitions must state the nationality of all beneficiaries, whether or not named, even if there are beneficiaries from more than one country."[669] Also, USCIS

---

[661] 8 CFR §214.2(h)(2)(i)(F)(3).

[662] 8 CFR §214.2(h)(2)(i)(F)(1).

[663] 73 Fed. Reg. 78104 (Dec. 19, 2008).

[664] 20 CFR §655.15(e). *See also* 8 CFR §214.2(h)(2)(ii).

[665] "AILA/CSC Liaison Practice Pointer: Multiple Beneficiary H-2B Petitions," AILA Doc. No. 10020168.

[666] 73 Fed. Reg. 78104 (Dec. 19, 2008).

[667] *Id.*

[668] 8 CFR §214.2(h)(2)(iii).

[669] *Id.*

Copyright © 2017. American Immigration Lawyers Association. All rights reserved.

"may require the petitioner to name H-2B beneficiaries where the name is needed to establish eligibility for H-2B status."[670] Any beneficiaries who are not from a country designated for participation, as discussed later in this chapter, must be named.[671]

The regulations do not require that an H-2B petition be filed on behalf of the same number of workers for which the temporary labor certification was approved. In the event that H-2B beneficiaries remain unidentified when the H-2B petition is filed, "multiple petitions for subsequent beneficiaries may be filed at different times but must include a copy of the same temporary labor certification."[672] Any subsequently filed H-2B petitions "must reference all previously filed petitions associated with that temporary labor certification,"[673] to allow USCIS to keep count of the H-2B workers. The practitioner should note, however, that the high demand for H-2B visa numbers usually exhausts the quota very soon after H-2B petitions may be filed. Because H-2B beneficiaries need not be named on the petition, the petitioner may wish to file the H-2B petition as early as possible, with evidence of the temporary need for the requested number of workers.

Beneficiaries may be substituted for named or unnamed beneficiaries who have not been admitted to the United States.[674] The petitioner must "demonstrate that the total number of beneficiaries will not exceed the number of beneficiaries certified in the original temporary labor certification."[675] Substitution is available only for openings where the beneficiaries "were previously approved for consular processing but have not been admitted."[676] It is not possible to request substitution of a beneficiary to replace an H-2B worker who has already been admitted to the United States in H-2B status.[677] Instead, a new labor certification and new petition would be necessary.[678]

A substitution request for a new beneficiary who is outside the United States should be filed with the U.S. consulate where the foreign national will apply for a visa or the port of entry where the foreign national will apply for admission.[679] The petitioner should "notify" DOS or CBP with a letter requesting substitution and a copy of the H-2B petition approval notice.[680] If the temporary labor certification stipulated requirements for the job opening, the petitioner should also include

---

[670] *Id.*

[671] *Id.*

[672] *Id.*

[673] *Id. See also* "CSC External Stakeholders Liaison Meeting Minutes" (May 6, 2009), AILA Doc. No. 09050767.

[674] 8 CFR §214.2(h)(6)(viii); 9 FAM 402.10-10(D).

[675] *Id.*

[676] *Id.*

[677] AFM 31.5.

[678] 8 CFR §214.2(h)(6)(viii).

[679] 8 CFR §214.2(h)(6)(viii)(A).

[680] *Id.*; "VSC Helpful Filing Tips" (Aug. 12, 2009), AILA Doc. No. 09112363.

Copyright © 2017. American Immigration Lawyers Association. All rights reserved.

evidence that the beneficiaries meet the minimum requirements.[681] This evidence may be in the form of letters or other statements from the H-2B petitioner or other employers "attesting to the beneficiaries' work experience."[682]

If the new beneficiary is in the United States, however, an amended petition, including filing fees, must be filed with the same USCIS Service Center where the original H-2B petition was filed.[683] The following documents must be included:

- A copy of the original H-2B petition approval notice;

- "[A] statement explaining why the substitution is necessary";

- Evidence of the immigration status of the beneficiaries;

- "Evidence of the qualifications of the beneficiaries"; and

- "[E]vidence that the number of beneficiaries will not exceed the number allocated on the approved temporary labor certification, such as employment records or other documentary evidence to establish that the number of visas sought in the amended petition were not already issued."[684]

On the amended H-2B petition, the petitioner must request "a period of employment within the same half of the same fiscal year as the original petition."[685] If the petitioner desires an employment period in the other half of the fiscal year, then the employer must obtain "a new temporary labor certification" and file a new H-2B petition.[686]

D. Petitioner Notification Requirements for No-Show, Termination, and Abscondment

As previously discussed, if an H-2B nonimmigrant's employment ends prior to the end date specified in the temporary labor certification application, the employer must notify DOL and DHS in writing within two work days after the employment cessation.[687] The two agencies articulate the triggers for this requirement somewhat differently, with the DOL regulation pointing in general to any separation from employment,[688] while the DHS regulation points to the following events:[689]

The H-2B labor or services are "completed more than 30 days early";

The H-2B employee fails to report for the assignment within five work days of the start date of the approved H-2B petition;

---

[681] 8 CFR §214.2(h)(6)(viii)(A).

[682] *Matter of [name not provided]*, EAC 08 030 51332 (AAO June 19, 2008), http://bit.ly/jun081d3.

[683] 8 CFR §214.2(h)(6)(viii)(B); "VSC Helpful Filing Tips" (Aug. 12, 2009), AILA Doc. No. 09112363.

[684] 8 CFR §214.2(h)(6)(viii)(B).

[685] *Id.*

[686] *Id.*

[687] 8 CFR §214.2(h)(6)(i)(F); 20 CFR §655.20(y).

[688] 20 CFR §655.20(y).

[689] 8 CFR §214.2(h)(6)(i)(F)(1).

Copyright © 2017. American Immigration Lawyers Association. All rights reserved.

The H-2B worker is terminated prior to completion of the "labor or services for which he or she was hired"; or

The H-2B employee "absconds from the worksite."[690]

Both DHS and DOL state that, if the employee fails to report to work for five consecutive work days without the consent of the employer, that would be considered an "abscondment."[691]

As stated by USCIS guidance:

"USCIS defers to the DOL's definition of 'workday' which, according to the Fair Labor Standards Act, in general, means the period between the time on any particular day when an employee commences his/her 'principal activity' and the time on that day at which he/she ceases such principal activity or activities."[692]

A similar principle was stated in the preamble to DHS's 2008 regulation.[693] This clarification seems to cover most, if not all, work schedules, including those that differ from the Monday through Friday, 9:00 am through 5:00 pm work day. The practitioner may wish to advise the client that the notification time period may occur on a weekend, when the petitioner's corporate offices are closed but when employees are sent to worksites for H-2B assignments. The practitioner may also wish to counsel the client to inform supervisors or other, non-H-2B employees working at individual worksites about the notification requirement and advise the client to develop an internal notification procedure, so that the petitioner may comply with this requirement even on the weekends or other nontraditional workdays. In the context of the H-2A classification, DOL stated that it was "using a purely temporal (5 day) calculation to provide clarity," although the practitioner should note that the NPRM did "not include[] an express exception to abandonment or abscondment of a short-term absence."[694]

As discussed above, the employment start date must be the start date of the H-2B petition, which in turn must match the "date of need" stipulated on the labor certification application.[695] Therefore, if the H-2B employee does not report to work within five work days of this date, he or she should be deemed an absconder, and DHS must be notified within two additional work days. Although DOL also notes that an employee "may be terminated for cause,"[696] the practitioner may wish to emphasize the notification requirement for employees who abscond either at the start of or during the H-2B assignment.

---

[690] 8 CFR §214.2(h)(6)(i)(F)(1).

[691] 8 CFR §214.2(h)(6)(i)(F)(2); 20 CFR §655.20(y).

[692] AFM 31.5.

[693] 73 Fed. Reg. 78104 (Dec. 19, 2008).

[694] 74 Fed. Reg. 45906 (Sept. 4, 2009).

[695] 8 CFR §214.2(h)(6)(iv)(D).

[696] 73 Fed. Reg. 78120 (Dec. 19, 2008).

Copyright © 2017. American Immigration Lawyers Association. All rights reserved.

Notification to DOL may be emailed at *TLC.Chicago@dol.gov.*[697] DHS notification should be sent to the USCIS office that approved the petition. "[E]mail notification is strongly recommended to ensure timely notification." The email address for the California Service Center (CSC) is *CSC-X.H-2BAbs@dhs.gov,* and the email for the Vermont Service Center (VSC) is *VSC.H2BABS@dhs.gov.*[698]

The following information should be included in the DHS notification:

- "The reason for the notification (for example, explain that the worker was either a "no show," "absconder," "termination," or "early completion")
- The reason for untimely notification and evidence for good cause, if applicable
- The USCIS receipt number of the approved H-2B petition
- The petitioner's information, including:
  - Name
  - Address
  - Phone number
  - Employer identification number (EIN)
- The employer's information (if different from that of the petitioner):
  - Name
  - Address
  - Phone number
- The H-2B worker's information:
  - Full Name
  - Date of birth
  - Place of birth
  - Last known physical address and phone number

Additionally, to help USCIS identify the H-2B worker, submit the following for each H-2B worker, if available:

- Social Security number, and
- Visa number"[699]

It is highly recommended that the employer retain evidence of such notification in case of later investigation or audit.

---

[697] DOL, "H-2B Temporary Non-agricultural Program," https://www.foreignlaborcert.doleta.gov/2015_H-2B_IFR.cfm. To launch an email from this webpage, select "Additional Resources" under "Helpful Links" and click on "Report Terminations & Job Abandonment."

[698] USCIS, "H-2B Temporary Non-Agricultural Workers" (updated Nov. 8, 2016), http://bit.ly/USCISh2b.

[699] *Id.*

Copyright © 2017. American Immigration Lawyers Association. All rights reserved.

DHS acknowledged that certain employment or personal situations may be exceptions to or unaddressed by the language of the notification requirement.[700] One example involved an H-2B employee "who is hospitalized due to an accidental injury and is unable to communicate, then at a later date contacts the employer and returns to work upon completion of the treatment for the injury."[701] DHS indicated that a petitioner must notify DHS of the abscondment, but may reinstate such an H-2B employee.[702] Although it is only a strong suggestion and not a requirement to notify DHS of the reinstatement, such subsequent notification could be made by the means used for the initial notification. DHS stated that the "information will be updated accordingly," but nevertheless directs the petitioner to maintain documentation of "such an incident to support a claim during any future inspection."[703] The practitioner may wish to advise the client to use and retain the delivery receipts, as indicated above. In addition, as a practical matter, if the H-2B worker experiences difficulty in obtaining an extension or visa, then the documents may serve as evidence that the petitioner and the employee complied with the requirements.

DHS also acknowledged that H-2B workers may terminate their employment without informing the petitioner, such as by accepting another H-2B assignment with a different employer or by returning abroad.[704] In such situations, the employee could be considered an absconder and the petitioner could need to report the abscondment.[705] To avoid delay and/or denial of a subsequent H-2B petition for the same beneficiary, the foreign national should obtain and maintain documents confirming his or her departure from the United States and arrival in the home country or in another foreign country, such as passport exit and entry stamps, boarding passes, flight itineraries, and foreign immigration certificates, or USCIS approval notice for the H-2B extension(s). These documents may then be submitted to USCIS in response to an RFE or proactively with an initial H-2B petition filing.

However, DHS also cautioned that employers should not threaten employees with notification in order "to keep them in an abusive work situation."[706] DHS and other government agencies may investigate and pursue enforcement against employers who engage in "improper reporting, abuse and/or intimidation," and "such employer will be, at a minimum, in violation of the terms and conditions of its H-2B petition and therefore subject to having its petition revoked on notice."[707]

---

[700] 73 Fed. Reg. 78104 (Dec. 19, 2008).

[701] *Id.*

[702] *Id.*

[703] *Id.*

[704] *Id.*

[705] *Id.*

[706] *Id.*

[707] 73 Fed. Reg. 78104 (Dec. 19, 2008).

Copyright © 2017. American Immigration Lawyers Association. All rights reserved.

E. Return Transportation Obligation

If the employer dismisses an H-2B worker's employment before the end of the H-2B assignment, then under DHS regulations, the employer is responsible for providing the reasonable cost of transportation to the worker's last place of foreign residence.[708] This requirement does not apply if the worker voluntarily terminates the employment, but the employer will be responsible for return transportation for dismissal "for any reason."[709] Notably, the "provision applies to any employer whose offer of employment became the basis for the alien obtaining or continuing H-2B status,"[710] which means that H-2B employers who file extension/change of employer petitions may be responsible for these costs as well as initial H-2B petitions.

DOL regulations also require that employers cover the cost of transportation, but in addition to costs of return, also include costs related to travel to the place of employment. The obligation for costs for travel to the job attaches once the employee has completed 50 percent of the period of employment covered by the job order. If the employer is covered by the Fair Labor Standards Act, then the reimbursement for transportation costs must be paid within the first week of employment.[711]

Under the DOL regulations, the cost of transportation includes meals and lodging during travel to the place of employment.[712] As discussed previously under "Transportation Costs," the DOL regulations provide substantial detail as to how and when transportation costs are to be paid.

With respect to return costs, the DOL regulations are essentially the same as DHS's, albeit with much more detail. The employer must provide or pay at the time of departure for expenses for return "to the place from which the worker, disregarding intervening employment, departed to work for the employer," if the worker completes the period of employment covered by the job order or if the worker is dismissed "for any reason" before that date, unless the worker has immediate subsequent H-2B employment.[713] "However, if separation from employment is due to voluntary abandonment by an H-2B worker or a corresponding worker, and the employer provides appropriate notification…, the employer is not responsible for providing or paying for return transportation and subsistence expenses of that worker."[714] If the subsequent employer has not agreed in the job order to pay for the transportation from the initial employer's worksite, the initial employer must pay for that

---

[708] 8 CFR §214.2(h)(6)(vi)(E).

[709] *Id.*

[710] *Id.*

[711] DOL, Wage and Hour Division, Fact Sheet #78F, "Inbound and Outbound Transportation Expenses, and Visa and Other Related Fees under the H-2B Program," https://www.dol.gov/whd/regs/compliance/whdfs78f.htm.

[712] 20 CFR §655.20(j).

[713] 20 CFR §655.20(j)(1)(ii).

[714] 80 Fed. Reg. 24042 (Apr. 29, 2015).

Copyright © 2017. American Immigration Lawyers Association. All rights reserved.

transportation. If the subsequent employer has agreed in the job order to cover those costs, then the initial employer has no obligation in that regard.[715]

The DHS regulation directs the beneficiary to "advise the Service Center which adjudicated the petition in writing" and notes that the complaint will be retained in the file relating to the petition."[716] While this provision once lacked teeth,[717] the addition of DOL's extensive regulatory and enforcement scheme, discussed above under "Enforcement of Obligations," with respect to transportation costs now subjects the employer to substantial sanctions, particularly where the failure is willful.

F. Citizens of Certain Named Countries

The H-2B classification is available only to citizens and nationals of "participating countries,"[718] which in turn have been named by publication in the Federal Register. As of January 2017, nationals of the following countries may be beneficiaries of H-2B petitions:

> Andorra; Argentina; Australia; Austria; Barbados; Belgium; Belize; Brazil; Brunei; Bulgaria; Canada; Chile; Colombia; Costa Rica; Croatia; Czech Republic; Denmark; Dominican Republic; Ecuador; El Salvador; Estonia; Ethiopia; Fiji; Finland; France; Germany; Greece; Grenada; Guatemala; Haiti; Honduras; Hungary; Iceland; Ireland; Israel; Italy; Jamaica; Japan; Kiribati; Latvia; Lichtenstein; Lithuania; Luxembourg; Macedonia; Madagascar; Malta; Mexico; Monaco; Montenegro; Nauru; The Netherlands; New Zealand; Nicaragua; Norway; Panama; Papua New Guinea; Peru; Philippines; Poland; Portugal; Romania; Samoa; San Marino; Serbia; Singapore; Slovakia; Slovenia; Solomon Islands; South Africa; South Korea; Spain; St. Vincent and the Grenadines; Sweden; Switzerland; Taiwan; Thailand; Timor-Leste; Tonga; Turkey; Tuvala; Ukraine; United Kingdom; Uruguay; and Vanuatu.[719]

The first 28 countries were selected in 2009 because they "are important for the operations of the H-2B program[,] ... are cooperative in the repatriation of their nationals[, and] ... the countries whose nationals contributed the vast majority of the total beneficiaries of the H-2B program during the last three fiscal years."[720] In considering these factors, DHS moved away from the harsher language of the proposed rule, which would have denied H-2B petitions filed on behalf of beneficiaries who are nationals of "countries that consistently deny or unreasonabl[y] delay the prompt return of citizens ... who are subject to a final order of removal

---

[715] 20 CFR §655.20(j)(1)(ii).

[716] 8 CFR §214.2(h)(6)(vi)(E).

[717] Legacy INS, P. Virtue, "Liability for Return Transportation Costs," (Aug. 17, 1992), 1 INS and DOJ Legal Opinions §92-44.

[718] 8 CFR §214.2(h)(6)(i)(E).

[719] 81 Fed. Reg. 74468 (Oct. 26, 2016); "USCIS Announces Addition of St. Vincent and the Grenadines to Eligible Countries for the H-2A and H-2B Visa Programs" (Nov. 8, 2016), AILA Doc. No. 16110834.

[720] 73 Fed. Reg. 78104 (Dec. 19, 2008).

Copyright © 2017. American Immigration Lawyers Association. All rights reserved.

from the United States."[721] DHS stated the change was in response to requests to "make the process more positive and to encourage countries to improve cooperation in the repatriation of their nationals ... to ensure that the H-2B program will be available to other nationals of their countries in the future" as an "incentive."[722]

A foreign national who is not a citizen or national of a participating country may nevertheless be the beneficiary of an approved H-2B petition, as long as DHS decides that participation in an H-2B program by such a foreign national "is in the U.S. interest."[723] Each beneficiary who is not a citizen of a designated country must be named.[724] To make such a determination and to allow the exception "*in the discretion of the Secretary of Homeland Security,*"[725] the following factors will be considered:

- "Evidence from the petitioner demonstrating that a worker with the required skills is not available either from among U.S. workers or from workers from a country currently on the list of eligible countries for participation in the program";

- Evidence that the proposed beneficiary previously held H-2B status;

- The level of risk for "abuse, fraud, or other harm to the integrity of the H-2B visa program through the potential admission of a beneficiary" who is not a citizen of an approved participating country; and

- "[S]uch other factors as may serve the U.S. interest."[726]

USCIS should consider the totality of the circumstances: "Although USCIS will consider any evidence submitted to address each factor, USCIS has determined that is it not necessary for a petitioner to satisfy each and every factor."[727] Included within the analysis of the potential risk of abuse or fraud is whether the country "cooperates with the repatriation of its nationals."[728] Evidence of "other factors" to serve the U.S. interest "include evidence substantiating the degree of harm that a particular U.S. employer, U.S. industry, and/or U.S. government entity might suffer without the services of ... H-2B workers from non-eligible countries," although these "circumstances ... are given weight, but are not binding."[729] If the H-2B petition does

---

[721] *Id.*

[722] *Id.*

[723] 8 CFR §214.2(h)(6)(i)(E)(2).

[724] 8 CFR §214.2(h)(2)(iii).

[725] USCIS, B. Velarde, "Clarification of evidence required to satisfy the U.S. interest requirement for beneficiaries from countries not listed on the H-2A or H-2B Eligible Countries List" (June 1, 2009), AILA Doc. No. 09061766 (emphasis in original). *See also* 8 CFR §214.2(h)(6)(i)(E)(2).

[726] 8 CFR §214.2(h)(6)(i)(E)(2).

[727] USCIS, B. Velarde, "Clarification of evidence required to satisfy the U.S. interest requirement for beneficiaries from countries not listed on the H-2A or H-2B Eligible Countries List" (June 1, 2009), AILA Doc. No. 09061766; AFM 31.5.

[728] *Id.*

[729] *Id.*

Copyright © 2017. American Immigration Lawyers Association. All rights reserved.

address the U.S. interest exception, then an RFE should be issued,[730] providing 30 days to respond.[731]

H-2B petitions filed on behalf of beneficiaries who are not citizens of participating countries must be filed separately from petitions on behalf of citizens of designated countries, so as to avoid delaying the adjudication of the latter H-2B petitions.[732] As stated by USCIS guidance: "Adjudicating officers will issue a request for evidence when petitions filed on behalf of a combination of aliens from both H-2B eligible and non-eligible countries lack sufficient evidence to establish whether the beneficiaries from non-eligible countries qualify for H-2B classification."[733] Denial of a petition for failure to establish the U.S. interest "may be appealed to the AAO" but "there is no *judicial* appeal available to challenge such a discretionary denial."[734]

Although the rule does not state this specifically, it seems that the inapplicability of the provision would only apply while the H-2B nonimmigrant remains in the United States pursuant to previously granted H-2B status, and that seeking an H-2B extension on behalf of a foreign national who currently holds H-2B status, but who is not a citizen of a participating country, would be subject to the U.S. interest exception. This approach is supported by USCIS guidance, which states: "A petition filed on behalf of H-2B workers who are not from a country that has been designated as an eligible country may be approved *only* if USCIS determines that it is in the U.S. interest for that alien to be a beneficiary of such petition."[735] Reports indicate that USCIS has in fact required evidence that the U.S. interest exception applies, whether with the initial H-2B petition or in response to an RFE.

G. Nonimmigrant Intent

The foreign national must demonstrate that he or she has a residence abroad that he or she has no intention of abandoning.[736] Appropriate evidence may include copies of property titles or deeds, mortgages, or lease agreements. These documents may be supplemented with evidence of continued enrollment in school or other programs in the home country, arrangements for sabbatical, bank statements, and evidence of family or community ties. Finally, a foreign employer may provide a statement confirming an employment offer following completion of temporary U.S. employment.

An H-2B nonimmigrant may not have the dual intent to hold nonimmigrant status and simultaneously seek permanent residence:

"In the case of an H-2 beneficiary, the employer previously submitted satisfactory representations that the need for the skills or labor was temporary. If the

---

[730] *Id.*

[731] AFM 31.5.

[732] 73 Fed. Reg. 78104 (Dec. 19, 2008); AFM 31.5.

[733] AFM 31.5.

[734] *Id.* (emphasis in original).

[735] AFM 31.5 (emphasis in original).

[736] INA §101(a)(15)(H)(iii); 9 FAM 402.10-9(C).

Copyright © 2017. American Immigration Lawyers Association. All rights reserved.

employer's need has changed, the beneficiary no longer qualifies for H-2 classification in the same job. To avoid abuses of the H-2 classification, examiners should not accept representations that the permanent service would be in a different job when the labor certification or preference petition is filed by the same employer."[737]

Being the beneficiary of an approved labor certification application or of a filed employment-based immigrant visa petition sponsored by the same H-2B petitioner "is a basis for denying a new petition,"[738] as this would indicate a desire to immigrate permanently to the United States.[739] This remains the case even if the petitioner files the labor certification application or immigrant visa petition for a different position than the temporary H-2B assignment: "Petitioners will not be permitted to circumvent the[] requirement[] [of nonimmigrant intent] by applying for permanent status on behalf of the alien in a different job."[740] Even a statement regarding the petitioner's hopeful desire that the job may become permanent is grounds for denial of an H-2B petition.[741]

It may be possible to obtain approval of an H-2B petition if the permanent labor certification application or immigrant visa petition was filed by an entity other than the H-2B petitioner or by a family member,[742] but the practitioner should explain in detail to the client that the foreign national will have to demonstrate that, despite the pursuit of U.S. permanent residence, he or she will maintain the foreign residence for the duration of the H-2B assignment. Given the prohibition on dual intent for H-2B workers, the practitioner should advise the client that even if the H-2B petition is approved, the foreign national's visa application may be denied by the U.S. consulate.

An H-2B petition and visa application may address these issues by providing explicit details of definite plans, such as ongoing payments of the mortgage, property taxes, or rent; offer of employment from a foreign entity upon conclusion of the temporary H-2B assignment and until the foreign national is able to obtain permanent residence; and evidence that the permanent position differs from the temporary H-2B assignment, if applicable. Nevertheless, the practitioner should advise the client that this situation presents a good deal of risk of denial, whether from USCIS or DOS. For a detailed discussion of strategies to contrast a future desire to immigrate with a temporary desire to visit the United States, see Volume 1: Chapter Three, "B Visas and Status and the Visa Waiver Program."

---

[737] OI 214.2; *see also* 55 Fed. Reg. 2606 (Jan. 26, 1990).

[738] OI 214.2.

[739] 8 CFR §214.2(h)(16)(ii); 55 Fed. Reg. 2606 (Jan. 26, 1990).

[740] 55 Fed. Reg. 2606 (Jan. 26, 1990).

[741] *Matter of [name not provided]*, WAC 92 181 51334 (AAU Apr. 19, 1993), 11 Immig. Rptr. B2-62.

[742] *Cf.* 8 CFR §214.2(h)(16)(ii).

Copyright © 2017. American Immigration Lawyers Association. All rights reserved.

IV. Managing Client Expectations: Increased Scrutiny and Special Processing for Certain Situations

Certain facts may trigger increased scrutiny by government agencies, and it may be helpful to manage client expectations and to prepare the client for potential issues by discussing these situations in greater detail.

Although the 2015 joint regulation removed a provision authorizing DOL to create new special procedures, the agency indicated that it "will continue to accept H-2B applications for professional athletes, tree planting and related reforestation, and professional/outdoor entertainers under the existing special procedures. However, the Department is in the process of expeditiously reviewing special procedures applicable to the H-2B program."[743] To date, those procedures have remained intact, but the practitioner should watch DOL developments in case of change.

A. The H-2B Nonimmigrant Will Provide Training

If the foreign national's services are necessary to provide training to U.S. workers, then additional requirements to establish the temporary need apply.[744] First, the H-2B nonimmigrant should provide only training or vocational instruction;[745] the foreign national should not perform hands-on work.[746] Second, the H-2B petition should include the following details:

Training program and schedule;

Information on the hiring or recruitment of foreign nationals;

"[A]ny other persuasive indicator of [the petitioner's] ability to retain the services of a full-time … instructor";[747] and

Evidence that the petitioner will be able to "operate simultaneously a training program and a viable commercial enterprise."[748]

These documents should demonstrate how the foreign national's time will be spent providing training. An H-2B petition may be denied if "the majority of the time of both the beneficiary and the remaining staff would have to be devoted to productive employment" for the petitioner to remain in business.[749] If the instructor will provide training infrequently, such as only one class per week, and the foreign national will "engage in practical training" for the remainder of the work week, then

---

[743] DOL, "OFLC Frequently Asked Questions and Answers" (May 2015), https://www.foreignlaborcert.doleta.gov/faqsanswers.cfm#q!75. Scroll down to "H-2B Temporary Labor Certification Program" and select "H-2B Special Processes" from the drop-down menu. *See also* 80 Fed. Reg. 24042, 24051 (Apr. 29, 2015).

[744] *Matter of Golden Dragon Chinese Restaurant*, 19 I&N Dec. 238 (Comm'r 1984). *See also* 9 FAM 402.10-4(E).

[745] *Id.*; *Matter of Samarius Industries, Inc.*, 15 I&N Dec. 608 (Reg'l Comm'r 1976).

[746] *Matter of Golden Dragon Chinese Restaurant*, 19 I&N Dec. 238.

[747] *Id.*

[748] *Matter of [name not provided]*, LIN 92 259 50517 (AAU June 18, 1993), 12 Immig. Rptr. B2-21.

[749] *Matter of Golden Dragon Chinese Restaurant*, 19 I&N Dec. 238.

Copyright © 2017. American Immigration Lawyers Association. All rights reserved.

the adjudicator is likely to deny the H-2B petition for failing to establish the temporary need for the beneficiary's training services.[750]

In general, an H-2B petition for a trainer or instructor will be based on a one-time need, as seasonal, peakload, or intermittent needs would indicate ongoing training programs, which in turn would be considered to demonstrate a permanent position.[751] Similarly, the fact that a beneficiary may provide training to some degree as a "vocational instructor" does not automatically mean that the job opportunity is temporary:[752] "[A] cook coming to train other cooks or organize a kitchen may be classified H-2B, but a cook coming to assume a job of a permanent nature may not be accorded H-2B ... status."[753] As with all H-2B petitions, the nature of the petitioner's need, as well as the petitioner's business purpose, will be evaluated.[754]

One H-2B petition was approved to allow a foreign national to train a U.S. citizen on medical equipment that was not generally available in the United States and that was available to the petitioner only as a donation from the manufacturer.[755] But the fact that the training will be technical does not guarantee approval of the H-2B petition absent evidence that the other requirements will be met.[756]

B. Restrictive Requirements: Professional Certifications, Combination of Occupations, Foreign Languages, and the Business Necessity Justification

Qualifications and requirements on the labor certification and job order "must be bona fide and consistent with the normal and accepted qualifications and requirements imposed by non-H-2B employers in the same occupation and area of intended employment."[757] Qualification is defined as "a characteristic that is necessary to an individual's ability to perform the job," while requirement "means a term or condition of employment which a worker is required to accept in order to obtain the job."[758]

DOL will carefully evaluate temporary labor certification applications for job opportunities where the "requirements are unduly restrictive or represent a combination of duties not normal to the occupation."[759] The practitioner should caution the client that a NOD is highly likely and that certification ultimately may not

---

[750] *Matter of [name not provided]*, EAC 93 165 51527 (AAU Aug. 26, 1994), 13 Immig. Rptr. B2-113.

[751] *Matter of [name not provided]*, LIN 92 259 50517 (AAU June 18, 1993), 12 Immig. Rptr. B2-21.

[752] *Matter of Golden Dragon Chinese Restaurant*, 19 I&N Dec. 238.

[753] 9 FAM 402.10-4(E).

[754] *Matter of Golden Dragon Chinese Restaurant*, 19 I&N Dec. 238 (stating that the "need of a Chinese restaurant for a Chinese specialty chef is clearly a permanent one").

[755] *Matter of [name not provided]*, LIN 94 040 50642 (AAU Jan. 28, 1994), 12 Immig. Rptr. B2-158.

[756] *Matter of [name not provided]*, EAC 93 165 51527 (AAU Aug. 26, 1994), 13 Immig. Rptr. B2-113.

[757] 20 CFR §655.20(e).

[758] *Id.*

[759] 72 Fed. Reg. 38621, 38623-4 (July 13, 2007). For a discussion of a combination of duties that are considered to be normal for the occupation, see "Logging, Tree Planting, and Reforestation Occupations," below.

Copyright © 2017. American Immigration Lawyers Association. All rights reserved.

be granted for certain situations. To determine whether a job requirement or qualification is "normal," DOL generally refers to the O*NET for specific occupations.[760]

> "For other qualifications and requirements not addressed by the O*NET (*e.g.*, criminal background checks, licensing requirements, or drug tests), [DOL] relies on its own historical experience with case-by-case application review as well as information received from outside sources (*e.g.*, information on non-H-2B job requirements and qualifications available to the State Workforce Agency, other employers in the industry or occupation, or interest groups with knowledge of the industry or occupation) to identify job requirements and qualifications that do not appear consistent with the regulatory standard."[761]

A professional certification requirement may be deemed restrictive, especially if the certification is only available in a country outside the United States, as this would "eliminate[] from consideration for the job all members of the United States workforce.... In visa petition proceedings for alien employment in the United States, requirements for petitions are always judged in terms of U.. standards."[762] An employer may justify such requirements as necessary because of business necessity, as discussed in Volume 2: Chapter Two, "The Labor Certification Application."

DOL may permit an employer to obtain temporary labor certification for a position that involves a combination of occupations, but the employer must provide evidence that the combination of duties was normally required, that the employer normally employed workers for such a combined occupation, that workers in the area of intended employment normally perform the combined duties, or that the combination of duties is a business necessity.[763] The employer must also pay the prevailing wage that is the higher of the two occupations, "regardless of the amount of time the worker will spend performing each respective duty."[764] Helpful evidence to document the business necessity includes "position descriptions and relevant payroll records, and/or letters from other employers stating their workers normally perform the combination of occupations in the area of intended employment.[765]

If the job requires fluency or proficiency in a foreign language, then the practitioner should inform the client that DOL will closely scrutinize the labor

---

[760] DOL, "2015 H-2B Interim Final Rule FAQs, Round 5," https://www.foreignlaborcert.doleta.gov/pdf/H-2B_2015_IFR_FAQs_Round5.pdf. The O*Net can be found at https://www.onetonline.org/.

[761] *Id.*

[762] 20 CFR §656.17(h)(1). This provision applies to permanent labor certification applications, but the principle should apply equally in the temporary context.

[763] DOL, "OFLC Frequently Asked Questions and Answers," https://www.foreignlaborcert.doleta.gov/faqsanswers.cfm#q!75. Select "Job Requirements/Duties" from the drop-down menu. This FAQ applies to permanent labor certification applications, but the principle should apply equally in the temporary context.

[764] *Id.*

[765] 20 CFR §656.17(h)(3). This provision applies to permanent labor certification applications, but the principle should apply equally in the temporary context.

Copyright © 2017. American Immigration Lawyers Association. All rights reserved.

certification application.[766] DOL considers a foreign language requirement as restrictive or excessive unless it is an intrinsic part of the job, such as with a translator or foreign-language teacher, and the employer typically must demonstrate the business necessity for the requirement.[767] "Needing to communicate with co-workers or subordinates who cannot effectively communicate in English and/or having a working environment where safety considerations would support a foreign language requirement" can support business necessity for a foreign language requirement.[768] An example of an approved labor certification application involved musicians performing songs in the foreign language.[769] In contrast, the requirement that an applicant speak a particular dialect of English was rejected as restrictive.[770] For a discussion of how to document the business necessity of a foreign language requirement, see Volume 2: Chapter Two, "Labor Certification Application."

C. Temporary Labor Certification Applications Filed by Job Contractors

A "job contractor" is defined as:

"[A] person, association, firm, or a corporation that meets the definition of an employer and who contracts services or labor on a temporary basis to one or more employers, which is not an affiliate, branch or subsidiary of the job contractor, and where the job contractor will not exercise any supervision or control in the performance of the services or labor to be performed other than hiring, paying, and firing the workers."[771]

A client of a job contractor, *i.e.* an "employer-client," is defined as:

"[A]n employer that has entered into an agreement with a job contractor and that is not an affiliate, branch, or subsidiary of the job contractor, under which the job contractor provides services or labor to the employer on a temporary basis and will not exercise substantial, direct day-to-day supervision and control in the performance of the services or labor to be performed other than hiring, paying and firing the workers."

A job contractor must demonstrate, "such as through the provision of payroll records,"[772] its own temporary need for the services or labor to be performed, "not that of its employer-client(s)."[773] Also, a job contractor is allowed to use only

---

[766] 20 CFR §656.17(h)(2); DOL, "OFLC Frequently Asked Questions and Answers," https://www. foreignlaborcert.doleta.gov/faqsanswers.cfm#q!75. Select "Job Requirements/Duties" from the drop-down menu This provision and the FAQ apply to permanent labor certification applications, but the principle should apply equally in the temporary context.

[767] *Id.*

[768] *Id.*

[769] *Matter of [name not provided]*, EAC 90 195 00722 (AAU Jan. 18, 1991), 9 Immig. Rptr. B2-13.

[770] *Matter of [name not provided]*, HHW N 5989 (AAU Nov. 10, 1987), 5 Immig. Rptr. B2-68.

[771] 20 CFR §655.5.

[772] 20 CFR §655.11(a).

[773] 20 CFR §§655.6(c) and 655.11(d) and (e).

Copyright © 2017. American Immigration Lawyers Association. All rights reserved.

seasonal and one-time occurrences as temporary need; it cannot use peakload or intermittent need.[774]

In explaining why it was requiring contractors to demonstrate their own temporary need, DOL seemed to contradict the requirement by emphasizing that contractors do not have their own need for workers:

> "We generally conclude that a person or entity that is *a job contractor ... has no individual need for workers.* Rather, its need is based on the underlying need of its employer clients. Job contractors generally have an ongoing business of supplying workers to other entities, even if the receiving entity's need for the services is temporary. However, we recognize that we should exclude from the program only those job contractors who have a definitively permanent need for workers, and that job contractors who only have a need for the services or labor to be performed several months out of the year have a genuine temporary need and should not be excluded.... *Contractors have no temporary need apart from the underlying need of the employer on whose behalf they are filing the Application for Temporary Employment Certification.* When considering any employer's H-2B Registration, DOL will require that employer to substantiate its temporary need by providing evidence required to support such a need."[775]

As an example of a temporary need by a contractor, DOL cites "a job contractor that regularly supplies workers for ski resorts from October to March but does not supply any workers performing the same services or labor needed by the ski resorts outside of those months." Such a contractor "would qualify as having a temporary need that is seasonal for such workers."[776]

DOL regards job contractors as joint employers with their employer-clients. Joint employment is defined as "where two or more employers each have sufficient definitional indicia of being an employer to be considered the employer of a worker."[777] DOL indicates that "some factors relevant to the determination of employment status include, but are not limited to, the following: The right to control the manner and means by which work is accomplished; the skill required to perform the work; the source of the instrumentalities and tools for accomplishing the work; the location of the work; discretion over when and how long to work; and whether the work is part of the regular business of the employer or employers."[778]

A job contractor may submit a temporary labor certification application jointly with an employer-client. The contractor must have separate contracts with each

---

[774] 20 CFR §655.6(c).

[775] 80 Fed. Reg. 24042, 24055 (Apr. 29, 2015) (emphasis added).

[776] *Id.*

[777] 20 CFR §655.5.

[778] 80 Fed. Reg. 24042, 24064 (Apr. 29, 2015).

Copyright © 2017. American Immigration Lawyers Association. All rights reserved.

employer-client, and each contract may support only one application for each job opportunity within a single area of intended employment.[779]

Either entity may submit the prevailing wage determination request, but each entity is separately responsible for ensuring that the required wage is advertised and paid.[780]

The regulation is not explicit as to which party submits the temporary labor certification application, but seems to assume that it will be submitted by the contractor. That application must:

- Clearly identify both the job contractor and the employer-client;

- Explain the employment relationship and specify the actual worksite;

- Be signed by both the job contractor and the employer-client, by which both entities are independently attesting to the conditions of employment and assuming responsibility for the accuracy of the application's representations and all employer responsibilities under the H-2B program; and

- Be accompanied by a copy of the contract or agreement between the two entities.[781]

Either entity may place the SWA job order and conduct the recruitment.[782] In either event, both entities are responsible for satisfying the content requirements of both, and that content must clearly identify both entities by name and clearly state the worksite location(s) where the job will be performed.[783]

The job contractor is allowed to combine more than one of its employer-clients' jobs in one advertisement, provided they are all in the same occupation, have the same requirements and terms and conditions (including dates of employment), and are all in the same area of intended employment. A combined advertisement must not only identify the job contractor by name, but also must disclose the joint employment relationships and the number of workers sought for each employer-client, which also must be identified by name. A combined advertisement is required to include this statement:

> "Applicants may apply for any or all of the jobs listed. When applying, please identify the job(s) (by company and work location) you are applying to for the entire period of employment specified."[784]

If an applicant does not specify a particular company and location, he or she is presumed to have applied for all that are listed, and must be treated as such.[785]

---

[779] 20 CFR §655.19(a) and (b).

[780] 20 CFR §655.19(c).

[781] 20 CFR §655.19(d).

[782] 20 CFR §655.19(e).

[783] *Id.*

[784] 20 CFR §655.19(e)(3)(ii).

[785] *Id.*

Copyright © 2017. American Immigration Lawyers Association. All rights reserved.

Both entities must sign the recruitment report.[786] Either may fulfill the requirement of updating the report throughout the recruitment period.[787]

An approved certification will be sent to the job contractor, with a courtesy copy sent to the employer-client.[788] If the application was filed electronically, the contractor must ensure that the original signatures of both the contractor and client are on the certification when it is submitted to USCIS with the H-2B petition.[789]

D. Tree Planting, Reforestation, and Logging Occupations

Temporary labor certification for tree planting and "related reforestation occupations" involve special processing for a number of reasons.[790] First, despite the fact that some of these occupations, such as "Tree Planter, Forest Worker and Laborer, and Brush Clearer," may be considered agricultural, H-2A classification is inappropriate because "they are not so classified under either the Internal Revenue Code" or the FLSA.[791] DOL proposed that reforestation, "pine straw activities," and logging occupations be classified as agricultural and therefore under the H-2A classification,[792] but only logging occupations are now classifiable as H-2A.[793] Similarly, activities are considered agricultural if they involve "the planting, raising, cultivating, and harvesting of Christmas trees when such services are performed on a farm."[794]

Second, these occupations "may have elements of both agricultural and non-agricultural occupations,"[795] which would be similar to having a combination of occupations that are generally impermissible for labor certification. Third, federal circuit court decisions have "directed the Department to cover migrant and seasonal forestry workers under the Migrant and Seasonal Agricultural Worker Protection Act (MSPA)."[796] Finally, these occupations frequently require itineraries that cover

---

[786] 20 CFR §655.48(b).

[787] Id.; 20 CFR §655.20(t).

[788] 20 CFR §655.19(f).

[789] 20 CFR §655.19(g).

[790] 72 Fed. Reg. 36504 (July 3, 2007); "H-2B Temporary Labor Certification Process Stakeholder Briefing" (Sept. 2009), AILA Doc. No. 09092568.

[791] 72 Fed. Reg. 36504 (July 3, 2007). Although an act that would classify these occupations as agricultural was introduced in 2009, it remains with the House sub-committee. "H-2B Program Reform Act of 2009," H.R. 4381 (Dec. 16, 2009), AILA Doc. No. 09121774; "Bill Summary and Status," available at http://loc.gov (search by bill number).

[792] 74 Fed. Reg. 45906 (Sept. 4, 2009).

[793] Id.; 75 Fed. Reg. 6884 (Feb. 12, 2010).

[794] 75 Fed. Reg. 6884 (Feb. 12, 2010).

[795] 72 Fed. Reg. 36504 (July 3, 2007).

[796] Id. (citing Bresgal v. Brock, 833 F.2d 763 (9th Cir. 1987) and Bracamantes v. Weyerhauser Co., 840 F.2d 271 (5th Cir. 1988)).

Copyright © 2017. American Immigration Lawyers Association. All rights reserved.

worksites in multiple states,[797] which are not permissible on a single H-2B temporary labor certification.

In addition, it is permissible to "require tree planter workers to perform minor related reforestation job activities such as tree seedling pulling, thinning, seed cone gathering, and pine straw gathering," even though this might ordinarily be considered a combination of occupations.[798] The temporary labor certification application and related recruitment documents should note the requirement, in order to "apprise workers of the full scope of possible job duties."[799]

1. Temporary Need

As with all H-2B temporary labor certification applications, the employer must demonstrate that the need is a one-time occurrence or is based on seasonal, peakload, or intermittent need.[800] DOL notes, however, that the seasonal standard may be the most appropriate, because the job duties "are predominantly seasonal activities determined by climatic conditions occurring once, or in some locations, twice a year," though certain "applications for relatively short itineraries can be justified under the peakload standard."[801]

Indeed, the general concern that a seasonal employment period for "a major portion of the year" is temporary does not apply to these applications, as it is common for employers to "bid on a sequence of work contracts linking each seasonal activity into an itinerary for such a long duration.[802] Instead, "the MSPA definition of 'on a seasonal or other temporary basis'" provides guidance for determining whether the job offer is for temporary employment:[803]

> "Labor is performed on a seasonal basis, where, ordinarily, the employment pertains to or is of the kind exclusively performed at certain seasons or periods of the year and which, from its nature, may not be continuous or carried on throughout the year. A worker, who moves from one seasonal activity to another, while employed in agriculture or performing agricultural labor, is employed on a seasonal basis even though he may continue to be employed during a major portion of the year."[804]

"Temporary basis," in turn is defined as follows: "[E]mployment where a worker is employed for a limited time only or where performance is contemplated for a

---

[797] 72 Fed. Reg. 36504 (July 3, 2007).

[798] Id.

[799] Id.

[800] Id.

[801] Id.

[802] Id.

[803] Id.

[804] Id.

Copyright © 2017. American Immigration Lawyers Association. All rights reserved.

particular piece of work, usually of short duration. Generally, employment which is contemplated to continue indefinitely is not temporary."[805]

Therefore, DOL guidance indicates that temporary labor certification may be granted for tree planters or related reforestation workers, even if the H-2B beneficiaries will be employed for the majority of the year by accepting continuous assignments in multiple states and even if the wages are based on a piece rate.[806] DOL will evaluate whether the job opportunity is temporary "by examining the employer's need for such workers for the duration of the itinerary."[807] In addition, the general prohibition on an employment period of longer than 10 months based on a peakload need remains applicable and "will not be certified" by DOL.[808] For seasonal, recurring employment for a period longer than 10 months, the employer must demonstrate through "compelling evidence … that the employer's need for such work and the job opportunity itself are not ongoing or otherwise permanent."[809]

In addition, the job opportunity may entail payment of wages "on a piece rate basis," as long as the employer "also guarantee[s] the required hourly wage rate per pay period."[810] This means that the employer must supplement the wage to pay the hourly wage if the worker's piece rate earnings, averaged for the duration of the pay period, were not at least equal to the hourly wage.[811] If the pay scale will be on a piece rate basis, then "the job offer must identify the piece rate, the length of the pay period and the ending day of the week of the payroll period and date, and the minimum productivity required for job retention."[812]

2. Temporary Labor Certification Applications Filed by Farm Labor Contractors

Temporary labor certification may be requested by a Farm Labor Contractor (FLC) for these tree planting and reforestation occupations,[813] whereas these parties would be precluded from certification for other H-2B occupations since the H-2B classification is for temporary nonagricultural services or labor.[814] Such an FLC must meet the MSPA definition of a Farm Labor Contractor (FLC): "[A]ny person … who for any money or other valuable consideration paid or promised to be paid, performs … recruiting, soliciting, hiring, employing, furnishing, and/or transporting workers.[815] However, the following entities may not be FLCs:

---

[805] Id.

[806] Id.

[807] Id.

[808] Id.

[809] Id.

[810] 72 Fed. Reg. 36504 (July 3, 2007).

[811] Id.

[812] Id.

[813] Id.

[814] 8 CFR §214.2(h)(1)(ii)(D).

[815] 72 Fed. Reg. 36504 (July 3, 2007).

Copyright © 2017. American Immigration Lawyers Association. All rights reserved.

An "[a]gricultural employer," which is "any person who owns or operates a farm, ranch, processing establishment, cannery, gin, packing shed, or nursery, or who produces or conditions seed";

An "[a]gricultural association," which is "any nonprofit or cooperative association of farmers, growers, or ranchers incorporated or qualified under applicable State law";

An employee of an agricultural employer; and

An employee of an agricultural association.[816]

In addition, the FLC "must register as a[n] FLC with the Department of Labor's Employment Standards Administration (ESA) before filing an H-2B application for workers who will be performing predominantly manual work, which includes, but is not limited to, tree planting, brush clearing, and precommercial tree thinning."[817] The FLC must also, at the time of filing the temporary labor certification application, "provide proof of current registration, including proof of the registration of any Farm Labor Contractor Employees" (FLCEs) employed when the application is filed,[818] as discussed below. The certificate(s) of registration for the FLC and for any FLCEs "must be valid for the entire period of need."[819] In the event that either or both certificates will expire "at any point during the period of need," then the FLC "must submit a signed written assurance that an application for renewing FLC and FLCE certificate(s) will be submitted timely to ESA in order to attempt to ensure that the certificate(s) are valid during the entire period of need."[820]

An FLCE is defined as a "person ... who is not an independent farm labor contractor who would be required to register under the Act in his own right" and as a person who performs activities to solicit, recruit, furnish, hire, employ, and/or transport "solely on behalf of" an FLC, who in turn holds a valid registration certificate.[821] If the proposed employer "is not properly registered as a FLC," then the application will be rejected: "[T]he SWA must promptly return the application with a notification that the SWA cannot accept a job opportunity for a reforestation related occupation when the employer is not registered as a FLC."[822]

A registered FLC has the following additional responsibilities:

- To state in the temporary labor certification application "[e]ach facility or real property used to house and each vehicle used to transport workers";

- To obtain authorization to use the "[h]ousing and transport vehicles for MSPA-covered workers ... on the FLC's certificate of registration prior to use";

---

[816] *Id.*

[817] *Id.*

[818] *Id. See also* 74 Fed. Reg. 45906 (Sept. 4, 2009).

[819] 72 Fed. Reg. 36504 (July 3, 2007). *See also* 74 Fed. Reg. 45906 (Sept. 4, 2009).

[820] 72 Fed. Reg. 36504 (July 3, 2007).

[821] *Id.*

[822] *Id.*

Copyright © 2017. American Immigration Lawyers Association. All rights reserved.

- To obtain an FLC or FLCE certification of registration for "[e]ach driver of a vehicle transporting MSPA-covered workers … that specifically authorizes driving"; and

- To "submit a signed, written assurance that all registrations, permits, and/or other required licenses for vehicles, housing, or drivers will remain valid during the entire period of use."[823]

An FLC is permitted to file either "a single master application covering multiple itineraries or separate applications for each itinerary where the tree planting or related reforestation work will begin."[824] An FLC may also file an application for a multi-state itinerary, as discussed below. If the FLC wishes to file a single master application for multiple itineraries, then the following conditions apply:

- "[T]he master application must be filed with the SWA where the largest number of job opportunities is being requested as stipulated on the itineraries," and DOL will "examin[e] the starting locations of each itinerary";

- A master application may not be filed if the assignment "crosses NPC jurisdictions as well," because if the itineraries stipulate worksites that are located in both NPC jurisdictions, then the application must be processed by "the NPC that has jurisdiction over the SWA where the employment will begin";

- The H-2B employees must work "for a single employer"; and

- The start dates of the H-2B assignments for each of the beneficiaries "cannot be more than 14 calendar days apart."[825]

Multi-state itineraries may not include Hawaii, Alaska, or the U.S. territories, and worksite locations that cross multiple SWAs "must be contiguous or located within close geographic proximity to one another," because itineraries with worksites in "widely separated geographic areas … are not normal to reforestation occupations and will not be permitted," in part because DOL then finds it difficult to establish the unavailability of U.S. workers.[826] If the employer desires temporary labor certification for H-2B workers for "one or more remote 'downstream' states," then individual temporary labor certifications must be filed.[827]

The following conditions apply for a master application covering multiple worksites:

- If the worksites are located in multiple SWAs, then the FLC should submit the master application "to the SWA where the itinerant employment will begin";

---

[823] Id.

[824] Id.

[825] Id.

[826] Id.

[827] Id.

Copyright © 2017. American Immigration Lawyers Association. All rights reserved.

- If the worksites are located in multiple SWAs, but the start dates for each assignment are identical, then the master application may be submitted "to any one of the SWAs covered by the itinerary"; and

- If the worksites are located in multiple SWAs that also are located in different NPC jurisdictions, then the master application must be filed with "the NPC that has jurisdiction over the SWA where the employment will begin."[828]

When requesting temporary labor certification for these reforestation occupations, the employer must provide "a signed and dated itinerary," including the following information:

- The employer's name;

- The employer's physical address and telephone number at each worksite, but if the physical address and/or telephone number are unavailable, then "the employer must provide as much geographic detail as possible (*e.g.*, county/city/township/state corresponding to the itinerary time-frame) regarding the location of the crews performing the work";

- The "wages offered in each worksite location";

- The total number of teams to be placed at each worksite;

- The "total number of workers in each crew" to be placed at each worksite; and

- "The estimated start and end dates of work in each worksite location,"[829] as discussed below.

Importantly, DOL recognized that these occupations "are dependent on climatic conditions" and acknowledged that the proposed H-2B employment period may not be "precise" because "subsequent contracts may not be defined at the time of placing a job order."

3. Filing the Temporary Labor Certification Application

Temporary labor certification applications for tree planting and reforestation occupations must be filed with the Chicago NPC[830] or through iCert.[831] Processing of temporary labor certification applications for these occupations does not differ from regular processing, except that DOL may establish special procedures "when employers can demonstrate, upon written application to the OFLC Administrator, that special procedures are necessary."[832]

When filing the temporary labor certification, the following documents and information should also be provided:

---

[828] *Id.*

[829] *Id.*

[830] 73 Fed. Reg. 78020 (Dec. 19, 2008).

[831] 77 Fed. Reg. 59670 (Sept. 28, 2012).

[832] *Id.*

Copyright © 2017. American Immigration Lawyers Association. All rights reserved.

- If the application will be filed by an agent, then "a copy of the 'Agent Agreement' or similar document to substantiate that specific authority has been granted to the agent" must also be provided;

- If the agent also qualifies as an FLC, then proof of registration must be submitted, as discussed above:

- "If the employer is represented by an attorney, the attorney must file a Notice of Appearance (G-28) with the application package";

- "[M]aximum number of hours required for overtime," with overtime pay at time and a half; and

- Production standards, with supplemental evidence, such as "past production records, improved equipment, [and] statement of how terrain will impact production rate," if the standard will be "higher than the prevailing practice in the industry."[833]

DOL will "review all itineraries to ensure each is normal to tree planting and related reforestation occupations," such as whether "it is prevailing practice to start in a particular area" and whether the type of itinerary is "normal for contracts and the H-2B program."[834] The practitioner may consider the new definition of normal as "not uncommon," as discussed above. Although the former special processing stated that the SWA would perform this review, the review is now conducted by the Chicago NPC.

The job order and advertisements should include the same information as for other H-2B applications, as well as the following:

- Direction to potential applicants to report or send résumés to the SWA for referral to the employer;

- Address of the local SWA office;

- Job order number for reference;

- Job description, including itinerary summary;

- Total number of job openings;

- "Starting locations and wages at each crew's starting location," if applicable;

- Availability of any benefits, such as housing, meals, or transportation, if applicable;

- Wage offered, including any incentive wages, such as piece rate wages;

- Notification that "employees must purchase or rent tools" for the job opportunity, if applicable, as well as whether pay deductions will be taken for the cost of tools and whether the employer is related in any way to the business from which tools much be purchased or rented;

---

[833] 72 Fed. Reg. 36504 (July 3, 2007).

[834] *Id.*

Copyright © 2017. American Immigration Lawyers Association. All rights reserved.

- Housing accommodations to be provided by the employer, as well as whether pay deductions will be taken, if applicable; and

- Wage offered, including any incentive wages, such as piece rate wages;[835]

In contrast to other occupations, job-related deductions, "including housing, transportation, meals, tools, [and] safety equipment," will be reviewed "to determine if they are allowable in accordance with" the FLSA.[836] Therefore, petitioners of tree planting and reforestation occupations remain responsible for these transportation costs, because "an employer subject to the FLSA may not make deductions that would violate the FLSA."[837] In addition, the MSPA requires that "transportation, housing, and any other employee benefits to be provided and any costs to be charged for each of them must be disclosed to the workers."

DOL may request information from the "appropriate office of the ESA Wage and Hour Division" on whether the deduction is reasonable, proper, and/or the prevailing practice in the industry: "Consultation with the Wage and Hour Division is extremely important for those deductions which are for tools of the trade and other materials and services incidental to carrying on the employer's business."[838, 839]

E. Professional Athletes

A professional athlete who does not qualify for O-1 or P-1 status may seek H-2B status. "Professional athlete" is defined as "an individual who is employed as an athlete by" either of the following sports teams:

- "A team that is a member of an association of six or more professional sports teams whose total combined revenues exceed $10,000,000 per year, if the association governs the conduct of its members and regulates the contests and exhibitions in which its member teams regularly engage; or

- "Any minor league team that is affiliated with such an association."[840]

Calculation of the prevailing wage for professional athletes may also differ from other H-2B temporary labor certification applications; if "the job opportunity is covered by professional sports league rules or regulations," then the wage stated in the rules or regulations is the prevailing wage.[841] Temporary labor certification

---

[835] 72 Fed. Reg. 36504 (July 3, 2007).

[836] *Id.* In the H-2A context, employers must "provide to the worker, without charge, all tools, supplies and equipment necessary to complete the job." 75 Fed. Reg. 6884 (Feb. 12, 2010); 74 Fed. Reg. 45906 (Sept. 4, 2009). *Cf.* "Wage & Hour Division H-2B Workers' Rights Cards," AILA Doc. No. 09090266. The information is translated from Spanish into English in the document.

[837] 73 Fed. Reg. 78120 (Dec. 19, 2008).

[838] 72 Fed. Reg. 36504 (July 3, 2007).

[839] "Wage & Hour Division H-2B Workers' Rights Cards," AILA Doc. No. 09090266. The information is translated from Spanish into English in the document.

[840] INA §212(a)(5)(A)(iii)(II); 73 Fed. Reg. 78120 (Dec. 19, 2008).

[841] INA §212(p)(2); 22 CFR §655.10(i).

Copyright © 2017. American Immigration Lawyers Association. All rights reserved.

applications for professional athletes must be directly filed with the Chicago NPC,[842] or through iCert.[843] The H-2B petition must also include a copy of the employment contract.[844]

In addition, the H-2B status of a professional athlete does not terminate upon being "traded from one organization or another organization."[845] Instead, the H-2B status and "employment authorization for the player will automatically continue for a period of 30 days after the player's acquisition by the new organization, within which time the new organization is expected to file" a new H-2B petition.[846] If the new H-2B petition is filed within 30 days, then "the professional athlete shall be deemed to be in valid H-2B status, and employment shall continue to be authorized, until the petition is adjudicated."[847] Only if a new H-2B petition is not filed within 30 days of the trade or if the new H-2B petition is denied will employment authorization be terminated.[848]

F. Entertainers

These cases are processed differently because of the "unique characteristics of the entertainment industry."[849] Legacy INS guidance indicates that the H-2B classification may be used for entertainers who do not have international or national renown and therefore do not qualify for O-1 status and for entertainers who do not "have exceptional skills in a unique or traditional art."[850] "Entertainers" include "performers and all technical and support personnel involved with a performance, including carnival workers."[851]

Temporary labor certification applications on behalf of entertainers must comply with the general regulatory requirements for a prevailing wage determination, recruitment period, recruitment requirements (SWA job order, advertisements, and notification to a union, if applicable), and preparation and submission of the recruitment report.[852] H-2B temporary labor certification applications on behalf of entertainers are no longer filed with Offices Specializing in Entertainment but instead

---

[842] 73 Fed. Reg. 11954 (Mar. 5, 2008).

[843] 77 Fed. Reg. 59670 (Sept. 28, 2012).

[844] OI 214.2.

[845] 8 CFR §214.2(h)(6)(vii).

[846] Id.

[847] Id.

[848] Id.

[849] "Special Guidelines for Processing H-2B Temporary Labor Certification in the Entertainment Industry" (May 31, 2006), AILA Doc. No. 06053190; "H-2B Temporary Labor Certification Process Stakeholder Briefing" (Sept. 2009), AILA Doc. No. 09092568.

[850] OI 214.2.

[851] "FAQs—Implementation of Final H-2B Regulations for Temporary Labor Certifications in the Entertainment Industry" (June 19, 2009), AILA Doc. No. 09063060.

[852] Id.

Copyright © 2017. American Immigration Lawyers Association. All rights reserved.

with the Chicago NPC[853] or via iCert. For paper applications, the practitioner may wish to mark the envelope "ATTN: CNPC Certifying Officer, H-2B Application for Entertainers."[854]

One exception is that "Canadian musicians who enter the U.S. to perform within a 50-mile area adjacent to the Canadian border for a period of 30 days or less are pre-certified and are not subject to these procedures," which means that the employer may file the H-2B petition with USCIS without "pre-recruitment."[855] Also qualifying for the pre-certification are "stagehands, drivers, and equipment handlers coming to the United States in connection with such musicians' employment, and such supporting workers may be included in the H-2B petition."[856] If the U.S.-Canada border follows a body of water, then the 50-mile boundary "extends inland from the United States shore of that body of water."[857] But if the musicians' service is required "for longer than 30 days, the prospective employer must file with the DOL for the required temporary labor certification and, upon receipt thereof, shall file a petition with the appropriate Service Center."[858]

The employer may file one application with an itinerary, listing "locations and duration of work in each location," as well as the prevailing wage of each worksite.[859] Just as for general prevailing wage determinations, an employer "submitting a prevailing wage determination covering itinerary locations will receive a wage determination for each location listed on the itinerary for work to be performed in that location."[860] When asked about the effect of a qualified applicant being able to work in only one state of a multi-state itinerary, DOL responded that an employer "may reject that worker, unless he is in fact willing to work for the rest of the itinerary."[861] If the employer is "willing to have [the applicant] join in only that state," then the employer may offer the applicant the position.[862] But importantly, "the certification

---

[853] *Id.* ("Employers are no longer required to submit applications for H-2B temporary employment of foreign workers to one of the Offices Specializing in Entertainment (OSEs) in New York, New York; Austin, Texas; or Sacramento, California") (emphasis in original).

[854] *Id.* The mailing address provided in this document is not the current address. The current address is: U.S. Department of Labor

Employment and Training Administration, Office of Foreign Labor Certification

Chicago National Processing Center

11 West Quincy Court

Chicago, IL 60604-2105.

[855] *Id.*; AFM 31.5(c)(3).

[856] AFM 31.5(c)(3).

[857] *Id.*

[858] *Id.*

[859] "FAQs—Implementation of Final H-2B Regulations for Temporary Labor Certifications in the Entertainment Industry," AILA Doc. No. 09063060.

[860] *Id.*

[861] *Id.*

[862] *Id.*

Copyright © 2017. American Immigration Lawyers Association. All rights reserved.

will be reduced accordingly for the entire itinerary."[863] The practitioner should discuss the impact of this reduction on the overall itinerary, as it may be difficult to find one qualified applicant in each state of the itinerary to compensate for the diminution.

G. Emergency Boilermakers

Temporary labor certification applications for emergency boilermakers have special procedures because the need arises from "emergencies ... generally precipitated by unscheduled outages in utility, petro-chemical and paper industries."[864] The National Association of Construction Boilermaker Employers and the International Brotherhood of Boilermakers coordinated with DOL and USCIS for expedited processing of these petitions,[865] on behalf of workers "from the Canadian boilermaker's union when there are insufficient U.S. boilermakers to meet contract needs."[866] Although the Manpower Optimization Stabilization and Training Fund (MOST) in Kansas City, Kansas, "will not be the petitioner" or the signatory on H-2B petitions, it will "serve[] as the clearinghouse for the employers and workers and will submit all of the paperwork required for temporary labor certification and [H-2B] petition approval."[867]

Processing of temporary labor certification applications for these occupations does not differ from regular processing, except that DOL may establish special procedures "when employers can demonstrate, upon written application to the OFLC Administrator, that special procedures are necessary."[868] The temporary labor certification applications must be filed directly with the Chicago NPC[869] or via iCert.

Individual temporary labor certification applications and H-2B petitions must be filed for each employer.[870] Similarly, individual H-2B petitions, including a copy of the approved temporary labor certification application, are required if the beneficiaries will seek U.S. admission at different ports of entry.[871] The H-2B petition need not include the names or qualifications of the Canadian boilermaker beneficiaries.[872] As stated by USCIS guidance:

> "Service center directors shall expedite adjudication of such petitions under emergent procedures.... On approval, [USCIS] shall send the petition to the

---

[863] Id.

[864] 60 Fed. Reg. 7216 (Feb. 7, 1995), AILA Doc. No. 95020730; "H-2B Temporary Labor Certification Process Stakeholder Briefing" (Sept. 2009), AILA Doc. No. 09092568.

[865] OI 214.2.

[866] AFM 31.5(j).

[867] Id.

[868] 73 Fed Reg. 78020 (Dec. 19, 2008).

[869] 73 Fed. Reg. 11954 (Mar. 5, 2008).

[870] AFM 31.5(j).

[871] Id.

[872] Id.

Copyright © 2017. American Immigration Lawyers Association. All rights reserved.

designated port of entry. MOST will provide the port of entry the names and evidence of the qualifications of beneficiaries before they apply for admission. The port director shall be responsible for nonimmigrant control. When an approved petition involves replacement, MOST will provide the port with the names of beneficiaries to be replaced, the date they departed the United States, and the names and evidence of the qualifications of new beneficiaries who will apply for admission."[873]

H. Seafood Workers

While seafood workers do not fall into the category of special processing, there are provisions regarding their admission dates that are unique to this group. DOL generally requires that, when an employer has more than one date of need in its season, it must file a separate temporary labor certification application for each separate date of need.[874] However, employers in the seafood industry may bring in H-2B workers on a staggered basis,[875] namely at any time during the 120 days beginning on the start date of need on the temporary labor certification.[876]

It is important to note, however, that if a seafood worker is to enter the United States in the period 90 to 120 days after the certified start date of need, the employer must conduct a new test of the labor market during the period that begins at least 45 days after the certified start date of need and ends before the 90th day after the certified start date of need. That test requires listing the job in local newspapers on two separate Sundays, placing new job orders with the SWA, posting the job opportunity at the place of employment for at least 10 days, and offering the job to an equally or better qualified U.S. worker applicant who will be available at the time and place of need.[877]

The employer does not need to file anything with DOL at this point, but the employer must have signed, when filing the initial labor certification application, DOL's attestation form[878] certifying that it will comply with this requirement. It also must provide each H-2B worker with a copy of the signed form to present to DOS when applying for a visa and/or to CBP upon applying for admission into the United States. Seafood industry employers must retain the additional recruitment documentation with its other required recruitment documentation for three years from the date of certification.[879]

---

[873] *Id.*

[874] 20 CFR §655.15(f); 80 Fed. Reg. 24042, 24060 (Apr. 29, 2015).

[875] Consolidated Appropriations Act of 2017, Pub. Law No. 115–31, §108.

[876] 20 CFR §655.15(f)(1).

[877] 20 CFR §655.15(f)(2)

[878] DOL, "Attestation for Employers Seeking Staggered Border Crossings of H-2B Nonimmigrants Working in the Seafood Industry" (exp. Dec. 31, 2018), https://www.foreignlaborcert.doleta.gov/pdf/2015_Seafood_Attestation.pdf.

[879] 20 CFR §655.15(f)(3).

Copyright © 2017. American Immigration Lawyers Association. All rights reserved.

Seafood is defined as "fresh or saltwater finfish, crustaceans, other forms of aquatic animal life, including, but not limited to, alligator, frog, aquatic turtle, jellyfish, sea cucumber, and sea urchin and the roe of such animals, and all mollusks."[880]

V. Forms and Filing Packages

A. Prevailing Wage Determination

As discussed above, the employer must obtain a prevailing wage determination (PWD) from the National Prevailing Wage Center (NPWC)[881] on Form ETA-9141, the Prevailing Wage Determination Request (PWDR).[882] "Electronic filing is strongly recommended," and is done through DOL's iCert portal.[883] The PWDR also may be filed by mail.[884] The physical form is available as a document online,[885] together with instructions.[886]

1. Parts A through C

The H-2B visa classification, requestor (practitioner) information, and employer information should be provided. The FEIN is the employer's tax identification number from the Internal Revenue Service (IRS).[887] The North American Industry Classification System (NAICS) code should "best describe[] the employer's business, not the alien's job,"[888] and may be identified online.[889]

2. Part D

The choices here are to identify the source for the prevailing wage. It is rare that an ACWIA wage will apply to an H-2B and, as discussed earlier, DBA and SCA wages cannot be used for H-2Bs. Also as discussed, if the position is covered by a collective bargaining agreement, the amount in that agreement will be the prevailing wage.

---

[880] 20 CFR §655.5.

[881] 20 CFR §655.10(c).

[882] 20 CFR §655.5, definition of Prevailing Wage Determination (PWD).

[883] DOL, "Welcome to the iCERT Visa Portal System," https://icert.doleta.gov/.

[884] "National Prevailing Wage and Helpdesk Center Prevailing Wage Frequently Asked Questions" (Mar. 2010), AILA Doc. No. 10032662.

[885] Department of Labor (DOL), "Application for Prevailing Wage Determination," https://www.foreignlaborcert.doleta.gov/pdf/ETA_Form_9141.pdf.

[886] DOL, "ETA Form 9141—General Instructions for the 9141," http://www.foreignlaborcert.doleta.gov/pdf/ETA_Form_9141_General_Instructions.pdf.

[887] Id.

[888] Id.

[889] U.S. Census Bureau, "North American Industry Classification System (NAICS)," http://www.census.gov/eos/www/naics/.

Copyright © 2017. American Immigration Lawyers Association. All rights reserved.

As also discussed earlier under "Prevailing Wage," circumstances under which an employer-provided survey can be used are usually limited. If a survey is being submitted for consideration, the employer must also file Form ETA-9165.[890]

If the answer is "no" to all of the choices, DOL will use the OES wage survey.

3. Part E

Information about the proposed job should be provided. The job title in #1 is the internal title used by the employer. The "suggested" SOC code and occupation title for #2 and #2a may be identified from the Foreign Labor Certification Data Center Online Wage Library, available at *www.flcdatacenter.com*, by selecting the FLC Wage Search Wizard, the state of intended employment from the drop-down menu, the county of intended employment, and the job code from the drop-down list (or searching by keyword). As stated by DOL: "The number on the left is the SOC code and the title to the right is the Occupation Title."[891] The job description should be reviewed to ensure it is a good match to the job duties of the H-2B assignment.

Details about the working conditions should be provided: number of hours per workweek, including overtime, if applicable; work schedule; supervisor's job title within the company; supervisory responsibilities; and number of employees supervised by the H-2B worker(s).

The job description should detail the proposed duties and connect the activities to any job requirements. "Pertinent working conditions" also should be included here.[892]

The practitioner may also wish to include the job requirements in this section as well as in Part E, Section b. The "Job Duties" section should also be used to request any special processing for a particular industry.[893]

Specifically, for special processing requests, "after the description of the job duties, include the following statement surrounded by asterisks: '***This position is for H-2B temporary employment in the <particular H-2B special procedure industry>. An itinerary is attached.***'"[894] The itinerary in turn "must include the following" information:

- "The place of employment with full address if available; use the name of the area covered if there is no street address such as George Washington National Forest;

- "The county of equivalent for that address;

---

[890] DOL, "Employer-Provided Survey Attestations to Accompany H-2B Prevailing Wage Determination Request Based on a Non-OES Survey" (exp. Dec. 31, 2018), https://www.foreignlaborcert.doleta.gov/pdf/Form_ETA-9165_rev_DOL_Appropriations_Act.pdf.

[891] "FAQs on H-2B Final Rule: Round One" (Apr. 20, 2009), AILA Doc. No 09042066.

[892] DOL, "ETA Form 9141—General Instructions for the 9141," http://www.foreignlaborcert. doleta.gov/pdf/ETA_Form_9141_General_Instructions.pdf.

[893] "National Prevailing Wage and Helpdesk Center Prevailing Wage Frequently Asked Questions" (Mar. 2010), AILA Doc. No. 10032662; "National Prevailing Wage and Helpdesk Center Prevailing Wage Frequently Asked Questions" (Dec. 2009), AILA Doc. No. 10010466.

[894] *Id.*

Copyright © 2017. American Immigration Lawyers Association. All rights reserved.

- "Any additional work sites in that area;
- "The begin and end dates for each work site"; and
- On each page, the employer's name, trade or d/b/a name, if applicable; job title; and date of the PWDR, as this information is stated on the actual PWDR itself.[895]

Travel may be required, for example, if the assignment requires visiting client worksites, but if so, the travel should be described in Question 6a. If the travel rises to the level of there being different worksites, the prevailing wage should be calculated based on these multiple worksites, as discussed above, and Part C should be completed for each site.

The job requirements section should be completed as discussed in Volume 2: Chapter Two, "The Labor Certification Application." The practitioner should be aware that a requirement of more than one diploma or degree may be considered to be restrictive, as discussed above. In addition, training should not include a duplication of educational or experience requirements: "Training may include, but is not limited to: programs, coursework, or training experience (other than employment)."[896]

The worksite information should be provided, even if the worksite is the same as the company headquarters stated in Part C. As noted above, multiple worksite information, including MSAs,[897] should be provided.

B. Temporary Labor Certification Application

The temporary labor certification application can be filed on Form ETA-9142B through the DOL's iCert system,[898] or by mail or overnight courier to:[899]

> U.S. Department of Labor
> Employment and Training Administration
> Office of Foreign Labor Certification
> Chicago National Processing Center
> 11 West Quincy Court
> Chicago, IL 60604-2105
> Attn: H-2B Application

If the application is filed by mail, it must contain the original signature of the employer and the attorney or agent, if there is one.[900] If filed electronically via iCert, the application is signed when the employer receives the approval.[901] The application

---

[895] Id.

[896] DOL, "ETA Form 9141—General Instructions for the 9141," http://www.foreignlaborcert. doleta.gov/pdf/ETA_Form_9141_General_Instructions.pdf.

[897] Id.

[898] DOL, "Welcome to the iCERT Visa Portal System," https://icert.doleta.gov/.

[899] DOL, "H-2B Temporary Non-agricultural Program" (updated Oct. 4, 2016), https://www. foreignlaborcert.doleta.gov/2015_H-2B_IFR.cfm.

[900] 20 CFR §655.15(d).

[901] Id.; 20 CFR §655.52.

Copyright © 2017. American Immigration Lawyers Association. All rights reserved.

must be accompanied by a copy of the job order that is being submitted concurrently to the SWA, a valid prevailing wage determination, Appendix B, and copies of all contracts or agreements with agents or recruiters used in connection with the positions.[902]

1. Parts A and B

Indicate in Part A that the application is for the H-2B classification.

The job title in #1 in Part B is the internal title used by the employer. The SOC Code and Occupation Title are stated on the issued PWD.[903] The position must be full time to qualify, as previously discussed. Also see discussion earlier in the chapter regarding the period of intended employment.

The total number of workers requested must be the aggregate of each number of workers in the different types of employment, with "0" marked in boxes as applicable.[904] Certain types of employment may, however, be more likely to be denied, as these categories are similar to the ones stated on the Form I-129. If an employer requests "[c]ontinuation of previously approved employment without change with the same employer," and the total employment period exceeds nine months, then temporary labor certification may be denied, as discussed above. Such a continuation might also be construed as permanent employment, rather than the temporary period that is required for H-2B assignments. Similarly, "[n]ew concurrent employment" may be rare for practical reasons; all job opportunities must be full time, as discussed above, and DOL may consider it unlikely that a worker would hold two full-time jobs, even though the form does not require the proposed workers to be named.

"Change in previously approved employment" may be appropriate, for example, where the employer's previous intermittent need developed into a seasonal need. "Change in employer" is for foreign nationals who hold valid H-2B status for employment with another company and who wish to extend H-2B status in order to be employed with a second company.

It remains unclear which workers would be stated for an "[a]mended petition." USCIS permits amended petitions to be filed to substitute H-2B beneficiaries, as discussed above, but that is a process separate from the temporary labor certification. The temporary labor certification application form may be amended in certain circumstances, but those minor revisions do not constitute an amended petition, as discussed above. The practitioner is advised to mark this box "0" until further clarification is provided by DOL.

---

[902] 20 CFR §655.15(a).

[903] For a discussion of how to identify this information before a PWD is obtained, see Volume 2: Chapter Two, "The Labor Certification Application."

[904] DOL, "Instructions to Form ETA 9142B" (exp. Dec. 31, 2018) https://www.foreignlaborcert. doleta.gov/pdf/ETA_Form_9142B_General_Instructions.pdf.

Copyright © 2017. American Immigration Lawyers Association. All rights reserved.

As discussed previously, the item 9 "[s]tatement of temporary need" should "clearly explain the nature of the employer's business or operations, why the job opportunity and number of workers being requested for certification reflect a temporary need, and how the request … meets one of the four DHS regulatory standards of temporary need."[905] In essence, the practitioner should produce on this form the contents of what is planned to be submitted to USCIS at the petitioning stage. Detail is necessary on the form, because DOL no longer asks the employer to submit documentation of temporary need with the application. [906]

Item 9 is likely to change once DOL has implemented the employer registration, discussed earlier in this chapter.

2. Part C

The employer name and contact information should be provided, and the FEIN is an absolute requirement, as discussed above. For a discussion of how to identify the appropriate NAICS code for the employer's business, see Volume 2: Chapter Two, "The Labor Certification Application." Importantly, DOL cautions: "The code selected by the employer should reflect the nature of the employer's business, not the job for which certification is sought."[907]

3. Part D

As stated on the form, the name and contact information should be for an employee "who is authorized to act on behalf of the employer in labor certification matters."[908] It is inappropriate for the attorney to provide his or her own contact details in this section and in Part E, unless the attorney is also an employee of the company.

4. Part E

If the employer was assisted or will be represented by an agent or attorney, then this section should be completed. As with the employer's FEIN, the FEIN for the law firm must be provided. For states that do not provide bar numbers to attorneys, "N/A" may be stated on a paper filing, or the field left blank on the electronic form.[909]

5. Part F

This section requires information about the job duties and requirements, as well as the work locations. As discussed above, the hours of overtime required must be completed, with pay at time-and-a-half. DOL may review the work schedules to ensure that they are normal to the occupation. The job description should also include

---

[905] DOL, "H-2B Temporary Nonimmigrant Visa Program/Announcement of Procedural Change to Streamline the H-2B Process for Non-Agricultural Employers: Submission of Documentation Demonstrating 'Temporary Need'" (Sept. 1, 2016), http://bit.ly/h2btempdoc.

[906] *Id.*

[907] "FAQs on H-2B Final Rule: Round One," AILA Doc. No 09042066.

[908] DOL, "Instructions to Form ETA 9142B" (exp. Dec. 31, 2018) https://www.foreignlaborcert. doleta.gov/pdf/ETA_Form_9142B_General_Instructions.pdf.

[909] *Id.*

Copyright © 2017. American Immigration Lawyers Association. All rights reserved.

discussion of "any equipment to be used and pertinent working conditions."[910] If there will be multiple worksites, they should all be listed and the list continued on a separate form if necessary. Contractors sending workers to multiple worksites and/or filing under one of the special procedures should list the first worksite on items 1-7 and include an attachment providing the business names and addresses of all physical locations where work will be performed. Item 7a should give the business name for the first worksite and then say "see attached worksites."[911]

6. Part G

The information on the wage offered should be identical to the PWD obtained previously. DOL stated that "employers are *strongly encouraged* to list all valid prevailing wage determinations … in support of the application as well as all corresponding wage offers."[912]

7. Part H

The details of the recruiting efforts should be provided here, with dates in the format of MM/DD/YYYY. For advertisements that ran for only one day, the same date should be stated in the "From" and "To" boxes.[913]

8. Part I and Appendix B

The H-2B employer should check "N/A" for #1. The second question, which should be marked "Yes," entails the attestations discussed above. The attestations are also stated in Appendix B, which must be signed and dated by the employer and the attorney or agent.[914]

9. Preparer

This section is completed only if the application was prepared by someone other than the employer point of contact or the attorney or agent.

C. H-2B Petition

The approved temporary labor certification application should be filed, together with the H-2B petition, in duplicate, with original signatures,[915] with the USCIS Service Center with jurisdiction over the place of employment (and not the headquarters of the U.S. company, if different), as discussed in Volume 1: Chapter Two, "Basic Nonimmigrant Concepts." The practitioner may also find it helpful to write the following in large block letters across the side of the Form I-129: "DUPLICATE PETITION; PLEASE FORWARD TO KCC."

---

[910] *Id.*

[911] *Id.*

[912] *Id.* (emphasis in original).

[913] *Id.*

[914] DOL, "Form ETA-9042B, Appendix B" (exp. Dec. 31, 2018), https://www.foreignlaborcert. doleta.gov/pdf/ETA_Form_9142B_APPENDIX.pdf.

[915] "TSC Liaison Minutes" (Aug. 13, 2000), AILA Doc. No. 00090703.

Copyright © 2017. American Immigration Lawyers Association. All rights reserved.

The second set of original documents will be forwarded to the U.S. consulate where the beneficiary will apply for an H-2B visa as supplementary evidence for the Petition Information Management Service (PIMS), as discussed in Volume 1: Chapter Two, "Basic Nonimmigrant Concepts."[916] Following approval of an H-2B petition, USCIS forwards approval notification to the Kentucky Consular Center (KCC), which in turn creates an electronic record to confirm the petition approval,[917] so that the information becomes available to a consular officer to verify the petition approval. Although duplicate original documents are not required, preparing and providing them may facilitate the foreign national's visa application in the future.[918]

The following documents should be submitted:

- Cover letter;

- Form G-28;

- Form I-907, if applicable;

- Form I-129;

- Supplement H;

- Support statement from U.S. company, including an explanation of the basis for the temporary need;

- Supplemental evidence of temporary need;

- Approved temporary labor certification;

- Evidence that the foreign national meets the minimum requirements for the job opening as stated on the temporary labor certification, if applicable, such as "employment letters and training certificates, showing that each named alien met the minimum job requirements stated in the certification at the time the application was filed";[919]

- Evidence of the foreign national's lawful immigration status, if applicable;

- Fraud fee of $500;[920] and

- Filing fee, which at the time of this writing is $460.[921]

---

[916] DOS, "Accessing NIV Petition Information Via the CCD" (Nov. 2007), AILA Doc. No. 08040331; "PIMS Processing Update" (Mar. 21, 2008), AILA Doc. No. 08032132.

[917] "PIMS Update" (Aug. 15, 2008), AILA Doc. No. 08081564; "PIMS Processing Update" (Mar. 21, 2008), AILA Doc. No. 08032132.

[918] "PIMS Processing Update" (Mar. 21, 2008), AILA Doc. No. 08032132.

[919] USCIS, "Instructions for Form I-129, Petition for a Nonimmigrant Worker" (exp. Dec. 31, 2018), https://www.uscis.gov/sites/default/files/files/form/i-129instr.pdf (discussing evidence of possessing the required minimum qualifications). For further discussion of evidence of possessing minimum qualifications, see Volume 2: Chapters Two and Three, "The Labor Certification Application" and "The Immigrant Visa Petition," respectively.

[920] USCIS, "Instructions for Form I-129, Petition for a Nonimmigrant Worker" (exp. Dec. 31, 2018), https://www.uscis.gov/sites/default/files/files/form/i-129instr.pdf (discussing the fraud fee).

[921] USCIS, "Our Fees" (updated Jan. 5, 2017), https://www.uscis.gov/forms/our-fees.

Copyright © 2017. American Immigration Lawyers Association. All rights reserved.

For the temporary labor certification application, the practitioner should "submit all pages including [the] final determination letter from DOL."[922] The labor certification must bear the original signatures of the employer and the attorney or agent.[923]

USCIS guidance indicates that the petitioner's ability to pay the wage offered may also be evaluated when an H-2B petition is adjudicated:

"This issue is most commonly associated with small enterprises that do not necessarily have the assets required to pay the salary guaranteed in the petition. Such a petition may be an accommodation to a relative or friend who will seek other employment or there may be an agreement to work for lower wages.

"It is not necessary that complete financial data be submitted with every petition. However, if the financial condition of the petitioner calls into question whether the petitioner really intends to employ the alien as claimed, evidence of financial ability may be requested at the discretion of the adjudicating officer in order to determine whether there exists a bona fide job offer.

"Other factors that may be examined include, but are not limited to, the nature of the petitioner's business, the relationship between the beneficiary and the owners/officers of the petitioning entity, and the petitioner and beneficiary's immigration histories."[924]

For further discussion of the ability to pay the wage, see Volume 2: Chapter Three, "The Immigrant Visa Petition."

USCIS may provide partial petition approval:

"A partial approval can occur with petitions for multiple beneficiaries when only some of the beneficiaries included on the petition are found to be approvable and some must be denied. For example, a partial approval may result in cases where a petition is filed for a combination of beneficiaries from H-2B eligible and non-eligible countries and the petitioner is unable to provide sufficient evidence in response to a USCIS request for evidence that the beneficiaries from non-eligible countries meet the U.S. interest requirements."[925]

1. Form G-28

If the petition is being submitted without a request for action on a beneficiary's status, such as a request for change or extension or status, the petition is exclusively that of the employer, and thus the U.S. company's information is what is provided in Questions 5 through 12 on the Form G-28. If a change or extension of status is also being requested for the beneficiary, and the attorney is also representing the

---

[922] "VSC Helpful Filing Tips" (Aug. 12, 2009), AILA Doc. No. 09112363.

[923] USCIS, "H-2A and H-2B Signature Requirement for Electronically Filed Temporary Labor Certifications and the H Classification Supplement to Form I-129" (May 4, 2013), AILA Doc. No, 13040440.

[924] AFM 31.5(k)(1).

[925] AFM 31.5(h)(3).

Copyright © 2017. American Immigration Lawyers Association. All rights reserved.

beneficiary, a separate G-28 should be submitted for him or her, and Questions 5 through 12 should be completed with the beneficiary's information on that form. The instructions require that signatures be in black.[926] In practice, however, the USCIS mailroom sometimes rejects forms signed in black ink because the signatures are incorrectly concluded to be photocopies, so signing in blue ink can be beneficial despite the USCIS instructions.

If there is limited time to prepare and file the petition before the U.S. assignment is to begin, such as if the forms are emailed to and printed out by the client, this form may be printed on plain white paper. However, as discussed in Volume 1: Chapter Two, "Basic Nonimmigrant Concepts," the Forms G-28 should be printed on blue paper whenever possible, in order to avoid processing delays.[927]

2. Form I-907

If the client wishes a response (approval, denial, or RFE) within 15 calendar days, then the client may pay USCIS an additional $1,225 for premium processing. This request may be filed concurrently with the H-2B petition, or the attorney or the client may request premium processing after the petition has been filed, by submitting Form I-907 with the petition's receipt notice, as discussed in Volume 1: Chapter Two, "Basic Nonimmigrant Concepts."

3. Form I-129

Part 1: Information on the U.S. company, including name, address, contact person, contact person's telephone number and email address, and Federal Employer Identification Number (FEIN), should be provided.

Part 2: For most H-2B petitions, "New employment" should be checked and consular notification should be requested, as discussed above. As discussed in Volume 1: Chapter Two, "Basic Nonimmigrant Concepts," USCIS should then notify the KCC, and the consulate abroad should then be able confirm petition approval when the foreign national applies for an H-2B visa.

Change of status may be requested on behalf of foreign nationals who hold lawful immigration status in the United States, as discussed above. In addition, the expiration date of the foreign national's current status should be calendared, so that a request to extend status may be timely filed. Ideally, the H-2B change of status petition will be approved before the beneficiary's underlying status expires, and premium processing may make this scenario possible. The practitioner may wish to advise the client on the intricacies of situations in which the initial status expires before the change of status petition is approved, as discussed in Volume 1: Chapter Two, "Basic Nonimmigrant Concepts." For more information on the eligibility requirements for change of status, accrual on unlawful presence, and filing an

---

[926] "Instructions for Notice of Entry of Appearance as Attorney or Accredited Representative" (exp. Mar. 31, 2018), https://www.uscis.gov/sites/default/files/files/form/g-28instr.pdf.

[927] VSC Practice Pointer: G-28s (Sept. 4, 2008), AILA Doc. No. 08090469.

Copyright © 2017. American Immigration Lawyers Association. All rights reserved.

extension while a change of status petition is pending, see Volume 1: Chapter Two, "Basic Nonimmigrant Concepts."

The total number of H-2B workers cannot exceed the number of workers approved on the temporary labor certification.

Parts 3 and 4: Information about the beneficiar(ies), including name, alternate names, date of birth, country of birth, country of birth and country of nationality, and passport information, should be provided. If there will be multiple named beneficiaries, then the practitioner should complete the Attachment 1 sheet with the required information. Names should be alphabetized and "should be listed as they appear on passport."[928] The practitioner is encouraged to use a larger font when listing multiple beneficiaries on an addendum.[929] If there will be multiple unnamed beneficiaries, then "N/A – Multiple Unnamed Beneficiaries" may be typed in the box for "Family Name," and Attachment 1 with the nationalities of the unnamed beneficiaries should be provided as well. However, as discussed above, if the petition covers any workers who are nationals of a country not designated to participate in the H-2B program, or if the beneficiary is in the United States, the beneficiary must be named.[930]

An individual must have a passport that is valid for at least six months from the petition's expiration date; otherwise, he or she is inadmissible and ineligible for nonimmigrant status.[931] If the beneficiary does not have such a passport, then the following options are available: either delay filing the H-2B petition until he or she obtains a renewed passport, or file the petition, have the beneficiary apply for a renewed passport in the interim, wait for an RFE, and then submit a photocopy of the biographic page of the renewed passport once it is available. For nationals of countries where passport renewal takes months, the second strategy can prevent the petition from being significantly delayed. If the client is willing to pay an additional $1,225 fee to USCIS, the delay caused by the RFE, which might also be several months, can be addressed by requesting premium processing when submitting the documentation of the renewed passport.

If the beneficiary is present in the United States when the petition is filed, then the I-94 card information should be provided, even if he or she will depart the United States during pendency of the petition. In this case, consular notification should be requested in Part 2, as discussed above. But it is no longer necessary to request cable notification to multiple U.S. consulates if there are multiple H-2B beneficiaries,

---

[928] "VSC Helpful Filing Tips" (Aug. 12, 2009), AILA Doc. No. 09112363.

[929] "TSC Liaison Teleconference" (Nov. 3, 2003), AILA Doc. No. 03112544.

[930] USCIS, "Instructions for Form I-129, Petition for a Nonimmigrant Worker" (exp. Dec. 31, 2018), https://www.uscis.gov/sites/default/files/files/form/i-129instr.pdf.

[931] INA §212(a)(7)(B)(i). The exceptions to this rule in INA §212(a)(d)(4) are discussed in Volume 1: Chapter Two, "Basic Nonimmigrant Concepts."

Copyright © 2017. American Immigration Lawyers Association. All rights reserved.

because consular confirmation of petition approval is electronic through PIMS,[932] as discussed below.

Parts 5 through 7: Information about the job title, description of proposed job duties, location, compensation, and general information about the petitioner should be provided. The "LCA Case Number" is the case number assigned to the temporary labor certification by DOL. The form should be signed by the petitioner's representative and the practitioner.

4. H Supplement

Only the introduction section and Section 2 of this form need to be completed. In Section 2, Questions 1 through 3 should be very similar to the information provided on the temporary labor certification application. If any beneficiaries have previously held H or L status, then the names and periods of stay should be provided, as well as evidence such as Forms I-797 and I-94 cards.

In Section 2, the countries of citizenship of the H-2B workers should be stated in Question 4. Question 5 addresses an H-2B petition filed on behalf of beneficiaries who are not nationals of a designated country, as discussed above. If there are multiple beneficiaries in this situation, the requested information for each should be provided in an attachment. Question 6 requests information on a beneficiary's previous H-2 status and compliance "with the terms of their status."[933] Evidence of such compliance may be in the form of proof of departure from the United States and/or proof of having maintained lawful U.S. immigration status. It remains unclear whether other types of evidence are necessary, as it seems that USCIS should be more concerned with compliance with the immigration laws. As a practical matter, it is difficult to prove that an individual did not engage in any violations. For a discussion of violations of status in the context of change of status requests, extensions, and of third country national visa applications, which may have some cross-applicability, see Volume 1: Chapter Two, "Basic Nonimmigrant Concepts."

If the employer used or "plan[s] to use a staffing, recruiting, or similar placement service or agent" to identify H-2B nonimmigrants, then the name and address of the organization of the individual should be provided.[934] The remaining questions address the attestation requirements and request confirmation that the employer has not accepted any prohibited fees. If the answer to any question is "yes," then an explanation should be provided in an addendum; an explanation may also be provided in the H-2B support statement. As discussed above, the employer must reimburse the employee for transportation and visa fees, contrary to the language on the form.[935]

---

[932] "VSC Helpful Filing Tips" (Aug. 12, 2009), AILA Doc. No. 09112363.

[933] USCIS, "I-129, Petition for a Nonimmigrant Worker" (exp. Dec. 31, 2018), www.uscis.gov/files/form/i-129.pdf.

[934] *Id.*

[935] *Id.*

Copyright © 2017. American Immigration Lawyers Association. All rights reserved.

The form must be signed by the petitioner, the employer if the petitioner is a separate entity, and any joint employers, if applicable.[936]

5. Support Statement

The petitioner's support statement should summarize the basis for the temporary need and the job duties. The statement should be on the U.S. company's letterhead and signed by a representative of the U.S. company. One format of a support statement is as follows:

- Introduction;
- Information about the petitioner;
- Discussion of the temporary need;
- Discussion of the job duties and requirements;
- Discussion of the foreign national's educational and experience background, if applicable; and
- Thank you and conclusion.

The concluding paragraph may contain the necessary information of the amount of remuneration and confirmation of compliance with the terms and conditions of the H-2B program.

VI. Post-Approval Processes

A. Visa Application

Upon approval of the H-2B petition, USCIS will send the attorney or representative a Form I-797 approval notice and the company representative will receive a courtesy copy. The beneficiary applying for a visa should be given the original, or if there are multiple beneficiaries a certified copy, of the approval notice.

Following approval of the H-2B petition, the foreign national, and his or her dependent spouse and family members, if applicable, may apply for H visas at a U.S. consulate abroad. In addition to the general visa application documents discussed in Volume 1: Chapter Two, "Basic Nonimmigrant Concepts," the following documents should be presented, and individual consulates frequently have additional requirements:

- Original or certified copy of Form I-797 approval notice from USCIS;
- Statement from the petitioner confirming that the foreign national continues to perform the H-2B assignment, if the foreign national obtained change of status from another nonimmigrant category;
- Certified copy of the H-2B petition, to be presented only if specifically requested; and
- Evidence of the visa applicant's foreign residence and nonimmigrant intent.

---

[936] *Id.*

Copyright © 2017. American Immigration Lawyers Association. All rights reserved.

Because an H-2B petition must be approved by USCIS in order for a foreign national to apply for an H-2B visa, and because the "DHS regulations governing adjudication of H petitions are complex," consular officers have been directed to "rely on the expertise DHS … in this area."[937] This means that the consular officer should not readjudicate the H-2B petition, as the H-2B petition approval "is prima facie evidence of entitlement to H classification," although the consular officer may inquire about eligibility for the visa,[938] such as to confirm that the visa applicant has the proper nonimmigrant intent, as discussed above. Dependents of H-2B foreign nationals must also establish nonimmigrant intent by maintaining "a residence abroad to which they intend to return."[939] H-4 dependents are not authorized to accept employment "unless they qualify independently for a classification in which employment is, or can be, authorized."[940]

While a consular officer may rely on the Form I-797 to schedule an appointment, it cannot issue a visa until it has verified the petition approval through PIMS. "If no record of the petition is found in PIMS, [the officer] may use the Person Centric Query Service (PCQS), via the Consolidated Consular Database (CCD), to verify that the petition has been approved. If post finds a petition approval in PCQS that was is not in PIMS, then post should" notify DOS so that the KCC's Fraud Prevention Unit can research approval of the petition and, "if able to confirm its approval, will make the details available through the CCD within two working days. [An officer] may not authorize a petition-based NIV without verification of petition approval either through PIMS or through PCQS."[941]

Certain U.S. consulates may issue H-2B visas well in advance of the assignment start date, in order to manage a "possible flood of applicants" seeking visas in September,[942] although the visa application may not be made until 90 days before the employment start date.[943] Visas issued earlier than 10 days before the employment start date will be annotated with the following statement: "[N]ot valid until (ten days prior to petition validity date)."[944]

B. Admission to the United States

A foreign national may seek H-2B admission up to 10 days before the start date of the petition and may remain in the United States for 10 days after expiration of the

---

[937] 9 FAM 402.10-7(A).

[938] 9 FAM 402.10-7(B).

[939] Id.

[940] 9 FAM 402.10-14(C).

[941] 9 FAM 402.10-9(A).

[942] "DOS Cable Encourages Issuance of H-1B and H-2B Visas with Deferred Validity Dates," AILA Doc. No. 04040862.

[943] 9 FAM 402.10-11.

[944] Id.; "DOS Cable Encourages Issuance of H-1B and H-2B Visas with Deferred Validity Dates," AILA Doc. No. 04040862.

Copyright © 2017. American Immigration Lawyers Association. All rights reserved.

petition,[945] although experience has shown that, to receive the 10 days at the end, the individual must ask for it at the time of entry. It is rarely included automatically in the I-94 record. The foreign national is not authorized to work during these 10-day grace periods.[946]

When seeking admission to the United States, the foreign national should present his or her passport, with the H-2B visa, and the H-2B petition approval notice from USCIS. The foreign national should be admitted in H-2B status valid until the end date of the petition, as stated on the approval notice, plus the extra 10 days noted above, if requested. If entering by land, the foreign national will be issued an I-94 card. If entering by sea or air, the individual will receive a stamp in the passport, and the I-94 will be recorded electronically.[947] Practitioners should advise clients who receive the passport stamp rather than the paper I-94 to check their I-94s on the online look-up[948] to ensure that it is correct and that the expiration date of their status is noted.

Due to the visa reciprocity schedules,[949] as discussed in Volume 1: Chapter Two, "Basic Nonimmigrant Concepts," a foreign national may receive a visa valid for a shorter period than the H-2B petition, but the expiration of H-2B status should match the end date of the H-2B petition and not the end date of the H-2B visa.

For example, Timor-Leste citizens are eligible for H visas valid for no longer than three months. Therefore, even though the underlying petition was approved for 24 months, a citizen of Timor-Leste will be able to obtain an H visa that is valid for only three months from the date of visa issuance. The Petition Expiration Date (PED) provided in the lower right corner of the visa should, however, match the dates of validity of the petition as stated on the Form I-797 approval notice. For applicants for admission with visas valid for a shorter period than the petition, the practitioner may wish to reiterate the need to present the Form I-797 approval notice to ensure that the period of authorized stay stated on the I-94 card matches the dates of the petition validity. The practitioner may also wish to contact clients with these employees well in advance of the visa expiration date to strategize subsequent applications for visas, so that the foreign national may travel internationally and re-enter the U.S. during the remaining time of petition validity.

The CBP inspector may also "insert H-2B worker rights cards prepared [by] USDOL's Wage & Hour Division into the passports of foreign temporary seasonal workers entering the US in H-2B Status."[950] The "card provides an informative

---

[945] 8 CFR §214.2(h)(13)(i)(A); 9 FAM 402.10-12.41.53 N10.

[946] 8 CFR §214.2(h)(13)(i)(A).

[947] 78 Fed. Reg. 18457 (Mar. 27, 2013). *See also* CBP Fact Sheet, "I-94 Automation" (Nov. 2015), https://www.cbp.gov/sites/default/files/assets/documents/2016-Mar/i-94-automation-fact-sheet.pdf.

[948] CBP, "I-94 Website," https://i94.cbp.dhs.gov/I94/#/home.

[949] DOS, "Reciprocity and Civil Documents by Country," https://i94.cbp.dhs.gov/I94/#/home.

[950] "Wage & Hour Division H-2B Workers' Rights Cards," AILA Doc. No. 09090266. The information is translated from Spanish into English in the document.

Copyright © 2017. American Immigration Lawyers Association. All rights reserved.

summary about the legal protections for H-2B workers," and offers DOL's contact information of 1-866-4US-WAGE (1-866-487-9243) and *www.wagehour.dol.gov*.[951] The card notes that H-2B nonimmigrants "have at minimum the right to the same salary protections as American workers," and provides information on minimum wage payments, overtime, illegal deductions, the employer's need to maintain documentation of hours worked and wages paid, and the worker's need to "keep documentation" of hours worked, wages paid, and the name, address, and phone number of the H-2B employer.[952]

For all foreign nationals, good follow-up should include requesting copies of visas and I-94 cards to ensure that all the information is correct, and calendaring the expiration dates to monitor the foreign national's status, as discussed below.

1. Admission of H-4 Dependents in B-2 Status

The spouse and children of an H-2B nonimmigrant may also use a B visa when seeking admission to the United States, if the "planned period of stay is to be brief," or "if the spouse or child already has a valid B-2 visa and it would be inconvenient or impossible for him or her to apply for an H-4 visa."[953] The practitioner should carefully discuss this approach with the client and the foreign national, however, as the dependents should make no misrepresentation when seeking admission in B-2 status at the port of entry. In particular, the practitioner may wish to have the dependents gather evidence of the brief stay, such as round-trip airfare, enrollment or admission in educational programs in the home country or elsewhere abroad, evidence of continued employment abroad, or other evidence of the reasons why the dependents will not remain in the United States for an extended period of time.

2. Canadian and Mexican Citizens

As discussed in Volume 1: Chapter Two, "Basic Nonimmigrant Concepts," Canadian citizens do not require visas in order to enter the United States.[954] Canadian nationals may apply for admission with the H-2B approval notice and Canadian passport at the port of entry.[955] As discussed above, it is also critical to note that H-2B admission may be denied if the foreign national's admission to the United States "would adversely affect the wages and working conditions of U.S. citizens and lawful resident workers."[956] For a more in-depth discussion of applications for admission in non-immigrant status by Canadian citizens, see Volume 1: Chapter Two, "Basic Nonimmigrant Concepts."

---

[951] *Id.*

[952] *Id.*

[953] 9 FAM 402.10-14(D).

[954] 1 legacy INS Examinations Handbook, Part V, 15-1, 1 legacy INS Inspector's Field Manual (IFM) ch. 15: Nonimmigrants and Border Crossers, 14-1 INS Manuals 15.4.

[955] 9 FAM 402.10-8(F).

[956] 8 CFR §214.2(h)(17)(i).

Copyright © 2017. American Immigration Lawyers Association. All rights reserved.

Unfortunately, Mexican citizens applying for H-2B visas may no longer obtain visas valid for up to two years by paying the reciprocity fee of $100 for each year of visa validity.[957]

VII. Additional Follow-up

After a foreign national has obtained H-2B status, the practitioner should follow up to request copies of the I-94 cards and the visas, if applicable, to ensure that all the information is correct and to calendar the expiration dates to monitor the foreign national's status, as discussed in Volume 1: Chapter Two, "Basic Nonimmigrant Concepts."

A. Extensions, Renewals, and Change of Status

A foreign national who has held H-2B status for the maximum period may not seek readmission, change of status, or H-2B extension until he or she has resided outside the United States for the immediate preceding three months.[958] The practitioner should note that time in L or other H statuses (other than H-4[959]) counts toward the H-2B limitation.[960]

The exceptions to this limitation are: (1) if the H-2B nonimmigrant did not reside continually in the United States and if his or her employment was seasonal, intermittent, or for an aggregate of six months or less per year; or (2) if the temporary worker resides abroad and regularly commutes to the United States to engage in part-time employment.[961] In these situations, the H-2B maximum periods of stay may not apply, as the temporary worker may not accrue a single year in H-2B status and therefore may not be subject to the three-year limitation.[962] The exception is unavailable if the H-4 dependents have resided continuously in the United States in H-4 status.[963] For a discussion of what may qualify as "part-time employment," see Volume 1: Chapter Eleven, "L Visas and Status."

The petitioner and foreign national bear the burden to provide "clear and convincing proof" of qualifying for these exceptions: "Such proof shall consist of evidence such as arrival and departure records, copies of tax returns, and records of employment abroad."[964] The practitioner may wish to supplement these documents with copies of property titles, mortgage or lease agreements, utility bills for the foreign residence, and credit card statements for purchases made outside the United States.

---

[957] DOS, "Mexico Reciprocity Schedule," https://travel.state.gov/content/visas/en/fees/reciprocity-by-country/MX.html. *Cf.* former DOS website, "Mexico Reciprocity Schedule," formerly available at http://travel.state.gov/visa/frvi/reciprocity/reciprocity_3622.html#B (link no longer works).

[958] 8 CFR §214.2(h)(13)(iv).

[959] 9 FAM 402.10-12.

[960] *Id.*

[961] 8 CFR §214.2(h)(13)(v); 9 FAM 402.10-13(C).

[962] 8 CFR §214.2(h)(13)(v).

[963] 9 FAM 402.10-13(C).

[964] 8 CFR §214.2(h)(13)(v); 9 FAM 402.10-13(C).

Copyright © 2017. American Immigration Lawyers Association. All rights reserved.

It is possible to obtain H-2B extensions for the remainder of the validity of the temporary labor certification application or for up to one year.[965] However, DOL regulations limit the period of validity of the labor certification to nine months for all but a one-time need, and obtaining time on a labor certification for more than nine months can occur only in "extraordinary circumstances,"[966] as discussed earlier in this chapter.

In addition, the foreign national's total period of H-2B stay must not exceed the three-year limitation.[967] But if the foreign national is the beneficiary of an approved permanent labor certification application or of an employment-based immigrant visa petition filed by the current H-2B employer, this is "a reason, by itself," to deny the extension request.[968]

The H-2B extension may be necessary if the foreign national entered the United States later than originally anticipated,[969] or if the initial H-2B petition was approved after the requested start date. The support statement should clearly explain why the extension is necessary and include details on the continued need for the foreign national's services as one-time, seasonal, peakload, or intermittent. To document the late start date, the practitioner should include copies of visa and entry stamps in the passport in the extension. However, the end date will still be limited to the end date of the underlying labor certification.

Conversely, it may be difficult to obtain temporary labor certification and H-2B extension approval for the same petitioner and beneficiary if the need is seasonal or peakload, because these temporary needs are considered connected to the physical seasons and not the majority of the year or more than one year, as discussed above. One possible exception to this general rule is if the petitioner has seasonal or peakload needs for workers in different fields or industries, such as hotel workers during the ski season and amusement park workers during the summer.

B. Interruptions to Accrual of H-2B Time

If an H-2B worker remains physically present outside the United States for certain periods of time, that time spent abroad should not count toward the accrual of H-2B time.[970] If the foreign national held H-2B status for 18 months or less, then he or she must spend at least 45 days outside the United States for the time abroad to interrupt the continued accrual of H-2B time.[971] For a foreign national who held H-2B status

---

[965] 8 CFR §214.2(h)(15)(ii)(C).

[966] 20 CFR §655.60.

[967] 8 CFR §214.2(h)(15)(ii)(C).

[968] 8 CFR §214.2(h)(16)(ii).

[969] *Matter of [name not provided]*, EAC 93 090 52290 (AAU June 23, 1993), 12 Immig. Rptr. B2-10; *Matter of [name not provided]*, SRC 91 026 00588 (AAU *[date not provided]*), 9 Immig. Rptr. B2-63.

[970] 8 CFR §214.2(h)(13)(v).

[971] *Id.*

Copyright © 2017. American Immigration Lawyers Association. All rights reserved.

for more than 18 months, only a period of at least two months is considered interruptive.[972]

Previous H-2B Status	Required Residence Abroad
Three years	Three months
Between 18 months and three years	Two months
18 months or less	45 days

C. Sponsoring an H-2B Worker for Permanent Residence

In most cases, employment-based sponsorship for permanent residence on behalf of H-2B nonimmigrants is extremely difficult, because the aggregate processing time for approval of the labor certification application, approval of the immigrant visa petition, and availability of an immigrant visa number is highly likely to take longer than the foreign national's current period of authorized stay.[973] But as stated by legacy INS guidance:

"Under the statutory requirements for [H-2B] classification[], a simultaneously temporary and permanent intent on the part of the petitioner and the beneficiary is inconsistent with Congressional intent. Continuing H-2 status requires the employer's need for the services to remain temporary.... Petitioners will not be permitted to circumvent this policy by applying for permanent status on behalf of the alien in a different job. Approval of a permanent labor certification or the filing of a preference petition for an H-2 ... beneficiary in the same or a different job or training position with the same employer is a basis for denying a new petition or the alien's application for an extension of stay."[974]

Similarly, DOL characterized the H-2B classification as follows:

"Any foreign workers who ultimately are brought in under the [H-2B] program are permitted to work only on a temporary basis, with no possibility of the job becoming permanent no matter how well the employees perform or what skills they acquire.... At the conclusion of the specified work period, the workers must leave the country and they are not permitted to seek subsequent work from another U.S. employer, unless that subsequent employer also is certified under the H-2B program."[975]

---

[972] Id.

[973] For an overview of the permanent residence process, see Volume 2: Chapter Two, "The Labor Certification Application"; Volume 2: Chapter Three, "The Immigrant Visa Petition"; and Volume 2: Chapter Four, "Consular Processing, Adjustment of Status, and Permanent Residence Issues."

[974] OI 214.2.

[975] 75 Fed. Reg. 6884 (Feb. 12, 2010).

Copyright © 2017. American Immigration Lawyers Association. All rights reserved.

The delays in immigrant visa availability for the EB-3 classification will most likely mean that the foreign national will be unable to apply to adjust status before expiration of the H-2B maximum time limitation, even if an H-2B extension is granted.[976] One exception would be if the foreign national qualified for EB-2 classification, by holding a master's degree or having five years of post-baccalaureate experience. The practitioner should take care, however, to caution the client of the prohibition on dual intent and to note how the legacy INS guidance refers to "simultaneously temporary and permanent intent on the part of the petitioner and the beneficiary."[977] It is possible that DHS could take into account the petitioner's "permanent intent" when considering whether the petitioner complied with the obligations of the H-2B program, as discussed above—perhaps, if not for a single case, then when evaluating the petitioner's history of program compliance in the course of an investigation.

Although one immigrant visa petition was approved on behalf of an H-2B employee, that case was unique for two reasons.[978] First, the immigrant visa petition was approved by a federal court, as opposed to USCIS or legacy INS;[979] it may be less likely that a petitioner will wish to seek judicial review. Second, the court held that the legacy INS's Operations Instructions (OIs) contradicted the legislative intent of the immigration statute, but those OIs differed from the most recent version of legacy INS OIs, which prohibit a foreign national from seeking employment-based permanent residence while in H-2B status.[980]

It may be possible to request consular processing, so the foreign national may remain outside the United States and pursue a career abroad while awaiting issuance of an immigrant visa. The practitioner should counsel the client, however, that the foreign national would most likely be unable to obtain an H-2B visa to enter the United States while the immigrant visa petition and consular processing are pending, as such steps would be construed as immigrant intent and most likely result in visa denial under INA §214(b). In addition, during the immigrant visa interview, the U.S. consulate may question whether the initial H-2B petition truly represented a temporary opportunity, especially if the job duties are similar. The practitioner may wish to document how the H-2B assignment represented a temporary need and how the permanent position differs from the previous temporary position. Further, if the temporary need became permanent because of a change in the petitioner's circumstances, the practitioner may wish to provide an explanation, taking care to note that neither the petitioner nor the former H-2B worker violated the immigration laws.

---

[976] For a discussion of the immigrant visa petition classifications and visa retrogression, see Volume 2: Chapter Three, "The Immigrant Visa Petition."

[977] OI 214.2.

[978] *North American Industries, Inc. v. INS*, 722 F.2d 893 (1st Cir. 1983).

[979] *Id.*

[980] OI 214.2.

Copyright © 2017. American Immigration Lawyers Association. All rights reserved.

CHAPTER NINE

H-3 VISAS AND STATUS

I. Executive Summary

The H-3 nonimmigrant classification allows foreign nationals to receive training in the United States, as long as the training is not available in the home country, the training will benefit the foreign national in pursuing a career outside the United States, the foreign national will only engage in productive employment that is incidental and necessary to the training, and the trainee job is not in the normal operation of the U.S. business or in a position in which citizens and permanent resident workers are regularly employed. The foreign national must also demonstrate nonimmigrant intent through the maintenance of a foreign residence. An H-3 petition approval may be valid for up to two years. There are no extensions beyond two years, and recapture of H-3 time is not available. Dependent spouses and children of H-3 trainees hold H-4 status.

A. Checklist of Requirements

Proper training program:

- Unavailable in home country
- No placement in a position in the business's normal operation where U.S. workers are regularly employed
- Productive employment is incidental to and necessary for the training
- Will benefit pursuit of a career abroad

B. Documents Necessary to Prepare the Petition

- Description of U.S. training program
- Copies of the foreign national's educational degrees, including transcripts
- Copy of foreign national's résumé
- Basic information about the company
- Copy of biographic page(s) of passport(s) of the foreign national and any dependent spouse and children

C. Checklist of Questions to Ask the Client

- What are the purpose, scope, and phases of the training program?
- Is the training unavailable in the foreign national's home country?
- Will the trainee be placed in a role that is in the business's normal operation and where U.S. workers are regularly employed?
- If there will be productive employment, is it incidental and necessary to the training?
- How will the training benefit the foreign national in pursuing a career abroad?

801

Copyright © 2017. American Immigration Lawyers Association. All rights reserved.

- Is the training for a medical student or nurse?
- Is there a labor dispute at the worksite of the proposed H-3 training program?
- Will the foreign national maintain a foreign residence for the duration of the training program?
- Is the foreign national a beneficiary of an immigrant visa petition or labor certification application?

II. Introduction

The H-3 classification allows a U.S. entity to provide specific training to a foreign national for his or her career development abroad. There are two types of H-3 training programs:

- A program "of an organization or individual" to provide "training in any field of endeavor, such as agriculture, commerce, communications, finance, government, transportation, or the professions, as well as training in a purely industrial establishment";[1] and

- A "special education exchange visitor program which provides for practical training and experience in the education of children with physical, mental, or emotional disabilities."[2]

For brevity, this chapter will refer to the first type of training program as a general H-3 training program. A general H-3 training program may be no longer than two years.[3] An H-3 special education training program may be valid for up to 18 months.[4] If the requested period of stay exceeds the time limitation, then "the petition shall be approved only up to the limit."[5]

As a practical matter, the foreign national may be unable to fully complete the planned training program because he or she is delayed in arriving in the United States. Reports indicate that some petitioners request "additional time on the petition validity to address unforeseen travel and visa contingencies," but that U.S. Citizenship and Immigration Services (USCIS) "officers are now limiting the time solely to the actual training dates."[6] In response, USCIS indicated that "given that there is no grace period," the petitioner may be able to "build this need into the program," although USCIS could not "provide specific guidance."[7] USCIS

---

[1] 8 Code of Federal Regulations (CFR) §214.2(h)(7)(i).

[2] 8 CFR §214.2(h)(1)(ii)(E)(2).

[3] 8 CFR §214.2(h)(9)(iii)(C)(1).

[4] 8 CFR §214.2(h)(9)(iii)(C)(2).

[5] 8 CFR §214.2(h)(9)(ii)(C).

[6] "CSC Stakeholders Meeting" (Apr. 29, 2010), AILA Doc. No. 10062988.

[7] Id. ("We will have to get back on that" and "we're sure it can be done").

Copyright © 2017. American Immigration Lawyers Association. All rights reserved.

specifically declined to include H-3s in the nonimmigrant categories to which it was adding a 10-day grace period in 2016.[8]

There is an annual numerical limitation of 50 H-3 visas per year for participants in special education exchange programs.[9] If the H-3 trainee is transferred to a different worksite, but will remain employed by the same U.S. entity and will receive the same training, a new H-3 petition should not be necessary.[10]

In practice, there are many similarities between the H-3 and the J-1 training visa detailed in Volume 1: Chapter Ten, "J-1 Visas and Status," and many training assignments could be accomplished on either a J-1 or an H-3. The J-1 visa process is typically faster, since no petition approval is needed from USCIS in advance of the consular appointment to obtain the visa. In addition, with the J-1 there is no requirement to show that the training is not available in the applicant's home country. However, an H-3 nonimmigrant is not subject to the two-year home residence requirement that applies to some J-1 trainees, even if the training program would otherwise be on the J-1 Skills List for the foreign national's home country. Moreover, some individuals coming to the United States for training may not meet the requirements to be classified as a J-1 trainee or J-1 intern, and the H-3 may be the only option as a result.

III. Requirements and Interpretations

A. Nonimmigrant Intent

The foreign national must demonstrate that he or she has a residence abroad that he or she has no intention of abandoning.[11] Appropriate evidence may include copies of property titles or deeds, mortgages, or lease agreements. These documents may be supplemented with a statement from a foreign employer confirming an employment offer following completion of the H-3 training program, evidence of continued enrollment in school or other programs in the home country, arrangements for sabbatical, bank statements, and evidence of family or community ties.

An H-3 nonimmigrant may not have dual intent, where he or she may pursue permanent residence while in H-3 status: "H-3 status should terminate when the beneficiary's training is not for the purpose of continuing a career outside the United States."[12]

Being the beneficiary of an approved labor certification application or of a filed employment-based immigrant visa petition sponsored by the same H-3 petitioner "is a basis for denying a new petition,"[13] as this would indicate a desire to immigrate

---

[8] 81 Fed. Reg. 82398, 82436 (Nov. 18, 2016).

[9] 8 CFR §214.2(h)(8)(i)(D).

[10] Legacy Immigration and Naturalization Service (INS) Operations Instruction (OI) 214.2.

[11] Immigration and Nationality Act (INA) §101(a)(15)(H)(iii).

[12] OI 214.2; *see also* 55 Fed. Reg. 2606 (Jan. 26, 1990).

[13] OI 214.2.

Copyright © 2017. American Immigration Lawyers Association. All rights reserved.

permanently to the United States.[14] Such sponsorship also raises a negative presumption: "When that same employer obtains a labor certification or files a preference petition for the beneficiary, it can be presumed that the purpose of the training was to recruit and train the alien to ultimately staff a position in the United States."[15] This remains the case even if the petitioner files the labor certification application or immigrant visa petition for a different position than the training program: "Petitioners will not be permitted to circumvent the[] requirement[] [of nonimmigrant intent] by applying for permanent status on behalf of the alien in a different job."[16]

It may be possible to obtain approval of an H-3 petition if the labor certification application or immigrant visa petition was filed by an entity other than the H-3 petitioner or by a family member,[17] but the practitioner should discuss the following issues in detail with the client. First, the foreign national would have to demonstrate that, despite the pursuit of U.S. permanent residence, he or she will maintain the foreign residence for the duration of the H-3 training program. Second, the pursuit of U.S. permanent residence may undermine the foreign national's ability to establish satisfaction of the requirement that the U.S. training will benefit him or her in pursuing a career abroad, as discussed below. Third, the adjudicator may determine that the H-3 petition filed on behalf of a foreign national who desires to ultimately seek permanent residence is a means to train the foreign national "for the ultimate staffing of domestic operations in the United States," as discussed below.

An H-3 petition may address these issues by providing explicit details of definite plans, such as ongoing payments of the mortgage, property taxes, or rent; offer of employment from a foreign entity upon conclusion of the H-3 training program; and evidence that the H-3 petitioner does not seek to employ the foreign national upon completion of the training program or evidence of the relationship between the H-3 petitioner and the foreign entity, if applicable. Nevertheless, the practitioner should advise the client that the H-3 petition runs a higher than normal risk of denial. For a detailed discussion of strategies to contrast a future desire to immigrate with a temporary desire to visit the United States, see Volume 1: Chapter Three, Visitors: "B Visas and Status and the Visa Waiver Program."

B. General H-3 Training Programs

The requirements of the H-3 classification are strict and preclude use of the H-3 visa for general employment; the foreign national should participate "in a training program that is not designed primarily to provide productive employment."[18]

---

[14] 8 CFR §214.2(h)(16)(ii); 55 Fed. Reg. 2606 (Jan. 26, 1990).

[15] OI 214.2.

[16] 55 Fed. Reg. 2606 (Jan. 26, 1990).

[17] Cf. 8 CFR §214.2(h)(16)(ii).

[18] INA §101(a)(15)(H)(iii).

Copyright © 2017. American Immigration Lawyers Association. All rights reserved.

Specifically, an H-3 training program must satisfy the following conditions, which are provided as evidentiary requirements in the regulations:

- "The proposed training is not available in the alien's own country;

- "The beneficiary will not be placed in a position which is in the normal operation of the business and in which citizens and resident workers are regularly employed;

- "The beneficiary will not engage in productive employment unless such employment is incidental and necessary to the training; and

- "The training will benefit the beneficiary in pursuing a career outside the United States."[19]

Each of these conditions is discussed below, as well as the interrelated requirements of the training program, which must specifically describe the following:

- The type of training to be provided and the type(s) of supervision to be provided;[20]

- The "structure of the training program,"[21] including:

  - The "proportion of time that will be devoted to productive employment";[22] and

  - The "number of hours that will be spent, respectively, in classroom instruction and in on-the-job training";[23]

- The "career abroad for which the training will prepare the alien";[24]

- The "reasons why such training cannot be obtained in the alien's country and why it is necessary for the alien to be trained in the United States";[25] and

- The "source of any remuneration received by the trainee and any benefit which will accrue to the petitioner for providing the training."[26]

The practitioner should also consider the following restrictions, as an H-3 petition which raises these issues will be denied:

---

[19] 8 CFR §214.2(h)(7)(ii)(A).

[20] 8 CFR §214.2(h)(7)(ii)(B)(*1*); *Matter of Treasure Craft of California*, 14 I&N Dec. 190 (Reg'l Comm'r 1972).

[21] 8 CFR §214.2(h)(7)(ii)(B)(*1*).

[22] 8 CFR §214.2(h)(7)(ii)(B)(*2*); *Matter of Frigon*, 18 I&N Dec. 164 (Comm'r 1981); *Matter of Koyama*, 11 I&N Dec. 425 (Reg'l Comm'r 1965).

[23] 8 CFR §214.2(h)(7)(ii)(B)(*3*); *Matter of Masauyama*, 11 I&N Dec. 157 (Acting Reg'l Comm'r 1965); *Matter of Frigon*, 18 I&N Dec. 164 (H-3 petition denied when classroom training comprised approximately five percent of the overall period of training).

[24] 8 CFR §214.2(h)(7)(ii)(B)(*4*).

[25] 8 CFR §214.2(h)(7)(ii)(B)(*5*).

[26] 8 CFR §214.2(h)(7)(ii)(B)(*6*); *Matter of Kraus Periodicals*, 11 I&N Dec. 63 (Reg'l Comm'r 1964); *Matter of St. Pierre*, 18 I&N Dec. 308 (Reg'l Comm'r 1982).

Copyright © 2017. American Immigration Lawyers Association. All rights reserved.

- The H-3 petition and training program describes only "generalities with no fixed schedule, objectives, or means of evaluation";[27]

- The proposed training program is "incompatible with the nature of the petitioner's business or enterprise";[28]

- The H-3 petition is filed on behalf of a foreign national "who already possesses substantial training and expertise in the proposed field of training";[29]

- The training program is "in a field in which it is unlikely that the knowledge or skill will be used outside the United States";[30]

- Approval of the H-3 petition "[w]ill result in productive employment beyond that which is incidental and necessary to the training";[31]

- The H-3 program is "designed to recruit and train aliens for the ultimate staffing of domestic operations in the United States";[32]

- The H-3 petition fails to "establish that the petitioner has the physical plant and sufficiently trained manpower to provide the training specified";[33] or

- The H-3 program is "designed to extend the total allowable period of practical training previously authorized [to] a nonimmigrant student."[34]

On a positive note, when considering whether the foreign national has previously gained substantial training and expertise in the field, USCIS may consider the nature of the field and the years of training ordinarily required for an individual to become a professional.[35]

These restrictions and requirements exist because of legacy Immigration and Naturalization Service's (INS) concern about misuse of the H-3 classification: "Operating experience has shown that when the alien is not of distinguished merit and ability or the petitioner cannot obtain a temporary labor certification, H-3 classification

---

[27] 8 CFR §214.2(h)(7)(iii)(A); *Matter of Kraus Periodicals*, 11 I&N Dec. 63.

[28] 8 CFR §214.2(h)(7)(iii)(B).

[29] 8 CFR §214.2(h)(7)(iii)(C); *Matter of Miyazaki Travel Agency, Inc.*, 10 I&N Dec. 644 (Reg'l Comm'r 1964); *Matter of Masauyama*, 11 I&N Dec. 157; *Matter of Sasano*, 11 I&N Dec. 363 (Reg'l Comm'r 1965); *Matter of Frigon*, 18 I&N Dec. 164.

[30] 8 CFR §214.2(h)(7)(iii)(D).

[31] 8 CFR §214.2(h)(7)(iii)(E); *Matter of Sasano*, 11 I&N Dec. 363.

[32] 8 CFR §214.2(h)(7)(iii)(F); *Matter of Glencoe Press*, 11 I&N Dec. 190 (Reg'l Comm'r 1966); *Matter of St. Pierre*, 18 I&N Dec. 308.

[33] 8 CFR §214.2(h)(7)(iii)(G).

[34] 8 CFR §214.2(h)(7)(iii)(H); *Matter of [name not provided]*, NYC N 10670 (AAU Oct. 15, 1985), 3 Immig. Rptr. B2-16 ("[a]lthough the petitioner states that 60% of the beneficiary's time will be spent in classroom or direct tutorial instruction, we are not persuaded that the beneficiary has not already taken some or all of the courses listed on the training program outline due to his extensive background as a law student").

[35] *Matter of [name not provided]*, LIN 94 196 51915 (AAU Aug. 26, 1994), 14 Immig. Rptr. B2-1 ("[a]lthough the record reflects that the beneficiary has received initial training at the [redacted], to characterize such training as 'substantial' greatly oversimplifies the training process for ballet dancers").

Copyright © 2017. American Immigration Lawyers Association. All rights reserved.

is sometimes requested to enable the alien to engage in actual employment under the guise of a training program."[36] Other legacy INS guidance stated:

"[T]he H-3 category appears to offer a relatively easy and immediately available form of relief. The petitioner decides to simply call the job 'a training position' and drafts a program which might suggest the beneficiary is going to be learning a job skill, usually with the intent of finding a way to enter the United States and work while exploring the possibilities of permanent immigration to this country."[37]

The practitioner should note that, unlike other nonimmigrant visa classifications, which require supplemental evidence that the requirements have been satisfied, an H-3 petition may be submitted without objective evidence of satisfying the requirements. For example, an L-1 petition requires evidence of the corporate relationship between the two companies as well as evidence of the qualifying employment by the transferee.[38] In contrast, however, the supplemental evidence of an H-3 petition generally will be the training program description from the petitioner.

In response, legacy INS guidance directed adjudicators to adhere to the following standard: "[T]he examiner should be satisfied that the purpose of the program is genuinely to train the beneficiary for a career abroad (even though the petitioner may derive benefits from the alien's training), and that the beneficiary intends to return abroad for employment after termination of the training program."[39] Or, as more succinctly stated by USCIS: "Officers must carefully review each petition for an H-3 trainee to ensure compliance with the intent of the H-3 category to train foreign nationals who will return to their home countries."[40] To this end, the practitioner should explore with the client the availability of objective evidence to corroborate how the H-3 training program complies with the requirements.

Foreign nationals may not participate in a general H-3 training program in order to receive "graduate medical education or training, or training provided primarily at or by an academic or vocational institution."[41] In addition, physicians "are statutorily ineligible to use H-3 classification in order to receive any type of graduate medical education or training,"[42] except as discussed below. For a discussion of H-3 programs for medical students and nurses, see below.

---

[36] OI 214.2; *see also Matter of Treasure Craft of California*, 14 I&N Dec. 190 (Reg'l Comm'r 1972) (calling the H-3 petition a "thinly veiled allegation … [of] a training program"); *see also* 55 Fed. Reg. 2606 (Jan. 26, 1990) (stating that legacy INS "has not found it credible that facilities which do not have significant programs for the training of U.S. nurses will not use scarce resources to train foreign nurses for a career abroad").

[37] 1 Legacy INS Examinations Handbook, Part II, 15-1.

[38] 8 CFR §214.2(*l*)(3)(ii).

[39] OI 214.2.

[40] USCIS Policy Manual, Vol. 2, Pt. J, Ch. 6.

[41] 8 CFR §214.2(h)(1)(ii)(E)(*1*).

[42] 8 CFR §214.2(h)(7)(i).

Copyright © 2017. American Immigration Lawyers Association. All rights reserved.

1. The Training Is Unavailable in the Home Country

As noted above, the H-3 program must entail training that is unavailable in the home country. Importantly, availability of the training abroad does not preclude H-3 petition approval, as long as the training is not available in the foreign national's home country.[43] The unavailability may be because the field has been more fully developed in the United States as compared to other countries, such as in response to U.S. statutes and regulations,[44] because the field or industry does not exist in the home country,[45] or because the petitioner's previous attempts to provide training in the home country may have been unsuccessful.[46] It also could be because the petitioner has developed "a new product for which training is unavailable in another country. The U.S. company may petition to train people to use that product, which will enable the trainees to train others to use the new product in their home country."[47]

Alternatively, the size of the petitioner's operations may mean that only a U.S. office has the capacity to offer such training,[48] or that the petitioner's training has been consolidated to one location in the United States. In these situations, however, USCIS may consider the "size of the petitioner, the scope of its operations, and [whether] the beneficiary will rotate through several of the petitioner's departments."[49] Another reason may be a change in the industry or marketplace, such as a shift in how work is allotted or performed, in response to the introduction of American techniques and models through foreign direct investment.

It is "irrelevant" that the training is available through other sources, such as the "utilization of personnel, materials, foreign educational/training programs, and the Internet," "unless those resources are in the beneficiary's own country."[50] Despite this guidance, however, it seems less likely that a petitioner could claim that the Internet is not available in the home country; this may be true only of a tiny handful of countries like North Korea.[51] And if such resources are available in the home country, questions can arise regarding whether the training truly is unavailable in the

---

[43] *Matter of [name not provided]*, EAC 04 252 53153 (AAO Apr. 11, 2005), http://bit.ly/apr051d5.

[44] *Matter of St. Pierre*, 14 I&N Dec. 190 (Reg'l Comm'r 1972). *Cf. Matter of [name not provided]*, EAC 07 021 53665 (AAO Sept. 17, 2007), http://bit.ly/sep071d5.

[45] *Matter of [name not provided]*, SRC 02 236 71198 (AAO Jan. 19, 2006), http://bit.ly/jan061d5.

[46] *Matter of International Transportation Corp.*, 12 I&N Dec. 389 (Reg'l Comm'r 1967) (stating "more credence is lent thereto by the petitioner's prior unsuccessful attempts to accord such training abroad").

[47] USCIS Policy Manual, Vol. 2, Pt. J, Ch. 6.

[48] *Matter of [name not provided]*, NYC N 111350 (AAU Apr. 25, 1986), 3 Immig. Rptr. B2-104.

[49] *Id.*

[50] *Matter of [name not provided]*, EAC 04 258 53391 (AAO Jan. 6, 2006), http://bit.ly/jan061d5.

[51] "The Last Places on Earth Without Internet" (Feb. 14, 2014), BBC, http://www.bbc.com/future/story/20140214-the-last-places-without-internet; "These Countries Have the World's Worst Internet Access" (Oct. 16, 2015), Fortune International, http://fortune.com/2015/10/06/worst-internet-access/.

Copyright © 2017. American Immigration Lawyers Association. All rights reserved.

home country.[52] Also, the practitioner should be cautioned that "[i]n cases where the program is entirely online, officers must review each case and ensure that the petitioner has met their burden of proof (preponderance of the evidence) demonstrating that the training cannot be made available in the beneficiary's home country."[53]

Submitting that the equipment necessary for the training is only available in the United States is also likely to result in denial of the H-3 petition, as USCIS may take the position that the equipment may be moved.[54] Importantly, if the advanced equipment is unavailable outside the United States, USCIS may question how training on such equipment will benefit the foreign national's career abroad: "[T]he petitioner has failed to establish why such training is necessary if the beneficiary cannot apply such 'high technology' skills and knowledge to the equipment presently available in that country."[55] In addition, it is possible that "administrative notice" will be taken regarding facts of the field's development in the home country.[56]

Additionally, USCIS may perform Internet searches to identify whether the training is available in the home country.[57] If such external information serves as a basis for denial of the H-3 petition, however, USCIS should issue a Request for Evidence (RFE) to provide "the opportunity to rebut any information discovered by an adjudicator from an external source."[58]

2. The Trainee's Role vis-à-vis Positions for U.S. Workers

The H-3 classification does not permit trainees to "be employed in a position or work which is in the normal operation of a business and for which citizens and resident aliens are regularly employed."[59] One successful H-3 petition demonstrated that the foreign national would not displace a U.S. worker because he would "tag along" as "the third man on a normal two man crew which would only need two men."[60]

Conversely, statements that the trainee will "shadow" senior staff and "participate solely in an ancillary manner in actual planning, decision making, and problem

---

[52] *Matter of I-USAE-LLC*, ID# 16842 (AAO June 1, 2016) (AAO remanded where "the availability of at least some of [a tennis academy's training program's] coaching methods through DVDs on sale on the Internet provide a reasonable basis for further inquiry as to whether the substantive techniques and methods comprising the Petitioner's have been incorporated into similar training programs available in Israel, such that it might not be necessary for the Beneficiary to come to the United States for the proposed training").

[53] USCIS Policy Manual, Vol. 2, Pt. J, Ch. 6.

[54] *Matter of Frigon*, 18 I&N Dec. 164 (Comm'r 1981).

[55] *Matter of [name not provided]*, NEW N 33181 (AAU Dec. 11, 1985), 3 Immig. Rptr. B2-41.

[56] *Matter of Treasure Craft of California*, 14 I&N Dec. 190 (Reg'l Comm'r 1972).

[57] *Matter of I-USAE-LLC*, ID# 16842 (AAO June 1, 2016).

[58] "AILA/USCIS Liaison Minutes" (Oct. 28, 2008), AILA Doc. No. 08110767. *See also* USCIS, D. Neufeld, "Removal of the Standardized Request for Evidence Processing Timeframe (June 1, 2007), AILA Doc. No. 07062171.

[59] *Matter of Miyazaki Travel Agency, Inc.*, 10 I&N Dec. 644 (Reg'l Comm'r 1964).

[60] *Matter of St. Pierre*, 18 I&N Dec. 308 (Reg'l Comm'r 1982).

Copyright © 2017. American Immigration Lawyers Association. All rights reserved.

solving," such that the trainee will not "have any meaningful impact on a practical or productive level," may be weakened if other evidence indicates that the foreign national will perform productive work.[61] USCIS guidance notes, under the heading of "Shadowing" that "[t]here are limited circumstances where a proposed training program that consists largely or entirely of on-the-job training may be approved. Officers should carefully evaluate the totality of the evidence against a preponderance of the evidence standard, including whether a U.S. worker is being displaced and if the on-the-job training would allow the trainee to be placed into a position which is in the normal operation of the business and in which U.S. citizens and legal residents are regularly employed."[62]

Similarly, an H-3 petition where the beneficiary will "engage in 'hands-on experience'" and "apply" skills learned from the training program may be denied, as such activities would constitute work "in the petitioner's normal operation of business."[63] USCIS may also deem the training program to be customary for all new hires, rather than specifically for an H-3 trainee.[64]

3. Productive Employment May Only Be Incidental and Necessary to the Training Program

The Immigration Act of 1990 (IMMACT90) imposed the requirement that the trainee engage in productive employment only as is incidental and necessary to the training.[65] Productive employment may be incidental and necessary if it is required to evaluate the trainee's progress, or if the trainee would be assigned "extra or 'make-work' for his use and benefit only."[66] In general, an H-3 program should provide "training of an individual rather than giv[e] him further experience by day-to-day application of his skills."[67] To determine whether the trainee will engage in productive employment, USCIS may consider the number of petitioner's other employees,[68] the daily and weekly hours of the program,[69] whether "the phases of the training will be repetitious,"[70] the length of the program, "the amount and nature of supervision," and "the inherent productivity of the beneficiary's proposed duties."[71]

---

[61] *Matter of [name not provided]*, EAC 07 021 53665 (AAO Sept. 17, 2007), http://bit.ly/sep071d5.

[62] USCIS Policy Manual, Vol. 2, Pt. J, Ch. 6.

[63] *Matter of [name not provided]*, WAC 06 054 50929 (AAO Sept. 17, 2007), http://bit.ly/sep072d5.

[64] *Id.*

[65] 9 Foreign Affairs Manual (FAM) 402.10-4(F); USCIS Policy Manual, Vol. 2, Pt. J, Ch. 6.

[66] *Matter of St. Pierre*, 18 I&N Dec. 308 (Reg'l Comm'r 1982).

[67] *Matter of Matsauyama*, 11 I&N Dec. 157 (Acting Reg'l Comm'r 1965).

[68] *Matter of Sasano*, 11 I&N Dec. 363 (Reg'l Comm'r 1965).

[69] *Id.*; *Matter of Koyama*, 11 I&N Dec. 425 (Reg'l Comm'r 1965).

[70] *Matter of Koyama*, 11 I&N Dec. 425.

[71] *Matter of [name not provided]*, WAC93 084 50156 (AAU Apr. 20, 1994), 13 Immig. Rptr. B2-22 (noting that "any production by the beneficiary was more than offset by time spent in training him" (citing *Matter of International Transportation Corp.*, 12 I&N Dec. 389 (Reg'l Comm'r 1967)).

Copyright © 2017. American Immigration Lawyers Association. All rights reserved.

In addition, if the proposed trainees have been previously or are currently employed by the petitioner, the H-3 petition is likely to be denied, especially if the beneficiaries previously performed "purely productive labor."[72] Productive employment also may not be excused by stating that the trainee may not receive training in managerial duties without first performing the hands-on duties of subordinates, even if the managerial duties will be performed abroad following the H-3 program; "Counsel cannot claim that the beneficiary's on-the-job training will not be of a productive nature, while simultaneously claiming that the beneficiary must receive certain productive training" in order to train subordinates in the home country.[73]

Even if there is a labor shortage of qualified U.S. workers in the occupation, USCIS may consider whether the foreign national will engage in work that is more than incidental or necessary to the training: "The central issue here is the effect or potential effect of productive employment upon United States workers balanced against the petitioner's need or purpose in training the alien beneficiary."[74] Productive employment is prohibited even if the petitioner has unsuccessfully attempted to recruit U.S. workers through advertisements in numerous cities.[75]

4. Benefit to Trainee in Pursuing a Career Outside the United States

The H-3 petition may demonstrate satisfaction of this condition by stating that the trainee will subsequently be employed abroad by an affiliated company or entity in a position that utilizes the training received in the United States.[76] Alternatively, the trainee may return abroad to a position with a "closely associated" entity, such as a company with a business or contractual relationship with the petitioner,[77] or a company with which the U.S. petitioner plans to create a joint venture.[78] In these situations, it may be helpful to note how "the overall purpose of such training is to improve the affiliate's operation [abroad] so that the United States firm can offer better service ... and that an understanding of the United States operation is essential thereto,"[79] as well as a copy of the job description for the foreign position.

In addition, the H-3 petition should include evidence that the foreign business currently exists or evidence of a plan to establish such a business.[80] Appropriate evidence may include an officer's certificate, copies of certificates of incorporation, copies of corporate tax returns, a copy of the blanket L petition with the page noting

---

[72] *Matter of Treasure Craft of California*, 14 I&N Dec. 190 (Reg'l Comm'r 1972).

[73] *Matter of [name not provided]*, EAC 07 021 53665 (AAO Sept. 17, 2007), http://bit.ly/sep071d5. In this case, performance of restaurant wait-staff duties was deemed to be productive employment.

[74] *Matter of Frigon*, 18 I&N Dec. 164 (Comm'r 1981).

[75] *Matter of Miyazaki Travel Agency, Inc.*, 10 I&N Dec. 644 (Reg'l Comm'r 1964).

[76] *Matter of [name not provided]*, NYC N 111350 (AAU Apr. 25, 1986), 3 Immig. Rptr.B2-104.

[77] *Matter of International Transportation Corp.*, 12 I&N Dec. 389 (Reg'l Comm'r 1967).

[78] *Matter of [name not provided]*, EAC 87 150 0096 (AAU July 31, 1987), 5 Immig. Rptr. B2-26.

[79] *Matter of International Transportation Corp.*, 12 I&N Dec. 389.

[80] *Matter of [name not provided]*, SRC 02 236 71198 (AAO Jan. 19, 2006), http://bit.ly/jan061d5.

Copyright © 2017. American Immigration Lawyers Association. All rights reserved.

the foreign entity tabbed, copies of contracts evidencing the business relationship between the H-3 petitioner and the foreign entity, print-outs from the foreign entity's website, a copy of the property title, a mortgage or lease agreement for the foreign entity's premises, and photographs of the foreign entity's premises. And although a nonprecedent decision notes the absence of "any evidence of an agreement or contract ... for future employment,"[81] there are reports of H-3 petition approval without this evidence, particularly where it is not the employer's normal business practice to enter into employment contracts for future employment.

The benefit may tie in with the unavailability of the training in the home country, such as if the field is newly developing in the home country and/or abroad and the foreign national will become a pioneer in his or her home country following the training program.[82] It does not seem necessary that the trainee subsequently use the training abroad in a hands-on manner; in one approved H-3 petition, the trainee planned to return to his position as a university professor.[83]

If evidence of the current careers of foreign nationals who participated in the previous training programs is submitted, then the practitioner should also be prepared to explain how the foreign nationals have utilized the training by obtaining foreign employment in the field.[84] The practitioner is advised against stating that the previous trainees chose "their desired field of employment," as this does not demonstrate how the current H-3 trainee's career abroad will be benefited.[85]

In addition, the foreign national must be prepared for a career abroad after completing the training program. It is insufficient for the training program to prepare the foreign national for admission or enrollment in an educational program necessary "to pursue [the] chosen field abroad."[86] Finally, if the training is "costly" to the U.S. entity, the adjudicator may consider it "highly unlikely that the beneficiary will return to his home country," and decide that the proposed training is "for the purpose of staffing the petitioner's own domestic operations."[87]

5. Specific Training Program

As noted above, the H-3 petition should include a comprehensive and detailed training program that must discuss certain specific points. A strong H-3 petition may have an "actual structured, sequential training program supported by formal training materials, books, syllabi of any academic or classroom instruction, or testing instruments or other evaluation methods,"[88] as required by Administrative Appeals

---

[81] Id.

[82] Matter of St. Pierre, 18 I&N Dec. 308 (Reg'l Comm'r 1982).

[83] Id.

[84] Matter of [name not provided], EAC 07 021 53665 (AAO Sept. 17, 2007), http://bit.ly/sep071d5.

[85] Id.

[86] Matter of [name not provided], EAC 04 236 51176 (AAO Jan. 19, 2006), http://bit.ly/jan062d5.

[87] Matter of [name not provided], NEW N 33181 (AAU Dec. 11, 1985), 3 Immig. Rptr. B2-41.

[88] Matter of [name not provided], WAC93 084 50156 (AAU Apr. 20, 1994), 13 Immig. Rptr. B2-22.

Copyright © 2017. American Immigration Lawyers Association. All rights reserved.

Unit (AAU) decisions predating the 1990 regulations; but the current standard requires only that the H-3 petition provide more than "generalities with no fixed schedule, objectives, or means of evaluation."[89] One approach is to provide a training program in a timeline format, with separate sections for each topic, and then broken down into significantly more discrete segments, with more information about how the time would be utilized. The practitioner may wish to include evidence of previous training programs conducted by the petitioner, if applicable, as this may help to demonstrate how previous H-3 training programs have been helpful to the petitioner's business.

Current USCIS guidance indicates that the statement setting forth the training program should cover the following:

- "Describe[] the type of training and supervision to be given, and the structure of the training program;

- "Set[] forth the proportion of time that will be devoted to productive employment;

- "Show[] the number of hours that will be spent, respectively, in classroom instruction and in on-the-job training;

- "Describe[] the career abroad for which the training will prepare the nonimmigrant;

- "Indicate[] the reasons why such training cannot be obtained in the trainee's country and why it is necessary for the foreign national to be trained in the United States; and

- "Indicate[] the source of any remuneration received by the trainee and any benefit which will accrue to the petitioner for providing the training."[90]

It should be noted that "having classroom instruction does not, in and of itself, mean the proposed program meets the necessary requirements where the purpose of the beneficiary's proposed presence in the United States is to obtain experience instead of training."[91] The foreign national may provide training to other individuals, as long as his or her "primary role" is as a trainee.[92]

If there will be on-the-job training as well as classroom instruction, the practitioner may wish to highlight how the on-the-job training builds upon the classroom instruction and is not productive employment.[93] In the context of the J-1 classification for trainees, DOS provided the following definition of on-the-job training: "an individual's observation of and participation in given tasks

---

[89] 8 CFR §214.2(h)(7)(iii)(A); *Matter of Kraus Periodicals*, 11 I&N Dec. 63 (Reg'l Comm'r 1964).

[90] USCIS Policy Manual, Vol. 2, Pt. J, Ch. 3.

[91] *Matter of [name not provided]*, WAC93 084 50156 (AAU Apr. 20, 1994), 13 Immig. Rptr. B2-22.

[92] *Matter of [name not provided]*, EAC 04 236 51176 (AAO Jan. 19, 2006), http://bit.ly/jan062d5 (accepting foreign national's role as teaching assistant trainee, because he "would attend numerous classes and … be either in class or in the studio 50-60 hours per week").

[93] *Matter of [name not provided]*, EAC-87-150-0096 (AAU July 31, 1987), 5 Immig. Rptr. B2-26.

Copyright © 2017. American Immigration Lawyers Association. All rights reserved.

demonstrated by experienced workers for the purpose of acquiring competency in such tasks."[94]

The adjudicator may consider, however, whether the classroom instruction may be completed in a time period that is shorter than the requested H-3 period of stay, and may believe that the foreign national will spend the remainder of the time in impermissible productive employment.[95] Experience has shown that H-3 petitions where the classroom instruction and on-the-job training are divided into separate phases regarding the different areas of training are more successful than H-3 petitions where the foreign national receives only one set period of classroom instruction and then another distinct period of on-the-job training.

An H-3 program consisting primarily of on-the-job training is likely to be closely scrutinized: "When a training program is characterized as on-the-job training, it is difficult to establish that the training is not principally productive employment."[96] The practitioner may provide details on how the skills to be learned are "practical" and why the training must be on the job, if applicable.[97] For example, the principles may be learned only through field work.[98] Alternatively, on-the-job training may be necessary because training on only modeling, forecasting, or hypothetical scenarios would not fully prepare the trainee for a career abroad, or because the industry changes so frequently that training solely on equipment or tools is insufficient to evaluate the trainee's ability to respond to new situations.

It is insufficient, however, to merely state that the nature of the petitioner's business precludes any classroom instruction.[99] The practitioner should discuss with the client any other reasons for the absence of classroom instruction. If possible, the H-3 petition should highlight how the on-the-job training will not constitute productive employment and state the small percentage of productive employment.

There is perhaps one exception to the requirement of a structured training program, but the practitioner should note that this exception is mentioned in a nonprecedent decision and advise the client accordingly:

> "In instances involving cultural, scientific, or educational institutions which offer uncompensated internships to be sustained by grants, fellowships, or paid sabbaticals offered by other than the petitioning organization, classification under

---

[94] 22 CFR §62.2.

[95] *Matter of [name not provided]*, EAC 91 009 50376 (AAU Aug. 31, 1992), 10 Immig. Rptr. B2-74.

[96] 55 Fed. Reg. 2606 (Jan. 26, 1990).

[97] *Matter of [name not provided]*, WAC93 084 50156 (AAU Apr. 20, 1994), 13 Immig. Rptr. B2-22 (stating "in some instances a training program of short duration with no formal academic or classroom instruction may meet the requirements of section 101(a)(15)(H)(iii) of the Act").

[98] *Matter of St. Pierre*, 18 I&N Dec. 308 (Reg'l Comm'r 1982).

[99] *Matter of [name not provided]*, EAC 04 258 53391 (AAO Jan. 6, 2006), http://bit.ly/jan061d5.

Copyright © 2017. American Immigration Lawyers Association. All rights reserved.

the statute at issue may be granted without regard to the training format to be utilized."[100]

It seems that the rationale behind the exception is that these H-3 petitions do not run afoul of the prohibitions on productive labor or displacement of U.S. workers, because the petitioner incurs no costs and the foreign national essentially is paid by an entity other than the petitioner for a training program that would not otherwise exist.[101] To qualify for the exception, the following conditions must be met:

- "The petitioner must be engaged in cultural or scientific research and development rather than the manufacture or sale of goods or services"; and

- "The internship must be financially sustained by outside sources."[102]

The Administrative Appeals Office (AAO) approved one H-3 petition filed by a nonprofit performing arts company for a "young artist trainee," stating that evaluations or progress reviews are "not relevant to the particular type of training proposed."[103] But the practitioner is advised against relying upon this nonprecedent decision, because there was no mention of whether remuneration was provided by an outside source, so it does not clearly fall within the narrow exception.

6. Source of Remuneration and Benefit to the Petitioner

The source of remuneration must also be disclosed in the H-3 petition. In most cases, the H-3 petitioner will also pay the trainee's salary or wages, and experience has shown that this is not typically an issue. Based on the language of legacy INS precedent decisions, it seems that the source of remuneration is considered to determine whether the trainee would displace a U.S. worker and/or whether there will be productive employment.[104] If the foreign national's salary or wages will be paid by the foreign affiliate or "closely related" entity, this fact could be helpful in demonstrating the bona fides of the H-3 training program.

One precedent decision noted the complete absence of remuneration from the H-3 petitioner, but that case presented the unique situation where the trainee obtained a sabbatical, with pay, from his foreign employer in order to receive the training.[105] Another nonprecedent decision noted that the foreign national had been awarded a grant from the provincial government of her home country.[106] These situations seem

---

[100] *Matter of [name not provided]*, ATL N 14351 (AAU Oct. 23, 1986), 4 Immig. Rptr. B2-79.

[101] *Id.*

[102] *Id.*

[103] *Matter of [name not provided]*, EAC 04 252 53153 (AAO Apr. 11, 2005), http://bit.ly/apr051d5.

[104] *Matter of Kraus Periodicals, Kraus Periodicals*, 11 I&N Dec. 63 (Reg'l Comm'r 1964); *Matter of Treasure Craft of California, Treasure Craft of California*, 14 I&N Dec. 190 (Reg'l Comm'r 1972); *Matter of Sasano*, 11 I&N Dec. 363 (Reg'l Comm'r 1965).

[105] *Matter of St. Pierre*, 18 I&N Dec. 308 (Reg'l Comm'r 1982).

[106] *Matter of [name not provided]*, ATL-N-14351 (AAU Oct. 23, 1986), 4 Immig. Rptr. B2-79.

Copyright © 2017. American Immigration Lawyers Association. All rights reserved.

uncommon, so while the source of remuneration will be considered, the focus may be on whether the salary will be "substantial."[107]

In one case, the AAO stated: "A salary of $52,000 per year indicates that the beneficiary would likely be engaged in productive employment."[108] If the foreign national will receive more than a token salary or stipend for basic living expenses, the practitioner may wish to provide information on wages normally paid to individuals holding full positions after completion of the same or similar training and evidence that the wage paid to the proposed trainee is "some smaller percentage … as might be expected of a trainee."[109] The practitioner may also wish to provide information on the foreign national's standard of living while in the United States in the metropolitan statistical area of the worksite, and on the needs of any accompanying dependent family members, if applicable.

The H-3 petition must also include an explanation of any benefit the petitioner may gain. This benefit may ultimately accrue to the overall group of companies or to a foreign company, rather than the specific U.S. petitioner, such as if the trainee will subsequently be employed by an affiliated company abroad. The AAO has also accepted a petitioner's statement that "increasing the international representation of its staff increases its ability to accommodate members from a variety of global communities."[110] Other reasons may include increased awareness of the global community and international diversity within the U.S. company, increased brand awareness in the home country upon the foreign national's return, development of relationships with future leaders in the home country, or investment in the industry's future through research and development.

7. Other Considerations

This section will discuss other potential pitfalls and types of evidence to comply with the requirements and restrictions.

a. Size and Nature of the Petitioner's Business

If the petitioner has only a small number of employees, USCIS may question whether there is "sufficient staff to provide the training described in the petition."[111] If there are no dedicated trainers, then the practitioner may wish to provide information on how training is part of the job descriptions of the supervisors and the reasons why training is a focus in the petitioner's business; these reasons may interrelate to the benefit gained by the petitioner, discussed above. The H-3 petition should also include evidence of how the staff are trained and will be able to provide

---

[107] *Matter of Kraus Periodicals*, 11 I&N Dec. 63; *Matter of [name not provided]*, EAC 05 043 52724 (AAO Sept. 16, 2005), http://bit.ly/sep058d.

[108] *Matter of [name not provided]*, EAC 05 043 52724 (AAO Sept. 16, 2005), http://bit.ly/sep058d.

[109] *Id.*

[110] Matter of [name not provided], EAC 07 021 53665 (AAO Sept. 17, 2007), http://bit.ly/sep071d5.

[111] USCIS Policy Manual, Vol. 2, Pt. J, Ch. 3.

Copyright © 2017. American Immigration Lawyers Association. All rights reserved.

the H-3 training,[112] such as copies of job descriptions, educational documents, professional certifications and licenses, and résumés of the petitioner's staff.

b. The Beneficiary Has Education and/or Experience in the Field or a Related Field

An H-3 petition may be denied if the beneficiary already possesses substantial training or expertise in the field, where the training may have been in the form of several years of classroom instruction in pursuit of a degree, diploma, or certificate,[113] or "in the same position as that of the proposed training."[114] Such a determination from USCIS may be rebutted with evidence of how the previous training or experience did not address a particular set of skills in the field of training.[115] In one case, the AAO remanded an H-3 petition to USCIS because, although the petitioner had asserted that the beneficiary lacked certain skills in sales, supporting documentation of the assertion was needed.[116]

Similarly, the education and/or experience may have been general and served as the necessary basis for the specific training program, which in turn may be needed to hold a more senior position abroad. In one case, USCIS considered the nature of the field and the years of training ordinarily required for an individual to become a professional.[117] For example, the foreign national may have a degree and several years of experience in chemical engineering, which is essential to understand the principles of translating laboratory experiments to industrial scale production; analyzing heat and mass transfer, thermodynamics, and reaction rates; and designing continuous improvement initiatives of products and processes, but the foreign national may nevertheless require specific H-3 training on how to apply these principles to the petitioner's proprietary or unique products. Anecdotal evidence indicates that this approach may even add credibility to the H-3 petition, such as if the training is sophisticated and could not have been gained through prior education or experience, and especially if, after completing the H-3 training, the foreign national will accept a position abroad that requires the services of an individual who has gained this training. Supporting evidence may include descriptions of the proprietary or unique products or processes, copies of transcripts and course descriptions to show

---

[112] *Id.* (noting that a training program may not be approved if it "[d]oes not establish that the petitioner has the physical plant and sufficiently trained workforce to provide the training specified").

[113] USCIS Policy Manual, Vol. 2, Pt. J, Ch. 3; *Matter of [name not provided]*, EAC 07 021 53665 (AAO Sept. 17, 2007), http://bit.ly/sep071d5.

[114] *Matter of [name not provided]*, EAC 05 043 52724 (AAO Sept. 16, 2005), http://bit.ly/sep058d.

[115] *Matter of [name and case number not provided]*, (AAO Jan. 6, 2015), http://bit.ly/jan151d5.

[116] *Id.*

[117] *Matter of [name not provided]*, LIN 94 196 51915 (AAU Aug. 26, 1994), 14 Immig. Rptr. B2-1 (stating "[a]lthough the record reflects that the beneficiary has received initial training at the [redacted], to characterize such training as 'substantial' greatly oversimplifies the training process for ballet dancers").

Copyright © 2017. American Immigration Lawyers Association. All rights reserved.

that the techniques could not have been taught during the degree program,[118] and experience letters from previous employers with descriptions of the former job duties.

Alternatively, the foreign national's education may have been in a related but different field from the proposed training; in another case, the AAO determined that a beneficiary with an associate's degree in culinary arts did not have substantial training and expertise in restaurant management.[119] Conversely, a statement that the educational training lacked a "hands-on and real-life aspect" is likely to be considered a statement that the trainee will engage in productive employment, especially if there is no explanation of the specifics of on-the-job training vis-à-vis other types of training to be provided.[120]

c. The Beneficiary Previously Received Practical Training in F-1 Status

If the foreign national gained expertise or received training through practical training while in F-1 status as an international student, then the H-3 petition may be denied. As noted above, the regulations prohibit use of the H-3 classification to extend the training of an international student, so requesting change of status from F-1 may result in denial of the H-3 petition.[121]

One strategy, reported to be successful from anecdotal evidence, is to demonstrate how the petitioner's training program was intended to have a two-year duration from the start, such that the H-3 change of status petition is necessary to complete the originally planned training program that the foreign national began while holding F-1 status. In this situation, the H-3 petition should explain how the petitioner initially intended a program involving two years of training and should include the detailed H-3 petition documents, including a specific training program and syllabus, to cover the entire two-year time period.

There are several issues with this approach, however. First, the practitioner is reminded that the other H-3 requirements must nevertheless be satisfied and indeed may be scrutinized more closely; it seems likely that USCIS will want confirmation that the specific aspects of the training provided during the first year, while the foreign national had Optional Practical Training (OPT) employment authorization, were not available in the home country, did not entail productive employment except that which was necessary and incidental to the training, and did not entail placement in a job in the business's normal operation where U.S. workers are regularly employed. Second, the H-3 petition may be construed as an attempt to extend the

---

[118] *Matter of [name not provided]*, NYC N 10670 (AAU Oct. 15, 1985), 3 Immig. Rptr. B2-16. These documents may overcome the suspicion that "the beneficiary has not already taken some or all of the courses listed on the training program outline" during previous educational programs.

[119] *Matter of [name not provided]*, EAC 04 258 53391 (AAO Jan. 6, 2006), http://bit.ly/jan0601d5.

[120] *Matter of [name not provided]*, EAC 07 021 53665 (AAO Sept. 17, 2007), http://bit.ly/sep071d5.

[121] 8 CFR §214.2(h)(7)(iii)(H); *Matter of [name not provided]*, WAC 06 054 50929 (AAO Sept. 17, 2007), http://bit.ly/sep072d5; *Matter of [name not provided]*, NYC N 10670 (AAU Oct. 15, 1985), 3 Immig. Rptr. B2-16").

Copyright © 2017. American Immigration Lawyers Association. All rights reserved.

U.S. training or employment of an international student, as noted above, so the H-3 petition should address how the training will benefit the foreign national's career abroad and substantiate the explanations with corroborating evidence wherever possible. Third, the practitioner is advised against preparing an H-3 petition that requests an additional two years for the training, as such a request is likely to undermine the contention that the training program was initially conceived as a two-year training program. The practitioner is advised to discuss these issues in detail with the client and to caution that the H-3 petition may still be denied.

Even if extension and change of status is not requested, however, the petition must "sufficiently differentiate" the proposed H-3 training program from the OPT that the foreign national received while in F-1 status.[122] Appropriate evidence may include descriptions of the duties of the OPT program; descriptions of the equipment or technologies for both programs;[123] evidence that the OPT training was received at a different entity than the H-3 petitioner; evidence of how the primary business purposes of the two entities differ; and names, job titles, and job descriptions of the different trainers and supervisors. The practitioner may wish to prepare a chart, similar to the "substantive differences chart" for a labor certification application, as discussed in Volume 2: Chapter Two, "The Labor Certification Application," to highlight the differences between the training programs.

C. Special Education Exchange Visitor Program

This subset of the H-3 classification was established by IMMACT90.[124] It is notable that the restrictions of participants of general H-3 training programs do not apply to these H-3 nonimmigrants,[125] including the prohibition on productive employment.[126] There are similarities with the J-1 classification, such as this H-3 subset being termed an "exchange visitor program," but the two classifications are different. First, an H-3 nonimmigrant is not subject to the two-year home residence requirement, even if the training program would otherwise be on the J-1 Skills List for the foreign national's home country.[127] Second, the scope of the H-3 program is extremely narrow and must entail training on special education for children with disabilities, as discussed below. Third, the H-3 subset has an annual quota of 50 visas, as noted above. Fourth, although the J-1 classification is appropriate to promote exposure to and an understanding of American culture, as discussed in

---

[122] *Matter of [name not provided]*, WAC 06 054 50929 (AAO Sept. 17, 2007), http://bit.ly/sep072d5.

[123] *Id.*

[124] Immigration Act of 1990 (IMMACT 90), Pub. L. 101-649, 104 Stat. 4978 (Nov 29, 1990); USCIS Policy Manual, Vol. 2, Pt. J, Ch. 1.

[125] 8 CFR §214.2(h)(7)(iv)(A)(*3*); 9 FAM 402.10-4(F).

[126] 9 FAM 402.10-4(G).

[127] For a discussion of the Skills List and the two-year foreign residence requirement, see Volume 1: Chapter Ten, "J Visas and Status."

Copyright © 2017. American Immigration Lawyers Association. All rights reserved.

Volume 1: Chapter Ten, "J-1 Visas and Status," this reason is likely to be less persuasive for H-3 petitions.[128]

The requirements for this H-3 classification are as follows:

- The foreign national will participate in "a special education training program" that is "structured" and "provides for practical training and experience in the education of children with physical, mental, or emotional disabilities";[129] and

- "The petition must be filed by a facility which has professionally trained staff and a structured program for providing education to children with disabilities, and for providing training and hands-on experience to participants in the special education exchange visitor program."[130]

Appropriate evidence for this special education exchange visitor program should include the following:

- A detailed description of the proposed training program, including descriptions of the following:

  - The facility's professional staff, such as details of professional, educational, and experience qualifications, details of any other professional training which would qualify the staff to provide the H-3 training, and details of previous supervision of H-3 special education training programs; and

  - The foreign national's participation in the training program, where "any custodial care of children must be incidental to the training";[131] and

- Evidence of the foreign national's professional qualifications, such as:

  - Possession of a bachelor's degree or higher degree in special education;

  - Evidence that the foreign national "is nearing completion of a baccalaureate or higher degree in special education," such as a letter from the foreign national's university or university transcripts; or

  - Evidence of "extensive prior training and experience in teaching children with physical, mental, or emotional disabilities,"[132] such as experience letters from the foreign national's previous employers or entities where the foreign national received training in special education.

---

[128] *Matter of [name not provided]*, EAC 07 021 53665 (AAO Sept. 17, 2007), http://bit.ly/sep071d5.

[129] 8 CFR §214.2(h)(7)(iv)(A)(*1*).

[130] 8 CFR §214.2(h)(7)(iv)(A)(*2*).

[131] 8 CFR §214.2(h)(7)(iv)(B)(*1*).

[132] 8 CFR §214.2(h)(7)(iv)(B)(*2*).

Copyright © 2017. American Immigration Lawyers Association. All rights reserved.

IV. Managing Client Expectations: Increased Scrutiny in Certain Situations

A. Training Programs for Medical Students

A medical student may participate in an H-3 training program, if it is offered by a "hospital approved by the American Medical Association or the American Osteopathic Association for either an internship or residency program."[133] The trainee must be "attending a medical school abroad" and "engage in employment as an extern during his or her medical school vacation."[134] These regulations should be distinguished from the rule that physicians may not use the H-3 classification for a residency program.[135]

B. Training Programs for Nurses

An H-3 petition on behalf of a foreign nurse may be approved if the following conditions are met:

- The nurse is not eligible for H-1 status;[136]

- The petition demonstrates that "there is a genuine need for the nurse to receive a brief period of training that is unavailable in the alien's native country and such training is designed to benefit the nurse and the overseas employer upon the nurse's return to the country of origin";[137]

- "The beneficiary has obtained a full and unrestricted license to practice professional nursing in the country where the beneficiary obtained a nursing education, or such education was obtained in the United States or Canada";[138] and

- "The petitioner provides a statement certifying that the beneficiary is fully qualified under the laws governing the place where the training will be received to engage in such training, and that under those laws the petitioner is authorized to give the beneficiary the desired training."[139]

Nevertheless, the practitioner is advised to provide evidence of the beneficiary's licensure and the petitioner's qualification and authorization to provide training under the laws of the location of the proposed training program.

C. Impact of Labor Disputes

A U.S. entity may not provide H-3 training if the Secretary of Labor certifies to the Attorney General that "a strike or other labor dispute involving a work stoppage

---

[133] 8 CFR §214.2(h)(7)(i)(A).

[134] *Id.*

[135] *Matter of Bronx Municipal Hospital Center*, 12 I&N Dec. 768 (Reg'l Comm'r 1968).

[136] 8 CFR §214.2(h)(7)(i)(B). For a discussion of the requirements for H-1 status, see Volume 1: Chapter Seven, "H-1B Visas and Status."

[137] 8 CFR §214.2(h)(7)(i)(B).

[138] 8 CFR §214.2(h)(7)(i)(B)(*1*).

[139] 8 CFR §214.2(h)(7)(i)(B)(*2*).

Copyright © 2017. American Immigration Lawyers Association. All rights reserved.

of workers is in progress in the occupation" at the training location and that the H-3 training "would adversely affect the wages and working conditions of U.S. citizens and lawful resident workers."[140] If both of these conditions are satisfied, then the H-3 petition will be denied.[141] If an H-3 petition has been approved, but the foreign national "has not yet entered the United States, or has entered the United States but not yet commenced employment," then the petition approval "is automatically suspended, and the application for admission on the basis of the petition shall be denied."[142] The practitioner should note that the strike or labor dispute must be certified by the Secretary of Labor.[143]

An H-3 trainee "shall not be deemed to be failing to maintain his or her status solely on account of past, present, or future participation in a strike or other labor dispute involving a work stoppage of workers," whether the strike or labor dispute is certified by the Secretary of Labor or not.[144] However, the H-3 trainee will "remain subject to all applicable provisions" of the immigration laws and regulations;[145] the H-3 status "is not modified or extended in any way by virtue of his or her participation,"[146] and a foreign national who remains in the United States beyond the expiration of authorized stay is subject to deportation, although participation in a strike or labor dispute should not be a ground for deportation.[147]

V. Preparing the H-3 Petition

This section discusses the documents of the H-3 petition. As discussed in Volume 1: Chapter Two, "Basic Nonimmigrant Concepts," all documents should be signed in black or blue ink.[148] The following documents should be prepared and filed for the H-3 petition:

- Cover letter
- Form G-28
- Form I-907, if applicable

---

[140] 8 CFR §214.2(h)(17)(i).

[141] 8 CFR §214.2(h)(17)(i)(A).

[142] 8 CFR §214.2(h)(17)(i)(B).

[143] 8 CFR §214.2(h)(17)(ii).

[144] 8 CFR §214.2(h)(17)(iii).

[145] 8 CFR §214.2(h)(17)(iii)(A).

[146] 8 CFR §214.2(h)(17)(iii)(B).

[147] 8 CFR §214.2(h)(17)(iii)(C).

[148] While USCIS previously advised signing documents in blue ink (*See, e.g.*, "TSC Liaison Minutes" (Aug. 13, 2000), AILA Doc. No. 00090703, in recent years it has more frequently stated a preference for black ink (*See, e.g.*, "Instructions for Notice of Entry of Appearance as Attorney or Accredited Representative" (May 5, 2106), https://www.uscis.gov/sites/default/files/files/form/g-28instr.pdf; "USCIS FY2016 H-1B Webpage Updated" (Mar. 12, 2015), AILA Doc. No. 15031362. In practice, however, the USCIS mailroom sometimes rejects forms signed in black ink because the signatures are incorrectly concluded to be photocopies, so signing in blue ink can be beneficial despite the USCIS instructions.

Copyright © 2017. American Immigration Lawyers Association. All rights reserved.

- Form I-129
- Supplement H
- Support statement from U.S. company
- Detailed training program

A. Form G-28

The U.S. company is the "petitioner" and the trainee is the "beneficiary" of an H-3 petition. The U.S. company's full address should be provided, and the trainee's foreign address should also be provided. If there is limited time to prepare and file the petition before the U.S. assignment is to begin, such as if the forms are emailed to and printed by the client, this form may be printed on plain white paper. However, as discussed in Volume 1: Chapter Two, "Basic Nonimmigrant Concepts," the Forms G-28 should be printed on blue paper whenever possible, in order to assist the USCIS mailroom in identifying the G-28.[149]

B. Form I-907

If the client wishes a response (approval, denial, or RFE) within 15 calendar days, then the client may pay USCIS an additional $1,225 for premium processing. This request may be filed concurrently with the H-3 petition, or the attorney or the client may request premium processing after the petition has been filed, by submitting Form I-907 with the petition's receipt notice, as discussed in Volume 1: Chapter Two, "Basic Nonimmigrant Concepts."

C. Form I-129

Part 1: Information on the U.S. company, including name, address, contact person, contact person's telephone number and email address, and Federal Employer Identification Number (FEIN), should be provided.

Part 2: For most H-3 petitions, "New employment" should be checked and consular notification should be requested, because change of status to H-3 is frequently problematic, as discussed above. As discussed in Volume 1: Chapter Two, "Basic Nonimmigrant Concepts," USCIS should then notify the Kentucky Consular Center (KCC), and the consulate abroad should then be able to confirm petition approval when the trainee applies for an H-3 visa.

If change of status is nevertheless requested, the practitioner should carefully review the approval notice to ensure that both the H-3 petition and the change of status request were approved, as failure to do so could result in the foreign national's accruing unlawful presence for the duration of the training program.[150] In addition, the expiration date of the foreign national's current status should be calendared, so that a request to extend status may be timely filed. Ideally, the H-3 change of status petition will be approved before the beneficiary's underlying status expires, and premium processing

---

[149] "VSC Practice Pointer: G-28s" (Sept. 4, 2008), AILA Doc. No. 08090469.

[150] "AILA/NSC Meeting Minutes" (July 27, 2006), AILA Doc. No. 06080269.

Copyright © 2017. American Immigration Lawyers Association. All rights reserved.

may make this scenario possible. The practitioner may wish to advise the client on the intricacies of situations where the initial status expires before the change of status petition is approved, as discussed in Volume 1: Chapter Two, "Basic Nonimmigrant Concepts." For more information on the eligibility requirements for change of status, accrual on unlawful presence, and filing an extension while a change of status petition is pending, see Volume 1: Chapter Two, "Basic Nonimmigrant Concepts."

Parts 3 and 4: Information about the beneficiary, including name, alternate names, date of birth, country of birth, country of birth and country of nationality, and passport information, should be provided.

An individual must have a passport that is valid for at least six months from the petition's expiration date; otherwise, he or she is inadmissible and ineligible for nonimmigrant status.[151] If the trainee does not have such a passport, the following options are available: either delay filing the H-3 petition until he or she obtains a renewed passport, or file the H-3 petition with a notation that the passport will be renewed, have the trainee apply for a renewed passport in the interim, wait for an RFE if one is issued, and then submit a photocopy of the biographic page of the renewed passport once it is available. For nationals of countries where passport renewal takes months, the second strategy can prevent the petition from being significantly delayed. If the client is willing to pay an additional $1,225 fee to USCIS, the delay caused by the RFE, which might also be several months, can be addressed by requesting premium processing when submitting the documentation of the renewed passport.

If the trainee is present in the United States when the petition is filed, the I-94 card information should be provided, even if the trainee will depart the United States during pendency of the H-3 petition. In this case, consular notification should be requested in Part 2, as discussed above.

Parts 5 through 7: Information about the title, description of training activities, location, compensation, and general information about the petitioner should be provided. Part 6 need not be completed for an H-3 petition. The form should be signed by the petitioner's representative and the practitioner.

D. H Supplement

Only the introduction section and Section 3 of this form must be completed. In Section 3, Question 1 addresses the requirements of the H-3 classification. If the answer to any question is "yes," an explanation should be provided in an addendum. An explanation may also be provided in the H-3 support statement. For example, if the beneficiary already possesses experience or education related to the proposed field of training, evidence of how this experience or education should not be considered "substantial expertise or training" should be provided.

---

[151] INA §212(a)(7)(B)(i). The exceptions to this rule in INA §212(a)(d)(4) are discussed in Volume 1: Chapter Two, "Basic Nonimmigrant Concepts."

Copyright © 2017. American Immigration Lawyers Association. All rights reserved.

A petitioner may answer "no" to Question 6, but then explain that a parent, subsidiary, affiliate, or another closely affiliated company will employ the foreign national upon completion of the training. If no arrangements have been made for subsequent employment, the petitioner should explain how training the foreign national will benefit the U.S. entity, as discussed above.

E. Support Statement

The support statement from the petitioner is very important, because it connects the training program to the petitioner's business and to the foreign national's background. The statement may also provide information required by the regulations but not included in a general training program template, as discussed below, and it may explain any acronyms used in the template training program so that the adjudicator understands the scope and objective of the H-3 training program. The statement should be on the U.S. company's letterhead and signed by a representative of the U.S. company. One format of a support statement is as follows:

- Introduction;

- Information about the petitioner;

- Discussion of the training program, including a discussion of why neither the training program nor a similar training program is available in the foreign national's home country;

- Discussion of the duties of the training program, including confirmation that the trainee will not be placed in a position that is in the normal operation of the petitioner's business and where U.S. workers are regularly employed, and possibly discussion of the proportion of productive employment, the number of hours of classroom instruction and on-the-job training, the supervision given, and the means of evaluation;

- Discussion of the foreign national's educational and experience background, including a discussion of how previous education and experience do not constitute substantial training and expertise in the field of proposed training, if applicable; and

- Thank you and conclusion.

Because the template training program should provide more detailed information on the structure of the training program, the H-3 support statement should focus on explaining the objectives of the training program as they relate to the nature of the petitioner's business (to rebut the conclusion that the training is "incompatible" with the petitioner's business), the proposed role of the trainee, and why the training is unavailable in the home country.

For example, the international group of companies may rely upon the U.S. training program to identify future managers and require that such individuals receive training on the methodologies and internal procedures of the U.S. headquarters before assuming managerial positions abroad. Alternatively, business plans for research and development activities may be developed by the U.S. operation but conducted abroad

Copyright © 2017. American Immigration Lawyers Association. All rights reserved.

because of lower overhead costs, thereby requiring a foreign national to receive training in the sophisticated technologies in the United States before performing the tests and creating the prototypes abroad. In each of these situations, the purpose of the training program should be highlighted, and any relevant information on the business plans to be managed abroad by the foreign national and the amount of financial investment should be included.

Either the H-3 support statement or the training program template may discuss the proportion of productive employment, the number of hours of classroom instruction and on-the-job training, the supervision given, and the means of evaluation; however, it may be best to only mention these points in the support statement and discuss them more fully in the template training program, for the reasons discussed below.

If the foreign national has already earned a degree or diploma in the field of proposed training or in a related field, or if the foreign national has already gained at least a few years of experience, the practitioner may wish to explain how the previous education and experience should not be considered substantial training and experience in the specific areas of training, as discussed above.

The final conclusion paragraph may contain the necessary information of the amount of remuneration for the professional services and any benefit to the petitioner.

F. Training Program and Index of Exhibits

The training program is the best place to explain the proportion of productive employment, the number of hours of classroom instruction and on-the-job training, the supervision given, and the means of evaluation, because then each of these points may be attached to a distinct and discrete phase of the training program, such that the adjudicator may see how the training program is specific, with a "fixed schedule, objectives, [and] means of evaluation."[152] In addition, if the training program is divided into rotations or segments, as is recommended above, then it is less likely that the adjudicator will view any on-the-job training as a solid block of time during which the training will rise to productive employment. The template training program may also provide individual objectives and different supervisors for each phase of the training, to underscore how each rotation covers a separate area.

Presentation of the training program in phases also makes it more likely that the adjudicator will see the connection between classroom instruction and any on-the-job training and see how any productive employment is incidental, such as if it is necessary as an evaluation to ensure that the foreign national understood the training. Experience has shown that the following types of evaluation may be acceptable, and typically, successful H-3 petitions have used more than one type of evaluation:

- Examination of the topics and materials covered by the training;
- Regular meetings with the supervisor(s), whether monthly, weekly, or following completion of each phase of the training;

---

[152] 8 CFR §214.2(h)(7)(iii)(A); *Matter of Kraus Periodicals*, 11 I&N Dec. 63 (Reg'l Comm'r 1964).

Copyright © 2017. American Immigration Lawyers Association. All rights reserved.

- Presentation of a completed project to senior managers or executives, where the productive employment would be necessary to evaluate the trainee's performance;

- Performance evaluations similar to those provided to regular staff employees; and

- Feedback from participants of the training program.

The practitioner may find that an index of exhibits helps to demonstrate that the requirements and restrictions have been met, especially if the training program is a template developed for use by the U.S. petitioner, as internal training programs and schedules will most likely not contain the information required by the regulations. If this is the case, then the template training program may be supplemented with additional evidence of compliance with the regulations, such as the job description for a foreign position following completion of the H-3 training program, evidence that the foreign operations exist, the absence of a similar training program at the foreign operations or in the home country, an explanation of the benefit to the H-3 petitioner in sponsoring the training program, an explanation of how the foreign national lacks substantial training and expertise in the narrow field of the H-3 program, copies of the credentials and résumés of the H-3 petitioner's staff, and photographs of the premises of the H-3 petitioner. The practitioner may also wish to organize the index of exhibits in the order of the regulations, with separate tabs for each requirement or restriction and sub-tabs for each document.

The section on H-3s in USCIS's Policy Manual contains a chart that is useful as a checklist of the issues and documentation that should be included with an H-3 petition.[153]

VI. Process

A. The H-3 Petition

After preparing the H-3 petition, it should be filed in duplicate, with original signatures,[154] with the USCIS Service Center with jurisdiction over the place of employment (and not the headquarters of the U.S. company, if different), as discussed in Volume 1: Chapter Two, "Basic Nonimmigrant Concepts." Practitioners may also find it helpful to write the following in large block letters across the side of the Form I-129: "DUPLICATE PETITION; PLEASE FORWARD TO KCC." If, however, the training program will take place in more than one location, the H-3 petition should be filed with the Service Center with jurisdiction over the state where the petitioning entity is based.[155]

---

[153] USCIS Policy Manual, Vol. 2, Pt. J, Ch. 6.

[154] USCIS, "Direct Filing Addresses for Form I-129, Petition for Nonimmigrant Worker," https://www.uscis.gov/i-129-addresses; "TSC Liaison Minutes" (Aug. 13, 2000), AILA Doc. No. 00090703.

[155] USCIS, "Direct Filing Addresses for Form I-129, Petition for Nonimmigrant Worker," https://www.uscis.gov/i-129-addresses.

Copyright © 2017. American Immigration Lawyers Association. All rights reserved.

The second set of original documents will be forwarded to the U.S. consulate where the trainee will apply for an H-3 visa as supplementary evidence for the Petition Information Management Service (PIMS), as discussed in Volume 1: Chapter Two, "Basic Nonimmigrant Concepts."[156] Following approval of an H-3 petition, USCIS forwards approval notification to the KCC, which in turn creates an electronic record to confirm the petition approval,[157] so the information becomes available to a consular officer to verify the petition approval.[158] Although duplicate original documents are not required, preparing and providing them may facilitate the trainee's visa application in the future.[159]

Multiple beneficiaries may be listed on the H-3 petition, if the foreign nationals will all receive "the same training, for the same period of time and in the same location."[160] However, if the foreign national will receive training from more than one U.S. entity, each entity must file an H-3 petition.[161] The practitioner should note that, unlike other H classifications, an agent may not file an H-3 petition.[162]

B. Visa Application

Upon approval of the H-3 petition, USCIS will send the attorney or representative an approval notice and the company representative will receive a courtesy copy. With the approval notice, the trainee may make an appointment to apply for an H-3 visa at a U.S. consulate abroad. Consular officers are instructed not to require Form I-797 as evidence of petition approval. Instead, "[a]ll petition approvals must be verified through the PIMS or through the PCQS [Person Centric Query Service]."[163] Nevertheless, the Form I-797 approval notice is needed to make the visa interview appointment, and it is generally preferable for the foreign national to present the original approval notice instead of the courtesy copy or a copy. The original approval notice will also be needed by the trainee at the time he or she is inspected by the CPB officer at the port of entry when entering the United States on the H-3 visa. Providing detailed instructions on how to apply for an H-3 visa, including a certified copy of the H-3 petition, is frequently very helpful to the client and the employee.

Following approval of the H-3 petition, the trainee, and his or her dependent spouse and family members, if applicable, may apply for H visas at a U.S. consulate

---

[156] DOS, "Accessing NIV Petition Information Via the CCD" (Nov. 2007), AILA Doc. No. 08040331; "PIMS Processing Update," AILA Doc. No. 08032132.

[157] DOS, "Temporary Worker Visas," https://travel.state.gov/content/visas/en/employment/temporary. html; "PIMS Update," AILA Doc. No. 08081564; "PIMS Processing Update," AILA Doc. No. 08032132.

[158] DOS, "Accessing NIV Petition Information Via the CCD," (Nov. 2007), AILA Doc. No. 08040331.

[159] "PIMS Processing Update," AILA Doc. No. 08032132.

[160] 9 FAM 402.10-10(B).

[161] 9 FAM 402.10-10(C).

[162] OI 214.2.

[163] 9 FAM 402.10-9(B). PIMS stands for Petition Information Management System and PCQS for Person Centric Query Service.

Copyright © 2017. American Immigration Lawyers Association. All rights reserved.

abroad. In addition to the general visa application documents discussed in Volume 1: Chapter Two, "Basic Nonimmigrant Concepts," the following documents should be presented, and individual consulates frequently have additional requirements:

- Original Form I-797 approval notice from USCIS;

- Statement from the petitioner confirming that the trainee continues to receive training, if the trainee obtained change of status from another nonimmigrant category;

- Certified copy of the H-3 petition, to be presented only if specifically requested; and

- Evidence of the visa applicant's foreign residence and nonimmigrant intent.

Because an H-3 petition must be approved by USCIS in order for a foreign national to apply for an H-3 visa, and because the "DHS regulations governing adjudication of H petitions are complex," consular officers have been directed to "rely on the expertise of DHS, specifically USCIS, in this area."[164] This means that the consular officer should not readjudicate the petition, as the H-3 petition approval "is prima facie evidence that the requirements for H classification which are examined in the petition process have been met," although in the interview "questions may arise as to the beneficiaries' eligibility,"[165] such as to confirm that the visa applicant has the proper nonimmigrant intent, as discussed above. Where "evidence which was not available to USCIS" emerges, the consular officer "may request any additional evidence which bears a reasonable relationship to this issue.[166] Disagreement with USCIS interpretation of the law or the facts, however, is not sufficient reason to ask USCIS to reconsider its approval of the petition."[167]

Dependents of H-3 trainees must also establish nonimmigrant intent by maintaining "a residence abroad to which they intend to return."[168] H-4 dependents are not authorized to accept employment "unless they qualify independently for a classification in which employment is, or can be, authorized."[169]

C. Admission to the United States

A foreign national may seek H-3 admission up to 10 days before the start date of the petition and may remain in the United States for 10 days after expiration of the petition, but the H-3 nonimmigrant may receive training only while the petition is valid.[170]

---

[164] 9 FAM 402.10-7(A).
[165] 9 FAM 402.10-7(B).
[166] Id.
[167] Id.
[168] 9 FAM 402.10-14.
[169] 9 FAM 402.10-14(C).
[170] 8 CFR §214.2(h)(13)(i)(A).

Copyright © 2017. American Immigration Lawyers Association. All rights reserved.

When seeking admission to the United States, the trainee should present his or her passport, with the H-3 visa, and the H-3 petition approval notice from USCIS. If entering by land, the trainee will be issued an I-94 card. If entering by sea or air, the individual will receive a stamp in the passport, and the I-94 will be recorded electronically.[171] Practitioners should advise clients who receive the passport stamp rather than the paper I-94 to check their I-94s on the online look-up[172] to ensure that it is correct and that the expiration date of their status is noted.

Due to the visa reciprocity schedules,[173] as discussed in Volume 1: Chapter Two, "Basic Nonimmigrant Concepts," a trainee may receive a visa valid for a shorter time period than the H-3 petition, but the expiration of H-3 status should match the end date of the H-3 petition and not the end date of the H-3 visa.

For example, Chinese citizens are eligible for H visas valid for no longer than 12 months. Therefore, even though the underlying H-3 petition was approved for 24 months, a Chinese citizen will be able to obtain an H visa that is valid for only 12 months from the date of visa issuance. The Petition Expiration Date (PED) provided in the lower right corner of the visa should, however, match the dates of validity of the H-3 petition as stated on the Form I-797 approval notice. For applicants for admission with visas valid for a shorter period of time than the H-3 petition, the practitioner may wish to reiterate the need to present the original Form I-797 approval notice, to ensure that the period of authorized stay stated on the I-94 record matches the dates of the petition validity. The practitioner may also wish to contact clients with these employees well in advance of the visa expiration date to strategize subsequent applications for visas, so that the trainees may travel internationally and re-enter the United States during the remaining time of petition validity.

For all trainees, good follow-up should include requesting copies of visas and I-94 cards to ensure that all the information is correct, and calendaring the expiration dates to monitor the trainees' status, as discussed below.

1. Admission of H-4 Dependents in B-2 Status

The spouse and children of an H-3 trainee may also use a B visa when seeking admission to the United States if the "planned period of stay is to be brief," or "if the spouse or child already has a valid B-2 visa and it would be inconvenient or impossible for him or her to apply for an H-4 visa."[174] The practitioner should carefully discuss this approach with the client and the foreign national, however, as the dependents should make no misrepresentations when seeking admission in B-2

---

[171] 78 Fed. Reg. 18457 (Mar. 27, 2013). *See also* CBP Fact Sheet, "I-94 Automation" (Nov. 2015), https://www.cbp.gov/sites/default/files/assets/documents/2016-Mar/i-94-automation-fact-sheet.pdf.

[172] CBP, "I-94 Website," https://i94.cbp.dhs.gov/I94/#/home.

[173] DOS, "Reciprocity and Civil Documents by Country," https://travel.state.gov/content/visas/en/fees/reciprocity-by-country.html.

[174] 9 FAM 402.10-14(D).

Copyright © 2017. American Immigration Lawyers Association. All rights reserved.

status at the port of entry. In particular, the practitioner may wish to have the dependents gather evidence of the brief stay, such as round-trip airfare, enrollment or admission in educational programs in the home country or elsewhere abroad, evidence of continued employment abroad, or other evidence of the reasons why the dependents will not remain in the United States for an extended period of time.

2. Canadian and Mexican Citizens

As discussed in Volume 1: Chapter Two, "Basic Nonimmigrant Concepts," Canadian citizens do not require visas in order to enter the United States.[175] Canadian nationals may apply for admission with the H-3 approval notice and Canadian passport at the port of entry.[176] As discussed above, it is also critical to note that H-3 admission may be denied if the trainee's admission to the United States "would adversely affect the wages and working conditions of U.S. citizens and lawful resident workers."[177] For a more in-depth discussion of applications for admission in nonimmigrant status by Canadian citizens, see Volume 1: Chapter Two, "Basic Nonimmigrant Concepts."

Unfortunately, Mexican citizens applying for H-3 visas may no longer obtain visas valid for up to two years by paying the reciprocity fee of $100 for each year of visa validity.[178]

VII. Additional Follow-up

After a foreign national has obtained H-3 status, the practitioner should follow up to request copies of the I-94 records and the visas, if applicable, to ensure that all the information is correct and to calendar the expiration dates to monitor the foreign national's status, as discussed in Volume 1: Chapter Two, "Basic Nonimmigrant Concepts."

A. Extensions, Renewals, and Change of Status

A foreign national who has held H-3 status for the maximum time period may not seek readmission, change of status, or H-3 extension until he or she has resided outside the United States for six months.[179] The practitioner should note that time in H-1, H-2, and/or L status counts toward the H-3 limitation.[180] In addition, any periods of unauthorized stay in the United States will not count toward the six months.

---

[175] 8 CFR §212.1(a).

[176] 9 FAM 402.10-8(F).

[177] 8 CFR §214.2(h)(17)(i).

[178] DOS, "Mexico Reciprocity Schedule," https://travel.state.gov/content/visas/en/fees/reciprocity-by-country/MX.html. *Cf.* former DOS website, "Mexico Reciprocity Schedule," formerly http://travel.state.gov/visa/frvi/reciprocity/reciprocity_3622.html#B (link no longer works).

[179] 8 CFR §214.2(h)(13)(iv).

[180] *Id.*

Copyright © 2017. American Immigration Lawyers Association. All rights reserved.

The practitioner should note that this rule should not apply if the foreign national does not accrue the maximum period of stay.[181] Therefore, a foreign national who has held H-3 status for a period that is less than the respective 24 or 18 months should be eligible for an H-3 extension, as discussed below, or change of status. The practitioner should discuss this availability with the client when strategizing options for longer-term employment authorization, if applicable. But the practitioner also should highlight how USCIS may nevertheless question the authenticity of the H-3 petition, especially whether the petitioner wished to train the foreign national for staffing of its domestic operations, and should caution the client that the petition for change of status from H-3 may be denied.

The exceptions to this rule are: (1) if the trainee did not reside continually in the United States and the trainee's "employment" was seasonal, intermittent, or for an aggregate of six months or less per year; or (2) if the trainee resides abroad and regularly commutes to the United States to engage in part-time "employment."[182] The practitioner should note that, although the regulations prohibit the "productive employment" of H-3 trainees, as discussed above, this regulation uses the term "employment." In these situations, the H-3 maximum periods of stay may not apply, as the trainee may not accrue a single year in H-3 status and therefore not be subject to the two-year or 18-month limitations.[183] The exception is unavailable if the H-4 dependents have resided continuously in the United States in H-4 status.[184] For a discussion of what may qualify as "part-time employment," see Volume 1: Chapter Eleven, "L-1 Visas and Status."

The petitioner and trainee bear the burden to provide "clear and convincing proof" of qualifying for these exceptions: "Such proof shall consist of evidence such as arrival and departure records, copies of tax returns, and records of employment abroad."[185] The practitioner may wish to supplement these documents with copies of property titles, mortgage or lease agreements, utility bills for the foreign residence, and credit card statements for purchases made outside the United States.

1. H-3 Extensions

It is possible to obtain H-3 extensions, as long as the total period of H-3 stay does not exceed the two-year or 18-month limitation.[186] But if the foreign national is the beneficiary of an approved labor certification application or of a filed employment-based immigrant visa petition filed by the current H-3 employer, this is "a reason, by itself," to deny the extension request.[187]

---

[181] 8 CFR §214.2(h)(13)(iv).

[182] 8 CFR §214.2(h)(13)(v).

[183] Id.

[184] 9 FAM 402.10-13(C).

[185] 8 CFR §214.2(h)(13)(v).

[186] 8 CFR §214.2(h)(15)(ii)(D).

[187] 8 CFR §214.2(h)(16)(ii).

Copyright © 2017. American Immigration Lawyers Association. All rights reserved.

The H-3 extension may be necessary if the foreign national entered the United States later than originally anticipated,[188] or if the initial H-3 petition was approved after the requested start date. The support statement should clearly explain why the extension is necessary and should include details on the remaining phases of the training program, if available. The support statement should also demonstrate how the purpose is not to "extend an organized training program that [the petitioner] had previously indicated was of a certain duration."[189]

Alternatively, a petitioner may request an H-3 extension in order for the trainee to receive advanced training.[190] However, when requesting such an extension, the practitioner should note that the following factors are likely to be considered:

- The approval and existence of the initial training program;
- The "content of the new program in comparison with that of the old"; and
- The "duration of the programs."[191]

To maximize approval of the extension, the H-3 petition and support statement should explain how the new H-3 training program is advanced and different from the initial training program. The practitioner is also advised to demonstrate that despite the request for an extension, the new training program is not an effort to allow the foreign national to engage in productive employment or to train the foreign national for the U.S. company's domestic staff.

In addition, the H-3 extension request may result in an inquiry into the bona fides of the H-3 petition regarding the trainee's performance of productive employment, the trainee's pursuit of a career outside the United States, and the international presence of the petitioner's operations.[192] In one case, the AAU made specific mention of how "the majority of the restaurants and hotels which [the petitioner] operates are in the United States."[193]

2. Change of Status from H-3

In practice, change of status requests from H-3 to another nonimmigrant classification are frequently denied, as the initial H-3 petition would have had to demonstrate how the foreign national's career abroad would benefit from the U.S. training. If the petitioner subsequently requests change of status from H-3, USCIS may question the veracity of the initial H-3 petition and determine that the foreign national did not intend to further his or her career abroad and that the H-3 petitioner wished to train the foreign national for staffing of its domestic operations.

---

[188] *Matter of [name not provided]*, EAC 87 150 0096 (AAU July 31, 1987), 5 Immig. Rptr. B2-26.

[189] *Matter of [name not provided]*, NYC N 98456 (AAU May 15, 1986), 3 Immig. Rptr. B2-132.

[190] *Id.*

[191] *Id.*

[192] *Id.*

[193] *Id.*

Copyright © 2017. American Immigration Lawyers Association. All rights reserved.

Experience has also shown that the H-3 nonimmigrant visa classification is frequently considered by petitioners and practitioners as an alternative to the largely unavailable H-1B visa classification.[194] For example, a U.S. company may wish to continue to provide training to a foreign national in F-1 OPT status, although this situation is typically closely scrutinized by USCIS, as discussed, above. For these situations, the practitioner is advised to discuss how H-3 status differs from H-1B status, including how OPT extensions or "cap-gap" measures are not available to foreign nationals seeking H-3 change of status.[195]

If the client nevertheless wishes to seek H-1B status on behalf of a trainee who holds H-3 status, then the option remains for the foreign national to apply for an H-1B visa at a U.S. consulate abroad. The practitioner should advise the client that, even if the petition is awarded an H-1B visa number,[196] the visa application may be closely scrutinized regarding the bona fides of the H-3 petition, especially regarding the representations made about the foreign national's pursuit of a career abroad, the foreign national's maintenance of a residence abroad for the duration of the H-3 petition, and the petitioner's desire to train the foreign national for its domestic staff, as discussed above.

In one nonprecedent decision, an O-1 petition was approved on behalf of a foreign national who had been initially admitted to the United States in H-3 status.[197] It is not clear, however, whether the petitioner requested a change of status from H-3 to O-1. Given that a previous petition filed by the petitioner was denied, both by USCIS and by the AAU, it seems more likely that change of status was not requested, as the foreign national would not have held valid H-3 status following denial of the second petition.[198] And although the decision did not address the issue of whether the H-3 training program was used to train the foreign national in order to ultimately staff the petitioner's business,[199] the practitioner is advised to address this point if the client nevertheless wishes to request change of status.

B. Sponsoring an H-3 Trainee for Permanent Residence

In most cases, employment-based sponsorship for permanent residence on behalf of H-3 nonimmigrants is extremely difficult, because the aggregate processing time for approval of the labor certification application, approval of the immigrant visa petition, and availability of an immigrant visa number are highly likely to be more than two

---

[194] For a discussion of the numerical limitation on H-1B visa numbers, see Volume 1: "Chapter Seven, H-1B Visas and Status."

[195] For a discussion of OPT extensions for students in Science, Technology, Engineering, and Mathematics (STEM) fields and "cap-gap" measures to allow F-1 students seeking H-1B status to remain in the United States, see Volume 1: Chapter Seven, "H-1B Visas and Status."

[196] For a discussion of the difficulty in obtaining an H-1B visa number, see Volume 1: Chapter Seven, "H-1B Visas and Status."

[197] *Matter of [name not provided]*, WAC 94 180 51386 (AAU Oct. 13, 1994), 13 Immig. Rptr. B2-224.

[198] *Id.*

[199] *Id.*

Copyright © 2017. American Immigration Lawyers Association. All rights reserved.

years.[200] Typically, the foreign national will not be eligible for EB-2 classification, because holding a master's degree or having five years of post-baccalaureate experience is likely to be considered substantial training and expertise that would likely result in denial of the H-3 petition. The delays in immigrant visa availability for the EB-3 classification will most likely mean that the foreign national will be unable to apply to adjust status before expiration of the H-3 maximum time limitation.[201]

It may be possible to request consular processing so that the foreign national may remain outside the United States and pursue a career abroad while awaiting issuance of an immigrant visa. The practitioner should counsel the client, however, that the U.S. consulate may question whether the initial H-3 petition was filed in order to train the foreign national in order to ultimately staff the U.S. operations, as discussed above. The practitioner may wish to provide the foreign national with evidence of how the H-3 training was unrelated to the position sponsored for permanent residence, such as if the training was for development of management skills but the permanent position is for a professional who will have no management responsibilities. Alternatively, the foreign national may have gained experience or qualifications abroad that made him or her a candidate for permanent residence sponsorship, such as if following the training and employment abroad, the foreign national attained extraordinary ability.[202]

In addition, a foreign national should not claim that he or she gained necessary experience required for the labor certification application and immigrant visa petition while in the United States in H-3 status:

> "The petitioner cannot go on record in one proceeding on a date certain (upon the filing of a nonimmigrant trainee petition) by stating that the beneficiary's services are sought as a trainee and consequently establish with any credibility in another proceeding that the time spent in that trainee capacity was not actually training but work experience."[203]

---

[200] For an overview of the permanent residence process, see Volume 2: Chapter Two, "The Labor Certification Application"; Volume 2: Chapter Three, "The Immigrant Visa Petition"; and Volume 2: Chapter Four, "Consular Processing, Adjustment of Status, and Permanent Residence Issues."

[201] For a discussion of the immigrant visa petition classifications and visa retrogression, see Volume 2: Chapter Three, "The Immigrant Visa Petition."

[202] *Matter of [name not provided]*, WAC 94 180 51386 (AAU Oct. 13, 1994), 13 Immig. Rptr. B2-224.

[203] *Matter of [name not provided]*, A23 541 030 (AAU Apr. 11, 1985), 2 Immig. Rptr. B2-103.

Copyright © 2017. American Immigration Lawyers Association. All rights reserved.

CHAPTER TEN

J-1 TRAINEES AND INTERNS

I. Executive Summary

The J-1 classification allows foreign nationals to visit the United States as exchange visitors, in order to receive training or participate in internships, among other programs offered by sponsors designated by the Department of State (DOS). The J-1 program sponsor must approve the proposed training or internship program as a career development opportunity for the J-1 participant. Afterward, the J-1 sponsor issues a DS-2019, Certificate of Eligibility, which allows the foreign national to apply for a J-1 visa or status. The foreign national must document his or her nonimmigrant intent, and, in order to emphasize the importance of ties abroad, J-1 trainee or intern status requires current enrollment in or prior completion of a qualifying foreign university degree and/or foreign employment experience. A J-1 program may be valid for up to 18 months for trainees and up to 12 months for interns. Extensions or subsequent J-1 intern and trainee programs may be obtained in certain limited circumstances. Dependent spouses and children of J-1 exchange visitors hold J-2 status and are eligible to apply for employment authorization, provided that the employment is not necessary to support the principal exchange visitor.

A. Checklist of Requirements

- Training or internship must be specific, supervised, and evaluated, with little or no time performing clerical tasks
- Approval of the training or internship program by a designated J-1 sponsor
- Nonimmigrant intent on the part of the foreign national
- Sufficient funds to cover expenses during the J-1 program

B. Documents Necessary to Prepare the Application (Filed with J-1 Program Sponsor)

- Description of U.S. training program or internship
- Copies of the foreign national's educational degrees and/or transcripts from foreign university
- Copy of foreign national's résumé
- Foreign national's experience letters from foreign employer(s)
- Basic information about the company
- Copy of biographic page(s) of passport(s) of the foreign national and any dependent spouse and children

C. Checklist of Questions to Ask the Client

- What are the purpose, scope, and phases of the training or internship program?
- Who will supervise each phase of the training or internship?
- Is the training in the field of "Agriculture" or "Hospitality and Tourism"?

Copyright © 2017. American Immigration Lawyers Association. All rights reserved.

- Does the foreign national have permanent ties to his or her country of permanent residence?

- If pursuing J-1 intern status, is the foreign national an enrolled student in a degree-granting, post-secondary program outside the United States? Is the student receiving credit for the U.S. internship?

- Is the foreign national a beneficiary of an immigrant visa petition or labor certification application?

- Does the foreign national have other countries of citizenship or permanent residence?

- Has the host organization previously provided a training or internship opportunity to a foreign national in J-1 status?

- How many individuals does the host organization employ?

- What is the host organization's annual revenue?

II. Introduction

The J-1 visa classification allows foreign nationals to reside temporarily in the United States as exchange visitors, "to increase mutual understanding between the people of the United States and the people of other countries" and "to further the foreign policy objectives of the United States."[1] The foreign national must have nonimmigrant intent, as discussed below. The United States Information Agency (USIA), the predecessor to DOS for purposes of the exchange visitor program, noted the clear congressional intent that "the private sector was to have a major role in ... cultural exchange activities ... and provide assistance for those exchange activities which are in the broadest national interests."[2]

The J-1 visa is available to "a bona fide student, scholar, trainee, teacher, professor, research assistant, specialist, or leader in a field of specialized knowledge or skill, or other person of similar description," and foreign medical graduate,[3] but this chapter will focus on J-1 programs for interns and trainees, where the practitioner's client is a U.S. company and will be a "host organization" for a J-1 program, which, in turn, is sponsored by a J-1 "sponsor" or "program sponsor" designated by DOS.[4] For brevity, the J-1 "program application" means the documents submitted to a designated J-1 program sponsor when requesting issuance of a Form DS-2019, Certificate of Eligibility. The practitioner may find the DOS list of J-1 intern and trainee sponsors, noted below, helpful when determining the appropriate "umbrella" J-1 program sponsor to which to send the J-1 program application, as J-1 program sponsors often limit their programs to specific industries and/or fields.

---

[1] 22 Code of Federal Regulations (CFR) §62.1(a).

[2] 58 Fed. Reg. 15180 (Mar. 19, 1993).

[3] Immigration and Nationality Act (INA) §101(a)(15)(J).

[4] Issues related to foreign medical graduates can alone comprise a book. *See Immigration Options for Physicians* (AILA, 3d Ed., 2009), https://agora.aila.org/product/detail/71.

Copyright © 2017. American Immigration Lawyers Association. All rights reserved.

In addition, this chapter will not discuss the eligibility requirements for J-1 sponsors,[5] the process of obtaining J-1 sponsor designation,[6] the complete obligations of J-1 sponsors and responsible officers,[7] the potential sanctions against J-1 program sponsors,[8] and the termination of designation,[9] for the reasons discussed in the Preface, although there is some discussion of the duties and obligations of J-1 program sponsors below. The practitioner may find that a client company has been designated as a J-1 program sponsor,[10] and this chapter may be helpful when approaching how to develop Form DS-7002, Training/Internship Placement Plan, and any supporting documents.

It is inappropriate for a J-1 internship or training program to involve certain activities, and J-1 sponsors should not approve them:

- Programs involving "unskilled or casual labor positions";[11]

- Programs that "require or involve child care or elder care," or "clinical or any other kind of work that involves patient care or patient contact, including any work that would require trainees or interns to provide therapy, medication, or other clinical or medical care (*e.g.*, sports or physical therapy, psychological counseling, nursing, dentistry, veterinary medicine, social work, speech therapy, and early childhood education)"[12]

- Programs that "involve more than 20 per cent clerical work,"[13] which is defined as "routine administrative work generally performed in an office or office-like setting, such as data entry, filing, typing, mail sorting and distribution, and other general office tasks";[14]

- Programs that "[p]lace trainees or interns in positions, occupations, or businesses that could bring the Exchange Visitor Program or the Department into notoriety or disrepute";[15] and

- Training programs "in the field of aviation,"[16] as discussed below.

---

[5] 22 CFR §62.3.

[6] 22 CFR §§62.5–.6.

[7] 22 CFR §§62.8–.15.

[8] 22 CFR §62.50.

[9] 22 CFR §§62.60–.63.

[10] Department of State (DOS), "Designated Sponsor Organizations," https://j1visa.state.gov/participants/how-to-apply/sponsor-search/?program=Intern (noting J-1 program sponsor designation for companies such as General Electric International, Inc., Hewlett-Packard Company, Intel Corporation, and PricewaterhouseCoopers LLC).

[11] 22 CFR §62.22(j)(1). For a list of "unskilled occupations" previously designated by DOS, *see* former 22 CFR §514.22(c)(1), 58 Fed. Reg. 15180 (Mar. 19, 1993).

[12] 22 CFR §62.22(j)(1).

[13] 22 CFR §62.22(j)(4).

[14] 22 CFR §62.2.

[15] 22 CFR §62.22(j)(2).

Copyright © 2017. American Immigration Lawyers Association. All rights reserved.

In addition, the J-1 training and intern categories should not be used simply to staff U.S. entities. Thus, designated J-1 programs are not permitted to "[e]ngage or otherwise cooperate or contract with a Staffing/Employment Agency to recruit, screen, orient, place, evaluate, or train trainees or interns, or in any other way involve such agencies in" a J-1 internship or training program,[17] as discussed below.

DOS terminated J-1 sponsor designation for all sponsors of flight training programs, effective June 1, 2010,[18] because DOS "does not have the expertise and resources to fully monitor flight training programs and insure their compliance with the national security concerns expressed in the PATRIOT Act."[19] Designated J-1 sponsors "will not be able to initiate new programs after December 31, 2009," although exchange visitors already in the United States were permitted to complete their training programs.[20]

The practitioner may wish to note two points. First, there are separate J-1 subsets for a number of different pursuits, including graduate medical education that involves specialized training available only to certain foreign medical graduates.[21] Second, internship and training programs should provide a career development opportunity and not merely additional experience. Accordingly, DOS understands that such programs may entail "work," as discussed below. However, J-1 trainees and interns should not be engaging in regular employment, as discussed below.

The spouse and minor children of a J-1 exchange visitor qualify for J-2 status,[22] and may request an Employment Authorization Document (EAD) once in the United States in J-2 status.[23]

Finally, certain information relating to "national security or law enforcement matters" gathered about J-1 program sponsors and exchange visitors is exempt from the Privacy Act, "in order to ensure that these [exchange visitors] comply with the requirements of their admission."[24]

III. Requirements and Interpretations

A. Internships and Training Programs

The two types of J-1 training programs discussed in this chapter are for interns and for trainees.[25] "Intern" is defined as "a foreign national participating in a structured

---

[16] 9 Foreign Affairs Manual (FAM) 402.5-6(E)(14).

[17] 22 CFR §62.22(j)(3).

[18] 73 Fed. Reg. 40008 (July 11, 2008).

[19] 71 Fed. Reg. 3913 (Jan. 24, 2006).

[20] 73 Fed. Reg. 40008 (July 11, 2008).

[21] 22 CFR §62.27.

[22] 22 CFR §41.62(b).

[23] 8 CFR §274a.12(c)(5).

[24] 73 Fed. Reg. 63507 (Oct. 23, 2008). For a discussion of the Privacy Act, see Volume 1: Chapter Two, "Basic Nonimmigrant Concepts."

[25] 22 CFR §62.22(a).

Copyright © 2017. American Immigration Lawyers Association. All rights reserved.

and guided work-based internship program in his or her specific academic field and who either":

- "Is currently enrolled full-time in and actively pursuing studies at a foreign ministerially-recognized degree or certificate-granting post-secondary academic institution outside the United States[;] or

- "Graduated from such an institution no more than 12 months prior to the exchange visitor program begin date reflected on Form DS-2019."[26]

Such an intern should participate in an "Internship Program," which is defined as:

"[A] structured and guided work-based learning program as set forth in an individualized Training/Internship Placement Plan (T/IPP) that reinforces a student's or recent graduate's academic study, recognizes the need for work-based experience, provides on-the-job exposure to American techniques, methodologies, and expertise, and enhances the Intern's knowledge of American culture and society."[27]

"Trainee," in turn, is defined as "a foreign national participating in a structured and guided work-based training program in his or her specific occupational field (in an occupational category for which a sponsor has obtained designation) who has either:

- "A degree or professional certificate from a foreign ministerially-recognized post-secondary academic institution and at least one year of prior related work experience in his or her occupational field acquired outside the United States[;] or

- "Five years of work experience in his or her occupational field outside the United States."[28]

A trainee should participate in a "Training Program," which is defined as "a structured and guided work-based learning program for a trainee as set forth in an individualized Trainee/Internship Placement Plan (Form DS-7002) that develops new and advanced skills in a trainee's occupational field through exposure to American techniques, methodologies, and technologies, and enhances a trainee's understanding of American culture and society."[29]

For brevity, this chapter will refer to the first type of program as an internship and the second type of program as a training program. A J-1 program must be full time, which is defined as a "minimum of 32 hours a week."[30] All J-1 programs should be at least three weeks in duration.[31]

---

[26] 22 CFR §62.4(h)(7).
[27] 22 CFR §62.2.
[28] 22 CFR §62.4(c).
[29] 22 CFR §62.2.
[30] 22 CFR §62.22(f)(1)(iv).
[31] 22 CFR §62.8(b).

Copyright © 2017. American Immigration Lawyers Association. All rights reserved.

A J-1 internship may be no longer than 12 months.[32] A J-1 training program may be valid for up to 18 months, except that training programs in "Agriculture" and in "Hospitality and Tourism" may be no longer than 12 months,[33] because DOS believes that "12 months is sufficient time to train a person in these occupational fields or categories."[34] In addition, any internship or training program lasting six months or more in the field of Hospitality and Tourism must contain at least "three departmental or functional rotations."[35]

Although training programs in the field of Agriculture typically have a maximum time period of 12 months, a J-1 program may be approved for 18 months if the additional six months of the program is "related classroom participation and studies," provided the classroom element was included in the original Trainee/Internship Placement Plan (T/IPP).[36] It may not be added at the end when the program extension is requested.

J-1 programs in the fields of Agriculture or Hospitality and Tourism that are management programs (e.g., "restaurant management, turf management") may last up to 18 months.[37] In contrast, programs at hotels or restaurants that rotate the trainee or intern through numerous departments and culminate "in a single supervisory position ... would fall under the 'Hospitality and Tourism' occupational category and be limited to 12 months."[38]

In addition, the J-1 program sponsor and/or host organization must "[c]ertify that training and internship programs in the field of agriculture meet all the requirements of the Fair Labor Standards Act ... and the Migrant and Seasonal Agricultural Worker Protection Act."[39] The practitioner may wish to caution the U.S. host company and foreign national that consular officials and/or immigration inspectors may question whether the proposed U.S. activities constitute employment rather than training or an internship, as discussed below.

The practitioner should also note the differing terms used in the definitions of the intern and trainee categories. Generally, internships should build upon the interns' academic study through work experience and on-the-job exposure to work activities "to develop practical skills that will enhance their future careers,"[40] whereas training programs seek to develop the trainees' previously acquired skills in a specific occupational field. The trainee category is geared toward allowing "foreign nationals

---

[32] 22 CFR §62.22(k).

[33] Id.

[34] 72 Fed. Reg. 33669 (June 19, 2007).

[35] 22 CFR §62.22(j)(5).

[36] 22 CFR §62.22(k).

[37] 9 FAM 402.5-6(E)(15); 72 Fed. Reg. 33669 (June 19, 2007).

[38] 9 FAM 402.5-6(E)(15).

[39] 22 CFR §62.22(f)(2)(vi); 75 Fed. Reg. 48555 (Aug. 11, 2010).

[40] 22 CFR §62.22(b)(2).

Copyright © 2017. American Immigration Lawyers Association. All rights reserved.

with significant experience in their occupational field [to] have the opportunity to receive training in the United States in such field."[41] For interns, "[p]rior work experience is not an eligibility requirement for participation."[42] As stated by DOS, "work-based learning" is appropriate for interns, and trainees should receive "bona fide training."[43]

To qualify for J-1 status:

- Trainees must have either

  - "a degree or professional certification from a foreign post-secondary academic institution and at least one year of prior related work experience in their occupational field acquired outside the United States, or

  - "five years of work experience in their occupational field acquired outside the United States." [44]

- Interns must be

  - "currently enrolled and full-time and pursuing studies in their advanced chosen career field at a degree- or certificate-granting post-secondary academic institution outside the United States, or

  - "graduated from such an institution no more than 12 months prior to their exchange visitor program begin date."[45]

In 2007, when DOS promulgated an interim final rule to re-engineer the trainee category to create two separate categories, one for interns and one for trainees, it also took the opportunity to "eliminate the distinction among 'non-specialty occupations'[,] … 'specialty occupations,' and 'unskilled' occupations."[46] As stated by DOS: "Time has proven that the distinctions among these three occupational categories are conceptually artificial and do not adequately describe the types of training that the Department desires to promote in the national interest."[47] Therefore, the focus of the inquiry shifted from the "artificial categorization of the type of training" to "the amount of prior experience" held by the foreign national.[48] The educational and/or experience requirements should better "ensure[] that prospective

---

[41] 22 CFR §62.22(a).

[42] 73 Fed. Reg. 35066 (June 20, 2008).

[43] 22 CFR §62.22(i)(2).

[44] 22 CFR §62.22(d)(2) (bulleting added). Although the lack of punctuation in this regulatory section leaves ambiguous what is an alternative to what, the preamble to the final rule makes clear that five years of work experience is the alternative to a degree/certification plus one year of experience. 75 Fed. Reg. 48555, 48556 (Aug. 11, 2010).

[45] 22 CFR §62.22(d)(3) (bulleting added).

[46] 72 Fed. Reg. 33669 (June 19, 2007). *See also* final rule at 75 Fed. Reg. 48555 (Aug. 11, 2010).

[47] *Id.*

[48] *Id.*

Copyright © 2017. American Immigration Lawyers Association. All rights reserved.

participants have an established connection with their home country at the time of application for participation in a training program."[49]

DOS intended that internships would allow students and recent graduates to "[b]ridg[e] the gap between formal education and practical work experience."[50] However, DOS also stated: "It is imperative that the new internship program be a true learning experience for the participant, one that is an integral part of the on-going education of the participant and one that is in harmony with what the Congress intended when it enacted the Fulbright-Hays Act."[51]

Both the internship and training programs "must not be used as substitutes for ordinary employment or work purposes; nor may they be used under any circumstances to displace American workers."[52] In particular, the J-1 program must entail bona fide training. The J-1 should not be used "merely [to] gain[] additional work experience" or for unskilled labor,[53] as discussed below. The practitioner should note that although the regulation only specifically prohibits an internship from involving unskilled labor, it seems very likely that training programs also should not entail unskilled labor.[54] It is worth emphasizing that the regulations are explicit that neither interns nor trainees may spend more than 20 percent of their time on clerical tasks,[55] which can be considered a subset of the unskilled labor concept.

B. Special Programs for Certain Nationalities

The Bureau of Educational and Cultural Affairs (ECA) has established programs specifically for Korean and Irish citizens. Korean citizens are eligible for the "Work, English Study, Travel" (WEST) program, where university students and recent graduates may visit the United States "for a period of 18 months on J-1 exchange visitor visas that will allow them to study English, participate in internships, and travel independently" to receive training on "American business practices and business procedures, U.S. corporate culture, and general office management issues."[56] The program, which became effective on October 31, 2008, and as of this writing is extended until 2018, has an annual limit of 2,000.[57] As of February 2015, about 2,000

---

[49] Id.

[50] 22 CFR §62.22(b)(2).

[51] 72 Fed. Reg. 33669 (June 19, 2007).

[52] 22 CFR §62.22(b)(1)(ii).

[53] Id.

[54] Id.

[55] 22 CFR §62.22(j)(4).

[56] DOS, "The WEST (Work, English Study, Travel) Program," http://2001-2009.state.gov/r/pa/prs/ps/2008/sept/110083.htm (archived document).

[57] Alliance for International Exchange, "U.S. and Korea Sign MOU to extend WHP and WEST exchange programs" (Oct. 30, 2013), http://www.alliance-exchange.org/policy-monitor/10/30/2013/us-and-korea-sign-mou-extend-whp-and-west-exchange-programs.

Copyright © 2017. American Immigration Lawyers Association. All rights reserved.

Korean nationals had used the program since its inception,[58] so there seems little immediate danger of exceeding the quota. J-1 sponsors approved to participate in the program issue Forms DS-2019 for these trainees and interns.[59] A host organization may be a corporate, nonprofit, academic, or other employer.[60] The foreign national must meet the following requirements:

- Be a citizen of South Korea;

- Be approved for participation by the government of South Korea;

- Be enrolled in or have graduated from a university in the immediate preceding 12 months;

- Not be a vocational student "pursuing studies at a tertiary level accredited academic institution";

- Have "proof of sufficient financial resources, prior to coming to the United States, to support [him/herself] throughout [the] program and for [the] return home"; and

- Not be accompanied to the United States by dependents.[61]

Similarly, DOS announced the "Intern Work and Travel (IWT) Program" for Irish citizens, through which students and recent graduates may visit the United States for up to 12 months to participate in internships and travel independently.[62] The program was initially authorized for five years, effective October 31, 2008, and, as of this writing, has been extended to 2019.[63] It is not clear whether there is a numerical limitation but it has been stated that "1,300 Irish participants come to the United States each year" under the program.[64] IWT participants must meet the following requirements:

- Be a citizen of Ireland;

- Be a student at or have graduated from a university in his or her home country in the immediate preceding 12 months;

---

[58] U.S. Embassy and Consulate in Korea, "Mark Lippert Remarks at Korea Employers Federation 38th Top Management Forums" (Feb. 5, 2015), http://bit.ly/Lippertremarks.

[59] DOS, "Guidelines for Administration of the WEST (Work, English Study, and Travel) Program" (Sept. 25, 2008), https://j1visa.state.gov/wp-content/uploads/2012/09/pilot-program-west.pdf.

[60] Id.

[61] Id.

[62] DOS, "Guidelines for Administration of the Intern Work and Travel Pilot Program with Ireland" (Oct. 31, 2008), https://j1visa.state.gov/wp-content/uploads/2012/09/pilot-program-irish-iwt.pdf; U.S. Embassy in Ireland, "United States and Ireland sign three year extension to the Ireland Work and Travel Program" (Dec. 6, 2006), https://ie.usembassy.gov/united-states-ireland-sign-three-year-extension-ireland-work-travel-iwt-program/.

[63] U.S. Embassy in Ireland, "United States and Ireland sign three year extension to the Ireland Work and Travel Program" (Dec. 6, 2016), https://ie.usembassy.gov/united-states-ireland-sign-three-year-extension-ireland-work-travel-iwt-program/.

[64] Id.

Copyright © 2017. American Immigration Lawyers Association. All rights reserved.

- Not be a vocational student "pursuing studies at a tertiary level accredited academic institution … unless such vocational study is part of a structured program leading to a degree or other credential recognized as equivalent to Level VI of the Irish Higher Education System";

- Have "proof of sufficient financial resources, prior to coming to the United States, to support [him/herself] throughout [the] exchange visitor program and for [the] return home"; and

- Not be accompanied to the United States by dependents.[65]

In contrast to other J-1 programs, IWT exchange visitors need not have an approved internship with a host organization in order to apply for a J-1 visa or seek U.S. admission; they may seek placement with a host organization after being admitted to the United States. The Form DS-2019 should note the absence of a host organization in the Subject/Field Code Remarks Box (*e.g.*, IWT participant).[66] The Form DS-7002, the Training/Internship Placement Plan, which is described in detail below, need not be completed until the exchange visitor informs the J-1 sponsor of the internship location.[67] However, within 10 days of arriving in the United States, the IWT participant must notify the J-1 sponsor of the arrival and of a U.S. residential address, and must also confirm that he or she has begun the J-1 program and/or begun searching for an internship.[68] When the program was extended in 2016, it became "a regular Private Sector program and no longer a pilot program," thus enabling more sponsors for the interns.[69]

In addition to the general J-1 program obligations, J-1 sponsors for IWT participants must validate the appropriate Student and Exchange Visitor Information System (SEVIS) record and update the residence and internship location information with every change.[70] J-1 sponsors must then "continue to contact participants and host organizations every 60 days thereafter throughout the duration of their participation in the sponsor's program."[71] There are no extensions beyond the maximum 12-month period for IWT programs.[72] For further discussion of the Forms

---

[65] DOS, "Guidelines for Administration of the Intern Work and Travel Pilot Program with Ireland" (Oct. 31, 2008), https://j1visa.state.gov/wp-content/uploads/2012/09/pilot-program-irish-iwt.pdf.

[66] *Id.*

[67] *Id.*

[68] *Id.*

[69] U.S. Embassy in Ireland, "United States and Ireland sign three year extension to the Ireland Work and Travel Program" (Dec. 6, 2016), https://ie.usembassy.gov/united-states-ireland-sign-three-year-extension-ireland-work-travel-iwt-program/.

[70] DOS, "Guidelines for Administration of the Intern Work and Travel Pilot Program with Ireland" (Oct. 31, 2008), https://j1visa.state.gov/wp-content/uploads/2012/09/pilot-program-irish-iwt.pdf.

[71] *Id.*

[72] Irish Times, "Guide to applying for 12 month U.S. visa" (July 18, 2012), http://www.irishtimes.com/blogs/generationemigration/2012/07/18/guide-to-applying-for-12-month-us-visa/.

Copyright © 2017. American Immigration Lawyers Association. All rights reserved.

DS-2019 and DS-7002, as well as the SEVIS system and J-1 sponsor obligations, see below.

C. Training Programs and Internships vs. Employment

It is not permissible to use the J-1 trainee or intern categories for regular employment or to fill full– or part-time positions that "are or could be occupied by American workers":

> "While training programs overall have been highly successful in meeting the goals of the Fulbright-Hays Act, both the Department and the GAO have found there have been occasions where training programs were being misused by some sponsors (*e.g.*, trainees were actually being used as 'employees' and the J visa was being used in lieu of the H visa or as a stepping stone for another longer-term non-immigrant or immigrant classification that may have been unavailable at the time of visa application).... Regulations strictly prohibit the use of the trainee category for ordinary employment purposes, stating in particular that sponsors must not place trainee participants in positions that are filled or would be filled by full-time or part-time employees."[73]

Thus, DOS places a duty on program sponsors to ensure that J-1 trainees or interns "do not displace full- or part-time or temporary or permanent American workers or serve to fill a labor need.[74]

There have been recurring concerns about abuse of the J-1 program for employment.[75] The J-1 program should not be used as "work programs designed to meet the staffing needs of an employer,"[76] to "exploit[] the J-1 trainees for cheap labor," or as a substitute for the H-2B program.[77] Certain occupational categories may receive additional scrutiny to confirm that the training program or internship is an appropriate use of the J-1 visa classification. For example, DOS stated:

> "Agricultural training programs were found to be particularly problematic because of the potential for fraud. Abuses of the training regulations were not hidden; there were cases where there was not even an attempt to represent jobs as training, and which certain employers referred to their program participants as employees, rather than trainees.... There were questions as to whether such programs were

---

[73] 72 Fed. Reg. 33669 (June 19, 2007); 58 Fed. Reg. 15180 (Mar. 19, 1993).

[74] 22 CFR §62.22(f)(2)(v).

[75] 72 Fed. Reg. 33669 (June 19, 2007) (citing Government Accountability Office (GAO), "Stronger Action Needed to Improve Oversight and Assess Risks of the Summer Work Travel and Trainee Categories of the Exchange Visitor Program" (Oct. 2005), http://www.gao.gov/new.items/d06106.pdf); Office of Inspector General (OIG), "The Exchange Visitor Program Needs Improved Management and Oversight" (Sept. 2000), https://oig.state.gov/system/files/8539.pdf.

[76] 58 Fed. Reg. 15180 (Mar. 19, 1993).

[77] OIG, "The Exchange Visitor Program Needs Improved Management and Oversight" (Sept. 2000), https://oig.state.gov/system/files/8539.pdf.

Copyright © 2017. American Immigration Lawyers Association. All rights reserved.

merely utilizing trainees for cheap labor and whether the trainees were simply receiving enough training to perform their work."[78]

To assist in determining what activities may constitute a proper training program or internship rather than prohibited employment, DOS offered the following guidance:

"[T]he Department recognizes that work is an essential component of on-the-job training, and that in many respects there are no conceptual or legal distinctions between an employee and a trainee. These two perspectives are not inconsistent. While a trainee is performing work as a component of his/her training experience, the work is only a part of the learning program that is designed to enhance the trainee's skills in his/her occupational specialty through exposure to American techniques, methodologies, and expertise."[79]

Therefore, it seems that DOS recognizes that work is a permissible and expected part of the J-1 trainee and intern categories,[80] as long as it is part of "on-the-job training" that is necessary for the exchange visitor's specific training program or internship, as evidenced on the DS-7002 form, which should clearly explain the "justification for the use of on-the-job training."[81] "On-the-job training" is defined as "an individual's observation of and participation in given tasks demonstrated by experienced workers for the purpose of acquiring competency in such tasks."[82] The practitioner may also find it helpful to review the standard of work that is "necessary and incidental" to a training program in the context of H-3 trainee petitions, as discussed in Volume 1: Chapter Nine, "H-3 Visas and Status."

Because of the concerns regarding abuse, the importance of a detailed training program or internship, including sufficient staff in numbers and type to provide supervision and evaluation, should be stressed to the U.S. host organization employer, especially if the J-1 program sponsor is not the host organization.[83] Moreover, the training offered should not be merely the same training or orientation offered to new employees.[84] The practitioner should note that of the approximately 90 designated J-1 trainee programs and 95 designated J-1 intern programs, discussed below, most J-1 program sponsors do not provide the training or internship directly. Instead, they place foreign nationals with U.S. host organization employers. Thus,

---

[78] 71 Fed. Reg. 3914 (Jan. 24, 2006).

[79] 72 Fed. Reg. 33669 (June 19, 2007).

[80] *See* 22 CFR §62.2(f)(2)(iii), including "on-the-job training" as among the methods that program sponsors should use to ensure that trainees and interns obtain the "skills, knowledge, and competencies" appropriate to their programs.

[81] 58 Fed. Reg. 15180 (Mar. 19, 1993).

[82] 22 CFR §62.2.

[83] 71 Fed. Reg. 3914 (Jan. 24, 2006).

[84] OIG, "The Exchange Visitor Program Needs Improved Management and Oversight" (Sept. 2000), https://oig.state.gov/system/files/8539.pdf.

Copyright © 2017. American Immigration Lawyers Association. All rights reserved.

each J-1 program sponsor has a special obligation to review very carefully the DS-7002 to ensure that a detailed training program or internship is being offered.

Employment pursuant to an approved J-1 program "at the sponsor's worksite, does not require issuance of an employment authorization document (EAD)."[85] Any other employment in the United States is unauthorized and is prohibited.[86]

A J-1 nonimmigrant may receive a salary from the J-1 sponsor or the host organization "when [the] activities are part of the exchange visitor's program."[87] It is important to note, however, that on-the-job training pursuant to a J-1 program differs from regular employment, as discussed above. Although neither a labor condition application nor a labor certification application is necessary for approval of a J-1 program, one J-1 program sponsor had its program designation revoked in part because "of evidence indicating that a U.S. citizen was replaced by exchange visitors," despite statements from the Department of Labor that "it is not likely that the exchange programs will have any effect on the U.S. labor market because of the small number of J-1 exchange visitors."[88]

D. J-1 Program Sponsors

As noted above, this chapter focuses on J-1 status pursuant to approval and issuance of a Form DS-2019 by an organization that has been designated by DOS as a J-1 program sponsor. In these cases, the U.S. entity will often be a "Host Organization," which "conducts training or internship programs on behalf of [a] designated program sponsor[] pursuant to an executed written agreement between the two parties."[89] The sponsor in these circumstances is sometimes referred to as an umbrella organization. These relationships entail responsibilities for both parties, although it seems that the J-1 program sponsor is held more accountable, as the J-1 program sponsor "must ensure" that the host organization complies with the following requirements:

- Signature on a complete Form DS-7002 to confirm "that all placements are appropriate and consistent" with the purpose and objectives of the internship or training program detailed in the J-1 program applications and descriptions, as discussed below;

- Prompt notification to the J-1 sponsor about the following events:
  - "[C]hanges in, or deviations from" the internship or training program submitted to the J-1 sponsor; and/or
  - "[A]ny emergency involving trainees or interns";

---

[85] 1 U.S. Customs and Border Protection (CBP) Inspector's Field Manual (IFM) ch.15: Nonimmigrants and Border Crossers, 14-1 Agency Manuals 15.4.

[86] 22 CFR §62.16(b).

[87] 9 FAM 402.5-6(H)(1); 22 CFR §62.16(a).

[88] OIG, "The Exchange Visitor Program Needs Improved Management and Oversight" (Sept. 2000), https://oig.state.gov/system/files/8539.pdf.

[89] 22 CFR §62.2.

Copyright © 2017. American Immigration Lawyers Association. All rights reserved.

- Compliance with any federal, state, and/or local occupational health and safety laws;

- Compliance with "all program rules and regulations set forth by the sponsor, including the completion of all mandatory program evaluations"; and

- Because "interns are seeking entry-level training and experience…, all placements must be tailored to the skills and experience level of the individual intern."[90]

A J-1 sponsor has the following additional responsibilities regarding administration of the J-1 programs:

- "Ensure that trainees and interns are appropriately selected, placed, oriented, supervised, and evaluated;

- "Be available to trainees and interns (and host organizations, as appropriate) to assist as facilitators, counselors, and information resources;

- "Ensure that training and internship programs provide a balance between the trainees' and interns' learning opportunities and their contributions to the organizations in which they are placed;

- "Ensure that the training and internship programs are full-time (minimum 32 hours a week); and

- "Ensure that any host organizations and third parties involved in the recruitment, selection, screening, placement, orientation, evaluation for, or the provision of training and internship programs are sufficiently educated on the goals, objectives, and regulations of the Exchange Visitor Program" and comply with applicable regulations, "as well as all additional terms and conditions governing Exchange Visitor Program administration that [DOS] may from time to time impose."[91]

With respect to the relationship between a J-1 sponsor and a host organization, the J-1 sponsor must perform the following actions:

- "[A]dequately screen all potential host organizations at which a trainee or intern will be placed by obtaining the following information:

  - Federal Employer Identification Number;

  - "Third party verification of telephone number, address, and professional activities, *e.g.*, via advertising, brochures, Web site, and/or feedback from prior participants; and

---

[90] 22 CFR §62.22(h). The practitioner should note that a similar consideration most likely applies to training programs, even if the particular regulation on host organization obligations does not explicitly state so. 22 CFR §62.22(f)(1)(i).

[91] 22 CFR §62.22(f)(1).

Copyright © 2017. American Immigration Lawyers Association. All rights reserved.

- "Verification of Worker's Compensation Insurance Policy or equivalent in each state or, if applicable, evidence of state exemption from requirement of coverage."

▪ Perform a site visit of the host organization, if required, as discussed below.[92]

Regardless of whether the J-1 programs are provided by the J-1 sponsor directly or by a host organization, a J-1 sponsor has the following duties:

▪ Ensure that there are "sufficient resources, plant, equipment, and trained personnel available to provide the specified training and[/or] internship program";

▪ Ensure that "experienced and knowledgeable staff" supply "continuous on-site supervision and mentoring of trainees and interns";

▪ "Ensure that trainees and interns obtain skills, knowledge, and competencies through structured and guided activities such as classroom training, seminars, rotation through several departments, on-the-job training, attendance at conferences, and similar learning activities, as appropriate in specific circumstances";

▪ Ensure that the exchange visitors are evaluated periodically, as discussed below;

▪ Ensure that U.S. workers, whether full– or part-time or temporary or permanent, are not displaced by the exchange visitor;

▪ Ensure that exchange visitors do not "serve to fill a labor need";

▪ "[E]nsure that the positions that trainees and interns fill exist solely to assist trainees and interns in achieving the objectives of their participation in training and internship programs";

▪ "Certify that training and internship programs in the field of agriculture meet all the requirements of the Fair Labor Standards Act … and the Migrant and Seasonal Agricultural Worker Protection Act…";[93]

▪ Ensure that potential interns and trainees are screened thoroughly, whether by the sponsor or by a third party, such as a host organization, "including a documented interview conducted by the sponsor either in-person or by videoconferencing, or by telephone if videoconferencing is not a viable option";[94]

▪ Retain all documents relating to the sponsor's obligations "for at least three years following the completion of all training and internship programs … in either hard copy or electronic format";[95]

---

[92] 22 CFR §§62.22(g)(3) and (4).

[93] 22 CFR §62.22(f)(2). For a discussion of these statutes, see Volume 1: Chapter Eight, "H-2B Visas and Status."

[94] 22 CFR §62.22(f)(3). For a discussion of third parties that are not host organizations, see below.

[95] 22 CFR §62.22(f)(4).

Copyright © 2017. American Immigration Lawyers Association. All rights reserved.

- Update SEVIS with the new legal name and/or address of the J-1 exchange visitor,[96] after the foreign national informs the J-1 sponsor of the move, as discussed below; and

- Ensure that the exchange visitors have health insurance to cover "sickness or accident during the period of time that an exchange visitor participates in the sponsor's exchange visitor program."[97]

DOS has published lists of designated J-1 sponsors for interns[98] and for trainees.[99] While it is not required that the program sponsor provide the health insurance, it is not uncommon for the program sponsor to provide access to the required insurance for an additional fee, since the sponsor must verify insurance coverage. Individual J-1 sponsors may also have additional eligibility requirements, such as age limitations for trainees and interns, stipend cap, or company statistics, for host organizations. The practitioner should consult the website or call the J-1 sponsor.

1. Site Visits of Host Organizations

Prior to issuing a Form DS-2019, the J-1 sponsor must also conduct a site visit of the host organization if the host organization has "not previously participated successfully in the sponsor's training and internship programs" and either of the following conditions apply:

- The host organization has "fewer than 25 employees"; or

- The host organization earns "less than three million dollars in annual revenue."[100]

DOS indicates that the site visits are necessary for the J-1 sponsor in order "to collect sufficient evidence to support a finding that participants are properly placed with host organizations that meet [the] standards"[101] for two reasons. First, the J-1 sponsor should confirm that the host organization "possess[es] and maintain[s] the ability and resources to provide structured and guided work-based learning experiences," such as the experienced personnel, resources, and equipment, as explained in the internship or training program submitted to the J-1 sponsor.[102] Second, the J-1 sponsor should ensure "that host organizations understand and meet their obligations" of the J-1 program.[103] If the host organization using an umbrella

---

[96] 8 CFR §214.2(j)(1)(viii).

[97] 22 CFR §62.14(a).

[98] DOS, "Designated Sponsor Organizations," https://j1visa.state.gov/programs/trainee/. Select "Find an Intern Sponsor."

[99] DOS, "Designated Sponsor Organizations," https://j1visa.state.gov/programs/trainee/. Select "Find a Trainee Sponsor."

[100] 22 CFR §62.22(g)(4).

[101] 72 Fed. Reg. 33669 (June 19, 2007).

[102] 22 CFR §62.22(g)(4).

[103] Id.

Copyright © 2017. American Immigration Lawyers Association. All rights reserved.

program is an "academic institution[]" or an office of the "federal, state, or local government," then the site visit is not required.[104]

2. Issuance of Form DS-2019

A J-1 sponsor may approve a program and issue a Form DS-2019 only if it has been designated to offer a program in the specified occupational category.[105] The following is a list of the available occupational categories:

- "Agriculture, Forestry, and Fishing;
- "Arts and Culture;
- "Construction and Building Trades;
- "Education, Social Sciences, Library Science, Counseling and Social Services;
- "Health Related Occupations;
- "Hospitality and Tourism;
- "Information Media and Communications;
- "Management, Business, Commerce and Finance;
- "Public Administration and Law; and
- "The Sciences, Engineering, Architecture, Mathematics, and Industrial Occupations."[106]

The practitioner should confirm that the J-1 sponsor is authorized to provide training in the particular category before submitting a J-1 internship or training program application,[107] and should also note that a single organization may be approved for differing occupational categories. For example, the International Exchange Center of the American Immigration Council may offer training and internship programs in the following categories:

- Arts and Culture;
- Social Sciences, Library Science, Non-Clinical Counseling, and Social Services;
- Tourism;
- Information, Media and Communications;
- Management, Business, Commerce and Finance;
- Public Administration and Law;
- Tourism (management level only); and

---

[104] Id.

[105] 22 CFR §62.22(c)(1).

[106] 22 CFR §62.22(c)(2).

[107] Id.

Copyright © 2017. American Immigration Lawyers Association. All rights reserved.

- The Sciences, Engineering, Architecture, Mathematics and Industrial Occupations.[108]

Before approving a program and issuing the Form DS-2019, the J-1 sponsor must obtain a complete and signed Form DS-7002 for each intern or trainee,[109] and the description of the training program or internship should not be a "boilerplate,"[110] as discussed below. The executed Form DS-2019 may not be forwarded to the intern or trainee "unless the individualized Form DS-7002 … has been completed and signed by all requisite parties,"[111] although electronic and faxed signatures will be accepted by DOS.[112] In addition, the J-1 sponsor must confirm that the foreign national has "verifiable English language skills sufficient to function on a day-to-day basis in their training environment," as confirmed by "a recognized English language test, by signed documentation from an academic institution or English language school, or through a documented interview conducted by the sponsor either in person or by videoconferencing, or by telephone if videoconferencing is not a viable option."[113] The J-1 sponsor must also confirm the foreign national's educational and experience qualifications, to ensure that he or she meets the requirements stated above.[114] Finally, the J-1 sponsor must be satisfied with the description of the proposed internship or training program, as discussed below.

A Form DS-2019 may not be issued, however, if any of the following conditions apply:

- A host organization has not been selected or the host organization representative has not signed the Form DS-7002, with the exception of the IWT program, as discussed above;

- The foreign national does not "have sufficient finances to support [him– or herself] for [the] entire stay in the United States, including housing and living expenses"; or

- The program "duplicate[s] the participants' prior work experience or training received elsewhere."[115]

These steps may be considered part of the J-1 sponsor's responsibility to have a method to "screen and select prospective exchange visitors to ensure that they are

---

[108] American Immigration Council, "Cultural Exchange," https://exchange.americanimmigration council.org/am-i-eligible.

[109] 22 CFR §62.22(i)(1).

[110] 72 Fed. Reg. 33669 (June 19, 2007).

[111] 22 CFR §62.22(m).

[112] 9 FAM 402.5-6(D)(7).

[113] 22 CFR §62.22(d)(1).

[114] 22 CFR §§62.22(d)(2) and (3).

[115] 22 CFR §62.22(e).

Copyright © 2017. American Immigration Lawyers Association. All rights reserved.

eligible for program participation" and to ensure that the J-1 "program is suitable to the exchange visitor's background, needs, and experience."[116]

The Form DS-2019 must be issued through the SEVIS system, discussed below; be two pages; possess the "SEVIS ID number" of the foreign national;[117] be signed in blue ink by an officer of the J-1 program,[118] who is physically present in the United States when the form is issued;[119] and have "a two-dimensional bar code on the top right side of the form."[120]

3. The SEVIS System

The SEVIS system allows U.S. Citizenship and Immigration Services (USCIS) U.S. Customs and Border Protection (CBP), and U.S. Immigration and Customs Enforcement (ICE) to monitor the immigration status of J-1 exchange visitors,[121] by sharing information among Department of Homeland Security (DHS), DOS, and J-1 program sponsors,[122] and to "collect and make accessible to authorized users major events associated with ... exchange visitors' status."[123] J-1 principal exchange visitors and their dependents have separate, individual SEVIS records.[124] Questions regarding the SEVIS system and the Student Exchange Visitor Program (SEVP) may be directed to the SEVP Response Center, which is "staffed by three highly trained SEVP employees knowledgeable on a variety of issues" relating to J-1 programs at (703) 603-3400 or at *SEVIS.Source@dhs.gov*.[125] The mailing address is:

Student and Exchange Visitor Program
DHS/ICE
500 12th Street SW, Stop 5600
Washington, DC 20536-5600[126]

When a foreign national applies for a J visa, the consular official must "verify the provenance of SEVIS-generated forms..., DS-2019 against SEVIS data in the Consular Consolidated Database CCD"; and the J-1 visa may not be issued until this

---

[116] 22 CFR §62.10(a).

[117] 9 FAM 402.5-6(D)(1).

[118] 9 FAM 402.5-6(J)(1).

[119] 22 CFR §62.71(a).

[120] 1 CBP IFM ch. 15: Nonimmigrants and Border Crossers, 14-1 Agency Manuals 15.4.

[121] 73 Fed. Reg. 55683 (Sept. 26, 2008); 1 CBP IFM ch. 15: Nonimmigrants and Border Crossers, 14-1 Agency Manuals 15.16.

[122] 67 Fed. Reg. 76307 (Dec. 12, 2002).

[123] DOS, "SEVIS and New Student and Exchange Visitor Forms" (June 12, 2002), AILA Doc. No. 02062444.

[124] 1 CBP IFM ch. 15: Nonimmigrants and Border Crossers, 14-1 Agency Manuals 15.16.

[125] U.S. Immigration and Customs Enforcement (ICE), "Students/Exchange Visitors," https://www. ice.gov/sevis/index.htm; "ICE SEVP Response Center Now in Operation" (updated 2/6/09), AILA Doc. No. 09012766.

[126] ICE, "Contact Information" (Aug. 10, 2010), AILA Doc. No. 10081264. ICE/SEVP, "Contact Us," https://www.ice.gov/sevis/contact.

Copyright © 2017. American Immigration Lawyers Association. All rights reserved.

verification is performed.[127] This is because information in the SEVIS record "supersedes information on the printed Form DS-2019."[128]

4. Detailed Internship or Training Program and Form DS-7002

The J-1 program application should contain a detailed description of the proposed internship or training program on Form DS-7002, because the J-1 sponsor must be satisfied that there will be no impermissible "unskilled or casual labor."[129] The following information must be provided for internship and training programs:

- The "specific goals and objectives of the training [or] internship program," including discussion of "each phase or component, if applicable";

- Specific details about "the knowledge, skills, or techniques to be imparted to the trainee or intern," including discussion of "each phase or component, if applicable"; and

- Explanation of "the methods of performance evaluation" and the supervision to be provided to the exchange visitor, including discussion of the evaluation and supervision "for each phase or component, if applicable."[130]

In addition, the internship program must also describe how the internship will "be divided into specific and various phases or components."[131] Then, "for each phase or component," the training program must provide the following information:

- Description of "the methodology of training"; and

- Explanation of the "chronology or syllabus,"[132] including any departmental rotations.

An internship program, in turn, must provide the following information:

- Description of the intern's "role ... in the organization";

- Identification of the "various departments or functional areas in which the intern will work," if applicable; and

- Statement of "the specific tasks and activities the intern will complete."[133]

As a general rule, the practitioner should ensure that the Form DS-7002 clearly explains how the trainee or intern will develop practical skills and how the progress of the trainee or intern will be evaluated, because this form was created in order to address concerns of abuse of the J-1 program, as discussed above. For example, the program application may specify the ways that the foreign national will receive training—such as by shadowing or performing informational interviews with

---

[127] 70 Fed. Reg. 7853 (Feb. 16, 2005).

[128] 9 FAM 402.5-6(J)(1).

[129] 22 CFR §62.22(i)(2).

[130] *Id.*

[131] 22 CFR §62.22(i)(3).

[132] *Id.*

[133] 22 CFR §62.22(i)(4).

Copyright © 2017. American Immigration Lawyers Association. All rights reserved.

experienced professionals; attending classes, seminars, or workshops; undertaking discrete research projects; and receiving on-the-job training—with each phase followed by an evaluation of progress, debriefing, or discussion of the training received by the foreign national.[134] A strong J-1 program application generally represents a cohesive whole, where the length of the training program or internship is supported by the chronology of specific rotations to allow the exchange visitor to develop practical skills in the field of the foreign national's education.

Contact information for the trainee or intern must be stated on the Form DS-7002, but the host organization's information may be provided if the foreign national does not yet have a U.S. address.[135]

5. J-1 Program Evaluations

J-1 program evaluations, whether conducted by the J-1 sponsor or the host organization, are mandatory: "In order to ensure the quality of training and internship programs, sponsors must develop procedures for evaluating all trainees and interns."[136] Although experience has shown that a J-1 sponsor may accept the evaluation method proposed by the host organization in the internship or training program application, the practitioner may wish to advise the client host organization that the J-1 sponsor may have an existing evaluation procedure with which the host organization must comply.

For all J-1 programs, an evaluation must be completed before the internship or training program concludes, with the evaluation form signed by the exchange visitor and his or her immediate supervisor.[137] If the J-1 program will have a duration that is longer than six months, "at a minimum, midpoint and concluding evaluations are required."[138] As noted above, the J-1 sponsor must retain the evaluations, whether electronic or paper, "for a period of at least three years following the completion of each training and internship program."[139] The practitioner may wish to explore with the client whether to describe the specific evaluation components at the conclusion of each phase of the internship or training program, for the benefit of the J-1 program sponsor as well as the host organization and trainees and interns.

6. Use of Third Parties by J-1 Sponsors

As noted above, host organizations are considered third parties, but other entities may have third-party relationships with J-1 program sponsors, such as "partners, local businesses, governmental entities, academic institutions, and other foreign or

---

[134] American Immigration Council, "Writing a Dynamic Training Plan," https://exchange.americanimmigrationcouncil.org/sites/default/files/cultural_exchange/dynamictrain_plan.pdf.

[135] 9 FAM 402.5-6(D)(7).

[136] 22 CFR §62.22(*l*).

[137] *Id.*

[138] *Id.*

[139] *Id.*

Copyright © 2017. American Immigration Lawyers Association. All rights reserved.

domestic agents."[140] These third parties may "assist [J-1 sponsors] in the conduct of their designated training and internship programs," but the J-1 program sponsor then bears additional duties and responsibilities.[141]

Perhaps most importantly, the use of a third party's assistance by a J-1 sponsor "does not relieve the sponsor of its obligations to comply with" the relevant regulations,[142] including the obligations discussed above. Indeed, the J-1 sponsor must also "ensure third party compliance with Exchange Visitor Program regulations,"[143] just as the J-1 sponsor must ensure that the host organization complies with the program's requirements. In addition, if the third party fails to comply with the regulations "or with any additional terms and conditions governing Exchange Visitor Program administration that [DOS] may from time to time impose," then DOS may impute that failure to the J-1 sponsor.[144]

If the J-1 sponsor nevertheless requests assistance from a third party, including a host organization, then the two parties must execute a "written agreement," where the third party is authorized "to act on behalf of the sponsor in the conduct of the sponsor's program," and the "agreement must outline the obligations and full relationship between the sponsor and third party on all matters involving the administration of their exchange visitor program."[145] It is worth repeating that staffing and placement agencies may not be third parties with any role whatsoever with J sponsors, as discussed above. There are also additional screening duties if the third party is located outside the United States.[146]

E. Nonimmigrant Intent

As stated by DOS: "A key goal of the Fulbright-Hayes Act, which authorizes these programs, is that participants will return to their home countries and share their experiences with their countrymen."[147] Accordingly, at the time of visa application, the J-1 visa applicant and any J-2 dependents must individually demonstrate that he or she has a residence abroad which he or she has no intention of abandoning.[148] Appropriate evidence may include copies of property titles or deeds, mortgages, or lease agreements. These documents may be supplemented with evidence of continued enrollment in school or other programs in the home country, arrangements for sabbatical, bank statements, and evidence of family or community ties.

---

[140] 22 CFR §62.22(g)(1).

[141] *Id.*

[142] *Id.*

[143] *Id.*

[144] *Id.*

[145] *Id.*

[146] 22 CFR §62.22(g)(2).

[147] 22 CFR §62.22(b)(1)(i).

[148] INA §101(a)(15)(J); 9 FAM 402.5-6(C).

Copyright © 2017. American Immigration Lawyers Association. All rights reserved.

Importantly, however, nonimmigrant intent in the context of J visa applicants "inherently" differs from the strict standard imposed on applicants for other visa categories, such as B-1 and B-2.[149] As stated by DOS: "The statute clearly presupposes that the natural circumstances and conditions of being an exchange visitor do not disqualify that applicant from obtaining a J visa. It is natural that the exchange visitor proposes an extended absence from his homeland."[150]

Parallel language can be found in the student visa context, in which DOS goes on to note that, rather than considering "exclusively" the foreign national's ties to the home country, the consular officer "should focus on the applicant's immediate intent."[151] Further, the "immediate intent" inquiry has a flexible standard that considers whether the foreign national "possesses the present intent to depart the United States at the conclusion of his or her program."[152] As stated by DOS with respect to students:

"[T]ypical youth often means they do not necessarily have a long-range plan, and hence are relatively less likely to have formed an intent to abandon their homes. That this intention is subject to change or even likely to change is not a sufficient reason to deny a visa."[153]

The above special considerations supplement the typical three-prong test used by the consular officer to assess intent, which is to consider whether:

- The foreign national has a residence in a foreign country;

- The foreign national does not have the "immediate intention of abandoning that residence"; and

- The foreign national "[i]ntends to depart from the United States upon completion of the program."[154]

The Immigration and Nationality Act (INA) does not provide for dual intent for a J-1 nonimmigrant who pursues permanent residence.[155] If the foreign national is the beneficiary of an approved labor certification application or of a filed employment-based immigrant visa petition, then the individual will almost certainly have difficulty obtaining a J-1 visa stamp in his or her passport.

It may be possible to obtain a J-1 visa if the labor certification application or immigrant visa petition was filed by an entity other than the J-1 sponsor or host company or was a family-based petition,[156] but the practitioner should discuss the

---

[149] 9 FAM 402.10-6(F).

[150] *Id.*

[151] 9 FAM 402.5-5(E)(1).

[152] 9 FAM 402.10-6(F).

[153] 9 FAM 402.5-5(E)(1).

[154] 9 FAM 402.5-6(F).

[155] 64 Fed. Reg. 29208 (June 1, 1999).

[156] *Cf.* 8 CFR §214.2(h)(16)(ii) with respect to H-3 trainees.

Copyright © 2017. American Immigration Lawyers Association. All rights reserved.

following issues in detail with the client. First, the foreign national would have to demonstrate that despite the pursuit of U.S. permanent residence, he or she will maintain a foreign residence for the duration of the J-1 training program. Second, the pursuit of U.S. permanent residence may undermine the foreign national's ability to establish nonimmigrant intent. Third, the consular office may determine that the J-1 program is for ordinary employment, rather than training, as discussed below.

A J-1 visa applicant may address these issues by providing explicit details of definite plans, such as ongoing payments of the mortgage, property taxes, or rent; offer of employment from a foreign entity upon conclusion of the J-1 training program; and evidence that the host organization does not seek to employ the foreign national upon completion of the training program. Additional evidence may include proof of the relationship between the host organization and a foreign entity that will employ the foreign national after the J-1 program is completed, if applicable. Nevertheless, the practitioner should advise the client that the J-1 visa application runs a higher than normal risk of denial. For a detailed discussion of strategies to contrast a future desire to immigrate with a temporary desire to visit the United States, see Volume 1: Chapter Three, Visitors: "B Visas and Status and the Visa Waiver Program."

F. Sufficient Funds

The exchange visitor must also demonstrate that he or she possesses "sufficient funds to cover expenses or has made other arrangements to provide for expenses" for the duration of the training program or internship.[157] This may also be evaluated by the J-1 program sponsor to ensure that each J-1 participant will be able to cover his or her transportation, room and board, and daily living expenses while living in the United States.[158] If the foreign national will receive a stipend for participating in the J-1 program, then the amount of the stipend should be stated on the issued Form DS-2019, and experience has shown that these funds may be deemed sufficient. The practitioner should be aware, however, that a J-1 sponsor may consider a high stipend to be indicative of employment rather than training or interning.[159]

Other evidence of sufficient funds includes bank statements, proof of assets, or proof of financial support from a third party, such as a relative. As discussed below, it is also inappropriate to present evidence that the prospective J-2 dependent(s) will engage in employment to cover these expenses.

---

[157] 22 CFR §41.62(a)(2).

[158] 22 CFR §62.22(e)(2).

[159] *See, e.g.*, American Immigration Council, "Host Organization," https://exchange.american immigrationcouncil.org/host-organization. Select "Financial and Non-Monetary Compensation" from the drop-down menu.

Copyright © 2017. American Immigration Lawyers Association. All rights reserved.

IV. Process

A. Preparing the J-1 Training Program or Internship Application

This section discusses the documents of the J-1 application to be submitted to the J-1 program sponsor. It is suggested that all documents be signed in blue ink,[160] as black ink sometimes results in rejection based on the belief that the document is a photocopy. The following documents should be prepared and/or provided to the J-1 sponsor:

- Form DS-7002, signed by the host company and the foreign national;
- Signed third-party agreement, which must satisfy the requirements discussed above, and an individual J-1 sponsor may have additional conditions, a specified format, or a specific form to be completed;
- Copies of the biographic page of the foreign national's passport and the biographic pages of the passports of any dependents;
- Copy of the foreign national's résumé;
- Copies of the foreign national's educational documents, with translations;
- Copies of experience confirmation letters, with translations, if applicable; and
- Check to cover the application fee to the J-1 sponsor, which may include the costs of health insurance and the SEVIS fee for the foreign national if permitted by the J-1 sponsor.

Individual J-1 sponsors may require additional documents, such as the following:

- Proof of enrollment in a foreign university for an intern, such as a letter from the university;
- Form providing information about the host organization;
- Form confirming health insurance coverage;
- Form specifying the financial support and budget for the foreign national, or proof that the foreign national possesses sufficient funds;
- Evidence of residing outside the United States for at least two years, if the proposed trainee previously participated in a J-1 program;
- Letter of offer of training or internship program;
- Declaration regarding compliance with obligations; and
- Form providing biographic information about the J-2 dependents.

The J-1 sponsor may offer expedited processing of the J-1 program application for an additional fee. In addition, the J-1 sponsor may contact the host organization with questions about the proposed training or internship program, or about the foreign national's background. It may be necessary to revise the documents as requested by the J-1 sponsor. Experience has shown that it is possible to submit a subsequent J-1

---

[160] *E.g.*, 9 FAM 402.5-6(J)(1), indicating that the DS-2019 must be signed in blue ink.

Copyright © 2017. American Immigration Lawyers Association. All rights reserved.

program application to a different J-1 sponsor if the initial J-1 application is denied, but the practitioner is advised to caution the client that the first J-1 sponsor may not refund all of the filing fees. The practitioner is reminded to ensure that the subsequent J-1 program application meets the requirements of the second J-1 sponsor.

1. The Form DS-7002[161]

As noted above, individual J-1 program sponsors may have requirements for completing, formatting, and submitting the Form DS-7002, so the practitioner should prepare the form according to those requirements. For the sake of brevity, this section addresses the content of the Form DS-7002, because if a program sponsor prefers to receive the information in a different format, such as a text document, then the same information should be provided in any event. Following approval of the internship or training program, the J-1 sponsor should provide "an executed copy of Form DS-7002" to the representative of the host organization and to the foreign national.[162]

Section 1: Exchange Visitor Information

The name and email address of the foreign national should be provided. If the foreign national does not have an email, then the information for the U.S. host company may be provided. The program category to indicate whether the application is for a trainee or for an intern should be selected, as should the occupational category of the training program or internship. The foreign national should provide his or her number of years of experience in that field or in a field that is relevant to the field of the training program or internship. The highest educational degree level should be stated. If the foreign national has not yet completed a degree program, then the current number of years completed and the projected date of completion should be provided. The field of the degree or educational studies should be provided, as should the anticipated dates of the training or internship program.

Section 2: Compensation

The title of this section is a bit of a misnomer, as most of the questions seek information about the host entity, such as its annual revenue and the number of full-time employees at the location where the J-1 will be placed. The name and address of the host organization should be provided. If the foreign national will be training or interning at a location that is different than the company's U.S. headquarters, then the address of the other location should be stated. If the trainee or intern will receive training or will be interning at multiple locations, then the address of the U.S. headquarters should be provided, and the J-1 sponsor may require an attachment stating the other locations.

---

[161] DOS, "Training/Internship Placement Plan" (exp. Mar. 31, 2018), https://eforms.state.gov/Forms/ds7002.pdf.

[162] 22 CFR §62.22(i)(1).

Copyright © 2017. American Immigration Lawyers Association. All rights reserved.

With regard to compensation, the section asks whether a stipend will be paid—and if so, how much—as well as the frequency of payment. It also probes whether the host has a workers' compensation policy, and whether the policy or an equivalent covers exchange visitors.

Section 3: Certifications

The first part of this section must be signed by the foreign national, who affirms that he or she understands and will abide by the conditions of the status and program, and declares under penalty of perjury that the statements made in the form are true "to the best of my knowledge, information and belief." This section should be signed at the consular interview if there is one.[163]

The second part is completed and signed by the Responsible Officer for the program sponsor—*i.e.*, the umbrella organization.

Section 4: Training/Internship Placement Plan

The name, contact information, and job title of the direct supervisor at the host entity should be provided. Whether the J-1 will be an intern or trainee must once again be indicated.

The training or internship program "should consist of definite phases of training or tasks performed,"[164] and thus the host entity will need to complete the "Phase Information" for each such phase. The host will need to provide a name and number for each phase, along with the name and address of the site where the phase will take place; the intended start and end dates of each phase; and the name, title, and contact information for each phase of the program. The practitioner should note that individual J-1 program sponsors may have different requirements for the length of individual phases and/or the total number of phases.

The information for the remaining boxes (exchange visitor's role; goals and objectives; names, titles, and qualifications of supervisors; cultural activity plans; skills and knowledge to be imparted; methodology for teaching; and method and measurements for evaluation) should be detailed and specific, where the information for each individual phase should relate to the goals of the overall training or internship program, as well as to the particular phase. Each phase section should address each of the topics, in order to illustrate a complete training program that makes chronological sense and flows from subject to subject of training.

The completed form should be signed and dated by the direct supervisor. Experience has shown that certain J-1 program sponsors may allow a human resources representative to sign the form in place of the supervisor, as long as the representative participates in evaluating the intern or trainee, as discussed below. However, the practitioner should confirm with the individual J-1 program sponsor

---

[163] 9 FAM 402.5-6(D)(2).

[164] DOS, "Training/Internship Placement Plan" (exp. Mar. 31, 2018), https://eforms.state.gov/Forms/ds7002.pdf; 73 Fed. Reg. 35066 (June 20, 2008).

Copyright © 2017. American Immigration Lawyers Association. All rights reserved.

before forwarding the form to the J-1 sponsor to avoid a potential delay while the appropriate signature is obtained and the original document forwarded to the J-1 sponsor again.

2. Sample Descriptions

This section will provide examples of descriptions for the initial phase of a training program in the field of Design Engineering named "Design and Simulation," with a manufacturer of information technology networking and communication devices. The trainee's role for this phase may be stated as follows: "During this phase of the program, the trainee will study and receive initial training on block level circuitry design techniques and methodologies for the company's high-speed networking and communication devices. The trainee will outline the methodologies for each of these devices, including power-magnet integrated products, and then perform simulations to determine if the methodologies are functional."

The goals and objectives could be "To heighten the trainee's awareness of current circuitry designs for networking and communication technologies." The knowledge, skills, or techniques to be learned section would then be stated as follows: "Block level circuitry, including utilization and evaluation of design techniques for networking and communication devices, as well as analysis and summarization of the methodologies for each product."

The section on how the skills will be taught is particularly important, as the J-1 sponsor may closely scrutinize any on-the-job training. One example of justifying such training is: "The trainee will learn skills and develop knowledge of practices, techniques, requirements, and policies which are unique to the Information Systems business environment in the United States. Therefore, this phase requires hands-on teaching to enable the trainee to experience the American and U.S. corporate culture on a day-to-day basis as he is exposed to the company's products and processes." To continue with our Design Engineering example:

"The Trainee will shadow multiple engineers performing the design and circuitry of many of the company's products. He will also participate in sessions dealing with block level circuitry of specific block circuits. Through a series of assigned tasks and projects, the trainee will participate in the design, simulation, and layout of analog circuits. This will include participating in the system level analysis and circuit level design performed on two types of power management integrated circuits, including the low dropout regulator and the switching regulator. He will also be trained on the specific design techniques and methodologies used on the power management integrated circuits along with the logic and reasoning for the design."

The method of teaching should relate to the chronology of the phases of training. For instance, if the phase states that the foreign national will shadow professionals, then there should be feedback from the professionals. One example of the description of teaching methods is as follows: "The trainee will interact with multiple expert engineers of the product to provide technical assistance and receive feedback relating to the product. In addition, the trainee will participate in

Copyright © 2017. American Immigration Lawyers Association. All rights reserved.

daily meetings with his supervisor and technical advisers to evaluate the trainee's performance."

3. Experience Confirmation Letters

As discussed above, a trainee must have either at least one year of foreign experience in the occupational field if he or she has earned a post-secondary degree or professional certificate abroad, or at least five years of experience in the occupational field if he or she has not earned a degree or certificate. This experience may be documented in the form of experience confirmation letters from previous employers or, if permitted by the J-1 sponsor, through evidence of self-employment.[165] An intern may also provide experience letters, if he or she graduated up to 12 months before the start date of the J-1 internship, although the letters are not as necessary.

Experience has shown that J-1 sponsors typically review the experience letters to confirm that the foreign national has experience in the same or related occupational field and not necessarily to determine whether the J-1 program will be duplicative of experience gained abroad. Nevertheless, the practitioner is reminded to verify any documentary requirements with the individual J-1 sponsor.

4. Letter of Offer of Training or Internship Program

An individual J-1 sponsor may require a statement confirming the offer of training or internship in addition to the program. The statement should be on the letterhead of the host organization and signed by a representative of that company. Depending on the requirements of the J-1 sponsor, the letter may simply confirm the offer of a training or internship program, location, and stipend.

Alternatively, a more detailed letter may be helpful to highlight how the proposed J-1 program is connected to the host organization's business and to the foreign national's background. The statement may also provide information required by the J-1 sponsor, but not included on the Form DS-7002, as discussed below. One format for a more detailed letter is as follows:

- Introduction;

- Information about the host organization;

- Discussion of the activities of the proposed J-1 program;

- Discussion of the foreign national's educational and experience background; and

- Thank you and conclusion, including amount of the stipend.

5. Declaration Regarding Compliance with Obligations

Experience has shown that, before issuing the Form DS-2019, an individual J-1 sponsor may require a separate and additional document or form confirming compliance with J-1 program obligations and/or conditions stipulated by the J-1

---

[165] For a discussion of evidence of self-employment, see Volume 1: Chapter Fourteen, "TN Visas and Status."

Copyright © 2017. American Immigration Lawyers Association. All rights reserved.

sponsor. Other conditions imposed by J-1 sponsors include agreeing not to apply to USCIS for change of status from J-1 to another nonimmigrant visa category, although the foreign national may travel abroad and apply for the visa shortly after completing the J-1 program. If the J-1 sponsor has additional requirements, then a statement about compliance may also be incorporated into the letter of offer of training or internship program, discussed above.

B. Visa Application

Following approval of the internship or training program, the J-1 sponsor should provide "a properly executed Form DS-2019, Certificate of Eligibility for Exchange Visitor (J-1) Status,"[166] and "an executed copy of Form DS-7002" to the foreign national, for use in applying for a J-1 visa.[167] Providing detailed instructions on how to apply for a J-1 visa is very helpful to the client and the employee. Because requirements for visa applications can vary among individual consular posts, the practitioner should confirm the current procedures required by the specific post.

The J-1 visa application may be made "at any time as long as the Form DS-2019 … and [the] SEVIS record are in INITIAL or ACTIVE status," but an initial J-1 visa may not be issued earlier than 90 days before the J-1 program start date.[168] Importantly, J-1 visa applications should be expedited by U.S. consulates to maximize the likelihood that exchange visitors obtain visas before the start date of the J-1 program.[169] First-time visa applicants should receive higher priority than "repeat applicants."[170]

In addition to the general visa application documents discussed in Volume 1: Chapter Two, "Basic Nonimmigrant Concepts," the following documents should be presented, and individual consulates frequently have additional requirements:

- Original Form DS-2019, executed by the J-1 program sponsor and the foreign national;

- Evidence of payment of the SEVIS fee, as discussed below;

- Original executed Form DS-7002;[171]

- Completed Form DS-160, Nonimmigrant Visa Application, for the foreign national;[172]

---

[166] 22 CFR §402.5-6(I)(4).

[167] 22 CFR §62.22(i)(1).

[168] DOS, "(A) 04 STATE 70079 (B) 03 STATE 349930 (C) 03 STATE 279071 (D) 03 STATE 144850 (E) 03 STATE 144850" (Aug. 2004), AILA Doc. No. 04080965.

[169] DOS, "Student (F and M Visa) and Exchange Visitor (J Visa) Annual Update" (Mar. 2008), AILA Doc. No. 08040255; DOS, "(A) 04 STATE 70079 (B) 03 STATE 349930 (C) 03 STATE 279071 (D) 03 STATE 144850 (E) 03 STATE 144850" (Aug. 2004), AILA Doc. No. 04080965.

[170] DOS, "Student (F and M Visa) and Exchange Visitor (J Visa) Annual Update" (Mar. 2008), AILA Doc. No. 08040255; DOS, "Student and Exchange Visitor Update" (Feb. 2009), AILA Doc. No. 09051963.

[171] 9 FAM 402.5-6(D)(7), (E)(5), and (E(14); 74 Fed. Reg. 5968 (Feb. 3, 2009).

Copyright © 2017. American Immigration Lawyers Association. All rights reserved.

- Evidence that the foreign national possesses the appropriate educational and/or professional qualifications for the training program or internship;[173]

- Evidence of possessing sufficient comprehension of the English language to participate in the program, such as test scores, educational certificates, or other documents, as discussed above;

- Evidence of sufficient funds, as discussed above; and

- Evidence of the visa applicant's foreign residence and nonimmigrant intent, as discussed above.

The consular officer may evaluate whether the foreign national's "qualifications or planned activities fit within the Exchange Visitor Program."[174] In addition, if the consular officer finds that the "start date specified in the applicant's Form DS-2019 … is already past or there is reason to believe the applicant will be unable to meet that date, [the officer] may assume the applicant may encounter difficulty at the port of entry [and] should determine whether the sponsor has amended the electronic SEVIS record to change the program start date, and make a case note to that effect to alert CBP. If this has not been done, [the officer] should direct the visa applicant to alert the designated U.S. program sponsor to the situation. The sponsor may choose to amend the electronic record or may choose other solutions. [The officer] should not intervene directly with designated U.S. sponsors on behalf of visa applicants."[175]

As stated by DOS guidance to consular officers:

"If there are minor errors on the form (*e.g.*, a program start date that is off one day) you can process the case using that form. However, if the form indicates an unrealizable program start date, or has a typographic error in the bio data, you must verify that the information is correct in SEVIS. You should then consider whether the error on the form would cause the traveler difficulty at the port of entry. If it would, you should request that the applicant travel with a corrected hard copy of the form."[176]

Following the visa interview, the consular officer "must return the completed Form DS-2019, Certificate of Eligibility for Exchange Visitor (J-1) Status to the exchange visitor … for presentation to the United States Customs and Border Protection (CBP) officer at the United States port of entry (POE)."[177] In addition, the consular officer will confirm:

"[T]he visa applicant understands all conditions of the stay in the United States in J status and understands also that a consular or immigration officer will make a

---

[172] DOS, "Exchange Visitor Visas," https://travel.state.gov/content/visas/en/study-exchange/exchange.html.

[173] 9 FAM 402.5-6(I)(1).

[174] *Id.*

[175] 9 FAM 402.5-6(I)(3).

[176] DOS, "Student and Exchange Visitor Update" (Feb. 2009), AILA Doc. No. 09051963.

[177] 9 FAM 402.5-6(D)(5).

Copyright © 2017. American Immigration Lawyers Association. All rights reserved.

preliminary determination as to whether the applicant is subject to the 2-year home country physical presence requirement. The applicant then must sign the bottom of page one of the Form DS-2019 confirming that he or she agrees to comply with that requirement if it is determined to be applicable."[178]

Although the preliminary determination of the two-year home residence requirement may result in annotation of the J visa, that determination is not definitive. There may also be a determination from CBP "at the time of inspection,"[179] and, as discussed later in this chapter, from USCIS when adjudicating an application in which the applicability of the requirement comes into issue.[180]

The issued J-1 visa must have the following annotations:

- Name and program number of the J-1 training program or internship;
- The foreign national's SEVIS number;[181]
- The name of the J-1 program sponsor; and
- "Subject to INA 212(e)" or "Not subject to INA 212(e)."[182]

J-2 dependents must present individual Forms DS-2019 at the visa interview,[183] with the J-2 classification indicated above the bar code, the name of the J-1 principal stated,[184] and biographical information for the principal and the dependent.[185] J-2 dependents may apply for EADs, as discussed below.

1. The SEVIS Fee

There is a $180 SEVIS fee that must be paid,[186] unless the J-1 program is "sponsored by the Federal government," as indicated by program identifier prefixes of G-1, G-2, G03, or G-7.[187] The SEVIS fee should be accompanied by a completed Form I-901.[188] The form and fee may be paid by mail, as a "check, money order, or foreign draft drawn on a financial institution in the United States and payable in United States currency,"[189] submitted electronically by credit card,[190] through the

---

[178] 9 FAM 402.5-6(D)(2). *See also* 22 CFR §41.62(d).

[179] 1 CBP IFM ch. 15: Nonimmigrants and Border Crossers, 14-1 Agency Manuals 15.4.

[180] Adjudicators Field Manual (AFM) 45.2(b)(1).

[181] 9 FAM 402.5-6(I)(2).

[182] 9 FAM 402.5-6(I)(7); DOS, "Student (F and M Visa) and Exchange Visitor (J Visa) Annual Update" (Mar. 2008), AILA Doc. No. 08040255.

[183] 9 FAM 402.5-6(D)(4).

[184] DOS, "SEVIS and New Student and Exchange Visitor Forms," SEVIS and New Student and Exchange Visitor Forms" (June 12, 2002), AILA Doc. No. 02062444.

[185] 1 CBP IFM ch. 15: Nonimmigrants and Border Crossers, 14-1 Agency Manuals 15.4.

[186] 8 CFR §§214.13(a)(2), 214.2(j)(5); ICE, "I-901 SEVIS Fee," https://www.ice.gov/sevis/i901/faq.

[187] 8 CFR §214.13(b)(1).

[188] 8 CFR §214.13(g)(1).

[189] 8 CFR §214.13(g)(1)(i).

[190] DOS, "State 162300" (Aug. 2004), AILA Doc. No 04092160.

Copyright © 2017. American Immigration Lawyers Association. All rights reserved.

U.S. Immigration and Customs Enforcement (ICE) website *FMJFee.com*,[191] or through Western Union.[192]

This section will refer to payment of the SEVIS fee by the foreign national for the sake of brevity, but it is permissible for a third party, such as the J-1 program sponsor or another individual, to pay the fee on behalf of the foreign national.[193] Importantly, "failure to pay the required fee is grounds for denial of … J nonimmigrant status or status-related benefits."[194] In addition, merely paying the fee will not "preserve" a foreign national's lawful J-1 status if he or she "has violated his or her status in some other manner,"[195] and failure to pay the fee is not a "minor or technical infraction" of J-1 status for purposes of J status reinstatement.[196]

A foreign national may schedule a visa appointment before paying the SEVIS fee, but it "must be paid prior to visa application."[197] Although the documents submitted with the visa application should include evidence of having paid the fee, the J-1 visa must not be issued until confirmation of payment is made through the SEVIS database by the consular officer.[198] It should be noted when scheduling the visa appointment that the system does have a "lapse … of approximately 10 days" between when the fee is paid and when the payment may be confirmed within the SEVIS system.[199] Foreign nationals who are visa-exempt, such as Canadian citizens, must pay the fee to DHS before applying for U.S. admission to begin "initial participation in a [DOS]-designated exchange visitor program"[200] through the methods discussed above. The SEVIS fee is also required in the following circumstances:

- The foreign national seeks change of status to J-1, except as described below;[201]

- The foreign national applies "for a change of program category,"[202] as discussed below;

- The foreign national applies for a J-1 visa or admission in connection with a subsequent J-1 program following denial of a visa or admission for the initial J-1 program, and the two programs have different J-1 program categories;[203]

---

[191] 8 CFR §214.13(g)(1)(ii).

[192] 8 CFR §214.13(g)(1)(iii). For instructions on how to pay at Western Union, see ICE, "I-901 SEVIS Fee," https://www.ice.gov/sevis/i901/faq.

[193] 8 CFR §214.13(g)(4).

[194] 8 CFR §214.13(h).

[195] *Id.*

[196] 8 CFR §214.13(h)(2).

[197] 9 FAM 402.5-6(K)(2).

[198] 22 CFR §41.62(a)(5).

[199] 1 CBP IFM ch. 15: Nonimmigrants and Border Crossers, 14-1 Agency Manuals 15.4.

[200] 8 CFR §214.13(d)(2).

[201] 8 CFR §214.13(d)(3).

[202] 8 CFR §214.13(d)(4).

Copyright © 2017. American Immigration Lawyers Association. All rights reserved.

- The foreign national holds J-1 status to participate in a program sponsored by the federal government and applies for a J-1 program change to one that is not sponsored by the federal government;[204] and

- The foreign national previously held J-1 status and seeks reinstatement "after a substantive violation of status" or after having been out of status "for longer than 120 days but less than 270 days during the course of his/her program."[205]

In contrast, the SEVIS fee need not be paid in the following situations:

- A J-1 nonimmigrant applies for an extension of the J-1 program in the same category,[206] as discussed below; or

- A J-1 nonimmigrant applies to transfer program sponsors,[207] as discussed below;

- The foreign national paid the SEVIS fee in connection with an application to change status to J-1 nonimmigrant and applies for a J-1 visa or admission as a "continuing … exchange visitor in a single course of study, so long as the nonimmigrant is not otherwise required to pay a new fee,"[208] as discussed above;

- The foreign national paid the SEVIS fee in connection with a denied "initial" J-1 visa application "in a particular program category," and "is reapplying for … the same J-1 exchange visitor category, within 12 months following the initial notice of denial";[209]

- The foreign national paid the SEVIS fee in connection with a denied initial request for change of status for a particular J-1 program category, and the motion to reopen the denied application is granted "within 12 months of receipt of initial notice of denial";[210] and

- J-2 dependents, whether applying for visas or admission, are not required to pay the SEVIS fee.[211]

DHS will provide the foreign national with a receipt evidencing payment of the SEVIS fee, until notice is published in the Federal Register "that paper receipts will no longer be necessary."[212] Expedited delivery of the receipt is available, "upon request and receipt of an additional fee."[213] Both DHS and DOS should accept an electronically printed receipt instead of the DHS-issued receipt if the payment was

---

[203] *Id.* and 8 CFR §214.13(e)(5).

[204] 8 CFR §214.13(d)(5).

[205] 8 CFR §214.13(d)(6).

[206] 8 CFR §214.13(e)(2)(i).

[207] 8 CFR §214.13(e)(2)(ii).

[208] 8 CFR §214.13(e)(3).

[209] 8 CFR §214.13(e)(5).

[210] 8 CFR §214.13(e)(6).

[211] 8 CFR §214.13(b)(2); 9 FAM 402.5-6(K)(2).

[212] 8 CFR §214.13(g)(2).

[213] 8 CFR §214.13(g)(2)(i).

Copyright © 2017. American Immigration Lawyers Association. All rights reserved.

made electronically.[214] Similarly, DHS and DOS should accept a receipt from Western Union if payment was made through Western Union.[215] In addition, if the foreign national "lost or did not receive a receipt" for payment of the SEVIS fee, then the foreign national may still be issued a J-1 visa or admitted to the United States, because DHS must "maintain an electronic record of payment for the alien as verification of receipt of the required fee."[216] Therefore, "[i]f DHS records indicate that the fee has been paid," then the foreign national "will not be denied an immigration benefit, including visa issuance or admission to the United States, solely because of a failure to present a paper receipt of fee payment."[217] DOS will verify through SEVIS or FMJFee.com that the fee has been paid.[218] Nevertheless, the practitioner is advised to stress the importance of presenting the receipt when the foreign national applies for a visa or admission, as discussed below, because failure to do so may cause delay in visa issuance or U.S. admission.

C. Admission to the United States

A J-1 nonimmigrant and any J-2 dependents may apply for initial admission up to 30 days before the "report date or start of the approved program listed on the Form DS-2019 ... for purposes of travel";[219] but the J-1 nonimmigrant may participate in the J-1 program only during the validity dates of the Form DS-2019.[220] It is very important that, if the initial entry of the J-1 principal is delayed for any reason, the program sponsor must change the program start date and reissue the Form DS-2019. The J-1 visitor's status and presence in the United States must be validated by the program sponsor within 30 days of the program start date listed on the Form DS-2019, which is also noted in SEVIS.[221] Although a CBP officer may admit an exchange visitor "in those instances where incoming flights are limited and the exchange visitor is arriving a few days early,"[222] the practitioner should discuss the risks of denial of admission with the client host organization.[223]

In addition, a J-2 dependent "may not be admitted for longer than the principal exchange visitor,"[224] and may not be admitted before the J-1 principal is admitted to the United States.[225] If the foreign national wishes to enter the United States earlier, then he or she "must qualify for, and obtain, a B-2 visitor visa," and then obtain

---

[214] 8 CFR §214.13(g)(2)(ii); ICE, "I-901 SEVIS Fee," https://www.ice.gov/sevis/i901/faq.

[215] 8 CFR §214.13(g)(2)(iii).

[216] 8 CFR §214.13(g)(3).

[217] *Id.*

[218] 9 FAM 402.5-6(K)(2).

[219] 8 CFR §214.2(j)(1)(ii).

[220] 8 CFR §214.2(h)(13)(i)(A).

[221] 22 CFR §62.70(d).

[222] 1 CBP IFM ch.15: Nonimmigrants and Border Crossers, 14-1 Agency Manuals 15.4.

[223] 9 FAM 402.5-6(I)(3).

[224] 8 CFR §214.2(j)(1)(ii).

[225] 1 CBP IFM ch.15: Nonimmigrants and Border Crossers, 14-1 Agency Manuals 15.4.

Copyright © 2017. American Immigration Lawyers Association. All rights reserved.

approval of a J-1 change of status application from DHS.[226] A foreign national may have a B visa and a J visa "in [the] passport at the same time," but the U.S. consulate should inform the foreign national of the probable need to depart the United States and re-enter in J-1 status before starting the J-1 program.[227]

When seeking admission to the United States, the foreign national should present his or her passport with the J-1 visa and Form DS-2019 "issued in his or her own name."[228] It also is a good idea for the foreign national to carry all of the documents presented at the visa interview, discussed above, as well as the contact information for the J-1 sponsor. A foreign national entering by land will receive an I-94 card indicating admission to the United States. If the individual is entering by air or sea, a stamp will be placed in his or her passport to indicate admission—no physical I-94 will be provided.[229] If a physical copy of the I-94 is wanted, which it almost inevitably will be, it is available through a portal on CBP's website.[230] In either event, the I-94 should be checked to ensure that the name is identical on the I-94 card and passport, and is marked with J-1 status for a period of "'D/S' (Duration of Status)."[231] The Form DS-2019 should also be endorsed with the admission stamp.[232] Due to the visa reciprocity schedules,[233] as discussed in Volume 1: Chapter Two, "Basic Nonimmigrant Concepts," a trainee may receive a visa valid for a shorter time period than the J-1 program, but the I-94 card should have the "D/S" notation.

For example, Sudanese citizens are eligible for J visas valid for no longer than six months. Therefore, even though the underlying J-1 training program or internship will be 12 months or longer, a citizen of Sudan will be able to obtain a J visa that is valid for only six months from the date of visa issuance. For applicants for admission with visas valid for a shorter period of time than the J-1 program, the practitioner may wish to reiterate the need to present the original Form DS-2019. The practitioner may also wish to contact clients with these exchange visitors well in advance of the visa expiration date to strategize subsequent applications for visas, so the trainees and interns may travel internationally and re-enter the United States during the remaining time of the J-1 program.

---

[226] 9 FAM 402.5-6(I)(4).

[227] DOS, "(A) 04 STATE 70079 (B) 03 STATE 349930 (C) 03 STATE 279071 (D) 03 STATE 144850 (E) 03 STATE 144850" (Aug. 2004), 04 STATE 70079 (B) 03 STATE 349930 (C) 03 STATE 279071 (D) 03 STATE 144850 (E) 03 STATE 144850" (Aug. 2004), AILA Doc. No. 04080965.

[228] 8 CFR §214.2(j)(1)(i).

[229] "American Immigration Lawyers Association CBP Liaison Committee Meeting Agenda" (Apr. 11, 2013), AILA Doc. No. 13051655, p. 8.

[230] "Official Site for Travelers Visiting the United States: Apply for or Retrieve I-94," https://i94.cbp.dhs.gov/I94/#/home.

[231] 9 FAM 402.5-6(I)(6).

[232] 1 CBP IFM ch.15: Nonimmigrants and Border Crossers, 14-1 Agency Manuals 15.4; OI 214.2.

[233] DOS, "Reciprocity and Civil Documents by Country," https://travel.state.gov/content/visas/en/fees/reciprocity-by-country.html.

Copyright © 2017. American Immigration Lawyers Association. All rights reserved.

1. *Canadian Citizens*

As discussed in Volume 1: Chapter Two, "Basic Nonimmigrant Concepts," Canadian citizens generally do not require visas in order to enter the United States.[234] Canadian nationals may apply for admission with the Form DS-2019, Form I-797, Notice of Action, or Internet receipt to prove payment of the SEVIS fee,[235] and Canadian passport.[236] If the foreign national lacks a receipt evidencing payment of the SEVIS fee, the CBP officer may consult the SEVIS database.[237] As noted above, a CBP officer may also determine whether the foreign national is subject to the two-year home residence requirement, but the practitioner should note that Canadian citizens are not subject to the requirement based on the Skills List,[238] which is discussed below. For a more in-depth discussion of applications for admission in nonimmigrant status by Canadian citizens, see Volume 1: Chapter Two, "Basic Nonimmigrant Concepts."

V. Additional Follow-up

After a foreign national has obtained J-1 status, the practitioner should follow up to request copies of the I-94 cards, endorsed Forms DS-2019, and visas, if applicable, to ensure that all the information is correct and calendar the program expiration dates to monitor the foreign national's status, as discussed in Volume 1: Chapter Two, "Basic Nonimmigrant Concepts."

The Form DS-2019, together with the I-94, is evidence of the foreign national's valid immigration status. DOS guidance states: "The exchange visitor must safeguard the form at all times. If the exchange visitor loses the Form DS-2019, he or she must obtain a replacement copy from the designated sponsor."[239]

The foreign national may engage in approved J-1 program activities, and termination of exchange visitor status may arise from the following events:

- Failure to engage in appropriate J-1 activities;
- Violation of J-1 program regulations and/or the J-1 sponsor's rules;
- Willful failure to maintain the mandatory insurance coverage, as discussed above; or
- Engaging in unauthorized employment.[240]

As discussed above, the host organization should notify the J-1 sponsor of any change in program participation. The practitioner is also advised to discuss with the

---

[234] 1 legacy INS Examinations Handbook, Part V, 15-1; 1 legacy INS IFM ch. 15: Nonimmigrants and Border Crossers, 14-1 INS Manuals 15.4.

[235] 1 CBP IFM ch.15: Nonimmigrants and Border Crossers, 14-1 Agency Manuals 15.4.

[236] *Id.*

[237] *Id.*

[238] 74 Fed. Reg. 20108 (Apr. 30, 2009).

[239] 9 FAM 402.5-6(D)(5).

[240] 22 CFR §62.40.

Copyright © 2017. American Immigration Lawyers Association. All rights reserved.

client how the J-1 sponsor should be informed if the foreign national departs the United States even a few days earlier than expected, whether because the program was completed early or because of personal emergencies, so that the J-1 sponsor may update the SEVIS system accordingly.[241] Complications may arise if a foreign national applies for U.S. admission under another nonimmigrant visa classification during the original validity dates of the J-1 program, because the immigration inspector may retrieve outdated information from the SEVIS system.[242]

The regulatory authority is unclear whether J-2 dependents may enroll in a full-time course of study without approval of change of status to F-1, J-1, or M-1.[243] The regulations themselves are silent on the question. The preamble to DOS's 2002 SEVIS rule did make the following statement:

> "INS has determined that monitoring of non-immigrants being educated and trained in the United States is of vital importance to the national security of the United States. Accordingly, any J-2 spouse or dependent child wishing to pursue fulltime study in the United States (other than avocational or recreational) is required to petition the INS for a change of status to that of an F-1, J-1 or M-1 non-immigrant."[244]

However, the regulatory sections being amended and added in that rulemaking made no mention of a need to change status with respect to J-2s, nor did the regulation issued the day before by what was then Immigration and Naturalization Service (INS). That INS rule, however, did specify that spouses of F-1 and M-1 students could not attend school, other than for avocational or recreational purposes, and that children of F-1s and M-1s could attend elementary or secondary schools on their F-2 or M-2 statuses, but not post-secondary school.[245]

However, current DOS guidance states that a J-1's "minor children are permitted to attend school while in the United States on J-2 visas and are not required to obtain student (F) visas."[246] And, the USCIS website goes further, stating: "You do not need to apply to change your nonimmigrant status if you wish to attend school in the United States, and you are the spouse or child of someone who is currently in the United States in any of the following nonimmigrant visa categories:…Exchange Visitors (J visa)."[247]

---

[241] DOS, "Guidelines for Administration of the Intern Work and Travel Pilot Program with Ireland," (Oct. 31, 2008), https://j1visa.state.gov/wp-content/uploads/2012/09/pilot-program-irish-iwt.pdf.

[242] Id.

[243] 67 Fed. Reg. 76256 (Dec. 11, 2002); 67 Fed. Reg. 76307 (Dec. 12, 2002).

[244] 67 Fed. Reg. 76307, 76312 (Dec. 12, 2002).

[245] 67 Fed. Reg. 76256 (Dec. 11, 2002); 8 CFR §§214.2(f)(15)(ii) and 214.2(m)(17)(ii).

[246] DOS, "Exchange Visitor Visas," https://travel.state.gov/content/visas/en/study-exchange/exchange.html. See also 9 FAM 402.5-6(D)(4).

[247] USCIS, "Change My Nonimmigrant Status," https://www.uscis.gov/visit-united-states/change-my-nonimmigrant-status-category/change-my-nonimmigrant-status.

Copyright © 2017. American Immigration Lawyers Association. All rights reserved.

Following completion of the J-1 training program or internship, the J nonimmigrant is granted an additional 30-day period of authorized stay "for domestic travel and/or to prepare for and depart from the United States, and for no other purpose."[248] As discussed in Volume 1: Chapter Two, "Basic Nonimmigrant Concepts," foreign nationals admitted for "Duration of Status" do not accrue unlawful presence and are not subject to visa voidance under INA §222(g), unless and until DHS or an immigration judge finds a status violation.[249]

A. Name and/or Address Changes

If the foreign national legally changes his or her name or changes residences, then he or she "must inform" USCIS and the J-1 program sponsor "within 10 days of the change in a manner prescribed by the program sponsor."[250] As discussed in Volume 1: Chapter Two, "Basic Nonimmigrant Concepts," nonimmigrants must inform USCIS of any address change on Form AR-11. A J-1 exchange visitor may "satisfy the requirement" by providing the change of address information to the J-1 sponsor, "who in turn shall enter the information in SEVIS within 21 days of notification by the exchange visitor."[251]

The address provided must be the "actual physical location where the exchange visitor resides rather than a mailing address."[252] The one exception is if the J-1 nonimmigrant "cannot receive mail where he or she resides," in which case a mailing address may be provided, but the J-1 sponsor "must maintain a record of, and must provide upon request from the Service, the actual physical location where the exchange visitor resides."[253]

B. Extensions, Subsequent J-1 Programs, and Program Transfers

It is possible to obtain a J-1 extension, as long as the total period of J-1 stay does not exceed the 18-month limitation for trainees or 12-month limitation for interns and as long as "the need for an extended training or internship program is documented by the full completion and execution of a new Form DS-7002."[254] However, agricultural training and internship programs have the following limitation:

"12-month training programs in the field of agriculture may not be extended to 18 months by adding six months of classroom participation and studies at the end of the original 12-month program duration.... [T]he six months of related classroom participation and studies must have been part of the trainee's original T/IPP."[255]

---

[248] 9 FAM 402.5-6(I)(6).

[249] Legacy INS, M. Pearson, "Section 222(g) of the Immigration and Nationality Act (Act)" (Jan.14, 1999), AILA Doc. No. 99011590; DOS, "98-State-051296" (Mar. 23, 1998), AILA Doc. No. 98032392.

[250] 8 CFR §214.2(j)(1)(viii).

[251] *Id.*

[252] *Id.*

[253] *Id.*

[254] 22 CFR §62.22(k).

[255] *Id.*

Copyright © 2017. American Immigration Lawyers Association. All rights reserved.

The issuance of the new DS-2019 before the end date of the first DS-2019 is solely in the discretion of the J-1 program sponsor. Revised program dates extend the foreign national's status in SEVIS, such that the Form I-94 (marked D/S at the time of entry) is not reissued or extended. Such an extension may be necessary, for example, if the foreign national entered the United States later than originally anticipated because of delays in visa issuance. The practitioner may wish to supplement the extension application with evidence of the late admission and an explanation of the situation.

When USIA administered the program for waivers of the two-year home residency requirement, it took the position that a program sponsor may not grant an extension if a favorable recommendation for a waiver of the requirement had been sent to the then-INS, even if the foreign national would have been eligible for an extension within the maximum 12– or 18-month program period if the waiver application had not been made.[256] In contrast, if the waiver application had been denied, then the foreign national would be eligible for an extension within the applicable 12– or 18-month maximum period.[257] It is unclear if this is still the government's position, given that the responsibility for waivers now rests with DOS, and a provision in the Foreign Affairs Manual (FAM) reflecting this position[258] no longer can be found in that document.

In any event, an extension request filed by a foreign national who is the beneficiary of an approved labor certification application or of a filed employment-based immigrant visa petition is likely to be denied, as discussed below.

In contrast to previous guidance which prohibited additional training programs or internships,[259] DOS regulations now permit repeat participation in certain circumstances, and "[i]f the participants meet these selection criteria and fulfill these conditions, there will be no limit to the number of times they may participate in a training and internship program."[260] As stated by regulation: "For both trainees and interns, additional training and internship programs must address the development of more advanced skills or a different field of expertise."[261]

Interns may accept subsequent J-1 internships, whether with the same or a different J-1 sponsor or host organization, "as long as they maintain student status or begin a new internship program within 12 months of graduation."[262] Alternatively, a "new internship is also permissible when a student has successfully completed a recognized course of study (i.e., associate, bachelors, masters, Ph.D., or their

---

[256] See also "USIA Letter Discusses Policy on J-1 Status Extensions" (Dec. 18, 1995), AILA Doc. No. 96011690.

[257] Former 9 FAM 41.62 N10.2.

[258] Former 9 FAM 41.62 N10.2.

[259] "DOS Prohibits Second J-1 Training Programs" (Oct. 1, 2003), AILA Doc. No. 03100640.

[260] 22 CFR §62.22(n)(2).

[261] 22 CFR §62.22(n).

[262] 72 Fed. Reg. 33669 (June 19, 2007). See also 22 CFR §62.22(n).

Copyright © 2017. American Immigration Lawyers Association. All rights reserved.

recognized equivalents) and has enrolled and is pursuing studies at the next higher level of academic study."[263]

If the intern no longer meets the intern eligibility criteria because he or she graduated more than 12 months before the anticipated program start date, then the foreign national is eligible for a J-1 training program after residing abroad for two years following completion of the internship.[264] Trainees must reside abroad for at least two years in order to be eligible for a subsequent J-1 training program.[265] Although the residence need not be in the foreign national's home country, the practitioner should be aware that only residence in the country stated on the Form DS-2019 will satisfy the two-year home residence requirement, if it applies, as discussed below.

For a discussion of strategies to explain how the subsequent internship or training program seeks to provide more advanced training, as well as the potential issues surrounding such a request, see Volume 1: Chapter Nine, "H-3 Visas and Status," because the considerations should be similar. An internship or training program may involve the development of practical skills in a different field of expertise if the occupational category differs from the occupational category of the initial J-1 program.[266]

The practitioner is advised to inform the client that participation in a subsequent J-1 program does not remove the home residence requirement, if applicable, although such participation is permissible because the regulations only prohibit obtaining H, L, or permanent resident status after completing a J-1 program.[267]

It is also possible for a foreign national to change J-1 program categories, such as from trainee to research scholar, but the application must be approved by DOS,[268] and either be "clearly consistent with the original OR a closely related objective."[269] J-1 program sponsors may also allow a foreign national "to transfer from one designated program to another designated program" in the same category of activity by issuing a new Form DS-2019, securing release from the previous J-1 sponsor, and notifying DOS.[270]

C. International Travel

When traveling internationally to destinations other than to other North American countries or adjacent islands, the foreign national should obtain a travel endorsement

---

[263] 22 CFR §62.22(n)(2).

[264] *Id.*; 9 FAM 402.5-6(E)(5).

[265] 22 CFR §62.22(n).

[266] For a list of the occupational categories, see above.

[267] INA §212(e).

[268] 22 CFR §62.41.

[269] OI 214.2 (emphasis in original).

[270] 22 CFR §§62.42, 62.76.

Copyright © 2017. American Immigration Lawyers Association. All rights reserved.

in blue ink on the Form DS-2019 and present it when applying for readmission,[271] but the Form DS-2019 should not be stamped again.[272]

Similar to some other nonimmigrant visa classifications, a J-1 exchange visitor "may be readmitted to the United States for the remainder of the time authorized on Form I-94" following international travel to "foreign contiguous territory or adjacent islands after an absence of less than 30 days," as long as the original I-94 card is presented at the port of entry.[273] A foreign national may be readmitted even if the J-1 visa has expired, if he or she presents the original I-94 card or a Form DS-2019 with valid J-1 program dates.[274] Despite the language of the regulation and CBP and ICE guidance indicating that the foreign national should present either an I-94 card "endorsed by DHS to show an unexpired period of initial admission or extension of stay" or a valid Form DS-2019 "indicating the period of initial admission or extension of stay authorized by DHS,"[275] the practitioner should advise the client that the foreign national should nevertheless obtain a travel endorsement and present the Form DS-2019 at the port of entry for several reasons.

First, DOS guidance states: "At each time of admission to the United States, an exchange visitor must present the Form DS-2019 along with the visa to the CBP officer."[276] Second, a J nonimmigrant's I-94 does not state an end date or any other amount of time; the J nonimmigrant is admitted for duration of status, as discussed above. Therefore, even though the CBP officer may consult the SEVIS system to confirm the foreign national's J status,[277] the immigration inspector may be reluctant to readmit the foreign national without the Form DS-2019 to state the duration of the J-1 training program or internship. Third, the regulation sometimes refers to the Form IAP-66, which was the previous form issued to J nonimmigrants, although most other references to the Form IAP-66 were revised to reflect the new Form DS-2019.[278] Fourth, traveling without the Form DS-2019 may subject the foreign national to additional difficulties at the port of entry and potential denial of admission, even if the immigration inspector is willing and able to confirm the J-1 program date through SEVIS.

D. Change of Status

Change of status to J-1 from another nonimmigrant visa classification is available,[279] and the foreign national should be able to obtain a J visa during a

---

[271] 8 CFR §214.2(j)(1)(iii); 1 CBP IFM ch. 15: Nonimmigrants and Border Crossers, 14-1 Agency Manuals 15.4

[272] 1 CBP IFM ch. 15: Nonimmigrants and Border Crossers, 14-1 Agency Manuals 15.4.

[273] 8 CFR §214.2(j)(1)(iii).

[274] 1 CBP IFM ch. 15: Nonimmigrants and Border Crossers, 14-1 Agency Manuals 15.4.

[275] 1 CBP IFM ch. 15: Nonimmigrants and Border Crossers, 14-1 Agency Manuals 15.3: Visas.

[276] 9 FAM 402.5-6(D)(5).

[277] 1 CBP IFM ch. 15: Nonimmigrants and Border Crossers, 14-1 Agency Manuals 15.16.

[278] *See generally* 8 CFR §214.2(j); 72 Fed. Reg. 10060 (Mar. 7, 2007).

[279] 9 FAM 402.5-6(I)(4).

Copyright © 2017. American Immigration Lawyers Association. All rights reserved.

subsequent trip abroad.[280] However, the practitioner should note that the simpler strategy may be for the foreign national to depart the United States, apply for a J-1 visa, and apply for U.S. admission in J-1 status.[281] This is because the foreign national may not engage in training or interning until the change of status application is approved,[282] a process that can take several months.[283] Moreover, as a practical matter, experience has shown that many J-1 program sponsors in the trainee and intern category will not issue a Form DS-2019 to a foreign national who is in the United States unless he or she holds valid nonimmigrant status that already authorizes the individual to temporarily live in the United States, such as H-4 or TD status.

The practitioner should also advise the client that even after filing a J-1 change of status application, the foreign national may be required to travel internationally in order to begin the J-1 program as scheduled, in which case the application would be deemed abandoned, as discussed in Volume 1: Chapter Two, "Basic Nonimmigrant Concepts," and the filing fee would be forfeited. If the J-1 change of status is nevertheless desired, the request should be made on Form I-539, Application to Extend/Change Nonimmigrant Status,[284] as discussed in Volume 1: Chapter Two, "Basic Nonimmigrant Concepts." It is inappropriate, however, to seek change of status from F-1 to J-1, if the intent is to gain additional practical training[285] or to allow the dependent spouse to obtain employment authorization.[286]

Change of status is permissible from J-1 to certain nonimmigrant visa classifications, as long as the foreign national is not subject to the two-year home residence requirement[287] or obtains a waiver of the requirement, as discussed below. Even if the foreign national is subject to the home residence requirement, it is possible to obtain status in another nonimmigrant classification, as long as the status is not H, K, or L,[288] and as long as the foreign national does not request a change of status in the United States.[289] Therefore, a J-1 trainee or intern could later obtain O-1,[290] TN,[291] or E-3 status.[292]

---

[280] 9 FAM 402.5-6(I)(8).

[281] DOS, "(A) 04 STATE 70079 (B) 03 STATE 349930 (C) 03 STATE 279071 (D) 03 STATE 144850 (E) 03 STATE 144850" (Aug. 2004), AILA Doc. No. 04080965.

[282] *Id.*

[283] *See, e.g.,* USCIS, "USCIS Processing Time Information" https://egov.uscis.gov/cris/process TimesDisplay.do; DOS, "(A) 04 STATE 70079 (B) 03 STATE 349930 (C) 03 STATE 279071 (D) 03 STATE 144850 (E) 03 STATE 144850" (Aug. 2004), AILA Doc. No. 04080965.

[284] AFM 30.3(a).

[285] *Matter of Kalia*, 14 I&N Dec. 559 (Reg'l Comm'r 1974).

[286] OI 248.5.

[287] 8 CFR §§248.2(a)(3) and (4).

[288] INA §212(e).

[289] 8 CFR §§248.2(a)(3) and (4).

[290] *See, e.g., Matter of [name not provided]* LIN 02 184 53385 (AAU Sept. 17, 2002), 26 Immig. Rptr. B2-92.

[291] 9 FAM 402.17-13.

Copyright © 2017. American Immigration Lawyers Association. All rights reserved.

If the trainee or intern was not subject to the two-year home residency requirement, then this could be pursued through a change of status in the United States before USCIS, unless the J-1 program sponsor required that the foreign national and host organization attest that change of status would not be pursued, as discussed above. For foreign nationals who are not restricted by the home residence requirement, the practitioner is reminded that the eligibility requirements for the H or L category must be met. For example, as a practical matter, H-1B change of status is available only to trainees and interns who have earned the equivalent of a U.S. bachelor's degree.[293]

USCIS has the authority to extend the authorized stay of J-1 and J-2 nonimmigrants who are beneficiaries of timely filed H-1B and H-4 change of status petitions "by notice in the Federal Register" for a given fiscal year.[294] The foreign nationals "shall be considered to be maintaining lawful nonimmigrant status for all purposes under the Act," either until the H-1B petition is adjudicated[295] or until the H-1B employment start date of October 1 of the fiscal year.[296] The foreign national "must not have violated the terms of his or her nonimmigrant stay."[297] International travel nullifies the extension and the foreign national must then apply for a visa at a U.S. consulate abroad. Employment is not authorized during this "extension of the … grace period."[298] The practitioner should note, however, that each authorization is valid only for the specific fiscal year;[299] the most recent authorization was in 2004,[300] the parallel provision for F-1s has been made permanent,[301] and USCIS has evinced little interest in reviving this benefit for J-1s.[302] Therefore, the practitioner should advise the client that this extension will likely not be available.

The practitioner should note that an application to change status from J-1 or J-2 to F-1 or F-2 is likely to be closely scrutinized to determine whether the application was filed as an attempt "merely to extend the stay."[303] In addition, change from J-1 to J-2

---

[292] "New England Chapter: Minutes of the New England Chapter Monthly Meeting" (Oct. 20, 2005), AILA Doc. No. 06022351.

[293] INA §214(i)(2)(B). For further discussion of the requirements for H-1B status, see Volume 1: Chapter Seven, "H-1B Visas and Status."

[294] 8 CFR §214.2(j)(1)(vi).

[295] Id.

[296] 65 Fed. Reg. 15178 (Mar. 21, 2000); 69 Fed. Reg. 44044 (July 23, 2004).

[297] 8 CFR §214.2(j)(1)(vi).

[298] 69 Fed. Reg. 44044 (July 23, 2004).

[299] 8 CFR §214.2(j)(1)(vi).

[300] 69 Fed. Reg. 44044 (July 23, 2004).

[301] 73 Fed. Reg. 18944 (Apr. 8, 2008) and 81 Fed. Reg. 13040 (Mar. 11, 2016).

[302] "USCIS National Stakeholder Meeting" (Jan. 26, 2010), AILA Doc. No. 10012963 (indicating that USCIS had no plans for the coming year to make this provision for J-1s).

[303] AFM 30.3(c)(7); 1 legacy INS Examinations Handbook, Pt. II, 15-1 Examinations Handbook Application.

Copyright © 2017. American Immigration Lawyers Association. All rights reserved.

or vice versa may be problematic.[304] USIA, which administered the J-1 program before DOS, stated a concern that a "'flip-flop' of status could continue back and forth for years, even decades, at the expense of program effectiveness and integrity."[305] Although USCIS guidance acknowledges that "changing from J-1 to J-2 is not regarded as a change of status" for purposes of INA §212(e) and is permissible,[306] other legacy INS guidance also noted similar concerns: "The Department of State generally does not look favorably upon a request by a J-1 principal for a change to J-2 status because it expects such principal to return abroad upon completion of the program."[307] In addition, changing between J-1 and J-2 statuses does not eliminate the two-year home residence requirement; in fact, such a change may subject a foreign national to the requirement, depending on the field or other characteristics of the new J-1 program, such as if the new J-1 program is funded by the government of the United States or home country.[308] An "indirect" change of status from J to F, where the foreign national held another nonimmigrant status after entering the United States in J status, is also inappropriate,[309] and "a prohibited action."[310]

E. EADs for J-2 Dependents

Dependent spouses and minor children of J-1 exchange visitors are eligible to apply for EADs.[311] A J-2 dependent may wish to obtain an EAD solely in order to apply for a Social Security number. The funds earned by the J-2 dependent "may be used to support the family's customary recreational and cultural activities and related travel, among other things."[312] It is important to note, however, that "[e]mployment will not be authorized if this income is needed to support the J-1 principal alien,"[313] so anticipated wages of the J-2 dependent(s) may not be used to demonstrate possession of sufficient funds to cover the expenses of the U.S. stay, as discussed above.

The EAD will be issued and valid only "for the duration of the J-1 principal alien's authorized stay as indicated on Form I-94 or a period of four years, whichever

---

[304] The problem of the "flip-flop" between J-1 and J-2 has largely been eliminated by DOS rules on J-1 participant selection, especially in the category of researcher, where an individual who has held J status (either J-1 or J-2) in the last 12 months usually cannot be selected for participation by a J-1 researcher program. 22 CFR §62.20(d).

[305] 61 Fed. Reg. 29285 (June 10, 1996).

[306] AFM 30.3(b)(2).

[307] OI 248.5.

[308] AFM 30.3(b)(7). See also Matter of Baterina, 16 I&N Dec. 127 (BIA 1977); Matter of Tuakoi, 19 I&N Dec. 341 (BIA 1985).

[309] Matter of Kim, 13 I&N Dec. 315 (Reg'l Comm'r 1968).

[310] AFM 30.3(c)(5).

[311] 8 CFR §214.2(j)(1)(v)(A); see also Social Security Administration (SSA), "RM 10211.420 Employment Authorization for Non-immigrants" (Mar. 15, 2017), http://policy.ssa.gov/poms.nsf/lnx/0110211420.

[312] 8 CFR §214.2(j)(1)(v)(A).

[313] Id.

Copyright © 2017. American Immigration Lawyers Association. All rights reserved.

is shorter," and only while the J-1 exchange visitor maintains lawful J-1 status.[314] An EAD application may not be filed until the foreign national holds valid J-2 status. If the dependent needs to obtain an extension and a new Form DS-2019 from the J-1 program sponsor of stay, then the EAD renewal application should be filed after the new Form DS-2019 is issued.

The following documents should be prepared and filed:

- Form G-28;
- Form I-765;
- Statement from host organization, confirming the J-1 program of the principal foreign national;
- Copies of Forms DS-2019 for the J-1 principal and the J-2 dependent;
- Copy of the principal J-1 nonimmigrant's J-1 visa;
- Copy of biographic page of passport of the J-2 dependent;
- Copy of J-2 visa and I-94 card;
- Copy of marriage and/or birth certificate of J-1 exchange visitor and the dependent(s); and
- Statement from the foreign national confirming that any income from employment "is not necessary to support the J-1 but is for other purposes."[315]

USCIS may expedite an EAD application if the J-2 dependent submits evidence of an employment offer "with an immediate start date."[316] In the event that a J-2 dependent applies for an EAD renewal based on a J-2 extension application with a new Form DS-2019, then USCIS hopes to avoid "unnecessary" Requests for Evidence (RFE) to confirm the dependent's valid immigration status, even though there is no guarantee that the extension application and EAD renewal application will "be worked concurrently."[317] The practitioner should note that this guidance seems to contradict the language of the regulation, as discussed above, and, therefore, should caution the client that the J-2 dependent may nevertheless not receive the EAD until the J-2 extension is approved.

F. Two-Year Home Residence Requirement

USCIS guidance indicates that the home residence requirement exists because the J-1 program was designed to "enable aliens to acquire skills and knowledge which would be valuable in their home countries..., [but] Congress became concerned that program participants were subverting the goals of the program by immigrating to the

---

[314] 8 CFR §214.2(j)(1)(v)(B).

[315] USCIS, "Instructions for I-765, Application for Employment Authorization," www.uscis.gov/files/form/I-765instr.pdf.

[316] "AILA Liaison/NSC Q&As on 'Other' Product Line Issues (July 26, 2007), AILA Doc. No. 07080769.

[317] "AILA Liaison/VSC Meeting Minutes" (Sept. 17, 2007).

Copyright © 2017. American Immigration Lawyers Association. All rights reserved.

United States (thereby creating a 'brain drain' in the very countries the program was designed to help)."[318]

1. Whether the Requirement Applies

A foreign national may be subject to the requirement following completion of the J-1 program if:

- The program was "financed in whole or in part, directly or indirectly, by an agency of the Government of the United States or by the government of the country of his nationality or his last residence";

- The "country of residence and intended field of endeavor or skill appear on the Skills List" when the application for J-1 visa or U.S. admission is made, or when J-1 change of status is granted;[319] or

- The individual held J-1 status "in order to receive graduate medical education or training."[320].

If the foreign national was not subject to the home residence requirement at the time of admission or change of status, he or she may nevertheless become subject if the Skills List changes and he or she performs one of the following actions:

- Departs the United States. and is later admitted to the United States "based on a new nonimmigrant visa"; or

- "Falls out of status for any reason and is later reinstated to the exchange classification."[321]

The foreign national bears the burden of establishing that the home residence requirement does not apply.[322] The residence requirement applies even if the foreign national obtained J-1 status through fraud and never participated in the J-1 program,[323] or if the foreign national should have received an F-1 international student visa,[324] "objected" to the J-1 visa at the U.S. consulate, and was stateless at the time the waiver application was made.[325]

J-2 dependents are also subject to the requirement if the principal J-1 foreign national is subject.[326] Despite concerns of unfairness because the term "exchange visitor" does not explicitly include the principal foreign national's family members,[327] the Board of Immigration Appeals (BIA) stated that the requirement is

---

[318] AFM 45.1(a).

[319] OI 214.2; 22 CFR §41.62(c)(1)(ii); INA §212(e).

[320] INA §212(e). Issues related to this category are a book in themselves, and thus are not treated in this book.

[321] AFM 45.1(a).

[322] *Matter of O–*, 19 I&N Dec. 871 (Comm'r 1989).

[323] *Matter of Park*, 15 I&N Dec. 436 (BIA 1975).

[324] *Matter of Koryzma*, 13 I&N Dec. 358 (BIA 1969); *Matter of Wojcik*, 11 I&N Dec. 608 (BIA 1966).

[325] *Matter of Koryzma*, 13 I&N Dec. 358 (BIA 1969).

[326] 8 CFR §212.7(c)(4); 22 CFR §41.62(c)(4).

[327] 22 CFR §62.2.

Copyright © 2017. American Immigration Lawyers Association. All rights reserved.

imposed because the dependents also "derived benefits" from the J-1 program,[328] except as discussed below.

If it is unclear whether the requirement applies, an advisory opinion may be requested from DOS or by the foreign national, an attorney, or the J-1 program's officer,[329] although USCIS makes the final determination of the requirement, as discussed below. The request should be in writing and include legible copies of all Forms DS-2019 or IAP-66 ever received by the individual.[330] A foreign national should be issued a DOS case number upon submitting the request for an advisory opinion, and this case number should be used in any subsequent waiver application.[331] Alternatively, DOS provides a "survey" that may be completed online to determine if the requirement applies.[332] The practitioner is encouraged to carefully analyze whether the requirement applies before submitting a waiver application. In at least one instance, a foreign national learned that the requirement did not apply only upon appeal to the Administrative Appeals Office (AAO) after a waiver application was submitted to and denied by USCIS.[333]

2. Satisfying the Home Residency Requirement

A foreign national may satisfy the residency requirement by being physically present in the country of which the individual "is a national or resident, or, if not a national, a legal permanent resident (or has status equivalent thereto)" for two years[334] in the aggregate.[335] Thus, "physical presence need not be continuous and may be cumulative."[336] Also, "[i]f the country of nationality differs from the country of last residence at the time of admission, or acquisition of, J status, then the alien is required to fulfill the two years in the country of last residence."[337]

The home residence requirement may not be satisfied through residence in a third country,[338] unless that residence was pursuant to service in the home country's "military service or in its career foreign service … at the behest of [the] home country's

---

[328] *Matter of Tabcum*, 14 I&N Dec. 113 (Reg'l Comm'r 1972).

[329] DOS, "Advisory Opinions," https://travel.state.gov/content/visas/en/general/advisory-opinions.html.

[330] *Id.*

[331] DOS, "Frequently Asked Questions: Waiver of the Exchange Visitor Two-Year Home-Country Physical Presence Requirement," https://travel.state.gov/content/visas/en/study-exchange/student/residency-waiver/ds-3035-faqs.html.

[332] DOS, "Welcome to J Visa Online!", https://j1visawaiverrecommendation.state.gov/.

[333] *Matter of [name and case number not provided]* (AAO Dec. 29, 2008), http://bit.ly/dec083h.

[334] 22 CFR §41.62(c)(3).

[335] 22 CFR §41.63(a)(1)(iii); 9 FAM 302.13-2(B)(1).

[336] 9 FAM 302.13-2(B)(1).

[337] *Id.*

[338] 9 FAM 302.13-2(B)(1).

Copyright © 2017. American Immigration Lawyers Association. All rights reserved.

government."[339] If this is the case, then DOS requires a statement from "an official of the home government (through the home country's embassy in Washington, D.C.)."[340]

The home residency requirement cannot be satisfied in another European Union (EU) country if the foreign national is an EU citizen.[341] This rule applies even if the reason for being subject to requirement is that the individual received funding from the EU: "Given that the EU is funded by its member states, EU funding of an exchange visitor from an EU member state comes in part, indirectly, from the exchange visitor's country of nationality or country of last residence."[342]

As noted previously in this chapter, even if the foreign national is subject to the home residence requirement, it is possible to obtain status in another nonimmigrant classification, as long as the status is not H, K, or L,[343] and as long as the foreign national does not request a change of status in the United States.[344]

3. The Skills List

The Skills List is organized by country and occupational fields.[345] The easiest way to interpret the Skills List may be to first find the home country and then compare the fields stated in that country's category against the field of the proposed or completed J-1 program. The practitioner may also wish to compare the fields stated on the Skills List against the master list of fields at the beginning of the document.

DOS guidance indicated that the occupational fields should not be exclusively considered as job fields: "The skills list does not necessarily list particular job or occupations and the 212(e) determination is made on whether the alien's exchange program involves 'a designated field of specialized knowledge or skill.'"[346] In addition, the occupational field "must be selected from the Department of Education's 'Classification of Instructional Programs' (CIP),"[347] which are available online.[348]

---

[339] DOS, "Frequently Asked Questions: Waiver of the Exchange Visitor Two-Year Home-Country Physical Presence Requirement," https://travel.state.gov/content/visas/en/study-exchange/student/residency-waiver/ds-3035-faqs.html.

[340] *Id.*

[341] "DOS Answers to AILA Questions" (Oct. 26, 2001), AILA Doc. No. 01103032; "DOS Answers to AILA Questions" (Oct. 13, 2004), AILA Doc. No. 04120760; USCIS Listening Session on J-1 Exchange Visitor Waivers" (Dec. 21, 2011), AILA Doc. No. 11101833.

[342] "DOS Agenda – J Visa Questions, AILA DOS Liaison Committee Fall Meeting" (Oct. 6, 2016), AILA Doc. No. 16100706.

[343] INA §212(e).

[344] 8 CFR §§248.2(a)(3) and (4).

[345] 74 Fed. Reg. 20108 (Apr. 30, 2009).

[346] "DOS Answers to AILA Questions" (Oct. 13, 2004), AILA Doc. No. 04120760.

[347] *Id.*

[348] U.S. Department of Education, "Classification of Instructional Programs (CIP 2000)," http://nces.ed.gov/pubs2002/cip2000/.

Copyright © 2017. American Immigration Lawyers Association. All rights reserved.

The most recent Skills List became effective on June 28, 2009,[349] and DOS has indicated that, "because this is a very burdensome exercise," it is done at "approximately 12 to 13 year intervals."[350] To identify which Skills List applies, the practitioner should review the J-1 program dates, as the determination should be made on the basis of "the skills list that was in effect when [the exchange visitor] first obtained the J-1 visa,"[351] or "on the basis of the most current skills list at the beginning of the J-1's program."[352] Therefore, a foreign national should not be subject to the residence requirement based on a Skills List that was effective for a time period before the J-1 program, unless the foreign national changes the program objective[353] or begins a new J-1 program with a new J-1 visa or is reinstated to J-1 status after falling out of status,[354] as discussed above. Similarly, a foreign national should not become subject to the residence requirement by applying a newer Skills List: "If a skill is added to a country's list, an [Exchange Visitor] EV is not subject retroactively since the skills list was not in effect when the EV began his or her exchange program."[355]

Legacy INS guidance stated, and USIA agreed, that "advancing to a higher level of study in the field of study is not considered a change of program objective."[356] USIA also indicated that international travel and/or issuance of a new J-1 visa should not change the applicable Skills List, as long as the foreign national re-enters the United States to continue participation in the same J-1 program.[357] If a country requests removal from the Skills List, then citizens and permanent residents of that country "are retroactively no longer required, on the basis of the skills list, to comply with the two-year home residence requirement."[358]

Macau, Taiwan, and the Hong Kong Special Administrative Region (Hong Kong SAR) are "considered independent of" the People's Republic of China (PRC) for section 212(e) purposes, and do not have a Skills List of their own.[359] Thus, "J visa recipients from those regions cannot be subject to 212(e) based on the PRC's Skills

---

[349] 74 Fed. Reg. 20108 (Apr. 30, 2009).

[350] "DOS Agenda – J Visa Questions, AILA DOS Liaison Committee Fall Meeting" (Oct. 6, 2016), AILA Doc. No. 16100706.

[351] DOS, "STATE 057336" (June 2009), AILA Doc. No. 09080362.

[352] OI 214.2.

[353] Id.

[354] AFM 45.1(a).

[355] "AILA Liaison/DOS Meeting Minutes" (Nov. 11, 2008), AILA Doc. No. 09022660.

[356] OI 214.2.

[357] "USIA Clarifies Application of Skills List to Exchange Visitors," 74 Interpreter Releases 832–33 (May 19, 1997).

[358] 62 Fed. Reg. 67431 (Dec. 24, 1997). See also DOS, "STATE 057336" (June 2009), AILA Doc. No. 09080362.

[359] "DOS Agenda – J Visa Questions, AILA DOS Liaison Committee Fall Meeting" (Oct. 6, 2016), AILA Doc. No. 16100706.

Copyright © 2017. American Immigration Lawyers Association. All rights reserved.

List."[360] However, those individuals still can be subject to the home residency requirement if they received government funding or engaged in clinical medical training, and would have to fulfill the requirement in their place of last residence.[361]

A foreign national must be either a "national and resident or, if not a national, a legal permanent resident (or [have] status equivalent thereto) of a country which the Secretary of State has designated … as clearly requiring the services of persons engaged in the field of specialized knowledge or skill" of the J-1 program.[362] As previously noted, "If the exchange visitor's country of nationality differs from his or her country of legal permanent residence, then he or she is required to return to the country of his or her legal permanent residence at the time the J-1 visa was issued or J status obtained."[363] For a further discussion of citizenship and permanent residence for purposes of fulfilling the home residence requirement, see below.

4. Strategies to Avoid the Home Residence Requirement and/or Avoid a Waiver Application

The following strategies may be considered either to avoid imposition of the home residence requirement at the outset, or after the foreign national has completed the J-1 program.

a. The Field Is Not on the Skills List for the Foreign National's Home Country

Although certain countries require the return of all J-1 exchange visitors, regardless of the occupational field of the J-1 program because these countries require all of the occupational fields on the Skills List, most countries list a selection of specific fields within each subject area.[364] The training or internship program offered by the host organization need not be an exact match to the business activities and objectives of the host organization. However, there should be a recognizable relationship between the two, and DOS or USCIS may consider the J-1 program activities.[365] For example, a company that engages in manufacturing automobiles may offer training or internship programs in the fields of "Labor Union Administration" and "Labor and Industrial Relations," so the foreign national may learn how to negotiate with worker unions; the U.S. company is not limited to J-1 programs in the field of "Mechanical Engineering." Therefore, the practitioner should strategize with the client and the J-1 sponsor to ensure that the occupational field is properly

---

[360] *Id.*

[361] *Id.*

[362] 22 CFR §41.62(c)(1)(ii).

[363] 9 FAM 302.13-2(B)(1).

[364] 74 Fed. Reg. 20108 (Apr. 30, 2009).

[365] "DOS Answers to AILA Questions" (Oct. 13, 2004), AILA Doc. No. 04120760 (stating "in [one] specific case banking did not appear on the skills list for the alien's sending country. However, the alien did submit an attachment that went into great detail about the exchange program activities that were on the skills list, thus rendering the EV subject to 212(e)").

Copyright © 2017. American Immigration Lawyers Association. All rights reserved.

classified, but should also consider if the field of the host organization's business is stated on the Skills List for the foreign national's home country.[366]

In addition, the occupational field of the J-1 program should be considered vis-à-vis the Skills List. For example, the 2009 Skills List states that Indian citizens are subject to the residence requirement if they participate in a program for any type of engineering except "Metallurgical Engineering," which is not subject to the requirement. In such a situation, care should be taken to highlight how the training or internship involves metallurgical skills, rather than other types of engineering activities, to avoid the complications of correcting a Form DS-2019 with the improper occupational field. The practitioner may also wish to contact the J-1 sponsor to discuss the proposed occupational field before submitting the J-1 program application in order to address in advance any concerns the J-1 sponsor may have about the training or internship program.

If the J-1 sponsor nevertheless states an erroneous occupational field on the Form DS-2019, then the practitioner should advise the client that the foreign national should not apply for a J-1 visa until a corrected Form DS-2019 is issued and liaise with the J-1 sponsor to resolve the issue.[367] Experience has shown that the J-1 sponsor may require additional information on the training or internship program or a revised application in order to issue a second Form DS-2019. However, the practitioner should advise the client that the short delay in this process may be preferable to imposition of the home residence requirement, which would preclude any application to change or adjust status until the residence requirement is fulfilled or waived; it is generally difficult and/or involves devotion of time and financial resources to obtain a waiver, as discussed below.

If an erroneous waiver approval does not give rise to a claim for estoppel, as discussed below, then it seems unlikely that the government would be estopped from imposing the residence requirement because the J-1 sponsor issued an incorrect Form DS-2019.[368] Although reports indicate that DOS's Waiver Review Division (WRD) may correct the erroneous field code on the Form DS-2019 and issue an advisory opinion that the foreign national is not subject to the home residence requirement, the practitioner may wish to avoid depending on such late assistance. For these reasons, it is advisable to request the corrected Form DS-2019 from the J-1 sponsor, and if the delay means that the J-1 program start date must be revised, then this change may be requested at the same time.

b. Only a Related Field Is Stated on the Skills List

The fact that a field is stated on the Skills List should not mean that another related field, which is not stated on the Skills List, should be incorporated by default. If the foreign national has already completed the J-1 program, change of status to H

---

[366] Id.

[367] Id.

[368] Id.

Copyright © 2017. American Immigration Lawyers Association. All rights reserved.

or L classifications may nevertheless be obtained without a waiver application by explaining in the petition package that the specific field of the J-1 program is not included on the Skills List.

For example, the fields of "Chemical Engineering," "Industrial Engineering," and "Genetic and Biomedical Engineering" are on the Master Skills List, but the field of "Food Engineering" is not. If the J-1 program focused on food engineering activities, such as developing new products and processes for refrigeration and storage, then the residence requirement could not apply, and therefore a waiver would be unnecessary. The practitioner should also confirm, however, that the foreign national would not be subject to the requirement because the J-1 program falls under another field which is on the Skills List for the foreign national's home country. In this example, an adjudicator could determine that the foreign national was nevertheless subject to the residence requirement because the J-1 program was in the field of "Food Science and Technology."

Appropriate evidence for this strategy includes statements from the J-1 sponsor, independent evaluators, and professional associations, as well as an advisory opinion from WRD. The practitioner may wish to caution the client, however, that the result may be that WRD and/or USCIS question why the J-1 program was classified under the incorrect occupational field. The answer may be that the correct field is a newly developing or newly developed specialization, such that it was impossible to classify the J-1 program in any other field. Alternatively, the field may be recognized on the Skills List, but not as a skill required by the home country, in which case the J-1 sponsor may have made an error.

c. The Foreign National Holds Dual Citizenship or Citizenship and Permanent Residence in Two Different Countries

For foreign nationals who hold dual citizenship or who hold citizenship in one country and permanent residence in another country, it may be feasible to contend that the home residence requirement does not apply because the Skills List does not require the foreign national's return to the other country of the foreign national's citizenship or status as a permanent resident. The statute provides that the home residence may be completed "in the country of his nationality or his last residence."[369] As a practical matter, USCIS is the entity that will respond to a change of status petition or application to adjust status by requesting evidence that the requirement was fulfilled or waived. Therefore, it is possible to file an application to change status to the H or L classifications or to apply to adjust status without first completing the home residence requirement or obtaining a waiver. However, approval is dependent upon USCIS rejecting DOS guidance.

The DOS guidance, which states that the foreign national must return to the country of permanent residence at the time the J-1 visa was issued or J-1 status was

---

[369] INA §212(e).

Copyright © 2017. American Immigration Lawyers Association. All rights reserved.

obtained, was most recently updated on December 20, 2016,[370] and should override much earlier guidance stating that residence in either country may satisfy the requirement. The practitioner should counsel the client about the risk of denial of the petition or application and forfeiture of the filing fees.

The same risk applies to a foreign national who seeks to obtain a "no objection" letter from a country that differs from the country of the foreign national's citizenship or permanent residence at the time that the J-1 visa is issued or J-1 change of status is granted, even though the statute states that the "no objection" letter may be issued by "the foreign country of the alien's nationality or last residence."[371] This analysis is supported by the imposition of the requirement upon an individual who was stateless at the time of visa issuance, though he or she obtained the J-1 visa in the country where he or she resided and not his or her country of citizenship,[372] as discussed above. DOS generally treats the country shown on the DS-2019 as the last residence as the place of obligation. The practitioner may wish to show that the country listed on the DS-2019 as the "legal permanent residence" is wrong. A program sponsor might incorrectly put a country of temporary residence (perhaps where the individual is studying) in the block on the form.

d. Impossibility of Fulfillment

It may be impossible for the foreign national to fulfill the requirement because his or her status as a citizen or permanent resident has been revoked, but this does not mean that the foreign national is automatically relieved from the obligation. The USIA, which administered the J-1 program before DOS, refused to accept this "impossibility of fulfillment" concept as policy, noting also that the foreign national could obtain a nonimmigrant visa from the former country of citizenship or permanent residence in order to complete the requirement.[373] The USIA suggested that a foreign national should not become exempt from the requirement based on his or her voluntary actions to acquire "citizenship or legal permanent residence in another country."[374]

Therefore, rather than a blanket exemption, USIA stated the following:

"The Agency will review, on a case by case basis, those extraordinarily few instances where fulfillment of the Section 1182(e) requirement is impossible due to facts totally beyond the control of the waiver applicant and which were not the predictable consequences of action on the part of the applicant. Compelling and probative evidence of such impossibility of performance, furnished by the alien, is necessarily a prerequisite to Agency review. Such evidence may be, for example,

---

[370] 9 FAM 302.13-2(B)(1); OI 214.8 (stating "REMOVED, TM1, June 24, 1997").

[371] INA §212(e).

[372] *Matter of Koryzma*, 13 I&N Dec. 358 (BIA 1969). To a certain extent, this case is viewed as an anomaly, however.

[373] 63 Fed. Reg. 42233 (Aug. 7, 1998).

[374] *Id.*

Copyright © 2017. American Immigration Lawyers Association. All rights reserved.

proof of denial of a request for a nonimmigrant visa from the home country or denial of a request to restore home country citizenship."[375]

DOS has stated that this policy "remains in effect," and that foreign nationals who seek an exemption based on impossibility of fulfillment should present the case in the form of a waiver application.[376] DOS did not, however, articulate a new policy regarding foreign nationals whose home countries no longer exist because of the "changed political landscape," stating instead that USIA's policy had been to allow such foreign nationals to apply for waivers and that DOS had "not yet been confronted with such a question."[377]

G. Waiver of Two-Year Home Residence Requirement

A foreign national need not reside abroad for two years if a "waiver of that requirement has been favorably recommended by [DOS] and then approved by [DHS]."[378] A waiver request may be made based on five grounds:

- Exceptional hardship to a U.S. citizen or permanent resident spouse or child;

- Fear of persecution based on race, religion, or political opinion;

- Request by an Interested Government Agency (IGA);[379]

- No objection from the home country's government;[380] and

- Request by an IGA or a State Department of Health on behalf of a foreign medical graduate who received graduate medical education or training in the United States and who will provide medical care in a Health Professional Shortage Area, a Medically Underserved Area, or a Mental Health Professional Shortage Area.[381]

The Form DS-3035, J-1 Visa Waiver Recommendation Application, must be completed online.[382] For waiver applications where the foreign national received a Form IAP-66 instead of the Form DS-2019, the SEVIS number should be "N0000000000 (must have 10 zeros)," and the "Subject/Field Code" should be the USIA field code, preceded by "00."[383] Also, if the individual entered the United

---

[375] *Id.*

[376] "DOS Answers to AILA Questions" (Oct. 26, 2001), AILA Doc. No. 01103032.

[377] *Id.*

[378] 9 FAM 302.13-2(B)(1). *See also* "AILA Liaison/DOS Meeting Minutes" (Nov. 11, 2008), AILA Doc. No. 09022660 (stating that DOS "only makes recommendations in 212(e) waiver applications, the final waiver authority rests with the Department of Homeland Security").

[379] 22 CFR §41.63(a)(2).

[380] 22 CFR §41.63(a)(3).

[381] 22 CFR §41.63(a)(4).

[382] DOS, "How to Apply Instructions – Waiver of the Exchange Visitor Two-Year Home-Country Physical Presence Requirement," https://travel.state.gov/content/visas/en/study-exchange/student/residency-waiver/ds-3035-instructions.html.

[383] *Id.*

Copyright © 2017. American Immigration Lawyers Association. All rights reserved.

States on a J-1 prior to February 1, 1999, the date in item 17 should be February 1, 1999.[384]

The case number and barcode are issued immediately upon completion of the online form after the form is completed.[385] The Form DS-3035 and the barcode, printed only in black and white, must be submitted with the fee payment, as well as copies of all Forms DS-2019 and/or Forms IAP-66 and two stamped, self-addressed envelopes;[386] a statement demonstrating why the exchange visitor is eligible to receive a waiver; Form G-28; and a copy of the biographic page of the exchange visitor's current passport. A prepaid express courier may be enclosed with the documents for WRD to use when forwarding the recommendation to USCIS, as long as the address and account number sections are completed.[387]

DOS states that the online system is the best way to check the status of a case and to confirm that DOS has received documents, such as the "no objection" letter.[388] The Public Inquiries Division should be contacted at *212ewaiver@state.gov* "only to correct an error or for matters not otherwise covered by the website."[389] DOS should be informed of changes in address or other personal information.[390] DOS provides estimated processing times for waiver applications online.[391]

Applicants who apply based on exceptional hardship or persecution must first complete both the online Form DS-3035 for DOS,[392] and then file Form I-612, Application for Waiver of the Foreign Residence Requirement, with USCIS. DOS does not consider the waiver application unless and until USCIS has made a determination of exceptional hardship or persecution and forwarded its internal Form I-613 to WRD with all documentation filed.[393] The Form DS-3035 may be filed either before the Form I-612 is filed or after DHS has issued a favorable recommendation,[394] but it is preferable to obtain the WRD waiver application number first so that it may be included in documents submitted to USCIS, particularly since

---

[384] *Id.*

[385] *Id.*

[386] *Id.*

[387] "DOS Answers to AILA Questions" (Oct. 26, 2001), AILA Doc. No. 01103032.

[388] DOS, "How to Apply Instructions – Waiver of the Exchange Visitor Two-Year Home-Country Physical Presence Requirement," https://travel.state.gov/content/visas/en/study-exchange/student/residency-waiver/ds-3035-instructions.html.

[389] *Id.*

[390] DOS, "Welcome to J Visa Online!", https://j1visawaiverrecommendation.state.gov/.

[391] DOS, "How to Apply Instructions – Waiver of the Exchange Visitor Two-Year Home-Country Physical Presence Requirement," https://travel.state.gov/content/visas/en/study-exchange/student/residency-waiver/ds-3035-instructions.html.

[392] DOS, "Welcome to J Visa Online!", https://j1visawaiverrecommendation.state.gov/.

[393] DOS, "How to Apply Instructions – Waiver of the Exchange Visitor Two-Year Home-Country Physical Presence Requirement," https://travel.state.gov/content/visas/en/study-exchange/student/residency-waiver/ds-3035-instructions.html.

[394] *Id.*

Copyright © 2017. American Immigration Lawyers Association. All rights reserved.

generally there is no notification when a favorable recommendation is issued, so the practitioner may not know when to file the form. The WRD recommendation is forwarded electronically to the California Service Center (CSC).[395]

If USCIS determines that there would be no exceptional hardship or no fear of probable persecution, or "a finding that the applicant's admission to the United States is 'in the public interest'" has not been established, then the waiver application will be denied.[396] Denials of I-612 applications are appealed to the USCIS Administrative Appeals Office.[397] USCIS, in turn, may not approve a waiver application without a favorable recommendation from WRD.[398] If the WRD recommendation "appears to rely on faulty information," then USCIS may prefer to request reconsideration of a WRD recommendation "rather than to deny the application for such reasons."[399] WRD, in turn, should not "re-adjudicate DHS's finding of hardship or persecution,"[400] but rather should balance the persecution or hardship against foreign policy and program considerations.[401]

Despite guidance from USCIS that the grounds are not mutually exclusive, so a foreign national may "base his waiver request on more than one of them,"[402] DOS states that a J-1 "may only apply under one waiver basis,"[403] and advises that "[i]f you believe that you qualify for a waiver of the two-year home-country physical presence requirement under both persecution and exceptional hardship to your U.S. citizen (or legal permanent resident) spouse or child, you may apply for a waiver recommendation under only one of these two bases." However, it also states that, if a waiver recommendation is denied, a new application can be submitted in another category.

Thus, it appears that waivers can be requested on multiple grounds, but DOS will only review one at a time. Indeed, where a foreign national may be eligible in more than one category, some practitioners submit applications on different bases simultaneously. DOS has indicated that, when faced with multiple waiver applications, "the WRD adjudicates the first complete application (meaning all required documents are in the case file). If an applicant receives a favorable recommendation, the WRD will not consider another application.... However, if the

---

[395] "I-612, Application for Waiver of the Foreign Residence Requirement," https://www.uscis.gov/i-612.

[396] 1 legacy INS Examinations Handbook, 15-1 Examinations Handbook Waiver.

[397] USCIS, "When to Use I-290B, Notice of Appeal or Motion," https://www.uscis.gov/i-290b/jurisdiction.

[398] AFM 45.3(f).

[399] 1 legacy INS Examinations Handbook, 15-1 Examinations Handbook Waiver.

[400] "DOS Answers to AILA Questions" (Mar. 17, 2005), AILA Doc. No. 05062117.

[401] DOS, "Frequently Asked Questions: Waiver of the Exchange Visitor Two-Year Home-Country Physical Presence Requirement," https://travel.state.gov/content/visas/en/study-exchange/student/residency-waiver/ds-3035-faqs.html.

[402] AFM 45.1(c).

[403] DOS, "Frequently Asked Questions: Waiver of the Exchange Visitor Two-Year Home-Country Physical Presence Requirement," https://travel.state.gov/content/visas/en/study-exchange/student/residency-waiver/ds-3035-faqs.html.

Copyright © 2017. American Immigration Lawyers Association. All rights reserved.

applicant receives an unfavorable recommendation, the WRD will consider another waiver application."[404] Note that a foreign medical graduate seeking a waiver may only request one waiver at a time from a State Department of Health or an IGA, and the applicant must certify that only one State or IGA waiver is pending or being sought.

The WRD filing fee is required for any subsequent waiver applications based on different grounds, but the initial case number should be used.[405] The DOS online system will generate a new number and bar code when the DS-3035 is updated, but the applicant should include a copy of the previous barcode.

Legacy INS guidance states that while a waiver application is pending, "[n]o action shall be taken to enforce the alien's departure,"[406] but the practitioner should be aware that the current environment of increased enforcement may mean that the legacy guidance is disregarded. After the foreign national applies for the waiver on Form DS-3035, pays the fee, and obtains a case number,[407] the status of the application may be monitored on the DOS J visa website.[408]

There is no USCIS filing fee for waiver applications based on sponsorship from an IGA or based on no objection from the home country's government, as the Form I-612 should not be filed.[409] As discussed below, these applications are initiated by a request from an IGA or the embassy of the foreign national's country of obligation, rather than by filing Form I-612 with USCIS. DOS forwards the recommendation to USCIS electronically.[410]

There is no appeal from WRD's recommendation to deny a waiver application, and most applications are denied "because the reasons given for requesting the waiver do not outweigh the program and the foreign policy considerations" of the J-1 program.[411] However, the USCIS decisions on exceptional hardship or fear of persecution may be appealed.[412] If the waiver application is denied after USCIS

---

[404] "DOS Agenda – J Visa Questions, AILA DOS Liaison Committee Fall Meeting" (Oct. 6, 2016), AILA Doc. No. 16100706. *See also* "Agenda Items for AILA DOS Liaison Meeting with Waiver Review Division" (Oct. 18, 2011), AILA Doc. No. 11102423.

[405] *Id.*

[406] OI 214.2.

[407] DOS, "How to Apply Instructions – Waiver of the Exchange Visitor Two-Year Home-Country Physical Presence Requirement," https://travel.state.gov/content/visas/en/study-exchange/student/residency-waiver/ds-3035-instructions.html.

[408] 9 FAM 302.13-2(b)(1); DOS, "Welcome to J Visa Online!", https://j1visawaiver recommendation.state.gov/.

[409] USCIS, "Instructions for Application for Waiver of the Foreign Residence Requirement," https://www.uscis.gov/sites/default/files/files/form/i-612instr.pdf; 1 legacy INS Examinations Handbook, 15-1 Examinations Handbook Waiver.

[410] "AILA Liaison/DOS Meeting Minutes" (Nov. 11, 2008), AILA Doc. No. 09022660.

[411] DOS, "Frequently Asked Questions: Waiver of the Exchange Visitor Two-Year Home-Country Physical Presence Requirement," https://travel.state.gov/content/visas/en/study-exchange/student/residency-waiver/ds-3035-faqs.html.

[412] AFM 45.3(f) and (h).

Copyright © 2017. American Immigration Lawyers Association. All rights reserved.

found hardship because DOS did not concur, and the foreign national obtains "new relevant information," he or she may file a new I-612 (including the fee) with USCIS. The application should include the original DOS waiver number.[413]

Before adjudicating the waiver application, the government official must confirm that the foreign national is, in fact, subject to the home residence requirement.[414] This remains the case, even if:

> "[A]nother officer so indicated during a prior proceeding on the IAP-66 [or Form DS-2019].... An alien erroneously determined to be subject to 212(e) by an American consular officer or immigration inspector is not made subject thereto because of the officer's error. Likewise, an alien who was erroneously determined *not* to be subject to 212(e) is not exempt from the requirement due to the officer's error. In other words, whatever is indicated on the IAP-66 [or Form DS-2019] is not necessarily correct and [the adjudicator] should verify that alien's obligations for [himself/herself] when adjudicating the waiver application."[415]

An approved waiver application means only that the foreign national does not need to return to his or her country of obligation; the waiver does not provide a means to remain in the United States. However, the foreign national may then apply for permanent residence or for a nonimmigrant change of status to H or L status.[416]

In the event that the waiver is erroneously approved, the government is not estopped from taking action to rescind or revoke any subsequent application for change or adjustment of status, as "this equitable relief should not be applied to accord the applicant a benefit for which he clearly was not eligible."[417] Failure to follow legacy INS Operations Instructions is also insufficient grounds for obtaining the relief of estoppel.[418]

An approved waiver application for a J-1 exchange visitor is also valid for the J-2 dependents,[419] as long as the dependent did not, in turn, participate in a separate J-1 program that would make him or her subject to the requirement,[420] in which case the dependent would require a waiver of his or her own.[421] This cannot be handled in one waiver—the dependent's obligation must be waived with the J-1 spouse's, and in a

---

[413] DOS, "Frequently Asked Questions: Waiver of the Exchange Visitor Two-Year Home-Country Physical Presence Requirement," https://travel.state.gov/content/visas/en/study-exchange/student/residency-waiver/ds-3035-faqs.html.

[414] AFM 45.2(b); 1 legacy INS Examinations Handbook, 15-1 Examinations Handbook Waiver.

[415] AFM 45.2(b) (emphasis in original).

[416] AFM 45.2.

[417] *Matter of Tayabji*, 19 I&N Dec. 264 (BIA 1985).

[418] *Matter of Tuakoi*, 19 I&N Dec. 341 (BIA 1985).

[419] DOS, "Frequently Asked Questions: Waiver of the Exchange Visitor Two-Year Home-Country Physical Presence Requirement," https://travel.state.gov/content/visas/en/study-exchange/student/residency-waiver/ds-3035-faqs.html.

[420] AFM 45.1.

[421] AFM 45.6.

Copyright © 2017. American Immigration Lawyers Association. All rights reserved.

separate application the individual must seek a waiver for his or her own J-1 program.[422]

A duplicate approval notice will be issued only after a Form I-824, Application for Action on an Approved Application or Petition, is filed, even if the initial approval notice was not received because the attorney and/or foreign national changed addresses.[423] The practitioner is strongly advised to "complete the DS-3035 correctly, as this form is scanned and transmitted electronically to the USCIS."[424] DOS should be informed of the new address through the SEVIS program and affirmatively by the foreign national by telephone at (202) 485-7828), by email at *212ewaivers@state.gov*, or in writing to:

Waiver Review Division, U.S. Department of State
CA-VO-L-W
SA-17 11th Floor
Washington, D.C. 20522

Or, for overnight services

Waiver Review Division, U.S. Department of State
CA-VO-L-W
SA-17 11th Floor
600 19th St. NW
Washington, D.C. 20522[425]

The same contact information may be used to update the attorney's address. If DOS already issued a waiver recommendation letter, then the foreign national "should contact [his or her] J-1 Program Officer and submit a Form AR-11 to USCIS," and the attorney should submit to USCIS a new Form G-28, Notice of Entry of Appearance of Attorney or Accredited Representative, "with a copy of the waiver recommendation attached."[426]

Although former J-2 dependents typically may not independently apply for waivers, such a waiver application may be made in certain circumstances. If the marital relationship is terminated by death or divorce, or if the child marries or reaches the age of 21, and the former dependent wishes to obtain a waiver of the home residence requirement, then "a full report of the circumstances surrounding the case may be submitted by the J-2 alien requesting that the State Department act on his or her behalf for a waiver recommendation." In this instance, DOS is acting as the

---

[422] "Agenda Items for AILA DOS Liaison Meeting with Waiver Review Division" (Oct. 18, 2011), AILA Doc. No. 11102423.

[423] "AILA/VSC Practice Pointer: When Your I-612 Has Gone Astray, Revisited " (Sept. 24, 2012), AILA Doc. No. 09083168.

[424] *Id.*

[425] "Practice Alert: Updated Contact Information for DOS Waiver Review Division" (July 9, 2015), AILA Doc. No. 14020303.

[426] "AILA/VSC Practice Pointer: When Your I-612 Has Gone Astray ... the Sequel" (Dec. 30, 2009), AILA Doc. No. 09123061.

Copyright © 2017. American Immigration Lawyers Association. All rights reserved.

IGA,[427] and the documents should be sent to the chief of WRD. DOS encouraged the dependents "to explain why no other IGA stepped forward and what are the particular merits of the case."[428] The practitioner should, however, advise the client that DOS "will act on behalf of such applicants only rarely and for humanitarian circumstances,"[429] or when the request "merits special consideration,"[430] and that the involvement of DOS as an IGA "is totally a discretionary function."[431] These requests should be accompanied with the relevant Forms DS-2019, as well as birth, marriage, death, and/or divorce certificates.[432]

For the purpose of brevity, this section will refer to the CA/VO/L/W office of DOS as DOS. Because this chapter focuses on J-1 programs for trainees and interns, this section will not address waivers for foreign nationals who received funding from the U.S. government for their J-1 programs or waivers for foreign medical graduates, including waivers for employment in a designated health care shortage area.[433] In addition, as both USCIS and DOS may make determinations on the merits of the waiver application, this section of the chapter will refer to the adjudicating officer as "the government official" for the sake of brevity.

1. Exceptional Hardship to U.S. Citizen or Permanent Resident Spouse or Child

The waiver application should be filed with USCIS on Form I-612.[434] The applicant has the option either to file the DS-3035, with fee, with DOS before submitting the I-612 to USCIS, or to make the DOS filing after USCIS has made its exceptional hardship finding.[435] In the latter case, if USCIS denies the I-612 application, the DOS fee will not be refunded.[436]

The following documents should be submitted to USCIS:

- Birth, marriage, and/or divorce certificates to evidence the familial relationship;

---

[427] 9 FAM 302.13-2(B)(2). *See also Matter of J-U-L-*, ID# 14006 (AAO Sept. 28, 2015).

[428] "DOS Answers to AILA Questions" (Oct. 26, 2001), AILA Doc. No. 01103032.

[429] 9 FAM 302.13-2(B)(2).

[430] DOS, "Frequently Asked Questions: Waiver of the Exchange Visitor Two-Year Home-Country Physical Presence Requirement," https://travel.state.gov/content/visas/en/study-exchange/student/residency-waiver/ds-3035-faqs.html.

[431] "DOS Answers to AILA Questions" (Oct. 26, 2001), AILA Doc. No. 01103032.

[432] DOS, "Frequently Asked Questions: Waiver of the Exchange Visitor Two-Year Home-Country Physical Presence Requirement," https://travel.state.gov/content/visas/en/study-exchange/student/residency-waiver/ds-3035-faqs.html.

[433] 22 CFR §§41.63(c)(4) and (e). For an overview of waivers for foreign medical graduates, *see* CRS Report for Congress, K. Ester, "Immigration: Foreign Physicians and J-1 Visa Waiver Program" (updated June 14, 2004), AILA Doc. No. 04062167.

[434] 22 CFR §41.63(b)(1).

[435] DOS, "How to Apply Instructions – Waiver of the Exchange Visitor Two-Year Home-Country Physical Presence Requirement," https://travel.state.gov/content/visas/en/study-exchange/student/residency-waiver/ds-3035-instructions.html.

[436] *Id.*

Copyright © 2017. American Immigration Lawyers Association. All rights reserved.

- Copies of permanent resident cards, birth certificates, copies of biographic pages of U.S. passports, and/or certificate of naturalization to evidence the status of the relative;[437]

- The original I-94 card of the foreign national, if he or she is physically present in the United States when the waiver application is filed;[438] and

- Supporting financial documents.

If USCIS finds that the application makes a prima facie case of exceptional hardship, USCIS will request a recommendation from DOS's WRD on Form I-613.[439] If it finds a lack of a prima facie case, it will issue a denial on Form I-292. Such a denial is appealable to the AAO.[440]

The application must "establish the hardship to the spouse or child while remaining in the U.S. without the applicant and if the applicant's spouse or child went abroad for two years."[441] The BIA noted the history of the standard of exception hardship: "[T]he finding of exceptional hardship was predicated upon the physical condition of the one United States citizen child with a history of heart disorders and the adverse effect such foreign residence would have upon him."[442] As stated by the AAU:

> "[B]y far the largest number of applications for waivers … come from nationals of countries who are in urgent need for expansion and improvement of their technological establishments and their health facilities. It is believed to be detrimental to the purposes of the program and to the national interests of the countries concerned to apply a lenient policy in the adjudication of waivers including cases where marriage occurring in the United States, or birth of a child or children, is used to support the contention that the exchange alien's departure from this country would cause personal hardship."[443]

With respect to the factors considered in a waiver application based on exceptional hardship, legacy INS stated the following regarding a "totality of the circumstances" analysis:

> "[A]n exceptional hardship claim must be considered under the circumstances of both relocation abroad and separation on the qualifying spouse or children…. [W]hile a determination of exceptional hardship is not fixed or inflexible, a number of common factors may be considered in examining a claim of exceptional hardship. No single factor would normally be determinative, but all relevant factors should be considered in the aggregate in order to render a

---

[437] AFM 45.3.

[438] USCIS, "Instructions for Application for Waiver of the Foreign Residence Requirement," http://www.uscis.gov/i-612.

[439] AFM 45.3(b) and (f).

[440] AFM 45.3(f).

[441] AFM 45.3(c).

[442] *Matter of Amin*, 13 I&N Dec. 209 (Reg'l Comm'r 1969).

[443] *Matter of [name not provided]* A23 267 428 (AAU Apr. 25, 1985), 2 Immig. Rptr. B2-115.

Copyright © 2017. American Immigration Lawyers Association. All rights reserved.

determination of exceptional hardship. Exceptional hardship to the qualifying family members must be that which is beyond the normal hardship expected from a temporary relocation or separation."[444]

Specifically, the waiver application must demonstrate hardship to the spouse and/or child if he or she remained in the United States and if he or she accompanies the foreign national abroad:

"[I]t must first be determined whether or not such hardship would occur as the consequence of [the spouse or child] accompanying [the foreign national] abroad, which would be the normal course of action to avoid separation. The mere election by the spouse to remain in the United States, absent such determination, is not a governing factor since any inconvenience or hardship which might thereby occur would be self-imposed. Further, even though it is established that the requisite hardship would occur abroad, it must also be shown that the spouse would suffer as the result of having to remain in the United States. Temporary separation, even though abnormal, is a problem many families face in life and, in and of itself, does not represent exceptional hardship as contemplated by section 212(e)."[445]

In addition, one district court noted that "the degree of hardship expected [must be] greater than the anxiety, loneliness, and altered financial circumstances ordinarily anticipated from a two-year sojourn abroad."[446] The practitioner should also note legacy INS guidance regarding the need for an adjustment period if the family moves to the home country:

"Adjustment factors will usually be present if the spouse and child proceeds abroad to a country where the customs, language, and mode of living are strange. Similarly, in most cases, an exchange alien will require a considerable length of time to reestablish himself there and begin earning income which would enable him to adequately support himself and the members of his family. These factors must then be considered the *usual* hardships which might be anticipated by the spouse and children of an exchange visitor who is required to comply with the foreign residence requirement."[447]

Successful cases typically demonstrate hardship through a number of factors, to demonstrate how the totality of circumstances merits approval,[448] even though "[a]ny[]one [factor] standing alone might not reach the level of exceptional hardship":[449]

"[A]n analysis of a given application must look at the entire situation rather than merely at certain items or facts common to most cases. In reaching a

---

[444] AFM 45.3(*l*).

[445] *Matter of Mansour*, 11 I&N Dec. 306 (BIA 1965).

[446] *Keh Tong Chen v. Att'y Gen. of the United States*, 546 F. Supp. 1060 (D.D.C. 1982).

[447] *Matter of Amin*, 13 I&N Dec. 209 (Reg'l Comm'r 1969) (emphasis in original).

[448] *See, e.g., Matter of [name not provided]*, A29 516 186 (AAU Oct. 13, 1995), 15 Immig. Rptr. B2-53.

[449] *Matter of [name not provided]*, A27 599 530 (AAU Feb. 19, 1991), 9 Immig. Rptr. B2-4.

Copyright © 2017. American Immigration Lawyers Association. All rights reserved.

determination, attention is limited to major, extraordinary disruptions, which disruptions are considered in their cumulative effect. Minor disturbances, or results which would normally result from accompanying a party abroad for a two-year period or from a separation for that term, are not considered, either individually or cumulatively, for to do so would effectively eliminate the bar where a qualifying spouse or child existed, a result contrary to Congressional intent. Further, disturbances which can be ameliorated by voluntary actions are not given weight, and dislocations or impacts which result from circumstances in existence at the time the applicant voluntarily became subject to the bar, or repercussions which could have reasonably been anticipated at that time, are dismissed. Hardships which result from voluntary actions taken by one or more of the parties involved in a waiver proceeding subsequent to full knowledge of the applicability of the bar are given less effect since the actions were taken voluntarily, knowing the extent of hardships which would result."[450]

In general, medical considerations tend to be more persuasive, especially if they are potentially "life-threatening"[451] or "go beyond the normal,"[452] such as if a condition would deteriorate in the foreign national's home country[453] or without the foreign national's financial support or health insurance, if applicable,[454] or if "continuing treatment" is necessary in the United States and unavailable abroad.[455] However, if a medical procedure is necessary because of delay on the part of the foreign national, then it is less likely that the waiver will be approved.[456] Supplementary evidence may include documents describing recent or upcoming medical surgeries or procedures[457] and any related rehabilitative programs,[458] or "a physician's diagnosis and prognosis."[459] Letters from doctors, psychologists, or other counselors may be given less weight or deemed to be "speculative," however, if "based on a single interview" and not an "established relationship."[460]

---

[450] *Matter of [name not provided]*, A23 208 973 (AAU Aug. 26, 1985), 2 Immig. Rptr. B2-170.

[451] *Matter of [name not provided]*, A20 618 336 (AAU Oct. 20, 1994), 13 Immig. Rptr. B2-234.

[452] *Matter of [name not provided]*, A29 516 186 (AAU Oct. 13, 1995), 15 Immig. Rptr. B2-53; *Matter of [name not provided]*, A28 326 515 (AAU Mar. 9, 1995), 14 Immig. Rptr. B2-105.

[453] *Matter of [name and case number not provided]*, (AAO Jan. 30, 2008), http://bit.ly/dec082h; *Matter of [name and case number not provided]*, (AAO May 12, 2014), AILA Doc. No. 14061333.

[454] *Matter of [name and case number not provided]*, (AAO Feb. 7, 2007), 34 Immig. Rptr. B2-7.

[455] AFM 45.3; *Matter of [name not provided]*, A20618336 (AAU Oct. 20, 1994), 13 Immig. Rptr. B2-234; *Matter of [name and case number not provided]*, (AAO May 12, 2014), AILA Doc. No. 14061333.

[456] *Matter of [name not provided]*, A24 066 703 (AAU June 26, 1995), 15 Immig. Rptr. B2-11.

[457] *Matter of [name not provided]*, A21 156 359 (AAU June 28, 1989), 7 Immig. Rptr. B2-77.

[458] *Matter of [name not provided]*, A28 444 774 (AAU Aug. 5, 1991), 9 Immig. Rptr. B2-64.

[459] AFM 45.3.

[460] *Matter of [name and case number not provided]*, (AAO Jan. 30, 2008), http://bit.ly/dec082h.

Copyright © 2017. American Immigration Lawyers Association. All rights reserved.

Economic factors may also be considered,[461] but mere financial difficulties or being "burdened by bills" is insufficient,[462] as is financial difficulty combined with only familial separation.[463] The prospect of career interruption alone is also insufficient to warrant approval of the application, especially if the salary earned by the foreign national and/or the spouse are adequate to support themselves and any children.[464] If the financial burdens are particularly high, then evidence of the debts, student loans, or medical bills should be provided.[465] Economic hardship may also be based on the need for occupational training that is unavailable in the foreign national's home country and that is necessary due to an underlying medical condition.[466] If the foreign national also financially supports the spouse's dependents, then the affidavits from the spouse's dependents should be submitted,[467] together with any evidence of why no other options exist for their care while the foreign national resides abroad.[468]

Finally, emotional and psychological hardship may be documented with statements from psychiatrists, psychologists, or other counselors,[469] especially if the spouse or child is particularly dependent upon the foreign national for a specific reason, such as mental retardation,[470] depression,[471] post-traumatic stress disorder,[472] or severe separation anxiety.[473] The Country Conditions Report, Consular Information Sheet, or any Travel Warning issued by DOS may also be provided, such as if the home country espouses anti-American practices, specifically and frequently targets Americans for crimes, or supports or is subject to terrorist activity.[474] These

---

[461] *Matter of [name not provided]*, A27 691 996 (AAU Dec. 6, 1994), 14 Immig. Rptr. B2-35.

[462] *Matter of [name not provided]*, A72 138 890 (AAU Nov. 21, 1994), 14 Immig. Rptr. B2-15.

[463] *Matter of [name not provided]*, A19 492 887 (AAU Nov. 27, 1987), 5 Immig. Rptr. B2-74.

[464] *Matter of [name not provided]*, A23 267 428 (AAU Apr. 25, 1985), 2 Immig. Rptr. B2-115.

[465] *Matter of [name and case number not provided]*, (AAO Feb. 21, 2008), http://bit.ly/feb083h; *Matter of S-M-Y-A*, ID# 73618 (AAO Nov. 14, 2016); *Matter of [name and case number not provided]*, (AAO Feb. 7, 2007), 34 Immig. Rptr. B2-7; *Matter of [name not provided]*, A29 516 186 (AAU Oct. 13, 1995), 15 Immig. Rptr. B2-53.

[466] *Matter of [name not provided]*, A28 444 774 (AAU Aug. 5, 1991), 9 Immig. Rptr. B2-64.

[467] AFM 45.3.

[468] *Matter of [name not provided]*, A24 066 703 (AAU June 26, 1995), 15 Immig. Rptr. B2-11; *Matter of [name not provided]*, A29 516 186 (AAU Oct. 13, 1995), 15 Immig. Rptr. B2-53.

[469] *Matter of [name not provided]*, A27 599 530 (AAU Feb. 19, 1991), 9 Immig. Rptr. B2-4; *Matter of [name and case number not provided]*, (AAO Feb. 21, 2008), http://bit.ly/feb083h; *Matter of [name not provided]*, A26 307 369 (AAU Sept. 30, 1986), 4 Immig. Rptr. B2-81.

[470] *Matter of [name not provided]*, A28 472 323 (AAU Oct. 31, 1990), 8 Immig. Rptr. B2-95.

[471] *Matter of [name and case number not provided]*, (AAO Feb. 7, 2007), 34 Immig. Rptr. B2-7.

[472] *Matter of [name and case number not provided]*, (AAO Feb. 21, 2008), http://bit.ly/feb083h.

[473] *Matter of [name not provided]*, A21 156 359 (AAU June 28, 1989), 7 Immig. Rptr. B2-77.

[474] *Matter of S-M-Y-A*, ID# 73618 (AAO Nov. 14, 2016); *Matter of [name and case number not provided]*, (AAO Jan. 30, 2008), http://bit.ly/dec082h; *Matter of [name and case number not provided]*, (AAO Feb. 21, 2008), http://bit.ly/feb083h; *Matter of [name and case number not provided]*, (AAO Feb. 7, 2007), 34 *Immig. Rptr.* B2-7.

Copyright © 2017. American Immigration Lawyers Association. All rights reserved.

documents may also describe other relevant social concerns, such as potential discrimination against U.S. citizens or permanent residents, or against interfaith or interracial marriages.[475]

The practitioner may also consider the guidance and interpretation of exceptional hardship in connection with an application for a suspension of deportation under pre-1996 law, as the government official may apply these standards,[476] to require that exceptional and extreme hardship involve "other factors such as advanced age, severe illness, family ties, etc. combine[d] with economic detriment,"[477] despite AAO guidance that the home residence waiver applications "require the lesser standard of exceptional hardship."[478]

The practitioner should also consider legacy INS guidance stating that the U.S. Public Health Service (USPHS) "is unable to provide expert advice concerning the availability of facilities for medical treatment abroad," although USPHS may provide information on "whether specified dangerous diseases are endemic in a certain country."[479] Such information would be helpful, for example, if an underlying medical condition would be aggravated by exposure to a particular disease or environmental condition that is widespread in the home country.[480] In the absence of corroborating evidence from USPHS, a statement from a doctor in the home country should be submitted.[481] While it is rarely if ever done, the government official may require a personal interview of the foreign national and the spouse, and the spouses may be interviewed separately "to better assess the validity of their statements," although legacy INS guidance states that "[t]he change from joint to separate interviews should be made as tactfully as possible."[482] Separate interviews should have "a written record or summary of the testimony."[483]

It is possible that a "more liberal attitude" may be applied if the foreign national has resided in the home country for a lengthy period of time,[484] especially if the J-1

---

[475] *Matter of Mansour*, 11 I&N Dec. 306 (BIA 1965); *Matter of [name not provided]*, A21 156 359 (AAU June 28, 1989), 7 Immig. Rptr. B2-77.

[476] AFM 45.3 (citing precedent decision *Matter of Anderson*, 16 I&N Dec. 596 (BIA 1978)).

[477] *Matter of Anderson*, 16 I&N Dec. 596 (BIA 1978).

[478] *Matter of [name and case number not provided]*, (AAO Feb. 7, 2007), 34 Immig. Rptr. B2-7.

[479] AFM 45.3.

[480] *Matter of [name and case number not provided]*, (AAO Jan. 30, 2008), http://bit.ly/dec082h.

[481] *Matter of Gupta*, 13 I&N Dec. 477 (Dep. Assoc. Comm'r 1970).

[482] 1 legacy INS Examinations Handbook, 15-1 Examinations Handbook Waiver.

[483] *Id.*

[484] *Matter of Coffman*, 13 I&N Dec. 206 (Dep. Assoc. Comm'r 1969); *Matter of [name not provided]*, A26 307 369 (AAU Sept. 30, 1986), 4 Immig. Rptr. B2-81.

Copyright © 2017. American Immigration Lawyers Association. All rights reserved.

program was short and the foreign national visited the United States not to gain skills but rather to train U.S. workers.[485]

Waiver applications based on exceptional hardship have been approved in the following situations:

- A U.S. citizen would suffer social ostracization and economic discrimination due to the waiver applicant's "Jewish background" and the anti-Semitic practices of the home country's government and population, documented by a statement from a local DOS office and by articles from major U.S. newspapers, despite the fact that the applicant's parents, who were also part-Jewish, resided in the home country at the time of the application;[486]

- A U.S. citizen spouse would suffer socially and emotionally in the foreign national's home country because of her Christian faith in a "predominantly" Muslim culture and because of fears that the family would not be permitted to depart the home country and would suffer from anxiety if she remained in the United States because of the recent death of a child at birth, where medical testimony recommended another pregnancy as soon as possible to overcome "shock and fear" caused by the first child's death;[487]

- A 3-year-old U.S. citizen child is "too young to be separated from his parents" and would suffer because of an existing medical condition that makes a smallpox vaccination "dangerous," but smallpox is "endemic" in the home country;[488]

- A U.S. citizen child of the "tender age" of 4 years suffered allergy and asthma attacks during a previous visit to the home country "because of the climatic conditions," documented by statements from doctors who treated her then, whereas a statement from a U.S. doctor stated the absence of these conditions in the United States, as "[i]t appears reasonable to assume that her return to [the home country] would again impose exceptional hardship";[489]

- A permanent resident spouse's career would suffer if he accompanied the waiver applicant, and if the spouse remained in the United States, he would "face[] the unusual hardship of maintaining two households," while a U.S. citizen child would

---

[485] *Matter of Coffman*, 13 I&N Dec. 206 (Dep. Assoc. Comm'r 1969). In this case, the foreign national would have resided in the home country for 23 months before the planned date of travel to the United States and held J-1 status for only 90 days.

[486] *Matter of Lejman*, 13 I&N Dec. 379 (Reg'l Comm'r 1969). As discussed below, this waiver application was not based on persecution, as the waiver applicant himself must suffer the persecution and not a spouse or child.

[487] *Matter of Mansour*, 11 I&N Dec. 306 (BIA 1965).

[488] *Matter of Ambe*, 13 I&N Dec. 3 (D.D. 1968).

[489] *Matter of Gupta*, 13 I&N Dec. 477 (Dep. Assoc. Comm'r 1970). It seems unlikely, however, that the "lack of availability of food to which [the child] was accustomed" discussed in this case would arise to the standard of exceptional hardship today.

Copyright © 2017. American Immigration Lawyers Association. All rights reserved.

suffer the "depriv[ation] of the affection, emotional security and direction of its father which is most important during its formative years";[490]

- A U.S. citizen spouse who the Social Security Administration (SSA) has determined to be disabled based on multiple medical conditions has a child whose non-custodial father has stated that he will not allow to be moved to another country could not join the applicant in his home country of Iraq. If she remains in the United States, she would fear for his safety, as he already is in Iraq and while there has been kidnapped and stalked. His employer has not been paying him, and she cannot work, creating severe financial hardships, particularly as the family has high medical bills.[491]

- Two U.S. citizen children would have to accompany the waiver applicant to the home country "as they are too young to be separated from their mother," and then would "be denied the special care and attention of their mother during her hours of employment," while the applicant's husband's occupation in the U.S. Navy prohibited his being able to accompany the family to the home country, impeded his ability to pay for the transportation abroad and maintenance of two households, and did not offer commissary privileges to family members when the military service person is not stationed abroad;[492] and

- A U.S. citizen spouse with a rare genetic disorder for which there are no treatment centers in the applicant's home country of Ukraine would be separated from his family, employment, community, and physicians familiar with his treatment; would face hardship in dealing with the unfamiliar culture and language; and would be unable to obtain proper medical care should he move to Ukraine. If he were to remain in the United States apart from his wife, he would be stressed over her safety, as she is a journalist critical of the government in a country where there has been violence against journalists, to the point where his functioning could become impaired.[493]

USCIS made favorable recommendations in the following cases:

- A U.S. citizen spouse suffered allergies, a rash, fever, and swollen limbs in reaction to the "insect life and hot weather conditions" during a previous visit to the home country, documented by letters from doctors in the home country and in the United States; feared that the medical technologies in the home country were inferior to those in the United States for an expected newborn child; and would suffer a disruption to her career whether she accompanied her husband or remained in the United States without his financial support;[494]

---

[490] *Matter of Savetamal*, 13 I&N Dec. 249 (Reg'l Comm'r 1969).

[491] *Matter of S-M-Y-A*, ID# 73618 (AAO Nov. 14, 2016).

[492] *Matter of Vicedo*, 13 I&N Dec. 33 (D.D. 1968).

[493] *Matter of [name and case number not provided]*, (AAO May 12, 2014), AILA Doc. No. 14061333.

[494] *Matter of Ibarra*, 13 I&N Dec. 277 (Acting Reg'l Comm'r 1968).

Copyright © 2017. American Immigration Lawyers Association. All rights reserved.

- A U.S. citizen spouse would experience heightened anxiety about the foreign national's safety and ability to return to the United States after two years due to the dangerous country conditions and anti-American sentiments, would face "likely suspension" of her professional license if she sought psychiatric treatment in response, and was deemed emotionally and psychologically dependent on the foreign national because of the stress of her competitive occupation;[495]

- A U.S. citizen spouse was diagnosed with hypothyroidism, depression, and basal cell carcinoma, which "requires lifetime surveillance" because of the "high likelihood of development of future cancers," and "her medical conditions are exacerbated by psychological stress," and she would suffer if the foreign national returned home alone because of fears over his safety due to his connections to the United States, his interfaith marriage, and mandatory military service;[496]

- Two U.S. citizen children suffered from congenital heart defects, which had to be monitored closely, and the applicant's spouse earned approximately only $30,000 per year;[497] and

- The U.S. citizen spouse could not accompany the foreign national while her mother was expected to succumb to cancer and could not be separated from the foreign national because she was experiencing a difficult pregnancy and had a history of depression.[498]

In contrast, waiver applications have been denied in the following circumstances:

- Two U.S. citizen children would not suffer exceptional hardship when the foreign national spouse of the waiver applicant had a medical condition that was indigenous to the home country and treatable there, even with the risk of multiple X-ray treatments because of resistance to drug therapies, because the application did not demonstrate that the children have previously suffered exceptional hardship due to the spouse's inability to care for the children during a recurrence;[499] and

- A U.S. citizen child would not suffer exceptional hardship from difficulty in learning the language of the home country, from the "lesser educational opportunities" offered in the home country, or from a lower standard of life, because the expected lower salary in the home country would be offset by a lower cost of living.[500]

If a waiver application is submitted based on hardship to a spouse and children, then the application may be approved based on one rather than both family members,

---

[495] *Matter of [name and case number not provided]*, (AAO Feb. 21, 2008), http://bit.ly/feb083h.

[496] *Matter of [name and case number not provided]*, (AAO Feb. 7, 2007), 34 Immig. Rptr. B2-7.

[497] *Matter of [name not provided]*, A29 516 078 (AAU Dec. 23, 1991), 9 Immig. Rptr. B2-79.

[498] *Matter of [name not provided]*, A23 208 973 (AAU Aug. 26, 1985), 2 Immig. Rptr. B2-170.

[499] *Matter of Amin*, 13 I&N Dec. 209 (Reg'l Comm'r 1969).

[500] *Matter of Lai*, 13 I&N Dec. 188 (Reg'l Comm'r 1969).

Copyright © 2017. American Immigration Lawyers Association. All rights reserved.

as the application must establish that each family member must individually suffer hardship.[501] If USCIS agrees that the spouse and/or child would suffer exceptional hardship, then the determination on Form I-613, "together with a summary of the details of expected hardship," will be forwarded by USCIS to WRD.[502] WRD, in turn, may consult with the J-1 program sponsor and will "review the program, policy, and foreign relations aspects of the case, make a recommendation, and forward it to the appropriate office at DHS."[503] The foreign national has a "continuing obligation to inform the Department of Homeland Security of changed circumstances material to his or her pending application."[504] If the waiver application is denied because exceptional hardship has not been established, then USCIS should "clearly explain why the alleged hardship does not meet the exception[al] hardship standard of the statute."[505]

2. Fear of Persecution Based on Race, Religion, or Political Opinion

The waiver application should be filed with USCIS on Form I-612, for a "finding of probable persecution," [506] and on the online Form DS-3035 to DOS.[507] The waiver application should "include a detailed statement of the basis for the applicant's belief that he or she would be persecuted," with supporting "affidavits by persons with direct knowledge of the alleged facts,"[508] as well as the foreign national's I-94 card if he or she is physically present in the United States when the waiver application is filed.[509]

Although immigration law uses the term "persecution" for both asylum applications and applications to waive the home residence requirement, it is important to note that the standards for these applications are not identical and that waiver applications have "a higher standard."[510] First, these waiver applications require that the foreign national demonstrate that he or she *would be subject to persecution* upon a return to the home country," whereas an asylum application requires only a *"well-founded fear of persecution."*[511] Second, the foreign national must be persecuted based on race,

---

[501] *Matter of [name and case number not provided],* (AAO Jan. 30, 2008), http://bit.ly/dec082h.

[502] 22 CFR §41.63(b)(2)(i).

[503] 22 CFR §41.63(b)(2)(ii).

[504] 22 CFR §41.63(f).

[505] 1 legacy INS Examinations Handbook, 15-1 Examinations Handbook Waiver.

[506] 22 CFR §41.63(b)(1).

[507] DOS, "How to Apply Instructions – Waiver of the Exchange Visitor Two-Year Home-Country Physical Presence Requirement," https://travel.state.gov/content/visas/en/study-exchange/student/residency-waiver/ds-3035-instructions.html.

[508] AFM 45.3(d). Although this section of the AFM is labeled "Waiver Based on Exceptional Hardship to USC or LPR Spouse or Child," it discusses several aspects of the waiver based on persecution as well.

[509] USCIS, "Instructions for Application for Waiver of the Foreign Residence Requirement," www.uscis.gov/files/form/i-612instr.pdf.

[510] AFM 45.4. For more information on asylum applications, see *AILA's Asylum Primer* (AILA 7th Ed. 2015), https://agora.aila.org/product/detail/2521.

[511] AFM 45.5 (emphasis added).

Copyright © 2017. American Immigration Lawyers Association. All rights reserved.

religion, or political opinion; the additional asylum grounds of nationality or membership in a particular social group are not grounds for a waiver application.[512]

The government official may also consult DOS's Country Reports on Human Rights Practices to evaluate the claim of persecution.[513] It is important to note that the persecution must be suffered by the foreign national,[514] and not by any U.S. citizen or permanent resident spouse or children, as this would constitute an impermissible intertwining of the claims of fear of persecution and exceptional hardship, as discussed above. Evidence that the applicant was previously a victim of persecution is persuasive.[515] However, the applicant must demonstrate that the persecution would be at the hands of the government or government officials, and not "by a minority, although forceful faction, within the country which the government is unable or unwilling to control."[516]

If USCIS agrees that compliance with the home residence requirement would subject the foreign national to persecution, then the determination on Form I-613,[517] "together with a summary of the details of expected ... persecution" will be forwarded by USCIS to WRD.[518] WRD, in turn, will "review the program, policy, and foreign relations aspects of the case, including consultation if deemed appropriate with the Bureau of Human Rights and Humanitarian Affairs of the United States Department of State, make a recommendation, and forward such recommendation" to DHS.[519] The foreign national has a "continuing obligation to inform the Department of Homeland Security of changed circumstances material to his or her pending application."[520]

3. Request by an Interested Government Agency (IGA)

An agency of the U.S. government may request a waiver on behalf of a foreign national "if such exchange visitor is actively and substantially involved in a program or activity sponsored by or of interest to such agency."[521] The request must be made in writing,[522] "be signed by the head of the agency, or his or her designee,"[523] and

---

[512] *Id.*

[513] 1 legacy INS Examinations Handbook, 15-1 Examinations Handbook Waiver.

[514] *Id.*

[515] *Matter of [name not provided]*, A26 928 029 (AAU Oct. 30, 1992), 11 Immig. Rptr. B2-67.

[516] *Matter of [name not provided]*, A29 771 581 (AAU Feb. 29, 1991), 8 Immig. Rptr. B2-127.

[517] DOS, "How to Apply Instructions – Waiver of the Exchange Visitor Two-Year Home-Country Physical Presence Requirement," https://travel.state.gov/content/visas/en/study-exchange/student/residency-waiver/ds-3035-instructions.html.

[518] 22 CFR §41.63(b)(2)(i).

[519] 22 CFR §41.63(b)(2)(iii).

[520] 22 CFR §41.63(f).

[521] 22 CFR §41.63(c)(1).

[522] 22 CFR §41.63(c)(2).

[523] *Id.*

Copyright © 2017. American Immigration Lawyers Association. All rights reserved.

sent directly to DOS.[524] DOS previously maintained a list on its website of agencies' officials designated for signatures, but has ceased to do so, stating "[a]ny U.S. government agency potentially may act as an 'interested government agency' … and so the Department is not able to provide a list of agencies that might act as interested government agencies, nor of contact information for the designated signatories at each agency."[525]

The request must be accompanied by copies of all relevant Forms DS-2019, as well as the foreign national's current address and country of nationality or last legal permanent residence.[526] The request also must "fully explain why the grant of such waiver request would be in the public interest and the detrimental effect that would result to the program or activity of interest to the requesting agency if the exchange visitor is unable to continue his or her involvement with the program or activity."[527] The foreign national's services must be "essential to a program or activity of official interest to that U.S. Government agency,"[528] and the foreign national must be offered full-time employment by the IGA or by a public or private employer, as long as "the primary work of the alien directly supports the mission of the IGA."[529] Whether the foreign national will be employed by the IGA or a third party, "[t]he IGA must certify that the waiver would directly benefit its mission, or programs of significant interest to its mission, and certify that the employment benefits the public interest."[530] The decision of the WRD "shall constitute the recommendation of the Department of State and … be forwarded to the Secretary of DHS."[531]

4. No Objection Statement from the Home Country's Government

As stated by DOS, "The No Objection Statement is a diplomatic note from the alien's home government stating that it has no objection to the exchange visitor's not returning home for two years to fulfill the INA 212(e) requirement and to the possibility of the alien's remaining in the United States and becoming a resident."[532] The foreign national must request the "no objection" statement or letter directly from his or her home country's government,[533] after completing the DOS waiver application online and obtaining a case number.[534] The home country may be the

---

[524] 9 FAM 302.13-2(D)(4).

[525] "Visa Office Responds to AILA Questions" (Apr. 9, 2014), AILA Doc. No. 14041600.

[526] 22 CFR §41.63(c)(3).

[527] 22 CFR §41.63(c)(2).

[528] 9 FAM 302.13-2(D)(4).

[529] AFM 45.6.

[530] *Id.*

[531] 22 CFR §41.63(c)(5).

[532] 9 FAM 302.13-2(D)(1).

[533] *Id.*

[534] DOS, "Frequently Asked Questions: Waiver of the Exchange Visitor Two-Year Home-Country Physical Presence Requirement," https://travel.state.gov/content/visas/en/study-exchange/student/residency-waiver/ds-3035-faqs.html.

Copyright © 2017. American Immigration Lawyers Association. All rights reserved.

foreign national's country of citizenship or country of "last legal permanent residence,"[535] as discussed above. The government agency, such as an embassy in Washington, D.C., or a diplomatic mission, must forward the letter directly to WRD.[536] The practitioner may wish to warn the client that the embassy or diplomatic mission may decline to provide the "no objection" letter, as countries vary widely in their willingness to issue the letters and their criteria for doing so.

If the home country sends a "no objection" letter, it should also include copies of the Form DS-2019 and the DOS waiver case number and barcode, and the letter must include the following information:

- "Full name of exchange visitor, date and place of birth,"[537] and current address;[538]

- "Date of entry into the United States;

- "List of exchange visitor program or programs and program numbers, if known, in which the alien participated;

- "The exchange visitor's alien registration number, if known; and

- "The name of the foreign government official with whom the case can be discussed, if necessary."[539]

Obtaining a "no objection" letter does not guarantee approval of the waiver application:[540] "It should be emphasized that the submission of such a statement by a foreign government serves only to initiate the consideration of the alien's request for a waiver."[541] WRD may request further information regarding the waiver application from the J-1 sponsor(s) "[i]f deemed appropriate,"[542] and may also consider "the program, policy, and foreign relations aspects of the case."[543] If WRD recommends approval of the waiver application, then it should be granted by USCIS.[544] There is no recourse for reconsideration if the waiver application is denied because of an unfavorable recommendation from WRD.[545]

USCIS guidance indicates that an application to adjust status may be filed with a favorable waiver recommendation from DOS, and the final approval of the waiver

---

[535] 22 CFR §41.63(d)(1).

[536] *Id.*; 9 FAM 302.13-2(D)(1).

[537] 9 FAM 302.13-2(D)(1).

[538] 22 CFR §41.63(d)(1).

[539] 9 FAM 302.13-2(D)(1).

[540] *See also Matter of Musharraf*, 17 I&N Dec. 462 (BIA 1980) (noting that a no-objection letter is not in and of itself a waiver).

[541] 9 FAM 302.13-2(D)(1).

[542] 22 CFR §41.63(d)(1).

[543] 22 CFR §41.63(d)(2).

[544] AFM 45.5; 22 CFR §41.63(d)(3).

[545] DOS, "Frequently Asked Questions: Waiver of the Exchange Visitor Two-Year Home-Country Physical Presence Requirement," https://travel.state.gov/content/visas/en/study-exchange/student/residency-waiver/ds-3035-faqs.html.

Copyright © 2017. American Immigration Lawyers Association. All rights reserved.

application may be granted together with approval of the application to adjust status.[546] The practitioner may wish to discuss with the client how waiting for approval of the waiver application is a better strategy. However, if the waiver application is denied, then the filing fee for the application to adjust status is lost.[547]

H. Sponsoring a J-1 Intern or Trainee for Permanent Residence

As noted above, a foreign national who has begun the permanent residence process as the beneficiary of an approved labor certification application or of a filed employment-based immigrant visa petition is eligible for J-1 extensions only if he or she also demonstrates the intent to return to the "residence abroad despite the petition approval or certification issuance."[548]

In most cases, employment-based sponsorship for permanent residence on behalf of J-1 trainees and interns will not be completed during the J-1 program, because the aggregate processing time for the labor certification application, the immigrant visa petition, and availability of an immigrant visa number is highly likely to be more than 18 months.[549] A foreign national with a master's degree or five years of post-baccalaureate experience may be eligible for EB-2 classification, but ineligible for an internship and a training program, because the J-1 sponsor may question why the internship or training is necessary for an individual with a high level of education or many years of experience. Delays that frequently occur in immigrant visa availability for the EB-3 classification will most likely mean that the foreign national will be unable to apply to adjust status before completion of the J-1 program.[550]

It may be possible to request consular processing so that the foreign national may remain outside the United States until an immigrant visa is issued.[551] The practitioner should counsel the client, however, that the U.S. consulate may question whether the initial J-1 program was for ordinary employment rather than training, especially if the duties of the two jobs are similar. The practitioner may wish to provide the foreign national with evidence of how the J-1 training was unrelated to the position sponsored for permanent residence, such as if the training was on American business practices, but the permanent position draws upon international business experience that the foreign national gained in positions abroad after completing the J-1 program. Alternatively, the foreign national may have gained experience or qualifications

---

[546] AFM 45.5.

[547] For a discussion of the filing fees, see Volume 1: Chapter Two, "Basic Nonimmigrant Concepts."

[548] OI 214.2.

[549] For an overview of the permanent residence process, see Volume 2: Chapter Two, "The Labor Certification Application," Volume 2: Chapter Three, "The Immigrant Visa Petition," and Volume 2: Chapter Four, "Consular Processing, Adjustment of Status, and Permanent Residence Issues."

[550] For a discussion of the immigrant visa petition classifications and visa retrogression, see Volume 2: Chapter Three, "The Immigrant Visa Petition."

[551] OI 214.2.

Copyright © 2017. American Immigration Lawyers Association. All rights reserved.

abroad that made him or her a candidate for permanent residence sponsorship, such as attaining extraordinary ability following the training and employment abroad.[552]

Legacy INS expressed an interest in expanding the concept of "dual intent" to apply to J-1 nonimmigrants, so that they may travel internationally using the issued visas without obtaining advance parole documents in connection with applications to adjust status, and requested public comments.[553] Unfortunately, there have been no further developments, so the practitioner is advised to inform the client that advance parole will be necessary for international travel while an adjustment of status application is pending.

A foreign national may be eligible for permanent residence based on a family relationship or other grounds, but the practitioner should confirm that the foreign national is not subject to the home residence requirement or that he or she has fulfilled that requirement, as discussed above.

---

[552] *Matter of [name not provided]*, WAC 94 180 51386 (AAU Oct. 13, 1994), 13 Immig. Rptr. B2-224. Although this case involved a foreign national who had previously held H-3 status, the considerations should be similar, as both the H-3 and J-1 classifications may be for training in the United States.

[553] 64 Fed. Reg. 29208 (June 1, 1999).

Copyright © 2017. American Immigration Lawyers Association. All rights reserved.

CHAPTER ELEVEN

L-1 VISAS AND NONIMMIGRANT STATUS

I. Executive Summary

The L-1 visa and nonimmigrant status allows for the intracompany transfer of employees of foreign entities to U.S. parent, affiliate, and subsidiary companies. In this way, key employees may contribute executive, managerial, or specialized knowledge skills to the U.S. business, and companies may ensure that their international operations are aligned in objectives and processes.

There are two types of L-1 status. Employees performing managerial or executive assignments in the United States hold L-1A status, with a maximum validity period of seven years, for an initial petition of three years and two extensions of two years each. Employees performing specialized knowledge assignments hold L-1B status, with a maximum validity period of five years, for an initial petition of three years and one extension of two years. Transferees may recapture any time spent physically present outside the United States, as this time should not count toward the maximum time limitations. Limited exceptions exist to the maximum periods of authorized stay for employment that requires only an intermittent presence in the United States. Dependent spouses and minor children of L-1 nonimmigrants obtain L-2 status, and L-2 spouses may obtain employment authorization.

A. Checklist of Requirements

- Qualifying corporate relationship between the foreign company and the U.S. company

- Qualifying (executive, managerial, or specialized knowledge) employment abroad by the transferee

- Managerial, executive, or specialized knowledge assignment in the United States

B. Documents and Information Necessary to Prepare L-1 Petition

- Job description for U.S. assignment

- Job description for foreign position(s) or updated, chronologically organized, detailed résumé from employee

- Information on corporate relationship between the qualifying foreign and intended U.S. employer companies

- Basic information about the U.S. and foreign companies

- Basic biographic information about the employee and his or her family, if applicable

- Copies of biographic pages of passports of employee and his or her family, if applicable

Copyright © 2017. American Immigration Lawyers Association. All rights reserved.

- Copies of any U.S. visa previously issued to the employee and each family member, whether current or expired

C. Checklist of Questions to Ask Client

- What is the relationship between the two companies? Has that relationship had any change in the last three years?
- Was the employee employed by the foreign company in the immediate preceding three years? For how long? Was the employment full-time and continuous? Was any of this time spent in the United States and, if so, in what status?
- What was the nature of his or her role at the foreign company? (Can explore numerous roles, if applicable.)
- What will be the nature of his or her role at the U.S. company?
- Will the employee be sent to the worksite of another company?
- Does the employee have at least a bachelor's degree?
- Is the transferee coming to the United States to open a new office?

II. Requirements and Definitions

A. Qualifying Relationship

The entity abroad and the entity in the United States must have a qualifying relationship; *i.e.*, they must be parent and subsidiary, parent and branch, or affiliates.[1] The qualifying relationship must exist at the time the petition is filed; it need not have existed throughout the transferee's qualifying employment.[2] While there must be a related foreign entity doing business while the beneficiary is in L-1 status, it need not be the same one through which the L-1 nonimmigrant initially qualified.[3] Changes in corporate relationships, such as mergers, acquisitions and spin-offs, do not preclude eligibility for L-1 status,[4] but U.S. Citizenship and Immigration Services (USCIS) will look to whether a qualifying relationship continues to exist after the reorganization.[5]

---

[1] 8 Code of Federal Regulations (CFR) §214.2(*l*)(1)(ii)(G)–(L).

[2] G. Rees III, "Petition for L-1 Nonimmigrant Classification,"1 INS and DOJ Legal Opinions §93-12 (Feb. 17, 1993).

[3] "Separate FOIA Requests Uncover L-1 Training Materials and Correspondence" (undated, posted Apr. 26, 2013), AILA Doc. No. 13042663, at 170: "Example: L-1A was a manager for Company A in Italy, L-1A transfers to work for affiliated Company B. After L-1A transfers, Company A ceases to do business and becomes a dormant company. Company B still has foreign affiliate, Company C, that is doing business in Japan. Therefore, the petition remains valid." Nevertheless, this analysis may not apply in the permanent residence multinational manager petition context.

[4] *Id.*

[5] U.S. Citizenship and Immigration Services (USCIS), "Adjudicators Field Manual" (AFM) 32.6(b).

Copyright © 2017. American Immigration Lawyers Association. All rights reserved.

It is also possible to obtain L-1 status for an employee who will open a new office in the United States, as long as the qualifying relationship exists, as discussed later in this chapter.

Documentation of the qualifying relationship is discussed under "Process" later in this chapter.

1. Parent/Subsidiary

A parent/subsidiary relationship exists in three types of scenarios, all of which can involve direct or indirect ownership:

- One of the entities owns more than half of the other entity;

- One entity is a 50 percent partner in the other entity, which is a joint venture, as long as the parent entity has equal control and veto power over the venture; or

- One of the entities owns less than half of the other, but in fact controls the other entity.[6]

USCIS looks for indicia of both ownership and control, applying concepts of de jure (by law) and de facto (in fact) control.[7] Control is defined by USCIS as "the right and authority to direct the management and operations of the business entity."[8] The first scenario involves de jure control, and thus rarely needs further documentation of control. However, if there is a circumstance that might raise a question of whether the majority owner does control the subsidiary, such as a stockholder agreement vesting control elsewhere or a franchise agreement that gives the franchisor some indicia of control, the practitioner may wish to document control more heavily than one might otherwise in a majority ownership scenario.[9]

For a joint venture, control can be said to be intrinsic in the ownership structure. The fact that a venture partner owns half the venture indicates that it has negative control over the entity: It can prevent action through what is effectively a veto power. However, because it is possible that other documents may distribute control differently, any petition involving a 50/50 joint venture should include all agreements "relating to voting of the shares, management and direction of the subsidiary, and similar factors which affect actual control over 50 percent of the subsidiary. Unless

---

[6] 8 CFR §214.2(*l*)(1)(ii)(I) and (K).

[7] "Separate FOIA Requests Uncover L-1 Training Materials and Correspondence" (undated, posted Apr. 26, 2013), AILA Doc. No. 13042663, at 83.

[8] Adjudicator's Field Manual (AFM) 32.6(b).

[9] *See Matter of I-I, Inc.*, ID# 15137 (AAO Apr. 25, 2016). In this instance, a franchisor that had no ownership interest required adherence to its rules and protocols, obtaining of authorization for the location of the store, and purchase of its trademark products. However, it was able to show that it conducts its business independently of the franchisor, has hiring and firing authority, and otherwise controls its own business operations.

Copyright © 2017. American Immigration Lawyers Association. All rights reserved.

such agreements restrict actual control of one parent, the 50-percent ownership will be deemed per se control."[10]

For a circumstance where less than half the other entity is owned, documentation can be more vexing. Situations with the potential to qualify under this alternative include where the remaining stock is dispersed among a large number of other stockholders, leaving a dominant but not majority stockholder with the ability to appoint the board of directors.[11] Suggested documentation of control has included evidence such as voting proxies or agreements among shareholders to vote in concert so as to establish a controlling interest.[12]

As a general rule, a franchise relationship will not be viewed as parent/subsidiary when it is based on an agreement or licensing arrangement, as no ownership is involved even if some control is present.[13] However, some franchise structures do involve ownership and can result in a qualifying relationship[14] if the proportions of ownership are sufficient and control can be shown.

2. Branch Office

A branch office is, in essence, the same company as the parent. It is "an operating division or office of the same organization housed in a different location."[15] USCIS takes the view that the office must be registered as a foreign corporation operating in the United States if the branch is the U.S. petitioner.[16] Documentation that has been suggested includes:

- State business license establishing that the foreign corporation is authorized to engage in business activities in the United States;

- Copies of Internal Revenue Service (IRS) Form 1120-F, U.S. Income Tax Return of a Foreign Corporation;

- IRS Form 941, Employer's Quarterly Federal Tax Return, listing the branch office as the employer; and

---

[10] *Matter of Siemen's Medical Systems*, 19 I&N Dec. 362 (Comm'r 1986).

[11] *See Matter of Hughes*, 18 I&N Dec. 289 (Comm'r 1982).

[12] See *Matter of [name not provided]*, WAC 00 054 50730 (AAO Apr. 4, 2005).

[13] "Separate FOIA Requests Uncover L-1 Training Materials and Correspondence" (undated, posted Apr. 26, 2013), AILA Doc. No. 13042663, at 78. *See also Matter of Church Scientology International*, 19 I&N Dec. 593 (AAO 1988).

[14] *See* USCIS Draft Template for Comment, Request for Evidence, "I-129 L-1 Intracompany Transferee: Qualifying Relationship/Ownership and Control/Doing Business" (Dec. 15, 2011), AILA Doc. No. 11121520. Among suggested documentation to request on the issue of ownership and control is "franchise purchase agreement, and documentation as evidence of the right and authority to direct the management and operation of the U.S. entity."

[15] 8 CFR §214.2(*l*)(1)(ii)(J).

[16] "Separate FOIA Requests Uncover L-1 Training Materials and Correspondence" (undated, posted Apr. 26, 2013), AILA Doc. No. 13042663, p. 63.

Copyright © 2017. American Immigration Lawyers Association. All rights reserved.

- State tax forms that demonstrate that the petitioner is a branch office of a foreign entity.[17]

If the entity is found to be incorporated or otherwise organized separately under law, it will not be treated as a branch office.[18]

USCIS will seek evidence that the U.S. company is authorized to operate in the foreign country if it is the foreign entity that is the branch.[19]

3. Affiliate

Three scenarios meet the definition of affiliate:

- Two subsidiaries, both of which are owned and controlled by the same parent or individual;

- Two entities owned and controlled by the same group of individuals, with each person owning and controlling approximately the same proportion of each entity; or

- Certain multinational accounting firms.[20]

With respect to the first scenario, see the discussion above regarding parent/subsidiary, since the same considerations will apply in this affiliate context.

In the second scenario, USCIS will look to both ownership and control. If one owner's share in one of the companies is disproportionately higher than in the other, such that he or she has effective control of one but not the other, the petition is unlikely to be successful.[21] It is not sufficient that groups from the same family own both companies; individual family members must own both companies in approximately the same proportions.[22]

For the third scenario, the accounting firm must meet very specific criteria. A United States partnership that provides accounting services "along with managerial and/or consulting services" and that markets its accounting services "under an internationally recognized name under an agreement with a worldwide coordinating organization that is owned and controlled by the member accounting

---

[17] *Matter of [name not provided]* (AAO, June 25, 2015), AILA Doc. No. 16082231.

[18] *Id.*

[19] USCIS Draft Template for Comment, Request for Evidence, "I-129 L-1 Intracompany Transferee: Qualifying Relationship/Ownership and Control/Doing Business" (Dec. 15, 2011), AILA Doc. No. 11121520, including a request for documentation that "the U.S. entity is authorized to operate as a branch office in (foreign country) by the appropriate (foreign nationality) agency."

[20] 8 CFR §214.2(*l*)(1)(ii)(L).

[21] *See Mahalaxmi Amba Jewelers v. Johnson*, Case No. 14-2321-JTM (D.Kan, 2015).

[22] *Ore v. Clinton*, 675 F. Supp. 2d 217 (D. Mass. 2009). Three family members owned the U.S. company, with two of them holding 90 percent. Six family members owned the Nigerian company, each in equal shares, so that the two owners of 90 percnt of the U.S. company held only 40 percent of the Nigerian company.

Copyright © 2017. American Immigration Lawyers Association. All rights reserved.

firms"[23] falls under this umbrella. Thus, an accounting partnership or the equivalent organized outside the United States would qualify if it markets its services under the same name under the described agreement.[24] Many of the better-known international accounting firms fall under this rubric.[25]

B. Qualifying Employment by the Transferee

The employee must have been continuously employed full-time by the foreign company,[26] in an executive, managerial, or specialized knowledge capacity, for at least one year in the immediate preceding three years before filing the L petition.[27] Although the statute seems to indicate that an individual need only have the year of qualifying employment by the intended date of admission to the United States and the start date of the assignment, if the beneficiary has had less than 365 days of qualifying employment abroad at the time of filing the L-1 petition, then it may be difficult to establish satisfaction of this requirement.[28] As a practical matter, the foreign company will be unable to confirm completion of one year of qualifying employment until the individual actually performs the employment for an entire year, so the client may need to re-evaluate the start date of the petition, the date of petition filing, and the start date of the assignment.

The qualifying employment may have been gained at any time during the immediately preceding three years. The employee may currently be employed by another company, or in a non-managerial and non-specialized knowledge capacity. For employees who have held various positions within a company, this may be helpful when positioning the petition for L-1A status instead of L-1B status, as discussed below.

The continuous employment requirement has some flexibility. If the transferee visited the United States in lawful status, either for business while employed abroad or for pleasure, then those visits are not considered to break the continuous nature of the employment.[29] However, any time spent in the United States does not count toward the year of qualifying employment.[30] Therefore, it may be necessary to delay filing the L-1 petition until the transferee has a total of 365 days of qualifying employment while physically present outside the United States at the time of filing the L-1 petition, as discussed above.

---

[23] 8 CFR §214.2(*l*)(1)(ii)(L)(3).

[24] *Id.*

[25] "Separate FOIA Requests Uncover L-1 Training Materials and Correspondence" (undated, posted Apr. 26, 2013), AILA Doc. No. 13042663, at 81-82.

[26] Note that employment in B-1 status in the United States with payment of salary by the foreign company does not meet this requirement. *Matter of Kloeti*, 18 I&N Dec. 295 (Reg'l Comm'r 1982).

[27] Immigration and Nationality Act (INA) §101(a)(15)(L) and 8 CFR §214.2(*l*)(1)(ii)(A).

[28] *Matter of Michelin Tire Corp.*, 17 I&N Dec. 248 (Reg'l Comm'r 1978).

[29] 8 CFR §214.2(*l*)(1)(ii)(A).

[30] *Id.*

Copyright © 2017. American Immigration Lawyers Association. All rights reserved.

In addition, an individual who was present in the United States for periods longer than a few weeks, and who held nonimmigrant status other than B-1 or B-2 during those trips, may still have maintained continuity of employment abroad with the foreign employer. The qualifying employment may be comprised of two distinct periods of employment abroad, separated by a period of stay, up to a few months, in the United States. Provided that the individual held a valid nonimmigrant status in the United States[31] to engage in short training periods, conferences and similar functions on behalf of the foreign company, such presence in the United States would not interrupt the worker's continuous employment abroad.[32] In such instances, the one year of qualifying employment may also be satisfied in the aggregate.[33]

The employment abroad must have been full time; several years of part-time employment, which comprise one year of full-time employment in the aggregate, do not satisfy the requirement.[34] The one exception is if the beneficiary provided part-time services to a number of affiliated companies and if the aggregate time of this part-time employment "meets or exceeds the hours of a full-time position."[35] As discussed in the next section, the employment abroad must have been in an executive, managerial, or specialized knowledge capacity, but the capacity abroad and the capacity in the United States need not be the same.[36]

C. Executive, Managerial, or Specialized Knowledge Capacity

The transferee's U.S. assignment must be in an executive, managerial, or specialized knowledge capacity. The definitions of the terms "executive," "managerial," and "specialized knowledge" are the same for both the position abroad and the U.S. assignment.

1. Different Duties or Capacities in the United States and Abroad

While it is common for an individual to be coming to the United States to fill essentially the same position as was performed abroad, it also is not unusual for the two positions to be somewhat or even drastically different. Indeed, it is not necessary in most cases for the position abroad and the U.S. assignment even to be in the same

---

[31] *Matter of Continental Grain Co.*, 14 I&N Dec. 140 (D.D. 1972). In that case, the beneficiary had gained over one year of qualifying employment abroad, entered the United States for a training program in H-3 status "in pursuit of further training related to his qualifying employment" for 28 months, and resumed qualifying employment abroad for an additional seven months. The beneficiary did not have a full continuous year of qualifying employment directly with the foreign company in the immediate preceding three years. The district director held that the training program did not disrupt the continuity of the qualifying employment abroad.

[32] *See Matter of Kloeti*, 18 I&N Dec. 295 (Reg'l Comm'r 1982).

[33] *Matter of Continental Grain Co.*, 14 I&N Dec. 140 (D.D. 1972). The district director allowed the year of qualifying employment totaled in the aggregate, by adding the seven-month period of employment following the training program in the United States to five months of qualifying employment that was gained before the training program.

[34] 9 Foreign Affairs Manual (FAM) 402.12-13(b).

[35] *Id.*

[36] 8 CFR §214.2(*l*)(3)(iv); AFM 32.3(b).

Copyright © 2017. American Immigration Lawyers Association. All rights reserved.

capacity. One position can be in a specialized knowledge capacity and the other a managerial or executive,[37] except in the case of a new office petition, where a transferee whose U.S. assignment is managerial or executive must also have served in a managerial or executive capacity abroad.[38]

In instances in which the capacity abroad and the capacity in the United States are different, care should be taken to demonstrate how the transferee will apply his or her specialized knowledge to manage subordinates or the essential function in the United States, as discussed below, or to demonstrate how the managerial or executive experience abroad provided the requisite specialized knowledge.[39] USCIS applies a higher level of scrutiny when the position abroad and the assignment in the United States seem to be "substantially different."[40]

The client may plan a managerial assignment for an individual who held a specialized knowledge position abroad.[41] This transferee is eligible for L-1A status, because the nature of the U.S. assignment determines the L-1A or L-1B classification. To maximize the likelihood of obtaining approval of an L-1A petition, however, the documents should clearly demonstrate the connection between the specialized knowledge gained abroad and the managerial duties of the U.S. assignment. The key is to show how the transferee will infuse the U.S. operations with his or her specialized knowledge gained abroad, by managing activities that will apply the specialized knowledge and by leading the implementation of new processes or procedures that involve the specialized knowledge, as opposed to applying specialized knowledge to perform similar duties as those performed abroad.

For example, the foreign company could have been the first to implement a new IT system, and the transferee could have gained advanced hands-on knowledge of

---

[37] 8 CFR §214.2(*l*)(3)(iv); U.S. Citizenship and Immigration Services (USCIS), W. Yates, "Re: Changes to the L Nonimmigrant Classification made by the L-1 Reform Act of 2004" (July 28, 2005), AILA Doc. No. 05080566, including AFM 32.3(b). *See also Matter of Vaillancourt*, 13 I&N Dec. 654 (1970).

[38] 8 CFR §214.2(*l*)(3)(v)(B); "Separate FOIA Requests Uncover L-1 Training Materials and Correspondence" (undated, posted Apr. 26, 2013), AILA Doc. No. 13042663, p. 53.

[39] For an overview of the legislative history of the L-1 category, *see* R. Skinner, "Review of Vulnerabilities and Potential Abuses of the L-1 Visa Program," Department of Homeland Security, Office of Inspector General (Jan. 2006), AILA Doc. No. 06021310; https://www.oig.dhs.gov/assets/Mgmt/OIG_06-22_Jan06.pdf.

[40] "Separate FOIA Requests Uncover L-1 Training Materials and Correspondence" (undated, posted Apr. 26, 2013), AILA Doc. No. 13042663, at 54-55, USCIS PowerPoint states "if the ... beneficiary will be transferring laterally to *the same position* in the United States, the Officer's review may not need to be as extensive as a situation where the beneficiary is transferring to the United States to occupy a different position, involving a different set of job duties." (italics in original). Conversely, the training PowerPoint indicates that "if the position in the United States appears to be substantially different than the one that the beneficiary occupied abroad, Officers should review the petition to ensure that the beneficiary's prior education, training and employment qualify him/her for the position in the United States."

[41] 8 CFR §214.2(*l*)(3)(iv). *See also* USCIS, W. Yates, "Re: Changes to the L Nonimmigrant Classification made by the L-1 Reform Act of 2004" (July 28, 2005), AILA Doc. No. 05080566; 1 INS Examinations Handbook, Part II, 15-1.

Copyright © 2017. American Immigration Lawyers Association. All rights reserved.

how the new IT system works, how the system should be deployed, how the system is integrated with the existing IT system, and how to address problems that arise with the deployment, implementation, and integration. The transferee could then apply his or her knowledge of the "ins and outs" of the system to manage all subordinate staff and/or all activities relating to the system's deployment, implementation, and integration, without primarily engaging in hands-on performance of the deployment, implementation, and integration.

The practitioner should note, however, that although such a transferee may be eligible for L-1A status, in most cases, he or she would not meet the requirements for a multinational manager immigrant visa petition.[42] The one exception would be if the transferee held another managerial position with the foreign entity. In such a situation, the transferee may qualify for the L-1A assignment based on a specialized knowledge position and then qualify for a multinational manager immigrant visa petition based on another, separate managerial position with the foreign entity that occurred within the three years immediately preceding the foreign national's transfer to the United States.[43]

2. The L-1A Manager or Executive

There is a tendency when discussing the L-1A to conflate the concepts of managerial and executive capacities, but in fact the respective criteria are somewhat different. USCIS adjudicators are trained that "an employee's job description must fulfill all four criteria of the definition of either manager or all four criteria of the definition of executive."[44] According to the training materials, mixing the points of the two standards can result in denial.[45] That being said, many of the issues that arise with respect to the capacity of the L-1A assignment apply to both managers and executives, and USCIS and the courts frequently discuss them interchangeably.

A central tenet of USCIS's examination of any L-1A petition, be it for executive or managerial capacity, is that the beneficiary must "be primarily engaged in a managerial (or executive) function."[46] The core of virtually every examination of executive or managerial capacity is the extent to which the position involves hands-on performance

---

[42] 8 CFR §204.5(j)(3)(i).

[43] Id.

[44] "Separate FOIA Requests Uncover L-1 Training Materials and Correspondence" (undated, posted Apr. 26, 2013), AILA Doc. No. 13042663, p. 101.

[45] Id.

[46] USCIS, M. Aytes, "AFM Update: Chapter 22: Employment-based Petitions (AD03-01)" (Sept. 12, 2006), AILA Doc. No. 06101910. Although this guidance was written for immigrant visa petitions for multinational managers and executives, due to the statutory similarities between the requirements for a manager or executive of an L-1A petition and an immigrant visa petition for a multinational manager or executive, USCIS has cross-applied guidance and interpretations. See, e.g., AILA/TSC Meeting Minutes (Mar. 6, 2006), AILA Doc. No. 06032213 (stating that the "same standard is applied to L-1A and I-140 cases"). But see "AAO/AILA Liaison Meeting" (Mar. 15, 2007), AILA Doc. No. 07051068 ("[w]e see INA Section 204 as a more exacting standard").

Copyright © 2017. American Immigration Lawyers Association. All rights reserved.

of day-to-day operations versus management of those operations. "An employee who primarily performs the tasks necessary to produce a product or to provide services" is not considered to be employed in a managerial or executive capacity.[47]

If the U.S. company has only a few employees, then USCIS currently tends to presume that the manager or executive is required to spend so much time on day-to-day operational activities that he or she cannot be "primarily" engaged in managerial or executive duties.[48] The statute dictates that, if staffing levels are used as a factor in determining executive or managerial capacity, the "reasonable needs of [the entity] in light of the overall purpose and stage of development" of the entity must be taken into account.[49] While the small size of a company, in and of itself, does not automatically lead to a conclusion that an individual is not serving in a managerial or executive capacity, "size is nevertheless a relevant 'factor in assessing whether [an organization's] operations are substantial enough to support a manager."[50] However, the "sole employee of a company may qualify as an executive or manager, for L visa purposes, provided his or her primary function is to plan, organize, direct and control an organization's major functions through other people."[51] See the discussion below regarding management of non-employees.

While USCIS acknowledges that "[i]f a small or medium-sized business supports a position wherein the duties are primarily executive or managerial the position may qualify under the L category,"[52] it notes that "neither the title of a position nor ownership of the business are, by themselves, indicators of managerial or executive capacity."[53] An example of a beneficiary who would be found ineligible is the professional who opens an office in the United States, hires and supervises office staff, and uses his or her professional skills to engage in that profession.[54]

The "reasonable needs" factors are often used to find a lack of managerial capacity. Denials of appeals by AAO frequently contain this boilerplate language:

"We note that a company's size alone, without taking into account the reasonable needs of the organization, may not be the determining factor in denying a visa

---

[47] *Matter of Church Scientology Int'l*, 19 I&N Dec. 593 (Comm'r 1988).

[48] *Id. See also Matter of [name not provided]*, SRC 03 199 53751 (AAO May 4, 2005), AILA Doc. No. 07011067, noting "[w]hen a company has a limited number of employees, it becomes questionable as to whether the operator of the business will be engaged in primarily managerial or executive duties" and "[a]bsent the evidence of a store manager, it is assumed that the beneficiary performs [the] task [of assistant manager/cashier] himself"). It is permissible for a transferee to perform certain non-managerial or non-executive duties, but the duties must be primarily managerial or executive. *Id.*

[49] INA §101(a)(44)(C).

[50] *Brazil Quality Stones, Inc. v. Chertoff*, 531 F.3d 1063 (9th Cir. 2008), quoting *Family, Inc. v. USCIS*, 469 F.3d 1313 (9th Cir. 2006).

[51] 9 FAM 402.12-14(B)(e).

[52] AFM 32.6(d).

[53] *Id.*

[54] *Id.*

Copyright © 2017. American Immigration Lawyers Association. All rights reserved.

petition for classification as a multinational manager or executive… However, it is appropriate for users to consider the size of the petitioning company in conjunction with other relevant factors, such as the absence of employees who would perform the non-managerial or non-executive operations of the company, or a 'shell company' that does not conduct business in a regular and continuous manner. *See, e.g., Family Inc. v. USCIS*, 469 F.3d 1313; *Systronics Corp. v. INS*, 153 F. Supp. 2d 7, 15 (D.D.C. 2001). The size of a company may be especially relevant when USCIS notes discrepancies in the record and fails to believe that the facts asserted are true."[55]

Strategies to deal with problems faced by small companies in this context are discussed below in "Petitioner is a Small Company in the United States."

While holding firm to the precept that an L-1A must engage primarily in managerial or executive activities, USCIS does allow that a qualified beneficiary "may be required to perform some operational or administrative tasks from time to time."[56] In non-precedent decisions, USCIS's Administrative Appeals Office (AAO) has been known to apply various lines of examination to the question of whether the petitioner has demonstrated that the duties are primarily executive or managerial. One line of analysis requires that the petitioner establish "that the non-qualifying tasks the beneficiary would perform are only incidental to the proposed position."[57] Another line takes a "majority of time" approach, analyzing whether more than 50 percent of the beneficiary's time and/or duties are to be devoted to managerial or executive functions.[58] The practitioner is advised to document for both approaches, as it cannot be known which will be applied to a given case.

Experience has shown that USCIS will frequently ask petitioners to provide a percentage of the time a beneficiary will devote to managerial or executive functions. Businesses of any size often encounter a challenge when attempting to quantify the percentage of time to be devoted to specific duties performed by managerial or executive-level personnel. Job responsibilities tend to be organized around the requirements of the business. For example, budgetary planning may comprise most of the day at certain times of the year but involve virtually no activity at other times. Rather than relying on a specific formula to document managerial or executive-level responsibilities, petitioners may provide a narrative explanation of the manner in which the duties are performed on a daily, monthly, or yearly basis.

---

[55] *E.g., Matter of S-C-B-, Inc.*, ID# 17930 (AAO July 27, 2016); *Matter of D-D- Inc.*, ID# 17704 (AAO July 26, 2016).

[56] *Matter of Z-A-, Inc.*, Adopted Decision 2016-02 (AAO Apr. 14, 2016).

[57] Matter of R-F-P-US Inc., ID# 16545 (AAO May 2, 2016). See also *Matter of [name not provided]* (AAO Aug. 27, 2014), AILA Doc. No. 16082200.

[58] *See, e.g., Matter of [name not provided]* (AAO Nov. 10, 2014), AILA Doc. No. 14112603; *Matter of [name not provided]*, WAC 10 081 50986 (AAO Jan. 19, 2011), AILA Doc. No. 11012430; *Matter of [name not provided]*, WAC 10 072 50477 (AAO Nov. 23, 2012), AILA Doc. No. 13032155.

Copyright © 2017. American Immigration Lawyers Association. All rights reserved.

It is possible to obtain L-1A status on behalf of an executive or manager even if there are no subordinate employees and even if the beneficiary will be the sole employee of the U.S. company, provided the hands-on activities are in some way performed primarily by other people.[59] For managers, the beneficiary may qualify as a "function manager," discussed in detail below under "The Function Manager." The function manager option is not, however, available to qualify as an executive. But both managers and executives may be able to qualify if the operational activities are carried out through non-employees.[60] Functions performed through contractors are generally accepted,[61] as is supervision of, or support from, employees of related companies abroad.[62]

In those cases in which USCIS considers the number of employees in the petitioning U.S. company when determining managerial or executive capacity,[63] it must evaluate this factor in conjunction with the "reasonable needs of the organization, in light of the overall purpose and stage of the development of the organization."[64]

---

[59] 9 FAM 402.12-14(B); *Matter of Irish Dairy Board, Inc.*, A28 845 421 (AAU Nov. 16, 1989), AILA Doc. No. 89111641, 66 Interpreter Releases 1329 (Dec. 4, 1989). This was an unpublished decision and is not precedent, although it may be cited to provide reasonable criteria that may be considered by USCIS when adjudicating an L-1 petition. One Service Center has stated: "[W]e have no objection to your citing reasonable criteria from unpublished, nonbinding decisions such as … the so-called *Matter of Irish Dairy Board* relating to intracompany transferees. To the extent that criteria make good sense, they are usable, in our view, regardless of whether they are official or unofficial. To the extent that criteria are unofficial, they may lack some degree of authority or weight, whether they are used by our adjudicators or by your members." "VSC Liaison Teleconference Minutes" (Dec. 17, 1997), AILA Doc. No. 98029681. *See also Matter of [name not provided]*, LIN 95 019 50617 (AAU Jan. 31, 1996), 16 Immig. Rptr. B2-29 (noting that L-1 position "followed the guidelines of *Matter of Irish Dairy Board*"). For an explanation of the types of decisions of the AAO, *see* USCIS, "Precedent and Non-Precedent Decision of the Administrative Appeals Office (AAO)," PM-602-0086.1 (Nov. 13, 2013), AILA Doc. No. 13112145.

[60] "Separate FOIA Requests Uncover L-1 Training Materials and Correspondence" (undated, posted Apr. 26, 2013), AILA Doc. No. 13042663, at 172, USCIS PowerPoint stating "[t]here is no regulation requiring that the employees supervised must be on the company's payroll."

[61] *Id.* at 172, stating "In determining whether and employee meets the criteria of a manager, the persons who the manager supervises abroad or will supervise in the United States may include independent contractors." *See also Matter of Irish Dairy Board, Inc.*, A28 845 421 (AAU Nov. 16, 1989), AILA Doc. No. 89111641, 66 Interpreter Releases 1329 (Dec. 4, 1989), with respect to an executive; *Matter of [name and case number not provided]* (AAO Nov. 18, 2014), AILA Doc. No. 14120206.

[62] *Matter of Z-A-, Inc.*, Adopted Decision 2016-02 (AAO Apr. 14, 2016). *See also Matter of [name and case number not provided]* (AAO Dec. 15, 2011), AILA Doc. No. 11122324; *Matter of [name and case number not provided]* (AAO Nov. 10, 2014), AILA Doc. No. 14112603.

[63] INA §101(a)(44)(C).

[64] 8 CFR §204.5(j)(4)(ii). *See also Matter of [name and case number not provided]* (AAO Apr. 1, 2005), AILA Doc. No. 08013060. *Cf.* California Service Center (CSC), "Written Answers to AILA Liaison Questions" (Aug. 7, 2002), AILA Doc. No. 02080842 (noting that although staffing levels of the U.S. company may be considered to determine the need for an executive, "[r]esponsible need for an executive is not an issue normally discussed in L-1 adjudications," even in the context of smaller companies).

Copyright © 2017. American Immigration Lawyers Association. All rights reserved.

One strategy to address issues related to performance of day-to-day activities versus management of operations is to provide the following detailed information and documents:

- Contracts for services to be provided to clients or products to be manufactured and/or provided to clients, both in the United States and abroad, may demonstrate that the U.S. company is well-established and does business in the United States, and may demonstrate that the group of companies has ongoing international business. If contracts are unavailable, then examples of other evidence include articles, correspondence (mail or email), website print-outs, press releases, conference sponsorships, or advertisements.

- Organizational charts, with job titles, details on the job descriptions, and educational backgrounds of other employees, may demonstrate that other employees will perform the administrative and operational activities of the company's business. The objective is to demonstrate that other employees will free the transferee from the day-to-day responsibilities of the company, so that the transferee may focus on managerial or executive activities.

- If there are no other employees of the U.S. entity, then the petitioner could submit evidence of how the administrative and operational activities will be handled by individuals other than the transferee. For example, part-time employees, independent contractors, or foreign-based employees may perform these duties, or the U.S. entity may have outsourced all administrative functions to a single service provider.[65]

- A detailed job description, including percentages of time to be spent on individual activities, where the aggregate time of managerial or executive duties comprises a majority of the overall job duties, may demonstrate that the transferee will be primarily engaged in managerial or executive activities.

It is best to strategize with the client to position the petition as either managerial or executive, because a hybrid "manager/executive" L-1A petition may require demonstrating that the petition satisfies the requirements for both "managers" and "executives" under Immigration and Nationality Act (INA) §§101(a)(44)(A) and 101(a)(44)(B), respectively.[66] As previously explained, it is not permissible to qualify for L-1A status by cobbling together "partial sections of the two statutory definitions."[67]

---

[65] 9 FAM 402.12-14(B)(e). The existence of only a few part-time employees or independent contractors may, however, be insufficient to demonstrate that the transferee's duties will be primarily managerial or executive. *Matter of [name not provided]*, LIN 94 193 50721 (AAU Mar. 27, 1995), 14 Immig. Rptr. B2-114. To prevent a denial on these grounds, the petition could provide job titles for the independent contractors or part-time employees, as well as detailed job descriptions that demonstrate how the supervised employees will relieve the transferee of administrative and operational duties. *See, e.g., Matter of [name not provided]*, LIN 94 117 52032 (AAU Oct. 25, 1994), 13 Immig. Rptr. B2-274.

[66] *Matter of [name not provided]*, SRC 03 199 53751 (AAO May 4, 2005), AILA Doc. No. 07011067.

[67] *Id.*

Copyright © 2017. American Immigration Lawyers Association. All rights reserved.

3. Standards Specific to the L-1A Executive

An "executive" has similar duties to those of a manager but on a broader scale, by exercising more senior-level responsibility for directing numerous departments, divisions, and business units.[68] For example, a Human Resources Manager has responsibility for all benefits and employment activities for a team of Sales Representatives and directs those activities through teams of Human Resources Associates and Assistants. In contrast, a Vice President – Human Resources would manage all Human Resources Managers, direct the establishment and implementation of company-wide Human Resources policies, direct the short-term and long-term activities of the Human Resources Managers, and have hiring and firing power for the Human Resources Managers, Human Resources Associates, and Human Resources Assistants.

The regulatory definition of executive has four components:

- Directing the management of the organization or a major component or function of it;

- Establishing the goals and policies of the entity;

- Exercising wide latitude in discretionary decision-making; and

- Receiving only general direction or supervision from higher-level executives, the board of directors, or stockholders.[69]

Thus, hallmarks of an executive, as opposed to a manager, include the following:

- Managing, through subordinate staff, all activities of the entire company, or all activities of a significant division of the company;

- Reporting directly to another senior executive, such as the Chief Executive Officer, or to the Board of Directors;

- Developing the overall budget for the entire company or the entire division;

- Developing the business objectives and implementation programs for the entire company or the entire division; and

- Exercising hiring and firing authority for direct subordinate staff, as well as the subordinate employees managed in turn by the subordinate staff.

The petitioner bears the burden of proof to establish, by a preponderance of the evidence,[70] that the assignment and the beneficiary meet the requirements for L-1 status, as discussed in Volume 1: Chapter Two, "Basic Nonimmigrant Concepts."[71]

---

[68] 8 CFR §214.2(*l*)(1)(ii)(C).

[69] *Id.*

[70] *Matter of Chawathe*, 25 I&N Dec. 369 (AAO Oct. 20, 2010), AILA Doc. No. 10102030; also at https://www.justice.gov/sites/default/files/eoir/legacy/2014/07/25/3700.pdf. The evidence submitted should be "relevant, probative and credible" and should lead USCIS "to believe that the claim is 'probably true' or 'more likely than not.'"

[71] INA §291.

Copyright © 2017. American Immigration Lawyers Association. All rights reserved.

USCIS requires specificity in the information provided in order to determine whether the assignment qualifies as an executive.[72] Because an executive's duties encompass a wider scope of departments or divisions, it is important to specify the executive responsibilities and clearly connect them to the company's business objectives and to the executive's role in directing and guiding the business practices. General descriptions, which only note the existence of the departments, may be less helpful. The key is to link the activities to the executive's responsibilities in developing and achieving the senior-level business objectives for the company overall or for a major department or initiative, as opposed to solely for a lesser function, division, or project.

4. Standards Specific to the L-1A Manager

For purposes of the L-1A visa category, a "manager" is an individual with responsibility for exercising discretion over the activities of a department, subdivision, or component of an organization, through subordinate managers, supervisors, or degreed professionals, while exercising authority to make or recommend personnel actions for such subordinates and exercises.[73] A transferee may also qualify as an L-1A manager without subordinate employees, however, if he or she manages an "essential function" within the organization.

a. Manager of Other Workers

The following are elements of duties performed by an L-1A manager with responsibility for managing other workers:[74]

- Manages the organization, or a department, subdivision, function, or component of the organization;

- Exercises discretionary authority with respect to managing all day-to-day activities of the department, division, or business unit; and

- Exercises discretionary authority to make or recommend personnel actions concerning subordinate staff, including hiring and firing power.[75]

---

[72] 8 CFR §214.2(*l*)(3)(ii). *See, e.g., Matter of S-O- LLC, ID# 17938 (Aug. 1, 2016)* (citing *Fedin Bros. Co., Ltd. v. Sava*, 724 F. Supp. 1103 (E.D.N.Y. 1989), *aff'd*, 905 F.2d 41 (2d Cir. 1990)); *Matter of [name not provided]*, SRC 03 199 53751 (AAO May 4, 2005), AILA Doc. No. 07011067 (the general description of "'managing the company' … is too broad to provide an understanding of what actual tasks the beneficiary will perform").

[73] 8 CFR §214.2(*l*)(1)(ii)(B).

[74] USCIS, M. Aytes, "AFM Update: Chapter 22: Employment-based Petitions (AD03-01)" (Sept. 12, 2006), AILA Doc. No. 06101910, drawing a distinction between "personnel managers" who manage subordinate staff and "function managers" who manage all activities relating to an essential function. Although this guidance was written for immigrant visa petitions for multinational managers and executives, USCIS has cross-applied the considerations for multinational manager immigrant visa petitions to L-1A manager petitions. *See, e.g., Matter of [name not provided]*, LIN 95 019 50617 (AAU Jan. 31, 1996), 16 Immig. Rptr. B2-29 (noting that L-1 position "followed the guidelines of *Matter of Irish Dairy Board*").

[75] 8 CFR §214.2(*l*)(1)(ii)(B); legacy Immigration and Naturalization Service (INS) Memorandum, F. Ohata, "Definition of Manager" (Dec. 20, 2002), AILA Doc. No. 03020549.

Copyright © 2017. American Immigration Lawyers Association. All rights reserved.

As discussed in "The L-1A Manager and Executive" section above, the managed personnel need not necessarily be employees of the U.S. company. They can be employees of companies in the affiliated group,[76] or can even be independent contractors.[77] However, those situations may be better analyzed as function management, discussed below. While a function manager may not have authority to hire and fire the personnel of a contractor, he or she may be responsible for deciding whether to engage or retain the services of a contractor. Such authority tends to demonstrate functional managerial authority.

Except where the supervised staff includes professionals, it is not enough that a manager be a supervisor of other workers;[78] he or she must manage non-professional staff through subordinate supervisors or managers.[79] "Front-line supervisors, such as those who plan, schedule, and supervise the day-to-day work of nonprofessional employees, are not employed in an executive or managerial capacity, even though they may be referred to as managers in their particular organization. In addition, individuals who primarily perform the tasks necessary to produce the product(s) or provide the service(s) of an organization are not employed in an executive or managerial capacity."[80]

USCIS applies analyses similar to those used in the H-1B context to determine whether the subordinates are to be considered professionals. Accordingly, subordinates must not only possess a specialized bachelor's degree or the equivalent, but their positions also must require such a degree.[81]

b. Function Manager

A "function manager" may qualify for classification as an L-1A "manager" even without subordinate staff, by virtue of the transferee having managerial responsibility for all aspects of a particular department, division, or business unit.[82] This transferee must operate "at a senior level within the organizational hierarchy or with respect to the function managed."[83] A function manager L-1A petition will "primarily" engage in managerial duties.[84] USCIS will examine the petition to see if it demonstrates that

---

[76] *Matter of [name and case number not provided]* (AAO Nov. 10, 2014), AILA Doc. No. 14112603.

[77] USCIS PowerPoint, "Separate FOIA Requests Uncover L-1 Training Materials and Correspondence" (undated, posted Apr. 26, 2013), AILA Doc. No. 13042663, p. 172.

[78] INA §101(44)(A); 8 CFR §214.2(*l*)(1)(B)(4).

[79] 8 CFR §214.2(*l*)(1)(B)(2).

[80] AFM 32.6(d), citing *Matter of Church Scientology International,* 19 I&N Dec. 593 (Comm. 1988).

[81] See, e.g., *Matter of [name and case number not provided]* (AAO Jan. 19, 2011), AILA Doc. No. 11012430. AAO rejected the Director's finding based on the "Occupational Outlook Handbook" that the subordinates' positions did not require degrees, and instead looked to documentation of client communications showing discussions at a level that would require engineering degrees.

[82] 8 CFR §214.2(*l*)(1)(ii)(B).

[83] 8 CFR §214.2(*l*)(1)(ii)(B)(3).

[84] USCIS, M. Aytes, "AFM Update: Chapter 22: Employment-based Petitions (AD03-01)" (Sept. 12, 2006), AILA Doc. No. 06101910. AFM 22.2(i)(3)(E)(1).

Copyright © 2017. American Immigration Lawyers Association. All rights reserved.

"the beneficiary will primarily *manage*, as opposed to *perform*, the essential function"[85] (emphasis in original).

- The examination of whether a beneficiary qualifies as a function manager is comprised of:[86]

- Identification of the essential function. It could be "finance, marketing, personnel, accounting, or sales,"[87] or some other function such as engineering[88] or project management.[89] It could be the president, vice president, chief operating officer, or some other senior title with responsibility over the U.S. operation's specified functions.[90]

- Details of the duties to be performed in managing that function. Those duties might include such tasks as budget development, establishment of goals, monitoring of plan execution, implementing policies and strategies, coordinating with related companies, assigning work to professionals, preparing performance appraisals, determining resource requirements, acquiring necessary resources, defining deliverables, etc.[91]

- Determining whether the duties are primarily managerial in nature. To this end, USCIS must "consider the totality of the record and weigh all relevant factors,"[92] such as:

  - Nature and scope of the business;

  - Organizational structure;

  - Staffing levels;

  - Beneficiary's position in the organizational hierarchy;

  - Scope of beneficiary's authority;

  - Work performed by other staff;

  - Whether other personnel relieve the beneficiary from operational and administrative duties.[93]

---

[85] *Matter of Z-A-, Inc.*, Adopted Decision 2016-02 (AAO Apr. 14, 2016).

[86] *Id.*

[87] USCIS, M. Aytes, "AFM Update: Chapter 22: Employment-based Petitions (AD03-01)" (Sept. 12, 2006), AILA Doc. No. 06101910. AFM 22.2(i)(3)(E)(1).

[88] *Matter of [name and case number not provided]* (AAO Nov. 10, 2014), AILA Doc. No. 14112603.

[89] *Matter of [name and case number not provided]* (AAO Nov. 23, 2012), AILA Doc. No. 13032155.

[90] *See Matter of Z-A-, Inc.*, Adopted Decision 2016-02 (AAO Apr. 14, 2016); *Matter of [name and case number not provided]* (AAO Nov. 18, 2014), AILA Doc. No. 14120206.

[91] *See, e.g., Matter of [name and case number not provided]* (AAO Dec. 15, 2011), AILA Doc. No. 11122324; *Matter of Z-A-, Inc.*, Adopted Decision 2016-02 (AAO Apr. 14, 2016); *Matter of [name and case number not provided]* (AAO Nov. 23, 2012), AILA Doc. No. 13032155.

[92] *Matter of Z-A-, Inc.*, Adopted Decision 2016-02 (AAO Apr. 14, 2016).

[93] *Id.*

Copyright © 2017. American Immigration Lawyers Association. All rights reserved.

USCIS may look not just at the U.S. company, but also at the entire international organizational structure, and take into consideration the needs of related foreign components.[94] Thus, if the international organization is to be presented as part of the picture, evidence of its needs and their materiality to the beneficiary's position in the United States should be included. As previously discussed with respect to managers and executives alike, "when analyzing whether the Beneficiary will primarily manage the function, [USCIS] must consider evidence presented by the Petitioner of personnel employed by another related entity within the qualifying organization who perform day-to-day non-managerial tasks for the petitioning entity."[95]

Other factors that USCIS considers in determining whether a transferee qualifies as a function manager may include the following:

- Whether the transferee will have the authority to initiate and veto activities relating to the function managed;

- Whether the transferee will have the authority to provide managerial guidance to employees "outside the formal chain of command"; and

- Whether the transferee will have the authority to commit the company, department, or division "to a course of action or expenditure of funds."[96]

A function manager should provide managerial guidance and direction to other employees regarding activities relating to the function, because otherwise USCIS may question whether the transferee will undertake the duties rather than manage their performance.[97] It is helpful if they are managerial, supervisory, and/or professional employees.[98] The function manager may also exercise discretionary authority for the recommendation of personnel actions for those employees.[99]

If, however, there are no managers, supervisors, or professionals who receive guidance from the function manager, then it may be wise to affirmatively describe who else will perform the function's activities and why the function manager will not have to undertake hands-on work, such as if another department has responsibility for the function's activities or if there are outside contractors that supply the services. It is also possible to describe how the function manager has both function manager

---

[94] Id.

[95] Id.

[96] Id.

[97] USCIS, M. Aytes, "AFM Update: Chapter 22: Employment-based Petitions (AD03-01)" (Sept. 12, 2006), AILA Doc. No. 06101910 (noting that "[i]t must be clearly demonstrated, however, that the 'essential function' being managed is not also being directly performed by the alien beneficiary").

[98] A first-line supervisor of nonprofessional personnel does not qualify as a manager. INA §101(a)(44)(A). In a petition where managerial guidance is not provided to managers, supervisors, or professionals, it may be difficult to establish that the function manager will serve "at a senior level within the organizational hierarchy or with respect to the function managed." 8 CFR §214.2(l)(ii)(B)(3).

[99] Although not required, this would be consonant with functioning "at a senior level within the organizational hierarchy or with respect to the function managed." 8 CFR §214.2(l)(ii)(B)(3).

Copyright © 2017. American Immigration Lawyers Association. All rights reserved.

responsibilities as well as first-line supervisory responsibilities over non-professional personnel, as the supervised employees could perform the hands-on work. But because an employee does not qualify as a manager merely by having first-line supervisory responsibilities,[100] care should be taken to emphasize the managerial responsibilities over the function, to underscore that the transferee is not just a first-line supervisor, to express that these supervisory responsibilities comprise only a small portion of the function manager's duties, and to provide detailed information on how the majority of the function manager's time is devoted to managerial responsibilities.

For example, a Quality Assurance Manager may have no direct reports, but he or she may still provide managerial guidance and direction to many managers and professionals in other departments with respect to quality assurance activities, such as to the Production Manager of the manufacturing plant, to the Marketing Manager, and to the Engineering Manager, as well as to the subordinate professionals and technical specialists managed by these managers. The L-1A petition for this case could describe how the actual quality assurance activities are performed by employees of the manufacturing plant as part of the manufacturing process or how the quality assurance activities are outsourced to an independent vendor.

Alternatively, the petition could explain that non-professional employees perform the hands-on quality assurance work, that the function manager spends limited time in supervising the work by reviewing computer-generated reports on accuracy, and that the function manager's responsibilities are primarily to manage the planning and implementation of quality assurance procedures, policies, goals, and objectives in order to ensure compliance with ever-changing government regulations.

As with an L-1A petition for an executive, the key is to link the function manager's responsibilities to the company's business practices and business objectives. Providing estimates of fiscal control and responsibility exercised by the function manager may be helpful in demonstrating the scope of the managerial duties. In this example, the Quality Assurance Manager's role is important because it protects the company from product recalls, penalties for non-compliance with federal regulations, and negative media reports.

Further, the Quality Assurance Manager may bear fiscal control and responsibility over the department's budget, for equipment and upgrade expenditures. Even without subordinate staff, the Quality Assurance Manager would be the sole authority on quality assurance activities, and other employees would need to follow his or her guidance. Moreover, in the event of a product recall, the Quality Assurance Manager may hold ultimate responsibility for recommending investments for new equipment and response strategies to restore consumer faith. Weaving these points into the L-1A petition can illustrate why the direction provided to other employees is an essential part of the worker's duties and

---

[100] INA §101(a)(44)(A).

Copyright © 2017. American Immigration Lawyers Association. All rights reserved.

should help to emphasize the critical nature of the function manager's role within the company.

In the event that USCIS issues a Request for Evidence (RFE) for an L-1A petition for a function manager requesting information about the subordinate employees supervised, the practitioner should point out the error, while responding to other valid points of the RFE.[101]

5. L-1B Specialized Knowledge

"Specialized knowledge" is "special knowledge of the company product and its application in international markets" or "an advanced level of knowledge of processes and procedures of the company."[102] The L-1B visa category may be understood as allowing a transferee to infuse the U.S. operations with specialized knowledge gained abroad.

In a stroke of understatement, the U.S. Department of State (DOS) has noted that "the statutory language defining 'specialized knowledge' is not simple or clear," and quotes an unnamed district court opinion that "specialized knowledge is a relative and empty idea which cannot have a plain meaning."[103] But the L-1B is too important to international commerce and the American economy to throw up our hands and go home, so meaning we must find. And the search for it has been long and convoluted.

a. History

For years, USCIS (and Immigration and Naturalization Services (INS) before it), as well as the State Department, the courts, attorneys, and international businesses, have searched for ways to give meaning to the term "specialized knowledge." When the category was enacted in 1970,[104] Congress did not define the term, though a reference to specialized knowledge L-1s as "key personnel" appeared in the legislative history.[105] Thereafter, a series of precedent decisions[106] attempted to develop a definition, as did a 1983 legacy INS regulation[107] that was largely based on those decisions, as well as a 1987 regulation[108] that attempted to refine the definition.

---

[101] "VSC Liaison Minutes" (Aug. 25, 2000), AILA Doc. No. 00082504.

[102] INA §214(c)(2)(B).

[103] DOS, "Guidance on L Visas and Specialized Knowledge," State 002016 (Jan. 2011), AILA Doc. No. 11012433. While the patent exasperation with the concept of specialized knowledge that this memo reflects is amusing and understandable, the memo's attempt to provide guidance on it is misguided at best. It relies on the notion derived from the legislative history of the now-superseded L-1 provisions of the Immigration Act of 1970 (Pub. L. 91-225, 84 Stat. 117) that the L-1B must be a "key employee" and, while weakly acknowledging that proprietary knowledge is not required, goes on to suggest that consular officers look for proprietary knowledge.

[104] Immigration Act of 1970 (Pub. L. 91-225, 84 Stat. 117).

[105] H.R. Rep. No. 91-851.

[106] E.g., *Matter of Raulin*, 13 I&N Dec. 654 (Reg. Comm'r 1970); *Matter of LeBlanc*, 13 I&N Dec. 816 (Reg. Comm'r 1971); *Matter of Michelin Tire*, 17 I&N Dec. 248 (Reg. Comm'r 1978); *Matter of Penner*, 18 I&N Dec. 49 (Comm'r 1982); and *Matter of Colley*, 18 I&N Dec. 117 (Comm'r 1982).

[107] 48 Fed. Reg. 41142 (Sept. 14, 1983).

[108] 52 Fed. Reg. 5738 (Feb. 26, 1987).

Copyright © 2017. American Immigration Lawyers Association. All rights reserved.

This was followed by another precedent decision that required "advanced knowledge, and an advanced level of expertise not readily available in the United States job market, with the petitioner having a proprietary right to the knowledge or its product."[109] That decision was then followed by a clarifying memo that described "proprietary knowledge" as "special knowledge possessed by an employee of the organization's product, service, research, equipment, techniques, management, or other interests that is different from or surpasses the ordinary or usual knowledge of an employee in the particular field."[110]

In 1990, Congress made a course correction, amending the INA to its current language:

"For purposes of section 101(a)(15)(L), an alien is considered to be serving in a capacity involving specialized knowledge with respect to a company if the alien has a special knowledge of the company product and its application in international markets or has an advanced level of knowledge of processes and procedures of the company."[111]

This statutory change engendered a new round of guidance that made clear that specialized knowledge is "uncommon" and "advanced,"[112] but is not necessarily "proprietary"[113] or closely held.[114] It noted that an L-1B petition should not require a test of the U.S. labor market,[115] and indicated that an L-1B petition may be successful if:

"The petitioner is able to show:

"(1) that the individual's set of skills or knowledge of the company's processes and procedures is so complex that it contributed directly to the success of the foreign entity ... and

---

[109] *Matter of Sandoz Crop Protection*, 19 I&N Dec. 666 (Comm'r 1988).

[110] Legacy INS, R. Norton, "Interpretation of Specialized Knowledge Under the L Classification, File No. CO 214.2L-P" (Oct. 27, 1988), AILA Doc. No. 11102730.

[111] Immigration Act of 1990, Pub. L. No. 101-649 (IMMACT 90), §206(b)(2), codified at INA §214(c)(2)(B).

[112] Legacy INS, J. Puleo, "Interpretation of Specialized Knowledge" (Mar. 9, 1994), AILA Doc. No. 01052171; USCIS, F. Ohata, "Interpretation of Specialized Knowledge for Chefs & Specialty Cooks Seeking L-1B Status" (Sept. 9, 2004), AILA Doc. No.04091666.

[113] Legacy INS, J. Puleo, "Interpretation of Specialized Knowledge" (Mar. 9, 1994), AILA Doc. No. 01052171. *See also* "AILA-TSC Liaison Meeting Minutes" (Jan. 26, 1999), AILA Doc. No. 9bb173; facsimile correspondence, D. Grabast, AILA Doc. No. 02012731; *Matter of [name not provided]*, WAC 07 277 53214 (AAO July 22, 2008).

[114] Legacy INS, J. Puleo, "Interpretation of Specialized Knowledge" (Mar. 9, 1994), AILA Doc. No. 01052171.

[115] IMMACT90, Pub. L. 101-649, Sec. 206(b)(2)(B). *See also* "AILA-TSC Liaison Meeting Minutes" (Jan. 26, 1999), AILA Doc. No. 9bb173; facsimile correspondence, D. Grabast, (Jan. 27, 2002); AILA Doc. No. 02012731 *Matter of [name not provided]*, WAC 07 277 53214 (AAO July 22, 2008).

Copyright © 2017. American Immigration Lawyers Association. All rights reserved.

"(2) that the company now wishes to replicate this success in the United States by transferring this person to its United States affiliate and using the person to establish a substantially similar operation in this country."[116]

This approach to specialized knowledge continued until the early 2000s, when concerns arose of perceived abuse of the L-1B category, and when some commentators claimed that L-1 transferees were being imported to replace U.S. workers,[117] particularly in instances where petitioners were providing labor for hire to an unaffiliated third-party company. The result was enactment of the L-1 Visa Reform Act of 2004, which provided:

"An alien who will serve in a capacity involving specialized knowledge ... and will be stationed primarily at the worksite of an employer other than the petitioning employer or its affiliate, subsidiary, or parent shall not be eligible for classification under section 101(a)(15)(L) if (i) the alien will be controlled and supervised principally by such unaffiliated employer; or (ii) the placement of the alien at the worksite of the unaffiliated employer is essentially an arrangement to provide labor for hire for the unaffiliated employer, rather than a placement in connection with the provision of a product or service for which specialized knowledge specific to the petitioning employer is necessary."[118]

After this, practitioners began to notice a retrenchment in USCIS adjudications on the definition of specialized knowledge, largely ignoring the post-IMMACT 90 guidance and returning to earlier standards, despite the fact that the 2004 legislation did not address the meaning of the term. This trend culminated in a 2008 AAO nonprecedent decision known as *Matter of GST*,[119] the reasoning behind which became widely used by USCIS as a standard for USCIS adjudications.

Attorneys and employers, noting this trend, pushed back on the practice. The Citizenship and Immigration Services (CIS) Ombudsman found that the decision was not consistent with USCIS guidance and "that adjudicators are incorrectly using the non-precedential *GST* decision as policy guidance in adjudicating L-1B petitions."[120] In response, USCIS stated its belief "that the *GST* decision does not conflict" with the then-existing USCIS guidance.[121] USCIS took the position that the denial was based in part because the petitioner failed to establish that the "beneficiary's knowledge is substantially different from the knowledge possessed by similar workers generally

---

[116] USCIS, F. Ohata, "Interpretation of Specialized Knowledge for Chefs & Specialty Cooks Seeking L-1B Status" (Sept. 9, 2004), AILA Doc. No.04091666.

[117] R. Wasem, "Immigration Policy for Intracompany Transfers (L Visa): Issues and Legislation" (May 15, 2006), http://www.fosterglobal.com/policy_papers/L-1IntracompanyTransferee.pdf.

[118] Pub. L. No. 108-447, 118 Stat. 3351, §412.

[119] *Matter of GST*, WAC 07 277 53214 (AAO, Jul. 22, 2008), AILA Doc. No. 08081964.

[120] USCIS, "USCIS Response to the Citizenship and Immigration Services Ombudsman's 2010 Annual Report to Congress" (Nov. 9, 2010), AILA Doc. No. 10112460.

[121] *Id.*

Copyright © 2017. American Immigration Lawyers Association. All rights reserved.

throughout the industry or by other employees of the petitioning organization," which USCIS in turn characterized as "the same standard described in the Puleo and subsequent L-1B Agency memoranda."[122]

USCIS agreed that the "*GST* decision is not a precedent decision and therefore should never be cited by adjudicators," but cautioned: "This point does not mean that USCIS adjudicators may not employ the rationale used in the *GST* decision,"[123] primarily an examination of whether the beneficiary's knowledge substantially differs from that "possessed by similar workers generally throughout the industry or by other employees of the petitioning organization."[124]

USCIS also heard from other users of the system about the issues with L-1B adjudications.[125] The American Immigration Lawyers Association (AILA) challenged USCIS's adjudicatory trends in this regard, presenting an analysis of the history of the standard, critiquing how it was currently being applied, and recommending a course for going forward.[126]

b. Current Standards

In August 2015, USCIS issued a memorandum[127] rescinding and superseding the three primary post-IMMACT 90 memos[128] and a 2005 memo that had implemented the 2004 L-1 Reform Act.[129] The 2015 memo describes itself as "consistent with those policy memoranda" but providing "consolidated and authoritative guidance."[130]

In the months immediately following publication of this memo, AAO sustained appeals based on de novo review in a series of at least 15 specialized knowledge cases. The decisions were brief, with little to no facts given, simply stating "the

---

[122] *Id.*

[123] *Id.*; "AILA Liaison Report from the CSC Stakeholder Meeting" (Oct. 27, 2010), AILA Doc. No. 10112462. ("CSC does review all AAO decisions to determine which decisions have been overturned and which ones have been sustained. CSC reviews the analysis because it finds this useful for adjudications. However, nonprecedent decisions, such as the 2008 [*GST*] decision, are not binding on CSC and CSC does not treat them as such").

[124] USCIS, "USCIS Response to the Citizenship and Immigration Services Ombudsman's 2010 Annual Report to Congress" (Nov. 9, 2010), AILA Doc. No. 10112460 (citation for quotation only); "AILA Liaison Report from the CSC Stakeholder Meeting" (Oct. 27, 2010), AILA Doc. No. 10112462 ("CSC is looking for a preponderance of information relating the particular industry, company and beneficiary").

[125] *See, e.g.*, "USCIS Stakeholder Engagement: L-1B Interpretation of the term Specialized Knowledge" (June 14, 2001), AILA Doc. No. 11042965.

[126] "Interpretation of the Term 'Specialized Knowledge' in the Adjudication of L-1B Petitions" (Jan. 24, 2012), AILA Doc. No. 12012560.

[127] USCIS, "L-1B Adjudications Policy," PM-602-0111 (Aug. 17, 2015).

[128] USCIS, J. Puleo, "Interpretation of Specialized Knowledge" (Mar. 9, 1994), AILA Doc. No. 01052171; F. Ohata, "Interpretation of Specialized Knowledge" (Dec. 20, 2002), AILA Doc. No. 03020548; F. Ohata, "Interpretation of Specialized Knowledge for Chefs & Specialty Cooks Seeking L-1B Status" (Sept. 9, 2004), AILA Doc. No.04091666.

[129] USCIS, W. Yates, "Re: Changes to the L Nonimmigrant Classification Made by the L-1 Reform Act of 2004" (July 28, 2005), AILA Doc. No. 05080566.

[130] USCIS, "L-1B Adjudications Policy," PM-602-0111 (Aug. 17, 2015).

Copyright © 2017. American Immigration Lawyers Association. All rights reserved.

totality of the record establishes by a preponderance of the evidence that the beneficiary possesses specialized knowledge and that [s]he has been and will be employed in a qualifying capacity."[131] The memo was not cited in any of these decisions, and no analysis was provided, so it is not certain that the memo is what generated these results, but the volume of positive decisions in a short time frame, combined with the coincidence of their timing, leads the observer to speculate that the memo may have, at least for a while, led to a broader view of specialized knowledge than had been seen in recent years.

USCIS acknowledges in the memo that the statute provides two alternative standards for what constitutes specialized knowledge. USCIS reads the first, "special knowledge of the company product and its application in international markets," as meaning "distinct or uncommon in comparison to that generally found in the particular industry." This means examining the beneficiary's knowledge of how the company "manufactures, produces, or develops" its products or services, and requires evidence that the individual's knowledge is "distinct or uncommon" as compared to that of "similarly employed workers in the particular industry."[132]

The second alternative standard, an "advanced level of knowledge of the processes and procedures of the company," is defined by USCIS as knowledge or expertise in the company's "specific" processes and procedures that is "not commonly found in the relevant industry" and is "greatly developed or further along in progress, complexity and understanding than that generally found within the employer."[133] Although the memo seems to acknowledge that the two standards are separate, USCIS here adds the standard for special (uncommon in the industry) to that of advanced (more progressed or complex compared to others the company), making the standard that applies to knowledge of processes and procedures more onerous than the one that applies to the company's product and application in international markets. While USCIS says that the focus is primarily on how advanced is the knowledge of "processes and procedures *used specifically by the petitioning organization*" (italics in original), the evidence must set the beneficiary's knowledge apart not only from basic knowledge held by others in the company, but also by that held by others in the relevant industry.[134]

c. Demonstrating How the Standards Are Met

Under either standard, USCIS emphasizes comparison of the beneficiary's knowledge against that of others.[135] But how is this comparison to be proven? The

---

[131] *See, e.g., Matter of S-R-A-T-, Inc.,* ID# 12521 (AAO Sept. 15, 2015); *Matter of M-, Inc.,* ID# 14885 (AAO Oct. 1, 2015); *Matter of CMCS-T- Inc.,* ID# 15266 (AAO Jan, 28, 2016).

[132] USCIS, "L-1B Adjudications Policy," PM-602-0111, at 7 (Aug. 17, 2015).

[133] *Id.*

[134] *Id.* at 8.

[135] *See, e.g., Matter of E-US LLC,* ID# 15238 (AAO Jan. 29, 2016); *Matter of N-C-O-A-,* ID# 15359 (AAO Feb. 8, 2016).

Copyright © 2017. American Immigration Lawyers Association. All rights reserved.

starting point is the detailed description required by the regulations of the services to be performed in the United States.[136] Details of the nature of the knowledge in question are needed, and should be accompanied by information as to how and when the knowledge was obtained. An explanation of why it would be difficult to impart the knowledge to others "without significant cost or disruption" to the petitioner's business also could be helpful.[137]

This information can be contained in the statement from the petitioner. While USCIS acknowledges that such a statement, if detailed and credible, could be persuasive evidence, it implies that acceptance of that evidence alone would not be the norm.[138] Other possible evidence includes:

- Documentation of the number of years the beneficiary has been using or developing the knowledge. The practitioner may wish to look to employment records, training records, statements by individuals familiar with the beneficiary's work, or contracts or correspondence reflecting past use of the body of knowledge;

- Evidence of the impact on the U.S. entity's operations of the transfer of the beneficiary. Apart from inclusion in the petitioner statement, documentation might also be found in business plans, budgets, contracts, schedules, or other future-facing planning documents;

- Documents showing how the beneficiary's knowledge has already benefited the international group by increasing productivity, competitiveness, revenues, etc.; and

- Patents, licenses, trademarks, or contracts that exist based on the beneficiary's work or knowledge.[139]

- Correspondence, work papers, or other such documents showing a high degree of sophistication or complexity of the body of knowledge; and/or

- Pay records, resumes, organizational charts, or other documents comparing the beneficiary to "parallel employees" in the entity.[140]

Additional factors that USCIS could consider include whether the beneficiary's knowledge of foreign operating conditions will be of significant value to the U.S.

---

[136] 8 CFR §214.2(*l*)(3)(ii).

[137] USCIS, "L-1B Adjudications Policy," PM-602-0111 (Aug. 17, 2015), pp.11-12.

[138] USCIS, "L-1B Adjudications Policy," PM-602-0111, at 11-12 (Aug. 17, 2015), stating "Adjudicators may, in appropriate cases, however, request further evidence to support a petitioner's statement, bearing in mind that there may be cases involving circumstances that may be difficult to document other than through a petitioner's own statement." *See also Matter of E-US LLC,* ID# 15238 (AAO Jan. 29, 2016), where the petition was denied in large part because of the lack of evidence corroborating the U.S. and foreign employers' statements.

[139] It is not enough to simply identify patents held by the company. One must show how the beneficiary's role and expertise relate to those patents. *Matter of T-S-, Inc,* ID#15186 (AAO Jan. 20, 2016).

[140] USCIS, "L-1B Adjudications Policy," PM-602-0111, 12-13 (Aug. 17, 2015).

Copyright © 2017. American Immigration Lawyers Association. All rights reserved.

operations, whether the beneficiary's employment abroad has enhanced that company's position in the marketplace, whether the knowledge can be gained only through prior experience with that organization, whether the knowledge cannot be transferred easily to someone else without significant cost or inconvenience,[141] time sensitivity of the need for that knowledge, sophistication or complexity of the knowledge, benefit to the petitioner's competitiveness, or other similar factors.[142]

USCIS cannot categorically ignore knowledge obtained through "cultural traditions, upbringing or 'life experiences.'"[143] USCIS has acknowledged that "knowledge and skills gained through cultural experience may be relevant," but asserts that cultural knowledge alone is not enough to show specialized knowledge. Skills "grounded in cultural knowledge" may suffice "depending on the length and complexity of in-house training required to perform such duties."[144]

All factors are to be viewed in the totality of the circumstances.[145]

USCIS also has offered some insights as to what specialized knowledge does not necessarily require:[146]

- While significant cost or inconvenience can be a factor in establishing specialized knowledge, this element is not required if such knowledge is otherwise established.

- It need not be "proprietary or unique to the petitioning organization," though the petitioner may provide evidence to this effect. This means that, if proprietary knowledge is claimed, the petition must still provide evidence of special or advanced knowledge—the proprietary claim, in and of itself, may not provide much help.[147]

- A petitioner does not need to show a lack of readily available U.S. workers. Instead, the inquiry goes to whether there are so many workers, within or

---

[141] "[T]he amount of in-house training a company's employees would have to receive to acquire the knowledge in question" is among "natural proxies for economic inconvenience." *Fogo De Chao (Holdings) Inc. v. DHS*, 769 F.3d 1127, 1142 (D.C. Cir. 2014). *But see* USCIS's decision on remand, *Matter of Fogo De Chao (Holdings) Inc.*, EAC 10 085 51371 (AAO June 12, 2015), AILA Doc. No. 15081106, at 26, stating "Economic inconvenience is not the only relevant factor; the petitioner must also demonstrate 'the complexity of the knowledge and the fact that the knowledge is not generally found in the industry.'"

[142] USCIS, "L-1B Adjudications Policy," PM-602-0111, at 8 (Aug. 17, 2015).

[143] *Fogo De Chao (Holdings) Inc.* v. DHS, 769 F.3d 1127 (D.C. Cir. 2014).

[144] *Matter of Fogo De Chao (Holdings) Inc.*, EAC 10 085 51371 (AAO June 12, 2015), AILA Doc. No. 15081106, p. 8.

[145] USCIS, "L-1B Adjudications Policy," PM-602-0111, at 8 (Aug. 17, 2015).

[146] USCIS, "L-1B Adjudications Policy," PM-602-0111, at 9-11 (Aug. 17, 2015).

[147] *See, e.g., Matter of E-US, LLC*, ID # 15238 (AAO, Jan. 29, 2016).

Copyright © 2017. American Immigration Lawyers Association. All rights reserved.

outside the company, with such knowledge that it could be considered commonly held and thus not specialized.[148]

- The knowledge "need not be narrowly held within the petitioning organization…. The mere existence of other employees with similar knowledge should not, in and of itself, be a ground for denial." Indeed, "[s]ome companies may use technologies or techniques that are so advanced or complex that nearly all employees working on the relevant products or services possess specialized knowledge." If the practitioner is relying on these statements, care should be taken to show why yet another person with this knowledge is needed.[149] This can include showing the difficulty in transferring the knowledge to another person, how the beneficiary's duties will differ from the others' duties, potential economic inconvenience or disruption to operations, and/or whether the beneficiary's total compensation is comparable to or higher than that of others with similar knowledge.

- The beneficiary need not be a supervisor or otherwise hold an elevated rank in the company, and need not draw a higher pay than others similarly situated[150] (but note that the latter may be helpful if relying on the proviso directly above).

- It does not matter if the beneficiary might also be eligible for another nonimmigrant classification.

Some examples of specialized knowledge provided a couple of decades ago by DOS appear to still be applicable (or be applicable once again) under the newer USCIS guidance. They include the following:

- "The foreign firm manufactures a product no one else does and the alien is familiar with the various procedures involved in such manufacture, use, or service of such product.

- "The foreign company manufactures a product which is significantly different from others in the industry. Although the product has some similarities to others, the knowledge required to sell, manufacture, or service the product is different from other products to the extent the U.S. or foreign firm would experience significant interruption of business in order to train a new worker to assume the duties to be assigned to the applicant.

- "The applicant has knowledge of a foreign firm's business procedures or methods of operation, to the extent that the U.S. firm would experience a

---

[148] See *Fogo De Chao (Holdings) Inc. v. DHS*, 769 F.3d 1127 (D.C. Cir. 2014); *Matter of Fogo De Chao (Holdings) Inc.*, EAC 10 085 51371 (AAO June 12, 2015), AILA Doc. No. 15081106.

[149] *See, e.g., Matter of K-I, Inc.*, ID#13257 (AAO Sept. 10, 2015), noting that, where all team members had the same specialized knowledge but a small number held advanced knowledge, the beneficiary was not sufficiently distinguished from the others.

[150] *See Matter of N-C-O-A-*, ID#15359 (AAO Feb, 8, 2016), which noted but disregarded in denying the petition the fact that the beneficiary's pay was significantly higher than that of others.

Copyright © 2017. American Immigration Lawyers Association. All rights reserved.

significant interruption of business in order to train a U.S. worker to assume his duties.

- "The applicant has knowledge of a process or a product which is of a sophisticated nature, although not unique to the foreign firm, which is not generally known in the U.S."[151]

While the factors provided by the DOS guidance above are helpful in preparing an L-1B petition, citation to such dated policy guidance is not recommended in view of the more current policy authority provided by USCIS.

d. Placement at Worksite of Another Company

As previously noted, in the early 2000s, concerns arose over claims that L-1 transferees were being imported to replace U.S. workers, particularly where petitioners were providing labor for hire to an unaffiliated third-party company.[152] In response, Congress enacted the L-1 Visa Reform Act of 2004, which prohibited use of the specialized knowledge category for individuals who "will be stationed primarily at the worksite of an employer other than" the petitioner or its related companies if "(i) the alien will be controlled and supervised principally by such unaffiliated employer; or (ii) the placement of the alien at the worksite of the unaffiliated employer is essentially an arrangement to provide labor for hire for the unaffiliated employer, rather than a placement in connection with the provision of a product or service for which specialized knowledge specific to the petitioning employer is necessary."[153]

USCIS guidance puts the burden on the petitioner to show that the beneficiary meets these statutory criteria when the beneficiary is stationed at an unaffiliated entity's site. Thus, where a third-party site is involved, a petitioner will need to show that it is going to supervise and control the beneficiary. To do this, it must demonstrate that it has a business relationship with the third-party company that involves the provision of products and services, and not just the supply of workers. The third-party worksite company may give the beneficiary day-to-day assignments, provided that "in the totality of the circumstances" it does not principally supervise the beneficiary's activities.[154] Indicia that the petitioner, and not the third-party company, control the beneficiary can include showing that the petitioner will dictate the manner in which the work is to be done, will reward or discipline the beneficiary, and will provide the beneficiary's salary and benefits.[155]

---

[151] Department of State (DOS), "L-1 Visa Specialized Knowledge" (Oct. 4, 1995), AILA Doc. No. 95100490.

[152] For a discussion of the perceived abuse of the L-1 visa category and the L-1 Visa Reform Act of 2004, *see* A.J. Vazquez-Azpiri & D. Horne, "The Impotence of Being Earnest: Revisiting the L-1 Controversy," 8 Bender's Immigr. Bull. 1607 (Oct. 15, 2003).

[153] Pub. L. No. 108-447, 118 Stat. 3351, §412. INA §214(c)(2)(F).

[154] USCIS, "L-1B Adjudications Policy," PM-602-0111 (Aug. 17, 2015), at 14.

[155] *Id.*

Copyright © 2017. American Immigration Lawyers Association. All rights reserved.

The key to demonstrating that the assignment does not run afoul of the labor for hire prohibition is to show that the beneficiary "will be using the specialized knowledge that served as the basis of the L-1B petition ... while working at the off-site location."[156] One strategy, which would also connect the two requirements, is to explain how the transferee must remain primarily under the control and supervision of the petitioning U.S. entity because the assignment requires applying specialized knowledge to create or deliver work product that is unique to the U.S. entity, such as installation of advanced software developed by the petitioner.[157] Application of general knowledge, skills, or services associated with generic products, that does not require knowledge of the petitioning company's product or processes, will typically be considered "labor for hire" by a "job shop."[158] Alternatively, the L-1B petition may highlight how the transferee will not be under the control and supervision of the worksite company because the transferee will be devoted to applying specialized knowledge of the petitioning company's internal processes and because employees of the third-party worksite cannot provide direction on these processes.

In particular, petitions that involve third-party placement for transferees in the Information Technology (IT) industry may be subject to additional scrutiny, as several commentators have noted abuse of the L-1B category for IT "job shops."[159] These petitions would benefit from additional details on how the software application is unique (and hopefully designed by no other company in the IT industry), how the knowledge to be applied during the L-1B assignment is uncommon within the IT industry, and how the foreign company is legitimate, to demonstrate that the transferee will not engage in labor for hire as merely an IT consultant.[160]

Great care must be taken in the language used to describe an IT assignment and the knowledge required for its execution, as adjudicators can be quick to find a "job shop" arrangement where none exists. For example, rather than saying "client-specific custom tools," one might wish to speak of tools based on software designed by the petitioning company to be customized for the applications being sold to the customer.[161]

Exploring the relationship between the U.S. company and the worksite may elicit key information on the business needs that drive the placement. For example, the petitioning company has a contract with the worksite company to manufacture automobile brake parts, and the transferee is required to apply specialized knowledge

---

[156] Id.

[157] DOS, "L-1 Visas and the H-1B Cap" (Feb. 14, 2004), AILA Doc. No. 04022410.

[158] Id.

[159] R. Wasem, "Immigration Policy for Intracompany Transfers (L Visa): Issues and Legislation" (May 15, 2006), http://www.fosterglobal.com/policy_papers/L-1IntracompanyTransferee.pdf.

[160] Id.

[161] See Matter of N-C-O-A-, ID#15359 (AAO Feb. 8, 2016), in which the AAO discounted the petitioner's argument that the beneficiary would be customizing its software to meet the client's needs by pointing to what it perceived as a contradiction in documentation that discussed "client-specific software tools."

Copyright © 2017. American Immigration Lawyers Association. All rights reserved.

of the group's proprietary manufacturing processes to gather the necessary requirements and specifications onsite where the rest of the automobile is manufactured. In another scenario, the petitioning company has designed a cutting-edge software application to monitor manufacturing activities and highlight inefficiencies, the worksite company has purchased the application, and the specialized knowledge transferee needs to provide installation and integration services that cannot be performed by an individual who is not intimately familiar with every aspect of the application.[162] A third example is where an international law firm has developed an uncommon, streamlined, and cost-effective process to respond to regulatory actions deriving from the Directives of the European Union, which in turn are similar to requirements of the U.S. Environmental Protection Agency for the relevant matter, and the transferee will apply this specialized knowledge to spearhead the client's strategy for ensuring compliance at the client's worksite by reviewing existing practices and recommending solutions.

In all of these examples, the transferee remains under the control of the petitioning company, whose employees alone have the advanced knowledge necessary for the assignment. These petitions may be strengthened with monetary estimates of the investment in the products or services, of the project, or of the value of the contract or account, as well as the overall business goals that the transferee would further or achieve, such as increase in market share and competitiveness in the marketplace, visibility and reputation within the industry, and consumer loyalty.[163]

In addition, it may be helpful to discuss the investment to train a U.S. worker, including time, resources, and lost productivity, that would be necessary if the transferee could not perform the specialized knowledge assignment at the third company's worksite, as this would demonstrate the "interruption of business" and "undue hardship" the U.S. petitioning company would suffer if unable to transfer the specialized knowledge employee.[164] Given that RFEs have been issued requesting this information, it may be helpful to affirmatively provide this information, as it may be probative in establishing that the specialized knowledge is truly necessary for the third-party placement.[165]

III. Key Issues

A. Planning Ahead for Permanent Resident Status

It is advisable to carefully consider the petitioner's and beneficiary's long-term goals from the outset so as to best position the petition and ongoing strategy to achieve those goals. The choice between L-1A and L-1B can have major implications down the road for a variety of reasons.

---

[162] *Id.*

[163] *Id.*

[164] *Id.*

[165] *See, e.g.,* "AILA/TSC Liaison Minutes" (Jan. 12, 2004), AILA Doc. No. 04022566.

Copyright © 2017. American Immigration Lawyers Association. All rights reserved.

1. Period of Authorized Stay

The L-1A category has several advantages over the L-1B category. First, a transferee may hold L-1A status for up to seven years, as opposed to the maximum five years of L-1B status. Exceptions to these maximum periods of authorized stay are available for part-time, intermittent, seasonal employment or for transferees who are physically present in the United States for an aggregate of less than six months per year, as discussed later in this chapter. However, if the individual is not eligible for one of these exceptions, the employer should carefully evaluate whether there will be a need for the services of the employee beyond the fifth or seventh year of L-1 eligibility.

Persons in L-1 status are not eligible for the American Competitiveness in the Twenty-First Century Act (AC21) extensions.[166] Consequently, such employees must either obtain permanent resident status or file an application to adjust status before exhausting all available L-1 time. The L-1 worker and any dependents may be eligible for employment authorization in "compelling circumstances"[167] once the immigrant visa petition is approved, but, as discussed in Volume 2: Chapter Three, "The Immigrant Visa Petition," the availability of this option is so limited, and the pitfalls surrounding it so severe, that it is rarely useful.

It may be possible for a transferee in L-1B status to change to another nonimmigrant status, if he or she meets the requirements for that status, and continue residing and working in the United States beyond the five-year maximum. For example, the transferee may hold H-1B status for up to six years, as discussed below, though the time spent in L-1 status will count toward those six years.[168] The practitioner should be aware, however, that statutory dual intent is permissible only for H-1 and L-1 nonimmigrants and their dependents. Changing to another status may cause complications in the permanent resident process, as discussed in Volume 1: Chapter Two, "Basic Immigrant Concepts." For example, the foreign national may be eligible to change nonimmigrant status from L-1 to TN, if he or she is a citizen of Canada or Mexico, but a TN nonimmigrant must possess nonimmigrant intent, as discussed in Volume 1: Chapter Fourteen, "TN Visas and Status." Therefore, a TN change of status request may be denied if the foreign national is the beneficiary of an immigrant visa petition.

2. Possible Eligibility for EB-1 Classification

Once an employer has demonstrated that a worker satisfies the requirements for L-1A classification, obtaining U.S. permanent resident status through the employment-based, first preference (EB-1) category as a multinational manager should be

---

[166] For a discussion of AC21 extensions, see Volume 1: Chapter Seven, "H-1B Status."

[167] 8 CFR §204.5(p).

[168] 8 CFR §§214(h)(13)(B) and 214(l)(12); 9 FAM 402.12-16(C).

Copyright © 2017. American Immigration Lawyers Association. All rights reserved.

considered if the need for the worker's services in the United States will change from temporary to indefinite.[169]

However, differences between L-1A qualification and EB-1 qualification must be kept in mind. Unlike the requirements for the L-1A nonimmigrant category, in order to qualify for the EB-1 immigrant category, the employee must have been a manager or executive abroad for at least one year in the three years immediately preceding the individual's transfer to the United States in addition to being a manager or executive in the United States. Employment abroad in a specialized knowledge capacity is not sufficient.[170]

Merely because a worker is maintaining L-1B status, however, does not preclude approval of an EB-1 immigrant visa petition. USCIS will make a separate determination of eligibility for EB-1 classification based on the evidence presented with a multinational manager petition. An employer may have filed an L-1B nonimmigrant worker petition to bring the worker to the United States for his or her specialized knowledge. In carrying out the duties of the position, however, the worker may also be performing managerial duties. This is particularly true for employees who may reasonably be classified as either a specialized knowledge worker or as a function manager, as discussed above. It is not necessary to file an application to change the nonimmigrant status of the worker from L-1B to L-1A status prior to filing an immigrant worker petition to classify the worker as a multinational manager under the EB-1 visa category. That being said, making such a change before filing the immigrant petition could help with how the adjudicator might ultimately view the immigrant petition, as discussed below.

If the foreign entity that employed the beneficiary has ceased operation or is no longer related to the U.S. entity, USCIS takes the position that the beneficiary is not eligible under the EB-1 category.[171] USCIS argues that because the INA defines executive or manager under the regulations governing the immigrant visa category as seeking entry "in order to *continue* to render services to the same employer or to a subsidiary or affiliate thereof…" (emphasis in original), the foreign company must continue to be in existence,[172] even though it suffices for L-1 purposes that there is a related company doing business somewhere in the world.[173] However, this is not a problem if the defunct foreign employer was a branch office of a company that still

---

[169] For a discussion of the preference classifications, see Volume 2: Chapter One, "Basic Immigrant Visa Concepts."

[170] INA §203(b)(1)(C); 8 CFR §204.5(j)(3)(i)(A) and (B).

[171] USCIS, M. Aytes, "AFM Update: Chapter 22: Employment-based Petitions (AD03-01)" (Sept. 12, 2006), AILA Doc. No. 06101910, at AFM 22.2(i)(C)(1).

[172] *Matter of [name not provided]*, LIN 06 189 52335 (AAO Nov. 7, 2008), AILA Doc. No. 16082330.

[173] "Separate FOIA Requests Uncover L-1 Training Materials and Correspondence" (undated, posted Apr. 26, 2013), AILA Doc. No. 13042663, p. 170.

Copyright © 2017. American Immigration Lawyers Association. All rights reserved.

exists and is related to the petitioner, since a branch office is, by definition, the "same employer" as the still-operating company.[174]

USCIS also takes the curious position that a branch office in the United States cannot be a petitioner for the EB-1 category, arguing that "an unincorporated branch office of a foreign employer [is not] competent to offer permanent employment to a beneficiary for the purpose of obtaining an immigrant visa for the beneficiary under section 203(b)(1)(C) of the Act. … The petitioner must be a U.S. citizen, corporation, partnership, or other legal entity to file this immigrant visa petition. Thus, a U.S. corporation with an overseas branch may file an E13 petition, but a foreign corporation with a branch office in the United States may not."[175] This position relies for authority upon a 1981 precedent decision, by the commissioner of what was then the INS, finding that an individual in nonimmigrant status was ineligible to petition on behalf of a household worker because, as a nonimmigrant, he could not offer permanent employment.[176]

This position and its reliance on the 1981 decision is nonsensical. First, a company's status is not subject to an expiration date, and thus the company is not incapable of offering permanent employment. Second, not only is there no statutory or regulatory language to justify USCIS's position, the plain language of the statute contradicts it, in that the INA requires that the beneficiary be seeking entry to render services to *"the same employer* or to a subsidiary or affiliate thereof" (emphasis added).[177] As discussed above, in the L-1 context, "same employer" essentially means "branch office."[178] That being said, USCIS may not always apply this position in practice.[179] Nevertheless, the practitioner should be prepared to make the statutory argument if the issue should arise.

In addition, as a practical matter, USCIS generally appears to apply a greater level of scrutiny in the adjudication of EB-1 multinational manager petitions. It is not uncommon to see an L-1A approved but an EB-1 petition providing the same facts and documentation denied.

3. Bypassing Labor Certification and the EB-2/EB-3 Categories

Being eligible for the EB-1 category means that labor certification is not necessary,[180] so the U.S. company may proceed directly to filing an immigrant visa

---

[174] *Matter of [name not provided]*, LIN 06 189 52335 (AAO Nov. 7, 2008), AILA Doc. No. 16082330.

[175] USCIS, M. Aytes, "AFM Update: Chapter 22: Employment-based Petitions (AD03-01)" (Sept. 12, 2006), AILA Doc. No. 061019l0, at AFM 22.2(i)(3)(B)(3).

[176] *Matter of Thornhill*, 18 I&N Dec. 34 (Comm. 1981).

[177] INA §203(b)(1)(C).

[178] 8 CFR §214.2(*l*)(1)(ii)(J).

[179] *See, e.g., Matter of [name not provided]*, LIN 06 189 52335 (AAO Nov. 7, 2008), AILA Doc. No. 16082330. While this case's approval turned on the fact that the foreign employer was a branch office, the U.S. employer also was a branch office, and that fact was not commented upon as a negative in the decision.

[180] 8 CFR §204.5(j)(5).

Copyright © 2017. American Immigration Lawyers Association. All rights reserved.

petition. In the event that the worker does not qualify for either EB-1 classification as a multinational manager or a national interest waiver under the employment-based, second preference (EB-2) immigrant visa category, obtaining labor certification will be necessary if the individual's services will be retained indefinitely.[181] The labor certification process, governed by U.S. Department of Labor (DOL) regulations, is a test of the labor market.[182] The preparation time and processing time associated with the labor certification process may add a year or more to the overall time of obtaining permanent residence status.

An employee who requires labor certification will qualify only for the EB-2 or the employment-based, third preference (EB-3) immigrant visa categories. As these categories can be severely impacted by immigrant visa retrogression,[183] depending on the employee's country of birth, there may be an additional delay of months or years from the date that the immigrant petition is approved to the date that the application to adjust status may be filed. As discussed in Volume 2: Chapter Four, "Consular Processing, Adjustment of Status and Permanent Residence Issues," an application for adjustment of status allows the worker, along with any dependents, to apply for interim employment and international travel authorization documents.[184] Furthermore, once the worker has a pending application for adjustment of status and has obtained an interim employment authorization document (EAD) he or she may remain lawfully present in the United States and continue to engage in employment if his or her period of L-1 eligibility runs out.

4. Changing from L-1B to L-1A

A client may plan initially for an L-1B assignment, but careful review of the transferee's background and the job duties of the U.S. assignment may reveal eligibility for the more preferable L-1A category. Although a worker maintaining L-1B status may qualify for EB-1 classification if the job duties entail managerial duties as well as specialized knowledge, there may be tactical reasons for filing an application to change the status of the worker from L-1B to L-1A.

---

[181] A national interest waiver allows an individual to bypass the labor certification requirement because his or her work in the United States will have substantial intrinsic merit and will be of great importance in national scope, such that waiving the usual labor certification requirement would be in the national interest. For a detailed discussion of national interest waivers, see Volume 2: Chapter One, "Basic Immigrant Visa Concepts."

[182] 20 CFR, Part 656.

[183] Immigrant visa retrogression occurs when demand for an immigrant visa classification exceeds the available supply of numbers. In this situation, there is a delay between the date that the immigrant visa petition is approved and the date that the foreign national beneficiary is eligible to apply for permanent residence because an immigrant visa number is available. For certain classifications, this delay may be several years or more. The DOS issues a monthly Visa Bulletin, https://travel.state.gov/content/visas/en/law-and-policy/bulletin.html, which provides information on which classifications are currently retrogressed. For a detailed discussion of immigrant visa retrogression, as well as strategies to lessen its negative impact, see Volume 2: Chapter One, "Basic Immigrant Visa Concepts."

[184] Although L-2 spouses are eligible for employment authorization pursuant to INA §214(c)(2)(E), there is no similar provision for L-2 children, who may not apply for employment authorization until the adjustment of status stage.

Copyright © 2017. American Immigration Lawyers Association. All rights reserved.

If the worker did not have at least 12 months of managerial experience abroad prior to beginning the assignment in the United States, then he or she will not qualify for the classification as an EB-1multinational manager, and the employer will need to pursue the lengthier labor certification process. Filing an application to change the worker's status from L-1B to L-1A will allow the employee to remain in nonimmigrant status up to seven years, rather than five years. This additional time may be sufficient to complete the labor certification process and allow the worker to become a permanent resident before running out of eligibility for nonimmigrant L-1 status.

If the job duties of an intracompany transferee change from primarily those of a specialist to those of a manager, an amended L-1A petition must be filed with USCIS to obtain authorization for the new position.[185] If an L-1B worker is approaching the end of his or her fifth year of L-1 eligibility, the status can be extended up to the maximum time of seven years at the same time that the amended petition is filed.[186]

When a worker admitted in L-1 status based on specialized knowledge is subsequently promoted to become a manager, the employer must file an amended petition to change from L-1B to L-1A status no later than six months before the worker reaches his or her fifth year of L-1 status.[187] USCIS has indicated that the requirement that the beneficiary begins performing managerial or executive duties for at least six months before reaching the end of the fifth year of L-1B status is imposed to prevent fraud and to ensure that the assignment is legitimately managerial.[188] Although the language of the regulation is ambiguous, USCIS may take the position that the amended L-1A petition to authorize performance of managerial duties must be *approved,* not merely filed, prior to the final six months of L-1B status.[189] In the event that the managerial promotion occurs in the final days before the last six months of the maximum five years of L-1B status, premium processing should be requested to maximize the likelihood that USCIS will not deny the extension on this basis. As a practice pointer, attorneys should alert clients to these issues well in advance of the final six months of a worker's L-1B status.[190]

In the event that no promotion has occurred before the last six months of a worker's L-1B status but the transferee performs both managerial and specialized

---

[185] 8 CFR §214.2(l)(7)(i)(C).

[186] 8 CFR §214.2(l)(15)(ii).

[187] *Id.*

[188] AILA-USCIS Liaison Meeting (Mar. 23, 2006), AILA Doc. No. 06060761.

[189] 8 CFR §214(*l*)(15)(ii); 9 FAM 402.12-16(C). *See also* "AILA-USCIS Liaison Meeting" (Mar. 23, 2006), AILA Doc. No. 06060761. The AAO (at that time called the AAU) has approved an L-1 extension of two years where the transferee assumed managerial duties and where the L-1 extension was filed six months and two days before the transferee would have exhausted his five years in L-1B status, but this may be an isolated case. *Matter of [name not provided],* LIN 00 074 53328 (AAU Oct. 30, 2000), 23 Immig. Rptr. B2-32.

[190] For an additional discussion of suggestions by AILA to resolve inconsistencies with L-1B to L-1A amended petitions, *see* the Appendix of "AILA-USCIS Liaison Meeting" (Mar. 23, 2006), AILA Doc. No. 06060761.

Copyright © 2017. American Immigration Lawyers Association. All rights reserved.

knowledge duties, another strategy is to file the amended L-1A petition with a discussion of how the petition could have been originally filed and approved for the L-1A classification rather than the L-1B classification. That is, the argument would be that there is no need to demonstrate a promotion or other change in job duties, since the original position already involved both specialist and managerial duties. This approach seeks to "re-characterize" the L-1 assignment as managerial. The practitioner should discuss the strategy, including the potential for petition denial, with the client in detail, as USCIS may question why L-1B classification was initially sought and accepted and/or why the petitioner did not request L-1A classification prior to the final six months or year of L-1B status. Also note that, if the L-1B was initially admitted as an L-1A and later changed to L-1B, a change back to L-1A can be requested at any time within the five years of the L-1B's stay without regard to the six-month rule.[191]

5. Filing an EB-1 While in L-1B Status

An alternative and perhaps more risky strategy is to file the immigrant visa petition for the multinational manager without first filing an amended L-1A petition. No statute or regulation requires that an L-1A petition first be approved in order for a multinational manager immigrant visa petition to be approved, although approval of the L-1A petition is a relevant factor considered by USCIS when adjudicating the immigrant visa petition.[192]

The client should be advised of the potential pitfalls of this strategy. First, as of this writing, premium processing is not available for multinational manager/executive immigrant visa petitions,[193] so the client may wait up to one year before being notified of the denial of the immigrant visa petition. If the transferee remains in the United States while the immigrant visa petition is pending, then this time would count toward the five-year maximum time limitation, potentially impacting the transferee's continued employment authorization for the preparation and processing times for the labor certification application, immigrant visa petition, and application to adjust status. Second, the client will not be able to recoup the legal and filing fees for a denied petition. Third, USCIS may question why the transferee holds L-1B status if the duties are managerial and why L-1B classification was initially sought and accepted.

6. Dual Intent Considerations

One key advantage of L status is that it permits a worker to simultaneously pursue permanent resident status while continuing to intend to comply with the terms of the

---

[191] "Separate FOIA Requests Uncover L-1 Training Materials and Correspondence" (undated, posted Apr. 26, 2013), AILA Doc. No. 13042663, p. 163.

[192] USCIS, "SOPs for I-140 Processing" (undated, posted Aug. 30, 2007), AILA Doc. No. 07083067.

[193] USCIS, "How Do I Use the Premium Processing Service?" (updated Oct. 26, 2015), https://www.uscis.gov/forms/how-do-i-use-premium-processing-service.

Copyright © 2017. American Immigration Lawyers Association. All rights reserved.

temporary nonimmigrant worker category.[194] As discussed in Volume 1: Chapter Two, "Basic Nonimmigrant Concepts," many nonimmigrant visa categories impose a presumption that a foreign national applying for an immigration benefit intends to immigrate permanently to the United States. For many nonimmigrant visa categories, visa applicants must establish eligibility by demonstrating a foreign residence and strong ties abroad. In contrast, a nonimmigrant in L status may be the beneficiary of an immigrant visa petition or labor certification application without risking denial of an L-1 petition or extension of L status on that basis.[195] An application for an L visa also should not be denied solely because the applicant is the beneficiary of an immigrant visa petition or labor certification application.[196]

Although L nonimmigrants are statutorily permitted to have the dual intent to hold nonimmigrant status and pursue labor certification or immigrant visas, the regulations require that L-1A petitions for owners and major stockholders demonstrate that the transferee's services will be used for a temporary period and that the transferee will be assigned abroad after completion of the U.S. assignment.[197] Further, USCIS has indicated that new office petitions for specialized knowledge employees are reviewed to confirm that the foreign entity remains in operation for the duration of the L-1 petition.[198] For both of these situations, the rationale seems to be to ensure that individual foreign nationals do not abuse the L-1 category by entering the United States "with an intent of closing down the business abroad."[199]

However, the long-standing agency policy has been that a statement of the temporary intent of the petitioner and the transferee is sufficient,[200] and that "adherence to the time limits on a temporary stay in the United States is sufficient to demonstrate temporary intent."[201] The practitioner who receives an RFE on these points may submit a statement, confirming the temporary intent of the petitioner and the transferee and documenting adherence to the L-1 time limitations.[202] The practitioner should also note that, in evaluating the credibility of the statement, USCIS may apply legacy INS policy and consider whether the petitioner has previously sponsored a high proportion of L-1 transferees for permanent residence

---

[194] INA §214(h); 8 CFR §214.2(*l*)(16); 9 FAM 402.12-15.

[195] 8 CFR §214.2(*l*)(16).

[196] DOS Cable No. 91-State 171115 (May 4, 1991), 68 Interpreter Releases 681 (June 3, 1991); 9 FAM 402.12-15.

[197] 8 CFR §214.2(*l*)(3)(vii).

[198] Department of Homeland Security (DHS), Office of Inspector General (OIG), Appendix E, "Comments on OIG Draft Report: A Review of Vulnerabilities and Potential Abuses of the L-1 Visa Program" (Jan. 2006), https://www.oig.dhs.gov/assets/Mgmt/OIG_06-22_Jan06.pdf.

[199] *Id.*

[200] 52 Fed. Reg. 5738 (Feb. 26, 1987).

[201] 56 Fed. Reg. 31553 (July 11, 1991).

[202] *Matter of [name not provided]*, SRC 99 041 54850 (AAU Oct. 30, 2000), 23 Immig. Rptr. B2-25; *Matter of [name not provided]*, LIN 99 174 51090 (AAU Sept. 26, 2000), 23 Immig. Rptr. B2-15.

Copyright © 2017. American Immigration Lawyers Association. All rights reserved.

and whether the petitioner employs many foreign nationals without employment authorization.[203]

7. International Travel While Permanent Residence Is Pursued

USCIS guidance indicates that international travel is permitted for L nonimmigrants and their dependents in any stage of sponsorship for permanent residence.[204] Previously, L-1 transferees could not travel internationally during the time period between filing an application to adjust status and receipt of a USCIS receipt notice for the application to adjust status, as failure to present the USCIS receipt notice for the application to adjust status, together with the passport and L visa, when applying for admission to the United States was considered to be abandonment of the application to adjust status.[205] However, the current policy indicates that there should be no restriction of international travel and re-admission to the United States in L status during this time period, and applicants for admission in L status are no longer required to present receipt notices for the applications to adjust status.[206]

The practitioner should note, however, that parole of a foreign national into the United States pursuant to advance parole is treated differently than admission of a foreign national in L-1 status. If presented with both an advance parole and an L-1 visa, a U.S. Customs and Border Protection (CBP) inspector, not the foreign national, will make the decision as to whether the traveler will be admitted as an L-1 or paroled in to the United States.[207] An individual who has both an L visa and an advance parole need only present one or the other.[208] Thus, the attorney should consider the relative advantages of the L-1 versus the advance parole, and advise the foreign national accordingly.

Unless the individual has no or limited eligibility left on L status, the L visa will usually be the better choice. First, if for any reason the adjustment of status application is denied, he or she will then be left without a status if the last entry was under an advance parole. Second, if the L-1 principal is traveling alone, and L-2 dependents are still in the United States, once the principal enters on an advance parole, it can call into question whether the dependents have any status left, since their statuses derive from the principal's. Third, "[a]ll persons presenting an Advance

---

[203] 52 Fed. Reg. 5738 (Feb. 26, 1987).

[204] 72 Fed. Reg. 61791 (Nov. 1, 2007), AILA Doc. No. 07103165.

[205] Former 8 CFR §245.2(a)(4)(ii)(C).

[206] 72 Fed. Reg. 61791 (Nov. 1, 2007).

[207] "AILA Liaison CBP Meeting Minutes with Supplemental Committee Notes" (Nov. 21, 2014), AILA Doc. No. 15020541; "AILA/CBP Liaison Meeting Minutes" (Apr. 16, 2105), AILA Doc. No. 16021030.

[208] "AILA/CBP Liaison Meeting Minutes" (Apr. 16, 2105), AILA Doc. No. 16021030, p. 6 ("If the person does not wish to use [advance parole], he should not present it").

Copyright © 2017. American Immigration Lawyers Association. All rights reserved.

Parole ... are routinely referred to secondary for verification of the document and to verify their validity."[209]

B. The Transferee Was a Contractor Abroad

In most cases, the transferee should have been directly employed by the foreign company and on that company's payroll. But the transferee may still have gained the qualifying employment when employed as a contractor to the foreign company. The best scenario is if the transferee was an independent contractor placed with the foreign company, or if the contractor established a company solely for his or her own contracting activities, and during the contract assignments, the transferee remained completely under the control of the foreign company.[210] In this situation, the contracting company is not a stand-alone business, but merely administers accounts receivable, payroll, and benefits on behalf of the one employee.[211]

It is also possible to obtain L-1 status if the contractor was employed by an outside company, which is not wholly owned and controlled by the contractor.[212] The contractor's services must have been continuously and exclusively provided to the foreign transferring company. Also, the foreign transferring company, not the consulting company that placed the individual, must have had right of control over the consultant.[213] Other factors that may be considered include selection and engagement of the individual, source of remuneration, and power of dismissal.[214] It is advisable to discuss this issue in depth with the client and warn the client that the L-1 petition may be denied, as USCIS may determine that the contractor was an employee of the consulting company and not of the foreign transferring company,[215] because the consulting company hired and placed the consultant, paid the consultant's wages, and had authority to terminate the placement.[216] In addition, a determination that there was no employment relationship between the consultant and the foreign

---

[209] "AILA Liaison CBP Meeting Minutes with Supplemental Committee Notes" (Nov. 21, 2014), AILA Doc. No. 15020541, p. 16.

[210] 8 CFR §274a.1(j); *Matter of Smith*, 12 I&N Dec. 772 (1968) (holding that direct employment relationship between the sponsoring company and the employee is necessary); 9 FAM 402.12-12; M*atter of [name not provided]*, A27 422 499 (AAU Dec. 15, 1987), 5 Immig. Rptr. B2-103.

[211] *Matter of Smith*, 12 I&N Dec. 772 (1968) (noting that direct payment by a company, that is responsible for all payroll deductions and taxes, is indicative of proper employment relationship).

[212] 8 CFR §274a.1(j).

[213] *Matter of Pozzoli*, 14 I&N Dec. 569 (Reg'l Comm'r 1974) (holding that the right of control is the most important factor in determining whether an employment relationship exists).

[214] *Id.*

[215] NAFTA Handbook (Nov. 1999), "L-1 Nonimmigrant Pursuant to NAFTA, Requirements for Admission,"14-1 INS Manuals Scope (stating that the "most common types of business relationships which are not qualifying under the L category are those based on contractual, licensing, and franchise agreements"); *Matter of Church Scientology Int'l*, 19 I&N Dec. 593 (BIA 1988).

[216] A. Paparelli, A. Tafapolsky, T. Chiappari, S. Cohen, and S. Yale-Loehr, "It Ain't Over Till It's Over: Immigration Strategies in Mergers, Acquisitions and Other Corporate Changes" (Oct. 15, 2000), 5 Bender's Immigr. Bull. 848.

Copyright © 2017. American Immigration Lawyers Association. All rights reserved.

transferring company may arise from reverse application of the guidance of the L-1 Visa Reform Act of 2004, where an L-1B petition may be approved for a transferee who will be placed at a third-party worksite only if control and supervision remain with the petitioner.[217] If the L-1 petition must clearly demonstrate an employment relationship only between the transferee and the U.S. petitioner, then it may also be said that an L-1 petition where the beneficiary was a contractor for the foreign company must clearly demonstrate the employment relationship between the contractor and the foreign company, including the "right of control," the "authority to engage," and the "authority to discharge."[218]

C. The Transferee Will Be Employed in a New Office

If the transferee will come to the United States to open or work in a new office that has been "doing business" in the United States through a parent, branch, affiliate, or subsidiary for less than one year,[219] then additional requirements apply.[220] These petitions may be subjected to closer scrutiny,[221] and a higher proportion of RFEs may be issued by USCIS for these petitions.[222]

Therefore, for new office L-1 petitions, strategy and timing considerations should be discussed with the client to ensure that the transferee's services are immediately required in the United States, given the increased scrutiny of new office L-1 petitions. If the transferee does not need to work in the United States in the near future,[223] then it may be wise to prepare to file the L-1 petition after the U.S. entity has been in operation and "doing business" for at least one year, so the new office requirements do not apply. However, where the business is not yet up and running, or is only barely developed, the new office provisions can help to qualify for the L-1 where otherwise the situation may not meet the standards.

1. Doing Business for Less Than One Year

In discussing whether the U.S. entity has been doing business in the United States for at least one year, the practitioner should confirm that there has been "regular, systematic, and continuous provision of goods and/or services by a qualifying organization," and not only the "presence of an agent or office."[224] A business that is

---

[217] USCIS Policy Memorandum, "L-1B Adjudications Policy," PM-602-0111 (Aug. 17, 2015).

[218] 9 FAM 402.12-12.

[219] 8 CFR §214.2(l)(1)(ii)(F).

[220] 8 CFR §214.2(l)(3)(v) and (v).

[221] "Minutes of INS/AILA Adjudications Liaison Meeting" (Sept. 30, 1997), AILA Doc. No. 97110459.

[222] AILA Liaison/VSC Agenda Item Q&As (Jan. 24, 2007), AILA Doc. No. 07021465.

[223] For a discussion of what constitutes "employment" in the U.S., see Volume 1: Chapter Two, "Basic Nonimmigrant Concepts."

[224] 8 CFR §214.2(l)(1)(ii)(H).

Copyright © 2017. American Immigration Lawyers Association. All rights reserved.

older than one year, but had stopped operations for a long period and then was reactivated, may be treated as a new office.[225]

However, USCIS has taken the position that a business that had been in operation for more than one year, but had not previously been related to the foreign company, may not be treated as a new office, even if the company is newly acquired and not yet strong enough to support a manager or executive,[226] and its adjudicators have been trained to that effect.[227] That being said, the wording of the training materials leaves some room for interpretation: "If the petitioner purchases and takes over the management of an established business *that is already staffed and supporting an executive or managerial employee*, the petition should not be treated as that for a 'new office'...."[228] (emphasis added). This phrasing suggests that, if the business is not staffed and capable of supporting an executive or manager, new office treatment might still be available.

The regulatory definition can be cited to support treatment of a newly acquired existing business as a new office if the organization of which the foreign entity is a part has not otherwise been operating in the United States: "New office means an *organization* which has been doing business in the United States through a parent, branch, affiliate, or subsidiary for less than one year"[229] (emphasis added). It could be said that, while the petitioner has been doing business for longer, the organization has not.

In determining whether the L-1 petition is for a new office, USCIS will consider the number of employees, the date the entity was established, and the gross and net incomes,[230] as evidenced by tax returns, audited financial statements, or other financial documents.[231] Other helpful evidence include documents that detail the goods or services provided, such as contracts, documents that demonstrate payment for goods or services, names of the companies or clients to which the petitioner provides goods or services,[232] invoices, letters of credit,[233] documents that detail

---

[225] "Separate FOIA Requests Uncover L-1 Training Materials and Correspondence" (undated, posted Apr. 26, 2013), AILA Doc. No. 13042663, p. 159.

[226] *Matter of [name and file number not provided]* (AAO, Jan. 29, 2003) AILA Doc. No. 16090607.

[227] "Separate FOIA Requests Uncover L-1 Training Materials and Correspondence" (undated, posted Apr. 26, 2013), AILA Doc. No. 13042663, p. 158.

[228] *Id.*

[229] 8 CFR §214.2(*l*)(1)(F).

[230] "NSC Liaison Q and As" (Feb. 1999), AILA Doc. No. 99031841. USCIS indicated that import/export companies in particular frequently document few employees and lower income, and that therefore USCIS closely evaluates whether the U.S. entity has been "doing business."

[231] *Matter of [name not provided]*, A29 662 740 (AAU Nov. 3, 1993), 12 Immig. Rptr. B2-101.

[232] *Matter of [name not provided]*, LIN 99 174 51090 (AAU Sept. 26, 2000), 23 Immig. Rptr. B2-15.

[233] S. Wehrer and A. Paparelli, "From the Beginning: Agile Immigration Advocacy for New Businesses" (undated), http://www.seyfarth.com/dir_docs/publications/AttorneyPubs/From%20the%20Beginning.pdf.

Copyright © 2017. American Immigration Lawyers Association. All rights reserved.

business activities undertaken by the U.S. entity,[234] payroll records, or letters from chambers of commerce or foreign investment associations.

Further, the business activities undertaken by the U.S. entity may have been for the benefit of the foreign parent company,[235] as consulting or liaison services to a foreign company.[236] These activities should be explored with the client as well, as they may provide a satisfactory explanation and background of meeting the "doing business" requirement.[237]

Moreover, there are concerns of abuse of the L-1 category for new offices and concerns of abuse of the L-1 category overall:

> "USCIS adjudicators we interviewed expressed a desire for more written guidance on how to adjudicate L-1 petitions. When questioned in more detail, however, it became clear that the underlying issue troubling them is their perception that the category is subject to fraud and abuse, rather than lack of guidance.... An adjudicator cannot be certain that a beneficiary will work as a personnel manager if approved, or as just another salesperson. No document can be requested that will prove the future activities of the beneficiary. A beneficiary's entitlement to the classification is based on, among other factors, their future conduct.... [T]he appearance of foreign companies establishing branches in the United States offices and then driving American workers out of their jobs with transplanted competitors led Congress to address the body shop issues in the L-1 Visa Reform Act of 2004."[238]

2. Documenting a Business Plan

Frequently, adjudicators closely scrutinize new office petitions,[239] so this type of L-1 petition should be strengthened by providing details, if applicable, regarding how the U.S. business will provide products or services other than outsourced labor at third-party worksites, how it plans to staff the new office with U.S. workers, and how the L-1 assignment benefits the long-term goals of the U.S. business.

The following is a non-exhaustive list of the factors considered by USCIS in new office L-1 petitions:

- "Amount of investment;
- "Intended personnel structure;
- "Product or service to be provided;

---

[234] *Matter of [name not provided]*, LIN 94 028 50814 (AAU Nov. 30, 1994), 14 Immig. Rptr. B2-26.

[235] *Id.*

[236] 52 Fed. Reg. 5738 (Feb. 26, 1987).

[237] *Matter of [name not provided]*, LIN 94 028 50814 (AAU Nov. 30, 1994), 14 Immig. Rptr. B2-26.

[238] R. Skinner, "Review of Vulnerabilities and Potential Abuses of the L-1 Visa Program," Department of Homeland Security, Office of Inspector General (Jan. 2006), https://www.oig.dhs.gov/assets/Mgmt/OIG_06-22_Jan06.pdf.

[239] *Id.*

Copyright © 2017. American Immigration Lawyers Association. All rights reserved.

- "Physical premises; and
- "Viability of the foreign operation."[240]

As L-1 petitions for transferees who will open or work at new offices are subject to closer scrutiny, in part because the "analysis in a new office situation … is inherently prospective,"[241] practitioners are advised to provide detailed information on these considerations. Although the regulations require that the petition explain the personnel structure, nature of the intended business, and physical premises of the U.S. office, in contrast, the amount of investment and viability of the foreign operations are not mentioned by the implementing regulations.[242] These details are factors that may, nonetheless, be evaluated by the adjudicating officer. In order to maximize the likelihood of L-1 petition approval, practitioners should gather this information from the client and provide it to USCIS when filing the petition in an effort to avoid an RFE or petition denial. In particular, the lease agreements for the office space of the new U.S. business must be for at least one year,[243] and virtual offices and post office boxes are unacceptable.[244] The heightened review of L-1 petitions for new offices may continue through the visa application phase, as consular officers may investigate the legitimacy of the foreign company through site visits.[245]

Further, newly established technology companies are subject to the same type of review as other new office L-1 petitions, so the L-1 petition should document its "comprehensive business plan, adequate investment by the foreign company, and sufficient physical premises to support a managerial/executive position within the next year," if applicable.[246] Despite their "great potential," technology petitioners and "start-ups" do not receive any additional favorable consideration, "because the benefit being sought is based on proposed business activity."[247] But "an adjudicator may exercise his discretion when accepting varying forms of documentation to establish the burdens set forth above."[248]

---

[240] "NSC Processing Guidelines" (June 9, 2000), AILA Doc. No. 00060909.

[241] Department of Homeland Security (DHS), Office of Inspector General (OIG), Appendix E, "Comments on OIG Draft Report: A Review of Vulnerabilities and Potential Abuses of the L-1 Visa Program" (Jan. 2006), https://www.oig.dhs.gov/assets/Mgmt/OIG_06-22_Jan06.pdf.

[242] 8 CFR §214.2(*l*)(3)(v).

[243] "AILA/ISD Liaison Q&As" (Oct. 15, 1998), AILA Doc. No. 98101958; "AILA-TSC Liaison Meeting Minutes" (Jan. 26, 1999), AILA Doc. No. 99021758; "Michigan AILA-CBP Liaison Q&As" (May 5, 2006*)*, AILA Doc. No. 06052650.

[244] "Michigan AILA-CBP Liaison" Q&As (May 5, 2006), AILA Doc. No. 06052650.

[245] "AILA-DOS Visa Office Liaison Meeting Agenda" (Oct. 15, 2003), AILA Doc. No. 03102043; DHS OIG, "A Review of Vulnerabilities and Potential Abuses of the L-1 Visa Program" (Jan. 2006), https://www.oig.dhs.gov/assets/Mgmt/OIG_06-22_Jan06.pdf.

[246] "AILA-VSC Liaison Minutes" (Mar. 28, 2000), AILA Doc. No. 00040671.

[247] *Id.*

[248] *Id.*

Copyright © 2017. American Immigration Lawyers Association. All rights reserved.

As a practical matter, having a well-written and detailed business plan is becoming increasingly important to obtain approval of a new office L-1 petition. This will either need to be produced by the client, or an outside vendor company can be engaged to assist with drafting the business plan. The plan needs to have detailed strategies and targets, as well as growth timelines, in order for the petition to be successful. In addition, it is important that the client understand the importance of growing the business in accordance with the business plan set forth in the new office petition. If hiring and other planned activities have not taken place during the initial one-year approval provided in new office L-1 petitions, USCIS will often deny the L-1 extension petition as discussed in more detail below.

Although USCIS had previously taken the position that "any newly incorporated business, even a subsidiary of an established company, is subject to the new office regulations," even for "subsidiaries of well-established, major corporations,"[249] this may no longer be the case. New offices created by established businesses may not be required to comply with all of the new office requirements stipulated in 8 CFR §214.2(*l*)(3)(v), as long as the petitioning company can demonstrate that it is already able to "support the services of a full-time manager or executive."[250] New offices that "are fully staffed and fully operational may be processed as 'normal' L-1 petitions in the discretion of the Center Director."[251] The new office may be part of an initiative to seek business diversification, so the foreign company and new U.S. office may manufacture different products or provide different services.[252] If the transferee will work in a new office created by an established business or group of companies, then evidence of the history and ongoing existence of the international business, as well as evidence of how the U.S. company can support a manager or executive, should be provided. The existence of this guidance, as well as the understanding that a new office transferee may be responsible for some day-to-day activities of the U.S. business discussed below, demonstrates, to a certain degree, how the new office petition is a more liberal provision of the immigration laws.

3. Documentation for a Manager or Executive Coming to a New Office

For a managerial or executive assignment, the petition should include documents to evidence the following considerations, at a minimum:

- "Sufficient physical premises to house the new office have been secured";

- The transferee has a year of qualifying employment as a manager or executive;

- The transferee's U.S. assignment will involve executive or managerial authority over the new operation; and

---

[249] "AILA/ISD Liaison Q&As" (Oct. 15, 1998), AILA Doc. No. 98101958.

[250] P. Zulkie and E. McGovern, "Practice Advisory—New Company L-1 Petitions" (Feb. 10, 1999), AILA Doc. No. 99021057.

[251] *Id.*

[252] "Michigan AILA-CBP Liaison Q&As" (May 5, 2006), AILA Doc. No. 06052650.

Copyright © 2017. American Immigration Lawyers Association. All rights reserved.

- Within a year of the petition's approval, the United States operation will support an executive or manager. This requirement must be met with documents that provide the following evidence:

  - The intended nature of the new U.S. office, with descriptions of the scope of the entity, its organizational structure, and its financial goals;
  - The size of the financial investment in the United States and the financial ability of the foreign company to pay the beneficiary and to commence doing business in the United States; and
  - The organizational structure of the foreign company. [253]

The requirements of an L-1A manager or executive of a new office differ from those of a standard L-1A manager or executive. First, the new office manager or executive must have been employed as a manager or executive during the qualifying employment abroad; a specialized knowledge employee may not obtain L-1A status to open or work at a new office.[254] Second, the government has acknowledged that an L-1A manager or executive at a new office "will be more than normally involved in day-to-day operations during the initial phases of the business."[255] Indeed, the regulations indicate an understanding that the requirement that the L-1A manager or executive of a new office perform primarily managerial or executive duties is unrealistic.[256] Nevertheless, the manager or executive "must also have authority and plans to hire staff and have wide latitude in making decisions about the goals and management of the organization,"[257] and the petitioning company must demonstrate that it will be able to support a manager or executive, within one year of L-1 petition approval, through evidence of "the proposed nature of the office describing the scope of the entity, its organizational structure and its financial goals."[258]

However, USCIS has previously denied new office L-1 petitions for failure to establish sufficient staff to perform the non-managerial and non-executive job duties, even when the petition indicates that the new office will employ additional staff within the first year of active operation, because the number of staff to be hired was deemed to be insufficient to allow the transferee to focus on managerial or executive

---

[253] 8 CFR §214.2(*l*)(3)(v).

[254] 8 CFR §214.2(*l*)(3)(v).

[255] 9 FAM 402.12-11(B).

[256] 52 Fed. Reg. 5738, 5740 (Feb. 26, 1987); Department of Homeland Security (DHS), Office of Inspector General (OIG), Appendix E, "Comments on OIG Draft Report: A Review of Vulnerabilities and Potential Abuses of the L-1 Visa Program" (Jan. 2006), https://www.oig.dhs.gov/assets/ Mgmt/OIG_06-22_Jan06.pdf, recognizing the "'anomaly' with respect to the opening of new offices in the U.S. since 'foreign companies will be unable to transfer key personnel to start-up operations if the transferees cannot qualify under the managerial or executive definition.'" *See also Matter of Z-C-, LLC*, ID# 16354 (AAO Apr. 28, 2016), noting that "the regulations recognize that a designated manager or executive responsible for setting up operations will be engaged in a variety of activities not normally performed" at that level.

[257] 9 FAM 402.12-11(B). *Accord., Matter of Z-C-, LLC*, ID# 16354 (AAO Apr. 28, 2016).

[258] "AILA Liaison/VSC Agenda Item Q&As" (Jan. 24, 2007), AILA Doc. No. 07021465.

Copyright © 2017. American Immigration Lawyers Association. All rights reserved.

duties after the first year.[259] USCIS has also denied a new office L-1 petition by requiring that the petitioner demonstrate how the manager or executive will primarily perform managerial or executive duties, instead of the new office standard of being able to support a manager or executive within a year's time.[260] Therefore, the L-1 new office petition should clearly explain how the hiring of additional staff within the first year of operation will be achieved, how these employees will relieve the manager or executive of administrative and/or operations duties, and how the manager or executive will focus on managerial or executive duties, such as overall business planning and expansion, as otherwise the L-1 petition may be denied.[261]

4. Documentation for a Specialized Knowledge Employee Coming to a New Office

For a specialized knowledge assignment, the petition should include documents to evidence the following considerations, at a minimum:

- "Sufficient physical premises to house the new office have been secured";
- The U.S. entity is or will be a parent, branch, affiliate, or subsidiary of the foreign entity; and
- The U.S. petitioner has the financial ability to pay the beneficiary and to commence doing business in the United States.[262]

Of these requirements, the final requirement may be most closely reviewed by USCIS, as it is feasible to secure the physical premises and establish the qualifying relationship before the U.S. business commences operations. If payment of the salary depends on the success of the U.S. business, however, the "inherently prospective" nature of the new office petition could be emphasized, and USCIS could determine that the projections of the L-1 petition are unsatisfactory.[263] To avoid such a determination, the evidence provided to demonstrate the amount of investment in the U.S. business may also demonstrate the U.S. company's ability to commence operations and pay the transferee's salary, such as if the investment structure has already incorporated the salary as a cost of doing business and as a liability in the balance sheet.[264] In contrast, relying upon accounts receivable from the new business to pay the salary may be detrimental in demonstrating that the transferee's employment in the United States is sustainable.[265]

5. Sufficient Physical Premises

---

[259] "AILA/INS Texas Service Center Liaison Meeting Minutes" (Sept. 8, 1998), AILA Doc. No. 99021758.

[260] *Matter of [name not provided]*, LIN 94 193 50721 (AAU Mar. 27, 1994), 14 Immig. Rptr. B2-114.

[261] "AILA/INS Texas Service Center Liaison Meeting Minutes" (Sept. 8, 1998), AILA Doc. No. 99021758.

[262] 8 CFR §214.2(*l*)(3)(vi).

[263] *Matter of [name not provided]*, LIN 94 193 50721 (AAU Mar. 27, 1995), 14 Immig. Rptr. B2-114.

[264] *Matter of [name not provided]*, LIN 94 237 51240 (AAU Oct. 4, 1995), 15 Immig. Rptr. B2-30.

[265] Department of Homeland Security (DHS), Office of Inspector General (OIG), Appendix E, "Comments on OIG Draft Report: A Review of Vulnerabilities and Potential Abuses of the L-1 Visa Program" (Jan. 2006), https://www.oig.dhs.gov/assets/Mgmt/OIG_06-22_Jan06.pdf.

Copyright © 2017. American Immigration Lawyers Association. All rights reserved.

Both managerial/executive and specialized knowledge new office documentation must include evidence that sufficient physical premises have been secured to house the new office.[266] Recent years have seen a marked trend toward personnel that work from their homes,[267] but USCIS regulations and adjudications have yet to embrace this change, at least in the new office context. While noting that "[t]here may be cases in which residential premises or home office would satisfy the regulatory requirements," commercial zoning, license to operate a business from a dwelling, or evidence of the landlord having authorized business use is still demanded.[268] If a petitioner is intent upon relying on a home office as its premises, it will still need to specify the amount and type of space needed to operate the business, describe its proposed staffing levels, and show how the space will accommodate those levels. If the plan does not anticipate a growth in staffing such that, for a manager or executive, the beneficiary will be relieved from day-to-day duties, the petition is unlikely to succeed.[269]

6. Continued Existence of Foreign Company

An additional point of concern to USCIS for L-1B new office petitions is the continued existence of a foreign company, to which the transferee could return following the U.S. assignment.[270] This issue is inconsistent with the concept of dual intent, to hold nonimmigrant status and pursue permanent residence, which is permitted for L-1 transferees,[271] as discussed below. The policy rationale for this requirement seeks to prevent "complete relocation of foreign businesses to the United States," so that the transferee has a foreign company to which to return following completion of the U.S. assignment, such as if the U.S. company fails to become viable after one year.[272] For these petitions, it is necessary to provide evidence of the ongoing business presence and activity of the foreign company, such as contracts of sale or service, employment contracts, and long-term leases or property deeds to house the foreign company. In addition, the U.S. petitioner and foreign entity must remain qualifying organizations in order for an L-1 extension to be approved, as discussed below.

The owner or stockholder of a petitioning company is eligible for L-1 status, as such ownership and remuneration in commission or dividends do not preclude a bona fide employment relationship with the U.S. company as a separate legal entity.[273] For

---

[266] 8 CFR §214.2(*l*)(3)(v)(A) and (vi)(A).

[267] M. Jacoby, "The Trend Toward Working from Almost Anywhere" (Sept, 8, 2015), http://www.huffingtonpost.com/margaret-jacoby/the-trend-toward-working-_b_8106428.html.

[268] *Matter of Z-C-, LLC*, ID# 16354 (AAO Apr. 28, 2016).

[269] *Id.*

[270] *Id.*

[271] 8 CFR §214.2(*l*)(16).

[272] 52 Fed. Reg. 5738 (Feb. 26, 1987).

[273] *Matter of [name not provided]*, EAC 87 096 0107 (AAU Feb. 26, 1988), 5 Immig. Rptr. B2-125. *See also Matter of M*, 8 I&N Dec. 24 (A.G. 1958) (rejecting position that sole owner of sponsoring company of visa
Cont'd

Copyright © 2017. American Immigration Lawyers Association. All rights reserved.

such assignments, "the petition must be accompanied by evidence that the beneficiary's services are to be used for a temporary period and evidence that the beneficiary will be transferred to an assignment abroad upon the completion of the temporary services in the United States."[274] This regulatory requirement also conflicts with the dual intent permitted for L-1 transferees, as discussed below.[275]

7. Extensions of New Office Petitions

After initial approval of this L-1 petition for one year,[276] the petitioner may file an extension, with the following documents:

- Evidence that the U.S. and foreign entities remain qualifying companies;

- Evidence that the United States entity has been doing business, by providing goods and/or services on a regular, systematic, and continuous basis;

- A statement of the duties performed by the transferee during the previous year and the duties the beneficiary will perform under the extended petition;

- "A statement describing the staffing of the new operation, including the number of employees and types of positions held accompanied by evidence of wages paid to employees when the beneficiary will be employed in a managerial or executive capacity; and

- "Evidence of the financial status of the United States operation."[277]

An L-1 extension on behalf of a transferee who was employed at a new office differs from an extension filed by a U.S. entity that has been doing business for at least one year. The regulations require that the specific foreign company that previously employed the transferee remain in operation and remain a qualifying organization in order for an L-1 extension to be approved on behalf of a transferee

---

petition, when visa petition is executed by another executive of the sponsoring company, is identical to individual filing visa petition on his own behalf; noting absence of statutory prohibition against corporation filing visa petition on behalf of foreign national who is owner of corporation; rejecting position that approval of such a petition frustrates the purpose of the immigration statute; and stating the "general rule ... that a corporation is a legal entity distinct from its sole stockholder" (citing *Dalton v. Bowers*, 287 U.S. 404, 408, 410 (1932))); *Matter of Tessel, Inc.*, 17 I&N Dec. 631 (Acting Assoc. Comm'r 1981) (noting that qualification for one preference category, such as an investor, does not preclude qualifying for another status, such as multinational manager); *Matter of Aphrodite*, 17 I&N Dec. 530 (Comm'r 1980) (commenting that although *Matter of M* addressed an immigrant visa petition, "its conclusions are equally valid in other areas of concern where an employer/employee relationship needs to be examined by the Service"; noting that the term used in the immigration statute for L-1 petitions is "employed" as opposed to "employee"; and approving the L-1 petition).

[274] 8 CFR 214.2(*l*)(3)(vii). *See also Matter of [name not provided]*, WAC 05 014 54339 (AAO Mar. 24, 2005), AILA Doc. No.

[275] *Cf. Matter of [name not provided]*, EAC 87 096 0107 (Feb. 26, 1988), 5 Immig. Rptr. B2-125, where the decision did not mention or discuss the temporary nature of the assignment or the intent to transfer the stockholder abroad following the U.S. assignment.

[276] 9 FAM 402.12-11(D).

[277] 8 CFR §214.2(*l*)(14)(ii).

Copyright © 2017. American Immigration Lawyers Association. All rights reserved.

who opens or works at a new office in the United States.[278] This provision seeks to deter complete transfer of the company's operations from abroad to the United States, as if the U.S. business is ultimately unsuccessful, the transferee should be able to return abroad.[279]

During adjudication of the extension, USCIS may "compare the business plan presented in the new office petition with the company's track record during this one-year start-up period, and require the petitioner to explain to the agency's satisfaction any deviations from the business plan presented in the original L-1 new office petition."[280]

For L-1A extensions after the first year, the U.S. company must demonstrate adequate staff to perform the operational and administrative tasks, such that the transferee is able to focus on managerial or executive duties.[281] In particular, the existence of other managerial, executive, or senior-level staff at the new office after the initial year of doing business may weaken the extension, as USCIS may take the position that these employees squeeze out the transferee from performing managerial or executive duties.[282] However, an L-1A extension petition may also be challenged for lack of other managers or other personnel to show that the transferee is, after the one-year period, free from performing primarily hands-on duties. At this point, the same analysis as with L-1A petitions in general applies, including demonstrating that the individual is a function manager and/or that the regular operations are performed through other personnel that can include contractors or staff located abroad.[283]

However, USCIS has sometimes demonstrated flexibility and favorable consideration when adjudicating new office extensions. For example, there is no statutory extension of the initial "start-up" period, but such an extension has been granted in "fairness to petitioner."[284] An extension may also be approved for a U.S.

---

[278] 8 CFR §214.2(*l*)(14)(ii)(A).

[279] 52 Fed. Reg. 5738 (Feb. 26, 1987).

[280] Department of Homeland Security (DHS), Office of Inspector General (OIG), Appendix E, "Comments on OIG Draft Report: A Review of Vulnerabilities and Potential Abuses of the L-1 Visa Program" (Jan. 2006), https://www.oig.dhs.gov/assets/Mgmt/OIG_06-22_Jan06.pdf.

[281] Department of Homeland Security (DHS), Office of Inspector General (OIG), Appendix E, "Comments on OIG Draft Report: A Review of Vulnerabilities and Potential Abuses of the L-1 Visa Program" (Jan. 2006), https://www.dhs.gov/xoig/assets/katovrsght/OIG_06-22_Jan06.pdf.

[282] *Matter of [name not provided]*, LIN 94 117 52032 (AAU Oct. 25, 1994), 13 Immig. Rptr. B2-274 (stating that "as the petitioning entity already employs a president and an executive assistant, it cannot be found that the United States operation, at this time, can support an additional executive or managerial position").

[283] *Matter of [name and file number not provided]* (AAO Sept. 13, 2013), AILA Doc. No. 13091857.

[284] Although there is no such statutory provision, because beneficiary was "the leader of a small but viable enterprise," a 12-month extension was granted following approval of the initial new office L-1 petition. *Matter of [name not provided]*, PHO-N-4883 (AAU Feb. 20, 1987), 4 Immig. Rptr. B2-172. Note that in this case, the petitioner employed 11 individuals and had a gross annual income of $450,000, and the decision stated that additional extensions would not be approved without "evidence of employment in a qualifying capacity and a substantial expansion of the enterprise outlined above." *See also Matter of [name not provided]*, LOS-N-54995 (AAU Feb. 11, 1987), 4 Immig. Rptr. B2-163.

Copyright © 2017. American Immigration Lawyers Association. All rights reserved.

business that initially had financial difficulties during the first year of operation but then experienced an increase in business towards the end of the first year.[285] Alternatively, a second new office L-1 petition may be approved for one year, to allow a second U.S. business to get started and become operational,[286] although such petitions have been denied where the first business did not fully develop during the initial year.[287] However, the risks of requesting such extensions should be discussed in detail with the client, as extensions of new office L-1 petitions have been denied for failure to demonstrate that the U.S. entity has been doing business for the previous year.[288]

For new office extensions where the U.S. business has not developed as much as anticipated, the approaches discussed above may also be helpful. The extension petitions should provide detailed information to demonstrate business activity, continued viability of the U.S. operation, and continued ability to pay the salaries of transferees who will remain in the United States. Such evidence may be in the form of contracts of sale or services, wire transfers of additional investment funds (whether from the foreign company or from private investors), and revised business plans and proposals. In addition, the business activities undertaken by the U.S. entity may have been for the benefit of the foreign parent company.[289] If that was the case, then the extension petition should demonstrate how the business activities fit within the vision or initiatives of the parent company or the overall group of companies and how the business activities would take root in the United States.

Because it is possible for an L-1 extension to be denied without an RFE, even after the initial L-1 new office petition was approved, it is critical to provide documentation that adequately demonstrates satisfaction of each of these requirements.[290] It is important to note that if the evidence submitted with the L-1 extension "clearly establishes that a substantive requirement cannot be met," then the extension may be denied without an RFE.[291] Therefore, although this type of denial is not common, the practitioner should not rely upon issuance of an RFE that will request additional information to correct deficiencies; the practitioner should prepare in advance to gather and present probative evidence for each material element with the initial extension filing to avoid an immediate denial.[292] Practitioners also should bear in mind that the initial new office L-1 petition may not be part of the record an adjudicator is given when adjudicating the L-1 extension.

---

[285] "Michigan AILA-CBP Liaison Q&As" (May 5, 2006), AILA Doc. No. 06052650.

[286] Id.

[287] Matter of [name not provided], SRC 05 161 50948 (AAO Apr. 5, 2007).

[288] Matter of [name not provided], WAC 04 103 54305 (AAO Aug. 17, 2005).

[289] Matter of [name not provided], LIN 94 028 50814 (AAU Nov. 30, 1994), 14 Immig. Rptr. B2-26.

[290] "NSC Teleconference Q&As on Business Product Line" (Apr. 27, 2006), AILA Doc. No. 06050510.

[291] Id.

[292] Id.

Copyright © 2017. American Immigration Lawyers Association. All rights reserved.

D. Petitioner Is a Small Company

Small companies that wish to transfer a foreign national employee to the United States face several additional difficulties. Anecdotal evidence indicates that this is frequently true whether the U.S. or foreign entity is small or a new office. First, as noted above, small companies, such as technology companies and "start-ups," do not receive any favorable consideration merely for being a small company or for having an entrepreneurial or adventurous business model.

Although USCIS in 2011 initiated a program titled Entrepreneurs in Residence (EIR) to, among other things, help adjudicators attain a better understanding of the needs and challenges of small and start-up ventures,[293] it is not clear that that goal was achieved.[294] Indeed, both statistics on denial rates for L-1 petitions during and immediately after the initiative[295] and the experience of practitioners indicate little to no positive impact on adjudications, with denials continuing to increase. It appears that USCIS's takeaway from the experience was more that the law needs to change than that any adjustment in adjudicative attitude was needed.[296]

Second, the difficulty in verifying the proper corporate relationship between the petitioner and the foreign entity is heightened when the petitioner is not a large company: "Unless the company is well-known, adjudicators might find the submitted documents insufficient to establish the facts" of the corporate relationship.[297] The corporate relationship must be confirmed in order to "prevent individuals or groups from creating shell companies in one country or the other, or falsifying the relationship between two legitimate companies, to transfer otherwise ineligible aliens

---

[293] USCIS, "Entrepreneurs in Residence Initiative Summary" (May 2013), https://www.uscis.gov/sites/default/files/USCIS/About%20Us/EIR/EntrepreneursinResidence.pdf.

[294] CIS Ombudsman, "Annual Report 2013" (June 27, 2013), AILA Doc. No. 13062846, https://www.dhs.gov/sites/default/files/publications/cisomb_2013_annual_report%20508%20final_1.pdf, noting "it is difficult to measure the impact of the EIR initiative on the quality and consistency of USCIS employment-based adjudications."

[295] National Foundation for American Policy, "L-1 Denial Rates Increase Again for High Skill Foreign Nationals" (Mar. 2015), AILA Doc. No. 15031861, http://nfap.com/wp-content/uploads/2015/03/NFAP-Policy-Brief.L-1-Denial-Rates-Increase-Again.March-20151.pdf, indicating that the L-1 denial rate for the first year of the program, fiscal year 2012, was 30 percent, rising to 34 percent in fiscal year 2013, and 34 percent in fiscal year 2014 (fiscal year 2014 ran from October 1, 2013, to September 30, 2014, and thus was the first full year after conclusion of the initiative). The denial rate had been rising for the past eight years, jumping from 7 percent in fiscal year 2007 to 22 percent in fiscal year 2008, and steadily rising each year ever since. However, the statistics do not differentiate based on company size.

[296] USCIS, "Entrepreneurs in Residence Initiative Summary" (May 2013), https://www.uscis.gov/sites/default/files/USCIS/About%20Us/EIR/EntrepreneursinResidence.pdf, stating "each existing immigration pathway contains unique challenges for entrepreneurs. Though proposed changes to regulations and statutes were beyond the scope of USCIS's EIR effort, the team's work highlighted barriers that should be addressed to ensure the United States continues to attract and retain the world's most innovative entrepreneurs."

[297] R. Skinner, "Review of Vulnerabilities and Potential Abuses of the L-1 Visa Program," Department of Homeland Security, Office of Inspector General (Jan. 2006), https://www.oig.dhs.gov/assets/Mgmt/OIG_06-22_Jan06.pdf.

Copyright © 2017. American Immigration Lawyers Association. All rights reserved.

to the United States," but adjudicators expressed concern that documents were falsified and that regulatory authorities abroad could not be contacted to authenticate the documents or the corporate existence of the foreign entity.[298] It is not difficult to understand how an adjudicator may wish to err on the side of caution and deny an L-1 petition filed by a small company rather than request that resources be expended to investigate the foreign company's existence.[299]

Third, experience has shown that USCIS reviews the petitioner's information on Form I-129, including gross and net revenues, number of employees, and type of business, to confirm that the company is established and viable. Experience has also shown that petitioners with low numbers of employees, low revenues, or net losses instead of net profits are questioned as to the authenticity of the need for the transferee's services and as to the availability of funds to pay the wage offered.

In a general sense, the heart of the issue may be credibility.[300] As stated by one commenter, "There is a widespread belief that the L visa was created so that large American companies with international operations could move foreign executive talent into the pre-existing U.S. offices of those companies."[301] Smaller companies are disadvantaged by this "widespread belief," as the same commenter noted abuse of "windows of opportunity," whereby petitioners may "transfer themselves to the United States."[302] A petitioner that is a large company may not transfer itself, as its corporate identity would be well-established and separate from its corporate officers, but the corporate identity of a small company may not be as reputable, recognized, or believable to a USCIS adjudicator. While a large company will not fall under suspicion of having been "created solely for the purpose of establishing an L-1 qualifying intra-company relationship,"[303] something that adjudicators are trained as being prohibited, a small company may be seen this way.

Finally, as a practical matter, the credibility issue may be intertwined with branding or name-recognition of a known, successful, established brand-name, business, or product. An adjudicator may be less inclined to believe that a large corporation would risk its brand name status for a single transferee but may accept

---

[298] *Id.*

[299] *Id.*

[300] *Matter of [name not provided]* EAC 87 219 0379 (AAU Feb. 24, 1988), 5 Immig. Rptr. B2-131; R. Skinner, "Review of Vulnerabilities and Potential Abuses of the L-1 Visa Program," Department of Homeland Security, Office of Inspector General (Jan. 2006), https://www.oig.dhs.gov/assets/ Mgmt/OIG_06-22_Jan06.pdf.

[301] R. Skinner, "Review of Vulnerabilities and Potential Abuses of the L-1 Visa Program," Department of Homeland Security, Office of Inspector General (Jan. 2006), https://www.oig.dhs.gov/assets/ Mgmt/OIG_06-22_Jan06.pdf.

[302] *Id.*

[303] "Separate FOIA Requests Uncover L-1 Training Materials and Correspondence" (undated, posted Apr. 26, 2013), AILA Doc. No. 13042663, p. 96. No citation is given, so it is not clear why USCIS believes this to be prohibited.

Copyright © 2017. American Immigration Lawyers Association. All rights reserved.

that a smaller company has little or nothing to lose in requesting L-1 status on behalf of an employee who comprises a significant portion of the combined workforce of the petitioner and the foreign entity. For this reason, L-1 petitions filed by smaller companies should take care to explain the nature of the service or product to be provided or produced and should specifically mention contracts or relationships with established businesses, if possible.

For example, an L-1 petitioner is small and less known as a provider of supply chain solutions through the application of proprietary algorithms, but it was awarded a test contract with a Fortune 500 company that is a retailer of non-perishable and grocery goods. The L-1 petition should explain the nature of the contract, the results-based demands of the Fortune 500 company, the value of the initial contract, the estimated value of any renewed contracts, and the specific reasons why the beneficiary's services are necessary to satisfy the Fortune 500 company and to ensure that a subsequent contract will be awarded.

The closer scrutiny is increased for new office petitions filed by smaller companies. As noted by a commenter, "[a]ny foreign company can use the L visa to send employees to the United States to open a new office. This opens a window of opportunity for the owners of a business abroad to send themselves and their families to the United States to live, work, and study."[304] One U.S. embassy reports:

> "L-1 applicants claim they are being sent to open new offices or subsidiaries in the United States. It is impossible to verify these claims as the new company need only show to DHS [the Department of Homeland Security] that it has a leased business space and possesses company registration. When we subsequently investigate 'existing' U.S. entities, we often find that the U.S. office never actually existed in the true sense, or that it is no longer doing business."[305]

L-1 extensions for transferees who opened new offices may be challenging as well, because the petitioner must also demonstrate that the new office has developed into being able to support a full-time manager or executive,[306] as discussed under "The Transferee Will Open a New Office," above.

E. Impact of Closure of a Foreign Entity

The regulations require that the U.S. petitioner and a foreign entity do business as an employer in the United States and abroad for the duration of the L-1 petition.[307] But the foreign entity need not be the same foreign company that previously employed the transferee; the transferring company may be closed, as long as there

---

[304] R. Skinner, "Review of Vulnerabilities and Potential Abuses of the L-1 Visa Program," Department of Homeland Security, Office of Inspector General (Jan. 2006), https://www.oig.dhs.gov/assets/Mgmt/OIG_06-22_Jan06.pdf.

[305] Id.

[306] Matter of [name not provided], LOS-N-54995 (AAU Feb. 11, 1987), 4 Immig. Rptr. B2-163.

[307] 8 CFR §214.2(l)(1)(ii)(G)(2).

Copyright © 2017. American Immigration Lawyers Association. All rights reserved.

remains a foreign qualifying organization to which the transferee could later be assigned following expiration of the L-1 petition.[308] Although an L-1 petition has been approved for a petitioner that did not have foreign parent, subsidiary, affiliate, or branch operations,[309] USCIS has retreated from this generous interpretation.[310] The existence of a foreign entity must be established for an initial L-1 petition and for any subsequent extensions to cover the duration of the transferee's stay in the United States.[311] In promulgating the regulations, legacy INS commented that "Congress did not intend the L category to accommodate the complete relocation of foreign businesses to the United States."[312]

It is important to note, however, that the requirements differ for new office L-1 petitions and extensions. For new office L-1 extensions, the specific foreign entity that employed the transferee abroad must remain in business throughout the initial year and during the pendency of any L-1 extension.[313]

It also is important to note that USCIS views closure of the transferring company differently for purposes of eligibility for permanent residence under the employment-based, first preference category for multinational managers and executives, as discussed under "Planning for Permanent Residence" above.

F. Employment That Is Other Than Full-Time Employment in L-1 Status

While USCIS regulations require that the one continuous year of qualifying employment abroad have been full time,[314] they do not contain an explicit requirement of full-time employment for the U.S. assignment. The State Department has indicated a belief that "the intent of the L-1 classification" is full-time employment,[315] but it clearly is permissible to engage in L-1 employment even if the employment is not full time under a variety of scenarios. As stated by regulation, a transferee may "reside abroad and regularly commute to the United States to engage in part-time employment,"[316] and a transferee in this situation may be exempted from the limitations of L-1 maximum period of stay, as discussed below. The practitioner should note that the regulation seems to liken residence abroad and commuting with part-time employment, an

---

[308] 52 Fed. Reg. 5738 (Feb. 26, 1987); *See also* "Separate FOIA Requests Uncover L-1 Training Materials and Correspondence" (undated, posted Apr. 26, 2013), AILA Doc. No. 13042663, at 170, stating that the "foreign qualifying entity need not be the exact same one as the one that employed the L-1 while he or she was abroad."

[309] *Matter of Chartier*, 16 I&N Dec. 285 (BIA 1977).

[310] A. Paparelli, A. Tafapolsky, T. Chiappari, S. Cohen, and S. Yale-Loehr, "It Ain't Over Til It's Over: Immigration Strategies in Mergers, Acquisitions and Other Corporate Changes" (Oct. 15, 2000), 5 Bender's Immigr. Bull. 848.

[311] 52 Fed. Reg. 5738 (Feb. 26, 1987).

[312] *Id.*; 9 FAM 402.12-10(C).

[313] 8 CFR §214.2(*l*)(14)(A).

[314] 8 CFR §214.2(*l*)(1)(i).

[315] 9 FAM 402.12-14(G).

[316] 8 CFR §214.2(*l*)(12)(ii). *See also* 9 FAM 402.12-14(G).

Copyright © 2017. American Immigration Lawyers Association. All rights reserved.

interpretation which may contradict the general interpretation of "part-time" employment. In the context of H-2A and H-2B petitions, DOL defines part-time employment as "a job requiring hours or days of work less than those normal or prevailing for the occupation in the area of intended employment, *e.g.*, less than seven hours a day or 35 hours a week."[317]

In addition, an L-1 transferee, who has been granted maternity leave and who intends to gradually resume a full-time work schedule, may return to work on a part-time basis.[318] Further, a transferee may maintain valid nonimmigrant status while not performing full-time work, such as during vacation, family leave, or medical leave, as long as the transferee remains employed by the L-1 company.[319] In these situations, the L-1 employer does not need to notify USCIS of the change.[320]

G. Impact of Labor Disputes on Canadian and Mexican Transferees

A U.S. company may not use the L-1 category to transfer a Canadian or Mexican national to the United States if the Secretary of Labor certifies or otherwise informs the Attorney General that "a strike or other labor dispute involving a work stoppage of workers is in progress" at the worksite,[321] and if the transferee's entry would "adversely affect the settlement of a labor dispute" or "the employment of any person involved in the dispute."[322] If both of these conditions are satisfied, then the L-1 petition on behalf of a Canadian or Mexican national transferee may be denied.[323] If an L-1 petition has been approved already, but the transferee "has not yet entered the United States, or has entered the United States but not yet commenced employment," then the petition approval "may be suspended, and an application for admission on the basis of the petition may be denied."[324]

The United States must consider and apply the "strikebreaker" provision when the L-1 petition is adjudicated by USCIS, when the transferee applies for an L-1 visa, and when the transferee applies for admission to the United States at a port of entry.[325]

---

[317] Appendix to legacy INS Operations Instruction (OI) 214.2(h)(1). *See also* Department of Labor (DOL) Memorandum, B. Farmer, "Standards to Determine Full Time Employment" (Apr. 13, 1993), http://www.aila.org/Content/default.aspx?docid=14903.

[318] USCIS, E. Hernandez (Mar. 9, 2004), AILA Doc. No. 04031165. Note that Mr. Hernandez's discussion referenced the Family and Medical Leave Act of 1993. The letter did not prohibit other part-time L-1 employment, if such employment is permitted pursuant to another federal law.

[319] *Id.*

[320] *Id.*

[321] 8 CFR §214.2(*l*)(18); "INS Final Rule on Entry under NAFTA," 63 Fed. Reg. 1331 (Jan. 9, 1998), AILA Doc. No. 98010960.

[322] INA §214(j); NAFTA Implementation Act, Pub. L. No. 103-182, 107 Stat. 2057.

[323] 8 CFR §214.2(*l*)(18)(i).

[324] *Id.*

[325] Legacy INS, "NAFTA Implementation of Strikebreaker Provisions" (Oct. 17, 1994), AILA Doc. No. 94101780.

Copyright © 2017. American Immigration Lawyers Association. All rights reserved.

The certification or notification from the Secretary of Labor "may include the locations and occupations affected by the strike."[326]

The intent of the provision is to "protect[] the domestic labor force and permanent employment in all three countries" that are signatory to the North American Free Trade Agreement (NAFTA) Treaty.[327] An L-1 petition may not be denied because of a strike or labor dispute if the Secretary of Labor does not certify or otherwise inform the Attorney General of the strike or labor dispute,[328] and L-1 transferees may be admitted "to engage in activities which do not affect adversely a labor dispute."[329] Moreover, a transferee who engages in authorized L-1 employment and subsequently participates in the strike or labor dispute cannot be deemed to be failing to maintain lawful L-1 status because of past, present, or future participation, whether or not the strike or labor dispute has been certified by the Department of Labor.[330] Such a transferee should, however, comply with the terms and conditions of L-1 status, as violation of status and physical presence in the United States following the expiration of the authorized period of stay are grounds for removal, and the transferee's status and authorized period of stay "is not modified or extended in any way by virtue of his or her participation in a strike or other labor dispute involving a work stoppage of workers."[331]

H. Calendar Expiration and Follow-Up

A practitioner should request and obtain copies of all visas, entry stamps, and I-94s from the transferee and dependent family members, if applicable, as soon as possible after admission to the United States. This allows the practitioner to review the status documents, verify them for accuracy, and arrange for corrections of any erroneous status documents.

Calendaring and monitoring the petition start and end dates for clients allows a practitioner to proactively notify clients well in advance of the expiration dates. By opening the discussion for extensions and/or amendments, additional value is provided to the client. This also allows the practitioner to ensure that there is enough time to strategize, gather necessary information, and prepare and file the petition, and therefore avoid crises under a fast-approaching deadline. Various software programs that are commercially available to support immigration law practice provide scheduling capabilities. If the immigration software program does not have a status monitoring function, a database program that provides reports for all upcoming expirations should be used. Reports for the upcoming six months should provide

---

[326] *Id.*

[327] Legacy INS, "Final Rule on Entry under NAFTA," 63 Fed. Reg. 1331 (Jan. 9, 1998), AILA Doc. No. 98010960.

[328] 8 CFR §214.2(*l*)(18)(ii).

[329] Legacy INS, "NAFTA Implementation of Strikebreaker Provisions" (Oct. 17, 1994*)*, AILA Doc. No. 94101780.

[330] 8 CFR §214.2(*l*)(18)(iii).

[331] *Id.*

Copyright © 2017. American Immigration Lawyers Association. All rights reserved.

enough time for the practitioner and the client to plan a course of action. If it is not technologically possible to run the reports this way, maintenance of a "tickler" folder (the "tickler" folder should be checked regularly) or setting reminders in an email calendar system may work as an alternative.

I. Finding More Time in the United States

1. Grace Periods

On November 18, 2016, DHS promulgated a final regulation that adds two types of grace periods for L nonimmigrants. The first is a 10-day grace period to the beginning and the end of the validity period of the L-1 authorized stay,[332] similar to what has long existed for the H-1B category.[333] Employment is not authorized during this period—it is strictly a consideration to allow the nonimmigrant to make preparations for starting life in the United States and for departing or changing status.[334] It should be noted that DHS currently requires in the H-1B context that the grace period be specified by CBP on the I-94 admission record in order to be effective.[335] The final rule is silent on this point, but presumably the same qualification would apply to nonimmigrants admitted in L status. Anecdotally, the grace period is rarely added to the period of authorized stay indicated on Form I-94, unless the nonimmigrant insists upon it at entry. Accordingly, the additional 10-day grace period should not be presumed. It is important to review the I-94 record to confirm that the period of admission includes the grace period added. Assuming that it was included, it is also important to ensure that both the employer and the L-1 nonimmigrant understand that employment during that period is prohibited.

The second type of grace period added to the L category by the November 18, 2016, regulation provides a transitionary period allowing nonimmigrants to manage interruptions in their L employment. This second form of grace period can be used only once during each approved petition validity. It allows individuals whose employment ends prior to the expiration of their authorized stay to remain in the United States lawfully for the shorter of 60 days or to the end of the existing period of authorized stay indicated on the I-94 record.[336] This allows the beneficiary to wind up affairs and depart or, if desired, to seek other employment and request a change of status if needed and eligible. The individual is not able to work during this grace period, unless otherwise authorized.[337]

---

[332] 81 Fed. Reg. 82398 (Nov. 18, 2016).

[333] 8 CFR §214.2(h)(13)(i)(A).

[334] *Id.*

[335] Inspector's Field Manual, 15(h)(1).

[336] 80 Fed. Reg. 81899 (Dec. 31, 2015), adding 8 CFR §214.1(*l*)(ii).

[337] *Id.*

Copyright © 2017. American Immigration Lawyers Association. All rights reserved.

2. Recapture of L-1 Time

When calculating the maximum period of authorized stay in L-1 status, only dates that the transferee has been physically present in the United States should be included.[338] Any time period of at least 24 hours spent outside the United States, for whatever reason, may be recaptured. The employer may request an extension of the worker's L-1 status to recapture this time.[339] A petition to recapture and extend L-1 time should provide independent documentary evidence of presence outside the United States. Examples of such evidence may include copies of entry and exit stamps in the passport, copies of I-94 records, and copies of flight itineraries, plane tickets, or boarding passes.[340] Providing a chart that details the date of departure, date of return, and type of corroborating evidence should assist the USCIS adjudicating officer.[341]

The L-1 extension may be approved for all periods where physical presence outside the United States is confirmed by independent evidence, and ineligibility for recapture of a particular time period should not affect eligibility for recapture of another time period.[342] USCIS will not issue an RFE concerning the time periods without satisfactory evidence,[343] so care should be taken to provide all available documentation when filing the L-1 extension to recapture time.

Dependents are also eligible for L-2 extensions to match the period of stay of the L-1 principal foreign national, as long as the dependents "are accompanying or following to join the beneficiary in the U.S."[344] Therefore, it is possible that L-2 dependents will have more than five or seven years of physical presence in the United States if the family members remained in the United States while the L-1 transferee traveled extensively for business.

An L-1 worker cannot "park" dependent L-2 family members in the United States while spending most of his or her work time outside the United States. If it appears to USCIS that L-2 dependents are not accompanying or joining the transferee in the United States or that the L-2 dependents are seeking to evade the limitations of the L nonimmigrant category, then L-2 extension may be denied, limited, or revoked.[345]

---

[338] USCIS, M. Aytes, "Procedures for Calculating Maximum Period of Stay Regarding the Limitations on Admission for H-1B and L-1 Nonimmigrants (AFM Update AD 05-21)" (Oct. 21, 2005), AILA Doc. No. 05110363.

[339] Id.

[340] Id. Note that the burden of proof remains with the petitioner to establish eligibility for the L-1 recapture and extension.

[341] Id.

[342] Id.

[343] Id.

[344] Id.

[345] Id.

Copyright © 2017. American Immigration Lawyers Association. All rights reserved.

3. H-1B Change of Status for L-1B Transferees

A nonimmigrant worker in L-1B status whose services will be retained indefinitely in the United States may require immigration procedures that take significant periods of time to complete. This may be due to the delay inherent in obtaining labor certification or by immigrant visa retrogression, as discussed above, and in Volume 2: Chapter One, "Basic Immigrant Visa Concepts." Accordingly, an L-1B worker may be unable to file the applications to adjust status before the maximum five years ends and may have to depart the United States. Employers should explore filing an H-1B change of status petition for such workers. If the worker is maintaining H-1B status instead of L-1B status and the labor certification application is filed before the fifth-year anniversary in H-1B status, the employee should be eligible for continued H-1B extensions pursuant to AC21 until obtaining permanent residence.[346]

It is advisable to plan and prepare for this strategy well in advance for two reasons. First, time spent in L-1 status counts towards the six-year maximum of H-1B status,[347] so the important fifth-year H-1B anniversary is identical to the fifth year expiration of L-1B status. Second, the significant demand for H-1B visa numbers, as well as the lottery system for determining which petitions receive these numbers,[348] means that there is no guarantee that the employee will be granted H-1B status at all. Starting to request the H-1B change of status while the employee is in the third or fourth year in L-1B status will allow for multiple opportunities to be selected in the H-1B lottery, if needed. The lottery is run in each individual fiscal year, however, so filing numerous change of status petitions over consecutive years does not increase the likelihood of one particular employee being selected in the H-1B lottery in a given year.

Another strategy to explore is recapturing L-1 time to extend the fifth-year deadline. This approach also allows an L-1B worker to continue temporary employment in the United States for a period that extends beyond five years from the transferee's initial admission to the United States in L-1 status. As discussed above, the transferee may recapture L-1B time for any days spent physically present outside the United States. For more details on the requirements of the H-1B category, see Volume 1: Chapter Seven, "H-1B Visas and Status."

---

[346] For a detailed discussion on AC21 extensions, see Volume 1: Chapter Seven, "H-1B Status," and Volume 2: Chapter One, "Basic Immigrant Visa Concepts."

[347] 8 CFR §214.2(*l*)(12)(i).

[348] There is a statutory cap on the number of available H-1B visa numbers. When the demand for H-1B visa numbers exceeds the supply of available numbers, USCIS selects which petitions will receive a number by a random lottery system. For a detailed discussion of the H-1B category, including the lottery system, see Volume 1: Chapter Seven, "H-1B Visas and Status."

Copyright © 2017. American Immigration Lawyers Association. All rights reserved.

4. Other Strategies After the Maximum Period of Authorized Stay Has Been Exhausted

If these other strategies are unavailable, then it may be possible to file an application to adjust status concurrently with the immigrant visa petition.[349] The labor certification must be approved, and the concurrent petition and application must be filed before the transferee reaches the end of his or her five-year period of eligibility for L-1B status. The transferee would then be able to remain lawfully present in the United States as an applicant for adjustment of status and, once the authorized period of L status expires, would no longer hold nonimmigrant status.

If the transferee has not filed an application to adjust status by the time of exhausting the seven– or five-year maximum period of authorized stay, then the transferee must depart and remain outside the United States for at least one year before being eligible to apply for L-1 status again.[350]

The practitioner should note that, as with the initial L-1 petition, "brief trips" to the United States will not interrupt the continuity of employment and physical presence, but time spent in the United States may not count toward the one-year absence requirement.[351] Although there is no standard for what constitutes a "brief trip," the USCIS Vermont Service Center (VSC) has indicated that a two-week stay is more likely to be considered a "brief trip" than a six-week stay.[352] In the event that an individual needs to visit the Unites States for six weeks, such as for a training program, the VSC suggests that the training program be divided into three two-week long programs.[353]

5. Exceptions to the Maximum Period of Stay Rule

The exceptions to the five– and seven-year maximum stay rule are as follows:

- The transferee did not reside continually in the United States and the transferee's L-1 employment was seasonal, intermittent, or for an aggregate of six months or less per year; or

- The transferee resides abroad and regularly commutes to the United States to engage in part-time employment.[354]

The petitioner and transferee bear the burden to provide "clear and convincing proof" of qualifying for these exceptions, and the exceptions are not available to the L-1 transferee if his or her L-2 dependents have resided continuously in the United

---

[349] 67 Fed. Reg. 49561 (July 31, 2002); USCIS, M. Aytes, "AFM Update: Chapter 22: Employment-based Petitions (AD03-01)" (Sept. 12, 2006), AILA Doc. No. 06101910.

[350] 8 CFR §214.2(*l*)(12)(i); "NSC Processing Guidelines" (June 9, 2000), AILA Doc. No. 00060909.

[351] 8 CFR §214.2(*l*)(12)(i).

[352] "Minutes of AILA-VSC Liaison Teleconference" (Mar. 1, 2006), AILA Doc. No. 06052617.

[353] *Id.*

[354] 8 CFR §214.2(*l*)(12)(ii); 9 FAM 402.12-16(E).

Copyright © 2017. American Immigration Lawyers Association. All rights reserved.

States in L-2 status.[355] In these situations, the L-1 maximum periods of stay may not apply, as the transferee would never accrue a single year in L-1 status and therefore not be subject to the seven– or five-year limitations.[356]

IV. Process

A. Preparing and Filing the Individual Petition

The following documents should be prepared and filed for the L-1 petition:

- Cover letter
- Form G-28
- Form I-907, if applicable
- Form I-129
- Supplement L
- Support statement from U.S. company
- Foreign company statement
- Evidence of the qualifying relationship between the companies

For all forms, "N/A" should be filled in for all questions left blank. As discussed in Volume 1: Chapter Two, "Basic Nonimmigrant Concepts," all documents should be signed in black or blue ink.[357]

1. Form G-28

The L-1 petition is a petition filed by the employer, and therefore the employer's information must be provided in Questions 5 through 12 on the G-28.[358]

If there is limited time to prepare and file the petition before the U.S. assignment is to begin, such as if the forms are emailed to and printed by the client, this form may be printed on plain white paper. However, as discussed in Volume 1: Chapter Two, "Basic Nonimmigrant Concepts," some practitioners prefer to submit the Form

---

[355] FAM 402.12-16(E); *Matter of [name not provided]*, WAC 89 213 00349 (AAU Sept. 24, 1992), 10 Immig. Rptr. B2-85. *Cf. Matter of [name not provided]*, EAC 87 219 0379 (AAU Feb. 24, 1988), 5 Immig. Rptr. B2-131.

[356] 8 CFR §214.2(*l*)(12)(ii).

[357] While USCIS previously advised signing documents in blue ink (*See, e.g.,* "TSC Liaison Minutes" (Aug. 13, 2000), AILA Doc. No. 00090703), in recent years it has more frequently stated a preference for black ink (*See, e.g.,* "Instructions for Notice of Entry of Appearance as Attorney or Accredited Representative" (May 5, 2106), https://www.uscis.gov/sites/default/files/files/form/g-28instr.pdf; "USCIS FY2016 H-1B Webpage Updated" (Mar. 12, 2015), AILA Doc. No. 15031362). In practice, however, the USCIS mailroom sometimes rejects forms signed in black ink because the signatures are incorrectly concluded to be photocopies, so signing in blue ink can be beneficial despite the USCIS instructions.

[358] "Instructions for Notice of Entry of Appearance as Attorney or Accredited Representative" (May 5, 2106), https://www.uscis.gov/sites/default/files/files/form/g-28instr.pdf.

Copyright © 2017. American Immigration Lawyers Association. All rights reserved.

G-28 on blue paper in order to help the G-28 be identified more easily in the USCIS mailroom.[359]

2. Form I-907

If the client wishes a response on an L-1 petition (approval, denial, or RFE) within 15 calendar days, then the client may pay USCIS an additional $1,225 for premium processing. This request may be filed concurrently with the L-1 petition, or the attorney or the client may request premium processing after the petition has been filed, by submitting Form I-907 with the petition's receipt notice, as discussed in Volume 1: Chapter Two, "Basic Nonimmigrant Concepts."

In 1990, the INA was amended to require USCIS review of L-1 petitions within 30 days,[360] but processing times for L-1 petitions frequently significantly exceed this time frame.[361] USCIS may provide a response to the L-1 petition within 30 days, but the response may be an RFE. In this case, adjudication should be completed within 30 days after the requested evidence has been received.[362] It may be possible to file a mandamus action against USCIS for failing to comply with the statutory mandate to adjudicate L petitions within 30 days,[363] but the costs of the action may significantly exceed the cost of the premium processing fee.

As discussed above, USCIS has not always complied with the statutory requirement[364] to adjudicate L-1 petitions in 30 days, and the 30 days would not include mailing time of the approval notice from USCIS to the attorney or the mailing time from the attorney to the transferee. The practitioner should discuss the timing considerations with the client and plan accordingly to ensure that the L-1 assignment may begin on schedule.

3. Form I-129

Part 1: L-1 petitioners will invariably be companies or organizations, so item 2, "Company or Organization Name" rather than item 1, "Legal Name of Individual Petitioner," should be completed. Other information on the U.S. company, including address, contact person, contact person's telephone number and email address, and Federal Employer Identification Number (FEIN), should be provided.

Part 2: In item 1, designate either "L-1A" or "L-1B." For initial L-1 petitions, "New employment" should be checked in item 2, and for most cases, consular notification should be requested in item 4. As discussed in Volume 1: Chapter Two, "Basic

---

[359] "VSC Practice Pointer: G-28s" (Sept. 4, 2008), AILA Doc. No. 08090469.

[360] IMMACT90, Pub. L. No. 101-649, §206(b)(2); 9 FAM 402.12-7(B).

[361] *See, e.g.,* USCIS "Vermont Processing Time Reports," http://www.aila.org/infonet/processing-time-reports/vsc; "AILA Liaison/VSC Agenda Item Q&As" (Sept. 20, 2006), AILA Doc. No. 06092266.

[362] "Report of AILA-NSC Teleconference" (Dec. 5, 2001), AILA Doc. No. 02011738.

[363] Additional mandamus documents can be found in AILA's *Immigration Litigation Toolbox* (AILA 5th Ed. 2016), https://agora.aila.org/product/detail/2890.

[364] INA §214(c)(2)(C) added by IMMACT90, Pub. L. No. 101-649, Sec. 206(b)(2).

Copyright © 2017. American Immigration Lawyers Association. All rights reserved.

Nonimmigrant Concepts," USCIS should then notify the Kentucky Consular Center (KCC), and the consulate abroad should then be able confirm petition approval when the transferee applies for an L-1 visa. A duplicate photocopy of the entire petition must be included in the filing for USCIS to notify KCC of the approval.

Change of status from another nonimmigrant status may be available to beneficiaries of L petitions. A request may be made to amend and extend the transferee's status if, for example, he or she is present in the United States on a business or pleasure trip when the petition is filed. Change of status is available only to those nonimmigrants who have continuously maintained the previous nonimmigrant status.[365] Violation of the terms and conditions of nonimmigrant status, such as unauthorized employment while in B status, is considered to be failure to maintain valid nonimmigrant status.[366] In addition, USCIS may raise fraud and misrepresentation concerns if a change of status application is filed less than 30 days after entry into the United States in B status or if there has been unauthorized employment. Strategies and issues relating to change of status petitions are discussed in more detail in Volume 1: Chapter Two, "Basic Nonimmigrant Concepts." For further discussion of the accrual of unauthorized employment, its impact on subsequent petitions, and strategies to address accrual of unauthorized employment, see Volume 1: Chapter Two, "Basic Nonimmigrant Concepts."

If change of status is requested, however, the expiration date of the beneficiary's B status should be calendared. Ideally, the L-1 change of status petition will be approved before the beneficiary's B status expires, and premium processing may make this scenario possible. The practitioner may wish to advise the client on the intricacies of situations in which the initial status expires before the change of status petition is approved. As discussed in Volume 1: Chapter Two, "Basic Nonimmigrant Concepts," a timely filed request for change of status will allow the beneficiary to remain lawfully present during pendency of the change of status petition, but a change of status petition will not extend the beneficiary's nonimmigrant status.[367] If the change of status petition is approved, then the transferee will be accorded a new period of authorized stay. The beneficiary would not have accrued unlawful presence.[368]

In the event that a change of status petition is ultimately denied because the beneficiary engaged in unauthorized employment or because the petition is deemed

---

[365] 8 CFR §§248.1(a) and (b).

[366] 8 CFR §214.1(e). *See also* "USCIS's SOPs for I-539 Processing" (undated, posted Sept. 7, 2007), AILA Doc. No. 07090760.

[367] Legacy INS, J. Podolny, "Interpretation of 'Period of Stay Authorized by the Attorney General' in determining 'unlawful presence' under INA section 212(a)(9)(B)(ii)" (Mar. 27, 2003), AILA Doc. No. 03042140.

[368] Legacy INS, M. Pearson, "Period of stay authorized by the Attorney General after 120-day tolling period for purposes of section 212(a)(9)(B) of the Immigration and Nationality Act (the Act). (AD 00-07)" (Mar. 3, 2000), AILA Doc. No. 00030774; AFM 40.9(b)(2)(G) and (b)(3)(B).

Copyright © 2017. American Immigration Lawyers Association. All rights reserved.

frivolous, then all of the time that the foreign national remained in the United States after expiration of the initial grant of admission will be considered unlawful presence.[369] Due to lengthy processing times, it is possible for a foreign national to accrue 180 days of unlawful presence while awaiting adjudication of a change of status petition. Accrual of more than 180 days of unlawful presence will trigger the three-year bar to re-entry to the United States upon departure from the United States. Accrual of more than 365 days of unlawful presence will trigger the 10-year ban to re-entry to the United States upon departure from the United States. For a detailed discussion of the three– and 10-year bars, see Volume 1: Chapter Two, "Basic Nonimmigrant Concepts," and Volume 2: Chapter One, "Basic Immigrant Visa Concepts." Even if the denial is not based upon unauthorized employment or the petition being deemed frivolous, there is a possibility of accrual of at least a few days of unlawful presence during the time required for the decision to arrive in the mail. Premium processing of the L-1 petition may be requested to address this issue.

A request for extension of B status may be filed while awaiting adjudication of an L-1 petition, but practitioners should be aware that USCIS may question the validity of a B-1 extension request and whether a legitimate B purpose is being served or fulfilled.[370] Nevertheless, if this strategy is pursued, then following expiration of the initial nonimmigrant status, the change of status petition should be updated with the receipt notice for the timely filed extension request, to evidence that the beneficiary has not failed to maintain lawful nonimmigrant status.[371]

Part 3: Information about the beneficiary, including name, alternate names, date of birth, Social Security number if any, country of birth, country of birth and country of nationality, and passport information, should be provided.

The transferee must have a passport that is valid for at least six months from the petition's expiration date; otherwise, he or she is inadmissible and ineligible for nonimmigrant status.[372] If the transferee does not have a passport with sufficient validity, then the following options are available: either delay filing the L-1 petition until a renewed passport is obtained, or file the L-1 petition, have the transferee apply for a renewed passport in the interim, wait for an RFE, and then submit a photocopy of the biographic page of the renewed passport once it is available. For nationals of countries where passport renewal takes months, the second strategy can prevent the petition from being significantly delayed. If the client is willing to pay an additional $1,225 fee to USCIS, the delay caused by the RFE, which might also

---

[369] *Id.*

[370] "AILA-VSC Conference Call Minutes" (Mar. 5, 2008), AILA Doc. No. 08031331.

[371] *Id.* Note that it is not current USCIS policy to apply the "last action rule," as discussed in Volume 1: Chapter Two, "Basic Nonimmigrant Concepts."

[372] INA §212(a)(7)(B)(i). The exceptions to this rule in INA §212(a)(d)(4) are discussed in Volume 1: Chapter Two, "Basic Nonimmigrant Concepts."

Copyright © 2017. American Immigration Lawyers Association. All rights reserved.

be several months, can be addressed by requesting premium processing when submitting the documentation of the renewed passport.

If the transferee is present in the United States on a business trip when the petition is filed, then the I-94 information should be provided, even if the transferee will depart the United States during pendency of the L-1 petition. In this case, consular notification should be requested in Part 2, as discussed above.

Part 4: Regardless of whether consular notification is requested, the foreign address and consular or port of entry information should be completed, in case USCIS decides that a change or extension of status is not warranted. If the petition is requesting change or extension of status, and the beneficiary's family is also present in the United States and requesting the same action, answer "yes" to item 5 and submit a Form I-539 for the dependents with the petition.

With respect to items 8 and 9, keep in mind that, if the beneficiary previously held L-1 or H-1B status, the time in that status will be counted against the total maximum allowable stay unless he or she has been outside the United States for at least one year. Also, because statutory dual intent applies to L-1 status, checking "yes" to item 7 that the employer has ever filed an immigrant petition for the beneficiary should not adversely impact the worker's eligibility for L-1 classification,[373] as discussed above, notwithstanding the parallel intent to eventually seek permanent residence. If the transferee is an owner of the company,[374] however, it may become necessary to document an intent to return abroad, as discussed earlier in this chapter.

Part 5: Information regarding third-party worksites, compensation, dates of intended employment, and business and financial data about the petitioner are included in this section. If the status requested is L-1B, and the beneficiary will be located at an unrelated company's worksite, see the discussion earlier in this chapter about "Placement at Worksite of Another Company."

Part 6: See the discussion in Volume 1: Chapter Two, "Basic Nonimmigrant Concepts," on export control requirements.

Part 7: The petitioner's representative will need to sign the petition, certifying his or her authority to sign on the company's behalf;, certifying under penalty of perjury that he or she has reviewed the petition and it is complete, true, and correct; and acknowledging that a site visit may be made. It is advisable for the attorney to call particular attention to these certifications, and to advise the company's representative to carefully review the petition for accuracy.

Part 8: The attorney completes and signs the preparer's declaration. There is some disagreement among the legal community as to whether an attorney who is submitting a G-28 needs to complete and sign this section, as it refers to "preparers"

---

[373] 8 CFR §214.2(*l*)(16).

[374] 8 CFR §214.2(*l*)(3)(vii).

Copyright © 2017. American Immigration Lawyers Association. All rights reserved.

and an attorney provides much more than preparation, but completing and signing it is the prevalent practice.

4. L Supplement

Information about the sponsoring company and the foreign company, including the corporate relationship between them, should be provided, as well as descriptions of the transferee's foreign and U.S. duties. As discussed earlier in this chapter, if the petitioner must answer "no" to Section 1, item 11, regarding whether the companies currently have the same qualifying relationship as they did during the qualifying employment abroad, this may not be detrimental to the petition, but must be explained and documented.

If the transferee will open a new office in the United States or will be placed at a different company's worksite, then these facts should be disclosed on the form and then explained in detail in the U.S. company statement.

Note that, while a list of prior stays in L or H status is required, the periods in which the beneficiary was in an L-2 or H-4 dependent status need not be listed.

The information requested about the number of employees in the United States, and in H-1B or L-1 status, is to determine whether the employer is subject to additional fees, as discussed under "Fees" below.

5. U.S. Company Statement

This statement should form the bulk of the L-1 petition, as it explains the motivation and reason for the U.S. assignment, as well as how the transferee is qualified for the assignment. The statement should be on the U.S. company's letterhead and signed by a representative of the U.S. company. One format of a support statement is as follows:

- Introduction
- Information about the petitioner
- Discussion of the driving reason for the U.S. assignment
- Discussion of the duties of the U.S. assignment, including an explanation of the percentage of time spent on each duty
- Discussion of the transferee's educational and experience background, including explanation of how the transferee has the critical skills necessary for the assignment, and dates of employment with the foreign employer, as well as an explanation of the percentage of time spent on each duty with the foreign employer
- A statement of the dates for which the L authorization is requested
- A statement of the source and amount of remuneration
- Thank you and conclusion

As discussed above for L-1A petitions, it is important to provide a detailed description of the personnel, functions, and activities managed. Support statements

Copyright © 2017. American Immigration Lawyers Association. All rights reserved.

for L-1B petitions should detail the specialized knowledge held by the transferee, how this specialized knowledge will be applied in the United States, and why the specialized knowledge is needed in the United States.

6. Foreign Company Statement

The foreign company statement serves to confirm that the transferee gained the required year of qualifying employment, so it should be sufficient to copy and paste that section from the U.S. company's support statement. It should be on the letterhead of the foreign company and signed by an appropriate official of that company. Experience has shown that a facsimile or scanned copy of this document is sufficient.

Although USCIS guidance indicates that confirmation of the transferee's qualifications in the petitioner's statement may suffice, the same guidance allows USCIS adjudicators to request additional evidence of qualifying employment in the form of wage and earning statements or an official statement from the foreign company.[375] Practitioners may wish to proactively submit the foreign company statement and/or wage statements demonstrating the qualifying one year of experience to avoid the delay caused by an RFE or by the investigation of the transferee's qualifications by a consular representative abroad.

7. Evidence of the Qualifying Relationship

"Large, established organizations" may submit a statement describing the ownership and control of each company.[376] The statement may be executed by the company's president, corporate secretary, corporate attorney, or another authorized official. The statement may be accompanied by other evidence, such as a copy of the most recent annual report (if the company is publicly traded), copies of filings to the Securities and Exchange Commission, or other documentation that lists the parent and its subsidiaries, such as a report from Dun and Bradstreet, Inc. The blanket L certification may be also presented, if the company has blanket L certification. Blanket L petitions are discussed in detail below.

L-1 petitions for smaller businesses should provide the statement detailed above, as well as additional evidence of the ownership and control of the two organizations.[377] This may be in the form of "records of stock ownership, profit and loss statements or other accountant's reports, tax returns, or articles of incorporation, by-laws, and minutes of board meetings."[378]

L-1 petitions for new offices should provide the statement of ownership and control, as well as "evidence of capitalization of the company or evidence of financial resources committed by the foreign company, articles of incorporation, by-laws, and minutes of board of directors' meetings, corporate bank statements, profit and loss

---

[375] AFM 32.3(e).

[376] AFM 32.3(d).

[377] Id.

[378] Id.

Copyright © 2017. American Immigration Lawyers Association. All rights reserved.

statements or other accountant's reports, or tax returns."[379] A detailed business plan should also be included in the L-1 petition for a new office.

8. Filing Fees

The basic filing fee for a Form I-129, Petition for a Nonimmigrant Worker, is $460. If the petition is accompanied by an extension or change of status request on behalf of dependents, Form I-539 also must be filed, and the fee for that is $370.[380] In addition, a $500 fraud prevention and detection fee is required for the first L-1 petition filed by an employer on behalf of a new employee. The $500 fee is not applicable to extension or amended petitions.

An additional $4,500 fee is required of L petitioners who employ at least 50 employees in the United States, more than 50 percent of whom hold H-1B, L-1A, or L-1B nonimmigrant status.[381] For extended discussion of the application and administration of this fee, see Volume 1: Chapter Seven, "H-1B Visas and Status." The fee is scheduled to sunset on September 30, 2025.[382] This fee should be submitted in a separate check from the filing fee.[383]

9. Bundling of Petitions

If a company is transferring multiple specialized knowledge personnel for a particular project, the L-1B petitions can be submitted to USCIS in a single bundle for consideration together. The petitions must all be from the same petitioner, and the beneficiaries must all be coming from the same foreign entity and working on the same project at the same location, performing the same specialized knowledge duties. L-1A managers' petitions can be included if they will be managing the L-1B personnel on the project.[384]

Each petition in the bundle should be packaged separately with its own fees and supporting materials, with a cover sheet on each clearly labeled "L-1 Bundle" that contains any information to help the adjudicator relate the petitions to one another. Each should be numbered, as in "1 of 10," "2 of 10," etc.[385]

The practitioner should carefully consider the advisability of using this process. Experience in recent years has shown a strong element of randomness to adjudications, particularly of L-1B petitions, resulting in inconsistent results for near-identical situations. The benefit of bundling is that the results are more likely to be consistent. The drawback is that, if the bundle is processed by an adjudicator with a

---

[379] Id.

[380] USCIS, "Filing Fees," https://www.uscis.gov/fees.

[381] Pub. L. No. 114-113 (Dec. 18, 2015).

[382] "Public Law 114-113, Consolidated Appropriations Act, 2016" (Dec. 18, 2016), AILA Doc. No. 15121601.

[383] USCIS, "H and L Filing Fees for Form I-129, Petition for a Nonimmigrant Worker" (Feb. 3, 2016), https://www.uscis.gov/forms/h-and-l-filing-fees-form-i-129-petition-nonimmigrant-worker.

[384] "USCIS Announces Ability to Bundle Filings of L-1 Petitions" (Nov. 3, 2011), AILA Doc. No. 1110330.

[385] Id.

Copyright © 2017. American Immigration Lawyers Association. All rights reserved.

negative view of L-1Bs, the entire project could be scuttled because all the petitions will be denied and none of the needed personnel can be transferred. Moreover, the adjudicator may be less convinced that the position involves specialized knowledge if multiple petitions are submitted simultaneously where each of the beneficiaries holds the same specialized knowledge. Bundling can therefore backfire, weakening the specialized knowledge claim rather than improving the adjudication.

B. Petition Approval

The L-1 petition should be filed in duplicate either with original signatures or an original and a photocopy, with the USCIS Service Center with jurisdiction over the place of employment (and not the headquarters of the U.S. company, if different), as discussed in Volume 1: Chapter Two, "Basic Nonimmigrant Concepts." Practitioners may also find it helpful to write the following in large block letters across the side of the Form I-129: "DUPLICATE PETITION; PLEASE FORWARD TO KCC."

The second set of original documents will be scanned by USCIS and forwarded to DOS to be entered into the Petition Information Management Service (PIMS), as discussed in Volume 1: Chapter Two, "Basic Nonimmigrant Concepts."[386] Following approval of an L petition, USCIS forwards approval notification to the KCC, which in turn creates an electronic record to confirm the petition approval. Although duplicate original documents are not required, preparing and providing them will facilitate the transferee's visa application in the future.[387]

Upon approval of the L-1 petition, USCIS will send the attorney or representative a Form I-797, Notice of Action, confirming approval of the petition, and the company representative will receive a courtesy copy.

C. Visa Application Based on Individual Petition

Following approval of the L-1 petition, the transferee, and any dependent spouse and family members, may apply for L visas at a U.S. consulate abroad, as discussed in Volume 1: Chapter Two, "Basic Nonimmigrant Concepts." The following documents are required for all L visa applications:

- Passport valid for at least six months from the date of visa application and with at least two blank pages;[388]

- Two passport-style photographs;

- Completed and signed electronic version of Form DS-160, Nonimmigrant Visa Application;

---

[386] DOS, "Accessing NIV Petition Information Via the CCD" (Nov. 2007), AILA Doc. No. 08040331; PIMS Processing Update, AILA Doc. No. 08032132.

[387] "PIMS Processing Update" (Mar. 21, 2008), AILA Doc. No. 08032132.

[388] Anecdotal evidence indicates that two blank pages are necessary for a visa application. As a practical matter, this allows room for the visa and the entry stamp to the United States, or, if the first visa is incorrect, room for a second visa after the first visa is cancelled without prejudice.

Copyright © 2017. American Immigration Lawyers Association. All rights reserved.

- Visa application fee;

- Reciprocity fee, if applicable;

- Statement from the petitioner confirming the transferee's continued L-1 employment, if the transferee obtained change of status from another nonimmigrant category; and

- Evidence of familial relationships of dependent spouse and children.

Individual consulates frequently have additional requirements. The website of the U.S. consulate where the applicant will apply for the visa should be consulted prior to scheduling the application interview appointment. DOS does not require that applicants for L visas present either an original Form I-797 approval notice or a copy of the petition and its supporting documents.[389]

The visa will be valid for the period of time prescribed by the visa reciprocity schedules,[390] which can be found on the State Department website.[391] This may mean that the transferee could receive a visa valid for a shorter time period than the L-1 petition, but in many cases it could mean that the visa will be valid for longer than the petition's validity.[392] In either event, CBP at the port of entry should admit the individual until the end date of the L-1 petition and not through the validity date of the L-1 visa, unless his or her passport expires earlier.[393] The individual can apply for admission into the United States only while the petition is valid, even if the visa is valid for a longer period.[394]

For example, Brazilian nationals are eligible for L visas valid for no longer than 24 months. Therefore, even though the underlying L petition may be approved for 36 months, a Brazilian national will be able to obtain an L visa that is valid for only 24 months from the date of visa issuance. Upon application for admission to the United States, however, the Brazilian citizen may be admitted through the petition expiration date up to 36 months.

By contrast, nationals of the United Kingdom are eligible for L visas valid for 60 months, even though an L petition approval will be valid for, at most, 36 months. Upon applying for admission to the United States, British citizens may be admitted through the validity of the L petition, up to 36 months.

---

[389] 9 FAM 402.12-5(B)(a) and 402.12-6(C); "AILA DOS Liaison Q&As" (Apr. 6, 2017), AILA Doc. No. 17041234.

[390] 22 CFR §41.112(b).

[391] State Dept., "Reciprocity and Civil Documents by Country," https://travel.state.gov/content/visas/en/fees/reciprocity-by-country.html.

[392] State Dept., "Visas: Issuance of Full Validity L Visas to Qualified Applicants" 77 Fed. Reg. 8119 (Feb. 14, 2012).

[393] CBP, "Processing of L-1 Nonimmigrants" (Mar. 16, 2009), AILA Doc. No. 10041564.

[394] State Dept., "Visas: Issuance of Full Validity L Visas to Qualified Applicants" 77 Fed. Reg. 8119 (Feb. 14, 2012).

Copyright © 2017. American Immigration Lawyers Association. All rights reserved.

The Petition Expiration Date (PED) provided in the lower right corner of the visa should, however, match the dates of validity of the L petition as stated on the Form I-797 approval notice. The PED helps guide the CBP officer at the port of entry to admit the worker for the correct period of time regardless of whether the L visa will expire earlier or later than the petition approving eligibility for L-1 classification. The practitioner should emphasize to the petitioner and the beneficiary the importance of presenting the original Form I-797 approval notice to the CBP officer at the port of entry.

Upon being admitted to the United States by CBP, the transferee should receive a stamp in the passport indicating L-1 status valid until the end date of the petition, as stated on the approval notice. As discussed in Volume 1: Chapter Two, "Basic Nonimmigrant Concepts," a paper Form I-94 is no longer issued for entries other than by land. Attorneys should advise petitioners and beneficiaries to check the CBP website to obtain the I-94 number and ensure that the worker and any dependents were admitted in the proper category and for an amount of time that matches the date of the petition validity.[395] For all transferees, attorneys should request copies of visas, passport stamps, and I-94 records for all nonimmigrants to ensure that all the admission information is correct. This also allows the attorney to calendar the expiration dates to monitor the status of the worker and the dependents, if any.

The practitioner may also wish to contact clients with employees with shorter visa validity dates well in advance of the visa expiration date to strategize subsequent visa applications, so the transferees may travel internationally and re-enter the United States during the remaining time of petition validity. Those with longer dates will not need to renew their visas after the L petition has been extended, as long as the visa is still valid.[396]

D. Canadian Citizens

As discussed in Volume 1: Chapter Two, "Basic Nonimmigrant Concepts," Canadian citizens do not require visas in order to enter the United States.[397] Canadian citizens may apply for admission with the L-1 approval notice and Canadian passport at the port of entry.[398] Alternatively, under the NAFTA Treaty, Canadian citizens may present a petition for L-1 classification concurrently with an application for admission in L-1 status.[399] In this process, the transferee files the L-1 petition with CBP at a Class A port of entry located on the U.S.-Canada border or at a U.S. pre-flight or pre-clearance station in Canada. An L-1 petition may not be submitted to

---

[395] CBP, "Arrival/Departure Forms: I-94 and I-94W," https://www.cbp.gov/i94.

[396] *Id.*, noting that those with visas valid longer than the initial petition "would not need to apply again for an L visa … if they were to travel outside the United States during the period indicated in the applicable reciprocity schedule."

[397] 8 CFR §212.1(a).

[398] 9 FAM 402.12-7(C).

[399] 8 CFR §214.2(*l*)(17)(i).

Copyright © 2017. American Immigration Lawyers Association. All rights reserved.

CBP at a port of entry in advance of the intended start date of the employment. When presenting a petition to CBP at a Preclearance Office port of entry, the transferee should allow ample time for the petition to be adjudicated before departure of the flight.[400] The CBP officer at the port of entry should confirm the transferee's Canadian citizenship and adjudicate the qualifying relationship between the U.S. company and the foreign company, confirm the transferee gained the year of qualifying employment, confirm the qualifying assignment at the U.S. company, and admit the transferee in L-1 status.[401]

If the CBP officer finds that documentation is lacking, the L-1 petition should be returned, and the beneficiary/applicant should be provided with instructions to obtain the missing documents. The filing fees should not be collected by CBP until the documentary deficiency is overcome. However, if the petition is "clearly deniable," CBP has the authority to collect the fees and deny the petition. If the denial cannot be issued at the port of entry, the petition with a recommendation for denial will be sent to USCIS, which will issue the formal denial.[402]

If the L-1 petition is approved at the port of entry, the transferee's passport will be stamped and, if it is a land port, a paper I-94 will be issued. The approved Form I-129 (or Form I-129S, if an L-1 petition is presented under a blanket L petition, as discussed below) is forwarded to USCIS, where a Form I-797 approval notice is generated,[403] although this process is sometimes delayed.[404] USCIS has stated that:

> "Generally, the I-797 approval notices are issued within a few weeks of receipt of the approved petition from the Border/Port of Entry, but in some instances the petitions are returned to the Border/Port of Entry for specific updates. If 30 days have elapsed, however, since the petition was granted, you may contact the NCSC at 800-375-5283 to follow-up."[405]

Approval notices may not be issued by USCIS for several months.[406] To maximize the likelihood that USCIS will receive the approved petition from CBP in the shortest period of time, L petitions filed with CBP at a port of entry should be accompanied by a pre-paid, U.S. Postal Service Express Mail envelope pre-addressed to the appropriate USCIS Service Center with jurisdiction over the location where the

---

[400] 1 INS Examinations Handbook, Part V, 15-1, 1 legacy INS Inspector's Field Manual (IFM) ch. 15: Nonimmigrants and Border Crossers, 14-1 INS Manuals 15.4

[401] CBP, "NAFTA Guide for TN and L Applicants" (June 2012), AILA Doc. No. 13091643.

[402] CBP, "CBP Standards for Accepting and Adjudicating I-129 Petitions for L-1 Intracompany Transferee Petitions for Canadian Citizens under the North American Free Trade Agreement (NAFTA)" (Jan. 3, 2012), AILA Doc. No. 12011168.

[403] "NSC Liaison Q and As" (Feb. 1999), AILA Doc. No. 99031841.

[404] "AILA Liaison/VSC Teleconference Minutes" (May 30, 2007), AILA Doc. No. 07061171.

[405] "AILA Liaison/VSC Stakeholder Q&A" (Sep. 20, 2010 and updated Oct. 19, 2010), AILA Doc. No. 10101471.

[406] *Id.*

Copyright © 2017. American Immigration Lawyers Association. All rights reserved.

transferee will work.[407] CBP should use the Express Mail envelope to send the approved petition to USCIS.

The practitioner should discuss these timing considerations with the client. The client may wish to postpone any subsequent international travel by the transferee until the approval notice is received, so that the transferee may travel with the approval notice rather than merely a passport stamp, which may come into question particularly for travel to countries other than Canada or Mexico.

The delay in approval notice issuance can also complicate admission of dependent spouses and children who are not traveling with the beneficiary at the time the petition is submitted. This is a particular problem for non-Canadian family members who will need to apply for a visa, as consular posts require confirmation of the L-1 approval through an entry into PIMS. The CBP inspector is supposed to fax a copy of the approved I-129 directly to the KCC for entry into PIMS. However, it is advisable that the inspector be reminded to do this, both by having the beneficiary request the fax at the time the petition is submitted and by including a colored sheet with the request in the petition package.[408]

The client should be advised of the advantages and disadvantages of filing an L-1 petition at the port of entry under NAFTA. Although the adjudication time of this process is typically much faster, there are drawbacks. The client should also consider the stress experienced by the transferee in seeking initial admission to the United States without an approval notice from USCIS. As always, there is the possibility that the L-1 petition might ultimately be denied by the CBP officer at the port of entry. In the short term, the transferee would not be admitted to the United States, and in the long term, subsequent petitions for L-1 status would have to disclose the previous L-1 petition denial. Because of these considerations, a client should be advised of the option to file the L-1 petition at a USCIS Service Center. While adjudication standards at USCIS Service Centers are sometimes quite stringent, this process has the advantage of allowing counsel to participate in responding to a Request for Evidence rather than having the L-1 applicant try to answer unanticipated questions at the port of entry without the benefit of consultation with counsel.

As discussed above, it is also critical to note that the L-1 petition may be denied if the transferee's admission to the United States might adversely affect "the settlement of a labor dispute that is in progress at the place or intended place of employment or

---

[407] CBP, "CBP Standards for Accepting and Adjudicating I-129 Petitions for L-1 Intracompany Transferee Petitions for Canadian Citizens under the North American Free Trade Agreement (NAFTA)" (Jan. 3, 2012), AILA Doc. No. 12011168.

[408] "Practice Pointer: PIMS, L-2, and TD Visa Issuance for Non-Canadian Spouses and Children," (Apr. 1, 2013), AILA Doc. No. 11012063. *See also* CBP, "CBP Standards for Accepting and Adjudicating I-129 Petitions for L-1 Intracompany Transferee Petitions for Canadian Citizens under the North American Free Trade Agreement (NAFTA)" (Jan. 3, 2012), AILA Doc. No. 12011168.

Copyright © 2017. American Immigration Lawyers Association. All rights reserved.

the employment of any person who is involved in such dispute."[409] For a more in-depth discussion of applications for admission in nonimmigrant status by Canadian nationals, see Volume 1: Chapter Two, "Basic Nonimmigrant Concepts."

E. Blanket L Petition

If a client frequently uses the L-1 visa category, it may be helpful to explore obtaining approval of a blanket L petition. This will allow certain transferees to apply for L-1 visas at the consulates, without first having to wait for approval of an individual L-1 petition by USCIS.[410] Nonprofit organizations and companies that do not meet the criteria below are not eligible for blanket L certification and must continue to file individual petitions with USCIS.[411]

In order to qualify to request blanket L certification, the petitioning U.S. company and all other entities in the group of companies must satisfy the following criteria:[412]

- The petitioner and each of those entities are engaged in commercial trade or services;

- The petitioner has an office in the United States that has been doing business for at least one year;

- The petitioner has three or more domestic and foreign branches, subsidiaries, or affiliates; and

- The petitioner and the other qualifying organizations have obtained approval of petitions for at least 10 "L" managers, executives, or specialized knowledge professionals during the previous 12 months, have U.S. subsidiaries or affiliates with combined annual sales of at least $25 million. or have a U.S. work force of at least 1,000 employees.

1. Obtaining Blanket L Certification

For the blanket L-1 petition for the group of companies, the following documents should be prepared and filed with the USCIS Service Center with jurisdiction over the U.S. headquarters:

- Form G-28
- Form I-129
- Supplement L
- Support statement from U.S. company
- List of qualifying companies

---

[409] North American Free Trade Agreement – U.S.–Can.-Mex. (Dec. 17, 1992), 32 I.L.M. 289 (entered into force Jan. 1, 1994), Chap. 16, Article 1608.

[410] 8 CFR §214.2(*l*)(4).

[411] 9 FAM 402.12-8(B).

[412] 8 CFR §214.2(*l*)(4)(i).

Copyright © 2017. American Immigration Lawyers Association. All rights reserved.

- Evidence of satisfying the requirements listed above[413]

On the Form I-129 and the L Supplement, only information about the U.S. company should be provided, as there is no foreign national beneficiary. The support statement from the U.S. company should provide information on the group of companies and the reasons why blanket L certification is requested.

Initial blanket L certification is valid for three years. A blanket L petition will be valid indefinitely upon its first extension.[414] Extensions of the blanket L petition may be requested up to six months before the petition's expiration, and it is important to ensure that the request for an indefinite extension is filed prior to expiration of the initial three-year blanket L certification, because the regulations state:

"If the petitioner in an approved blanket petition fails to request indefinite validity or if indefinite validity is denied, the petitioner and its other qualifying organizations shall seek L classification by filing individual petitions until another three years have expired; after which the petitioner may seek approval of a new blanket petition."[415]

The list of qualifying companies may be amended with the blanket L extension, or a separate petition to amend may be filed at any time.[416]

It is important to monitor the usage of the blanket petition. If none of the entities listed in the blanket petition have used the blanket procedure for three consecutive years, USCIS may revoke the blanket petition on notice.[417]

2. L-1 Visa Applications Under the Blanket L Petition

Transferees who will open or work in a new office are not eligible to apply for L visas under the blanket L petition, and instead an individual L petition must be filed with USCIS.[418] Managers, executives, and "specialized knowledge professionals" may apply for L-1 visas under a blanket L petition,[419] but only "clearly approvable applications" may be approved by a consular officer.[420]

---

[413] Experience has shown that, increasingly, USCIS is not satisfied with simply receiving an Officer's Certificate confirming the appropriate relationship exists between the qualifying companies. Instead, even for larger organizations, USCIS will frequently request underlying corporate documentation showing the required relationship.

[414] 9 FAM 402.12-8(A) This section of the FAM also discusses the requirements for extending the blanket L petition.

[415] 8 CFR §214.2(*l*)(14)(iii)(B).

[416] 8 CFR §214.2(*l*)(7)(B)–(C).

[417] 8 CFR §214.2(*l*)(14)(iii)(A)(6).

[418] 9 FAM 402.12-8(C).

[419] 8 CFR §214.2(*l*)(4)(ii).

[420] 9 FAM 402.12-8(F).

Copyright © 2017. American Immigration Lawyers Association. All rights reserved.

"Specialized knowledge professionals" are those individuals who possess specialized knowledge and who are "members of the professions."[421] The statute names only architects, engineers, lawyers, medical doctors, and teachers as members of "professions," but the list is not exhaustive.[422] In practice, the interpretation of the term "profession" appears to overlap the requirements of "specialty occupation" for H-1B status, where the position should require a "baccalaureate degree for academic study in a specific discipline or narrow range of disciplines for entry into the occupation," and where the position should require "theoretical and practical application of a body of highly specialized knowledge to fully perform the occupation" in fields such as mathematics, physical sciences, social sciences, business, accounting, law, theology, and the arts.[423] Copies of educational degrees, diplomas, transcripts, and training certificates may be requested to confirm that the transferee is a professional.[424]

In limiting use of the blanket L petition to managers, executives, and "specialized knowledge professionals," legacy INS sought to prevent misuse of the L-1 category for workers who "should be subject to the H-2 labor certification requirements."[425] For specialized knowledge transferees who lack bachelor's degrees, an individual L-1 petition must be filed with USCIS even if the group of companies has blanket L certification.[426]

A petitioner "may not seek L classification for the same alien under both procedures."[427] A petitioner may choose to file an individual L-1 petition with USCIS on behalf of a transferee who would qualify for an L-1 visa under the blanket L petition, but if the individual petition is filed with USCIS, then the petitioner must certify that the transferee will not also apply for an L-1 visa under the blanket L petition.[428] Conversely, if a consular officer denies an L-1 visa application under the blanket L petition, then the U.S. company may subsequently file an individual petition with USCIS.

A transferee who obtained L classification under a blanket L petition may provide services or "be reassigned to any organization listed in the approved petition during his or her authorized stay, without referral to DHS, if the alien will be performing virtually the same job duties."[429] If, however, the transferee's job duties are different than those stated on the initial Form I-129S, or if the new U.S.

---

[421] 8 CFR §214.2(*l*)(1)(ii)(E).

[422] INA §101(a)(32).

[423] 55 Fed. Reg. 2606 (Jan. 26, 1990).

[424] AFM 32.5(a).

[425] 52 Fed. Reg. 5738 (Feb. 26, 1987).

[426] 9 FAM 402.12-8(C).

[427] *Id.*

[428] 9 FAM 402.12-8(H).

[429] 9 FAM 402.12-8(I).

Copyright © 2017. American Immigration Lawyers Association. All rights reserved.

entity that will receive the transferee's services is not listed on the blanket L petition, then the new U.S. organization must file a petition with the USCIS Service Center that approved the blanket L petition, including Form I-129S,[430] as well as Form I-129 and Supplement L.[431]

Once the group of companies has obtained blanket L certification, beneficiaries will need to submit the following documents to apply for an L-1 visa at a U.S. consulate under a blanket L petition:

- Cover letter
- Form G-28
- Form I-129S, in triplicate (A transferee may apply for the visa at any time during the six months after the date of the Form I-129S.[432])
- Support statement from U.S. company
- Foreign company statement confirming employment of the beneficiary
- Three certified copies of the approval notice for the blanket L petition for the group of companies. (It may be helpful to highlight the transferring and U.S. company on the list of companies and tab those pages.)

If the I-129S is approved for an initial applicant, its validity period will be the lesser of three years or the period reflected in the petition's "dates of intended employment,"[433] and it should be endorsed with validity dates. However, as discussed above and in Volume 1: Chapter Two, "Basic Nonimmigrant Concepts," the issued L-1 visa should be valid for the maximum period allowable under the visa reciprocity schedules.[434] Because an L visa may be valid for longer than the validity of the corresponding I-129S, a number of complications have arisen, as discussed below.

The L-1 visa should be annotated with "the name of the company or subsidiary that the applicant will be primarily working for, even though the subsidiary as named on Form I-129S…, may or may not be the company named in PIMS."[435] In addition to the visa, the transferee should also receive two identical sets of documents: the Form I-129S (which should be endorsed by the consular officer) and the blanket L petition approval notice.[436]

3. Filing Fees

---

[430] 8 CFR §214.2(*l*)(5)(ii)(G); 9 FAM 41.54 N14.9.

[431] 8 CFR §214.2(*l*)(14)(i).

[432] 8 CFR §214.2(*l*)(5)(ii)(B).

[433] 9 FAM 402.12-8(F).

[434] State Dept., "Visas: Issuance of Full Validity L Visas to Qualified Applicants" 77 Fed. Reg. 8119 (Feb. 14, 2012).

[435] DOS, "9 FAM Update for L Visa Annotation" (May 2010), AILA Doc. No. 10070233.

[436] 9 FAM 402.12-8(F).

Copyright © 2017. American Immigration Lawyers Association. All rights reserved.

All first-time blanket L-1 filings on Form I-129S are subject to a $500 "fraud detection fee."[437] The fee is also collected if a subsequent L-1 visa application is based on a new Form I-129S.[438] Also, for most nationalities, a reciprocity fee is charged.[439] However, the $500 fee is deducted from the reciprocity fee,[440] so that if the reciprocity fee is $500 or less, that fee would be $0. In addition, the processing fee, which as of this writing is $190, is required.[441] Further, an additional $4,500 fee is required of L petitioners who employ at least 50 employees in the United States, more than 50 percent of whom hold H-1B, L-1A, or L-1B nonimmigrant status.[442]

4. Admission to the United States with L-1 Visa Issued Under a Blanket L Petition

When seeking initial admission to the United States, the transferee should present both sets of documents to the CBP officer, together with the passport containing the L-1 visa, if applicable. The CBP officer determines the individual's eligibility for the L classification and authorizes a period of admission. The officer should stamp the Forms I-129S to confirm validity of the blanket L-1 approval, return one set of documents to the transferee, and forward the final set of documents to USCIS.[443] The transferee should retain the remaining Form I-129S and be prepared to present it on any subsequent application for admission in blanket L status.[444]

Historically, CBP (and legacy INS) admitted blanket L workers for a uniform period of three years from the date of admission.[445] Although it has not released any public guidance, CBP appears to have abandoned uniform three-year blanket L admissions and adopted a new policy. The correct period of admission for a blanket L-1 beneficiary is up to three years, provided the following conditions are met:

- The applicant for admission has the requisite passport validity;
- The application has the requisite authorization on Form I-129S for the period of admission; and
- The applicant will not exceed the regulatory maximum period of admission in the United States for the L-1 class of admission (five years for L-1B; seven years for L-1A).[1446]

---

[437] INA §214(c)(12)(B).

[438] 9 FAM 402.12-8(J).

[439] State Dept., "Reciprocity and Civil Documents by Country," https://travel.state.gov/content/visas/en/fees/reciprocity-by-country.html.

[440] 9 FAM 402.12-8(K).

[441] DOS, "Fees for Visa Services," https://travel.state.gov/content/visas/en/fees/fees-visa-services.html.

[442] Pub. L. No. 114-113 (Dec. 18, 2015); 9 FAM 402.12-8(J).

[443] Id.

[444] 8 CFR §214.2(l)(13)(ii).

[445] See CBP Inspector's Field Manual 15.4 (l)(1)(C); FAM 32.4(c); USCIS, T. Cook, "L-1 Blanket Petitions" (Feb. 20, 2001), AILA Doc. No. 01022003.

[446] "Practice Alert: Blanket L From I-129 Endorsement Policy" (Oct. 30, 2015), AILA Doc. No. 15103066, citing "AILA/CBP Liaison Q&As" (Nov. 21, 2104), AILA Doc. No. 14121746.

Copyright © 2017. American Immigration Lawyers Association. All rights reserved.

Local CBP officers have stated that initial blanket L admissions should be for three years, with subsequent admissions not to exceed the I-129S endorsement dates.[447] Notwithstanding these statements, anecdotal reports indicate that CBP officers "frequently admit blanket L nonimmigrants for seemingly random periods of time, such as three years from the date of admission, until the I-129S expiration date, or until the visa expiration date. As a result, it is common to see a blanket L nonimmigrant with a CBP-issued I-94 with an expiration date that extends beyond the I-129S endorsement date."[448]

The practitioner may wish to reiterate the recommendation to carry the documents for employees who, due to reciprocity schedules, obtain visas that have a shorter or longer validity period than the L-1 petition. The endorsed Form I-129S and the Form I-797 approval notice for the blanket L certification should be presented.[449]

Once the I-129S expires, there are two procedural options to extend the validity of the worker's L classification. An employer can either file a petition with USCIS to extend the L status of the worker, or it can prepare a new Form I-129S for the worker to present at a U.S. consulate abroad. An L visa will be valid for a period of five years unless the worker is a citizen of a country that has a shorter period of L visa validity based on the reciprocity schedule. Even though the L visa in the worker's passport may still be valid, it is possible to file an application for a new blanket L visa in order to obtain a new endorsed Form I-129S.[450]

As an alternative to having a blanket L employee travel abroad to obtain a new endorsed Form I-129S, a petitioner may choose to file an I-129 and I-129S with USCIS to seek an extension of stay. This undermines the efficiency of the blanket process. It also subjects the beneficiary to risk and the petitioner to potential disruption of business, as USCIS does not give deference to State Department prior adjudications.[451]

As discussed in Volume 1: Chapter Two, "Basic Nonimmigrant Concepts," Canadian nationals need not apply for L-1 visas abroad. Pursuant to the terms of the NAFTA Treaty, they may apply for L-1 status under a blanket L petition at a port of entry by presenting the documents listed above.[452] The port of entry should be a Class A port of entry on a land border, or a U.S. pre-clearance or pre-flight station.[453]

---

[447] "Practice Alert: Blanket L From I-129 Endorsement Policy" (Oct. 30, 2015), AILA Doc. No. 15103066, citing "CBP Liaison Meeting Minutes for Chicago Chapter" (May 5, 2015), AILA Doc. No. 15061675.

[448] "Practice Alert: Blanket L From I-129 Endorsement Policy" (Oct. 30, 2015), AILA Doc. No. 15103066.

[449] 8 CFR §214.2(*l*)(13).

[450] "AILA/Department of State Liaison Meeting Q&As" (Oct. 9, 2014), AILA Doc. No. 14101042.

[451] USCIS, "L-1B Adjudications Policy," PM-602-0111, at 15 (Aug. 17, 2015).

[452] 9 FAM 402.12-8(E).

[453] 8 CFR 214.2(l)(17); 9 FAM 402.12-8(E).

Copyright © 2017. American Immigration Lawyers Association. All rights reserved.

An L-1 petition under the blanket on behalf of a Canadian transferee need not be filed with the port of entry. Instead, a U.S. company may file an individual petition for a Canadian citizen with a USCIS Service Center for a Form I-797 or an individual petition with the port of entry under NAFTA, as discussed above.[454]

F. EADs for L-2 Spouses

Spouses of L-1 transferees are eligible to apply for employment authorization documents (EADs).[455] The statutory provision authorizing the employment of spouses, however, does not extend to dependent children in L-2 status.[456] Practitioners may wish to advise clients that USCIS takes the position that, unlike the principal L-1 nonimmigrant, the L-2 spouse does not automatically have employment authorization following admission to the United States. Instead, USCIS requires an L-2 spouse wishing to engage in employment to affirmatively file an application, despite contrary guidance from the Social Security Administration (SSA), as discussed below. The following documents should be prepared and filed:

- Form G-28
- Form I-765
- Statement from U.S. company, confirming the L-1 employment of the transferee
- Copy of biographic page of L-2 spouse's passport
- Copy of L-2 visa
- Copies of I-94 records for the L-1 and L-2 nonimmigrants
- Copy of the principal alien's L-1 visa
- Copy of biographic page of the L-1 transferee's passport
- Copy of marriage certificate of transferee and spouse

An L-2 spouse may wish to obtain an EAD solely in order to apply for a Social Security number (SSN). It may be possible to obtain an SSN from the Social Security Administration, however, without first obtaining an EAD. SSA guidance takes the position that L-2 spouses are eligible for employment authorization incident to status and need not apply for EADs.[457] To receive a SSN, an L-2 spouse should show an EAD or an admission stamp in the passport or I-94 admission record and marriage document.

---

[454] 9 FAM 402.12-8(E).

[455] INA §214(c)(2)(E).

[456] *Id.*; USCIS, W. Yates, "Guidance on Employment Authorization for E and L Nonimmigrant Spouses" (Feb. 22, 2002), AILA Doc. No. 2022832.

[457] Social Security Administration, "Section RM 10211.420 Employment Authorization for Nonimmigrants" (Aug. 9, 2016), https://secure.ssa.gov/poms.nsf/lnx/0110211420.

Copyright © 2017. American Immigration Lawyers Association. All rights reserved.

Practitioners should note the discrepancy between this guidance and the general position of the SSA, as stated in the Frequently Asked Questions (FAQs), as well as a discrepancy between the SSA guidance and the policy of DHS with respect to employment authorization for L-2 spouses. Contrary to the SSA guidance, DHS clearly requires L-2 spouses to obtain EAD cards for employment authorization.[458]

G. Extensions

An extension of L-1 status may be filed up to six months in advance of the L-1 status expiration.[459] An extension petition will be timely filed provided that it is received on or before the date that the worker's L-1 status expires.[460] For a discussion of how to address, prepare, and file untimely extensions of status, see Volume 1: Chapter Two, "Basic Nonimmigrant Concepts." Extensions of L-2 status for any dependent family members should also be prepared and filed. The transferee and any family members must be physically present in the United States when the extensions are filed.[461]

A timely filed L-1 petition extension will provide an additional 240 days of employment authorization with the petitioning employer, during pendency of the L-1 extension filing and after expiration of the current L-1 status.[462] Once the original L-1 petition expires, however, the transferee should not travel internationally, as he or she would not have a valid L-1 petition to support readmission. The worker would need to remain outside the United States until the petition extension is approved in order to be able to reapply for admission in L-1 status.

If the L visa in the worker's passport remains valid, it is not necessary to apply for a new visa. In order to be readmitted to the United States, the individual would need to present a copy of the new petition approval notice, Form I-797, along with the existing, unexpired L visa. Even though the original L visa may have a PED that is expired, the visa may be used through its validity date provided that the individual also presents a valid, unexpired Form I-797.

If the transferee and any family members need to travel internationally for business or personal reasons while the extensions are pending, the petitioner may

---

[458] USCIS, M. Yates, "Guidance on Employment Authorization for E and L Nonimmigrant Spouses" (Feb. 22, 2002), AILA Doc. No. 2022832. For a discussion of the contradictory guidance, see "AILA-Social Security Administration Liaison Committee Meeting Minutes" (May 8, 2006), AILA Doc. No. 06082360; "SSA Liaison Committee Practice Tip: EADs and SSNs for E and L Spouses" (Aug. 25, 2006), AILA Doc. No. 06082560; D. Horne, "Requests for Evidence: Do E-2 and L-2 Spouses Need EAD Cards Before They Start Working?" 13-12 Bender's Immigr. Bull. 2 (June 15, 2002).

[459] USCIS, "Instructions for Form I-129, Petition for a Nonimmigrant Worker," https://www.uscis.gov/files/form/i-129instr.pdf.

[460] 8 CFR §214.2(*l*)(14)(i); see also "DOS on Unlawful Presence During EOS/COS Application" (June 2, 2000), AILA Doc. No. 00060202 and 5 Bender's Immigr. Bull. 590 (June 15, 2000).

[461] 8 CFR §214.2(*l*)(14)(i).

[462] 8 CFR §274a.12(b)(20).

Copyright © 2017. American Immigration Lawyers Association. All rights reserved.

request consular notification of the extension approval.[463] The transferee and any family members may then apply for visas. If international travel needs demand it, premium processing may be requested for the L-1 extension, and the L-2 extensions should be adjudicated concurrently. The client should be advised, however, of the possibility that the transferee and any family members may need to remain outside the United States for an extended period of time in order to await approval of the extensions and to apply for visas.

Alternatively, if international travel is required of the transferee and the company has a valid blanket L petition, the transferee may make a new application for an L-1 visa under the blanket instead of filing an individual extension with USCIS. Because a petitioner must certify that an L-1 visa application under a blanket L petition will not be made after filing the individual extension with USCIS,[464] this strategy should be explored with the client in advance. This renewal would require the same documents as the initial visa application under the blanket. Upon approval of the new blanket L visa application, the consular officer will endorse a new Form I-129S, cancel the previous L visa, and issue a new one that the transferee may use to apply for readmission to the United States. If the international travel is to a country other than the transferee's home country or country of permanent residence or alternate citizenship, then the practitioner should confirm that the U.S. consulate in that country accepts visa applications by third-country nationals.

When filing an L-1 extension petition, practitioners should be aware that adjudicators of the L-1 extension frequently do not have access to the initial L-1 petition. The extension petition should completely re-document the nature and scope of the U.S. assignment.[465] This is particularly true for L-1B extensions, where the documents should explicitly detail how the transferee will apply specialized knowledge for the benefit of the U.S. company.[466] An L-1B extension may receive an RFE requesting documentation of the qualifying employment abroad, even though the question of qualifying employment should have been addressed in the initial L-1B petition.[467] Practitioners filing L-1B extensions may find it helpful to reiterate the nature of the specialized knowledge gained abroad, as well as how the specialized knowledge will be applied for the benefit of the U.S. company, and to provide a copy of the foreign company statement to USCIS in the L-1B extension filing. For a detailed discussion of the issues surrounding a petition to extend status, see Volume 1: Chapter Two, "Basic Nonimmigrant Concepts."

USCIS adjudicators are instructed to give deference in extension requests to prior adjudications involving the same parties and same facts unless there was a material

---

[463] 8 CFR §214.2(*l*)(14)(i).

[464] 9 FAM 402.12-8(H).

[465] "VSC Answers Liaison Questions" (Aug. 27, 2002), AILA Doc. No. 02091271.

[466] *Id.*

[467] "VSC Stakeholder Q&A" (Apr. 6, 2010), AILA Doc. No. 10040832.

Copyright © 2017. American Immigration Lawyers Association. All rights reserved.

error with respect to the previous approval, there has since been a substantial change in circumstances, or there is new material information that adversely affects eligibility.[468] Under current USCIS practices, however, such deference is rarely accorded.[469] Adjudicators are trained, however, to review the specialized knowledge to ascertain whether, with the passage of time and advent of technological advances, the knowledge has become general or no longer advanced.[470] Indeed, denial rates for extensions of L-1B status have been known to be higher than the rates for initial petitions.[471] Also, deference does not necessarily extend to determinations by other agencies: "USCIS will take note of a previous determination...made by the Department of State or U.S. Customs and Border Protection, but will make a determination on the instant petition based on the record before it."[472]

In addition, for L-1 extensions where the transferee will be assigned to a "new office," additional documents should be provided to establish eligibility for the L-1 category under the "new office" regulations, as discussed above.

VI. Practice Pointers

Below are some practice pointers for an L-1A petition:

- Providing monetary estimates of budgets, investments, projects, or cost savings can demonstrate the manager's scope of fiscal responsibility. Responsibility for developing and managing a budget, or achieving cost savings, may also underscore the managerial nature of the transferee's role.

- Providing job titles of managers, professionals, or technical specialists managed by the transferee can demonstrate the senior-level nature of the role.

- Providing detailed organizational charts and detailed job descriptions for the transferee's role and for other job functions can demonstrate how the manager, executive, or function manager will be able to focus on managerial or executive job duties.

---

[468] USCIS, "L-1B Adjudications Policy," PM-602-0111 (Aug. 17, 2015) at 15; USCIS, W. Yates, "The Significance of a Prior CIS Approval of a Nonimmigrant Petition in the Context of a Subsequent Determination Regarding Eligibility for Extension of Petition Validity," HQPRD 72/11.3 (Apr. 23, 2004), AILA Doc. No. 04050510.

[469] CIS Ombudsman Annual Report, 2015, http://bit.ly/2015Ombudsman.

[470] "Separate FOIA Requests Uncover L-1 Training Materials and Correspondence" (undated, posted Apr. 26, 2013), AILA Doc. No. 13042663, p. 126-127.

[471] National Foundation for American Policy, "L-1 Denial Rates Increase Again for High Skill Foreign Nationals" (Mar. 2015), AILA Doc. No. 15031861, http://nfap.com/wp-content/uploads/2015/03/NFAP-Policy-Brief.L-1-Denial-Rates-Increase-Again.March-20151.pdf, noting "USCIS denies L-1B petitions at a higher rate for employees already working in the U.S. and extending their status (41 percent in FY 2014) than initial applications (32 percent)."

[472] USCIS, "L-1B Adjudications Policy," PM-602-0111, at 15 (Aug. 17, 2015).

Copyright © 2017. American Immigration Lawyers Association. All rights reserved.

- Providing evidence of the ongoing international nature of the business of a smaller U.S. company can demonstrate that the U.S. company is able to support an executive.

- Exploring whether a transferee may qualify as a function manager, as opposed to a specialized knowledge transferee, may result in long-term advantages, including a longer period of authorized stay.

- Identifying and providing a detailed description of all managerial duties into the role of the transferee can strengthen a petition.

- Having the job title of "manager" without consonant managerial duties, is typically insufficient for approval of an L-1A petition.

Here are some practice pointers for an L-1B petition:

- Connect the transferee's specialized knowledge to the U.S. operations, to show how the U.S. operations will benefit from the knowledge gained abroad.

- Provide monetary estimates of budgets, investments, projects, or cost savings, to demonstrate the transferee's scope of fiscal responsibility. This, in turn, can underscore how important the application of specialized knowledge is to the company's overall business goals and objectives.

- Provide information and insight on the company's business goals and objectives with respect to the specialized knowledge, to highlight the important motivation for requiring the transferee's specialized knowledge in the United States.

- Provide job titles of managers, professionals, or technical specialists who receive direction from the transferee, to demonstrate the sophisticated nature of the role.

- Provide information on the number of employees who hold the specialized knowledge (or a similar quantification, such as a percentage of the company's workforce), to emphasize the uncommonness of the knowledge.

Copyright © 2017. American Immigration Lawyers Association. All rights reserved.

CHAPTER TWELVE

O VISAS AND STATUS

I. Executive Summary

The O-1 classification allows foreign nationals who have demonstrated extraordinary ability in the sciences, education, business, athletics, the arts, or in the motion picture or television industries to visit the United States temporarily to work in the field. The O-2 classification is available to support staff accompanying the O-1 principal to assist with artistic or athletic events or performances. Spouses and dependent children of O-1 and O-2 principals are eligible for O-3 status in the United States and are ineligible to apply for work authorization. An O petition may be approved for up to three years, and extensions may be granted indefinitely for long-term projects or assignments or for a group of related performances or activities. There is currently no annual limit on O visa numbers.

A. Checklist of Requirements

- Assignment, performance, or event requiring the foreign national's extraordinary ability;

- Contacts within the foreign national's field or independent authorities capable of providing the required advisory opinion and recommendations; and

- Documentation of the foreign national's extraordinary ability in the sciences, education, business, athletics, the arts, or in the motion picture or television industries.

B. Documents Necessary to Prepare the Petition

- Basic information about the employer;

- Description of the assignment, event, or performance;

- Copies of the foreign national's educational degrees and/or transcripts;

- Copy of foreign national's résumé;

- Copy of employment contract;

- Information from the foreign national regarding his or her accomplishments in the field;

- Information on contacts who can provide an advisory opinion and recommendation letters; and

- Copy of biographic page(s) of passport(s) of the foreign national and any dependent spouse and children.

C. Checklist of Questions to Ask the Client

- What is the nature of the petitioner's activity in the United States?

- What is the nature of the assignment, performance, or event in the United States?

Copyright © 2017. American Immigration Lawyers Association. All rights reserved.

- Can the foreign national demonstrate, through independent evidence and recommendation letters, attainment of a level of expertise and renown indicative of an individual of extraordinary ability?

- Does the foreign national meet at least three criteria of the list for his or her particular field of endeavor (attach list of criteria)?

- Has the foreign national risen to the very top of his or her field of endeavor?

- Will the petitioner be the only employer?

- Is the petitioner in business as an agent?

II. Introduction

The O-1 classification is appropriate for a foreign national who has "extraordinary ability" in his or her field, which may be science, education, business, athletics, art, or the motion picture and television industries,[1] or "any field of endeavor."[2] Importantly, the "provisions of this visa classification are intended to be highly restrictive," such that evidence that may be adequate for approval of an H-1B petition is generally insufficient for approval of an O-1 petition.[3] There is no annual numerical limitation on O visa numbers.[4]

As a practical matter, the O-1 classification is typically very document heavy,[5] so the practitioner may wish to caution the client of the need for sufficient time to gather, prepare, and assemble the petition. Support personnel of O-1 nonimmigrants may obtain O-2 status,[6] as discussed below. Only one O-1 beneficiary may be named on the petition, and any O-2 petition must be filed separately from the O-1 petition.[7] It is possible to have multiple O-2 beneficiaries, as long as each beneficiary will "assist[] the same O-1 alien for the same events or performances, during the same period of time, and in the same location."[8]

The petition may be filed by a U.S. employer, a U.S. agent, or a foreign employer through a U.S. agent, but not by the foreign national,[9] as discussed below. It is not

---

[1] Immigration and Nationality Act (INA) §101(a)(15)(O)(i).

[2] Legacy Immigration and Naturalization Service (INS), L. Weinig, "Policy Guidelines for the Adjudication of O and P Petitions" (June 25, 1992), 69 Interpreter Releases 1084–87 (Aug. 31, 1992) (stating that legacy INS "has interpreted the O-1 classification to apply to any field of endeavor").

[3] *Matter of [name not provided]*, EAC 07 138 51199 (AAO Feb. 2, 2009), http://bit.ly/feb0912d (citing 137 Cong. Rec. S18247 (daily ed. Nov. 16, 1991).

[4] U.S. Citizenship and Immigration Services (USCIS) Office of Business Liaison, Employer Information Bulletin 15, "Aliens with Extraordinary Ability (O-1) and Accompanying/Assisting Aliens (O-2)" (Dec. 8, 2004), 82 Interpreter Releases 180–84 (Jan. 17, 2005); Legacy INS, J. Bednarz (Sept. 29, 1992), 69 Interpreter Releases 1471–72 (Nov. 16, 1992).

[5] INA §101(a)(15)(O)(i) (noting that the individual's "achievements [must] have been recognized in the field through extensive documentation").

[6] INA §101(a)(15)(O)(ii).

[7] 8 Code of Federal Regulations (CFR) §214.2(o)(2)(i).

[8] 8 CFR §214.2(o)(2)(iv)(F).

[9] 8 CFR §214.2(o)(2)(i).

Copyright © 2017. American Immigration Lawyers Association. All rights reserved.

mandatory that the O-1 employer file the O-2 petition.[10] If the beneficiary will "work in more than one location," then the petition "must include an itinerary with the dates and locations of work."[11] Substitution of O-1 or O-2 beneficiaries is not permitted.[12]

Petitions for O-1 and O-2 status must be filed with and approved by U.S. Citizenship and Immigration Services (USCIS), "even in emergency situations," although the petition may be filed up to one year before the date of need.[13] Although a Notice of Proposed Rulemaking (NPRM) suggested revising the regulations to require the filing of an O petition at least six months in advance of the date of need, USCIS declined to adopt that proposed rule after numerous comments from industry insiders about the difficulty in identifying the beneficiary six months in advance, the rarity of making an employment offer six months before a start date, and the common delays in negotiating an employment contract.[14] USCIS recommends, "To avoid delays, the Form I-129 should be filed at least 45 days before the date of employment."[15]

As discussed in more detail below, the standard for the fields of science, art, education, business, and athletics entails "sustain[ing] national or international acclaim," whereas the standard for motion picture and television production is "a demonstrated record of extraordinary achievement."[16] These standards are meant to determine if an individual, rather than a group, has extraordinary ability.[17]

Experience has shown that a foreign national may hold O-1 status for long periods of time, even 10 or 15 years, as long as other requirements are met.[18] O-1 status is a nonimmigrant option for foreign nationals who are subject to the two-year foreign residence requirement,[19] as discussed in Volume 1: Chapter Ten, "J-1 Visas and Status." A dependent spouse or child of an O-1 nonimmigrant holds O-3 status,[20] and

---

[10] Legacy INS, L. Weinig, "Policy Guidelines for the Adjudication of O and P Petitions," (June 25, 1992), 69 Interpreter Releases 1084–87 (Aug. 31, 1992).

[11] 8 CFR §214.2(o)(2)(iv)(A).

[12] 9 Foreign Affairs Manual (FAM) 402.13-7.

[13] 8 CFR §§214.2(o)(1)(i), (o)(2)(i); 72 Fed. Reg. 18856 (Apr. 16, 2007).

[14] 72 Fed. Reg. 18856 (Apr. 16, 2007).

[15] USCIS, "O-1 Visa: Individuals with Extraordinary Ability or Achievement" (updated Sept. 14, 2015), http://bit.ly/2cCoXRa.

[16] INA §101(a)(15)(O)(i); 8 CFR §214.2(o)(1)(i).

[17] Legacy INS, L. Weinig, "Policy Guidelines for the Adjudication of O and P Petitions," (June 25, 1992), 69 Interpreter Releases 1084–87 (Aug. 31, 1992). The P classification is more appropriate for an "outstanding" group. Legacy INS, P. Virtue, "O-1 and P Nonimmigrant Visa Classifications" (Sept. 29, 1993), 1 INS and DOJ Legal Opinions §93-76. For a discussion of this strategy, see Volume 1: Chapter Thirteen, "P Visas and Status."

[18] USCIS Office of Business Liaison, Employer Information Bulletin 15, "Aliens with Extraordinary Ability (O-1) and Accompanying/Assisting Aliens (O-2)" (Dec. 8, 2004), 82 Interpreter Releases 180–84 (Jan. 17, 2005) (stating that "[t]here is no limitation on the duration of stay in the United States of an O nonimmigrant").

[19] INA §212(e); 9 FAM 402.5-6(L).

[20] INA §101(a)(15)(O)(iii); 8 CFR §214.2(o)(1)(i).

Copyright © 2017. American Immigration Lawyers Association. All rights reserved.

may not "accept employment unless he or she has been granted employment authorization."[21]

III. Requirements and Interpretations

A. The O-1 Assignment

Although it is not mandatory that the O-1 assignment require an individual with extraordinary ability,[22] such that "an operatic diva may come to the U.S. to sing in the opera chorus for a community opera,"[23] the "O-1 petition must be accompanied by evidence that the work which the alien is coming to the United States to continue is in the area of extraordinary ability."[24] Importantly, in one case, the Administrative Appeals Office (AAO) stated: "[T]he director [of legacy Immigration and Naturalization Service] erred in requiring the petitioner to establish that the position offered the beneficiary requires the services of an alien of extraordinary ability or achievement. The statute requires only that the O-1 alien be coming to perform services in the area of extraordinary ability."[25] Although included in the NPRM, the requirement was "eliminated" in the final rule,[26] and an erroneous denial based on this reason was reversed by the AAO.[27] Stated another way: "To establish that a position requires the services of an alien of extraordinary ability or achievement, the position to be filled must meet the following criteria: The alien must be coming to the United States to perform services in his or her area of expertise."[28]

---

[21] 8 CFR §214.2(o)(6)(iv).

[22] USCIS Office of Business Liaison, Employer Information Bulletin 15, "Aliens with Extraordinary Ability (O-1) and Accompanying/Assisting Aliens (O-2)" (Dec. 8, 2004), 82 Interpreter Releases 180–84 (Jan. 17, 2005) (stating that the "O-1 nonimmigrant may be admitted even if the work to be performed in the United States does not require a person of extraordinary ability or achievement"); Adjudicator's Field Manual (AFM) 33.4 (stating that "[i]n support of all O-1 petitions, the petitioner must establish that the beneficiary has met the standards or demonstrated that he or she possesses sustained national or international acclaim and recognition in his or her particular field and that the alien is coming to work in that field (but not necessarily that the particular duties to be performed require someone of such extraordinary ability)"). The practitioner should note, however, that certain sections of the regulations still reference how the assignment or event must require the services of an individual with extraordinary ability. 8 CFR §214.2(o)(2)(iv)(D) (stating that "a petitioner may add additional performances or engagements during the validity period of the petition without filing an amended petition, provided the additional performances or engagements require an alien of O-1 caliber"). See also 8 CFR §§214.2(o)(5)(ii)(A) and 214.2(o)(5)(iii).

[23] USCIS Office of Business Liaison, Employer Information Bulletin 15, "Aliens with Extraordinary Ability (O-1) and Accompanying/Assisting Aliens (O-2)" (Dec. 8, 2004), 82 Interpreter Releases 180–84 (Jan. 17, 2005).

[24] 8 CFR §214.2(o)(3)(i).

[25] Matter of [name not provided], EAC 96 058 51556 (AAO June 25, 1998), 19 Immig. Rptr. B2-62.

[26] Matter of [name not provided], WAC 95 042 52458 (AAO Jan. 12, 1995), 14 Immig. Rptr. B2-43 (citing 59 Fed. Reg. 41818 (Aug. 15, 1994)).

[27] Matter of [name not provided], LIN 02 184 53385 (AAO Sept. 17, 2002), 26 Immig. Rptr. B2-92.

[28] 9 FAM 402.13-4(A).

Copyright © 2017. American Immigration Lawyers Association. All rights reserved.

1. Field of Endeavor

The petitioner should "clearly indicate[] what it considers to be the beneficiary's field of endeavor."[29] The practitioner should confirm that the field in which the foreign national has extraordinary ability will be the field of endeavor for the U.S. assignment, as a "beneficiary can only *continue* work in a given area if he/she has *already* been working in that area."[30] The previous and proposed duties should be in fields that are identical or as similar as possible.[31] For example, the petitioner should not claim that the beneficiary will work in the field of athletics if: "The petitioner seeks to employ the beneficiary as a general manager at its ski and snowboarding school; therefore, the petitioner must establish that the beneficiary is an alien of extraordinary ability in management."[32] As another example, an individual who has extraordinary ability in playing a sport is not automatically eligible for O-1 classification as a coach of that sport, as discussed below.

In addition, the AAO commented on the inappropriateness of overly restricting the field: "[C]ounsel cannot narrow the beneficiary's field to such an extent that it excludes any meaningful comparison to other artists engaged in similar work."[33] If the petition identifies multiple fields, USCIS may be unable to identify what is the field of endeavor, or may choose one for the petitioner,[34] a situation unlikely to result in approval.

The industry of the petitioner's business should not be dispositive, but it is relevant in determining whether the beneficiary will continue to provide services in his or her field of endeavor.[35] For example, if the business is limousine and tour services, but the beneficiary's services are sought as an art curator, then USCIS may investigate whether the petitioner does in fact own an art gallery.[36]

2. Event

O-1 status is inappropriate if the beneficiary will freelance in the United States,[37] or be self-employed with no employment relationship between the petitioner and the

---

[29] *Matter of [name not provided]*, WAC 07 800 12235 (AAO Feb. 9, 2009), http://bit.ly/feb092d.

[30] *Matter of [name not provided]*, WAC 07 006 52866 (AAO Mar. 5, 2008), http://bit.ly/mar081d.

[31] *Matter of [name not provided]*, EAC 07 224 51635 (AAO June 23, 2009), http://bit.ly/jun091d (stating that "the beneficiary's duties associated with this project are far removed from those he will perform in the United States as a project architect, to the extent that the work is in 'the same field' using only the broadest interpretation of the term").

[32] *Matter of [name not provided]*, LIN 04 157 52612 (AAO May 3, 2005), http://bit.ly/may051d.

[33] *Matter of [name not provided]*, EAC 04 187 50327 (AAO Oct. 4, 2006), http://bit.ly/oct061d. *See also Matter of AM-*, ID# 15019 (AAO Jan. 8, 2016) ("Petitioner may not narrow the Beneficiary's field to include only other artists working in a small, niche movement").

[34] *Matter of [name and case number not provided]*, (AAO Mar. 14, 2014), http://bit.ly/mar141d.

[35] *Matter of [name not provided]*, SRC 05 100 50633 (AAO Nov. 10, 2005), http://bit.ly/nov051d.

[36] *Id.*

[37] USCIS Office of Business Liaison, Employer Information Bulletin 15, "Aliens with Extraordinary Ability (O-1) and Accompanying/Assisting Aliens (O-2)" (Dec. 8, 2004), 82 Interpreter Releases 180–84 (Jan. 17, 2005); *Matter of [name not provided]*, WAC 07 006 52866 (AAO Mar. 5, 2008),
Cont'd

Copyright © 2017. American Immigration Lawyers Association. All rights reserved.

beneficiary.[38] The beneficiary's purpose in entering the United States must be to participate in an "event," but the term is not limited to the typical interpretation of a one-time occurrence:

"An event is defined as an activity such as, but not limited to, a scientific project, conference, convention, lecture series, tour, exhibit, business project, academic year, or engagements. In addition, a job which may not have a specific engagement or project may also fall under this definition if the job is the 'activity' within the alien's area of extraordinary ability. Activities such as these may include short vacations, promotional appearances, and stopovers which are incidental and/or related to the main event."[39]

"A group of related activities may also be considered to be an event. In the case of an O-1 athlete, the event could be the alien's contract."[40]

In areas such as business and science, where the proposed activities cannot be broken down into specific events, it is still possible to satisfy this requirement:

"In order to facilitate us in proper adjudication, we would ask that members explain how the related activities make up an event or support the event. In the case of professors, it can be established through contractual terms identifying the semester or school year. The researcher could identify his event under the terms of the research project or terms of the grant. The business executive could define event through the project she is heading such as a roll out of a product, expansion. In each example the concept of event remains intact while providing flexibility based on the field of endeavor.

"Please note that although the [Request for Evidence] RFE might appear to be requesting evidence that might most easily be identified or associated with artists or performers, these evidentiary requirements can be met with other professions. It is an articulation of the nature of the event or activity that suffices. It must be noted that the law maintains the need for an event regardless of the field of expertise for the alien."[41]

The AAO has noted that:

---

http://bit.ly/mar081d; *Matter of [name not provided]*, WAC 10 018 51674 (AAO Oct. 1, 2010), AILA Doc. No. 11022363; USCIS, "Clarifying Guidance on 'O' Petition Validity Period; Revisions to the Adjudicator's Field Manual (AFM) Chapter 33.4(e)(2); AFM Update AD10-36," PM-602-0003 (July 20, 2010), AILA Doc. No. 10072061; AFM 33.4 (stating that "speculative employment and/or freelancing are not allowed").

[38] *Matter of [name not provided]*, LIN 93 176 51248 (AAO Jan. 25, 1994), 12 Immig. Rptr. B2-156; USCIS, "Clarifying Guidance on 'O' Petition Validity Period; Revisions to the Adjudicator's Field Manual (AFM) Chapter 33.4(e)(2); AFM Update AD10-36," PM-602-0003 (July 20, 2010), AILA Doc. No. 10072061; AFM 33.4 (stating that "speculative employment and/or freelancing are not allowed").

[39] USCIS, "Clarifying Guidance on 'O' Petition Validity Period; Revisions to the Adjudicator's Field Manual (AFM) Chapter 33.4(e)(2); AFM Update AD10-36," PM-602-0003 (July 20, 2010), AILA Doc. No. 10072061. *See also* 8 CFR §214.2(o)(3)(ii).

[40] 8 CFR §214.2(o)(3)(ii).

[41] "CSC Answers to AILA Liaison Questions" (Sept. 2001), AILA Doc. No. 01090734.

Copyright © 2017. American Immigration Lawyers Association. All rights reserved.

"[A] narrow interpretation of what constitutes a qualifying 'event' is untenable as it would essentially prohibit private sector employers from hiring O-1 scientists, engineers, and business leaders. Rather, such persons would be limited to either working in academia or coming to the United States only for conventions, conferences, to deliver lectures, or to work on scientific or business 'projects.' Given that the regulations allow for an initial three-year period of stay…it is reasonable to believe that the "engagement" included in the regulatory definition of 'event' may include a three-year offer of employment in the alien's area of extraordinary ability, including the 'normal' duties of one's profession. Of course, petitioner must still provide a detailed description of the nature of the activities and provide a copy of its written contract or a summary of the terms of its oral agreement with the alien."[42]

This means that the O-1 assignment may be longer term, and even up to three years, as discussed below, if that is the length of the contract,[43] or the planned assignment.[44]

Similarly, a business project may be comprised of more than one part,[45] but employing the beneficiary on multiple discrete projects so that the petitioner may "serve its client in the normal course of business" may be deemed not specific enough for a qualifying event.[46] The start and end dates of the assignment or event should be stated on the petition.[47] For longer-term assignments, the O-1 petition should contain evidence supporting the proposed employment dates,[48] because the "examples

---

[42] *Matter of [name not provided]*, WAC 10 018 51674 (AAO Oct. 1, 2010), AILA Doc. No. 11022363.

[43] *Matter of [name not provided]*, WAC 07 001 54685 (AAO July 29, 2008), http://bit.ly/jul081d (AAO withdrew USCIS's ground for denial).

[44] *Matter of [name not provided]*, EAC 02 127 52263 (AAO Sept. 16, 2002), 26 Immig. Rptr. B2-26 (AAO accepted a five-year term for an event based on the employer's anticipated need for the beneficiary's services and stated "[w]hile this is an unusual circumstance for an alien seeking O-1 classification in the arts, it is concluded that such a temporary stay satisfies the intent of a specific event found in the regulations").

[45] *Matter of [name not provided]*, WAC 93 168 50373 (AAO Aug. 3, 2002), 26 Immig. Rptr. B2-84 (stating that "it may be concluded that the opening of a new restaurant, as part of a series of restaurants around the world, may be considered a business project satisfying the temporary intent of entering the United States for a specific event").

[46] *Matter of [name not provided]*, WAC 01 250 52367 (AAO Aug. 4, 2002), 26 Immig. Rptr. B2-87 (noting that graphic designer's work on "projects includ[ing] the design of a book cover, a business card, several textile wall hangings," and a few websites "is not the type of specific event contemplated for the temporary employment of a[n] alien with extraordinary ability in the arts and does not represent continuing work in the area of extraordinary ability").

[47] "CSC Answers to AILA Liaison Questions" (Sept. 2001), AILA Doc. No. 01090734.

[48] *Cf. Matter of [name not provided]*, WAC 06 262 52536 (AAO Oct. 9, 2007), http://bit.ly/oct071d (petition denied where petitioner requested approval for three-year period and submitted project schedule covering only 18 week,s because "the petitioner failed to submit the requisite explanation and documentation of the project or other event(s) which would require the beneficiary's services for the three-year period"); *Matter of [name not provided]*, WAC 06 167 50726 (AAO Mar. 6, 2007), http://bit.ly/mar071d.

Copyright © 2017. American Immigration Lawyers Association. All rights reserved.

provided by the regulation suggest occurrences or phenomena of definite and finite duration."[49]

An event may be described in the contract.[50] As another example, if the event is a filming of a motion picture, then television appearances and post-production services, such as "voice over work and filming additional scenes to be used in the DVD edition of the motion picture," could be considered "related to the event."[51] Legacy Immigration and Naturalization Service (INS) provided additional examples:

"The concept of activities is also attached to these activities being associated with and in support of the event…. [I]f an architect is working on a project that is the event, then it is feasible that several buildings could comprise that project. However, the event as such should be defined in the project. If the architect was to commence a new project that is not associated with this previous project, then the Service's position would be that there is in fact a new event.

"In the case of those areas in the sciences, business, academia or the arts, it is not unrealistic to expect a definition of event in the petition. It is not unreasonable to require the petitioner to define the terms under which the alien is being sought for employment. Clearly these terms would be defined by contract or oral agreement that would identify what scientific project, length of academic stay, business endeavor and artistic engagement the alien is coming in to perform."[52]

Recent USCIS policy guidance explains the totality of the circumstances approach to determine whether a "continuous 'event'" is described even if there is a "length of time between the [multiple] scheduled events, also known as a 'gap.'"[53] Although in the past, adjudicators seemed to rely upon such a gap to approve a petition only for "the length of time needed to accomplish what appeared to be the initial specific event," the guidance noted:

"There is no statutory or regulatory authority for the proposition that a gap of a certain number of days in an itinerary automatically indicates a new event. The regulations speak in terms of tours and multiple appearances as meeting the 'event' definition…. Adjudicators should evaluate the totality of the evidence submitted to determine if the activities described in the itinerary are related in such a way that they would be considered an 'event' for purposes of the validity period."[54]

---

[49] *Matter of [name not provided]*, EAC 04 204 50274 (AAO Feb. 21, 2006), http://bit.ly/feb062d.

[50] *Matter of [name not provided]*, WAC 02 238 54702 (AAO Feb. 27, 2003), 27 Immig. Rptr. B2-35.

[51] 8 CFR §214.2(o)(3)(ii); *Matter of [name not provided]*, WAC 02 238 54702 (AAO Feb. 27, 2003), 27 Immig. Rptr. B2-35.

[52] "CSC Answers to AILA Liaison Questions" (Sept. 2001), AILA Doc. No. 01090734.

[53] USCIS, "Clarifying Guidance on 'O' Petition Validity Period; Revisions to the Adjudicator's Field Manual (AFM) Chapter 33.4(e)(2); AFM Update AD10-36," PM-602-0003 (July 20, 2010), AILA Doc. No. 10072061

[54] *Id.*

Copyright © 2017. American Immigration Lawyers Association. All rights reserved.

Specifically, "[t]here is no requirement for a 'single' event in the statute," and:

"[T]here is a clear indication in the regulations that a petition may be approved to cover not only the actual event or events but also services and/or activities in connection with that event or events.... Unlike other nonimmigrant categories that have a specified time limit, a temporal period is not specified for the Os.... A group of related activities may also be considered to be an event.... A petitioner must establish that there are events or activities in the alien's field of extraordinary ability for the validity period requested, *e.g.*, an itinerary for a tour, contract or summary of the terms of the oral agreement under which the beneficiary will be employed, contracts between the beneficiary and employers if an agent is being utilized in order to establish the events."[55]

Therefore, a beneficiary may engage in "short vacations, promotional appearances, and stopovers which are incidental and/or related to the event" and such activities should not break the continuity of the O event.[56] Stated simply, the "gaps" may be considered "incidental to the original 'event.'"[57]

The analysis should focus on whether "the activities on the itinerary are related in such a way that they could be considered an 'event,'" and if so, then "the petition should be approved for the requested validity period."[58] The guidance provided the example of "a series of events that involve the same performers and the same or similar performance, such as a tour by a performing artist in venues around the United States."[59] Further, the fact that the beneficiary will return abroad to engage in activities that are "incidental and/or related to the work performed in the United States" during "a break in between events" in the United States, such as international travel "does not necessarily interrupt the original 'event.'"[60] Any gaps involving activities performed abroad "should not by themselves be used to limit a validity period."[61]

The petitioner bears the burden "to demonstrate that the activities listed on the itinerary are related to the event despite gaps in which the beneficiary may travel abroad and return to the United States."[62] An RFE may be issued if "a review of the itinerary does not establish an event or activity, or a series of connected events and activities which would allow the validity period requested, or if the petitioner is requesting a validity period beyond the last established event or activity."[63]

---

[55] USCIS, "Clarifying Guidance on 'O' Petition Validity Period; Revisions to the Adjudicator's Field Manual (AFM) Chapter 33.4(e)(2); AFM Update AD10-36," PM-602-0003 (July 20, 2010), AILA Doc. No. 10072061; AFM 33.4.

[56] *Id.*

[57] *Id.*

[58] *Id.*

[59] *Id.*

[60] *Id.*

[61] *Id.*

[62] *Id.*

[63] *Id.*

Copyright © 2017. American Immigration Lawyers Association. All rights reserved.

An approved O-1 petition may be valid for up to three years,[64] or for a period of time determined by the director to be necessary to accomplish the event or activity, whichever is less.[65] An approved O-2 petition "shall be valid for a period of time determined to be necessary to assist the O-1 alien to accomplish the event or activity, not to exceed 3 years."[66]

If the O-1 petition is approved before the start date of the assignment or event, then the petition will be valid for the "actual dates requested by the petitioner."[67] If the start date of the assignment or event has already occurred by the time the petition is approved, then the petition will be valid from the date of approval to the end date requested by the petitioner.[68]

B. O-1 Petitioners; Agents

A petition for O-1 or O-2 status may be filed by a U.S. employer, a U.S. agent, or a foreign employer through a U.S. agent, but not by the foreign national.[69] A U.S. employer should be established as a business or other legal entity, have an official business address, and have a business license or proof of doing business in the United States.[70]

If the beneficiary "will work concurrently for more than one employer within the same time period," then separate petitions must be filed by each employer.[71] Alternatively, "an established agent" may file a single petition on behalf of the employers,[72] as discussed below.

A U.S. agent may file both O-1 and O-2 petitions, and the regulations acknowledge that these services are typically required for "workers who are traditionally self-employed or workers who use agents to arrange short-term employment on their behalf with numerous employers,"[73] although not concurrently,[74] as well as for foreign employers,[75] as discussed below. A U.S. agent may be one of the following:

- The "actual employer" of the foreign national;

---

[64] 8 CFR §214.2(o)(6)(ii)(C).

[65] 8 CFR §214.2(o)(6)(iii)(A).

[66] 8 CFR §214.2(o)(6)(iii)(B).

[67] 8 CFR §214.2(o)(6)(ii)(A).

[68] 8 CFR §214.2(o)(6)(ii)(B).

[69] 8 CFR §214.2(o)(2)(i).

[70] *Matter of [name not provided]*, WAC 07 236 52246 (AAO Feb. 18, 2009), http://bit.ly/feb091d (USCIS revocation; company administratively dissolved by the state of Arizona).

[71] 8 CFR §214.2(o)(2)(iv)(B).

[72] *Id.*

[73] 8 CFR §214.2(o)(2)(iv)(E).

[74] USCIS Office of Business Liaison, Employer Information Bulletin 15, "Aliens with Extraordinary Ability (O-1) and Accompanying/Assisting Aliens (O-2)" (Dec. 8, 2004), 82 Interpreter Releases 180–84 (Jan. 17, 2005).

[75] 8 CFR §214.2(o)(2)(iv)(E).

Copyright © 2017. American Immigration Lawyers Association. All rights reserved.

- A "representative of both the employer and the beneficiary"; or
- A "person or entity," who has authorization from the employer "to act for" or "in place of" the employer.[76]

Any petition filed by a U.S. agent must meet certain conditions. First, "[a]n agent performing the function of an employer must provide the contractual agreement between the agent and the beneficiary which specifies the wage offered and the other terms and conditions of employment of the beneficiary."[77] As discussed later in this chapter, an oral agreement covering those specifics is acceptable if a written contract does not exist, provided a summary of the terms of the agreement is submitted.[78] The summary does not need to be signed by both parties.[79] No particular wage structure is required; a "detailed description of the wage offered or fee structure and that the wage offered/fee structure was agreed upon may satisfy" the requirement that the wage be specified.[80] But note that the description of the wage offered must be detailed. Vague descriptions like "compensation based on commission from sales of art and projects—varies" are insufficient, and may be found not to satisfy the criteria for an agent filing.[81]

Second, if the agent will file the petition because the beneficiary will work concurrently for more than one employer during the same period of time, then the agent should be "the representative of both the employers and the beneficiary."[82] This petition must include "a complete itinerary of the event or events," with specific details on "the dates of each service or engagement, the names and addresses of the actual employers, and the names and addresses of the establishments, venues, or locations where the services will be performed."[83] And since there must also be a "contract between the petitioner and the beneficiary,"[84] the practitioner should ensure that a copy of the contract or summary of the agreement is also included, and that any "terms and conditions of the employment" are explained and supported by supplementary evidence, if applicable.[85]

---

[76] *Id.*

[77] 8 CFR §214.2(o)(2)(iv)(E)(1); "USCIS Clarifies Requirements for Agents Filing as Petitioners for the O and P Visa Classification" (Oct. 7, 2009), AILA Doc. No. 09100861.

[78] USCIS, "'O' Nonimmigrant Visas—Agents as Petitioners Stakeholder Teleconference," (Apr. 13, 2011), AILA Doc. No. 11030437.

[79] *Id.*

[80] USCIS, "O Nonimmigrant Classifications Question and Answers" (Mar. 16, 2011), http://bit.ly/2cYANkO.

[81] *Matter of Z-P-*, ID# 15020 (AAO Mar. 25, 2016) (denied for failure to state wage as "exact amount or percentage of commission").

[82] 8 CFR §214.2(o)(2)(iv)(E)(2).

[83] *Id.*

[84] 8 CFR §214.2(o)(2)(iv)(E)(2).; USCIS, "O-1 Visa: Individuals with Extraordinary Ability or Achievement" (updated Sept. 14, 2015), http://bit.ly/2cCoXRa.

[85] *Id.*

Copyright © 2017. American Immigration Lawyers Association. All rights reserved.

The regulations also indicate that the agent may be "[a] person or company in business as an agent,"[86] to clarify that an agent "need not be limited to a person or entity who has entered into a formal agency agreement with the employer," although the "general legal agency relationship" is acceptable.[87] It seems that one petitioner may not file an O petition as the "representative" of multiple petitioners and as the agent of the beneficiary unless the petitioner "establish[es] that it is in 'business' as an agent,"[88] which in turn is based on a case-specific assessment of whether:

> "[I]t is more likely than not that the petitioner is in business as an agent for the series of event, services, or engagements that is the subject of the petition. The focus should be on whether the petitioner can establish that it is authorized to act as an agent for the other employers *for purposes of filing the petition*. This means that the petitioner does not have to demonstrate that it normally serves as an agent outside the context of this petition."[89]

> "Please note that a petitioner who will be filing as an agent for multiple employers must establish that it is duly authorized to act as an agent for the other employers."[90]

To address this issue, the petitioner may submit "a document signed by the beneficiary's other employer(s) which states that the petitioner is authorized to act in that employer's place as an agent for the limited purpose of filing the ... petition ... with USCIS," but USCIS should not require specific form language or issue an RFE for this reason.[91] Alternatively, other appropriate evidence includes a statement, signed by the petitioner and the other employers confirming the itinerary of events, as well as the names and addresses of all employers; copies of "other types of agency representation contracts," such as if the petitioner's business is as an agent; and "statements from the other employers regarding the nature of the petitioner's representation of the employers and beneficiary."[92] "Contracts between the agent and the employers" may be submitted;[93] although the guidance states that such documents "must" be included,[94] it remains unclear whether it is a true requirement, as discussed

---

[86] 8 CFR §214.2(o)(2)(iv)(E)(2).

[87] 72 Fed. Reg. 18508 (Apr. 16, 1997).

[88] "USCIS Clarifies Requirements for Agents Filing as Petitioners for the O and P Visa Classification" (Oct. 7, 2009), AILA Doc. No. 09100861. USCIS, D. Neufeld, "Requirements for Agents and Sponsors Filing as Petitioners for the O and P Visa Classifications" (Nov. 20, 2009), AILA Doc. No. 09113064.

[89] USCIS, D. Neufeld, "Requirements for Agents and Sponsors Filing as Petitioners for the O and P Visa Classifications" (Nov. 20, 2009), AILA Doc. No. 09113064 (emphasis in original).

[90] USCIS, "O-1 Visa: Individuals with Extraordinary Ability or Achievement" (updated Sept. 14, 2015), http://bit.ly/2cCoXRa.

[91] USCIS, D. Neufeld, "Requirements for Agents and Sponsors Filing as Petitioners for the O and P Visa Classifications" (Nov. 20, 2009), AILA Doc. No. 09113064.

[92] *Id.*

[93] USCIS, "O-1 Visa: Individuals with Extraordinary Ability or Achievement" (updated Sept. 14, 2015), http://bit.ly/2cCoXRa.

[94] *Id.*

Copyright © 2017. American Immigration Lawyers Association. All rights reserved.

below. Copies of fee arrangements may also be submitted, but USCIS has noted that "compensation is not a requirement to establish an agency."[95] As long as the agent-petitioner's authority to represent the other employers for purposes of filing the petition is established, an approved petition will have a validity period that covers all of the qualifying events for employment with all of the employers.[96] Otherwise, the petition will be approved only for the period of employment with the agent-petitioner, and an RFE may be issued before the petition is adjudicated.[97]

This November 2009 USCIS guidance appears to supercede October 2009 guidance that had required evidence that the other employers are clients of the petitioner.[98] The previous guidance required copies of contracts between the petitioner and the other employers, and evidence of the agency relationship between the petitioner and the other employers, or else the O petition would be approved only for the employment with the agent-petitioner.[99] This approach seems to resolve the conflict between the regulations and the previous guidance, which would have required contracts between the agent-petitioner and other employers in order to approve a petition filed by the agent as the representative of the employer and beneficiary and as the person or entity with authorization to act for and on behalf of the employer.[100] This interpretation is supported by the discussion in the rule's promulgation, discussed above, and by the fact that the three subparts of the regulation on "[a]gents as petitioners" indicate that all three types of parties may file O petitions as agents,[101] in contrast with the specific mention of the "person or company in business as an agent" when requiring a complete itinerary.[102]

It also seems likely that the new guidance supersedes a once oft-repeated AAO statement that not every individual or business entity may declare itself to be an "agent" and thereby claim standing to file O petitions,[103] although USCIS may nevertheless assess whether the agent is established, and "being 'established in the

---

[95] USCIS, D. Neufeld, "Requirements for Agents and Sponsors Filing as Petitioners for the O and P Visa Classifications" (Nov. 20, 2009), AILA Doc. No. 09113064.

[96] *Id.*

[97] *Id.*

[98] *Id.* (clarifying USCIS Update, "USCIS Clarifies Requirements for Agents Filing as Petitioners for the O and P Visa Classification" (Oct. 7, 2009) AILA Doc. No. 09100861). Note that the November 2009 guidance is linked to from USCIS's main web page on O-1s, while the October 2009 guidance is not: "O-1 Visa: Individuals with Extraordinary Ability or Achievement" (updated Sept. 14, 2015), http://bit.ly/2cCoXRa.

[99] "USCIS Clarifies Requirements for Agents Filing as Petitioners for the O and P Visa Classification" (Oct. 7, 2009) AILA Doc. No. 09100861.

[100] 8 CFR §214.2(o)(2)(iv)(E).

[101] *Id.*

[102] *Id.*

[103] *See, e.g., Matter of [name not provided]*, EAC 08 134 51786 (AAO May 4, 2009), http://bit.ly/may091d. *See also Matter of [name not provided]*, WAC 07 015 50561 (AAO Nov. 7, 2007), http://bit.ly/nov072d. Searches of both the USCIS website and the Premium Fastcase AAO non-precedent decision databases on AILALink (http://ailalink.aila.org) produced no examples of this language in an AAO decision since the November 2009 guidance.

Copyright © 2017. American Immigration Lawyers Association. All rights reserved.

arts community'" or another industry may be deemed "not equivalent to being 'established' as an agent."[104] USCIS may also review whether the named agent provided any services.[105]

A foreign employer, which is defined as "any employer who is not amenable to service of process in the United States," may not petition directly for an O-1 or O-2 nonimmigrant "but instead must use the services of a United States agent to file a petition for an O nonimmigrant alien."[106] The U.S. agent, in turn, "must be authorized to file the petition, and to accept services of process in the United States in proceedings ... on behalf of the foreign employer."[107] Even if an agent files the O-1 or O-2 petition on behalf of a foreign employer, the foreign employer is, nevertheless, through the U.S. agent,[108] "responsible for complying with all of the employer sanctions provisions" regarding verifying the identity and employment authorization of workers in the United States.[109]

C. Industry-Specific Requirements

The O-1 classification provides U.S. employment authorization for many different types of individuals and fields, which may be grouped into two categories with respect to the required standard of evidence:

- For the fields of science, education, business, athletics, or art, the foreign national beneficiary must be able to demonstrate "sustained national or international acclaim,"[110] and must be "coming temporarily to the United States to continue work in the area of extraordinary ability";[111] and

- For the fields of motion picture or television production, the foreign national must have "a demonstrated record of extraordinary achievement,"[112] and must be " oming temporarily to the United States to continue work in the area of extraordinary achievement."[113]

USCIS generally refers to the first group of fields, other than the arts, as O-1A, and the second group plus the arts as O-1B.[114]

---

[104] *Matter of [name not provided]*, EAC 08 134 51786 (AAO May 4, 2009), http://bit.ly/may091d. *See also Matter of [name not provided]*, WAC 07 015 50561 (AAO Nov. 7, 2007), http://bit.ly/nov072d.

[105] *Matter of [name not provided]*, EAC 08 134 51786 (AAO May 4, 2009), http://bit.ly/may091d.

[106] 8 CFR §214.2(o)(2)(i); 72 Fed. Reg. 18508 (Apr. 16, 1997).

[107] 8 CFR §214.2(o)(2)(i).

[108] 72 Fed. Reg. 18508 (Apr. 16, 1997).

[109] 8 CFR §214.2(o)(2)(iv)(E)(3).

[110] INA §101(a)(15)(O)(i); 8 CFR §214.2(o)(3)(iii).

[111] 8 CFR §214.2(o)(1)(ii)(A)(1).

[112] INA §101(a)(15)(O)(i); 8 CFR §214.2(o)(1)(i).

[113] 8 CFR §214.2(o)(1)(ii)(A)(2).

[114] USCIS, "O-1 Visa: Individuals with Extraordinary Ability or Achievement" (updated Sept. 14, 2015), https://www.uscis.gov/working-united-states/temporary-workers/o-1-visa-individuals-extraordinary-ability-or-achievement.

Copyright © 2017. American Immigration Lawyers Association. All rights reserved.

The INA defines extraordinary ability in the arts for O-1 purposes as "distinction."[115] A legacy INS memorandum states that "distinction" in the arts, for artists and entertainers,[116] is similar to "prominence" as that term was previously defined for H-1B classification,[117] for foreign nationals "of distinguished merit and ability."[118] Generally, the factors to establish prominence included "expert opinions, including critical reviews, popularity, box office appeal, sales of records, and contractual arrangements, including remuneration,"[119] and the gist of these criteria have been stated in the regulations, although there are differences in the types of evidence.[120] However, other USCIS guidance states:

> "Neither of these terms precisely equates to the term 'distinguished merit and ability' found in the former H-1 category and cited in numerous precedent decisions published prior to the 1990 amendments. Accordingly, those decisions should not be cited in decisions or used as references for O-1 petition adjudication."[121]

The likely reason for this approach seems to be:

> "Although Congress intended these two categories of aliens [of O-1 nonimmigrants and H-1B nonimmigrants under the previous regulations] to be 'essentially the same,' and the regulatory definitions of these two classifications are essentially the same, the evidentiary standards for establishing eligibility for O-1 nonimmigrant classification differ from those for H-1B prominent aliens under previous law."[122]

The practitioner may nevertheless wish to review the case history as it may assist in identifying "other comparable evidence" for establishing extraordinary ability,[123] as discussed below. Another relevant factor is that popularity in the arts, and especially the performing arts, may be subject to fads: "While one of [the beneficiary's] songs has reached the pinnacle of success in Britain, their popularity

---

[115] INA §101(a)(46).

[116] AFM 33.9.

[117] Legacy INS, L. Weinig, "Policy Guidelines for the Adjudication of O and P Petitions," (June 25, 1992), 69 Interpreter Releases 1084–87 (Aug. 31, 1992) (stating that legacy INS "has interpreted the term 'distinction' as it relates to O-1 artists to be identical to the prior H-1B standard for prominent aliens"); Legacy INS, P. Virtue, "O-1 and P Nonimmigrant Visa Classifications" (Sept. 29, 1993), 1 INS and DOJ Legal Opinions §93-76.

[118] *Matter of Caron International, Inc.*, 19 I&N Dec. 791 (Comm'r 1988).

[119] *Matter of Shaw*, 11 I&N Dec. 277 (Dist. Dir. 1965).

[120] Legacy INS, P. Virtue, "O-1 and P Nonimmigrant Visa Classifications" (Sept. 29, 1993), 1 INS and DOJ Legal Opinions §93-76.

[121] AFM 33.2.

[122] Legacy INS, P. Virtue, "O-1 and P Nonimmigrant Visa Classifications" (Sept. 29, 1993), 1 INS and DOJ Legal Opinions §93-76.

[123] *Id.*

Copyright © 2017. American Immigration Lawyers Association. All rights reserved.

has been strictly ephemeral, as is characteristic of most songs, and even performers, in this idiom."[124]

Similarly, the standard for extraordinary ability in science, business, education, or athletics is "extremely high" and requires more than "prominence" as that term was interpreted for the previous H-1B classification: "The vast majority of the aliens seeking O-1 classification will be eligible for H-1B classification as most of the occupations will probably be specialty occupations."[125] In contrast, as stated by the AAO:

"It should be noted that under the statute, the standard for an O-1 artist is significantly lower than the standard for an alien of extraordinary ability in the fields of science, education, business, or athletics. Petitioners are required to establish only that the O-1 artist is prominent in his or her field of endeavor. Eligibility for O-1 classification in the field of arts is not limited to those aliens who have reached the very top of their professions as is required in the fields of science, business, education, or athletics."[126]

USCIS guidance also indicates that a higher standard is imposed for individuals who work in motion picture or television production than is imposed for individuals who have extraordinary ability in the arts,[127] although the "regulations do not limit these individuals to the small percentage who have risen to the top of their field."[128] Specifically:

"Until August 15, 1994, [legacy INS] likened the standard for aliens of extraordinary achievement in the motion picture and television industry to the standard for aliens of extraordinary ability in the arts. This has been modified by a final rule, however, which currently provides that an alien of extraordinary achievement in motion pictures or television must now meet a higher standard than that necessary for aliens of extraordinary ability in the arts."[129]

Therefore, the standard of "prominence" should no longer be applied to individuals who will work in the field of motion picture and television production, and foreign nationals who are "merely well-known" will generally not qualify.[130]

---

[124] *Matter of Shaw*, 11 I&N Dec. 277 (Dist. Dir. 1965).

[125] Legacy INS, L. Weinig, "Policy Guidelines for the Adjudication of O and P Petitions," (June 25, 1992), 69 Interpreter Releases 1084–87 (Aug. 31, 1992).

[126] *Matter of [name not provided]*, EAC 96 058 51556 (AAO June 25, 1998), 19 Immig. Rptr. B2-62; *Matter of [name not provided]*, SRC 03 237 50782 (AAO Apr. 13, 2005), http://bit.ly/apr051d (stating that the "AAO concurs that the less rigorous standard for arts ('distinction') applies").

[127] USCIS Office of Business Liaison, Employer Information Bulletin 15, "Aliens with Extraordinary Ability (O-1) and Accompanying/Assisting Aliens (O-2)" (Dec. 8, 2004), 82 Interpreter Releases 180–84 (Jan. 17, 2005) (noting "high level of achievement" vs. "very high level of accomplishment," respectively (emphasis in original)).

[128] AFM 33.9.

[129] *Matter of [name not provided]*, WAC 95 042 52458 (AAO Jan. 12, 1995), 14 Immig. Rptr. B2-43 (citing 59 Fed. Reg. 41818, 41832 (Aug. 15, 1994)).

[130] *Matter of [name not provided]*, WAC 95 042 52458 (AAO Jan. 12, 1995), 14 Immig. Rptr. B2-43.

Copyright © 2017. American Immigration Lawyers Association. All rights reserved.

For each of these categories, the regulations allow extraordinary ability to be established either by a one-time major award or by at least three types of evidence, as discussed below. A petitioner may not pick and choose the standard and types of evidence.[131] When determining which standard to apply, USCIS and/or the AAO may evaluate the proposed job duties of the assignment, and the business activity of the petitioner is not as important.[132] If the incorrect standard is applied by USCIS, then the petitioner may appeal and the AAO should remand the case.[133]

With the exception of sections that specifically address O-1 and O-2 petitions on behalf of individuals involved in motion picture and television production, in the interest of brevity, this chapter will reference the "extraordinary ability" of the foreign national beneficiary.

1. Extraordinary Ability in Science, Education, Business, or Athletics (O-1A)

The regulations state: "Extraordinary ability in the field of science, education, business, or athletics means a level of expertise indicating that the person is one of the small percentage who have arisen to the very top of the field of endeavor."[134]

For truly outstanding individuals, evidence of "[r]eceipt of a major, internationally recognized award, such as the Nobel Prize,"[135] or "major league MVP,"[136] may suffice. Alternatively, a superior level of achievement and renown may be demonstrated by submitting at least three of the following types of evidence:

- Evidence that the beneficiary received "nationally or internationally recognized prizes or awards for excellence in the field of endeavor";

- Evidence that the beneficiary holds membership in a professional industry association, "which require outstanding achievements of their members, as judged by recognized national or international experts in their disciplines or fields";

- "Published material in professional or major trade publications or major media about the alien," which describe the beneficiary's work and/or achievements and

---

[131] *Matter of [name not provided]*, WAC 07 273 54624 (AAO Mar. 11, 2009), http://bit.ly/mar091d (stating that the "petitioner cannot choose to submit evidence applicable to the criteria for the athlete category and then argue for the lesser standard applicable to aliens in the arts field").

[132] *Matter of [name not provided]*, LIN 06 103 50190 (AAO Dec. 13, 2006), http://bit.ly/dec061d (stating that "[w]hile the services offered by the petitioning center may involve 'spiritual' teachings, the beneficiary' position and duties are business related," and did not fall under the requested field of art).

[133] *Matter of [name not provided]*, WAC 06 163 50719 (AAO Nov. 15, 2006), http://bit.ly/nov061d; *Matter of [name not provided]*, WAC 03 193 52043 (AAO Nov. 22, 2006), http://bit.ly/110601d; *Matter of [name not provided]*, WAC 03 193 52043 (AAO Mar. 24, 2006), http://bit.ly/mar064d.

[134] 8 CFR §214.2(o)(3)(ii); *Matter of [name not provided]*, SRC 98 066 50295 (AAO Aug. 2, 1998), 19 Immig. Rptr. B2-77 (accepting "testimonials assert[ing] that the beneficiary is in the top 5% of his field").

[135] 8 CFR §214.2(o)(3)(iii)(A).

[136] AFM 33.4; *Matter of [name not provided]*, LIN 01 245 54595 (AAO Oct. 16, 2002), 26 Immig. Rptr. B2-81 (beneficiary voted most valuable player in five different basketball tournaments).

Copyright © 2017. American Immigration Lawyers Association. All rights reserved.

"which shall include the title, date, and author of such published material, and any necessary translation," as discussed below;

- Evidence that the beneficiary served "as a judge of the work of others in the same or in an allied field of specialization to that for which classification is sought," either individually or as a member of a panel;

- "Evidence of the alien's original scientific, scholarly, or business-related contributions of major significance in the field," as discussed below;

- "Evidence of the alien's authorship of scholarly articles in the field, in professional journals, or other major media";

- Evidence that the beneficiary is or was "employed in a critical or essential capacity for organizations and establishments that have a distinguished reputation," as discussed below; and

- "Evidence that the alien has either commanded a high salary or will command a high salary or other remuneration for services, evidenced by contracts or other reliable evidence."[137]

Chess[138] and competitive ballroom dance have been viewed as within the field of athletics, especially since the International Olympic Committee "has formally recognized" the latter as "a sport under consideration for inclusion in the Olympic games, although it is not yet a medal sport."[139] Horse or other animal training may be considered to be in the field of athletics if the training is for competitive sports such as polo, racing, or "cutting"; however, if the training is for entertainment, such as for circuses or for television or film, it may be considered to be in the arts.[140]

2. Extraordinary Ability in the Arts (O-1B)

The regulation defines "arts" as "any field of creative activity or endeavor such as, but not limited to, fine arts, visual arts, culinary arts, and performing arts."[141] Architecture is also included in the arts,[142] as is acrobatic circus performance.[143]

---

[137] 8 CFR §214.2(o)(3)(iii)(B).

[138] *Matter of [name not provided]*, WAC 04 058 51676 (AAO Jan. 17, 2006), http://bit.ly/jan062d.

[139] *Matter of [name not provided]*, WAC 07 273 54624 (AAO Mar. 11, 2009), http://bit.ly/mar091d. *See also Matter of [name and case number not provided]* (AAO June 19, 2014), AILA Doc. No. 14121644, finding competitive ballroom dancing to be a sport and not an art because of the competitive element.

[140] *Matter of T-H-C-A-I-A-C-H-,* ID# 10527 (AAO Dec. 16, 2015) (horse trainer for "cutting" is subject to criteria for athletics rather than arts, notwithstanding the specific inclusion of animal trainers in the definition of arts at 8 CFR §214.2(o)(3)(ii). AAO distinguishes the regulatory provision on the basis that the mention is in the context of "other essential personnel" related to the creative arts).

[141] 8 CFR §214.2(o)(3)(ii).

[142] *Matter of [name not provided]*, EAC 96 058 51556 (AAO June 25, 1998), 19 Immig. Rptr. B2-62 (reversing denial of petition, *inter alia*, where legacy INS required "the beneficiary to meet the standards of extraordinary ability in the sciences, education, business or athletics").

[143] *Matter of [name not provided]*, WAC 07 054 53346 (AAO May 1, 2009), http://bit.ly/may0901d. Circus personnel with extraordinary ability who seek O-1 status "are not subject to the international recognition and 'sustained and substantial' group relationship requirements" of P-1 status. Legacy INS, P. Virtue,
Cont'd

Copyright © 2017. American Immigration Lawyers Association. All rights reserved.

An individual who will coach other people in sporting activities may nevertheless be considered an artist as long as the other individuals will not compete in sporting events.[144]

An individual need not be a "principal" creator or performer in order to qualify for O-1 classification; "other essential persons such as, but not limited to, directors, set designers, lighting designers, sound designers, choreographers, choreologists, conductors, orchestrators, coaches, arrangers, musical supervisors, costume designers, makeup artists, flight masters, stage technicians, and animal trainers,"[145] or fight masters,[146] may also obtain O-1 status,[147] although the petition would need to demonstrate the individual's extraordinary ability in the particular field, such as in animal training. As noted above, however, other animal training may be considered to be in the field of arts only if the training is for entertainment uses, such as for circuses or for television or film; otherwise, it may be considered to be in athletics if the training is for competitive sports such as polo, racing, or "cutting."[148]

To establish extraordinary ability in arts, the petition should demonstrate how the individual has achieved "distinction," which, in turn, is defined as "a high level of achievement in the field of arts evidenced by a degree of skill and recognition substantially above that ordinarily encountered to the extent that a person described as prominent is renowned, leading, or well-known in the field of arts."[149] This definition excludes not only the "struggling artist," but also an artist who is an amateur,[150] or only locally known, as the individual must be "prominent"[151] and not merely "a successful artist able to make a living from the sale of her works," even if exhibitions of the beneficiary's artwork are shown at "highly selective" galleries.[152] As a practical matter, renown in the field should be shown by industry articles and recommendations from industry experts, as discussed below.

If the beneficiary has been nominated for and/or received "significant national or international awards or prizes in the particular field such as an Academy Award, an Emmy, a Grammy, or a Director's Guild Award," then this evidence may suffice.[153]

"Classification for Circus Performers" (Mar. 3, 1994), 1 INS and DOJ Legal Opinions §94-16. For a discussion of P-1 status, see Volume 1: Chapter Thirteen, "P Visas and Status."

[144] *Matter of [name not provided]*, WAC 07 054 53346 (AAO May 1, 2009), http://bit.ly/may0901d. *Cf. Matter of [name not provided]*, WAC 07 273 54624 (AAO Mar. 11, 2009), http://bit.ly/mar091d (petitioner sought classification for an artist but AAO stated that "the director should have evaluated the instant petition for classification of the beneficiary as an alien of extraordinary ability in athletics").

[145] 8 CFR §214.2(o)(3)(ii).

[146] *Matter of [name not provided]*, WAC 95 042 52458 (AAO Jan. 12, 1995), 14 Immig. Rptr. B2-43.

[147] 8 CFR §214.2(o)(3)(ii).

[148] *Matter of T-H-C-A-I-A-C-H-*, ID# 10527 (AAO Dec. 16, 2015).

[149] *Id.*

[150] AFM 33.9.

[151] 8 CFR §214.2(o)(3)(iv).

[152] *Matter of [name not provided]*, EAC 08 134 51786 (AAO May 4, 2009), http://bit.ly/may091d.

[153] 8 CFR §214.2(o)(3)(iv)(A).

Copyright © 2017. American Immigration Lawyers Association. All rights reserved.

Alternatively, distinction and prominence may be shown by submitting at least three of the following types of evidence:

- "Evidence that the alien has performed, and will perform, services as a lead or starring participant in productions or events which have a distinguished reputation as evidenced by critical reviews, advertisements, publicity releases, publications contracts, or endorsements,"[154] or "by articles in newspapers, trade journals, publications, or testimonials";[155]

- Evidence that the beneficiary "has achieved national or international recognition" for his or her artistic work in the form of "critical reviews or other published materials by or about the individual in major newspapers, trade journals, magazines, or other publications";

- "Evidence that the alien has performed, and will perform, in a lead, starring, or critical role for organizations and establishments that have a distinguished reputation," as documented "by articles in newspapers, trade journals, publications, or testimonials";

- Evidence that the beneficiary "has a record of major commercial or critically acclaimed successes," based on "such indicators as title, rating, standing in the field, box office receipts, motion picture or television ratings, and other occupational achievements reported in trade journals, major newspapers, or other publications";

- Evidence of "significant recognition for achievements from organizations, critics, government agencies, or other recognized experts in the field," where the "testimonials must be in a form which clearly indicates the author's authority, expertise, and knowledge of the alien's achievements," similar to the recommendation statements or affidavits discussed below; or

- "Evidence that the alien has either commanded a high salary or will command a high salary or other substantial remuneration for services in relation to others in the field, as evidenced by contracts or other reliable evidence."[156]

In addition, the O-1 petition may be supplemented with other, "comparable" documentary evidence that satisfies the standard for other types of individuals with extraordinary ability.[157]

3. Extraordinary Ability in Motion Picture or Television Production (O-1B)

As stated in the regulations:

---

[154] 8 CFR §214.2(o)(3)(iv)(B).

[155] USCIS Office of Business Liaison, Employer Information Bulletin 15, "Aliens with Extraordinary Ability (O-1) and Accompanying/Assisting Aliens (O-2)" (Dec. 8, 2004), 82 Interpreter Releases 180–84 (Jan. 17, 2005).

[156] 8 CFR §214.2(o)(3)(iv)(B).

[157] 8 CFR §214.2(o)(3)(iv)(C).

Copyright © 2017. American Immigration Lawyers Association. All rights reserved.

"Extraordinary achievement with respect to motion picture and television productions, as commonly defined in the industry, means a very high level of accomplishment in the motion picture or television industry evidenced by a degree of skill and recognition significantly above that ordinarily encountered to the extent that the person is recognized as outstanding, notable, or leading in the motion picture or television field."[158]

Although the field is stated as "motion picture or television production," O-1 classification is not limited to actual producers; individuals who will be "in the motion picture and television industry,"[159] and "others,"[160] may also obtain O-1 status: "Neither the statute nor regulations preclude certain occupations within the field of motion pictures or television from the classification sought in this matter."[161] The practitioner should note, however, that it may be difficult for individuals in occupations of lesser acclaim, such as assistant directors and associate producers, to qualify.[162]

Similarly, motion picture or television production may include work on "corporate videos and commercials,"[163] or composing music and writing screenplays.[164] But work in the field of motion picture or television production should not automatically mean that an individual should be held to this standard if work is performed for other industries.[165] The practitioner should, however, clearly state that classification is sought based on extraordinary ability in another field and caution the client that the extraordinary achievement standard may nevertheless be imposed, as in one case, the AAO stated: "Because the petitioner seeks to employ the beneficiary in motion picture and television productions, it was reasonable for the director to consider the petition in the context of 'motion picture and television productions' rather than under the category of 'arts.'"[166]

Evidence that the beneficiary was nominated for and/or received "significant national or international awards or prizes in the particular field such as an Academy Award, an Emmy, a Grammy, or a Director's Guild Award" may be sufficient, in its own, for approval of the O-1 petition. In the more common event that the beneficiary has not earned such a nomination or award, the O-1 petition may include at least three of the following types of evidence:

---

[158] 8 CFR §214.2(o)(3)(ii).

[159] 9 FAM 402.13(A).

[160] AFM 33.2.

[161] *Matter of [name not provided]*, WAC 95 042 52458 (AAO Jan. 12, 1995), 14 Immig. Rptr. B2-43.

[162] *Id.*

[163] *Matter of [name not provided]*, WAC 07 006 52866 (AAO Mar. 5, 2008), http://bit.ly/mar081d.

[164] *Matter of [name not provided]*, WAC 03 193 52043 (AAO Nov. 22, 2006), http://bit.ly/nov0601d.

[165] *Matter of [name not provided]*, WAC 07 006 52866 (AAO Mar. 5, 2008), http://bit.ly/mar081d (for a graphic artist and design editor whose work was "not limited to film and television," AAO accepted that USCIS applied the wrong standard but there was "no prejudicial error" where the "RFE requested evidence to establish that the beneficiary is an alien of extraordinary ability in the arts").

[166] *Id.*

Copyright © 2017. American Immigration Lawyers Association. All rights reserved.

- "Evidence that the alien has performed, and will perform, services as a lead or starring participant in productions or events which have a distinguished reputation as evidenced by critical reviews, advertisements, publicity releases, publications contracts, or endorsements";

- Evidence that the beneficiary "has achieved national or international recognition" for his/her production work in the form of "critical reviews or other published materials by or about the individual in major newspapers, trade journals, magazines, or other publications";

- "Evidence that the alien has performed, and will perform, in a lead, starring, or critical role for organizations and establishments that have a distinguished reputation," as documented "by articles in newspapers, trade journals, publications, or testimonials";

- Evidence that the beneficiary "has a record of major commercial or critically acclaimed successes," based on "such indicators as title, rating, standing in the field, box office receipts, motion picture or television ratings, and other occupational achievements reported in trade journals, major newspapers, or other publications";

- Evidence of "significant recognition for achievements from organizations, critics, government agencies, or other recognized experts in the field," where the "testimonials must be in a form which clearly indicates the author's authority, expertise, and knowledge of the alien's achievements," similar to the recommendation statements or affidavits discussed below; or

- Evidence that the alien has either commanded a high salary or will command a high salary or other substantial remuneration for services in relation to others in "the field, as evidenced by contracts or other reliable evidence."[167]

While the regulations virtually mirror each other when discussing the field of art and the field of motion picture and television production,[168] the regulations do not allow for submission of "comparable evidence" for the latter.[169] In practice, however, submission of "comparable evidence" can strengthen a filing even though the regulations do not explicitly allow it.

D. Criteria to Establish Extraordinary Ability

As discussed in Volume 1: Chapter Two, "Basic Nonimmigrant Concepts, AAO decisions, unlike Board of Immigration Appeals (BIA) decisions,[170] and the

---

[167] 8 CFR §214.2(o)(3)(v)(B).

[168] *Matter of [name not provided]*, WAC 07 006 52866 (AAO Mar. 5, 2008), http://bit.ly/mar081d (stating that "the enumerated evidentiary criteria to establish eligibility under either of these standards are exactly the same").

[169] 8 CFR §214.2(o)(3)(v)(B). *See also* the USCIS website, which states that the comparable evidence "exception does not apply to the motion picture or television industry," https://www.uscis.gov/working-united-states/temporary-workers/o-1-visa-individuals-extraordinary-ability-or-achievement.

[170] 8 CFR §§103.37(g) and 1003.1(g).

Copyright © 2017. American Immigration Lawyers Association. All rights reserved.

Adjudicator's Field Manual, are not binding on USCIS,[171] unless they are adopted as precedent decisions.[172] The AAO decisions are, however, mentioned frequently in the foregoing sections, to inform the practitioner about adjudicatory trends, potential grounds for petition denial, and strategies to resolve the underlying concern stated by the AAO. Similarly, although "extraordinary ability" criteria for O-1 petitions and for immigrant visa classification are very similar, this does not automatically mean that guidance is absolutely cross-applicable between the two. For example, when asked about a federal court decision for the EB-1 immigrant visa classification (*Kazarian v. USCIS*), USCIS responded with awareness of the decision, but indicated that it would "continue to adjudicate as [it] ha[s] previously."[173] A few months after that discussion, USCIS issued a policy memorandum that applied the *Kazarian* decision to other immigrant categories that involved providing documentation from multiple categories of evidence, such as exceptional ability and outstanding professors and researchers, but made no mention of nonimmigrant categories with the same type of evidence structure, namely Os and Ps.[174]

That being said, experience has shown that, while USCIS rarely explicitly references *Kazarian* in RFEs and denials for O-1 cases, it does often seem to apply a *Kazarian*-type approach, at least in broad terms, to them.[175] The AAO does, from time to time, directly cite and apply *Kazarian* in O-1 cases,[176] but often simply uses the two-step analysis derived from that case without direct reference to it.[177]

Kazarian is discussed in greater detail in Volume 2: Chapter 3, "The Immigrant Visa Petition." But, briefly by way of background, the *Kazarian* court criticized USCIS's prior approach to EB-1 extraordinary ability, in which USCIS imposed standards on the categories of evidence that were not contained in the regulations, such as looking to the research community's reaction to published articles to determine whether the category for authorship of scholarly articles was satisfied.[178] The court found that USCIS could not impose such additional standards on the already-detailed evidentiary requirements, and suggested instead that that "analysis might be relevant to a final merits determination."[179]

---

[171] "AILA/USCIS Liaison Minutes" (Mar. 19, 2009), AILA Doc. No. 09031920.

[172] *See, e.g.*, USCIS, J. Scharfen, "Re: *Matter of Vazquez*" (July 31, 2007), http://bit.ly/2druXxy.

[173] "CSC Stakeholders Meeting" (Apr. 29, 2010), AILA Doc. No. 10062988, with respect to applicability of *Kazarian v. USCIS*, 596 F.3d 1115 (9th Cir. 2010), AILA Doc. No. 10030420, to the O-1 category.

[174] USCIS, "Evaluation of Evidentiary Criteria in Certain Form I-140 Petitions (AFM Update AD-11-14)" PM-602-0005.1 (Dec. 22, 2010), AILA Doc. No. 11020231.

[175] *E.g., Matter of AM-,* ID# 15019 (AAO Jan. 8, 2016), in which the AAO noted, without directly citing *Kazarian*, that the petitioner's framing of the evidentiary question in a two-step approach (which is the approach used in *Kazarian*) was correct.

[176] *E.g., Matter of [name and case number not given],* (AAO Jan. 10, 2012), http://bit.ly/jan122d; *Matter of [name and case number not given],* (AAO June 14, 2013), http://bit.ly/jun131d.

[177] *E.g., Matter of AM-,* ID# 15019 (AAO Jan. 8, 2016).

[178] *Kazarian v. USCIS*, 596 F.3d 1115 (9th Cir. 2010), AILA Doc. No. 10030420.

[179] *Id.,* at 1121-1122.

Copyright © 2017. American Immigration Lawyers Association. All rights reserved.

From that suggestion, USCIS extrapolated a new, two-step adjudicative approach.[180] First, the evidence required by the regulations is evaluated to see if the required number of categories is fulfilled. While the "quality and caliber" of the evidence should be evaluated, no determination is made at this step regarding whether the individual has risen to the top of the field and/or has sustained national or international acclaim.[181] This is followed by a "final merits determination" by which the quality of the evidence is considered, and the evidence evaluated together to determine if the definition of extraordinary ability is met.[182]

USCIS asserts that, post-*Kazarian*, "objective evaluation of the evidence listed at 8 CFR 204.5(h)(3) will continue as before; what changes is when the determination of extraordinary ability occurs in the adjudicative process." Thus, the evidence submitted, while supposed to be initially evaluated within the exact language of the regulations, nevertheless needs to meet the other tests imposed by the agency over the years, as those tests are now applied at the second, final merits, step.

The result for the petitioner is that what needs to be submitted remains largely unchanged. While, for example, it no longer is necessary to show that an award reflects sustained acclaim to count as having fulfilled the prizes or awards category, if the adjudicator cannot find evidence *somewhere* in the package that the beneficiary's acclaim is sustained, the petition still will be denied. The difference is that it will be denied for failing to demonstrate sustained acclaim rather than for failing to fulfill the evidentiary criteria.[183] Thus, one must ensure that, if the award does not show sustained acclaim, documentation in other categories does. Moreover, the application of a *Kazarian*-type analysis in adjudication of O-1 petitions means that it is valuable to show that the O-1 beneficiary meets as many of the criteria as possible, even though just three of the criteria are required. By showing that the beneficiary meets additional criteria, even if the argument for those criteria is not overly strong, the second step of the *Kazarian* analysis that will occur as part of the adjudication can be satisfied.

Although a "petitioner is not required to demonstrate that [the beneficiary] meets all possible criteria listed in the regulations,"[184] USCIS "cannot make a favorable determination simply because the petitioner has submitted three of the forms of documentation mentioned."[185] The general adjudicatory approach to O-1 petitions

---

[180] USCIS, "Evaluation of Evidentiary Criteria in Certain Form I-140 Petitions (AFM Update AD-11-14)" PM-602-0005.1 (Dec. 22, 2010), AILA Doc. No. 11020231.

[181] AFM 22.2(i)(1)(A).

[182] AFM 22.2(i)(1)(A). Extra-regulatory standards previously considered as part of the evaluation of the evidentiary categories are now considered in this step, for example "whether the judging responsibilities were internal and whether the scholarly articles ... are cited by others in the field."

[183] *Rijal v. USCIS*, 683 F.3d 1030 (9th Cir. 2012), AILA Doc. No. 12061356, adopting the district court opinion at 772 F. Supp. 2d 1339 (W.D. Wash. 2011).

[184] "TSC Approved Minutes" (June 3, 2002), AILA Doc. No. 02082742. Although the guidance relates to extraordinary ability immigrant visa petitions, the principle should remain the same.

[185] AFM 33.4(d).

Copyright © 2017. American Immigration Lawyers Association. All rights reserved.

seems to be that USCIS's "decision in a particular case is dependent upon the quality of the evidence submitted by the petitioner, not just the quantity of the evidence."[186] Therefore, the analysis is typically articulated as a totality of the circumstances evaluation:[187]

"A petitioner cannot establish eligibility for this classification merely by submitting evidence that simply relates to the criterion. In determining whether a [beneficiary] meets a specific criterion, the evidence must itself be evaluated in terms of whether it establishes that the [beneficiary] has sustained national or international acclaim."[188]

"However, examiners have discretion to consider all the evidence submitted with respect to each qualifying criteria. A petition may be approved by conclusively satisfying three criteria or, if the evidence is less conclusive, the alien may need to meet the threshold for approval by submitting evidence addressing additional criteria set forth in the regulations."[189]

"Sustained national or international acclaim" and a "demonstrated record of extraordinary achievement" are generally interpreted as being based on a history of multiple achievements, rather than "a single achievement."[190] For a strong O-1 petition, the pattern should start at least several years before the O-1 petition is filed,[191] and continue up through the year the O-1 petition is filed.[192] Petitions should contain current evidence of the beneficiary's achievements, rather than old evidence from when he or she was a junior competitor, as USCIS may deem the latter to be insufficient.[193] Therefore, the practitioner should take care that any evidence and/or testimonials submitted with the petition are recent.[194]

---

[186] *Matter of [name not provided]*, SRC 98 066 50295 (AAO Aug. 2, 1998), 19 Immig. Rptr. B2-77.

[187] AFM 33.4(d); "NSC Business Product Line Teleconference Q&As" (May 26, 2005), AILA Doc. No. 05052761.

[188] *Matter of [name not provided]*, LIN 03 239 51646 (AAO May 25, 2005), http://bit.ly/may0501d.

[189] "AILA/TSC Liaison Minutes" (Oct. 7, 2002), AILA Doc. No. 02121641. Although the discussion relates to extraordinary ability immigrant visa petitions, the principle should remain the same.

[190] *Matter of [name not provided]*, EAC 07 224 51635 (AAO June 23, 2009), http://bit.ly/jun091d.

[191] *Matter of [name not provided]*, LIN 06 039 53131 (AAO June 29, 2006), http://bit.ly/jun091d (noting that almost all of the beneficiary's competitions "took place within one year of the filing of the petition").

[192] *Matter of [name not provided]*, SRC 06 138 52302 (AAO Nov. 7, 2007), http://bit.ly/nov0701d (stating that the "dearth of recent documentary evidence indicates that whatever acclaim the beneficiary may have earned in the past has not been sustained"); *Matter of [name not provided]*, EAC 04 800 31656 (AAO June 1, 2007), http://bit.ly/jun071d; *Matter of [name not provided]*, WAC 07 055 52449 (AAO Mar. 21, 2008), http://bit.ly/mar0801d (membership in an industry association "appears to have occurred six or more years before the petition was filed and so does not demonstrate the requisite sustained acclaim," and articles submitted were published seven years before the petition was filed).

[193] *Matter of [name not provided]*, SRC 05 099 50283 (AAO Mar. 24, 2006), http://bit.ly/mar065d; *Matter of [name not provided]*, LIN 04 114 52837 (AAO Jan. 26, 2005), http://bit.ly/jan052d.

[194] *Matter of [name not provided]*, EAC 05 028 52811 (AAO Jan. 9, 2007), http://bit.ly/jan071d (beneficiary had won numerous awards but approximately seven years before the petition was filed); *Matter of [name not provided]*, LIN 04 156 52532 (AAO July 11, 2005), http://bit.ly/jul052d (numerous awards earned six years

Cont'd

Copyright © 2017. American Immigration Lawyers Association. All rights reserved.

Similarly, especially for more youthful beneficiaries, testimonials indicating that the beneficiary "shows promise," "is just beginning in the field,"[195] an emerging talent,[196] or "is in the relative infancy of her career,"[197] or discussing expertise and accomplishments in the context of "limited professional experience," have been construed by USCIS as indicative of the fact that the beneficiary has not yet attained extraordinary ability.[198] For example, in an athlete petition, the AAO commented on the beneficiary's status as a "rising competitor who is just beginning to compete among the sport's most established and successful [competitors]."[199] The AAO has noted that "documented recognition of achievements, not talent, is the standard by which extraordinary ability is measured."[200] Therefore, the practitioner may wish to encourage the petitioner to include a detailed discussion of the beneficiary's achievements, "career and employment history."[201] If relevant developments or products are in the experimental stage, then USCIS may determine that this only establishes the beneficiary's potential and prospective achievements because "the beneficiary's contribution has not yet had an impact."[202]

In addition, less helpful are articles or other independent evidence that acknowledge that the beneficiary "is not widely known,"[203] indicate the beneficiary entered the field only a short time before the petition was filed,[204] "mention[] that the beneficiary 'followed the work'" of others in the field,[205] or "acknowledge" the beneficiary's professional skill without detailing aspects of extraordinary ability.[206]

Instead, the supporting evidence should connect the beneficiary's previous accomplishments with the assignment to be performed in the United States. For example, an O-1 petition was denied where:

---

or longer before the O-1 petition was filed); *Matter of [name not provided]*, LIN 04 114 52837 (AAO Jan. 26, 2005), http://bit.ly/jan052d (numerous awards earned 15 years before the petition was filed).

[195] *Matter of [name not provided]*, WAC 07 055 52449 (AAO Mar. 21, 2008), http://bit.ly/mar0801d; *Matter of [name not provided]*, LIN 01 245 54595 (AAO Oct. 16, 2002), 26 Immig. Rptr. B2-81 (reversed on AAO appeal); *Matter of [name not provided]*, WAC 06 273 55205 (AAO Oct. 11, 2007), http://bit.ly/oct0701d.

[196] *Matter of [name not provided]*, EAC 08 134 51786 (AAO May 4, 2009), http://bit.ly/may091d.

[197] *Matter of Shaw*, 11 I&N Dec. 277 (Dist. Dir. 1965). *See also Matter of [name not provided]*, WAC 07 015 50561 (AAO Nov. 7, 2007), http://bit.ly/nov072d ("newcomer").

[198] *Matter of [name not provided]*, WAC 07 006 52866 (AAO Mar. 5, 2008), http://bit.ly/mar081d (USCIS denial notice); *Matter of [name not provided]*, SRC 05 088 50358 (AAO Mar. 1, 2006), http://bit.ly/mar061d.

[199] *Matter of [name not provided]*, WAC 06 224 53958 (AAO May 4, 2009), http://bit.ly/may091d.

[200] *Matter of [name not provided]*, WAC-01-250-52367 (AAO Aug. 4, 2002), 26 Immig. Rptr. B2-87.

[201] *Id.*

[202] *Matter of [name not provided]*, LIN 04 131 54595 (AAO Aug. 16, 2005), http://bit.ly/aug051d.

[203] *Matter of [name not provided]*, LIN 93 176 51248 (AAO Jan. 25, 1994), 12 Immig. Rptr. B2-156.

[204] *Matter of Shaw*, 11 I&N Dec. 277 (Dist. Dir. 1965) (noting that the "evidence of record shows that barely one year ago the beneficiary was unknown as a performer"); *Matter of [name not provided]*, LIN 04 156 52532 (AAO July 11, 2005), http://bit.ly/jul052d.

[205] *Matter of [name not provided]*, EAC 07 224 51635 (AAO June 23, 2009), http://bit.ly/jun091d.

[206] *Matter of [name not provided]*, WAC 07 800 12235 (AAO Feb. 9, 2009), http://bit.ly/feb092d.

Copyright © 2017. American Immigration Lawyers Association. All rights reserved.

"The director observed that the skills required to create a virtual reconstruction of ancient buildings [for which the beneficiary had received recognition in articles] are not of the same nature required to perform the beneficiary's proposed duties as a project architect in the United States…. The AAO does not entirely concur with the director's assessment that the beneficiary's work on the [virtual reconstruction] project is *wholly* unrelated to the proffered position as a project architect responsible for designing retail stores, and this not 'in the area of extraordinary ability.' … [T]he AAO will not entirely discount the beneficiary's accomplishments and recognition earned as a result of [the virtual reconstruction project]. However, it is reasonable to expect that an alien with extraordinary ability in architecture, who is coming to the United States to assume a traditional position as an architect, to submit evidence clearly relating to his achievements and recognition by his peers in the field of architecture…. Furthermore, as discussed above, the beneficiary's duties associated with this project are far removed from those he will perform in the United States as a project architect, to the extent that the work is in 'the same field' using only the broadest interpretation of the term."[207]

Evidence of satisfying the criteria may be stated in recommendation letters, and USCIS has stated that it "will continue to recognize … especially expert opinions from other authorities in the field who are familiar with the alien's contributions."[208] However, testimonials alone are generally insufficient for petition approval, so the practitioner should work with the client to identify and present independent evidence,[209] which should ideally be primary[210] and objective,[211] to corroborate the statements made in the testimonials:[212]

"NSC also notes however, that these supporting letters alone are not sufficient to establish extraordinary ability. They may be helpful to understand the nature of

---

[207] *Matter of [name not provided]*, EAC 07 224 51635 (AAO June 23, 2009), http://bit.ly/jun091d (USCIS denial) (emphasis in original).

[208] "TSC Approved Minutes" (June 3, 2002), AILA Doc. No. 02082742.

[209] *Matter of [name not provided]*, WAC 07 006 52866 (AAO Mar. 5, 2008), http://bit.ly/mar081d (USCIS RFE); *Matter of [name not provided]*, WAC 07 021 53980 (AAO Mar. 11, 2009), http://bit.ly/mar092d (USCIS denial); *Matter of [name not provided]*, SRC 06 138 52302 (AAO Nov. 7, 2007), http://bit.ly/nov0701d; *Matter of [name not provided]*, LIN 05 262 51156 (AAO Nov. 7, 2007), http://bit.ly/nov073d (only a letter from an individual who "personally witnessed" the beneficiary judge an event); *Matter of [name not provided]*, LIN 04 114 52837 (AAO Jan. 26, 2005), http://bit.ly/jan052d.

[210] *Matter of [name not provided]*, EAC 05 251 50742 (AAO Oct. 25, 2007), http://bit.ly/oct071d8 (petitioner failed to present any primary evidence of the beneficiary's membership on athletic teams; the claim was made by counsel, and an untranslated website page print-out was provided); *Matter of [name not provided]*, SRC 03 059 50346 (AAO Apr. 13, 2005), http://bit.ly/apr052d (petition lacked any independent evidence of the beneficiary's selection as the chief Nephrology Fellow at a university).

[211] *Matter of [name not provided]*, EAC 05 167 53726 (AAO Mar. 24, 2006), http://bit.ly/mar066d.

[212] *Matter of [name and receipt number not provided]*, (AAO June 20, 2005), http://bit.ly/jun051d (noting that in "the absence of corroborating evidence, this letter cannot be given much weight").

Copyright © 2017. American Immigration Lawyers Association. All rights reserved.

the beneficiary's accomplishments or research, but the letters alone do not establish the necessary qualifications."[213]

"[T]he opinions of individuals in the field cannot form the cornerstone of a successful claim for this classification.... An individual with sustained national or international acclaim should be able to produce ample unsolicited materials reflecting that acclaim."[214]

"Opinions from witnesses whom the petitioner has selected do not represent extensive documentation. Independent evidence that already existed prior to the preparation of the visa petition package carries greater weight than new materials prepared especially for submission with the petition.... The opinions of experts in the field, while not without weight, cannot form the cornerstone of a successful claim of sustained national or international acclaim, however.... USCIS may even give less weight to an opinion that is not corroborated, in accord with other information or is in any way questionable."[215]

For example, the AAO reversed denial of a petition when the petitioner submitted independent evidence of the beneficiary's award; the petition had initially included only a statement that the beneficiary won the award, without proof.[216]

On the other hand, a lack of testimonials may make it appear that the foreign national does not have extraordinary ability.[217] USCIS and/or the AAO may review the beneficiary's employment history to determine if submitted evidence is contradictory with his or her role or position within the field.[218] In practice, some testimonial letters are a necessity even for very accomplished O-1 beneficiaries.

And although as a practical matter certainly preferable, it is not absolutely necessary that every critic, reviewer, and recommender concur on the beneficiary's abilities, especially in the field of art: "It is recognized that such determinations often lead to controversey [sic]—professional concert and drama critics and book reviewers

---

[213] "AILA Liaison/Nebraska Service Center Liaison Teleconference Q&As" (June 25, 2009), AILA Doc. No. 09070864. Although the discussion relates to extraordinary ability immigrant visa petitions, the principle should remain the same.

[214] *Matter of [name not provided]*, WAC 07 006 52866 (AAO Mar. 5, 2008), http://bit.ly/mar081d (USCIS RFE). *See also Matter of [name not provided]*, EAC 07 224 51635 (AAO June 23, 2009), http://bit.ly/jun091d (petitioner failed to present "independent evidence" of an award referenced in a testimonial).

[215] *Matter of [name not provided]*, EAC 05 167 53726 (AAO Mar. 24, 2006), http://bit.ly/mar066d.

[216] *Matter of [name not provided]*, WAC 02 196 50736 (AAO Sept. 16, 2002), 26 Immig. Rptr. B2-23. *See also Matter of [name not provided]*, EAC 07 224 51635 (AAO June 23, 2009), http://bit.ly/jun091d ("Absent additional documentary evidence, [redacted] third-party statement that the beneficiary participated in award-winning projects is insufficient to meet this criterion").

[217] *Matter of [name not provided]*, WAC 92 194 51841 (AAO Nov. 8, 1993), 12 Immig. Rptr. B2-106 (initial evidence, including articles from Austrian and Japanese newspapers discussing the beneficiary's work, "was not sufficient to establish that the beneficiary is a person of extraordinary ability in the arts").

[218] *Matter of [name not provided]*, WAC 07 800 12235 (AAO Feb. 9, 2009), http://bit.ly/feb092d (beneficiary was working as an intern when the article was published); *Matter of [name not provided]*, SRC 05 100 50633 (AAO Nov. 10, 2005), http://bit.ly/nov051d (secondary positions of sous chef and chef de partie are not consistent with a lead, starring, or critical role in a restaurant).

Copyright © 2017. American Immigration Lawyers Association. All rights reserved.

are seldom in total agreement. Very often completely divergent opinions pertaining to the same event are authored by the 'experts.'"[219] Another relevant factor is that popularity in the arts, and especially the performing arts, may be subject to fads: "While one of [the beneficiary's] songs has reached the pinnacle of success in Britain, their popularity has been strictly ephemeral, as is characteristic of most songs, and even performers, in this idiom."[220]

If the beneficiary states that additional evidence that would satisfy the following criteria is forthcoming, then the practitioner may wish to discuss with the client the strategy of delaying filing the O-1 petition until the additional evidence is available, as the "petitioner must establish the beneficiary's eligibility as of the date of filing the petition."[221]

1. Awards and Prizes (O-1A and B)

If an individual in a field of science, education, business, or athletics (O-1A) demonstrates receipt of a "major, internationally recognized award, such as the Nobel Prize,"[222] no further documentation is required. For the arts and for the motion picture or television industry (O-1B), evidence that the person has "been nominated for, or has been the recipient of, significant national or international awards ... such as an Academy Award, an Emmy, a Grammy, or a Director's Guild Award,"[223] is sufficient in and of itself. Without such an award, the petition must include evidence from at least three of the categories discussed below.

While the awards named are only examples, as stated by the AAO: "The regulatory reference to 'the Nobel Prize' gives some indication of the caliber of prize that would merit consideration under the 'major award' clause."[224] Thus, very few awards other than the ones named have been found to qualify for this rarified category.

For the fields of science, education, business, or athletics, lesser awards can demonstrate sustained national or international acclaim and recognition. Those awards must be nationally or internationally recognized and be for excellence in the field of endeavor.[225] In the arts, including motion pictures and television, there is no

---

[219] *Matter of Shaw*, 11 I&N Dec. 277 (Dist. Dir. 1965).

[220] *Id.*

[221] *See, e.g., Matter of [name not provided]*, SRC 02 202 54837 (AAO Nov. 3, 2003), 28 Immig. Rptr. B2-84; *Matter of [name not provided]*, LIN 06 052 52226 (AAO Nov. 29, 2007), http://bit.ly/nov071d (nomination for induction into U.S. Martial Arts Association International Hall of Fame occurred after the O-1 petition was filed); *Matter of [name not provided]*, WAC 06 160 52954 (AAO May 31, 2007), http://bit.ly/may071d; *Matter of [name not provided]*, WAC 03 209 54393 (AAO June 13, 2005), http://bit.ly/jun052d (appearance on television program eight months after the petition was filed).

[222] 8 CFR §214.2(o)(3)(iii)(A). Note that, for these particular fields, the award must be internationally recognized—national recognition alone will not suffice.

[223] 8 CFR §214.2(o)(3)(iv)(A) and (v)(A).

[224] *Matter of [name not provided]*, SRC 06 138 52302 (AAO Nov. 7, 2007), http://bit.ly/nov0701d.

[225] 8 CFR §214.2(o)(3)(iii)(B)(1).

Copyright © 2017. American Immigration Lawyers Association. All rights reserved.

documentation category for lesser awards,[226] though lesser awards may be used to buttress other evidentiary categories.[227] USCIS will examine awards to see if they are "comparable in stature" to the ones named.[228]

For awards, such as the Emmy, that are bestowed upon a show or production as opposed to an individual, USCIS and/or the AAO may consider the beneficiary's actual contribution to the show.[229] Generally, an award—major or lesser—to an employer is not considered an award to the individual,[230] but USCIS may look for whether the individual "played a primary or principal role in the success."[231]

A copy of the award should be provided,[232] or newspaper or magazine articles discussing the beneficiary's receipt of the award,[233] as independent primary evidence of the award, should be given.[234] Photographs of medals may be deemed insufficient if they do not clearly state the beneficiary's name as the recipient.[235] There should be a connection between the award, the beneficiary's field of endeavor, and the activities to be performed in the United States.[236] The authority of the organization offering the

---

[226] 8 CFR §214.2(o)(3)(iv)(B) and (v)(B).

[227] *Matter of K-IP, LLC,* ID# 156221 (AAO Apr. 28, 2016) (nominations for national video awards evidenced critically acclaimed successes).

[228] *Matter of Z-P-,* ID# 15020 (AAO Mar. 22, 2016).

[229] *Matter of [name not provided],* WAC 06 167 50726 (AAO Mar. 6, 2007), http://bit.ly/mar071d (stating that the "beneficiary's limited contribution to just one short segment of only one episode indicates that the Emmy Award received for the 'Classical Baby' program as a whole was not largely or substantially attributable to the beneficiary's work").

[230] *Matter of G-L-, Inc.,* ID# 16732 (AAO June 15, 2016).

[231] *Matter of H-M-H-, LLC,* ID# 15897 (AAO Mar. 22, 2016).

[232] *Matter of [name not provided],* WAC 07 055 52449 (AAO Mar. 21, 2008), http://bit.ly/mar0801d (petitioner's counsel merely asserted that the beneficiary received the award).

[233] *Matter of BCMHV-, LLC,* ID# 16546 (AAO May 26, 2016); *Matter of [name not provided],* WAC 06 197 52823 (AAO Mar. 4, 2008), http://bit.ly/mar0801d8. *Cf. Matter of [name not provided],* EAC 07 224 51635 (AAO June 23, 2009), http://bit.ly/jun091d (petitioner failed to present "independent evidence" of an award referenced in a testimonial); *Matter of [name not provided],* WAC 07 273 54624 (AAO Mar. 11, 2009), http://bit.ly/mar091d; *Matter of [name not provided],* EAC 05 028 52811 (AAO Jan. 9, 2007), http://bit.ly/jan071d.

[234] *Cf. Matter of [name not provided],* WAC 06 163 50719 (AAO Sept. 13, 2007), http://bit.ly/sep071d (criterion not satisfied where a testimonial discussed the award but the petition contained no independent evidence).

[235] *Matter of [name not provided],* EAC 05 251 50742 (AAO Oct. 25, 2007), http://bit.ly/oct071d8.

[236] *Matter of [name not provided],* WAC 06 197 52823 (AAO Mar. 4, 2008), http://bit.ly/mar0801d (Miss Hawaiian Tropic International award not related to the "field of endeavor, *i.e.,* the marketing and sales of skin care products and services"); *Matter of [name not provided],* SRC 02 202 54837 (AAO Nov. 3, 2003), 28 Immig. Rptr. B2-84 (beneficiary "was appointed in recognition of 'his valuable contributions and dedication to the Republican Party' rather than due to his achievements in the practice of medicine"); *Matter of [name not provided],* LIN 04 157 52612 (AAO May 3, 2005), http://bit.ly/may051d (awards earned in athletic competitions not relevant to petition for general manager); *Matter of [name not provided],* LIN 04 216 53865 (AAO Mar. 11, 2005), http://bit.ly/mar051d.

Copyright © 2017. American Immigration Lawyers Association. All rights reserved.

award may also be considered,[237] or contacted independently by USCIS for verification.[238]

For awards that lack universal name recognition, the practitioner should explain how the award qualifies as major and internationally recognized and should "establish the significance" of the award and "and its importance within the sport" or industry.[239] For example, the AAO accepted "the premiere juggler award at Circus Fest, an annual competition of circus performers in Monaco."[240] It may also be necessary to provide an explanation of the authority of the organization providing the assessment if it is not well-known,[241] with corroborating evidence.[242] As another example, the AAO accepted a statement from the Croatian Tennis Association confirming that an award is "nationally recognized by the Croatian Tennis Association, the governing institution for tennis sport in Croatia."[243] The practitioner should note, however, the AAO's statement that a "competition or event does not achieve this status [of a nationally or internationally recognized award] simply by identifying itself as a 'national' or 'international' event."[244] USCIS may also independently review the website of an award-giving organization, to confirm that the award is prestigious.[245]

---

[237] *Matter of [name not provided]*, SRC 06 138 52302 (AAO Nov. 7, 2007), http://bit.ly/nov071d (award "presented by the [member] club under the [US Polo Association's] authority, rather than directly by the USPA as a national organization" deemed local "and does not establish recognition beyond the individual club that presented the award").

[238] *Matter of [name not provided]*, WAC 06 163 50719 (AAO Sept. 13, 2007), http://bit.ly/sep071d.

[239] *Matter of [name not provided]*, WAC 07 055 52449 (AAO Mar. 21, 2008), http://bit.ly/mar0801d; *Matter of [name not provided]*, SRC 06 138 52302 (AAO Nov. 7, 2007), http://bit.ly/nov0701d; *Matter of [name not provided]*, LIN 06 052 52226 (AAO Nov. 29, 2007), http://bit.ly/nov071d; *Matter of [name not provided]*, LIN 05 262 51156 (AAO Nov. 7, 2007), http://bit.ly/nov073d (gold medal at Taekwondo World Cup not accepted because of lack of explanation); *Matter of [name not provided]*, SRC 06 095 50306 (AAO Jan. 24, 2007), http://bit.ly/jan0701d (same for silver medals from the South American Games and the Central American Games); *Matter of [name not provided]*, WAC 06 167 50726 (AAO Mar. 6, 2007), http://bit.ly/mar071d (award not accepted because there were only 60 international entries); *Matter of [name not provided]*, LIN 04 037 54758 (AAO Jan. 9, 2006), http://bit.ly/jan063d (gold medal in U.S. Open Taekwondo Championship); *Matter of [name not provided]*, LIN 04 184 52913 (AAO Aug. 17, 2005), http://bit.ly/aug052d (award from the Kuwait Tennis Federation); *Matter of [name not provided]*, LIN 04 156 52532 (AAO July 11, 2005), http://bit.ly/jul052d; *Matter of [name not provided]*, LIN 02 296 53935 (AAO Jan. 26, 2005), http://bit.ly/jan0501d.

[240] *Matter of [name not provided]*, WAC 02 196 50736 (AAO Sept. 16, 2002), 26 Immig. Rptr. B2-23.

[241] *Matter of [name not provided]*, SRC 06 138 52302 (AAO Nov. 7, 2007), http://bit.ly/nov0701d (noting lack of "background information about the *Robb Report*") (italics in original).

[242] *Matter of [name not provided]*, LIN 04 037 54758 (AAO Jan. 9, 2006), http://bit.ly/jan063d (statement from vice president of the U.S. Taekwondo Union stating that the U.S. Open Championship is an "internationally acclaimed competition" deemed insufficient without corroborating evidence).

[243] *Matter of [name not provided]*, EAC 05 064 52917 (AAO June 12, 2006), http://bit.ly/jun061d (internal formatting omitted).

[244] *Matter of [name not provided]*, WAC 04 058 51676 (AAO Jan. 17, 2006), http://bit.ly/jan062d.

[245] *Matter of [name not provided]*, SRC 06 138 52302 (AAO Nov. 7, 2007), http://bit.ly/nov0701d (noting lack of mention of the beneficiary's award on the website of the U.S. Polo Association); *Matter of [name not*

Cont'd

Copyright © 2017. American Immigration Lawyers Association. All rights reserved.

Examples of athletic awards that have been found acceptable include major league MVP,[246] MVP of the European Junior Championship, selection as a member of a national All-Star Team, and being named as European Player of the Year.[247]

Awards for other than first place also should be acceptable.[248] For example, the AAO accepted an "award as one of twenty of America's Most Promising Biomedical Researchers by the Pew Scholars in the Biomedical Sciences."[249] It is preferable to present a fourth place award for a more prestigious competition than a first place prize for a regional competition,[250] as "city, regional or state awards" are not usually nationally or internationally recognized awards.[251] Awards may also be in the form of a national or worldwide competitive ranking for athletes,[252] and it may be necessary to submit the methodology of ranking.[253] The level or class of competition for which the beneficiary received an award may also be evaluated, such that receipt of an award for a lower ranked competition may be deemed not a major award.[254] Even for artists, finishing in the top 15 percent or in 22nd place out of 237 competitors may not establish that the beneficiary has extraordinary ability.[255]

Research grants from the U.S. federal government may also comprise a nationally recognized award.[256] The practitioner should be aware, however, that several AAO cases attempt to impose a limitation. In one case, the AAO stated that "[r]esearch funding through competitive grants is inherent to many fields within the basic and applied sciences," where the "prestigious grants may indicate the

---

provided], WAC 04 058 51676 (AAO Jan. 17, 2006), http://bit.ly/jan062d (noting lack of mention of the beneficiary "among the top fifty women players" on the website of the World Chess Federation).

[246] AFM 33.4(d).

[247] *Matter of [name not provided]*, LIN 01 245 54595 (AAO Oct. 16, 2002), 26 Immig. Rptr. B2-81.

[248] *Matter of [name not provided]*, WAC 94 180 51386 (AAO Oct. 13, 1994), 13 Immig. Rptr. B2-224 (jury's special prize award).

[249] *Matter of [name not provided]*, SRC 02 245 52561 (AAO Nov. 1, 2002), 26 Immig. Rptr. B2-17.

[250] *Matter of [name not provided]*, WAC 94 180 51386 (AAO Oct. 13, 1994), 13 Immig. Rptr. B2-224 (fourth place ranking in the "prestigious Moscow International Ballet Competition, which Bonnie Brooks, President and Executive Director of Dance/USA, considers to be 'by far the most important ballet competition in the world'"); *Matter of [name not provided]*, WAC 07 026 52214 (AAO May 12, 2008), http://bit.ly/may081d (rejecting a regional championship).

[251] *Matter of [name not provided]*, WAC 07 273 54624 (AAO Mar. 11, 2009), http://bit.ly/mar091d; *Matter of [name not provided]*, LIN 04 037 54940 (AAO June 13, 2005), http://bit.ly/jun053d.

[252] *Matter of [name not provided]*, WAC 07 026 52214 (AAO May 12, 2008), http://bit.ly/may081d; *Matter of [name not provided]*, WAC 07 001 54685 (AAO July 29, 2008), http://bit.ly/jul081d (ranking of 41 in the world and 80 for Australian squash players deemed insufficient); *Matter of [name not provided]*, WAC 04 058 51676 (AAO Jan. 17, 2006), http://bit.ly/jan062d.

[253] *Matter of [name not provided]*, WAC 07 001 54685 (AAO July 29, 2008), http://bit.ly/jul081d; *Matter of [name not provided]*, WAC 06 224 53958 (AAO May 4, 2009), http://bit.ly/may092d.

[254] *Matter of [name not provided]*, LIN 06 039 53131 (AAO June 29, 2006), http://bit.ly/jun0601d.

[255] *Id.*

[256] *Matter of [name not provided]*, SRC 98 066 50295 (AAO Aug. 2, 1998), 19 Immig. Rptr. B2-77 (accepting research grants "originat[ing] from the Department of Energy, the Department of Commerce and the Environmental Protection Agency").

Copyright © 2017. American Immigration Lawyers Association. All rights reserved.

recognized value of the recipient's research, [so] they are not prizes or awards for documented achievements."[257] In two other cases, the AAO noted that fellowships and research grants that do not comprise financial aid also may not qualify, because these honors are "granted generally to fund future research rather than to award an achievement in the field," and that USCIS will not presume that "any recognition by a renowned organization is, or should be, a nationally or internationally recognized award for excellence":[258]

"While the fellowship committee will take the recipient's accomplishments into account, such consideration ensures that the fellowship funds will advance the project and is not an award for excellence in the field.… Further, it is noted that research grants simply fund a scientist's work. The past achievements of the principal investigator are factors in grant proposals. The funding institution has to be assured that the investigator is capable of performing the proposed research. Nevertheless, a research grant is principally designed to fund future research, and is not an award to honor or recognize past achievement."[259]

To avoid an RFE or rejection of evidence of research grants as honors, the practitioner may wish to provide a statement from an official of the awarding institution, explaining the factors considered when providing research grants and emphasizing how the research grant constitutes an award, if applicable.

Generally, awards may be rejected as not internationally or nationally recognized where competition is only with other employees of the same entity or where the beneficiary did not compete for the awards with "others in his field,"[260] or where the competition was open only to students,[261] or apprentices,[262] including academic scholarships, fellowships, and "other forms of competitive financial aid."[263] Other types of acknowledgements rejected for this criterion include "selection for a

---

[257] *Matter of [name not provided]*, WAC 06 160 52954 (AAO May 31, 2007), http://bit.ly/may071d.

[258] *Matter of [name not provided]*, EAC 04 236 53319 (AAO Mar. 1, 2006), http://bit.ly/mar063d; *Matter of [name not provided]*, SRC 04 112 51533 (AAO Jan. 9, 2006), http://bit.ly/jan0602d.

[259] *Matter of [name not provided]*, EAC 04 236 53319 (AAO Mar. 1, 2006), http://bit.ly/mar063d (fellowship from the National Institutes of Health and research grant by the Ministry of Science and Technology); *Matter of [name not provided]*, LIN 04 131 54595 (AAO Aug. 16, 2005), http://bit.ly/aug051d.

[260] *Matter of [name not provided]*, SRC 02 202 54837 (AAO Nov. 3, 2003), 28 Immig. Rptr. B2-84 (stating that it "appears that the beneficiary competed only with other physicians, residents and fellows at the University of Wisconsin"). The practitioner should note that the other awards, which included the Honorary West Virginian Award from the state of West Virginia, an award from the governor of Kentucky, and the National Leadership Award from the National Republican Congressional Committee, sounded prestigious but were rejected by the AAO. *See also Matter of [name not provided]*, LIN 04 143 53690 (AAO Aug. 17, 2005), http://bit.ly/aug0501d; *Matter of [name not provided]*, SRC 04 181 53036 (AAO Apr. 21, 2005), http://bit.ly/apr055d; *Matter of [name not provided]*, SRC 03 236 51017 (AAO Apr. 21, 2005), http://bit.ly/apr0502d.

[261] *Matter of [name not provided]*, WAC 06 167 50726 (AAO Mar. 6, 2007), http://bit.ly/mar071d; *Matter of [name not provided]*, LIN 03 239 51646 (AAO May 25, 2005), http://bit.ly/may0501d.

[262] *Matter of [name not provided]*, EAC 04 240 52613 (AAO July 13, 2005), http://bit.ly/jul0502d.

[263] *Matter of [name not provided]*, EAC 06 014 52770 (AAO Sept. 29, 2006), http://bit.ly/sep061d; *Matter of [name not provided]*, SRC 04 112 51533 (AAO Jan. 9, 2006), http://bit.ly/jan062d; *Matter of [name not provided]*, SRC 03 236 51017 (AAO Apr. 21, 2005), http://bit.ly/apr0502d.

Copyright © 2017. American Immigration Lawyers Association. All rights reserved.

competitive slot at an esteemed institution,"[264] earning "a promotion within the ranks of the sport,"[265] being certified for a profession,[266] attending a professional program,[267] being nominated for an award,[268] and merely participating in competitions or presentations,[269] unless the competition itself is established to be prestigious,[270] such as the Olympic Games. Similarly, the AAO stated that a "travel award is not an award or prize for excellence in the field of endeavor," because it is "to help the beneficiary defray the expense of attending the symposium," even if the travel award is provided only to a few attendees based on "review[] by the scientific committee and only those that have a high scientific merit may be able to win one of the limited number of Travel Awards."[271]

If the award was given to a product developed or created by the beneficiary, then USCIS and/or the AAO may consider whether they "are indeed awards or simple recognition by the organizations as their games [or other products] of choice in certain categories."[272] Publication in the premier professional journal or presentation of work at a leading conference for the industry may be considered an award, although the evidence should be corroborated by statement(s) from expert(s) in the field discussing the prestige of the publication or symposium.[273]

If a field has no awards because of "the specialized area" of a subfield,[274] then the practitioner may wish to include a statement to this effect, such as in the petitioner's support statement. Similarly, if an industry commonly does not bestow awards on individuals because awards are given to teams, products, or organizations, then independent evidence of this fact should be provided.[275]

---

[264] *Matter of [name not provided]*, LIN 04 131 54595 (AAO Aug. 16, 2005), http://bit.ly/aug051d; *Matter of [name not provided]*, LIN 03 239 51646 (AAO May 25, 2005), http://bit.ly/may0501d.

[265] *Matter of [name not provided]*, LIN 05 262 51156 (AAO Nov. 7, 2007), http://bit.ly/nov073d.

[266] *Matter of [name not provided]*, LIN 06 103 50190 (AAO Dec. 13, 2006), http://bit.ly/dec061d.

[267] *Matter of [name not provided]*, SRC 06 039 50380 (AAO May 10, 2006), http://bit.ly/2may061d (language immersion programs for businessman); *Matter of [name not provided]*, LIN 04 143 53690 (AAO Aug. 17, 2005), http://bit.ly/aug0501d (board certification for a medical doctor).

[268] *Matter of [name not provided]*, WAC 06 163 50719 (AAO Sept. 13, 2007), http://bit.ly/sep071d.

[269] *Matter of [name not provided]*, EAC 07 224 51635 (AAO June 23, 2009), http://bit.ly/jun091d; *Matter of [name not provided]*, WAC 07 273 54624 (AAO Mar. 11, 2009), http://bit.ly/mar091d; *Matter of [name not provided]*, SRC 06 138 52302 (AAO Nov. 7, 2007), http://bit.ly/nov0701d.

[270] *Matter of [name not provided]*, SRC 06 138 52302 (AAO Nov. 7, 2007), http://bit.ly/nov0701d.

[271] *Matter of [name not provided]*, EAC 04 236 53319 (AAO Mar. 1, 2006), http://bit.ly/mar063d (internal formatting omitted).

[272] *Matter of [name not provided]*, WAC 03 024 54644 (AAO Jan. 17, 2006), http://bit.ly/jan0603d.

[273] "INS Liaison Teleconference Minutes" (Feb. 15, 2000), AILA 00032802.

[274] *Matter of [name not provided]*, WAC 92 194 51841 (AAO Nov. 8, 1993), 12 Immig. Rptr. B2-106.

[275] *Matter of [name not provided]*, WAC 03 024 54644 (AAO Jan. 17, 2006), http://bit.ly/jan0603d; *Matter of G-L-, Inc.*, ID#16732 (AAO June 15, 2016).

Copyright © 2017. American Immigration Lawyers Association. All rights reserved.

2. Membership in a Prestigious Industry Association (O-1A)

If the petition will present evidence of the beneficiary's membership in an industry association that, in turn, "require[s] outstanding achievements of their members, as judged by recognized national or international experts in their disciplines or fields,"[276] then the practitioner should ensure that there is also evidence of the requirements for attaining the prestigious membership,[277] such as copies of membership criteria or bylaws.[278] An exception may exist if the organization is universally known, such as selection for an Olympics team or for a national All-Star team.[279] The industry of the association should be the same or related to the beneficiary's endeavor.[280] Membership in merely professional associations is generally insufficient,[281] as is a professional credential or licensure,[282] even if the beneficiary was among a handful of individuals to possess the credential,[283] if the beneficiary holds membership in numerous associations,[284] and if the "requisites for membership are rigorous," but not based upon outstanding achievements.[285]

---

[276] 8 CFR §214.2(o)(3)(iii)(B)(2).

[277] *Matter of [name not provided]*, WAC 07 055 52449 (AAO Mar. 21, 2008), http://bit.ly/mar0801d; *Matter of [name not provided]*, SRC 02 202 54837 (AAO Nov. 3, 2003), 28 Immig. Rptr. B2-84; *Matter of [name not provided]*, EAC 06 075 53028 (AAO Oct. 4, 2006), http://bit.ly/oct062d (AAO reversed USCIS's acceptance of this criterion); *Matter of [name not provided]*, LIN 04 156 52532 (AAO July 11, 2005), http://bit.ly/jul052d (no evidence of achievements necessary to become a member of the National Ukrainian Figure Skating team).

[278] *Matter of [name not provided]*, LIN 06 052 52226 (AAO Nov. 29, 2007), http://bit.ly/nov071d; *Matter of [name not provided]*, LIN 06 103 50190 (AAO Dec. 13, 2006), http://bit.ly/dec061d; *Matter of [name not provided]*, LIN 04 216 53865 (AAO Mar. 11, 2005), http://bit.ly/mar051d. *Cf.* "INS Liaison Teleconference Minutes" (Feb. 15, 2000), AILA Doc. No, 00032802 (possibly allowing for acceptance of expert's statement regarding the prestige of the association).

[279] *Matter of [name not provided]*, LIN 01 245 54595 (AAO Oct. 16, 2002), 26 Immig. Rptr. B2-81.

[280] *Matter of [name not provided]*, LIN 04 157 52612 (AAO May 3, 2005), http://bit.ly/may051d (membership in prestigious athletic team not relevant to petition for general manager).

[281] *See, e.g., Matter of [name not provided]*, SRC 02 202 54837 (AAO Nov. 3, 2003), 28 Immig. Rptr. B2-84 (membership in the American College of Surgeons (Initiate Group), the Kentucky Medical Association, the Lexington Medical Society, the International Society of Heart Lung Transplantation, the American Medical Association, the South Eastern Surgical Congress, the Heart Failure Society, and the International Society of Heart Research deemed inadequate); *Matter of [name not provided]*, WAC 06 160 52954 (AAO May 31, 2007), http://bit.ly/may071d (24,000 members in the American Association for Cancer Research); *Matter of [name not provided]*, EAC 06 014 52770 (AAO Sept. 29, 2006), http://bit.ly/sep061d; *Matter of [name not provided]*, LIN 04 143 53690 (AAO Aug. 17, 2005), http://bit.ly/aug0501d; *Matter of [name not provided]*, WAC 02 038 51106 (AAO May 24, 2005), http://bit.ly/may051d8.

[282] *Matter of [name not provided]*, SRC 05 175 50496 (AAO July 25, 2006), http://bit.ly/jul061d8; *Matter of [name not provided]*, LIN 04 184 52913 (AAO Aug. 17, 2005), http://bit.ly/aug052d; *Matter of [name and receipt number not provided]*, (AAO June 20, 2005), http://bit.ly/jun0502d; *Matter of [name not provided]*, LIN 03 239 51646 (AAO May 25, 2005), http://bit.ly/may0501d.

[283] *Matter of [name not provided]*, SRC 05 200 51253 (AAO July 23, 2007), http://bit.ly/jul071d.

[284] *Matter of [name not provided]*, EAC 04 236 53319 (AAO Mar. 1, 2006), http://bit.ly/mar063d.

[285] *Matter of [name not provided]*, SRC 04 181 53036 (AAO Apr. 21, 2005), http://bit.ly/apr055d ("prospective members must be sponsored by at least three members, have studied at an ASTS [association] approved institution and have at least three publications in the transplantation literature" and then applications must be approved by the membership committee, another council, and two-thirds vote of the general membership).

Copyright © 2017. American Immigration Lawyers Association. All rights reserved.

This is because the adjudicatory trend seems to require "documentation which specifically states that their membership is limited to those who have completed meritorious outstanding research [or other activities] relating to the beneficiary's field of endeavor,"[286] or "evidence that 'outstanding achievement' is a pre-requisite" to taking a qualifying examination for membership.[287] Even the statement that membership is "restricted only to those physicians whose achievements have merited such national and international attention as to bring their extraordinary abilities to the attention of the membership" was rejected as failing to provide the necessary details on how the association "requires outstanding achievements of their members, as judged by recognized national or international experts in his field of endeavor."[288] The AAO determined that judging a few international competitions did not constitute an outstanding achievement for purposes of being considered for membership in a prestigious organization.[289] The AAO also stated that probative value of membership in a prestigious association may be weakened if the association has differing levels of membership and the beneficiary holds the lowest level.[290]

3. Published Materials Describing the Beneficiary's Achievements (O-1A)

Published materials describing the beneficiary's achievements should be from "professional or major trade publications in the field,"[291] or major media,[292] not from local "newspapers and tabloid magazines,"[293] or from official public records.[294] As noted above, information regarding the publication title, date, and author should be provided, especially if the article was published abroad.[295] In addition, publications,

---

[286] *Matter of [name not provided]*, SRC 98 066 50295 (AAO Aug. 2, 1998), 19 Immig. Rptr. B2-77. *See also Matter of [name not provided]*, WAC 06 224 53958 (AAO May 4, 2009), http://bit.ly/may092d.

[287] *Matter of [name not provided]*, WAC 07 026 52214 (AAO May 12, 2008), http://bit.ly/may081d.

[288] *Matter of [name not provided]*, SRC 02 202 54837 (AAO Nov. 3, 2003), 28 Immig. Rptr. B2-84. *Cf. Matter of [name not provided]*, LIN 95 131 50963 (AAO Nov. 3, 1995), 15 Immig. Rptr. B2-61 (accepting statement that membership "is reserved only for those culinarians who have established an outstanding reputation for excellence in the culinary arts").

[289] *Matter of [name not provided]*, SRC 06 095 50306 (AAO Jan. 24, 2007), http://bit.ly/jan0701d.

[290] *Id.*

[291] 8 CFR §214.2(o)(3)(iii)(B)(3); *Matter of [name not provided]*, SRC 02 202 54837 (AAO Nov. 3, 2003), 28 Immig. Rptr. B2-84 (*Lexington Herald-Ledger* deemed major media); *Matter of [name not provided]*, WAC 93 168 50373 (AAO Aug. 3, 2002), 26 Immig. Rptr. B2-84 (accepting "reviews of the beneficiary's London restaurant in distinguished publications such as the *Times of London* and *Gourmet* magazine").

[292] 8 CFR §214.2(o)(3)(iii)(B)(3).

[293] *Matter of [name not provided]*, WAC 06 197 52823 (AAO Mar. 4, 2008), http://bit.ly/mar0801d; *Matter of [name not provided]*, SRC 02 202 54837 (AAO Nov. 3, 2003), 28 Immig. Rptr. B2-84 (locally distributed newspapers rejected).

[294] *Matter of [name not provided]*, SRC 02 202 54837 (AAO Nov. 3, 2003), 28 Immig. Rptr. B2-84.

[295] *Matter of [name not provided]*, WAC 07 026 52214 (AAO May 12, 2008), http://bit.ly/may081d (without information about the Swedish publications, the AAO could not determine if they would qualify as "major media").

Copyright © 2017. American Immigration Lawyers Association. All rights reserved.

especially those from outside the United States, should be accompanied with evidence of how the newspaper, magazine, or journal qualifies as major media:[296]

"[T]he petitioner's assertion that the articles appeared in publications with 'international distribution and audiences' is insufficient to establish that the articles should be considered 'major media,' as the petitioner submitted no concrete evidence to support its claims. The burden is not on USCIS to find support for the petitioner's claim that the publications should be considered 'major media.'"[297]

The AAO has accepted "circulation figures,"[298] "web traffic" for online articles,[299] or other evidence that the media "are relied upon by those" in the industry,[300] but rejected a statement from the publisher of the newspaper or magazine.[301] In practice, however, even if articles have appeared in publications that may not qualify as "major media," it is still helpful to the strength of the O-1 petition to include them as they can help to bolster the overall profile of the O-1 beneficiary.

Evidence submitted for this criterion should specifically discuss the beneficiary's achievements,[302] awards,[303] and/or publicity,[304] even if the beneficiary appeared on the cover.[305] If the publications represent only publicity that does not discuss the foreign national's ability or accomplishments,[306] or publicity about a final product upon which

---

[296] *Matter of [name not provided]*, EAC 04 187 50327 (AAO Oct. 4, 2006), http://bit.ly/oct061d (no evidence that the *Pittsburgh Tribune-Review* is major media).

[297] *Matter of [name not provided]*, EAC 07 224 51635 (AAO June 23, 2009), http://bit.ly/jun091d.

[298] *Matter of [name not provided]*, WAC 06 273 55205 (AAO Oct. 11, 2007), http://bit.ly/oct0701d (USCIS RFE); *Matter of [name not provided]*, SRC 04 225 52570 (AAO July 19, 2005), http://bit.ly/jul051d; *Matter of [name not provided]*, LIN 04 156 52532 (AAO July 11, 2005), http://bit.ly/jul052d.

[299] *Matter of [name not provided]*, SRC 04 112 51533 (AAO Jan. 9, 2006), http://bit.ly/jan0602d.

[300] *Id.*

[301] *Matter of [name not provided]*, LIN 06 103 50190 (AAO Dec. 13, 2006), http://bit.ly/dec061d.

[302] *Cf. Matter of [name not provided]*, WAC 06 163 50719 (AAO Sept. 13, 2007), http://bit.ly/sep071d; (petition denied due in part to the lack of discussion of beneficiary's achievements).

[303] *Matter of [name not provided]*, LIN 01 245 54595 (AAO Oct. 16, 2002), 26 Immig. Rptr. B2-81.

[304] *Matter of [name not provided]*, SRC 02 202 54837 (AAO Nov. 3, 2003), 28 Immig. Rptr. B2-84 (articles discussed "the lives of two of the beneficiary's patients, rather than … the beneficiary and his work"); *Matter of [name not provided]*, WAC 93 168 50373 (AAO Aug. 3, 2002), 26 Immig. Rptr. B2-84 (for an executive chef who would open a U.S. restaurant, AAO accepted industry reviews and critical reviews of the beneficiary's restaurants).

[305] *Matter of [name not provided]*, WAC 06 224 53958 (AAO May 4, 2009), http://bit.ly/may092d.

[306] *Matter of Shaw*, 11 I&N Dec. 277 (Dist. Dir. 1965) (stating that many of the newspaper articles "are minutia or essentially biographical items offering so little specific information with respect to the beneficiary's performances or serious critical appraisal of her talents as to be virtually immaterial"); *Matter of [name not provided]*, SRC 06 138 52302 (AAO Nov. 7, 2007), http://bit.ly/nov0701d (only "brief, passing references to the beneficiary" and "little more than team rosters"); *Matter of [name not provided]*, EAC 04 187 50327 (AAO Oct. 4, 2006), http://bit.ly/oct061d (article discussed the beneficiary's role "in selling the religious figurines made by Christian families" rather than his own achievements); *Matter of [name not provided]*, LIN 04 216 53865 (AAO Mar. 11, 2005), http://bit.ly/mar051d (stating that the "article is clearly a human-interest piece rather than about the beneficiary's acclaim in his field of endeavor").

Copyright © 2017. American Immigration Lawyers Association. All rights reserved.

the beneficiary worked, which only discusses the final product and not the beneficiary's contributions,[307] then the evidence may be rejected. Similarly, merely being a "celebrity" is generally inadequate unless such status was achieved as a result of the beneficiary's contributions to the field of endeavor, as opposed to notoriety.[308]

Appropriate evidence may include articles in major trade publications or copies of newspaper articles where the beneficiary is quoted,[309] ideally as an industry expert, or heralding the beneficiary's achievements.[310] Alternatively, a chapter in an industry textbook citing the beneficiary's achievements may be submitted.[311] Also relevant is the number of articles about the beneficiary, as three articles "about the beneficiary during a 20-year career" were rejected by the AAO as not being "evidence of sustained acclaim."[312] Participation in television newscasts may qualify as other major media, but the broadcasts should discuss the beneficiary's achievements.[313] Similarly, exhibition of the beneficiary's work in a museum may be relevant, as long as the display focuses on the beneficiary's achievements.[314]

Also rejected as insufficient by the AAO are photographs, DVDs, Internet searches for the beneficiary's name,[315] advertisements,[316] citation histories,[317] mention of an athlete beneficiary's competition statistics,[318] or "[m]ere mention in a

---

[307] *Matter of [name not provided]*, WAC 07 006 52866 (AAO Mar. 5, 2008), http://bit.ly/mar081d.

[308] *Matter of [name not provided]*, WAC 06 197 52823 (AAO Mar. 4, 2008), http://bit.ly/mar0801d (articles focused on television appearances and "rumors regarding her social life and relationships"); *Matter of Shaw*, 11 I&N Dec. 277 (Dist. Dir. 1965) (newspaper articles "merely tend to establish a certain degree of popularity or notoriety").

[309] *Matter of [name not provided]*, SRC 98 066 50295 (AAO Aug. 2, 1998), 19 Immig. Rptr. B2-77.

[310] *Matter of [name not provided]*, WAC 95 042 52458 (AAO Jan. 12, 1995), 14 Immig. Rptr. B2-43 (article from *Screen International* indicated that "no other first assistant director has worked with so many of Australia's most acclaimed film directors").

[311] *Matter of [name not provided]*, WAC 95 042 52458 (AAO Jan. 12, 1995), 14 Immig. Rptr. B2-43.

[312] *Matter of [name not provided]*, EAC 05 064 52917 (AAO June 12, 2006), http://bit.ly/jun061d. *See also Matter of [name not provided]*, SRC 04 112 51533 (AAO Jan. 9, 2006), http://bit.ly/jan0602d (stating that "publicity about two articles in a four-year period and spanning a career of over 11 years following the beneficiary's receipt of her bachelor of nursing degree is not indicative of sustained acclaim in her field of endeavor").

[313] *Matter of [name not provided]*, SRC 02 202 54837 (AAO Nov. 3, 2003), 28 Immig. Rptr. B2-84. *See also Matter of [name not provided]*, EAC 07 224 51635 (AAO June 23, 2009), http://bit.ly/jun091d (documentary focused on technology of a virtual reconstruction project rather than on the beneficiary's architectural work).

[314] *Matter of [name not provided]*, EAC 07 224 51635 (AAO June 23, 2009), http://bit.ly/jun091d (exhibition "focused on the art, culture and history of ancient Persia").

[315] *Matter of [name not provided]*, LIN 06 052 52226 (AAO Nov. 29, 2007), http://bit.ly/nov071d; *Matter of [name not provided]*, EAC 05 251 50742 (AAO Oct. 25, 2007), http://bit.ly/oct071d8; *Matter of [name not provided]*, LIN 06 039 53131 (AAO June 29, 2006), http://bit.ly/jun0601d.

[316] *Matter of [name not provided]*, SRC 05 150 50069 (AAO Nov. 28, 2005), http://bit.ly/nov053d.

[317] *Matter of [name not provided]*, SRC 05 088 50358 (AAO Mar. 1, 2006), http://bit.ly/mar061d; *Matter of [name not provided]*, LIN 04 131 54595 (AAO Aug. 16, 2005), http://bit.ly/aug051d (stating that "[c]itations are not about the alien or his work, rather, they are references to his work").

[318] *Matter of [name not provided]*, WAC 04 058 51676 (AAO Jan. 17, 2006), http://bit.ly/jan062d.

Copyright © 2017. American Immigration Lawyers Association. All rights reserved.

publication."[319] Publications authored by the beneficiary also may not qualify,[320] but book reviews may qualify, as long as the review references the beneficiary as an author.[321] As a practical matter, however, this evidence may also be included in the category of original and significant contributions to the field and/or authorship of published articles in the field, discussed below, as long as the beneficiary is credited as the author.[322]

Care should be taken with articles in languages other than English to ensure that they are accompanied by "a full English language translation which the translator has certified as complete and accurate, and that he or she is competent to translate from the foreign language into English."[323] Summary translations,[324] and articles that have been translated using an online translation tool,[325] have been criticized as having "diminished" or "limited" probative value, respectively.

Even where the published materials describing the beneficiary's achievements do not rise to the level contemplated by the regulations, however, there is often still value in including them. From a practical standpoint, obtaining approval of an O-1 petition requires not just that the petition meet the specific regulatory requirements, but also that the USCIS adjudicator is persuaded that the O-1 beneficiary in fact possesses extraordinary ability. Experience has shown that this can sometimes be best achieved by including not just materials that meet the specific regulatory requirements, but additional materials as well to bolster the overall case.

4. Beneficiary's Role as a Judge of the Work of Others (O-1A)

Service as the judge of the work of other individuals[326] may be in the form of peer reviewing articles for professional publications,[327] refereeing or editing a professional journal,[328] judging competitions,[329] evaluating research proposals for well-regarded

---

[319] *Matter of [name and receipt number not provided]*, (AAO June 20, 2005), http://bit.ly/jun0502d.

[320] *Matter of [name not provided]*, SRC 02 202 54837 (AAO Nov. 3, 2003), 28 Immig. Rptr. B2-84 (chapter of a medical textbook); *Matter of [name not provided]*, LIN 06 103 50190 (AAO Dec. 13, 2006), http://bit.ly/dec061d.

[321] *Matter of [name not provided]*, SRC 02 202 54837 (AAO Nov. 3, 2003), 28 Immig. Rptr. B2-84 (chapter of a medical textbook).

[322] *Id.*

[323] 8 CFR §103.2(b)(3).

[324] *Matter of F-I-T-T-*, ID# 16838 (AAO June 23, 2016).

[325] *Matter of C-B-&F-, Inc.*, ID# 13701 (AAO Sept. 28, 2015).

[326] 8 CFR §214.2(o)(3)(iii)(B)(4).

[327] "TSC Approved Minutes" (June 3, 2002), AILA Doc. No. 02082742. Although the discussion relates to extraordinary ability immigrant visa petitions, the principle should remain the same. *See also Matter of [name not provided]*, SRC 02 202 54837 (AAO Nov. 3, 2003), 28 Immig. Rptr. B2-84; *Matter of [name not provided]*, SRC 98 066 50295 (AAO Aug. 2, 1998), 19 Immig. Rptr. B2-77; *Matter of [name not provided]*, SRC 02 245 52561 (AAO Nov. 1, 2002), 26 Immig. Rptr. B2-17.

[328] "INS Liaison Teleconference Minutes" (Feb. 15, 2000), AILA 00032802.

[329] *Matter of [name not provided]*, SRC 06 095 50306 (AAO Jan. 24, 2007), http://bit.ly/jan0701d.

Copyright © 2017. American Immigration Lawyers Association. All rights reserved.

institutions,[330] and "providing official direction for a thesis or dissertation."[331] The work reviewed and judged must be in the beneficiary's field of endeavor.[332] Appropriate evidence includes a statement from an editor of the professional publication, which ideally should state that the beneficiary "was selected to perform peer review based on his expertise in the subject matter,"[333] or a statement from the organization that held the competition, confirming that the beneficiary was a judge.[334] Failure to "establish the basis for the beneficiary's selection to review" the work of others may result in rejection of the evidence for this criterion, as may a selection to review made by the beneficiary's supervisor rather than "by an independent editor."[335] Similarly, being selected as a more senior judge based on a record of judging other competitions may be insufficient, as USCIS and/or the AAO may state that the beneficiary should be chosen "on the basis of national or international acclaim and recognition for his achievements,"[336] although if a *Kazarian*-type analysis were to be applied, it is more likely that the selection as a judge would be accepted as satisfying this category, but the individual still found in the final merits analysis not to be of extraordinary ability.[337]

The articles reviewed should be in "recognized scholarly or scientific journal[s]," and not "vanity presses."[338] The number of articles reviewed may be considered,

---

[330] *Matter of [name not provided]*, SRC 02 245 52561 (AAO Nov. 1, 2002), 26 Immig. Rptr. B2-17 (beneficiary judged research proposals "at the behest of the National Institute for Health (NIH), NASA and the U.S. Department of Veteran's Affairs Medical Research Service"); "Legacy INS Liaison Teleconference Minutes" (Feb. 15, 2000), AILA Doc. No. 00032802. *See also* "AILA/TSC Liaison Minutes" (Oct. 7, 2002), AILA Doc. No. 02121641 (stating that "one may be deemed a judge of the work of others in the scientific and academic community ... by serving as a reviewer for significant research grants such as those administered in the various fields of science"). Although the discussion relates to extraordinary ability immigrant visa petitions, the principle should remain the same.

[331] "TSC Approved Minutes" (June 3, 2002), AILA Doc. No. 02082742. *See also* "AILA/TSC Liaison Minutes" (Oct. 7, 2002), AILA Doc. No. 02121641 (accepting "providing thesis direction in the scientific and academic community"). Although the discussion relates to extraordinary ability immigrant visa petitions, the principle should remain the same.

[332] *Matter of [name not provided]*, LIN 06 103 50190 (AAO Dec. 13, 2006), http://bit.ly/dec061d.

[333] *Matter of [name not provided]*, SRC 02 202 54837 (AAO Nov. 3, 2003), 28 Immig. Rptr. B2-84; *Matter of [name not provided]*, SRC 04 112 51533 (AAO Jan. 9, 2006), http://bit.ly/jan0602d (no evidence that the request for review was due to her "outstanding reputation in her field").

[334] *Matter of [name not provided]*, EAC 06 075 53028 (AAO Oct. 4, 2006), http://bit.ly/oct062d (criterion not established where the statement only noted that the beneficiary was a panelist).

[335] *Matter of [name not provided]*, SRC 03 236 51017 (AAO Apr. 21, 2005), http://bit.ly/apr0502d. *See also Matter of [name not provided]*, SRC 03 059 50346 (AAO Apr. 13, 2005), http://bit.ly/apr052d (professional association asked all clinician-members to review examination questions).

[336] *Matter of [name not provided]*, LIN 04 216 53865 (AAO Mar. 11, 2005), http://bit.ly/mar051d.

[337] *Matter of P-K-*, ID# 15915 (AAO Aug. 8, 2016) (scientist acted as judge of work of others in multiple ways, but the final merits analysis noted that none were indicative of sustained acclaim). Although the decision relates to an extraordinary ability immigrant visa petition, the principle should remain the same.

[338] "AILA/TSC Liaison Minutes" (Oct. 7, 2002), AILA Doc. No. 02121641. Although the discussion relates to extraordinary ability immigrant visa petitions, the principle should remain the same.

Copyright © 2017. American Immigration Lawyers Association. All rights reserved.

especially for scientists and researchers, because at least the AAO believes this is "a professional obligation of scientists who themselves publish in scientific journals":

"Occasional participation in peer review ... does not automatically demonstrate that the beneficiary has earned sustained national or international acclaim at the very top of his field.... Without evidence that sets the [beneficiary] apart from others in his field..., such as evidence that he has peer-reviewed an unusually large number of manuscripts for publication in various scientific journals, received multiple independent requests for his services from a substantial number of journals, or served in an editorial position for a distinguished journal, we cannot conclude that the beneficiary meets this criterion."[339]

When a *Kazarian*-type analysis is applied, a small number of reviewed articles can be found to meet the judge of the work of others criterion, but the end result is the same—the individual is not found to be of extraordinary ability:

"[T]he record reflects that the beneficiary had, as of the date of filing, reviewed a total of three articles ... thus satisfying the plain language of the evidentiary criterion.... However, he has served as a peer reviewer for only three articles during the course of his career, and has reviewed articles for a single journal. While it may be true that not every scientist has an opportunity to serve as a peer reviewer, the AAO finds insufficient support for a finding that any peer review experience places a beneficiary among the small percentage of scientists at the very top of the field. The beneficiary's experience may distinguish him from other junior scientists who have not yet been invited to review the work of their peers. However, the petitioner must distinguish the beneficiary from all scientists in his field, including those who regularly review articles for multiple scholarly journals and sit on editorial boards." [340]

Pictures of the beneficiary acting as a judge are typically rejected by USCIS and the AAO.[341] Other AAO cases state that review of the work of others should be differentiated from reviewing "the merit of grant proposals,"[342] assisting another individual in peer reviewing articles,[343] participating in a panel that does not judge the work of others,[344] evaluating a "student's academic progress"[345] and evaluating the

---

[339] *Matter of [name not provided]*, SRC 05 088 50358 (AAO Mar. 1, 2006), http://bit.ly/mar061d.; *Matter of [name not provided]*, SRC 04 112 51533 (AAO Jan. 9, 2006), http://bit.ly/jan0602d (only one article reviewed).

[340] *Matter of [name and case number not provided]* (AAO Oct. 14, 2010), http://bit.ly/oct102d.

[341] *Matter of [name not provided]*, WAC 06 163 50719 (AAO Sept. 13, 2007), http://bit.ly/sep071d; *Matter of [name not provided]*, SRC 04 065 50565 (AAO Jan. 9, 2006), http://bit.ly/jan0601d.

[342] *Matter of [name not provided]*, SRC 02 202 54837 (AAO Nov. 3, 2003), 28 Immig. Rptr. B2-84.

[343] *Matter of [name not provided]*, EAC 06 014 52770 (AAO Sept. 29, 2006), http://bit.ly/sep061d.

[344] *Matter of [name not provided]*, LIN 03 239 51646 (AAO May 25, 2005), http://bit.ly/may0501d; *Matter of [name not provided]*, EAC 06 075 53028 (AAO Oct. 4, 2006), http://bit.ly/oct062d (criterion not established where the statement only noted that the beneficiary was a panelist).

[345] *Matter of [name not provided]*, LIN 06 103 50190 (AAO Dec. 13, 2006), http://bit.ly/dec061d; *Matter of [name not provided]*, EAC 05 047 51751 (AAO Jan. 17, 2006), http://bit.ly/jan064d. *See also Matter of [name not provided]*, LIN 04 037 54758 (AAO Jan. 9, 2006), http://bit.ly/jan063d (stating that "it is an
Cont'd

Copyright © 2017. American Immigration Lawyers Association. All rights reserved.

BUSINESS IMMIGRATION: LAW & PRACTICE, 2ND ED.

work of staff members if the beneficiary holds a supervisory position.[346] The AAO has gone both ways with respect to whether refereeing an athletic competition constitutes judging the work of others.[347] The AAO has asserted that judging competitions for amateurs, children, or teenagers was insufficient.[348] USCIS may also require that competitions in turn be national or international, in order to "demonstrate[] national or international (as opposed to regional) acclaim."[349]

Finally, in practice USCIS has been receptive to the argument that O-1 beneficiaries in the field of business whose roles have involved judging and evaluating the work of other employees can meet this criterion, particularly where it can be shown that substantial business decisions are based upon judgments made by the O-1 beneficiary. For instance, where an investment fund manager assesses and judges investment recommendations made by investment analysts and ultimately determines whether to invest tens of millions of dollars into a particular stock as a result of that judgment, an argument can be made that this kind of activity satisfied this particular O-1 criterion.

5. Original and Significant Contributions to the Field (O-1A)

Any evidence of original and significant contributions to the field[350] should be accompanied by documents that specifically explain how the beneficiary's work benefited the field.[351] Submitting the beneficiary's work without an explanation of the impact is generally insufficient,[352] and does not provide the necessary context of the

---

inherent part of an instructor's job to judge the work of his or her students"); *Matter of [name not provided]*, LIN 04 184 52913 (AAO Aug. 17, 2005), http://bit.ly/aug052d.

[346] *Matter of [name not provided]*, LIN 04 143 53690 (AAO Aug. 17, 2005), http://bit.ly/aug0501d; *Matter of [name not provided]*, LIN 04 131 54595 (AAO Aug. 16, 2005), http://bit.ly/aug051d (evaluating medical residents as a chief resident); *Matter of [name not provided]*, LIN 04 157 52612 (AAO May 3, 2005), http://bit.ly/may051d; *Matter of [name not provided]*, SRC 03 059 50346 (AAO Apr. 13, 2005), http://bit.ly/apr052d.

[347] *Compare Matter of [name not provided]*, LIN 05 193 53002 (AAO July 18, 2006), http://bit.ly/jul061d (stating that a taekwondo coach "does not evaluate or judge the skills or qualifications of the participants" when refereeing because "the responsibility of the referee is to ensure that rules and procedures are being followed and that the match is safe and fair") *with Matter of BCMHV, LLC,* ID# 126546 (AAO May 26, 2016) (finding that a jiu-jitsu coach's refereeing of matches was judging the work of others). Ironically, the O-1 petition in the former case was approved, because enough other criteria were met, whereas the O-1 petition in the latter case was denied, because judging the work of others was the only criterion met. *Cf.* "AILA/TSC Liaison Minutes" (Oct. 7, 2002), AILA Doc. No. 02121641 (discussing the "referee[ing] for a notable journal" in the context of reviewing articles). Although the discussion relates to extraordinary ability immigrant visa petitions, the principle should remain the same.

[348] *Matter of [name not provided]*, WAC 07 273 54624 (AAO Mar. 11, 2009), http://bit.ly/mar091d.

[349] *Matter of [name not provided]*, LIN 05 262 51156 (AAO Nov. 7, 2007), http://bit.ly/nov073d.

[350] 8 CFR §214.2(o)(3)(iii)(B)(5).

[351] *Matter of [name not provided]*, WAC 06 197 52823 (AAO Mar. 4, 2008), http://bit.ly/mar0801d; *Matter of [name and receipt number not provided]*, (AAO June 20, 2005), http://bit.ly/jun0502d.

[352] *Matter of [name not provided]*, WAC 07 800 12235 (AAO Feb. 9, 2009), http://bit.ly/feb092d (stating that the "documents submitted appear to be standard promotional marketing materials similar to what any person in the beneficiary's profession would be expected to produce for their clients"); *Matter of [name not provided]*, LIN 06 103 50190 (AAO Dec. 13, 2006), http://bit.ly/dec061d.

Copyright © 2017. American Immigration Lawyers Association. All rights reserved.

achievement. The petition should include proof of "why this is an original contribution of major significance" to the beneficiary's field of endeavor,[353] such as "documentary evidence of any new protocols or strategies" developed by the beneficiary,[354] evidence of how other industry insiders "used or relied upon" the beneficiary's work,[355] or a detailed explanation of any new products or technologies. For example, this criterion was deemed established and summarized by the AAO with the following statements:

> "The stem cell transplantation that the beneficiary is involved in exclusively utilizes hematopoietic stem cells which are produced by the patient's own body, as opposed to the more controversial use of embryonic stem cells. The transplant procedure involves destroying a patient's own faulty immune system with chemotherapy and immunosuppressive drugs and then using the hematopoietic stem cells to reproduce a new healthy immune system. The beneficiary and his colleagues have made significant advances using this procedure to treat patients with such debilitating and potentially fatal diseases as multiple sclerosis, Crohn's disease and lupus.... The beneficiary has been working in the field of hematopoietic stem cell transplantation for autoimmune diseases, a novel area of clinical medicine. He has participated in some of the pioneering early studies of stem cell transplantation for rheumatoid arthritis, systemic lupus erythematosis, Crohn's disease, and multiple sclerosis. The beneficiary helped to organize the first major international conference in hematopoietic transplantation for autoimmune diseases. The record shows that the beneficiary's research is of major significance in relation to other similar work being performed."[356]

The practitioner should note that information was provided on the practical application of the beneficiary's scientific innovations, that the area of research was "novel," and that the beneficiary's work was distinguished from other methodologies. Such benefits may be pioneering,[357] ground-breaking,[358] revolutionary,[359] state-of-the-art,[360] or a matter of public interest to the United States.[361] Also relevant are life-

---

[353] *Matter of [name not provided]*, SRC 04 181 53036 (AAO Apr. 21, 2005), http://bit.ly/may055d.

[354] *Matter of [name not provided]*, SRC 04 112 51533 (AAO Jan. 9, 2006), http://bit.ly/jan0602d.

[355] *Matter of [name not provided]*, WAC 03 024 54644 (AAO Jan. 17, 2006), http://bit.ly/jan0603d.

[356] *Matter of [name not provided]*, LIN 02 184 53385 (AAO Sept. 17, 2002), 26 Immig. Rptr. B2-92.

[357] *Matter of [name not provided]*, SRC 02 202 54837 (AAO Nov. 3, 2003), 28 Immig. Rptr. B2-84 (recommender "wrote that the beneficiary successfully implemented the 'first ever outpatient ventricular assist program in Eastern and Southern Kentucky'"); *Matter of [name not provided]*, LIN 02 184 53385 (AAO Sept. 17, 2002), 26 Immig. Rptr. B2-92.

[358] *Matter of [name not provided]*, EAC 06 075 53028 (AAO Oct. 4, 2006), http://bit.ly/oct062d.

[359] *Matter of [name not provided]*, SRC 02 245 52561 (AAO Nov. 1, 2002), 26 Immig. Rptr. B2-17 (beneficiary discovered a master gene "that regulates bone development and a brain bone connection through the molecule leptin").

[360] *Matter of [name not provided]*, SRC 98 066 50295 (AAO Aug. 2, 1998), 19 Immig. Rptr. B2-77 ("the anticipated final product" of a "coupled physical-biological model" held to be "of primary scientific and socio-economic importance for the United States").

Copyright © 2017. American Immigration Lawyers Association. All rights reserved.

saving measures,[362] research efforts,[363] or achievements that optimize or increase the effectiveness of already existing technology,[364] as well as evidence of how the beneficiary's "continued presence on the projects he is involved with is vital."[365]

In contrast, O-1 petitions were denied, among other reasons, in the following cases:

> "None of this evidence sets the documentaries apart from the countless other documentaries produced and released each year, each of which presumably has been shaped by one or more editors.... [I]nvolvement with these festivals does not amount to a lead, starring or critical role therein, and the petitioner has not shown that the beneficiary stood out in any way from the hundreds of other individuals who contributed to the many films shown at those festivals."[366]

> "Although counsel asserts that the beneficiary's project brought attention for 'its cutting edge architectural design' she provides no description of how the design is original. Further, while counsel also asserts that the project carries the highest seismic loads in Spain, there is no evidence that this is the first building to carry such loads or that the beneficiary used new or innovative design or engineering techniques. The record contains no evidence that the beneficiary's project brought new techniques, ground-breaking designs, or other innovations to his field."[367]

In short, the evidence for a strong O-1 petition should demonstrate and explain how the beneficiary's work "is of major significance in relation to other similar work being performed,"[368] as opposed to being of value to a small number of people, such as the beneficiary's patients:[369]

---

[361] *Matter of [name not provided]*, SRC 98 066 50295 (AAO Aug. 2, 1998), 19 Immig. Rptr. B2-77 (accepting that the "National Science Foundation has found [the beneficiary's] research to be in the public interest").

[362] *Matter of [name not provided]*, SRC 02 202 54837 (AAO Nov. 3, 2003), 28 Immig. Rptr. B2-84 (recommender "wrote that the beneficiary 'has been personally responsible for saving the lives of hundreds of patients who otherwise would have no hope of surviving'").

[363] *Matter of [name not provided]*, SRC 98 066 50295 (AAO Aug. 2, 1998), 19 Immig. Rptr. B2-77 (holding that research results pursued through federal funding "has yielded results of major significance").

[364] *Matter of [name not provided]*, SRC 02 202 54837 (AAO Nov. 3, 2003), 28 Immig. Rptr. B2-84 (stating that "the beneficiary has made a significant contribution to his field of endeavor by discerning a heart device defect, reporting it to the manufacturer that implemented the design changes and to his peers who took necessary steps to avoid injuring patients, thereby impacting his field"). The reporting occurred through publication in a professional medical journal, the *Journal of Thoracic and Cardiovascular Surgery*.

[365] *Matter of [name not provided]*, SRC 98 066 50295 (AAO Aug. 2, 1998), 19 Immig. Rptr. B2-77.

[366] *Matter of [name not provided]*, WAC 07 006 52866 (AAO Mar. 5, 2008), http://bit.ly/mar081d.

[367] *Matter of [name not provided]*, EAC 06 075 53028 (AAO Oct. 4, 2006), http://bit.ly/oct062d.

[368] *Matter of [name not provided]*, EAC 04 236 53319 (AAO Mar. 1, 2006), http://bit.ly/mar063d; *Matter of [name not provided]*, WAC 02 038 51106 (AAO May 24, 2005), http://bit.ly/may051d8; *Matter of [name not provided]*, SRC 03 059 50346 (AAO Apr. 13, 2005), http://bit.ly/apr052d.

[369] *Matter of [name not provided]*, LIN 03 239 51646 (AAO May 25, 2005), http://bit.ly/may0501d.

Copyright © 2017. American Immigration Lawyers Association. All rights reserved.

"By definition, all professional research must be original and significant in order to warrant publication in a professional journal.[370]

"However, to satisfy the 'original scientific contribution' criteria, a petitioner should explain the role of the beneficiary in the research effort.[371]

"TSC recognizes the importance of group research within the scientific community. The alien may satisfy this criteri[on] for adjudication by demonstrating that he or she has made critical contributions to significant research accomplishments. The alien does not necessarily need to be solely responsible for the achievement."[372]

"Contributions of major significance in the field" requires "evidence of an impact beyond one's employer and clients or customers."[373]

As another example, in one case both USCIS and the AAO accepted that the beneficiary had gained recognition for the contribution of a virtual reconstruction project, but found that the "petitioner has not provided evidence of any original contributions of major significance made by the beneficiary to the field of architecture or architectural design, outside the area of visual reconstruction and modeling of ancient cities."[374]

The beneficiary's role as the co-inventor of patents may be evidence of an original and significant contribution to the field of endeavor.[375] However, owning patents does not automatically satisfy this criterion: "The granting of a patent documents that an invention or innovation is original, but not every patented invention or innovation constitutes a significant contribution in one's field."[376] Merely having "exceptional technical qualifications" may not necessarily mean that the beneficiary has made an original and significant contribution to the field.[377] USCIS may dismiss evidence for this criterion as only demonstrating the high value of the beneficiary's work to a

---

[370] *Matter of [name not provided]*, EAC 04 236 53319 (AAO Mar. 1, 2006), http://bit.ly/mar063d; *Matter of [name not provided]*, SRC 05 088 50358 (AAO Mar. 1, 2006), http://bit.ly/mar061d; *Matter of [name not provided]*, LIN 04 143 53690 (AAO Aug. 17, 2005), http://bit.ly/aug0501d; *Matter of [name not provided]*, LIN 04 131 54595 (AAO Aug. 16, 2005), http://bit.ly/aug051d; *Matter of [name not provided]*, LIN 03 239 51646 (AAO May 25, 2005), http://bit.ly/may0501d.

[371] "AILA/TSC Liaison Minutes" (Oct. 7, 2002), AILA Doc. No. 02121641 (discussing the multiple authors of scholarly articles for the criterion of original and significant contribution). Although the discussion relates to extraordinary ability immigrant visa petitions, the principle should remain the same.

[372] "TSC Approved Minutes" (June 3, 2002), AILA Doc. No. 02082742. Although the discussion relates to extraordinary ability immigrant visa petitions, the principle should remain the same.

[373] *Matter of G-L-, Inc.*, ID# 16732 (AAO June 15, 2016).

[374] *Matter of [name not provided]*, EAC 07 224 51635 (AAO June 23, 2009), http://bit.ly/jun091d.

[375] *Matter of [name not provided]*, SRC 02 245 52561 (AAO Nov. 1, 2002), 26 Immig. Rptr. B2-17.

[376] *Matter of [name not provided]*, SRC 05 088 50358 (AAO Mar. 1, 2006), http://bit.ly/mar061d; *Matter of [name not provided]*, SRC 04 225 52570 (AAO July 19, 2005), http://bit.ly/jul051d.

[377] *Matter of [name not provided]*, SRC 05 200 51253 (AAO July 23, 2007), http://bit.ly/jul071d.

Copyright © 2017. American Immigration Lawyers Association. All rights reserved.

small number of industry insiders,[378] so the practitioner should work with the client to identify independent sources of corroborating evidence whenever possible:

"While these testimonials speak highly of the beneficiary, letters written by those with professional ties to the beneficiary do not establish that the beneficiary is well-known beyond his immediate circle of colleagues, as one might expect of a person who had made an original contribution of major significance in the field."[379]

A citation history of published articles may also be submitted as evidence of the beneficiary's original and significant contributions,[380] as a new development in a field would be discussed by other industry experts.[381] However, the practitioner should be aware that USCIS and/or the AAO may require that the beneficiary's articles are "unique or cited as being one of major significance to the field" and not only reflect "the prospect of a finding of major significance."[382] The number of citations may also be considered:

"Ten citations to a person's work, in and of themselves, are not evidence of the originality or significance of an individual's contribution. It is the nature of scientific research to build upon the work of other researchers, and citations to other scientists are common in the field. While large numbers of citations by one's peers may reflect the communities' reaction to the research as original and of major significance, ten citations are not sufficient evidence of the major impact this work has had on the field."[383]

For a further discussion of citation histories, see below.

The AAO noted that the "omission of 'athletic contributions' is a realistic reflection of the nature of athletic competition":

"Winning a competition is not an 'original contribution;' it is expected that any given athletic event will have a winning athlete or team that outscores or outperforms rival competitors. Similarly, possessing a high level of the skills needed to succeed in a particular sport is generally a matter of degree, rather than an 'original contribution' to the sport."[384]

---

[378] *Matter of [name not provided]*, EAC 06 014 52770 (AAO Sept. 29, 2006), http://bit.ly/sep061d.

[379] *Matter of [name not provided]*, LIN 04 143 53690 (AAO Aug. 17, 2005), http://bit.ly/aug0501d; *Matter of [name not provided]*, LIN 04 131 54595 (AAO Aug. 16, 2005), http://bit.ly/aug051d; *Matter of [name not provided]*, WAC 03 209 54393 (AAO June 13, 2005), http://bit.ly/jun052d; *Matter of [name not provided]*, WAC 02 038 51106 (AAO May 24, 2005), http://bit.ly/may051d8.

[380] *Matter of [name not provided]*, SRC 02 202 54837 (AAO Nov. 3, 2003), 28 Immig. Rptr. B2-84.

[381] *Matter of [name not provided]*, EAC 06 014 52770 (AAO Sept. 29, 2006), http://bit.ly/sep061d.

[382] *Matter of [name not provided]*, SRC 04 112 51533 (AAO Jan. 9, 2006), http://bit.ly/jan0602d (stating that the beneficiary's study work merely "revealed some important public misperceptions").

[383] *Matter of [name not provided]*, SRC 04 181 53036 (AAO Apr. 21, 2005), http://bit.ly/apr055d.

[384] *Matter of [name not provided]*, WAC 06 224 53958 (AAO May 4, 2009), http://bit.ly/may092d; *Matter of [name not provided]*, LIN 02 296 53935 (AAO Jan. 26, 2005), http://bit.ly/jan0501d.

Copyright © 2017. American Immigration Lawyers Association. All rights reserved.

6. Authorship of Published Scholarly Articles in the Field (O-1A)

The articles[385] should be published in refereed publications,[386] "recognized scholarly or scientific journal[s]," or "top international publications,"[387] as opposed to "vanity presses."[388] The articles should be accompanied by evidence about the publication's stature.[389]

"[A] peer reviewed scientific journal would not be considered a 'vanity press.' An article published in a ranked scientific or academic journal is the type of publication referenced in the EB-1 and O-1 regulations. The journal does not have to be in the highest tier of ranked publications, but the examiners maintain discretion in weighing the totality of the evidence."[390]

Generally, the higher the number of published articles, the better,[391] because the adjudicatory focus is typically on whether the articles "have significantly influenced other [industry members] in his field or related specialties in a manner consistent with sustained national or international acclaim."[392] USCIS and/or the AAO have considered whether the beneficiary was the lead author of the article,[393] although legacy INS provided the following guidance:

"Qualifying publications, like original scientific contributions, often requires the joint efforts of researchers in the field. Publications would not normally require only one author to satisfy the publication criteria for EB-1 and O-1 cases. Publication of research in scientific journals usually indicates that the research is deemed significant. However, to satisfy the 'original scientific contribution' criteria, a petitioner should explain the role of the beneficiary in the research effort."[394]

---

[385] 8 CFR §214.2(o)(3)(iii)(B)(6).

[386] "INS Liaison Teleconference Minutes" (Feb. 15, 2000), AILA 00032802.

[387] "TSC Approved Minutes" (June 3, 2002), AILA Doc. No. 02082742. Although the guidance relates to extraordinary ability immigrant visa petitions, the principle should remain the same.

[388] "AILA/TSC Liaison Minutes" (Oct. 7, 2002), AILA Doc. No. 02121641.

[389] "INS Liaison Teleconference Minutes" (Feb. 15, 2000), AILA Doc. No. 00032802.

[390] "AILA/TSC Liaison Minutes" (Oct. 7, 2002), AILA Doc. No. 02121641; "TSC Approved Minutes" (June 3, 2002), AILA Doc. No. 02082742. Although the discussion relates to extraordinary ability immigrant visa petitions, the principle should remain the same.

[391] *Matter of [name not provided]*, SRC 02 202 54837 (AAO Nov. 3, 2003), 28 Immig. Rptr. B2-84 (25 scholarly articles); *Matter of [name not provided]*, SRC 98 066 50295 (AAO Aug. 2, 1998), 19 Immig. Rptr. B2-77 (47 scholarly articles); *Matter of [name not provided]*, SRC 02 245 52561 (AAO Nov. 1, 2002), 26 Immig. Rptr. B2-17 (22 articles and 20 abstracts); *Matter of [name not provided]*, LIN 02 184 53385 (AAO Sept. 17, 2002), 26 Immig. Rptr. B2-92 (28 articles published in professional journals or presented at professional conferences); *Matter of [name and receipt number not provided]*, (AAO June 20, 2005), http://bit.ly/jun0502d.

[392] *Matter of [name not provided]*, WAC 06 160 52954 (AAO May 31, 2007), http://bit.ly/may071d.

[393] *Id.*

[394] "AILA/TSC Liaison Minutes" (Oct. 7, 2002), AILA Doc. No. 02121641.

Copyright © 2017. American Immigration Lawyers Association. All rights reserved.

However, technical guides or articles, such as those providing advice on sports techniques, have been deemed not scholarly by the AAO.[395] It is not necessary to submit the entire article: "Title pages or the first page with the title, author and publication data are sufficient."[396]

Although a citation history of published articles may also be submitted as evidence of published materials in major media discussing the beneficiary's achievements, a citation history should also be presented for this criterion where possible:[397] "In the absence of citation histories, the AAO cannot evaluate the impact of the beneficiary's work on the field of endeavor."[398] A citation history "from services such as SciFinder, PubMed, Google Scholar, are useful and will be accepted," and the "relevant parts of the listed articles citing the works should be included."[399] Alternatively, the full article citing the beneficiary's work may "be included and highlighted to make it easier for the examiner to find the reference,"[400] and the practitioner should also tab the page with the citation.

USCIS "is looking for independent citations and does not give additional credibility to authors who cite their own works."[401] Similarly, "footnoted references with no positive comment offer little value."[402] The number of citations is also pertinent, as discussed above. For example, five articles being cited up to three times each and one article being cited 12 times was deemed insufficient.[403]

Another adjudicatory trend is to reject articles published by scientists, so the practitioner is encouraged to also submit a citation history:

"Duties or activities which nominally fall under a given regulatory criterion … do not demonstrate national or international acclaim if they are inherent or routine to the occupation itself. As frequent publication of research findings is inherent to success as a research scientist, publications alone do not necessarily indicate the sustained acclaim requisite to classification as an alien with extraordinary ability."[404]

---

[395] *Matter of [name not provided]*, SRC 06 071 50688 (AAO June 2, 2006), http://bit.ly/jun0601d8.

[396] "AILA Liaison/Nebraska Service Center Liaison Teleconference Q&As" (June 25, 2009), AILA Doc. No. 09070864. Although the discussion relates to extraordinary ability immigrant visa petitions, the principle should remain the same.

[397] *Matter of [name not provided]*, SRC 02 202 54837 (AAO Nov. 3, 2003), 28 Immig. Rptr. B2-84.

[398] *Matter of [name not provided]*, LIN 04 143 53690 (AAO Aug. 17, 2005), http://bit.ly/aug0501d.

[399] "AILA Liaison/Nebraska Service Center Liaison Teleconference Q&As" (June 25, 2009), AILA Doc. No. 09070864. Although the discussion relates to extraordinary ability immigrant visa petitions, the principle should remain the same.

[400] *Id.*

[401] *Id.*

[402] "TSC Approved Minutes" (June 3, 2002), AILA Doc. No. 02082742. Although the discussion relates to extraordinary ability immigrant visa petitions, the principle should remain the same.

[403] *Matter of [name not provided]*, LIN 04 131 54595 (AAO Aug. 16, 2005), http://bit.ly/aug051d.

[404] *Matter of [name not provided]*, WAC 06 160 52954 (AAO May 31, 2007), http://bit.ly/may071d.

Copyright © 2017. American Immigration Lawyers Association. All rights reserved.

In other words, the AAO contends that in "the scientific research community, publication of one's work is expected, even among researchers who are still in an academic training environment."[405] Therefore, petitions for scientists should also contain a citation history of the beneficiary's articles, as "[p]ublished articles by the beneficiary that have been cited by others would more meaningfully establish that the beneficiary enjoys a measure of influence through his publications":[406]

"Publication alone may serve as evidence of originality, but it is difficult to conclude that a published article is important or influential if there is little evidence that other researchers have relied upon the [beneficiary's] findings. Frequent citation by independent researchers, however, would demonstrate widespread interest in, and reliance on, the beneficiary's work. If, on the other hand, there are few or no citations of an alien's work, suggesting that the work has gone largely unnoticed by the greater research community, then it is reasonable to conclude that the alien's work is not nationally or internationally acclaimed."[407]

"However, all published articles in professional journals are presumed to be of original work and designed to advance knowledge in the field."[408]

As with many of the other criteria, when a *Kazarian*-type analysis is applied, the mere fact of publication of the articles is generally accepted as fulfilling this criterion regardless of their reception in the field, but found in the final merits analysis not to show national or international acclaim, thus creating the same result through a somewhat different route.[409]

These published articles may also include books, book reviews, or a textbook chapter, even if co-authored.[410] For a discussion of "major media," see above.

7. Employment in a Critical or Essential Capacity for Organizations with Distinguished Reputations (O-1A)[411]

In rare instances, such as when the organizations are commonly known, it may not be necessary to provide evidence of the distinguished reputation;[412] however, the practitioner is advised to err on the side of caution and to encourage the client and/or beneficiary to provide this information, as what is well known to an industry insider may not be well known to a USCIS adjudicator. The organization should have a

---

[405] *Matter of [name not provided]*, EAC 04 236 53319 (AAO Mar. 1, 2006), http://bit.ly/mar063d.

[406] *Id.*

[407] *Matter of [name not provided]*, SRC 05 088 50358 (AAO Mar. 1, 2006), http://bit.ly/mar061d; *Matter of [name not provided]*, LIN 03 239 51646 (AAO May 25, 2005), http://bit.ly/may0501d.

[408] *Matter of [name not provided]*, SRC 04 112 51533 (AAO Jan. 9, 2006), http://bit.ly/jan0602d.

[409] *Matter of [name and case number not provided]* (AAO Oct. 14, 2010), http://bit.ly/oct102d.

[410] *Matter of [name not provided]*, SRC 02 202 54837 (AAO Nov. 3, 2003), 28 Immig. Rptr. B2-84.

[411] 8 CFR §214.2(o)(3)(iii)(B)(7).

[412] *Matter of [name not provided]*, SRC 98 066 50295 (AAO Aug. 2, 1998), 19 Immig. Rptr. B2-77 (accepting the distinguished reputations of the Department of Energy, United Nations organizations, and Louisiana State University, among others).

Copyright © 2017. American Immigration Lawyers Association. All rights reserved.

distinguished reputation in the beneficiary's field of endeavor.[413] A distinguished reputation may be due to outstanding achievements by the owner(s), executives, members, and/or employees,[414] status in history,[415] or prestige within the industry.[416]

Generally, statements from independent sources regarding the distinguished reputation of the petitioner are more favorably received than statements from "individuals either directly or indirectly involved in the petitioning organization and its parent corporation."[417] However, merely being employed by such an organization is insufficient, as the distinguished or national reputation of an organization may not be imputed to a beneficiary's work.[418]

The AAO has stated that the "terms critical and essential are synonymous with crucial and indispensable,"[419] so the practitioner is encouraged to provide evidence regarding how the beneficiary's role was integral,[420] during his or her period of previous employment,[421] such as by describing "the beneficiary's specific duties and where he fits in the hierarchy of his own firm's team."[422] The former positions held should be in the same field of endeavor for which the O-1 petition is filed.[423] USCIS should not, however, focus exclusively upon the beneficiary's job titles when

---

[413] Matter of [name not provided], EAC 05 028 52811 (AAO Jan. 9, 2007), http://bit.ly/jan071d (stating that the "petitioner submitted evidence that [the organization] has been noticed for its cuisine and atmosphere, but it submitted no evidence that it has a distinguished reputation in the field of music," which was the beneficiary's field of endeavor).

[414] Matter of [name not provided], LIN 01 245 54595 (AAO Oct. 16, 2002), 26 Immig. Rptr. B2-81 (champion basketball teams).

[415] Matter of [name not provided], LIN 93 124 51276 (AAO Jan. 23, 1995), 14 Immig. Rptr. B2-128 (indicating that status as a historic site may mean that an "old church" has a distinguished reputation). Cf. Matter of [name not provided], EAC 04 204 50274 (AAO Feb. 21, 2006), http://bit.ly/feb062d (newspaper article referring to an organization as a "respected business" deemed insufficient).

[416] Matter of [name not provided], EAC 05 028 52811 (AAO Jan. 9, 2007), http://bit.ly/jan071d.

[417] Matter of [name not provided], SRC 03 237 50782 (AAO Apr. 13, 2005), http://bit.ly/apr051d.

[418] Matter of [name not provided], WAC 07 006 52866 (AAO Mar. 5, 2008), http://bit.ly/mar081d (stating that "while the evidence shows national recognition of the ensemble itself, there is no evidence to establish a comparable reputation of the documentary or of the entity that produced it"). See also Matter of [name not provided], WAC 07 015 50561 (AAO Nov. 7, 2007), http://bit.ly/nov072d (stating the "[p]articipating in an ensemble dance performance for course credit at a university does not convey on the beneficiary a level of recognition proportional to the reputation of the university as a whole"). Although these cases addressed the criterion of achievement of national or international recognition, the principle should remain the same.

[419] Matter of [name not provided], WAC 02 038 51106 (AAO May 24, 2005), http://bit.ly/may051d8.

[420] Matter of [name not provided], SRC 02 202 54837 (AAO Nov. 3, 2003), 28 Immig. Rptr. B2-84 (petitioner failed to provide evidence of how research programs had distinguished reputations, even though the beneficiary was the "principal investigator" on clinical trials).

[421] Matter of [name not provided], SRC 05 200 51253 (AAO July 23, 2007), http://bit.ly/jul071d (stating that "[p]roposed employment in the future will not suffice").

[422] Matter of [name not provided], EAC 06 075 53028 (AAO Oct. 4, 2006), http://bit.ly/oct062d.

[423] Matter of [name not provided], LIN 04 157 52612 (AAO May 3, 2005), http://bit.ly/may051d (noting that participation on athletic teams "is not related to her future field of endeavor, management; therefore, the beneficiary does not satisfy this criterion").

Copyright © 2017. American Immigration Lawyers Association. All rights reserved.

evaluating whether he or she held a critical and/or essential role.[424] An RFE on this issue should not inquire whether the beneficiary's "expertise exceeds that of all other experts at the company":

> "The alien need only demonstrate that he or she is at the top of the very specialized field. TSC recognizes that a company may have numerous extraordinarily talented experts, and the alien's expertise does not have to exceed that of all other extraordinary employees within the company. Likewise, a company may not have any extraordinarily gifted professionals, so being the best at such a company offers no real adjudication value. This has been discussed with examiners and was part of a training issue. Examiners should not be sending any more RFEs of this nature."[425]

Another way to view this factor is as "prior employment in [a] key role on major projects,"[426] as long as "the petitioner can establish that these projects have a distinguished reputation."[427] The practitioner should encourage the recommender to explain the magnitude or impact of the beneficiary's achievements in the context of the industry and/or of practical application in the real world. If such information is not forthcoming from the recommender, then the practitioner should request this information from the client and/or beneficiary and confirm that it is included in the petitioner's support statement.

For example, being the principal investigator or co-principal for federally funded research projects may be deemed an essential or critical role,[428] as may being the head of a research team and laboratory, especially if funding for the research project has a high monetary value.[429] Alternatively, distinguished companies may have utilized the beneficiary's skills on high profile and major projects.[430] As a third example, a petition for an athlete may include media articles describing how the beneficiary "led his team" to an international title or to a national championship or

---

[424] *Matter of [name not provided]*, WAC 02 038 51106 (AAO May 24, 2005), http://bit.ly/may051d8 (withdrawing the portion of the USCIS decision that stated the criterion was not satisfied because the beneficiary has not served as a chief operating officer for any of the organizations, and stating that "we do not believe that the job title is necessarily determinative of whether an alien meets this criterion").

[425] "TSC Approved Minutes" (June 3, 2002), AILA Doc. No. 02082742. Although the discussion relates to extraordinary ability immigrant visa petitions, the principle should remain the same.

[426] AFM 33.4.

[427] *Matter of [name not provided]*, SRC 03 236 51017 (AAO Apr. 21, 2005), http://bit.ly/apr0502d.

[428] *Matter of [name not provided]*, SRC 98 066 50295 (AAO Aug. 2, 1998), 19 Immig. Rptr. B2-77.

[429] *Matter of [name not provided]*, SRC 02 245 52561 (AAO Nov. 1, 2002), 26 Immig. Rptr. B2-17 (beneficiary was the lead investigator of a project awarded $800,000 in funding from the National Institutes of Health).

[430] *Matter of [name not provided]*, EAC 96 058 51556 (AAO June 25, 1998), 19 Immig. Rptr. B2-62 (for an Architect/Urban Designer, previous architectural firms employed her for important projects).

Copyright © 2017. American Immigration Lawyers Association. All rights reserved.

how performance during an important competition was outstanding,[431] or may include evidence that the beneficiary coached his home country's Olympic team.[432]

Merely being on an important team, without holding a leadership role, such as director or president,[433] or without being the leader of the team, the "department head, senior researcher or principal investigator,"[434] may be rejected as insufficient, so the practitioner should provide a detailed explanation of how the role was critical or essential.[435] AAO cases also rejected being selected to represent a region in a "one-time athletic event,"[436] and "association with persons of distinguished reputation."[437] In particular, testimonial letters submitted in support of this criterion should include a detailed discussion of several examples of the O-1 beneficiary's role on key projects or initiatives, and the reason that these projects were particularly important or valuable for the company.

It remains unclear whether being appointed to faculty of a top educational or research institution would qualify. Legacy INS guidance indicates this may be acceptable as long as there is independent evidence of the preeminence of the institution, such as national ranking from *U.S. News and World Report*;[438] but the employment may be construed as only employment, with the distinguished or national reputation of an organization not imputed to a beneficiary's work,[439] as noted above. To avoid an RFE or denial, the practitioner may wish to also provide appointment criteria for the institution to demonstrate how the employment constituted an achievement in and of itself.

---

[431] *Matter of [name not provided]*, LIN 01 245 54595 (AAO Oct. 16, 2002), 26 Immig. Rptr. B2-81 (beneficiary played "on the 2000 Russian Olympic Team where he saw action in all seven games (3 starts), averaging 9.4 points, second-best on the team").

[432] *Matter of [name not provided]*, LIN 05 193 53002 (AAO July 18, 2006), http://bit.ly/jul061d.

[433] *Matter of [name not provided]*, SRC 06 039 50380 (AAO May 10, 2006), http://bit.ly/may061d; *Matter of [name not provided]*, LIN 03 239 51646 (AAO May 25, 2005), http://bit.ly/may0501d.

[434] *Matter of [name not provided]*, EAC 06 014 52770 (AAO Sept. 29, 2006), http://bit.ly/sep061d.

[435] *Cf. Matter of [name not provided]*, SRC 02 202 54837 (AAO Nov. 3, 2003), 28 Immig. Rptr. B2-84 (role deemed not critical or essential). *See also Matter of [name not provided]*, WAC 06 160 52954 (AAO May 31, 2007), http://bit.ly/may071d; *Matter of [name not provided]*, EAC 06 075 53028 (AAO Oct. 4, 2006), http://bit.ly/oct062d.

[436] *Matter of [name not provided]*, WAC 07 273 54624 (AAO Mar. 11, 2009), http://bit.ly/mar091d.

[437] *Matter of [name not provided]*, SRC 06 138 52302 (AAO Nov. 7, 2007), http://bit.ly/nov0701d.

[438] "INS Liaison Teleconference Minutes" (Feb. 15, 2000), AILA Doc. No. 00032802.

[439] *Matter of [name not provided*, WAC 07 006 52866 (AAO Mar. 5, 2008), http://bit.ly/mar081d (stating that "while the evidence shows national recognition of the ensemble itself, there is no evidence to establish a comparable reputation of the documentary or of the entity that produced it"). *See also Matter of [name not provided]*, WAC 07 015 50561 (AAO Nov. 7, 2007), http://bit.ly/nov072d (stating that "[p]articipating in an ensemble dance performance for course credit at a university does not convey on the beneficiary a level of recognition proportional to the reputation of the university as a whole"). Although these cases addressed the criterion of achievement of national or international recognition, the principle should remain the same.

Copyright © 2017. American Immigration Lawyers Association. All rights reserved.

A testimonial may be analyzed to determine if the beneficiary served in an essential or critical role for the organization, rather than a team or laboratory.[440] Earning patents on behalf of an organization may be accepted, but USCIS may require that the petitioner establish that "the beneficiary is the sole employee conducting research and filing patent applications."[441] The practitioner is encouraged to submit evidence of the impact of the patent to the organization, such as its practical application or importance to the organization's research or business efforts.

The employment should have been for a significant period of time, and in one case, the AAO deemed serving as a team captain as not "employment" for purposes of this criterion.[442] Similarly, nontraditional employment relationships and entities may be evaluated to determine if they qualify as employment or an organization or establishment, respectively,[443] such as through payroll records, employment confirmation letters, or USCIS employment authorization.[444]

Employment recommendation letters that are merely "complimentary"[445] are not helpful in establishing this criterion. Such letters need to provide specific details on how the beneficiary's duties were in an essential or critical capacity. In other words, these letters must go beyond conveying "that the beneficiary is a talented [professional] who performed his duties satisfactorily during his employment."[446] If a statement from a previous employer is provided, the signatory should provide details regarding his or her credentials and the beneficiary's period of employment, as discussed below. Similarly, merely providing a copy of the beneficiary's résumé does not conclusively establish that he or she held critical or essential roles within distinguished organizations,[447] most likely based on the same rationale that a résumé is insufficient to establish a foreign national's education and experience for purposes of proving eligibility for an immigrant visa petition based on a labor certification application.[448]

---

[440] *Matter of [name not provided]*, EAC 06 014 52770 (AAO Sept. 29, 2006), http://bit.ly/sep061d; *Matter of [name not provided]*, SRC 04 181 53036 (AAO Apr. 21, 2005), http://bit.ly/apr055d.

[441] *Matter of [name not provided]*, SRC 05 088 50358 (AAO Mar. 1, 2006), http://bit.ly/mar061d.

[442] *Matter of [name not provided]*, WAC 07 055 52449 (AAO Mar. 21, 2008), http://bit.ly/mar0801d (six weeks of employment is insufficient).

[443] *Matter of [name not provided]*, EAC 07 224 51635 (AAO June 23, 2009), http://bit.ly/jun091d (AAO indicated it was "unclear" whether work on a virtual reconstruction is considered employment "or whether the project itself constitute[d] an 'organization or establishment'").

[444] *Matter of [name not provided]*, WAC 06 224 53958 (AAO May 4, 2009), http://bit.ly/may091d.

[445] *Matter of [name not provided]*, WAC 07 273 54624 (AAO Mar. 11, 2009), http://bit.ly/mar091d; *Matter of [name not provided]*, WAC 07 800 12235 (AAO Feb. 9, 2009), http://bit.ly/feb092d.

[446] *Matter of [name not provided]*, EAC 07 224 51635 (AAO June 23, 2009), http://bit.ly/jun091d.

[447] *Matter of [name not provided]*, WAC 07 800 12235 (AAO Feb. 9, 2009), http://bit.ly/feb092d; *Matter of [name not provided]*, EAC 04 236 53319 (AAO Mar. 1, 2006), http://bit.ly/mar063d.

[448] For a discussion of labor certification applications and immigrant visa petitions, see Volume 2: Chapters Two and Three, "The Labor Certification Application" and "The Immigrant Visa Petition," respectively.

Copyright © 2017. American Immigration Lawyers Association. All rights reserved.

8. High Salary or Remuneration (O-1A and O-1B) [449]

AAO cases on this criterion require a showing that the remuneration "is substantially higher than that paid to" others performing the same occupation[450] through some type of quantitative comparison.[451] The remuneration should be paid to the beneficiary rather than allotted for an overall project.[452] The AAO accepted a salary that was almost double the average starting salary,[453] but a salary that was less than that of the 75th percentile was rejected,[454] as was a wage 12 percent more than the average wage.[455]

Salary surveys may be provided as evidence,[456] but the history of acceptance of salary surveys remains unclear. The AAO has stated: "[T]o evaluate whether the salary is high, USCIS would need a wage survey that specifies the median and highest wages offered nationwide or internationally."[457] On the other hand, multiple anecdotal reports indicate that salary surveys are frequently rejected.[458] If the beneficiary's previous income was through self-employment, then use of prevailing wage data may be less helpful.[459] Although not explicitly stated in the regulations, USCIS seems to construe this requirement as "rel[ying] on past income history."[460]

---

[449] 8 CFR §214.2(o)(3)(iii)(B)(8), (iv)(B)(6), and (v)(B)(6).

[450] *Matter of [name not provided]*, WAC 07 055 52449 (AAO Mar. 21, 2008), http://bit.ly/mar0801d; *Matter of [name not provided]*, LIN 01 245 54595 (AAO Oct. 16, 2002), 26 Immig. Rptr. B2-81 (remuneration of $831,120 per year not discussed, perhaps because this figure may not be comparatively high for the field of professional basketball players with the NBA).

[451] *Matter of [name not provided]*, WAC 07 273 54624 (AAO Mar. 11, 2009), http://bit.ly/mar091d (no "documentary evidence supporting the claim that 210,000 rubles is a high salary for a ballroom dance instructor").

[452] *Matter of [name not provided]*, SRC 05 200 51253 (AAO July 23, 2007), http://bit.ly/jul071d.

[453] *Matter of [name not provided]*, EAC 96 058 51556 (AAO June 25, 1998), 19 Immig. Rptr. B2-62 ($38,000 and $22,125 per year, respectively). *See also Matter of [name not provided]*, LIN 95 131 50963 (AAO Nov. 3, 1995), 15 Immig. Rptr. B2-61 ($37,000 and $60,000 per year, respectively).

[454] *Matter of [name not provided]*, SRC 05 088 50358 (AAO Mar. 1, 2006), *available at www.uscis.gov* (select "Laws," "Administrative Decisions" link on the right toolbar under "More Information," D8, and then search by date and for "01D8101").

[455] *Matter of [name not provided]*, LIN 04 114 52837 (AAO Jan. 26, 2005), *available at www.uscis.gov* (select "Laws," "Administrative Decisions" link on the right toolbar under "More Information," D8, and then search by date and for "02D8101").

[456] *Matter of [name not provided]*, LIN 95 131 50963 (AAO Nov. 3, 1995), 15 Immig. Rptr. B2-61 (survey of "Compensation for Salaried Personnel in Food Service").

[457] *Matter of [name not provided]*, LIN 04 184 52913 (AAO Aug. 17, 2005), http://bit.ly/aug052d; *Matter of [name not provided]*, LIN 04 143 53690 (AAO Aug. 17, 2005), http://bit.ly/aug0501d; *Matter of [name not provided]*, SRC 04 225 52570 (AAO July 19, 2005), http://bit.ly/jul051d; *Matter of [name and receipt number not provided]*, (AAO June 20, 2005), http://bit.ly/jun0502d; *Matter of [name not provided]*, WAC 03 209 54393 (AAO June 13, 2005), http://bit.ly/jun052d; *Matter of [name not provided]*, SRC 04 181 53036 (AAO Apr. 21, 2005), http://bit.ly/apr055d.

[458] *Matter of [name and case number not provided]* (AAO July 13, 2012) http://bit.ly/jul121d.

[459] *Matter of [name not provided]*, EAC 08 134 51786 (AAO May 4, 2009), http://bit.ly/may091d.

[460] *Matter of [name not provided]*, EAC 02 127 52263 (AAO Sept. 16, 2002), 26 Immig. Rptr. B2-26. *See also Matter of [name not provided]*, EAC 07 224 51635 (AAO June 23, 2009), http://bit.ly/jun091d.

Copyright © 2017. American Immigration Lawyers Association. All rights reserved.

An RFE may be issued to request evidence of earning a high salary for a sustained period of time.[461] Reliance on past history can be helpful where it is unclear whether the present offer could be considered to be for high remuneration, but the beneficiary has a history of elevated pay.[462]

The data should be appropriate for the occupational industry[463] and for the type and level of the position.[464] It may also be prudent to mention how the beneficiary's salary is comparable to others with similar levels of education and experience,[465] or degree of specialization: "To broaden the petitioner's field to mechanical engineering in general, and only for the purpose of assessing the beneficiary's eligibility under this criterion, is thus disingenuous and inconsistent."[466] Even if the appropriate salary survey is presented, it may be rejected on the ground that it provides local data, based on the AAO's rationale that the O-1 petition "must demonstrate that the beneficiary's salary places her at the top of her field at the national level, not simply at what her work would command at the local level."[467] The practitioner should note that certain publications, such as the Occupational Outlook Handbook (OOH), may offer salaries for "the top 10%" of an occupation.[468] Also, USCIS will generally look at the top levels of wage surveys for comparisons,[469] rather than at the median or mean, arguing that an individual with extraordinary ability should be compared with the top earners.[470] And for athlete petitions, USCIS and/or the AAO may compare the beneficiary's monetary winnings with other competitors.[471]

USCIS may also look to what the petitioner is paying others of similar years of experience, if the company employs multiple people in that occupation.[472]

---

[461] "CSC Answers AILA Questions" (Feb. 13, 2001), AILA Doc. No. 01031401. Although the discussion relates to extraordinary ability immigrant visa petitions, the principle should remain the same.

[462] *Matter of [name and case number not provided]* (AAO Mar. 11, 2013), http://bit.ly/mar131d.

[463] *Matter of [name not provided]*, SRC 05 088 50358 (AAO Mar. 1, 2006), http://bit.ly/mar061d (salary survey for education industry rejected because the beneficiary would not work in the education industry); *Matter of [name not provided]*, WAC 03 024 54644 (AAO Jan. 17, 2006), http://bit.ly/jun0603d.

[464] *Pellizzari v. Zuchowski*, No. 15-2527 (D.C.N.J., Feb. 8, 2016), AILA Doc. No. 16021203.

[465] *Matter of [name not provided]*, EAC 07 224 51635 (AAO June 23, 2009), http://bit.ly/jun091d (AAO rejected offer of high entry-level salary where the beneficiary had 10 years of experience); *Matter of [name not provided]*, WAC 03 201 50250 (AAO July 8, 2005), http://bit.ly/jul0510d.

[466] *Matter of [name not provided]*, SRC 05 200 51253 (AAO July 23, 2007), http://bit.ly/jul081d.

[467] *Matter of [name not provided]*, EAC 04 204 50274 (AAO Feb. 21, 2006), http://bit.ly/feb062d; *Matter of [name not provided]*, EAC 04 240 52613 (AAO July 13, 2005), http://bit.ly/jul0502d.

[468] *Matter of [name not provided]*, SRC 04 112 51533 (AAO Jan. 9, 2006), http://bit.ly/jan0602d.

[469] *See, e.g., Matter of [name and case number not provided]* (AAO Mar. 11, 2013), http://bit.ly/mar131d.

[470] *See, e.g., Matter of [name and case number not provided]* (AAO Aug. 25, 2014), http://bit.ly/aug141b, citing *Matter of Price*, 20 I&N Dec. 953, 954 (Assoc. Comm'r 1994). Although the case relates to extraordinary ability immigrant visa petitions, the principle should remain the same.

[471] *Matter of [name not provided]*, WAC 06 224 53958 (AAO May 4, 2009), http://bit.ly/may092d.

[472] *Matter of [name and case number not provided]* (AAO Mar. 11, 2013), http://bit.ly/mar131d.

Copyright © 2017. American Immigration Lawyers Association. All rights reserved.

Use of this criterion can be problematic in some fields, such as entertainment, publishing, and athletics, where remuneration is comprised of such forms as appearance fees, advances, or a percentage of sales.[473] Surveys rarely cover this type of income, and USCIS is loath to accept uncorroborated statements that the remuneration is high:[474]

> "[W]e acknowledge the ... claim that there are no 'published studies' of track and field athletes' earnings. Such claim does not exempt the petitioner from providing some other form of corroborating evidence.... The regulation simply requires that the petitioner's claims be supported by 'reliable evidence.' The petitioner could have sought other published articles from reputable sources, letters from the sponsors of the races in which the beneficiary will participate setting forth the range of participation fees paid to athletes, a letter from the governing body of the sport attesting to the unavailability of published wage information, the opinions of other experts in the field, or any form of other 'reliable evidence' to corroborate its claims. [Name redacted] opinion that the beneficiary will receive a high salary is simply insufficient to meet this evidentiary requirement."[475]

The practitioner should note that although a high salary may be indicative of extraordinary ability, a low salary should not automatically mean that the beneficiary lacks extraordinary ability: "[T]he fact that some services may be performed with low salary or remuneration, or services performed gratis, does not, in and of itself, disqualify an alien for this classification."[476] However, this factor has nevertheless been considered.[477]

9. Performance in a Lead, Starring, or Critical Role in Productions or Events for Entities with Distinguished Reputations (O-1B)

A lead or starring role can fulfill two different criteria, depending upon the type of evidence submitted and the type of entity for which the role will be or has been performed. Since the two criteria are similar, it is possible to get a "twofer" and cover two of the three needed categories with one set of evidence.[478]

As stated in the regulations, primary evidence of performing in a lead or starring role for distinguished "productions or events" includes critical reviews, publicity releases, publications, contracts, advertisements, or endorsements,[479] where the

---

[473] *Matter of [name and case number not provided]* (AAO July 11, 2011), http://bit.ly/jul112d; *Matter of [name and case number not provided]* (AAO Sept. 9, 2013), http://bit.ly/sep131d.

[474] *Matter of [name and case number not provided]* (AAO July 11, 2011), http://bit.ly/jul112d.

[475] *Matter of [name and case number not provided]* (AAO Feb. 3, 2011), http://bit.ly/feb111d.

[476] USCIS Office of Business Liaison, Employer Information Bulletin 15, "Aliens with Extraordinary Ability (O-1) and Accompanying/Assisting Aliens (O-2)" (Dec. 8, 2004), 82 Interpreter Releases 180–84 (Jan. 17, 2005).

[477] *Matter of Shaw*, 11 I&N Dec. 277 (Dist. Dir. 1965) (stating that the petitioner "may not realistically be expected to be able to secure the services of a performer of 'distinguished merit and ability' at the salary offered").

[478] *Matter of [name and case number not provided]* (AAO July 11, 2011), http://bit.ly/jul112d.

[479] 8 CFR §214.2(o)(3)(iv)(B)(1) and (v)(B)(1).

Copyright © 2017. American Immigration Lawyers Association. All rights reserved.

beneficiary is mentioned by name.[480] A separate category for lead or critical roles for "organizations and establishments" with distinguished reputations provides for evidence from "newspapers, trade journals, publications, or testimonials."[481]

For a strong O-1 petition, the documents should discuss more than one performance or event, as the AAO stated: "Clearly, favorable reviews from a single engagement is not sufficient to establish the requisite extraordinary ability in the performing arts."[482]

A lead or starring role has been construed as more than a "limited contribution to just one short segment of only one episode," so even if a program earned the Emmy Award, USCIS and/or the AAO may determine that the distinguished reputation garnered from the award "was not largely or substantially attributable to the beneficiary's work."[483] Similarly, the AAO stated that a musician does not hold a lead or starring role if he or she performs "as part of an orchestra, ensemble or musical duo," instead of as a "solo performer, principal musician or featured soloist,"[484] even if the musician was first chair.[485] For athletic and artistic competitors, the AAO noted that "[b]eing a finalist is not equivalent to being a lead or starring participant," and even placing first may be deemed insufficient, if details "about the stature of the competitions, or how the beneficiary could be characterized as playing a lead or starring role in competitions" is not provided,[486] so the practitioner should provide this information.

The display and sale of products "may be considered productions or events."[487] Similarly, exhibition of an artist's work may also qualify, as long as evidence of the exhibition's distinguished reputation is provided, such as information on "the number of participants and the attendance."[488] A starring role in one art show has been found insufficient.[489]

---

[480] *Matter of [name not provided]*, SRC 04 204 53136 (AAO Apr. 29, 2005), http://bit.ly/apr0501d (beneficiary's name not stated in several critical reviews). *But see Matter of [name and case number not provided]* (AAO July 11, 2011), http://bit.ly/jul112d (from the overall discussion in the decision, it appears that the beneficiary was not mentioned by name, or at most was mentioned in passing, in favorable reviews of his band).

[481] 8 CFR §214.2(o)(3)(iv)(B)(3) and (v)(B)(3).

[482] *Matter of [name not provided]*, WAC 02 196 50736 (AAO Sept. 16, 2002), 26 Immig. Rptr. B2-23.

[483] *Matter of [name not provided]* WAC 06 167 50726 (AAO Mar. 6, 2007), http://bit.ly/mar071d.

[484] *Matter of [name not provided]*, WAC 06 177 52596 (AAO Jan. 24, 2007), http://bit.ly/jan071d8; *Matter of [name not provided]*, SRC 04 048 51779 (AAO Jan. 17, 2006), http://bit.ly/jan0601d8; *Matter of [name and case number not provided]*, (AAO June 20, 2005), http://bit.ly/jun051d (soloist performance of a ballet dancer accepted by the AAO). *But see Matter of [name and case number not provided]* (AAO July 11, 2011), http://bit.ly/jul112d (drummer in alt-rock band had lead role).

[485] *Matter of S-Y-P-A-, Inc.*, ID# 15674 (AAO Mar. 1, 2016) (first horn in orchestra not a lead or starring role).

[486] *Matter of [name not provided]*, LIN 02 296 53935 (AAO Jan. 26, 2005), http://bit.ly/jan0501d.

[487] *Matter of [name not provided]*, EAC 04 187 50327 (AAO Oct. 4, 2006), http://bit.ly/oct061d.

[488] *Matter of [name not provided]*, EAC 05 047 51751 (AAO Jan. 17, 2006), http://bit.ly/jan064d.

[489] *Matter of T-H-G-A-S-, LLC*, ID# 15858 (AAO Mar. 22, 2016).

Copyright © 2017. American Immigration Lawyers Association. All rights reserved.

Importantly, the regulations require that the beneficiary has performed and will perform in a leading, starring, or critical role,[490] so merely providing evidence of past performance has been deemed insufficient.[491] Appropriate evidence includes copies of the documents (critical reviews, advertisements, publicity releases, publications contracts, or endorsements), copies of awards, copies of articles discussing the production or events, and the professional credit history of the beneficiary. The beneficiary should be mentioned by name in these documents, as well.[492] In the context of O-1 petitions for individuals involved in film and television production, the organization may be a film or television agency, a renowned director, or an actual film or television show, and the beneficiary's professional credits may be submitted as evidence.[493] For a discussion of what may qualify as a distinguished reputation, see above.

Similar to evidence of employment in a critical or essential capacity, letters from previous and current employers may be submitted, but they should be supplementary to independent evidence: "While such letters are important in providing details about the [beneficiary's] role in various organizations, they cannot by themselves establish the beneficiary has achieved distinction in his field of endeavor."[494] As discussed above, experience confirmation letters from the beneficiary's previous employers are typically insufficiently detailed to establish satisfaction of this criterion, as they may simply provide dates of employment and job duties or only generally describe the duties of an occupation.[495]

As noted above, evidence of performance in a leading, starring, or critical role for a distinguished organization should be documented "by articles in newspapers, trade journals, publications, or testimonials,"[496] which should mention the beneficiary by name and discuss his or her performance.[497] As obvious as it seems, the evidence should discuss how "the beneficiary performed a lead, starring or critical role" and should demonstrate how the entity has a well-regarded reputation.[498] For more obscure or lesser-known occupations, the petition should contain an explanation of

---

[490] 8 CFR §§214.2(o)(3)(iv)(B)(3) and (o)(3)(iv)(B)(1); *Matter of [name not provided]*, EAC 05 028 52811 (AAO Jan. 9, 2007), http://bit.ly/jan071d.

[491] *Matter of [name not provided]*, EAC 05 028 52811 (AAO Jan. 9, 2007), http://bit.ly/jan071d; *Matter of [name not provided]*, EAC 04 024 52731 (AAO Feb. 4, 2005), http://bit.ly/feb052d.

[492] *Matter of [name not provided]*, WAC 03 201 50250 (AAO July 8, 2005), http://bit.ly/jul0501d.

[493] *Matter of [name not provided]*, WAC 95 042 52458 (AAO Jan. 12, 1995), 14 Immig. Rptr. B2-43.

[494] *Matter of [name not provided]*, SRC 05 100 50633 (AAO Nov. 10, 2005), http://bit.ly/nov051d.

[495] *Matter of [name not provided]*, SRC 03 237 50782 (AAO Apr. 13, 2005), http://bit.ly/apr051d (stating that it "is not enough to assert generalities about Executive Chefs in the hotel industry").

[496] 8 CFR §214.2(o)(3)(iv)(B)(3).

[497] *Matter of [name not provided]*, SRC 04 048 51779 (AAO Jan. 17, 2006), http://bit.ly/jan061d8 (AAO rejected photographs where the identification of the beneficiary was made by the petitioner rather than by the newspaper).

[498] *Matter of [name not provided]*, EAC 05 800 13985 (AAO Mar. 10, 2008), http://bit.ly/mar081d8 (petitioner's counsel merely asserted that several organizations were "sources of high national regard," without any independent evidence to support the contention).

Copyright © 2017. American Immigration Lawyers Association. All rights reserved.

how the role is lead, starring, or critical.[499] Status as a "lead participant" may be based on senior "responsibilities and operative functions of the position."[500] If the materials submitted from the institution do not reference the beneficiary's role, then USCIS may presume that "the organization itself does not consider the beneficiary's role to be leading, starring, or critical."[501]

10. National or International Recognition as Evidenced by Critical Reviews or Publications (O-1B)

As noted above, evidence of this recognition should be in the form of "critical reviews or other published materials by or about the individual in major newspapers, trade journals, magazines, or other publications,"[502] which mention the beneficiary by name and which discuss his or her achievements,[503] rather than only "indicat[ing] that the beneficiary has received some publicity based on his own and his employer's reputation."[504] The absence of such written materials means this criterion will not be satisfied.[505] The name and date of publication should also be stated.[506]

The practitioner should note that a beneficiary may document this criterion through either national or international recognition. It is not necessary to have attained national *and* international recognition. Therefore, recognition in the beneficiary's home country may suffice, either within the industry,[507] or for the nation at large.

Any recognition should be a result of the beneficiary's achievements, rather than for another reason, such as the "historical and cultural significance of the project,"[508] and the discussion of the beneficiary should be more than as among a list "of many competitors."[509] Without independent evidence, the distinguished or national

---

[499] *Matter of [name not provided]*, WAC 07 006 52866 (AAO Mar. 5, 2008), http://bit.ly/mar081d (stating that "the petitioner has not shown that a film editor plays a lead, starring or critical role" for exhibitions presented at internationally known museums).

[500] *Matter of [name not provided]*, WAC 95 042 52458 (AAO Jan. 12, 1995), 14 Immig. Rptr. B2-43.

[501] *Matter of [name not provided]*, WAC 07 006 52866 (AAO Mar. 5, 2008), http://bit.ly/mar0801d.

[502] 8 CFR §214.2(o)(3)(iv)(B)(2) and (v)(B)(2); *Matter of [name not provided]*, EAC 05 047 51751 (AAO Jan. 17, 2006), http://bit.ly/jan064d.

[503] *Matter of [name and receipt number not provided]*, (AAO June 20, 2005), http://bit.ly/jun051d; *Matter of [name and case number not provided]* (AAO July 11, 2011), http://bit.ly/jul112d.

[504] *Matter of [name not provided]*, SRC 05 100 50633 (AAO Nov. 10, 2005), http://bit.ly/nov051d.

[505] *Matter of [name not provided]*, SRC 03 237 50782 (AAO Apr. 13, 2005), http://bit.ly/apr051d.

[506] *Matter of [name not provided]*, EAC 04 024 52731 (AAO Feb. 4, 2005), http://bit.ly/feb052d.

[507] *Matter of [name not provided]*, WAC 95 042 52458 (AAO Jan. 12, 1995), 14 Immig. Rptr. B2-43 (excerpt from *An Encyclopedia of Australian Film*, among other evidence that the "beneficiary has achieved at least national recognition in Australia").

[508] *Matter of [name not provided]*, EAC 07 224 51635 (AAO June 23, 2009), http://bit.ly/jun091d. The case involved extraordinary ability in the field of architecture, and the standard for business was applied rather than the standard for art.

[509] *Matter of [name not provided]*, LIN 06 039 53131 (AAO June 29, 2006), http://bit.ly/jun0601d.

Copyright © 2017. American Immigration Lawyers Association. All rights reserved.

reputation of an organization will not generally be imputed to a beneficiary's work.[510] Similarly, evidence should be provided of how an organization, performance, or event "enjoys more than a regional reputation."[511]

The particular nature of a field may also be taken into account:

"[T]he statements of ten top experts in the field of the culinary arts may be considered to establish the requisite distinction defined as renown in the field of the culinary arts. The fact that a private chef is known to so many top commercial chefs demonstrates a degree of recognition substantially above that ordinarily encountered."[512]

11. Record of Major Commercial or Critical Acclaimed Successes (O-1B)

The regulations state that the indicators "such as title, rating, standing in the field, box office receipts, motion picture or television ratings, and other occupational achievements" should be "reported in trade journals, major newspapers, or other publications."[513]

This is a category into which lesser awards could fit.[514] Although awards are not specifically named, the "such as" language indicates that the list is not exclusive, and thus other types of indicators might be accepted. However, when it comes to the evidence itself, there is no broadening language; the indicators must be reported in publications. Thus, testimonials and recommendation letters are not acceptable in this category; the evidence must be in published form.[515]

Submitting only evidence of a recording is generally insufficient; there must also be evidence of commercial or critical success.[516] USCIS and/or the AAO may also determine that such a record is not established if the publications generally discuss the beneficiary's technique without exploring his or her achievements, such as statements for a competitive dancer that the beneficiary's "foot alignments are improved" and that she "kept looking at the floor."[517]

---

[510] *Matter of [name not provided]*, WAC 07 006 52866 (AAO Mar. 5, 2008), http://bit.ly/mar081d (stating that "while the evidence shows national recognition of the ensemble itself, there is no evidence to establish a comparable reputation of the documentary or of the entity that produced it"). *See also Matter of [name not provided]*, WAC 07 015 50561 (AAO Nov. 7, 2007), http://bit.ly/nov072d (stating that "[p]articipating in an ensemble dance performance for course credit at a university does not convey on the beneficiary a level of recognition proportional to the reputation of the university as a whole").

[511] *Matter of [name not provided]*, WAC 07 006 52866 (AAO Mar. 5, 2008), http://bit.ly/mar081d.

[512] *Matter of [name not provided]*, EAC 02 127 52263 (AAO Sept. 16, 2002), 26 Immig. Rptr. B2-26.

[513] 8 CFR §214.2(o)(3)(iv)(B)(4) and (v)(B)(4).

[514] *Matter of K-IP, LLC*, ID# 16221 (AAO Apr. 28, 2016).

[515] *Matter of T-H-G-A-S-, LLC*, ID# 15858 (AAO Mar. 22, 2016).

[516] *Matter of [name not provided]*, EAC 05 028 52811 (AAO Jan. 9, 2007), http://bit.ly/jan071d.

[517] *Matter of [name not provided]*, LIN 06 039 53131 (AAO June 29, 2006), http://bit.ly/jun061d.

Copyright © 2017. American Immigration Lawyers Association. All rights reserved.

12. Significant Recognition for Achievements from Government Organizations or Experts in the Field (O-1B)[518]

Any evidence of recognition from a government organization or an industry expert should be accompanied by evidence of how the recognition is significant and a result of the beneficiary's accomplishments.[519] Similar to testimonials about employment in a critical capacity, discussed above, merely complimentary statements do not usually comprise significant recognition within the industry.[520] As with all testimonials, discussed below, the signatory should state his or her "authority, expertise, or knowledge" of the field,[521] and ideally the reputation of the writer should be more than local or regional.[522]

In one case, the AAO accepted testimonials from "teachers, peers, art gallery owners, and from one art critic/curator," discussing solo and two-person art exhibitions in different countries, as establishing that the beneficiary had garnered "significant recognition for her work as an artist."[523] Although critical reviews are generally submitted as evidence of being a lead or starring participant in a production or event with a distinguished reputation, as discussed above, they may also serve as evidence of recognition from experts in the field, especially if the reviewer is well-regarded.[524]

13. Comparable Evidence

With respect to the fields of science, education, business, athletics, and art, if the beneficiary's occupation is such that the regulatory criteria "do not readily apply, the petitioner may submit comparable evidence to establish the beneficiary's eligibility."[525] As previously noted, while the regulations for the field of art and the

---

[518] 8 CFR §214.2(o)(3)(iv)(B)(5) and (v)(B)(5).

[519] *Matter of [name not provided]*, WAC 07 006 52866 (AAO Mar. 5, 2008), http://bit.ly/mar081d (honorary citizenship award from a city governmental entity).

[520] *Matter of [name and case number not provided]* (AAO Jan. 6, 2015), http://bit.ly/jan151d (letters must describe the "recognition and achievement in factual terms"); *Matter of [name not provided]*, WAC 06 177 52596 (AAO Jan. 24, 2007), http://bit.ly/jan071d8; *Matter of [name not provided]*, EAC 04 187 50327 (AAO Oct. 4, 2006), http://bit.ly/oct061d; *Matter of [name not provided]*, LIN 06 039 53131 (AAO June 29, 2006), http://bit.ly/jun0601d; *Matter of [name not provided]*, SRC 04 225 52570 (AAO July 19, 2005), http://bit.ly/jul051d; *Matter of [name not provided]*, LIN 02 296 53935 (AAO Jan. 26, 2005), http://bit.ly/jan0501d.

[521] *Matter of [name not provided]*, WAC 06 273 55205 (AAO Oct. 11, 2007), http://bit.ly/oct0701d (statement from New York General Consul of the Dominican Republic did not address his expertise in the field); *Matter of [name not provided]*, EAC 04 187 50327 (AAO Oct. 4, 2006), http://bit.ly/oct061d; *Matter of [name not provided]*, EAC 04 240 52613 (AAO July 13, 2005), http://bit.ly/jul0502d (explanation of testimonial writer's qualifications required of First Vice Chairman of The James Beard Foundation).

[522] *Matter of [name not provided]*, SRC 04 048 51779 (AAO Jan. 17, 2006), http://bit.ly/jan0601d8.

[523] *Matter of [name not provided]*, EAC 05 047 51751 (AAO Jan. 17, 2006), http://bit.ly/jan064d.

[524] *Matter of [name not provided]*, WAC 94 180 51386 (AAO Oct. 13, 1994), 13 Immig. Rptr. B2-224 (critical reviews from *The San Francisco Chronicle, The Mercury News,* and *The San Francisco Examiner*).

[525] 8 CFR §§214.2(o)(3)(iii)(C) and (iv)(C).

Copyright © 2017. American Immigration Lawyers Association. All rights reserved.

field of motion picture and television production virtually mirror each other,[526] the regulations do not allow for submission of "comparable evidence" for motion picture and television production.[527]

USCIS looks at comparable evidence on a "criterion-by-criterion" basis, meaning that a petitioner must show why a specific criterion on the list of 10 does not apply and provide comparable evidence with respect to that criterion.[528] It is not necessary "to show that all or a majority of the criteria do not readily apply before comparable evidence may be considered."[529] In other words, USCIS views comparable evidence as substituting for one of the eight (or six for the arts) other specified criteria, not creating a separate criterion that can substitute for all the specified criteria—at least three must still be fulfilled.

For example, comparable evidence may include election to a national all-star team (comparable with evidence of membership in an association), or that a coach's athlete won an Olympic medal (comparable with lesser nationally or internationally recognized awards for coach).[530]

In such a case, it is important to explain why the specific regulatory criterion does not apply and to provide evidence of this, such as a letter from an expert, although "claims that USCIS should accept witness letters as comparable evidence are not persuasive."[531] It is also important to identify which criterion the evidence is "comparable" with and how it is comparable.[532] Broad statements "that the ... objective criteria .... do not readily apply to the alien's occupation are not probative and should be discounted."[533]

Care should be taken to consider whether the evidence would indeed fit into a particular existing criterion other than the one being argued. For example, the AAO rejected the argument that proprietary patents on a sensitive subject that could not be publicized should be considered comparable to authorship of scholarly articles, finding that the patents would generally fit into the original scientific contributions of major significance criterion: "Innovations that do not rise to the level of contributions

---

[526] *Matter of [name not provided]*, WAC 07 006 52866 (AAO Mar. 5, 2008), http://bit.ly/mar081d (stating that "the enumerated evidentiary criteria to establish eligibility under either of these standards are exactly the same").

[527] 8 CFR §214.2(o)(3)(v)(B). *See also* the USCIS website, which states that the comparable evidence "exception does not apply to the motion picture or television industry," https://www.uscis.gov/working-united-states/temporary-workers/o-1-visa-individuals-extraordinary-ability-or-achievement.

[528] USCIS Interim Policy Memorandum, "Comparable Evidence Provision for O Nonimmigrant Visa Classifications," PM-602-0123 (Jan. 21, 2016), AILA Doc. No. 16012132.

[529] *Id.*

[530] AFM 22.2(i)(1)(A). USCIS, "Evaluation of Evidentiary Criteria in Certain Form I-140 Petitions (AFM Update AD-11-14)," PM-602-0005.1 (Dec. 22, 2010), AILA Doc. No. 11020231, p. 12. Although the guidance relates to extraordinary ability immigrant visa petitions, the principle should remain the same.

[531] *Id.*

[532] *Id.*

[533] *Id.*

Copyright © 2017. American Immigration Lawyers Association. All rights reserved.

of major significance ... need not be considered in the alternative as comparable evidence of scholarly articles."[534]

Similarly, an award that does not meet the standards of the awards criteria cannot be used: "Where a beneficiary is simply unable to meet or submit documentary evidence meeting a criterion, the plain language of the regulation at 8 CFR §214.2(o)(3)(iii)(C) does not allow for the submission of comparable evidence."[535]

While practitioners should endeavor to ensure that comparable evidence matches the particular regulatory criteria to the extent possible, experience has shown that including evidence that does not nicely fit a specific criterion can still be helpful to the case overall. Where documentation shows that the O-1 beneficiary has achieved a significant accomplishment, that evidence should normally be included in the petition even if it does not neatly fall within one of the regulatory categories or a category that is precisely comparable.

E. O-2 Petitions

The O-2 classification[536] is for an "accompanying alien"[537] coming to the United States "solely to assist in the artistic or athletic performance by an O-1."[538] O-2 is not available to those individuals accompanying O-1s "in the fields of science, business or education."[539]

The O-2 accompanying an artist or athlete of extraordinary ability (*i.e.*, not in the motion picture or television industry) must:

- Be coming to assist in the O-1's performance;
- Be an integral part of the actual performance; and
- Have critical skills and experience with the O-1 that:
  - Are "not of a general nature," and
  - Are "not possessed by a U.S. worker."[540]

An O-2 accompanying an O-1 of extraordinary achievement (*i.e.*, in the motion picture or television industry) must:

- Hold skills and experience with the O-1 that:
  - Are not of a general nature; and
  - Which are critical, either because:

---

[534] *Matter of [name and case number not provided]* (AAO Mar. 15, 2015), http://bit.ly/mar151d.

[535] *Matter of G-L-, Inc.,* ID# 16732 (AAO June 15, 2016).

[536] INA §101(a)(15)(o)(ii).

[537] 8 CFR §§214.2(o)(1)(ii)(B) and 214.2(o)(4).

[538] *Id.*

[539] 8 CFR §214.2(o)(4)(i).

[540] 8 CFR §214.2(o)(4)(ii)(A).

Copyright © 2017. American Immigration Lawyers Association. All rights reserved.

- They are based on a pre-existing and longstanding working relationship with the O-1; or

- If in connection with a specific production, significant production will take place both inside and outside the United States (including pre– and post-production), and the continuing participation of the O-2 is essential to successful completion.[541]

Although "an O-2 alien must be petitioned for in conjunction with the services of the O-1 alien,"[542] it is not required that the O-2 petition be filed concurrently with the O-1 petition.[543] Indeed, the petitioner for the O-1 and the O-2 need not necessarily be the same entity, though if filings from different petitioners are submitted simultaneously, it is a good idea to mark them as related petitions so that the USCIS mailroom does not separate them. [544]

If the practitioner is not filing O-1 and O-2 simultaneously, the O-1 should be filed first, and the I-797C receipt notice or the I-797B approval notice should be included in the O-2 package.[545] If the O-1 was denied, USCIS will automatically deny the O-2.[546] If an RFE is outstanding on the O-1, the O-2 petition's viability will, at a minimum, be called into question.[547] The fact that the O-2 beneficiary is already in the United States in another status should not, in and of itself, be a bar to O-2 eligibility.[548]

The supporting evidence submitted with an O-2 petition must "establish the current essentiality, critical skills, and experience of the O-2 alien with the O-1 alien and that the alien has substantial experience performing the critical skills and essential support services for the O-1 alien."[549] Experience letters and copies of educational documents may provide this information.[550]

Typical administrative or managerial duties, such as coordinating, scheduling, maintaining profit margins, or developing vendor relationships, ordinarily will be viewed as general in nature, not critical skills integral to the O-1's "actual performance, and/or skills that would be possessed by a U.S. worker."[551] USCIS

---

[541] 8 CFR §214.2(o)(4)(ii)(B).

[542] 8 CFR §214.2(o)(4)(i).

[543] *Matter of [name and case number not provided]* (AAO Dec. 8, 2010), http://bit.ly/dec101d.

[544] "Practice Pointer: Different Petitioners for O-1 and Accompanying O-2 Petitions" (Dec. 14, 2015), AILA Doc. No. 15121405.

[545] *Id.*

[546] *Matter of [name and case number not provided]* (AAO Oct. 8, 2014), http://bit.ly/oct141d.

[547] *Matter of [name and case number not provided]* (AAO Dec. 8, 2010), http://bit.ly/dec101d.

[548] *Id.*

[549] 8 CFR §214.2(o)(4)(ii)(C).

[550] For a discussion of experience letters, see Volume 2: Chapter Two, "The Labor Certification Application."

[551] *Matter of [name and case number not provided]* (AAO Dec. 8, 2010), http://bit.ly/dec101d; *Matter of [name not provided]*, WAC 03 044 52545 (AAO July 25, 2006), http://bit.ly/jul062d.

Copyright © 2017. American Immigration Lawyers Association. All rights reserved.

guidance indicates that being an "integral part" means "provid[ing] direct support to the O-1 principal,"[552] which may be similar to the direct support provided by a Scientific Technician/Technologist in Trade NAFTA (TN) status to a professional.[553] Freeing the O-1 to focus on his or her area of ability is not sufficient to show criticality.[554]

There is no specified bright line test for length of association with the O-1 to qualify as having the required experience with him or her.[555] Guidance issued by U.S. Customs and Border Protection (CBP) indicates that the O-2 beneficiary must have at least one year of experience working with the O-1 beneficiary,[556] but it remains unclear whether this requirement is imposed by USCIS. However, as a practical matter, the shorter the time with the O-1, the more difficult the argument. If the O-2 beneficiary's experience with the O-1 is relatively brief, it would be important to document the quality and intensity of the experience.

If the O-2 nonimmigrant's services are necessary for a "specific motion picture or television production, the evidence shall establish that significant production has taken place outside the United States, and will take place inside the United States, and that the continuing participation of the alien is essential to the successful completion of the production."[557] This evidence may take the form of executed contracts and permits for filming and/or production work.

The O-2 classification "does not entitle [the beneficiary] to work separate and apart from the O-1 alien to whom he or she provides support."[558] In other words, the O-2's eligibility is tied up with the specific O-1. If the O-1 leaves the entity that employed both the O-1 and O-2, it would be very difficult to substitute another O-1 individual as the primary because, even if the O-2 has extensive skills critical to the entity, the O-2 would not have critical skills and experience with that particular O-1 individual.[559]

The practitioner should be aware that the "O category relates to individual aliens, not groups," and so legacy INS guidance noted the previous attempts of O-1 individuals "to bring a large group of accompanying aliens with them in order to

---

[552] USCIS Office of Business Liaison, Employer Information Bulletin 15, "Aliens with Extraordinary Ability (O-1) and Accompanying/Assisting Aliens (O-2)" (Dec. 8, 2004), 82 Interpreter Releases 180-184 (Jan. 17, 2005).

[553] For a discussion of this topic, see Volume 1: Chapter Fourteen, "TN Visas and Status."

[554] *Matter of [name and case number not provided]* (AAO Dec. 8, 2010), http://bit.ly/dec101d.

[555] *Matter of [name and case number not provided]* (AAO Dec. 8, 2010), http://bit.ly/dec101d (denied because the experience was found not to have been documented, but implied that six months may not be enough).

[556] 1 U.S. Customs and Border Protection (CBP) Inspector's Field Manual (IFM) 15, 14-1 Agency Manuals 15.4.

[557] 8 CFR §214.2(o)(4)(ii)(C).

[558] 8 CFR §214.2(o)(4)(i).

[559] *Matter of [name and case number not provided]* (AAO Oct. 21, 2011), http://bit.ly/oct111d.

Copyright © 2017. American Immigration Lawyers Association. All rights reserved.

circumvent the individual nature of the category."[560] Therefore, the practitioner may wish to prepare the client for the possibility that only some, and not all, named O-2 beneficiaries "may be classified as accompanying aliens."[561]

To further highlight the individual nature of the O-1 classification, legacy INS guidance states how it may be appropriate to request O-1 status for "a solo artist or entertainer" and O-2 status for the "back-up band" or "back-up singers or musicians,"[562] if the entire group is unable to petition for P status,[563] since it "is unlikely that many individual members of 'outstanding' entertainment groups would be able to meet the stringent requirements for O-1 classification as aliens with extraordinary ability in the arts."[564]

Although typically multiple O-2 beneficiaries may be named on a single petition, individual petitions must be filed if the beneficiaries will apply for O visas at different U.S. consulates or will apply for O admission at different ports of entry,[565] or if different actions are requested for different beneficiaries (such as requesting change of status for one and consular processing for another).[566] As discussed above, an O-2 nonimmigrant must have a foreign residence that he or she has no intention of abandoning.[567]

F. Supporting Evidence for O-1 and O-2 Petitions

The following supporting evidence must be submitted to USCIS with the O-1 and/or O-2 petition:

- Evidence that the O-1 beneficiary possesses extraordinary ability or has extraordinary achievement, as applicable;[568]

- Evidence that the O-2 beneficiary is an integral part of the performances or events and possesses critical, non-general skill and experience with the O-1, or that the O-2 in the television or motion picture field has non-general and critical skills and experience with the O-1 based on a longstanding relationship or significant production that will take place inside and outside the United States;[569]

---

[560] Legacy INS, L. Weinig, "Policy Guidelines for the Adjudication of O and P Petitions," (June 25, 1992), 69 Interpreter Releases 1084–87 (Aug. 31, 1992).

[561] Id.

[562] Id.

[563] For a discussion of P status, see Volume 1: Chapter Thirteen, "P Visas and Status."

[564] Legacy INS, P. Virtue, "O-1 and P Nonimmigrant Visa Classifications" (Sept. 29, 1993), 1 INS and DOJ Legal Opinions §93-76.

[565] AFM 33.4.

[566] "Tips for Filing O-1 and P-1 Petitions at VSC" (Dec. 12, 2015), AILA Doc. No. 15120231.

[567] INA §101(a)(15)(O)(ii)(IV).

[568] 8 CFR §§214.2(o)(2)(ii)(A) and 214.2(o)(3)(i).

[569] 8 CFR §§214.2(o)(2)(ii)(B).

Copyright © 2017. American Immigration Lawyers Association. All rights reserved.

- "Copies of any written contracts between the petitioner and the alien beneficiary or, if there is no written contract, a summary of the terms of the oral agreement under which the alien will be employed,"[570] as discussed below;

- "An explanation of the nature of the events or activities, the beginning and ending dates for the events or activities, and a copy of any itinerary for the events or activities";[571] and

- "A written advisory opinion(s) from the appropriate consulting entity or entities,"[572] as discussed below.

Any document, such as an affidavit, contract, or award, that demonstrates the beneficiary's accomplishment(s) "must reflect the nature of the alien's achievement and be executed by an officer or responsible person employed by the institution, firm, establishment, or organization where the work was performed."[573] Importantly, the signatory to the document need not be "the person in charge" of the organization, firm, institution, or establishment.[574] As a practical matter, it seems that the term "where the work was performed" covers two different types of scenarios: first, the performance or showing of an artistic, entertainment, or athletic work or event; and second, work product created while employed or affiliated with a business entity.

For example, if the beneficiary won an award from an international film festival, then a copy of the official award, with seal and signature by an executive of the award-granting institution, may be submitted. Alternatively, an executive of the film festival organization may provide a signed statement attesting to the beneficiary's award. In this instance, the work performed would be the screening of the film that received an award. As another example, the beneficiary could have been listed as the inventor of record on patent applications for technologies developed while he or she was employed with a business entity. Then, appropriate evidence would be either a copy of the patent application or approval, with the beneficiary's name highlighted, or a statement from the beneficiary's employer, which should also meet the guidelines discussed below.

Photocopies of original documents may be filed with USCIS, but the original must be submitted if USCIS requests it.[575] All documents in a foreign language should be accompanied by certified translations[576] that are *full and complete.*[577] As previously

---

[570] 8 CFR §214.2(o)(2)(ii)(B).

[571] 8 CFR §214.2(o)(2)(ii)(C).

[572] 8 CFR §214.2(o)(2)(ii)(D).

[573] 8 CFR §214.2(o)(2)(iii)(A).

[574] 59 Fed. Reg. 41818 (Aug. 15, 1994), AILA Doc. No. 94081560.

[575] 8 CFR §214.2(o)(2)(iii)(C).

[576] 8 CFR §214.2(o)(3)(iii)(B). *See, e.g., Matter of [name not provided]*, EAC 07 224 51635 (AAO June 23, 2009), http://bit.ly/jun091d (petitioner failed to provide a translation of an article, instead only handwriting the name of the magazine and "prize-winning competition," so "the AAO cannot determine whether the evidence supports the petitioner's claims"); *Matter of [name not provided]*, WAC 07 273 54624 (AAO Mar. 11, 2009), http://bit.ly/mar091d; *Matter of [name not provided]*, WAC 07 800 12235 (AAO Feb. 9, 2009), http://bit.ly/feb092d.

Copyright © 2017. American Immigration Lawyers Association. All rights reserved.

noted, summary translations[578] and articles that have been translated using an online translation tool[579] have been criticized as having "diminished" or "limited" probative value, respectively. USCIS "can not accept documentation in electronic format for security reasons."[580]

1. Testimonials from Industry Experts

Any statements or affidavits "written by present or former employers or recognized experts certifying to the recognition and extraordinary ability of the alien … shall specifically describe the alien's recognition and ability or achievement in factual terms and set forth the expertise of the affiant and the manner in which the affiant acquired such information."[581] Put more simply, the individual providing the recommendation should not merely make conclusory statements that the beneficiary "has extraordinary ability,"[582] or be "couched in generalities,"[583] but should provide extensive details about the beneficiary's achievements and accomplishments that demonstrate extraordinary ability.[584] In particular, the statements or affidavits should provide specific examples of particular accomplishments of the O-1 beneficiary, and should detail how those accomplishments are extraordinary.

Similarly, the practitioner should avoid submitting testimonials that merely "indicate that the beneficiary is well-respected by … individuals with whom she worked closely in the past,"[585] or that "do not demonstrate that the alien's work is of major significance in his field beyond the limited number of individuals with whom he has worked directly."[586] Instead, the statements should describe the beneficiary's previous accomplishments,[587] their impact on a final product[588] if applicable, and the

---

[577] *Matter of [name not provided]*, EAC 05 251 50742 (AAO Oct. 25, 2007), http://bit.ly/oct071d8 (emphasis in original).

[578] *Matter of F-I-T-T-*, ID# 16838 (AAO June 23, 2016).

[579] *Matter of C-B-&F-, Inc.*, ID# 13701 (AAO Sept. 28, 2015).

[580] "AILA Liaison/Nebraska Service Center Liaison Teleconference Q&As" (June 25, 2009), AILA Doc. No. 09070864. Although the discussion relates to extraordinary ability immigrant visa petitions, the principle should remain the same.

[581] 8 CFR §214.2(o)(2)(iii)(B).

[582] *Matter of [name not provided]*, EAC 05 800 13985 (AAO Mar. 10, 2008), http://bit.ly/mar081d8; *Matter of [name not provided]*, SRC 02 202 54837 (AAO Nov. 3, 2003), 28 Immig. Rptr. B2-84; *Matter of [name not provided]*, EAC 04 118 50468 (AAO Feb. 22, 2006), http://bit.ly/feb0602d; *Matter of [name not provided]*, LIN 04 092 50085 (AAO May 25, 2005), http://bit.ly/may055d; *Matter of [name not provided]*, SRC 03 236 51017 (AAO Apr. 21, 2005), http://bit.ly/apr0502d.

[583] *Matter of [name not provided]*, LIN 04 131 54595 (AAO Aug. 16, 2005), http://bit.ly/aug051d.

[584] *Matter of [name not provided]*, WAC 02 038 51106 (AAO May 24, 2005), http://bit.ly/may051d8 (testimonials were "insufficiently specific" petition denied); *Matter of [name not provided]*, SRC 03 236 51017 (AAO Apr. 21, 2005), http://bit.ly/apr0502d (testimonials "are conclusory rather than specific in detailing the beneficiary's contributions").

[585] *Matter of [name not provided]*, EAC 05 800 13985 (AAO Mar. 10, 2008), http://bit.ly/mar081d8; *Matter of [name not provided]*, EAC 05 800 13985 (AAO Apr. 19, 2007), http://bit.ly/apr071d.

[586] *Matter of [name not provided]*, WAC 06 160 52954 (AAO May 31, 2007), http://bit.ly/may071d.

[587] *Matter of [name not provided]*, LIN 02 184 53385 (AAO Sept. 17, 2002), 26 Immig. Rptr. B2-92.

Copyright © 2017. American Immigration Lawyers Association. All rights reserved.

proposed job duties.[589] It is also helpful if the testimonials demonstrate the nexus between the beneficiary's achievements and his or her status as an individual with extraordinary ability,[590] as opposed to praising the beneficiary's character.[591] Ideally, these explanations should be written in plain English, rather than bogged down with many technical terms, in a manner that puts the job in context. For example, in describing the duties of an assistant director, one individual stated: "The first assistant director is fully responsible for organizing and preparing for each and every scene filmed. He is also responsible for directing the myriad of activities taking place behind the camera to enable the director to solely focus his attention on the scene being filmed."[592] It is also preferable to have the statements supported by independent evidence where possible:[593]

> "Even when written by independent experts, letters solicited by an alien in support of an immigration petition carry less weight than preexisting, independent evidence of major contributions that one would expect of an alien who has achieved sustained national or international acclaim."[594]

The statement or affidavit should also state any relevant qualifications of the recommender, such as educational and/or professional degrees; years of experience in the industry; receipt of awards; membership in professional organizations; service as the judge of others; and authorship of articles. The practitioner may note that these points correlate to the extraordinary ability criteria, discussed above; this is because, as a practical matter, a recommendation letter from an industry member who is recognized for his or her own achievements tends to be granted more weight than a statement from an unknown individual.[595] In addition, possession of long-term experience in the field

---

[588] *Matter of [name not provided]*, WAC 95 042 52458 (AAO Jan. 12, 1995), 14 Immig. Rptr. B2-43 (stating that "ability of the first assistant to direct these operations and effectively prepare for each scene is certainly reflected in the quality of the picture on the screen").

[589] *Id.* (detailed description of job duties of an assistant director).

[590] *Id.* (testimonial stated that the beneficiary "is one of the finest first assistant directors in the world—no mean achievement as it is a job that requires tremendous organizational, technical, artistic and diplomatic skills").

[591] *Matter of [name not provided]*, WAC 06 224 53958 (AAO May 4, 2009), http://bit.ly/may092d.

[592] *Matter of [name not provided]*, WAC 95 042 52458 (AAO Jan. 12, 1995), 14 Immig. Rptr. B2-43.

[593] *Matter of [name not provided]*, WAC 95 042 52458 (AAO Jan. 12, 1995), 14 Immig. Rptr. B2-43 (statements were corroborated by a textbook on filmmaking); *Matter of [name and receipt number not provided]*, (AAO June 20, 2005), http://bit.ly/jun051d.

[594] *Matter of [name not provided]*, SRC 05 200 51253 (AAO July 23, 2007), http://bit.ly/jul071d; *Matter of [name not provided]*, WAC 06 160 52954 (AAO May 31, 2007), http://bit.ly/may071d.

[595] *Matter of [name not provided]*, SRC 02 202 54837 (AAO Nov. 3, 2003), 28 Immig. Rptr. B2-84 (statement from the "World Governor of the International College of Surgeons"); *Matter of [name not provided]*, WAC 93 168 50373 (AAO Aug. 3, 2002), 26 Immig. Rptr. B2-84 (testimonials of celebrities and business leaders); *Matter of [name not provided]*, SRC 98 066 50295 (AAO Aug. 2, 1998), 19 *Immig. Rptr.* B2-77 ("several affidavits from prominent scientists, from universities and the Federal Government"); *Matter of [name not provided]*, LIN 95 131 50963 (AAO Nov. 3, 1995), 15 Immig. Rptr. B2-61 (the individual providing the recommending consultation was the President of the "world's largest organization of culinary professionals which is composed of 52 member countries and 1.5 million chefs and cooks around the globe" and "Manager of the Culinary Team USA which is the United States competitive team of chefs that

Cont'd

Copyright © 2017. American Immigration Lawyers Association. All rights reserved.

may strengthen both the recommender's status as an individual qualified to provide a testimonial and the beneficiary's petition.[596] The recommender should also state how he or she is familiar with the work or achievements of the beneficiary,[597] with the dates of employment by the same entity, if applicable, or through review of the O-1 petition and other work of the beneficiary.[598] However, obtaining a recommendation letter from a well-known industry leader and/or a well-respected industry organization does not guarantee approval of the O-1 petition:[599]

> "[L]etters from independent references who were previously aware of the beneficiary through his reputation are far more persuasive than letters from independent references who were not previously aware of the beneficiary and are merely responding to a solicitation to review the beneficiary's statement regarding his work and provide an opinion based solely on that review."[600]

At the same time, the practitioner should proceed with caution if the recommenders' credentials are significantly superior to the credentials of the beneficiary. Experience has shown that USCIS is fond of pointing out large gaps between acknowledged leaders and the beneficiary to argue that the beneficiary is still only junior in the field, while the recommenders are the people who have reached the requisite level of acclaim.[601]

---

represents the food … profession of the Americas in all international and world championship competitions"; had been awarded 15 international gold medals, including four Culinary Olympic gold medals, as well as 10 national gold medals; and had been awarded an Honorary Doctorate Degree in Culinary Arts); *Matter of [name not provided]*, WAC 95 042 52458 (AAO Jan. 12, 1995), 14 Immig. Rptr. B2-43 (testimonials from two-time nominee for Academy Awards for Best Director, an Academy Award winner for Best Picture, and three-time Academy Award nominee); *Matter of [name not provided]*, WAC 92 194 51841 (AAO Nov. 8, 1993), 12 *Immig. Rptr.* B2-106 (testimonial from Olympic Gold Medalist, among others). *Cf. Matter of [name not provided]*, LIN 93 176 51248 (AAO Jan. 25, 1994), 12 Immig. Rptr. B2-156 (noting that "petitioner has not shown that the authors of these testimonials are well-known or leading experts in the field").

[596] *Matter of [name not provided]*, WAC 95 042 52458 (AAO Jan. 12, 1995), 14 Immig. Rptr. B2-43 (testimonial stated that "[h]aving directed films in the U.S., Europe and elsewhere for 30 years, I have never found a better first assistant director than [the beneficiary").

[597] *Matter of [name and receipt number not provided]*, (AAO June 20, 2005), http://bit.ly/jun051d (noting that the "letter fails to state the basis for [redacted] knowledge of the beneficiary and provide sufficient details to support her conclusion").

[598] *Matter of [name not provided]*, EAC 07 224 51635 (AAO June 23, 2009), http://bit.ly/jun091d.

[599] *Matter of [name not provided]*, WAC 07 006 52866 (AAO Mar. 5, 2008), http://bit.ly/mar081d (petition denied, even with recommendation letter from the Video Production Editor at MTV Networks discussing beneficiary's work on recreation of scenes from the film "The Matrix Re-Loaded").

[600] *Matter of [name not provided]*, EAC 04 118 50468 (AAO Feb. 22, 2006), http://bit.ly/feb0602d. *See also* "Questions and Answers from NSC Liaison Meeting" (Oct. 17, 2001), AILA Doc. No. 01101833 (one commenter critiquing the trend of requiring testimonials from "'non-colleagues, non-collaborators' in and out of the field"). Although the discussion relates to extraordinary ability immigrant visa petitions, the principle should remain the same.

[601] *Matter of [name and case number not provided]* (AAO Oct. 14, 2010), http://bit.ly/oct102d (pointing out one recommender's 249 peer reviews vs. the beneficiary's three, and another recommender's 142 publications vs. the beneficiary's one article and five abstracts).

Copyright © 2017. American Immigration Lawyers Association. All rights reserved.

With respect to testimonials from the petitioner, the AAO has stated: "CIS gives credence to testimonials written by employees of the petitioner, but such testimonials are given less weight than those from independent sources, which would tend to demonstrate sustained national or international acclaim in the field."[602] However, the support statement from the petitioner, discussed in detail below, may highlight how the beneficiary was selected for the assignment because of his or her extraordinary ability and underscore the critical need for the beneficiary's services on the project.[603] For example, in the context of the performing arts, the lead or starring role will in most cases be offered to an individual who is prominent and has remarkable ability.[604] In another case, the AAO stated that the "petitioner's prestige and leadership role in the field of entertainment on ice must be given significant weight in this proceeding," especially since the "petitioner was the leading ice show in the U.S. since 1940 and required a distinguished costume designer to maintain its high standards."[605]

Because the testimonials must be extremely detailed, the practitioner should discourage the client from submitting general employment confirmation or recommendation letters, such as those frequently provided to individuals upon termination of employment,[606] or statements prepared for another petition.[607] The testimonials also should not contain the "identical content,"[608] as "repetition indicates that the language of many of these letters is not the authors' own and greatly detracts from the documents' probative value."[609]

2. Advisory Opinion from a Peer Group, Labor Organization, or Management Organization

Almost every O-1 and O-2 petition must contain an advisory opinion from a peer group, labor organization, or management organization,[610] "with expertise in the specific field involved,"[611] whichever is most applicable to the industry and/or

---

[602] *Matter of [name not provided]*, SRC 02 202 54837 (AAO Nov. 3, 2003), 28 Immig. Rptr. B2-84; *Matter of [name not provided]*, SRC 03 237 50782 (AAO Apr. 13, 2005), http://bit.ly/apr051d.

[603] *Matter of [name not provided]*, WAC 95 042 52458 (AAO Jan. 12, 1995), 14 Immig. Rptr. B2-43.

[604] *Matter of [name not provided]*, WAC 94 180 51386 (AAO Oct. 13, 1994), 13 Immig. Rptr. B2-224.

[605] *Matter of [name not provided]*, WAC 92 194 51841 (AAO Nov. 8, 1993), 12 Immig. Rptr. B2-106.

[606] *Cf. Matter of [name not provided]*, EAC 07 224 51635 (AAO June 23, 2009), http://bit.ly/jun091d (general employment recommendation letters did not provide sufficient details about employment in a critical or essential capacity).

[607] *Matter of [name not provided]*, WAC 07 800 12235 (AAO Feb. 9, 2009), http://bit.ly/feb092d.

[608] *Id.*

[609] *Matter of [name not provided]*, WAC 06 224 53958 (AAO May 4, 2009), http://bit.ly/may092d. *See also Matter of [name not provided]*, WAC 07 800 12235 (AAO Feb. 9, 2009), http://bit.ly/feb092d; *Matter of [name not provided]*, EAC 04 800 31656 (AAO June 1, 2007), http://bit.ly/jun071d; *Matter of [name not provided]*, EAC 05 800 13985 (AAO Apr. 19, 2007), http://bit.ly/apr071d; *Matter of [name not provided]*, EAC 04 240 52613 (AAO July 13, 2005), http://bit.ly/jul0502d.

[610] INA §214(c)(3); 8 CFR §§214.2(o)(5)(i)(A), (C) and (D).

[611] INA §214(c)(6)(A); 8 CFR §214.2(o)(5)(i)(B).

Copyright © 2017. American Immigration Lawyers Association. All rights reserved.

occupation. Otherwise, the petition will be denied.[612] As stated by legacy INS: "Labor organizations are very sensitive to the consultation process and [legacy INS] must ensure that such entities are consulted at all costs…. This statutory provision provides organized labor with input on any petition filed with the Service."[613] However, the impact on American workers is not the only reason for requiring the advisory opinion:

> "While the desire of unions to ban or limit the employment of foreign entertainers utilized to the detriment of unemployed American performers is appreciated, the opinions of such organizations must be given some weight because of their pertinency in matters involving an assessment of the merit and availability of performers in areas in which they are of necessity experienced and knowledgeable."[614]

The advisory opinion must be written,[615] "must be signed by an authorized official of the group or organization,"[616] should discuss "the nature of the work to be done,"[617] and should discuss the beneficiary's outstanding qualifications.[618] An email communication may be insufficient.[619] Although the opinion is not binding upon USCIS,[620] no O-1 petition may be approved without such an advisory opinion,[621] except as discussed below.

Submitting a fraudulent advisory opinion may be deemed to "constitute[] a willful misrepresentation of two material facts, *i.e.*, the claim that the beneficiary is an alien of extraordinary ability … and that the petitioner has obtained a valid consultation."[622] There may be a finding of fraud, and the petitioner may be required to present within 30 days independent corroborating evidence of the beneficiary's eligibility for O-1 status, since USCIS and/or the AAO "cannot accord any of [the petitioner's] other claims any weight, without original evidence that indisputably

---

[612] Legacy INS, L. Weinig, "Policy Guidelines for the Adjudication of O and P Petitions," (June 25, 1992), 69 Interpreter Releases 1084–87 (Aug. 31, 1992).

[613] *Id.*

[614] *Matter of Shaw*, 11 I&N Dec. 277 (Dist. Dir. 1965).

[615] 8 CFR §§214.2(o)(5)(i)(B), (C), and (D).

[616] 8 CFR §214.2(o)(5)(i)(C).

[617] *Matter of [name not provided]*, WAC 06 167 50726 (AAO Mar. 6, 2007), http://bit.ly/mar071d.

[618] 8 CFR §214.2(o)(5)(i)(A).

[619] *Matter of [name not provided]*, WAC 06 262 52536 (AAO Oct. 9, 2007), http://bit.ly/oct071d (stating "electronic mail message does not constitute a consultation"). But the practitioner should note that the preceding discussion focused on the deficiencies of the statement's content, rather than the form, so it remains unclear if email statements are unacceptable.

[620] *Matter of [name not provided]*, EAC 10 057 51177 (AAO Apr. 5, 2011), http://bit.ly/apr111d; *Matter of [name not provided]*, EAC 04 009 53707 (AAO May 25, 2005), http://bit.ly/may053d (petition denied even with favorable consultation); *Matter of [name not provided]*, SRC 04 204 53136 (AAO Apr. 29, 2005), http://bit.ly/apr0501d (same).

[621] 8 CFR §214.2(o)(5)(i)(D).

[622] *Matter of [name not provided]*, LIN 03 178 50282 (AAO June 17, 2005), http://bit.ly/jun052d8.

Copyright © 2017. American Immigration Lawyers Association. All rights reserved.

proves those claims," and withdrawing the petition may not necessarily "negate or prevent a finding of fraud."[623]

A "peer group" is defined as "a group or organization which is comprised of practitioners of the alien's occupation."[624] Experience has shown that this may include, for example, a professional organization devoted to the beneficiary's field of expertise,[625] and even a subset of a larger industry or field, such as a society within a professional association,[626] as this society would represent "a person or persons with expertise in the field,"[627] or "an individual or several individuals engaged in the occupation."[628] It may be necessary to provide details on how the peer group is "appropriate" or how "its opinions are in any way authoritative."[629] The peer group should be American,[630] and not an international or foreign organization with affiliation with U.S. organizations.[631]

A peer group need not be an organization, association or other such entity.[632] It can be "a person or persons with expertise in the field."[633] However, if an individual expert is used, that expertise must be shown.[634]

A peer group may also be a union, such as if the O-1 "employer's employees in the occupational classification" in which the beneficiary will perform duties are represented by a collective bargaining representative,[635] or "a labor organization, a professional or management organization."[636] As discussed below, however, "in some fields, there may not be an organized, identifiable peer group."[637]

---

[623] *Id.*

[624] 8 CFR §214.2(o)(3)(ii).

[625] *Matter of [name not provided]*, LIN 95 131 50963 (AAO Nov. 3, 1995), 15 Immig. Rptr. B2-61 ("world's largest organization of culinary professionals which is composed of 52 member countries and 1.5 million chefs and cooks around the globe").

[626] For example, the Institute of Electrical and Electronics Engineers has 38 societies. Institute of Electrical and Electronics Engineers, "IEEE Society Memberships," http://www.ieee.org/web/membership/societies/index.html.

[627] 8 CFR §214.2(o)(5)(i)(A).

[628] AFM 33.2.

[629] *Matter of [name not provided]*, LIN 93 124 51276 (AAO Jan. 23, 1995), 14 Immig. Rptr. B2-128; *Matter of [name not provided]*, SRC 06 138 52302 (AAO Nov. 7, 2007), http://bit.ly/nov0701d (details evidence of individual's expertise that was accepted by the AAO).

[630] *Matter of [name not provided]*, EAC 04 187 50327 (AAO Oct. 4, 2006), http://bit.ly/oct061d.

[631] *Matter of [name not provided]*, WAC 06 187 51596 (AAO Sept. 19, 2007), http://bit.ly/sep072d (Brazilian organization had international headquarters in the United States but AAO nevertheless rejected it as non-U.S. organization).

[632] *Matter of [name and case number not provided]* (AAO Feb. 15, 2011), http://bit.ly/feb1101d.

[633] 8 CFR §214.2(o)(5)(i)(A).

[634] *Matter of [name and case number not provided]* (AAO Dec. 29, 2014), http://bit.ly/dec143d (statement from an individual in the same occupation was found not to provide enough detail of her expertise).

[635] 8 CFR §214.2(o)(3)(ii).

[636] AFM 33.2.

[637] *Id.*

Copyright © 2017. American Immigration Lawyers Association. All rights reserved.

A union may also be a labor organization.[638] If an umbrella labor organization has been "recognized" by USCIS, then it may be inappropriate to limit the occupational field to a narrow subfield.[639] The practitioner may find it helpful to provide the following documents to the labor union:

- Cover letter with the practitioner's contact information;

- Copy of the O petition, including the Form I-129, O Supplement, employer's support statement, and selected documents evidencing the beneficiary's extraordinary ability or qualifications as "essential support" personnel;

- Copy of the employment contract or summary of the terms of the employment agreement;

- Copy of the itinerary of events, performances, and/or activities; and

- Check to cover the cost of the advisory opinion, including any fee for expedited processing of the opinion, if applicable.[640]

An advisory opinion from a labor organization should be valid for two years, so the practitioner may submit the same consultation on behalf of the beneficiary during that time period.[641] The list of documents may also be helpful when submitting a request for an advisory opinion to a peer group or a management organization.

A list of approximately 75 peer groups, labor organizations, and management organizations that have agreed to provide consultation letters in an array of disciplines is available to AILA members on the AILA website.[642] A somewhat older list can also be found on the USCIS website.[643] It should be noted that many of these organizations charge a fee, generally in the range of $250 to $500,[644] and some have strictly followed guidelines for how a request is to be presented.[645] In addition, the petitioner or beneficiary may be aware of entities that can serve as peer groups for purposes of the advisory opinion.

---

[638] 8 CFR §214.2(o)(5)(i)(F).

[639] *Matter of [name not provided]*, EAC 02 127 52263 (AAO Sept. 16, 2002), 26 Immig. Rptr. B2-26 (petitioner claimed there was no labor organization for private chefs, but the AAO held that a labor organization existed for the culinary arts).

[640] "AILA/VSC Committee Practice Pointer: O-1: How to Obtain a Labor Union Consultation" (July 29, 2009), AILA Doc. No. 09072962.

[641] *Id.*

[642] "Updated Address Index for I-129 O & P Consultation Letters" (updated June 3, 2016), AILA Doc. No. 16060305.

[643] USCIS, "Address Index for I-129 O & P Consultation Letters" (updated Mar. 11, 2013), http://bit.ly/2dHkz1O.

[644] "ACES Practice Alert: New Fee for Advisory Opinions from the Directors Guild of America" (Apr. 12, 2016), AILA Doc. No. 16041231; "Updated Address Index for I-129 O & P Consultation Letters" (updated June 3, 2016), AILA Doc. No. 16060305, under column headed "Covered Occupations & Notes").

[645] "Practice Alert: AMPTP Revises O-1/O-2 Consultation Instructions" (Mar. 10, 2014), AILA Doc. No. 14031049; "Updated Address Index for I-129 O & P Consultation Letters" (updated June 3, 2016), AILA Doc. No. 16060305, under column headed "Covered Occupations & Notes".

Copyright © 2017. American Immigration Lawyers Association. All rights reserved.

If the O-1 petition is submitted with an advisory opinion from an organization "other than a labor organization, USCIS must submit a copy of the petition and supporting documents to the appropriate union (if any exists) for a second opinion."[646] Although the regulations provide for the following procedure, the practitioner is encouraged to provide the advisory opinion from the labor organization in order to avoid processing delays:

"In a routine processing case where the petition is accompanied by a written opinion from a peer group, but the peer group is not a labor organization, the Director will forward a copy of the petition and all supporting documentation to the national office of the appropriate labor organization within 5 days of receipt of the petition."[647]

The labor organization is granted 15 days "from receipt of the petition and supporting documents" to respond with "a written advisory opinion, comment, or letter of no objection." Otherwise, USCIS will adjudicate the petition without the advisory opinion.[648] If a statement is provided, then USCIS "shall adjudicate the petition in no more than 14 days," although this processing time may be shortened "for emergency reasons, if no unreasonable burden would be imposed on any participant in the process."[649]

The practitioner should note that, despite this stated two-week time period, neither the statute nor the regulation provide for any penalty for failure to adjudicate the petition within 14 days.[650] As a practical matter, relying upon USCIS to request the advisory opinion may delay adjudication of the petition, as even USCIS states: "[B]e advised that a petition filed without the actual advisory opinion will require substantially longer processing time."[651] Even USCIS acknowledged when promulgating the rule permitting filing of an O petition one year in advance of the date of need that the rule would allow petitioners to "be better assured that they will receive a decision on their petitions in a timeframe that will allow them to secure the services of the O or P nonimmigrant when such services are needed."[652]

If the O-1 beneficiary will work in the field of motion picture or television production, then the advisory opinions must be provided from "the appropriate union representing the alien's occupational peers and a management organization in the

---

[646] AFM 33.3.

[647] 8 CFR §214.2(o)(5)(i)(F). *See also* INA §214(c)(6)(B).

[648] INA §214(c)(6)(D); 8 CFR §214.2(o)(5)(i)(F).

[649] *Id.*

[650] INA §214(c)(6)(D).

[651] USCIS, "Instructions for Form I-129, Petition for a Nonimmigrant Worker" (updated Aug. 13, 2015), https://www.uscis.gov/sites/default/files/files/form/i-129instr.pdf, at 24.

[652] 72 Fed. Reg. 18856 (Apr. 16, 2007).

Copyright © 2017. American Immigration Lawyers Association. All rights reserved.

area of the alien's ability."[653] Importantly, opinions from both organizations must be provided, as otherwise an RFE will be issued.[654]

The written statement from the peer group or labor/management organization should have one of the following structures:

- "If the advisory opinion is favorable to the petitioner, it should describe the alien's ability and achievements in the field of endeavor, describe the nature of the duties to be performed, and state whether the position requires the services of an alien of extraordinary ability,"[655] with details on how the assessment or evaluation was made;[656]

- If an advisory opinion on behalf of an individual who will work in the field of motion picture or television production is "favorable to the petitioner, the written advisory opinion from the labor and management organizations should describe the alien's achievements in the motion picture or television field and state whether the position requires the services of an alien of extraordinary achievement";[657]

- "If the advisory opinion is not favorable to the petitioner, the advisory opinion must set forth a specific statement of facts which supports the conclusion reached in the opinion";[658] or

- Statement of "no objection" if the organization "has no objection to the approval of the petition,"[659] although it remains unclear whether a state of no objection must include a "statement of facts in support of this conclusion."[660]

A consultation also is required for a petition for an O-2.[661] If the O-2 will be working on a motion picture or television production, consultations with "a labor organization *and* a management organization in the area of the alien's ability is required."[662] An unfavorable opinion must "set forth a specific statement of facts which supports the conclusion reached."[663]

A favorable opinion for an O-2 accompanying an artist or athlete should:

- "Describe the alien's essentiality to, and working relationship with, the O-1; and

---

[653] 8 CFR §214.2(o)(5)(iii); *Matter of [name not provided]*, WAC 95 042 52458 (AAO Jan. 12, 1995), 14 Immig. Rptr. B2-43 (advisory opinions from the Directors Guild of America, the Alliance of Motion Picture and Television Producers, and the Producers Guild of America).

[654] "AILA/VSC Liaison Practice Pointer: O and P Visas" (Dec. 23, 2009), AILA Doc. No. 09122335.

[655] 8 CFR §214.2(o)(5)(ii)(A).

[656] *Matter of [name not provided]*, LIN 93 124 51276 (AAO Jan. 23, 1995), 14 Immig. Rptr. B2-128.

[657] 8 CFR §214.2(o)(5)(iii).

[658] 8 CFR §§214.2(o)(5)(i)(C), (ii)(A) and (iii).

[659] 8 CFR §214.2(o)(5)(ii)(A) and (iii).

[660] *Matter of [name not provided]*, WAC 94 180 51386 (AAO Oct. 13, 1994), 13 Immig. Rptr. B2-224.

[661] 8 CFR §214.2(o)(5)(i)(A) and (o)(5)(iv).

[662] 8 CFR §214.2(o)(5)(iv) (emphasis added).

[663] 8 CFR §214.2(o)(5)(iv).

Copyright © 2017. American Immigration Lawyers Association. All rights reserved.

- "State whether there are available U.S. workers who can perform the support services."[664]

A favorable opinion for an O-2 accompanying an O-1 in the motion picture or television industry should address:

- The O-2's skills and experience with the O-1, and whether the O-2 has a longstanding, pre-existing relationship with the O-1; or

- Whether significant production will take place in the United States and abroad, and whether continuing participation of the O-2 is essential to the successful completion of the production.[665]

A consulting entity may submit a letter of no objection in lieu of a favorable or unfavorable advisory opinion on an O-2.[666]

An unfavorable advisory opinion does not necessarily mean that the O-1 or O-2 petition will be denied,[667] but the practitioner is encouraged to work with the organization to identify the reasons for the statements and to provide information or documents that may address those concerns. Otherwise, the supporting evidence must more firmly establish the beneficiary's eligibility for O status:

"A negative consultation does not automatically result in the denial of the petition, as decisions must be based on the totality of the evidence. Accordingly, if the petitioner can submit evidence that overcomes a negative advisory opinion and which establishes the merits of the alien, USCIS may approve the petition."[668]

USCIS guidance provides a list of peer groups and labor and management organizations "which have agreed to provide advisory opinions."[669] Because the list is neither "exclusive" nor "exhaustive," USCIS "and petitioners may use other sources, such as publications, to identify appropriate peer groups, labor organizations, and management organizations."[670] The practitioner should confirm that the appropriate office receives the request, as "many of the consulting entities are sensitive about their jurisdictions."[671] The practitioner should also ensure that an advisory opinion is

---

[664] *Id. See also Matter of [name and case number not provided]* (AAO Oct. 21, 2011), http://bit.ly/oct111d.

[665] 8 CFR §214.2(o)(5)(iv).

[666] *Id.*

[667] *Matter of [name not provided]*, WAC 95 042 52458 (AAO Jan. 12, 1995), 14 Immig. Rptr. B2-43 (one advisory opinion from the Directors Guild of America "categorically oppose[d] the granting of O-1 status in this matter" and opined that the "Guild has gone on record with INS previously that it is impossible for unit production managers and assistant directors to attain the recognition and experience necessary for O-1 visas," but AAO approved the petition).

[668] AFM 33.3.

[669] 8 CFR §214.2(o)(5)(v). USCIS, "Address Index for I-129 O & P Consultation Letters" (updated Mar. 11, 2013), http://bit.ly/2dHkz1O.

[670] *Id.*

[671] Legacy INS, L. Weinig, "Policy Guidelines for the Adjudication of O and P Petitions" (June 25, 1992), 69 Interpreter Releases 1084–87 (Aug. 31, 1992).

Copyright © 2017. American Immigration Lawyers Association. All rights reserved.

obtained "for each type of occupation listed on the petition, if the occupations are represented by different unions."[672]

An opinion that discusses a different role or occupation than that named on the O-1 petition, because it was obtained for another petition, should not be submitted.[673] USCIS may request evidence that the signatory of the advisory opinion has authority to provide the statement.[674] An advisory opinion from an organization that was co-created or co-founded by the beneficiary may be considered "self-serving, and therefore inadequate to satisfy the requirement for a written advisory opinion from a peer group or labor organization."[675]

Legacy INS guidance, issued shortly after the O visa category was created, stated:

"Due to the novelty of the O and P classifications, it is suggested that officers involved in the adjudication of O and P petitions adopt a lenient policy towards accepting consultations submitted by petitioners, as long as they appear reasonable.... Petitioners should not be penalized because of the inability of the consulting entity to provide the appropriate consultation."[676]

It appears, however, that such leniency may be a thing of the past, at least as far as the AAO is concerned.[677] Therefore, the practitioner is encouraged to educate the consulting entity of the points that must be stated in an advisory opinion.

3. Exceptions to, and Waivers of, the Advisory Opinion Requirement

There are two main exceptions to the requirement to submit an advisory opinion. First, if the petitioner establishes that no "appropriate peer group" and/or labor organization exists, then USCIS "shall render a decision on the evidence of record."[678] As noted by legacy INS: "This evidence will probably take the form of affidavits or statements from individuals employed in the beneficiary's field of endeavor. Common sense will dictate whether the evidence submitted establishes the

---

[672] *Id.*

[673] *Matter of [name not provided]*, SRC 06 138 52302 (AAO Nov. 7, 2007), http://bit.ly/nov0701d.

[674] *Matter of [name not provided]*, SRC 06 138 52302 (AAO Nov. 7, 2007), *available at www.uscis.gov* (select "Laws," "Administrative Decisions" link on the right toolbar under "More Information," D8, and then search by date and for "01D8101") (USCIS RFE).

[675] *Matter of [name not provided]*, EAC 08 178 51729 (AAO Jan. 30, 2009), http://bit.ly/jan091d. Notably, the petition also included evidence of the beneficiary's role in co-creating the organization "not long before the instant petition was filed."

[676] Legacy INS, L. Weinig, "Policy Guidelines for the Adjudication of O and P Petitions" (June 25, 1992), 69 Interpreter Releases 1084–87 (Aug. 31, 1992).

[677] *E.g., Matter of [name and case number not provided]* (AAO Dec. 29, 2014), http://bit.ly/dec143d (finding that no qualifying advisory opinion was submitted despite submission of an unfavorable advisory opinion that did not contain a specific statement of the facts to support the negative conclusion, and of a statement from an individual in the same occupation that was found not to provide enough detail of her expertise); *Matter of D-,* ID# 13836 (AAO Oct. 5, 2015) (letter from teacher in the field did not contain specifics required by the regulations); *Matter of V-M-D-, Inc.,* ID# 15267 (AAO May 16, 2016) (no consultation submitted).

[678] INA §214(c)(6)(C); 8 CFR §214.2(o)(5)(i)(G).

Copyright © 2017. American Immigration Lawyers Association. All rights reserved.

nonexistence of a labor organization."[679] A statement by the petitioner that no appropriate group exists is generally not sufficient.[680]

As discussed above, a petitioner should not claim that there is no appropriate organization by narrowly limiting the field of endeavor.[681] If an organization exists, but it no longer provides advisory opinions, then the practitioner should endeavor to present independent evidence from the organization as substantiation.[682]

Second, USCIS affirmatively "shall contact the appropriate labor and/or management organization and request an advisory opinion if one is not submitted by the petitioner," as long as the petition is for a beneficiary who will work in the field of art, entertainment, or athletics, and as long as USCIS "has determined that a petition merits expeditious handling,"[683] "based on the merits of the case, such as an overriding humanitarian concern."[684] Importantly, "[e]xpedited processing should not be confused with premium processing," where a response is provided in 15 days because of an additional fee,[685] as discussed below. In such a situation, a response must be provided by the labor and/or management organization within 24 hours, and the advisory opinion(s) must be provided within an additional five days "of the initiating request."[686] Both communications may be made by telephone.[687] USCIS will adjudicate the petition without the advisory opinion if the labor and/or management organization fails to respond within 24 hours.[688]

The required advisory opinion may be waived if the O-1 beneficiary will work in the field of art "in those instances where the alien seeks readmission to the United States to perform similar services within 2 years of the date of a previous consultation."[689] The practitioner should, on behalf of the O-1 employer, "submit a copy of the prior consultation with the petition and advise the Director of the waiver request."[690] It is advisable to highlight the waiver request, as it is often overlooked.[691] Then, after the waiver is granted, USCIS will "forward a copy of the petition and

---

[679] Legacy INS, L. Weinig, "Policy Guidelines for the Adjudication of O and P Petitions" (June 25, 1992), 69 Interpreter Releases 1084–87 (Aug. 31, 1992).

[680] *Matter of D-*, ID# 13836 (AAO Oct. 5, 2015).

[681] *Matter of [name not provided]*, EAC 02 127 52263 (AAO Sept. 16, 2002), 26 Immig. Rptr. B2-26.

[682] *Matter of [name not provided]*, SRC 06 138 52302 (AAO Nov. 7, 2007), http://bit.ly/nov0701d.

[683] 8 CFR §214.2(o)(5)(i)(E).

[684] AFM 33.8.

[685] *Id.*

[686] 8 CFR §214.2(o)(5)(i)(E).

[687] AFM 33.8.

[688] 8 CFR §214.2(o)(5)(i)(E).

[689] 8 CFR §214.2(o)(5)(ii)(B); INA §214(c)(3); USCIS, "O-1 Visa: Individuals with Extraordinary Ability or Achievement" (updated Sept. 14, 2015), http://bit.ly/2cCoXRa.

[690] 8 CFR §214.2(o)(5)(ii)(B); USCIS, "O-1 Visa: Individuals with Extraordinary Ability or Achievement" (updated Sept. 14, 2015), http://bit.ly/2cCoXRa.

[691] "AILA VSC Liaison Practice Pointer: Obtaining a Waiver of the Consultation Requirement for an O-1B" (Sept. 7, 2012), AILA Doc. No. 12090745.

Copyright © 2017. American Immigration Lawyers Association. All rights reserved.

supporting documentation to the national office of an appropriate labor organization."[692]

Similarly, O-1 petitions on behalf of major league baseball players should not need to have an advisory opinion, because it has already "been furnished to Headquarters."[693] The statement "from the Major League Baseball Players Association (MLBPA) states that all foreign baseball players who have signed a major league contract have in the opinion of the MLBPA, established eligibility for either P-1 or O-1 classifications," and adjudicating officers have been directed "to accept this letter as the required consultation."[694]

Advisory opinions are also theoretically not required for O extensions to continue the same event or activity unless requested by USCIS.[695] However, as discussed under "Extensions" later in this chapter, USCIS has increasingly been requesting full documentation as a routine matter. Also, AAO has suggested that the plain language of the regulations requires an advisory opinion for every petition other than the exceptions and waivers discussed above.[696]

4. Employment Contracts and Summaries of Terms of the Oral Agreement Under Which the Beneficiary Will Be Employed

Failure to submit contract documents is grounds for denial of the O-1 petition.[697] In practice, however, USCIS does not require contracts for an O-1A petition in the business context for a regular employee of a company and recognizes that such employment may be at-will. Any contracts or summaries should contain the start and end dates of employment, be signed by the beneficiary,[698] and be dated before the O petition is filed. Otherwise it may be "not relevant to a determination of the beneficiary's eligibility,"[699] since it would "not indicate that a contract was in effect at the time the petition was filed."[700] An exception may exist if "the written contract represents the terms of a pre-existing oral agreement between the two parties."[701] In order for a summary of an oral agreement to be acceptable, it must specify "what was

---

[692] 8 CFR §214.2(o)(5)(ii)(B).

[693] AFM 33.10.

[694] *Id.*

[695] 8 CFR §214.2(o)(11).

[696] *Matter of [name and case number not provided]* (AAO Mar. 11, 2011), http://bit.ly/mar111d, citing 8 CFR §214.2(o)(5)(i)(D).

[697] 8 CFR §214.2(o)(2)(ii)(B); *Matter of [name not provided]*, WAC 06 224 53958 (AAO May 4, 2009), http://bit.ly/may092d; *Matter of [name not provided]*, WAC 07 236 52246 (AAO Feb. 18, 2009), http://bit.ly/feb091d (approval revoked).

[698] *Matter of [name not provided]*, EAC 08 178 51729 (AAO Jan. 30, 2009), http://bit.ly/jan091d.

[699] *Matter of [name not provided]*, EAC 05 800 13985 (AAO Mar. 10, 2008), http://bit.ly/mar081d8.

[700] *Matter of [name not provided]*, WAC 07 236 52246 (AAO Feb. 18, 2009), http://bit.ly/feb091d; *Matter of [name not provided]*, EAC 05 800 13985 (AAO Apr. 19, 2007), http://bit.ly/apr071d.

[701] *Matter of [name not provided]*, WAC 07 236 52246 (AAO Feb. 18, 2009), http://bit.ly/feb091d.

Copyright © 2017. American Immigration Lawyers Association. All rights reserved.

offered by the employer" and "what was accepted by the employee."[702] USCIS provided the following guidance regarding oral agreements:

"USCIS will accept an oral contract, as evidenced by the summation of the elements of the oral agreement. Such evidence may include but is not limited to: emails between the contractual parties, a written summation of the terms of the agreement, or any other evidence which demonstrates that an oral agreement was created.... The summary does not have to be signed by both parties to establish the oral agreement. However, it must document the terms of the employment offered and that the beneficiary has agreed to the offer."[703]

The AAO stated that an offer of employment is insufficient as a contract or summary.[704] Any dates of employment on the contract should be consistent with the dates of need stated on the Form I-129, and supported by a relevant event,[705] as discussed above:

"It is not the CSC standard to require separate contracts to outline each 'event' if … the event is for a series of concerts at various venues as long as the broader concept of the event is defined as a concert series and supported by contract.... Therefore, a request for a contract is appropriate and supported under Regulations as part of the evidentiary requirements for the O classification and will be requested. The request can be met by incorporating these 'sub' events into the terms of the contract or oral agreement.

"In some instances we have seen incomplete contracts and itineraries that do not identify dates, venues and other essential elements to support the petition. It is unclear in these instances what the alien will be doing or how the requested period of stay is substantiated. In these cases, an RFE generally will be issued to seek clarification on these points."[706]

5. Explanation of Services and Itinerary

The supporting documents for the O-1 petition should explain how the beneficiary's services are necessary for "already-planned specific events," and not merely "to enable the beneficiary to be available for engagements that may occur during the intended period covered by the petition,"[707] or for freelance work.[708] In

---

[702] USCIS, "O-1 Visa: Individuals with Extraordinary Ability or Achievement" (updated Sept. 14, 2015), http://bit.ly/2cCoXRa.

[703] Id.

[704] Matter of [name not provided], EAC 05 800 13985 (AAO Mar. 10, 2008), http://bit.ly/mar081d8.

[705] Matter of [name not provided], WAC 06 262 52536 (AAO Oct. 9, 2007), http://bit.ly/oct071d.

[706] "CSC Answers to AILA Liaison Questions" (Sept. 2001), AILA Doc. No. 01090734.

[707] Matter of [name not provided], EAC 05 800 13985 (AAO Mar. 10, 2008), http://bit.ly/mar081d8.

[708] Matter of [name not provided], WAC 07 006 52866 (AAO Mar. 5, 2008), http://bit.ly/mar081d; USCIS, "Clarifying Guidance on 'O' Petition Validity Period; Revisions to the Adjudicator's Field Manual (AFM) Chapter 33.4(e)(2); AFM Update AD10-36," PM-602-0003 (July 20, 2010), AILA Doc. No. 10072061; AFM 33.4.

Copyright © 2017. American Immigration Lawyers Association. All rights reserved.

addition, the explanation of services or itinerary should be consistent with the event, as discussed above:

> "Clearly there are cases where an itinerary would not be appropriate. The RFE as such is not demanding an itinerary if it is not appropriate or where a contract would suffice. In some instances the itinerary would be defined as the academic year, the semester, the performance season or concert halls where the alien would be perform, the business enterprise, the product roll out, the lecture series and venues of lectures."[709]

A petition for an artist or entertainer should discuss with specificity the event or events for which the beneficiary's services are necessary, and merely naming possible performances may be inadequate.[710] For a discussion of how multiple events may nevertheless be considered a single "event" for purposes of O classification, see above. Reports indicate that O petitions on behalf of university professors,[711] researchers, and other individuals who do not engage in performance events have been denied for lack of an itinerary. In such cases, the practitioner may wish to include a document titled "Itinerary" that sets forth the schedule of activities, such that the petition is not denied due to elevating form over substance.

For O-1 petitions that will involve a series of performances by the beneficiary, the itinerary should name the beneficiary as the performer, rather than the name of the group.[712] Otherwise, USCIS and/or the AAO may conclude that the petitioner seeks "to have the beneficiary available for bookings that may occur during the intended period covered by the petition."[713] If the petitioner is the beneficiary's agent, then the O-1 petition must include an itinerary of events and the contract between the beneficiary and his or her employer,[714] as noted in the section about agents, above.

G. Nonimmigrant Intent

As stated by the Department of State (DOS):

> "An applicant for an O-1 visa does not have to have a residence abroad which he or she does not intend to abandon… There must be a temporary intent to remain on the part of the O-1 visa holder. Thus, dual intent is permissible for O-1 visa holders."[715]

Specifically, being the beneficiary of an approved labor certification application or immigrant visa petition "shall not be a basis for denying an O-1 petition, a request to

---

[709] "CSC Answers to AILA Liaison Questions" (Sept. 2001), AILA Doc. No. 01090734.

[710] *Matter of [name not provided]*, LIN 04 131 51238 (AAO Feb. 24, 2006), http://bit.ly/feb061d (petition mentioned "entertainment events such as half time shows for NBA, WNBA, and NHL" but did not name specific events or provide an itinerary).

[711] "CSC Stakeholders Meeting" (Apr. 29, 2010), AILA Doc. No. 10062988.

[712] *Matter of [name not provided]*, WAC 06 273 55205 (AAO Oct. 11, 2007), http://bit.ly/oct0701d.

[713] *Id.*

[714] *Matter of [name not provided]*, LIN 04 092 50085 (AAO May 25, 2005), http://bit.ly/may055d.

[715] 9 FAM 402.13-10(B) (citations omitted).

Copyright © 2017. American Immigration Lawyers Association. All rights reserved.

extend such a petition, or the alien's application for admission, change of status, or extension of stay."[716] As stated by the regulations: "The alien may legitimately come to the United States for a temporary period as an O-1 nonimmigrant and depart voluntarily at the end of his or her authorized stay and, at the same time, lawfully seek to become a permanent resident of the United States."[717] USCIS guidance explicitly states: "O-1 aliens may have *dual intent*, meaning that they may admitted to the U.S. to work temporarily but are permitted to have petitions pending during that time for permanent residence."[718]

O-2 support personnel, however, must demonstrate "having a residence in a foreign country which he or she has no intention of abandoning."[719] Appropriate evidence may include copies of property titles or deeds, mortgages, or lease agreements, as well as evidence of continued enrollment in school or other programs in the home country, arrangements for sabbatical, bank statements, and evidence of family or community ties. And since the purpose of a U.S. visit by support personnel should be to "com[e] to assist in the artistic or athletic performance" of an O-1 nonimmigrant,[720] other evidence could include a statement by a foreign employer confirming an employment offer after the U.S. event or performance. Therefore, a foreign national who seeks O-2 status and who is the beneficiary of an approved labor certification application or of a filed immigrant visa petition may find the O-2 petition denied, as this would indicate a desire to immigrate permanently to the United States.

It may be possible to obtain approval of an O-2 petition if the labor certification application or immigrant visa petition was filed by an entity other than the O-2 petitioner or by a family member, but practitioners should thoroughly discuss the issue with the client. This is because the foreign national would have to demonstrate that, despite the pursuit of U.S. permanent residence, he or she will maintain the foreign residence for the duration of the O-2 assignment.

An O-2 petition may address these issues by providing explicit details of definite plans, such as ongoing payments of the mortgage, property taxes, or rent; offer of employment from a foreign entity upon conclusion of the O-2 assignment; and evidence of the relationship between the O-2 petitioner and the foreign entity, if applicable. Nevertheless, the practitioner should advise the client that the O-2 petition runs a higher than normal risk of denial, as discussed below. For a detailed discussion of strategies to contrast a future desire to immigrate with a temporary desire to visit

---

[716] 8 CFR §214.2(o)(13). *See also* 9 FAM 402.13-5(C).

[717] 8 CFR §214.2(o)(13); 9 FAM 402.13-5(C).

[718] USCIS Office of Business Liaison, Employer Information Bulletin 15, "Aliens with Extraordinary Ability (O-1) and Accompanying/Assisting Aliens (O-2)" (Dec. 8, 2004), 82 Interpreter Releases 180–84 (Jan. 17, 2005) (emphasis in original).

[719] 8 CFR §214.2(o)(1)(i); 9 FAM 402.13-10(B).

[720] 8 CFR §214.2(o)(1)(i).

Copyright © 2017. American Immigration Lawyers Association. All rights reserved.

the United States, see Volume 1: Chapter Three, "Visitors: B Visas and Status and the Visa Waiver Program."

The standard of nonimmigrant intent, or lack thereof, of O-3 dependents applies respective of the standard of the O-1 or O-2 principal beneficiary.[721]

IV. Managing Client Expectations: Increased Scrutiny in Certain Situations

A. Coaches, Trainers, and Instructors of Athletic Competitors

The practitioner should not presume that an individual with extraordinary ability as a competitor also possesses extraordinary ability as a coach, trainer, or instructor of that sport.[722] As stated by a federal court and the AAO:

> "It is reasonable to interpret continuing to work in one's 'area of extraordinary ability' as working in the same profession in which one has extraordinary ability, not necessarily in any profession in that field. For example, Lee's extraordinary ability as a baseball player does not imply that he also has extraordinary ability in all positions or professions in the baseball industry such as a manager, umpire or coach. The regulations regarding this preference classification are extremely restrictive, and not expanding 'area' to include everything within a particular field cannot be considered unreasonable."[723]

> "Competitive athletics and sports instruction are not the same area of expertise and the USCIS will not assume that an alien with extraordinary ability as an athlete has the same level of expertise as a coach or instructor of his or her sport. However, given the nexus between athletic competition and coaching or sports instruction, in a case where an alien has clearly achieved national or international acclaim as an athlete and has sustained that acclaim in the field of coaching at a national or international level, an adjudicator may consider the totality of the evidence as establishing an overall pattern of sustained acclaim and extraordinary ability such that it can be concluded that coaching is within the beneficiary's area of expertise. Specifically, in such a case, USCIS will consider the level at which the alien acts as a coach.... In an RFE issued on December 22, 2006, the director advised the petitioner that while USCIS recognizes a nexus between playing and coaching a given sport, it would not be assumed that every extraordinary ability athlete's area of expertise includes coaching.... While a competitive tennis player and a tennis

---

[721] 9 FAM 402.13-10(B).

[722] Legacy INS, L. Weinig, "Policy Guidelines for the Adjudication of O and P Petitions," (June 25, 1992), 69 Interpreter Releases 1084–87 (Aug. 31, 1992) (noting that "most coaches would not qualify"); *Matter of [name not provided]*, WAC 07 055 52449 (AAO Mar. 21, 2008), http://bit.ly/mar0801d (beneficiary deemed to have extraordinary ability as a tennis player but, with only one year of experience in coaching other tennis players, not as a tennis coach); *Matter of [name not provided]*, WAC 07 026 52214 (AAO May 12, 2008), http://bit.ly/may081d. *See also Lee v. Ziglar*, 237 F. Supp. 2d 914 (N.D. Ill. 2002) (immigrant visa petition); *Matter of [name not provided]*, WAC 07 273 54624 (AAO Mar. 11, 2009), http://bit.ly/mar091d (beneficiary cannot qualify for O-1 status as a ballroom dance instructor based solely on achievements as a competitive ballroom dancer); *Matter of [name not provided]*, WAC 07 001 54685 (AAO July 29, 2008), http://bit.ly/jul081d.

[723] *Lee v. Ziglar*, 237 F. Supp. 2d 914 (N.D. Ill. 2002).

Copyright © 2017. American Immigration Lawyers Association. All rights reserved.

coach share knowledge of tennis, the two rely on different sets of basic skills. Thus, competitive tennis and tennis coaching and instruction are not the same area of expertise."[724]

"To assume that every extraordinary athlete's area of expertise includes coaching, however, would be too speculative…. Specifically, in such a case, we will consider the level at which the alien acts as a coach."[725]

For these petitions, the adjudicatory trend indicates that USCIS will evaluate the totality of the circumstances.[726] If applicable, the petition may also include evidence of the beneficiary's achievements while competing in the sport he or she now coaches, trains, or instructs,[727] as it is credible that an acclaimed athlete could translate and/or apply the skills to teach others.[728] However, the adjudicatory trend also reflects that the "longer the time since the [beneficiary] switched from competing to training, the less relevance [USCIS and/or the AAO] accord to the [beneficiary's] accomplishments as a competitor."[729]

This trend is borne out in recent guidance and cases emerging from USCIS in connection with the parallel permanent category of EB1-1 Extraordinary Ability. USCIS guidance in that arena states:

"[I]f a beneficiary has clearly achieved *recent* national or international acclaim as an athlete and has sustained that acclaim in the field of coaching/managing at a national level, adjudicators can consider the totality of the evidence as establishing an overall pattern of sustained acclaim and extraordinary ability such that we can conclude the coaching is within the beneficiary's area of expertise."[730]

USCIS may not allow such consideration of non-coaching acclaim if the beneficiary has "had an extended period of time to establish his or her reputation as a coach *beyond the years* in which he or she had sustained national or international acclaim as an athlete."[731] Thus, a 2007 petition on behalf of a women's gymnastics

---

[724] *Matter of [name not provided]*, WAC 07 055 52449 (AAO Mar. 21, 2008), http://bit.ly/mar0801d; *Matter of [name not provided]*, WAC 07 273 54624 (AAO Mar. 11, 2009), http://bit.ly/mar091d (same statements regarding an instructor); *Matter of [name not provided]*, WAC 07 001 54685 (AAO July 29, 2008), http://bit.ly/jul081d.

[725] *Matter of [name not provided]*, EAC 05 064 52917 (AAO June 12, 2006), http://bit.ly/jun061d.

[726] *Matter of [name not provided]*, WAC 07 055 52449 (AAO Mar. 21, 2008), http://bit.ly/mar0801d; *Matter of [name not provided]*, WAC 07 273 54624 (AAO Mar. 11, 2009), http://bit.ly/mar091d.

[727] *Matter of [name not provided]*, WAC 07 055 52449 (AAO Mar. 21, 2008), http://bit.ly/mar0801d; *Matter of [name not provided]*, WAC 06 224 53958 (AAO May 4, 2009), http://bit.ly/may092d; *Matter of [name not provided]*, WAC 07 273 54624 (AAO Mar. 11, 2009), *available at www.uscis.gov* (select "Laws," "Administrative Decisions" link on the right toolbar under http://bit.ly/mar091d.

[728] *Lee v. Ziglar*, 237 F. Supp. 2d 914 (N.D. Ill. 2002) (immigrant visa petition denied, but USCIS "observed that Lee, as an ex-player, might be well-suited for a coaching position, but that the visa classification demands a much higher showing than simply being well-equipped for a given occupation").

[729] *Matter of [name not provided]*, SRC 05 175 50496 (AAO July 25, 2006), http://bit.ly/jul061d.

[730] AFM 22.2(i)(1)(B) (emphasis in original).

[731] *Id.* (emphasis in original).

Copyright © 2017. American Immigration Lawyers Association. All rights reserved.

gold medalist in the 1988 Olympics, whose last competition was in 1991, was denied on the basis that coaching was not her area of expertise.[732]

Conversely, a judo champion whose petition was filed within seven months of his last major competitive achievement was found to have "presented a sufficient nexus between his ability as an athlete and his work as a coach, such that we conclude that he seeks to enter the United States to continue to work in his area of extraordinary ability." The evidence of extraordinary ability related to the beneficiary's achievements as a participating athlete, but the AAO also highlighted the beneficiary's "progression of education, experience, and licensing" as positioning him to "continue in his area of expertise as a judo coach." It viewed his university-level coaching, his master's thesis on athletes' anxiety, and his licensing as a judo sports coach as indicators that "coaching is within his area of expertise."[733]

For individuals seeking O-1 classification as sports coaches, "USCIS will consider the success of athletes coached by the alien as comparable evidence," such as evidence "that the beneficiary has instructed, trained or coached any tennis players [or athletes] who have won major, internationally recognized awards" and a list of the successful athletes coached.[734] A strong O-1 petition for an instructor should contain evidence of "an established history of instructing dancers [or other competitors] who compete regularly at the national level."[735] The extraordinary ability of trainers may be "measured by the results of the horses [or other beings trained] he trains."[736] However, the AAO indicated that the individuals coached, trained, or instructed should achieve "significant recognition" or have extraordinary ability of their own.[737]

The AAO has noted that the dates of coaching, training, or instruction, as well as the dates of awards won by those pupils, should be recent.[738] Copies of the awards

---

[732] *Integrity Gymnastics & Pure Power Cheerleading*, LLC v. USCIS, 131 F. Supp. 3d 721 (S.D. Ohio, 2015). The court noted that the AAO had acknowledged that "there exists a nexus between playing and coaching a given sport" requiring "a balanced approach … in the final merits determination," but that while a gymnast and coach share knowledge of the sport, "the two rely on very different sets of basic skills." *See also Lee v. Ziglar*, 237 F. Supp. 2d 914, 918 (N.D. Ill. 2002) (petition denied for beneficiary who was "one of the most famous baseball players in Korean history," but sought to work in the United States as a Chicago White Sox coach and had not established extraordinary ability as a coach); *Matter of S-F-F-C-*, ID# 17919 (AAO Sept. 7, 2016) (O-1 for coaching denied where a long time has passed since the beneficiary competed and he hasn't reached the level of extraordinary ability in coaching).

[733] *Matter of K-S-Y-*, ID# 14269 (AAO, Mar. 9, 2016), AILA Doc. No. 16042961.

[734] *Matter of [name not provided]*, WAC 07 055 52449 (AAO Mar. 21, 2008), http://bit.ly/mar0801d.

[735] *Matter of [name not provided]*, WAC 07 273 54624 (AAO Mar. 11, 2009), http://bit.ly/mar091d. *See also Matter of [name not provided]*, EAC 04 024 52731 (AAO Feb. 4, 2005), http://bit.ly/feb052d (stating that "this office recognizes a nexus between performing an art and instructing that art form").

[736] *Matter of [name not provided]*, WAC 06 224 53958 (AAO May 4, 2009), http://bit.ly/may092d.

[737] *Matter of [name not provided]*, LIN 04 216 53865 (AAO Mar. 11, 2005), http://bit.ly/mar051d (athletes coached had won awards but this was insufficient). *See also Matter of BCMHV-, LLC*, ID# 16546 (AAO May 26, 2016) (evidence of students' standings not sufficiently explained to show their significance).

[738] *Matter of [name not provided]*, SRC 06 095 50306 (AAO Jan. 24, 2007), http://bit.ly/jan0701d (criterion not satisfied where the athlete won an award a decade before the petition was filed).

Copyright © 2017. American Immigration Lawyers Association. All rights reserved.

won by the competitors should be submitted, as well as a list of names.[739] In addition, any testimonials from athletes who have benefited from the beneficiary's services should specify the dates of coaching, training, or instruction.[740] If photographs of the beneficiary with other elite athletes are submitted, then they should show the parties playing together: "[A]n 'affiliation' does not compel the inference that the two individuals played together."[741] For example, when one petitioner submitted photographs of the beneficiary with a famous actor and the Prince of Wales, the AAO stated:

> "[I]t does not necessarily follow that a polo player who plays on the same team with [these celebrities] must, himself, rank among 'the most elite polo players of the world.' The photographs do not show how the beneficiary ranks when compared to individuals who became famous by playing polo (rather than famous people who happen to play polo)."[742]

Not all coaches will coach athletes who will compete in sports; a coach may train a performing artist: "While competitive gymnasts and circus acrobats may possess similar skills, the fields are clearly different, and the AAO finds it reasonable to classify the former as athletes and the latter as artists."[743]

The AAO has noted that "we do not mean to imply that [athletics] is the only career transition that may occur within an individual's area of expertise. Because the case before us concerns the very athlete-coach transition contemplated by the AFM, we need not address what other career transition scenarios might warrant a similar analysis (e.g., athlete-to-broadcaster or musician-to-instructor)."[744] The AAO has also stated that "the mere inclusion of the work 'coaches' in the definition of 'arts'…, however, does not mean that all coaches in other fields, including athletic coaches, may be classified as aliens with extraordinary ability in the arts."[745]

In addition, USCIS and/or the AAO may reject the coaching, training, or instruction of amateurs or child competitors, as "an international award received by a 9-year-old student would not carry the same evidentiary weight as an international award received by a competitor at the adult, professional level, without some additional explanation as to how the sport is governed at the junior level."[746] Merely

---

[739] *Matter of [name not provided]*, WAC 07 273 54624 (AAO Mar. 11, 2009), http://bit.ly/mar091d; *Matter of [name not provided]*, WAC 07 001 54685 (AAO July 29, 2008), http://bit.ly/jul081d; *Matter of [name not provided]*, LIN 02 296 53935 (AAO Jan. 26, 2005), http://bit.ly/jan0501d.

[740] *Matter of [name not provided]*, WAC 07 001 54685 (AAO July 29, 2008), http://bit.ly/jul081d; *Matter of [name not provided]*, LIN 05 262 51156 (AAO Nov. 7, 2007), http://bit.ly/nov073d; *Matter of [name not provided]*, LIN 02 296 53935 (AAO Jan. 26, 2005), http://bit.ly/jan0501d.

[741] *Matter of [name not provided]*, SRC 06 138 52302 (AAO Nov. 7, 2007), http://bit.ly/nov0701d.

[742] *Id.*

[743] *Matter of [name not provided]*, WAC 07 054 53346 (AAO May 1, 2009), http://bit.ly/may0901d.

[744] *Matter of K-S-Y-,* ID# 14269 (AAO, Mar. 9, 2016), AILA Doc. No. 16042961, footnote 4.

[745] *Matter of [name not provided]*, WAC 06 163 50719 (AAO Sept. 13, 2007), http://bit.ly/sep071d.

[746] *Matter of [name not provided]*, WAC 07 273 54624 (AAO Mar. 11, 2009), http://bit.ly/mar091d.

Copyright © 2017. American Immigration Lawyers Association. All rights reserved.

possessing certificates for coaching, training, or instruction are not considered, in and of themselves, evidence of being the judge of the work of others.[747]

B. Impact of Labor Disputes

A U.S. employer may not use the O category to employ a foreign national in the United States if the Secretary of Labor certifies or otherwise informs the Attorney General that:

"[A] strike or other labor dispute involving a work stoppage of workers is in progress in the occupation at the place where the beneficiary is to be employed, and that the employment of the beneficiary would adversely affect the wages and working conditions of U.S. citizens and lawful resident workers."[748]

If such a certification is made, then the O-1 and/or O-2 petition will be denied.[749] If an O-1 or O-2 petition has been approved already, but the foreign national "has not yet entered the United States, or has entered the United States but not yet commenced employment," then the petition approval "is automatically suspended" and any application for admission based on the petition will be denied.[750] The practitioner should note that the strike or labor dispute must be certified by the Secretary of Labor; a petition may not be denied or suspended without such certification.[751]

With respect to visa applications, DOS will "defer visa issuance and follow whatever instructions are given regarding the disposition of the suspended petition," whether the consular officer is informed of the strike or labor dispute by the Department of Homeland Security (DHS), DOS, or "another official source."[752]

An O-1 or O-2 nonimmigrant "shall not be deemed to be failing to maintain his or her status solely on account of past, present, or future participation in a strike or other labor dispute involving a work stoppage of workers," whether the strike or labor dispute is certified by the Secretary of Labor or not.[753] The following conditions also apply:

- The O-1 or O-2 nonimmigrant remains "subject to all applicable provisions" of the immigration laws and regulations "in the same manner as are all other O nonimmigrants";

- O-1 or O-2 status and period of authorized stay "is not modified or extended in any way by virtue of his or her participation in a strike or other labor dispute involving a work stoppage of workers"; and

---

[747] *Matter of [name not provided]*, WAC 07 001 54685 (AAO July 29, 2008), http://bit.ly/jul081d.

[748] 8 CFR §214.2(o)(14)(i).

[749] 8 CFR §214.2(o)(14)(i)(A).

[750] 8 CFR §214.2(o)(14)(i)(B).

[751] 8 CFR §214.2(o)(14)(ii).

[752] 9 FAM 402.13-5(E).

[753] 8 CFR §214.2(o)(14)(iii).

Copyright © 2017. American Immigration Lawyers Association. All rights reserved.

- "Although participation by an O nonimmigrant alien in a strike or other labor dispute involving a work stoppage of workers will not constitute a ground for deportation, an alien who violates his or her status or who remains in the United States after his or her authorized period of stay has expired will be subject to deportation."[754]

C. Return Transportation Obligation

If the O-1 and/or O-2 employment terminates, then the practitioner should inform the client of the duty to pay "for the reasonable cost of return transportation of the alien abroad," which is defined as the beneficiary's "last place of residence prior to his or her entry into the United States."[755] The obligation applies if the termination of the employment relationship is for any reason other than voluntary resignation by the beneficiary.[756] If the employer and the O-1 petitioner are different entities, then both parties "are jointly and severally liable."[757]

V. Preparing the O-1 or O-2 Petition

This section discusses the documents of the O-1 and O-2 petition. As discussed in Volume 1: Chapter Two, "Basic Nonimmigrant Concepts," all documents should be signed in black or blue ink.[758] The following documents should be prepared:

- Cover letter
- Form G-28
- Form I-907, if applicable
- Form I-129
- Supplement O
- Support statement from U.S. company
- Index of exhibits

Although AAO may remand a petition back to USCIS if the denial notice does not provide "adequate notice of the deficiencies in the evidence" or if the petition is denied without an RFE,[759] USCIS may also deny a petition without an RFE if the submitted initial evidence "does not demonstrate eligibility."[760] The client will most

---

[754] *Id.*

[755] 8 CFR §214.2(o)(16); 9 FAM 402.13-12.

[756] 8 CFR §214.2(o)(16).

[757] *Id.*

[758] While USCIS previously advised signing documents in blue ink (*See, e.g.*, "TSC Liaison Minutes" (Aug. 13, 2000), AILA Doc. No. 00090703, in recent years it has more frequently stated a preference for black ink (*See, e.g.*, "Instructions for Notice of Entry of Appearance as Attorney or Accredited Representative" (May 5, 2106), https://www.uscis.gov/sites/default/files/files/form/g-28instr.pdf; "USCIS FY2016 H-1B Webpage Updated" (Mar. 12, 2015), AILA Doc. No. 15031362.) In practice, however, the USCIS mailroom sometimes rejects forms signed in black ink because the signatures are incorrectly concluded to be photocopies, so signing in blue ink can be beneficial despite the USCIS instructions.

[759] *Matter of [name not provided]*, WAC 07 021 53980 (AAO Mar. 11, 2009), http://bit.ly/mar092d.

[760] 8 CFR §103.2(b)(8)(ii).

Copyright © 2017. American Immigration Lawyers Association. All rights reserved.

likely be displeased with the cost and delay of filing an AAO appeal, so the practitioner should provide as many relevant documents as possible in order to present the most comprehensive picture of the beneficiary's extraordinary ability.[761] For example, an initial O-1 petition was denied and appealed, and then a second O-1 petition filed by the same petitioner on behalf of the same beneficiary was approved while the appeal for the first petition was pending.[762] This situation could have been avoided, as well as payment of the filing fees for the appeal and the second petition, by presenting comprehensive evidence when the initial petition was filed.

A. Form G-28

If the petition is being submitted without a request for action on the beneficiary's status, such as a request for change or extension or status, the petition is exclusively that of the employer, and thus the U.S. company's information is what is provided in Questions 5 through 12 on the G-28. If a change or extension of status is also being requested for the beneficiary, and the attorney is also representing the beneficiary, a separate G-28 should be submitted for him or her, and Questions 5 through 12 should be completed with the beneficiary's information on that form.

If there is limited time to prepare and file the petition before the U.S. assignment is to begin, such as if the forms are emailed to and printed by the client, this form may be printed on plain white paper. However, as discussed in Volume 1: Chapter Two, "Basic Nonimmigrant Concepts," the Forms G-28 should be printed on blue paper whenever possible, in order to help the USCIS mailroom easily identify the G-28.

B. Form I-907

If the client wishes a response (approval, denial, or an RFE) within 15 calendar days, then the client may pay USCIS an additional $1,225 for premium processing. This request may be filed concurrently with the O petition, or the attorney or the client may request premium processing after the petition has been filed, by submitting Form I-907 with the petition's receipt notice, as discussed in Volume 1: Chapter Two, "Basic Nonimmigrant Concepts."

C. Form I-129

Part 1: Item 2, "Company or Organization Name," rather than item 1, "Legal Name of Individual Petitioner," should be completed if the petitioner is a business entity. Other information on the U.S. company, including address, contact person, contact person's telephone number and email address, and Federal Employer Identification Number (FEIN), should be provided. If the petitioner uses a residential address as its mailing address, USCIS may question whether a private residence

---

[761] "CSC Liaison Minutes" (Aug. 1, 2000), AILA 00091103 (urging practitioners "to make sure that all supporting documents are includ[ed] at the time of filing the initial petition so that the file is complete").

[762] *Matter of [name not provided]*, WAC 06 214 50193 (AAO Sept. 14, 2007), http://bit.ly/sep0701d.

Copyright © 2017. American Immigration Lawyers Association. All rights reserved.

may serve as the worksite.[763] Thus, the practitioner may wish to confirm whether the petitioner has a business address in addition to the residential address.

Part 2: For most O-1 and O-2 petitions, "New employment" should be checked and consular notification should be requested. As discussed in Volume 1: Chapter Two, "Basic Nonimmigrant Concepts," USCIS should then notify the Kentucky Consular Center (KCC), and the consulate abroad should then be able confirm petition approval when the beneficiary applies for an O visa.

If change of status is nevertheless requested, the practitioner should carefully review the approval notice to ensure that both the O petition and the change of status request were approved, as failure to do so could result in the foreign national accruing unlawful presence.[764] In addition, the expiration date of the foreign national's current status should be calendared, so that a request to extend status may be timely filed. Ideally, the O change of status petition will be approved before the beneficiary's underlying status expires, and premium processing may make this scenario possible. The practitioner may wish to advise clients on the intricacies of situations where the initial status expires before the change of status petition is approved, as discussed in Volume 1: Chapter Two, "Basic Nonimmigrant Concepts." For more information on the eligibility requirements for change of status, accrual on unlawful presence, and filing an extension while a change of status petition is pending, see Volume 1: Chapter Two, "Basic Nonimmigrant Concepts."

Parts 3 and 4: Information about the beneficiary, including name, alternate names, date of birth, country of birth, Social Security number if any, country of birth and country of nationality, and passport information, should be provided.

An individual must have a passport that is valid for at least six months from the petition's expiration date. Otherwise, he or she is inadmissible and ineligible for nonimmigrant status.[765] If the beneficiary does not have such a passport, then the following options are available: (1) either delay filing the O petition until he or she obtains a renewed passport, or (2) file the O petition, have the beneficiary apply for a renewed passport in the interim, wait for an RFE, and then submit a photocopy of the biographic page of the renewed passport once it is available. For nationals of countries where passport renewal takes months, the second strategy can prevent the petition from being significantly delayed. If the client is willing to pay an additional $1,225 fee to USCIS, the delay caused by the RFE, which might also be several months, can be addressed by requesting premium processing when submitting the documentation of the renewed passport.

If the beneficiary is present in the United States when the petition is filed, then the I-94, Arrival/Departure Record, information should be provided, even if he or she

---

[763] *Matter of [name not provided]*, WAC 06 163 50719 (AAO Nov. 15, 2006), http://bit.ly/nov061d (USCIS denial).

[764] "AILA/NSC Meeting Minutes" (July 27, 2006), AILA Doc. No. 06080269.

[765] INA §212(a)(7)(B)(i). The exceptions to this rule in INA §212(a)(d)(4) are discussed in Volume 1: Chapter Two, "Basic Nonimmigrant Concepts."

Copyright © 2017. American Immigration Lawyers Association. All rights reserved.

will depart the United States during pendency of the O petition. In this case, consular notification should be requested in Part 2, as discussed above. However, it is no longer necessary to request cable notification to multiple U.S. consulates if there are multiple O beneficiaries, because consular confirmation of petition approval is electronic through the Petition Information Management Service (PIMS),[766] as discussed below.

Regardless of whether consular notification is requested, the foreign address and consular or port of entry information should be completed, in case USCIS decides that a change or extension of stay is not warranted. If the petition is requesting change or extension of status, and the beneficiary's family is also present in the United States and requesting the same action, answer "yes" to item 5 and submit a Form I-539 for the dependents with the petition.

Parts 5 through 7: Information about the job title, description of proposed job duties, location, compensation, and general information about the petitioner should be provided. The information in Part 6 should be completed for O-1A petitions only. It is not required for O-1B or O-2 petitions. See the discussion in Volume 1: Chapter Two, "Basic Nonimmigrant Concepts," on export control requirements.

The form should be signed by the petitioner's representative and the practitioner. There is some disagreement within the legal community as to whether an attorney who is submitting a G-28 needs to complete and sign this section, as it refers to "preparers" and an attorney provides much more than preparation. However, completing and signing it is the prevalent practice.

D. O and P Supplement

The name of the petitioner and the name of the beneficiary or the number of beneficiaries should be stated, and the appropriate box should be checked for the type of O worker. The petitioner should then briefly summarize the type of event and the duties of the O assignment. For an O-2 petition, any dates of previous employment with the principal O-1 foreign national should be stated. If the answer is "yes" to item 7, USCIS could question whether the O-1 petition is an attempt at self-employment similar to the use of an L-1 petition by a company solely owned by the L-1 beneficiary. The practitioner should therefore fully explain a "yes" answer to this question. Finally, information on the required advisory opinion and peer group, labor organization, or management organization should be provided. If there is no advisory opinion because there is no appropriate organization, then the practitioner may wish to type in a phrase to that effect and to attach the statement(s) from industry experts attesting to the lack of such an organization. An addendum may be included to provide information on additional O-2 beneficiaries.

E. Support Statement

The support statement from the petitioner is very important because it allows the petitioner to frame, address, and connect the issues of the beneficiary's extraordinary

---

[766] "AILA/VSC Liaison Practice Pointer: O and P Visas" (Dec. 23, 2009), AILA Doc. No. 09122335.

Copyright © 2017. American Immigration Lawyers Association. All rights reserved.

ability, the job duties of the proposed assignment, and the qualifying event. The statement may also include a summary of the terms of employment if there is no formal employment contract, and it may explain any acronyms or technical terms used in the testimonials so that the adjudicator understands the scope and practical application of the beneficiary's achievements.

The statement should be on the U.S. company's letterhead and signed by a representative of the U.S. company. One format of a support statement is as follows:

- Introduction;

- Information about the petitioner;

- Discussion of the assignment, including a discussion of why the beneficiary's particular expertise is required and of how the beneficiary's extraordinary ability will be applied to the assignment or performance;

- Discussion of the duties of the assignment, including explanation of technical terms, business objectives to be achieved through the project(s), and estimated financial impact, if applicable;

- Discussion of the foreign national's educational and experience background, including a summary of achievements; and

- Thank you, including mention of remuneration and terms of employment, and conclusion.

One strategy is to weave phrases or sentences from the testimonials or articles in the support statement to highlight the beneficiary's achievements and their potential applicability to the O assignment. The support statement in this way can serve as a "summary" of the O-1 argument, which has been shown to improve the odds of petition approval by making the review easier for the USCIS adjudicator.

For major league baseball players, the support statement may be "bare bones" or even excluded, as "a league letter (which describes the process for establishing the level of competition in the league) has been furnished to Headquarters."[767]

F. Index of Exhibits

Given the large volume of evidence typically necessary for O petitions, the practitioner is strongly advised to prepare an index of exhibits, grouped by the criteria, and tabbed on the bottom: "No particular order is required but an index and tabs make it easier. Tabs should be placed at the bottom. Examiners find it helpful if the evidence follows the regulations and criteria. Unpublished manuscripts are not considered important."[768]

Therefore, the practitioner may find that an index of exhibits helps to demonstrate the beneficiary's eligibility for the O classification, with tabs organized in the order

---

[767] AFM 33.10.

[768] "AILA Liaison/Nebraska Service Center Liaison Teleconference Q&As" (June 25, 2009), AILA Doc. No. 09070864. Although the discussion relates to extraordinary ability immigrant visa petitions, the principle should remain the same.

Copyright © 2017. American Immigration Lawyers Association. All rights reserved.

of the regulations and sub-tabs for each document that addresses the particular criterion. Experience has shown that documents may be copied and included in more than one section. For example, an article discussing how the beneficiary developed a new procedure for blood transfusion could be included in the publications about the beneficiary section and in the original and significant contribution section. The practitioner is strongly encouraged to highlight any places where the beneficiary is mentioned or discussed, in order to ease the adjudicator's task. Practitioners are cautioned against including every possible exhibit with an O-1 petition, or including entire full-length copies of all articles written by the O-1 beneficiary. Including too much documentation can make the petition unwieldy and difficult for the USCIS officer to review.

For major league baseball players, the index of exhibits may be "bare bones" or even excluded, as legacy INS guidance states that "the major league baseball club would not need to submit anything more than the major league contract when filing their petition."[769]

VI. Process

A. The O Petition

After preparing the O petition, it should be filed in duplicate, with original signatures,[770] with the USCIS Service Center with jurisdiction over the place of employment (and not the headquarters of the U.S. company, if different), as discussed in Volume 1: Chapter Two, "Basic Nonimmigrant Concepts." "The practitioner may also find it helpful to write the following in large block letters across the side of the Form I-129: "DUPLICATE PETITION; PLEASE FORWARD TO KCC."

If, however, the O assignment will take place in more than one location, then the O petition should be filed with the Service Center with jurisdiction over the state where the petitioning entity is based.[771] If the petitioner is an agent, the petition is filed with the Service Center with jurisdiction over the place where the agent is based, though USCIS instructions are silent on this point. Since this will be the address on the I-129 form, the case will typically be rejected by the mailroom if another Service Center is chosen. If multiple employers will each file O petitions, then those petitions should be filed with the Service Center with jurisdiction over the place where the services will be provided.[772] However, an established agent may file on behalf of multiple employers, as discussed earlier in this chapter. Again, USCIS instructions are silent as to where the agent should file, but presumably it is the Service Center with jurisdiction over the place where the agent is located.

---

[769] AFM 33.10.

[770] "TSC Liaison Minutes" (Aug. 13, 2000), AILA Doc. No. 00090703.

[771] USCIS, "Direct Filing Addresses for Form I-129, Petition for Nonimmigrant Worker" (updated July 1, 2016), https://www.uscis.gov/i-129-addresses; 9 FAM 402.13-6.

[772] Id.

Copyright © 2017. American Immigration Lawyers Association. All rights reserved.

The second set of original documents will be forwarded to the U.S. consulate where the beneficiary will apply for an O visa as supplementary evidence for PIMS, as discussed in Volume 1: Chapter Two, "Basic Nonimmigrant Concepts."[773] Following approval of an O petition, USCIS forwards approval notification to the KCC, which in turn creates an electronic record to confirm the petition approval,[774] so the information becomes available to a consular officer to verify the petition approval. Although duplicate original documents are not required, preparing and providing them may facilitate the foreign national's visa application in the future.[775]

If certain nonprofit petitioners require approval of the O petition in a short period of time, but do not request premium processing, then expedited processing may be requested, as discussed in Volume 1: Chapter Two, "Basic Nonimmigrant Concepts." The practitioner may write the performance date "on the front of the application in large red letters" and provide an explanation "of why the case could not be filed earlier, to ensure that counsel made a good faith effort to avoid requesting an expedite."[776] Again, as discussed in Volume 1: Chapter Two, "Basic Nonimmigrant Concepts," expedited processing is available only to certain nonprofit organizations.

B. RFEs

The practitioner may wish to prepare the client for the possibility that an RFE will be issued, even if the most comprehensive picture of the beneficiary's eligibility is presented, as legacy INS acknowledged that RFEs may "request information already submitted and/or excessive and irrelevant information,"[777] and multiple anecdotal reports confirm this fact. An RFE should not merely state the qualifying criteria, but should "state specific deficiencies of a filing."[778] Unfortunately, this is not always the case.

C. Visa Application

Upon approval of the O petition, USCIS will send the attorney or representative an approval notice, and the company representative will receive a courtesy copy. The foreign national and any dependents may then apply for a visa at a U.S. consulate abroad. Although consuls have been instructed that they should no longer require the Form I-797 approval notice or a copy of the approved petition,[779] procedures do vary across consulates. Experience has shown that providing detailed instructions on how

---

[773] DOS, "Accessing NIV Petition Information Via the CCD" (Nov. 2007), AILA Doc. No. 08040331; "PIMS Processing Update" (Mar. 21, 2008), AILA Doc. No. 08032132.

[774] "PIMS Update" (Aug. 15, 2008), AILA Doc. No. 08081564; "PIMS Processing Update" (Mar. 21, 2008), AILA Doc. No. 08032132.

[775] "PIMS Processing Update" (Mar. 21, 2008), AILA Doc. No. 08032132.

[776] "CSC Liaison Minutes" (Aug. 1, 2000), AILA 00091103.

[777] Id.

[778] "TSC Approved Minutes" (Aug. 26, 2002), AILA Doc. No. 02112043; "TSC Approved Minutes" (June 3, 2002), AILA Doc. No. 02082742. Although the discussion relates to extraordinary ability immigrant visa petitions, the principle should remain the same.

[779] 9 FAM 402.13-5(B).

Copyright © 2017. American Immigration Lawyers Association. All rights reserved.

to apply for an O visa, including a certified copy of the O-1 or O-2 petition, is frequently very helpful to the employer and the employee.[780] Moreover, the CBP officer will normally want to see the original Form I-797 approval notice as part of the admission process, so it is important that the O-1 beneficiary have the approval notice by the time he or she travels to the United States to enter in O-1 status.

A visa application may be made up to 90 days before the start date of the validity period.[781]

In addition to the general visa application documents discussed in Volume 1: Chapter Two, "Basic Nonimmigrant Concepts," the following documents should be presented, and individual consulates frequently have additional requirements:

- Original Form I-797 approval notice from USCIS;[782]

- Statement from the petitioner confirming that the foreign national continues to provide services in the field of extraordinary ability, if he or she obtained change of status from another nonimmigrant category;

- Certified copy of the O-1 or O-2 petition, to be presented only if specifically requested;

- For an O-2 visa application, evidence of the visa applicant's foreign residence and nonimmigrant intent; and

- For O-3 dependents, evidence of the familial relationship and evidence of financial support from the principal beneficiary, as discussed below, as well as copies of the I-94 card and O visa of the principal beneficiary, especially if the O-3 visa applications are made after the principal beneficiary has already obtained O-1 or O-2 status.[783]

DOS directs consular officers to accept the O-1 approval by USCIS as verified through PIMS or the Person Centric Query Service (PCQS): "Once you have verified approval ... consider this as prima facie evidence that the requirements for O classification...have been met. Other than instances involving obvious errors, consular officers do not have the authority to question the approval of O petitions without specific evidence, unavailable to DHS at the time of petition approval that the beneficiary may not be entitled to status."[784] However, the petition approval "does not relieve the alien of the burden of establishing visa eligibility in the course of which questions may arise as to ... eligibility to O classification."[785] Thus, the consul may request additional evidence that "bears a reasonable relationship" to the

---

[780] Because requirements for visa applications vary among individual consular posts, the practitioner should confirm on the post's website the current procedures required by the particular consulate.

[781] 9 FAM 402.13-8.

[782] 8 CFR §214.2(o)(15).

[783] 9 FAM 402.13-11.

[784] 9 FAM 402.13-5(B).

[785] Id.

Copyright © 2017. American Immigration Lawyers Association. All rights reserved.

issue that arose in the interview, but disagreement with DHS's interpretation of law or facts "is not sufficient reason to ask DHS to reconsider its approval."[786]

The issued O visa should be annotated with the receipt number of the O petition, "followed by the name and location of the alien's employer."[787] If the foreign national is the beneficiary of more than one O petition and "does not plan to depart from the United States between engagements," then DOS "may issue a single O visa valid until the expiration date of the last expiring petition, reciprocity permitting," with annotations for both receipt numbers, as well as names and locations of both O employers.[788] If the visa's validity is limited, such as because of the reciprocity schedules or because of a shorter validity period for a waiver of inadmissibility, then the visa should also be annotated with the following statement: "PETITION VALID TO (Date)."[789] If the reciprocity schedules require that a visa have a validity period that is shorter than the petition validity period, then "consular officers may issue the visa any number of times within the allowable period," although any reciprocity fees must be paid with each visa issuance.[790]

O-3 visas for dependents of O-1 and O-2 principal beneficiaries will be subject to "the same visa validity, period of admission, and limitations as the O-1 or O-2 principal alien."[791] Because O-3 dependents may not engage in employment unless they independently qualify for a work-authorized nonimmigrant status, the consular officer may also "take this into account in evaluating whether family members have furnished adequate evidence of their support while in the United States."[792] However, experience has shown that evidence of the remuneration to be paid to the principal beneficiary is generally sufficient.

D. Admission to the United States

1. Generally

A foreign national may seek admission up to 10 days before the start date of the O-1 or O-2 petition and may remain in the United States for 10 days after the petition expiration, but the nonimmigrant may "engage in employment" only while the petition is valid.[793] O-2 beneficiaries may seek admission to the United States before the O-1 principal in order "to prepare for the event."[794]

When seeking admission to the United States, the foreign national should present his or her passport, with the O-1 or O-2 visa, and the O petition approval notice from

---

[786] *Id.*

[787] 9 FAM 402.13-10(F).

[788] 9 FAM 402.13-10(G).

[789] 9 FAM 402.13-10(H).

[790] 9 FAM 402.13-10(I).

[791] 9 FAM 402.13-11(a).

[792] 9 FAM 402.13-11(b).

[793] 8 CFR §214.2(o)(10).

[794] CBP IFM 15, 14-1 Agency Manuals 15.4..

Copyright © 2017. American Immigration Lawyers Association. All rights reserved.

USCIS.[795] The foreign national should be admitted in O-1 or O-2 status valid until the end date of the petition, as stated on the approval notice. Due to the visa reciprocity schedules,[796] as discussed in Volume 1: Chapter Two, "Basic Nonimmigrant Concepts," a foreign national may receive a visa valid for a shorter time period than the O petition, but the expiration of O-1 or O-2 status should match the end date of the O petition and not the end date of the visa.

For example, citizens of East Timor are eligible for O visas valid for no longer than three months. Therefore, even though the underlying O petition was approved for 36 months, an East Timorian citizen will be able to obtain an O visa that is valid for only 12 months from the date of visa issuance. The Petition Expiration Date (PED) provided in the lower right corner of the visa should, however, match the dates of validity of the O petition as stated on the Form I-797 approval notice, and the visa should be annotated with the petition expiration date also, as discussed above. For applicants for admission with visas valid for a shorter period of time than the O petition, the practitioner may wish to reiterate the need to present the original Form I-797 approval notice to ensure that the period of authorized stay stated on the passport stamp and in the I-94 record matches the dates of the petition validity. The practitioner may also wish to contact clients with these employees well in advance of the visa expiration date to strategize subsequent applications for visas, so the foreign nationals may travel internationally and re-enter the United States during the remaining time of petition validity.

If entering by land, the foreign national will be issued an I-94 card. If entering by sea or air, the individual will receive a stamp in the passport, and the I-94 will be recorded electronically.[797] Practitioners should advise clients who receive the passport stamp rather than the paper I-94 to check their I-94s on the online look-up[798] to ensure that it is correct and that the expiration date of their status is noted.

2. Canadian and Mexican Citizens

As discussed in Volume 1: Chapter Two, "Basic Nonimmigrant Concepts," Canadian citizens do not require visas in order to enter the United States.[799] Canadian nationals may apply for admission with the O-1 or O-2 approval notice and Canadian passport at the port of entry.[800] For a more in-depth discussion of applications for admission in nonimmigrant status by Canadian citizens, see Volume 1: Chapter Two, "Basic Nonimmigrant Concepts."

---

[795] 8 CFR §214.2(o)(15); CBP IFM 15, 14-1 Agency Manuals 15.4.

[796] The Visa Reciprocity Tables, searchable by country, are available at https://travel.state.gov/content/visas/en/fees/reciprocity-by-country.html.

[797] 78 Fed. Reg. 18457 (Mar. 27, 2013). *See also* CBP Fact Sheet, "I-94 Automation" (Nov. 2015), https://www.cbp.gov/sites/default/files/assets/documents/2016-Mar/i-94-automation-fact-sheet.pdf.

[798] CBP, "I-94 Website," https://i94.cbp.dhs.gov/I94/#/home.

[799] 1 legacy INS Examinations Handbook, Part V, 15-1, 1 legacy INS IFM ch. 15 Nonimmigrants and Border Crossers, 14-1 INS Manuals 15.4.

[800] 8 CFR §214.2(o)(15).

Copyright © 2017. American Immigration Lawyers Association. All rights reserved.

Mexican citizens are now eligible for O visas valid for up to 12 months;[801] formerly, the reciprocity schedule limited O visas to six months of validity.[802] Unfortunately, Mexican citizens applying for O visas may not obtain visas valid for up to three years by paying the reciprocity fee of $100 for each year of visa validity, as was previously the case.[803]

VII. Additional Follow-Up

After a foreign national has obtained O status, the practitioner should follow up to request copies of the I-94 records and the visas, if applicable, to ensure that all the information is correct and calendar the expiration dates to monitor the foreign national's status, as discussed in Volume 1: Chapter Two, "Basic Nonimmigrant Concepts."

O-3 dependents may attend school while accompanying the principal O-1 or O-2 beneficiary to the United States,[804] whether full– or part-time.[805]

A. Extensions

If the foreign national's services are required after the expiration of the approved petition, "in order to continue or complete the same activities or events specified in the original petition," an O-1 and/or O-2 extension application may be filed, with documents similar to those necessary for the initial O petition, as long as the initial O petition remains valid.[806] An extension may be granted to allow the beneficiary to "complete the activities described in the original petition and to extend the original petition where it did not include certain engagements," although "[p]etition extensions to cover additional performances or engagements must merit the services of an O-1 caliber individual."[807]

The beneficiary should be physically present in the United States when the extension application is filed; if the foreign national must depart the United States for personal or business reasons while the extension is pending, then "the petitioner may request the Director to cable notification of approval of the petition extension to the consular office abroad where the alien will apply for a visa."[808] O extensions may be

---

[801] DOS, "Mexico Reciprocity Schedule," https://travel.state.gov/content/visas/en/fees/reciprocity-by-country/MX.html.

[802] Former DOS website, "Mexico Reciprocity Schedule," formerly available at http://travel.state.gov/visa/frvi/reciprocity/reciprocity_3622.html#B (link no longer works).

[803] DOS, "Mexico Reciprocity Schedule," https://travel.state.gov/content/visas/en/fees/reciprocity-by-country/MX.html. *Cf.* former DOS website, "Mexico Reciprocity Schedule," formerly available at http://travel.state.gov/visa/frvi/reciprocity/reciprocity_3622.html#B (link no longer works).

[804] 9 FAM 402.13-11; 1 CBP IFM ch. 15, 14-1 Agency Manuals 15.4.

[805] USCIS, "O-1 Visa: Individuals with Extraordinary Ability or Achievement" (updated Sept. 14, 2015), http://bit.ly/2cCoXRa.

[806] 8 CFR §214.2(o)(11).

[807] USCIS Office of Business Liaison, Employer Information Bulletin 15, "Aliens with Extraordinary Ability (O-1) and Accompanying/Assisting Aliens (O-2)" (Dec. 8, 2004), 82 Interpreter Releases 180–84 (Jan. 17, 2005).

[808] 8 CFR §214.2(o)(12)(i).

Copyright © 2017. American Immigration Lawyers Association. All rights reserved.

granted in yearly increments, "plus an additional 10 days to allow the beneficiary to get his or her personal affairs in order."[809]

The application should be "accompanied by a statement explaining the reasons for the extension."[810] Importantly, the practitioner should note that, despite the regulation text, which states that "[s]upporting documents are not required unless requested by the Director,"[811] multiple anecdotal reports indicate that USCIS has been issuing RFEs for O extensions, requesting essentially the same index of supporting documents that were necessary for the initial O petition. There has also been a history of denials of O-1 extensions,[812] and the AAO states that neither USCIS nor the AAO are bound by previous approval of an O-1 petition filed by the same petitioner on behalf of the same beneficiary:[813] "The prior approvals do not preclude USCIS from denying an extension of the original visa based on reassessment of petitioner's [or beneficiary's] qualifications."[814] Therefore, the practitioner may wish to avoid the delay of an RFE by submitting the extensive documents, including recent evidence available since the initial petition was filed,[815] with the extension filing. Legacy INS had taken the view that a new advisory opinion should not be necessary,[816] but it does not appear that USCIS still holds that position.[817]

Alternatively, instead of filing three yearly extensions, the practitioner and client may wish to discuss whether it is more cost-effective and efficient to file another new O petition requesting a validity period of three years. This option is available as long as the O petitions are filed either by a new employer or by the same employer but

---

[809] 8 CFR §214.2(o)(12)(ii).

[810] 8 CFR §214.2(o)(12)(i).

[811] 8 CFR §214.2(o)(11).

[812] *Matter of [name not provided]*, SRC 02 202 54837 (AAO Nov. 3, 2003), 28 Immig. Rptr. B2-84 (USCIS denial); *Matter of [name not provided]*, WAC 02 238 54702 (AAO Feb. 27, 2003), 27 Immig. Rptr. B2-35 (USCIS denial); *Matter of [name not provided]*, SRC 03 059 50346 (AAO Apr. 13, 2005), http://bit.ly/apr052d.

[813] *Matter of [name not provided]*, WAC 07 015 50561 (AAO Nov. 7, 2007), http://bit.ly/nov072d (citing *Matter of Church Scientology International*, 19 I&N Dec. 593 (Comm'r 1988); *Sussex Engg. Ltd. v. Montgomery*, 825 F.2d 1084 (6th Cir. 1987), *cert. denied*, 485 U.S. 1008 (1988) (stating that an agency is not bound by "acknowledged errors"); and *Texas A&M Univ. v. Upchurch*, 99 Fed. Appx. 556, 2004 WL 1240482 (5th Cir. 2004)); *Matter of [name not provided]*, LIN 04 143 53690 (AAO Aug. 17, 2005), http://bit.ly/aug0501d; *Matter of [name not provided]*, WAC 02 038 51106 (AAO May 24, 2005), http://bit.ly/may051d8.

[814] *Matter of [name not provided]*, LIN 04 131 54595 (AAO Aug. 16, 2005), *available at www.uscis.gov* (select "Laws," "Administrative Decisions" link on the right toolbar under "More Information," D8, and then search by date and for "01D8101") (citing *Texas A&M Univ. v. Upchurch*, 99 Fed. Appx. 556, 2004 WL 1240482 (5th Cir. 2004)).

[815] *Cf. Matter of [name not provided]*, WAC 07 015 50561 (AAO Nov. 7, 2007), *available at www.uscis.gov* (select "Laws," "Administrative Decisions" link on the right toolbar under "More Information," D8, and then search by date and for "02D8101") (the AAO "note[d] that much of the evidence of record is several years old, duplicated from an ealier petition filed on the beneficiary's behalf").

[816] Legacy INS, J. Bednarz (Sept. 29, 1992), 69 Interpreter Releases 1471–72 (Nov. 16, 1992).

[817] *Matter of [name and case number not provided]* (AAO Mar. 11, 2011), http://bit.ly/mar111d.

Copyright © 2017. American Immigration Lawyers Association. All rights reserved.

"for a new event or activity."[818] Although a new advisory opinion will be necessary, both the practitioner and the client may agree that the delay in obtaining this document is far outweighed by the cost and resource savings of not having to pay for or prepare two extension applications.

The O extension may be necessary if the foreign national entered the United States later than originally anticipated, or if the initial O petition was approved after the requested start date. The support statement should clearly explain why the extension is necessary and include details on the remaining activities or events, if applicable.

B. Amended and Change of Employer Petitions

A change of employer may be filed if the O-1 beneficiary wishes to be employed by an entity other than the one named on the initial O-1 petition:[819] "The new petitioner/employer cannot step into the shoes of the prior petitioner/employer to request an extension of the validity of the previously approved petition. As a new employer, the petitioner must file its own petition."[820] If the petition is erroneously denied because the event is not a continuation, then an appeal may be filed, although the same standard will be applied to determine if there is a qualifying event or events,[821] as discussed above.

A change of employer petition for an O-2 beneficiary may be filed "only in conjunction with a change of employers by the principal O-1 alien."[822] If an agent will file the change of employer petition, then "evidence relating to the new employer" must be provided.[823]

An amended O petition is appropriate and necessary if there are "any material changes in the terms and conditions of employment or the beneficiary's eligibility as specified in the original approved petition."[824] An amended petition is not necessary, however, if the beneficiary is an artist or entertainer and the employer wishes to "add additional performances or engagements during the validity period of the petition," as long as the added events "require an alien of O-1 caliber."[825] Similarly, if the O-1 nonimmigrant is promoted "to a higher level position within an organization," an amended petition should not be required, because the promotion should not "constitute[] a material change in the terms and conditions of the alien's

---

[818] "ISD Liaison Teleconference" (Oct. 3, 2002), AILA Doc. No. 02110470; *Matter of [name not provided]*, WAC 02 238 54702 (AAO Feb. 27, 2003), 27 Immig. Rptr. B2-35 (new employer and new activities of promotion of a film and post-production services, although counsel for the petitioner mischaracterized the petition as an extension).

[819] 8 CFR §214.2(o)(2)(iv)(C).

[820] *Matter of [name not provided]*, LIN 04 131 54595 (AAO Aug. 16, 2005), http://bit.ly/aug051d.

[821] *Matter of [name not provided]*, WAC 01 250 52367 (AAO Aug. 4, 2002), 26 Immig. Rptr. B2-87.

[822] 8 CFR §214.2(o)(2)(iv)(C); 9 FAM 402.13-6.

[823] *Id.*

[824] 8 CFR §214.2(o)(2)(iv)(D).

[825] *Id.*

Copyright © 2017. American Immigration Lawyers Association. All rights reserved.

employment," "provided that the requirements of the new position are related to the former position."[826]

If there are "any changes in the terms and conditions of employment of a beneficiary which may affect eligibility" for O status, but "the petitioner no longer employs the beneficiary, the petitioner shall send a letter explaining the change(s) to the Director who approved the petition" and no amended petition is necessary.[827]

There is additional flexibility for a "professional O-1 athlete who is traded from one organization to another organization."[828] After such a trade, "employment authorization for the player will automatically continue for a period of 30 days after acquisition by the new organization."[829] The regulations were revised to "codify [legacy INS's] longstanding policy" because "a single athlete can have a significant impact on a team's performance."[830] The flexibility is not limited to "'U.S.-based' organizations" and applies to "a minor league affiliate in the United States of a foreign major league franchise."[831]

The new organization "is expected to file" an O-1 change of employer petition during this 30-day period. As long as the new petition is filed, the O-1 athlete may be employed by the new organization. "[T]he professional athlete shall be deemed to be in valid O-1 status, and employment shall continue to be authorized, until the petition is adjudicated."[832] The employment authorization will terminate, however, if the new petition is not filed or if the O-1 change of employer petition is denied.[833]

C. If Employment Ceases

O-1 nonimmigrants whose employment ends prior to the expiration of their authorized stay are able to remain in the United States lawfully for the shorter of 60 days or when the existing validity period ends.[834] This can be used only once during each "authorized validity period." The purpose is to allow the beneficiary to wind up affairs or to seek other employment and request a change of status if needed and eligible.[835] The individual is not able to work during this period, unless otherwise authorized.[836]

---

[826] Legacy INS, J. Brown (Oct. 14, 1997), 75 Interpreter Releases 155 (Jan. 26, 1998) (promotion from Senior Vice President to President).

[827] 8 CFR §214.2(o)(8)(i)(A).

[828] 8 CFR §214.2(o)(2)(iv)(G).

[829] Id.

[830] 72 Fed. Reg. 18508 (Apr. 16, 1997).

[831] Id.

[832] 8 CFR §214.2(o)(2)(iv)(G).

[833] Id.

[834] 8 CFR §214.1(l)(ii).

[835] 80 Fed. Reg. 81923 (Dec. 31, 2015).

[836] Id.

Copyright © 2017. American Immigration Lawyers Association. All rights reserved.

D. Sponsoring an O-1 Beneficiary for Permanent Residence

As noted above, neither the statute nor the regulations prohibit O-1 nonimmigrants from pursuing permanent residence while holding nonimmigrant status. USCIS guidance also indicates that an employment-based, first preference immigrant visa petition is typically appropriate for O-1 nonimmigrants: "Generally, aliens who qualify for O-1 classification will also meet the standards for employment-based permanent residence in the U.S. under the first preference."[837] However, the practitioner should note that the O-1 regulations "mirror" the immigrant visa petition regulations "only in the instance of an alien of extraordinary ability in the fields of science, education, business, or athletics."[838]

It is possible for an EB-1 immigrant visa petition to be approved even when an O-1 petition is denied,[839] but, as a practical matter, the immigrant visa petition may be strengthened if the beneficiary already holds O-1 status: "While a prior approval for the alien in O1 … nonimmigrant status helps support an E11 … approval, it is not dispositive."[840] However, merely holding current O-1 status does not guarantee approval of the immigrant visa petition for the extraordinary ability classification.[841] The practitioner is therefore advised to provide as much updated and independent evidence of the foreign national's eligibility for the extraordinary ability immigrant visa classification as possible:

"Generally, adjudicators are to take notice of a beneficiary's current or prior O-1 nonimmigrant status (in science, education, business or athletics), but are otherwise instructed to adjudicate the I-140 based on the evidence filed with it (Sec. 291 of the Act; 8 CFR 103.2(b)(1)). Also note that the I-140 filing must contain its own documentation. We cannot incorporate the prior nonimmigrant case file into the I-140 case file. Another important consideration is that the beneficiary must meet eligibility criteria AT THE TIME OF FILING, so evidence that s/he met the criteria some time prior must be accompanied by evidence that s/he continues to do so.…

"[A]n adjudicator would have no way of knowing what was claimed or what evidence was submitted in any earlier proceeding. Moreover, the statute itself at Sec. 203(b)(A)(i) requires 'extensive documentation' and adjudicators cannot grant the requested immigrant benefit absent such documentation.

"Even assuming identical evidence, a Form I-140 adjudicator could conclude that the prior approval was erroneous (consistent with HQ guidance of April 23, 2004, regarding extensions of nonimmigrant classifications) and find the I-140 deniable.

---

[837] USCIS Office of Business Liaison, Employer Information Bulletin 15, "Aliens with Extraordinary Ability (O-1) and Accompanying/Assisting Aliens (O-2)" (Dec. 8, 2004), 82 Interpreter Releases 180–84 (Jan. 17, 2005).

[838] "VSC Liaison Minutes" (Nov. 10, 1999), AILA Doc. No. 99120171.

[839] *Matter of [name not provided]*, SRC 06 116 53293 (AAO Nov. 3, 2008), http://bit.ly/nov081d.

[840] "VSC Liaison Minutes" (Nov. 10, 1999), AILA Doc. No. 99120171.

[841] *Matter of [name not provided]*, LIN 05 262 51156 (AAO Nov. 7, 2007), http://bit.ly/nov073d.

Copyright © 2017. American Immigration Lawyers Association. All rights reserved.

"Finally, regarding 'established facts,' it often happens that Form I-140 adjudicators do not face the same facts as presented in the initial nonimmigrant petition. An example is that of a nonimmigrant worker who, for whatever reason, did not continue to receive acclaim in the field in the years following admission into the U.S. In other words, a Form I-140 adjudicator often faces new additional facts that may or may not be favorable to the beneficiary."[842]

For a further discussion of this topic, see Volume 2: Chapter Three, "The Immigrant Visa Petition."

Employment-based sponsorship for permanent residence on behalf of O-2 nonimmigrants, however, is extremely difficult, because of the requirement that the O-2 nonimmigrant provide essential support to an O-1 principal. In addition, the aggregate processing time for approval of the labor certification application, approval of the immigrant visa petition, and availability of an immigrant visa number are highly likely to be more than two years.[843] Typically, the foreign national will not be eligible for EB-2 classification because holding a master's degree or having five years of post-baccalaureate experience are not common requirements for a position that entails supporting an athlete, artist, or entertainer. The delays in immigrant visa availability for the EB-3 classification will most likely mean that the foreign national will be unable to apply to adjust status before expiration of the O-2 maximum time limitation.[844]

It may be possible to request consular processing, so the foreign national may remain outside the United States and pursue a career abroad while awaiting issuance of an immigrant visa. The practitioner should counsel the client, however, that the lengthy processing time may mean that the foreign national is unable to obtain an immigrant visa in time for the planned event and that the foreign national would be unable to obtain an O-2 visa in the interim.[845] For a discussion of how to differentiate nonimmigrant intent for the U.S. visit and the pursuance of permanent residence, see Volume 1: Chapter Three, "Visitors: B Visas and Status and the Visa Waiver Program."

---

[842] "NSC Teleconference Q&As on Business Product Line" (Apr. 27, 2006), AILA Doc. No. 06050510 (emphasis in original).

[843] For an overview of the permanent residence process, see Volume 2: Chapter Two, "The Labor Certification Application"; Volume 2: Chapter Three, "The Immigrant Visa Petition"; and Volume 2: Chapter Four, "Consular Processing, Adjustment of Status, and Permanent Residence Issues."

[844] For a discussion of the immigrant visa petition classifications and visa retrogression, see Volume 2: Chapter Three, "The Immigrant Visa Petition."

[845] 9 FAM 402.13-10(B).

Copyright © 2017. American Immigration Lawyers Association. All rights reserved.

CHAPTER THIRTEEN

P VISAS AND STATUS

I. Executive Summary

The P classification is generally for athletes and entertainment groups. P-1 status allows foreign nationals who have earned international recognition to visit the United States temporarily to compete in an athletic event, either individually or as part of a team. P-1 status is also available for entertainment groups who will perform in the United States. P-2 status is appropriate for reciprocal exchange entertainment groups. P-3 status is available for entertainment groups who provide culturally unique performances. P-1, P-2, and P-3 status is also available for essential support personnel accompanying the P principal to assist with athletic events or entertainment performances. Spouses and dependent children of P nonimmigrants are eligible for P-4 status in the United States and are ineligible to apply for work authorization.

A P-1 petition on behalf of an individual athlete may be approved for up to five years; the athlete is eligible for another extension of five years, and there is a lifetime maximum of 10 years. P-1 petitions on behalf of athletic teams and entertainment groups, P-2 petitions, P-3 petitions, and petitions on behalf of essential support personnel may be approved for the time period necessary to complete the event or for one year, whichever is less. Extensions may be granted for longer-term events or performances. There is currently no annual limit on P visa numbers.

A. Checklist of General Requirements

- Competition, performance, or event requiring the foreign national's athletic or entertainment participation
- P-1: independent evidence of the foreign national's international recognition
- P-2: reciprocal exchange agreement
- P-3: culturally unique performance
- Advisory opinion from a labor organization
- Employment contract
- Itinerary or schedule of activities

B. Documents Necessary to Prepare the Petition

- Basic information about the employer
- Description of the competition, performance, or event
- Copy of employment contract
- Independent evidence of the foreign national's international recognition
- Information from the foreign national regarding his or her accomplishments
- Copy of foreign national's résumé or other summary of achievements
- Copies of the foreign national's educational degrees and/or transcripts

Copyright © 2017. American Immigration Lawyers Association. All rights reserved.

- Copy of biographic page(s) of passport(s) of the foreign national and any dependent spouse and children

C. Checklist of General Questions to Ask the Client

- What is the nature of the competition, performance, or event in the United States?
- For P-1 petitions, can the foreign national demonstrate, through independent evidence and testimonials, international recognition?
- For P-1 petitions, does the foreign national meet the minimum number of criteria of the list for his or her field of endeavor (attach list of criteria for athletes or performance groups)?
- Have at least 75 percent of the P-1 entertainment group's members performed with the group for at least one year?
- Will the P principals require essential support personnel?
- Will the petitioner be the only employer?
- Is the petitioner an agent or a sponsoring organization?
- Is there a labor dispute at the worksite of the proposed P assignment?

II. Introduction

The P-1 classification is appropriate for a foreign national who is a professional athlete or performer in an entertainment group, as long as certain conditions are satisfied,[1] or for essential support personnel,[2] as discussed below. Artists and entertainers, whether performing individually or as part of a group, may obtain P-2 status, and the performance may be through "a reciprocal exchange program" between organizations in the United States and abroad,[3] as discussed below. P-2 status is also available for individuals who will provide essential support, as "an integral part of the performance of such a group."[4] P-3 status is appropriate for artists and entertainers, whether performing individually or as part of a group, who will perform, coach, or teach "under a commercial or noncommercial program that is culturally unique,"[5] and for essential support personnel who are "an integral part of the performance of such a group," as discussed below. There is no numerical limitation on P visas.[6]

Multiple beneficiaries may be named for P-1 petitions for athletes;[7] for P-1, P-2, and P-3 petitions for "members of a group seeking classification based on the

---

[1] Immigration and Nationality Act (INA) §101(a)(15)(P)(i).

[2] 8 Code of Federal Regulations (CFR) §214.2(p)(1)(ii)(A)(2).

[3] INA §101(a)(15)(P)(ii).

[4] Id.

[5] INA §101(a)(15)(P)(iii).

[6] Miscellaneous and Technical Immigration and Naturalization Amendments of 1991 (MTINA), §202(a)(3), Pub. L. No. 102-232, 105 Stat. 1737, eliminating previous annual limitation of 25,000 in former INA §214(g)(1)(C).

[7] INA §214(c)(4)(G).

Copyright © 2017. American Immigration Lawyers Association. All rights reserved.

reputation of the group as an entity"; and for foreign nationals who "will provide essential support to P-1, P-2, or P-3 beneficiaries performing in the same location and in the same occupation."[8] Any P petition for essential support personnel must be filed separately from the petition for the principal P beneficiary.[9] All beneficiaries must be named on the P petition.[10] Substitution of beneficiaries for groups is permitted,[11] as discussed below.

The petition may be filed by a U.S. employer, a U.S. agent, a foreign employer through a U.S. agent, a U.S. sponsoring organization, or the U.S. labor organization that negotiated the P-2 reciprocal exchange agreement. If the beneficiary will "work in more than one location," the petition "must include an itinerary with the dates and locations of the performances."[12]

Petitions for P status must be filed with and approved by U.S. Citizenship and Immigration Services (USCIS), "even in emergency situations," although the petition may be filed up to one year before the date of need.[13] Even USCIS acknowledged that the rule would allow petitioners to "be better assured that they will receive a decision on their petitions in a timeframe that will allow them to secure the services of the O or P nonimmigrant when such services are needed."[14] Although a Notice of Proposed Rulemaking (NPRM) suggested revising the regulations to require filing of a P petition at least six months in advance of the date of need, USCIS declined to adopt that proposed rule after numerous comments from industry insiders about the difficulty in identifying the beneficiary six months in advance, the rarity of making an employment offer six months before a start date, and the common delays in negotiating an employment contract.[15]

Dependents of principal P nonimmigrants hold P-4 status,[16] "subject to the same period of admission and limitations as the alien beneficiary," and may not "accept employment."[17]

---

[8] 8 CFR §214.2(p)(2)(iv)(F).

[9] 8 CFR §214.2(p)(2)(i); 9 Foreign Affairs Manual (FAM) 402.14-7(A); USCIS, "2003 CSC Guidelines," (Feb. 6, 2003), AILA Doc. No. 03040440; *Matter of [name not provided]*, EAC 08 054 51251 (AAO May 1, 2009), http://bit.ly/may093d.

[10] 8 CFR §214.2(p)(2)(iv)(G); 9 Foreign Affairs Manual (FAM) 402.14-7(F).

[11] 8 CFR §214.2(p)(2)(iv)(H); 9 FAM 402.14-7(F).

[12] 8 CFR §214.2(p)(2)(iv)(A).

[13] 8 CFR §214.2(p)(2)(i); 72 Fed. Reg. 18856 (Apr. 16, 2007).

[14] 72 Fed. Reg. 18856 (Apr. 16, 2007).

[15] *Id.*

[16] INA §101(a)(15)(P)(iv); 8 CFR §214.2(p)(8)(iii)(D).

[17] 8 CFR §214.2(p)(8)(iii)(D).

Copyright © 2017. American Immigration Lawyers Association. All rights reserved.

III. Requirements and Definitions

A. Competition, Performance, or Event of the P Assignment

The beneficiary's purpose in entering the United States must be to participate in a competition, performance, tour, or event, and the duration may be longer term:

"Competition, event, or performance means an activity such as an athletic competition, athletic season, tournament, tour, exhibit, project, entertainment event, or engagement. Such activity could include short vacations, promotional appearances for the petitioning employer relating to the competition, event, or performance, and stopovers which are incidental and/or related to the activity. An athletic competition or entertainment event could include an entire season of performances. A group of related activities will also be considered an event. In the case of a P-2 petition, the event may be the duration of the reciprocal exchange agreement. In the case of a P-1 athlete, the event may be the duration of the alien's contract."[18]

Generally, the duration of the P assignment will be governed by the contract, especially for athletes.[19] For purposes of the P nonimmigrant classification, "contract" is defined as "the written agreement between the petitioner and the beneficiary(ies) that explains the terms and conditions of employment."[20] Every contract must "describe the services to be performed, and specify the wages, hours of work, working conditions, and any fringe benefits."[21] Despite the flexibility of the regulations, the term "event" has nevertheless been interpreted by the Administrative Appeals Office (AAO) "as a finite period, rather than as employment of indefinite (permanent) duration."[22] The start and end dates of the assignment or event should be stated on the petition and substantiated by independent evidence, such as an itinerary or signed contracts for performances by the beneficiary during the stated time period.[23] A petition may be denied if the duties stated in the contract are inappropriate for the P classification.[24]

---

[18] 8 CFR §214.2(p)(3).

[19] Adjudicator's Field Manual (AFM) 33.10; *Matter of [name not provided]*, LIN 04 175 51125 (AAO June 13, 2005), http://bit.ly/jan061d9.

[20] 8 CFR §214.2(p)(3).

[21] *Id.*

[22] *Matter of [name not provided]*, WAC 04 010 50133 (AAO Jan. 10, 2006), http://bit.ly/jan061d9 (beneficiaries had held P-3 status for at least five years).

[23] *Matter of [name not provided]*, WAC 07 038 50648 (AAO Oct. 27, 2008), http://bit.ly/oct081d (noting that "[m]erely stating an intent to 'manage' a professional boxer for an unspecified period of time is not sufficient to satisfy the ... requirements"); *Matter of [name not provided]*, WAC 05 076 51609 (AAO Mar 8, 2006), http://bit.ly/mar0601d; *Matter of [name not provided]*, EAC 05 146 50600 (AAO Mar. 1, 2006), http://bit.ly/mar061d9.

[24] *Matter of [name not provided]*, LIN 92 172 50725 (AAU Apr. 30, 1993), 11 Immig. Rptr. B2-64 (petition for athlete denied where the contract described competitive events but also promotional activities for the petitioner's water ski products).

Copyright © 2017. American Immigration Lawyers Association. All rights reserved.

P-1 athletes may not use the P classification "solely to make guest appearances or to give camps,"[25] unless these activities are specifically included in the broader contract.[26] Similarly, P status is not appropriate solely for promotional and non-performing guest appearances, although these activities are permissible if they are "related to an actual event in which [the beneficiaries] are going to perform in the United States."[27]

The regulations require that P-1 athletes and entertainment groups be coming to the United States to "perform services which require an internationally recognized" athlete, team, or entertainment group.[28] The statute does not contain such a requirement, specifying only that the P-1 possess such international recognition and that the individual be coming for a specific event or competition.[29] Contrast this with the position long taken by USCIS, and legacy Immigration and Naturalization Service (INS) before it, that it is not mandatory that an O-1 assignment require an individual with extraordinary ability.[30] The statute there also does not specify that the event must require extraordinary ability, but rather only that the nonimmigrant be coming to continue work in the area of his or her extraordinary ability.[31]

An approved P-1 petition for an individual athlete may be valid for up to five years.[32] Petitions for P-1 athletic teams, P-1 entertainers or entertainment groups, P-2 and P-3 nonimmigrants, and essential support personnel may be valid for the period of time determined by USCIS to be necessary to complete the U.S. competition, performance, activity, or event, or for one year, whichever is less.[33] Although not explicitly stated in the regulations, it seems highly likely that the validity period of an

---

[25] Legacy Immigration and Naturalization Service (INS), L. Weinig, "Policy Guidelines for the Adjudication of O and P Petitions" (June 25, 1992), 69 Interpreter Releases 1084 (Aug. 31, 1992); AFM 33.10.

[26] AFM 33.10 (indicating that baseball players may participate in off-season camps if these activities are described in the contract).

[27] Legacy INS, L. Weinig, "Policy Guidelines for the Adjudication of O and P Petitions," (June 25, 1992), 69 Interpreter Releases 1084 (Aug. 31, 1992).

[28] 8 CFR §214.2(p)(4)(i). See also Matter of F-F-S-, LLC, ID# 126527 (AAO Sept. 26, 2016) (competition does not necessarily require international recognition just because it is open to competitors from different countries); Matter of R-S-T-A-, ID# 18220 (AAO Aug 30, 2016); Matter of T-L-A-, ID# 11763 (AAO Dec. 30, 2015).

[29] INA §§214(c)(4)(A) and 101(a)(15)(p).

[30] USCIS Office of Business Liaison, Employer Information Bulletin 15, "Aliens with Extraordinary Ability (O-1) and Accompanying/Assisting Aliens (O-2)" (Dec. 8, 2004), 82 Interpreter Releases 180–84 (Jan. 17, 2005) (stating that the "O-1 nonimmigrant may be admitted even if the work to be performed in the United States does not require a person of extraordinary ability or achievement"); AFM 33.4 (stating that "[i]n support of all O-1 petitions, the petitioner must establish that the beneficiary has met the standards or demonstrated that he or she possesses sustained national or international acclaim and recognition in his or her particular field and that the alien is coming to work in that field (but not necessarily that the particular duties to be performed require someone of such extraordinary ability)"). See Volume 1, Chapter 12: "O Visas and Status," for a more detailed discussion.

[31] INA §101(a)(15)(o).

[32] 8 CFR §214.2(p)(8)(iii)(A).

[33] INA §214(a)(2)(B); 8 CFR §§214.2(p)(8)(iii)(A), (B), (C), and (E).

Copyright © 2017. American Immigration Lawyers Association. All rights reserved.

approved P petition for essential support personnel should coincide with the petition approval dates for the principal P nonimmigrant.[34]

If the petitioner requests petition validity that exceeds these limitations, then the "petition shall be approved only up to the limit."[35] If the itinerary or schedule of activities submitted with the petition "only depict[s] a limited amount of time," rather than covering the entire time period requested by the petitioner, the petition may be approved for a shorter period of time that is supported by the itinerary.[36]

If the P-1 petition is approved before the start date of the assignment, performance, competition, or event, then the petition will be valid for the "actual dates requested by the petitioner."[37] If the start date stated on the petition has already occurred by the time the petition is approved, then the petition will be valid from the date of approval to the end date requested by the petitioner.[38]

B. P Petitioners

A P-1 petition may be filed by a U.S. employer, a U.S. sponsoring organization, a U.S. agent, or a foreign employer through a U.S. agent.[39] A P-2 petition may be filed by a U.S. employer, the U.S. "labor organization which negotiated the reciprocal exchange agreement," or the sponsoring organization.[40] A P-3 petition may be filed by a U.S. employer or the sponsoring organization.[41]

If the beneficiary "will work concurrently for more than one employer within the same time period," then separate petitions must be filed by each employer.[42] Alternatively, "an established agent" may file a single petition on behalf of the employers,[43] as discussed below. If, however, the petitioner files the petition as the single employer and the beneficiary accepts employment with other entities, then the beneficiary may be deemed to have violated his or her immigration status.[44]

A U.S. employer should be established as a business or other legal entity, have an official business address, and have a business license or proof of doing business in

---

[34] 8 CFR §214.2(o)(6)(iii)(B) (discussing validity period of essential support personnel in O-2 status).

[35] 8 CFR §214.2(p)(8)(ii)(C).

[36] "NSC Liaison Questions & Answers" (Nov. 11, 1999), AILA Doc. No. 99111672; *Matter of [name not provided]*, EAC 08 054 51251 (AAO May 1, 2009), http://bit.ly/may093d (USCIS RFE).

[37] 8 CFR §214.2(p)(8)(ii)(A).

[38] 8 CFR §214.2(p)(8)(ii)(B).

[39] 8 CFR §214.2(p)(2)(i).

[40] *Id.*

[41] *Id.*

[42] 8 CFR §214.2(p)(2)(iv)(B); *Matter of [name not provided]*, SRC 05 800 32163 (AAO Apr. 28, 2009), http://bit.ly/apr0901d.

[43] 8 CFR §214.2(p)(2)(iv)(B).

[44] *Matter of [name not provided]*, EAC 03 207 50044 (AAO Aug. 17, 2005), http://bit.ly/aug052d9.

Copyright © 2017. American Immigration Lawyers Association. All rights reserved.

the United States.[45] A U.S. sponsoring organization is the same as a sponsor,[46] which is defined as "an established organization in the United States which will not directly employ a P-1, P-2, or P-3 alien but will assume responsibility for the accuracy of the terms and conditions specified in the petition."[47] If the petitioner will directly employ the beneficiary, the petitioner may not file as a sponsoring organization.[48] The practitioner is encouraged to submit "evidence, such as a written contract between [the sponsoring organization] and the beneficiary ... guarantee[ing] the terms and conditions of employment of the beneficiary."[49]

A foreign employer, which is defined as "any employer who is not amenable to service of process in the United States," may not petition directly for a P-1 nonimmigrant "but instead must use the services of a United States agent."[50] The U.S. agent in turn "must be authorized to file the petition, and to accept services of process in the United States in proceedings ... on behalf of the foreign employer."[51] Even if an agent files the P-1 petition on behalf of a foreign employer, the foreign employer is nevertheless, through the U.S. agent,[52] "responsible for complying with all of the employer sanctions provisions" regarding verifying the identity and employment authorization of workers in the United States.[53]

1. Agent-Petitioners

A U.S. agent may file a P-1 petition on behalf of "workers who are traditionally self-employed or workers who use agents to arrange short-term employment on their behalf with numerous employers,"[54] as well as on behalf of a foreign employer.[55] A U.S. agent may be one of the following:

- The "actual employer" of the foreign national;
- A "representative of both the employer and the beneficiary"; or
- A "person or entity" who has authorization from the employer "to act for, or in place of the employer as its agent."[56]
- Any petition filed by a U.S. agent must meet certain conditions. First:

---

[45] *Matter of [name not provided]*, WAC 07 236 52246 (AAO Feb. 18, 2009), http://bit.ly/feb091d (USCIS revocation; company administratively dissolved by the state of Arizona). Although the case addresses U.S. employers for O-1 petitions, the principle should remain the same.

[46] 8 CFR §214.2(p)(1)(i).

[47] 8 CFR §214.2(p)(3).

[48] USCIS, D. Neufeld, "Requirements for Agents and Sponsors Filing as Petitioners for the O and P Visa Classifications" (Nov. 20, 2009), AILA Doc. No. 09113064.

[49] *Id.*

[50] 8 CFR §214.2(p)(2)(i); 72 Fed. Reg. 18508 (Apr. 16, 1997).

[51] 8 CFR §214.2(p)(2)(i).

[52] 72 Fed. Reg. 18508 (Apr. 16, 1997).

[53] 8 CFR §214.2(p)(2)(iv)(E)(*3*).

[54] 8 CFR §214.2(p)(2)(iv)(E).

[55] *Id.*

[56] *Id.*

Copyright © 2017. American Immigration Lawyers Association. All rights reserved.

- "An agent performing the function of an employer must specify the wage offered and the other terms and conditions of employment by contractual agreement with the beneficiary or beneficiaries. The agent/employer must also provide an itinerary of definite employment and information on any other services planned for the period of time requested."[57]

Second, if the agent will file the petition because the beneficiary will work for more than one employer during the same period of time, then the agent should be "the representative of both the employers and the beneficiary or beneficiaries."[58] This petition must include "a complete itinerary of services or engagements," with specific details on "the dates of each service or engagement, the names and addresses of the actual employers, the names and addresses of the establishment, venues, or locations where the services will be performed."[59] In addition, in "questionable cases, a contract between the employer(s) and the beneficiary or beneficiaries may be required,"[60] so the practitioner should ensure that a copy of the contract is also included whenever possible, as discussed below, and that any "terms and conditions of the employment" are explained and supported by supplementary evidence, if applicable, as the agent-petitioner bears the burden to do so.[61]

The regulations also indicate that the agent may be "[a] person or company in business as an agent,"[62] to clarify that an agent "need not be limited to a person or entity who has entered into a formal agency agreement with the employer," although the "general legal agency relationship" is acceptable.[63] It seems that a petitioner may not file a P petition as the "representative" of multiple petitioners and as the agent of the beneficiary unless the petitioner "establish[es] that it is in 'business' as an agent,"[64] which in turn is based on a case-specific assessment of whether:

"It is more likely than not that the petitioner is in business as an agent for the series of event, services, or engagements that is the subject of the petition. The focus should be on whether the petitioner can establish that it is authorized to act as an agent for the other employers *for purposes of filing the petition*. This means

---

[57] 8 CFR §214.2(p)(2)(iv)(E)(*1*); "USCIS Clarifies Requirements for Agents Filing as Petitioners for the O and P Visa Classification" (Oct. 7, 2009), AILA Doc. No. 09100861; *Matter of [name not provided]*, WAC 05 231 52139 (AAO Mar. 8, 2006), http://bit.ly/mar064d9.

[58] 8 CFR §214.2(p)(2)(iv)(E)(*2*).

[59] *Id.*; *Matter of [name not provided]*, WAC 05 231 52139 (AAO Mar. 8, 2006), http://bit.ly/mar064d9.

[60] 8 CFR §214.2(p)(2)(iv)(E)(*2*).

[61] *Id.*

[62] *Id.*

[63] 72 Fed. Reg. 18508 (Apr. 16, 1997); *Matter of [name not provided]*, WAC 05 231 52139 (AAO Mar. 8, 2006), http://bit.ly/mar064d9 (withdrawing ground of USCIS denial based on purported lack of evidence that the agent was an "established agent" and citing 72 Fed. Reg. 18508 (Apr. 16, 1997)).

[64] "USCIS Clarifies Requirements for Agents Filing as Petitioners for the O and P Visa Classification" (Oct. 7, 2009), AILA Doc. No. 09100861; USCIS Memorandum, D. Neufeld, "Requirements for Agents and Sponsors Filing as Petitioners for the O and P Visa Classifications" (Nov. 20, 2009), AILA Doc. No. 09113064.

Copyright © 2017. American Immigration Lawyers Association. All rights reserved.

that the petitioner does not have to demonstrate that it normally serves as an agent outside the context of this petition."[65]

To address this issue, the petitioner may submit "a document signed by the beneficiary's other employer(s) which states that the petitioner is authorized to act in that employer's place as an agent for the limited purpose of filing the ... P petition ... with USCIS," but USCIS should not require specific form language or issue a Request for Evidence (RFE) for this reason.[66] Alternatively, other appropriate evidence includes a statement, signed by the petitioner and the other employers, confirming the itinerary of events, as well as the names and addresses of all employers; copies of "other types of agency representation contracts," such as if the petitioner's business is as an agent; and "statements from the other employers regarding the nature of the petitioner's representation of the employers and beneficiary."[67] Copies of fee arrangements may also be submitted, and USCIS noted that "compensation is not a requirement to establish an agency."[68] As long as the agent-petitioner's authority to represent the other employers for purposes of filing the P petition is established, an approved petition will have a validity period that covers all of the qualifying events for employment with all of the employers.[69] Otherwise, the petition will be approved only for the period of employment with the agent-petitioner, and an RFE may be issued before the petition is adjudicated.[70]

This November 2009 USCIS guidance appears to supersede October 2009 guidance that had required evidence that the other employers are clients of the petitioner.[71] The previous guidance required copies of contracts between the petitioner and the other employers and evidence of the agency relationship between the petitioner and the other employers, or else the P petition would be approved only for the employment with the agent-petitioner.[72] The newer approach seems to resolve the conflict between the regulations and the previous guidance, which would have required contracts between the agent-petitioner and other employers in order to approve a petition filed by the agent as the representative of the employer and beneficiary and as the person or entity with authorization to act for and on behalf of

[65] USCIS, D. Neufeld, "Requirements for Agents and Sponsors Filing as Petitioners for the O and P Visa Classifications" (Nov. 20, 2009), AILA Doc. No. 09113064 (emphasis in original).

[66] *Id.*

[67] *Id.*

[68] *Id.*

[69] *Id.*

[70] *Id.*

[71] *Id.* (clarifying "USCIS Clarifies Requirements for Agents Filing as Petitioners for the O and P Visa Classification" (Oct. 7, 2009), AILA Doc. No. 09100861). The later guidance is linked from the USCIS web pages regarding P-1s, but this earlier guidance is not shown there. *See, e.g.,* "P-1A Internationally Recognized Athlete" (updated July 15, 2015), https://www.uscis.gov/working-united-states/temporary-workers/p-1a-internationally-recognized-athlete.

[72] "USCIS Clarifies Requirements for Agents Filing as Petitioners for the O and P Visa Classification" (Oct. 7, 2009), AILA Doc. No. 09100861.

Copyright © 2017. American Immigration Lawyers Association. All rights reserved.

the employer.[73] This interpretation is supported by the discussion in the rule's promulgation, discussed above, and by the fact that the three subparts of the regulation on "[a]gents as petitioners" indicate that all three types of parties may file P petitions as agents,[74] in contrast with the specific mention of the "person or company in business as an agent" when requiring a complete itinerary.[75]

It also seems likely that the new guidance supersedes a once oft-repeated AAO statement that not every individual or business entity may declare itself to be an "agent" and thereby claim standing to file P petitions:

> "The director noted that the petitioning individual or company must be an established entity or 'else any U.S. immigrant or citizen can petition for a nonimmigrant worker by just identifying himself or herself as a U.S. agent.' The director noted that in most cases, one year of experience in the profession is sufficient to be considered an established agent."[76]

But a P-1 petition was denied by both USCIS and the AAO before the guidance was issued, where "the director has specifically and repeatedly requested documentary evidence to establish that the petitioner in this matter is actively doing business *as an agent*."[77] Although the inquiry was likely triggered by the absence of information on the Form I-129, Petition for a Nonimmigrant Worker, regarding the petitioner's number of employees and gross and net annual income, the AAO noted that it was insufficient to only provide evidence that the petitioner existed as a legal entity. Despite the petitioner's claims that the requested evidence was not relevant, the AAO noted:

> "The regulation states that the petitioner shall submit additional evidence as the director, in his or her discretion, may deem necessary. The purpose of the request for evidence is to elicit further information that clarifies whether eligibility for the benefit sought has been established, as of the time the petition is filed.... As noted by the director, it is simply insufficient for the petitioner to identify itself as an agent and then be unwilling or unable to provide any documentary evidence to corroborate its statements."[78]

It seems, therefore, that important factors in this case were the absence of an itinerary, the absence of an "'employer' per se, the beneficiary ha[d] no guaranteed salary, and instead [was] required to give a significant share of his earnings to the petitioner under the terms of the agreement."[79] Therefore, the practitioner may wish to prepare the client for the need to submit a business license, federal tax returns, "an

---

[73] 8 CFR §214.2(p)(2)(iv)(E).

[74] *Id.*

[75] 8 CFR §214.2(p)(2)(iv)(E)(*2*).

[76] *See, e.g., Matter of [name not provided]*, WAC 07 082 50689 (AAO Mar. 11, 2009), http://bit.ly/mar093d.

[77] *Id.* (emphasis in original).

[78] *Id.* (internal citations omitted).

[79] *Id.* (emphasis in original).

Copyright © 2017. American Immigration Lawyers Association. All rights reserved.

affidavit by the agent that he or she has been in the business of working as an agent in the United States, which states when he or she started working as an agent," and "evidence of wages paid to employees."[80]

C. P-1 Petitions

To qualify for P-1 status, the individual athlete, athletic team, or entertainment group must be "internationally recognized," which is defined as "having a high level of achievement in a field evidenced by a degree of skill and recognition substantially above that ordinarily encountered, to the extent that such achievement is renowned, leading, or well-known in more than one country."[81] Legacy INS noted specifically regarding P-1 entertainers and performers:

> "This definition is essentially the same as the one used by the Service with respect to O-1 nonimmigrants with extraordinary ability in the arts as well as the one previously used for 'prominent' alien entertainers in the old H-1B classification. Nevertheless, ... the evidence a petitioner must submit in order to establish eligibility for P-1 classification differs from that previously required with respect to H-1B prominent entertainers."[82]

As discussed in more detail in the following sections, the international recognition may be based on the achievements of an individual, athletic team, or entertainment group, with different types of evidence for the respective beneficiary or beneficiaries. For a discussion of the totality of circumstances analysis and how merely submitting the minimum number of types of evidence may be insufficient, see Volume 1: Chapter Twelve, "O Visas and Status."

1. P-1 Athletes

A foreign national may qualify as a professional athlete if he or she meets one of the following definitions:

- "Performs as an athlete, individually or as part of a group or team, at an internationally recognized level of performance," as discussed below;[83]
- Is "employed as an athlete by" either of the following sports teams:
  - "A team that is a member of an association of 6 or more professional sports teams whose total combined revenues exceed $10,000,000 per year, if the association governs the conduct of its members and regulates the contests and exhibitions in which its member teams regularly engage; or
  - "Any minor league team that is affiliated with such an association."[84]

---

[80] Id.

[81] 8 CFR §214.2(p)(3).

[82] Legacy INS, P. Virtue, "O-1 and P Nonimmigrant Visa Classifications" (Sept. 29, 1993), 1 INS and DOJ Legal Opinions §93-76.

[83] INA §214(c)(4)(A)(i)(I).

[84] Id. and INA §204(i)(2).

Copyright © 2017. American Immigration Lawyers Association. All rights reserved.

- Performs as an athlete or coach, "as part of a team or franchise that is located in the United States and a member of a foreign league or association of 15 or more amateur sports teams," as long as:
  - The "foreign league or association is the highest level of amateur performance of that sport in the relevant foreign country";
  - Membership or "participation in such league or association renders players ineligible, whether on a temporary or permanent basis, to earn a scholarship in, or participate in, that sport at a college or university in the United States under the rules of the National Collegiate Athletic Association"; and
  - A major sports league or a minor league affiliate of such a sports league drafts "a significant number of the individuals who play in such league or association";[85] or
- Is a professional or amateur athlete "who performs individually or as part of a group in a theatrical ice skating production."[86]

The latter three definitions were codified in 2006[87] to "expand the reach of the P-1 classification" by identifying three classes of athletes, but the statute did not remove the requirement that an athlete who does not seek to qualify under one of the three new definitions have earned international recognition.[88]

A "team" is defined as "two or more persons organized to perform together as a competitive unit in a competitive event."[89] The beneficiary must seek "to enter the United States temporarily and solely for the purpose of performing" as an athlete in "a specific athletic competition" or, if the individual is an ice skater, "in a specific theatrical ice skating production or tour,"[90] "at an internationally recognized level of performance."[91] This seems to preclude a P assignment where "some of the beneficiary's job duties involve teaching, coaching, training and conditioning individuals and teams,"[92] as then the beneficiary would not be "solely" competing in a "specific" athletic contest.[93] Thus, the petition's supporting documents should

---

[85] INA §214(c)(4)(A)(i)(III).

[86] INA §214(c)(4)(A)(i)(IV).

[87] USCIS, M. Aytes, "'Creating Opportunities for Minor League Professional, Entertainers, and Teams through Legal Entry Act of 2006 (COMPETE Act of 2006)' – Admission as P-1 Nonimmigrant" (Dec. 28, 2006), AILA Doc. No. 07010865.

[88] *Matter of [name not provided]*, WAC 07 082 50689 (AAO Mar. 11, 2009), http://bit.ly/mar093d.

[89] 8 CFR §214.2(p)(3). *See also* 8 CFR §214.2(p)(4)(i)(B).

[90] INA §214(c)(4)(A)(ii).

[91] 8 CFR §214.2(p)(1)(ii)(A)(*1*).

[92] *Matter of [name not provided]*, LIN 04 175 51125 (AAO June 13, 2005), http://bit.ly/jun051d9.

[93] INA §214(c)(4)(A)(ii); *Matter of I-R-A-*, ID# 16608 (AAO May 25, 2016); *Matter of [name not provided]*, WAC 07 011 52367 (AAO May 1, 2009), http://bit.ly/may092d9; *Matter of [name not provided]*, WAC 07 073 52093 (AAO Aug. 1, 2008), http://bit.ly/aug084d; *Matter of [name not provided]*, EAC 04 252 53882 (AAO Nov. 30, 2005), http://bit.ly/nov051d9.

Copyright © 2017. American Immigration Lawyers Association. All rights reserved.

describe the competitive event in detail where possible,[94] and the employment contract, if any, should also address the athletic contest.[95] P-1 petitioners should not omit non-qualifying duties such as teaching or coaching, however, as such omission could be seen as a material misstatement.

The practitioner should note that an athlete may qualify for P-1 status as an individual or as a member of a team. Individual and team member P-1 nonimmigrants "must be coming to the United States to participate in an athletic competition which has a distinguished reputation and which requires participation of an athlete or athletic team that has an international reputation."[96] Therefore, the petition should include evidence of the distinguished reputation of the competition and evidence of how the contest(s) requires an athlete or athletes with international recognition.[97] Experience has shown that USCIS can be skeptical of the level of the competition where participants can pay to compete. If all the competitors do not "derive their livelihood" from the sport, then USCIS and/or the AAO may conclude that the sport is not recognized in the United States.[98]

To qualify for P-1 status as an individual athlete, whether he or she "will compete individually or as a member of a U.S. team," the foreign national must be internationally recognized "in the sport,"[99] "based on his or her own reputation and achievements as an individual," and "must be coming to the United States to perform services which require an internationally recognized athlete."[100] One key advantage to filing a P-1 petition on behalf of an individual athlete is that the beneficiary may have employment authorization even if he or she is traded to another team, as long as a change of employer petition is filed within 30 days of the trade. In contrast, a reason to file the petition for a team, if applicable, is if the foreign national does not "have an internationally recognized reputation as an international athlete."[101]

Qualification based on being a member of a team, in turn, requires that the team is "internationally recognized as outstanding in the discipline."[102] Competitors training at, or representing, an athletic center are not considered part of a team if the athletes

---

[94] *Matter of [name not provided]*, WAC 07 011 52367 (AAO May 1, 2009), http://bit.ly/may092d9.

[95] *Matter of [name not provided]*, WAC 07 073 52093 (AAO Aug. 1, 2008), http://bit.ly/aug084d.

[96] 8 CFR §§214.2(p)(4)(ii)(A), 214.2(p)(4)(i)(A), and 214.2(p)(4)(i)(B); *Matter of [name not provided]*, WAC 05 076 51609 (AAO Mar. 8, 2006), http://bit.ly/mar0601d.

[97] *Matter of [name not provided]*, WAC 05 191 50035 (AAO Mar. 7, 2006), http://bit.ly/mar063d9; *Matter of [name not provided]*, SRC 05 075 50527 (AAO Feb. 24, 2006), http://bit.ly/feb061d9.

[98] *Matter of [name not provided]*, SRC 04 243 53449 (AAO Mar. 1, 2006), http://bit.ly/mar065d9 (USCIS denial).

[99] 8 CFR §214.2(p)(4)(ii)(B).

[100] 8 CFR §214.2(p)(4)(i)(A).

[101] 8 CFR §214.2(p)(4)(ii)(A).

[102] 8 CFR §214.2(p)(4)(i)(B).

Copyright © 2017. American Immigration Lawyers Association. All rights reserved.

compete on an individual basis or if their accomplishments are listed individually and not as team results.[103]

While USCIS seems to take the view that coaches are not athletes and thus do not qualify for P-1s as individuals,[104] coaches may be eligible for a P-1 as part of a Creating Opportunities for Minor League Professionals, Entertainers, and Teams Through Legal Entry (COMPETE) Act[105] qualifying team. To qualify, a coach must "perform as part of a team or franchise that is located in the United States and a member of a foreign league or association of 15 or more amateur sports teams"[106] if: "1) the foreign league is operating at the highest level of amateur performance in the relevant foreign country, 2) participation in that foreign league renders the players ineligible, whether on temporary or permanent basis, to earn a scholarship or participate in the sport at a college or university in the United States under the rules of the National Collegiate Athletic Association; and 3) where a significant number of players who play in the foreign leagues are drafted by major league or minor league affiliates of such sports leagues in the United States."[107]

It is insufficient that participation in the foreign league renders a player National Collegiate Athletic Association (NCAA)-ineligible only by winning—the ineligibility must derive from merely playing.[108] The AAO also has found that play that renders an athlete NCAA-ineligible if it occurs during the academic year does not constitute NCAA ineligibility, because not all play makes an athlete ineligible. It also found in the same case that there was no foreign league where the league is U.S.-based with teams in Canada.[109] It should be noted, however, that in that case, the petitioner's attorney had cited 11 other instances in which petitions for coaches had been approved under the exact same facts, so it could be said that results may vary on these two issues.

A P-1 petition filed on behalf of an athletic team has the advantage that the members need not individually be internationally recognized: "Each member of the team is accorded P-1 classification based on the international reputation of the

---

[103] *Matter of C-D-M-, Inc.*, ID# 11695 (AAO Feb. 25, 2016) (tennis academy found not to be a team); *Matter of I-G-C-*, ID# 16551 (AAO May 16, 2016) (gymnastics center not considered a team).

[104] *Matter of [name not provided]*, WAC 06 800 08950 (AAO Oct. 2, 2008), http://bit.ly/oct081d9; *Matter of [name not provided]*, WAC 06 256 51370 (AAO May 30, 2008), http://bit.ly/may081d9 (USCIS denial stated that "P-1 classification is not available to aliens seeking employment as coaches or instructors at an academy or school devoted to the sport"); *Matter of [name not provided]*, LIN 04 175 51125 (AAO June 13, 2005), http://bit.ly/jun051d9.

[105] Creating Opportunities for Minor League Professional, Entertainers, and Teams through Legal Entry Act of 2006, Public Law 109-463, codified at INA §214(c)(4)(A)(i)(III).

[106] *Id.*

[107] USCIS, M. Aytes, "'Creating Opportunities for Minor League Professional, Entertainers, and Teams through Legal Entry Act of 2006 (COMPETE Act of 2006)' – Admission as P-1 Nonimmigrant" (Dec. 28, 2006), AILA Doc. No. 07010865.

[108] *Matter of C-D-M-, Inc.*, ID# 11695 (AAO Feb. 25, 2016).

[109] Matter of D-T-S- LLC, ID# 73133 (AAO Sept. 30, 2016).

Copyright © 2017. American Immigration Lawyers Association. All rights reserved.

team."[110] But this is balanced by the fact that the individual team members "may not perform services separate and apart from the ... athletic team."[111]

The petitioner or foreign national beneficiary may request other nonimmigrant status, such as H-2B or O-1, on behalf of a foreign national, as long as the beneficiary qualifies; professional athletes are not limited only to P-1 status.[112]

a. Evidence for P-1 Athlete Petitions

First and foremost, the P-1 petition must include a "tendered contract with a major United States sports league or team."[113] Alternatively, if it is common and normal in a sport to execute "a tendered contract in an individual sport commensurate with international recognition in that sport," then a copy of that contract may be submitted.[114]

The supporting documents for a P-1 athlete petition should include evidence of the international recognition of the individual athlete or the "team as a unit," whichever is applicable.[115] The evidence should comprise at least two of the following criteria:

- Evidence that the beneficiary "participated to a significant extent in a prior season with a major United States sports league";

- Evidence that the beneficiary "participated in international competition with a national team";

- Evidence that the beneficiary "participated to a significant extent in a prior season for a U.S. college or university in intercollegiate competition";

- A written statement, "detail[ing] how the alien or team is internationally recognized," from either an official of a major U.S. sports league or an official of the governing body of the sport;

- A written statement, "detail[ing] how the alien or team is internationally recognized," from a member of the sports media or a recognized expert in the sport;

- "Evidence that the individual or team is ranked if the sport has international rankings"; or

- Evidence that the foreign national or team has received a significant honor or award in the sport.[116]

---

[110] 8 CFR §214.2(p)(4)(ii)(B).

[111] 8 CFR §214.2(p)(4)(i)(B).

[112] INA §214(c)(4)(H).

[113] 8 CFR §214.2(p)(4)(ii)(B)(*1*).

[114] *Id.*

[115] 8 CFR §214.2(p)(4)(ii)(B).

[116] 8 CFR §214.2(p)(4)(ii)(B)(*2*).

Copyright © 2017. American Immigration Lawyers Association. All rights reserved.

The practitioner should bear in mind that, for most P-1 athlete petitions, the standard requires international recognition, but "[n]ot every athlete that plays at an international level is internationally recognized."[117]

In 2010, the Ninth Circuit Court of Appeals issued the *Kazarian* decision criticizing USCIS's prior approach to EB-1 extraordinary ability, in which USCIS imposed standards on the categories of evidence that were not contained in the regulations, such as looking to the research community's reaction to published articles to determine whether the category for authorship of scholarly articles was satisfied, and suggested instead that that "analysis might be relevant to a final merits determination."[118] While USCIS has issued guidance that, on its own initiative, applied the *Kazarian* decision to other immigrant categories that involved providing documentation from multiple categories of evidence, such as exceptional ability and outstanding professors and researchers, it made no mention of nonimmigrant categories with the same type of evidence structure, namely Os and Ps.[119]

Since then, USCIS has been known to sometimes apply *Kazarian* to O-1 cases, either in broad terms[120] or explicitly,[121] but experience and a search of AAO decision databases[122] have shown no instances in which *Kazarian* was overtly applied in the P-1 context, although the AAO has used a *Kazarian*-type two-step approach in the P-1 context at least once without identifying it as such.[123]

(1) Significant Participation in a Prior Season with a Major U.S. Sports League

Evidence to address this criterion may be in the form of an experience letter from a major U.S. sports league, confirming the beneficiary's dates of employment and position on the team. Experience has shown that the statement should discuss in detail how the beneficiary's participation was significant. For example, statistics, such as number of goals or points scored or number of assists, may be helpful and should

---

[117] *Matter of [name not provided]*, WAC 05 191 50035 (AAO Mar. 7, 2006), http://bit.ly/mar063d9 (accepting beneficiary's participation in the Olympic Games but finding that his international recognition was not established).

[118] *Kazarian v. USCIS*, 596 F.3d 1115 (9th Cir. 2010), AILA Doc. No. 10030420. *Kazarian* is discussed in greater detail in Volume 2, Chapter Three: "The Immigrant Visa Petition."

[119] USCIS, "Evaluation of Evidentiary Criteria in Certain Form I-140 Petitions (AFM Update AD-11-14)" PM-602-0005.1 (Dec. 22, 2010), AILA Doc. No. 11020231.

[120] *E.g., Matter of AM-*, ID# 15019 (AAO Jan. 8, 2016), in which the AAO noted, without directly citing *Kazarian*, that the petitioner's framing of the evidentiary question in a two-step approach (which is the approach used in *Kazarian*) was correct.

[121] *E.g., Matter of [name and case number not given]*, (AAO Jan. 10, 2012), http://bit.ly/jan122d; *Matter of [name and case number not given]*, (AAO June 14, 2013), http://bit.ly/jun131d.

[122] AAO nonprecedent decisions can be found both on the USCIS website, at https://www.uscis.gov/about-us/directorates-and-program-offices/administrative-appeals-office-aao/aao-non-precedent-decisions (though the search functionality is highly limited), and on Fastcase Premium, as part of a subscription to AILALink, https://agora.aila.org/Product/Subscription/166.

[123] *Matter of T-L-A-*, ID# 11763 (AAO Dec. 30, 2015) (finding that the petitioner had provided the requisite two forms of evidence, but that, on a review of the "totality of the record," the evidence did not demonstrate that the tennis player had achieved international recognition).

Copyright © 2017. American Immigration Lawyers Association. All rights reserved.

ideally be supported by independent evidence, such as newspaper articles, photographs, or league performance charts or reports. Alternatively, the beneficiary may have benefited the team's performance at a critical moment, such as by scoring the final goal or assisting in the play that sent an important game into overtime, and newspaper articles may corroborate the statement. For a discussion of the requirements of published materials, see below. For a further discussion of experience letters and testimonials, see Volume 2: Chapter Two, "The Labor Certification Application," and Volume 1: Chapter Twelve, "O Visas and Status," respectively.

(2) Participation in International Competition with a National Team •

In most cases, the petition should be accompanied by independent "background information" explaining how the competitions are ones "at which athletes compete on national teams."[124] For example, the AAO accepted as appropriate evidence statements from two individuals and two published articles, one written by the beneficiary.[125] One exception is the Olympic Games; this criterion was deemed satisfied where the petitioner submitted "a translated excerpt from the Mexican Olympic Delegation handout," including "the beneficiary's biography and photographs," and "the beneficiary's Olympic Village badge from the 2004 Olympic summer games."[126]

Generally, participation in an international competition on a national team at the junior or youth level seems insufficient to establish international recognition,[127] as opposed to ranking from junior level competitions, as discussed below.

(3) Significant Participation in a Prior Season for a U.S. College or University in Intercollegiate Competition

For a discussion of significant participation, see the first category of documentation above. But in one case, USCIS and the AAO rejected as insufficient a testimonial from the Director of Tennis at a U.S. university, which stated that the beneficiary played for the university's team and provided the years of participation;[128] also rejected as unsubstantiated was counsel's statement that the beneficiary had played in the NCAA Division I Tennis tournaments for the university.[129]

---

[124] *Matter of [name not provided]*, WAC 07 011 52367 (AAO May 1, 2009), http://bit.ly/may092d9.

[125] *Matter of [name not provided]*, SRC 05 075 50527 (AAO Feb. 24, 2006), http://bit.ly/feb061d9 (statements written by Office Manager of the Paint Horse Association of Australia and the Director of Shows and Performance Department Head of an organization whose name was redacted).

[126] *Matter of [name not provided]*, WAC 05 191 50035 (AAO Mar. 7, 2006), http://bit.ly/mar063d9.

[127] *Matter of [name not provided]*, EAC 04 238 53587 (AAO Nov. 28, 2005), http://bit.ly/nov051d91.

[128] *Id. Cf. Matter of [name not provided]*, LIN 92 172 50725 (AAU Apr. 30, 1993), 11 Immig. Rptr. B2-64 (for an athlete, petition denied where the contract described competitive events but also promotional activities for the petitioner's water ski products).

[129] *Matter of [name not provided]*, EAC 04 238 53587 (AAO Nov. 28, 2005), http://bit.ly/nov051d91.

Copyright © 2017. American Immigration Lawyers Association. All rights reserved.

(4) Statement of the International Recognition of the Beneficiary or Team by Governing Body or Official of the Sport

This criterion is satisfied by a written statement from either an official of a major U.S. sports league or an official of the governing body of the sport, "detail[ing] how the alien or team is internationally recognized."[130] USCIS may review the petition's supporting evidence to determine whether the appropriate sports league or governing body provided the statement.[131] A governing body "is not synonymous with a league."[132] The governing body need not be international in scope or be a U.S. body, but its statement must detail how the athlete is internationally recognized.[133]

A strong statement should provide an "explanation of the significance of the beneficiary's accomplishments in specific tournaments, or how such results conveyed international recognition on the beneficiary."[134] Merely providing a list of achievements and "summarily" stating that the beneficiary has international recognition, "without explaining the significance or scope of the tournaments or the international recognition conveyed on the beneficiary as a result of her performance," may be insufficient.[135] Instead, the statement(s) should focus on "provid[ing] … information regarding the specific international tournaments in which the beneficiary has participated" and their importance in the sport.[136] For example, an invitation to compete in an event may be limited only to internationally recognized athletes, as discussed below.

(5) Statement of International Recognition from Sports Media or Recognized Expert

This criterion requires a written statement, "detail[ing] how the alien or team is internationally recognized," from a member of the sports media or a recognized expert in the sport.[137] The individual should state his or her credentials to inform USCIS of his or her role in sports media or of how he or she is recognized as an expert, as in one case, a statement from the Chief Inspector of the California State

---

[130] 8 CFR §214.2(p)(4)(ii)(B)(*2*).

[131] *Matter of [name not provided]*, WAC 07 011 52367 (AAO May 1, 2009), http://bit.ly/may092d9 (President of the Massachusetts States Taekwondo Association, but the AAO noted that "a bid manual for the U.S. Open Taekwondo Championships[] indicates that the United States Olympic Committee (USOC) recognizes USA Taekwondo as the National Governing Body (NGB) for the sport of Taekwondo in the United States"); *Matter of [name not provided]*, SRC 05 008 53511 (AAO Nov. 23, 2005), http://bit.ly/nov0501d (AAO affirmatively researched the national governing body for the sport of taekwondo).

[132] *Matter of I-G-C-*, ID #16551 (AAO May 16, 2016).

[133] *Matter of F-F-S-, LLC*, ID# 126527 (AAO Sept. 26, 2016).

[134] *Matter of [name not provided]*, WAC 07 011 52367 (AAO May 1, 2009), http://bit.ly/may092d9; *Matter of [name not provided]*, SRC 05 075 50527 (AAO Feb. 24, 2006), http://bit.ly/feb061d9.

[135] *Matter of [name not provided]*, EAC 08 054 50732 (AAO Aug. 18, 2008), http://bit.ly/aug083d; *Matter of [name not provided]*, SRC 04 243 53449 (AAO Mar. 1, 2006), http://bit.ly/mar065d.

[136] *Id.*

[137] 8 CFR §214.2(p)(4)(ii)(B)(*2*).

Copyright © 2017. American Immigration Lawyers Association. All rights reserved.

Athletic Commission was rejected on this ground.[138] As with the statement from an official of the sports league or U.S. governing body of the sport, a strong statement from the sports media member or an expert should "explain the significance of the accomplishments and how the beneficiary's achievements are renowned, leading, or well-known in more than one country."[139]

(6) International Ranking

Because a petitioner need not "establish that the beneficiary has played as a professional in [his/]her sport,"[140] amateur rankings are acceptable, even if the athlete recently turned professional.[141] A high ranking from junior or youth competitions may be relevant, as long as the ranking is recent:

"[A] distinction can be made between a 17-year old who has recently competed in junior tournaments and is currently ranked as a youth or junior player, and a 27-year old player whose only achievements and rankings were achieved at the junior level. Evidence of a beneficiary's accomplishments as a junior or youth level athlete will carry greater weight when it reflects the contemporaneous accomplishments of an athlete."[142]

If official handicaps are used in the sport, then the petition should include evidence of how the handicap is a ranking system.[143] The practitioner should also be aware that a handicap that is well respected in the sport may nevertheless be "not consistent with a high level of achievement in the field evidenced by a degree of skill and recognition substantially above that ordinarily encountered, to the extent that such achievement is renowned, leading, or well-known in more than one country."[144]

(7) Significant Honor or Award

The petition should include independent evidence of the significance of the honor or award,[145] such as participation requirements,[146] or evidence of how setting a new record in a sport was honored or recognized by the sport or its competitors.[147] A demonstrated record of first–, second–, and third-place finishes among distinguished competitors can be considered a significant honor or award.[148] This is a more flexible

---

[138] *Matter of [name not provided]*, WAC 05 191 50035 (AAO Mar. 7, 2006), http://bit.ly/mar063d9.

[139] *Matter of [name not provided]*, WAC 07 011 52367 (AAO May 1, 2009), http://bit.ly/may092d9.

[140] *Matter of [name not provided]*, EAC 08 054 50732 (AAO Aug. 18, 2008), http://bit.ly/aug083d.

[141] *Matter of T-L-A-*, ID# 11763 (AAO Dec. 30, 2015).

[142] *Matter of [name not provided]*, EAC 08 054 50732 (AAO Aug. 18, 2008), http://bit.ly/aug083d.

[143] *Matter of [name not provided]*, SRC 04 243 53449 (AAO Mar. 1, 2006), http://bit.ly/mar065d9.

[144] *Id.* (handicap of four goals on a scale from negative one to 10 goals).

[145] *Matter of [name not provided]*, WAC 05 191 50035 (AAO Mar. 7, 2006), http://bit.ly/mar063d9 (petitioner stated awards won by the beneficiary but failed to provide corroborating evidence of the awards or their significance).

[146] *Matter of [name not provided]*, WAC 07 011 52367 (AAO May 1, 2009), http://bit.ly/may092d9; *Matter of [name not provided]*, SRC 05 008 53511 (AAO Nov. 23, 2005), http://bit.ly/nov0501d.

[147] *Matter of [name not provided]*, WAC 05 144 51666 (AAO Mar. 1, 2006), http://bit.ly/mar062d.

[148] *Matter of F-F-S-, LLC*, ID# 126527 (AAO Sept. 26, 2016) (horse jumping rider; denied on other grounds).

Copyright © 2017. American Immigration Lawyers Association. All rights reserved.

standard than the O-1 prizes or awards criterion, discussed in Volume 1: Chapter Twelve, "O Visas and Status." If competition in a tournament is by invitation and reserved only for internationally recognized athletes, the statement should explain this fact[149] and provide corroborating evidence of the participation requirements. But merely qualifying for an event with international competitors may not automatically mean that the beneficiary also qualifies for P-1 status.[150] All published materials describing the significance of the honor or award should state the title and date of publication,[151] and be translated if in a language other than English.

b. No P-1 Visas to Beneficiaries Who Are Nationals of Countries That Are State Sponsors of International Terrorism

A P-1 visa will not be issued to a foreign national "who is a national of a country that is a state sponsor of international terrorism,"[152] which is defined as "any country the government of which has been determined by the Secretary of State … to have repeatedly provided support for acts of international terrorism," under any of the following laws:[153]

- Section 6(j)(1)(A) of the Export Administration Act of 1979 (or successor statute).
- Section 40(d) of the Arms Export Control Act.
- Section 620A(a) of the Foreign Assistance Act of 1961.[154]

The prohibition was codified in 2006.[155] The one exception is if the Secretary of State determines, in consultation with the Secretary of Homeland Security and the heads of other appropriate U.S. agencies, that such foreign national does not pose a threat to the safety, national security, or national interest of the United States, based on the applications of "standards developed by the Secretary of State, in consultation with the Secretary of Homeland Security and the heads of other appropriate United States agencies, that are applicable to the nationals of such states."[156]

2. P-1 Arts and Entertainment Groups

The regulations define the term "arts" as including "fields of creative activity or endeavor such as, but not limited to, fine arts, visual arts, and performing arts."[157]

---

[149] *Matter of [name not provided]*, EAC 08 054 50732 (AAO Aug. 18, 2008), http://bit.ly/aug083d.

[150] *Id.*

[151] *Matter of [name not provided]*, SRC 04 243 53449 (AAO Mar. 1, 2006), http://bit.ly/mar065d9.

[152] INA §214(c)(4)(F)(i).

[153] INA §214(c)(4)(F)(ii).

[154] INA §214(c)(4)(F)(iii) (citing 50 USC App. §2405(j)(1)(A), 22 USC §2780(d), and 22 USC §2371(a), respectively).

[155] Creating Opportunities for Minor League Professional, Entertainers, and Teams through Legal Entry Act of 2006, Public Law 109-463, codified at INA §214(c)(4)(A)(i)(III). *See also* USCIS, M. Aytes, "'Creating Opportunities for Minor League Professional, Entertainers, and Teams through Legal Entry Act of 2006 (COMPETE Act of 2006)' – Admission as P-1 Nonimmigrant" (Dec. 28, 2006), AILA Doc. No. 07010865.

[156] INA §214(c)(4)(F)(i).

[157] 8 CFR §214.2(p)(3).

Copyright © 2017. American Immigration Lawyers Association. All rights reserved.

The practitioner may note that this definition differs from that for arts in the context of extraordinary ability petitions, which includes culinary arts as well.[158] Circus arts are also included, as noted by legacy INS:

> "Congress considered a circus to be an entertainment group for P-1 purposes ... [and] Congress clearly indicated its intent to extend the P-1 classification both to circus personnel who are members of a circus act, as well as circus personnel coming individually to perform as part of, or who will be an integral and essential part of, a circus."[159]

An artist or entertainer may obtain P-1 status if he or she will perform with or be "an integral and essential part of the performance of an entertainment group that has ... been recognized internationally as being outstanding in the discipline for a sustained and substantial period of time,"[160] as long as he or she "has had a sustained and substantial relationship with that group (ordinarily for at least one year) and provides functions integral to the performance of the group."[161] Specifically, P-1 status is appropriate only for "members of foreign-based entertainment groups, not individual entertainers."[162]

a. Standards for Entertainment Groups

A "group" is defined as "two or more persons established as one entity or unit to perform or to provide a service,"[163] and a "member of a group" is "a person who is actually performing the entertainment services,"[164] to differentiate a group member from essential support personnel,[165] as discussed below. The P petition should contain "evidence that the beneficiaries are established as one entity or unit to perform," such as evidence of previous performances together,[166] if the group is comprised only of the named beneficiaries. But the other members of the entertainment group may be U.S. citizens, because "[t]here are no statutory or regulatory requirements that beneficiaries comprise a group in their own right,"[167] and because the focus of the inquiry is on whether the group is internationally recognized. "The fact that two

---

[158] 8 CFR §214.2(o)(3)(ii).

[159] Legacy INS, P. Virtue, "Classification for Circus Performers" (Mar. 3, 1994), 1 INS and DOJ Legal Opinions §94-16.

[160] INA §214(c)(4)(B)(i)(I); 8 CFR §§214.2(p)(1)(ii)(A)(2) and 214.2(p)(4)(iii)(A).

[161] INA §214(c)(4)(B)(i)(II); 8 CFR §§214.2(p)(1)(ii)(A)(2) and 214.2(p)(4)(iii)(A).

[162] AFM 33.5.

[163] 8 CFR §§214.2(p)(3) and 214.2(p)(4)(i)(B); legacy INS Memorandum, L. Weinig, "Policy Guidelines for the Adjudication of O and P Petitions" (June 25, 1992), 69 Interpreter Releases 1084 (Aug. 31, 1992).

[164] 8 CFR §214.2(p)(3).

[165] Legacy INS, L. Weinig, "Policy Guidelines for the Adjudication of O and P Petitions," (June 25, 1992), 69 Interpreter Releases 1084 (Aug. 31, 1992).

[166] Matter of [name not provided], WAC 06 172 52572 (AAO June 23, 2008), http://bit.ly/jun081d.

[167] Matter of [name not provided], EAC 04 233 53201 (AAO Sept. 21, 2006), http://bit.ly/sep061d9.

Copyright © 2017. American Immigration Lawyers Association. All rights reserved.

members of [redacted] are United States citizens does not preclude the remaining alien members from receiving P-1 classification."[168]

However, while it is clear that the rest of the group can be comprised of U.S. citizens, whether the group must be foreign-based, or can be U.S.-based, remains ambiguous:

> "An individual entertainer may be a member of *a foreign-based 'group'* which is recognized internationally even if the rest of the group is from (but not based in) the United States and not filing. For example, if the group is based in London, England and consists of three American expatriates and one British subject, the British subject can be petitioned for as a P-1. Likewise, if an individual entertainer is to join or rejoin his or her *foreign-based group* which is already touring in the United States as P-1 nonimmigrants, he or she can be petitioned for as an individual P-1."[169]

Contrast the Adjudicator's Field Manual (AFM) passage above with this AAO finding:

> "[T]the regulation in question makes no specific restriction with regard to whether the internationally recognized group in which the alien is coming to join be based in the United States or abroad."[170]

A 2011 draft memo acknowledged that "the statute and regulations do not limit the P-1B classification to individual entertainers coming to the United States to join only foreign-based entertainment groups," and would have changed the AFM to state, "The P-1B classification for entertainers applies to an internationally recognized group, which can be based in the United States or abroad."[171] However, that memo was never released in final form, leaving this issue in question.

The "entertainment group must have been established for a minimum of 1 year," and 75 percent of the total beneficiary-group members "must have had a sustained and substantial relationship with the group,"[172] by "performing entertainment services for the group for a minimum of 1 year,"[173] and "under the same name as shown on the petition."[174] The latter requirement, discussed below, is often called "the 75 percent rule."[175] A group can be comprised of as few as two people,[176] but it must

---

[168] *Id.*

[169] AFM 33.5(a). (emphasis added).

[170] *Matter of [name not provided]*, WAC 06 266 55302 (AAO Dec. 16, 2008), http://bit.ly/dec081d (AAO withdrew USCIS's ground of denial based on the fact that the group was based in the United States).

[171] Draft USCIS, "Clarifying Guidance on Definition of 'Internationally Recognized' for the P-1 Classification; Revisions to the Adjudicator's Field Manual (AFM) Chapter 33.5(a) AFM Update AD 11-03" (Jan. 14, 2011), AILA Doc. No. 11011860.

[172] 8 CFR §214.2(p)(4)(iii)(A).

[173] 8 CFR §214.2(p)(4)(i)(B).

[174] AFM 33.2.

[175] AFM 33.5.

[176] 8 CFR §214.2(p)(3), definition of "group."

Copyright © 2017. American Immigration Lawyers Association. All rights reserved.

be shown that the two have performed together for the requisite one year, and a member of the group having performed with others may be seen as an indication that this is not a group.[177] Where only a few members of a large band are coming to the United States on tour, USCIS will look at the history of the relationship of those who are coming, rather than at the group as a whole.[178]

The group must come to the United States "to perform services which require an internationally recognized entertainment group."[179] Importantly, the group members need not individually be internationally recognized: "A P-1 classification shall be accorded to an entertainment group to perform as a unit based on the international reputation of the group,"[180] because "the focus in P-1 cases is on whether the sum parts of the group (*i.e.*, the group members) amount to an 'outstanding' whole."[181] But, the group members "may not perform services separate and apart from the entertainment group."[182]

For P-1 petitions for entertainment groups, the practitioner should note the following guidance:

"In addition, a P-1 petitioner, unlike an O-1 or H-1B petitioner [under the former prominent standard], must show that the group, as opposed to the individual alien, has an 'outstanding' international reputation. This obviously necessitates the submission of different documentation than in cases where an O-1 petition is filed on behalf of an alien coming to this country to perform in an individual capacity. Moreover, different documentation is required with respect to the prospective P-1 nonimmigrant as opposed to the petitioning group. Since only the group and not the alien must be internationally renowned in P-1 cases, it follows that, unlike the group itself, a P-1 group member need not have attained the distinction of an O-1 extraordinary alien or an H-1B prominent alien. Rather, a group member need only provide functions integral to the performance of the group, or, in the case of accompanying support personnel, functions that are integral and essential to the performance of the group."[183]

Legacy INS guidance notes that the establishment of the P classification "reflect[s] a carefully crafted compromise between the interests of employers and U.S. workers in the arts field":[184]

---

[177] *Matter of F-I-G-, Inc.*, ID# 11762 (AAO Sept. 3, 2015).

[178] *Id.*

[179] 8 CFR §214.2(p)(4)(i)(B).

[180] 8 CFR §214.2(p)(4)(iii)(A).

[181] Legacy INS, P. Virtue, "O-1 and P Nonimmigrant Visa Classifications" (Sept. 29, 1993), 1 INS and DOJ Legal Opinions §93-76 (emphasis in original).

[182] 8 CFR §§214.2(p)(4)(i)(B) and 214.2(p)(4)(iii)(A).

[183] Legacy INS, P. Virtue, "O-1 and P Nonimmigrant Visa Classifications" (Sept. 29, 1993), 1 INS and DOJ Legal Opinions §93-76.

[184] *Id.* (also noting the importance of reciprocity for U.S. performers).

Copyright © 2017. American Immigration Lawyers Association. All rights reserved.

"In enacting the P-1 provisions, Congress sought to protect both: (a) the interest of certain outstanding entertainment groups in maintaining a consistently high level of performance by allowing them to hire the most qualified performers, and (b) the interest of labor groups in the entertainment field in preventing the use of the P-1 nonimmigrant category to undercut qualified American performing artists.... In addition, the legislative history of the P-1 provisions demonstrates that Congress sought to protect the interest of the 'up-and-coming' American performers and entertainers seeking opportunities to perform abroad by affording similar opportunities to their foreign counterparts to perform in this country."[185]

Therefore, the P-1 requirements ensure that only "a small number of entertainment groups capable of establishing that they are 'outstanding'" may qualify, as less recognized groups would have to use the H-2B classification and obtain temporary labor certification from the Department of Labor (DOL) to confirm that there are no willing, able, and qualified U.S. workers who may perform with the group.[186] The legislative intent was that these outstanding entertainment groups should not be forced to "seriously compromise the group's ability to maintain its high standards, since the H-2B labor market test is an objective one which fails to take into account varying levels of technical proficiency and the highly individualized and less tangible personnel requirements of performing groups."[187] The high standards of "major arts institutions," symphonies, and recording companies should in turn protect U.S. labor interests because they "are not going to hire the cheapest available [f]oreign labor under the guise of artistic merit."[188] In addition, an entertainment group that has earned international recognition "has a vital interest in maintaining its outstanding reputation."[189]

Similarly, "requiring the P-1 alien to provide functions 'integral' to the performance of the group, was designed to ensure that a group would not be able to use the P-1 category merely as a means of hiring cheap foreign labor," even without the temporary labor certification.[190] The idea was that even if a person was not individually outstanding, he or she would "possess sufficient skill that his or her inclusion within the group will not adversely affect the overall outstanding quality of the group itself," such that the group's "standards [would] not be compromised,"[191]

---

[185] Legacy INS, P. Virtue, "O-1 and P Nonimmigrant Visa Classifications" (Sept. 29, 1993), 1 INS and DOJ Legal Opinions §93-76 (internal citations omitted).

[186] *Id.* (internal citation omitted). For a discussion of H-2B status and the temporary labor certification application process, see Volume 1: Chapter Eight, "H-2B Status and Visas."

[187] Legacy INS, P. Virtue, "O-1 and P Nonimmigrant Visa Classifications" (Sept. 29, 1993), 1 INS and DOJ Legal Opinions §93-76.

[188] *Id.* (internal citation omitted).

[189] *Id.* (internal citation omitted).

[190] *Id.* (internal citation omitted).

[191] *Id.*

Copyright © 2017. American Immigration Lawyers Association. All rights reserved.

and the group's performances would benefit.[192] Therefore "the scope of the P-1 category" would be restricted "to a limited number of highly talented performers," even as the entertainment group would "retain its ability to be selective in making its hiring decisions" and "the freedom to determine which performers could best enhance the performance and therefore the reputation of the group."[193]

Finally, the 75 percent rule was "designed to ensure that the petitioning group is essentially the same one as that which earned the outstanding reputation," in order "to prevent the use of the P-1 category by 'pick-up' and ad hoc bands."[194] As stated by legacy INS, "Congress intended that all internationally recognized entertainment groups, regardless of nationality, may utilize the P-1 category on behalf of prospective group members."[195]

If the exact dates of employment of each member of the entertainment group are not provided with the P petition, then USCIS will almost certainly request this information, as well as independent corroborating evidence,[196] so the practitioner should confirm that it is provided in order to avoid processing delays.[197] Approval notices for previous P petitions may also be compared with the information provided on the current P petition.[198]

However, legacy INS also acknowledged the challenge of petitioning for a group: "One of the most difficult decisions which the Service will be faced with is determining whether a group is, in fact, a group."[199] The recognition granted in the manner of billing is not an absolute determiner of whether the performers qualify as a group: "If a solo artist or entertainer traditionally performs on stage with the same group of aliens, *e.g.*, back-up singers or musicians, the act may be classified as a group."[200] The back-up singers and/or musicians would have to satisfy the 75 percent rule, or otherwise the solo artist or entertainer would have to obtain O-1 status, with O-2 status for the accompanying foreign nationals.[201]

---

[192] *Matter of [name not provided]*, WAV 06 266 55302 (AAO Dec. 16, 2008), http://bit.ly/dec081d (P-1 status inappropriate for beneficiaries to "rehearse, perform, and *teach* with their colleagues") (emphasis in original).

[193] Legacy INS, P. Virtue, "O-1 and P Nonimmigrant Visa Classifications" (Sept. 29, 1993), 1 INS and DOJ Legal Opinions §93-76.

[194] *Id.*

[195] *Id.*

[196] *Matter of [name not provided]*, EAC 05 146 50600 (AAO Mar. 1, 2006), http://bit.ly/mar061d9; *Matter of [name not provided]*, EAC 03 177 53938 (AAO Aug. 12, 2005), http://bit.ly/aug051d9.

[197] 8 CFR §214.2(p)(4)(iii)(B)(*2*).

[198] *Matter of [name not provided]*, EAC 03 177 53938 (AAO Aug. 12, 2005), http://bit.ly/aug051d9 ("discrepancies between the information provided on the Form I-129 petition and the 2002 approval notice as to the group's composition").

[199] Legacy INS, L. Weinig, "Policy Guidelines for the Adjudication of O and P Petitions" (June 25, 1992), 69 Interpreter Releases 1084 (Aug. 31, 1992).

[200] *Id.*

[201] *Id.* For a discussion of O status, see Volume 1: Chapter Twelve, "O Visas and Status."

Copyright © 2017. American Immigration Lawyers Association. All rights reserved.

b. Evidence for Artist and Entertainer P-1 Petitions

Initial evidence for a P-1 petition for an entertainment group should include documents demonstrating "that the group has been established and performing regularly for a period of at least 1 year."[202] Then, to satisfy the 75 percent rule, the petitioner should submit a statement "listing each member of the group and the exact dates for which each member has been employed on a regular basis by the group."[203]

Evidence that the entertainment group has been internationally recognized for a sustained and substantial period of time may be in the form of nominations and/or receipt of "significant international awards or prizes for outstanding achievement in its field."[204] For a discussion of the types of awards that are considered significant and international, see Volume 1: Chapter Twelve, "O Visas and Status." Alternatively, the petitioner may submit evidence that satisfies at least three of the following criteria:

- "Evidence that the group has performed, and will perform, as a starring or leading entertainment group in productions or events which have a distinguished reputation," as documented "by critical reviews, advertisements, publicity releases, publications, contracts, or endorsements";

- Evidence that the group has achieved and earned "international recognition and acclaim for outstanding achievement," as documented "by reviews in major newspapers, trade journals, magazines, or other published material";

- "Evidence that the group has performed, and will perform, services" as a starring or leading group "for organizations and establishments that have a distinguished reputation, as documented "by articles in newspapers, trade journals, publications, or testimonials";

- "Evidence that the group has a record of major commercial or critically acclaimed successes, as evidenced by such indicators as ratings; standing in the field; box office receipts; record, cassette, or video sales; and other achievements in the field as reported in trade journals, major newspapers, or other publications";

- Evidence of "significant recognition for achievements from organizations, critics, government agencies, or other recognized experts in the field," where the "testimonials must be in a form which clearly indicates the author's authority, expertise, and knowledge of the alien's achievements," similar to the testimonials or affidavits discussed below; or

- "Evidence that the group has either commanded a high salary or will command a high salary or other substantial remuneration for services comparable to others

---

[202] 8 CFR §214.2(p)(4)(iii)(B)(*1*).

[203] 8 CFR §214.2(p)(4)(iii)(B)(*2*).

[204] 8 CFR §214.2(p)(4)(iii)(B)(*3*).

Copyright © 2017. American Immigration Lawyers Association. All rights reserved.

similarly situated in the field as evidenced by contracts or other reliable evidence."[205]

(1) Performance as a Starring or Leading Entertainment Group in Productions or Events Which Have a Distinguished Reputation

Critical reviews, publications, contracts, advertisements, publicity releases, and endorsements may be submitted to demonstrate that the group has performed and will perform as a starring or leading entertainment group,[206] or a "featured group,"[207] in productions or events that have a distinguished reputation.[208] All published materials should state the title and date of publication.[209] For a further discussion of this criteria, see Volume 1: Chapter Twelve, "O Visas and Status."

(2) International Recognition and Acclaim for Outstanding Achievement

This criterion requires evidence that the group has achieved and earned "international recognition and acclaim for outstanding achievement," as documented "by reviews in major newspapers, trade journals, magazines, or other published material."[210] If the group has not performed internationally, then USCIS and/or the AAO may construe the absence to indicate that the group does not have international recognition.[211] For a further discussion of this criteria, see Volume 1: Chapter Twelve, "O Visas and Status."

(3) Performance as a Starring or Leading Group for Organizations and Establishments That Have a Distinguished Reputation

Articles in newspapers, trade journals, publications, and testimonials may describe how the entertainment group "has performed, and will perform, services" as a starring or leading group "for organizations and establishments that have a distinguished reputation."[212] All published materials should state the title and date of publication.[213] For a further discussion of this criteria, see Volume 1: Chapter Twelve, "O Visas and Status."

(4) Record of Major Commercial or Critically Acclaimed Success

The regulations state that the indicators of "ratings; standing in the field; box office receipts; record, cassette, or video sales; and other achievements in the field"

---

[205] 8 CFR §214.2(p)(4)(iii)(B)(*3*).

[206] *Id.*

[207] AFM 33.5.

[208] 8 CFR §214.2(p)(4)(iii)(B)(*3*).

[209] *Matter of [name not provided]*, EAC 04 233 53201 (AAO Sept. 21, 2006), http://bit.ly/sep061d9 ("two undated articles from unnamed publications").

[210] 8 CFR §214.2(p)(4)(iii)(B)(*3*).

[211] *Matter of [name not provided]*, WAV 06 266 55302 (AAO Dec. 16, 2008), http://bit.ly/dec081d.

[212] 8 CFR §214.2(p)(4)(iii)(B)(*3*).

[213] *Matter of [name not provided]*, EAC 04 233 53201 (AAO Sept. 21, 2006), http://bit.ly/sep061d9 ("two undated articles from unnamed publications").

Copyright © 2017. American Immigration Lawyers Association. All rights reserved.

should be "reported in trade journals, major newspapers, or other publications."[214] All published materials should state the title and date of publication.[215] For a further discussion of this criteria, see Volume 1: Chapter Twelve, "O Visas and Status."

(5) Significant Recognition from Organizations, Critics, Government Agencies, or Other Recognized Experts

If the entertainment group has earned "significant recognition for achievements from organizations, critics, government agencies, or other recognized experts in the field," then the "testimonials must be in a form which clearly indicates the author's authority, expertise, and knowledge of the alien's achievements," similar to the recommendation statements or affidavits discussed below.[216] An advertisement prepared by the group or by the group's management company will most likely be rejected, as it is not from an "objective" reviewer.[217] All published materials should state the title and date of publication.[218] For a further discussion of this criteria, see Volume 1: Chapter Twelve, "O Visas and Status."

(6) High Salary or Remuneration

This criterion allows for evidence "that the group has either commanded a high salary or will command a high salary or other substantial remuneration for services comparable to others similarly situated in the field as evidenced by contracts or other reliable evidence."[219] Other reliable evidence may include salary surveys and newspaper articles. All published materials should state the title and date of publication.[220] For a further discussion of this criteria, see Volume 1: Chapter Twelve, "O Visas and Status."

3. Exceptions

The practitioner should note several exceptions to general requirements for P-1 artists and performers. The first exception is that the "international recognition requirement" may be waived, "in consideration of special circumstances," as long as the "entertainment group that is recognized nationally as being outstanding in its discipline for a sustained and substantial period of time."[221] As stated in the regulations: "An example of a special circumstance would be when an entertainment

---

[214] 8 CFR §214.2(p)(4)(iii)(B)(*3*).

[215] *Matter of [name not provided]*, EAC 04 233 53201 (AAO Sept. 21, 2006), http://bit.ly/sep061d9 ("two undated articles from unnamed publications").

[216] 8 CFR §214.2(p)(4)(iii)(B)(*3*); *Matter of [name not provided]*, EAC 03 177 53938 http://bit.ly/aug051d9 (statements rejected because they were not in the form of affidavits and did not state the expertise of the signatory or "the manner in which the authors acquired such information provided").

[217] *Matter of [name not provided]*, WAC 06 266 55302 (AAO Dec. 16, 2008), http://bit.ly/dec081d.

[218] *Matter of [name not provided]*, EAC 04 233 53201 (AAO Sept. 21, 2006 http://bit.ly/sep061d9 ("two undated articles from unnamed publications").

[219] 8 CFR §214.2(p)(4)(iii)(B)(*3*).

[220] *Matter of [name not provided]*, EAC 04 233 53201 (AAO Sept. 21, 2006), http://bit.ly/sep061d9 ("two undated articles from unnamed publications").

[221] INA §214(c)(4)(B)(ii); 8 CFR §214.2(p)(4)(iii)(C)(*2*).

Copyright © 2017. American Immigration Lawyers Association. All rights reserved.

group may find it difficult to demonstrate recognition in more than one country due to such factors as limited access to news media or consequences of geography."[222]

The second exception allows individuals to be eligible for P-1 status, even if they have not had a relationship of at least one year with the group, for 25 percent of the performers and entertainers in an entertainment group.[223] This may be appropriate, for example, if a foreign national must replace a named P-1 beneficiary "because of illness or unanticipated and exigent circumstances replaces an essential member of the group" or if the foreign national will "augment[] the group by performing a critical role."[224] For substitution of beneficiaries, the Department of State (DOS) is authorized to "waive the 1-year relationship requirement."[225] But in both of these situations, the practitioner is strongly encouraged to provide detailed information regarding the exigent circumstances and/or regarding how the new beneficiary "replaced an essential member of the group."[226]

The third exception applies specifically and only to foreign national circus personnel, and essential support personnel who will assist circus performers,[227] because these individuals "have been accorded special treatment by Congress."[228] These individuals need not have had a relationship of one year with the petitioner's circus or circus group in order to qualify.[229] In addition, the petitioner's circus or circus group need only to have earned national recognition for being "outstanding for a sustained and substantial period of time"; international recognition is not necessary.[230] Further, there "is no requirement in the statute that the circus act itself has to have national or international renown," and the focus of the inquiry is on "the reputation of the circus" overall.[231] The individuals must seek U.S. admission "as a part of such a circus" or in order to join such a circus or circus group.[232]

D. P-2 Artists and Entertainers in Reciprocal Exchange Programs

P-2 status is appropriate for a foreign national who will "perform as an artist or entertainer, individually or as part of a group, or to perform as an integral part of the performance of such a group, and who seeks to perform under a reciprocal exchange

---

[222] 8 CFR §214.2(p)(4)(iii)(C)(2).

[223] INA §214(c)(4)(B)(iii)(I); 8 CFR §214.2(p)(4)(iii)(C)(2).

[224] INA §214(c)(4)(B)(iii)(II); 8 CFR §214.2(p)(4)(iii)(C)(2).

[225] 8 CFR §214.2(p)(4)(iii)(C)(2).

[226] *Matter of [name not provided]*, EAC 04 096 53634 (AAO July 29, 2008), http://bit.ly/jul081d9.

[227] INA §214(c)(4)(B)(iv); 8 CFR §214.2(p)(4)(iii)(C)(1).

[228] Legacy INS, L. Weinig, "Policy Guidelines for the Adjudication of O and P Petitions" (June 25, 1992), 69 Interpreter Releases 1084 (Aug. 31, 1992).

[229] INA §214(c)(4)(B)(iv); 8 CFR §214.2(p)(4)(iii)(C)(1).

[230] INA §214(c)(4)(B)(iv); 8 CFR §214.2(p)(4)(iii)(C)(1); Legacy INS, L. Weinig, "Policy Guidelines for the Adjudication of O and P Petitions" (June 25, 1992), 69 Interpreter Releases 1084 (Aug. 31, 1992).

[231] Legacy INS, L. Weinig, "Policy Guidelines for the Adjudication of O and P Petitions" (June 25, 1992), 69 Interpreter Releases 1084 (Aug. 31, 1992).

[232] INA §214(c)(4)(B)(iv); 8 CFR §214.2(p)(4)(iii)(C)(1).

Copyright © 2017. American Immigration Lawyers Association. All rights reserved.

program."[233] As discussed below, essential support personnel may obtain P-2 status "based on a support relationship to a P-2 artist or entertainer under a reciprocal exchange program."[234] There is "no requirement that P-2 entertainers be of exceptional ability."[235]

The reciprocal exchange program must be between one or more organizations in the United States, which may be management organizations or groups, and one or more organizations "in one or more foreign states" and must "provide[] for the temporary exchange of artists and entertainers, or groups of artists and entertainers."[236] USCIS guidance notes that there are four qualifying exchange programs, between:

- The American Federation of Musicians in the United States and the American Federation of Musicians in Canada;

- The Actor's Equity Association in the United States and the Canadian Actors' Equity Association in Canada;

- The Actor's Equity Association in the United States and the British Actors' Equity Association in the United Kingdom; and

- The International Council of Air Shows and the Canadian Air Show Association.[237]

USCIS no longer requires that adjudication of a P-2 petition based on another exchange program be reviewed by USCIS Headquarters "to determine if it meets the regulatory standards regarding reciprocal agreements":

"The regulations require that the petitioner submit evidence that an appropriate labor organization in the U.S. was involved in negotiating, or has concurred with, the reciprocal exchange of the U.S. and foreign artists or entertainers. Given that the Service Centers possess the entire record, they are capable of determining if the reciprocal agreement meets the regulatory requirements. Effective immediately, service centers are not required to contact Headquarters if they encounter a reciprocal agreement not previously approved."[238]

Therefore, if "a reciprocal agreement is submitted other than these four [listed above], the adjudicator must review the agreement to determine if the agreement adheres to the regulatory standard."[239] The exchange program should have procedures in place to ensure that the artists and entertainers exchanged are similar "in terms of

---

[233] 8 CFR §§214.2(p)(1)(ii)(B) and 214.2(p)(5)(i)(A).

[234] 8 CFR §214.2(p)(5)(i)(C).

[235] AFM 33.6.

[236] 8 CFR §§214.2(p)(1)(ii)(B) and 214.2(p)(5)(i)(A); 9 FAM 41.56 N5.

[237] AFM 33.6.

[238] USCIS, D. Neufeld, "Clarifying Guidance on Adjudicating Reciprocal Exchange Agreements Revisions to the Adjudicator's Field Manual (AFM) Chapter 33.6(d) AFM Update AD10-28" (undated, posted Mar. 16, 2010), AILA Doc. No. 10031663.

[239] Id.; AFM 33.6.

Copyright © 2017. American Immigration Lawyers Association. All rights reserved.

caliber" and number and to ensure that the "terms and conditions of employment, such as length of employment" are also similar, although "this requirement does not preclude an individual for group exchange."[240]

A P-2 petition should include the following evidence:

- "A copy of the formal reciprocal exchange agreement" between the U.S. organization(s) "which sponsor" the beneficiaries and the foreign organization(s) "which will receive the U.S. artist or entertainers";

- "A statement from the sponsoring organization describing the reciprocal exchange of U.S. artists or entertainers as it relates to the specific petition for which P-2 classification is being sought";

- Evidence that an appropriate U.S. labor organization "was involved in negotiating, or has concurred with, the reciprocal exchange of U.S. and foreign artists or entertainers"; and

- Evidence that the P-2 beneficiaries have skills that are comparable to those possessed by U.S. artists and/or entertainers subject to the reciprocal exchange agreement, as well as evidence "that the terms and conditions of employment are similar."[241]

As stated by legacy INS: "Since there are no qualitative standards for the P-2 classification, the consultation is the most essential part of the adjudication process. Therefore, the consultation must include all of the items described in the regulation without exception."[242] For a discussion of the advisory opinion, see below. For a discussion of the totality of circumstances analysis and merely submitting the minimum number of types of evidence, see Volume 1: Chapter Twelve, "O Visas and Status."

E. Culturally Unique P-3 Artists and Entertainers

The P-3 classification is available for an artist, entertainer, or entertainment group who will "perform, teach, or coach under a commercial or noncommercial program that is culturally unique."[243] Culturally unique is defined as "a style of artistic expression, methodology, or medium which is unique to a particular country, nation, society, class,

---

[240] 8 CFR §214.2(p)(5)(i)(B).

[241] 8 CFR §214.2(p)(5)(ii). *See also* AFM 33.6 ("Because there is no requirement that P-2 entertainers be of exceptional ability, supporting documents are limited to basic items: the consultation, a copy of the reciprocal agreement and evidence that the beneficiaries are subject to the reciprocal exchange"); USCIS Memorandum, D. Neufeld, "Clarifying Guidance on Adjudicating Reciprocal Exchange Agreements Revisions to the Adjudicator's Field Manual (AFM) Chapter 33.6(d) AFM Update AD10-28" (date unknown), AILA Doc. No. 10031663.

[242] Legacy INS, L. Weinig, "Policy Guidelines for the Adjudication of O and P Petitions" (June 25, 1992), 69 Interpreter Releases 1084 (Aug. 31, 1992).

[243] 8 CFR §§214.2(p)(1)(ii)(C) and 214.2(p)(6)(i)(B).

Copyright © 2017. American Immigration Lawyers Association. All rights reserved.

ethnicity, religion, tribe, or other group of persons."[244] A strong P-3 petition should address this issue, such as how a featured type of music is culturally unique, in depth.[245]

The purpose of the beneficiary's stay in the United States should be to interpret, represent, develop, coach, or teach "a unique or traditional ethnic, folk, cultural, musical, theatrical, or artistic performance or presentation,"[246] by "participat[ing] in a cultural event or events which will further the understanding or development of his or her art form."[247]

The performance may be by an individual or a group,[248] and " there is no requirement for P-3 aliens that the group have existed before their trip to the United States."[249] The regulations allow commercial programs, but "the performances must be sponsored primarily by educational, cultural or governmental agencies."[250] The P-3 classification is not a replacement option for entertainment groups who cannot satisfy the 75 percent rule, because the focus of the inquiry is on whether the performance is culturally unique.[251]

As stated by legacy INS: "Examples of such culturally unique art forms could include Georgian dancers, Irish harpists, or other traditional forms of expression representative of particular countries."[252] And as stated by the AAO: "There is no requirement in either the statute or the regulations that the beneficiary demonstrate the authenticity of [his or her] skills in the cultural art form."[253] In a precedent decision involving Jewish Argentinean musicians, the AAO reversed USCIS's denial, which was based on the rationale that a "hybrid or fusion style of music cannot be considered culturally unique to one particular country, nation, society, class, ethnicity, religion, tribe, or other group of persons."[254] Specifically, the AAO stated:

> "The AAO can find no justification for the director's exclusion from this definition an artistic expression that is derived from a hybrid or fusion of artistic styles or traditions from more than one culture or region. Rather, the fact that the regulatory definition allows its application to an unspecified 'group of persons'

---

[244] 8 CFR §214.2(p)(3).

[245] *Cf. Matter of [name not provided]*, EAC 08 038 51086 (AAO Mar. 11, 2009), http://bit.ly/mar092d9.

[246] 8 CFR §214.2(p)(6)(i)(A).

[247] 8 CFR §214.2(p)(6)(i)(B).

[248] 8 CFR §214.2(p)(1)(ii)(C).

[249] 9 FAM 402.14-5(C).

[250] Legacy INS, L. Weinig, "Policy Guidelines for the Adjudication of O and P Petitions" (June 25, 1992), 69 Interpreter Releases 1084 (Aug. 31, 1992).

[251] *Id.*

[252] Legacy INS, P. Virtue, "O-1 and P Nonimmigrant Visa Classifications" (Sept. 29, 1993), 1 INS and DOJ Legal Opinions §93-76 (internal citation and formatting omitted); *see also Matter of [name not provided]*, WAC 09 800 01866 (AAO Jan. 20, 2010), http://bit.ly/jan101d9 (traditional Ukrainian folk dance and music).

[253] *Matter of [name not provided]*, WAC 06 119 52449 (AAO July 25, 2006), http://bit.ly/2elr2mT.

[254] *Matter of Skirball Cultural Center*, 25 I&N Dec. 799 (AAO 2012), AILA Doc. No. 12051552.

Copyright © 2017. American Immigration Lawyers Association. All rights reserved.

makes allowances for beneficiaries whose unique artistic expression crosses regional, ethnic or other boundaries…. The regulations do not require that an art form be 'traditional' in order to qualify as culturally unique."[255]

While this precedent decision acknowledges that cultural fusion can result in something culturally unique, AAO still looks for performances that are "unique to an identifiable group of persons with a distinct culture."[256]

Documentation of cultural uniqueness needs to be strong and to be internally consistent:

> "[One testimonial] also explains how the beneficiaries, as South Americans born to Eastern European immigrants, came to be influenced by both cultures to create something new and unique to their experience. All three opinion letters recognize the existence of a distinct Jewish Argentine culture and identity that is expressed in the beneficiary group's music, and opine that the beneficiary group is a 'leading exponent and innovator of South American klezmer.'"[257]

Evidence should explain and emphasize what is culturally unique about the beneficiaries' performance, and experts providing supporting documentation should have knowledge of the cultural elements. For example, letters from rock music experts about a "Persian post-surf punk rock" band were dismissed because the experts displayed no knowledge of the Persian influence, only of the rock elements.[258] Similarly, letters that discuss the popularity of a band in its home country, but do not discuss the "cultural or traditional" elements of the performance, have been found meritless.[259]

The petition also should establish, based on the itinerary, that the beneficiary will continue to perform or present a culturally unique art form during the P assignment[260] on a regular basis, as USCIS and the AAO denied a petition where the performances were on an intermittent or occasional basis.[261]

Merely performing in a foreign language or "native dialect"[262] is insufficient to establish cultural uniqueness, because if this argument is accepted, then "all foreign singers who perform in their native language would qualify for the P-3 classification as 'culturally unique' performers,"[263] and "[t]he fact that the proposed programs

---

[255] *Id.*

[256] *Matter of D-C-M-, LLC*, ID# 17337 (AAO Mar. 9, 2016).

[257] *Matter of Skirball Cultural Center*, 25 I&N Dec. 799 (AAO 2012), AILA Doc. No. 12051552.

[258] *Matter of D-C-M-, LLC*, ID# 17337 (AAO Mar. 9, 2016).

[259] *Matter of U-A-E- Corp.*, ID# 14520 (AAO Nov. 30, 2015).

[260] *Matter of [name not provided]*, EAC 04 118 50432 (AAO Dec. 22, 2005), http://bit.ly/dec054d (decorative artwork for residential and organizational customers).

[261] *Matter of [name not provided]*, EAC 03 150 52118 (AAO Aug. 17, 2005), http://bit.ly/aug053d.

[262] *Matter of I-T-P- Inc.*, ID# 15426 (AAO Aug. 26, 2016) (Jamaican acting troupe performing in local dialect).

[263] *Matter of [name not provided]*, WAC 08 800 08004 (AAO Apr. 3, 2009), http://bit.ly/apr091d9; *Matter of [name not provided]*, WAC 06 159 50735 (AAO June 24, 2008), http://bit.ly/jun081d9.

Copyright © 2017. American Immigration Lawyers Association. All rights reserved.

would be in Russian does not necessarily mean that *all* of the proposed events would be culturally unique events anymore [sic] than all programs in English are culturally unique to England or the United States."[264] But note that experience has shown that if the performance will be in English, then it may be difficult to obtain a consultation letter and therefore P-3 status, as the organization may presume that a performance in English is not culturally unique.

Cultural uniqueness seems to be construed as more than an event with a theme that has "some national significance to the beneficiaries' home country,"[265] although "the regulations do not require that an alien's performance date from a certain period in order to be considered culturally unique."[266] That being said, performers of modern music popular in their home countries have not generally fared well in seeking the P-3 category.[267] Also, it seems generally insufficient to only submit documents describing a cultural performance without connecting the art form to the beneficiary's previous performances.[268]

Similarly, a beneficiary's mere connection to another culture's influence does not automatically mean that P-3 classification is appropriate: "It is unclear how the petitioner maintains that preparing floral arrangements for a bar mitzvah or a fundraiser for the American Heart Association will further the development and understanding of Flemish floral design."[269] Neither should cultural uniqueness be confused with popularity with a cultural or ethnic group, originality,[270] or international recognition.[271] In addition, distinguishing between a foreign culture's style or art form and the American style may be insufficient to establish cultural uniqueness.[272] Details regarding the beneficiary's job duties are necessary in order to demonstrate that he or she will perform the required performing, teaching, coaching, representing, or interpreting activities,[273] and directing and producing television plays may be rejected by USCIS.[274]

Similarly, the venues stated in the petition may be evaluated to determine if the performances will comprise culturally unique events, and copies of contracts between

---

[264] *Matter of [name not provided]*, WAC 03 210 50365 (AAO Mar. 7, 2006), http://bit.ly/mar0604d9.

[265] *Matter of [name not provided]*, WAC 06 159 50735 (AAO June 24, 2008), http://bit.ly/jun081d9; *Matter of [name not provided]*, WAC 06 172 52572 (AAO June 23, 2008), http://bit.ly/jun081d.

[266] *Matter of [name not provided]*, WAC 06 172 52572 (AAO June 23, 2008), http://bit.ly/jun081d.

[267] *E.g., Matter of U-A-E- Corp.*, ID# 14520 (AAO Nov. 30, 2015) (popular Albanian band); *Matter of D-C-M-, LLC*, ID# 17337 (AAO Mar. 9, 2016) (Iranian punk rock band).

[268] *Matter of [name not provided]*, WAC 06 159 50735 (AAO June 24, 2008), http://bit.ly/jun081d9.

[269] *Matter of [name not provided]*, WAC 07 042 52371 (AAO Aug. 1, 2008), http://bit.ly/aug088d.

[270] *Matter of [name not provided]*, WAC 06 119 52449 (AAO July 25, 2006), http://bit.ly/jul061d9.

[271] *Matter of [name not provided]*, EAC 05 021 52907 (AAO Dec. 22, 2005), http://bit.ly/dec051d.

[272] *Matter of [name not provided]*, WAC 07 042 52371 (AAO Aug. 1, 2008), http://bit.ly/aug088d.

[273] *Matter of [name not provided]*, EAC 06 041 51888 (AAO July 29, 2008), http://bit.ly/jul083d.

[274] *Matter of [name not provided]*, WAC 03 210 50365 (AAO Mar. 7, 2006), http://bit.ly/mar0604d9 (USCIS denial on this ground reversed by the AAO in part because the petitioner stated on appeal that the beneficiary would also act).

Copyright © 2017. American Immigration Lawyers Association. All rights reserved.

the venues and the petitioner may help to demonstrate this fact, as opposed to "perform[ing] pop songs in their native language for the entertainment of patrons of the nightclubs and casinos at which [the beneficiaries] will perform."[275] But generally, "[t]here is no statutory or regulatory requirement that P-3 entertainers present at venues that limit performances to only those that are culturally unique."[276]

A P-3 petition should include the following evidence:

- Statements, which may be in the form of affidavits, testimonials, or letters, "from recognized experts" in the field or industry, "attesting to the authenticity of the alien's or the group's skills in performing, presenting, coaching, or teaching the unique or traditional art form and giving the credentials of the expert, including the basis of his or her knowledge of the alien's or group's skill"; or

- Independent evidence, in the form of reviews in newspapers, journals, or other published materials, of how the performance is culturally unique; and

- "Evidence that all of the performances or presentations will be culturally unique events."[277]

For a discussion of the totality of circumstances analysis and merely submitting the minimum number of types of evidence, see Volume 1: Chapter Twelve, "O Visas and Status." The statements from experts must state the qualifications of the signatories and "the basis of [their] knowledge of the beneficiary's skill,"[278] and should explain how the entertainer or group has "experience in delivering a culturally unique performance,"[279] and "will prospectively perform in culturally unique programs."[280] If an RFE requests evidence of remunerating the beneficiary while he or she previously held P-3 status, then submitting only two checks may be insufficient.[281] The absence of the signatory's credentials may result in the statement being rejected.[282]

---

[275] *Matter of [name not provided]*, WAC 08 800 08004 (AAO Apr. 3, 2009), http://bit.ly/apr091d9.

[276] *Matter of [name not provided]*, WAC 04 010 50133 (AAO Jan. 10, 2006), http://bit.ly/jan061d9 (performances scheduled "at the San Francisco Fisherman's Wharf, various farmers markets, malls, and festivals").

[277] 8 CFR §214.2(p)(6)(ii); *Matter of [name not provided]*, WAC 06 800 12420 (AAO Aug. 1, 2008), http://bit.ly/aug081d (petition denied for failure to submit evidence for the first two criteria, as well as an advisory opinion from an appropriate labor organization); *Matter of [name not provided]*, WAC 07 023 50953 (AAO Aug. 1, 2008), http://bit.ly/aug085d (same).

[278] *Matter of [name not provided]*, WAC 03 211 53798 (AAO May 23, 2005), http://bit.ly/may0501d9.

[279] *Matter of [name not provided]*, WAC 08 800 08004 (AAO Apr. 3, 2009), http://bit.ly/apr091d9 (noting that the "beneficiaries appear to be a random assortment of well-known Vietnamese pop singers").

[280] *Matter of [name not provided]*, WAC 07 023 50953 (AAO Aug. 1, 2008), http://bit.ly/aug085d; *Matter of [name not provided]*, EAC 06 041 51888 (AAO July 29, 2008), http://bit.ly/jul083d.

[281] *Matter of [name not provided]*, EAC 03 260 51773 (AAO Mar. 2, 2006), http://bit.ly/mar0602d9.

[282] *Matter of U-A-E- Corp.*, ID# 14520 (AAO Nov. 30, 2015); *Matter of [name not provided]*, WAC 06 221 50605 (AAO Aug. 1, 2008), http://bit.ly/aug087d; *Matter of [name not provided]*, WAC 06 800 10474 (AAO July 29, 2008), http://bit.ly/jul082d; *Matter of [name not provided]*, EAC 05 021 52907 (AAO Dec. 22, 2005), http://bit.ly/dec051d.

Copyright © 2017. American Immigration Lawyers Association. All rights reserved.

A petitioner may not submit the required advisory opinion in place of the statements from industry experts,[283] especially if the advisory opinion is essentially a letter of no objection,[284] even if the labor organization emphatically states its belief that the beneficiaries qualify.[285] Neither may "professional biographies" and "CD covers" replace the expert statements.[286]

For the independent evidence criterion, the published materials should ideally confirm the statements from recognized experts,[287] but should at the very least mention the particular cultural art form of the beneficiary or entertainment group and discuss each of the named beneficiaries of a group.[288] Advertisements generally do not establish the cultural uniqueness of a performance,[289] and neither do copies of publications that do not mention the beneficiary even if they do describe the differing style or art form of a foreign culture.[290] USCIS and/or the AAO may note the absence of U.S. reviews or program brochures if the petition indicates that the beneficiary has been performing in the United States for some time.[291]

Evidence about the U.S. performances should specifically show how a culturally unique performance is incorporated "as a significant component."[292] For example, one P-3 petition was denied based on lack of this detail for a Chinese New Year Festival and an International Moon Festival, where the petitioner only mentioned multicultural performances.[293] The venues and dates of performances should be named.[294] As a practical matter, documents evidencing the cultural uniqueness of the performance should frequently be the same documents that describe the event or

---

[283] *Matter of [name not provided]*, EAC 08 038 51086 (AAO Mar. 11, 2009), http://bit.ly/mar092d9; *Matter of [name not provided]*, WAC 06 221 50605 (AAO Aug. 1, 2008), http://bit.ly/aug087d.

[284] *Matter of [name not provided]*, WAC 08 800 08004 (AAO Apr. 3, 2009), http://bit.ly/apr091d9.

[285] *Matter of [name not provided]*, EAC 08 038 51086 (AAO Mar. 11, 2009), http://bit.ly/mar092d9.

[286] *Id.*

[287] *Matter of [name not provided]*, WAC 06 800 10474 (AAO July 29, 2008), http://bit.ly/jul082d; *Matter of [name not provided]* WAC 10 003 51578 (AAO Dec. 19, 2009), http://bit.ly/dec091d.

[288] *Matter of [name not provided]*, EAC 03 266 553300 (AAO Dec. 22, 2005), http://bit.ly/dec053d (no mention of the style of music); *Matter of [name not provided]*, LIN 05 058 52346 (AAO Dec. 15, 2005), http://bit.ly/dec051d9 (same).

[289] *Matter of [name not provided]*, WAC 06 186 52752 (AAO Aug. 1, 2008), http://bit.ly/aug082d; *Matter of [name not provided]*, WAC 03 211 53798 (AAO May 23, 2005), http://bit.ly/may0501d9.

[290] *Matter of [name not provided]*, WAC 07 042 52371 (AAO Aug. 1, 2008), http://bit.ly/aug088d.

[291] *Matter of [name not provided]*, EAC 03 260 51773 (AAO Mar. 2, 2006), http://bit.ly/mar062d (three years).

[292] *Matter of [name not provided]*, EAC 06 041 51888 (AAO July 29, 2008), http://bit.ly/jul083d.

[293] *Id.*

[294] *Matter of [name not provided]*, WAC 06 800 10474 (AAO July 29, 2008), http://bit.ly/jul082d (venues not named).

Copyright © 2017. American Immigration Lawyers Association. All rights reserved.

performance for general P classification,[295] as discussed above, so a submitted contract should specify the type of cultural art form to be presented or performed.[296]

F. Supporting Evidence for P Petitions

The following supporting evidence must be submitted to USCIS with the P petition:

- Evidence appropriate to the particular nonimmigrant classification;[297]

- "Copies of any written contracts between the petitioner and the alien beneficiary or, if there is no written contract, a summary of the terms of the oral agreement under which the alien will be employed,"[298] as discussed below;

- "An explanation of the nature of the events or activities, the beginning and ending dates for the events or activities, and a copy of any itinerary for the events or activities";[299] and

- "A written consultation from a labor organization,"[300] as discussed below.

Any document, such as an affidavit, contract, or award, that demonstrates national or international recognition or the beneficiary's accomplishment(s) "must reflect the nature of the alien's achievement and be executed by an officer or responsible person employed by the institution, firm, establishment, or organization where the work was performed."[301]

Photocopies of original documents may be filed with USCIS, but the original must be submitted if USCIS requests it.[302] All documents in a foreign language should be accompanied by certified full translations[303] that translate the entire document rather than provide "a general description of the content of the articles."[304] All published

---

[295] *Matter of [name not provided]*, EAC 06 041 51888 (AAO July 29, 2008), http://bit.ly/jul083d (USCIS RFE requested "a complete description of engagements, itineraries and contracts to establish that the beneficiary is coming to the United States to participate in an entertainment event or engagement").

[296] *Matter of [name not provided]*, EAC 03 266 553300 (AAO Dec. 22, 2005), http://bit.ly/dec053d.

[297] 8 CFR §214.2(p)(2)(ii)(A).

[298] 8 CFR §214.2(p)(2)(ii)(B).

[299] 8 CFR §214.2(p)(2)(ii)(C); *Matter of [name not provided]*, WAC 05 231 52139 (AAO Mar. 8, 2006), http://bit.ly/mar064d9.

[300] 8 CFR §214.2(p)(2)(ii)(D).

[301] 8 CFR §214.2(p)(2)(iii)(A).

[302] 8 CFR §214.2(p)(2)(iii)(C).

[303] *See, e.g., Matter of [name not provided]*, WAC 08 800 06171 (AAO Feb. 20, 2009), http://bit.ly/feb091d9; *Matter of [name not provided]*, WAC 06 800 10474 (AAO July 29, 2008), http://bit.ly/jul082d; *Matter of [name not provided]*, WAC 06 159 50735 (AAO June 24, 2008), http://bit.ly/jun081d9; *Matter of [name not provided]*, EAC 03 266 52192 (AAO Aug. 23, 2005), http://bit.ly/aug0501d9; *Matter of [name not provided]*, EAC 03 177 53938 (AAO Aug. 12, 2005), http://bit.ly/aug051d9.

[304] *Matter of [name not provided]*, EAC 04 252 53882 (AAO Nov. 30, 2005), http://bit.ly/nov051d9.

Copyright © 2017. American Immigration Lawyers Association. All rights reserved.

materials should state the title and date of publication.[305] USCIS "can not accept documentation in electronic format for security reasons."[306]

1. Testimonials from Industry Experts

Any statements or affidavits "written by present or former employers or recognized experts certifying to the recognition ... of the alien ... shall specifically describe the alien's recognition and ability or achievement in factual terms" and "set forth the expertise of the affiant and the manner in which the affiant acquired such information."[307] Put more simply, the individual providing the recommendation should not merely make conclusory statements that the beneficiary has earned international recognition,[308] or is "a well respected competitor,"[309] but should provide extensive details about the beneficiary's achievements and accomplishments that demonstrate international recognition.[310] For example, the AAO noted that an individual "wrote that the beneficiary has won 'numerous prestigious awards with her horses,' but failed to assert, let alone establish, that the beneficiary is internationally recognized."[311] For a detailed discussion of testimonials, see Volume 1: Chapter Twelve, "O Visas and Status."

The statement or affidavit should also state any relevant qualifications of the recommender, such as educational and/or professional degrees, years of experience in the industry, receipt of awards, membership in professional organizations, service as the judge of others, and authorship of articles.[312] The practitioner may note that these points correlate to the extraordinary ability criteria, discussed in Volume 1: Chapter Twelve, "O Visas and Status"; this is because, as a practical matter, these tend to be the factors considered by USCIS when determining whether an individual qualifies as an expert.[313] The recommender should also state how he or she is familiar with the

---

[305] *Matter of [name not provided]*, EAC 04 233 53201 (AAO Sept. 21, 2006), http://bit.ly/sep061d9 ("two undated articles from unnamed publications"); *Matter of [name not provided]*, SRC 04 243 53449 (AAO Mar. 1, 2006), http://bit.ly/mar065d9; *Matter of [name not provided]*, SRC 05 075 50527 (AAO Feb. 24, 2006), http://bit.ly/feb061d9; *Matter of [name not provided]*, EAC 03 266 553300 (AAO Dec. 22, 2005), http://bit.ly/dec053d; *Matter of [name not provided]*, EAC 03 177 53938 (AAO Aug. 12, 2005), http://bit.ly/aug051d9.

[306] "AILA Liaison/Nebraska Service Center Liaison Teleconference Q&As" (June 25, 2009), AILA Doc. No. 09070864. Although the discussion relates to extraordinary ability immigrant visa petitions, the principle should remain the same.

[307] 8 CFR §214.2(p)(2)(iii)(B).

[308] *Matter of [name not provided]*, SRC 05 075 50527 (AAO Feb. 24, 2006), http://bit.ly/feb061d9.

[309] *Matter of [name not provided]*, EAC 04 238 53587 (AAO Nov. 28, 2005), http://bit.ly/nov051d91.

[310] *Matter of [name not provided]*, SRC 05 075 50527 (AAO Feb. 24, 2006), http://bit.ly/feb061d9.

[311] *Matter of [name not provided]*, SRC 05 075 50527 (AAO Feb. 24, 2006), http://bit.ly/feb061d9.

[312] *Matter of [name not provided]*, EAC 03 177 53938 (AAO Aug. 12, 2005), http://bit.ly/aug051d9; *Matter of [name not provided]*, WAC 10 003 51578 (AAO Dec. 19, 2009), http://bit.ly/dec091d.

[313] *Matter of [name not provided]*, EAC 05 021 52907 (AAO Dec. 22, 2005), http://bit.ly/dec051d. For a further discussion of credentials of experts, see Volume 1: Chapter Twelve, "O Visas and Status."

Copyright © 2017. American Immigration Lawyers Association. All rights reserved.

work or achievements of the beneficiary,[314] with the dates of employment by the same entity, if applicable.

The testimonials also should not contain the identical content to each other,[315] or to the petitioner's support statement, as repetition "indicates that the language of the letter is not the author's own and further detracts from its probative value."[316] If the statement is on personal letterhead, then USCIS and/or the AAO may question whether the testimonial is provided in the signatory's official capacity.[317] If a statement can only be obtained on personal letterhead, it can be helpful to affix a business card from the signatory to the signed statement.

2. Advisory Opinion from a Labor Organization

An advisory opinion "regarding the nature of the work to be done and the alien's qualifications,"[318] from a labor organization "with expertise in the specific field of athletics or entertainment involved" for P-1 and P-3 nonimmigrants,[319] "representing artists and entertainers in the United States" for P-2 petitions,[320] and for essential support personnel,[321] is "mandatory,"[322] and must be included in the initial P petition.[323] Unlike with the O visa, peer reviews are not acceptable—only a union advisory can be used.[324] Although the opinion is not binding upon USCIS, no P petition may be approved without such an advisory opinion,[325] except as discussed below.

As stated by legacy INS: "Labor organizations are very sensitive to the consultation process and [legacy INS] must ensure that such entities are consulted at all costs.... This statutory provision provides organized labor with input on any petition filed with the Service."[326] But the impact on American workers is not the only reason for requiring the advisory opinion:

---

[314] 8 CFR §214.2(p)(2)(iii)(B).

[315] *Matter of [name not provided]*, SRC 04 243 53449 (AAO Mar. 1, 2006), http://bit.ly/mar065d9.

[316] *Matter of [name not provided]*, EAC 06 041 51888 (AAO July 29, 2008), http://bit.ly/jul083d; *Matter of [name not provided]*, EAC 04 118 50432 (AAO Dec. 22, 2005), http://bit.ly/dec054d.

[317] *Matter of [name not provided]*, SRC 05 075 50527 (AAO Feb. 24, 2006), http://bit.ly/feb061d9.

[318] 8 CFR §214.2(p)(7)(i)(A).

[319] INA §§214(c)(4)(D) and 214(c)(6)(A)(iii).

[320] INA §214(c)(4)(E).

[321] 8 CFR §§214.2(p)(4)(iv)(B)(*1*), 214.2(p)(5)(iii)(B)(*1*), and 214.2(p)(6)(iii)(B)(*1*).

[322] 8 CFR §§214.2(p)(7)(i)(A) and 214.2(p)(7)(i)(C).

[323] 8 CFR §214.2(p)(7)(i)(D).

[324] *Matter of [name and case number not provided]* (AAO Mar. 3, 2011), http://bit.ly/mar111d9.

[325] 8 CFR §214.2(p)(7)(i)(D); legacy INS, L. Weinig, "Policy Guidelines for the Adjudication of O and P Petitions," (June 25, 1992), 69 Interpreter Releases 1084 (Aug. 31, 1992); *Matter of [name not provided]*, EAC 06 041 51888 (AAO July 29, 2008), http://bit.ly/jul083d; *Matter of [name not provided]*, WAC 06 166 50592 (AAO July 24, 2008), http://bit.ly/jul01d9.

[326] Legacy INS, L. Weinig, "Policy Guidelines for the Adjudication of O and P Petitions," (June 25, 1992), 69 Interpreter Releases 1084 (Aug. 31, 1992).

Copyright © 2017. American Immigration Lawyers Association. All rights reserved.

"While the desire of unions to ban or limit the employment of foreign entertainers utilized to the detriment of unemployed American performers is appreciated, the opinions of such organizations must be given some weight because of their pertinency in matters involving an assessment of the merit and availability of performers in areas in which they are of necessity experienced and knowledgeable."[327]

"Finally, the labor consultation requirement not only ensures that appropriate labor organizations will be informed about the group's hiring activities, but also that such labor organizations will have an opportunity to provide their input into the P-1 petition process…. For instance, a labor organization may conclude that, contrary to the petitioner[']s claim, a prospective P-1 nonimmigrant performer or entertainer will not provide functions integral to the performance of the group. While an advisory opinion is not binding on the Service, it can provide the Service with a perspective different from the petitioner[']s regarding the alien's qualifications for P-1 classification. As such, it can be an extremely valuable tool in assisting the Service to properly adjudicate P-1 petitions filed on behalf of alien performers and entertainers."[328]

The advisory opinion must be written,[329] "must be signed by an authorized official of the organization,"[330] "and must discuss "the nature of the work to be done," and the beneficiary's qualifications.[331] It is strongly encouraged that the advisory opinion be on the official letterhead of the labor organization, with contact information, so USCIS may "verify its contents."[332] If the signatory's job title does not clearly demonstrate his official role within the labor organization, the practitioner should provide information describing how the signatory served on the board of the organization "or held a similarly authoritative position of leadership" when the letter was written and signed.[333] For a discussion of fraudulent advisory opinions, see Volume 1: Chapter Twelve, "O Visas and Status."

USCIS guidance provides a list of labor organizations "which have agreed to provide advisory opinions."[334] A list of organizations that have agreed to provide consultation letters on O and P petitions is available to American Immigration

---

[327] *Matter of Shaw*, 11 I&N Dec. 277 (D.D. 1965). Although the case addressed a performer under the former H-1B standard of prominence, the principle should remain the same.

[328] Legacy INS, P. Virtue, "O-1 and P Nonimmigrant Visa Classifications" (Sept. 29, 1993), 1 INS and DOJ Legal Opinions §93-76 (internal citation omitted).

[329] 8 CFR §§214.2(p)(7)(i)(B), (C), and (D).

[330] 8 CFR §214.2(p)(7)(i)(C).

[331] 8 CFR §214.2(p)(7)(i)(A).

[332] *Matter of [name not provided]*, WAC 08 800 06171 (AAO Feb. 20, 2009), http://bit.ly/feb091d9.

[333] *Matter of [name not provided]*, SRC 05 204 50594 (AAO Oct. 13, 2006), *available at* https://www.uscis.gov (select "Laws," "Administrative Decisions" link on the right toolbar under "More Information," D9, and then search by date and for "01D9101").

[334] 8 CFR §214.2(p)(7)(vii).

Copyright © 2017. American Immigration Lawyers Association. All rights reserved.

Lawyers Association (AILA) members on the AILA website.[335] A somewhat older list can also be found on the USCIS website.[336] Because the list is neither "exclusive" nor "exhaustive," USCIS "and petitioners may use other sources, such as publications, to identify appropriate labor organizations."[337] The practitioner should confirm that the appropriate office receives the request, as "many of the consulting entities are sensitive about their jurisdictions."[338] The practitioner should also ensure that an advisory opinion is obtained "for each type of occupation listed on the petition, if the occupations are represented by different unions."[339] For a definition of labor organizations in the context of O petitions, see Volume 1: Chapter Twelve, "O Visas and Status."[340]

The practitioner may find it helpful to provide the following documents to the labor organization:

- Cover letter with the practitioner's contact information;

- Copy of the P petition, including the Form I-129, P Supplement, employer's support statement, and selected documents evidencing the achievements of the beneficiary, team, or group, or evidencing the beneficiary's qualifications as "essential support" personnel;

- Copy of the employment contract or summary of the terms of the employment agreement;

- Copy of the itinerary of events, performances, and/or activities; and

- Check to cover the cost of the advisory opinion, including any fee for expedited processing of the opinion, if applicable.[341]

The practitioner should follow up with the labor organization to ensure that the required advisory opinion is provided in a timely manner.[342] The written statement from the labor organization should have one of the following structures:

---

[335] "Updated Address Index for I-129 O & P Consultation Letters" (updated June 3, 2016), AILA Doc. No. 16060305.

[336] USCIS, "Address Index for I-129 O & P Consultation Letters" (updated Mar. 11, 2013), http://bit.ly/2dHkz1O.

[337] Id.

[338] Legacy INS, L. Weinig, "Policy Guidelines for the Adjudication of O and P Petitions," (June 25, 1992), 69 Interpreter Releases 1084 (Aug. 31, 1992).

[339] Id.

[340] The regulations for P petitions do not provide a definition of labor organization, but the definition for O petitions should be cross-applicable.

[341] "AILA/VSC Committee Practice Pointer: O-1: How to Obtain a Labor Union Consultation" (July 29, 2009), AILA Doc. No. 09072962. Although the discussion addressed consultations for O-1 petitions, the principle should remain the same, as the same labor organizations are on the list of appropriate organizations.

[342] *Matter of [name not provided]*, WAC 07 042 52371 (AAO Aug. 1, 2008), http://bit.ly/aug088d (no advisory opinion from labor organization 21 months after the request was mailed); *Matter of [name not provided]*, WAC 06 166 50592 (AAO July 24, 2008), http://bit.ly/jul0801d9 (counsel claimed in response to the RFE that the labor organizations were "backlogged").

Copyright © 2017. American Immigration Lawyers Association. All rights reserved.

- Detailed statement of favorable support for the P petition, as discussed below;

- "If the advisory opinion is not favorable to the petitioner, the advisory opinion must set forth a specific statement of facts which supports the conclusion reached in the opinion";[343] or

- Statement of "no objection" if the organization "has no objection to the approval of the petition," for P-1 and P-3 petitions on behalf of principal beneficiaries and essential support personnel,[344] though it remains unclear whether a statement of no objection must include a "statement of facts in support of this conclusion."[345]

A favorable advisory opinion for a P-1 athlete, entertainer, or entertainment group should explore the beneficiary or beneficiaries and the assignment in the following manner:

"[E]valuate and/or describe the alien's or group's ability and achievements in the field of endeavor, comment on whether the alien or group is internationally recognized for achievements, and state whether the services the alien or group is coming to perform are appropriate for an internationally recognized athlete or entertainment group."[346]

For P-1 circus personnel, the "advisory opinion provided by the labor organization should comment on whether the circus which will employ the alien has national recognition as well as any other aspect of the beneficiary's or beneficiaries' qualifications which the labor organization deems appropriate."[347] An advisory opinion for a P-2 petition should "verify the existence of a viable exchange program" and "comment on the bona fides of the reciprocal exchange program and specify whether the exchange meets the requirements."[348] An advisory opinion for a P-3 petition "should evaluate the cultural uniqueness of the alien's skills, state whether the events are cultural in nature, and state whether the event or activity is appropriate for P-3 classification."[349] For a discussion of an advisory opinion for essential support personnel, see below.

---

[343] 8 CFR §§214.2(p)(7)(i)(C), 214.2(p)(7)(ii)–(vi).

[344] 8 CFR §§214.2(p)(7)(i)(C), 214.2(p)(7)(ii), 214.2(p)(7)(iii), 214.2(p)(7)(v), and 214.2(p)(7)(vi).

[345] *Matter of [name not provided]*, WAC 08 800 08004 (AAO Apr. 3, 2009), http://bit.ly/fapr091d9 (labor organization's opinion provided general information, as opposed to specific information, and was not explicitly rejected by the AAO, but the AAO noted that it "is unclear how the [labor organization] reached [its] conclusion based on the evidence submitted with the petition"); *Matter of [name not provided]*, WAC 03 210 50365 (AAO Mar. 7, 2006), http://bit.ly/mar0604d9 (no objection letter rejected for failing to provide specifics required of P-3 consultations).

[346] 8 CFR §214.2(p)(7)(ii).

[347] 8 CFR §214.2(p)(7)(iii).

[348] 8 CFR §214.2(p)(7)(iv).

[349] 8 CFR §214.2(p)(7)(v); *Matter of [name not provided]*, WAC 03 210 50365 (AAO Mar. 7, 2006), http://bit.ly/mar0604d9.

Copyright © 2017. American Immigration Lawyers Association. All rights reserved.

An unfavorable advisory opinion does not necessarily mean that the P petition will be denied, since the consultation is not binding on USCIS,[350] but the practitioner is encouraged to work with the organization to identify the reasons for the statements and to provide information or documents that may address those concerns. Otherwise, the supporting evidence must more firmly establish the beneficiary's eligibility for P status:

"A negative consultation does not automatically result in the denial of the petition, as decisions must be based on the totality of the evidence. Accordingly, if the petitioner can submit evidence that overcomes a negative advisory opinion and which establishes the merits of the alien, USCIS may approve the petition."[351]

It is generally inappropriate and inadequate to submit an advisory opinion that discusses only one beneficiary when classification is requested for a group.[352] But an advisory opinion may also be "inadequate" if it is "outdated" or "a photocopy, very poorly worded, grammatically incorrect and suspect."[353] A statement from an entity that is not the appropriate labor organization, such as a company to whom the beneficiaries will be contracted for employment, may not serve as an advisory opinion.[354] For a further discussion of other inappropriate advisory opinions, see Volume 1: Chapter Twelve, "O Visas and Status."

The statute states that regulations will establish "expedited consultation procedures in the case of nonimmigrant artists or entertainers ... to accommodate the exigencies and scheduling of a given production or event" and "expedited consultation procedures in the case of nonimmigrant athletes ... in the case of emergency circumstances (including trades during a season),"[355] but it seems that there is no formal guidance, except for where the petitioner does not obtain an advisory opinion, as discussed below.

Legacy INS guidance, issued shortly after the P visa category was created, stated:

"Due to the novelty of the O and P classifications, it is suggested that officers involved in the adjudication of O and P petitions adopt a lenient policy towards accepting consultations submitted by petitioners, as long as they appear reasonable.... Petitioners should not be penalized because of the inability of the consulting entity to provide the appropriate consultation."[356]

It is doubtful that such leniency exists today, almost 20 years after the P visa category was created, as has been seen from AAO rejections of various advisory

---

[350] 8 CFR §214.2(p)(7)(i)(D); AFM 33.3.

[351] AFM 33.3.

[352] *Matter of [name not provided]*, WAC 04 010 50133 (AAO Jan. 10, 2006), http://bit.ly/jan061d9.

[353] *Matter of [name not provided]*, EAC 03 181 54109 (AAO May 25, 2005), http://bit.ly/may051d9.

[354] *Matter of [name not provided]*, WAC 06 229 53697 (AAO Aug. 1, 2008), http://bit.ly/aug089d.

[355] INA §214(c)(6)(E).

[356] Legacy INS, L. Weinig, "Policy Guidelines for the Adjudication of O and P Petitions," (June 25, 1992), 69 Interpreter Releases 1084 (Aug. 31, 1992).

Copyright © 2017. American Immigration Lawyers Association. All rights reserved.

opinions that do not meet the letter of the regulations.[357] Thus, the practitioner is encouraged to educate the consulting entity of the points that must be stated in an advisory opinion.

3. Exceptions to the Advisory Opinion Requirement

There are two main exceptions to the requirement to submit an advisory opinion. First, if the petitioner establishes that "an appropriate labor organization does not exist," then USCIS "shall render a decision on the evidence of record."[358] As noted by legacy INS: "This evidence will probably take the form of affidavits or statements from individuals employed in the beneficiary's field of endeavor. Common sense will dictate whether the evidence submitted establishes the nonexistence of a labor organization."[359] A petitioner may not take advantage of the exception merely by stating, without corroborating evidence, that there is no appropriate labor organization.[360] An "expert opinion" attesting to the absence of an appropriate labor organization may be accepted.[361]

Legacy INS guidance also states that a list of "those occupations or fields of endeavor where it has been determined by the Service that no appropriate labor organization exists" is available.[362] But because the list of labor organizations that do provide advisory opinions is neither exclusive nor exhaustive, as discussed above, the petitioner should not claim that there is no appropriate labor organization for the occupation simply because the occupation is not covered by the labor organizations stated on the list.[363] Neither may a petitioner avoid the advisory opinion requirement by stating that "the beneficiaries are non-unionized and would not be performing any equity performance union contracts."[364]

If an organization exists, but it no longer provides advisory opinions, then independent evidence, ideally from the organization, should be provided as substantiation.[365] Alternatively, the practitioner may need to explain why a labor

---

[357] *E.g., Matter of [name and case number not provided]* (AAO July 28, 2011), http://bit.ly/jul111d (rejecting advisory opinion from expert in the field where no union exists and letter was found not sufficiently detailed); *Matter of [name and case number not provided]* (AAO Aug. 27, 2014), http://bit.ly/aug14ld (opinion regarding essential support personnel addressed horse grooms generally and was not specific to the beneficiary).

[358] INA §214(c)(6)(C); 8 CFR §214.2(p)(7)(i)(F).

[359] Legacy INS, L. Weinig, "Policy Guidelines for the Adjudication of O and P Petitions," (June 25, 1992), 69 Interpreter Releases 1084 (Aug. 31, 1992).

[360] *Matter of [name not provided]*, SRC 05 163 50684 (AAO Dec. 13, 2005), http://bit.ly/dec052d9; *Matter of [name not provided]*, EAC 03 266 52192 (AAO Aug. 23, 2005), http://bit.ly/aug0501d9.

[361] *Matter of [name not provided]*, WAC 93 169 50795 (AAU Sept. 30, 1994), 13 Immig. Rptr. B2-180 (AAU accepted letter "from an official of the United States Surfing Federation" for a surfer).

[362] 8 CFR §214.2(p)(7)(vii).

[363] *Matter of [name not provided]*, WAC 05 191 50035 (AAO Mar. 7, 2006), http://bit.ly/mar063d9.

[364] *Matter of [name not provided]*, SRC 05 063 50385 (AAO Dec. 13, 2005), http://bit.ly/dec0501d9.

[365] *Matter of [name not provided]*, WAC 08 038 50550 (AAO May 1, 2009), http://bit.ly/may091d9 (counsel's submission of his or her own statement and an excerpt from an immigration text was rejected by
Cont'd

Copyright © 2017. American Immigration Lawyers Association. All rights reserved.

organization that is not a union "cannot be considered a labor organization with expertise in the beneficiary's field."[366] But if USCIS accepts that no appropriate labor organization exists, then USCIS should not request a consultation from a peer group as "alternate evidence."[367]

Second, USCIS affirmatively "shall contact the labor organization and request an advisory opinion if one is not submitted by the petitioner," as long as USCIS "has determined that a petition merits expeditious handling,"[368] "based on the merits of the case, such as an overriding humanitarian concern."[369] Importantly, "[e]xpedited processing should not be confused with premium processing," where a response is provided in 15 days because of an additional $1,225 fee,[370] as discussed below.

In such a situation, a response must be provided by the labor organization within 24 hours, USCIS should adjudicate the petition after receiving the labor organization's response, and the advisory opinion(s) must be provided within an additional five business days of the request.[371] Both communications may be made by telephone.[372] USCIS will adjudicate the petition without the advisory opinion if the labor organization fails to respond within 24 hours.[373]

P-1 petitions on behalf of major league baseball players should not need to have an advisory opinion, because it has already "been furnished to Headquarters."[374] The statement "from the Major League Baseball Players Association (MLBPA) states that all foreign baseball players who have signed a major league contract have in the opinion of the MLBPA, established eligibility for either P-1 or O-1 classifications," and adjudicating officers have been directed "to accept this letter as the required consultation."[375] Similarly, petitions filed on behalf of hockey players employed by the National Hockey League (NHL) need only have a "letter from the NHL Player's

---

the AAO and USCIS because the petitioner had obtained a consultation the year before the relevant petition was filed).

[366] *Matter of [name not provided]*, SRC 06 086 51969 (AAO Mar. 11, 2009), http://bit.ly/mar091d9 (questioning why the Jockey's Guild, self-described as "the only organization in the United States at this time that has the authority to represent jockeys in labor matters," could not provide the advisory opinion); *Matter of [name not provided]*, SRC 06 087 52651 (AAO Feb. 9, 2009), http://bit.ly/feb093d.

[367] *Matter of [name not provided]*, EAC 08 054 50732 (AAO Aug. 18, 2008), http://bit.ly/aug083d (calling the USCIS request "inappropriate").

[368] 8 CFR §214.2(p)(7)(i)(E).

[369] AFM 33.8.

[370] *Id.*

[371] 8 CFR §214.2(p)(7)(i)(E).

[372] AFM 33.8.

[373] 8 CFR §214.2(p)(7)(i)(E).

[374] AFM 33.10.

[375] *Id. See also* legacy INS, J. Bednarz, "P-1 Petitions for Professional Baseball Players" (Jan. 15, 1993), AILA Doc. No. 04110465 (see Related Resources link or simply go to http://www.aila.org/content/default.aspx?docid=11780).

Copyright © 2017. American Immigration Lawyers Association. All rights reserved.

Association," which is the relevant labor organization. "An individual consultation letter is NOT required."[376]

4. Employment Contracts and Summaries of Terms of the Oral Agreement Under Which the Beneficiary Will Be Employed

Failure to submit these document(s) is grounds for denial of the P petition.[377] Generally, an "unsigned, generic contract" is insufficient.[378] A "loosely structured contract" may be sufficient if the petitioner "demonstrate[s] that this contract is commensurate with international recognition in the sport."[379] If a summary of an oral agreement or contract, such as a memorandum of understanding,[380] is submitted, it must state the "proposed wages or compensation to be paid to the beneficiaries,"[381] as well as "the essential terms under which the beneficiary would be employed."[382] Information stated in the contract should be consistent with that stated on the documents for the P petition, as all the documents may be compared with each other.[383] The proposed job duties stated in the contract may also be evaluated to determine whether they describe an appropriate event,[384] as discussed above. For a further discussion of contracts, see Volume 1: Chapter Twelve, "O Visas and Status."

An employment contract for essential support personnel should demonstrate how the "beneficiary will perform support services for the P-1 alien and strictly for the principal alien under the terms of the written contract submitted," by naming the specific principal P nonimmigrant "for whom the beneficiary would work."[385]

5. Explanation of Services and Itinerary

The explanation of services or itinerary should be consistent with the event, as discussed above: "In some instances the itinerary would be defined as ... the performance season or concert halls where the alien would be perform."[386] As discussed above, the itinerary and/or explanation of services should cover the entire period of time requested for the P assignment, as otherwise it is highly likely that the

---

[376] AFM 33.10 (emphasis in original).

[377] *Matter of [name not provided]*, SRC 06 086 51969 (AAO Mar. 11, 2009), http://bit.ly/mar091d9.

[378] *Id.*

[379] *Matter of [name not provided]*, WAC 93 169 50795 (AAU Sept. 30, 1994), 13 Immig. Rptr. B2-180.

[380] *Matter of [name not provided]*, WAC 05 231 52139 (AAO Mar. 8, 2006), http://bit.ly/mar064d9.

[381] *Matter of [name not provided]*, LIN 03 116 51773 (AAO Apr. 3, 2008), http://bit.ly/apr082d.

[382] *Matter of [name not provided]*, WAC 05 231 52139 (AAO Mar. 8, 2006), http://bit.ly/mar064d9.

[383] *Matter of [name not provided]*, WAC 03 211 53798 (AAO May 23, 2005), http://bit.ly/may0501d9 (petition stated that the beneficiary would perform live concerts, but this activity was not stated in the employment contract).

[384] *Matter of [name not provided]*, LIN 92 172 50725 (AAU Apr. 30, 1993), 11 Immig. Rptr. B2-64 (for an athlete, petition denied where the contract described competitive events but also promotional activities for the petitioner's water ski products).

[385] *Matter of [name not provided]*, SRC 06 087 52651 (AAO Feb. 9, 2009), http://bit.ly/feb093d.

[386] "CSC Answers to AILA Liaison Questions" (Sept. 2001), AILA Doc. No. 01090734.

Copyright © 2017. American Immigration Lawyers Association. All rights reserved.

petition will be approved only for the time period addressed in the itinerary.[387] In addition, the contract may not be "accepted in lieu of the itinerary, as these two types of evidence are separate regulatory requirements."[388]

For P-2 petitions where the beneficiary must depart the United States between multiple events, USCIS indicated that the petition may be approved to include all events:

> "We would apply a totality of circumstances review to this type of case. We would look at the purpose to see what [the beneficiary is] doing here and abroad, and whether they are related. For example, you couldn't do a three-month stint in the U.S. and then leave for 9 months and achieve approval for a single event."[389]

A similar analysis is applied for P-3 petitions with breaks between performances: "We examine what the beneficiary will be doing between the events, to see if they are a series of events that could be considered close enough to constitute one event for the entire period that the petition requests."[390]

In the event that the venues for the particular sport do not publish competition schedules years in advance, the petitioner should submit evidence of "other venues at which the beneficiary would race [or compete] or provide any evidence documenting the typical racing [or sport] schedule in the sport, such as prior years' schedules for the events in which the beneficiary is expected to compete during the next three years."[391]

As a practical matter, it may be difficult to submit to USCIS a complete itinerary of events, as in many instances the booking cannot be completed until the foreign national is present in the United States. In this situation, the practitioner may wish to submit evidence that the venues for the type of performance do not select performers well in advance of the performance date(s), as well as evidence of other venues where the foreign national would perform; of a typical schedule of performances; or of previous tours. For a further discussion of itineraries on behalf of entertainment groups, see Volume 1: Chapter Twelve, "O Visas and Status."

G. Nonimmigrant Intent

As stated by DOS, "every P visa applicant must satisfy the consular officer that he or she has a residence abroad which he or she has no intention of abandoning."[392] But, except for essential support personnel, being the beneficiary of an approved labor certification application or a filed immigrant visa petition "shall not be a basis for denying a P petition, a request to extend such a petition, or the alien's admission,

---

[387] "NSC Liaison Questions & Answers" (Nov. 11, 1999), AILA Doc. No. 99111672; *Matter of [name not provided]*, SRC 05 800 32163 (AAO Apr. 28, 2009), http://bit.ly/apr0901d.

[388] *Matter of [name not provided]*, SRC 05 800 32163 (AAO Apr. 28, 2009), http://bit.ly/apr0901d.

[389] "CSC Stakeholders Meeting" (Apr. 29, 2010), AILA Doc. No. 10062988.

[390] *Id.*

[391] *Matter of [name not provided]*, SRC 05 800 32163 (AAO Apr. 28, 2009), http://bit.ly/apr0901d.

[392] 9 FAM 402.14-10(D).

Copyright © 2017. American Immigration Lawyers Association. All rights reserved.

change of status, or extension of stay."[393] As stated by the regulations: "The alien may legitimately come to the United States for a temporary period as a P nonimmigrant and depart voluntarily at the end of his or her authorized stay and, at the same time, lawfully seek to become a permanent resident of the United States."[394]

Residence in the United States for a significant period of time, however, may cause USCIS to question whether the beneficiary has the appropriate nonimmigrant intent.[395] As a practical matter, P-2 and P-3 nonimmigrants may face a stricter interpretation of nonimmigrant intent than P-1 nonimmigrants, perhaps because reciprocal exchange seems to indicate a temporary exchange rather than a foreign national pursuing permanent residence, and because neither P-2 nor P-3 status has a correlative immigrant provision in the same way that international recognition is similar to the extraordinary ability immigrant provision.

Essential support personnel, however, are not covered by the provision permitting pursuance of permanent residence.[396] Therefore, a foreign national who seeks status as a P essential support personnel and who is the beneficiary of an approved labor certification application or of a filed immigrant visa petition may find the P petition or visa[397] denied. Appropriate evidence may include copies of property titles or deeds, mortgages, or lease agreements, as well as evidence of continued enrollment in school or other programs in the home country, arrangements for sabbatical, bank statements, and evidence of family or community ties.[398] And since the purpose of a U.S. visit by essential support personnel should be to assist a principal P beneficiary, other evidence could include a statement by a foreign employer confirming an employment offer after the U.S. competition, event, or performance.

It may be possible to obtain approval of a P petition on behalf of essential support personnel if the labor certification application or immigrant visa petition was filed by an entity other than the P petitioner or by a family member, but the practitioner should discuss the issue in detail with the client. This is because the foreign national would have to demonstrate that despite the pursuit of U.S. permanent residence, he or she will maintain the foreign residence for the duration of the P assignment.

A P petition may address these issues by providing explicit details of definite plans, such as ongoing payments of the mortgage, property taxes, or rent; offer of employment from a foreign entity upon conclusion of the P assignment; and evidence

---

[393] 8 CFR §214.2(p)(15). *See also* 9 FAM 402.14-10(D).

[394] *Id.*

[395] *Matter of [name not provided]*, EAC 04 118 50432 (AAO Dec. 22, 2005), http://bit.ly/dec054d (beneficiary had held H-1B status for six years); *Matter of [name not provided]*, EAC 03 207 50044 (AAO Aug. 17, 2005), http://bit.ly/aug052d9 (beneficiary had held P-3 status for three years); *Matter of [name not provided]*, EAC 03 150 52118 (AAO Aug. 17, 2005), http://bit.ly/aug053d (beneficiaries had held P-3 status for 26 months).

[396] 8 CFR §214.2(p)(15).

[397] 9 FAM 402.14-10(D).

[398] For a further discussion of evidence of nonimmigrant intent, see Volume 1: Chapter Three, Visitors: "B Visas and Status and the Visa Waiver Program."

Copyright © 2017. American Immigration Lawyers Association. All rights reserved.

of the relationship between the P petitioner and the foreign entity, if applicable. Nevertheless, the practitioner should advise the client that the P petition runs a higher than normal risk of denial, as discussed below. For a detailed discussion of strategies to contrast a future desire to immigrate with a temporary desire to visit the United States, see Volume 1: Chapter Three, Visitors: "B Visas and Status and the Visa Waiver Program."

IV. Managing Client Expectations: Common Issues

A. Substitution of Beneficiaries

Beneficiaries may be substituted if the P petition was approved for a group.[399] There is no substitution of essential support personnel; a new petition must be filed to "add additional new essential support personnel."[400]

A substitution request for a new beneficiary who is outside the United States should be filed with the U.S. consulate where the foreign national will apply for a visa or the port of entry where the foreign national will apply for admission.[401] The request should include a letter, a copy of the approval notice,[402] and a statement, including the beneficiary's "date of birth, country of nationality, and position," and a certification "that the alien is qualified to fill the position described in the approved petition."[403] As discussed above, the consular officer may use this information to determine whether the beneficiary qualifies as a member of the athletic team or entertainment group.[404]

For entertainment groups who are already performing in the United States and who wish to add or substitute members, "the additions or substitutes should be petitioned as P-1s."[405] In addition, the practitioner should note the following guidance:

"Evidence of the original approval and the required consultation will need to be submitted, but the 75% rule is not relevant here, nor does documentation relating to the qualifications of the new members need to be submitted. This is due to the fact that it is the renown of the group which determines whether the new member is of P-1 caliber."[406]

B. Essential Support Personnel

A P nonimmigrant, whether an individual P-1 athlete, a P-1 athletic team, a P-1 entertainment group, a P-2 entertainer, a P-2 entertainment group, a P-3 entertainer,

---

[399] 8 CFR §214.2(p)(2)(iv)(H); 9 FAM 402.14-7(F).

[400] 8 CFR §214.2(p)(2)(iv)(H).

[401] Id.

[402] Id.

[403] 9 FAM 402.14-7(F).

[404] Id.

[405] AFM 33.5.

[406] Id.

Copyright © 2017. American Immigration Lawyers Association. All rights reserved.

or a P-3 entertainment group, may be accompanied and assisted by "essential support" personnel,[407] which is defined as:

> "[A] highly skilled, essential person determined by the Director to be an integral part of the performance of a P-1, P-2, or P-3 alien because he or she performs support services which cannot be readily performed by a United States worker and which are essential to the successful performance of services by the P-1, P-2, or P-3 alien."[408]

Although essential support personnel should be "an integral and essential part of the performance of the entertainment group," they should be differentiated from performers who are integral and essential to the performance.[409] The standard for essential support personnel may be similar to the direct support provided by a Scientific Technician/Technologist in TN status to a professional.[410]

Examples of P-1 essential support personnel for athletes include coaches, trainers, scouts, "other team officials,"[411] and managers.[412] Teams made up entirely of "United States citizens or United States athletes are clearly not eligible for P-1 status since [the essential support personnel] are not performing and they are not supporting a P-1 athlete."[413] Instead, there must be at least one P-1 athlete, although it is not necessary to establish that all the members of the entire team hold P-1 status.[414] P-1 status for essential support personnel is inappropriate for coaches of athletes competing at the amateur level,[415] or even the "top" junior level.[416]

In addition, "sports leagues which traditionally employ foreign referees, linesmen, or officials to conduct its [sic] games may petition for these aliens to support the P-1 aliens employed by the teams in the league."[417] The athletic league, rather than the

---

[407] 8 CFR §§214.2(p)(4)(iv)(A), 214.2(p)(5)(iii)(A), and 214.2(p)(6)(iii)(A).

[408] 8 CFR §214.2(p)(3).

[409] Legacy INS, P. Virtue, "O-1 and P Nonimmigrant Visa Classifications" (Sept. 29, 1993), 1 INS and DOJ Legal Opinions §93-76 (noting the absence of a prohibition against an "entertainment group from filing a P-1 petition on behalf of an alien performer or entertainer coming to this country to provide functions integral to the performance of the group" and the absence of a prohibition against an "entertainment group from filing P-1 nonimmigrant petitions on behalf of alien support personnel, provided the petitioner can establish that such persons are an integral and essential part of the performance of the entertainment group"). Although the guidance specifically addresses P-1 performers and essential support personnel, the principle should remain the same for P-2 and P-3 performers and essential support personnel.

[410] For a discussion of this topic, see Volume 1: Chapter Fourteen, "TN Visas and Status."

[411] Legacy INS, L. Weinig, "Policy Guidelines for the Adjudication of O and P Petitions," (June 25, 1992), 69 Interpreter Releases 1084 (Aug. 31, 1992).

[412] *Matter of [name not provided]*, WAC 07 004 51026 (AAO Nov. 20, 2006), http://bit.ly/nov061d9.

[413] Legacy INS, L. Weinig, "Policy Guidelines for the Adjudication of O and P Petitions," (June 25, 1992), 69 Interpreter Releases 1084 (Aug. 31, 1992).

[414] *Matter of [name not provided]*, WAC 07 004 51026 (AAO Nov. 20, 2006), http://bit.ly/nov061d9.

[415] *Matter of [name not provided]*, EAC 04 252 53882 (AAO Nov. 30, 2005), http://bit.ly/nov051d9.

[416] *Matter of [name not provided]*, EAC 03 181 54109 (AAO May 25, 2005), http://bit.ly/may051d9.

[417] Legacy INS, L. Weinig, "Policy Guidelines for the Adjudication of O and P Petitions," (June 25, 1992), 69 Interpreter Releases 1084 (Aug. 31, 1992).

Copyright © 2017. American Immigration Lawyers Association. All rights reserved.

individual team, must petition for linesmen, referees, and other game officials.[418] As with all P petitions, an advisory opinion from a labor organization is required, and for hockey essential support personnel, this may be "the current Collective Bargaining Agreement between the League and the National Hockey League Officials Association which bears the beneficiary's signature and the NHL Officials Association cover letter," and "there is no labor organization for trainers."[419] A horse trainer may also qualify as essential support personnel,[420] as long as the assistance is provided to at least one P-1 athlete or athletic team and not only to horses and ponies.[421]

Support personnel for entertainment groups include performance technicians, such as sound engineers, and managers.[422] As stated by legacy INS regarding entertainment groups: "It must be born in mind that the term 'group' relates only to the performing aliens. It does not include the individuals who assist in the presentation who are not on stage, such as lighting men or sound men. These individuals are properly classified as accompanying aliens."[423] The regulations do not permit naming performers and essential support personnel as multiple beneficiaries on the same petition.[424]

The beneficiary providing essential support "must have appropriate qualifications to perform the services, critical knowledge of the specific services to be performed, and experience in providing such support to the P-1, P-2, or P-3 alien."[425] Supporting evidence for P petitions on behalf of essential support personnel should include the following documents:

- A consultation and advisory opinion "from a labor organization with expertise in the area of the alien's skill," as discussed below;

- A statement detailing the beneficiary's "prior essentiality, critical skills, and experience with the principal alien(s)"; and

- "A copy of the written contract or a summary of the terms of the oral agreement between the alien(s) and the employer."[426]

A petition filed on behalf of essential support personnel must also be accompanied by an advisory opinion from a labor organization "with expertise in the skill area

---

[418] AFM 33.10.

[419] *Id.*

[420] *Matter of [name not provided]*, WAC 07 028 51404 (AAO Aug. 18, 2008), http://bit.ly/aug082d9.

[421] *Matter of [name not provided]*, WAC 06 800 08950 (AAO Oct. 2, 2008), http://bit.ly/oct081d9.

[422] *Matter of [name not provided]*, EAC 08 054 51251 (AAO May 1, 2009), http://bit.ly/may093d; *Matter of [name not provided]*, WAC 06 159 50735 (AAO June 24, 2008), http://bit.ly/jun081d9.

[423] Legacy INS, L. Weinig, "Policy Guidelines for the Adjudication of O and P Petitions," (June 25, 1992), 69 Interpreter Releases 1084 (Aug. 31, 1992).

[424] *Matter of [name not provided]*, EAC 08 054 51251 (AAO May 1, 2009), http://bit.ly/may093d (sound engineer included on same petition for performers).

[425] 8 CFR §214.2(p)(3).

[426] 8 CFR §§214.2(p)(4)(iv)(B), 214.2(p)(5)(iii)(B), and 214.2(p)(6)(iii)(B).

Copyright © 2017. American Immigration Lawyers Association. All rights reserved.

involved."[427] The structure of the advisory opinion(s) is similar to those for P principal nonimmigrants, as discussed above, regarding an unfavorable opinion or a statement of "no objection."[428] A favorable opinion should "evaluate the alien's essentiality to and working relationship with the artist or entertainer, and state whether United States workers are available who can perform the support services,"[429] and should be specific to the individual beneficiary, rather than to the field in general.[430]

Experience letters and copies of educational documents may provide the information necessary for the second requirement, but the former employer should specifically state the dates of employment,[431] the essential support skills utilized by the beneficiary, and preferably should state the exclusive employment relationship.[432] Statements that suggest that the skills necessary for the assignment are generic for the industry and not "specific to a certain" athlete or performer are less helpful, as they may be construed as indicative that a U.S. worker could perform the duties or that the skills are not integral, essential, or highly skilled.[433]

Instead, the statement(s) should specifically describe how the duties of the essential support personnel directly impact and influence the successful performance of the principal P nonimmigrant,[434] and how the beneficiary possesses the specific skills to provide the support.[435] For example, if the principal P nonimmigrant requires an assistant who will prepare meals, then it may be necessary to explain how the principal P nonimmigrant "has special dietary needs that must be met b[y] a specialized cook, chef or nutritionist" and how the "beneficiary is skilled or experienced in preparing foods that would meet such needs."[436]

If statements from other industry members are presented, the individuals should have "specific knowledge regarding the beneficiary or his prior relationship with or

---

[427] 8 CFR §214.2(p)(7)(vi).

[428] *Id.*

[429] 8 CFR §214.2(p)(7)(vi); AFM 33.3.

[430] *Matter of [name and case number not provided]* (AAO July 28, 2011), http://bit.ly/jul111d.

[431] *Matter of [name not provided]*, WAC 08 800 06171 (AAO Feb. 20, 2009), http://bit.ly/feb091d9; *Matter of [name not provided]*, SRC 06 122 52917 (AAO Feb. 9, 2009), http://bit.ly/feb092d9; *Matter of [name not provided]*, SRC 05 204 50594 (AAO Oct. 13, 2006), http://bit.ly/oct061d9.

[432] *Matter of [name not provided]*, SRC 06 086 51969 (AAO Mar. 11, 2009), http://bit.ly/mar091d9 (noting that the former employer "stopped short of stating that the beneficiary worked specifically for him or performed essential support services for him"); *Matter of [name not provided]*, WAC 06 186 50097 (AAO Mar. 11, 2009), http://bit.ly/mar094d; *Matter of [name not provided]*, SRC 06 122 52917 (AAO Feb. 9, 2009), http://bit.ly/feb092d9 (stating that "based on the letter, it appears that the beneficiary assisted the trainer as opposed to only assisting the principal alien"). For a discussion of experience letters, see Volume 2: Chapter Two, "The Labor Certification Application."

[433] *Matter of [name not provided]*, SRC 06 086 51969 (AAO Mar. 11, 2009), http://bit.ly/mar091d9.

[434] *Matter of [name not provided]*, WAC 06 186 50097 (AAO Mar. 11, 2009), http://bit.ly/mar094d; *Matter of [name not provided]*, SRC 05 204 50594 (AAO Oct. 13, 2006), http://bit.ly/oct061d9.

[435] *Matter of [name not provided]*, WAC 08 800 06171 (AAO Feb. 20, 2009), http://bit.ly/feb091d9; *Matter of [name not provided]*, SRC 05 204 50594 (AAO Oct. 13, 2006), http://bit.ly/oct061d9.

[436] *Matter of [name not provided]*, WAC 08 800 06171 (AAO Feb. 20, 2009), http://bit.ly/feb091d9.

Copyright © 2017. American Immigration Lawyers Association. All rights reserved.

prior essentiality to the principal P-1 athlete [or principal P beneficiary]."[437] U.S. Customs and Border Protection (CBP) guidance indicates that the essential support personnel must have at least one year of experience working with the principal P individual, team, or group, but it remains unclear whether this requirement is imposed by USCIS.[438]

USCIS may review template job descriptions from DOL to determine whether the job duties "require a highly skilled, essential person, or [whether] such duties cannot be readily performed by a United States worker."[439] Additional potential factors are whether the principal P nonimmigrant has been successful without the services of the essential support personnel, by "relying on local [assistants] to perform the proposed duties," or whether the beneficiary possesses "knowledge beyond that of other [assistants] that is specific to the performance of the principal alien."[440]

USCIS and/or the AAO may compare the stated dates of employment with other information relating to the beneficiary's employment relationships: "[T]he beneficiary was granted P-1 status as an internationally recognized athlete in 2003, a status he would not have been granted had he actually been working as a jockey valet for [redacted] in the year preceding the filing of his P-1 petition."[441] Therefore, in these situations, independent evidence of the employment relationship with the former should be provided to reconcile the differences in information.[442]

Essential support personnel should be named on a petition separate from the petition for the principal beneficiary or beneficiaries,[443] "with the appropriate consultation letters."[444] But if the petitions will be filed on the same day, then attention should be drawn to the "related cases so that they are not separated," especially if premium processing is requested to avoid delays.[445] Alternatively, the petition for essential support personnel may include evidence of the principal's valid

---

[437] *Matter of [name not provided]*, SRC 06 086 51969 (AAO Mar. 11, 2009), http://bit.ly/mar091d9. Although the case specifically addresses essential support personnel for a P-1 athlete, the rationale should remain the same for other principal P beneficiaries.

[438] 1 U.S. Customs and Border Protection (CBP) Inspector's Field Manual (IFM) 15: Nonimmigrants and Border Crossers, 14-1 Agency Manuals 15.4: Requirements and Procedures for Nonimmigrant Classes.

[439] *Matter of [name not provided]*, WAC 06 186 50097 (AAO Mar. 11, 2009), http://bit.ly/mar094d.

[440] *Id.*

[441] *Matter of [name not provided]*, SRC 06 086 51969 (AAO Mar. 11, 2009), http://bit.ly/mar094d. *See also Matter of [name not provided]*, SRC 06 122 52917 (AAO Feb. 9, 2009), http://bit.ly/feb092d9 (stating that if "the petitioner intended to indicate that the beneficiary had a prior working relationship with the principal athlete in England, then such claim would be contradicted by the letter from Ms. Badger, whose letter suggests that her only prior contact with the beneficiary occurred in the United States"); *Matter of [name not provided]*, SRC 05 204 50594 (AAO Oct. 13, 2006), http://bit.ly/oct061d9.

[442] *Matter of [name not provided]*, SRC 06 086 51969 (AAO Mar. 11, 2009), http://bit.ly/mar091d9.

[443] 8 CFR §214.2(p)(2)(i); 9 FAM 402.14-7(A); *Matter of [name not provided]*, WAC 06 800 12420 (AAO Aug. 1, 2008), http://bit.ly/aug081d.

[444] USCIS, "2003 CSC Guidelines" (Feb. 6, 2003), AILA Doc. No. 03040440.

[445] "AILA/TSC Liaison Minutes" (Oct. 18, 2004), AILA Doc. No. 04111219.

Copyright © 2017. American Immigration Lawyers Association. All rights reserved.

immigration status, if appropriate, but the requested dates of employment should coincide with the dates of petition approval for the principal beneficiary.[446]

USCIS guidance states that it is acceptable if a minor league hockey team does not employ a P-1 athlete when the petition for the essential support personnel is filed, as long as a P-1 athlete will be employed during the requested season:

> "They might not presently have a P-1 hockey player on the team, but if they can establish that they will have one during the up-coming season, this is okay. If this is the case, the team is to submit evidence of this. They can establish eligibility by submitting evidence that they have employed alien players with NHL contracts in the immediate prior season and that they have an affiliation with a major league team which will continue through the upcoming season."[447]

A petition on behalf of an essential support worker may be denied if the P-1 petition on behalf of the P-1 nonimmigrant is denied by USCIS and not sustained on appeal to the AAO.[448] Multiple essential support beneficiaries may be named on a single petition, even if the beneficiaries will apply for P visas at different U.S. consulates or will apply for P admission at different ports of entry.[449] As discussed above, essential support personnel must have a foreign residence which they have no intention of abandoning.[450]

C. Impact of Labor Disputes

A U.S. employer may not use the P category to employ a foreign national in the United States if the Secretary of Labor certifies or otherwise informs the Attorney General that:

> "[A] strike or other labor dispute involving a work stoppage of workers is in progress in the occupation at the place where the beneficiary is to be employed, and that the employment of the beneficiary would adversely affect the wages and working conditions of U.S. citizens and lawful resident workers."[451]

If such a certification is made, then the P petition will be denied.[452] If a P petition has been approved already, but the foreign national "has not yet entered the United States, or has entered the United States but not yet commenced employment," then the petition approval "is automatically suspended" and any application for admission based on the petition will be denied.[453] The practitioner should note that the strike or

---

[446] *Matter of [name not provided]*, SRC 06 086 51969 (AAO Mar. 11, 2009), http://bit.ly/mar091d9.

[447] AFM 33.10.

[448] *Matter of [name not provided]*, WAC 06 193 52819 (AAO Feb. 2, 2007), http://bit.ly/feb071d.

[449] "VSC Helpful Filing Tips" (Aug. 12, 2009), AILA Doc. No. 09112363.

[450] 8 CFR §214.2(p)(15).

[451] 8 CFR §214.2(p)(16)(i).

[452] 8 CFR §214.2(p)(16)(i)(A).

[453] 8 CFR §214.2(p)(16)(i)(B).

Copyright © 2017. American Immigration Lawyers Association. All rights reserved.

labor dispute must be certified by the Secretary of Labor; a petition may not be denied or suspended without such certification.[454]

With respect to visa applications, DOS will "defer visa issuance and follow whatever instructions are given regarding the disposition of the suspended petition," whether the consular officer is informed of the strike or labor dispute by the Department of Homeland Security (DHS), DOS, or "another official source."[455]

A P nonimmigrant "shall not be deemed to be failing to maintain his or her status solely on account of past, present, or future participation in a strike or other labor dispute involving a work stoppage of workers," whether the strike or labor dispute is certified by the Secretary of Labor or not.[456] The following conditions also apply:

- The P nonimmigrant remains "subject to all applicable provisions" of the immigration laws and regulations "in the same manner as are all other P nonimmigrant aliens";

- Any P status and period of authorized stay "is not modified or extended in any way by virtue of his or her participation in a strike or other labor dispute involving a work stoppage of workers"; and

- "Although participation by a P nonimmigrant alien in a strike or other labor dispute involving a work stoppage of workers will not constitute a ground for deportation, an alien who violates his or her status or who remains in the United States after his or her authorized period of stay has expired, will be subject to deportation."[457]

D. Return Transportation Obligation

If the P employment terminates, then the practitioner should inform the client of the duty to pay "for the reasonable cost of return transportation of the alien abroad,"[458] which is defined as the beneficiary's "last place of residence prior to his or her entry into the United States."[459] The obligation applies if the termination of the employment relationship is for any reason other than voluntary resignation by the beneficiary.[460] If the employer and the P petitioner are different entities, then both parties "are jointly and severally liable,"[461] and the petitioner must "provide assurance satisfactory to the Attorney General that the reasonable cost of that transportation will be provided."[462]

---

[454] 8 CFR §214.2(p)(16)(ii).
[455] 9 FAM 402.14-6(C).
[456] 8 CFR §214.2(p)(16)(iii).
[457] 8 CFR §§214.2(p)(16)(iii) and 214.2(p)(18).
[458] INA §214(c)(5)(B); 8 CFR §214.2(p)(18).
[459] 8 CFR §214.2(p)(18); 9 FAM 402.14-12.
[460] INA §214(c)(5)(B); 8 CFR §214.2(p)(18).
[461] INA §214(c)(5)(B); 8 CFR §214.2(p)(18).
[462] INA §214(c)(5)(B).

Copyright © 2017. American Immigration Lawyers Association. All rights reserved.

V. Preparing the P Petition

This section discusses the documents of the P petition. As discussed in Volume 1: Chapter Two, "Basic Nonimmigrant Concepts," all documents should contain original signatures.[463] The following documents should be prepared:

- Cover letter
- Form G-28
- Form I-907, if applicable
- Form I-129
- O and P Classifications Supplement to Form I-129
- Support statement from U.S. company
- Index of exhibits

The practitioner should be aware that USCIS may deny a petition without an RFE if the submitted initial evidence "does not demonstrate eligibility."[464] The client will certainly be displeased with the cost and delay of filing an AAO appeal or the need for a new filing, so the practitioner should provide as many relevant documents as possible in order to present the most comprehensive picture of the beneficiary's eligibility for P status.[465]

A. Form G-28

If the petition is being submitted without a request for action on the beneficiary's status, such as a request for change or extension or status, the petition is exclusively that of the employer, and thus the U.S. petitioner's information is what is provided in Questions 5 through 12 on the G-28. If a change or extension of status is also being requested for the beneficiary, and the attorney is also representing the beneficiary, a separate G-28 should be submitted for him or her, and Questions 5 through 12 should be completed with the beneficiary's information on that form. The instructions require that signatures be in black, but USCIS routinely accepts G-28 forms signed in blue ink.[466]

If there is limited time to prepare and file the petition before the U.S. assignment is to begin, such as if the forms are emailed to and printed by the client, this form

---

[463] While USCIS previously advised signing documents in blue ink (*See, e.g.,* "TSC Liaison Minutes" (Aug. 13, 2000), AILA Doc. No. 00090703, in recent years it has more frequently stated a preference for black ink (*See, e.g.,* "Instructions for Notice of Entry of Appearance as Attorney or Accredited Representative" (May 5, 2106), https://www.uscis.gov/sites/default/files/files/form/g-28instr.pdf; "USCIS FY2016 H-1B Webpage Updated" (Mar. 12, 2015), AILA Doc. No. 15031362. As a practical matter, however, signing documents in black ink can sometimes result in the USCIS mailroom incorrectly assuming the signature is a photocopy and rejecting the filing.

[464] 8 CFR §103.2(b)(8)(ii).

[465] "CSC Liaison Minutes" (Aug. 1, 2000), AILA Doc. No. 00091103 (urging practitioners "to make sure that all supporting documents are includ[ed] at the time of filing the initial petition so that the file is complete").

[466] "Instructions for Notice of Entry of Appearance as Attorney or Accredited Representative" (May 5, 2106), https://www.uscis.gov/sites/default/files/files/form/g-28instr.pdf.

Copyright © 2017. American Immigration Lawyers Association. All rights reserved.

may be printed on plain white paper. However, as discussed in Volume 1: Chapter Two, "Basic Nonimmigrant Concepts," the Forms G-28 should be printed on blue paper whenever possible, in order to assist the USCIS mailroom with identifying the inclusion of a Form G-28 in the filing.[467]

B. Form I-907

If the client wishes a response (approval, denial, or RFE) within 15 calendar days, then the client may pay USCIS an additional $1,225 for premium processing. This request may be filed concurrently with the P petition, or the attorney or the client may request premium processing after the petition has been filed, by submitting Form I-907 with the petition's receipt notice, as discussed in Volume 1: Chapter Two, "Basic Nonimmigrant Concepts."

C. Form I-129

Part 1: Item 2, "Company or Organization Name" rather than item 1, "Legal Name of Individual Petitioner," should be completed if the petitioner is a business entity. Other information on the U.S. company, including address, contact person, contact person's telephone number and email address, and Federal Employer Identification Number (FEIN), should be provided.

Part 2: For most P petitions, "New employment" should be checked and consular notification should be requested. As discussed in Volume 1: Chapter Two, "Basic Nonimmigrant Concepts," USCIS should then notify the Kentucky Consular Center (KCC), and the consulate abroad should then be able to confirm petition approval when the beneficiary applies for a P visa. If multiple beneficiaries will apply for visas at different consulates and/or ports of entry, then only one consulate or port of entry should be stated. It is not necessary to "indicate who is going where." because all petition approvals must be verified through the Petition Information Management Service (PIMS), in any event.[468]

If change of status is nevertheless requested, the practitioner should carefully review the approval notice to ensure that both the P petition and the change of status request were approved, as failure to do so could result in the foreign national's accruing unlawful presence.[469] In addition, the expiration date of the foreign national's current status should be calendared, so that a request to extend status may be timely filed. Ideally, the P change of status petition will be approved before the beneficiary's underlying status expires, and premium processing may make this scenario possible. The practitioner may wish to advise clients on the intricacies of situations where the initial status expires before the change of status petition is approved, as discussed in Volume 1: Chapter Two, "Basic Nonimmigrant Concepts." For more information on the eligibility requirements for change of status, accrual of

---

[467] "VSC Practice Pointer: G-28s" (Sept. 4, 2008), AILA Doc. No. 08090469.

[468] "VSC Helpful Filing Tips" (Aug. 12, 2009), AILA Doc. No. 09112363.

[469] "AILA/NSC Meeting Minutes" (July 27, 2006), AILA Doc. No. 06080269.

Copyright © 2017. American Immigration Lawyers Association. All rights reserved.

unlawful presence, and filing an extension while a change of status petition is pending, see Volume 1: Chapter Two, "Basic Nonimmigrant Concepts."

Parts 3 and 4: Information about the beneficiary, including name, alternate names, date of birth, country of birth, province of birth, Social Security number if any, country of nationality, and passport information, should be provided.

An individual must have a passport that is valid for at least six months from the petition's expiration date; otherwise, he or she is inadmissible and ineligible for nonimmigrant status.[470] If the beneficiary does not have such a passport, then the following options are available: either delay filing the P petition until he or she obtains a renewed passport, or file the P petition and note that a passport renewal is in process, have the beneficiary apply for a renewed passport in the interim, wait for an RFE, and then submit a photocopy of the biographic page of the renewed passport once it is available. For nationals of countries where passport renewal takes months, the second strategy can prevent the petition from being significantly delayed. If the client is willing to pay an additional $1,225 fee to USCIS, the delay caused by the RFE, which might also be several months, can be addressed by requesting premium processing when submitting the documentation of the renewed passport.

If the beneficiary is present in the United States when the petition is filed, then the I-94 information should be provided, even if he or she will depart the United States during pendency of the P petition. Regardless of whether consular notification is requested, the foreign address and consular or port of entry information should be completed, in case USCIS decides that a change or extension of stay is not warranted. If the petition is requesting change or extension of status, and the beneficiary's family is also present in the United States and requesting the same action, answer "yes" to item 5 and submit a Form I-539 for the dependents with the petition.

Parts 5 through 7: Information about the job title, description of proposed job duties, location, compensation, and general information about the petitioner should be provided. The information in Part 6 does not need to be completed for a P nonimmigrant. The form should be signed by the petitioner's representative and the practitioner.

D. P Supplement

The name of the petitioner and the name of the beneficiary or the number of beneficiaries should be stated, and the appropriate box checked for the type of P worker. The petitioner should then briefly summarize the type of event and the duties of the P assignment. For a petition on behalf of essential support personnel, any dates of previous employment with the principal P foreign national should be stated. Finally, information on the required advisory opinion and labor organization should be provided. If there is no advisory opinion because there is no appropriate organization,

---

[470] INA §212(a)(7)(B)(i). The exceptions to this rule in INA §212(a)(d)(4) are discussed in Volume 1: Chapter Two, "Basic Nonimmigrant Concepts."

Copyright © 2017. American Immigration Lawyers Association. All rights reserved.

then the practitioner may wish to type in a phrase to that effect and to attach the statement(s) from industry experts attesting to the lack of such an organization.

The second page of the P supplement may be used to provide information on additional P beneficiaries, including dates of birth, countries of citizenship, and countries of birth.[471] The names should be typed, alphabetized, and should match the spelling stated on the beneficiaries' passports.[472] USCIS encourages the practitioner to double check the spelling of the beneficiaries' names.[473] Attach a separate statement to the I-129 to request a waiver of the one-year relationship requirement and/or of the international recognition requirement for entertainment groups.[474] This statement should set forth the reasons why the waiver(s) should be granted.

E. Support Statement

The petitioner's support statement provides the opportunity to present and emphasize important facts regarding the beneficiary's eligibility for P status and to connect them to the criteria. One strategy is to weave phrases or sentences from the testimonials or articles in the support statement, in order to highlight the beneficiary's achievements and their potential applicability to the P assignment. For petitions in which there is no formal employment contract, this document will set forth the job duties of the proposed assignment and the qualifying event, summarize the terms of employment, and explain any acronyms or technical terms used in the testimonials so that the adjudicator understands the particular sport or entertainment field and the scope of the beneficiary's achievements.

The statement should be on the U.S. company's letterhead and signed by a representative of the U.S. company. One format of a support statement is as follows:

- Introduction;

- Information about the petitioner;

- Discussion of the assignment, including a discussion of the qualifying competition, performance, or event;

- Discussion of the duties of the assignment, including explanation of technical terms and estimated financial impact, if applicable;

- Discussion of the foreign national's educational and experience background, including a summary of achievements, which may be separated into sections relating to individual criteria; and

- Thank you, including mention of remuneration and terms of employment, and conclusion.

---

[471] "VSC Helpful Filing Tips" (Aug. 12, 2009), AILA Doc. No. 09112363.

[472] *Id.*

[473] *Id.*

[474] "Instructions for Petition for Nonimmigrant Worker" (updated Aug. 13, 2015), at 18, https://www.uscis.gov/sites/default/files/files/form/i-129instr.pdf.

Copyright © 2017. American Immigration Lawyers Association. All rights reserved.

For major league baseball players, the support statement may be "bare bones" or even excluded, as "a league letter (which describes the process for establishing the level of competition in the league) has been furnished to Headquarters."[475] Similarly, P-1 petitions filed on behalf of National Hockey League players may simply describe "the process of establishing the level of competition in the League."[476]

F. Index of Exhibits

Because P petitions, and especially P-1 petitions, typically require discrete types of evidence, the practitioner may wish to organize the documents in an index of exhibits, grouped by the criteria, and tabbed on the bottom: "No particular order is required but an index and tabs make it easier. Tabs should be placed at the bottom. Examiners find it helpful if the evidence follows the regulations and criteria."[477]

Therefore, the practitioner may find that an index of exhibits helps to demonstrate that the beneficiary's eligibility for the P classification, with tabs organized in the order of the regulations and sub-tabs for each document that addresses the particular criterion. Experience has shown that documents may be copied and included in more than one section. For example, for a P-1 petition, a newspaper review of the entertainment group's performance may serve as evidence of a performance in a leading role for a production with a distinguished reputation, evidence of international recognition, and evidence of a record of critical acclaim. The practitioner is strongly encouraged to highlight any places where the beneficiary is mentioned or discussed, in order to ease the adjudicator's task.

For major league baseball players, the index of exhibits may be "bare bones" or even excluded, as legacy INS guidance states that "the major league baseball club would not need to submit anything more than the major league contract when filing their petition."[478] P-1 petitions on behalf of National Hockey League players need only contain a copy of the major league contract, the NHL statement, and the advisory opinion from the NHL Player's Association,[479] as discussed above.

VI. Process

A. The P Petition

After preparing the P petition, it should be filed in duplicate, with original signatures,[480] with the USCIS Service Center with jurisdiction over the place of employment (and not the headquarters of the U.S. company, if different), as discussed

---

[475] AFM 33.10. *See also* legacy INS, J. Bednarz, "P-1 Petitions for Professional Baseball Players" (Jan. 15, 1993), AILA Doc. No. 04110465 (see Related Resources link).

[476] AFM 33.10.

[477] "AILA Liaison/Nebraska Service Center Liaison Teleconference Q&As" (June 25, 2009), AILA Doc. No. 09070864. Although the guidance relates to extraordinary ability immigrant visa petitions, the principle should remain the same.

[478] AFM 33.10.

[479] *Id.*

[480] "TSC Liaison Minutes" (Aug. 13, 2000), AILA Doc. No. 00090703.

Copyright © 2017. American Immigration Lawyers Association. All rights reserved.

in Volume 1: Chapter Two, "Basic Nonimmigrant Concepts." The practitioner may also find it helpful to write the following in large block letters across the side of the Form I-129: "DUPLICATE PETITION; PLEASE FORWARD TO KCC."

If, however, the P assignment will take place in more than one location, then the P petition should be filed with the Service Center with jurisdiction over the state where the petitioning entity is based.[481] If the petitioner is an agent, presumably this means that the petition is filed with the Service Center with jurisdiction over the place where the agent is based, though USCIS instructions are silent on this point. Finally, all P petitions filed by Major League Sports teams, including petitions for "major league athletes, minor league sports and any affiliates associated with the major leagues in baseball, hockey, soccer, basketball, and football," as well as "coaches, trainers, broadcasters, referees, linesmen, umpires, and interpreters," must be filed with the Vermont Service Center (VSC).[482]

The second set of original documents will be forwarded to the U.S. consulate where the beneficiary will apply for a P visa as supplementary evidence for PIMS, as discussed in Volume 1: Chapter Two, "Basic Nonimmigrant Concepts."[483] Following approval of a P petition, USCIS forwards approval notification to the KCC, which in turn creates an electronic record to confirm the petition approval, so the information becomes available to a consular officer to verify the petition approval.[484] Although duplicate original documents are not required, preparing and providing them may facilitate the beneficiary's visa application in the future.[485]

If the petitioner requires approval of the P petition in a short period of time but does not request premium processing, then expedited processing may be requested, as discussed in Volume 1: Chapter Two, "Basic Nonimmigrant Concepts." The practitioner may write the performance date "on the front of the application in large red letters" and provide an explanation "of why the case could not be filed earlier, to ensure that counsel made a good faith effort to avoid requesting an expedite."[486] If a beneficiary's name is misspelled on a receipt notice, USCIS directs the practitioner to "alert USCIS immediately."[487]

---

[481] 9 FAM 41.56 402.14-7(A); USCIS, "Direct Filing Addresses for Form I-129, Petition for Nonimmigrant Worker" (updated July 1, 2016), https://www.uscis.gov/i-129-addresses.

[482] USCIS, "Direct Filing Addresses for Form I-129, Petition for Nonimmigrant Worker," https://www.uscis.gov/i-129-addresses; USCIS, D. Neufeld, "Requirements for Agents and Sponsors Filing as Petitioners for the O and P Visa Classifications" (Nov. 20, 2009), AILA Doc. No. 09113064.

[483] DOS, "Accessing NIV Petition Information Via the CCD" (Nov. 2007), AILA Doc. No. 08040331; "PIMS Processing Update" (Mar. 21, 2008), AILA Doc. No. 08032132.

[484] "PIMS Update" (Aug. 15, 2008), AILA Doc. No. 08081564; "PIMS Processing Update" (Mar. 21, 2008), AILA Doc. No. 08032132.

[485] "PIMS Processing Update" (Mar. 21, 2008), AILA Doc. No. 08032132.

[486] "CSC Liaison Minutes" (Aug. 1, 2000), AILA Doc. No. 00091103.

[487] "VSC Helpful Filing Tips" (Aug. 12, 2009), AILA Doc. No. 09112363.

Copyright © 2017. American Immigration Lawyers Association. All rights reserved.

Petition denials may be appealed to the AAO.[488] See Volume 1: Chapter 2, "Basic Nonimmigrant Concepts," for a description of the appeal process. The practitioner may wish to monitor AAO decisions on P appeals, which are posted on the USCIS website,[489] to keep abreast of adjudicatory trends in P petitions.

B. Visa Application

Upon approval of the P petition, USCIS will send the attorney or representative an approval notice, and the company representative will receive a courtesy copy. The foreign national and any dependents may then apply for a visa at a U.S. consulate abroad. Although consuls have been instructed that they should no longer require the Form I-797 approval notice or a copy of the approved petition,[490] procedures do vary across consulates. Providing detailed instructions on how to apply for a P visa, including a certified copy of the P petition, is frequently very helpful to the petitioner and the employee.[491]

A visa application may be made up to 90 days before the start date of the validity period.[492] DOS also directed consular officers to "be sensitive to the needs of performers whose schedules may be disrupted by unforeseen events, and whenever possible, accommodate these groups through post's normal procedures for expediting visa applications," especially if "changes in a program or a group [are] compelled by illness, injury or other emergencies,"[493] for substitutions, as discussed above. Individual members of an entertainment group are not required to apply for P visas "at the same time and place."[494]

In addition to the general visa application documents discussed in Volume 1: Chapter Two, "Basic Nonimmigrant Concepts," the following documents should be presented, and individual consulates frequently have additional requirements:

- Original Form I-797 approval notice from USCIS;[495]

- Statement from the petitioner confirming that the foreign national continues to participate or perform in the qualifying event, if he or she obtained change of status from another nonimmigrant category;

- Certified copy of the P petition, to be presented only if specifically requested;

- Evidence of the visa applicant's foreign residence and nonimmigrant intent; and

---

[488] USCIS, "The Administrative Appeals Office (AAO)" (updated June 13, 2016), https://www.uscis.gov/about-us/directorates-and-program-offices/administrative-appeals-office-aao/administrative-appeals-office-aao.

[489] USCIS, "Administrative Decisions," http://bit.ly/AAOpDecs.

[490] 9 FAM 402.14-6(E) and 10(C).

[491] Because requirements for visa applications vary among individual consular posts, practitioners should confirm on the consul's website the current procedures required by the particular consulates.

[492] 9 FAM 402.14-10(F).

[493] DOS, "Visa Applications from Artists and Entertainers" (July 2005), AILA Doc. No. 05072661.

[494] Id.

[495] 8 CFR §214.2(p)(17).

Copyright © 2017. American Immigration Lawyers Association. All rights reserved.

- For P-4 dependents, evidence of the familial relationship and evidence of financial support from the principal beneficiary, as discussed below, as well as copies of the I-94 card and P visa of the principal beneficiary, especially if the P-4 visa applications are made after the principal beneficiary has already obtained P status.[496]

DOS directs consular officers to accept the P petition approval issued by USCIS: "You may not question the approval of P petitions without specific evidence, unavailable to DHS at the time of petition approval, that the beneficiary may not be entitled to status."[497] This means that the consular officer should not re-adjudicate the P petition, as the P petition approval "is prima facie evidence of entitlement to P classification."[498] The consular officer may, however, inquire about eligibility for the visa,[499] and may request "evidence of past activity" and "business records of the group, especially focusing on intended performances in the United States."[500]

For P petitions approved on behalf of athletic teams or entertainment groups, however, consular officers bear "responsibility to determine whether the team or group member applying for a P visa is qualified to fill the position described in the approved petition and is otherwise eligible for the visa," because USCIS "does not examine the individual qualifications of team or group members, other than verifying that 75 percent of the members have had a sustained and substantial relationship with the organization for at least one year."[501] However, the consular officer should not require an entertainment performance by the visa applicant in order to confirm that he or she is in fact a performer.[502]

The issued P visa should be annotated with the receipt number of the P petition, "followed by the name and location of the alien's employer."[503] If the foreign national is the beneficiary of more than one P petition and "does not plan to depart from the United States between engagement," then DOS "may issue a single P visa valid until the expiration date of the last expiring petition, reciprocity permitting," with annotations for both receipt numbers, as well as names and locations of both P employers.[504] If the visa's validity is limited, such as because of the reciprocity schedules or because of a shorter validity period for a waiver of inadmissibility, then the visa should also be annotated with the following statement: "PETITION VALID TO (Date)."[505] If the reciprocity schedules require that a visa have a validity period

---

[496] 9 FAM 402.14-11.

[497] 9 FAM 402.14-6(E).

[498] *Id.*; DOS, "Visa Applications from Artists and Entertainers" (July 2005), AILA Doc. No. 05072661.

[499] 9 FAM 402.14-6(E).

[500] DOS, "Visa Applications from Artists and Entertainers" (July 2005), AILA Doc. No. 05072661.

[501] 9 FAM 402.14-10(E).

[502] DOS, "Visa Applications from Artists and Entertainers" (July 2005), AILA Doc. No. 05072661.

[503] 9 FAM 402-14-10(J).

[504] 9 FAM 402-14-10(G).

[505] 9 FAM 402-14-10(H).

Copyright © 2017. American Immigration Lawyers Association. All rights reserved.

that is shorter than the petition validity period, then "consular officers may issue the visa any number of times within the period allowable," although any reciprocity fees must be paid with each visa issuance.[506]

P-4 visas for dependents of P principal beneficiaries will be subject to "the same visa validity, period of admission, and limitations as the P-1, P-2, or P-3 principal alien."[507] Because P-4 dependents may not engage in employment unless they independently qualify for a work-authorized nonimmigrant status, the consular officer may also "take this into account in evaluating whether family members have furnished adequate evidence of their support while in the United States."[508] But experience has shown that evidence of the remuneration to be paid to the principal beneficiary is generally sufficient.

C. Admission to the United States

A foreign national may seek admission up to 10 days before the start date of the P petition and may remain in the United States for 10 days after the petition expiration, but the nonimmigrant may engage in employment only while the petition is valid.[509]

When seeking admission to the United States, the foreign national should present his or her passport, with the P visa and the P petition approval notice from USCIS.[510] The foreign national should receive a passport stamp with P-1, P-2, or P-3 status valid until the end date of the petition, as stated on the approval notice. Due to the visa reciprocity schedules,[511] as discussed in Volume 1: Chapter Two, "Basic Nonimmigrant Concepts," a foreign national may receive a visa valid for a shorter time period than the P petition, but the expiration of P status should match the end date of the P petition and not the end date of the visa.

For example, Belarusian citizens are eligible for P visas valid for no longer than 12 months. Therefore, even though the underlying P-1 petition was approved for five years, a Belarusian citizen will be able to obtain a P visa that is valid for only 12 months from the date of visa issuance. The Petition Expiration Date (PED) provided in the lower right corner of the visa should, however, match the dates of validity of the P petition as stated on the Form I-797 approval notice, and the visa should be annotated with the petition expiration date also, as discussed above. For applicants for admission with visas valid for a shorter period of time than the P petition, the practitioner may wish to reiterate the need to present the original Form I-797 approval notice, to ensure that the period of authorized stay stated on the I-94 record matches the dates of the petition validity. The practitioner may also wish to contact

---

[506] 9 FAM 402-14-10(I).

[507] 9 FAM 402-14-11(a).

[508] 9 FAM 402-14-11(c).

[509] 8 CFR §214.2(p)(12).

[510] 1 CBP IFM 15: Nonimmigrants and Border Crossers, 14-1 Agency Manuals 15.4: Requirements and Procedures for Nonimmigrant Classes.

[511] 9 FAM 402.14-10(F). The Visa Reciprocity Tables, with a country-by-country look-up feature, are available at https://travel.state.gov/content/visas/en/fees/reciprocity-by-country.html.

Copyright © 2017. American Immigration Lawyers Association. All rights reserved.

clients with these employees well in advance of the visa expiration date to strategize subsequent applications for visas, so the foreign nationals may travel internationally and re-enter the United States during the remaining time of petition validity.

If entering by land, the foreign national will be issued an I-94 card. If entering by sea or air, the individual will receive a stamp in the passport, and the I-94 will be recorded electronically.[512] Practitioners should advise clients who receive the passport stamp rather than the paper I-94 to check their I-94s on the online look-up[513] to ensure that it is correct and that the expiration date of their status is noted.

1. Canadian and Mexican Citizens

As discussed in Volume 1: Chapter Two, "Basic Nonimmigrant Concepts," Canadian citizens do not require visas in order to enter the United States.[514] Canadian nationals may apply for admission with the P approval notice and Canadian passport at the port of entry.[515] Despite the regulations, which state that a "beneficiary of a P petition who does not require a nonimmigrant visa may present a copy of the approval notice at a Port-of-Entry to facilitate entry into the United States,"[516] the practitioner is advised to encourage the foreign national to present the original.

It is also critical to note that P admission may be denied if the foreign national's admission to the United States "would adversely affect the wages and working conditions of U.S. citizens and lawful resident workers."[517] For a more in-depth discussion of applications for admission in nonimmigrant status by Canadian citizens, see Volume 1: Chapter Two, "Basic Nonimmigrant Concepts."

Unfortunately, Mexican citizens applying for P visas may no longer obtain multiple entry visas by paying $125 instead of the usual $100 for a single entry visa, as was previously the case.[518] The validity period of a P visa for a Mexican citizen may not exceed 12 months.[519]

VII. Additional Follow-up

After a foreign national has obtained P status, the practitioner should follow up to request copies of the I-94 records and the visas, if applicable, to ensure that all the

[512] 78 Fed. Reg. 18457 (Mar. 27, 2013). *See also* CBP Fact Sheet, "I-94 Automation" (Nov. 2015), https://www.cbp.gov/sites/default/files/assets/documents/2016-Mar/i-94-automation-fact-sheet.pdf.

[513] CBP, "Get I-94 Information," https://i94.cbp.dhs.gov/I94/request.html.

[514] 1 legacy INS Examinations Handbook, Part V, 15-1; 1 Legacy INS IFM 15: Nonimmigrants and Border Crossers, 14-1 INS Manuals 15.4.

[515] 8 CFR §214.2(o)(15). Although this guidance applies to O-1 petitions, it is highly likely that it is cross-applicable to P-1 petitions in the absence of any other direction.

[516] 8 CFR §214.2(p)(17).

[517] 8 CFR §214.2(p)(16)(i)(B).

[518] DOS, "Mexico Reciprocity Schedule," https://travel.state.gov/content/visas/en/fees/reciprocity-by-country/MX.html. *Cf.* former DOS website, "Mexico Reciprocity Schedule," formerly at http://travel.state.gov/visa/frvi/reciprocity/reciprocity_3622.html#C (link no longer works).

[519] DOS, "Mexico Reciprocity Schedule," https://travel.state.gov/content/visas/en/fees/reciprocity-by-country/MX.html.

Copyright © 2017. American Immigration Lawyers Association. All rights reserved.

information is correct and to calendar the expiration dates to monitor the foreign national's status, as discussed in Volume 1: Chapter Two, "Basic Nonimmigrant Concepts."

P-4 dependents may attend school while accompanying the principal P beneficiary to the United States.[520] The beneficiary of a denied P petition may not appeal the decision to the AAO.[521]

A. Extensions

If the foreign national's services are required after the expiration of the approved petition, "in order to continue or complete the same activity or event specified in the original petition," a P extension application may be filed, with documents similar to those necessary for the initial P petition, as long as the initial P petition remains valid.[522] But because the term "event" has been interpreted "as a finite period, rather than as employment of indefinite (permanent) duration," the practitioner should be mindful of the beneficiary's immigration history, as an extension was denied where the beneficiaries had held P-3 status for at least five years:

"Congress did not intend to allow entertainers to circumvent the labor certification process and remain in the U.S. indefinitely.... The petitioner may not extend the classification by merely submitting a request for an extension with a new itinerary. The AAO finds that the beneficiary has completed the event or engagement specified in the original petition and is ineligible for an extension of his visa petition validity."[523]

The beneficiary should be physically present in the United States when the extension application is filed. If the foreign national must depart the United States for personal or business reasons while the extension is pending, then "the petitioner may request the Director to cable notification of approval of the petition extension to the consular office abroad where the alien will apply for a visa."[524]

An individual athlete and his or her essential support personnel are eligible for P-1 extension(s) valid for up to five years, "for a total period of stay not to exceed 10 years."[525] Neither the individual athletes nor their essential support personnel are subject to a "lifetime admission limit of 10 years" in the United States; they may apply for P-1 admission even after holding P-1 status for 10 years, although the application for admission must be based on a new approved P-1 petition and the

---

[520] 1 CBP IFM 15: Nonimmigrants and Border Crossers, 14-1 Agency Manuals 15.4: Requirements and Procedures for Nonimmigrant Classes.

[521] *Matter of [name not provided]*, WAC 05 089 51309 (AAO Mar. 1, 2006), http://bit.ly/mar063d9; *Matter of [name not provided]*, LIN 04 105 51932 (AAO Feb. 24, 2006), http://bit.ly/feb062d9.

[522] 8 CFR §214.2(p)(13).

[523] *Matter of [name not provided]*, WAC 04 010 50133 (AAO Jan. 10, 2006), http://bit.ly/jan061d9 (beneficiaries had held P-3 status for at least five years).

[524] 8 CFR §214.2(p)(14)(i).

[525] INA §214(a)(2)(B); 8 CFR §214.2(p)(14)(ii)(A).

Copyright © 2017. American Immigration Lawyers Association. All rights reserved.

individuals must first depart the United States "in order to be eligible for a new initial period of admission of up to 1 year."[526]

Unlike H-1B and L-2 nonimmigrants,[527] there is no mandatory period of time during which the foreign national must remain outside the United States.[528] This means that a P petition after the individual has already held P status for 10 years must be filed requesting consular or port of entry notification rather than an extension of stay.[529] Other applications for admission do not create a rolling computation of a five-year period of stay:

"USCIS believes that allowing P-1 nonimmigrants to restart their admission period after every departure and reentry into the United States is inconsistent with the statutory scheme under INA 214, contrary to congressional intent as reflected in the inclusion of time limits on the P-1 category in the first place, and administratively unfeasible."[530]

Other P nonimmigrants are eligible for extensions in yearly increments.[531] The lifetime admission guidance relating to P-1 individual athletes and their essential support personnel does not apply to P-1 entertainment groups, to P-2 and P-3 entertainers and entertainment groups, or to essential support personnel who assist these individuals or groups.[532] CBP guidance indicates that a foreign national who has held P-2 status for one year "ordinarily may not re-enter the U.S. on a new P-2 petition for 3 months" and that a "waiver is available as part of the petition process,"[533] but the basis for the statements is unclear, as there is no such requirement in the statute or regulations.

The application should be "accompanied by a statement explaining the reasons for the extension."[534] The practitioner should note that, despite the regulation text, which states that "[s]upporting documents are not required unless requested by the

---

[526] USCIS, D. Neufeld, "Procedures for Applying the Period of Authorized Stay for P-1S Nonimmigrant Individual Athletes' Essential Support Personnel" (July 14, 2009), AILA Doc. No. 09071660; USCIS Memorandum, D. Neufeld, "Procedures for Applying the Period of Authorized Stay for P-1 Nonimmigrant Individual Athletes" (Mar. 6, 2009), AILA Doc. No. 09030967.

[527] 8 CFR §§214.2(h)(13)(iii)(A) and 214.2(*l*)(12)(i).

[528] USCIS, D. Neufeld, "Procedures for Applying the Period of Authorized Stay for P-1S Nonimmigrant Individual Athletes' Essential Support Personnel" (July 14, 2009), AILA Doc. No. 09071660; USCIS, D. Neufeld, "Procedures for Applying the Period of Authorized Stay for P-1 Nonimmigrant Individual Athletes" (Mar. 6, 2009), AILA Doc. No. 09030967 (no mention of mandatory residence outside the United States).

[529] USCIS, D. Neufeld, "Procedures for Applying the Period of Authorized Stay for P-1S Nonimmigrant Individual Athletes' Essential Support Personnel" (July 14, 2009), AILA Doc. No. 09071660.

[530] USCIS, D. Neufeld, "Procedures for Applying the Period of Authorized Stay for P-1 Nonimmigrant Individual Athletes" (Mar. 6, 2009), AILA Doc. No. 09030967.

[531] 8 CFR §214.2(p)(14)(ii)(B).

[532] USCIS, D. Neufeld, "Procedures for Applying the Period of Authorized Stay for P-1S Nonimmigrant Individual Athletes' Essential Support Personnel" (July 14, 2009), AILA Doc. No. 09071660.

[533] 1 CBP IFM 15: Nonimmigrants and Border Crossers, 14-1 Agency Manuals 15.4: Requirements and Procedures for Nonimmigrant Classes.

[534] 8 CFR §214.2(p)(14)(i).

Copyright © 2017. American Immigration Lawyers Association. All rights reserved.

Director,"[535] an RFE may be issued requesting supporting documents. Therefore, the practitioner may wish to avoid the delay of an RFE by submitting extensive documents, including recent evidence available since the initial petition was filed, with the extension filing, although a new advisory opinion should not be necessary.[536]

The practitioner may wish to discuss with the client the need to obtain a new advisory opinion from a labor organization, especially if several years have passed since the initial P petition: "Considering the amount of time that has lapsed since the original petition, it is entirely reasonable for the director to question whether the beneficiary continues to be engaged in the same work."[537] Alternatively, the client may wish to wait to see if an RFE requesting the advisory opinion is requested by USCIS,[538] but the practitioner should warn the client that this may result in processing delays. If this approach is pursued, then the practitioner should include a copy of the previous advisory opinion in the supporting documents for the extension application, "as records of separate nonimmigrant proceedings are not combined."[539]

The practitioner and client should not rely upon the fact that the beneficiary previously obtained P status, because neither USCIS nor the AAO are bound by previous approval of a P petition filed by the same petitioner on behalf of the same beneficiary:[540]

"If the previous nonimmigrant petitions were approved based on the same unsupported assertions that are contained in the current record, the approval would constitute material and gross error on the part of the director. The AAO [or USCIS] is not required to approve applications or petitions where eligibility has not been demonstrated, merely because of prior approvals that may have been erroneous."[541]

Therefore, although the AAO reversed a USCIS denial of a P-3 extension which was based on the absence of supporting documents,[542] the practitioner is not advised to rely upon this nonprecedent decision.

---

[535] 8 CFR §214.2(p)(13).

[536] Legacy INS, J. Bednarz (Sept. 29, 1992), 69 Interpreter Releases 1471–72 (Nov. 16, 1992).

[537] *Matter of [name not provided]*, WAC 08 038 50550 (AAO May 1, 2009), http://bit.ly/mar091d9.

[538] *Id.* (USCIS RFE).

[539] *Id.*

[540] *See, e.g., Matter of [name not provided]*, SRC 05 800 32163 (AAO Apr. 28, 2009), http://bit.ly/apr0901d; *Matter of [name not provided]*, EAC 03 266 553300 (AAO Dec. 22, 2005), http://bit.ly/dec053d; *Matter of [name not provided]*, EAC 03 207 50044 (AAO Aug. 17, 2005), http://bit.ly/aug052d9; *Matter of [name not provided]*, EAC 03 150 52118 (AAO Aug. 17, 2005), http://bit.ly/aug053d9; *Matter of [name not provided]*, LIN 04 175 51125 (AAO June 13, 2005), http://bit.ly/jun051d9.

[541] *Matter of [name not provided]*, SRC 05 800 32163 (AAO Apr. 28, 2009), http://bit.ly/apr0901d; *Matter of [name not provided]*, EAC 08 038 51086 (AAO Mar. 11, 2009), http://bit.ly/mar092d9.

[542] *Matter of [name not provided]*, WAC 09 800 01866 (AAO Jan. 20, 2010), http://bit.ly/jan101d.

Copyright © 2017. American Immigration Lawyers Association. All rights reserved.

B. Amended and Change of Employer Petitions

An amended P petition is appropriate and necessary if there are "any material changes in the terms and conditions of employment or the beneficiary's eligibility as specified in the original approved petition."[543] An amended petition is not necessary, however, if the employer wishes to add "additional, similar or comparable performance[s], engagements, or competitions during the validity period of the petition."[544]

If there are "any changes in the terms and conditions of employment of a beneficiary which may affect eligibility" for P status, but "the petitioner no longer employs the beneficiary, the petitioner shall send a letter explaining the change(s) to the Director who approved the petition"; and no amended petition is necessary.[545]

A change of employer may be filed if the P beneficiary wishes to be employed by an entity other than the one named on the initial P petition.[546] The beneficiary "may not commence employment with the new employer or sponsor until the petition and request for extension have been approved."[547] As a practical matter, however, it is very likely that most change of employer petitions will be filed on behalf of P-1 beneficiaries.

There is additional flexibility for a "professional P-1 athlete who is traded from one organization to another organization."[548] After such a trade, "employment authorization for the player will automatically continue for a period of 30 days after acquisition by the new organization."[549] The regulations were revised to "codify [legacy INS's] longstanding policy" because "a single athlete can have a significant impact on a team's performance."[550] The flexibility is not limited to "'U.S.-based' organizations" and applies to "a minor league affiliate in the United States of a foreign major league franchise."[551]

The new organization "is expected to file" a P-1 change of employer petition during this 30-day period. As long as the new petition is filed, the P-1 athlete may be employed by the new organization, "the professional athlete shall be deemed to be in valid P-1 status, and employment shall continue to be authorized, until the petition is

---

[543] 8 CFR §§214.2(p)(2)(iv)(D) and 214.2(p)(10)(i)(A).

[544] 8 CFR §214.2(p)(2)(iv)(D).

[545] 8 CFR §214.2(p)(10)(i)(A).

[546] 8 CFR §214.2(p)(2)(iv)(C)(*1*).

[547] *Id.*

[548] 8 CFR §214.2(p)(2)(iv)(C)(*2*).

[549] *Id.*

[550] 72 Fed. Reg. 18508 (Apr. 16, 1997).

[551] *Id.*

Copyright © 2017. American Immigration Lawyers Association. All rights reserved.

adjudicated."[552] The employment authorization will terminate, however, if the new petition is not filed or if the P-1 change of employer petition is denied.[553]

C. Sponsoring a P Nonimmigrant for Permanent Residence

As noted above, neither the statute nor the regulations prohibit principal P nonimmigrants, except essential support personnel, from pursuing permanent residence while holding nonimmigrant status.[554] The employment-based, first preference (EB-1) immigrant visa petition may be appropriate, but USCIS guidance notes that only the criteria for P athletes are similar to the immigrant visa petition criteria.[555] Although the criteria for P-1 entertainment groups may be similar to the immigrant criteria for performing artists, the practitioner should note that in the immigrant visa petition context, the foreign national must have individual international recognition.[556] However, Schedule A, Group II exceptional ability might be viable for some P-1s, as might the national interest waiver for P-1s involved in activities such as promoting the field or youth development. See Volume 2: Chapter Three, "The Immigrant Visa Petition" for a discussion of the national interest waiver.

It is possible for an EB-1 immigrant visa petition to be approved even when a P-1 petition is denied, but, as a practical matter, the immigrant visa petition may be strengthened if the beneficiary already holds P-1 status. For a discussion of how approval of an immigrant visa petition is not guaranteed and of the need to provide as much updated and independent evidence of the foreign national's eligibility for the extraordinary ability immigrant visa classification as possible, see Volume 1: Chapter Twelve, "O Visas and Status." For a further discussion of the immigrant visa petition, see Volume 2: Chapter Three, "The Immigrant Visa Petition."

Employment-based sponsorship for permanent residence on behalf of essential support personnel, however, is extremely difficult, because of the requirement that support be provided to a P principal. In addition, the aggregate processing time for approval of the labor certification application, approval of the immigrant visa petition, and availability of an immigrant visa number is highly likely to be more than two years.[557] Typically, the foreign national will not be eligible for EB-2 classification, because holding a master's degree or having five years of post-baccalaureate experience are not common requirements for a position which entails supporting an athlete, artist, entertainer, or entertainment group. The delays in immigrant visa availability for the EB-3 classification will most likely mean that the foreign national will be unable to apply to adjust status before expiration of his or her

---

[552] 8 CFR §214.2(p)(2)(iv)(C)(2).

[553] Id.

[554] 8 CFR §214.2(p)(15).

[555] "VSC Liaison Minutes" (Nov. 10, 1999), AILA Doc. No. 99120171.

[556] 8 CFR §204.5(h)(3).

[557] For an overview of the permanent residence process, see Volume 2: Chapter Two, "The Labor Certification Application"; Volume 2: Chapter Three, "The Immigrant Visa Petition"; and Volume 2: Chapter Four, "Consular Processing, Adjustment of Status, and Permanent Residence Issues."

Copyright © 2017. American Immigration Lawyers Association. All rights reserved.

underlying nonimmigrant P status.[558] In advising the client of these issues, the practitioner should also counsel the client that premium processing is not always available for these immigrant visa petitions.[559]

It may be possible to request consular processing, so the foreign national may remain outside the United States and pursue a career abroad while awaiting issuance of an immigrant visa. The practitioner should counsel the client, however, that the lengthy processing time may mean that the foreign national is unable to obtain an immigrant visa in time for the planned event and that the foreign national may be unable to obtain a P visa in the interim.[560] For a discussion of how to differentiate nonimmigrant intent for the U.S. visit and the pursuance of permanent residence, see Volume 1: Chapter Three, "Visitors: B Visas and Status and the Visa Waiver Program."

---

[558] For a discussion of the immigrant visa petition classifications and visa retrogression, see Volume 2: Chapter Three, "The Immigrant Visa Petition."

[559] USCIS website, "How Do I Use the Premium Processing Service?" (updated Oct. 26, 2015), https://www.uscis.gov/forms/how-do-i-use-premium-processing-service.

[560] 9 FAM 402.14-10(D).

Copyright © 2017. American Immigration Lawyers Association. All rights reserved.

CHAPTER FOURTEEN
TN VISAS AND STATUS

I. Executive Summary

The TN classification is for Canadian and Mexican citizens who will perform professional assignments in the United States. With a few exceptions, discussed below, the Canadian and Mexican citizens must be professionals. The North American Free Trade Agreement (NAFTA) Treaty specifies the list of occupations, as well as the corresponding educational and/or licensure requirements. A TN (NAFTA Professional) petition may be valid for up to three years. For Canadian citizens, a petition can be filed with U.S. Citizenship and Immigration Services (USCIS)[1], or the individual may directly apply for admission at select ports of entry. Mexican citizens must apply for TN visas at U.S. consulates abroad, and do not have the option of obtaining a petition approval from USCIS in advance. Dependent spouses and children of TN professionals hold TD (NAFTA Dependent) status. An extension of TN status for Canadian or Mexican citizens may be filed with USCIS, or the beneficiary may apply for a new period of TN status at a port of entry or at a U.S. consulate abroad.

A. Checklist of Requirements

- Citizen or national of Canada or Mexico
- Professional assignment in the United States falling within one of the NAFTA list of occupations
- Bachelor's degree (with limited exceptions)
- Professional license (if applicable)

B. Documents and Information Necessary to Prepare TN Request

- U.S. job description
- Copies of the foreign national's educational degrees, including transcripts
- Copies of the foreign national's professional licenses
- Experience letters for the foreign national (for certain occupational categories)
- Copy of foreign national's résumé
- Basic information about the company (Annual Report, Company Brochure, etc.)
- Copy of biographic page(s) of passport(s) of the foreign national and any dependent spouse and children

---

[1] "USCIS Announces a New Filing Option on behalf of Canadian TN Nonimmigrants and Reminds Employers of the Current Filing Options on behalf of Canadian L-1 Nonimmigrants." (Sept. 28, 2012), AILA Doc. No. 12100343. *See also* the USCIS website by searching "USCIS NAFTA professionals."

Copyright © 2017. American Immigration Lawyers Association. All rights reserved.

C. Checklist of Questions to Ask Client

- Will the U.S. assignment be a professional assignment falling within one of the NAFTA list of occupations?

- Does the foreign national possess at least a bachelor's degree or other acceptable professional credentials?

- Does the foreign national have dependent family members who are not citizens of Canada or Mexico?

- Will the foreign national be an employee or independent contractor of the U.S. company?

- Is there a labor dispute at the worksite of the proposed TN assignment?

- Is the foreign national a management consultant, a scientific technician or technologist, or a health care worker?

- Is the foreign national a beneficiary of an immigrant visa petition or labor certification application?

- Is there past negative immigration or criminal history that may affect the admissibility of the candidate?

II. Requirements and Definitions

The eligibility requirements for a TN assignment are as follows:

- The assignment must be professional and listed on the Appendix to the NAFTA Treaty;[2]

- The foreign national must hold the proper educational degree closely related to the field of the offered position or license to be considered a professional as stated on the Appendix to the NAFTA Treaty and/or the foreign national must have the requisite professional experience, if applicable;[3]

- The foreign national must qualify as a business person as the term is defined in the NAFTA Treaty;[4]

- The foreign national must be a citizen of Canada or Mexico;[5] and

- The foreign national must seek temporary entry.[6]

---

[2] Immigration and Nationality Act (INA) §214(e)(2); North American Free Trade Agreement (NAFTA), U.S.-Can.-Mex. (Dec. 17, 1992), 32 I.L.M. 289 (entered into force Jan. 1, 1994), Chap. 16, Appendix 1603.D.1.

[3] North American Free Trade Agreement (NAFTA), U.S.-Can.-Mex. (Dec. 17, 1992), 32 I.L.M. 289 (entered into force Jan. 1, 1994), Chap. 16, Appendix 1603.D.1; 8 CFR §214.6(c).

[4] NAFTA, U.S.-Can.-Mex. (Dec. 17, 1992), 32 I.L.M. 289 (entered into force Jan. 1, 1994), Chap. 16, Article 1608.

[5] INA §214(e)(2).

[6] NAFTA, U.S.-Can.-Mex. (Dec. 17, 1992), 32 I.L.M. 289 (entered into force Jan. 1, 1994), Chap. 16, Annex 1603; 8 CFR §214.6(b).

Copyright © 2017. American Immigration Lawyers Association. All rights reserved.

Given the differences in the process of obtaining TN status for Canadian citizens and Mexican citizens, where Canadian citizens may apply for admission at a port of entry in contrast to Mexican citizens who must first apply for TN visas at a U.S. consulate abroad, as discussed below, this chapter will refer to the underlying documents to request TN status as the TN petition, rather than referring to the application for TN admission or for a TN visa. Similarly, immigration inspectors at the ports of entry and consular officers, who adjudicate TN petitions, are referred to as government officials.

A. Professional Assignment in the United States

All the permissible TN occupations are listed in the NAFTA Treaty.[7] A foreign national may not provide services in other unlisted occupations, although he or she may be the beneficiary of another employment-based petition.[8] In addition, performing one of these TN assignments does not automatically mean that the foreign national will qualify for an H-1B professional assignment.[9] The TN assignment must have a worksite in the United States, including the District of Columbia and Puerto Rico; the TN classification is not available for assignments located in Guam, the Northern Mariana Islands, American Samoa, or the U.S. Virgin Islands.[10] The TN classification may be used for part-time employment.[11] However, the TN may not be used for self-employment.[12]

When discussing the option of TN status with a client, the practitioner should review the proposed U.S. job description and ask questions to confirm that the U.S. job duties will entail one of the following professions and to confirm that the foreign national holds the necessary educational degree and/or has the necessary professional experience and professional licensure from abroad, if applicable.[13] A foreign national may seek TN admission or a TN visa in order to "perform training functions relating to the profession, including conducting seminars,"[14] as discussed below.

For ease of reference, the following chart provides the profession, as well as the educational, experience, and licensure requirements. The practitioner should note that not all professions require the TN employee to have educational degrees, professional licenses, and experience letters. The educational, licensure, and experience

---

[7] NAFTA, U.S.-Can.-Mex. (Dec. 17, 1992), 32 I.L.M. 289 (entered into force Jan. 1, 1994), Chap. 16, Appendix 1603.D.1.

[8] 1 legacy Immigration and Naturalization Service (INS) Inspector's Field Manual (IFM) ch. 15, "NAFTA Admissions," 14-1 INS Manuals 15.5.

[9] 9 Foreign Affairs Manual (FAM) 402.16-2(A).

[10] NAFTA Implementation Cable 010, 1 NAFTA Handbook (Nov. 1999), 14-1 INS Manuals Scope.

[11] 9 FAM 402.17-10(a).

[12] 8 Code of Federal Regulations (CFR) §214.6 (b); 9 FAM 402.17-5(A) and 402.17-10(b).

[13] 8 CFR §214.6(c).

[14] NAFTA, U.S.-Can.-Mex. (Dec. 17, 1992), 32 I.L.M. 289 (entered into force Jan. 1, 1994), Chap. 16, Appendix 1603.D.1; 58 Fed. Reg. 69205 (Dec. 30, 1993).

Copyright © 2017. American Immigration Lawyers Association. All rights reserved.

requirements are also stated in the Treaty,[15] and a detailed discussion is provided below.

Accountant	Baccalaureate or Licenciatura degree	**OR** CPA, CA, CGA, or CMA	
Architect	Baccalaureate or Licenciatura Degree	**OR** State/provincial license	
Computer Systems Analyst	Baccalaureate or Licenciatura Degree		**OR** Post-secondary certificate and three years of experience
Disaster Relief Insurance Claims Adjuster	Baccalaureate or Licenciatura Degree and successful completion of training in the appropriate areas of insurance adjustment pertaining to disaster relief claims		**OR** three years of experience in claims adjustment and successful completion of training in the appropriate areas of insurance adjustment pertaining to disaster relief claims
Economist	Baccalaureate or Licenciatura Degree		
Engineer	Baccalaureate or Licenciatura Degree	**OR** state or provincial license	
Forester	Baccalaureate or Licenciatura Degree	**OR** state or provincial license	

---

[15] NAFTA, U.S.-Can.-Mex. (Dec. 17, 1992), 32 I.L.M. 289 (entered into force Jan. 1, 1994), Chap. 16, Appendix 1603.D.1; 8 CFR §214.6(c).

Copyright © 2017. American Immigration Lawyers Association. All rights reserved.

Graphic Designer	Baccalaureate or Licenciatura Degree		**OR** Post-Secondary Diploma or Post-Secondary Certificate and three years of experience
Hotel Manager	Baccalaureate or Licenciatura Degree in hotel/restaurant management		**OR** Post-Secondary Diploma or Post-Secondary Certificate in hotel/restaurant management and three years of experience in hotel/restaurant management
Industrial Designer	Baccalaureate or Licenciatura Degree		**OR** Post-Secondary Diploma or Post-Secondary Certificate and three years of experience
Interior Designer	Baccalaureate or Licenciatura Degree		**OR** Post-Secondary Diploma or Post-Secondary Certificate and three years of experience
Land Surveyor	Baccalaureate or Licenciatura Degree	**OR** state, provincial, or federal license	
Landscape Architect	Baccalaureate or Licenciatura Degree		

Copyright © 2017. American Immigration Lawyers Association. All rights reserved.

Lawyer (including a Notary in the province of Quebec)	LL.B., J.D., LL.L., B.C.L. or Licenciatura Degree (five years)	**OR** membership in a state or provincial bar	
Librarian	M.L.S. or B.L.S. (for which another Baccalaureate or Licenciatura Degree was a prerequisite)		
Management Consultant	Baccalaureate or Licenciatura Degree	**OR** equivalent professional experience as established by statement or professional credential attesting to five years of experience as a management consultant	**OR** five years of experience in a field of specialty related to the consulting agreement
Mathematician (including Statistician)	Baccalaureate or Licenciatura Degree		
Range Manager or Range Conservationist	Baccalaureate or Licenciatura Degree		
Research Assistant	Baccalaureate or Licenciatura Degree		

Copyright © 2017. American Immigration Lawyers Association. All rights reserved.

Scientific Technician or Technologist	No degree required (but note that the TN worker must be directly supporting a degreed professional)	Possession of theoretical knowledge of any of the following disciplines: agricultural sciences, astronomy, biology, chemistry, engineering, forestry, geology, geophysics, meteorology, or physics	**AND** the ability to solve practical problems in any of those disciplines, or the ability to apply principles of any of those disciplines to basic or applied research
Social Worker	Baccalaureate or Licenciatura Degree		
Sylviculturist (including Forestry Specialist)	Baccalaureate or Licenciatura Degree		
Technical Publications Writer	Baccalaureate or Licenciatura Degree		**OR** Post-Secondary Diploma or Post-Secondary Certificate and three years of experience
Urban Planner (including Geographer)	Baccalaureate or Licenciatura Degree		
Vocational Counselor	Baccalaureate or Licenciatura Degree		

Copyright © 2017. American Immigration Lawyers Association. All rights reserved.

Dentist	D.D.S., D.M.D., Doctor en Odontologia or Doctor en Cirugia Dental	**OR** state or provincial license	
Dietician	Baccalaureate or Licenciatura Degree	**OR** state or provincial license	
Medical Laboratory Technologist or Medical Technologist	Baccalaureate or Licenciatura Degree		**OR** Post-Secondary Diploma or Post-Secondary Certificate and three years of experience
Nutritionist	Baccalaureate or Licenciatura Degree		
Occupational Therapist	Baccalaureate or Licenciatura Degree	**OR** state or provincial license	
Pharmacist	Baccalaureate or Licenciatura Degree	**OR** state or provincial license	
Physician (teaching or research only)	M.D. or Doctor en Medicina	**OR** state or provincial license	
Physiotherapist or Physical Therapist	Baccalaureate or Licenciatura Degree	**OR** state or provincial license	
Psychologist	Licenciatura Degree	**OR** state or provincial license	
Recreational Therapist	Baccalaureate or Licenciatura Degree		

Copyright © 2017. American Immigration Lawyers Association. All rights reserved.

Registered Nurse	Licenciatura Degree	**OR** state or provincial license	
Veterinarian	D.V.M., D.M.V. or Doctor en Veterinaria; or state/provincial license		
Agriculturist (including Agronomist)	Baccalaureate or Licenciatura Degree		
Animal Breeder	Baccalaureate or Licenciatura Degree		
Animal Scientist	Baccalaureate or Licenciatura Degree		
Apiculturist	Baccalaureate or Licenciatura Degree		
Astronomer	Baccalaureate or Licenciatura Degree		
Biochemist	Baccalaureate or Licenciatura Degree		
Biologist (including Plant Pathologist)	Baccalaureate or Licenciatura Degree		
Chemist	Baccalaureate or Licenciatura Degree		
Dairy Scientist	Baccalaureate or Licenciatura Degree		

Copyright © 2017. American Immigration Lawyers Association. All rights reserved.

Entomologist	Baccalaureate or Licenciatura Degree		
Epidemiologist	Baccalaureate or Licenciatura Degree		
Geneticist	Baccalaureate or Licenciatura Degree		
Geochemist	Baccalaureate or Licenciatura Degree		
Geologist	Baccalaureate or Licenciatura Degree		
Geophysicist (including Oceanographer)	Baccalaureate or Licenciatura Degree		
Horticulturist	Baccalaureate or Licenciatura Degree		
Meteorologist	Baccalaureate or Licenciatura Degree		
Pharmacologist	Baccalaureate or Licenciatura Degree		
Physicist (including Oceanographer)	Baccalaureate or Licenciatura Degree		
Plant Breeder	Baccalaureate or Licenciatura Degree		

Copyright © 2017. American Immigration Lawyers Association. All rights reserved.

Poultry Scientist	Baccalaureate or Licenciatura Degree		
Soil Scientist	Baccalaureate or Licenciatura Degree		
Zoologist	Baccalaureate or Licenciatura Degree		
College Teacher	Baccalaureate or Licenciatura Degree		
Seminary Teacher	Baccalaureate or Licenciatura Degree		
University Teacher	Baccalaureate or Licenciatura Degree		

In the event that the practitioner is unsure whether a U.S. assignment will be considered one of these stated TN professions, reference may be made to the template job descriptions of the Department of Labor (DOL).[16] As discussed in more detail below, the practitioner should ensure that the support statement highlights how the proposed U.S. duties fall within the standard duties of the profession and may wish to provide a copy of the template DOL job description to the foreign national when he or she presents the TN petition.

B. Qualification as a Professional

All but a handful of the TN classifications require that the foreign national hold either a baccalaureate or licenciatura degree, as "[b]usiness activities at a professional level means those undertakings which require that, for successful completion, the individual has at least a baccalaureate degree or appropriate credentials demonstrating status as a professional."[17] "A baccalaureate or Licenciatura [sic] degree is the

---

[16] O*Net, http://flcdatacenter.com/OesWizardStart.aspx (select the state from the drop-down menu and then type the job title into the search box or browse the drop-down menu); Dictionary of Occupational Titles, http://www.occupationalinfo.org/ (browse the occupational definitions); and http://www.oalj.dol.gov/PUBLIC/DOT/REFERENCES/DOTALPHA.HTM (search the alphabetical index).

[17] U.S. Customs and Border Protection (CBP) Office of Field Operations Admissibility & Passenger Programs Enforcement Programs, "NAFTA Guide for TN and L Applicants," p. 5 (June 2012), AILA Doc. No. 13091643. *See also* 1 legacy INS IFM ch.15, "NAFTA Admissions," 14-1 INS Manuals 15.5.

Copyright © 2017. American Immigration Lawyers Association. All rights reserved.

minimum requirement for these professions unless an alternative credential is otherwise specified."[18] A three-year degree is acceptable: "There is no requirement that the baccalaureate be gained in a four-year academic program."[19] Except for hotel managers, discussed below, the degree should be in the field of the TN classification or in a related field.[20]

If the degree was awarded by a university outside the United States, Canada, or Mexico, then the foreign national must also present a credentials evaluation, confirming that the degree is equivalent to an American, Canadian, or Mexican degree.[21] The same requirement applies to diplomas and certificates earned outside the United States, Canada, and Mexico.[22] Other evidence of professional credentials includes certificates, diplomas, professional licenses, or membership in a professional association.[23] As a practical matter, even where a credentials evaluation is not required, it can be beneficial to provide one, particularly where the degree is from a university that may not be known to the officers at the port of entry or consulate.

For 13 professions, the foreign national may present a valid state or provincial license instead of a degree. Such a license is defined as "any document issued by a state, provincial, or federal government, as the case may be, or under its authority, but not by a local government, that permits a person to engage in a regulated activity or profession."[24] The professions are architect, engineer, forester, land surveyor, dentist, dietician, occupational therapist, pharmacist, physician, physiotherapist or physical therapist, psychologist, registered nurse, and veterinarian. The practitioner should note that only the profession of land surveyor allows a foreign national to hold a federal license;[25] thus, even if Canada or Mexico issue federal licenses for other professions, such federal licenses should not be used to request TN admission or a TN visa.

Importantly, evidence of licensure for these professions is an alternative to educational documents and not a requirement for admission in addition to educational documents.[26] As stated by Department of State (DOS) guidance:

"The list of professions reveals requirements for admission into the United States under immigration provisions. Such requirements for admission or classification

---

[18] 58 Fed. Reg. 69205 (Dec. 30, 1993).

[19] Legacy INS Operations Instruction (OI) 214.6.

[20] Legacy INS, M. Cronin, "Guidance for Processing Applicants under the North American Free Trade Agreement (NAFTA)" (July 24, 2000), AILA Doc. No. 00101705.

[21] 8 CFR §214.6(d)(3)(ii).

[22] 9 FAM 402.17-5(C).

[23] Id.

[24] NAFTA, U.S.-Can.-Mex. (Dec. 17, 1992), 32 I.L.M. 289 (entered into force Jan. 1, 1994), Chap. 16, Appendix 1603.D.1.

[25] Id.; 8 CFR §214.6(c).

[26] 69 Fed. Reg. 60939 (Oct. 13, 2004).

Copyright © 2017. American Immigration Lawyers Association. All rights reserved.

as a NAFTA professional do not include licensure. Licensure to practice a given profession in the United States is a post-entry requirement subject to enforcement by the appropriate state or other sub-federal authority."[27]

The previous legacy Immigration and Naturalization Service (INS) guidance, which required foreign nationals to present evidence of satisfying the licensure requirements of the state of proposed employment, has been voided.[28] If the foreign national is denied TN admission or a TN visa for failure to present evidence of licensure when he or she presented the appropriate degree, then this should be considered an erroneous denial: "[A]dmission/classification should not be denied based solely on the fact that the applicant does not already hold a license to practice in the United States."[29] When re-applying for admission or for the visa, the foreign national should disclose the previous application and submit copies of the guidance.

Moreover, the licensure requirements should not apply in situations where the proposed duties do not require licensing and where the foreign national would not actually practice the profession in the United States, such as providing professional seminars or training for one of the TN occupations. Legacy INS guidance provides the examples of an architect who develops plans but does not sign the plans and a dentist who would lecture at a seminar on dentistry.[30] The final example involves a lawyer who will offer legal advice about Canadian law but who will not "practice before any state bar in the U.S." While this may be helpful with respect to approval of the TN, the practitioner should note that certain state bars would consider the provision of such legal advice to entail the practice of law.[31]

In addition, accountants may present evidence of professional certification in the alternative to educational documents: CPA (Certified Public Accountant), CA (Chartered Accountant), CGA (Certified General Accountant), or CMA (Certified Management Accountant).[32] Attorneys may present educational documents for a variety of degrees: LL.B (Bachelor of Laws), J.D. (Juris Doctor), LL.L (Licentiate of Laws), or a five-year licenciatura degree. Alternatively, an attorney may submit evidence of membership in a state or provincial bar.[33] A librarian must hold a Master of Library Science degree or a Bachelor of Library Science degree, for which another

---

[27] 9 FAM 402.17-4(B).

[28] 1 legacy INS IFM ch.15, "NAFTA Admissions," 14-1 INS Manuals 15.5.

[29] 9 FAM 402.17-4(B).

[30] 1 legacy INS IFM ch.15, "NAFTA Admissions," 14-1 INS Manuals 15.5.

[31] Laurel Terry, "Jurisdictions with Rules Regarding Foreign Lawyer Practice," American Bar Association (June 29, 2016), http://bit.ly/2kLdylv.

[32] NAFTA, U.S.-Can.-Mex. (Dec. 17, 1992), 32 I.L.M. 289 (entered into force Jan. 1, 1994), Chap. 16, Appendix 1603.D.1; 8 CFR §214.6(c).

[33] *Id.*

Copyright © 2017. American Immigration Lawyers Association. All rights reserved.

bachelor's degree was a requirement for admission to the educational program, and there are no alternative requirements.[34]

An additional seven professions allow the foreign national to qualify by presenting a post-secondary certificate or diploma and evidence of professional experience instead of a baccalaureate or licenciatura degree: computer systems analysts, graphic designers, hotel managers, industrial designers, interior designers, technical publications writers, and medical laboratory technologists and medical technologists.[35]

A "post-secondary diploma" is defined as "a credential issued, on completion of two or more years of post-secondary education, by an accredited academic institution in Canada or the United States."[36] A "post-secondary certificate" is defined as "certificate issued, on completion of two or more years of post-secondary education at an academic institution, by the federal government of Mexico or a state government in Mexico, an academic institution recognized by the federal government or a state government, or an academic institution created by federal or state law."[37] The post-secondary diploma or certificate must be issued in the United States, Canada, or Mexico.[38]

The evidence of professional experience "should be in the form of letters from former employers."[39] Although not specifically stated as requirements, the practitioner is advised that as a practical matter, it is preferable that the experience letters be on company letterhead and signed by an individual who has the authority to confirm the foreign national's experience, such as a former manager or supervisor, or a representative of the human resources department of the company. Experience has shown that this type of letter is granted the greatest weight of credibility. If detailed letters cannot be obtained on company letterhead, a detailed personal letter from a former supervisor combined with a generic letter on letterhead confirming the dates of employment is often accepted as an alternative. In the event that the foreign national wishes to use experience that he or she gained while self-employed, "business records must be submitted attesting to that self-employment."[40] These records may include invoices for payment for professional services rendered, evidence of payment, and service contracts with the entity. It is also helpful to obtain experience letters from the former client or clients who received the foreign national's services.

---

[34] Id.

[35] Id.

[36] NAFTA, U.S.-Can.-Mex. (Dec. 17, 1992), 32 I.L.M. 289 (entered into force Jan. 1, 1994), Chap. 16, Appendix 1603.D.1.

[37] Id.

[38] Legacy INS, M. Cronin, "Guidance for Processing Applicants under the North American Free Trade Agreement (NAFTA)" (Jul. 24, 2000), AILA Doc. No. 00101705.

[39] 9 FAM 402.17-5(C); 1 legacy INS IFM ch.15, "NAFTA Admissions," 14-1 INS Manuals 15.5.

[40] 9 FAM 402.17-4(B); 1 legacy INS IFM ch.15, "NAFTA Admissions," 14-1 INS Manuals 15.5.

Copyright © 2017. American Immigration Lawyers Association. All rights reserved.

Finally, the requirements for disaster relief insurance claims adjusters, hotel managers, management consultants, and scientific technicians and technologists have unique differences from other TN classifications, as discussed below.

C. Qualification as a Business Person

In order to be admitted in TN status or be issued a TN visa, the foreign national must be a business person, as that term is defined in the NAFTA Treaty: a Canadian or Mexican citizen "who is engaged in trade in goods, the provision of services or the conduct of investment activities."[41] The foreign national must seek to "engage in business activities at a professional level [which] means the performance of prearranged business activities for a U.S. entity, including an individual."[42] The TN petition should confirm satisfaction of these requirements, as the support statement should confirm that the foreign national will provide services as prearranged business activities to a company or individual. A foreign national in TN status may not engage in self-employment, as discussed below.

D. Canadian or Mexican Citizenship

Applicants for admission must submit proof of their Canadian or Mexican citizenship. Under the Western Hemisphere Travel Initiative, "Canadian citizens can present a valid passport, Enhanced Driver's License, or Trusted Traveler Program card (NEXUS, SENTRI or FAST)."[43] As a practical matter, a Canadian citizen should present a valid passport, as the TN entry stamp will be placed on a blank page of the passport and is helpful for future admissions to the United States in TN status.

For purposes of TN admission, the term "citizen of Mexico" means "a national or a citizen according to the existing provisions of Articles 30 and 34, respectively, of the Mexican Constitution."[44] Mexican citizens must present valid passports, as the required TN visas will be in the passports.

Dependent spouses and children of TN professionals need not, however, be citizens of Canada or Mexico.[45] They will require TD visa stamps. For dependent spouses and children of Canadian citizens, a TD visa stamp can be obtained at a U.S. consulate after the principal is admitted to the U.S. in TN status. For dependent spouses and children of Mexican citizens, a TD visa stamp can be obtained at the U.S. consulate at the same time as the principal applicant obtains his or her TN visa

---

[41] NAFTA, U.S.-Can.-Mex. (Dec. 17, 1992), 32 I.L.M. 289 (entered into force Jan. 1, 1994), Chap. 16, Article 1608.

[42] CBP Office of Field Operations Admissibility & Passenger Programs Enforcement Programs, "NAFTA Guide for TN and L Applicants," at 6 (June 2012), AILA Doc. No. 13091643. *See also* 1 legacy INS IFM ch.15, "NAFTA Admissions," 14-1 INS Manuals 15.5.

[43] CBP, "Western Hemisphere Travel Initiative," https://www.cbp.gov/travel/us-citizens/western-hemisphere-travel-initiative.

[44] NAFTA, U.S.-Can.-Mex. (Dec. 17, 1992), 32 I.L.M. 289 (entered into force Jan. 1, 1994), Chap. 16, Annex 1608.

[45] 9 FAM 402.17-11(d).

Copyright © 2017. American Immigration Lawyers Association. All rights reserved.

stamp. Persons holding permanent resident status in Canada or Mexico are not eligible for TN status.[46]

E. Temporary Entry

A TN professional should be granted "temporary entry" to the United States:

"Temporary entry, as defined in the NAFTA, means entry without the intent to establish permanent residence. The alien must satisfy the inspecting immigration officer that the proposed stay is temporary. A temporary period has a reasonable, finite end that does not equate to permanent residence. In order to establish that the alien's entry will be temporary, the alien must demonstrate to the satisfaction of the inspecting immigration officer that his or her work assignment in the United States will end at a predictable time and that he or she will depart upon completion of the assignment."[47]

Similarly, legacy INS stated that "while there is no specific limit on the total period of time a citizen of Canada or Mexico may remain in TN status, the TN classification is nevertheless for persons seeking temporary entry without the intent to establish permanent residence."[48] This provision distinguishes the TN classification from other employment-based nonimmigrant visa categories, such as L and H-1B, which impose maximum time limitations on foreign nationals, as discussed in Volume 1: Chapter Two, "Basic Nonimmigrant Concepts."

While demonstration of nonimmigrant intent remains a requirement of the TN category, with the promulgation of regulations extending the period of stay available to TN professionals from one year to three years,[49] a substantial inquiry into nonimmigrant intent may not take place until the second or even the third term of three years. This may be a more proper interpretation of the DOS guidance that "[a]n extended stay, even in terms of years, may be temporary, as long as there is no immediate intent to immigrate."[50] Nevertheless, in preparing the foreign national for the renewal application, the practitioner is advised to discuss in detail with the foreign national how to explain continued nonimmigrant intent to a government official, because the "circumstances surrounding an application should reasonably and convincingly indicate that the alien's temporary work assignment in the United States will end predictably and that the alien will depart upon completion of the assignment."[51]

---

[46] 9 FAM 402-17-2(B).

[47] 8 CFR §214.6(b); 22 CFR §41.59(c).

[48] 63 Fed. Reg. 1331 (Jan. 9, 1998).

[49] 73 Fed. Reg. 61332 (Oct. 16, 2008).

[50] 9 FAM 402-17.7.

[51] 9 FAM 402.17-7 22 CFR §41.59(c).

Copyright © 2017. American Immigration Lawyers Association. All rights reserved.

The foreign national's nonimmigrant intent will be considered at the time he or she applies for admission to the United States;[52] and the nonimmigrant intent of Mexican citizens will be considered during the visa interview as well.[53] For a further discussion of nonimmigrant intent, see Volume 1: Chapter Two, "Basic Nonimmigrant Concepts." Because of the nonimmigrant intent requirement, it is possible that the foreign national could be denied TN admission or a TN visa if he or she is the beneficiary of an immigrant visa petition, although certain strategies may maximize the likelihood of visa issuance and U.S. admission, as discussed below.

III. Managing Client Expectations: Increased Scrutiny in Certain Situations

The practitioner should be aware that eligibility for a TN assignment may require more than performance of professional duties and that certain TN classifications are subject to heightened inquiry from the government official. For certain TN classifications, there is clear guidance indicating the scope of the duties to be performed and stipulating conditions to the admission. Experience has shown that other applications for TN admission are reviewed carefully and face a higher than normal risk of denial.

For applications for Canadian citizens in these categories, it is often advisable to obtain advance approval of the TN petition in advance through the USCIS Service Center, and to then have the foreign national present the I-797 Approval Notice rather than having the application processed at the port of entry. While the government official retains the authority to make the final admission decision and may still question the foreign national about the details of the assignment, experience has shown that obtaining advance approval through the USCIS Service Center increases the chances of a problem-free admission.

A. Management Consultants

Legacy INS guidance indicates that management consultants are responsible "for provid[ing] services that are directed toward improving the managerial, operating, and economic performance of public and private entities by analyzing and resolving strategic and operating problems and thereby improving the entity's goals, objectives, policies, strategies, administration, organization, and operation."[54] In a general sense, the management consultant may not be a personnel manager or a "function manager," as discussed in Volume 1: Chapter Eleven, "L Visas and Status," but liaises with the regular management of the U.S. company as a consultant.

For several reasons, the TN petition for a management consultant should be prepared with careful attention to common issues, and the practitioner should thoroughly discuss the process of applying for admission or for a visa and advise the client of the higher likelihood that the TN petition may be denied.

---

[52] 1 legacy INS IFM ch.15, "NAFTA Admissions," 14-1 INS Manuals 15.5.

[53] 9 FAM 402.17-7.

[54] 1 legacy INS IFM ch.15, "NAFTA Admissions," 14-1 INS Manuals 15.5.

Copyright © 2017. American Immigration Lawyers Association. All rights reserved.

First, anecdotal evidence indicates that immigration inspectors and consular officers believe that this TN classification has been abused and/or is more subject to abuse by U.S. employers. This may be because the TN classification does not require that the foreign national hold a baccalaureate or licenciatura degree, or, in the alternative, professional licensure or a post-secondary certificate or diploma and several years of professional experience. The government officials may believe that unscrupulous employers used the classification to employ foreign nationals who were not degreed professionals and who did not truly have the appropriate experience background, because the government officials were unable to confirm the authenticity of the experience letters submitted with the TN petition. Although the increased scrutiny should apply most clearly in current situations where the foreign national does not have the baccalaureate or licenciatura degree, experience has shown that the entire TN classification may be tainted by this erroneous presumption. Experience has also shown that management consultant TN petitions on behalf of foreign nationals who hold baccalaureate or licenciatura degrees are subject to the same level of intense scrutiny, although government officials do not seem to demand experience letters. However a good practice would be to provide experience letters to be presented with the applicant in the event they are needed for review by the adjudicating government official.

Second, legacy INS guidance indicates that management consultants must be either independent consultants of the U.S. company or employees of a consulting company.[55] Specifically, the legacy INS guidance states:

> "Management consultants are usually independent contractors or employees of consulting firms under contracts to U.S. entities. They may be salaried employees of the U.S. entities to which they are providing services only when they are not assuming existing positions or filling newly created positions. As a salaried employee of such a U.S. entity, they may only fill supernumerary temporary positions. On the other hand, if the employer is a U.S. management consulting firm, the employee may be coming temporarily to fill a permanent position. Canadian or Mexican citizens may qualify as management consultants by holding a Baccalaureate or Licenciatura degree or by having five years of experience in a specialty related to the consulting agreement."[56]

Although the text of the Inspector's Field Manual (IFM) is not supported by treaty, statute, or regulation, reports indicate that government officials nevertheless have been requiring one of the enumerated employment relationships for TN status.[57] Experience and anecdotal evidence indicate that government officials have denied TN petitions for management consultants when the foreign national is neither an independent consultant nor an employee of a consulting firm. Therefore, the

---

[55] *Id.*

[56] *Id.*

[57] *See, e.g.*, D. Horne, "Requests for Evidence," 11-15 Bender's Immigr. Bull. 3 (Aug. 1, 2006) (stating in a footnote that the IFM is only "an internal manual designed to provide guidance on policies and procedures" (citing *Munyua v. U.S.*, 2005 U.S. Dist. LEXIS 11499 (N.D. Cal. Jan. 10, 2005)).

Copyright © 2017. American Immigration Lawyers Association. All rights reserved.

practitioner should counsel the client that such a management consultant may be questioned in detail and ultimately may be denied TN admission.

"And if the foreign national will fill a supernumerary temporary position, then the support statement should explicitly state this fact. The term supernumerary is defined as 'associated with a regular body or staff as an assistant or substitute in case of necessity.'[58] The supernumerary nature of the assignment may be stated in a consulting agreement, employment contract, or TN support statement."

Further, the issues may be due to the lack of a clear definition of the duties of a management consultant. Even 14 years after the NAFTA Treaty went into effect, comments received in response to the proposed rule to extend the term of TN admission to three years "requested a more comprehensive reform of the TN regulations to include ... [a] more extensive definition[] for the position[] of Management Consultant."[59] The final rule implementing the three-year period of TN admission declined to provide any more guidance on the occupation, as the rule did not seek to reform the TN program.[60] The practitioner may consult the definition provided by legacy INS guidance, as discussed above, as well as the DOL template job descriptions.[61] Upon seeking TN admission or visa, the foreign national should be able to articulate clearly the reason for the U.S. assignment, the daily job duties, and the employment relationship. Finally, the consulting agreement or employment contract should be valid for the entire period of requested stay, especially if the foreign national seeks TN admission for the maximum period of three years.

B. Scientific Technicians and Technologists

Scientific technicians and technologists are not eligible for TN admission for a discrete assignment. They must seek admission "for work in direct support of professionals."[62] This classification is unique, because it is the only TN profession for which the employee need not have gained any university-level or post-secondary education, need not have a state or provincial license, and need not have any professional experience. Instead, the focus of the inquiry is on the foreign national's theoretical knowledge and practical skill. But as a practical matter, the language is similar to the definition of a "specialty occupation," which requires "theoretical and practical application of a body of highly specialized knowledge" pursuant to H-1B status.[63]

---

[58] *Webster's Revised Unabridged Dictionary* (1998), http://dictionary.reference.com/browse/supernumerary.

[59] 73 Fed. Reg. 61332 (Oct. 16, 2008).

[60] *Id.*

[61] O*Net, "Summary Report for Management Analysts," http://online.onetcenter.org/link/summary/13-1111.00; Department of Labor (DOL), http://www.oalj.dol.gov/PUBLIC/DOT/REFERENCES/DOT01F.HTM (scroll down to 189.167-010).

[62] 1 legacy INS IFM ch.15, "NAFTA Admissions," 14-1 INS Manuals 15.5.

[63] 8 CFR §214.2(h)(4)(ii).

Copyright © 2017. American Immigration Lawyers Association. All rights reserved.

Perhaps because scientific technicians and technologists may not qualify as degreed professionals,[64] the foreign national must demonstrate that he or she will directly support a professional of the same field within which the proposed TN employees gained theoretical knowledge and practical skills: agricultural sciences, astronomy, biology, chemistry, engineering, forestry, geology, geophysics, meteorology, or physics.[65] The two-prong eligibility test focuses first on the theoretical knowledge in these disciplines and then on whether the foreign national has either "the ability to solve practical problems in any of those disciplines, or the ability to apply principles of any of those disciplines to basic or applied research."[66]

When determining whether the proposed assignment qualifies for the TN classification, legacy INS provided the following guidance, where scientific technician or technologist was abbreviated to "ST/T":

"The offer [of employment] must demonstrate that the work of the ST/T will be inter-related with that of the supervisory professional. That is, the work of the ST/T must be managed, coordinated and reviewed by the professional supervisor, and must also provide input to the supervisory professional's own work.

"The ST/T's theoretical knowledge should have been acquired through the successful completion of at least two years of training in a relevant educational program. Such training may be documented by presentation of a diploma, a certificate, or a transcript accompanied by evidence of relevant work experience.

"U.S. authorities will rely on the Department of Labor's Occupational Outlook Handbook to establish whether proposed job functions are consistent with those of a scientific or engineering technician or technologist. ST/Ts should not be admitted to perform job functions that are primarily associated with other job titles."[67]

"This TN classification is inappropriate for foreign nationals who will perform construction or building work, even if the trade is 'specialized' to a scientific industry."[68]

This legacy INS guidance is notable in several respects. First, it explicitly references job descriptions from the Occupational Outlook Handbook (OOH), so the practitioner should review the template job descriptions for more details on the appropriate job duties. Updated versions of the OOH job descriptions are available

---

[64] 1 legacy INS IFM ch.15, "NAFTA Admissions," 14-1 INS Manuals 15.5 (stating "[t]hese occupations do not ordinarily require a baccalaureate").

[65] North American Free Trade Agreement, U.S.- Can.–Mex. (Dec. 17, 1992), 32 I.L.M. 289 (entered into force Jan. 1, 1994), Chap. 16, Appendix 1603.D.1.

[66] 8 CFR §214.6(c).

[67] Legacy INS, J. Williams, "Field Guidance on the Admission of Scientific Technicians/Technologists under the North American Free Trade Agreement (IN 03-01)" (Nov. 7, 2002), AILA Doc. No. 02121331.

[68] Id.

Copyright © 2017. American Immigration Lawyers Association. All rights reserved.

online,[69] and the practitioner should compare them to the job description for the proposed assignment to confirm that the job duties are appropriate for the TN classification. The practitioner should also note that the legacy INS guidance seems to group all of the enumerated disciplines which are not engineering-related or teaching positions into the broad category of "scientific."[70] The practitioner may wish to highlight the scientific aspects of the job description in the TN support statement to maximize the likelihood of TN petition approval.

Second, the requirement that the theoretical knowledge be gained through an educational program contradicts earlier guidance from legacy INS, which stated: "Although no degree or post-secondary diploma is required for entry, the immigration officer must be satisfied that the applicant possesses the theoretical knowledge in one of those disciplines."[71] The older guidance indicated that there were discussions with U.S. "federal agencies and the Canadian and Mexican officials to develop common interpretative guidance and definitions for the terms 'possess theoretical knowledge' and 'works in direct support,'" and that further guidance would be issued once the negotiations were complete.[72] It appears that the subsequent memorandum is the negotiated guidance, as the subsequent memorandum comments that the "Scientific Technician/Technologist category has been problematic for all of the parties to NAFTA," and that "[i]n December 2001, the parties drafted and subsequently agreed to guidelines for evaluating applicants for Scientific Technician/Technologist positions."[73]

Therefore, the theoretical knowledge must have been gained from educational programs, such as those for professional certification, vocational programs, and/or degree coursework. Based on this guidance, it seems that the theoretical knowledge may not have been gained solely through previous employment experience or on-the-job training, although this experience may be the vehicle through which the foreign national gained the ability to solve practical problems or the ability to apply principles to basic or applied research. Indeed, in the event that the foreign national did not earn a degree, diploma, or certificate, then he or she must have evidence of work experience in order to document possession of the theoretical knowledge. Based on this guidance, the practitioner may wish to advise the client that the foreign national must present evidence of at least one relevant educational program in order to establish eligibility for the TN classification. One consideration may be that a scientific technician or technologist may use educational coursework even if he or she

---

[69] http://www.bls.gov/ooh/.

[70] Legacy INS, J. Williams, "Field Guidance on the Admission of Scientific Technicians/Technologists under the North American Free Trade Agreement (IN 03-01)" (Nov. 7, 2002), AILA Doc. No. 02121331.

[71] Legacy INS, M. Cronin, "Guidance for Processing Applicants under the North American Free Trade Agreement (NAFTA)" (July 24, 2000), AILA Doc. No. 00101705.

[72] Id.

[73] Legacy INS, J. Williams, "Field Guidance on the Admission of Scientific Technicians/Technologists under the North American Free Trade Agreement (IN 03-01)" (Nov. 7, 2002), AILA Doc. No. 02121331.

Copyright © 2017. American Immigration Lawyers Association. All rights reserved.

did not ultimately earn a degree, or a post-secondary certificate or diploma, as coursework may be successfully completed even without completion of the educational program.

The analysis regarding the weight of the subsequent memorandum also applies to the interpretation of the term "works in direct support" of a professional in one of the enumerated scientific fields. Thus, the TN foreign national must establish that he or she has an employment offer specifically to provide technical or technological services directly to a supervisory professional, and the "[i]ndividuals for whom scientific technicians/technologists wish to provide direct support must qualify as a professional in their own right."[74]

It is possible that it would be sufficient to have the USCIS equivalent of a degree through progressive experience as under the H-1B classification,[75] or that it would be sufficient to hold the educational and/or experience background for the relevant occupation under NAFTA.[76] For example, a TN engineer or forester may qualify as a professional either by having a baccalaureate or licenciatura degree or by holding a state or provincial license.[77] It is increasingly common that documentation of the professional credentials of the supervisory professional is requested when a foreign national applies for TN admission or for a TN visa, so as a practical matter, this documentation should be included as part of the TN application. Moreover, in preparing the TN support statement, the practitioner should provide details on how the supervisory professional's occupation is professional, including the job title and a brief description of the professional's job duties. The practitioner should counsel the client that a scientific technician or technologist who will support a professional, who in turn does not hold at least a bachelor's degree, may be denied TN admission or a TN visa even if the appropriate equivalency is held.

Further, as stated in the guidance, "[a] general offer of employment by such a professional is not sufficient, by itself, to qualify for admission."[78] Other legacy INS guidance states: "Supporting documents could be an attestation from the prospective U.S. employer or the Canadian employer, or other documents establishing the individual possesses the skills."[79] The support statement should confirm that the TN employee will work in direct support of a professional in one of the enumerated fields, as well as a detailed explanation of how the foreign national gained the theoretical knowledge and of how the foreign national has ability to solve practical problems

---

[74] Id.

[75] 8 CFR §214.2(h)(4)(iii)(D)(5).

[76] NAFTA, U.S.-Can.-Mex. (Dec. 17, 1992), 32 I.L.M. 289 (entered into force Jan. 1, 1994), Chap. 16, Appendix 1603.D.1; 8 CFR §214.6(c).

[77] NAFTA, U.S.-Can.-Mex. (Dec. 17, 1992), 32 I.L.M. 289 (entered into force Jan. 1, 1994), Chap. 16, Appendix 1603.D.1; 8 CFR §214.6(c).

[78] Legacy INS, J. Williams, "Field Guidance on the Admission of Scientific Technicians/Technologists under the North American Free Trade Agreement (IN 03-01)" (Nov. 7, 2002), AILA Doc. No. 02121331.

[79] 1 legacy INS IFM ch.15, "NAFTA Admissions," 14-1 INS Manuals 15.5.

Copyright © 2017. American Immigration Lawyers Association. All rights reserved.

and/or to apply principles to basic or applied research. The support statement should also provide details regarding the supervisory professional's job duties, as well as how the supervisory professional requires the services of a technician or technologist, how the technician or technologist's job duties are "inter-related" with the duties of the supervisory professional, and how the supervisory professional will manage, coordinate, and review the work of the technician or technologist.

Finally, the prohibition on performance of construction or building work by a foreign national admitted pursuant to NAFTA applies to scientific technicians and technologists, even if the construction or building work is "specialized to a particular industry (*e.g.*, aircraft, power distribution, etc.)."[80] For a detailed discussion of the history of this prohibition, see Volume 1: Chapter Three, "Visitors: B Visas and Status and the Visa Waiver Program."

Similar to the legacy INS guidance, DOS directs consular officers to consider the following factors and provides an example:

"[T]he position must involve the use of principles of science, research and development, and/or scientific observations and calculations. (This is from the DOL job description.) … The position must primarily include activity consistent with the support of a science professional…. The technician who assists the engineer in the lab to design and develop a new technology may qualify as a scientific technician, but the mechanic who repairs and maintains that same technology after it's built and used in everyday life, is not a scientific technician."[81]

In light of the example provided by DOS, it would appear at first blush that scientific technicians and technologists should not be responsible only for installation, repair, and maintenance of equipment but must be primarily responsible for designing or developing the technology. However, U.S. Customs and Border Protection (CBP) may be more open to technicians and technologists whose duties involve work on existing technology, noting that "CBP has its own internal guidance and does not follow DOS guidance. Scientific Technicians may enter the U.S. either to work on new equipment or to work on existing equipment, so long as they work in direct support of an engineer and otherwise qualify for the classification."[82] Thus, Canadian and Mexican applicants in this situation may encounter different results, as the Canadian will be processed by CBP while the Mexican national must first obtain a visa, and thus will fall under the DOS standards.

---

[80] Legacy INS, J. Williams, "Field Guidance on the Admission of Scientific Technicians/Technologists under the North American Free Trade Agreement (IN 03-01)" (Nov. 7, 2002), AILA Doc. No. 02121331.

[81] "DOS Guidance on Qualification as a 'Scientific Technician/Technologist' under NAFTA" (Jan. 4, 2008), AILA Doc. No. 08022774.

[82] "AILA CBP OFO Liaison Committee Meeting with U.S. Customs and Border Protection Office of Field Operations (OFO)" (Nov. 4, 2016), AILA Doc. No. 17010304.

Copyright © 2017. American Immigration Lawyers Association. All rights reserved.

Although it remains unclear which DOL job description is referenced by DOS, current versions of DOL template job descriptions are available online.[83] The practitioner should also review the OOH job descriptions discussed above, as those templates discuss how science and engineering technicians "apply theory and principles" of their scientific or engineering disciplines to solve technical problems in their fields.[84]

Indeed, there are separate template job descriptions for certain industries, such as electrical and electronics repairers, commercial and industrial equipment,[85] electricians,[86] and electronics engineering technicians,[87] as well as for industrial machinery mechanics[88] and industrial engineering technicians.[89] Further, a substantial proportion of the template job descriptions from DOL where "repair" or "maintain" is the keyword are construction and building occupations,[90] and this is an impermissible use of the TN classification, as discussed above.

Despite the requirement that the TN employee seek admission to work in direct support of a professional, experience has shown that the foreign national need not travel to the United States in the company of the professional. Indeed, there is no

---

[83] O*Net, "Summary Report for Forest and Conservation Technicians," http://online.
onetcenter.org/link/summary/19-4093.00; "Summary Report for Geophysical Data Technicians,"
http://online.onetcenter.org/link/summary/19-4041.01; "Summary Report for Geological Sample Test
Technicians," http://online.onetcenter.org/link/summary/19-4041.02; "Summary Report for Chemical
Technicians," http://online.onetcenter.org/link/summary/19-4031.00; "Summary Report for Biological
Technicians," http://online.onetcenter.org/link/summary/19-4021.00; "Summary Report for Agricultural
Technicians," http://online.onetcenter.org/link/summary/19-4011.01; "Summary Report for Mechanical
Engineering Technicians," http://online.onetcenter.org/link/summary/17-3027.00; "Summary Report for
Industrial Engineering Technicians," http://online.onetcenter.org/
link/summary/17-3026.00; "Summary Report for Environmental Engineering Technicians,"
http://online.onetcenter.org/link/summary/17-3025.00; "Summary Report for Electrical Engineering
Technicians," http://online.onetcenter.org/link/summary/17-3023.03; "Summary Report for Electronics
Engineering Technicians," http://online.onetcenter.org/link/summary/17-3023.01;
"Summary Report for Civil Engineering Technicians," http://online.onetcenter.org/link/summary/17-3022.00;
and "Summary Report for Aerospace Engineering and Operations Technicians,"
http://online.onetcenter.org/link/summary/17-3021.00.

[84] http://www.bls.gov/ooh/

[85] O*Net, "Summary Report for Electrical and Electronics Repairers, Commercial and Industrial Equipment,"
http://online.onetcenter.org/link/summary/49-2094.00.

[86] O*Net, "Summary Report for Electricians," http://online.onetcenter.org/link/summary/47-2111.00.

[87] O*Net, "Summary Report for Electronics Engineering Technicians," http://online.onetcenter.org/
link/summary/17-3023.01.

[88] O*Net, "Summary Report for Industrial Machinery Mechanics," http://online.onetcenter.org/
link/summary/49-9041.00.

[89] O*Net, "Summary Report for Industrial Engineering Technicians," http://online.onetcenter.org/link/
summary/17-3026.00.

[90]   DOL, "FLC Wage Search Wizard," http://flcdatacenter.com/OesWizardStep3.aspx?keyword1=
repair&area=33860&year=9&source=1 (providing many job codes that relate to construction and building
occupations), and "FLC Wage Search Wizard," http://flcdatacenter.com/OesWizard
Step3.aspx?keyword1=maintain&area=33860&year=9&source=1.

Copyright © 2017. American Immigration Lawyers Association. All rights reserved.

requirement that the professional be a foreign national seeking TN classification; the professional may be an employee of the U.S. company which seeks to hire the foreign national in TN status. But although guidance was requested from CBP as to whether the TN nonimmigrant may work at a different location from the professional, no response was provided.[91] If the TN nonimmigrant works at a different location than the professional that he or she directly supports, it is a good practice to have documentation (printed emails, memos or design schematics, etc.) on hand that may be reviewed by the CBP officer to demonstrate the interaction between the Scientific Technician and the professional that he or she directly supports in order to address the "direct support" element of this classification.

Finally, although reports indicated that CBP officers imposed a requirement that the scientific technicians or technologists work in a laboratory following issuance of the DOS guidance, senior CBP officials stated that this requirement was improper and confirmed: "CBP still follows Legacy INS guidance with respect to this issue."[92]

C. Medical and Health Care Professions

In addition to the requirements for TN status, certain foreign health care workers must present a health care certificate from an approved agency in order to be admissible:[93]

- "Licensed Practical Nurses, Licensed Vocational Nurses, and Registered Nurses.

- "Occupational Therapists.

- "Physical Therapists.

- "Speech Language Pathologists and Audiologists.

- "Medical Technologists (Clinical Laboratory Scientists).

- "Physician Assistants.

- "Medical Technicians (Clinical Laboratory Technicians)."[94]

The certification process entails the following activities by the credentialing agency:

- "Verification of the foreign national's education and training, as well as his or her license and/or experience, if applicable, in order to confirm that his or her professional qualifications satisfy the statutory and regulatory requirements for the class of admission 'are comparable with that required for an American health-care worker of the same type; and are authentic and,

---

[91] "AILA National's U.S. Customs and Border Protection (CBP) Liaison Committee Meeting Liaison Agenda" (Mar. 25, 2010), AILA Doc. No. 10072870.

[92] "AILA Liaison/CBP Meeting Minutes" (Aug. 26, 2008), AILA Doc. No. 08110768 .

[93] INA §212(a)(5)(C); 8 CFR §214.15(a).

[94] 8 CFR §212.15(c).

Copyright © 2017. American Immigration Lawyers Association. All rights reserved.

in the case of a license, unencumbered,'[95] which means the license is 'not burdened or affected'";[96]

- "Confirmation that the foreign national has the required level of English competency";[97] and

- "If a majority of U.S. states that license the health care profession 'recognize a test predicting the success on the profession's licensing or certification examination,' confirmation that the foreign national has passed such a test or examination,"[98] or 'confirmation that the foreign national has passed the occupation's licensing or certification examination.'"[99]

Importantly, the verification decision, stating that the foreign national's professional qualifications meet the statutory and regulatory requirements for admission to the United States, is "not binding on the DHS,"[100] even as it is required of the credentialing agency. The government official may use the interview to confirm that the foreign national has the necessary English competency and "appropriate knowledge of the certified health care field."[101] Therefore, the practitioner is advised to explain to the client that issuance of the certificate does not guarantee visa issuance or admission to the United States, as a government official will make the determination of whether the foreign national is eligible for TN status.

Similarly, the certificate should also be differentiated from a license: "A certificate or certified statement described in this section does not constitute professional authorization to practice in that health care occupation."[102] The practitioner should advise the client that, if the foreign national did not obtain a state or federal license for the certificate process, he or she will nevertheless need to obtain a license in order to practice the health care occupation after admission to the United States.

The issued certificate must provide the following information:

- Name, address, and telephone number of the credentialing agency, as well as "a point of contact to verify the validity of the certificate";

- Date of issuance;

- Health care occupation for which the certificate is issued; and

- Name, date of birth, and place of birth of the foreign national.[103]

---

[95] INA §212(a)(5)(C)(i).
[96] 73 Fed. Reg. 62197 (Oct. 20, 2008).
[97] INA §212(a)(5)(C)(ii).
[98] INA §212(a)(5)(C)(iii).
[99] 8 CFR §212.14(f)(1)(iv).
[100] 8 CFR §212.15(f)(1)(iii).
[101] 9 FAM 302.1-7(B)(6).
[102] 8 CFR §212.15(a)(3).
[103] 8 CFR §212.15(f)(2).

Copyright © 2017. American Immigration Lawyers Association. All rights reserved.

For Canadian citizens, the certificate must be valid at the time the foreign national applies for TN admission;[104] for Mexican citizens, the certificate must be valid at the time of visa application and at the time of application for TN admission.[105] The valid certificate must be presented during each application for admission and/or visa; it is not sufficient to rely upon an expired certificate that was valid at the time of a previous application for a visa or admission.[106] The certificate "or certified statement must be used within five years of the date that it was issued."[107]

The interim final rule of 2002 acknowledged that the certification requirement presented a "possible conflicting obligation of the United States under NAFTA."[108] The interim final rule indicated the joint intent by DOS and legacy INS to continue to exercise discretion under Immigration and Nationality Act (INA) §212(d)(3)(A) and stated that DOS would "continue to use its discretion to temporarily waive this inadmissibility for nonimmigrant health care workers until concerned Executive branch agencies resolve the apparent conflict."[109] The 2008 rule "adopt[ed] as final without change the Department's interim rule," but the final rule had no discussion of continuing to waive the ground of inadmissibility based on a conflict with the terms of the NAFTA Treaty, even though there does not seem to have been any resolution of the conflict.[110]

As stated by the interim rule that set forth the initial deadline for health care workers in all nonimmigrant classifications, as of July 26, 2004: "The legislative history of IIRIRA confirms that, in this instance, the DHS may not rely on the commenters' assertions regarding an alleged conflict with NAFTA to reach a different result."[111] Subsequently, the Department of Homeland Security (DHS) issued an interim rule granting an additional extension, until July 26, 2005, of the certification requirement to TN professionals, as long as the foreign nationals held TN status before September 23, 2003.[112] But this rule also had no discussion of the interrelation of the obligations of the NAFTA Treaty and the certification requirement.[113]

The most recent guidance on point is from August 17, 2004, and indicates that the blanket waiver was only available until July 26, 2004: "On and after July 26, 2004 discretion shall be applied on a case-by-case basis. This waiver also applies to Canadians seeking admission in Trade NAFTA (TN) status. Health-care workers who

---

[104] 8 CFR §212.15(d)(2).

[105] 8 CFR §212.15(d)(1).

[106] 8 CFR §§212.15(d)(1) and (2). *See also* 68 Fed. Reg. 43901 (July 25, 2003).

[107] 9 FAM 302.1-7(B)(7).

[108] 67 Fed. Reg. 77158 (Dec. 17, 2002).

[109] *Id.*

[110] 73 Fed. Reg. 62197 (Oct. 20, 2008).

[111] 68 Fed. Reg. 43901 (July 25, 2003) (citing H.R. Rep. No. 104-828, at 226–27 (1996) (Conf. Rep.)).

[112] 69 Fed. Reg. 43729 (July 22, 2004).

[113] *Id.*

Copyright © 2017. American Immigration Lawyers Association. All rights reserved.

receive waivers for INA 212(a)(5)(C) ineligibilities should be issued visas limited to a single entry with six-month validity."[114]

The practitioner is advised against relying upon the exercise of discretion on a case-by-case basis, as the government official is likely to note that the certificate requirement has been in place for several years. It is possible that a waiver may be granted if there are special circumstances, but it seems unlikely that a waiver would be granted as a matter of course as it was during the time period when the blanket waiver was authorized.

Not all medical professions require the certificate. Specifically excluded from the requirement are physicians in TN status, who may not engage in direct patient care.[115]

Also excluded from the certificate requirement are the following foreign nationals:

- Individuals who will work in "non-clinical health care occupation[s]," where the foreign nationals are "not required to perform direct or indirect patient care," such as "medical teachers, medical researchers, and managers of health care facilities";[116]

- Trainees in H-3, H-1, and J-1 status;[117]

- The dependent spouse and children of a foreign health care worker;[118]

- Employment-based immigrants who will provide services in an occupation "that does not fall under one of the covered health care occupations" and family-based immigrants;[119] and

- "[C]hiropractors, dentists, dental technicians, dental assistants, acupuncturists, psychologists, nutritionists … medical consultants to the insurance industry, etc."[120]

The confirmation of English competence is not required of graduates of programs in Australia, Canada (except certain schools in Quebec), Ireland, New Zealand, the United Kingdom, and the United States, where the language of instruction was English, so these foreign nationals need not take the English language test.[121] Graduates of certain accredited programs are "exempt from the educational comparability review and English language proficiency testing."[122] For a detailed discussion of the certification requirements for these graduates, see Volume 1:

---

[114] 9 FAM 302.1-7(D)(2).

[115] INA §212(a)(5)(C); 8 CFR §212.15(b)(1).

[116] 8 CFR §212.15(b)(2).

[117] 8 CFR §212.15(b)(3).

[118] 8 CFR §212.15(b)(4).

[119] 8 CFR §212.15(b)(5).

[120] 9 FAM 302.1-7(D)(2).

[121] 8 CFR §212.15(g)(2)(ii).

[122] 8 CFR §212.15(i).

Copyright © 2017. American Immigration Lawyers Association. All rights reserved.

Chapter Seven, "H-1B Visas and Status." The discussion in this chapter will focus on the TN professions that also happen to be health care occupations requiring certification.

Finally, it is not recommended that the foreign national present a certificate for one health care occupation while seeking TN admission or applying for a TN visa for another health care profession. Based on the statutory and regulatory language, the certificate should confirm that the foreign national has the appropriate professional credentials for the specific TN classification that is sought.[123] The practitioner should note that, with the exception of the "Certified Statement" for a nurse who holds a valid U.S. state license and has passed the National Council Licensure Examination-Registered Nurse (NCLEX-RN) examination, all certificates must state "the health care occupation for which the certificate is issued."[124]

1. Registered Nurses

To qualify for TN status as a registered nurse, the foreign national must present either a licenciatura degree or a state or provincial license, as well as the certificate, as discussed below. Notably, registered nurse constitutes one of only two TN classifications where only the licenciatura degree is stated as the educational requirement.[125] This seems strange, since Canadian universities offer baccalaureate degree programs in nursing,[126] but the practitioner is advised to inform the client that the state or provincial license is required of Canadian citizens. Even though the general minimum requirement for TN classification is a baccalaureate or licenciatura degree,[127] the practitioner is advised against sending the Canadian citizen to the port of entry with only a Canadian baccalaureate degree, as this would not satisfy the requirements stipulated by NAFTA. The practitioner should also note that although a foreign nurse seeking H-1B status must present the equivalent of a U.S. bachelor's degree,[128] a foreign nurse seeking TN status may present the alternate credential of a state or provincial license.[129] Experience has shown that applications for TN

---

[123] INA §212(a)(5)(C)(i)(I) (discussing the "statutory and regulatory requirements for entry into the United States under the classification specified in the application"); 8 CFR §§212.15(d)(1) and (2) (discussing the "foreign health care worker certification or certified statement for a particular health care occupation").

[124] 8 CFR §212.15(f)(2)(iii).

[125] NAFTA, U.S.-Can.-Mex. (Dec. 17, 1992), 32 I.L.M. 289 (entered into force Jan. 1, 1994), Chap. 16, Appendix 1603.D.1; 8 CFR §214.6(c). The other TN classification is Psychologists.

[126] See, e.g., McGill University School of Nursing, http://www.mcgill.ca/nursing/programs/bscn/; and University of British Columbia School of Nursing, https://nursing.ubc.ca/undergraduate-program/bachelor-science-nursing/.

[127] 58 Fed. Reg. 69205 (Dec. 30, 1993).

[128] "USCIS's Standard Operating Procedures (SOPs) for H-1B Adjudication" (document not dated; posted July 27, 2007), AILA Doc. No. 07072668; Legacy INS, J. Williams, "Guidance on Adjudication of H-1B Petitions Filed on Behalf of Nurses" (Nov. 27, 2002), AILA Doc. No. 02121746; Vintage Health Resources Inc. v. Meissner, 201 F.2d. 384 (5th Cir. 2000).

[129] NAFTA, U.S.-Can.-Mex. (Dec. 17, 1992), 32 I.L.M. 289 (entered into force Jan. 1, 1994).

Copyright © 2017. American Immigration Lawyers Association. All rights reserved.

admission by Canadian citizens with Canadian baccalaureate degrees and a valid nursing license from a U.S. state or a Canadian province have been approved with little difficulty.

With respect to the job duties, DOS guidance provides a template description:

"Nurse, Professional (Medical Service) [Alternate Titles: Nurse, Certified Nurse, Licensed, Registered]—applies to persons meeting the educational, legal, and training requirements to practice as professional nurses, as required by a State Board of Nursing. This individual performs acts requiring substantial specialized judgment and skill, care and counsel of ill, injured, or infirm persons and in promotion of health and prevention of illness. Classifications are made according to types of nursing activity such as:

"Director;

"Nursing Service (Medical Service);

"Nurse, General Duty (Medical Service)."[130]

The inclusion of the hierarchy of nursing duties indicates that the TN classification is available for more occupations than those entailing direct patient care activities in a hospital or clinic work environment. For these more senior nursing occupations, however, the practitioner is advised to highlight in the support statement how the foreign national will perform nursing duties, such as the "care and counsel of ill, injured, or infirm persons" through subordinate nurses as a nurse manager of supervisor of a nursing unit,[131] or such as activities performed "in promotion of health and prevention of illness" by "[i]nstruct[ing] individuals, families and other groups on topics such as health education, disease prevention and childbirth, and develop[ing] health improvement programs."[132]

Registered nurses may satisfy the certificate requirement with one of two documents issued by the Commission on Graduates of Foreign Nursing Schools (CGFNS), as CGFNS is currently the only approved agency.[133] The VisaScreen Certificate satisfies the standard statutory and regulatory requirements for certification, discussed above. There is also a VisaScreen streamlined process for graduates of entry-level programs accredited by the National League for Nursing Accreditation Commission (NLNAC) or the Commission on Collegiate Nursing Education (CCNE), as these foreign nationals are "exempt from the educational comparability review and English language proficiency testing."[134]

---

[130] 9 FAM 302.1-7(B)(1).

[131] O*Net, "Summary Report for Registered Nurses," http://online.onetcenter.org/link/summary/29-1111.00.

[132] Id.

[133] 8 CFR §212.15(e)(1); 9 FAM 302.1-7(B)(5).

[134] 8 CFR §212.15(i). See also CGFNS, "VisaScreen: Visa Credentials Assessment Application Handbook" (2009-2014), www.cgfns.org/wp-content/uploads/VSHandbook.pdf.

Copyright © 2017. American Immigration Lawyers Association. All rights reserved.

Alternatively, the foreign national may present the "Certified Statement," which confirms that the foreign national:

- Passed the NCLEX-RN examination;

- Possesses "a valid and unrestricted license as a nurse in a state where the alien intends to be employed and such state verifies that the foreign licenses of alien nurses are authentic and unencumbered"; and

- Graduated from a nursing program, which "was in operation on or before November 12, 1999," and was located in Australia, Canada (except certain schools in Quebec), Ireland, New Zealand, the United Kingdom, or the United States, where "the language of instruction was English."[135]

2. Medical Laboratory Technologists and Medical Technologists

Medical laboratory technologists and medical technologists must seek TN admission in order to "perform in a laboratory chemical, biological, hematological, immunologic, microscopic or bacteriological tests and analyses for diagnosis, treatment or prevention of disease."[136] The Foreign Affairs Manual (FAM) indicates that a medical technologist also can be titled clinical laboratory scientists service.[137] The FAM uses the title "medical laboratory technician" instead of the NAFTA term "technologist," and also indicates an alternative title of clinical laboratory technician.[138]

A curiosity in NAFTA's language results in some confusion as to whether and when professionals in these occupations are required to work in a laboratory. Because NAFTA's list of qualifying professions states "Medical Laboratory *Technologist* (Canada)/Medical Technologist (Mexico and the United States)"[139] (emphasis added), some practitioners and immigration inspectors have taken the view that technologists from Canada must work in a laboratory, while the laboratory requirement does not apply to technologists from Mexico. The fact that the FAM separates Medical Laboratory Technologist and Medical Technologist[140] only adds to the confusion.

It should be remembered that the footnote in NAFTA, quoted above, applies to both job titles and uses the phrase "perform in a laboratory" to modify all the activities described.[141] That being said, another footnote in NAFTA that applies to all listed professions indicates that the individual "may also perform training functions

---

[135] INA §212(r); 8 CFR §§212.15(h) and (a)(2).

[136] NAFTA, U.S.-Can.-Mex. (Dec. 17, 1992), 32 I.L.M. 289 (entered into force Jan. 1, 1994), Chap. 16, Appendix 1603.D.1, footnote 7; 8 CFR §214.6(c).

[137] 9 FAM 302.1-7(B)(1)(e).

[138] 9 FAM 302.1-7(B)(1) (f).

[139] NAFTA, U.S.-Can.-Mex. (Dec. 17, 1992), 32 I.L.M. 289 (entered into force Jan. 1, 1994), Chap. 16, Appendix 1603.D.1.

[140] 9 FAM 302.1-7(B)(1)(e) and (f).

[141] NAFTA, U.S.-Can.-Mex. (Dec. 17, 1992), 32 I.L.M. 289 (entered into force Jan. 1, 1994), Chap. 16, Appendix 1603.D.1, footnote 7; 8 CFR §214.6(c).

Copyright © 2017. American Immigration Lawyers Association. All rights reserved.

relating to the profession, including conducting seminars."[142] Consistent with this latter footnote, DOS guidance indicates that medical technicians may "train and supervise students."[143] Thus, the terms of NAFTA seem to direct that the focus of these TN employees should be to conduct laboratory activities and related training activities,[144] and not to provide services in the general environment of a hospital, clinic, doctor's office, or research center.

The professional credentials for this TN classification are a baccalaureate or licenciatura degree, or a post-secondary diploma or post-secondary certificate and three years of experience.[145] The experience letters should be in the format discussed above. It was previously unclear whether medical laboratory technologists and medical technologists were subject to the certification requirement, because it appears that only 10 U.S. states issue licenses: California, Florida, Hawaii, Louisiana, Montana, Nevada, North Dakota, Rhode Island, Tennessee, and West Virginia.[146] Foreign nationals who will work in these states will need to obtain a U.S. state license before commencing employment.[147] It is clear now, however, that these professionals must present VisaScreen certificates in order to be admissible.[148]

3. Occupational Therapists

An occupational therapist performs the activities "in hospital, institution, or community settings to facilitate development and rehabilitation of mentally, physically, or emotionally handicapped individuals ... to help patient or handicapped persons develop or regain physical and mental functioning."[149] He or she may also "[p]repare the individual for return to employment, assist[] in restoration of functions, and aid[] in adjustment to disability ... [and may] be designated director, occupational therapy (Medical Service)."[150]

The inclusion of a job title with more senior-level responsibility indicates that the TN classification is appropriate for such a managerial profession, rather than only foreign nationals who will provide hands-on occupational therapy and care. For such a TN petition, the practitioner may wish to include discussion of how the foreign

---

[142] Id.

[143] 9 FAM 302.1-7(B)(1)(e).

[144] NAFTA, U.S.-Can.-Mex. (Dec. 17, 1992), 32 I.L.M. 289 (entered into force Jan. 1, 1994), Chap. 16, Appendix 1603.D.1; 8 CFR §214.6(c).

[145] NAFTA, U.S.-Can.-Mex. (Dec. 17, 1992), 32 I.L.M. 289 (entered into force Jan. 1, 1994).

[146] "CGFNS Comment to Interim Rule on Certification of Foreign Health Care Workers" (Sept. 17, 2004), AILA Doc. No. 08080460.

[147] 9 FAM 402.17-4(B).

[148] INA §212(a)(5)(C); 9 FAM 302.1-7(B)(1), (B)(2), and (B)(5).

[149] 9 FAM 302.1-7(B)(1)(c).

[150] Id.

Copyright © 2017. American Immigration Lawyers Association. All rights reserved.

national's job duties focus on occupational therapy tasks, such as to "conduct, plan, direct, and coordinate training program and occupational therapy programs."[151]

The foreign national must present either a baccalaureate or licenciatura degree, or a state or provincial license.[152] In addition, occupational therapists must obtain either the VisaScreen certificate from CGFNS,[153] or a Visa Credential Verification Certificate from the National Board for Certification in Occupational Therapy (NCBOT).[154] The practitioner should note, however, that NBCOT "is authorized to issue certificates in the field of occupational therapy pending final adjudication of its credentialing status."[155] There is a streamlined process if the foreign national "graduated from a program accredited by the Accreditation Council for Occupational Therapy Education (ACOTE) of the American Occupational Therapy Association (AOTA)," because the educational comparability review and English language proficiency testing need not be performed.[156]

4. Physiotherapists and Physical Therapists

These professionals plan, coordinate, and provide "medically prescribed physical therapy treatment for patients suffering from injuries, or muscle, nerve joint and bone disease [to] restore function, relieve pain, and prevent disability."[157] The FAM guidance also states that physical therapists direct the "work activities of assistants, aides, and students" and provide "lectures and training programs on physical therapy and related topics for medical staff, students and community groups,"[158] indicating that standard physical therapist duties are not limited to those of providing direct patient care. The FAM guidance also states that the following may be appropriate physical therapist duties:

- "May teach physical therapy techniques and procedures in educational institutions; and

- "May write technical articles and reports for publications; may plan, direct, and coordinate physical therapy program and be the designated director."[159]

---

[151] Id.

[152] NAFTA, U.S.-Can.-Mex. (Dec. 17, 1992), 32 I.L.M. 289 (entered into force Jan. 1, 1994), Chap. 16, Appendix 1603.D.1; 8 CFR §214.6(c).

[153] 9 FAM 302.1-7(B)(5); CGFNS, "VisaScreen: Visa Credentials Assessment Application Handbook" (2009-2014), www.cgfns.org/wp-content/uploads/VSHandbook.pdf.

[154] 9 FAM 302.1-7(B)(5); National Board for Certification in Occupational Therapy (NBCOT), "Visa Credential Verification Certificate Handbook" (2016), http://www.nbcot.org/assets/candidate-pdfs/international-pdfs/vcvc-handbook.

[155] 8 CFR §212.15(e)(2).

[156] 8 CFR §212.15(i)(2). See also American Occupational Therapy Association (AOTA), "Accreditation" under "Education & Careers," http://www.aota.org.

[157] 9 FAM 302.1-7(B)(1)(b).

[158] Id.

[159] Id.

Copyright © 2017. American Immigration Lawyers Association. All rights reserved.

Should the client wish the TN physical therapist or physiotherapist to have these more senior-level duties, the practitioner may wish to connect these managerial activities to the field of physical therapy, such as if the techniques, articles, or programs are cutting-edge and contribute to the overall level of patient care or "integrate physical treatment with other aspect[s] of [the] patient's health care."[160]

The foreign national must present either a baccalaureate or licenciatura degree, or a state or provincial license.[161] For the foreign health care certificate, a VisaScreen Certificate from CGFNS or a Comprehensive Credentials Evaluation from the Foreign Credentialing Commission on Physical Therapy (FCCPT) will suffice.[162] The practitioner should note, however, that FCCPT "is authorized to issue certificates in the field of physical therapy pending final adjudication of its credentialing status."[163] The practitioner should note that at least one state requires a different type of certificate, even though the certificate is an application in addition to the state licensure application.[164] In addition, a foreign national who "graduated from a program accredited by the Commission on Accreditation in Physical Therapy Education (CAPTE) of the American Physical Therapy Association (APTA) is exempt from the educational comparability review and English language proficiency testing."[165]

5. Physicians

Physicians may perform TN assignments only as long as the activities are focused on teaching and research; they may not provide direct patient care.[166] It may be permissible for the TN physician to provide patient care that is "incidental" to his or her teaching and/or research activities.[167] Legacy INS guidance states:

> "Patient care is incidental when it is casually incurred in conjunction with the physician's teaching or research. To determine if the patient care will be incidental, factors such as the amount of time spent in patient care relative to teaching and/or research, whether the physician receives compensation for such services, whether the salary offer is so substantial in teaching and/or research that direct patient care is unlikely, or whether the physician will have a regular patient load, should be considered by the officer."[168]

---

[160] Id.

[161] NAFTA, U.S.-Can.-Mex. (Dec. 17, 1992), 32 I.L.M. 289 (entered into force Jan. 1, 1994), Chap. 16, Appendix 1603.D.1; 8 CFR §214.6(c).

[162] 8 CFR §212.15(e); 9 FAM 302.1-7(B)(5). See also Foreign Credentialing Commission on Physical Therapy (FCCPT), http://www.fccpt.org/.

[163] 8 CFR §212.15(e)(2).

[164] Foreign Credentialing Commission on Physical Therapy, http://www.fccpt.org/Getting-Started/Primary-Services/New-York-Credentials-Verification.

[165] 8 CFR §212.15(i)(3). See also "CAPTE Accreditation Handbook," http://www.capteonline.org/AccreditationHandbook/.

[166] 1 legacy INS IFM ch.15, "NAFTA Admissions," 14-1 INS Manuals 15.5.

[167] Id.

[168] Id.

Copyright © 2017. American Immigration Lawyers Association. All rights reserved.

In practice, the inquiry focuses on the proportion of patient care services vis-à-vis teaching and/or research duties. The TN physician should be "primarily" responsible for teaching and/or research duties, much as a manager or executive in L-1 status should be primarily responsible for managing and directing the activities of his or her subordinate personnel.[169] Physicians need not obtain or present the foreign health care worker certificate, as their duties should not entail direct patient care.[170]

D. Disaster Relief Insurance Claims Adjusters

Legacy INS guidance indicates that disaster relief insurance claims adjusters must meet very stringent requirements in order to be admitted. These professionals must present evidence that there is a disaster event; then, one of the following conditions must be met:

- The event is declared to be a disaster by the President of the United States, or a state statute, or a local ordinance;

- The event is "at a site which has been assigned a catastrophe serial number by the Property Claims Service of the American Insurance Services Group"; or

- "[A]n association of insurance companies representing at least 15 percent of the property casualty market in the U.S." must confirm that the "property damage exceeds $5 million and represents a significant number of claims,"[171] although the property damage may be an "estimated total amount."[172]

In addition, the foreign national either must be employed by an insurance company in Canada or Mexico or must be an independent claims adjuster.[173] The professional requirements for this TN classification are a baccalaureate or licenciatura degree and "successful completion of training in the appropriate areas of insurance adjustment pertaining to disaster relief claims."[174] Alternatively, the foreign national may present evidence of three years of experience in claims adjustment and successful completion of training in the appropriate areas of insurance adjustment pertaining to disaster relief claims.[175] Appropriate evidence to satisfy the requirements may include presidential, gubernatorial, or municipal Executive Orders, newspaper articles, statements from the American Insurance Services Group or from

---

[169] 8 CFR §214.2(*l*)(1)(ii)(B). For a detailed discussion of L-1A managers and executives, see Volume 1: Chapter Eleven, "L-1 Visas and Status."

[170] 8 CFR §§212.15(b)(1) and (2).

[171] 1 legacy INS IFM ch.15, "NAFTA Admissions," 14-1 INS Manuals 15.5.

[172] Operating Instructions (OI) 214.6.

[173] *Id.*

[174] NAFTA, U.S.-Can.-Mex. (Dec. 17, 1992), 32 I.L.M. 289 (entered into force Jan. 1, 1994), Chap. 16, Appendix 1603.D.1; 8 CFR §214.6(c).

[175] *Id*

Copyright © 2017. American Immigration Lawyers Association. All rights reserved.

an association of insurance companies, professional certifications, school transcripts, and experience letters. Template job descriptions from DOL are available online.[176]

E. Hotel Managers

The TN classification of hotel managers is the only profession where a degree must be earned in a specific field.[177] For the rest of the TN classifications, legacy INS guidance indicates that the degree should be in the field or in a related field.[178] But a TN hotel manager must have a baccalaureate or licenciatura degree in hotel management or restaurant management.[179] Alternatively, the foreign national may present a post-secondary certificate or diploma in hotel or restaurant management and evidence of three years of experience in hotel or restaurant management.[180] A DOL template job description is available online.[181]

F. Sylviculturists, Foresters, and Range Managers

Legacy INS guidance specifically provides brief job descriptions for these three occupations. "Sylviculturists and foresters plan and supervise the growing, protection, and harvesting of trees."[182] The practitioner may also wish to review the DOL job description for foresters.[183] There is no DOL job description for sylviculturists; one dictionary defines a sylviculturist as one "who cultivates forest trees, especially as a business."[184] NAFTA includes forestry specialists within the TN classification of sylviculturists.[185] Although the legacy INS guidance does not provide a job description for the occupation of a forestry specialist, the practitioner may review related template job descriptions from DOL.

Other forestry-related occupations can be more problematic. The practitioner should note that there is not a template job description specifically for a forestry

---

[176] O*Net, "Summary Report for Insurance Adjusters, Examiners, and Investigators," http://online.onetcenter.org/link/summary/13-1031.02, and "Summary Report for Claims Examiners, Property and Casualty Insurance," http://online.onetcenter.org/link/summary/13-1031.01.

[177] NAFTA, U.S.-Can.-Mex. (Dec. 17, 1992), 32 I.L.M. 289 (entered into force Jan. 1, 1994), Chap. 16, Appendix 1603.D.1; 8 CFR §214.6(c); Legacy INS, M. Cronin, "Guidance for Processing Applicants under the North American Free Trade Agreement (NAFTA)" (July 24, 2000), AILA Doc. No. 00101705.

[178] Legacy INS, M. Cronin, "Guidance for Processing Applicants under the North American Free Trade Agreement (NAFTA)" (July 24, 2000), AILA Doc. No. 00101705.

[179] NAFTA, U.S.-Can.-Mex. (Dec. 17, 1992), 32 I.L.M. 289 (entered into force Jan. 1, 1994), Chap. 16, Appendix 1603.D.1; 8 CFR §214.6(c).

[180] Id.

[181] O*Net, "Summary Report for Lodging Managers," http://online.onetcenter.org/link/summary/11-9081.00.

[182] 1 legacy INS IFM ch.15, "NAFTA Admissions," 14-1 INS Manuals 15.5.

[183] O*Net, "Summary Report for Foresters," http://www.onetonline.org/link/summary/19-1032.00.

[184] Dictionary, http://www.thefreedictionary.com/Sylviculturist.

[185] NAFTA, U.S.-Can.-Mex. (Dec. 17, 1992), 32 I.L.M. 289 (entered into force Jan. 1, 1994), Chap. 16, Appendix 1603.D.1; 8 CFR §214.6(c).

Copyright © 2017. American Immigration Lawyers Association. All rights reserved.

technician; the closest matches are for forest and conservation technicians,[186] and forester aides or forest technicians.[187] The other DOL job descriptions from other DOL websites are for "First-Line Supervisors/Managers of Agricultural Crop and Horticultural Workers,"[188] "First-Line Supervisors/Managers of Logging Workers,"[189] and "Forest and Conservation Workers."[190] The practitioner should, however, consider the alternative job descriptions in light of the prohibition on employing foreign nationals for building and construction work,[191] and should advise the client that performing logging or agricultural work is most likely inappropriate for TN professionals, as these activities would most likely be construed as labor for hire.[192] It seems that a TN forestry specialist professional may engage in the supervision or management of forestry activities, similar to a supervisor or management of construction or building personnel, as discussed in Volume 1: Chapter Three, "Visitors: B Visas and Status and the Visa Waiver Program." But TN classification does not seem to be appropriate to engage in forestry work of this kind: Even if there is no hands-on work that would constitute labor for hire and displace U.S. workers, the template job description is the same as for logging workers.[193] For this reason, it is not advised that TN status be pursued on behalf of these kinds of forest workers.[194]

Legacy INS guidance states that range managers "manage, improve, and protect rangelands to maximize their use without damaging the environment."[195] For the TN classifications of sylviculturist, forester, and range manager, legacy INS guidance stipulates the requirement of "a baccalaureate or licenciatura degree in forestry or a related field or a state/provincial license."[196]

---

[186] O*Net, "Summary Report for Forest and Conservation Technicians," http://online. onetcenter.org/link/summary/19-4093.00.

[187] Dictionary of Occupational Titles, http://www.oalj.dol.gov/PUBLIC/DOT/REFERENCES/ DOT04A.HTM (scroll down to 452.364.010).

[188] O*Net, "Summary Report for First-Line Supervisors/Managers of Agricultural Crop and Horticultural Workers," http://online.onetcenter.org/link/summary/45-1011.07.

[189] O*Net, "Summary Report for First-Line Supervisors/Managers of Logging Workers," http://online.onetcenter.org/link/summary/45-1011.05.

[190] Occupational Outlook Handbook (OOH), http://www.bls.gov/ooh/farming-fishing-and-forestry/forest-and-conservation-workers.htm.

[191] 51 Fed. Reg. 44266 (Dec. 9, 1986).

[192] Legacy INS, P. Virtue, "Admissibility of Canadian Log Loaders," 1 INS and DOJ Legal Opinions §93-86.

[193] Legacy INS, M. Cronin, "Guidance for Processing Applicants under the North American Free Trade Agreement (NAFTA)" (July 24, 2000), AILA Doc. No. 00101705.

[194] OOH, "Forest, Conservation, and Logging Workers," www.bls.gov/oco/ocos178.htm.

[195] 1 legacy INS IFM ch.15, "NAFTA Admissions," 14-1 INS Manuals 15.5.

[196] *Id.*

Copyright © 2017. American Immigration Lawyers Association. All rights reserved.

G. Computer Systems Analysts

The job description for computer systems analysts provided by legacy INS guidance states:

"A systems analyst is an information specialist who analyzes how data processing can be applied to the specific needs of users and who designs and implements computer-based processing systems. Systems analysts study the organization itself to identify its information needs and design computer systems which meet those needs."[197]

While many technology positions involve both systems analysis and programming, the Computer Systems Analyst TN classification should not be used for a pure programmer. As stated by the guidance, "[a]lthough the systems analyst will do some programming, the TN category has not been expanded to include programmers."[198] There are separate DOL job descriptions for computer systems analysts and computer programmers, but the DOL templates note how the job title programmer analyst may be used for computer systems analyst and computer programmer positions.[199] The TN support statement should emphasize the systems analysis duties, so that it is clear that the assignment is appropriate for TN classification. In addition, as discussed below, the practitioner should consider whether the position more appropriately falls into the category of Software Engineer rather than Computer Systems Analyst.

A computer systems analyst should present evidence of either baccalaureate or licenciatura degree, or a post-secondary diploma or post-secondary certificate and three years of experience.

H. Engineers and Software Engineers

The TN classification of engineer includes the many different types of engineering: "Since the appendix doesn't specify certain specialties, the three NAFTA partners interpret this to mean that all engineering specialties are included."[200] Moreover, the NAFTA Treaty does not specifically state "the types of engineering degrees (*e.g.*, civil, mechanical, electrical, etc.) that qualify for TN classification."[201]

In addition, the same guidance specifically states that software engineers should qualify for the TN classification of engineer.[202] As with the other TN classifications,

---

[197] *Id.*

[198] *Id.*

[199] O*Net, "Summary Report for Computer Systems Analyst," http://online.onetcenter. org/link/summary/15-1051.00, and "Summary Report for Computer Programmer," http://online.onetcenter.org/link/summary/15-1021.00.

[200] Legacy INS, M. Cronin, "Guidance for Processing Applicants under the North American Free Trade Agreement (NAFTA)" (July 24, 2000), AILA Doc. No. 00101705.

[201] *Id.*

[202] *Id.*

Copyright © 2017. American Immigration Lawyers Association. All rights reserved.

the baccalaureate or licenciatura degree must be in the field of software engineering or in a related field.[203] As stated by the guidance:

> "Returning to the 'software engineer' example, it is reasonable to require the TN applicant to provide evidence of a degree in engineering just as it is reasonable to require an engineering degree for admission as a TN to perform professional level duties as a civil engineer."[204]

Despite the focus of the guidance on the degree requirement, a TN engineer may present alternative evidence of a state or provincial engineering license.[205] As a practical matter, however, state or provincial licenses specifically for software engineers seem to be rare; the foreign national may need to present evidence of a professional engineer license instead.[206] The job duties of software engineers should be differentiated from computer systems analysts,[207] and from programmers, as discussed above.

In practice, as long as the position involves the design, development, and/or maintenance of computer software or hardware systems, adjudications of TN applications in this category typically are not problematic. The practitioner should emphasize in the TN support statement the way in which the TN beneficiary will draw on his or her engineering education to perform computer engineering duties. Referencing particular coursework and the way in which that coursework is applied in performing the computer engineering assignment can be helpful to strengthen the TN petition.

I. Animal and Plant Breeders

Two more occupations for which legacy INS provided job descriptions are animal breeders and plant breeders: "Animal and plant breeders breed animals and plants to improve their economic and aesthetic characteristics."[208] The practitioner may also review DOL template job descriptions.[209] Notably, only the old DOT classification system provided a template for plant breeders; under the new system, this occupation

---

[203] *Id.*

[204] *Id.*

[205] *Id.* (stating "[i]f there is an acceptable alternative credential to the educational requirement, it is also listed" in the Appendix to the NAFTA Treaty).

[206] *See, e.g.,* Professional Engineers Ontario, "Engineering Association Embraces Software Practitioners," http://www.peo.on.ca/index.php/ci_id/26350/la_id/1.htm; Association of Information Technology Professionals, "Licensing of Software Engineers in Texas" (Aug. 12, 2003), https://www.aitp.org/news/71043/Licensing-of-Software-Engineers-in-Texas.htm.

[207] O*Net, "Summary Report for Software Developers, Applications," https://www.onetonline.org/link/summary/15-1132.00, and "Summary Report for Software Developers, Systems Software," https://www.onetonline.org/link/summary/15-1133.00.

[208] 1 legacy INS IFM ch.15, "NAFTA Admissions," 14-1 INS Manuals 15.5.

[209] O*Net, "Summary Report for Animal Breeders," http://online.onetcenter.org/link/summaey/45-2021.00; DOL website, Dictionary of Occupational Titles, http://www.oalj.dol.gov/PUBLIC/DOT/REFERENCES/DOT01B.HTM (scroll down to 041.061.082).

Copyright © 2017. American Immigration Lawyers Association. All rights reserved.

falls under the broader position of soil and plant scientists,[210] and soil scientist is a separate TN classification.[211] Animal and plant breeders must present a baccalaureate or licenciatura degree to qualify for TN admission.

J. Actuaries

The TN classification of mathematician includes the occupation of statistician.[212] A DHS regulation then specifically included the occupation of actuary within the occupation of mathematician, because "it is generally accepted that an actuary is in fact a type of mathematician."[213] This addition was negotiated by the three parties to the NAFTA Treaty upon the request of the American Academy of Actuaries and the professional actuarial associations in Canada and Mexico.[214]

Although the proposed rule allowed for a foreign national to qualify as a professional actuary by holding a "Baccalaureate or Licenciatura degree in Actuarial Science or satisfaction of the necessary requirements to be recognized as an actuary by a professional actuarial association or society,"[215] the final rule notes the "one modification" of adding the footnote to the NAFTA Treaty to include actuaries in the TN classification of mathematician.[216] The footnote in the regulation states:

"An Actuary must satisfy the necessary requirements to be recognized as an actuary by a professional actuarial association or society. A professional actuarial association or society means a professional actuarial association or society operating in the territory of at least one of the Parties."[217]

There is no mention of a requirement of a baccalaureate or licenciatura degree in actuarial science; the only mention of a baccalaureate or licenciatura degree is in the general educational requirement for a mathematician.[218] Therefore, it seems that the general acceptance of a degree in the field or in a related field would apply,[219] and that a TN actuary must be recognized as an actuary by a professional actuarial association or society.

---

[210] O*Net, "DOT Crosswalk Search," http://online.onetcenter.org/crosswalk/DOT?s=041.061-082.

[211] NAFTA, U.S.-Can.-Mex. (Dec. 17, 1992), 32 I.L.M. 289 (entered into force Jan. 1, 1994), Chap. 16, Appendix 1603.D.1; 8 CFR §214.6(c).

[212] NAFTA, U.S.-Can.-Mex. (Dec. 17, 1992), 32 I.L.M. 289 (entered into force Jan. 1, 1994), Chap. 16, Appendix 1603.D.1, footnote 5; 8 CFR §214.6(c).

[213] 69 Fed. Reg. 60939 (Oct. 13, 2004); CBP, "Additional TN (Trade NAFTA) Occupations: Actuaries and Plant Pathologists" (Oct 26, 2004), AILA Doc. No. 05033173.

[214] 65 Fed. Reg. 79320 (Dec. 19, 2000).

[215] Id.

[216] 69 Fed. Reg. 60939 (Oct. 13, 2004).

[217] 8 CFR §214.6(c).

[218] Id.; 69 Fed. Reg. 60939 (Oct. 13, 2004).

[219] Legacy INS, M. Cronin, "Guidance for Processing Applicants under the North American Free Trade Agreement (NAFTA)" (July 24, 2000), AILA Doc. No. 00101705.

Copyright © 2017. American Immigration Lawyers Association. All rights reserved.

The regulation does not specifically require that the foreign national actually be recognized as an actuary by a professional actuarial association or society,[220] so it seems that the foreign national need only possess the professional credentials to be recognized as an actuary by a professional actuarial association or society. But as a practical matter, the practitioner is advised against having the foreign national apply for TN admission or for a TN visa without the credential, as the government official could deny the petition on the basis that the applicant has not met his or her burden of proof to demonstrate the credential has been obtained. Based on the language of the regulation, although the recognition may be likened to a license, it appears that TN actuaries must present evidence of the recognition, even though foreign nationals seeking TN status in other classifications need not present a license as a condition for admission or visa issuance.[221] The interpretation that the recognition is not a license is supported by the fact that the same final regulation incorporated the TN occupation of actuaries and stated that licensure is not required as a condition for TN admission.[222] DOL job descriptions for actuaries are available online.[223] The OOH website also names two U.S. professional actuarial associations that provide professional credentials: the Society of Actuaries (SOA) and the Casualty Actuarial Society (CAS).[224]

Practitioners should note that individuals who may qualify for TN status in the category of Actuary in many cases would also qualify in the category of Mathematician. Therefore, concerns about whether appropriate credentials are possessed by the applicant are sometimes most easily addressed by choosing the Mathematician category instead.

K. Training

The TN classification is also appropriate for a foreign national to "perform training functions relating to any of the cited occupations or professions, including conducting seminars."[225] There are, however, a few limitations:

"However, these training functions must be conducted in the manner of prearranged activities performed for a U.S. entity and the subject matter to be proffered must be at a professional level. The training function does not allow for the entry of a business person to conduct seminars which do not constitute the performance of prearranged activities for a U.S. entity."[226]

---

[220] 8 CFR §214.6(c).

[221] 69 Fed. Reg. 60939 (Oct. 13, 2004); DOS, "Mexican and Canadian NAFTA Professional Workers," https://travel.state.gov/content/visas/en/employment/nafta.html.

[222] 69 Fed. Reg. 60939 (Oct. 13, 2004).

[223] O*Net, "Summary Report for Actuaries," http://online.onetcenter.org/link/summary/15-2011.00; OOH, "Actuaries," http://www.bls.gov/ooh/math/actuaries.htm.

[224] OOH, "Actuaries," http://www.bls.gov/ooh/math/actuaries.htm.

[225] 1 legacy INS IFM ch.15, "NAFTA Admissions," 14-1 INS Manuals 15.5.

[226] Id.

Copyright © 2017. American Immigration Lawyers Association. All rights reserved.

For a discussion of what constitutes "prearranged services," see below. For a discussion of how a foreign national who will provide training or conduct a seminar may not need to present evidence of licensure in order to qualify for TN admission or a TN visa, because a license is not necessary if the foreign national will not practice the profession, see above.

Practitioners should also consider whether the nature of the activities in the United States will in fact rise to the level of formal training functions, or whether they are more akin to business meetings and discussions. For those activities that can be appropriately described as business meetings, B-1 status may be more appropriate, particularly where the duration of stay in the United States will be brief and where the foreign national will not be remunerated in the United States.

L. Impact of Labor Disputes on Canadian and Mexican Professionals

A U.S. employer may not use the TN category to employ a Canadian or Mexican citizen in the United States if the Secretary of Labor certifies or otherwise informs the Attorney General that "a strike or other labor dispute involving a work stoppage of workers is in progress."[227] If the TN worker's temporary entry would "adversely affect the settlement of any labor dispute or the employment of any person who is involved in such dispute,"[228] then the TN application for admission or application for a TN visa may be denied.[229] DOS regulations indicate that the dispute must be for the "occupational classification ... where the alien is, or intends to be, employed,"[230] but DHS regulations do not contain this qualification. Practitioners should be cautious about relying on DOS regulations in conjunction with matters before CBP, however, as CBP is part of DHS. Moreover, a strike or labor dispute as a general matter will almost always cause additional scrutiny of the application by the government official, even if the foreign national has previously been admitted to the United States in TN status.

If a TN petition or visa application has been approved already, but the foreign national "has not yet entered the United States, or has entered the United States but not yet commenced employment," then the petition approval "may be suspended."[231] The practitioner should note that the strike or labor dispute must be certified by the Secretary of Labor.[232]

The United States must consider and apply the "strikebreaker" provision when the TN petition is adjudicated, when the foreign national applies for a TN visa, and when

---

[227] 8 CFR §214.6(k)(1).

[228] 8 CFR §214.6(k).

[229] 8 CFR §§214.6(k)(1) and 214.2(k)(2); 9 FAM 402.17-8.

[230] 22 CFR §41.59(d).

[231] 8 CFR §214.6(k)(2).

[232] 8 CFR §214.6(k)(4).

Copyright © 2017. American Immigration Lawyers Association. All rights reserved.

the foreign national applies for admission to the United States at a port of entry.[233] The certification or notification from the Secretary of Labor "may include the locations and occupations affected by the strike."[234]

If the TN admission or visa is denied because of a certified labor dispute, the foreign national must be notified in writing of the reasons; the foreign national's home country government must also be notified.[235] A TN professional will not be considered to be "failing to maintain his or her status solely on account of past, present, or future participation in a strike or other labor dispute involving a work stoppage of workers,"[236] whether the strike or labor dispute is certified by the Secretary of Labor or not.[237] However, the professional remains subject to all other applicable provisions of the INA, and the period of stay is not extended by virtue of participation in the work stoppage.[238] For a further discussion of the intent of the provision and the protections afforded to treaty professionals, see Volume 1: Chapter Eleven, "L-1 Visas and Status."

M. Self-Employment Prohibited

As noted above, a foreign national may not seek TN admission or apply for a TN visa in order to engage in self-employment in the United States; the U.S. government views the E-1 or E-2 visa category to be more appropriate.[239] Self-employment in TN status conflicts with the purpose of the NAFTA Treaty,[240] although it was not discussed in the earlier Free Trade Agreement between the United States and Canada.[241] Upon the transition to the NAFTA Treaty from the earlier Free Trade Agreement between the United States and Canada, Canadian citizens who had been self-employed in the United States in TC Status were not eligible for automatic conversion to TN status.[242] Following implementation of the NAFTA Treaty, the agency of Citizenship and Immigration Canada instructed its field officers that TN professionals from the United States and Mexico "must ... provide pre-arranged services to a Canadian enterprise."[243]

---

[233] Legacy INS Cable, J. Puleo, "NAFTA Implementation 011 Strikebreaker Provisions" (Oct. 17, 1994), AILA Doc. No. 94101780.

[234] *Id.*

[235] 9 FAM 402.17-8(c).

[236] 8 CFR §214.6(k)(2).

[237] 9 FAM 402.17-8(b).

[238] 8 CFR §214.6(k)(2).

[239] 9 FAM 402.17-5(A) and 402.17-10(b); 1 legacy INS IFM ch.15, "NAFTA Admissions," 14-1 INS Manuals 15.5.

[240] 58 Fed. Reg. 69205 (Dec. 30, 1993) ("[a]s stated in the NAFTA Implementation Act Statement of Administrative Action at page 178, 'Section D of Annex 1603 does not authorize a professional to establish a business or practice in the United States in which the professional will be self-employed'").

[241] 58 Fed. Reg. 69205 (Dec. 30, 1993).

[242] *Id.*

[243] Legacy INS "NAFTA Implementation Cable 008" (Apr. 20, 1994), AILA Doc. No. 94042880.

Copyright © 2017. American Immigration Lawyers Association. All rights reserved.

But if a foreign national will "provide prearranged services for a U.S. entity," then this will not constitute self-employment,[244] even if the foreign national is self-employed abroad.[245] The U.S. entity "can take any legal form (as defined in Article 201 of the NAFTA), that is, 'any entity entirely constituted or organized under applicable law, whether or not for profit, and whether privately-owned or government-owned, including any corporation, trust partnership, sole proprietorship, joint venture or other association.'"[246] Legacy INS guidance states:

> "To constitute pre-arranged professional services, there must exist, prior to the time at which classification as a NAFTA professional is sought, a formal arrangement to render professional service to an individual or to an enterprise in the receiving NAFTA Party. The formal arrangement may be through an employee-employer relationship, or through a signed contract between the business person or the business person's employer and an individual or an enterprise in the receiving NAFTA Party."[247]

But a foreign national may not provide pre-arranged professional services to "a U.S. corporation or entity of which he or she is the sole or controlling shareholder or owner or over which he or she holds de facto control.... The enterprise must be substantively separate from the business person seeking entry."[248] A sole proprietorship operated by the foreign national in the United States is not a substantively separate entity.[249] Merely having a different and separate legal identity for the U.S. entity is also not substantively separate, "if the receiving enterprise is substantially controlled by that business person."[250]

In determining whether the foreign national has substantial control over the U.S. entity, legacy INS considered the following factors:

- "[W]hether the applicant has established the receiving enterprise;

- "[W]hether, as a matter of fact, the applicant has sole or primary control of the U.S. enterprise (regardless of the applicant's actual percentage of share ownership);

- "[W]hether the applicant is the sole or primary owner of the business; [and]

---

[244] Letter from Yvonne M. LaFleur, Chief, Nonimmigrant Branch, legacy INS Adjudications (Feb. 5 1995), 73 Interpreter Releases 248 (Feb. 26, 1996).

[245] 1 legacy INS IFM ch.15, "NAFTA Admissions," 14-1 INS Manuals 15.5.

[246] *Id.*

[247] Letter from Yvonne M. LaFleur, Chief, Nonimmigrant Branch, legacy INS Adjudications (Feb. 5 1995), 73 Interpreter Releases 248 (Feb. 26, 1996).

[248] 1 legacy INS IFM ch.15, "NAFTA Admissions," 14-1 INS Manuals 15.5. *See also* CBP Office of Field Operations Admissibility & Passenger Programs Enforcement Programs, "NAFTA Guide for TN and L Applicants," at 6 (June 2012), AILA Doc. 13091643 (self-employment involves "rendering services to a corporation or entity of which the professional is the sole or controlling shareholder or owner").

[249] *Id.*

[250] *Id.*

Copyright © 2017. American Immigration Lawyers Association. All rights reserved.

- "[W]hether the applicant is the sole or primary recipient of income of the business."[251]

Importantly, ownership share in the Canadian or Mexican entity is not relevant in determining whether a foreign national will engage in self-employment; the focus is on the services to be provided to a U.S. individual or entity, as long as the business activities do not entail establishment of a business in the United States through which the foreign national will be self-employed.[252]

Similarly, TN classification is not appropriate when the foreign national seeks to establish a business in the United States through which he or she will be self-employed. Legacy INS guidance states that the following factors are pertinent:

- If the foreign national has incorporated a company through which he or she will be self-employed;

- If the foreign national has initiated "communications (*e.g.*, by direct mail or by advertising) for the purpose of obtaining employment or entering into contracts for an enterprise in the United States"; or

- If the foreign national has "respond[ed] to advertisements for the purpose of obtaining employment or entering into contracts."[253]

The same guidance also helpfully provides a list of activities which "do not constitute the establishment of a business in which the business person will be self-employed in the United States:"[254]

- "[R]esponding to unsolicited inquiries about service(s) which the professional may be able to perform; or

- "[E]stablishing business premises from which to deliver pre-arranged service to clients.[255]

In essence, it seems that the foreign national should not initiate activities, whether to seek a U.S. entity to which to provide services or to establish such an enterprise, but he or she may be the recipient of recruiting efforts and he or she may set up a worksite from which to provide services pursuant to a contract or employment relationship.

---

[251] *Id.*

[252] Letter from Yvonne M. LaFleur, Chief, Nonimmigrant Branch, legacy INS Adjudications (Feb. 5 1995), 73 Interpreter Releases 248 (Feb. 26, 1996) (responding to a letter where an individual asked whether TN classification would be permissible if the foreign national owned various percentages, including 100 percent, of a Canadian entity).

[253] 1 legacy INS IFM ch.15, "NAFTA Admissions," 14-1 INS Manuals 15.5.

[254] *Id.*

[255] *Id.*

Copyright © 2017. American Immigration Lawyers Association. All rights reserved.

N. The Foreign National Is a Beneficiary of an Immigrant Visa Petition

An immigrant visa petition is a petition filed by a sponsoring U.S. company, U.S. citizen, or U.S. permanent resident to request an immigrant visa number for the foreign national beneficiary.[256] Therefore, a foreign national who is the beneficiary of an immigrant visa petition may risk denial of TN admission or a TN visa, as such pursuit of permanent residence might be considered indicative of the abandonment of "temporary intent" or indicative of the intent to remain in the United States beyond the end date of the completion of the TN assignment.[257] For a deeper discussion of dual intent, see Volume 1: Chapter Two, "Basic Nonimmigrant Concepts."

Foreign nationals applying for TN classification seek "temporary entry" and must demonstrate nonimmigrant intent. Early on, USCIS explicitly rejected the application of the concept of dual intent: "Congressional approval of this Article [1608] in the NAFTA Treaty indicates that Congress did not intend TNs to have dual intent."[258] Legacy INS also rejected allowing TN nonimmigrants to have dual intent, as that would be "clearly inconsistent" with the terms of the NAFTA Treaty,[259] despite the fact that dual intent had been permitted under the Free Trade Agreement between the United States and Canada.[260]

With time, this perspective became more refined. CBP guidance states the following:

"After reviewing applicable law for North American Free Trade Agreement (NAFTA) applicants for admission, it is our determination that the mere filing or approval of an immigrant petition does not automatically constitute intent on the part of the beneficiary to abandon his or her foreign residence…. Of course, a TN applicant could have the intent to immigrate or adjust status at a future time, but as long as his or her intent at the time of application for admission is to be in the United States for a temporary period pursuant to NAFTA and regulations at 8 CFR 214.6, he or she could be admitted. However, once a TN files an application for an immigrant visa or adjustment of status, then the TN would no longer be eligible for admission or an extension of stay as a TN nonimmigrant. The NAFTA professional must establish that the intent of entry is not for permanent residence."[261]

Although the situation involved a TN principal "riding on a spouse's immigrant petition," the guidance should be applicable to a foreign national holding TN status

---

[256] For a detailed discussion of the immigrant visa petition, see Volume 2: Chapter Three, "The Immigrant Visa Petition."

[257] Letter from Jackie Bednarz (June 18, 1996), 73 Interpreter Releases 978 (July 22, 1996).

[258] 73 Fed. Reg. 61332 (Oct. 16, 2008).

[259] 63 Fed. Reg. 1331 (Jan. 9, 1998).

[260] Letter from Jackie Bednarz (June 18, 1996), 73 Interpreter Releases 978 (July 22, 1996).

[261] Letter from Paul Morris, Executive Director, Admissibility and Passenger Programs, CBP (Apr. 21, 2008), AILA Doc. No. 09021280.

Copyright © 2017. American Immigration Lawyers Association. All rights reserved.

being the beneficiary of an immigrant visa petition. In addition, in practice the change to the standard period of stay in TN status from one year to three years that occurred in 2008[262] appears to have also had the effect of further lessening focus of the government official on the issue of nonimmigrant intent.

Despite this guidance and evolution of focus, however, the practitioner is advised to discuss the issue in detail with the client, especially since "the TN classification is nevertheless for persons seeking temporary entry without the intent to establish permanent residence,"[263] as discussed above. Being the beneficiary of a labor certification or immigrant visa petition could be construed by the government official as demonstrating "intent to establish permanent residence." Further, if TN admission is denied, a Canadian citizen may be put into expedited removal proceedings, as discussed below. The foreign national may also carry a copy of the letter when traveling, but the practitioner should provide caution that the letter is not binding upon the inspector, as discussed in Volume 1: Chapter Two, "Basic Nonimmigrant Concepts."

It may be possible for such a foreign national to be granted TN admission or issued a TN visa if the government official is provided with a clear explanation of how the foreign national possesses nonimmigrant intent specifically for the TN assignment, despite being the beneficiary of an immigrant visa petition, if the foreign national establishes to the satisfaction of the government official "that the proposed stay is temporary."[264] This approach is further supported by legacy INS guidance:

> "The fact that an alien is the beneficiary of an approved I-140 petition may not be, in and of itself, a reason to deny an application for admission, readmission, or extension of stay *if the alien's intent is to remain in the United States temporarily*. Nevertheless, because the Service must evaluate each application on a case-by-case basis with regard to the alien's intent, this factor may be taken into consideration *along with other relevant factors* every time that a TN nonimmigrant applies for admission, readmission or a new extension of stay.[265]

To prevail in these situations, the strategy is twofold. First, the duration of the TN petition should be clearly demarcated from the goal of immigrating in the future: "An intent to immigrate in the future which is in no way connected to the proposed immediate trip need not in itself result in a finding that the immediate trip is not temporary."[266] Second, care should be taken to provide evidence of the "other relevant factors." The objective is to demonstrate that there is a specific end date to the TN assignment and that the foreign national will depart the United States upon completion of the assignment. Appropriate evidence may include the following:

---

[262] 73 Fed. Reg. 61332 (Oct. 16, 2008).

[263] 63 Fed. Reg. 1331 (Jan. 9, 1998).

[264] 9 FAM 402.17-7.

[259] Letter from Jackie Bednarz (June 18, 1996), 73 Interpreter Releases 978 (July 22, 1996) (emphasis added).

[266] 9 FAM 402.17-7.

Copyright © 2017. American Immigration Lawyers Association. All rights reserved.

- Short-term service contract with the foreign national's Canadian or Mexican employer, with a specific end date for the TN assignment and a resumption of employment abroad;

- Employment contract between the U.S. entity and the foreign national, with a specific end date for the TN assignment;

- Programs, agendas, and itineraries for the training seminar that the foreign national will provide, with a specific end date for the seminar;

- Documents evidencing the short-term nature of the project on which the foreign national will work;

- Service or employment contract evidencing how the foreign national will provide services outside the United States following the end date of the TN assignment;

- Other documents evidencing why the foreign national must depart the United States following completion of the TN assignment, such as future plans and activities in Canada, Mexico, or another foreign country;

- If the TN nonimmigrant worker resides in a foreign country and commutes to the United States to work in a city that borders his or her home country, evidence such as a child's attendance records in the foreign country, mortgage, bills, etc. for the home in which the worker resides in the bordering country (Canada or Mexico); and

- Other documents evidencing how the foreign national will depart the United States upon completion of the TN assignment, such as a return airplane, train, or sea vessel ticket.

It is not advised that the foreign national present only the latter two types of evidence, as the other types of evidence better address the specific duration of the TN assignment. The objective in a situation in which a labor certification application or immigrant petition may indicate immigrant intent should be to demonstrate why the TN assignment must end by a certain date; experience has shown that it is insufficient to merely provide the end date of the TN assignment, with no substantiating evidence or explanation. The practitioner should also note that evidence of long-term plans in Canada or Mexico, such as an employment offer or date of closing on the purchase of a home, tend to be more persuasive than shorter-term plans, whether the events will occur in Canada, Mexico, or a third country, such as a wedding, other family event, or vacation. In addition, while submitting a return ticket does serve as evidence of the intent to depart the United States, without other substantiating documents, the government official may nevertheless be concerned that the foreign national will forfeit the price of the ticket and overstay in the United States. The practitioner should counsel the client to prepare and gather as much evidence as possible, rather than relying solely upon the return ticket.

Copyright © 2017. American Immigration Lawyers Association. All rights reserved.

Government inspectors will interview the applicant, often with a mind to potential contradictions.[267] Government inspectors may research the applicant or the sponsoring employer on the Internet and social media such as Linked In, Facebook, Instagram, or other profiles to verify claims made by the applicant during the interview.[268] The foreign national should be able to concisely articulate satisfaction of all the TN eligibility requirements during the application for admission or the visa interview; the practitioner may wish to prepare clients through the use of mock interviews. For a more detailed discussion of how to approach overcoming the presumption of immigrant intent when the foreign national is the beneficiary of an immigrant visa application, see Volume 1: Chapter Three, "Visitors: B Visas and Status and the Visa Waiver Program." See below in this chapter for a discussion of change of status from TN to H-1B so that a foreign national may possess dual intent. For a discussion of strategies if the foreign national is the beneficiary of an immigrant visa petition filed by the U.S. employer, see below.

IV. Process

The process of applying for TN status differs for Canadian and Mexican citizens, based on the statutory and regulatory requirements. The differences are addressed individually, below. However, both must ultimately apply for admission into the United States. Previously, if the foreign national received TN status at the port of entry, a paper "multiple-entry" Form I-94, Arrival/Departure Record, was issued, with an admission stamp and the nonimmigrant classification of "TN," which stands for "Trade NAFTA."[269]

In 2013, CBP began to roll out an automated process whereby the foreign national receives a stamp in the passport, and the I-94 is recorded electronically and not given to the individual.[270] The automated process is now standard procedure for arrivals by air and sea. For land entries, travelers have the option of obtaining an electronic I-94 by visiting CBP's I-94 website within seven days of their planned entry into the United States. They are able to pay the I-94 fee online and are then issued an electronic I-94 after they are admitted.[271]

In the automated process, CBP creates an I-94 record electronically, but does not give it to the nonimmigrant. Instead, an admission stamp is provided that is annotated

---

[267] "Final Questions and Answers: American Immigration Lawyers Association CBP Liaison Committee Meeting Questions" (Nov. 9, 2011), AILA Doc. No. 12020166. ("Denial of Admission may occur for a number of reasons, including if the individual is unable to explain the intended activities or if there is a discrepancy between the duties described by the applicant and the duties described in the prospective employer's letter supporting the application for TN classification").

[268] "DHS Privacy Policy for Operational Use of Social Media" (June 8, 2012), AILA Doc. No. 16081102.

[269] 58 Fed. Reg. 69205 (Dec. 30, 1993); 1 legacy INS IFM ch.15, "NAFTA Admissions," 14-1 INS Manuals 15.5.

[270] 78 Fed. Reg. 18457 (Mar. 27, 2013).

[271] CBP, "I-94 Website," https://i94.cbp.dhs.gov/I94/#/apply-document, select tab "Apply for New I-94."

Copyright © 2017. American Immigration Lawyers Association. All rights reserved.

with the date and class of admission and the expiration date of the status.[272] If a physical copy of the I-94 is desired, which it almost inevitably will be, it is supposed to be available through a portal on CBP's website.[273] Early experience with the site was less than perfect, but it has improved significantly. If the I-94 contains an error, it is important to seek a correction by contacting CBP, as the I-94 will generally be needed for such things as I-9 verification, obtaining a U.S. driver's license, and other circumstances where proof of status is needed. In any event, the foreign national and attorney should review the I-94 to ensure that it is accurate.

Where the old process is still in place, a paper I-94 is issued. The reverse of the I-94 card should be annotated with the employer and the TN profession, as legacy INS and USCIS must "share data specific to each occupation, profession or activity, with Canada and Mexico."[274] Legacy INS guidance also mentions that a "handout" discussing the terms and conditions of TN classification should be given to TN professionals.[275]

The practitioner should note that attorneys are generally not permitted to accompany foreign nationals into secondary inspection, unless the foreign national "has become the focus of a criminal investigation and has been taken into custody,"[276] as discussed in Volume 1: Chapter Two, "Basic Nonimmigrant Concepts." CBP stated that the change from previous practice was "in response to [a] need to increase security at our ports of entry,"[277] although the correspondence did not expand upon how security would be increased.[278]

The practitioner may wish to inform the client and foreign national that there is no right to attorney representation at the port of entry, although the practitioner may be in the "port of entry waiting area,"[279] especially because a Canadian citizen may be subject to expedited removal if he or she refuses to withdraw the application for admission, as discussed below.

The foreign national should be admitted for three years or for the duration of the TN assignment as indicated on the support statement, whichever is less.[280] Although

---

[272] CBP, "I-94 Automation" (Mar. 2016), https://www.cbp.gov/sites/default/files/assets/documents/2016-Mar/i-94-automation-fact-sheet.pdf.

[273] CBP, "I-94 Website," https://i94.cbp.dhs.gov/I94/#/apply-document, select tab "Get Most Recent I-94."

[274] 1 NAFTA Handbook, "Canadian TN Nonimmigrant pursuant to NAFTA," 14-1 legacy INS Manuals Scope.

[275] Id.

[276] 8 CFR §292.5(b).

[277] Letter from M. Ambrosia (Aug. 28, 2003), 8 Bender's Immigr. Bull. 1773 (Nov. 15, 2003).

[278] G. Boos and R. Pauw, "Reasserting the Right to Representation in Immigration Matters Arising at Ports of Entry," *Travel for Work and Business*, at 65–74 (Revised Ed. 2004).

[279] Letter from M. Ambrosia (Aug. 28, 2003), 8 Bender's Immigr. Bull. 1773 (Nov. 15, 2003).

[280] 8 CFR §214.6(e); "Update on New TN Regulation" (Oct. 22, 2008), AILA Doc. No. 08102261. See also "AILA/CBP Liaison Committee Practice Pointer: TN Admissions for Citizens of Mexico" (Aug. 30, 2013), AILA Doc. No. 12012347.

Copyright © 2017. American Immigration Lawyers Association. All rights reserved.

previously TN admission was valid for only one year at a time, USCIS promulgated a rule to extend the maximum validity period to three years in order to "reduce the administrative burden of TN classification on USCIS, and [to] ease the entry of eligible professionals to the United States."[281]

In November 2016, DHS extended a rule that had long applied to H-1Bs to make TNs eligible for a 10-day grace period added to the beginning and end of the validity period of the authorized stay.[282] Employment is not authorized during this period—it is strictly a consideration to allow the nonimmigrant to make preparations for starting life in the United States and for departing or changing status.[283] It should be noted that DHS has long required in the H-1B context that the grace period be specified by CBP on the I-94 to be effective.[284] The final rule regarding TNs is silent on this point, but presumably the same qualification would apply. Experience with H-1Bs has shown that the grace period is rarely added to the I-94 unless the nonimmigrant insists upon it at entry, so it should not be presumed. It is important to check the individual's I-94 record for the period of admission to see if the grace period was added and, if it was, to ensure that he or she understands that employment during that period is prohibited.

The "multiple-entry" I-94 should allow the foreign national to travel to Canada or Mexico and return to the United States during the validity period of the TN status, without needing to apply for admission with all of the TN petition documents with each visit.[285] If the I-94 is electronic, the foreign national should show the stamp in the passport, and the inspector should be able to access the I-94 electronically. If the I-94 is a physical card, the foreign national should have retained it in the passport, and should be admitted for the remaining duration of the TN assignment.[286] It should be noted that CBP views each application for admission as new, and thus it is not impossible that an inspector will probe the underlying status. However, "when a TN returns to the U.S. after travel during the approved period of stay, officers should generally not readjudicate the TN unless contradictory information has come to CBP's attention."[287]

Procedures for readmission where the foreign national does not possess the original I-94, such as when the foreign national has traveled outside continental North America, are discussed in the individual Canadian citizen and Mexican citizen sections below.

---

[281] 73 Fed. Reg. 61332 (Oct. 16, 2008).

[282] 81 Fed. Reg. 82398 (Nov. 18, 2016).

[283] Id.

[284] Inspector's Field Manual, 15(h)(1).

[285] 8 CFR §214.6(g)(1).

[286] Id.

[287] "AILA National Liaison Meeting with U.S. Customs and Border Protection Office of Field Operations" (Oct. 8, 2015), AILA Doc. No. 16031104.

Copyright © 2017. American Immigration Lawyers Association. All rights reserved.

It is possible to request a TN change of status or change of employer on Form I-129, Petition for a Nonimmigrant Worker, but this process seems to be utilized very rarely. This is most likely because processing times for these petitions are usually measured in months,[288] and because the foreign national may not engage in employment until USCIS approves the petition.[289]

Dependent spouses and children of TN professionals are eligible for TD (Trade Dependent) classification.[290] In most cases, CBP officers exercise discretion by requiring dependents of the TN nonimmigrant to physically reside in the United States with the TN nonimmigrant spouse or parent when considering issuance of TD classification to the TD applicant. Unless the dependents are also citizens of a visa-exempt country, they must present TD visas.[291] Dependents who are Canadian or Mexican citizens "should be issued multiple-entry visas valid for the maximum period authorized by reciprocity schedules or for the length of the principal alien's visa and/or authorized period of stay, whichever is less."[292] But because the reciprocity schedules provide the reciprocity fees for TN and TD visas only for Canadian and Mexican citizens,[293] "the number of entries, fees, and validity for non-Canadian or non-Mexican family members of a TN status holder seeking TD visas should be based on the reciprocity schedule of the TN principal alien."[294] For a discussion of how a Canadian citizen may need to apply for a TN visa for the benefit of his or her dependent family members, see below.

To apply for TD status or a TD visa, the dependents should present evidence of the relationship with the principal foreign national through marriage, birth, or adoption certificates and evidence of physical residence in the United States. If the dependent(s) will apply for TD admission or visa after the principal foreign national has already been granted TN status, the dependents should also present evidence of the principal foreign national's TN status, such as copies of the I-94 card,[295] the Form I-797 approval notice, the TN visa stamp (if applicable), and evidence of continued employment in TN status, such as an employment confirmation letter or several recent paystubs. Upon U.S. admission, the TD dependents "shall be issued confirming documentation bearing the legend 'multiple entry.'"[296] There are no

---

[288] *See, e.g.*, Vermont Service Center Processing Time Reports, http://www.aila.org/infonet/processing-time-reports/vsc.

[289] 8 CFR §214.6(i)(1).

[290] 8 CFR §214.6(j)(1).

[291] 8 CFR §214.6(j)(2).

[292] 9 FAM 402-17.11(c).

[293] DOS provides a reciprocity look-up on its website: https://travel.state.gov/content/visas/en/fees/reciprocity-by-country.html.

[294] 9 FAM 402-17.11(d).

[295] 9 FAM 402-17.11(a).

[296] 8 CFR §214.6(j)(3).

Copyright © 2017. American Immigration Lawyers Association. All rights reserved.

processing fees for TD admissions.[297] While in the United States, TD dependents may attend school,[298] but foreign nationals in TD status may not accept employment.[299]

A. Canadian Citizens

1. Application for U.S. Admission

Canadian citizens, who are visa exempt, have two options for requesting TN classification. They may submit the TN request when they apply for admission at "a United States Class A port of entry, at a United States airport handling international traffic, or at a United States pre-clearance/pre-flight station,"[300] or their employer may submit Form I-129 to USCIS on their behalf.[301] Despite this guidance, when a Canadian is considering applying at a location other than a major Canadian land port of entry or airport, the practitioner may wish to contact the airport or port of entry in advance to ensure that the TN application can be adjudicated and to obtain current information on any restrictions as to the days of the week or time of day when applications will be accepted.

When submitting a TN request for a Canadian citizen, the following evidence should be submitted:

- A valid Canadian passport, Enhanced Driver's License, or Trusted Traveler Program card (NEXUS, SENTRI. or FAST);

- Support statement from the U.S. employer evidencing the U.S. employment, as discussed below;

- Evidence of appropriate professional qualifications for the TN classification sought, as discussed above;

- If applicable for the TN category, experience or reference letters from the foreign national's previous employers; and

- Evidence of the foreign national's nonimmigrant intent, as discussed above.

If the foreign national is making the TN request at the port of entry, no form is required. If the request is being made by filing with USCIS, Form I-129 and the Form I-129 TN Supplement with fee should be submitted in accordance with the filing process discussed in Volume 1: Chapter 2, "Basic Nonimmigrant Concepts," accompanied by the documentation listed above.

---

[297] *Id.*

[298] 9 FAM 402-17.11(a).

[299] 8 CFR §214.6(j)(4).

[300] 8 CFR §214.6(d)(2).

[301] "USCIS Announces a New Filing Option on behalf of Canadian TN Nonimmigrants and Reminds Employers of the Current Filing Options on behalf of Canadian L-1 Nonimmigrants." (Sept. 28, 2012), AILA Doc. No. 12100343.

Copyright © 2017. American Immigration Lawyers Association. All rights reserved.

The primary disadvantages of filing beforehand with USCIS are the cost of the filing fee[302] and the wait for processing, which can take two months or more.[303] Premium processing is available (albeit for a substantial additional fee[304]), which can cut the processing time to 15 days. Once the petition is approved, the foreign national needs to take to the port of entry the approval notice from USCIS and proof of Canadian citizenship. In addition, USCIS indicates that the individual should have in his or her possession "a copy of the Form I-129 and all supporting documentation that was submitted to USCIS, to respond to questions about ... eligibility."[305]

The primary advantage of going first to USCIS is to have the petition adjudicated before the foreign national faces the vagaries of the port of entry. In addition, should there be any questions from USCIS about the petition, USCIS will issue a Request for Evidence (RFE), and counsel can assist with preparing a response. That being said, as is implied by the USCIS instruction to bring a copy of the I-129 and supporting documents, it is still possible that the inspector will re-visit the question of eligibility, and so the individual may yet face a full interview and another opportunity for denial. This occurs most frequently with TN petitions in the Management Consultant category, and is much less common with more straightforward categories such as Engineer, Mathematician, Economist, and Accountant. Therefore, even with advance USCIS approval, the foreign national should still be prepared to explain his or her planned job duties, background, and how he or she meets the requirements for the TN category. Foreign nationals have reported in-depth questioning in some circumstances, including being asked to write out their planned job duties and qualifications without referencing the petition materials.

In the hope of enhancing quality of adjudication at the ports of entry, CBP in September 2014 designated 14 ports, including four preclearance locations, for "optimized processing."[306] Officers and supervisors at these ports received additional training on TN (and L-1) processing from USCIS beyond what is received by inspectors at other ports.[307] However, applications still can be made at any port.[308]

---

[302] USCIS, "Form I-129, Petition for Nonimmigrant Worker" https://www.uscis.gov/i-129.

[303] *See, e.g.,* "Vermont Service Center Processing Time Report" (June 14, 2016), AILA Doc. No. 16061563.

[304] USCIS, "Form I-907, Request for Premium Processing," https://www.uscis.gov/i-907.

[305] USCIS, "TN NAFTA Professionals" (June 17, 2013), search "TN NAFTA professionals" on https://www.uscis.gov.

[306] CBP, "Traveling on a TN or L-1 Visa from Canada?" (Sept. 16, 2014), https://www.cbp. gov/travel/canadian-and-mexican-citizens/traveling-tn-or-ll-visa-canada. Also at AILA Doc. No. 14091645.

[307] "AILA National Liaison Meeting with U.S. Customs and Border Protection" (Nov. 21, 2014), AILA Doc. No. 14121746, Question 23.

[308] CBP, "Traveling on a TN or L-1 Visa from Canada?" (Sept. 16, 2014), https://www.cbp.gov/travel/canadian-and-mexican-citizens/traveling-tn-or-ll-visa-canada, AILA Doc. No. 14091645. *See also* "Final Questions and Answers, American Immigration Lawyers Association CBP Liaison Committee Questions" (Nov. 9, 2011), Question 7, AILA Doc. No. 12020166.

Copyright © 2017. American Immigration Lawyers Association. All rights reserved.

For a Canadian citizen, the "application for entry as a TN professional is an application for admission."[309] The practitioner should note that a Canadian citizen who does not withdraw his or her application for admission may be subject to expedited removal proceedings, as discussed below. In addition, if the Canadian citizen is denied TN classification, then this may be considered a denial of an application for admission, which in turn must be disclosed on subsequent applications for admission and any visa applications, as discussed below. The more risk-averse client and/or foreign national who does not have time to use the USCIS petitioning option may appreciate the practitioner taking the following actions to smooth the way:

- Calling the intended port of entry to discuss when the foreign national intends to apply to ensure applications can be processed by an experienced officer at that date and time;

- Providing copies of relevant regulations, Adjudicator's Field Manual, and other source material to support the application for TN admission; and

- Inquiring whether an attorney may accompany the foreign national during the inspection or may at least remain in the same room or area inside the airport.[310]

It should be noted that some Canadian citizens must apply for a visa because of ground(s) of inadmissibility. They should follow the procedure discussed in Volume 1: Chapter Two, "Basic Nonimmigrant Concepts."

2. Admission to the United States

In addition to the procedure detailed above, Canadian citizens must pay a $50.00 processing fee.[311] This fee is not applicable where the foreign national possesses an I-797 Approval Notice from the USCIS pre-adjudication process. Canadian citizens who apply for TN admission at a land port of entry will also need to pay a $6.00 fee for the Form I-94, even with an I-797 Approval Notice.[312] Canadian citizens should receive receipts evidencing payment of these fees.[313]

Canadian citizens who received a paper I-94 and travel outside the United States and who did not retain their original I-94 cards may nevertheless be readmitted, as long as the period of TN validity has not expired, upon presentation of a "confirming letter from the United States employer" and either the fee receipt(s) or "a previously issued admission stamp as TN in a passport."[314] The Canadian citizen should be

---

[309] CBP, "TN Processing at Ports of Entry" (Dec. 23, 2011), AILA Doc. No. 11122358.

[310] "New England Chapter – News & Updates" (Dec.18, 2009)" AILA Doc. 09231220.

[311] 8 CFR §103.7(b)(1)(ii)(K).

[312] 8 CFR §103.7(b)(1)(ii)(D).

[313] 8 CFR §214.6(e).

[314] 8 CFR §214.6(g)(2)(i).

Copyright © 2017. American Immigration Lawyers Association. All rights reserved.

readmitted to the United States for the remaining duration of the initially approved TN classification and issued another I-94 card "with the legend 'multiple entry.'"[315]

3. Denial of TN Petition and U.S. Admission

If the immigration inspector at the port of entry is not satisfied that the Canadian citizen is qualified for the TN assignment, then the Canadian citizen may be permitted to withdraw the application for admission, although there is no right to such a withdrawal.[316] Alternatively, if the immigration inspector believes that there is fraud or willful misrepresentation or that the applicant is an "intending immigrant," the Canadian citizen may be issued a Notice to Appear[317] and placed into expedited removal proceedings.[318]

Withdrawal of the admission application by a Canadian citizen is therefore wise, to avoid being placed in expedited removal proceedings based on the charge of being an intending immigrant, which could arise in a situation in which he or she fails to demonstrate nonimmigrant intent and lacks an immigrant visa. In addition, as stated by legacy INS guidance:

> "An applicant who withdraws his or her application for admission is not considered formally removed and therefore does not require permission to reapply for admission to the United States. Once the reason for the inadmissibility is overcome, the alien may be eligible to apply for a new visa or admission to reenter the United States."[319]

Practitioners should advise the foreign national of the application withdrawal option, and should counsel the foreign national that if he or she believes the CBP officer is unlikely to approve the TN application, he or should should request withdrawal rather than having the application denied. Withdrawal of the application for admission is especially encouraged in situations in which the ground(s) of inadmissibility may be overcome easily, such as lack of a valid passport or other documents.[320] There is no appeal from the denial of a TN petition at a port of entry.[321] CBP interprets the immigration law[322] as preventing immigration attorneys from representing Canadian applicants for admission at the port of entry,[323] as discussed

---

[315] 8 CFR §214.6(g)(2).

[316] INA §235(a)(4); 8 CFR §235.4.

[317] Michigan Chapter: Minutes/Q&A of CBP Liaison Meeting (Nov. 1, 2007), AILA Doc. No. 07111950.

[318] INA §§212(a)(6)(C), 212(a)(7), and 235(b)(1)(B)(iii). *See also* legacy INS, M. Pearson, "Denial of Applicants for Admission under the North American Free Trade Agreement (IN01-11)" (May 25, 2001), AILA Doc. No. 01070231.

[319] 1 legacy INS IFM ch.17, "Inadmissible Aliens," 14-1 INS Manuals 17.2.

[320] *Id.*

[321] Legacy INS, M. Pearson, "Denial of Applicants for Admission under the North American Free Trade Agreement (IN01-11)" (May 25, 2001), AILA Doc. No. 01070231.

[322] INA §292.

[323] "CBP Liaison Minutes" (Nov. 13, 2003), AILA Doc. No. 03123110 ("the statute authorizes access to counsel before an immigration judge, but not at primary or in secondary").

Copyright © 2017. American Immigration Lawyers Association. All rights reserved.

above. For a further discussion of applications for admission and of what constitutes fraud or willful misrepresentation, see Volume 1: Chapter Two, "Basic Nonimmigrant Concepts."

Legacy INS directed immigration inspectors to "maintain the highest standards of objectivity, courtesy and professionalism when processing applicants for admission," because the NAFTA Treaty "is an international agreement subject to scrutiny by the public, the media, other governments and the Temporary Entry Working Group."[324] Thus, if the Canadian citizen is denied TN classification, he or she should receive proper written notification of the reasons for denial.[325]

4. Dependents of Canadian Citizens

Although Canadian citizens are visa-exempt, the dependent spouse and/or children may be citizens of a country for which visas are required. If this is the case, the dependents should be issued TD visas.[326] Because there are no reciprocity tables for TNs and TDs other than Canadians and Mexicans, dependents who are citizens of countries other than Canada or Mexico are subject to the fees, numbers of entries, and validity period of the principal TN.[327] However, it appears that a Mexican citizen dependent of a Canadian principal TN nonimmigrant should be issued a TD visa pursuant to the reciprocity schedules of a Mexican citizen.[328] For a discussion of the Mexican reciprocity schedules, see below.

The Canadian citizen TN does not need to obtain a visa, but the non-Canadian spouse or child does need one. Thus, often the foreign national makes the initial entry into the United States in TN status, and the family joins him or her later after obtaining the visa. Problems have been encountered with consulates demanding notification from DHS through the Petition Information Management System (PIMS) that the two agencies use to communicate actions to one another. USCIS is the primary user of PIMS, and thus CBP has not routinely been part of the information flow. In order to resolve this problem, CBP agreed that it should fax the approved documents to the Kentucky Consular Center (KCC) for entry into PIMS, and recommended that the individual seeking TN status at the port of entry indicate to the inspector that derivatives will need to seek visas and ask that the approval be faxed to the KCC.[329]

However, the Canadian citizen and his or her family may need to travel together to the United States, and may need to come directly from a third country. Thus, the

---

[324] Legacy INS, R. Bach, "Processing of Applicants for Admission under The North American Free Trade Agreement" (Oct. 20, 1999), AILA Doc. No. 99110401.

[325] 1 legacy INS IFM ch.17, "Inadmissible Aliens," 14-1 INS Manuals 17.2.

[326] 9 FAM 402.17-11.

[327] 9 FAM 402.17-11(d).

[328] Id.

[329] "Practice Pointer: PIMS, L-2, and TD Visa Issuance for Non-Canadian Spouses and Children" (Apr. 1, 2013), AILA Doc. No. 11012063.

Copyright © 2017. American Immigration Lawyers Association. All rights reserved.

principal foreign national may "need a TN visa in order to confer derivative (TD) status on his or her dependents."[330] In this situation, the Canadian citizen should apply for a TN visa at a U.S. consulate abroad. A Canadian visa applicant must pay the visa application fee, but he or she will not need to pay the $50 processing fee, discussed above.[331] And although it is very likely that the majority of TN visas are issued from U.S. consulates located in Mexico, consular officers in third countries may refer to the FAM guidance, and DOS cables on the standards for TN visa issuance should be distributed to all consular posts.[332]

B. Mexican Citizens

1. Application for a TN Visa

The option for obtaining USCIS adjudication of an initial application for TN status applies only to Canadian citizens. Mexican citizens are required to have the initial TN application adjudicated at a U.S. consulate abroad. While Mexican citizens can obtain an extension of stay in TN status or a change of status to TN through a USCIS petition, the U.S. consulates will generally treat a visa application from a Mexican citizen as an application to be adjudicated at the consulate even with an approval notice from USCIS.

In addition to the visa application documents discussion in Volume 1: Chapter Two, "Basic Nonimmigrant Concepts," applicants for TN visas must present the following "requisite evidence to a consular officer for adjudication".[333]

- Evidence of Mexican citizenship with a valid Mexican passport;
- Support statement from the U.S. employer evidencing the U.S. employment, as discussed below;
- Evidence of appropriate professional qualifications for the TN classification sought, as discussed above;
- If applicable for the TN category, experience or reference letters from the foreign national's previous employers; and
- Evidence of the foreign national's nonimmigrant intent, as discussed above.

Individual U.S. consulates have differing requirements for the documents that must be submitted with the TN visa application. The practitioner should check the website of the U.S. consulate and prepare any additional documents requested.

Previously, TN petitions on Forms I-129 on behalf of Mexican citizens had to be filed with the Nebraska Service Center (NSC), but the petitioning requirement has

---

[330] 9 FAM 402.17-6(a).

[331] Department of State, search for "fees for visa services" at http://travel.state.gov.

[332] See, e.g., "DOS Issues Guidance on Processing Mexican TNs" (Jan. 4, 2004), AILA Doc. No. 04022562; "DOS Cable Updates the FAM To Account for Changes in Mexican TN Process" (Feb. 4, 2004), AILA Doc. No. 04020413.

[333] 9 FAM 402.17-6.

Copyright © 2017. American Immigration Lawyers Association. All rights reserved.

been removed, and the individual now applies directly to the consulate for a visa.[334] With respect to processing of TN petitions, DOS guidance states:

"Post processing procedures: As this visa classification is no longer petition based, it is recommended that posts process similar to procedures established to process Treaty Trader/Investor Visas. The United States is committed to facilitative processing of NAFTA visas, so posts are encouraged to be mindful of this commitment when setting procedures."[335]

The visa should be issued for the duration of the TN assignment or one year, whichever is less.[336] Unfortunately, Mexican citizens applying for TN visas may no longer obtain visas valid for up to three years by paying the reciprocity fee of $100 for each year of visa validity.[337] Note that while the visa stamp itself is issued valid for a maximum of only one year, the consular officer will often annotate the visa stamp with a Petition Expiration Date (PED) valid for up to three years[338] that facilitates future visa stamp renewal applications and the TN admission process.

As discussed in Volume 1: Chapter Two, "Basic Nonimmigrant Concepts," review of a visa denial is generally very limited, and neither the statutes nor the regulations stipulate a process for review of visa denials.[339] If the TN visa is denied, the foreign national will need to disclose this fact on all subsequent visa applications.[340]

2. Admission to the United States

Mexican citizens may apply for TN admission with a valid TN visa at a "Class A port of entry, at a United States airport handling international traffic, or at a United States pre-clearance/pre-flight station."[341] As stated by legacy INS: "In addition to the visa requirement, the Mexican citizen shall present at the time of application for initial admission a copy of the employer's statement,"[342] "regarding the nature of the applicant's duties in the United States"[343] and stating the anticipated length of employment.[344] Legacy INS believed that submission of the support statement would

---

[334] 69 Fed. Reg. 11287 (Mar. 10, 2004); 79 Fed. Reg. 7582 (Feb. 10, 2014).

[335] "DOS Issues Guidance on Processing Mexican TNs" (Jan. 4, 2004), AILA Doc. No. 04022562; see also "New Procedures for TN and E Visas at Matamoros Effective September 10, 2008" (Sept. 22, 2008), AILA Doc. No. 08092264 (grouping TN and E visa applications in the same processing category).

[336] DOS, "Mexico Reciprocity Schedule," https://travel.state.gov/content/visas/en/fees/reciprocity-by-country/MX.html.

[337] Id. Cf. former DOS website, "Mexico Reciprocity Schedule," formerly available at http://travel.state.gov/visa/frvi/reciprocity/reciprocity_3622.html#B (link no longer works).

[338] 8 CFR §214.6(e).

[339] INA §§104(a) and 221(a).

[340] Form DS-156, Nonimmigrant Visa Application.

[341] 8 CFR §214.6(d)(1).

[342] 58 Fed. Reg. 69205 (Dec. 30, 1993).

[343] 1 legacy INS IFM ch.15, "NAFTA Admissions," 14-1 INS Manuals 15.5.

[344] CBP "NAFTA Guide for TN and L Applicants" (June 2012), AILA Doc. No. 13091643.

Copyright © 2017. American Immigration Lawyers Association. All rights reserved.

"facilitate the inspection procedure."[345] In practice, CBP officers tend not to attempt to re-adjudicate the TN petition once a Mexican national has obtained a visa stamp, and instead focus on general questions of admissibility. There are no port of entry fees for TN admission of Mexican citizens, as these foreign nationals are charged fees for visa issuance.[346]

As noted above, although reciprocity limits the TN visa validity for a Mexican citizen to one year, admission can be for up to three years.[347] A shorter period may be granted if the documentation indicates that the assignment will be for less than three years,[348] or if the individual's passport is not valid for the entire period.[349] However, if the validity period is cut short because of an expiring passport, the TN nonimmigrant "can go to any port of entry upon receipt of a new passport and be given the remaining validity period in a new I-94. The TN will not be re-adjudicated (but may be reviewed) and the applicant should only have to pay $6.00 for a new I-94 card."[350] The individual should bring a copy of the prior TN application package.[351]

In addition, legacy INS guidance mentions only Canadian citizens when discussing how the application for TN classification is an application for admission.[352] However, the practitioner is reminded that a Mexican citizen with a TN visa may nevertheless be denied admission to the United States,[353] and this denial must be disclosed on all subsequent applications for visas and admission. The Mexican citizen may be permitted to withdraw the application, so long as there was no visa fraud or misrepresentation:

> "[I]n a situation where the alien may have innocently or through ignorance, misinformation, or bad advice obtained an inappropriate visa but has not concealed information during the course of the inspection, withdrawal should ordinarily be permitted."[354]

---

[345] 58 Fed. Reg. 69205 (Dec. 30, 1993).

[346] CBP "NAFTA Guide for TN and L Applicants" (June 2012), AILA Doc. No. 13091643.

[347] 8 CFR §214.6(e).

[348] *See, e.g.,* "DOS Practice Alert: TN Annotation at CDJ" (Aug. 30, 2012); CBP "NAFTA Guide for TN and L Applicants" (June 2012), AILA Doc. No. 13091643, p. 7.

[349] "AILA/CBP Liaison Committee Practice Pointer: TN Admissions for Citizens of Mexico" (Aug. 30, 2013), AILA Doc. No. 12012347.

[350] "AILA/U.S. CBP Office of Field Operations Meeting" (Apr. 6, 2016), AILA Doc. No. 16052700, pp. 10-11, response to Question 18.

[351] *Id.*

[352] Legacy INS, M. Pearson, "Denial of Applicants for Admission under the North American Free Trade Agreement (IN01-11)" (May 25, 2001), AILA Doc. No. 01070231; 1 legacy INS IFM ch.15, "NAFTA Admissions," 14-1 INS Manuals 15.5.

[353] DOS, "Mexican and Canadian NAFTA Professional Workers," http://travel.state.gov/visa/temp/types/types_1274.html.

[354] 1 legacy INS IFM ch.17, "Inadmissible Aliens," 14-1 INS Manuals 17.2.

Copyright © 2017. American Immigration Lawyers Association. All rights reserved.

Although the immigration laws allow the expedited removal of Mexican citizens seeking TN admission,[355] experience has shown that this occurs primarily when there has been visa fraud or willful misrepresentation in procuring the TN visa, as the Mexican citizen would have had to provide sufficient evidence of nonimmigrant intent to the consular officer in order to obtain the visa in the first place. For a discussion of expedited removal for TN nonimmigrants, see above.

Mexican citizens who did not retain their original I-94 cards may nevertheless be readmitted, as long as the period of TN validity has not expired, upon presentation of "a valid unexpired TN visa and evidence of previous admission,"[356] which should be the previously issued admission stamp. The Mexican citizen should be readmitted to the United States for the remaining duration of the initially approved TN classification and issued another I-94 card "with the legend 'multiple entry.'"[357] I-94 cards issued to Mexican TN visa holders can typically be retrieved from CBP's online I-94 system, however, so obtaining a duplicate is less likely to be a practical problem.

V. Preparing the TN Petition

This section discusses the documents of the TN petition.

A. Form I-129

The Form I-129 is filed only if the process for pre-filing with USCIS is being used, or if an extension of status, change of status, or change of employer is being requested. For initial requests for status, only Canadian citizens can use the pre-filing process.[358] The Trade Agreement Supplement to the I-129 is used.

Part 1: Information on the employer, including name, address, contact person, and contact person's telephone number and email address, should be provided. If the employer is a U.S. company, then the Federal Employer Identification Number (FEIN) should be provided. A private individual employer should provide his or her Social Security number. If the employer is a foreign company, then the individual tax identification number of the company in the country of incorporation should be provided.

Part 2: For an initial TN petition, "New employment" and "Notify the office" in Part 4 should be checked.

Part 3: Information about the beneficiary, including name, alternate names, date of birth, country of birth, country of nationality, and passport information, should be provided.

---

[355] INA §§212(a)(6)(C), 212(a)(7), and 235(b)(1)(B)(iii).

[356] 8 CFR §214.6(g)(2)(ii).

[357] 8 CFR §214.6(g)(2).

[358] "USCIS Announces a New Filing Option on behalf of Canadian TN Nonimmigrants and Reminds Employers of the Current Filing Options on behalf of Canadian L-1 Nonimmigrants." (Sept. 28, 2012), AILA Doc. No. 12100343. *See also* the USCIS website by searching "USCIS NAFTA professionals."

Copyright © 2017. American Immigration Lawyers Association. All rights reserved.

Part 4: As Canadians do not need a visa, generally either "Pre-flight inspection" or "Port of Entry" should be checked, depending on how the foreign national intends to enter, and the location of the port or inspection station should be noted. From a practical standpoint, it does not matter whether the port or inspection station noted matches the one where the Canadian ultimately enters the United States. However, as previously discussed, if the individual is in a third country and has non-Canadian dependents, consular notification may be needed.

An individual must have a passport that is valid for at least six months from the petition's expiration date; otherwise, he or she is inadmissible and ineligible for nonimmigrant status.[359] If the individual's passport expires during the expected period of stay, he or she should seek a new passport, or request the shortened period on the petition if the wait for the passport will be too long.

Parts 5 and 7 (Part 6 is not required for TN status): Information about the title, description of job activities, location, compensation, and general information about the petitioner should be provided. The form should be signed by the petitioner's representative and the practitioner.

Trade Agreement Supplement: The Trade Agreement Supplement allows the petitioner to designate itself as a foreign company; U.S. companies and private individual employers should mark this box "N/A."

B. Support Statement

For port of entry filings, the main document to be prepared for a TN petition is the U.S. employer support statement. The statement also is an important part of any filing with USCIS.

Because the government official should be provided with the information necessary to adjudicate the petition for approval, the practitioner is advised against having the foreign national submit only a contract for service, although a contract may serve as supplementary evidence.

The practitioner is advised to prepare a separate TN support statement in detail, to provide the following information:

- "The professional activities that the applicant will perform in the United States;
- "A summary of the applicant's daily responsibilities;
- "The length of time that the applicant's services are required (… must not exceed maximum allowable time for a TN). The applicant must also demonstrate [that the] assignment will be temporary and that he or she will depart upon completion…;

---

[359] INA §212(a)(7)(B)(i). The exceptions to this rule in INA §212(a)(d)(4) are discussed in Volume 1: Chapter Two, "Basic Nonimmigrant Concepts."

Copyright © 2017. American Immigration Lawyers Association. All rights reserved.

- "The educational requirement in the form of baccalaureate degree, licensing, years and type of experience, etc.;

- "The salary and employment benefits that the applicant will receive."[360]

The statement should be on the U.S. company's letterhead and signed by a representative of the U.S. company. One format of a support statement is as follows:

- Introduction;

- Information about the petitioner;

- Discussion of the project or reason for need of the foreign national's professional services for the U.S. assignment;

- Discussion of the duties of the U.S. assignment, with an emphasis on the way in which these duties match the TN classification sought;

- Discussion of the foreign national's educational and experience background; and

- Explanation of salary and employment benefits offered, intended duration of the TN assignment, and conclusion.

It is recommended that the practitioner include the requested TN classification in the "Re:" line of the support statement, as this should assist the adjudicating officer from the outset.

The most critical parts of the support statement are the paragraphs that address the need for the foreign national's professional services and the daily job duties. Experience has shown that the government official will most likely focus on this centerpiece first; only after being satisfied that there is a professional assignment will the government official consider whether the foreign national possesses the required professional credentials. Therefore, the support statement should provide details on the project(s) or initiative(s) that gave rise to the assignment and how the job duties will contribute to the successful completion of the employer's objectives. The practitioner may wish to review the employer's job description in conjunction with the DOL job description to ensure that the U.S. assignment is an appropriate fit with the TN classification and to prepare the support statement to highlight those job duties that match the template job description, as discussed above.

The final conclusion paragraph may contain the necessary information on the length of the U.S. assignment as the "anticipated length of stay," and the amount of remuneration for the professional services. In addition, for a TN management

---

[360] CBP Office of Field Operations Admissibility & Passenger Programs Enforcement Programs, "NAFTA Guide for TN and L Applicants," at. 5 (June 2012), AILA Doc. No. 13091643. The State Department, at 9 FAM 402.17-5(B), states these somewhat differently: "(1) A detailed listing of the activities in which the alien shall be engaged; (2) Purpose of entry; (3) Anticipated length of stay; (4) Educational qualifications or appropriate credentials demonstrating professional status; (5) Arrangements for remuneration."

Copyright © 2017. American Immigration Lawyers Association. All rights reserved.

consultant, the final paragraph may also reference the three-year validity of the consulting agreement or employment contract, as discussed above.

C. Form G-28

There are two ways to prepare the Form G-28: either to represent the employer and the foreign national or to represent only the foreign national. If there is limited time to prepare and file the petition before the U.S. assignment is to begin, such as if the forms are emailed to and printed by the client, this form may be printed on plain white paper. However, as discussed in Volume 1: Chapter Two, "Basic Nonimmigrant Concepts," the Forms G-28 should be printed on blue paper whenever possible, in order to avoid processing delays.[361]

For the first style, the "Re" box may be completed with the following language: "Company, Inc.—Petition for TN Status on behalf of Foreign National." The U.S. company is the "petitioner" and the foreign national is the "beneficiary" of a TN petition. Both addresses, for the U.S. company and for the foreign national abroad, should be provided. The U.S. company representative should sign this form in blue ink.[362]

For the second style, the "Re" box may be completed with the following language: "Foreign National—Application for TN Status." The foreign national is the "applicant" for admission is TN status, and his or her foreign address should be provided. The foreign national should sign this form in black ink.[363]

In determining which style of Form G-28 to prepare, the practitioner should consider the purpose of the representation. If the foreign national is also the client, then the second approach should be taken. But if the client is the U.S. company, then either style may be used, and the practitioner should consider the challenges of dual representation, as discussed in Volume 1: Chapter Two, "Basic Nonimmigrant Concepts." If the employer-client and/or practitioner are concerned about creating an attorney-client relationship with the foreign national, then it may be preferable to use the first style.

VI. Strategy: TN vs. H-1B

Because the TN classification was modeled after the H-1B nonimmigrant classification,[364] a foreign national may be eligible for both nonimmigrant categories. In this situation, the practitioner should strategize with the client to decide which classification is a better fit for the needs of the employer and the foreign national. In general, the H-1B category is preferred for situations in which the foreign national does not meet the eligibility requirements for TN status: when the foreign national is

---

[361] "VSC Practice Pointer: G-28s" (Sept. 4, 2008), AILA Doc. No. 08090469.

[362] Instructions to Form G-28, part 4. www.uscis.gove/sites/default/files/files/form/g-28instr.pdf. *See also* "AILA FAQ: Completing the New G-28 Form" (Oct. 11, 2013) AILA Doc. No. 13101144.

[363] *Id.*

[364] 9 FAM 402.17-2(A)(c).

Copyright © 2017. American Immigration Lawyers Association. All rights reserved.

pursuing permanent residence; when the position is not one of the enumerated TN professions; or when the foreign national lacks the required educational, licensure, or experience background. The TN classification is preferred for most other situations. But because of the numerical limitation on H-1B visa numbers and the lottery system for allotting H-1B visa numbers, discussed below, it may not be feasible for the employer to wait to employ the foreign national in H-1B status; it may be necessary to request TN status first and then consider at some point filing an H-1B change of status petition at a later date, as discussed below.

A. Numerical and Time Limitations

First and foremost, there is a numerical limitation on the number of new H-1B visas that are available each year,[365] whereas there is no such quota for the TN classification.[366] There was formerly a numerical limitation of 55,000 TN visas each year for Mexican citizens, but this quota was abolished in 2004.[367] Because of a historically high demand for H-1B visas, USCIS often conducts a random lottery each year to determine which foreign nationals will be able to claim an H-1B visa number, and in fiscal year 2017, only 36 percent of proposed H-1B beneficiaries were awarded H-1B visa numbers.[368] In addition, the high demand for H-1B visa numbers creates a situation in which only H-1B petitions filed during the first week of April for start dates of no earlier than October 1 can be considered for the lottery.[369] Therefore, as a practical matter, if the employer seeks to hire a foreign national in H-1B status for a start date earlier than October 1 of any given year, or if the employer and/or foreign national are not ready to file the H-1B petition in early April, the foreign national will be unable to claim an H-1B visa number. The exception is if H-1B filings are low in number, perhaps because of a downturn in the economy, as discussed in Volume 1: Chapter Seven, "H-1B Visas and Status."

Except in certain specific circumstances, a foreign national may hold H-1B status for a maximum of six years,[370] whereas a foreign national could hold TN status for a longer period of time.[371] As discussed above, the statutes do not set a maximum time period for TN status, but as a practical matter, foreign nationals requesting extensions beyond the initial three-year period of admission may be questioned about their nonimmigrant intent.

---

[365] INA §214(g)(1). For a detailed discussion of the requirements of the H-1B category, see Volume 1: Chapter Seven, "H-1B Visas and Status."

[366] 1 legacy INS IFM ch.15, "NAFTA Admissions," 14-1 INS Manuals 15.5; 69 Fed. Reg. 11287 (Mar. 10, 2004).

[367] 69 Fed. Reg. 11287 (Mar. 10, 2004).

[368] "USCIS Completes H-1B Cap Random Selection Process" (Apr. 12, 2016), https://www.uscis.gov/news/alerts/uscis-completes-h-1b-cap-random-selection-process-fy-2017; AILA Doc. No. 16041361.

[369] 73 Fed. Reg. 15389 (Mar. 24, 2008).

[370] INA §214(g)(4).

[371] 9 FAM 402.17-7.

Copyright © 2017. American Immigration Lawyers Association. All rights reserved.

B. Professional Occupations

The numerical limitation is unfortunate, as the H-1B classification is available to a wider group of professionals than the TN classification, whereas the professional occupations are specifically enumerated in the NAFTA Treaty.[372] If the foreign national's duties in the United States do not fall within one of the specified TN professions, then the H-1B classification may be the only way for the foreign national to gain U.S. employment authorization.[373] The employer and foreign national may be forced to wait to file the H-1B petition, hope that the H-1B petition is selected in the lottery, and wait for an employment start date of no earlier than October 1st of the upcoming fiscal year. The foreign national may also need to apply for H-1B status if he or she does not meet the minimum educational, licensure, and/or experience qualifications of the TN occupation, such as if he or she has the equivalent of a baccalaureate degree based on progressively more responsible experience.[374]

C. Timing and Cost Issues

In addition to the delays caused by the annual quota of H-1B visa numbers, the process of the H-1B petition will likely take longer as well. The lottery should first be conducted; then, the petition must be adjudicated by USCIS, whose processing times can range from two months to six months or more.[375] Premium processing may be requested for an additional fee of $1,225 for a response (approval, denial, or request for further evidence) within 15 days.[376] Upon approval of the H-1B petition, the foreign national may apply for H-1B admission or for an H-1B visa. In contrast, it is not necessary to file an initial TN petition with USCIS, so the foreign national may start the process by applying for admission or for a TN visa.

For employers of more than 25 employees, the filing fees for an H-1B petition currently total $2,460, not including the premium processing fee.[377] The costs for the TN petition are $56 for Canadian citizens.[378] If the USCIS advance petition process is

---

[372] NAFTA, U.S.-Can.-Mex. (Dec. 17, 1992), 32 I.L.M. 289 (entered into force Jan. 1, 1994), Chap. 16, Appendix 1603.D.1; 8 CFR §214.6(c).

[373] 8 CFR §214.2(h)(4)(ii).

[374] 9 FAM 402.17-4(A); 8 CFR §§214.2(h)(4)(iii)(C)(4) and 214.2(h)(4)(iii)(D).

[375] See, e.g., Vermont Service Center Processing Time Reports, http://www.aila.org/infonet/processing-time-reports/vsc.

[376] USCIS Will Temporarily Suspend Premium Processing for All H-1B Petitions starting April 3, 2017. See https://www.uscis.gov/news/alerts/uscis-will-temporarily-suspend-premium-processing-all-h-1b-petitions.

[377] USCIS, https://www.uscis.gov/forms/h-and-l-filing-fees-form-i-129-petition-nonimmigrant-worker. For smaller employers, the fee is $1,710, and for employers considered H-1B dependent, it is $6,460. For a discussion of the various filing fees for initial H-1B petitions, see Volume 1: Chapter Seven, "H-1B Visas and Status."

[378] 8 CFR §103.7(b)(ii)(D) and (K).

Copyright © 2017. American Immigration Lawyers Association. All rights reserved.

used, the fee is \$466, not including premium processing. For Mexican citizens, the costs include the \$160 visa application fee.[379]

Finally, in order to file an H-1B petition, a labor condition application must be certified by DOL, and the labor condition application must contain the employer's attestation that the foreign national will be paid 100 percent of the prevailing wage for the occupation in the metropolitan statistical area of the worksite.[380] If the foreign national will not be paid the prevailing wage, then the employer cannot petition for H-1B status. It was formerly a requirement that TN petitions on behalf of Mexican citizens also had to be accompanied by a certified labor condition application, but this is no longer required.[381]

D. State Licensure

The TN classification does not require that the foreign national hold a valid U.S. state license to practice his or her profession in the United States,[382] as opposed to the H-1B classification, where an H-1B petition for an occupation that requires a state or local license typically cannot be approved unless the foreign national holds a valid U.S. state license.[383] The H-1B licensure requirement may apply to occupations such as doctors, nurses, pharmacists, lawyers, occupational therapists, accountants, and teachers.[384] In contrast, legacy INS guidance regarding the licensure of TN nonimmigrants specifically directs immigration inspectors and consular officers to recognize that the licensure requirements should be administered by U.S. state authorities; immigration officials should not require that a foreign national hold a U.S. license, because the license is a post-admission requirement and not a condition precedent for admission.[385]

States have on some occasions attempted to deny licenses to nonimmigrants. However, a federal appellate court overturned on equal protection grounds attempts

---

[379] DOS, "Mexico Reciprocity Schedule," https://travel.state.gov/content/visas/en/fees/reciprocity-by-country/MX.html.

[380] 8 CFR §§214.2(h)(1)(ii)(B)(1) and 214.2(h)(4)(i)(B)(1); 20 CFR §§655.700(a)(3), 655.705(c)(1), and 655.730(c)(4).

[381] 69 Fed. Reg. 11287 (Mar. 10, 2004).

[382] 69 Fed. Reg. 60939 (Oct. 13, 2004).

[383] 8 CFR §214.2(h)(4)(v)(A). For a discussion of the exceptions to the licensure requirement, see Volume 1: Chapter Seven, "H-1B Visas and Status."

[384] *See, e.g.*, "USCIS' Standard Operating Procedures (SOPs) for H-1B Adjudication" (document undated, posted July, 26, 2007), AILA Doc. No. 07072668; "AILA Liaison/VSC Meeting Minutes" (Sept. 17, 2007), AILA Doc. No. 07100261.

[385] 69 Fed. Reg. 60939 (Oct. 13, 2004); DOS website, "Mexican and Canadian NAFTA Professional Workers," http://travel.state.gov/visa/temp/types/types_1274.html.

Copyright © 2017. American Immigration Lawyers Association. All rights reserved.

by New York State to limit licensing of certain medical professionals, such as pharmacists and veterinarians, to U.S. citizens and lawful permanent residents.[386]

E. Employment Relationships and Employer Responsibilities

The H-1B classification is not appropriate where the foreign national will be employed by a Canadian or Mexican company and will provide professional services in the United States.[387] It is permissible, however, for a Canadian or Mexican citizen in TN status to provide such services in the United States on behalf of a Canadian or Mexican entity.[388] If the foreign national is employed by a Canadian or Mexican entity and will provide services in the United States, the practitioner should discuss with the client how to demonstrate the relationship between the foreign entity and the U.S. company that will receive the foreign national's services. For example, if the two companies have a corporate relationship, as discussed in Volume 1: Chapter Eleven, "L Visas and Status," then the foreign national should be prepared to present the annual report or an officer's certificate attesting to that relationship. Alternatively, if the U.S. company is a client of the foreign company, the foreign national should have copies of the service contract, invoices, or other evidence of payment for services pursuant to an agreement between the two companies.

Conversely, although the foreign national may not be self-employed in the United States in TN status,[389] a self-employed foreign national may seek H-1B status by having a U.S. agent file the H-1B petition on his or her behalf.[390]

The regulations require that the employer of an H-1B nonimmigrant pay the return transportation costs to the home country if the foreign national's employment is terminated,[391] but there is no such requirement for TN employees.

F. Change in Duties or Work Location

The employer must file an amended TN petition with USCIS if there will be a material change in the job duties, or in the TN employer,[392] but an amended TN petition is not necessary if the work location changes, as long as the foreign national continues to perform the same duties for the same employer as stated on the initial TN petition.[393] For H-1B employees, USCIS must be notified with an amended H-1B

---

[386] *Dandamudi v. Tisch*, 686 F.3d 66 (2d Cir. 2012). *See also Kirk v. New York State Dept. of Education*, 644 F.3d 134 (2d Cir. 2011) (finding that the challengers to the law regarding veterinarians were prevailing parties for purposes of attorney's fees).

[387] 8 CFR §214.2(h)(4)(ii).

[388] 9 FAM 402.17-5(A) (stating that the TN nonimmigrant "must engage in prearranged business activity for a U.S. or foreign employer").

[389] 9 FAM 402.17-5(A).

[390] 8 CFR §214.2(h)(2)(i)(F)(3).

[391] 8 CFR §214.2(h)(4)(iii)(E).

[392] 8 CFR §214.6(i)(3); 9 FAM 402.17-10(c).

[393] *Id.*

Copyright © 2017. American Immigration Lawyers Association. All rights reserved.

petition if there is a change in the job duties and/or change in the job location.[394] The client should also be advised of the requirements of the H-1B labor condition application, where a new labor condition application may need to be filed if the foreign national works even temporarily in a new location.[395]

G. Dual Intent

Although it is permissible for a foreign national in H-1B status to pursue permanent residence, a TN professional must continue to maintain nonimmigrant intent and should be granted "temporary entry,"[396] as discussed above. Therefore, if the employer or a family member will sponsor the foreign national for permanent residence, the employer may wish to consider requesting a change of status to H-1B, as discussed below, although TN status may be granted prior to filing an application for an immigrant visa or adjustment of status, as discussed above. Nevertheless, the practitioner should discuss with the foreign national how to clearly demonstrate nonimmigrant intent despite the filing of a labor certification application or immigrant visa petition, particularly in the event the foreign national travels abroad, as discussed above.

VII. Additional Follow-up

After a foreign national has obtained TN status, the practitioner should follow up to request copies of the I-94 cards and the visas, if applicable, to ensure that all the information is correct and to calendar the expiration dates to monitor the foreign national's transferee status, as discussed in Volume 1: Chapter Two, "Basic Nonimmigrant Concepts."

A. Extensions

If the employer wishes to continue to employ the foreign national beyond the validity of the initial TN petition, an extension may be filed with USCIS. Alternatively, a Canadian citizen may present a new TN petition at a port of entry, and a Mexican citizen may present a new TN visa application at a U.S. consulate. For a discussion of the advantages and disadvantages of both approaches, see below.

1. TN Extensions Filed with USCIS

An employer may file an extension petition with USCIS, as long as the foreign national is currently in valid TN status,[397] and is physically present in the United States on the date the petition is filed.[398] The extension petition may be filed up to six

---

[394] 8 CFR §§214.2(h)(2)(i)(D) and (E). *See also Matter of Simeio Solutions, LLC*, 26 I&N Dec. 542 (AAO 2015); "USCIS Final Guidance on When to File an Amended or New H-1B Petition After *Matter of Simeio Solutions, LLC*," PM-602-0120 (July 21, 2015), AILA Doc. No. 15072105.

[395] 20 CFR §655.735.

[396] 9 FAM 402.17-7.

[397] 8 CFR §214.6(h)(1).

[398] 8 CFR §214.6(h)(1)(ii).

Copyright © 2017. American Immigration Lawyers Association. All rights reserved.

months in advance of the TN status expiration,[399] and it will be timely filed as long as it is received by the date that the TN status expires.[400] For a discussion of how to address, prepare, and file untimely extensions of status, see Volume 1: Chapter Two, "Basic Nonimmigrant Concepts." The extension may be approved for up to three years or for the duration of the assignment, whichever is less.[401]

Extensions of TD status for the dependent family members should also be prepared and filed. If a Mexican citizen and/or dependent family members need to travel internationally for business or personal reasons while the extensions are pending, the petitioner may request consular notification of the extension approval, so that the Mexican citizen and/or family members may apply for a visa.[402] The practitioner should note that even if USCIS approves the TN and TD extensions, Mexican citizens must apply for new visas in order to re-enter the United States after international travel.[403] In most instances, as a practical matter, consular officials will re-adjudicate the TN petition notwithstanding the fact that the foreign national has an approved extension petition. The petitioner may request that cable notification be sent to the port of entry where a Canadian citizen will apply for admission. It is also possible, although more expensive, to make an application for TN admission or visa after the TN extension has been filed with USCIS, as discussed below.

When filing a TN extension, the practitioner should be aware that the USCIS adjudicator likely does not have access to the initial TN petition.[404] If the USCIS adjudicator of an L-1B extension has difficulty reviewing the initial L-1B petition which was filed with USCIS, as discussed in Volume 1: Chapter Eleven, "L Visas and Nonimmigrant Status," then it seems highly likely that the TN extension adjudicator does not have access to the initial TN petition, which must have been filed with a port of entry or a U.S. consulate. The support statement for the TN extension should be very detailed, as discussed below, in particular, because there is no appeal from the denial of an application to extend stay.[405] For a detailed discussion of the issues surrounding a petition to extend status, see Volume 1: Chapter Two, "Basic Nonimmigrant Concepts."

A TN extension petition should contain the following documents:

- Cover letter;
- Form G-28;

---

[399] USCIS, "Instructions for Form I-129, Petition for a Nonimmigrant Worker," www.uscis.gov/files/form/i-129instr.pdf.

[400] "DOS on Unlawful Presence During EOS/COS Application" (May 30, 2000), AILA Doc. No. 00060202, and 5 Bender's Immigr. Bull. 590 (June 15, 2000).

[401] 8 CFR §214.6(h)(1)(iii).

[402] 8 CFR §214.2(h)(1)(ii).

[403] 8 CFR §214.6(h)(2).

[404] "VSC Answers Liaison Questions" (Aug. 27, 2002), AILA Doc. No. 02091271.

[405] 8 CFR §§214.1(c)(5) and 248.3(g).

Copyright © 2017. American Immigration Lawyers Association. All rights reserved.

- Form I-907 (if applicable);
- Form I-129;
- Trade Agreement Supplement;
- Support statement;
- Evidence of the foreign national's professional qualifications;
- Evidence of the foreign national's valid TN status, in the form of the I-94 card and the TN visa, if applicable;
- Evidence of continued employment in TN status, such as several recent paystubs; and
- Filing fee(s) for the TN extension and any TD extension(s), if applicable.[406]

a. Form G-28

The Form G-28 should be prepared with the employer as the petitioner and the foreign national as the beneficiary, as discussed above. A representative of the employer should sign the form in black ink.

b. Form I-907

If the client wishes a response (approval, denial, or RFE) within 15 calendar days, the client may pay USCIS an additional $1,225 for premium processing. This request may be filed concurrently with the TN extension petition, or the attorney or the client may request premium processing after the petition has been filed, by submitting Form I-907, Request for Premium Processing, with the petition's receipt notice, as discussed in Volume 1: Chapter Two, "Basic Nonimmigrant Concepts."

c. Form I-129

Part 1: Information on the employer, including name, address, contact person, and contact person's telephone number and email address, should be provided. If the employer is a U.S. company, then the FEIN should be provided. A private individual employer should provide his or her Social Security number. If the employer is a foreign company, then the individual tax identification number of the company in the country of incorporation should be provided.

Part 2: For TN extensions where the TN assignment remains the same as the initial TN petition, "Continuation of previously approved employment without change with the same employer" should be checked. Although Canadian citizens who present other types of nonimmigrant petitions at ports of entry later receive a Form I-797 approval notice from USCIS,[407] experience has shown that Form I-797 approval notices are not always issued for TN petitions filed at ports of entry. The blanks for Question 3 may be completed as follows for Canadian citizens: "N/A—POE

---

[406] 8 CFR §103.7(b).

[407] "NSC Liaison Questions and Answers" (Feb. 1999), AILA Doc. No. 99031841; "AILA Liaison/VSC Teleconference Minutes" (May 30, 2007), AILA Doc. No. 07061171.

Copyright © 2017. American Immigration Lawyers Association. All rights reserved.

Application." Similarly, Mexican citizens who obtain TN visas at U.S. consulates are not issued USCIS receipt notices, so the blanks should be completed as follows: "N/A—Consular Application."

If there will be a substantive change in job duties in the new TN assignment, then "Change in previously approved employment" should be checked. The practitioner should use good judgment in determining the amount of change in job duties or conditions necessary to mark this box instead of the "continuation" box. The practitioner should note that actions like a pay raise or change in worksite are typically considered minor changes, whereas it is appropriate to acknowledge a change in TN classification, such as from biologist to biochemist, or a major change in the daily job duties.

It is not recommended to request consular notification, as doing so would result in a Form I-797 approval notice that does not have a replacement I-94 card, the foreign national's status would not be extended, and he or she would need to depart the United States and seek admission in TN status again, thereby incurring the costs of international travel in addition to the filing fee(s). In addition, Mexican citizens and their families would encounter the timing issues discussed above, and Canadian citizens and their families would have to incur the costs of travel to depart the United States. Instead, the practitioner should request to "Extend the status of a nonimmigrant classification based on a Free Trade Agreement." But if consular notification is requested, as discussed in Volume 1: Chapter Two, "Basic Nonimmigrant Concepts," USCIS should notify the Kentucky Consular Center, and the consulate abroad should then be able confirm petition approval when the foreign national applies for a TN visa, if a visa is required.

Parts 3 and 4: Information about the beneficiary, including name, alternate names, date of birth, country of birth, country of nationality, and passport information, should be provided.

Because TN professionals receive multiple-entry I-94 cards, they do not need to surrender the I-94 with each departure from the United States. Therefore, the most recent date of entry to the United States may differ from the initial date of entry, when the I-94 card was issued. Despite the fact that the foreign national may not have a new I-94 card or admission stamp, the most recent date of entry should be provided and not the date of initial admission, if different.

An individual must have a passport that is valid for at least six months from the petition's expiration date; otherwise, he or she is inadmissible and ineligible for nonimmigrant status.[408] If the individual does not have such a passport, then the following options are available: either delay filing the TN petition until he or she obtains a renewed passport, or file the TN petition, note that the person is seeking a passport renewal, and have the person apply for a renewed passport in the interim.

---

[408] INA §212(a)(7)(B)(i). The exceptions to this rule in INA §212(a)(d)(4) are discussed in Volume 1: Chapter Two, "Basic Nonimmigrant Concepts."

Copyright © 2017. American Immigration Lawyers Association. All rights reserved.

USCIS does not always issue an RFE under these circumstances, but in the event of an RFE, it is then possible to submit a photocopy of the biographic page of the renewed passport once it is available. For nationals of countries where passport renewal takes months, the second strategy can prevent the petition from being significantly delayed. If the client is willing to pay an additional $1,225 fee to USCIS, the delay caused by the RFE, which might also be several months, can be addressed by requesting premium processing when submitting the documentation of the renewed passport.

If the beneficiary is present in the United States when the petition is filed, then the I-94 information should be provided, even if the professional will depart the United States during pendency of the TN petition. In this case, consular notification may be requested in Part 2, as discussed above.

The answer to Question 9 should be "yes," and in the addendum, the practitioner should explain that an application for TN admission or visa was made at a port of entry or U.S. consulate. The validity dates of the approved TN petition should also be provided.

Parts 5 and 7 (Part 6 is not required for TN status): Information about the title, description of job activities, location, compensation, and general information about the petitioner should be provided. The form should be signed by the petitioner's representative and the practitioner.

d. Trade Agreement Supplement

The Trade Agreement Supplement allows the petitioner to designate itself as a foreign company; U.S. companies and private individual employers should mark this box "N/A."

e. TN Extension Support Statement

As noted above, the TN extension should clearly describe the need for the extended TN assignment and the job duties. The practitioner may find it helpful to revise the initial TN support statement only to include reference to the extension and the reason for the extension, retaining the detailed description of the professional activities of the TN assignment and the foreign national's professional qualifications.

2. Filing a New TN Petition at a Port of Entry or U.S. Consulate

The client and/or foreign national may decide to submit a new application for TN admission or visa at a port of entry or U.S. consulate,[409] rather than filing the extension application with USCIS. This process would be very similar to the initial port of entry TN petition process, discussed above, with the exception of revisions to the TN support statement.[410]

---

[409] 8 CFR §214.6(h)(2).
[410] *Id.*

Copyright © 2017. American Immigration Lawyers Association. All rights reserved.

3. TN Extension Filed with USCIS vs. New TN Petition Filed with Port of Entry or U.S. Consulate

Because TN professionals have the option of either filing a TN extension with USCIS or submitting a new TN petition at a port of entry or U.S. consulate, the practitioner should strategize with the client the approach that best fits the needs of the employer, the foreign national, and the foreign national's dependent family members. The typical issues are discussed in this section. For both strategies, the foreign national must satisfactorily demonstrate nonimmigrant intent.[411] As a practical matter, however, USCIS rarely raises the issue of nonimmigrant intent when processing a TN extension petition.

a. Extension of Employment Authorization

A TN extension that is timely filed with USCIS will provide an additional 240 days of employment authorization with the petitioning employer, during pendency of the TN extension filing and after expiration of the current TN status.[412] This is helpful for TN professionals who do not have the time to depart the United States, seek a new visa (if applicable), and seek admission to the United States again. As a practical matter, however, the investment of time for this process will typically be less for a Canadian citizen than for a Mexican citizen, as the Mexican citizen must obtain a new TN visa, which is an additional step with a potentially long processing time, as discussed below.

As a practical matter, notwithstanding the automatic 240-day extension of work authorization, international travel is not possible once the underlying petition has expired. A Mexican citizen would have neither a TN visa as an entry document with which to re-enter the United States nor an approved TN extension with which to apply for a TN visa, and a Canadian citizen would not have the necessary TN extension approval notice with which to seek admission to the United States. The foreign national would then need to apply for new TN admission or visa, as discussed below, after having paid the costs of filing and legal fees for the TN extension, the TD extensions (if applicable), and the premium processing fee (if applicable).

In contrast, submitting a new TN petition to a port of entry or U.S. consulate does not confer an extension of employment authorization. The practitioner should advise the client that continuing U.S. employment beyond the expiration date of the current TN petition entails engaging in unauthorized employment, with associated potential negative ramifications. If a new TN petition will be submitted, the practitioner should counsel the client to have the foreign national depart the United States before the expiration date of the current TN petition, even if the new TN petition will not be submitted for some time after the departure, whether because of wait times for the next available visa appointment or because of business or personal reasons.

---

[411] 1 NAFTA Handbook, "Canadian TN Nonimmigrant pursuant to NAFTA," 14-1 INS Manuals Scope.
[412] 8 CFR §274a.12(b)(20).

Copyright © 2017. American Immigration Lawyers Association. All rights reserved.

b. Travel to the Port of Entry or U.S. Consulate

The foreign national need not travel outside the United States to obtain approval of the TN extension filed with USCIS.[413] In contrast, submission of a new TN petition to a port of entry or U.S. consulate necessarily entails international travel, as well as the costs associated with such travel. But this process nevertheless has several potential advantages.

First, the client and foreign national may save money by not having to pay the filing fees and premium processing fee, if applicable, although there may still be costs associated with traveling to the port of entry or U.S. consulate and airline tickets for the entire family may be costly as well. Second, Mexican citizens must obtain TN visas in order to travel internationally, so if the TN professional is Mexican and has international travel planned already, it may make more sense to bypass the USCIS extension process by seeking a new TN visa. Third, the processing times for TN petitions made at ports of entry and U.S. consulates are typically shorter than extensions filed with USCIS, which can take months to complete.[414]

If the client decides to have the Mexican citizen make a new application for a TN visa, then any family members would have to travel with the principal foreign national, or await approval of the TN visa and admission to the United States before being eligible to apply for TD extensions based on the approval of the Mexican citizen's TN status. If the Mexican citizen will apply for a new TN visa alone, it is advised that he or she do so well in advance of the expiration of the initial TN status, to allow for processing of the TN visa, admission to the United States, and filing of the TD extensions before their expiration.

Conversely, the foreign national may have no international travel planned for a while, and the employer and/or foreign national may not wish to bear the costs of the international travel necessary to submit such a new TN petition.

If there is an urgent need for international travel during the pendency of the TN extension, a Canadian citizen may travel to a port of entry and make a new application for TN admission: "VSC advises that if an individual travels back to Canada during the pendency of a TN Extension Application, she could process at the port of entry upon returning to the United States and make the application for an extension moot."[415] Similarly, a Mexican citizen may choose to abandon the extension request and apply for a TN visa at a U.S. consulate abroad. The practitioner should discuss with the client how the option is available for Canadian citizens and how TN processing differs in other situations for Canadian and Mexican citizens so that the client may make an informed decision. If the client decides to proceed with

---

[413] "VSC Practice Pointer: Filing TN Change or Extension of Status", AILA Doc. No. 08092364. *See also* "I-129 Nonimmigrant Classification Chart with Filing Locations," https://www.uscis.gov/i-129-addresses.

[414] Vermont Service Center Processing Time Reports, http://www.aila.org/infonet/processing-time-reports/vsc.

[415] "AILA Liaison/VSC Agenda Item Q&As" (Jan. 24, 2007), AILA Doc. No. 07021465.

Copyright © 2017. American Immigration Lawyers Association. All rights reserved.

this approach, for either a Canadian or Mexican employee, it is recommended that the TN extension petition be withdrawn from USCIS after approval of the application for TN admission or visa to avoid potential confusion of expiration dates. The practitioner should also discuss the timing issues with the TD extensions on behalf of any dependents of Mexican TN visa holders, as discussed above.

c. Processing Times

As noted above, processing times are typically longer for extensions filed with USCIS than for applications for new TN admission or visas. But the practitioner should also discuss with the client that the visa application may entail a significant period of time outside the United States for Mexican citizens. There may be delays in visa issuance, depending on the visa processing of the U.S. consulate, or for administrative processing of certain visa applications, as discussed in Volume 1: Chapter Two, "Basic Nonimmigrant Concepts."

d. Premium Processing

Premium processing is available for TN petitions filed with USCIS. If international travel needs demand it, premium processing may be requested for the TN extension, as discussed above, and the TD extensions should be adjudicated concurrently. The client should be advised, however, of the possibility that the foreign national and/or his or her family members may need to remain outside the United States for an extended period of time in order to await approval of the extensions and, if applicable, to apply for visas. This strategy should be explored with the client in advance for several reasons.

First, one must consider the costs of the TN extension and premium processing for Canadian and Mexican citizens; Mexican citizens would also have to pay the visa application and reciprocity fees, as well as for airfare to travel to a U.S. consulate for the principal foreign national and/or the family members, if applicable. Payment of the filing and premium processing fees could be avoided if the foreign national directly filed the TN petition with a port of entry or a U.S. consulate. Second, the time necessary for this process will in most circumstances be longer than filing the TN petition with a port of entry or U.S. consulate, as discussed above. Third, if the international travel is to a country other than the transferee's home country or country of permanent residence, then the practitioner should confirm that the U.S. consulate in that country accepts visa applications by third country nationals.

e. Review of Denials

The employer or foreign national may choose to file an extension with USCIS because of concern that a new TN petition may be denied by the port of entry or U.S. consulate, in which case the foreign national would be outside the United States with limited recourse for review of the denial.[416] An applicant for TN admission may be

---

[416] Legacy INS, M. Pearson, "Denial of Applicants for Admission under the North American Free Trade Agreement (IN01-11)" (May 25, 2001), AILA Doc. No. 01070231.

Copyright © 2017. American Immigration Lawyers Association. All rights reserved.

afforded the opportunity to withdraw the application or become subject to expedited removal proceedings, as discussed above, and review of a visa denial is limited at best, as discussed in Volume 1: Chapter Two, "Basic Nonimmigrant Concepts." Some have felt that, for those situations involving heightened scrutiny, filing an extension with USCIS would allow the opportunity for appeal to the Administrative Appeals Office (AAO). However, the regulations specify that there is no appeal of an extension of status.[417] Now, apparently, there also is no appeal of the underlying petition for TN status. A chart on the USCIS web page indicates that there is no appeal of an I-129 for treaty-based statuses such as E-1, E-2, TN, or H-1B1.[418] The regulations have been silent on this subject since DHS in 2003 deleted the previous section of law[419] that addressed AAO jurisdiction and left nothing in its place but a broad delegation of authority. [420]

The petitioner may, however, seek reopening or reconsideration of the denial of the TN petition.[421] The petitioner also has the option of filing a new TN petition with USCIS disclosing the prior denial and addressing how the new petition filing overcomes the grounds of the prior denial.

On a related note, the foreign national may have held TN status for a number of years, and the client may be concerned that the TN admission or visa may be denied for lack of nonimmigrant intent.[422] The client may prefer to file the TN extension with USCIS so that the foreign national does not receive a denial while physically outside the United States, in order to preserve the option of moving to reopen the denial of the TN petition.

B. If Employment Ceases

TN nonimmigrants whose employment ends prior to the expiration of their authorized stay are able to remain in the United States lawfully for the shorter of 60 days or when the existing validity period ends.[423] This can be used only once during each "authorized validity period." The purpose is to allow the beneficiary to wind up affairs or to seek other employment and request a change of status if needed and eligible.[424] The individual is not able to work during this period, unless otherwise authorized.[425] The rulemaking that put in place this grace period was silent as to what

---

[417] 8 CFR §§214.1(c)(5) and 248.3(g).

[418] "When to Use Form I-290B, Notice of Appeal or Motion" (Feb. 23, 2016), https://www.uscis.gov/i-129b/jurisdiction.

[419] Former 8 CFR §103.1(f)(3)(iii) (at Feb. 28, 2003).

[420] 68 Fed.Reg. 10922 (Mar. 6, 2011).

[421] "When to Use Form I-290B, Notice of Appeal or Motion" (Feb. 23, 2016), https://www.uscis.gov/i-129b/jurisdiction.

[422] 1 NAFTA Handbook, "Canadian TN Nonimmigrant pursuant to NAFTA," 14-1 INS Manuals Scope.

[423] 8 CFR §214.1(l)(ii).

[424] 80 Fed. Reg. 81923 (Dec. 31, 2015).

[425] Id.

Copyright © 2017. American Immigration Lawyers Association. All rights reserved.

would be an "authorized validity period" in the TN context, but presumably it means any given period of admission, or the validity period of the approved USCIS petition, whichever is in effect for the individual at the time.

C. Sponsoring a TN Professional for Permanent Residence

If the U.S. company wishes to sponsor a TN nonimmigrant for permanent residence, it is important to consider the conditions of "temporary entry," as discussed above. "Temporary entry" is granted to TN professionals upon admission to the United States,[426] and the foreign national's nonimmigrant intent is considered during the visa interview for Mexican citizens.[427] Therefore, the foreign national may, in many cases, prefer not to travel outside the United States or apply for a TN visa if he or she continues to be employed by the U.S. company in the United States and is the beneficiary of an immigrant visa petition filed by the same employer, unless the employer and/or foreign national wish to rely upon the CBP guidance discussed earlier in this chapter.[428]

Relying on that guidance may have its pitfalls where the foreign national resides and works in the United States, because the government official may not accept that the immigrant intent to be employed by the U.S. company "is in no way connected" to the U.S. assignment with the same U.S. company.[429] In addition, it is possible that the government official would be unpersuaded that the foreign national would "depart upon completion of the assignment."[430]

In the event that the foreign national must travel outside the United States for business or personal reasons, the practitioner may postpone filing of the immigrant visa petition until after the foreign national returns to the United States. Another strategy is to concurrently file the immigrant visa petition and an application to adjust status.[431] This may be done only if an immigrant visa number is immediately available to the foreign national,[432] and if the foreign national applies for an Advance Parole for international travel.[433] For a detailed discussion of strategies and timing considerations of immigrant visa petitions and concurrent filing, see Volume 2: Chapter Three, "The Immigrant Visa Petition." For a discussion of the Advance

---

[426] NAFTA, U.S.-Can.-Mex. (Dec. 17, 1992), 32 I.L.M. 289 (entered into force Jan. 1, 1994), Chap. 16, Article 1608.

[427] DOS, "INA 214(b) Basis of Refusal Not Equivalent to Inadmissibility or Immigrant Intent" (Dec. 2004), AILA Doc. No. 05032279.

[428] Letter from Paul Morris, Executive Director, Admissibility and Passenger Programs, CBP (Apr. 21, 2008), AILA Doc. No. 09021280.

[429] 9 FAM 402.17-7.

[430] Id.

[431] 8 CFR §245.2(a)(2)(i).

[432] 8 CFR §§245.1(g)(1) and 245.2(a)(2)(i).

[433] 8 CFR §245.2(a)(4)(ii)(B).

Copyright © 2017. American Immigration Lawyers Association. All rights reserved.

Parole document, see Volume 2: Chapter Four, "Consular Processing, Adjustment of Status, and Permanent Residence Issues."

The third option is to postpone filing the immigrant visa petition until the foreign national obtains H-1B status. As discussed above, this process may take up to several years, due to the high demand for H-1B visa numbers and due to the lottery system of selection of foreign nationals who are awarded H-1B visa numbers. But because a foreign national in H-1B status is not subject to the conditions of INA §214(b) and is not granted "temporary entry," an H-1B nonimmigrant may travel internationally throughout the permanent residence process. For a discussion of H-1B change of status petitions, see below.

This strategy is especially encouraged for foreign nationals for whom the immigrant visa petition will be classified as EB-3 (third employment-based preference), as visa retrogression may significantly delay the permanent residence process,[434] such that the foreign national is unable to apply to adjust status before expiration of the current TN petition. In addition, upon holding H-1B status, the foreign national could be eligible for American Competivieness in the Twenty-First Century Act (AC21) extensions until he or she obtains permanent residence.[435]

Conversely, given the extended delays caused by visa retrogression in the EB-3 classification for foreign nationals born in India and China, it may not be possible for a foreign national to file the application to adjust status even within the three-year validity of a newly approved TN extension.[436] For example, at the time of this writing, foreign nationals born in India face a wait time of 12 years for an immigrant visa number to become available, and foreign nationals born in other countries face constantly fluctuating wait times that can run several months to several years.[437] In advising the client of this potential delay, the practitioner should counsel the client that the processing time for the immigrant visa petition must also be considered.[438]

Foreign nationals who are beneficiaries of a labor certification application should not face the same level of difficulty, because, with the exception of Schedule A occupations,[439] that early-in-the-process application is filed with DOL and not with the DHS component agencies of USCIS and CBP. For a discussion of strategies and timing considerations of labor certification applications, see Volume 2: Chapter Two, "The Labor Certification Application."

---

[434] For a discussion of the immigrant visa petition classifications and visa retrogression, see Volume 2: Chapter Three, "The Immigrant Visa Petition."

[435] For a discussion of AC21 extensions, see Volume 1: Chapter Seven, "H-1B Visas and Status."

[436] DOS, "Visa Bulletin" http://www.travel.state.gov/visa/en/law-and-policy/bulletin.html.

[437] *Id.*

[438] USCIS, "How Do I Use the Premium Processing Service?" (Oct. 25, 2015), https://www.uscis.gov/forms/how-do-i-use-premium-processing-service.

[439] 20 CFR §656.15(a).

Copyright © 2017. American Immigration Lawyers Association. All rights reserved.

D. H-1B Change of Status Petitions

The client may decide to apply for H-1B change of status for several reasons. First, the client may anticipate that the immigrant visa petition will be classified as EB-3, and experience has shown that the permanent residence process for such a foreign national born in a country subject to immigrant visa retrogression very frequently takes five years or longer, as discussed above, and this is much longer than the maximum term of TN admission of three years. There are two related points to consider: Obtaining an H-1B change of status will grant the foreign national a new "clock" of six years of H-1B time,[440] for which only time of physical presence in the United States is counted,[441] and a foreign national in H-1B status is eligible for AC21 extensions until the foreign national obtains permanent residence.[442]

Second, the foreign national may need to travel extensively outside the United States for business or personal reasons. As discussed above, international travel triggers inquiry into the foreign national's nonimmigrant intent and qualification for "temporary entry" in TN status; if the foreign national cannot remain in the United States while the immigrant visa petition is pending and/or until an immigrant visa number is available and an application to adjust status can be filed, then H-1B change of status is recommended, unless the client feels comfortable relying upon the guidance discussed above.

Third, the foreign national may have spent many years in the United States in TN status, such that his or her ability to demonstrate nonimmigrant intent is of concern. For example, the foreign national may be the beneficiary of a labor certification application. Although this application is filed with DOL and not USCIS, if the immigration inspector or consular official asks the foreign national about whether he or she is pursuing permanent residence or is the beneficiary of such an application, the admission or visa may be denied, despite the CBP guidance discussed above. Experience has shown that these questions are more frequently asked of foreign nationals who have held nonimmigrant status for a number of years. The drawbacks to requesting H-1B change of status are discussed above. The practitioner should discuss all relevant points with the client, with particular attention to the cost and timing issues of H-1B petitions.

In the event that the underlying TN status will not expire on or around October 1 of a given year, the practitioner should also strategize with the client regarding the timing of the H-1B petition and how the foreign national will maintain TN status and enter the United States in H-1B status. For example, if the TN petition will expire

---

[440] INA §214(g)(4).

[441] USCIS, M. Aytes, "Procedures for Calculating Maximum Period of Stay Regarding the Limitations on Admission for H-1B and L-1 Nonimmigrants (AFM Update AD 05-21)" (Oct. 21, 2005), AILA Doc. No. 05110363.

[442] The American Competitiveness in the Twenty-First Century Act of 2000 (AC21) §106(a), Pub. Law 106-313 (enacted Oct. 18, 2000).

Copyright © 2017. American Immigration Lawyers Association. All rights reserved.

before October 1, then the practitioner should request notification to the consulate or port of entry and should not request change of status and extension on the Form I-129. Then, if an H-1B visa number is awarded, the foreign national may depart the United States, apply for an H-1B visa if necessary, and seek admission in H-1B status on or after October 1.[443] If an H-1B visa number is not awarded, then there should be no impact on the foreign national's current TN status, and the foreign national could apply to obtain a TN extension from USCIS or apply at a port of entry or U.S. consulate for TN admission or visa to cover the time between expiration of the current TN status and availability of the H-1B petition.

Requesting notification to the port of entry or U.S. consulate is also helpful in postponing the initial date of admission in H-1B status. If change of status and extension is requested, the H-1B time starts upon approval of the H-1B petition; as a practical matter, this start date must be in the first week of October, or the H-1B petition would not be eligible for the lottery, as H-1B petitions may be filed no more than 180 days before the requested start date, and the H-1B lottery includes only petitions filed during the first five business days of April.[444] In contrast, if change of status and extension is not requested, then the initial date of H-1B admission, which is used to calculate the six-year maximum time limitation for H-1B nonimmigrants, will be whenever the foreign national is physically admitted to the United States.

This admission may be sought at any time during the validity period of the H-1B petition, such as after the filing of an application to adjust status or an application for an immigrant visa, or even after filing an immigrant visa petition, when the foreign national should not seek TN admission because it could be denied for lack of nonimmigrant intent, as discussed above. This is a particularly important concern for foreign nationals whose immigrant visa petitions are classified as EB-3, as even the smallest durations of time may keep the U.S. employer from having to file an AC21 extension. Having the option of filing an AC21 extension is certainly helpful, but the client should appreciate avoiding the costs of filing and legal fees for H-1B extensions.

Conversely, if the foreign national has no international travel plans, if the employer and/or foreign national do not wish to bear the costs of international travel and visa applications (if applicable), or if the foreign national is likely to obtain permanent residence within the six-year maximum time limitation for H-1B nonimmigrants, then requesting H-1B change of status and extension may be appropriate.

---

[443] INA §214(g); 73 Fed. Reg. 15389 (Mar. 24, 2008).
[444] 73 Fed. Reg. 15389 (Mar. 24, 2008).

Copyright © 2017. American Immigration Lawyers Association. All rights reserved.

INTERNATIONAL ENTREPRENEUR RULE[1]

I. Introduction and Background

On January 17, 2017, the Department of Homeland Security (DHS) finalized its "International Entrepreneur Rule,"[2] with an effective date of July 17, 2017. The regulation, under the authority of Immigration and Nationality Act (INA) §212(d)(5), adds new provisions to 8 Code of Federal Regulations (CFR) permitting the use of parole for "entrepreneurs of start-up entities whose entry into the United States would provide a significant public benefit through the substantial and demonstrated potential for rapid business growth and job creation."[3] The rule is a product of November 2014 executive actions on immigration, particularly the DHS Secretary's November 21, 2014, direction to U.S. Citizenship and Immigration Services (USCIS) to "propose a program that will permit DHS to grant parole status, on a case-by-case basis, to inventors, researchers, and founders of start-up enterprises who may not yet qualify for a national interest waiver, but who have been awarded substantial U.S. investor financing or otherwise hold the promise of innovation and job creation through the development of new technologies or the pursuit of cutting-edge research."[4] DHS estimates that as many as 2,940 entrepreneurs could be eligible for parole under this program on an annual basis.[5]

II. Requirements for an Initial Grant of Parole

An entrepreneur may be considered for parole if he or she demonstrates that parole "will provide a significant public benefit to the United States based on his or her role as an entrepreneur of a start-up entity."[6] To do so, applicants must demonstrate that they:

- Meet the definition of "entrepreneur" and "start-up entity"; and
- Establish that the entity has:

---

[1] Adapted and updated from AILA's "Summary of Proposed International Entrepreneur Rule" (Sept. 6, 2016), AILA Doc. No. 16090603. **Editor's Note:** As of July 5, 2017, DHS is considering a delay in implementation of the rule.

[2] 82 Fed. Reg. 5238 (Jan. 17, 2017).

[3] 81 Fed. Reg. 60130 (Aug. 31, 2016) (proposed rule). INA §212(d)(5) provides the Secretary of Homeland Security with discretionary authority to grant parole to individuals on a case-by-case basis for "urgent humanitarian reasons" or "significant public benefit."

[4] DHS, "Policies Supporting U.S. Businesses and High-Skilled Workers," (Nov. 21, 2014), AILA Doc. No. 14112009.

[5] 82 Fed. Reg. 5238, 5242 (Jan. 17, 2017).

[6] 8 CFR §212.19(b)(2)(i).

Copyright © 2017. American Immigration Lawyers Association. All rights reserved.

- o Received within 18 months preceding the filing the application a qualified investment of at least $250,000 from one or more qualified investors; or

- o Received within 18 months preceding the filing of the application at least $100,000 through one or more qualified government awards or grants.[7]

An individual who meets the definition of "entrepreneur" and "start-up entity," but only partially meets one or both of the criteria for amount of investment, may still qualify if he or she can provide "other reliable and compelling evidence" of the entity's substantial potential for rapid growth and job creation.[8] DHS has not defined the type of evidence that might be deemed "reliable and compelling," but notes that such evidence would need to be "particularly persuasive."[9] DHS also notes that the necessary amount and weight of such evidence will depend on the degree to which the applicant meets one or both of the capital investment or government funding criteria—the lower the amount of investment, the higher the quantum of evidence needed.

In order to meet the definition of "entrepreneur," the applicant must possess "a substantial ownership interest in a start-up entity" and have "a central and active role in the operations of that entity, such that [he or she] is well-positioned, due to his or her knowledge, skills, or experience, to substantially assist the entity with the growth and success of its business."[10] To be considered "substantial," the applicant's ownership interest in the start-up entity must be at least 10 percent at the time of adjudication of the initial parole request and at least five percent at the time a re-parole is adjudicated.[11] In addition, the entrepreneur must continuously maintain at least a five percent ownership interest in the entity throughout the duration of the initial parole. The ownership percentage can continue to be reduced through the re-parole period, but some ownership interest must be maintained.[12]

In order to meet the definition of "start-up entity," the entity must be a "U.S. business entity" that was formed within the five years immediately preceding the filing of the initial parole application, must have lawfully done business "during any period of operation since its formation," and must have "substantial potential for rapid growth and job creation."[13] A "U.S. business entity" is any corporation, limited

---

[7] 8 CFR §212.19(b)(2)(ii).

[8] 8 CFR §212.19(b)(2)(iii).

[9] 81 Fed. Reg. 60130, 60141–60142 (Aug. 31, 2016).

[10] 8 CFR §212.19(a)(1).

[11] *Id.*

[12] *Id.*

[13] 8 CFR §212.19(a)(2). An entity may also "be considered recently formed if it was created within the 5 years immediately preceding the receipt of the relevant grant(s), award(s), or investment(s)."

Copyright © 2017. American Immigration Lawyers Association. All rights reserved.

liability company (LLC), partnership, or other entity organized under federal or state law that conducts business in the United States and is not an investment vehicle.[14] In other words, the entity must provide or seek to provide good or services.[15] Entities that will not qualify are businesses "with limited growth potential created by entrepreneurs for the sole or primary purpose of providing income to the entrepreneur and his or her family."[16]

A "qualified investment" is as an investment made in good faith of lawfully derived capital that is a purchase from the start-up entity of "equity, convertible debt, or other security convertible into its equity commonly used in financing" in the business's industry. Investments made by the entrepreneur or his or her parent, spouse, sibling, or child do not qualify, nor do investments made by a corporation, LLC, partnership, or other entity where the entrepreneur or his or her parent, spouse, sibling, or child has any direct or indirect ownership interest.[17]

A "qualified investor" is defined as a U.S. citizen (USC) or lawful permanent resident (LPR) or an organization located in the United States that operates through a legal entity organized under U.S. federal or state law, that is majority owned and controlled by USCs and/or LPRs.[18] In addition, the investor must, within the past five years:

- Have made investments in start-up entities in exchange for equity or convertible debt in at least three separate calendar years totaling no less than $600,000; and

- Subsequent to such investment, at least two such entities each created at least five qualified jobs or generated at least $500,000 in revenue with an average annualized revenue growth of at least 20 percent.[19]

A "qualified job" is defined as full-time employment (paid employment, at least 35 hours per week, may not combine part-time positions) located in the United States that has been filled for at least one year by a USC, LPR, or other immigrant lawfully authorized to be employed in the United States and who is not an independent contractor, or an entrepreneur of the start-up, or the parent, spouse, sibling, or child of such entrepreneur.[20]

---

[14] 8 CFR §212.19(a)(9).

[15] 81 Fed. Reg. 60130, 60137 (Aug. 31, 2016).

[16] 82 Fed. Reg. 5238, 5258 (Jan. 17, 2017).

[17] 8 CFR §212.19(a)(4).

[18] 8 CFR §212.19(a)(5). Excluded from the definition of "qualified investor" are individuals or organizations that have been found to have violated securities laws.

[19] *Id.*

[20] 8 CFR §212.19(a)(6)-(8).

Copyright © 2017. American Immigration Lawyers Association. All rights reserved.

A "qualified government award or grant" is an award or grant "for economic development, research and development, or job creation (or other similar monetary award typically given to start-up entities) made by a federal, state, or local government entity … that regularly provides such awards or grants to start-up entities." Contractual commitments for goods and services are excluded, as are grants or awards from foreign entities.[21]

III. Application Process for an Initial Grant of Parole

An applicant requesting an initial grant of parole would file Form I-941, Application for Entrepreneur Parole, along with supporting evidence, a biometrics fee, and a filing fee of $1,200.[22] Applicants who file while in the United States will have biometrics collected at an Application Support Center. Applicants who are outside the United States will have biometrics collected overseas, after parole is authorized but before the travel document is issued.[23]

Though not included in the text of the regulation itself, the Supplementary Information of the proposed rule included a useful list of evidence that may be submitted, in addition to evidence of the capital investment or government funding criteria, to meet the standards for definition of "entrepreneur" and "start-up entity." Such evidence may include:

- Evidence of capital investments from qualified investors, or government awards or grants, other than those relied on to satisfy proposed 8 CFR §212.19(b)(2)(i)(B);

- Letters from relevant government entities, qualified investors, or established business associations with knowledge of the entity's research, products, or services and/or the applicant's knowledge, skills, or experience that would advance the entity's business;

- Newspaper articles or other similar evidence that the applicant or entity has received significant attention or recognition;

- Evidence that the applicant or entity has been recently invited to participate in, is currently participating in, or has graduated from one or more established and reputable start-up accelerators;

- Evidence of significant revenue generation and growth in revenue;

- Patent awards or other documents indicating that the entity or applicant is focused on developing new technologies or cutting-edge research;

- Evidence that the applicant has played an active and central role in the success of prior start-up entities;

---

[21] 8 CFR §212.19(a)(3).

[22] 8 CFR §103.7(b)(1)(i)(KKK).

[23] 8 CFR §212.19(e); 82 Fed. Reg. 5238, 5280 (Jan. 17, 2017).

Copyright © 2017. American Immigration Lawyers Association. All rights reserved.

- Degrees or other documentation indicating that the applicant has knowledge, skills, or experience that would significantly advance the entity's business;

- Payroll, bookkeeping, salary, bank records. or other documents related to jobs created prior to filing the request for parole; and

- Any other relevant, probative, and credible evidence indicating the entity's potential for growth and/or the applicant's ability to advance the entity's business in the United States.[24]

For purposes of documenting the required ownership interest (10 percent for initial parole), the applicant should provide copies of legal or financial documents, "such as formation and organizational documents, equity certificates, equity ledgers, ownership schedules, or capitalization tables."[25]

IV. Adjudication of Initial Parole Application

In adjudicating the application, USCIS will "consider and weigh all evidence including any derogatory evidence" such as criminal activity or national security concerns, and may deny parole as a matter of discretion, even if the regulatory criteria are met.[26]

Initial parole may be granted for up to 30 months,[27] although DHS retains discretion to provide a shorter period of parole where appropriate.[28] Moreover, notwithstanding USCIS approval of the parole application, U.S. Customs and Border Protection (CBP) retains the authority to deny parole or to modify the parole period when the individual appears at the port of entry.[29] Parolees will be issued a multiple entry travel document to permit travel for the duration of the parole period.[30] CBP will assign a "PE-1" code of admission to entrepreneur parolees.[31] Once paroled, the entrepreneur parolee would be authorized for employment with the start-up entity incident to status.[32] The entrepreneur is not authorized for employment with any other entity.[33]

---

[24] 81 Fed. Reg. 60130, 60138 (Aug. 31, 2016).

[25] 81 Fed. Reg. 60130, 60139 (Aug. 31, 2016).

[26] 8 CFR §212.19(d)(1).

[27] 8 CFR §212.19(d)(2)

[28] 81 Fed. Reg. 60130, 60144 (Aug. 31, 2016).

[29] Id.

[30] Id.

[31] 81 Fed. Reg. 60130, 60145 (Aug. 31, 2016).

[32] 8 CFR §212.19(g).

[33] 8 CFR §274a.12(b)(37).

Copyright © 2017. American Immigration Lawyers Association. All rights reserved.

The Supplementary Information section of the final rule states that parole in place will not be available to entrepreneurs present in the United States.[34] Instead, the regulatory language indicates that a person approved for parole would need to "appear at a port of entry to be granted parole."[35] Moreover, DHS notes that a person lawfully admitted in a nonimmigrant status who is granted parole would be required to depart and apply for parole at a port of entry "as parole will not involve any direct change from other nonimmigrant status."[36]

V. Requirements for Re-Parole

In general, the parolee may be considered for re-parole if he or she demonstrates that a grant of parole will continue to provide a significant public benefit to the United States based on his or her role as an entrepreneur of a start-up entity.[37] To do so, applicants must demonstrate:

- That the foreign national continues to meet the definition of "entrepreneur" and the entity continues to meet the definition of "start-up entity"; and

- The entity has:

  o Received at least $500,000 in qualified investments, qualified government grants or rewards, or a combination of such funding during the initial parole period;

  o Created at least five qualified jobs with the start-up entity during the initial parole period; or

  o Reached at least $500,000 in revenue and averaged 20 percent annual growth during the initial parole period.[38]

For purposes of re-parole, the entrepreneur will be considered to possess a substantial ownership interest if he or she maintains at least a 10 percent ownership interest in the start-up entity during the initial parole period, and at least five percent at the time the re-parole is adjudicated.[39] In addition, the entrepreneur must continuously maintain at least a five percent ownership interest in the entity throughout the duration of the initial parole. The ownership percentage can continue to be reduced through the re-parole period, but some ownership interest must be maintained.[40]

---

[34] 82 Fed. Reg. 5238, 5265 (Jan. 17, 2017).

[35] 8 CFR §212.19(d)(2).

[36] 81 Fed. Reg. 60130, 60160. (Aug. 31, 2016).

[37] 8 CFR §212.19(c)(2)(i).

[38] 8 CFR §212.19(c)(2)(ii). See above for definitions of highlighted terms.

[39] 8 CFR §212.19(a)(1).

[40] *Id.*

Copyright © 2017. American Immigration Lawyers Association. All rights reserved.

A person who continues to meet the definition of "entrepreneur" and whose entity continues to meet the definition of "start-up entity," but who only partially meets one or all of the criteria for investment, may still qualify by providing "other reliable and compelling evidence" of the start-up entity's substantial potential for rapid growth and job creation.[41]

Beginning 90 days prior to the expiration of the initial grant of parole, the entrepreneur may submit a request for re-parole based on the same start-up entity by filing Form I-941 with all required fees (including biometrics fee) and supporting documents.[42] Re-parole may be granted for one additional period for up to 30 months.[43] If the parolee is in the United States when re-parole is approved, parole is automatically extended. If the parolee outside the United States, the parolee must appear at a port of entry to be granted re-parole.[44]

Employment authorization will be automatically extended for 240 days from the date of expiration of the initial parole period, or until USCIS makes a decision on the re-parole application, whichever is sooner, when a request for re-parole is timely filed by the entrepreneur.[45]

VI. Spouses and Minor Children

The spouse and minor children of the parolee must individually apply for parole by completing Form I-131, Application for Travel Document, and including evidence of the qualifying relationship to the entrepreneur as well as the I-131 filing fee and a biometrics fee.[46] Parole for spouses and children will also be considered on a case-by-case basis and may be denied as a matter of discretion.[47] The period of parole granted for the spouse and children may be no longer than the period of parole granted to the entrepreneur.[48]

After having been paroled into the United States (no concurrent filing), the spouse is eligible for employment authorization but must apply on Form I-765, Application for Employment Authorization, and include evidence of eligibility and relationship to the entrepreneur. Children are not permitted employment authorization.[49]

VII. Obligations and Limitations on Parole for Entrepreneurs

---

[41] 8 CFR §212.19(c)(2)(iii).

[42] 8 CFR §212.19(c)(1). The "90-day rule" is set forth in the instructions to Form I-941.

[43] 8 CFR §212.19(d)(3).

[44] *Id.*

[45] 8 CFR §274a.12(b)(37).

[46] 8 CFR §212.19(h)(1).

[47] 81 Fed. Reg. 60130, 60144 (Aug. 31, 2016).

[48] 8 CFR §212.19(h)(2).

[49] 8 CFR §§212.19(h)(3) and (4), and 274a.12(c)(34).

Copyright © 2017. American Immigration Lawyers Association. All rights reserved.

The parolee must maintain household income greater than 400 percent of the federal poverty line for his or her household size.[50] USCIS may impose "other such reasonable conditions" on the parolee in its discretion and may request proof of compliance with any such condition at any time.[51] Violation of any condition, including the household income condition, may lead to termination of parole.[52] USCIS may ask the applicant to verify his or her income at the time of application for re-parole, or upon notification to USCIS of a material change.[53] The parolee must "immediately" report any material changes to USCIS. If the entrepreneur continues to be employed by the entity and maintains a qualifying ownership interest, material changes are reported to USCIS by filing a new Form I-941 with fee (no biometrics fee) and supporting documentation of the material change. If the parolee no longer owns a qualifying ownership interest or ceases to be employed by the start-up entity, the parolee must notify USCIS of such in writing.[54]

"Material change" is defined as any change in facts that could reasonably affect the determination as to whether the parolee provides or continues to provide a significant public benefit to the United States. This includes, but is not limited to:

- Any criminal charge, conviction, no contest plea, or other criminal judicial determination concerning the entrepreneur or the entity;

- Any complaint, settlement, judgment, or other determination concerning the entrepreneur or entity in a judicial or administrative action brought by a government entity, or by a private individual or organization (other than proceedings involving claims for damages not exceeding 10 percent of the assets of the entrepreneur or entity);

- The sale or disposition of all or substantially all of the entity's assets;

- The liquidation, dissolution, or cessation of operations;

- The filing of a bankruptcy petition by or against the entity; or

- Any significant change to the entrepreneur's role in ownership and control, or any other significant changes in ownership and control of the entity.[55]

No more than three entrepreneurs from the same entity may be granted parole, and no more than five years of parole may be granted to any single entrepreneur based on the same entity.[56] There is no right to appeal the denial of parole, nor any right to a

---

[50] 8 CFR §212.19(i).

[51] Id.

[52] Id.

[53] 81 Fed. Reg. 60130, 60143 (Aug. 31, 2016).

[54] 8 CFR §212.19(j).

[55] 8 CFR §212.19(a)(10).

[56] 8 CFR §212.19(f).

Copyright © 2017. American Immigration Lawyers Association. All rights reserved.

motion to reopen or reconsider, though DHS retains its authority to reopen or reconsider a case on its own motion (sua sponte).[57]

DHS may terminate parole at any time without notice or opportunity to respond if it determines that parole no longer provides a significant public benefit.[58] Parole is automatically terminated without notice upon expiration of parole (unless a re-parole request is timely filed), if USCIS receives written notice from the parolee that he or she is no longer employed by the entity or no longer holds at least qualifying ownership interest. Parole of spouse and children is also automatically terminated, as is any Employment Authorization Document (EAD) of the spouse.[59]

USCIS may issue a notice of intent to terminate if it believes that the facts or information contained in the parole request were not true and accurate, the parolee failed to timely notify USCIS of a material change, the parolee is no longer employed in a central and active role with the entity or ceases to possess a qualifying ownership interest, the foreign national otherwise violated the terms and conditions of parole, or parole was erroneously granted.[60] The parolee will be provided 30 days to respond. Failure to timely respond will result in termination of parole. No appeal or motion to reopen and/or reconsider is available on a decision to terminate, except sua sponte.[61]

VIII. Miscellaneous

Investment and revenue amounts will be automatically adjusted every three years by the Consumer Price Index and posted on the USCIS website. Adjustments will apply to all applications filed on or after the beginning of the fiscal year for which the adjustment is made.[62]

The entrepreneur's valid foreign passport with I-94 Arrival/Departure record containing an unexpired "PE-1" endorsement would be acceptable evidence of identity and employment authorization for entrepreneur parolees.[63]

---

[57] 8 CFR §212.19(d)(4).

[58] 8 CFR §212.19(k)(1).

[59] 8 CFR §212.19(k)(2).

[60] 8 CFR §212.19(k)(3).

[61] 8 CFR §212.19(k)(4).

[62] 8 CFR §212.19(l).

[63] 8 CFR §274a.2(b)(1)(v)(A)(5).

Copyright © 2017. American Immigration Lawyers Association. All rights reserved.

TABLES OF CITATIONS
VOLUME 1
NONIMMIGRANT CONCEPTS

TABLE OF DECISIONS

Alphabetization is letter-by-letter (e.g., "Masters" precedes "Master Video").
References are to volume and page number.

Copyright © 2017. American Immigration Lawyers Association. All rights reserved.

Copyright © 2017. American Immigration Lawyers Association. All rights reserved.

Copyright © 2017. American Immigration Lawyers Association. All rights reserved.

Copyright © 2017. American Immigration Lawyers Association. All rights reserved.

Copyright © 2017. American Immigration Lawyers Association. All rights reserved.

Copyright © 2017. American Immigration Lawyers Association. All rights reserved.

Copyright © 2017. American Immigration Lawyers Association. All rights reserved.

Copyright © 2017. American Immigration Lawyers Association. All rights reserved.

Copyright © 2017. American Immigration Lawyers Association. All rights reserved.

A

Copyright © 2017. American Immigration Lawyers Association. All rights reserved.

Copyright © 2017. American Immigration Lawyers Association. All rights reserved.

B

Copyright © 2017. American Immigration Lawyers Association. All rights reserved.

Copyright © 2017. American Immigration Lawyers Association. All rights reserved.

Copyright © 2017. American Immigration Lawyers Association. All rights reserved.

Copyright © 2017. American Immigration Lawyers Association. All rights reserved.

D

Copyright © 2017. American Immigration Lawyers Association. All rights reserved.

E

Copyright © 2017. American Immigration Lawyers Association. All rights reserved.

F

Copyright © 2017. American Immigration Lawyers Association. All rights reserved.

Copyright © 2017. American Immigration Lawyers Association. All rights reserved.

H

Copyright © 2017. American Immigration Lawyers Association. All rights reserved.

Copyright © 2017. American Immigration Lawyers Association. All rights reserved.

I

J

Copyright © 2017. American Immigration Lawyers Association. All rights reserved.

K

Copyright © 2017. American Immigration Lawyers Association. All rights reserved.

L

Copyright © 2017. American Immigration Lawyers Association. All rights reserved.

Copyright © 2017. American Immigration Lawyers Association. All rights reserved.

M

Copyright © 2017. American Immigration Lawyers Association. All rights reserved.

Copyright © 2017. American Immigration Lawyers Association. All rights reserved.

N

Copyright © 2017. American Immigration Lawyers Association. All rights reserved.

O

Copyright © 2017. American Immigration Lawyers Association. All rights reserved.

Copyright © 2017. American Immigration Lawyers Association. All rights reserved.

Copyright © 2017. American Immigration Lawyers Association. All rights reserved.

Copyright © 2017. American Immigration Lawyers Association. All rights reserved.

Copyright © 2017. American Immigration Lawyers Association. All rights reserved.

Copyright © 2017. American Immigration Lawyers Association. All rights reserved.

Copyright © 2017. American Immigration Lawyers Association. All rights reserved.

T

Copyright © 2017. American Immigration Lawyers Association. All rights reserved.

U

Copyright © 2017. American Immigration Lawyers Association. All rights reserved.

V

Copyright © 2017. American Immigration Lawyers Association. All rights reserved.

Copyright © 2017. American Immigration Lawyers Association. All rights reserved.

Copyright © 2017. American Immigration Lawyers Association. All rights reserved.

TABLE OF INA CITATIONS

References are to volume and page number.

IMMIGRATION AND NATIONALITY ACT (INA)

Copyright © 2017. American Immigration Lawyers Association. All rights reserved.

Copyright © 2017. American Immigration Lawyers Association. All rights reserved.

Copyright © 2017. American Immigration Lawyers Association. All rights reserved.

Copyright © 2017. American Immigration Lawyers Association. All rights reserved.

Copyright © 2017. American Immigration Lawyers Association. All rights reserved.

Copyright © 2017. American Immigration Lawyers Association. All rights reserved.

Copyright © 2017. American Immigration Lawyers Association. All rights reserved.

Copyright © 2017. American Immigration Lawyers Association. All rights reserved.

Copyright © 2017. American Immigration Lawyers Association. All rights reserved.

Copyright © 2017. American Immigration Lawyers Association. All rights reserved.

TABLE OF U.S. CODE CITATIONS

References are to volume and page number.

UNITED STATES CODE (USC)

Copyright © 2017. American Immigration Lawyers Association. All rights reserved.

Copyright © 2017. American Immigration Lawyers Association. All rights reserved.

TABLE OF CFR CITATIONS

References are to volume and page number.

CODE OF FEDERAL REGULATIONS (CFR)

Copyright © 2017. American Immigration Lawyers Association. All rights reserved.

Copyright © 2017. American Immigration Lawyers Association. All rights reserved.

Copyright © 2017. American Immigration Lawyers Association. All rights reserved.

Copyright © 2017. American Immigration Lawyers Association. All rights reserved.

Copyright © 2017. American Immigration Lawyers Association. All rights reserved.

Copyright © 2017. American Immigration Lawyers Association. All rights reserved.

Copyright © 2017. American Immigration Lawyers Association. All rights reserved.

Copyright © 2017. American Immigration Lawyers Association. All rights reserved.

Copyright © 2017. American Immigration Lawyers Association. All rights reserved.

Copyright © 2017. American Immigration Lawyers Association. All rights reserved.

Copyright © 2017. American Immigration Lawyers Association. All rights reserved.

Copyright © 2017. American Immigration Lawyers Association. All rights reserved.

Copyright © 2017. American Immigration Lawyers Association. All rights reserved.

Copyright © 2017. American Immigration Lawyers Association. All rights reserved.

Copyright © 2017. American Immigration Lawyers Association. All rights reserved.

Copyright © 2017. American Immigration Lawyers Association. All rights reserved.

Copyright © 2017. American Immigration Lawyers Association. All rights reserved.

Copyright © 2017. American Immigration Lawyers Association. All rights reserved.

Copyright © 2017. American Immigration Lawyers Association. All rights reserved.

Copyright © 2017. American Immigration Lawyers Association. All rights reserved.

Copyright © 2017. American Immigration Lawyers Association. All rights reserved.

Copyright © 2017. American Immigration Lawyers Association. All rights reserved.

Copyright © 2017. American Immigration Lawyers Association. All rights reserved.

Copyright © 2017. American Immigration Lawyers Association. All rights reserved.

Copyright © 2017. American Immigration Lawyers Association. All rights reserved.

Copyright © 2017. American Immigration Lawyers Association. All rights reserved.

Copyright © 2017. American Immigration Lawyers Association. All rights reserved.

Copyright © 2017. American Immigration Lawyers Association. All rights reserved.

Copyright © 2017. American Immigration Lawyers Association. All rights reserved.

Copyright © 2017. American Immigration Lawyers Association. All rights reserved.

Copyright © 2017. American Immigration Lawyers Association. All rights reserved.

Copyright © 2017. American Immigration Lawyers Association. All rights reserved.

Copyright © 2017. American Immigration Lawyers Association. All rights reserved.

Copyright © 2017. American Immigration Lawyers Association. All rights reserved.

Copyright © 2017. American Immigration Lawyers Association. All rights reserved.

Copyright © 2017. American Immigration Lawyers Association. All rights reserved.

Copyright © 2017. American Immigration Lawyers Association. All rights reserved.

Copyright © 2017. American Immigration Lawyers Association. All rights reserved.

Copyright © 2017. American Immigration Lawyers Association. All rights reserved.

TABLE OF FAM CITATIONS

References are to volume and page number.

Copyright © 2017. American Immigration Lawyers Association. All rights reserved.

Copyright © 2017. American Immigration Lawyers Association. All rights reserved.

Copyright © 2017. American Immigration Lawyers Association. All rights reserved.

Copyright © 2017. American Immigration Lawyers Association. All rights reserved.

Copyright © 2017. American Immigration Lawyers Association. All rights reserved.

Copyright © 2017. American Immigration Lawyers Association. All rights reserved.

Copyright © 2017. American Immigration Lawyers Association. All rights reserved.

Copyright © 2017. American Immigration Lawyers Association. All rights reserved.

Copyright © 2017. American Immigration Lawyers Association. All rights reserved.

TABLE OF USCIS POLICY MANUAL CITATIONS

References are to volume and page number.

Copyright © 2017. American Immigration Lawyers Association. All rights reserved.

TABLE OF AFM CITATIONS

References are to volume and page number.

ADJUDICATOR'S FIELD MANUAL (AFM)

Copyright © 2017. American Immigration Lawyers Association. All rights reserved.

Copyright © 2017. American Immigration Lawyers Association. All rights reserved.

Copyright © 2017. American Immigration Lawyers Association. All rights reserved.

Copyright © 2017. American Immigration Lawyers Association. All rights reserved.

Copyright © 2017. American Immigration Lawyers Association. All rights reserved.

TABLE OF IFM CITATIONS

References are to volume and page number.

INSPECTOR'S FIELD MANUAL (IFM)

Copyright © 2017. American Immigration Lawyers Association. All rights reserved.

TABLE OF FEDERAL REGISTER CITATIONS

References are to volume and page number.

FEDERAL REGISTER (Fed. Reg.)

48 Fed. Reg.
41142 (Sept. 14, 1983) *1:* 932

51 Fed. Reg.
44266 (Dec. 9, 1986) *1:* 174, 201, 202, 204, 205, 206, 1209

52 Fed. Reg.
5738 (Feb. 26, 1987) *1:* 932, 949, 950, 954, 957, 959, 961, 966, 988
5740 (Feb. 26, 1987) *1:* 957

55 Fed. Reg.
2606 (Jan. 26, 1990) *1:* 511, 525, 526, 527, 528, 535, 537, 539, 540, 541, 543, 544, 572, 583, 663, 763, 803, 804, 807, 814, 988

56 Fed. Reg.
31553 (July 11, 1991) *1:* 949
60897 (Nov. 29, 1991) *2:* 421, 474
60899 (Nov. 29, 1991) *2:* 421

57 Fed. Reg.
1316 (Jan. 13, 1992) *1:* 429
1319 (Jan. 13, 1992) *1:* 429

58 Fed. Reg.
15180 (Mar. 19, 1993) *1:* 838, 839, 847
40024 (July 26, 1993) *1:* 168, 184
58982 (Nov. 5, 1993) *1:* 182
69205 (Dec. 30, 1993) *1:* 1175, 1184, 1201, 1215, 1221, 1231, 1232

59 Fed. Reg.
41818 (Aug. 15, 1994) *1:* 1000, 1012, 1063
41832 (Aug. 15, 1994) *1:* 1012

60 Fed. Reg.
7216 (Feb. 7, 1995) *1:* 780
24757 (May 9, 1995) *1:* 321
29771 (June 6, 1995) *2:* 474

61 Fed. Reg.
29285 (June 10, 1996) *1:* 881

62 Fed. Reg.
67431 (Dec. 24, 1997) *1:* 886

63 Fed. Reg.
1331 (Jan. 9, 1998) *1:* 215, 968, 1188, 1218, 1219
42233 (Aug. 7, 1998) *1:* 890

Copyright © 2017. American Immigration Lawyers Association. All rights reserved.

64 Fed. Reg.

65 Fed. Reg.

66 Fed. Reg.

67 Fed. Reg.

68 Fed. Reg.

69 Fed. Reg.

Copyright © 2017. American Immigration Lawyers Association. All rights reserved.

Copyright © 2017. American Immigration Lawyers Association. All rights reserved.

Copyright © 2017. American Immigration Lawyers Association. All rights reserved.

Copyright © 2017. American Immigration Lawyers Association. All rights reserved.

Copyright © 2017. American Immigration Lawyers Association. All rights reserved.

TABLE OF IMMIGRATION-RELATED ACTS

References are to volume and page number.

ACTS

Copyright © 2017. American Immigration Lawyers Association. All rights reserved.

Copyright © 2017. American Immigration Lawyers Association. All rights reserved.

Copyright © 2017. American Immigration Lawyers Association. All rights reserved.

TABLE OF AGENCY COMMUNICATIONS

References are to volume and page number.

DEPARTMENT OF STATE CABLES

MEMORANDA AND LETTERS

Ahern, J.

Aleinikoff, T.

Ambrosia, M.

Aytes, M.

Copyright © 2017. American Immigration Lawyers Association. All rights reserved.

Copyright © 2017. American Immigration Lawyers Association. All rights reserved.

Creppy, M.

INS Memorandum, "Documentation and Registration of Nonimmigrant Students" (Sept. 21, 1993) *1:* 249

Legacy INS memorandum, "Documentation and Registration of Nonimmigrant Students" (Dec. 21, 1993) ... *1:* 165

Crocetti, L.

Legacy INS Memorandum, "Processing of 245(i) adjustment applications on or after the October 1, 1997, sunset date; Clarification regarding the applicability of certain new grounds of inadmissibility to 245(i) applications" (May 1, 1997) *1:* 133

Cronin, M.

INS Memorandum, "AFM Update: Revision of March 14, 2000 Dual Intent Memorandum (HQADJ 70/ 2.8.6, 2.8.12, 10.18)" (May 16, 2000) *1:* 386

INS Memorandum, "Standard Employment Authorization: Prohibition on Local Variations: Use of Receipts: Timely Adjudication: Interim Employment Authorization" (Mar. 10, 1998) *1:* 201

Legacy INS Memorandum, "Guidance for Processing Applicants under the North American Free Trade Agreement (NAFTA)" (July 24, 2000) *1:* 1184, 1186, 1193, 1208, 1209, 1210, 1212

USCIS Memorandum, "Adjustment of status under section 245(i), as amended by the Legal Immigration Family Equity Act Amendments of 2000" (Jan. 26, 2001) *2:* 736

Cronin, M. and W. Yates

Legacy INS Memorandum, "Educational and Experience Requirements for Employment-Based Second Preference (EB-2) Immigrants" (Mar. 20, 2000) *2:* 283, 285, 286, 491, 492, 493, 515

DeRocco, E. Stover

DOL Memorandum, "Revised Prevailing Wage Determination Guidance" (May 17, 2005) with attached "Policy Guidance" (May 9, 2005) *2:* 81, 132

Divine, R.

Letter correspondence (July 14, 2006) *1:* 139

USCIS Memorandum, "Legal and Discretionary Analysis for Adjudication" (May 3, 2006) *1:* 35, 39, 56

DOS Memorandum, "Tips for U.S. Visas: Employment Based Visas" (Feb. 1998) *2:* 445

Farmer, B.

DOL Field Memorandum 48-94, "Policy Guidance on Alien Labor Certification Issues" (May 16, 1994) *2:* 56

DOL Memorandum, "Standards to Determine Full Time Employment" (Apr. 13, 1993) *1:* 967

Field Memorandum No. 48-94, "Policy Guidance on Alien Labor Certification Issues" (May 16, 1994) *2:* 56, 145, 281, 282, 303, 313, 366

Forman, M.

ICE Memorandum, "Worksite Enforcement Strategy" (Apr. 30, 2009) *2:* 303

Hernandez, E.

Letter correspondence (June 7, 2001) *1:* 465

Letter correspondence (Mar. 9, 2004) *1:* 967

Hrinyak, M.

CBP Memorandum, "Expired Form I-551 Cards Presented at the POE" (July 26, 2004) *2:* 816

CBP Memorandum, "New Nonimmigrant Visa Classification: E-3" (Sept. 19, 2005) *1:* 393

CBP Memorandum, "New Photo Requirement for USCIS Issued Documents" (Aug. 4, 2004) *2:* 790

Copyright © 2017. American Immigration Lawyers Association. All rights reserved.

Copyright © 2017. American Immigration Lawyers Association. All rights reserved.

Norton, R.

Odom, E.

Odom, H.

Ohata, F.

Pearson, M.

Copyright © 2017. American Immigration Lawyers Association. All rights reserved.

Copyright © 2017. American Immigration Lawyers Association. All rights reserved.

Copyright © 2017. American Immigration Lawyers Association. All rights reserved.

Copyright © 2017. American Immigration Lawyers Association. All rights reserved.

Copyright © 2017. American Immigration Lawyers Association. All rights reserved.

OPERATION INSTRUCTIONS

FACT SHEETS

CBP Fact Sheets

DHS Fact Sheets

DOL Fact Sheets

ICE Fact Sheets

USCIS Fact Sheets

Copyright © 2017. American Immigration Lawyers Association. All rights reserved.

Copyright © 2017. American Immigration Lawyers Association. All rights reserved.

requirements for adjustment, cont'd
available IV number, *2:*668–70
eligibility for immigrant visa, *2:*658–68
failure to maintain lawful status, *2:*666–68
lawful status on date AOS application is filed, *2:*668
unauthorized employment and §245(k), *2:*661–66
inspection and admission or parole, *2:*657–58
security checks and biometrics
biometrics information, *2:*790–93
clearances, *2:*793–800
FBI fingerprint check, *2:*794
FBI name check, *2:*794–99
other agencies, *2:*800
transferring AOS applications between bases of eligibility, *2:*718–22
travel abroad pending AOS, *2:*713–18
advance parole. *See* Advance parole
H and L nonimmigrants, *1:*950–951, *2:*717–18
administrative appeals
of denials of adjustment applications, *2:*812–13
of denials of IV petitions
appeals to AAO, *2:*579–80
of denials of NIV petitions
appeals to AAO, *1:*61–65
H-1B denials, *1:*636–38
motions to reopen or reconsider, *1:*60–61, *1:*65–69
of LCA violations, appeals to ARB, *1:*490–91
of LC denials/revocations. *See* Labor certification, *subhead:* Form ETA-9089 procedure
of prevailing wage determination, *2:*132–34
administrative processing, *1:*83–86, *2:*645–46. *See also* Security checks
admission, *1:*95–119. *See also* Consular processing; Inadmissibility; *specific visa types*
deferred inspection, *1:*111–15
documents required, *1:*98–100
waiver of requirements, *1:*108–11
Form I-94 Arrival/Departure Record. *See* Forms
Traveler Redress Inquiry Program (DHS-TRIP), *1:*117
US-VISIT, *1:*149–58
VWP participants. *See* Visa Waiver Program
withdrawal of application for admission, *1:*115–17
advance parole, *2:*713–17
adjudication of application, *2:*777–81
preparing Form I-131, *2:*756–59
after-sales service professions
B-1 visas for Canadians and Mexicans, *1:*226–28
aging-out children, *2:*32–47
adjustment of status, *2:*706–07
effective-date issues, *2:*43–47
example, *2:*42–43

final decision or final determination, *2:*33
notification to NVC of any aging-out children, *2:*605
"sought to acquire," *2:*36–41
AIDS / HIV
B visas for HIV-positive individuals, *1:*211–12
no longer ground of inadmissibility, *2:*675–76
airline employees
B-1 visas, *1:*264
American Competitiveness in the 21st Century Act (AC21)
H-1B extensions, *1:*655–67
animal and plant breeders
TN visas and status, *1:*1211–12
appeals. *See* Administrative appeals
applications
for NIVs. *See* Nonimmigrant visas
Armed Forces of the U.S.
dependents of foreign national member of U.S. Armed Forces
B-2 visas for, *1:*266
arrival/departure record. *See* Forms, *subhead:* I-94
artists. *See* P visas
athletes. *See also* O visas; P visas
B-1 visas for team member and other athletes, *1:*263–64
B-2 visas for amateurs, *1:*248–49
EB-2 petitions for, *2:*522–24
H-2B status for professionals, *1:*777–78
labor certification, *2:*319
attestation. *See* Labor certification; Labor condition application
attorneys and agents
consulates and embassies, relationship with attorneys, *2:*636–37
Form G-28. *See* Forms
H-1B petitions filed by agents, *1:*571–73
H-2B petitions filed by agents, *1:*750–53
labor certification
new attorney or agent after supervised recruitment, *2:*253
role of attorneys and agents, *2:*240–42
for H-2B temporary LCs, *1:*747–48
litigation by B-1 visitors, *1:*177–78
P petitions filed by agents, *1:*1107–11
practice aids. *See* Practice aids
au pairs. *See* Household employees
Australian special occupation visas. *See* E-3 visas
authorized period of stay. *See* Unlawful presence

Copyright © 2017. American Immigration Lawyers Association. All rights reserved.

Copyright © 2017. American Immigration Lawyers Association. All rights reserved.

engineers, *2:*442–43
experience in teaching or research, *2:*436–37
internationally recognized as outstanding, demonstration of, *2:*418–36
    authorship of scholarly articles or books, *2:*433–36
    awards and prizes, *2:*420–23
    contributions to field, *2:*430–33
    judge of peers, participation as, *2:*427–30
    membership in associations requiring outstanding achievement, *2:*423–25
    publications about beneficiary, *2:*425–27
    testimonials and letters of endorsement, *2:*441–42
product designers, *2:*442–43
qualified employment offer, *2:*437–40
    as professor or teacher, *2:*438–39
    as researcher with private employer, *2:*440
    as researcher with university or college, *2:*439–40

EB-2 and EB-3 petitions, *2:*488–516
athletes, EB-2 petitions for, *2:*522–24
checklists, *2:*489
EB-2, description of, *2:*490–95
    degree requirement, *2:*490–91
        equivalency in experience, *2:*490–91
    vs. EB-3, *2:*508–16
    exceptional ability, *2:*516–24
        distinguished from "extraordinary ability," *2:*521
        "in the sciences, arts, or business," *2:*517–19
        "in the sciences or arts" (Sch. A, Group II), *2:*519–22
    professional position, *2:*492–95
    progressive experience, *2:*491–92
EB-3, description of, *2:*495–97
    vs. EB-2, *2:*508–16
    filing dates, *2:*669
experience prior to master's degree completion, *2:*515–16
labor certification, *2:*497–502. *See also* Labor certification
    LC application as basis for IV classification, *2:*283–87
    new certification, when required, *2:*500–01
    revocation and invalidation, *2:*501–02
national interest waivers (NIWs)
    post-*NYSDOT* clinical-physician case studies, *2:*480
three-year bachelor's degrees, *2:*512–15

eligibility for benefits
establishment of, *1:*16–19

email delivery of audit letters, *2:*228

emergency boilermakers
H-2B visas, special considerations, *1:*780–81

Employ American Workers Act (EAWA)
TARP recipients, *1:*450

employees. *See specific type of employee and specific type of visa*

employment authorization. *See* Adjustment of status; *specific visa type*

engineers
EB-1 outstanding professor/researcher petitions, *2:*442–43
TN visas and status, *1:*1210–11

entertainers. *See also* O visas; P visas
B-1 visas for professional entertainers, *1:*261–62
B-2 visas for amateurs, *1:*248–49
H-2B status for entertainers without international or national renown, *1:*778–80

equivalencies. *See* Degrees, credentials, licensure, and equivalencies

ESTA (Electronic System for Travel Authorization)
for Visa Waiver Program participants, *1:*290–98

evidence. *See also specific visa types*
best evidence rule
    E visa applications, *1:*322
    USCIS's reliance on, *1:*37–39

exceptional ability
distinguished from "extraordinary ability," *2:*521
EB-2 petitions, *2:*516–24
PERM Sch. A Group II professions, *2:*519–22

exchange visitors
J visas. *See* J visas
special education exchange visitor program. *See* H-3 visas

exclusion grounds. *See* Inadmissibility

executives. *See* EB-1 multinational manager/executive petitions; L-1 visas

expedited processing, *1:*30–32. *See also* Premium processing

expedited removal, *1:*115–17

export control, *1:*158–62
federal regulations (ITAR and EAR), *1:*158–59

extension of status. *See also specific visa types*
nonimmigrant visas, *1:*119–28
    common issues, *1:*124–28
    Form I-539, *1:*123–24
    nunc pro tunc extensions, *1:*127–28

extraordinary ability
distinguished from "exceptional ability," *2:*521
IVs. *See* EB-1 extraordinary ability
NIVs. *See* O visas

F

F visas and status (academic students)
H-1Bs, changes of status to. *See* H-1B visas
parents of minor students, B-2 visas, *1:*267

Copyright © 2017. American Immigration Lawyers Association. All rights reserved.

Copyright © 2017. American Immigration Lawyers Association. All rights reserved.

Copyright © 2017. American Immigration Lawyers Association. All rights reserved.

Copyright © 2017. American Immigration Lawyers Association. All rights reserved.

J

 Copyright © 2017. American Immigration Lawyers Association. All rights reserved.

Copyright © 2017. American Immigration Lawyers Association. All rights reserved.

Copyright © 2017. American Immigration Lawyers Association. All rights reserved.

Copyright © 2017. American Immigration Lawyers Association. All rights reserved.

willful violators
  additional attestations, *1:*456–64
  displacement in course of willful violation, *1:*468
  identifying, *1:*454–55
labor disputes
  impact of labor dispute
    on E-1 and E-2 petitioners from Canada or
      Mexico, *1:*360–61
    on H-1Bs petitioners, *1:*582–84
    in H-3 trainees, *1:*821–22
    on L-1 transferees from Canada or Mexico,
      *1:*967–68
    on O-1 and O-2 petitioners, *1:*1084–85
    on P petitioners, *1:*1154–55
    on TN professionals, *1:*1214–15
  strike or lockout attestation in LCA, *1:*445–47
lawful permanent residents (LPRs). *See also*
    Adjustment of status; Consular processing;
    Numerical limitations; Priority dates
  B visa petition by member of LPR's family, *1:*210–
    11
  evidence of LPR status, *2:*650
  green cards. *See* Permanent resident cards (I-551)
  maintaining LPR status, *2:*817–29
    criminal convictions, *2:*829
    obligations of LPRs, generally, *2:*816–17
    re-entry permits, *2:*821–29
      biometrics, *2:*825–27
      USCIS decision, *2:*827–29
    rescission of status, *2:*836–41
licensure. *See* Degrees, credentials, licensure, and
    equivalencies
litigation
  by B-1 visitors, *1:*177–78
lockbox, filing with, *2:*559–63

M

"mailbox rule," *1:*13, *1:*121
maintenance of status. *See also specific visa types*
  nonimmigrant visas, generally, *1:*132–48
management consultants
  TN visas and status, *1:*1189–91
market researchers and analysts
  B-1 visas for Canadians and Mexicans, *1:*218
marriage and cohabitation
  common-law spouses, cohabitants, and
    nontraditional partners, *1:*129–30
  adjustment of status, *2:*705–06
  B-2 visas, *1:*238–48
  definition of spouse, *1:*129–30
medical and lab technologists
  TN visas and status, *1:*1203–04

medical conditions
  Visa Waiver Program participants, emergencies
    preventing departure, *1:*286
medical students. *See* Students
Mexico and Mexicans. *See also* NAFTA; TN visas;
    Western Hemisphere Travel Initiative (WHTI)
  Border Crossing Cards (BCCs), *1:*109–110, *1:*234–
    35
  FAST Program, *1:*108–09
  H-2B admission, *1:*796–97
  H-3 admission, *1:*831
  O-1 and O-2 admission, *1:*1094–95
  P admission, *1:*1165
  SENTRI Program, *1:*109
  TCN visa applications. *See* Third country national
    (TCN) applications
  waiver of documentary requirements for admission,
    *1:*109–10
minors. *See also* Aging-out children; Derivative
    beneficiaries
  unlawful presence, nonaccrual of, *1:*146
missionaries, *1:*256–60
models. *See* Fashion models
motion-picture production
  extraordinary-ability petitioners. *See* O visas
motions to reopen or reconsider
  denial of NIV petition, *1:*60–61, *1:*65–69

N

NAFTA (North American Free Trade
    Agreement). *See also* TN visas
  B-1 status for Canadians and Mexicans, *1:*213–35
    after-sales service, *1:*226–28
    buyers, *1:*220–21
    commercial transactions, *1:*228–29
    customs brokers, *1:*224–26
    harvester owners, *1:*216–17
    market researchers and analysts, *1:*218
    professionals, *1:*228
    public relations and advertising, *1:*229
    purchasing and production managers, *1:*217
    research and design, *1:*216
    sales representatives and agents, *1:*219–20
    tour bus operators, *1:*231–33
    tourism personnel, *1:*229–30
    trade fair and promotional personnel, *1:*218–19
    translators and interpreters, *1:*233–34
    transportation operators, *1:*221–24
  E status for Canadians and Mexicans, *1:*366–67
    effect of labor dispute, *1:*360–61
  L-1 transferees
    dual intent "inconsistent" with NAFTA, *1:*213
    labor disputes, impact on Canadian and Mexican
      transferees, *1:*967–68

Copyright © 2017. American Immigration Lawyers Association. All rights reserved.

O

Copyright © 2017. American Immigration Lawyers Association. All rights reserved.

P

Copyright © 2017. American Immigration Lawyers Association. All rights reserved.

R

Copyright © 2017. American Immigration Lawyers Association. All rights reserved.

Copyright © 2017. American Immigration Lawyers Association. All rights reserved.

Copyright © 2017. American Immigration Lawyers Association. All rights reserved.

tree-planting, reforestation, and logging occupations
  special considerations for classifying as H-2A, *1:*770–77
Troubled Asset Relief Program, *1:*450
two-year foreign-residence requirement. *See* Foreign-residence requirement

U

United Nations
  B-1 visas for interns with U.N. Institute for Training and Research, *1:*266
universities, *1:*424–26. *See also* Professors and instructors
unlawful presence, *1:*136–46
  authorized period of stay, *1:*137
  Canadian citizens, *1:*145–46
  exchange visitors, *1:*145
  minors, *1:*146
  students, *1:*145
  three– and ten-year bars, *1:*138–39
  vs. unlawful status, *1:*136–37
  visa waiver entrants, *1:*146
  voluntary departure, effect of, *1:*135, *1:*139–40
U.S. Citizenship and Immigration Services (USCIS)
  Case Status Online, *1:*53–54
  erroneous rejections by service centers, *1:*33–34
  Fraud Detection and National Security Directorate, *1:*615–21
  National Customer Service Center (NCSC), *1:*54–56
U.S. Department of Commerce
  Bureau of Industry and Security (BIS) and Export Administration Regulations (EAR), *1:*159
U.S. Department of Defense (DOD)
  H-1B visas for cooperative R&D project, *1:*503
U.S. Department of Labor (DOL)
  OES wage date, *1:*420–24
U.S. Department of State (DOS)
  Fraud Prevention Unit, *1:*621–23
  National Visa Center. *See* Consular processing
  Petition Information Management Service (PIMS), *1:*81–83
  Visa Office Inquiry Form, *1:*85–86
US-VISIT program, *1:*149–58

V

visa revalidation/reissuance. *See* Revalidation of visas
visas. *See* Immigrant visas (IVs); Nonimmigrant visas (NIVs); *specific visas and specific issues*
Visas Condor/Donkey/Mantis. *See* Security checks
Visa Waiver Program (VWP), *1:*279–314
  B visa vs. VWP, *1:*310–13
  countries eligible, *1:*282–84
  countries of concern, *1:*303–07
  departure, reporting after fact, *1:*302–03
  E-1 and E-2 visas applications, *1:*364
  E-3 visas applications, *1:*399
  Form I-94W, *1:*301
  land POE arrivals, *1:*301
  machine-readable passports, *1:*289–90
  online registration, ESTA program, *1:*290–98
  period of admission, *1:*284–89
    medical and other emergencies, *1:*286
  previous violations of VWP admission, *1:*308
  refusal of admission, effect of, *1:*313–14
  round-trip ticket requirement, *1:*298–301
  threats to U.S., persons posing, *1:*307–08
  unlawful presence, accrual of, *1:*146
  voluntary departure, effect of, *1:*287–88
  waiver of right to challenge inadmissibility/removal, *1:*308–10
visitors. *See* B-1 and B-2 visas
voluntary departure
  unlawful presence, effect on, *1:*135, *1:*139–40
  Visa Waiver Program participants, *1:*287–88

W

waivers
  of foreign residence requirement. *See* Foreign-residence requirement
  of inadmissibility grounds. *See* Inadmissibility
  NIWs. *See* National interest waivers
Western Hemisphere Travel Initiative (WHTI), *1:*149–52
  waiver of documentary requirements for admission, *1:*108–11
willful violators. *See* Labor condition application (LCA)
Work, English Study, Travel (WEST) program, *1:*844–45
work stoppages. *See* Labor disputes

Copyright © 2017. American Immigration Lawyers Association. All rights reserved.